PRENTICE HALL
2008-2009
Accounting Faculty Directory

Compiled by
James R. Hasselback

PEARSON
Prentice Hall

Upper Saddle River, New Jersey 07458

AVP/Executive Editor: Steve Sartori
Project Manager: Kerri Tomasso
Production Project Manager: Kevin Holm
Buyer: Michelle Klein
Printer/Binder: Courier/Kendallville

Pearson Prentice Hall[TM] **is a trademark of Pearson Education, Inc.**

10 9 8 7 6 5 4 3 2 1

ISBN-13: 978-0-13-600186-7
ISBN-10:   0-13-600186-6

COMPUTERIZED ACCOUNTING (www.prenhall.com/accounting)

COMPUTERIZED ACCOUNTING (www.prenhall.com/accounting)	ISBN	© Year	In-Stock Status
Brunsdon, *Learning Microsoft Office Accounting 2007 and Student CD Package*	0-13-158660-2	2008	Published
Brunsdon, *Learning Peachtree Complete 2007 and Peachtree Complete CD*	0-13-240557-1	2008	Published
Brunsdon, *Learning QuickBooks Pro 2007 and Student CD Package*	0-13-241938-6	2008	Published
Brunsdon, *Getting Started with Microsoft Small Business Accounting 2006*	0-13-223882-9	2007	Published
Brunsdon/Romney/Steinbart, *Introduction to Microsoft Great Plains 8.0: Focus on Internal Controls*	0-13-186064-X	2006	Published
Heldstab, *Getting Started with Peachtree and QuickBooks 2006*	0-13-175618-4	2007	Published
Horne, *QuickBooks Pro 2006 with Update 2007*	0-13-615025-X	2008	Published
Horne, *QuickBooks Pro 2006: A Complete Course*	0-13-178982-1	2007	Published
Horne, *QuickBooks Pro 2006: Simplified*	0-13-238057-9	2007	Published
Horne, *QuickBooks Pro 2004 with Update 2005, 7e*	0-13-242407-X	2006	Published
Osteraa/Horne, *Peachtree Complete Accounting 2006*	0-13-173537-3	2007	Published
Peachtree Complete 2007 CD	0-13-612869-6	2008	Published
Peachtree Complete 2006 CD	0-13-227509-0	2007	Published
Peachtree Complete 2005 Software	0-13-187747-X	2006	Published

COLLEGE ACCOUNTING

COLLEGE ACCOUNTING	ISBN	© Year	In-Stock Status
Slater, *College Accounting, 10e Chapters 1-25*	0-13-228638-6	2007	Published
Slater, *College Accounting, 10e Chapters 1-12*	0-13-156366-1	2007	Published

SURVEY OF ACCOUNTING

SURVEY OF ACCOUNTING	ISBN	© Year	In-Stock Status
Anthony/Breitner, *Essentials of Accounting, 9e*	0-13-149693-X	2007	Published
Anthony/Breitner, *Essentials of Accounting Review, 9e*	0-13-149695-6	2007	Published
Terrell/Terrell, *Survey of Accounting: Making Sense of Business*	0-13-091184-4	2005	Published
Werner/Jones, *Introduction to Accounting: A User Perspective, 2e*	0-13-032758-1	2004	Published

PRINCIPLES OF ACCOUNTING I & II

PRINCIPLES OF ACCOUNTING I & II	ISBN	© Year	In-Stock Status
Horngren/Harrison, *Accounting, 7e*	0-13-243960-3	2007	Published
Horngren/Harrison, *Accounting, 7e, Chapters 1-13*	0-13-224995-2	2007	Published
Horngren/Harrison, *Accounting, 7e, Chapters 12-25*	0-13-224996-0	2007	Published
Horngren/Harrison, *Accounting, 7e, Chapters 1-18*	0-13-239949-0	2007	Published
Pollard/Mills/Harrison, *Principles of Accounting*	0-13-230479-1	2007	Published

FINANCIAL ACCOUNTING

FINANCIAL ACCOUNTING	ISBN	© Year	In-Stock Status
Harrison/Horngren, *Financial Accounting, 7e*	0-13-612934-X	2008	Published
Reimers, *Financial Accounting, A Business Process Approach, 2e*	0-13-147386-7	2008	Published
Reimers, *Financial Accounting*	0-13-149201-2	2007	Published
Fraser/Ormiston, *Understanding Financial Statements, 8e*	0-13-187856-5	2007	Published
Schoenebeck, *Interpreting and Analyzing Financial Statements, 4e*	0-13-239109-2	2007	Published
Horngren/Sundem/Elliott, *Introduction to Financial Accounting, 9e*	0-13-147972-5	2006	Published

MANAGEMENT ACCOUNTING

MANAGEMENT ACCOUNTING	ISBN	© Year	In-Stock Status
Horngren/Sundem/Stratton/Schatzberg/Burgstahler, *Intro. to Management Accounting, 14e*	0-13-612921-8	2008	Published
Atkinson/Kaplan/Young/Matsumura, *Management Accounting, 5e*	0-13-173281-1	2007	Published
Bamber/Braun/Harrison, *Managerial Accounting-Class Test Edition*	0-13-228463-4	2007	Published
Young, *Readings in Management Accounting, 5e*	0-13-228022-1	2007	Published
Allen/Brownlee/Haskins/Lynch/Rotch, *Cases in Management Accounting and Control Systems, 4e*	0-13-570425-1	2005	Published
Werner/Jones, *Introduction to Management Accounting, 2e*	0-13-032750-6	2004	Published
Merchant/Van der Stede, *Management Control Systems*	0-273-65596-5	2003	Published

(continued)

COMPUTERIZED ACCOUNTING (www.prenhall.com/accounting)	ISBN	© Year	In-Stock Status
Brunsdon, *Learning Microsoft Office Accounting 2007 and Student CD Package*	0-13-158660-2	2008	Published
Brunsdon, *Learning Peachtree Complete 2007 and Peachtree Complete CD*	0-13-240557-1	2008	Published
Brunsdon, *Learning QuickBooks Pro 2007 and Student CD Package*	0-13-241938-6	2008	Published
Brunsdon, *Getting Started with Microsoft Small Business Accounting 2006*	0-13-223882-9	2007	Published
Brunsdon/Romney/Steinbart, *Introduction to Microsoft Great Plains 8.0: Focus on Internal Controls*	0-13-186064-X	2006	Published
Heldstab, *Getting Started with Peachtree and QuickBooks 2006*	0-13-175618-4	2007	Published
Horne, *QuickBooks Pro 2006 with Update 2007*	0-13-615025-X	2008	Published
Horne, *QuickBooks Pro 2006: A Complete Course*	0-13-178982-1	2007	Published
Horne, *QuickBooks Pro 2006: Simplified*	0-13-238057-9	2007	Published
Horne, *QuickBooks Pro 2004 with Update 2005, 7e*	0-13-242407-X	2006	Published
Osteraa/Horne, *Peachtree Complete Accounting 2006*	0-13-173537-3	2007	Published
Peachtree Complete 2007 CD	0-13-612869-6	2008	Published
Peachtree Complete 2006 CD	0-13-227509-0	2007	Published
Peachtree Complete 2005 Software	0-13-187747-X	2006	Published

COLLEGE ACCOUNTING

	ISBN	© Year	In-Stock Status
Slater, *College Accounting, 10e Chapters 1-25*	0-13-228638-6	2007	Published
Slater, *College Accounting, 10e Chapters 1-12*	0-13-156366-1	2007	Published

SURVEY OF ACCOUNTING

	ISBN	© Year	In-Stock Status
Anthony/Breitner, *Essentials of Accounting, 9e*	0-13-149693-X	2007	Published
Anthony/Breitner, *Essentials of Accounting Review, 9e*	0-13-149695-6	2007	Published
Terrell/Terrell, *Survey of Accounting: Making Sense of Business*	0-13-091184-4	2005	Published
Werner/Jones, *Introduction to Accounting: A User Perspective, 2e*	0-13-032758-1	2004	Published

PRINCIPLES OF ACCOUNTING I & II

	ISBN	© Year	In-Stock Status
Horngren/Harrison, *Accounting, 7e*	0-13-243960-3	2007	Published
Horngren/Harrison, *Accounting, 7e, Chapters 1-13*	0-13-224995-2	2007	Published
Horngren/Harrison, *Accounting, 7e, Chapters 12-25*	0-13-224996-0	2007	Published
Horngren/Harrison, *Accounting, 7e, Chapters 1-18*	0-13-239949-0	2007	Published
Pollard/Mills/Harrison, *Principles of Accounting*	0-13-230479-1	2007	Published

FINANCIAL ACCOUNTING

	ISBN	© Year	In-Stock Status
Harrison/Horngren, *Financial Accounting, 7e*	0-13-612934-X	2008	Published
Reimers, *Financial Accounting, A Business Process Approach, 2e*	0-13-147386-7	2008	Published
Reimers, *Financial Accounting*	0-13-149201-2	2007	Published
Fraser/Ormiston, *Understanding Financial Statements, 8e*	0-13-187856-5	2007	Published
Schoenebeck, *Interpreting and Analyzing Financial Statements, 4e*	0-13-239109-2	2007	Published
Horngren/Sundem/Elliott, *Introduction to Financial Accounting, 9e*	0-13-147972-5	2006	Published

MANAGEMENT ACCOUNTING

	ISBN	© Year	In-Stock Status
Horngren/Sundem/Stratton/Schatzberg/Burgstahler, *Intro. to Management Accounting, 14e*	0-13-612921-8	2008	Published
Atkinson/Kaplan/Young/Matsumura, *Management Accounting, 5e*	0-13-173281-1	2007	Published
Bamber/Braun/Harrison, *Managerial Accounting-Class Test Edition*	0-13-228463-4	2007	Published
Young, *Readings in Management Accounting, 5e*	0-13-228022-1	2007	Published
Allen/Brownlee/Haskins/Lynch/Rotch, *Cases in Management Accounting and Control Systems, 4e*	0-13-570425-1	2005	Published
Werner/Jones, *Introduction to Management Accounting, 2e*	0-13-032750-6	2004	Published
Merchant/Van der Stede, *Management Control Systems*	0-273-65596-5	2003	Published

(continued)

32nd ACCOUNTING FACULTY DIRECTORY

Compiled by
James R. Hasselback
Mary Ball Washington Eminent Scholar
6753 Thomasville Rd, PMB 108-321
Tallahassee, Florida 32312-3966
850-894-2244 Phone/Recorder/Fax

The following is a listing of the Deans and Accounting Faculty over 1,000 schools for the academic year 2007-2008. It is compiled from information provided by the respective schools. Only that information received by May 12, 2007, is included in the Directory. The Canadian and other foreign schools follow the American schools in the school listing.

The telephone area code is in parenthesis. The Fax number follows the area code in the first line for each school.

The years in the right-hand column of each school line are the AACSB Bachelors and Masters accreditation dates. The ß indicates that the school has a Beta Alpha Psi chapter. Programs with Accounting accreditation are indicated by a 1, 2, or 3 in parenthesis.
1 - Bachelors with concentration in Accounting
2 - MBA with concentration in Accounting
3 - Masters of Accounting

The school's E-Mail address is in the second line below the area code. At the end of the second line are the programs and degrees with emphasis or concentration in Accounting.

The third line for a school includes the department phone number, school street address, and departmental secretary/administrative assistant.

The columns are as follows:
Name   Rank   School-Phone   E-Mail   Area   Degree   CIA CMA CPA   Start

$ next to a Dean or Chairman indicates "Acting"
&   represents a CPA, CGA, or CA certificate
*   represents a CMA or RIA certificate
#   represents a CIA certificate

For the Chairman, the title and rank are:
C Chairman   Prof or Pr Professor
H Head   Assoc or Ac Associate
D Director   Asst or As Assistant

The electronic-mail column includes the individual's address. The individual address must be combined with the school's electronic-mail address; for instance, jhassel@cob.fsu.edu. When an individual address includes an "@", that individual has a different school address from the school address listed in the second line of the school; the individual's complete electronic-mail address is included in the electronic-mail column. However, if an individual electronic-mail address ends with a "." then the school's address must be added to the individual address provided. A + in a persons e-mail indicates a name too long to fit in the column. @a stands for aol.com.

The degree column represents the highest earned degree or "all but dissertation," date received, and school. A period between the year and the school indicates that the individual has a doctorate with an Accounting concentration from a U.S. school.

The start column is for the first year of employment at that school.

The area column is for the person's teaching/research interests.

A Auditing	J Ethics	S Systems
B Behavioral	K SEC	T Theory
C Cost	L Business Law	U Controllership
D Computer	M Managerial	V Advanced
E Education	N Not-For-Profit	W Social
F Financial	O Internal Audit	X Tax
G Governmental	P Principles	Y Agency
H History	Q Quantitative	Z Oil & Gas
I International	R CPA Review	

Individual teaching only Business Law are not included in the Accounting Directory.

Only four-year programs are included in this Directory. Joe Rhile, 1609 Normandy, Leesburg, Florida 32748, 352-787-4333 compiles information on the community colleges.

Any mistakes in the Directory are my responsibility. However, some of the misinformation belongs to schools not providing complete information.

Any corrections, additional information, and new schools should be sent directly to me. If your school is not included, send me your listing in a format similar to that in the Directory.

James R. Hasselback   www.jrhasselback.com

Schools Offering Doctorates or Concentrations in Accounting — Thru 2006 Doct

School	1st Degree	Pre88	88	89	90	91	92	93	94	95	96	97	98	99	00	01	02	03	04	05	06	Total	Prog
Alabama	1953	94	3	3	1	6	1	3	6	2	0	1	1	1	4	1	0	2	0	2	0	132	10
American	* 1966	12	0	0	0	0	0	0	0	0	0	0	0	0	0	0	0	0	0	0	0	12	*
Arizona	1970	29	2	4	5	1	2	4	4	7	6	2	4	0	0	7	1	3	3	3	3	90	13
Arizona St	1968	56	4	2	5	3	3	5	4	2	3	3	1	2	2	3	2	1	3	2	4	110	14
Arkansas	1961	134	2	5	0	2	4	0	4	2	2	3	0	5	3	1	1	1	0	3	2	174	7
Boston U	1986	3	4	3	1	2	4	1	0	0	3	1	0	4	0	0	1	1	3	3	2	36	7
Ca-Berkeley	1929	74	2	2	1	3	2	0	2	0	2	1	2	4	1	0	1	0	1	0	0	99	?
Calif-Irvine	1984	0	0	0	0	0	0	0	0	0	0	0	0	2	1	0	1	1	0	0	2	10	3
UCLA	1962	50	0	0	2	2	1	1	0	1	0	1	0	0	0	0	0	0	0	1	1	61	3
Carnegie Mel	1959	16	2	0	1	0	1	1	2	1	2	1	4	1	0	1	2	0	1	1	2	39	9
Case Western	1966	8	0	2	0	2	1	0	0	2	0	1	1	1	0	1	0	1	0	2	0	23	7
Central Fla	1991	0	0	0	0	1	0	0	0	4	3	2	0	0	0	1	0	0	0	3	0	14	?
Chicago	1922	57	2	1	3	1	1	1	1	2	1	1	0	2	0	0	1	0	1	1	1	78	12
Cincinnati	1970	27	2	0	1	1	2	2	2	0	0	1	0	1	0	1	0	0	0	0	0	40	11
CUNY-Baruch	1975	21	1	1	5	2	0	1	0	0	0	1	0	1	0	3	3	0	2	0	1	42	11
Cleveland St	* 1994	0	0	0	0	0	0	2	0	2	2	2	1	2	2	0	0	0	0	0	0	14	*
Colorado	1966	50	3	0	5	3	2	3	1	3	1	2	1	3	1	2	0	2	1	3	3	89	7
Columbia	1952	51	2	0	1	1	0	1	0	3	1	6	3	3	0	2	3	1	2	1	1	82	17
Connecticut	1992	0	0	0	0	0	1	0	3	1	2	4	3	3	0	0	2	0	3	1	0	23	11
Cornell	1968	23	0	2	3	2	2	1	0	3	1	0	2	1	1	1	3	1	0	2	2	50	4
Drexel	1985	3	1	1	2	2	2	4	2	2	2	0	1	1	2	2	2	0	0	0	3	32	6
Duke	1986	1	0	0	0	0	2	0	0	0	0	0	0	0	0	0	0	0	0	0	3	7	6
Emory		0																			0	0	12
Florida	1956	70	3	9	3	4	2	0	3	5	0	3	4	1	3	0	0	0	2	0	4	114	8
Fla Atl	1991	0	0	0	0	1	0	0	0	0	0	1	0	1	0	1	2	1	0	0	4	12	9
Fla Intl	1993	0	0	0	0	0	0	1	2	0	0	0	0	0	0	1	0	0	0	0	0	4	11
Fla State	1970	29	3	1	1	3	7	4	5	2	4	4	0	1	2	1	0	3	0	1	1	73	18
George Wash	1969	32	0	0	3	1	0	2	1	2	0	1	2	3	1	0	2	1	0	2	1	54	5
Georgia	1970	58	6	7	3	2	10	3	2	5	2	2	3	1	0	3	1	1	1	3	2	116	9
Georgia Tech	1986	1	1	0	0	0	1	0	0	1	0	0	0	0	0	0	0	0	0	0	0	4	4
Georgia St	1965	51	4	5	4	2	1	3	5	1	0	0	3	2	0	3	4	1	1	0	2	92	5
Harvard	1935	89	1	2	1	0	1	3	0	1	1	0	2	2	0	1	1	0	3	1	0	109	?
Hawaii	2004	0																	1			1	3
Houston	1973	52	5	5	2	5	4	5	5	3	4	5	2	1	1	0	1	0	2	3	3	105	18
Illinois	1939	285	5	5	5	3	6	6	3	3	3	3	1	3	2	1	0	1	3	3	1	345	22
Indiana	1950	110	2	5	1	5	9	0	3	3	3	0	1	3	2	1	0	1	1	3	1	154	9
Iowa	1951	37	0	4	1	1	0	2	2	0	5	1	2	2	2	3	0	1	1	3	0	67	14
Jackson State	2002	0																1	3			6	6
Kansas	1970	17	0	0	1	2	1	6	2	0	1	1	0	1	0	1	0	2	1	1	1	38	4
Kent State	1970	28	5	4	3	4	0	4	1	3	0	3	2	2	2	4	3	2	1	1	1	74	9
Kentucky	1973	63	4	5	3	10	3	4	4	6	3	3	6	1	0	6	1	3	3	1	0	129	10
Lehigh	* 1978	3	0	0	0	0	0	0	0	0	0	0	0	0	0	0	0	0	0	0	0	3	*
Louisiana St	1943	111	6	8	2	3	1	2	1	5	5	1	1	3	0	1	0	4	0	2		157	2
Louisiana Tech	1973	26	6	7	1	2	1	2	6	2	3	6	1	1	2	2	1	2	1	0		74	8
Maryland	1969	19	3	4	0	1	3	1	3	1	2	1	1	3	0	0	5	1	0	3	2	55	4
Massachusetts	1971	24	2	1	0	0	1	0	0	0	1	1	1	1	0	1	0	1	2	2	1	39	10
MIT	1960	3	1	0	0	0	1	0	0	0	0	1	1	1	0	1	0	1	0	2	1	16	3
Memphis	1982	7	3	4	2	2	2	6	0	4	2	0	7	0	0	0	1	1	0	0	0	41	5
U Miami	* 1996	0	0	0	0	0	0	0	0	2	0	0	0	0	0	0	0	0	0	0	0	2	3
Michigan	1939	85	7	1	2	2	0	1	3	4	4	4	1	3	3	1	0	4	3	3	2	134	10
Mich State	1959	130	2	8	4	2	5	5	4	2	3	4	2	5	2	1	3	0	5	2	1	188	10
Minnesota	1936	81	2	2	2	2	5	4	3	0	0	0	0	0	0	0	0	0	0	0	0	102	11
Mississippi	1964	40	5	4	4	3	3	6	4	4	4	2	6	3	1	4	2	0	1	2	4	106	12
Miss State	1968	35	4	2	4	7	3	2	7	2	2	0	2	2	1	0	2	2	3	0		81	6
Missouri	1941	150	5	0	3	1	6	2	0	2	0	2	0	2	1	1	4	1	1			184	8
Morgan State		0																			0	0	?
Nebraska	1943	84	5	6	6	6	6	3	0	1	2	4	3	3	0	1	0	0	4	2		139	10
New York U	1944	61	3	3	2	0	3	2	1	2	2	0	1	3	4	2	3	5	1	0		100	10
North Carolina	1957	51	3	2	3	1	1	1	1	2	2	1	2	1	2	1	1	4	5			85	10
North Texas	1969	62	6	4	1	2	6	8	5	1	7	3	5	1	2	1	1	0	3	3	1	119	12
Northwestern	1956	42	1	1	2	6	1	1	6	2	1	2	1	0	0	2	0	3	2	2		73	7
Ohio State	1950	95	2	3	4	4	4	1	3	4	3	2	1	0	0	4	2	1	0	2	2	138	7
Oklahoma	1967	33	1	1	2	2	3	1	2	1	1	0	2	0	0	4	2	1	0	2	0	61	7
Okla State	1971	66	0	2	4	3	4	6	1	6	0	3	2	0	1	5	3	1	4	0	0	111	15
Oregon	1964	26	1	0	2	2	2	2	1	1	1	3	1	1	1	3	2	1	1	2	0	53	4
Pennsylvania	1973	9	1	6	1	0	1	0	2	2	1	2	1	1	0	0	2	4	2			37	7
Penn State	1967	68	1	6	3	5	1	7	4	2	5	1	6	0	4	1	2	0	1	2	6	125	12
Pittsburgh	1932	28	1	2	4	3	4	4	2	1	0	1	4	1	2	3	0	0	1	1	1	62	5
Purdue	1969	14	1	1	0	1	2	0	6	1	2	0	1	0	1	0	3	1	1			38	7
Rensselaer	* 1973	1	0	0	0	0	0	0	0	0	0	0	0	0	0	0	0	0	0	0	0	1	*
Rice	* 1989	0	0	0	0	0	0	0	0	0	0	0	0	0	0	0	0	0	0	0	3	3	*
Rochester	1972	8	1	2	1	1	4	1	0	0	2	1	1	1	1	0	0	3	0	0	4	34	?
Rutgers	1992	0	0	0	1	2	8	2	3	0	1	0	2	0	5	4	2	5	5	2	0	42	16
St Louis	* 1966	19	0	1	2	4	2	0	0	1	0	0	1	2	4	0	0	0	0	0	0	39	*
Santa Clara	* 1972	11	0	0	0	0	0	0	0	0	0	0	0	0	0	0	0	0	0	0	0	11	*
South Carolina	1976	38	2	9	3	6	4	4	4	2	1	1	0	2	4	1	2	2	1	0	2	90	9
South Fla	1992	0	0	0	0	0	2	1	2	1	1	0	0	2	4	1	0	1	0	0	2	19	9
Southern Calif	1963	72	4	1	5	0	2	1	4	3	1	0	2	3	2	1	2	1	2	1		107	13
So Illinois	1988	1	0	1	4	1	0	1	5	0	2	0	0	2	1	2	1	2	1	1	1	28	14
Stanford	1939	49	3	2	3	1	0	5	2	1	2	4	2	2	1	1	1	0	2	2		85	9
SUNY-Binghamp	* 1999	0	0	0	0	0	0	0	0	0	0	0	0	1	0	1	0	0	0	0	0	4	*
SUNY-Buffalo	1957	18	2	1	1	1	0	1	0	3	0	0	0	1	3	1	2	0	1	1	1	39	7
Syracuse	1970	20	1	0	1	2	3	0	2	0	2	4	2	1	0	1	0	1	1	1	1	35	4
Temple	1981	13	4	1	1	0	3	3	0	2	1	2	4	2	1	0	1	0	1	2	2	44	9
Tennessee	1976	28	4	1	4	4	1	5	3	1	2	4	2	1	0	1	0	1	0	1	2	68	8
Tx-Arlington	1980	2	0	0	0	1	1	2	6	4	5	5	2	0	0	1	0	0	0	0		29	9
Texas-Austin	1934	188	5	6	6	7	3	3	4	5	6	8	0	3	3	0	3	0	4	3	2	261	20
Texas-Dallas		0																				2	9
Tx-San Antonio	2006	0																				2	9
Texas A&M	1972	60	6	5	1	6	7	7	4	2	0	2	6	7	6	2	3	0	6	2	2	139	17
Texas Tech	1969	40	3	3	0	5	3	2	4	3	0	3	2	2	0	3	2	3	2	3		82	7
Tulane	1976	1	0	0	0	0	0	0	0	0	0	0	0	0	0	0	0	0	0	0	0	9	?
Union	* 1989	0	0	0	0	0	0	0	0	0	0	0	0	0	0	0	0	0	0	0	0	10	*
Utah	1967	11	4	2	1	2	0	1	0	2	1	1	1	1	0	0	2	0	0	0	3	37	8
Vanderbilt	* 1990	0	0	0	0	0	0	0	0	0	0	0	0	0	0	0	0	0	0	0	0	1	?
Va Comm	1987	1	1	1	1	4	1	0	3	5	1	1	2	0	2	0	4	2	1	0		33	?
Va Tech	1976	30	7	4	5	6	3	3	3	1	3	3	6	1	2	3	2	4	1	4	2	93	14
U Washington	1956	78	7	6	5	2	4	1	3	4	3	3	1	0	3	0	3	1	1	0		130	16
Wash Univ	1964	19	0	0	1	1	2	2	0	1	0	1	0	3	0	1	1	0	0	0	0	32	4
Wash State	1989	0	0	2	0	1	1	3	2	0	3	1	1	1	5	0	1	0	0	0	0	23	6
Wisconsin	1953	92	10	4	7	5	4	3	2	4	1	5	1	1	2	2	4	4	0			154	6
Total inactive *		3785	207	216	175	196	199	204	200	168	164	153	152	127	104	122	110	99	134	122	123	6761	

2007-2008 PRENTICE-HALL ACCOUNTING FACULTY DIRECTORY
ALPHABETICAL BY SCHOOL

NAME	RANK	PHONE	Electronic Mail	AREA	Degr/Date/School		START
Abilene Christian Univ	Abilene, TX	79699-9305		(325) Fax=674-2564			2003,2003
Dept of Accounting Box 29305	College of Business			coba.acu.edu			BBA,MA-ACCT
Dept Phone: 674-2304	1600 Campus Court						Kim Turman
Homepage: www.acu.edu							
Lytle, Richard S.	Dean	674-2503	rick.lytle	Mktg	PHD	94 Ariz St	1991
Fowler, Bill	C-Ac	674-2080	bill.fowler	ACX	MBA	83 Walsh	1992
Griggs, Jack A.	Prof	674-2244	jack.griggs	F	PHD	71 Tx-Austin	1-91
Neill, John D. III	Prof	674-2053	john.neill	FAV	PHD	90. Florida	& 8-00
Wertheim, Paul	Prof	674-2071	paul.wertheim	FA	PHD	87. Kansas	& 8-00
Perkins, W. David	Assoc	674-2018	david.perkins	AC	PHD	91. Tx A&M	* &1999
Stovall, Scott	Assoc	674-2558	scott.stovall	AC	PHD	03. North Tx	&1998
Clements, Curtis E.	Asst	674-2047		AC	PHD	99. Tx A&M	&2005
email: csc05e@acu.edu							
Adams State College	Alamosa, CO	81102		(719) Fax=			
Department of Accounting	School of Business			adams.edu			BSBA
Dept Phone: 587-7838	208 Edgemont Street						
Homepage: www.adams.edu							
Keiser, Kurt J.	C	589-7161	kjkeiser		PHD	Colo St	2004
Corning, Gerald L.	Assoc	587-7838	glcornin		MBA	W NewMex	#*&
Coolbaugh, Carl W.	Asst	587-7172	cwcoolba		MBA	Colorado	&
Newell, Randall	Asst	587-7676	rbnewell		DBA	Nova SE	&
Reid, Linda W.	Asst	587-7576	lwreid	S	DBA	05 Nova SE	&
Adelphi University	Garden City, NY	11530		(516) Fax=877-4607			
Dept of Accounting and Law	School of Business Adm			adelphi.edu			BBA,MBA
Dept Phone: 877-4620	South Avenue						
Homepage: www.adelphi.edu							
Libertella, Anthony F.	Dean	877-4690	libertel	Mgt	PHD	72 Ohio St	2000
Baker, C. Richard	C-Pr	877-4628	baker	AF	PHD	75. UCLA	&2005
Conway, Grace M.	Assoc	877-4620	conway	CVGF	MA	77 NY Soc	&1978
Pandit, Ganesh M.	Assoc	877-4659	pandit	MF	DBA	94. La Tech	* &2004
Angel, Jack	Asst	877-4614	angel	X	MS	78 Lgls-Post	&1981
Kreitzman, Alan J.	Asst	877-4615	kreitzma	MA	MBA	69 Adelphi	&1977
Yang, Simon S. M.	Asst	877-4618	yang	MN	PHD	00 Houston	&2000
Adrian College	Adrian, MI	49221-2575		(517) Fax=264-3807			
Accounting Faculty	Dept of Atg & Bus Adm			adrian.edu			BBA,BS
Dept Phone: 265-5161	110 South Madison Street						
Homepage: www.adrian.edu							
265-5161 phone for all							
Quinlan, Patrick	C-Pr	264-3742	pquinlan	Mktg	JD	NW Cal	8-82
Coy, David G.	Prof	Ext 3940	dcoy	PCSV	MBA	83 Toledo	* & 8-88
Nalepka, William T.	Assoc	Ext 3941	bnalepka	PXDC	MBA	76 E Mich	& 8-96
University of Akron	Akron, OH	44325-4802		(330) Fax=972-8597	ß (123) 1966,1976		
G.W. Daverio Sch Accountancy	College of Business Adm			uakron.edu		BS,MBA,MX,MSA	
Dept Phone: 972-7586	259 S. Broadway					Sharlene Husk 972-7588	
Homepage: www.uakron.edu							
Aggarwal, Raj	Dean	972-7442	cbadean	Fnce	DBA	75 Kent St	9-06
Calderon, Thomas G.	C-Pr	972-6288	tcalder	CM	PHD	87. Va Tech	& 9-88
Chandra, Akhilesh	Prof	972-6230	ac10	DS	PHD	93. Memphis	* 9-01
Frank, Gary B.	Prof	972-7242	gfrank1	FMA	PHD	73 Illinois	* & 1-85
Kim, Il-Woon	Prof	972-7461	ikim	CMI	PHD	85. Nebraska	1-86
Cheh, John J.	Assoc	972-6091	cheh	S	PHD	86. Michigan	1999
Conrad, Edward J.	Assoc	972-6228	econrad	F	PHD	91. Fla St	* & 8-91
Emore, James R.	Assoc	972-7442	jemore	UMC	DBA	84. Kent St	9-73
KPMG Fellow; Associate Dean							
Keltyka, Pamela K.	Assoc	972-6745	pkeltyk	CM	PHD	99. Ca-Irvine	9-97
KPMG Fellow							
Kimmell, Sharon L.	Assoc	972-6088	skimmell	FV	DBA	86. Kent St	& 9-81
KPMG Teaching Fellow							
Lieberman, Alvin H.	Assoc	972-6229	lieberm	XF	JD	64 Akron	& 9-69
KPMG Fellow							
Ofobike, Emeka	Assoc	972-6228	ofobike	FVI	PHD	84. Oregon	* & 9-89
Hausman, Thomas	VAsst	972-5272	hausman	X	LLM	76 NYU	9-06
Wang, Li	Asst	972-7586		FA	PHD	06. Kent St	* & 9-07
Apple, Jerome E.	Inst	972-6912	jea1	XF	JD	70 Clev St	& 9-96
Gradisher, Suzanne	Inst	972-6606	shg16	FMX	JD	04 Akron	& 8-04
Welfley, Mark	Inst	972-7349	mmw20	D	MBA	04 CS-Domin	1-04

University of Alabama Tuscaloosa, AL   35487-0220   (205) Fax=348-8453   ß (13) 1929,1963
Culverhouse Sch of Acctncy Culverhouse C Comm & BA cba.ua.edu   BS,MACC,MTA,PHD
Dept Phone: 348-6131   310 Alston Hall   Ms. Tonta Mauter
Homepage: www.cba.ua.edu/accounting

Mason, J. Barry	Dean	348-7443	jbmason	Mktg	PHD	67	Alabama	1967
Stone, Mary S.	D-Pr	348-2915	mstone	FT	PHD	81.	Illinois	&1981
Hugh F. Culverhouse Professor								
Albright, Thomas L.	Prof	348-2908	talbrigh	M	PHD	90.	Tennessee	&1990
J. Reese Phifer Faculty Fellow								
DeZoort, F. Todd	Prof	348-6694	tdezoort	ABJS	PHD	95.	Alabama	6-01
Professional Advisory Board Fellow								
Dugan, Michael T.	Prof	348-2902	mdugan	FT	DBA	82.	Tennessee	&1985
Ernst & Young Professor								
Houston, Richard W.	Prof	348-8392	rhouston	AF	PHD	95.	Indiana	&1995
Y. Boozer Faculty Fellow								
Ingram, Robert W.	Prof	348-6694	ringram	FG	PHD	77.	Tx Tech	&1985
S. J. Ross-H. F. Culverhouse Chair								
Kee, Robert C.	Prof	348-2909	rkee	CS	DBA	80.	Fla St	* 9-78
Mason, John O. Jr.	Prof	348-2904	jomason	AD	PHD	69.	Missouri	&1968
Robbins, Walter A.	Prof	348-4598	wrobbins	NF	DBA	82.	Tennessee	&1981
Schnee, Edward J.	Prof	348-2910	eschnee	X	PHD	73.	Mich St	& 6-82
Culverhouse Professor of Accounting								
Dindon, Kathleen N.	Assoc	348-2911	kbindon	IX	PHD	81.	Penn St	&1979
Taylor, Gary K.	Assoc	348-4658	gtaylor	FT	PHD	96.	Ohio St	&1996
PricewaterhouseCoopers Fellow								
Chen, Keji	Asst	348-2917	kchen	F	PHD	03.	Ohio St	7-03
Hatfield, Richard C.	Asst	348-2908	rhatfiel	XA	PHD	98.	Florida	& 8-06
Reitenga, Austin L.	Asst	348-5780	areiteng	D	PHD	98.	Kentucky	* & 8-06
Fitzgibbon, Thomas	Inst	348-2903	tfitgib	F	MACC	06	Alabama	8-06
McKinney, Lisa	Inst	348-6679	lmckinne	F	MTA	95	Alabama	8-03
Trowbridge, Deborah W.	Adj	348-6131		AB	MACC	89	Alabama	&1992

email: dcabnis@bama.ua.edu

U of Alabama at Birmingham Birmingham, AL   35294-4460   (205) Fax=975-4429   ß (13) 1973,1977
Dept Accounting & Info Sys School of Business   uab.edu   BS,MAC
Dept Phone: 934-8820   1150 Tenth Avenue South   Tracey White
Homepage: www.business.uab.edu

Holmes, Robert E.	Dean	934-0055	holmesr	Mgt	PHD	71	Arkansas	1-99
Messina, Frank M.	C-Ac	934-8820	fmessina	SX	DBA	93.	Miss St	&1993
Ernst & Young Scholar								
Broom, Lowell S.	Prof	934-8820	lbroom	AN	DBA	80.	La Tech	&1988
Associate Dean								
Bryant, Keith Jr.	Emer	934-8820		1995	PHD	67	Alabama	* 1969
Edmonds, Thomas P.	Prof	934-8820	tedmonds	FP	PHD	79.	Geo St	1986
Alumni and Friends Professor of Accounting								
Rayburn, Frank R.	Emer	934-8820		1998	PHD	74.	Alabama	* &1990
Tanju, Deborah W.	Prof	934-8820	dtanju	FO	PHD	81.	Georgia	# * 1982
Tanju, Murat N.	Prof	934-8820	mtanju	FM	PHD	77.	Georgia	* &1977
Tsay, Bor-Yi	Prof	934-8820	bytsay	SM	PHD	86.	Houston	&1986
Adkins, Nell	Assoc	934-8828	nell6184	X	PHD	95.	Fla St	& 1-99
Grice, J. Stephen	Assoc	934-8820	sgrice	FA	PHD	97.	Alabama	&2007
Powers, Ollie S.	Assoc	934-8820	opowers	FV	MA	71	Alabama	* 1976
Singleton, Tommie W.	Assoc	934-8862	tsingleton	AEOS	PHD	95.	Miss	* &2003
Turpen, Richard A.	Assoc	934-8820	raturpen	FA	PHD	87.	Alabama	&1993
PricewaterhouseCoopers Scholar								
Watkins, Frank E. Jr.	Assoc	934-8820	fwatkins	X	PHD	73.	LSU	&1980
Springer, Elizabeth H.	Inst	934-8820	bspringer	F	MACC	82	Alabama	&2006

U of Alabama in Huntsville Huntsville, AL   35899   (256) Fax=824-2929   ß 1994,1994
Dept Accounting & Finance College of Adm Science uah.edu   BSBA,MACC
Dept Phone: 824-6159   ASB 350   Jeannie Mackay
Homepage: www.uah.edu/colleges/adminsci/index.html

Billings, C. David	Dean	824-6735	billind	Fnce	PHD	69	Missouri	1981
Evans, Dorla A.	C-Pr	824-6764	dorla.evans	Fnce	PHD	85	Arkansas	1991
Baldwin, Amelia A.	Assoc	824-6811	amelia.baldwin	S	PHD	91.	Va Tech	2006
Bryson, R. Eugene	Assoc	824-6567	brysong	FHV	PHD	76.	Geo St	&1976
Allport, Christopher D.	Asst	824-6582	allporc	FMA	PHD	05.	Va Tech	2005
Hickman, Charles	Asst	824-6598	charles.hickman		LLM	89	Mo-Ks Cty	2006
Pendley, John A.	Asst	824-7334	pendleyj	SFA	PHD	94	Georgia	&1998

Alabama A&M University Normal, AL   35762   (256) Fax=372-5972
Dept of Accounting Box 429 School of Business   aamu.edu   BS,MBA
Dept Phone: 372-4767   Linda Kelley Leslie
Homepage: http://www.aamu.edu/nsb/accounting1.htm

Name	Rank	Phone	Email	Area	Degree	Yr	School	Date
Sarkar, Amin	Dean	372-5092	amin.sarkar	Econ	PHD	88	Berkeley	2007
Anantharaman, Sekhar	C-Ac	372-4777	sekhar.ananth+	FSVP	PHD	96.	Cen Fla	8-96
Jain, Rohit	Prof	372-4778	rohit.jain	MFI	PHD	80.	Florida	* 8-96
Khanna, Haresh	Assoc	372-4790	haresh.khanna	PFM	DBA	80	Miss St	* 9-77
Gilmore, Rufus III	Asst	372-4776	rufus.gilmore	PCF	MBA	76	Atlanta	1976
McQuitter-Banks, Bonnie	Asst	372-4783	bonnie.banks	PM	MBA	84	Alab A&M	1984
Ohene-Nyako, Eric	Asst	372-4786	eric.ohene	CPMF	MBA	82	Alab A&M	1983
Wang, Hewei (Wendy)	Asst	372-4077	hewei.wang		DBA		Nova SE	
Gabre, Helen G.	Inst	372-4785	helen.gabre	PFXG	MBA	84	Alab A&M	& 9-99

Alabama State University
Dept of Accounting & Finance
Dept Phone: 229-4134
Homepage: cobanetwork.com
Montgomery, AL   36101-0271
College of Business Adm
915 S. Jackson Street
(334) Fax=229-6806
alasu.edu
BS,MACC

Name	Rank	Phone	Email	Area	Degree	Yr	School	Date
Vaughn, Percy J. Jr.	Dean	229-4123	pvaughn	Mktg	DBA	75	Tx Tech	1974
Crawford, Jean G.	C-Pr	229-4133	jcrawford	TAF	PHD	87.	Alabama	& 8-88
Watkins, Herbert N.	Assoc	229-6809	hwatkins	CGF	PHD	70.	Wisconsin	&1999
Bradford, Jorja F.	Asst	229-6802	jbradford	AF	MBA	98	Aub-Mont	1999
Montgomery, Walter	Asst	229-6807	wmontgomery	CFA	MBA	74	Atlanta	&1993

Univ of Alaska, Anchorage
Department of Accounting
Dept Phone: 786-4133
  email @1=cbpp.uaa.alaska.edu
Anchorage, AK   99508-8244
College of Bus & Pub Pl
3211 Providence Drive
(907) Fax=786-4115
uaa.alaska.edu
1995,1995
BBA
Fannie Slaten

Name	Rank	Phone	Email	Area	Degree	Yr	School	Date
Case, Thomas R.	Dean	786-4126	tcase	Sys	MS	76	S Calif	2002
Barbee, Ronald F.	C-Ac	786-1662	afrfb@1	SFMG	PHD	93.	Wash St	& 8-01
Boze, Ken M.	Prof	786-4144	afkmb	MCF	PHD	83	Arkansas	* &1989
Koshiyama, Lynn K.	Prof	786-4139	aflkk	FM	MBA	91	Ak Pacif	&1988
Maloney, Robert C.	Prof	786-4137	afrcm1	FE	MBA	72	Miami U	&1988
Fernandez, Rudy	Assoc	786-4141	afrff	FIX	JD	94	Colorado	&1988
Fort, C. Patrick	Assoc	786-4138	afcpf	FV	PHD	93.	Colorado	1993
Kilpatrick, Donna J.	Assoc	786-4112	djkilp@1	CMB	PHD	97.	U Wash	
Mason, J. David	Assoc			MX	PHD	93.	Colorado	&

Univ of Alaska Fairbanks
Accounting & Info Sys
Dept Phone: 474-7461
Homepage: uafsom.com/adegree.html
Fairbanks, AK   99775-6080
School of Management
201 Bunnell
(907) Fax=474-5219
uafsom.edu
(1) 1988,1988
BBA,MBA

Name	Rank	Phone	Email	Area	Degree	Yr	School	Date
Marr, Wayne	Dean	474-7916	ffmwm	Fnce	PHD	83	Tx Tech	8-04
Davis, Michael L.	D-Ac	474-5872	ffmld1	FV	PHD	86.	Mass	& 8-04
Robinson, E. Thomas	Emer	474-6526	ffetr	2005	MSA	71	Wisconsin	* & 8-74
Wichmann, Henry Jr.	Prof	474-7238	ffhw	GNMV	PHD	72	N Colo	& 1-86
Abramowicz, Kenneth F.	Assoc	474-7080	ffkfa	XF	PHD	91.	Missouri	&1994
Berry, Kevin T.	Assoc	474-1808	ffktb	MZF	PHD	95.	Okla St	8-07
Zhao, Yijiang	Asst	474-2476	ffyz	F	PHD	05.	Nebraska	8-06
Bartlett, Thomas E.	Clin	474-5136	ffteb	AF	MBA	69	Emory	& 8-07

Univ of Alaska Southeast
Accounting Faculty
Dept Phone: 796-6123
Homepage: uas.alaska.edu/business
Juneau, AK   99801-8672
School Bus & Public Adm
11120 Glacier Highway
(907) Fax=
uas.alaska.edu
BBA
Karen Cummins

Name	Rank	Phone	Email	Area	Degree	Yr	School	Date
Schmitt, Karen	Dean	796-6123	karen.schmitt		PHD			
Dye, Janet L.	C-Pr	465-6346	janet.dye		PHD	94	Colum Pac	& 8-93

Alaska Pacific University
Accounting Faculty
Dept Phone: 564-8234
Homepage: http://www.alaskapacific.edu/
Anchorage, AK   99508-4672
Business Admin Dept
4101 University Drive
(907) Fax=563-8255
alaskapacific.edu
BA
Tania Marsh

Name	Rank	Phone	Email	Area	Degree	Yr	School	Date
Thiru, Yaso	C-Ac	564-8260	yasot	MIEF	EDD	02	Fielding	* 1989

Albany State University
Atg, Bus Info Sys & Mktg
Dept Phone: 430-4773
Albany, GA   31705
College of Business
504 College Drive
(229) Fax=430-5119
asurams.edu
BS,MBA
Ramona Nealy

Name	Rank	Phone	Email	Area	Degree	Yr	School	Date
Ojemakinde, Abiodun	Dean	430-2749	aojemaki	Econ	PHD	89	LSU	9-89
Bennett, Cynthia F.	C-Pr$	430-4786	cynthia.bennett	Bus	PHD	92	OSU	1-94
Dean, Passard	Asst	430-1747	passard.dean		PHD	04	Argosy	8-06
Wright, William B.	Asst	430-4778	william.wright	PX	MBA	78	Valdosta	9-82

Albion College
Accounting Faculty
Dept Phone: 629-0419
Albion, MI   49224-1899
Dept of Economics & Mgt
611 E. Porter St
(517) Fax=629-0428
albion.edu
BA
Renee Harlow

Name	Rank	Phone	Email	Area	Degree	Yr	School	Date
Hooks, Jon A.	C-Pr$		jhooks	Fnce	PHD	89	Mich St	1989
Smith, Gaylord N.	Prof	629-0424	gsmith	FXA	MBA	67	Mich St	&1976
Bedient, John B.	Assoc	629-0343	jbedient	MFV	MBA	78	Indiana	&1985

Albright College
Department of Accounting
Dept Phone: 921-7538
Eguae-Obazee, Gertrude
Reilly, Terence J.
Wright, Gail E.

Reading, PA   19612-5234
Business Box 15234
13th N & Bern Streets

C-Ac	921-7703	tobazee	MCNG	MBA	80	JacksonSt		&1991
Prof	921-7705	treilly	F	MS	67	Northeas		&1975
Prof	921-7702	gwright	XAI	MBA	75	Pittsburgh	#	&1989

(610) Fax=921-7883
alb.edu   BS
Ms. Linda Reinhart

Alcorn State University
Div of Accounting & Finance
Dept Phone: 877-6450
Homepage: www.alcorn.edu
Wells, Steve C.
Kariuki-Mwangi, Benson
Gill, John W.
Posey, Clyde L.
Odaiyappa, Ramasamy
Dogar, Zulfiquar A.
Wilson, R. Tim

Alcorn State, MS   39096-7500
School of Business
1000 ASU Drive #90

Dean$	304-4308	steve	FX	PHD	94	Miss	*	&1996
C-As	877-6450	benson	FAN	DBA	00	Nova SE		&1986
Prof	629-3538	jgill	A	PHD	92.	Miss		&1998
Prof	304-4367	cposey	MA	PHD	78.	Okla St		&2005
Assoc	877-6450	ramasamy	CMP	PHD	85.	Florida		2000
Asst	877-6450	dogar	DS	MBA	87	NE La		&1987
Asst	877-6450	rwilson	AF	PHD	06.	Miss		&1975

(601) Fax=877-2326
alcorn.edu   BS
Mrs. Geraldine Varnado

Alderson-Broaddus College
Accounting Faculty
Dept Phone: 457-6338
Horacek, Thomas
Johnson, Elizabeth H.

Philippi, WV   26416-2095
Division of Social Sci
College Hill Road

C-Ac	457-6275	horacektl					
Asst	457-6338	johnsoneh	ACFX	MBA		* & 8-90

(304) Fax=457-6367
mail.ab.edu   BA
Nancy Zetty

Alfred University
Accounting Faculty, Saxon Dr
Dept Phone: 871-2294
Homepage: www.alfred.edu
Hall, William M.
Davidson, Sharon M.

Alfred, NY   14802-1205
College of Business
Saxon Drive

Dean	871-2124	fhall		PHD		Syracuse	1980
Asst	871-2826	fdavidson	A	MS	83	Roch Tech	&1983

(607) Fax=871-2114   1987,1987
alfred.edu   BS,MBA

Alma College
Accounting Faculty
Dept Phone: 463-7274
Homepage: www.alma.edu
Baleja, Gregory
Jacques, Randolph
Ealey, Thomas L.

Alma, MI   48801-1599
Business Adm Dept
614 West Superior Street

C-Pr	463-7274	baleja	Mktg	MBA		Mich St	1988
Prof	463-7149	jacques	FGIM	MBA	72	Wayne St	1977
Assoc	463-7135	ealey		MAC	76	Bowl Gr	&2006

(989) Fax=463-7277
alma.edu   BA
Barb Tripp

American University
Dept Accounting & Taxation
Dept Phone: 885-1942
Homepage: www.kogod.american.edu
Durand, Richard M.
Williamson, Donald T.
Sampson, Michael P.
Adhikari, Ajay
Duru, Augustine
Jacoby, Philip F.
Thompson, Robert B.
Marcum, Sue
Zhang, Yinqi

Washington, DC   20016-8044
Kogod School of Bus
4400 Massachusetts Ave NW

Dean	758-3485	durand	Mktg	PHD	75	Florida	1999
C-Pr	885-1942	dwillia	X	LLM	83	Geotown	& 9-85
Prof	885-1936	msampson	X	LLM	73	Geotown	& 9-83
Assoc	885-1993	aadhika	I	PHD	91.	Va Comm	9-91
Assoc	885-1937	aduru	MF	PHD	97.	Maryland	& 9-98
Assoc	885-1933	pjacoby	AFB	DBA	80.	Geo Wash	& 9-72
Assoc	885-1956	rthomps	F	PHD	84.	Florida	& 9-00
Asst	885-1935	smarcum	F	MST	86	American	& 9-06
Asst	885-3305	zhangyq	F	PHD	06.	Temple	& 9-06

(202) Fax=885-1992   1991,1991
american.edu   BSBA,MST,MBA,MS

American International Coll
Accounting Department
Dept Phone: 205-3230
Homepage: www.aic.edu
   Did Not Respond--2005-2006 Listing
Rogers, John W.
Gauthier, Keith G.
Manley, Michael

Springfield, MA   01109-3189
School of Business Adm
1000 State Street

Dean	205-3230			PHD			
C-As	205-3447	kgauthie	VX	MS	84	Hartford	&1986
Asst	205-3308	mmanley	F	MBA	93	Am Intl	&2003

(413) Fax=205-3943
aic.edu   BSBA,BBA,MSAT

Anderson University
Accounting Faculty
Dept Phone: 231-2003
Karnes, Carol L.
Anderson, H. Kyle
Davis, James R.

Anderson, SC   29621
College of Business
316 Boulevard

Dean	231-2003	ckarnes	Mgt	PHD	91	Clemson	1991
Prof	231-2478	kanderson	CPVX	MPA	84	Clemson	* &1997
Prof	231-2862	jdavis	CJS	PHD	74.	Geo St	* 2005

(864) Fax=231-2854
andersonuniversity.edu   BS
Stephanie McLees

Anderson University Anderson, IN 46012-3468 (765) Fax=641-4356
Accounting Faculty Falls Sch of Business anderson.edu BA,MBA
Dept Phone: 641-4358 1303 East 5th Street Carol Whetsel/Chris Smith
Homepage: www.anderson.edu/falls/index.html

Truitt, Terry C.	Dean	641-4354	tctruitt	Fnce	PHD	96	Miss St	1995
Peck, Cynthia L.	Assoc	641-4366	cjpeck	FAN	MBA	88	Indiana	&1984
Waters, John M. II	Assoc	641-3834	jmwaters	AF	PHD	88.	Tennessee	&2006
Motluck, Mark	Asst	641-4359	memotluck	FXLM	JD	85	U Miami	2000

Andrews University Berrien Spr, MI 49104-0024 (269) Fax=471-6158
Dept of Atg, Econ & Finance School of Business andrews.edu BBA,MBA
Dept Phone: 471-3429

Tidwell, Charles	Dean	471-3236	tidwell	Mgt	PHD	83	Calgary	1996
Gashugi, Leonard K.	C-Ac	471-3581	gashugi	Econ	PHD	92	Boston U	9-79
Gibson, Ann M.	Prof	471-3214	gibson	AJ	PHD	92.	Wash St	9-92
Geddes, Sheri	Inst	471-3583	geddes		MBA	99	Iowa	8-04

Angelo State University San Angelo, TX 76909 (325) Fax=942-2285
Accounting Faculty Box10908 Dept of Atg, Econ & Fin angelo.edu BBA,MBA,MPAC
Dept Phone: 942-2046 2601 W. Ave N Merrily Nelson
Homepage: www.angelo.edu/dept/aef/
phone: 942-2046

Bankston, Thomas	Dean$	942-2337	thomas.bankston	Fnce	PHD	75	Florida	1974
Buerger, Kurt H.	H-Pr$	Ext 245	kurt.buerger	FVGI	PHD	71	Kentucky	* &1983
Sunderman, Norman A.	Prof	Ext 245	norman.sund+	FCP	DMA	69	Michigan	&1987
DeCelles, Michael D.	Assoc	Ext 259	michael.decelles	PTF	PHD	83.	Oklahoma	2003
Lewis, Judy D.	Assoc	Ext 256	judy.lewis	AP	PHD	96.	North Tx	&1999
Ranganathan, Krishnan	Assoc	Ext 255	krishnan.rang+	XMP	PHD	90.	North Tx	* &1997
Brooks, Kelli	Lect		kelli.brooks		MPAC	04	AngeloSt	2005

Appalachian State Univ Boone, NC 28608-2013 (828) Fax=262-6640 β 1976,1981
Department of Accounting Walker College of Bus appstate.edu BS,MS
Dept Phone: 262-2036 416 Howard Street Ms. Sandra L. Everhart
Homepage: http://www.business.appstate.edu

Edwards, Randal K.	Dean	262-2058	edwardsrk	ANG	PHD	88	Tennessee	&1981
Forsyth, Timothy B.	C-Ac	262-6205	forsythtb	FM	PHD	91.	Alabama	1-89
Baker, William M.	Prof	262-6200	bakerwm	SCUR	PHD	87.	Va Tech	* 1991
Butts, F. Eugene	Emer	262-6208		1998	EDD	69	N Colo	&1977
Jones, James F.	Emer	262-6208	jonesjf	1992	MA	52	E Carol	1956
Kelley, Claudia L.	Prof	262-6216	kelleycl	X	PHD	91.	Alabama	&1994
Larson, Raymond L.	Emer	262-6204	larsonrl	2004	PHD	70.	Oregon	9-72
Marden, Ronald E.	Prof	262-6211	mardenre	AF	PHD	95.	S Fla	& 8-95
Martinelli, Alvaro	Prof	262-6201	martinellia	CHI	PHD	74.	North Tx	9-74
Peacock, Kenneth E.	Prof	262-2058	peacockke	XF	PHD	79.	LSU	&1983
University Chancellor								
Pollard, William B.	Prof	262-6206	pollardwb	XM	PHD	81.	S Carol	1981
Brackney, Kennard S. Jr.	Assoc	262-6210	brackneyks	FI	PHD	90.	N Carol	&2003
Kaenzig, Rebecca	Assoc	262-6207	kaenzigr	XP	PHD	87.	S Carol	1986
Kowalczyk, Tamara K.	Assoc	262-6226	kowalczykt	FXJ	PHD	96.	Tx A&M	&2005
Stallworth, H. Lynn	Assoc	262-6189	stallworthl	F	PHD	98.	LSU	&2006
Witmer, Philip R.	Assoc	262-6232	witmerpr	AF	PHD	93.	Geo Wash	&1992
DeBusk, Gerald K.	Asst	262-6204	debuskgk	M	PHD	04.	Va Tech	* & 8-04
Hofmann, Mary Ann	Asst	262-6288	hofmannma	FX	PHD	02.	Ariz St	* &2006
Roberts, F. Douglas	Asst	262-6213	robertsfd	S	PHD	02.	Tennessee	&2002
Buchanan, Keith	Lect	262-2688	buchannk	PX	MS	79	Appalach	&2006
Keller, Rachel	Lect	262-6240	kellerrd	P	MS	00	Appalach	&2006
Sheffield, Susie E.	Lect	262-6209	sheffields	P	MS	85	Appalach	&1998
Woods, Janet L.	Lect	262-6202	woodsjl	P	MS	00	Appalach	&2001

Aquinas College Grand Rapids, MI 49506-1799 (616) Fax=732-4489
Accounting Faculty Accounting Department aquinas.edu BS
Dept Phone: 632-8900 1607 Robinson Road SE
Homepage: www.aquinas.edu

VanGelderen, Cynthia G.	Dean	632-2922	vangecyn	XP	MBA	84	W Mich	&1980
Smith-Banks, Betty	C-Ac	632-2928	smithbet	AVN	MBA	75	Atlanta	&1994
Hogan, John	Asst	632-2927	hoganjoh	CS	MBA	00	Gr Valley	2002

Arcadia University Glenside, PA 19038-3295 (215) Fax=572-4489
Accounting Faculty Dept of Bus Adm & Econ arcadia.edu BS,BA
Dept Phone: 572-2891 450 S. Easton Road Lisa C. Scholly

Halpin, Annette L.	C-As	572-2849	halpin	Fnce	PHD	97	Drexel	9-84
Brinker, Thomas M.	Assoc	572-4039	brinker	AX	MST	93	St Joe	& 9-97

University of Arizona
Department of Accounting
Dept Phone: 621-2620
Homepage: accounting.eller.arizona.edu
email @1 = email.arizona.edu

Tucson, AZ 85721-0108
Eller College of Mgt
McClelland Hl 301 1130 Helen

(520) Fax = 621-3742
eller.arizona.edu
ß (13) 1948,1966
BS,MBA,MACC,PHD
Marion Levy 621-2366

Name	Rank	Phone	email		Degree		School	
Portney, Paul R.	Dean	621-2165	pportney	Econ	PHD		Nrthwstrn	7-05
Dhaliwal, Dan S.	H-Pr	621-2146	dhaliwal	FMT	PHD	77.	Arizona	1980
Louis A. Myers Professor								
Felix, William L. Jr.	Prof	621-2443	wfelix	A	PHD	70.	Ohio St	&1983
Eller Professor								
Schatzberg, Jeffrey W.	Prof	621-2238	jschatzberg	AM	PHD	86.	Iowa	& 1-87
Trombley, Mark A.	Prof	621-4805	trombley@1	F	PHD	90.	U Wash	* & 1-91
Beach Fleischman Profesor								
Waller, William S.	Prof	621-2351	wwaller	CA	PHD	81.	U Wash	&1981
Deloitte & Touche Professor								
Bens, Daniel A.	Assoc	621-4129	dbens	B	PHD	99.	Penn	8-05
Eldenburg, Leslie G.	Assoc	621-4585	eldenbur@1	M	PHD	91.	U Wash	&1993
Li, Oliver Zhen	Assoc	621-2366		FX	PHD	03.	Arizona	2007
Cheng, Mei	Asst	621-3786	meicheng@1	F	PHD	05.	S Calif	2006
Goodman, Theodore	Asst	621-1252	tgoodman	F	PHD	05.	Penn	8-05
Schwartz, William C.	Asst	621-4830	schwartz	F	PHD	01.	Iowa	2001
Stefanescu, Monica L.	Asst	621-3765	mis125@1	F	PHD	06.	Penn St	8-06
Blanchard, Phillip A.	SLect	621-2877	pblancha	M	MBA	77	Fairl Dick	& 1-98
Cohen, Leslie	SLect	621-2910	lcohen	F	MBA	90	Chicago	1994
Doing, Judith	SLect	621-2310	jdoing	FX	MSA	94	Arkansas	1-95
Associate Department Head								
Otto, Karen A.	SLect	621-2536	otto	FA	DBA	99.	Boston U	8-99
Cordova, Kathryn	Lect	621-3713	kcordova@1		MBA	00	Ariz St	2005
Plagman, Carol	Lect	621-3712	plagman@1		MAC	94	Arizona	2001

Arizona State University
School of Accountancy
Dept Phone: 965-3631
Homepage: www.wpcarey.asu.edu

Tempe, AZ 85287-3606
W.P Carey School of Bus
PO Box 873606

(480) Fax = 965-8392
asu.edu
ß (13) 1962,1964
BS,MAIS,MT,PHD
Julie Barnes

Name	Rank	Phone	email		Degree		School	
Mittelstaedt, Robert A.	Dean	965-2468	robert.mittel +		MBA	72	Penn	7-04
Christian, Charles W.	D-Pr	965-6632	charles.chris +	X	PHD	85.	Georgia	& 1-85
Boatsman, James R.	Prof	965-6616	james.boatsman	F	PHD	73.	Tx-Austin	&1986
KPMG Professor								
Kaplan, Steven E.	Prof	965-6498	steve.kaplan	M	PHD	82.	Illinois	1981
Ohlson, James A.	Prof	965-3693	james.ohlson	FT	PHD	72.	Berkeley	2004
W. P. Carey Chair in Accountancy								
Pany, Kurt J.	Prof	965-6849	kurt.pany	AF	PHD	78.	Illinois	& 1-78
Pei, Buck K. W.	Prof	965-6635	buck.pei	SBA	PHD	85.	North Tx	1986
Reckers, Philip M. J.	Prof	965-2283	philip.reckers	FAB	PHD	78.	Illinois	1980
Schultz, Joseph J. Jr.	Prof	965-7177	joe.schultz	ABM	PHD	74.	Tx-Austin	&1983
Drake, Philip D.	Assoc	965-7084	philip.drake	F	PHD	90.	Ohio St	&2006
Golen, Steven P.	Assoc	965-6617	steven.golen	F	PHD	79	Ariz St	1984
Hwang, Yuhchang	Assoc	965-7159	hwangy	FM	PHD	87.	Berkeley	8-95
Mercer, Molly	Assoc	965-3631		F	PHD	01.	Tx-Austin	2007
Regier, Philip R.	Assoc	965-4357	phil.regier	F	PHD	87.	Illinois	&1987
Whitecotton, Stacey M.	Assoc	965-8315	stacey.whitec +	MB	PHD	93.	Oklahoma	& 8-97
Brown, Jennifer L.	Asst	965-3631		X	PHD	07	Tx-Austin	2007
Comprix, Joseph	Asst	727-7187	joe.comprix	F	PHD	00.	Illinois	8-00
Fedyk, Tatiana	Asst	965-3631		M	PHD	07	Berkeley	&2007
Mikhail, Michael B.	Asst	727-7198	michael.mikhail	F	PHD	97	Chicago	&2006
Petersen, Michael J.	Asst	965-3631	michael.petersen	M	PHD	02.	Iowa	2001
Rowe, Casey	Asst	965-3631	casey.rowe	M	PHD	01.	Pittsburgh	2001
Geiger, Karen	SLect	965-0823	karen.geiger	M	MS	92	Ariz St	1997
Goldman, Donald	SLect	965-3631	donald.goldman	T	BS	74	Ariz St	2001
Maccracken, Harriet	SLect	965-6637	harriet.maccr +	F	MA	80	Ariz St	& 8-95
Munshi, Persy	SLect	965-9124	perseus.munshi	AS	MBA	88	Ohio St	7-03
Leshinski, Dianne L.	Lect	965-2393	dianne.leshinski	F	MBA	93	Dayton	&2006
Levendowski, Glenda	Lect	965-0143	glenda.levend +	FX	MS	83	Hou-CILk	&2004
West, Stephen L.	Lect	727-7249	slwest	M	MBA	78	Nova SE	2006

Arizona State University
Dept of Information Systems
Dept Phone: 965-3631

Tempe, AZ 85287
W.P. Cary School of Bus

(480) Fax = 965-8392
asu.edu

Name	Rank	Phone	email		Degree		School	
Mittelstaedt, Robert A.	Dean	965-2468	robert.mittel +		MBA	72	Penn	7-04
St. Louis, Robert D.	C-Ac	965-1440	st.louis	Sys	PHD	72	Purdue	1982
Steinbart, Paul John	Prof	965-8991	paul.steinbart	S	PHD	85.	Mich St	& 8-97
David, Julia Smith	Assoc	965-8603	julie.smith.da +	S	PHD	95.	Mich St	& 8-95
Iyer, Govind S.	Assoc	965-2382	govind.iyer	ST	PHD	94.	Geo St	&1998

Arizona State Univ West

Dept of Accounting 2451
Dept Phone: 543-6275
Homepage: www.west.asu.edu/sgml

Phoenix, AZ 85069-7100
School Mgt Box 37100
4701 West Thunderbird Rd

(602) Fax=543-6303 ß (1) 1994,1994
asu.edu

BS
Veronica Mize

Name	Rank	Phone	Email					
Waissi, Gary	Dean	543-6661	gary.waissi	Mgt	PHD	85	Michigan	2006
Baldwin, Bruce A.	C-Pr	543-1035	bruce.baldwin	F	PHD	79.	Ariz St	9-89
Vickrey, Don W.	Prof	543-6213	don.vickrey	TF	PHD	75.	Tx-Austin	& 8-92
Duncan, William A.	Assoc	543-6112	william.duncan	X	PHD	83.	Tx-Austin	& 9-91
Lowe, D. Jordan	Assoc	543-6148	jordan.lowe	AFM	PHD	92.	Ariz St	& 9-03
Prosch, Marilyn M.	Assoc	543-6219	marilyn.prosch	SF	PHD	91.	Temple	& 8-00
Swenson, Dan W.	Assoc	543-6226	dan.swenson	MC	PHD	93.	Miss	* & 8-00
Chen, Huyaing "Lucy"	Asst	543-6218	huajing.chen		PHD	05.	Temple	8-05
Chung, Hyeesoo "Sally"	Asst	543-6127	sally.chung		PHD	04.	Purdue	8-05
Samuels, Janet A.	Asst	543-6222	janet.samuels	SCM	PHD	04.	Ariz St	9-03
Dallmus, John	Lect	543-6144	john.dallmus	FS	MBA	94	Loyola	8-00
Finger, Catherine A.	Lect	543-6210	catherine.finger	FV	PHD	91.	Berkeley	2004
Muller, Barbara	SLect	543-6113	barbara.muller	TF	MBA	91	Ariz St	& 9-91
Wood, Robert	Lect	543-6111	robert.e.wood	SD	PHD	69	Berkeley	8-05

University of Arkansas

Department of Accounting
Dept Phone: 575-4051
Homepage: http://waltoncollege.uark.edu/acct

Fayetteville, AR 72701
Sam M. Walton Coll Bus
WCOB 401

(479) Fax=575-2863 ß (13) 1931,1963
walton.uark.edu BS,MACC,PHD
Suzanna Hicks

Name	Rank	Phone	Email					
Worrell, Dan L.	Dean			Mgt	PHD	78	LSU	8-05
Richardson, Vernon J.	C-Pr	575-6803	vrichardson	SF	PHD	97.	Illinois	&2005
Ralph L. McQueen Chair								
Bouwman, Marinus J.	Prof	575-6117	rbouwman	BEMS	PHD	79.	Car Mellon	6-92
Callahan, Carolyn M.	Prof	575-6126	ccallahan	FM	PHD	85.	Mich St	2001
Doris M. Cook Chair								
Finn, Don W.	Prof	575-4051	dfinn	BJM	PHD	82.	Arkansas	2003
Garrison/Wilson Chair								
Pincus, Karen V.	Prof	575-6119	kpincus	ABE	PHD	84.	Maryland	& 8-95
S. Robson Walton Chair								
Thomas, Deborah W.	Assoc	575-6132	dthomas	X	JD	78	Vanderbilt	&1983
Nolan E. Williams Lecturer								
West, Timothy D.	Assoc	575-5227	twest	MC	PHD	93.	Tennessee	&2002
Henderson, B. Charlene	Asst	575-6116	chenderson	XF	PHD	96.	Ariz St	&2005
BKD Lecturer								
Peters, Gary F.	Asst	575-4051	gfpeters	FA	PHD	98.	Oregon	&2003
Sanchez, Juan Manuel	Asst	575-6113	jsanchez	FMS	PHD	06.	Tx-SanAnt	2006
Shook, Carol L.	Inst	575-6096	cshook	FM	MBA	94	Arkansas	&1999
Leflar, Charles J. F.	Clin	575-6616	cleflar	FA	PHD	95.	Missouri	&1993

U of Arkansas at Fort Smith

Accounting Faculty
Dept Phone: 788-7801

Ft. Smith, AR 72913-3649
College of Business
5210 Grant Ave.

(479) Fax=
uafortsmith.edu

Name	Rank	Phone	Email					
Roderick, Roger	Dean	788-7801	rroderick	IndR	PHD	70	Illinois	
Dearman, David T.	Assoc	788-7633	ddearman	MCS	PHD	98.	Memphis	*
Tanner, Margaret M.	Assoc	788-7804	mtanner	F	PHD	92.	North Tx	&
Hayes, Thomas P. Jr.	Asst	788-7633	thayes	AP	PHD	06.	North Tx	&2006
Schmidt, George L.	Asst	788-7885	gschmidt	F	PHD	96.	North Tx	

U of Arkansas at Little Rock

Department of Accounting
Dept Phone: 569-3351

Little Rock, AR 72204-1099
College of Business Adm
2801 South University

(501) Fax=569-7021 ß (12) 1976,1982
ualr.edu BS,MBA
L. Boyer

Name	Rank	Phone	Email					
Sherman, Hugh D.	Dean	569-8892	hdsherman	Mgt	PHD	95	Temple	
Oliva, Robert R.	C-Pr	569-3352	rroliva	X	PHD	93	Fla Intl	& 7-05
Culpepper, Robert C.	Emer	569-8881	rcculpepper	1998	PHD	69.	Arkansas	& 6-75
Kusel, Jimie	Prof	569-8886	jxkusel	FM	PHD	73.	Mich St	& 9-81
Swingen, Judyth A.	Prof	569-8893	jaswingen	MX	PHD	84.	Wisconsin	& 6-01
Hamm, Jeffrey L.	Assoc	569-3309	jlhamm	FVX	PHD	95.	Tx Tech	& 7-00
Taylor, Cynthia	Assoc	569-8888	cltaylor	IG	PHD	98.	Okla St	8-99
Watts, Michael	Assoc	569-8890	mmwatts	XFP	JD	90	Ark-LtlR	& 9-79
Daily, Cynthia M.	Asst	569-8855	cadaily	A	PHD	02.	La Tech	& 6-04
Farewell, Stephanie M.	Asst	569-8888	smfarewell	SF	PHD	01	Oklahoma	7-01
Kumar, Gaurav	Asst	569-3051	gkumar	FTP	PHD	06.	Miss	& 8-06
Dorsey, Roger	Inst	683-7485	rwdorsey	XLP	LLM	03	Florida	& 7-06

U of Arkansas at Monticello

Accounting Faculty
Dept Phone: 460-1041
Homepage: www.uamont.edu

Monticello, AR 71656-3616
School of Business
Babin Business Center Rm 216

(870) Fax=460-1784
uamont.edu

Jan Stanley

Name	Rank	Phone	Email					
James, Louis J.	Dean	460-1041	jamesl	Fnce	PHD	70	Kansas	2003
Gulledge, Dexter E. (Gene)	Prof	460-1741	gulledge	NCFS	DBA	91.	Miss St	* &2001
Hammett, Ted M.	Assoc	460-1641	hammett	ACGF	DBA	94.	La Tech	&2000
Eichelberger, David L.	Asst	460-1111	eichelberger	X	MA	72	Ohio St	&2006
visiting from Austin Peay University								

U of Arkansas at Pine Bluff
Atg Faculty 1200 N Universit
Dept Phone: 575-8587
Homepage: hppt://www.uapb.edu.com

Pine Bluff, AR 71601
School of Bus & Mgt
1200 North University Drive

(870) Fax=543-4667
uapb.edu

BS
Alisa Davis

Name	Rank	Phone	Email		Deg	Yr	School	Year
Campbell, Hank	Dean$	575-8577	campbellh		PHD	77	Ohio St	2006
Henry, Matthew R.	C-Ac	575-8587	henrym	VA	MBA	65	Atlanta	&1968
Karlin, Arthur D.	Prof	575-8593	karlina	XF	PHD	64.	Illinois	1994
Marshall, Clifford L.	Assoc	575-8598	marshallc	F	PHD	83.	North Tx	2000
Hammons, Albert	Asst	575-8600	hammonsa	FV	MBA	76	Michigan	&1986

Arkansas State University
Dept of Accounting & Law
Dept Phone: 972-3038

State Univ, AR 72467-0550
Col of Bus PO Box 550
Caraway Road

(870) Fax=972-3868
astate.edu

1979,1985
BS,MACC
Sue Carver

Name	Rank	Phone	Email		Deg	Yr	School	Year
Frey, Len	Dean	972-3035	lfrey	Mgt	PHD	94	Memphis	2000
Quinn, Tina Steward	C-Ac	972-3038	tquinn	FX	PHD	96.	Miss	& 8-96
Moore, Louella	Prof	972-3038	lmoore	GHF	PHD	86.	Arkansas	* & 8-79
Dancer, Terry	Assoc	972-3038	dancer	CMF	PHD	88.	Miss	8-78
Robertson, John	Asst	972-3038	jfrobert	X	LLM	99	Alabama	2000
Carr, Rebecca	Inst	972-3038	rcarr	FXP	MS	86	Illinois	& 8-88

Arkansas Tech University
Department of Accounting
Dept Phone: 968-0354
Homepage: www.atu.edu

Russellville, AR 72801-2222
School of Business

(479) Fax=968-0677
atu.edu

2000,2000
BS

Name	Rank	Phone	Email		Deg	Yr	School	Year
Tyler, Thomas P.	Dean	968-0490	tom.tyler	Econ	PHD	80	Arkansas	1967
Carr, Pamela S.	H-Ac	968-0612	pam.carr	PX	PHD	01.	Okla St	&1991
Alexander, Sherman	Assoc	968-0357	sherman.alex+	CFM	PHD	95.	Kentucky	&1993
Goza, Nina M.	Asst	968-0495	nina.goza	GFM	PHD	05.	Miss	2004
McKnight, Constance	Asst	968-0611	connie.mcknight	FA	PHD	02.	Arkansas	&2003

Ashland University
Department of Bus Adm
Dept Phone: 289-5210
Homepage: www.ashland.edu/colleges/business/bushome.html

Ashland, OH 44805
Dauch Col Bus & Econ
410 College Avenue

(419) Fax=289-5910
ashland.edu

BS
Jolynn Lopeman, Adm Asst

Name	Rank	Phone	Email		Deg	Yr	School	Year
Pittenger, Khushwant K.	Dean$	289-5219	kpitten	Mgt	PHD	88	Cincinnati	8-87
Brenan, Kathleen	Assoc	289-5226	kbrenan	DP	MA	82	Bowl Gr	& 9-84
Parsons, Kristine	Assoc		kparsons	MSVC	PHD	95.	Kent St	* 2005
Piper, Beverly	Assoc	289-5230	bpiper	PMC	MS	78	Toledo	* & 9-79
Schloemer, Paul G.	Assoc	289-5210	pschloem	MVX	PHD	91.	Va Tech	& 8-01

Assumption College
Accounting Faculty
Dept Phone: 767-7255
Homepage: www.assumption.edu

Worcester, MA 01609-1296
Dept Business Studies
500 Salisbury Street

(508) Fax=767-7252
assumption.edu

BA,MBA
Maria Alicata

Name	Rank	Phone	Email		Deg	Yr	School	Year
McNett, Jeanne M.	C-Ac	767-7457	jmcnett	Mgt	PHD	80	Mass	1997
Foley, Joseph T.	Assoc	767-7456	jfoley	FTPR	MS	73	Northeas	&1979
Marino, Frank A.	Assoc	767-7461	fmarino	VAP	MST	82	Bentley	&1981
Niece, Jennifer M.	Asst	767-7245	jniece	CPS	MBA	98	Boston C	&2001
Sullivan, William N.	Asst	767-7458	wsulliva	XPF	MBA	75	Babson	& 9-80

Athens State University
Accounting Faculty
Dept Phone: 233-8211
Homepage: www.athens.edu

Athens, AL 35611
College of Business
300 North Beaty Street

(256) Fax=233-8151
athens.edu

BS
Molly Pepper

Name	Rank	Phone	Email		Deg	Yr	School	Year
Shonesy, Linda B.	Dean$	233-8174	linda.shonesy	Mgt	EDD		Alabama	1985
Hemingway, Linda J.	C-Ac	233-8162	linda.jhemingway	EGT	MACC	84	N Mex St	& 9-91
Whitley, William	Prof	233-8145	william.whitley	XVC	EDD	97	Alabama #	&1987
Brathwaite, Faye	Asst	216-3322	faye.brathwaite		DBA	06	Nova SE	2005
Hughes, Stacie R.	Asst	233-6543	stacie.hughes		ABD		Alabama	2005

Auburn University
School of Accountancy
Dept Phone: 844-5340
Homepage: www.business.auburn.edu/acct/
email @1=auburn.edu

Auburn, AL 36849-5247
College of Business
415 W. Magnolia Ave

(334) Fax=844-5875 ß (13) 1976,1980
business.auburn.edu
BS,MAC
Mrs. Julie Reece

Name	Rank	Phone	Email		Deg	Yr	School	Year
Bobrowski, Paul M.	Dean	844-4030		OprM	PHD		Indiana	2004
Godwin, Norman H.	D-Ac	844-6225	godwin	F	PHD	96.	Mich St	& 9-96
Alderman, C. Wayne	Prof	844-6209	alderman	FA	DBA	77.	Tennessee #	& 4-77
Clark, Ronald L.	Prof	844-6221	rclark	S	PHD	83.	Alabama	& 6-95
Tabor, Richard H.	Prof	844-6214	rtabor	CA	PHD	80.	Florida	& 9-85

Charles M. Taylor, Jr. Professor of Accounting

Wilson, Arlette C.   Prof   844-6218   awilson   FMA   PHD   83. Arkansas   # * & 6-85
   Charles M. Taylor Jr. Professor of Accounting
Jones, Jefferson P.   Assoc   844-6208   jjones   F   PHD   97. Fla St   & 9-97
Key, Kimberly G.   Assoc   844-6346   kkey   T   PHD   95. Mich St   & 9-99
Mueller, Jennifer M.   Assoc   844-6219   jmueller   FAS   PHD   00. Va Tech   8-00
Stanwick, Sarah A.   Assoc   844-6205   sstanwick   CW   PHD   93. Fla St   & 9-92
Brandon, Duane M.   Asst   844-6215   branddm@1   A   PHD   03. Va Tech   8-03
Loraas, Tina M.   Asst   844-6203   loraatm   S   PHD   04. Tx A&M
McClain, Guy   Asst   844-5340   gmcclain   FA   PHD   07. Arkansas   8-07
McLelland, Andrew J.   Asst   844-6217   mclelaj@1   FKAG   PHD   03. Tx A&M   * & 8-02
Searcy, DeWayne L.   Asst   844-5827   searcydl   CSM   PHD   02. Tennessee   # * & 8-05
Campbell, Amy B.   Lect   844-6207   campbell   F   MAC   92 Auburn   & 1-94
   Director of Graduate Programs and Internships

Auburn Univ, Montgomery   Montgomery, AL   36124-4023   (334) Fax=244-3792   1988,1988
Dept of Accounting & Finance   School of Business   mail.aum.edu   BSBA,MBA
Dept Phone: 244-3490   7300 University Drive   Melinda Ligeon
Goodson, Jane R.   Dean   244-3476   jgoodson   Mgt   PHD   86 Alabama   1986
Gurley, A. Lee   H-Ac   244-3227   lgurley   XF   PHD   96. Miss   &2000
Kamniker, Judith A.   Prof   244-3496   jkamnikar   FGN   PHD   82 Denver   &1985
Kim, Jeong Youn   VProf   244-3491   F   PHD   89. Wash St   2007
Marudas, Nicholas P.   Prof   244-3136   nmarudas   AND   PHD   01. Geo St   # &2002
Heier, Jan Richard   Assoc   244-3497   jheier   MHC   DBA   86. Miss St   &1986
Deal, Keren H.   Asst   244-3495   kdeal   FGM   PHD   07 Auburn   &2007
Leach, Maria A.   Asst   244-3490   mleach   CSIM   DBA   02. Miss St   &2004

Augsburg College   Minneapolis, MN   55454   (612) Fax=330-1607
Accounting Facultyu   Dept of Business Adm   augsburg.edu
Dept Phone: 330-1774   731 21St Ave South   Colleen Junnila
Cerrito, John C.   C-As   330-1768   cerriotj
LaFave, Steven J.   Prof   330-1542   lafave   EFC   MBA   89 Minnesota   &1991
Stoller, Stuart M.   Assoc   330-1772   stoller   MS   Long Isl

Augusta State University   Augusta, GA   30904-2200   (706) Fax=667-4064   1999,1999
Accounting Faculty   College of Business Adm   aug.edu   BBA,MBA
Dept Phone: 737-1560   2500 Walton Way   Ms. Loyd, Ms. Westjohn
Miller, Marc D.   Dean   737-1418   mmiller   Mis   PHD   94 Auburn
Jackson, Pamela Z.   Prof   737-1560   pjackson   ASFM   PHD   90. Georgia   & 1-89
Miller, Jeffrey R.   Assoc   737-1560   jmiller   ADFP   PHD   85. LSU   &1993
Styron, W. Joey   Assoc   737-1560   wstyron   FX   PHD   93. Tx A&M   &1991
Smalley, Robert   Asst   737-1560   rsmalley   MBA   73 Georgia   2002

Augustana College IL   Rock Island, IL   61201-2296   (309) Fax=794-7605
Accounting   Dept of Accounting   augustana.edu   BA
Dept Phone: 794-7470   639 38th Street   Reita Mason-Griffin
Abernathy, Jeff   Dean   794-7311   PHD   Fla St   9-04
Druger, Pamela J.   C-Pr   794-7394   pameladruger   FCV   MS   86 Iowa   * & 9-87
Delaney, John   Asst   794-7732   johndelaney   AGNO   MBA   95 Iowa   # &

Augustana College SD   Sioux Falls, SD   57197   (605) Fax=274-5229
Accounting Faculty   Dept of Business Adm   augie.edu   BA,BAPA
Dept Phone: 274-5220   2001 S. Summitt Avenue   MaryJane Minnig
Homepage: www.augie.edu/dept/bsad/index.html
Anderson, Craig   C-Ac   274-5306   canderson   Mgt   JD   80 S Calif   8-06
English, Richard D.   Assoc   274-5312   dick_english   EFJX   MBA   68 Wash U   &1974
Oppegard, Anne M.   Assoc   274-5220   anne_oppegard   DEFT   PHD   97 Nebraska   &1988
Bolen, Dennis I.   Asst   274-5308   dennis_bolen   CFMN   PHD   00 N Dakota   * &1988
Bueu, Kevin   Asst   274-4602   kevin.bueu   EFJX   MBA   86 USD   8-06

Aurora University   Aurora, IL   60506-4892   (630) Fax=844-7830
Atg, Fnce, Mktg, Mgt Program   Dunham Sch of Business   aurora.edu   BA
Dept Phone: 844-5410   347 South Gladstone Ave
Homepage: www.aurora.edu/sbps
Green, Shawn A.   Dir$ 844-5527   sgreen   Mktg   PHD   Union
Moran, Timothy   Asst   844-6500   moran   AFTW   MBA   99 St Johns   2003
Scholl, Leonard   Asst   844-6895   lschool   ACFT   MBA   62 Xavier   2001

Austin Peay State University   Clarksville, TN   37044   (931) Fax=221-7355
Department of Accounting   College of Business   apsu.edu   BBA
Dept Phone: 221-7556   Central Recv, 681 Summer St   Mary Waller
Rayburn, William   D   221-7355   rayburnw   MBA   82 Vanderbilt   1989
Clark, Roger W.   Assoc   221-7574   clarkr   PXI   PHD   92 Tennessee   &1992
Meyer, Dan W.   Assoc   221-7754   meyerdw   FMGP   PHD   88. Missouri   &2004
Said, Hassan A.   Assoc   221-7754   saidh   MFCX   PHD   94 Alabama
Francisco, William   Asst   franciscob   S   MS   75 S Miss   2006
Brown, Pennye   221-7755   brownp   PF   2005
Davidson, Leslie   davidsonl   PC   2004

Azusa Pacific University
Accounting Faculty
Dept Phone: 812-3085
Homepage: ww3.apu.edu/sbm/
Azusa, CA 91702-7000
School of Bus & Mgt
901 East Alosta Ave
(626) Fax=815-3802
apu.edu
BA,BS,MBA,MHOD
Heidi Capp

Name	Rank	Phone	Email		Degree	Yr	School	
Bezjian, Ilene L.	Dean	812-3090	ibezjian	Mktg	DBA	86	US Intl	9-91
Anderson, Paul V.	Asst	815-6000	pvanderson		MBA	75	UCLA	8-04
Deal, Stan	Asst	812-3092	sdeal	XT	MS		Golden Gt	& 9-84

Babson College
Div of Accounting & Law
Dept Phone: 239-4576
Homepage: www.babson.edu
Babson Park, MA 02457-0310
School of Management
Forest St
(781) Fax=239-5230
babson.edu
1980,1981
BS,MBA,MS
Beverly Balconi

Name	Rank	Phone	Email		Degree	Yr	School	
Fleischmann, Fritz	Dean	239-6317	fleischmann	Engl	PHD	83	Erlangen	1989
Nanni, Alfred J. Jr.	C-Pr	239-5137	nanni	UBMC	PHD	81.	Mass	1993
Ansari, Shahid L.	Prof	239-4277	sansari	BM	PHD	73.	Columbia	2005
Bell, Jan	Prof	239-4484	jbell	FM	PHD	80.	UCLA	&2006
Carr, Lawrence P.	Prof	239-5138	carr	CMU	PHD	89.	Union-NY	1989
Fetters, Michael L.	Prof	239-4378	fetters	F	PHD	73.	Wisconsin	& 9-77
Coyle, William H.	Assoc	239-4366	coyle	FAMI	PHD	93.	Tx A&M	* &1992
Halsey, Robert F.	Assoc	239-4347	halsey	F	PHD	97.	Wisconsin	1997
Lawler, William C.	Assoc	239-4364	lawler	CM	PHD	81.	Mass	1979
Turner, Robert M.	Assoc	239-4302	turnerr	FNE	DBA	92.	Boston U	1990
Williams, Joanne D.	Assoc	239-4278	williamsj	F	PHD	87.	Tx A&M	&1992
Soybel, Virginia E.	Asst	209-4241	soybel	FM	PHD	09.	Columbia	1995
Wain, Charles A.	Lect	239-5619	wain	FCM	MBA	70	Harvard	1999

Baldwin-Wallace College
Accounting Faculty
Dept Phone: 826-2392
Berea, OH 44017-2088
Div of Business Adm
275 Eastland Road
(440) Fax=826-3868
bw.edu
BA,MBA

Name	Rank	Phone	Email		Degree	Yr	School	
Kelly, J. Peter	C	826-2391	pkelly		JD	72	Duquesne	2-01
Felber, Michael J.	Assoc	826-2361	mfelber	FMX	MS	75	Akron	& 9-83
Grugle, Roger A.	Assoc	826-2363	rgrugle	CDM	ABD		Kent St	& 9-87
Chase, Linda	Asst	826-3039	lchase	AFC	MBA	97	Bald-Wal	9-01
Luli, Roger	Asst	826-2098	rluli	AFS	MBA	75	Bald-Wal	9-96

Ball State University
Department of Accounting
Dept Phone: 285-5100
Homepage: www.bsu.edu/cob/accounting
Muncie, IN 47306-0330
College of Business
2000 University Avenue
(765) Fax=285-4312 ß (13) 1978,1984
bsu.edu
BS,MS
Sylvia Ewert

Name	Rank	Phone	Email		Degree	Yr	School	
Richardson, Lynne D.	Dean	285-8192	lrichard	Mktg	PHD	89	Alabama	7-01
VanAlst, Lucinda L.	C-Ac	285-5100	lvanalst	FX	DBA	89.	Kentucky	& 3-86
Schmutte, James L.	Prof	285-5120	jschmutt	FA	DBA	83.	Kentucky	& 9-81
Duncan, James R.	Assoc	285-4976	jduncan	FA	PHD	97.	Kentucky	& 9-97
Myring, Mark J.	Assoc	285-5100	mmyring	FS	PHD	01.	Kent St	8-00
George and Franaes Ball Distinguished Professor of Accounting								
White, Gwendolen B.	Assoc	285-5116	gwhite	MA	PHD	89.	Indiana	& 9-86
Wrege, William T.	Assoc	285-5204	wwrege	FGN	DBA	84.	Kentucky	& 9-87
Ledbetter, John	Asst	285-5109	jledbett	FX	PHD	98.	Houston	& 9-99
Luchs, Christopher	Asst	285-5111	luchs	FM	PHD	03.	Kent St	8-06
Sun, Li	Asst	285-5107	lsun	FM	PHD	07.	Okla St	1-07
Yu, Minna	Asst	285-5108	myu	F	ABD		Kent St	8-06
Alley, Sheryl J.	Inst	285-5104	salley	FM	MA	79	Ball St	& 9-79
Culp, Richard I.	Inst	285-5113	riculp	F	BA	66	Fairmont	1-03
Shipley, Vicki	Inst	285-5114	vshipley	FM	MA	76	Ball St	3-79

University of Baltimore
Dept of Accounting & MIS
Dept Phone: 837-5083
Homepage: business.ubalt.edu/areas/acct
Baltimore, MD 21201-5779
Merrick Sch of Business
1420 North Charles Street
(410) Fax=837-5722 ß 1983,1989
ubalt.edu
BS,MST,MS
Cindy Tannebaum

Name	Rank	Phone	Email		Degree	Yr	School	
Zacur, Susan Rawson	Dean	837-4955	szacur	Mgt	PHD	74	Maryland	1975
Korb, Phillip J.	C-Ac	837-5080	pkorb	XVF	MBA	75	Maryland	&1976
Lynn, Susan A.	Assoc	837-5099	slynn	FBE	DBA	82.	Maryland	& 1-89
Sigler, John N.	Assoc	837-5107	jsigler	LXFS	JD	76	Maryland	&1970
Vermeer, Thomas E.	Assoc	837-5114	tvermeer	AFNS	PHD	98.	North Tx	&2000
Ernst & Young Distinguished Professor								
White, Lourdes Ferreira	Assoc	837-5090	lwhite	MBC	DBA	89.	Harvard	9-92
Williams, Jan L.	Asst	837-6593	jwilliams	EF	PHD	06	MorganSt	&2006

Barry University
Accounting Faculty
Dept Phone: 899-3500
Homepage: www.barry.edu/business
Miami Shores, FL 33161-6695
Andreas Sch of Business
11300 NE 2nd Ave
(305) Fax=892-6412
mail.barry.edu
2003,2003
BS,MBA,MSA

Name	Rank	Phone	Email		Degree	Yr	School	
Scarborough, Jack W.	Dean	899-3534	jscarborough	Mgt	PHD	88	Maryland	8-89
Broihahn, Michael A.	C-Ac	899-3506	mbroihahn	FAJ	MBA	73	Wisconsin	# * &8-88
Hudack, Lawrence R.	Prof	899-3528	lhudack	FNXG	PHD	89.	North Tx	* &8-98
McGee, Robert W.	Prof	899-3525	rmcgee	FJI	PHD	86	Warwick	# * &8-02
Tyler, Michael	Prof	899-3521	mtyler	FMT	PHD	95	Fla Intl	1-94

Barton College　Wilson, NC　27893-7000　(252) Fax=399-6571
Accounting Faculty　School of Business　barton.edu　BS
Dept Phone: 399-6418　400 Acc Drive NE　Nikita Allen
Bethune, John J.　Dean　399-6422　jbethune　Econ　PHD　87　Fla St　9-00
　Kennedy Chair in Business
Burrus, Patricia　Asst　399-6426　pburrus　FGVX　MBA　81　E Carol　& 8-94
Corbett, Rena　Asst　399-6419　rcorbett　FACM　MBA　94　N Carol　& 8-01

Baylor University　Waco, TX　76798-8002　(254) Fax=710-1067　ß (13) 1950,1969
Dept Atg & B Law- Box 98002　Hankamer Sch Business　baylor.edu　BBA,MT,MACC
Dept Phone: 710-3536　One Bear Place #98002　Shelly R. Herzog
Homepage: http://hsb.baylor.edu/acc/default.asp
Maness, Terry S.　Dean　710-1211　terry_maness　Fnce　DBA　76　Indiana　1977
Davis, Charles E.　C-Ac　710-6138　charles_davis　SMB　PHD　91.　N Carol　&1991
　Walter Plumhoff Professor of Accounting
Baldwin, Jane N.　Prof　710-6180　jane_baldwin　F　PHD　85.　Arkansas　&1986
　Ernst & Young Teaching Fellow
Davis, Elizabeth B.　Prof　710-4772　elizabeth_davis　MA　PHD　92.　Duke　&1992
Erickson, Paul R.　Prof　710-6171　paul_erickson　XL　JD　81　Idaho　&1981
　R. E. and Marilyn Reamer Professor of Accounting
Robinson, Michael A.　Prof　710-6129　michael_robinson　CM　PHD　81.　Illinois　1991
Thomas, C. William　Prof　710-4924　bill_thomas　A　PHD　78.　Tx-Austin　& 6-71
　J.E. Bush Professor of Accounting; KPMG-Thomas L. Holton Chair of Accounting
Cassell, Michael N.　Assoc　710-6133　mike_cassell　FG　PHD　76.　Georgia　9-80
Hurtt, David N.　Assoc　710-1327　david_hurtt　F　PHD　98.　Tx A&M　&2005
Stanley, Charles W.　Assoc　710-6228　charles_stanley　SA　PHD　84.　Okla St　& 1-83
Chevis, Gia　Asst　710-1328　gia_chevis　MFI　PHD　03.　Tx A&M　8-05
Ford, Caroline O.　Asst　710-1495　carie_ford　AB　PHD　06.　Tx Tech　2007
Hurtt, R. Kathy　Asst　710-4788　kathy_hurtt　S　PHD　99.　Utah　&2004
Kobelsky, Kevin　Asst　710-1155　kevin_kobelsky　SMDA　PHD　00　Ca-Irvine　&2004
MacGregor, Jason E.　Asst　　　A　PHD　07　Florida　2007
Stuebs, Martin T. Jr.　Asst　710-1329　marty_stuebs　JM　PHD　05.　Arkansas　2005
Wilkinson, Brett R.　Asst　710-6161　brett_wilkinson　X　PHD　02.　Tx Tech　9-02
　Roderick L. Holmes Chair of Accountancy
Abbe, Suzanne C.　Lect　710-4765　suzanne_abbe　P　MBA　　Baylor　1987
Bryant, Scott M.　Lect　710-7678　scott_m_bryant　P　MACC　03　Baylor　2003
Jones, Becky　Lect　710-4956　becky_jones　P　MBA　78　Baylor　& 8-78
Miller, Helen J.　Lect　710-6126　helen_miller　P　MBA　72　Baylor　& 8-73
Willis, Betsy　Lect　710-6132　betsy_willis　PX　MTAX　87　Baylor　&1983

Belhaven College　Jackson, MS　39202-1789　(601) Fax=968-8951
Accounting Faculty　School of Business Adm　belhaven.edu　BS
Dept Phone: 968-8945　1500 Peachtree St Box 310　Sarah Jo. Steffens
Homepage: www.belhaven.edu
Mason, Ralph A. (Chip)　Dean　968-8945　cmason　　PHD　　N Carol　1995
Goldsmith, Geoffrey　Assoc　968-8723　ggoldsmith　NPT　PHD　96.　Kent St　1993

Bellarmine University　Louisville, KY　40205　(502) Fax=452-8013　2004,2004
Department of Accounting　W. Fielding Rubel Sch　bellarmine.edu　BA
Dept Phone: 452-8240　2001 Newburg Road　Carol Huff
Bauer, Daniel L.　Dean　452-8026　dbauer　Fnce　PHD　96　Miss St　8-95
Richardson, Keith W.　C-Ac　452-8403　krichardson　PFB　PHD　95.　Oregon　& 8-97
Collins, David T.　Assoc　452-8248　dcollins　FIS　PHD　93.　Geo St　& 8-94
Deck, Alan B.　Assoc　452-8246　adeck　CFP　PHD　84.　Alabama　& 8-98
Schrader, Richard W.　Assoc　452-8443　rschrader　FGV　PHD　93.　Fla St　#　& 8-99
Selvy, Patricia M.　Assoc　452-8243　pselvy　FA　PHD　91　Geo St　& 8-86
Carver, Patricia　Inst　452-8165　pcarver　P　MBA　00　Bellarm　& 8-02

Bellevue University　Bellevue, NE　68005-3098　(402) Fax=293-3819
Accounting Area　College of Business　scholars.bellevue.edu　BS,BA,BBA,MBA
Dept Phone: 293-2001　1000 Galvin Rd South　Cynthia Payne 293-2001
McDaniel, Donna　Dean　557-7125　donna.mcdaniel　　JD　82　Creighton　1998
Dinville, Pamela　C-Ac　557-7561　pam.dinville　VA　MBA　83　NW Mo St　* &1985
McElhaney, Monica　Assoc　557-7562　monica.mcelhaney　TFSC　MBA　　95
Northeas　*　&　　　　　　8-96
Nye, Cynthia　Assoc　557-7563　cynthia.nye　MC　MS　84　S Calif　* &1995
Spivck, Dara　Asst　　dara.spivack　XGN　MPA　95　N Orleans　&1990

Belmont University　Nashville, TN　37212-3757　(615) Fax=460-6455　(13) 2001,2001
Accounting Faculty　Massey School Business　mail.belmont.edu　BS,MBA,MACC
Dept Phone: 460-6480　1900 Belmont Blvd　Linda Jenkins
Raines, J. Patrick　Dean　460-6422　rainesp　Econ　PHD　83　Alabama　2003
Finley, Jane B.　C-Ac　460-6478　finleyj　SM　PHD　95　Fla St　&1995
Childs, Bradley D.　Assoc　460-6485　childsb　FX　PHD　94.　Purdue　&2001

Coker, John W.	Assoc	460-6784	cokerj	PFC	PHD	90.	Miss	&1991
Dillard-Eggers, Jane	Assoc	460-6311	eggersj	FP	PHD	95.	Alabama	&1998
Warren, D. Lee	Assoc	460-6309	warrenl	MP	PHD	95.	Georgia	&1998
Wooten, Thomas C.	Assoc	460-6484	wootent	AP	PHD	94.	Geo St	&1994
Young, Marilyn N.	Assoc	460-5551	youngm	PX	PHD	00.	Miss	&2001
DeVries, Delwyn D.	Asst	460-6400	devriesd	SM	PHD	01.	Ariz St	&2007

Bemidji State University — Bemidji, MN 56601-2699 — (218) Fax=755-4100
Department of Accounting — Professional Studies — bemidjistate.edu — BS
Dept Phone: 755-2907 — 1500 Birchmont Drive NE — Lori Deering
Homepage: bemidjistate.edu/accounting

Nielsen, Carol	Dean	755-3732	cnielsen		JD		Wm Mitch	&1985
Bland, Sandra	C-Pr	755-3716	sbland	XPS	PHD	02	E Illinois	&1992
Gardner, George F.	Prof	755-3713	ggardner	GPVR	MBA		Minnesota	&1989
Mayer, Richard D.	Prof	755-3710	rmayer	CPMR	MBA		Iowa	&1981
Wick, Madalyn	Prof	755-3711	mwick	FP	PHD	93.	Nebraska	&1984
Massuglia, David	Asst	755-2906	dmassuglia	PAM	MBA		St Thomas	&2006

Benedict College — Columbia, SC 29204 — (803) Fax=
Department of Accounting — School of Bus & Econ — benedict.edu — BS
Dept Phone: 253-5187 — Harden & Blanding St — Ms. Fowler
Homepage: www.benedict.edu

Jackson, Peter	Dean	252-5212						
Mahdi, Syed I.	C-Pr$	253-5187	mahdis	Econ	PHD	76	Mass	1975
Gbenedio, Pender	Prof	253-5070	gbenediop	FIS	PHD	77	Cincinnati	1999
Alino, Nelson	Inst	253-5185		IF	MBA	98	Nigeria	&2002
Booth-Bell, Darlene	Inst	758-4492		M	MPM	95	Car Mellon	2000

Benedictine College — Atchison, KS 66002-1499 — (913) Fax=360-7301
Accounting Faculty — Dp Atg & Bus Adm & Entr — benedictine.edu — BA,MBA
Dept Phone: 360-7426 — 1020 North 2nd Street — Donna Bonnel
Homepage: benedictine.edu/business

Hoy, Donald A.	C	360-7425	dhoy	L	JD	66	Iowa	1999
Franklin, Paul	Asst	360-7426		S	MS	93	Mo-Ks Cty	&2003
Glenski, Christine	Asst	360-7426	cglenski	X	MS	93	Tx-Austin	* 2003
McClaflin, John	Inst	360-7486			EMBA	01	Benedict	&2002

Benedictine University — Lisle, IL 60532-0900 — (630) Fax=829-6226
Undergrad Business Dept — College of Business — ben.edu — BBA
Dept Phone: 829-6225 — 5700 College Road
Homepage: www.ben.edu

Gill, Sandra	Dean	829-6216	sgill		PHD			
Gahala, Charles	C-Pr	829-6471	cgahala	Fnce	EDD	83	N Illinois	8-84
Madura, Jeffrey M.	Prof	829-6467	jmadura		MBA	71	Nrthwstrn	&1971
Dibblee, David A.	Assoc	829-6469	ddibblee		MBA	79	N Illinois	&1982
Henschel, Don	Inst	829-6477	dhenschel		MBA		Chicago	& 9-02

Bentley College — Waltham, MA 02452-4705 — (781) Fax=891-2896 — ß (123) 1989,1989
Department of Accountancy — College of Business — bentley.edu — BSA,MBA,MSA
Dept Phone: 891-2134 — 175 Forest Street — Florence Jones
Homepage: www.bentley.edu

Olson, Margrethe E.	Dean	891-2921	molson	Sys	PHD	78	Minnesota	2002
Nixon, Mark R.	C-Ac	891-2087	mnixon	X	PHD	95.	Tx A&M	&1993
Abdolmohammadi, Mohammad	Prof	891-2976	mabdolmo	AMST	DBA	82.	Indiana	&1988
John E. Rhodes Chair in Accountancy								
Bedard, Jean C.	Prof	891-2410	jbedard	AF	PHD	85.	Wisconsin	&2005
Burnaby, Priscilla A.	Prof	891-2519	pburnaby	FO	PHD	82.	Tx A&M	&1976
Fedorowicz, Jane	Prof	891-3153	jfedorowicz	DS	PHD	81	Car Mellon	1994
Rae D. Anderson Chair in Accounting & Information Systems								
Gelinas, Ulric J. Jr. (Joe)	Prof	891-2264	ugelinas	SAO	PHD	78.	Mass	1981
Gujarathi, Mahendra R.	Prof	891-3408	mgujarathi	MFI	PHD	81	India	&1989
Hunton, James E.	Prof	891-2422	jhunton	SAB	PHD	94.	Tx-Arlin	&2002
Trustee Professor of Accounting								
Read, William J.	Prof	891-2525	wread	FA	PHD	84.	Va Tech	&1984
Schlorff, H. Lee	Prof	891-2661	hschlorff	FAE	PHD	73.	Missouri	1978
Cross, Richard L.	Assoc	891-2933	rcross	RFCV	MBA	72	Northeas	&1969
Earley, Christine E.	Assoc	891-2439	cearley	A	PHD	98.	Pittsburgh	2005
Feldmann, Dorothy A.	Assoc	891-2782	dfeldmann	F	DBA	92.	Boston U	&1991
Haselkorn, Michael	Assoc	891-2521	mhaselkorn	MF	PHD		Chicago	1974
Klein, Lawrence A.	Assoc	891-2776	lklein	MEUA	PHD	78.	Penn St	1984
Levy, Elliott S.	Assoc	891-2712	elevy	FAEP	MA	78	Florida	# * &1980
MacIver, Brian H.	Assoc	891-2510	bmaciver	FA	EDD		Mass	&1975

McQuade, Ralph J. Jr.	Assoc	891-2523	rmcquade	FTXE	MBA	72	Babson		&1975
Thibodeau, Jay C.	Assoc	891-2564	jthibodeau	A	PHD	97.	Conn		&1996
Baxter, Ryan	Asst		rbaxter	S	PHD	07	Case Wes		8-07
Boss, Scott	Asst		sboss	S	PHD	07	Pittsburgh		8-07
Hoitash, Rani	Asst		rhoitash	AS	PHD	03.	Rutgers	#	8-07
Malgwi, Charles	Asst	891-2774	cmalgwi	FMLI	PHD	93	Reading		1999
Noga, Tracy J.	Asst	891-2432	tnoga	X	PHD	01.	Tx Tech		&2005
Schwarzkopf, David L.	Asst	891-2783	dschwarzkopf	BFMA	PHD	02.	Conn		&1991
Howe, Martha	SLect	891-2573	mhowe	F	PHD	99.	Conn		1995
Levesque, Raymond J.	SLect	891-3486	rlevesque	XF	MST	78	Bentley		&1983
Nolder, Christine	Inst	891-2470	cnolder	F	MBA	01	Bentley		&2005
Osterheld, Karen	SLect	891-2724	kosterheld	FS	MBA	78	Wisconsin		&1990
Reed, Arthur E.	Inst	891-2919	areed	X	MST	85	Bentley		&1989

Berea College　Berea, KY　40404　(859) Fax=985-3906
Accounting Faculty　Dept of Econ & Business　berea.edu　　　　BS
Dept Phone: 985-3138　Chestnut Street　　　　Becky Grandgeorge
Homepage: www.berea.edu

Browner, Stephanie	Dean	985-3800	stephanie_brow+		PHD	94	Indiana		1994
Isaacs, Patricia	C-Pr	985-3174	trish_isaacs	EFJX	PHD	94.	Kentucky		&1989
McCormack, G. Edward	Prof	985-3175	ed_mccormack	AMD	MBA	88	Estrn Ky		&1986
Tolliver, R. Wayne	Assoc	985-3147	wayne_tolliver	FT	DBA	87	Kentucky		1976

Berry College　Mount Berry, GA　30149-5024　(706) Fax=238-7854　　2006
Accounting Faculty　Campbell School of Bus　berry.edu　　　BS,MBA
Dept Phone: 238-7908　2277 Martha Berry Hwy., NW　　　Lynda Eden

Grout, John	Dean	236-2233	jgrout	Mgt	PHD	90	Penn St		8-97
Bible, Lynn	Assoc	238-7908	lbible	FB	PHD	99.	Conn		& 8-05
Biggart, Timothy B.	Assoc	238-7908	tbiggart	CMS	PHD	97.	Fla St		8-05
Carnes, Thomas A.	Assoc	238-7908	tcarnes	F	PHD	97.	Fla St		& 8-05

Bethel College　Mishawaka, IN　46545-5591　(574) Fax=257-7617
Department of Business　School of Bus & Soc Sci　bethelcollege.edu　　BA
Dept Phone: 257-3488　1001 West McKinley Ave.　　　Mrs. Patsy Fish
Homepage: http://www.bethelcollege.edu/academics/undergra/business

Spivey, Norm	D	257-3420	spiveyn	EdPs	PHD	94	N Colo		1988
Jarusewic, Margaret	C-Ac	257-3488	jarusep	AFMX	MBA	89	Ind-S Bn		& 8-81

Bethune-Cookman College　Daytona Bch, FL　32115-3099　(386) Fax=481-2802
Accounting Area　School of Business　cookman.edu　　　BS
Dept Phone: 481-2800　640 Mary McLeod Bethune Blvd　　Mrs. Tijuana Orr-Anthony
Homepage: www.cookman.edu

Long, Aubrey E.	Dean	481-2800	longa	Bus	PHD	80	Ohio St		1988
Feimson, Carla	Asst	481-2876	feimsonc	XA	MBA	79	Pace		&2001
Forbes, Renee	Asst	481-2818	forbesr		PHD		Sarasota		2005
Cameron, Alan M.	SLect	463-5758	alan.cameron	LT	LLM	84	Victoria		1975
Fink, Calvin	Inst	481-2814	finkc	FMC	MBA	83	N Fla		2004

Biola University　LaMirada, CA　90639-0001　(562) Fax=906-4545
Accounting Faculty　School of Business　bubbs.biola.edu　　　BS
Dept Phone: 903-4770　13800 Biola Avenue　　　Tori Finley
Homepage: www.biola.edu/business

Strand, Larry D.	Dean	903-4770	larry.strand	Mgt	EDD	06	Pepperdi		1986
Woodward, Philip L.	Assoc	903-4770	phil.woodward	MPVX	MBT	81	S Calif		1990

Birmingham-Southern College　Birmingham AL　35254　(205) Fax=226-3080　2002,2002
Accounting Faculty　Dept of Business & Atg　bsc.edu　　　BS,MAC
Dept Phone: 226-4846　900 Arkadelphia Road　　　Nancy Parsons

Craft, Stephen	C-As			Mktg	PHD				2004
Stunda, Ronald A.	D-Ac	226-4826	rstunda	FXC	PHD	96.	Fla St	*	&1995
Klersey, George F.	Assoc	226-4809	gklersey	AFT	PHD	90.	S Calif		&1995

　EBSCO Professor of Accounting; on leave

Sudderth, Tara N.	Assoc	226-4817	tsuddert	FLX	PHD	99.	Miss	*	&1998

　Donald C. Brakston Professor of Accounting

Bloomsburg University　Bloomsburg, PA　17815-1301　(570) Fax=389-4912　2004,2004
Department of Accounting　College of Business　bloomu.edu　　BS,MBA,MAC
Dept Phone: 389-4755　400 East Second Street　　　Mrs. Veronica Breisch
Homepage: www.bloomu.edu

Martin, David G.	Dean	389-4019	dmarti2	Fnce	PHD	91	St Louis		2006
Baker, Richard L.	C-Pr	389-4561	rbaker	NFV	PHD	84.	Penn St	# *	&1987
Bealing, William E. Jr.	Prof	389-4386	wbealing	FV	PHD	91.	Penn St		&1999
Coulmas, Nancy E.	Prof	389-4755	ncoulmas	CPFM	PHD	89.	Penn St		1994

Hwang, Dennis	Prof	389-4817	hwang	FI	PHD	84	Oklahoma	* &1989
Shapeero, Mike P.	Prof	389-4913	mshapeer	ABPJ	PHD	96.	Va Tech	* &1997
Robson, Gary S.	Assoc	389-4519	gsrobson	CDFM	PHD	90.	Arizona	&2006
Rude, John A.	Assoc	389-4520	jrude	GITV	PHD	90.	Kent St	&1997
Russo, Charles J.	Assoc	389-4393	crusso	BX	PHD	02	Penn St	2003
Staley, Andrew B.	Assoc	389-4392	astaley	DFX	DBA	97	Nova SE	2003

Bluefield State College — Bluefield, WV 24701-2198 — (304) Fax=327-4571
Accounting Faculty — School of Business — bluefieldstate.edu — BSBA,BSACCT
Dept Phone: 327-4081 — 219 Rock Street

Halsey-Hunter, Deb	Dean	327-4081	dhunter		EDD	96	Va Tech	1984
Scott, Elaine D.	Dean	327-4317	escott	Econ	PHD	82	Purdue	2004
Goodman, William D.	Assoc	327-4107	wgoodman	CGNS	MA	77	Appalach	& 8-87

Bluffton University — Bluffton, OH 45817-1196 — (419) Fax=358-3074
Accounting Faculty — Dept of Econ, Bus & Atg — bluffton.edu — BA
Dept Phone: 358-3302 — 1 University Drive
Homepage: www.bluffton.edu/Dept/EBA

Lehman, George A.	C-Pr	358-3302	lehmang		EDM	00	Case Wes	1994
Young, Roger D.	Prof	358-3447	youngr		MBA	64	Xavier	&2001
Swartzlander, Jason	Asst		swartzlanderj		MBA	05	Tiffin	

Boise State University — Boise, ID 83725-1610 — (208) Fax=426-3637 — ß (123) 1979,1985
Department of Accountancy — College Business & Econ — boisestate.edu — BA,BBA,MS,MBA
Dept Phone: 426-3461 — 1910 University Drive — Pam Sorensen
Homepage: ac.boisestate.edu/

Smith, Howard L.	Dean	426-2321	hsmith	Mgt	PHD	76	U Wash	6-06
English, Denise M.	C-Pr	426-1322	denglish	FAEO	PHD	88.	Indiana	# & 1-88
Bahnson, Paul R.	Prof	426-2190	pbahnson	FTV	PHD	87.	Utah	&1999
English, Thomas J.	Prof	426-1261	tenglish	AOR	PHD	88.	Ariz St	& 9-87
Koeppen, David R.	Prof	426-3841	dkoeppen	FTVM	PHD	83.	Wisconsin	& 9-86
Lathen, William C.	Prof	426-1236	blathen	XE	PHD	82.	Ariz St	& 9-84
Krumwiede, Kip R.	Assoc	426-2288	kipkrumwiede	CM	PHD	96.	Tennessee	* &2003
Novak, E. Shawn	Assoc	426-1238	snovak	PXR	PHD	91.	Houston	& 9-96
Renner, Celia J.	Assoc	426-3461	crenner	SCM	PHD	95.	Colorado	&2002
Cowan, Mark	Asst	426-1565	mcowan	XL	JD	04	Conn	&2004
Christensen, Fred	Lect	426-1472	fchriste	PGAF	MBA	81	Utah	& 1-84
Ilett, Frank	Lect	426-1322	filett	PSC	MBA	69	Chicago	& 9-94
Shannon, Susan S.	Lect	426-1271	sshannon	PX	MBA	85	Boise St	&1985

Boston College — Chestnut Hl, MA 02467-3808 — (617) Fax=552-6345 — 1956,1975
Department of Accounting — Carroll Sch of Mgt — bc.edu — BS,MBA,MSA
Dept Phone: 552-3940 — 140 Commonwealth Avenue — Maureen Chancey

Boynton, Andrew C.	Dean	552-3925		Mis	PHD	87	N Carol	2004
Soo, Billy S.	C-Ac	552-3963	billy.soo	AFK	PHD	91.	Nrthwstrn	1990
O'Reilly, Vin	Exec	552-1933	oreillyv	HJI	MBA	59	Penn	&1997
Wilson, G. Peter	Prof	552-1963	wilsongp	FTE	PHD	85.	Car Mellon	1997
Joseph E. Sweeney Chair in Accounting								
Cohen, Jeffrey R.	Assoc	552-3165	cohen	BJIE	PHD	87.	Mass	* 1986
Corsini, Louis S.	Assoc	552-3951	corsini	FI	PHD	72.	LSU	&1971
Hammond, Theresa A.	Assoc	552-4525	hammonth	BWJE	PHD	90.	Wisconsin	* 1990
Ernst and Young Research Fellow in Diversity Studies								
Hutton, Amy P.	Assoc	552-1951	amy.hutton	F	PHD	92.	Rochester	2006
Manzon, Gil B. Jr.	Assoc	552-4637	manzong	FX	DBA	90.	Boston U	1989
Pawliczek, Ronald B.	Assoc	552-3948	pawlicze	FE	PHD	75.	Mass	1974
Schwartz, Kenneth B.	Assoc	552-3942	schwartk	FTK	PHD	82.	Syracuse	1986
Shu, Susan Z.	Assoc	552-1759	susan.shu	AKF	PHD	00.	Rochester	1999
Trompeter, Gregory M.	Assoc	552-0878	trompete	AEBF	PHD	88.	Wisconsin	* &1992
Brown, Helen	Asst	552-1632	helen.brown.2	ASF	PHD	03.	Wisconsin	2004
Roberts, Andrea Alston	Asst	552-1448	robertaf	FN	PHD	00.	Geo Wash	&1999
Zamora, Valentina L.	Asst	552-2240	zamorav	FM	PHD	03.	U Wash	2003
Bagnani, Betty S.	Lect	552-3994	elizabeth.bag+	F	PHD	86	Mass	2004
LaCombe, Amy	Lect	552-6827	lacombea	FS	MBA	00	Boston C	2001
Taylor, Ed	Lect	552-2302	taylored	FMX	MST	93	Bentley	1986

Boston University — Boston, MA 02215 — (617) Fax=353-6667 — ß 1921,1965
Department of Accounting — School of Management — bu.edu — BS,MBA,DBA
Dept Phone: 353-4613 — 595 Commonwealth Ave — Jeffrey Harrington

Lataif, Louis E.	Dean	353-2668	lelataif	Mgt	MBA	64	Harvard	9-91
Kirby Jones, Alison J.	C-Ac	353-2029	kirby	MC	PHD	86.	Stanford	7-94
Hagigi, Moshe	Prof	353-3374	mhagigi	FIVX	PHD	81	NYU	9-88
Menon, Krishnagopal	Prof	353-2661	kmenon	FM	PHD	82.	Penn St	9-82

Sivakumar, Kumar N.	Assoc	353-2035	kns	FH	PHD	89.	Rice	9-01
Smith, Michael J.	Assoc	353-6673	msmith22	FM	PHD	98.	Stanford	9-04
Albuquerque, Ana Maria	Asst	358-4185	albuquea	FM	PHD	06.	Rochester	9-05
Huang, Wenli	Asst	353-4985	wlhuang	FM	PHD	05.	Berkeley	9-05
Papadakis, George	Asst			F	PHD	07	MIT	9-07
Sinha, Nishi	Asst	353-2927	nishi	FM	PHD	94.	Purdue	9-01
Wu, Eng C.	Asst	358-4207	engwu	FCM	DBA	96.	Boston U	9-05
Doherty, Patricia A.	Inst	353-4415	pdoherty	FME	MS	77	Bentley	9-94

Bowling Green State Univ Bowling Gr, OH 43403-0262 (419) Fax=372-2875 ß (1) 1954,1966
Dept of Accounting & MIS College of Business cba.bgsu.edu BS,MAC
Dept Phone: 372-2767 East Wooster Street Cathy Smith
Homepage: www.cba.bgsu.edu/amis

Rogers, Rodney K.	Dean	372-2747	rrogers	FHS	PHD	95	Case Wes	& 7-06
Kowalski, Lawrence W.	C-As	372-2803	lwkowal	X	JD	75	Toledo	1978
Lord, Alan T.	Prof	372-8045	alord	ABS	PHD	89.	Case Wes	&1995
Ernst & Young Professor of Accounting								
Albrecht, W. David	Assoc	372-8016		FKA	PHD	91.	Va Tech	&1990
email: albrecht@profalbrecht.com								
Eckel, Norman L.	Assoc	372-8376	neckel	MCU	PHD	82,	W Ontario	1979
Essex, Patricia A.	Assoc	372-6073	pessex	MS	PHD	93.	Mich St	* &1993
Nicolaou, Andreas I.	Assoc	372-2767	anicol	MS	DBA	93.	S Illinois	&2000
Schauer, Paul C.	Assoc	372-2939	schauer	AFS	PHD	99.	Temple	&1999
Snead, Kenneth C.	Assoc	372-8160	ksnead	MB	PHD	88.	S Carol	1988
Stott, David	Assoc	372-2709	dstott	AF	PHD	00.	Wash St	&1999
Bajor, Lawrence H.	Asst	372-8074	bajorl	X	PHD	02.	Mich St	2001
Garcia, Andy	Asst	372-7812	garcia	FA	PHD	05.	Tx Tech	2005
Burba, David	Inst	372-2710	dburba	P	MBA	90	Toledo	
Rohrs, Brian	Inst	372-8313	brohrs	P	MBA	97	Indiana	&1998
Schurrer, Phillip	Inst	372-8046	pschurr	P	MBA	98	Toledo	8-03
Zeigler, James F.	Inst	372-2092	jzeigle	P	MBA	84	Toledo	&2001

Bradley University Peoria, IL 61625-0328 (309) Fax=677-3374 ß (123) 1978,1983
Department of Accounting Foster Coll of Bus Adm bradley.edu BS,BA,MSA
Dept Phone: 677-2288 1501 W. Bradley Ave Sue Tomsovic 677-2288
Homepage: http://www.bradley.edu/fcba/atg/

Baer, Robert B.	Dean	677-2255	rbb	SocP	PHD	81	Miami U	8-84
Gillett, John W.	C-Pr	677-2290	jwg	FTV	PHD	83.	North Tx	& 8-93
Krull, George W. Jr.	Prof	677-2289	gkrull	AFS	PHD	71.	Mich St	& 1-01
Executive in Residence								
Raiborn, Mitchell H.	Prof	677-2293	mhr	FM	PHD	70.	Missouri	* & 8-81
Petravick, Simon P.	Assoc	677-2286	simonp	AS	PHD	94	Il-Chicago	& 8-94
Troutman, Coleen S.	Assoc	677-3397	coleen	FX	PHD	93.	Okla St	& 8-92
Kerr, Stephen G.	Asst	677-2283	skerr	M	PHD	00	Alberta	* 8-07
Wilcox, William E.	Asst	677-2284	wwilcox	FTV	PHD	97.	Nebraska	& 8-99
Johnson, Shondra	Inst	677-2717	sljohnson	FMS	MPA	93	Tx-Austin	& 8-04
Wayron, Paul W.	Inst	677-2292	pwayron	FMJ	MBA	92	Mich St	& 1-04

Brescia University Owensboro, KY 42301-3023 (270) Fax=686-4266
Accounting Faculty Wm. Thompson Sch of Bus brescia.edu BS,MS
Dept Phone: 685-3131 717 Frederica Street Nancy Rhodes
Homepage: www.brescia.edu

Garvin, Jim	C-Ac	686-4310	james.garvin	QJ	ABD	75	Ohio St	&1985
Smith, S. Duane	Prof	686-4311	duanes	AFGM	PHD	91.	Tx A&M	* &2001
Payne, Ronald	Asst	686-4274	ron.payne		MS		Tulsa	2003

Briar Cliff University Sioux City, IA 51104-2100 (712) Fax=279-1698
Accounting Faculty Div Atg, Bus Adm & HR briarcliff.edu BA
Dept Phone: 279-5552 3303 Rebecca St
Frangedakis, George	C-Ac	279-1626	george.frang+	Econ	ABD		Nebraska	
Sorathia, Vali M.	Assoc	279-5552	sorathia	CGVX	ABD	72	Indiana	1974
Cornelsen, Erin	Asst	279-1626	erin.cornelsen		MPA		Nebraska	&

University of Bridgeport Bridgeport, CT 06601-2449 (203) Fax=576-4388
Department of Accounting School of Business bridgeport.edu BS
Dept Phone: 576-4384 230 Park Avenue Angela Pulley
Forgotson, Merrill Jay	Dean	576-4385	mforgots		JD	70	Boston U	2006
Kohn, S. David	C-Ac	576-4380	dskohn9021@a		PHD	95	NYU	&2002
Maron, Matthew	Asst	576-4008	mmaron	X	MS	97	NewHamp	2004

Bridgewater State College

Dept of Accounting & Finance	School of Management		bridgew.edu			BS,MA
Dept Phone: 531-1395	Harrington Hall					Stephanie Chaves
Morgan, Catherine L.	Dean			PHD		
Bancroft, Patricia C.	C-Ac	531-2477	pbancroft	FLX	DBA	& 9-98
Donchess, Carleton M.	Prof	531-1395	cdonchess		MSA	* 9-84
Sevigny, Kathleen	Prof	531-1395	ksevigny	CFTA	MBA	# * 1-83
Silverman, Harold	Prof	531-1395	hsilverman	FLX	LLM	& 8-83
Donovan, Shannon	Assoc	531-2684	s1donovan	M	PHD	

Bridgewater, MA 02325 (508) Fax=531-1121

Brigham Young University

Provo, UT 84602-3068 (801) Fax=422-0621 ß (123) 1963,1971

School of Accountancy	Marriott School of Mgt		byu.edu				BS,MACC
Dept Phone: 422-4195	540 N Eldon Tanner Bldg						Erin Bailey
Homepage: http://marriottschool.byu.edu/soa/							
Hill, Ned C.	Dean	422-6821	ned_hill	Fnce	PHD	76 Cornell	5-87
Joel C. Peterson Professor of Business Administration							
Stocks, Kevin D.	D-Pr	422-4613	kevin_stocks	MC	PHD	81 Okla St	& 6-83
Steve Albrecht Professor							
Albrecht, W. Steve	Prof	422-3154	steve_albrecht	FA	PHD	75 Wisconsin	# & 6-77
Arthur Andersen Professor							
Cottrell, David M.	Prof	422-3268	david_cottrell	FA	PHD	92 Ohio St	9-92
Gardner, Robert L.	Prof	422-3212	robert_gardner	X	PHD	79 Tx-Austin	9-79
Robert J. Smith Professor							
Glover, Steven M.	Prof	422-6080	steve_glover	FAB	PHD	94 U Wash	9-94
PricewaterhouseCoopers Research Fellow							
Nemrow, Norman R.	Prof	422-3029	norman_nemrow	F	MACC	79 Brighm Yg	9-92
Prawitt, Douglas F.	Prof	422-2351	douglas_prawitt	AB	PHD	93 Arizona	& 1-93
Warnick/Deloitte & Touche Research Fellow							
Radebaugh, Lee H.	Prof	422-4368	radebaugh	IFM	DBA	73 Indiana	9-80
KPMG Professor							
Randall, Boyd C.	Prof	422-2314	boyd_randall	X	PHD	72 Minnesota	9-74
Ernst & Young Professor							
Skousen, K. Fred	Prof	422-2640	kfs	F	PHD	68 Illinois	& 9-70
Vice President							
Spilker, Brian C.	Prof	422-4644	brian_spilker	XB	PHD	93 Tx-Austin	& 6-93
Glen Ardis Research Fellow							
Stewart, Dave N.	Prof	422-2365	dave_stewart	X	PHD	80 Florida	& 9-80
Rachel Martin Professor							
Stice, Earl K.	Prof	422-4176	eks	F	PHD	88 Cornell	9-98
PricewaterhouseCoopers Professor							
Stice, James D.	Prof	422-2455	jds	F	PHD	89 U Wash	9-88
Distinguished Professor							
Swain, Monte R.	Prof	422-3174	monte_swain	MSB	PHD	92 Mich St	* & 9-91
Deloitte & Touche Research Fellow							
Barrick, John A.	Assoc	422-9128	john_barrick	X	PHD	98 Nebraska	& 6-00
Black, Ervin L.	Assoc	422-1767	erv_black	F	PHD	95 U Wash	9-00
Budd, Cassy JH	Assoc	422-5012	cassybudd	FAX	MACC	02 Utah St	&2005
Burton, F. Greg	Assoc	422-8767	fgb	M	PHD	94 S Carol	& 7-01
Deloitte & Touche Research Fellow							
Christensen, Theodore E.	Assoc	422-1768	ted_christensen	M	PHD	95 Georgia	& 9-00
Hobson, L. Scott	Assoc	422-8196	shobson	FM	MACC	83 Brighm Yg	& 6-03
Summers, Scott L.	Assoc	422-9790	scott_summers	S	PHD	95 Tx A&M	6-99
Wilks, T. Jeffrey	Assoc	422-1728	jeff_wilks	F	PHD	00 Cornell	9-00
on leave until 9/08							
Worsham, Ronald G. Jr.	Assoc	422-2329	ron_worsham	X	PHD	94 Florida	1-94
LeAnn Albrecht Fellow							
Zimbelman, Mark F.	Assoc	422-1227	mz	A	PHD	96 Arizona	8-99
Selvoy J. Boyer Research Fellow							
Charles, Shannon	Asst	422-1877	shannon_charles	MF	PHD	00 Okla St	2001
Heninger, William G.	Asst	422-6899	heninger	S	PHD	97 Georgia	& 7-01
Johnson, Peter M.	Asst	422-3827	peter_johnson	FAM	PHD	03 Ariz St	& 7-02
Paik, Gyung H.	Asst	422-1969	paik	M	PHD	01 Illinois	1-01
Peterson, Fredric G.	Asst	422-3460	fredric_peterson	Q	PHD	73 Utah	9-75

Brigham Young University

Provo, UT 84602-3068 (801) Fax=

Information Systems	Marriott School of Mgt		byu.edu				
Dept Phone: 422-3247							Leesa Scott
Romney, Marshall B.	C-Pr	422-5704	marshall_romney	2006	PHD	77 Tx-Austin	& 9-77
John & Nancy Hardy Professor							
Hansen, James V.	Prof	422-2308	james_hansen	S	PHD	73 U Wash	9-82
McKell, Lynn J.	Prof	422-3834	lynn_mckell	SQMD	PHD	73 Purdue	8-74
Dean, Douglas L.	Assoc	422-1224	doug_dean	S	PHD	85 Arizona	6-99
David & Knight Research Fellow							
Hansen, Gary W.	Assoc	422-3880	gary_hansen	S	PHD	74 Indiana	9-83
Liddle, Stephen W.	Assoc	422-8792	liddle	S	PHD	95 Brighm Yg	6-95
Grant & David Research Fellow							

Meservy, Rayman D.	Assoc	422-2119	rayman_meservy	SADG	PHD	85.	Minnesota	9-89
Albrecht, Conan C.	Asst	422-1792	conan_albrecht	S	PHD	00	Arizona	1-01
Anderson, Bonnie B.	Asst	422-7880	bonnie_anderson	S	PHD	01	Car Mellon	9-01
Lowry, Paul B.	Asst	422-1215	paul_lowry	S	PHD	02	Arizona	5-02
Ball, Nicholas L.	Inst	422-4195	nick_ball	S	PHD	05	Minnesota	8-05
Lindstrom, Craig J.	AsTch	422-4602	craig_lindstrom	S	MS	01	Utah St	8-02

Brigham Young Univ-Hawaii Laie, HI 96762-1294 (808) Fax=293-3582
Department of Accounting School of Business byuh.edu BS
Dept Phone: 293-3580 55-220 Kulanui St Box 1956 Saralyn Lopez-Camit
Homepage: www.bus.byuh.edu

Hubner, Clayton	Dean	293-3580	hubnerc	Mgt	PHD	94	Michigan	2003
Tew, Glade K.	C-Ac	293-3590	tewg	IMF	PHD	97.	Okla St	& 8-96
Kimball, Kevin C.	Assoc	293-3584	kimballk	ASFD	MACC	90	Brighm Yg	& 8-97
Chen, Ching-Kuan	Asst	293-3586	chenj	FJWX	PHD	05.	Cen Fla	2005

Bryant University Smithfield, RI 02917-1284 (401) Fax=232-6319 1994,1994
Accounting Department College of Business bryant.edu BS,MBA,MST,MSA
Dept Phone: 232-6168 1150 Douglas Pike Amy Paul
Homepage: web.bryant.edu/accounting

Trifts, Jack W.	Dean	232-6227	jtrifts	Fnce	PHD	84	Florida	7-05
Bline, Dennis M.	C-Pr	232-6402	dbline	BVFI	PHD	85.	Arkansas	1-92
Beausejour, David	Prof	232-6219	dbeausej	XF	JD	89	Suffolk	& 8-84
Cullinan, Charles P.	Prof	232-6421	cullinan	AMF	PHD	91.	Kentucky	# * & 8-92
Filippelli, Michael F.	Prof	232-6066	mfilippe	FP	MBA	65	Rhode Isl	& 9-70
Hebert, Marcel G.	Prof	232-6339	mhebert	FNGC	PHD	87.	Tx Tech	* & 9-79
Lynch, Michael F.	Prof	232-6136	mlynch	X	JD	80	NE Law	& 1-77
Roohani, Saeed J.	Prof	232-6168	sroohani	SAF	DBA	92.	Miss St	8-91
Simons, Kathleen A.	Prof	232-6443	ksimons	F	DBA	91.	Boston U	& 8-84
Farrar, Robert H.	Assoc	232-6159	rfarrar	MUF	PHD	78.	Mass	8-86
Krumwiede, Timothy G.	Assoc	232-6394	krumwied	XF	PHD	93.	Tx Tech	& 8-92
Witner, Lawrence H.	Assoc	232-6290	lwitner	X	LLM	76	Geo Wash	& 8-92
Folami, L. Buky	Asst	232-6564	lfolami	FM	PHD	99.	Geo St	* &2006
Sinkin, Charlene	Asst				ABD		Okla St	

Bucknell University Lewisburg, PA 17837 (570) Fax=577-1338
Accounting Faculty Dept of Management bucknell.edu BS,MS
Dept Phone: 577-1306 Monroe Avenue Elaine Herrold

Allen, Douglas L.	C-Ac	577-1399			PHD	95	Iowa St	9-95
Bettner, Mark S.	Assoc	577-3569	mbettner	FM	PHD	88.	Tx Tech	9-89
Christian R. Lindback Chair								
Coyne, Michael P.	Assoc	577-3628	mcoyne	BHJW	PHD	02.	Conn	& 9-00
Jensen, David E.	Assoc	577-1105	djensen	FVX	PHD	87.	Penn St	&1987
Needham, Robert A.	Assoc	577-1066	needham	FM	MS	79	Youngstwn	& 9-94
Willits, Stephen D.	Assoc	577-3166	swillits	AF	PHD	86.	Tx Tech	& 1-86

Buena Vista University Storm Lake, IA 50588-1798 (712) Fax=749-1462
Accounting Faculty School of Business bvu.edu BA
Dept Phone: 749-2410 610 W. Fourth Street Cindy McDonough
Homepage: www.bvu.edu/academics/business

Ullerich, Stanton G.	Dean	749-2419	ullerich	Econ	PHD	95	Purdue	1994
Redenbaugh, Margaret	Assoc	749-2420	redenbaugh	PXCA	PHD	74	NW Mo St	* &1982
Biankers, Beth	Asst	749-2413	biankers	PMX	JD	03	Minnesota	* &2005

Buffalo State College Buffalo, NY 14222-1095 (716) Fax=878-5500
Accounting Faculty Business buffalostate.edu
Dept Phone: 878-4239 1300 Elmwood Avenue Carol Bradley
Homepage: http://www.buffalostate.edu/depts/business

Mulkahy, Kevin	C	878-3132	mulkahkf					
Ahiarah, Sol	C-Ac	878-4239	ahiarasc	FMGI	PHD	85	Pittsburgh	& 8-90
Janowsky, Dale	Asst		janowsdw	FMC	MS	75	Canisius	& 9-81
Ricigliano, Daniel	Asst		riciglds	FMX	MBA	75	SUNY-Buf	& 9-79

Butler University Indianapolis, IN 46208-3485 (317) Fax=940-9455 1998,1998
Accounting Area College of Business Adm butler.edu
Dept Phone: 940-9221 4600 Sunset Avenue Sharon Bratcher

Fetter, Richard E. Jr.	Dean	940-9836	rfetter	Mktg	PHD	93	Indiana	8-92
Mahenthiran, Sakthi	C-Ac	940-8024	smahenth	BCMS	PHD	91.	Temple	1995
Hicks, Harry E.	Prof	940-9261	hhicks	AXLJ	JD	79	Indiana	&1974
Kershaw, Russell	Assoc	940-9841	rkershaw	PMCS	PHD	96.	S Carol	1996
Carl K. Doty Professor of Accounting								
Sander, James F.	Assoc	940-9839	jsander	PFT	PHD	87.	Illinois	&1990
Updyke, Karel Ann	Assoc	940-9531	kaupdyke	FTM	PHD	87.	Purdue	&1986
Huang, Henry	Asst		hhuang	PFM	PHD	05.	Houston	8-05
Kelly, Anne S.	Asst	940-3049	akelly	APCF	PHD	86.	Cincinnati	&2006
Rouse, Pamela	Lect	940-8816	prouse	PF	MBA	88	Indiana	1996

Calif Univ of Pennsylvania
California, PA 15419-1394 (724) Fax=938-5908
Accounting Faculty Business & Econ Dept cup.edu BS,MBA
Dept Phone: 938-4371 250 University Avenue Shirley Elnikar

Colelli, Leonard	Dean	938-4169	colelli					
Brown, Burrell A.	C-Pr	938-5991	brown	Mgt	JD	73	Pittsburgh	1989
Roberts, Clyde A.	Prof	938-5996	roberts	CSX	DBA	88.	Kentucky	&1992
Blosel, William F.	Assoc	938-5735	blosel	CIP	MBA		Pittsburgh	1976
Jones, David T.	Assoc	938-5728	jones_dt	FMP	MS		W Virginia	1985
Mendola, Edward	Assoc	938-5994	mendola_e	PXG	MS	82	Rbt Morr	1989

U of California-Berkeley
Berkeley, CA 94720-1900 (510) Fax=642-4700 ß 1916,1963
Accounting Faculty Haas School of Business haas.berkeley.edu BS,MBA,PHD
Dept Phone: 642-0115 545 Student Srvs Bldg Joseph Cadora
Homepage: www.haas.berkeley.edu/accounting/

Campbell, Tom	Dean	643-2027	campbell	Econ	PHD	80	Chicago	8-02
Dutta, Sunil	C-Ac	643-1229	dutta	M	PHD	94.	Minnesota	1996
Egen and Joan von Kaschnitz Associate Professor of Atg & Intl Business								
Zhang, Xiao-Jun	C-Ac	642-4789	xzhang	F	PHD	98.	Columbia	1998
Emile R. Niemela Associate Professor of Accounting								
Cerf, Alan R.	Emer	642-4849	acerf	1993	PHD	56	Stanford	1955
Dechow, Patricia M.	Prof	642-2708	patricia_dechow	F	PHD	93.	Rochester	2007
Donald H. and Ruth F. Seiler Chair in Public Accounting								
Hakansson, Nils H.	Emer	642-1686	hakansso	2003	PHD	66	UCLA	&1969
Staubus, George J.	Emer	643-6623		1993	PHD	54.	Chicago	&1952
Fan, Quintao	Asst	642-2025	fan	FM	PHD	04.	Stanford	2003
Johnson, Nicole	Asst	642-6590	njohnson	M	PHD	05	Stanford	2005
Levi, Shai	Asst	643-4356	slevi	F	PHD	04.	NYU	2004
Nondorf, Maria E.	Asst	642-5372	nondorf	F	PHD	03.	N Carol	2003

Univ of California-Davis
Davis, CA 95616-8609 (530) Fax=752-2924 1992
Accounting Faculty Graduate School of Mgt ucdavis.edu MBA,PHD
Dept Phone: 752-4600 AOB4, Shields Avenue Kari Wilkinson
Homepage: www.gsm.ucdavis.edu

Biggart, Nicole W.	Dean	752-6366	nwbiggart	Mgt	PHD	81	Berkeley	9-81
Barber, Brad M.	Prof	752-0512	bmbarber	FQ	PHD	91	Chicago	1991
Griffin, Paul A.	Prof	752-7372	pagriffin	FT	PHD	74.	Ohio St	&1981
Maher, Michael W.	Prof	752-7034	mwmaher	MA	PHD	75.	U Wash	&1987
Yetman, Robert J.	Assoc	752-4600	rjyetman	FA	PHD	00.	N Carol	&2003
Yetman, Michelle H.	Asst	752-4600	mhyetman	FT	PHD	01.	N Carol	&2003

Univ of Calif, Irvine
Irvine, CA 92697-3125 (949) Fax=824-8469 1987
Accounting Faculty Paul Merage Sch of Bus uci.edu MBA,PHD
Dept Phone: 824-6855 GSM Bldg Denise Bonnell

Policano, Andrew J.	Dean	824-8470		Econ	PHD	75	Brown	8-04
Pincus, Morton	C-Pr	824-4062	mpincus	FX	PHD	82.	Wash U	& 7-05
Ho, Joanna L.	Prof	824-4041	jlho	FMB	PHD	86.	Tx-Austin	* & 7-86
Teoh, Siew Hong	Prof	824-9952	steoh	F	PHD	88.	Chicago	7-06
Karuna, Christo	Asst	824-9653	ckaruna	M	PHD	04.	Michigan	7-04
Shi, Charles	Asst	824-7017	cshi	M	PHD	00	Minnesota	7-00

Univ of Calif, Los Angeles
Los Angeles, CA 90095-1481 (310) Fax=267-2193 1939
Accounting Faculty Anderson Grad Sch Mgt anderson.ucla.edu MBA,PHD
Dept Phone: 825-3271 Box 951481 Dianthia Simon
Homepage: www.anderson.ucla.edu/acad_unit/accounting/

Olian, Judy D.	Dean	825-7982	judy.olien	Mgt	PHD	80	Wisconsin	1-06
Trueman, Brett	C-Pr	825-4720	brett.trueman	F	PHD	81	Columbia	2003
Hughes, John S.	Prof	794-9553	john.hughes	FMTY	PHD	74.	Purdue	& 7-99
Miller, Bruce L.	Prof	825-1814	bruce.miller	MF	PHD	67	Stanford	1984
Aboody, David	Assoc	825-3393	david.aboody	F	PHD	95.	Berkeley	1995
Benartzi, Shlomo	Assoc	206-9939	shlomo.benartzi	F	PHD	94.	Cornell	1996
Hayn, Carla K.	Assoc	206-9225	carla.hayn	F	PHD	87.	Michigan	1997
Liu, Jing	Assoc	206-5861	jing.liu	F	PHD	99.	Columbia	1999
Caskey, Judson	Asst	206-1503	judson.caskey	F	PHD	06.	Michigan	&2006
Saouma, Richard	Asst	825-7132	richard.saouma	M	PHD	06	Stanford	2006
Zhang, Li	Asst	825-7132	li.zhang	FM	PHD	99.	Car Mellon	7-99

Univ of Calif, Riverside
Riverside, CA 92521-0203 (951) Fax=827-3970 2003,2003
Accounting Faculty Graduate School of Mgt ucr.edu BSB,MBA
Dept Phone: 827-6329 900 University Avenue
Homepage: www.ucr.edu

Deolalikar, Anil	Dean$	827-4237	anilaqsm	Econ	PHD	81	Stanford	2002
Rodgers, Waymond	C-Pr	827-4786	waymond.rodg+	FBAJ	PHD	84.	S Calif	&1992
Liao, Woody M.	Prof	827-6451	woody.liao	MQY	PHD	74.	Florida	* &1991
Choy, Helen	Asst	827-2333	helen.choy	F	PHD	04.	Rochester	2003
Mishra, Birendra K. (Barry)	Asst	827-7707	barry.mishra	MS	PHD	96.	Tx-Austin	2003

U of Calif, Santa Barbara Santa BarbaraCA 93106-9210 (805) Fax=893-8830
Economics Department College of Letters & Sc econ.ucsb.edu BA
Dept Phone: 893-3670
Homepage: www.econ.ucsb.edu

Name	Rank	Phone	email					
Kuhn, Peter J.	C-Pr	893-3666	pjkuhn	Econ	PHD		Harvard	
Anderson, Robert W.	Lect	893-2143			MAC	92	Ca-SnBarb	2004
email rafs@sbcglobal.net								
Harmon, Coby	Lect	893-4333	harmon	VGFS	BA	82	Ca-SnBarb	&1988
Loster, Donald R.	Lect	893-2143	lobby	MA	BS	69	Woodbury	&1979
Maass, Lisa E.	Lect	893-5570	lisa	CFNP	BA	85	Ca-SnBarb	&1989
Owen, Glenn E.	Lect	893-4572	owen	SF	BA	75	UCLA	&1979
Sander, Henry C.	Lect	893-2984	bud	FXP	BA	76	Conn	&1980
Watson, Richard B.	Lect	893-4402	watson	TMC	PHD	81	Ca-SnBarb	1981

California Lutheran Univ Thousand Oaks CA 91360-2787 (805) Fax=493-3719
Accounting Faculty School of Business clunet.edu BS
Dept Phone: 493-3360 60 West Olson Road Ms. Erzsi Huffman

Name	Rank	Phone	email					
Maxey, Charles	Dean	493-3360	maxey	B	PHD	82	Illinois	1991
Julius, Edward H.	Prof	493-3363	julius	FTV	MS	75	Penn	&1981
Coman, Carol Lynn	Assoc	493-3376	coman	FMX	MS	84	CS-Nrthr	1986
Gunewald, Sandra	Asst	493-3893	sgurnewa	ACDF	MBA	91	Ca Luthr	&1992

Cal Poly State U-SLO SanLuisObispoCA 93407 (805) Fax=756-6347 1981,1987
Accounting Area Ortelea College of Bus calpoly.edu BS
Dept Phone: 756-1384
Homepage: http://www.cob.calpoly.edu/cob/areas/actg/

Name	Rank	Phone	email					
Christy, Dave	Dean	756-1411		Mgt	PHD	84	Georgia	9-04
Carr, Janice S.	Prof	756-1488	jcarr	FXE	PHD	85.	Ariz St	& 9-83
Cerf, Douglas C.	Prof	756-2871	dcerf	FM	PHD	91	Ca-Davis	& 9-90
Associate Dean								
Kalfayan, Garo	Prof	756-5327	kalfayan	X	JD	83	UCLA	& 9-06
Keller, Earl C.	Prof	756-2588	eckeller	FGKV	PHD	73.	U Wash	& 9-87
Miller, Charles R. (Tad)	Prof	756-2831	cmiller	FA	PHD	87.	Arizona	& 9-87
Mintz, Steven M.	Prof	756-1416	smintz	FJ	PHD	78.	Geo Wash	& 9-06
Dang, Li	Assoc	756-2987	ldang	F	PHD	04.	Drexel	7-06
Lancaster, Kathryn A. S.	Assoc	756-2922	klancast	EFMW	PHD	97.	Tx A&M	& 9-97
Savage, Arline	Assoc	756-2977	savage	SF	DCOM	99	Port Eliz	& 9-04

Calif State Poly U-Pomona Pomona, CA 91768-2557 (909) Fax=869-4511 1995,1995
Accounting Department College of Business Adm csupomona.edu BS,MBA
Dept Phone: 869-2365 3801 West Temple Avenue Leanne Hall
Homepage: http://www.csupomona.edu/~acc

Name	Rank	Phone	email							
Klock, David R.	Dean	869-2400		Fnce	PHD	71	Illinois			
Hefzi, Hassan	C-Pr	869-2364	hhefzi	FVM	PHD	88.	Ariz St			& 9-98
Mickey & Lee Segal Faculty Fellow										
Adamson, Willie D.	Prof	869-2382	badamson	XFC	EDD	84	Pepperdi			1973
on retirement, teaching Winter										
Ahadiat, Nasrollah	Prof	869-2434	nahadiat	CFM	PHD	83.	Arkansas	#	*	1991
Brock, Glenda C.	Prof	869-2369	gcbrock	XGN	PHD	89.	Miss		&	9-92
Hurt, Robert L.	Prof	869-2372	rlhurt	CMSU	PHD	91	Claremont		*	1987
Karayan, John E.	Prof	869-2367	jekarayan	MXIG	PHD	94	Claremont			1991
Kellner, Rochelle	Prof	869-4531	rakellner	FP	PHD	85	UCLA			1979
Martin, Rose	Prof	869-2376	rmmartin	FS	PHD	96.	S Calif		&	9-99
Pak, Hong S.	Prof	869-2377	hspak	F	PHD	91.	Memphis			&1991
Peden, Vicki	Prof	869-2707	vspeden	AFS	PHD	94.	Tx-Arlin			&1995
Salimi, Anwar Y.	Prof	869-2383	aysalimi	FSDM	PHD	84.	UCLA		*	1981
Chan, Hung C. (Leon)	Asst	869-2378	hungchan	MS	PHD	06.	Houston			2006
Betty & Hayward Taff Faculty Fellow										
Farag, Magdy	Asst	869-2365		F	PHD	07	Kent St			2007
Lee, Byunghwan	Asst	869-2365		F	PHD	05.	Houston			2007
Yan, Yun-chia	Asst	869-2365		FSA	PHD	07	Fla Intl			2007
Natarajan, Ashok	Lect	869-4539	anatarajan	FM	PHD	02.	Ca-Irvine			2004

Calif State U., Bakersfield Bakersfield, CA 93311-1099 (661) Fax=664-2438 1975,1982
Dept of Fnce & Accounting Sch of Bus & Public Adm csub.edu BS,MBA
Dept Phone: 664-3406 9001 Stockdale Highway Margaret Moorhead

Name	Rank	Phone	email							
Shakoori, Ken	C-Pr	664-3406	kshakoori	Fnce	PHD	80	Clark			1984
Bacon, Leonard A.	Prof	664-2186	lbacon	MFPC	PHD	73.	Miss	#	*	& 9-79
Doucet, Mary S.	Prof	664-3406	mdoucet	AJSF	PHD	83.	Arizona	#		& 9-98
Doucet, Thomas A.	Prof	664-3406	tdoucet	CFMS	PHD	92.	Georgia			9-98
Miller, Gary A.	Prof		gmiller5	FI	PHD	85.	Santa Cl			&2005
Ruiz, Janis	Prof	664-3480	jruiz	FMZ	PHD	86.	UCLA			3-89
Patten, James A.	Assoc	664-2339	jpatten	F	MBA	70	DePaul			& 9-82

Calif State Univ, Chico

Dept Accounting & Mgt Info S
Dept Phone: 898-6463
Homepage: www.csuchico.edu

Chico, CA   95929-0011
College of Business
Tehama 313

(530) Fax=898-4970
csuchico.edu

ß 1972,1976
BS,MBA,MS
Ronda McGrath/Jill Rice

Hopkins, Willie E.	Dean	898-6359	wehopkins	Mgt	PHD	84	Colorado		8-05
Corbitt, Gail F.	C-Pr	898-6463	gcorbitt	Sys	PHD	89	Colorado		9-91
Adams, Steven J.	Prof	898-6359	sjadams	SMU	PHD	81.	Cincinnati	*	& 9-82
DeBerg, Curtis L.	Prof	898-4824	cdeberg	FE	PHD	85.	Okla St		& 9-90
Leese, Wallace R.	Prof	898-5314	wleese	CFM	PHD	78.	Ariz St	*	9-78
Mensching, James R.	Prof	898-6405	jmensching	SF	PHD	76	Chicago		& 9-91
Milliron, Valerie C.	Prof	898-6286	vmilliron	XE	PHD	84.	S Calif		& 9-90
Murdoch, Brock G.	Prof	898-5832	bmurdoch	FT	PHD	84.	Ca-Irvine		& 9-85
Nissan, Samir I.	Prof	898-4831	snissan	IVFM	PHD	71	Illinois		& 9-80
Geddiz, Mary	Assoc	898-3636	mfgeddiz	FG	ABD		Houston		8-06
Kizirian, Timothy G.	Assoc	898-6463	tkizirian	SAM	PHD	01.	Arizona		7-01
Jones, Nancy	Inst	898-4822	njones	SM	MBA	01	CS-Chico		1-05

Calif St U-Dominguez Hills

Dept Accounting/Law/Finance
Dept Phone: 243-3556

Carson, CA   90747
Col of Bus Adm & Pub Pl
1000 East Victoria Street

(310) Fax=217-6964
csudh.edu

BS,MBA
Betty Castillo

Strong, James T.	Dean	243-3548	jstrong	Mktg	PHD	90	Drexel		2003
El-Badawi, Mohamed H.	C-Pr	243-3571	melbadawi	MF	PHD	80.	S Calif		&1986
Barnett, Donald J.	Prof	243-3565	dbarnett	BFM	PHD	73.	UCLA		1996
Chang, Chiou-Hsiung (Bear)	Prof	243-3577	cchang	MST	PHD	73.	LSU	*	1983
Malamud, Richard	Prof	243-2239	rmalamud	XL	LLM	79	NYU		&1990
Mazhin, Reza	Prof	243-3576	rmazhin	MF	PHD	84.	Indiana		&1984
Auerbach, Melvin P.	Assoc	243-3453	mauerbach	AF	MS	75	CS-Nrthr		&1977

Calif State Univ, East Bay

Dept of Accounting & Finance
Dept Phone: 885-3397
Homepage: www.csueastbay.edu

Hayward, CA   94542-3067
Col of Business & Econ
25800 Carlos Bee Blvd.

(510) Fax=885-4796
csueastbay.edu

ß 1973,1981
BS,MBA,MST

Kohl, John P.	Dean	885-3291	john.kohl	Mgt	PHD	82	Penn St		2005
Lubwama, Christopher W. K.	C-Pr	885-3397	clubwama	CIMU	PHD	89	Simon Fr		9-87
Duncan, Doris	Prof	885-3364	dduncan	SD	PHD	78	Golden Gt		4-76
Frankel, Micah P.	Prof	885-3327	mfrankel	FQV	PHD	91.	Arizona	*	& 9-91
Associate Dean									
Hagen, Will	Prof	885-3341	will.hagen	LX	SJD	04	Wisconsin		4-06
Kam, Vernon T.	Emer	885-4684	vkam	2000	PHD	68.	Berkeley		& 9-69
Lowenthal, Franklin	Prof	885-3417	flowenth	CMSQ	PHD	65	Stanford		9-78
Mangold, Nancy R.	Prof	885-3899	nmangold	MF	PHD	84.	Berkeley		9-84
Mashaw, Bijan	Prof	885-3899	bmashaw	SD	PHD	76	Clemson		9-84
McBride, Gary R.	Prof	885-3097	gmcbride	X	JD	81	Hastings		& 1-88
Ossman, Edward T.	Emer	885-4684		2001	PHD	71	Ill Tech		& 9-72
Pefkaros, Kenneth	Prof	885-2980	kpefkaro	SDQ	PHD	72	Delaware		9-84
Satin, Diane C.	Prof	885-3141	dsatin	FMC	PHD	92.	Berkeley		1990
Jan, Ching-Lih	Assoc	885-3340	cjan	FM	PHD	88.	Berkeley		9-95
Lin, Y. Robert	Assoc	885-3002	boblin	CFM	PHD	89.	UCLA	*	1-89
Du, Hongwei	Asst	885-3899	hdu	SD	PHD	94	Fla Tech		9-01
Shima, Kim	Asst		kim.shima	FI	PHD	07	Hawaii		9-07
Wan, Huishan	Asst		huishan	F	PHD	07	Iowa		9-97
Yang, Jing-Wen (Margaret)	Asst		jing.yang	F	PHD	07	Maryland		
Abendroth, Charlene	Lect	885-3298	cabendro	FT	MS	72	Brighm Yg		& 9-76
Busch, Suzanne M.	Lect	885-3265	sbusch	FA	MBA	77	CS-Haywa	*	& 9-74

Calif State Univ-Fresno

Department of Accountancy
Dept Phone: 278-2852
Homepage: craig.csufresno.edu/departments/acct/default.htm

Fresno, CA   93740-8001
Craig Sch of Business
5245 N Backer Avenue

(559) Fax=278-6931
csufresno.edu

ß 1959,1977
BS,MBA,MS
Debbie Koehler

Huff, Patricia Lee	C-Pr$	278-2021	patricia	CM	PHD	94	Arkansas		& 8-93
Baker, Dennis M.	Prof	278-2546	dennisb	SM	PHD	73.	UCLA		& 8-84
Harper, Robert M. Jr.	Prof	278-2852	roberth	PSFM	DBA	84.	Fla St		1-90
Osborn, John P.	Prof	278-4958	johno	XA	PHD	81.	Georgia		& 8-79
Patterson, Denise M.	Prof	278-3971	denisep	AF	PHD	94.	Geo St		& 8-94
Peyvandi, Ali A.	Prof	278-2921	alip	FCRI	PHD	80.	Missouri		8-80
Tai, Benjamin Y.	Prof	278-2217	benjamin	AF	PHD	81.	Missouri	*	& 8-85
Du, Chan	Asst	278-8055	chandu	PFM	DBA	06.	Boston U		8-06
Lin, Shu	Asst	278-5121	shulin	PFM	PHD	06	Tx		8-06
Baker, Timothy W.	Lect	278-3997	tbaker	PFMX	MSTX	93	San Joaq		& 8-00
Copeland, Cheryl	Lect	278-8555	copeland	PMC	MBA	03	CS-Fresno		8-03
Ude, Pamela	Lect	278-2979	pamelause	FM	MBA	02	CS-Fresno		& 1-05

Calif State Univ, Fullerton

Calif State Univ, Fullerton	Fullerton, CA	92834-6848		(714) Fax=278-4518		ß (123) 1965,1972			
Department of Accounting	College of Bus & Econ			fullerton.edu		BA,MSA,MST,MBA			
Dept Phone: 278-2225	800 State College Blvd					Carolyn Mathisen			
Homepage: http://business.fullerton.edu/accounting									
Puri, Anil K.	Dean	278-2592	apuri	Econ	PHD	77	Minnesota		1977
Chavis, Betty M.	C-Pr	278-2225	bchavis	FIX	PHD	90.	S Calif		&1996
Foote, Paul S.	Prof	278-2682	pfoote	SF	PHD	83.	Mich St		7-89
Grant, C. Terry	Prof	278-7206	tgrant	FI	PHD	92.	Fla St		&2005
Hardman, O. Clyde	Prof	278-2238	chardman	XFC	PHD	74.	Illinois		&1974
Hassan, Mahamood M.	Prof	278-2225	mhassan	CF	PHD	89	Arizona		& 2-90
Hirsch, A. Jay	Prof	278-2163	jhirsch	FM	PHD	62.	Illinois		1966
Hoth, Gerald B.	Prof	278-3465	ghoth	SMC	PHD	82.	Colorado	*	&1989
Kim, Kun J.	Prof	278-3835	kkim	MF	DBA	83.	Kentucky		&1986
Luzi, Andrew D.	Prof	278-3931	aluzi	S	PHD	78.	Kansas		1990
Mande, Vivek	Prof	278-7659	vmande	FI	PHD	91.	UCLA		&2002
Miller, Robert L. C.	Prof	278-3940	rmiller	FG	PHD	73.	Oregon		1974
Petruzzi, Christopher R.	Prof	278-7104	cpetruzzi	X	PHD	84	S Calif		7-89
Seth, Shirish B.	Prof	278-3938	sseth	MC	PHD	69.	Mich St		1976
Sharifi, Mohsen	Prof	278-2230	msharifi	SFM	PHD	75.	LSU	*	8-01
Smith, Ephraim P.	Prof	278-2615	esmith	X	PHD	68.	Illinois		8-90
Vice President; fax 714-278-5853									
Alali, Fatima A.	Assoc	278-2225	falali	AF	PHD	05	Rutgers		2007
Grant, Gerry H.	Assoc	278-3938	ggrant	SC	PHD	05	Miss		&2004
Son, Myungsoo	Assoc	278-2225	mson	FM	PHD	05.	Nebraska		2007
Tarantino, Kimberly A.	Lect	278-2225	ktarantino	AF	MS	83	Ca-SnDgo		&1993

Calif State Univ - Humboldt

Calif State Univ - Humboldt	Arcata, CA	95521-8299		(707) Fax=826-6666					
School of Business & Econ	College of Prof Studies			humboldt.edu			BS,MBA		
Dept Phone: 826-3224	1 Harpst Street					Gina Pierce 826-3224			
Homepage: http://www.humboldt.edu/~sbe									
Higgins, Susan	Dean	826-3961			EDD	77	Columbia		2002
Mortazavi, Saeed	C-Pr	826-3846	sm5	Fnce	PHD	83	Tx-Dallas		1983
Fults, Gail J.	Prof	826-6026	gjf2	FM	PHD	87	Claremont		1986
Kenyon, Peter B.	Prof	826-4762	pbk1	FC	PHD	85.	Santa Cl	*	1984
Thomas, Michael F.	Assoc	826-6022	mft5	M	PHD	85.	Wisconsin	*	2005

Calif State Univ, Long Beach

Calif State Univ, Long Beach	Long Beach, CA	90840-8504		(562) Fax=985-7586		ß 1971,1977			
Department of Accountancy	College of Business Adm			csulb.edu		BS,MBA			
Dept Phone: 985-4653	1250 Bellflower Blvd					Kellee Zbornak			
Homepage: www.csulb.edu/~accting									
Khan, Mo B.	Dean				PHD				
Fisher, Steven A.	C-Pr	985-7968	sfisher	CF	DBA	85.	Kent St	*	&1990
Chase, Michael D.	Prof	985-5754	mdchase	FVS	PHD	84.	S Calif		1982
Constas, Michael	Prof	985-5042	mconstas	CMLX	PHD	94	UCLA		1994
Davidson, David B.	Prof	985-5624	davidson	XFCA	PHD	82	N Colo		&1983
Grace, Debra M.	Prof	985-5758	dgrace	FX	PHD	80.	Okla St		&2001
Hunt, Herbert G.	Prof	985-2600	hhunt	XF	PHD	82.	Colorado		&2002
Lacey, John M.	Prof	985-4576	lacey	FTKJ	PHD	82.	UCLA		&1989
Ernst & Young Research Fellow									
Mahapatra, Sitikantha	Prof	985-8478	maha	FTM	PHD	74	Case Wes		1983
Shim, Jae K.	Prof	985-8609	jaeshim	CM	PHD	73	Berkeley		1981
Nguyen, Loc T.	Assoc	985-4831	loc	FXI	MST	89	SanDiego		&1986
Smith, Rodney E.	Assoc	985-4521	rsmith5	FMS	PHD	00.	Ca-Irvine	*	&2006
Lin, Ping	Asst	985-4560	plin2	CM	PHD	03.	Ca-Irvine	*	2006
Pearlman, Sy	Lect	985-5565	spearlma	FX	JD	66	DePaul		&1996
Todd, John	Lect	985-4446	jtodd	FA	MBA	64	UCLA		&1995
Valenzuela, John	Lect	985-4831	jvalenzu	FCM	MBA	81	CS-LgBch		&2000

Calif State U-Los Angeles

Calif State U-Los Angeles	Los Angeles, CA	90032-8121		(323) Fax=343-6439		ß 1960,1964			
Department of Accounting	College of Bus & Econ			calstatela.edu		BS,MBA,MS			
Dept Phone: 343-2830	5151 State Univ Dr St F517					Lyssa DePompa			
Lee, Dong-Woo	Dean	343-2800	dwlee	FI	PHD	95	Michigan		9-95
Kunkel, J. Gregory	C-Pr	343-2834	gkunkel	FV	PHD	81.	Berkeley		9-93
Abdeen, Adnan M.	Prof	343-2867	aabdeen	MCI	DBA	74.	Miss St		& 9-86
Donohoo, Jim	Prof	343-2848	jdonoho	FX	LLM	84	SanDiego		& 9-78
Hayes, Rick S.	Prof	343-2837	rhayes	FBA	PHD	89	London		9-90
Lau, Chor T.	Prof	343-2843	clau	MC	PHD	76.	Oregon		1985
Murphy, Dennis M.	Prof	343-2833	dmurphy	XFM	MBA	65	Michigan		&1975
Park, L. Jane	Prof	343-2839	jpark	F	PHD	65	Illinois		& 9-89
Warren, Hugh E.	Prof	343-2852	hwarren	FMC	PHD	66	Michigan		1-76
Elias, Rafik Z.	Assoc	343-2867	relias	FMC	DBA	97.	La Tech		& 9-93
Hansen, Kathryn A.	Assoc	343-2854	khansen3	FMG	PHD	96	Geo Wash		9-98
Kim, Neung-Jip	Assoc	343-2840	nkim	F	PHD	87.	Temple		6-88
Lau, Richard T.	Assoc	343-5253	rlau	FV	PHD	89.	LSU		9-89

El-Masry, Hussein	Asst	343-2848	helmasry	FS	PHD	03. S Fla	9-03
He, Haihong	Asst	343-5253	hhe	FM	PHD	04. Conn	9-04
Hossain, David	Asst	343-2847	dhossai2	FX	PHD	03. Rutgers	& 9-03
James, Marianne L.	Asst	343-5253	mjames2	FM	PHD	98 Fla Intl	9-98
Monsour, Edward L.	Asst	343-2843	emonsour	FX	JD	82 Clev St	& 9-02

Calif State Univ, Northridge — Northridge, CA 91330-8372 — (818) Fax=677-2456 — ß 2004,2004
Dept Accounting & Info Sys — Col of Business & Econ — csun.edu — BS
Dept Phone: 677-2461 — 18111 Nordhoff Street
Homepage: csun.edu/accounting

Jennings, William	Dean$	677-2455	william.jennings	Fnce	PHD	81 UCLA	1977
Driscoll, Donna A.	C-Pr	677-4840	donna.driscoll	S	PHD	84. S Calif	1980
AlHashim, Dhia D.	Emer	677-2427	dhia.alhashim	IT	PHD	71. Missouri	1974
Chen, Raymond S.	Emer	677-2429	raymond.chen	AFI	PHD	73. Missouri	&1971
Chiu, James S. H.	Prof	677-2424	james.chiu	LF	PHD	73. Missouri	* &1979
Gray, Glen L.	Prof	677-3948	glen.gray	S	PHD	88. S Calif	&1987
Kiani-Aslani, Rajabali	Prof	677-3975	rajabali.kiani	M	PHD	75. Oklahoma	1978
Kiddoo, Robert J.	Emer	677-3952	robert.kiddoo	C	DBA	78 S Calif	* 1970
Lundblad, Heidemarie	Prof	677-2440	hlundblad	MF	PHD	86. U Wash	1982
Reinstein, Todd R.	Emer	677-2428	todd.reinstein	X	JD	62 UCLA	&1967
Rogoff, Donald L.	Prof	677-2439	donald.rogoff	FM	DBA	64 Mich St	&1977
Sangeladji, Mohammad A.	Emer	677-2425	msangeladji	M	PHD	75. Oklahoma	* 1979
Stone, Ronald S.	Prof	677-2419	ronald.stone	AFPS	PHD	83. UCLA	&1986
Stout, Gary R.	Prof	677-2449	gary.stout	X	DBA	77. S Calif	&1985
Weiss, Earl	Prof	677-2466	earl.weiss	XF	JD	74 Southwes	&1984
Vedd Rishma	Asst	677-2437	rishma. vedd	PFMV	PHD		2006
Fountaine, Drew	Lect	677-3081	drew.fountaine	UFLM	MBA	97 CS-Nrthr	2007
Jeppson, Catherine T.	Lect	677-4505	cjeppson	XMCF	MS	75 CS-Nrthr	&1983
Macklin, James H.	Lect	677-3947	james.macklin	A	MA	66 Ohio St	& 1-83

Calif State Univ-Sacramento — Sacramento, CA 95819-6088 — (916) Fax= — ß 1963,1970
Accounting Faculty — College of Business Adm — csus.edu — BS,MS,MBA
Dept Phone: 278-6942 — 6000 J Street — Tamara Dunn

Varshney, Sanjay	Dean	278-6942	varshney	Fnce	PHD	94 LSU	2004
Ogilby, Suzanne M.	Prof	278-5577	ogilbysm	IFGH	PHD	91. Wisconsin	& 1-90
Associate Dean							
Beirne, Thomas J. Jr.	Prof	278-7135	beirne	FTR	PHD	81. Oklahoma	&1977
Brecht, H. David	Prof	278-7149		CM	PHD	74 Tx-Austin	& 9-75
email gomail5@pacbell.net							
Corless, John C.	Prof	278-7124	corlessj	AFTJ	PHD	71. Minnesota	# &1984
Crow, Steven R.	Prof	278-7129	crow	XM	PHD	90. S Calif	&1989
Davis, Charles J.	Prof	278-7145	daviscj	FM	PHD	79. Illinois	&1982
Kim, Jong H.	Prof	278-7396	kimjh	FM	PHD	88. Missouri	8-89
Mackey, James T.	Prof	278-7122	mackey	CM	PHD	81. Illinois	* & 9-87
Meyer, Kent W.	Prof	278-7125	meyerkw	XI	PHD	80. Tx-Austin	1980
Wunder, Haroldene F. (Deenie)	Prof	278-7134	wunderh	FX	PHD	78. S Carol	& 8-93
Liu, Caixing	Asst	278-7110	liuc	FA	PHD	04. Hawaii	2004
Pforsich, Hugh	Asst	278-7141	pforsich	C	PHD	95. Wash St	&2004
Xiong, Yan	Asst	278-7143	xiongy	S	PHD	03. Wash St	8-02

Calif St U-San Bernardino — S Bernardino, CA 92407-2397 — (909) Fax=537-7514 — ß 1994,1994
Dept of Accounting & Finance — Col of Bus & Public Adm — csusb.edu — BS,MBA
Dept Phone: 537-5704 — 5500 University Parkway — Andraew German

Bowerman, Karen Dill	Dean	537-5700		Mgt	PHD	79 Tx A&M	8-04
Sarwar, Ghulam	C-Pr	537-3398	gsarwar	Fnce	PHD	97 Oklahoma	1996
Benson, Frank D.	Prof	537-5706	fbenson	FMAO	PHD	84 Claremont	# * &1986
Chang, Otto H.	Prof	537-5700	ochang	FMX	PHD	84. Illinois	&1991
Dorocak, John R.	Prof	537-5750	jdorocak	X	LLM	90 Florida	&1991
Henry, Linvol G.	Prof	537-5710	lhenry	FCX	MS	73 Long Isl	& 9-85
Hoverland, Hal	Emer	537-5711	hhoverla	1999	PHD	63. Michigan	9-72
Huh, Sung-Kyoo	Prof	537-5712	huh	MC	PHD	88. Kent St	1987
Savich, Richard S.	Prof	537-5722	rsavich		PHD	73. Illinois	&
Scribner, John	Prof	537-5720	scribner	FP	MABA	74 Ca-Rivers	& 9-78
Shalchi, Hossein	Prof	537-5757	hshalchi	FTQ	PHD	81. Illinois	1989
Lillie, Rick		537-5158	rlillie				

Calif State U - San Marcos — San Marcos, CA 92096-0001 — (760) Fax=750-3107
Accounting & Finance — College of Business Adm — csusm.edu — BS
Dept Phone: 750-4264 — 333 South Twin Oaks Valley — Sharon bowen
Homepage: www.csusm.edu

Guseman, Dennis S.	Dean	750-4242	dguseman	Mktg	DBA	77 Colorado	2002
Detzel, F. Larry	C-Ac	750-4262	ldetzel	X	PHD	96. Cen Fla	&1999
Hwang, Nen-Chen Richard	Prof	750-4220	hwang	FAC	PHD	91. St Louis	* &1991
Styles, Alan K.	Assoc	750-4251	astyles	FIH	PHD	98. North Tx	1998
Wang, Zheng	Asst			F	PHD	06. Maryland	2007

Calif State U, Stanislaus
Dept of Accounting & Finance
Dept Phone: 667-3671
Homepage: panopticon.csustan.edu

Turlock, CA 95382
School of Business Adm
801 W Monte Vista Avenue

(209) Fax=667-3042
toto.csustan.edu

2003,2003
BS
Nancy Mardakis

Name	Rank	Phone	Email	Area	Degree	Yr	School	Notes
Elmallah, Amin A.	Dean	667-3287	elmallah	CIGS	PHD	74	Illinois	* &7-00
Lindsay, David H.	C-Pr	667-3296	dlindsay	F	PHD	92	Kent St	&1991
Campbell, Annhenrie	Prof	667-3454	acampbel	FC	PHD	91.	Colorado	* &1991
Garner, Don E.	Prof	667-3072	garner	AF	DBA	72.	S Calif	# &1987
Filling, Steven M.	Assoc	667-3773	sfilling	SF	PHD	96.	LSU	&1994
Johnson, Lynn	Assoc	667-3626	lyjohnso	F	PHD	98	Oregon	* &1995
McGhee, Thomas M. (Mitch)	Assoc	667-3891	tmcghee	XI	PHD	89.	S Carol	8-06
Tan, Kim B.	Asst	667-3573	kbtan	MF	PHD	98	Temple	&1998

Calvin College
Dept of Economics & Business
Dept Phone: 526-7191

Grand Rapids, MI 49546
Division of Social Sci
3201 Burton Street, SE

(616) Fax=526-8410
calvin.edu

BS
Susan M. Camp

Name	Rank	Phone	Email	Area	Degree	Yr	School	Notes
Ward, Dean	Dean	526-6203	ward		PHD	87	Virginia	
Cook, David	C-Pr	526-7025	dcook	FMX	MS	79	W Mich	& 9-85
Slager, Raymond L.	Prof	526-6098	slgr	SVAM	MS	70	W Mich	&1982
Medema, Robert	Assoc	526-6380	rmedema	FMP	MBA	72	Michigan	1999
Reynolds, Don	Assoc	526-6480	djr6		PHD	03	Sarasota	2003
Voskuil, Julie	Asst	526-6189	jvoskuil	MIF	MBA	02	W Mich	1999

Cameron University
Accounting Discipline
Dept Phone: 581-2267

Lawton, OK 73505-6377
School of Business
2800 W. Gore Blvd

(580) Fax=581-2253
cameron.edu

BS
Cindy Johnson

Name	Rank	Phone	Email	Area	Degree	Yr	School	Notes
Burgess, Sylvia M.	Dean	581-2267	sylviab	Law	LLM	84	So Meth	1995
Treadwell, Gregory	C-In	581-5528	gtreadwell	SACF	MSA	92	Oklahoma	1994
Cammack, Susan Missouri	Asst	581-5516	scammackmmack	FGPV	PHD	02.		2006
Helvey, Aubree L.	Asst	581-2853	aubreeh	LJ	JD	02	Oklahoma	&2002

Campbell University
Accounting Faculty
Dept Phone: 893-1410
Homepage: www.campbell.edu
   phone 893-1387

Buies Creek, NC 27506
Lundy-Fetterman Sch Bus

(910) Fax=893-1392
mailcenter.campbell.edu

BBA
April Hawkins

Name	Rank	Phone	Email	Area	Degree	Yr	School	Notes
Hawkins, Ben	Dean	893-1380	hawkinsb	Econ	PHD	79	Kentucky	2000
Witherspoon, James E.	C-Ac	893-1387	witherspoon	Law	JD	83	Wake For	1983
Berry, Joseph W.	Asst	893-1389	berry		MBA		Fayettev	1996
Butler, Robie S.	Asst	893-1388	butler		MBA		Campbell	&1995
Deutsch, Robert A.	Asst	893-1995	deutsch		PHD	91	Kentucky	&2000
Vaughan, Jo Ann	Asst	893-1394	vaughan		MA		N Carol	&1989

Canisius College
Department of Accounting
Dept Phone: 888-2870
Homepage: www.canisius.edu

Buffalo, NY 14208-1098
Wehle School of Bus
2001 Main Street

(716) Fax=888-2880
canisius.edu

1977,1982
BS,MBA,MBAA
Ms. Eva Dulski

Name	Rank	Phone	Email	Area	Degree	Yr	School	Notes
Alber, Antone F. (Joe)	Dean	888-2160	albera	Fnce	PHD	71	Penn St	2002
Redpath, Ian J.	C-Ac	888-2868	redpathi	XL	LLM	86	Wisconsin	1985
Gress, Edward J.	Prof	888-2865	gress	TFI	PHD	70.	Arizona	1976
Davis, Robert R.	Assoc	888-2866	davis	AF	PHD	82.	SUNY-Buf	&1967
Kermis, George F.	Assoc	888-2864	kermisg	FC	PHD	82.	Syracuse	&1978
O'Connor, Eugene	Assoc	888-2873	oconnore	LX	JD	59	SUNY-Buf	1976

Capital University
Accounting Faculty
Dept Phone: 236-6595

Columbus, OH 43209-2394
School of Management
1 College and Main

(614) Fax=236-6540
capital.edu

BA,MBA
Dana Blanke

Name	Rank	Phone	Email	Area	Degree	Yr	School	Notes
Moore, Keirsten	Dean$	236-6579	kmoore		PHD		Ohio St	1993
Mellum, Steven D.	C-Ac	236-6132	smellum	FGCM	MBA		Ohio St	&1991
Mittermaier, Linda J.	Prof	236-6130	lmitterm	FMX	PHD	87.	Indiana	&1994
Mittler, Dale L.	Prof	236-6598	dmittler	XAV	MBA		Capital	&1978
Martin, Steven	Asst	236-6545	smartin	LXM	JD		Ohio St	1994

Carnegie Mellon University
Accounting Faculty
Dept Phone: 268-2265

Pittsburgh, PA 15213-3890
Tepper School of Bus
5000 Forbes Ave

(412) Fax=
andrew.cmu.edu

1982,1957
BS,MS,PHD
Carol Salerno

Name	Rank	Phone	Email	Area	Degree	Yr	School	Notes
Dunn, Kenneth B.	Dean	268-2265	kbdunn	Fnce	PHD	79	Purdue	2002
Glover, Jonathan C.	Prof	268-8499	jglover	TMF	PHD	92.	Ohio St	&1992
Ijiri, Yuji	Prof	268-2303	ijiri	FM	PHD	63.	Car Mellon	&1967
Robert M. Trueblood University Professor of Accounting and Economics								
Gu, Zhaoyang	Assoc	268-3585	zygu	FM	PHD	99.	Tulane	&1999
Levine, Carolyn P.	Assoc	268-9543	clevine	FTM	PHD	96.	Car Mellon	2001
Liang, Pierre Jinghong	Assoc	268-3315	liangj	TMF	PHD	98.	Florida	1998
O'Brien, John R.	Assoc	268-5963	jo0x	FM	PHD	85.	Minnesota	1984
Nan, Lin	Asst	268-5709	linnan	FY	PHD	04.	Florida	2004

Carroll College
Accounting Faculty
Dept Phone: 524-7172
Waukesha, WI 53186-5593
Business, Atg & Econ
100 N. East Avenue
(262) Fax=524-7397
cc.edu
BS

Kunz, Jeffrey T.	D-As	524-7172	jkunz	FMPT	MS	76	Wisconsin	& 9-81
Olsen, Gary L.	Assoc	524-7171	golsen	SFAC	PHD	86	Marquette	& 9-75
Fredricks, Thomas P.	Lect	524-9035	tfredricks	FMT	MS	64	Wisconsin	9-97

Carson-Newman College
Dept of Business/Econ
Dept Phone: 471-3316
Homepage: www.cn.edu
Jefferson Cy, TN 37760
Division of Bus & Econ
1646 Russell Avenue
(865) Fax=471-3599
cn.edu
BS
Becky Dinkins

Sites, Millicent M.	C-Ac	471-3433	msites	Econ	PHD	85	Tennessee	1995
Driver, Phyllis N.	Assoc	471-3317	pdriver	PCFV	ABD		Tennessee	&1978

Carthage College
Accounting Faculty
Dept Phone: 551-5836
Homepage: www.carthage.edu/departments/business
Kenosha, WI 53140-1994
Dept of Business Adm
2001 Alford Drive
(262) Fax=551-6208
carthage.edu
BA
Kristin Walcott

Groleau, Thomas G.	C-Ac	551-5983	tgroleau	DSci	PHD	95	Kentucky	1999
Brunn, David	Prof	551-5961	dbrunn	FMCV	MBA	62	Nrthwstrn	* &1993
Rogers Palmer Distinquished Professor of Business Administration								
Schlichting, David K.	Assoc	551-5836	dschlichting	FMX	PHD	88.	Wisconsin	&1997
Dawson, Julie A.	Asst		jdawson	FMX	MSA	93	Wisconsin	&2007
Duffy, Cathy	Asst	551-5818	cduffy	FMAX	MST	96	DePaul	&2001

Case Western Reserve Univ
Department of Accountancy
Dept Phone: 368-4141
Cleveland, OH 44106-7235
Weatherhead Sch of Mgt
10900 Euclid Avenue
(216) Fax=368-6244 ß (13) 1979,1958
case.edu BS,MBA,MACC,PHD
Elaine Iannicelli

Reddy, N. Mohan	Dean	368-1156	mxr8	Mktg	PHD	85	Case Wes	7-85
Parker, Larry M.	C-Ac	368-2065	lmp3	ABFM	PHD	81.	Houston	& 7-85
Bricker, Robert J.	Prof	368-5355	rxb22	FABH	PHD	87.	Case Wes	& 8-90
Ernst & Young Faculty Fellow								
Fogarty, Timothy J.	Prof	368-3938	tjf	XABE	PHD	89.	Penn St	& 8-89
KPMG Peat Marwick Faculty Fellow								
Pearson, David B.	Prof	368-1057	dbp2	AF	DBA	64.	Indiana	& 1-99
Previts, Gary John	Prof	368-2074	gjp	FHKE	PHD	72.	Florida	& 7-79
Associate Dean								
Grant, Julia E. S.	Assoc	368-4158	jsg2	FMD	PHD	89.	Cornell	& 7-91
Braun, Karen Wilken	Asst	368-3532	kwb8	FM	PHD	96.	Conn	& 7-06
Jonas, Gregory	Asst			FMS	ABD		Va Comm	* 7-07
Blazey, Lee	Lect	368-2051	lxb46	X	BA	63	Case Wes	& 6-98

Catawba College
Accounting Faculty
Dept Phone: 637-4405
Salisbury, NC 28144-2488
Ketner School of Bus
2300 West Innes Street
(704) Fax=637-4422
catawba.edu
BS
Elaine Corothers

Thompson, Pamela L.	C-Ac	637-4223	pthompso		MBA		Jms Mad	
Trenchard, William H.	Prof	637-4483	btrencha	FPCE	MS	72	Va Comm	& 8-88
Spencer, Darin	Lect	637-4441	dsspenc	FPCE	MACC	99	NC-Charl	8-05

Catholic Univ of America
Dept of Business & Econ
Dept Phone: 319-5236
Homepage: http://www.cua.edu
Washington, DC 20064
Sch Arts and Sciences
620 Michigan Avenue NE
(202) Fax=319-4426
cua.edu
BA,MA
Ms. Brenda Nichols

Poos, Lawrence R.	Dean			Hst	PHD		Cambridge	
Forbes, Kevin F.	C-Ac	319-4794	forbes	Econ	PHD	82	Maryland	1983
Leung, Kwok Wai	Asst	319-4698	leungk	CF	PHD	99.	Maryland	9-00

Cedarville University
Busines Adm Deptartment
Dept Phone: 766-7910
Cedarville, OH 45314-0601
Sch Soc Sci & Prof Stds
251 North Main Street
(937) Fax=766-7925
cedarville.edu
BA
Vicki Edem

Wheeler, Bert G.	C-Pr	766-7714	wheelerb	Econ	PHD	85	Tennessee	1992
Hartman, Charles	Assoc	766-7914	hartmanc	LX	JD	97	Dayton	1989
Rich, Anne N.	Assoc	766-4992	richa	P	MS	78	Cen Fla	&2000
Smith, Sarah H.	Assoc	766-7913	smiths	GF	PHD	82.	Va Tech	1980
Anderson, Harry	Asst	766-7924	handerson	AMVS	MACC	69	Ohio St	2003

Centenary College
Accounting Faculty
Dept Phone: Ext 2287
Did Not Respond--2005-2006 Listing; phone 852-1400 Ex 2045
Hackettstown, NJ 07840-9989
Business
400 Jefferson Street
(908) Fax=813-1934
centenarycollege.edu
BS

Dunham, Heather	Dean	852-1400	dunhamh	Mktg	EDD	99	St Johns	8-82
Ippolito, Joseph V.	C-As	Ext 2045	ippolitoj	Law	JD	90		5-04
Greenberg, Daniel	Asst	852-1400	greenbergd	CPVX	MBA		Pace	& 8-00

Centenary College of LA Shreveport, LA   71134-1188   (318) Fax=869-5139
Accounting Faculty   Frost Sch of Business   centenary.edu
Dept Phone: 869-5141   2911 Centenary Blvd   BA,MBA
Homepage: centenary.edu/business
Martin, Christopher L.   Dean   869-5149 cmartin   PHD   Ga Tech
Davis, Barbara J.   Prof   869-5153 bdavis   F   DBA   95 La Tech   #   & 8-86
Sikes, Helen B.   Prof   869-5182 hsikes   T   DBA   95 La Tech   *   & 8-90

Central College   Pella, IA   50219   (641) Fax=628-5307
Accounting Faculty   Dept Econ, Atg & Mgt   central.edu
Dept Phone: 628-5183   812 University Street
Homepage: www.central.edu
Rundle, Jaclyn   C-Ac   628-5118 rundlej   Mgt   PHD
Den Adel, Kevin J.   Assoc   628-5258 denadelk   FAS   PHD   99. Iowa   2002
Maurer, Robert J.   Assoc   628-5121 maurerr   MBA   68 Indiana   1968

Univ of Central Arkansas Conway, AR   72035-0001   (501) Fax=450-5302   ß 1984,1990
Department of Accounting   College of Business Adm   mail.uca.edu   BBA,MBA
Dept Phone: 450-3108   201 Donaghey Street   Lauren Stout
Cantrell, Pat   Dean   450-3106 patc   Econ   PHD   83 So Meth   9-84
Mounce, Patricia H.   C-Ac$ 450-5333 pmounce   X   PHD   98. Miss   & 8-04
Atkinson, Keith E.   Prof   450-5311 keitha   AM   PHD   96. Miss   & 7-01
Jensen, Paul H.   Prof   450-5312 paulj   FM   DBA   95. Memphis   & 8-82
Moore, P. Michael   Prof   450-5332 mikem   F   PHD   82. Arkansas   * & 7-89
Oxner, Thomas H.   Prof   450-5314 toxner   AFS   PHD   77. Georgia   & 7-97
Spikes, Pamela A.   Prof   450-5315 pams   X   PHD   93. Miss   & 8-80
Smith, Donna   Asst   450-5313 donnas   CS   MBA   Okla St   *   8-78
Watson, Stephanie F.   Asst   450-5317 swatson   OSP   PHD   04. LSU   #   8-03
Vance, Danny   Inst   450-3108 dvance   FMA   BBA   70 Cen Ark   & 8-02
Young, Laura   Inst   450-3189 lyoung   F   MAC   81 Cen Ark   & 1-00

Central Connecticut St Univ New Britain, CT 06050-1140   (860) Fax=832-3219
Department of Accounting   School of Business   ccsu.edu   BS,MBA
Dept Phone: 832-3220   1615 Stanley Street   Donna Stewart
Homepage: www.ccsu.edu/business/accounting
Galligan, Christopher   Dean$ 832-3276 galliganc
Walo, Judith C.   C-Pr   832-3238 waloj   AFB   PHD   90. Mich St   &1994
Rich, Anne J.   Prof   832-3230 richannch FMT   PHD   78. Mass   * &2007
Roxas, Maria L.   Prof   832-3233 roxas   CMSJ   PHD   88. Georgia   &1992
Stoneback, Jane Y.   Prof   832-3235 stoneback CMBI   PHD   92. Kansas   1992
Crespi, Cheryl   Assoc   832-3239 crespichs FMX   JD   04 Conn   # &2005
Grasso, Lawrence P.   Assoc   832-3226 grassola   CMS   DBA   89. Boston U   &2003
Tomczyk, Stephen H.   Assoc   832-3324 tomczykst FIMS   DBA   76. Kentucky   * 2003
Shakun, Harlan J.   Asst   832-3234 shakun   FMX   MSPA 76 Hartford   & 9-81

Univ of Central Florida Orlando, FL   32816-1400   (407) Fax=823-3881   ß (13) 1975,1979
Dixon School of Accounting   College of Business Adm   bus.ucf.edu   BA,MSA,MST,PHD
Dept Phone: 823-2871   4000 Central Florida Blvd   Connie Dawson
Homepage: www.bus.ucf.edu/acc/
Keon, Thomas L.   Dean   823-2182 thomas.keon   Mgt PHD   79 Mich St   8-97
Roberts, Robin W.   D-Pr   823-6726 robin.roberts G   PHD   87. Arkansas   & 6-98
  Burnett Eminent Scholar Chair
Arnold, Vicky   Prof   vicky.arnold MAS PHD   89. Arkansas   & 8-05
  Ernst & Young Professor
Sutton, Steve G.   Prof   steve.sutton SAW PHD   87. Missouri   & 8-05
  KPMG Professor
Bobek, Donna D.   Assoc   823-3082 donna.bobek   FT   PHD   97. Florida   & 1-97
Dwyer, Peggy D.   Assoc   823-2588 peggy.dwyer   FA   PHD   88. Missouri   & 8-97
Goldwater, Paul M.   Assoc   823-5754 paul.goldwater MCQ PHD   89. LSU   * 7-89
Judd, Andrew J.   Assoc   823-2871 andrew.judd   X   PHD   85. Florida   & 8-87
Kelliher, Charles F.   Assoc   823-5128 charles.kelliher FBT PHD 90. Tx A&M   & 8-85
Roush, Pamela B.   Assoc   823-5664 pamela.roush FAO PHD   89. Geo St   * 7-89
Welch, Judith K.   Assoc   823-5659 judith.welch FGVS PHD   85. Fla St   & 9-88
Benford, Tanya S.   Asst   823-2965 tanya.benford S   PHD   00. S Fla   & 8-04
Lacy, Jo Y.   Asst   823-2150 jo.lacy   ABF PHD   02. Geo Wash   & 8-02
Robb, Sean W. G.   Asst   823-2966 sean.robb   F   PHD   95. Florida   & 8-05
Hampton, Marcye S.   Inst   823-5678 marcye.hampton F   MBA   96 Cen Fla   & 8-04
Smith, V. Scott   Inst   823-1459 scott.smith   M   MBA   83 Loyola   & 8-98
Veit, Marcia R.   Inst   823-5124 marcia.veit   FV   MBA   76 Arkansas   & 9-80
Allen, Darryl E.   Lect   823-0151 darryl.allen M   PHD   03. Geo Wash   &
Dennis, Lynda M.   Lect   823-5839 lynda.dennis FG   PHD   04 Cen Fla   & 8-05
Hornik, Steven R.   Lect   823-5739 steven.hornik FS   PHD   99 Fla Intl   & 5-06

Central Michigan University

School of Accounting
Dept Phone: 774-3796
Homepage: www.cmich.edu

Mt. Pleasant, MI 48859
College of Business Adm

(989) Fax=774-3999   ß (1) 1983,1989
cmich.edu   BS,MBA
                                   Janice Lee

Name	Rank	Phone	Email					
Fields, D. Michael	Dean	774-3337	mike.fields	Mktg	PHD	85	Arkansas	4-06
Kintzele, Philip L.	C-Pr	774-3796	kintz1pl	FGV	DBA	73.	Indiana	&1981
Arndt, Terry L.	Prof	774-1255	arndt1tl	FP	PHD	73	Arkansas	&1993
Bromley, Robert G.	Prof	774-3845	broml1rg	SA	PHD	84.	Nebraska	&1983
Cron, William R.	Prof	774-3393	cron1wr	FMV	PHD	73	Mich St	* 1982
Damitio, James W.	Prof	774-3699	damit1j	PM	PHD	88	Mich St	* 1983
Grant, Edward B.	Prof	774-3105	grant1eb	FM	PHD	77.	Mich St	&1977
Hayes, Randall B.	Prof	774-3939	hayes1rb	FM	PHD	78.	Michigan	1989
Hood, William C.	Prof	774-4466	hood1wc	X	JD	86	Cooley	&1981
Karmon, David J.	Prof	774-6506	karmo1d	FV	PHD	84.	Nebraska	&1979
Kwiatkowski, Vernon E.	Prof	774-3557	kwiat1v	GF	DBA	86.	Kentucky	&1986
McGilsky, Debra E.	Prof	774-3476	mcgil1da	X	PHD	86.	Mich St	&1989
Weirich, Thomas R.	Prof	774-3314	weiri1tr	AKF	PHD	76.	Missouri	&1976
Hayes, Gary W.	Asst	774-3142	hayes1gw	CM	DBA	94.	Miss St	&1993
Neurath, James H.	Inst	774-6509	neura1jh	PX	MS	84	Cen Mich	&1984
Rusch, Nancy E.	Inst	774-3994	rusch1ne	PF	MS	79	Cen Mich	&1981

Univ of Central Missouri

Department of Accounting
Dept Phone: 543-4631
Homepage: cmsu.edu/academic/accounting

Warrensburg, MO 64093-5070
Harmon Col of Bus Adm
Dockery 400

(660) Fax=543-8465   ß (123) 1995,1995
ucmo.edu   BSBA,MBA,MA
                              Sherry Adams

Name	Rank	Phone	Email					
Wilson, George W.	Dean$	543-4560	gwilson	Econ	PHD	76	Okla St	1972
Stone, Kenneth E.	C-Pr$	543-4816	kstone	PF	PHD	76.	Missouri	&1969
Joy, David W.	Prof	543-8566	joy	PCX	PHD	84.	Nebraska	&1990
Koehn, Jo Lynne	Prof	543-8562	koehn	AP	PHD	95.	Wisconsin	&1995
Niemeyer, Ronald D.	Prof	543-8561	niemeyer	PVT	DBA	74.	Miss St	1980
Delvecchio, Stephen C.	Assoc	543-8555	sdelvecchio	ASM	DBA	90.	S Illinois	&2000
Fessler, Nicholas J.	Asst	543-8567	nfessler	CM	PHD	98.	Indiana	* &2005
Klimek, Janice L.	Asst	543-4631	jklimek	FCX	PHD	96.	Nebraska	&2001
Showers, Robert	Asst	543-4946	showers	PM	MBA	82	S Dakota	&2001

Univ of Central Oklahoma

Department of Accounting
Dept Phone: 974-5272

Edmond, OK 73034-5209
College of Business Adm
100 North University Drive

(405) Fax=974-3853
ucok.edu   BS,MBA

Name	Rank	Phone	Email					
Shirley, Michael	Dean	974-2810	mshirley		PHD			
Terrell, Katherene P.	C-Pr	974-5272	kterrell	F	EDD	94	Okla St	& 8-90
Haskin, Daniel L.	Prof	974-2441	dhaskin	FU	PHD	82.	Tx Tech	& 8-93
Hora, Bambi A.	Prof	974-2156	bhora	XCMG	JD	98	Okla Cty	& 8-90
Sheets, Mary	Prof	974-2834	msheets	PSF	PHD	95	Oklahoma	& 9-88
Terrell, Robert L.	Prof	974-2814	rterrell	VAF	EDD	92	Okla St	# & 1-86
Parrish, Barbara K.	Assoc	974-3440	bparrish	FMPT	PHD	94.	Arkansas	& 8-99
Alltizer, Richard L.	Asst	974-5272	ralltizer	XF	PHD	94.	Oklahoma	& 8-07
Brownell, Wede	Asst	974-2815	wbrownell	CF	PHD	04.	Okla St	8-05
Calvert, Jane	Asst	974-2161	jcalvert	MPF	MAC	84	Oklahoma	& 9-84
Teal, Mary	Asst	974-2806	mteal	XZF	JD	05	Okla Cty	8-05
Pursifull, Charles	Inst	974-2823	cpursifull	PFM	MBA	58	Oklahoma	& 1-95
Stone, Joan	Inst	974-5336	jstone	FM	MBA	86	Cen Okla	& 8-05

Central State Univ-Ohio

Dept Financial Sys Box 1004
Dept Phone: 376-6428
Did Not Respond--2005-2006 Listing

Wilberforce, OH 45384
Col Business & Industry
1400 Brush Row Rd.

(937) Fax=376-6206
csu.ces.edu   BS
                        Alison Jobson

Name	Rank	Phone					
Showell, Charles H. Jr.	Dean	376-6441	BAdm	PHD	75	Ohio St	9-88
Vafaie, Massie S.	C-Ac	376-6421	Econ	PHD	79	Cincinnati	1991
Riechman, Edward J.	Assoc	376-6428	AXFM	MBA	66	Xavier	& 9-86
Rangarajan, A. V.	Inst	376-6426	VFDM	MS	69	Wash U	9-70

Central Washington Univ

Department of Accounting
Dept Phone: 963-3340
439 phone numbers have (206) area code; 640 numbers have (425)

Ellensburg, WA 98926-7484
College of Business
400 E. University Way

(509) Fax=963-2875
cwu.edu   BS,MPA
                        Sharon Damm

Name	Rank	Phone	Email					
Savoian, Roy T.	Dean	963-1955	savoianr	Econ	PHD	79	Ca-SnBarb	1998
Tidd, Ronald R.	C-As	963-2466	tiddr	AS	PHD	92.	Minnesota	&2001
Forsyth, Jay D.	Prof	439-3822	forsythj	CXTF	MS	64	Okla St	& 9-69
Gierlasinski, Norman J.	Prof	439-3825	normang	AEF	PHD	84	Nova SE	# & 3-86
Heesacker, Gary W.	Prof	963-3339	heesacke	FAJ	MBA	69	U Wash	& 9-72
Holtfreter, Robert E.	Prof	963-2144	holtfret	FMA	PHD	78.	Nebraska	&1993
Distinguished Professor of Accounting & Research								
Martinis, Karen	Prof	963-2031	martinis	FM	MBA	80	Puget Sd	& 9-79

Bae, Benjamin R.	Assoc	640-3798	baeb	S	PHD	98.	Temple		2004
Larson, Linda L.	Assoc		larsonl	SOB	DBA	97.	Clev St	#	& 8-06
Atkinson, MaryAnne	Asst	640-1313	atkinsom	AS	PHD	90.	Drexel		1997
Ruble, Michael R.	Asst	640-1570	rublem	AFG	PHD	84.	Ariz St		&1998
Sullivan, Carol E.	Asst	439-3826	sullivanc	AS	PHD	92.	Tx A&M	#	&2004
McDonald, Frederick	Lect	963-3330	mcdonalf	FX	MBA	91	Port St		2002

Chaminade University   Honolulu, HI   96816-1578   (808) Fax=440-4249
Accounting Faculty   School of Business   chaminade.edu   BS,MBA
Dept Phone: 440-4245   3140 Waialae Avenue   Ginger Miller

Schroeder, Scott J.	Dean	739-4601	sschroed	Mgt	PHD	98	UCLA		2001
Kido, Richard Y.	D-As	440-4245	rkido	EACN	MBA	97	Hawaii		& 8-02
Tanna, Wayne M.	Prof	739-4606	wtanna	LPNX	LLM	90	McGeorge		1-93
Kido, Nolan Y.	Lect	440-4269	nkido	P	MBA	03	Hawaii		8-05

Chapman University   Orange, CA   92866   (714) Fax=532-6081   1999,1999
Accounting Faculty   Argyros Sch Bus & Econ   chapman.edu   BS
Dept Phone: 997-6684   One University Drive   Jennifer Freebury 997-6707
Homepage: www.chapman.edu/argyros

Kraft, Arthur	Dean	997-2839	akraft	Econ	PHD	70	SUNY-Buf		
Pfeiffer, Glenn M.	C-Pr	997-6814	pfeiffer	FM	PHD	80.	Cornell		9-95
Dehning, Bruce	Assoc	997-6684	bdehning	FS	PHD	99.	Colorado		9-02
Lipman, Francine J.	Assoc	997-6705	lipman	FX	LLM	94	NYU		& 9-01
Sinha, Praveen	Assoc	744-7986	sinha	FM	PHD	92	Car Mellon		9-04
Virchick, John M.	Assoc	997-6996	virchick	ACFM	MBA	74	E New Mex		& 9-83
Adler, Hirschel (Hank)	Asst	628-7283	adler	FX	MBA	69	UCLA		9-04

College of Charleston   Charleston, SC   29424-0001   (843) Fax=953-0754   (13) 1988,1988
Dept of Atg & Legal Studies   Sch of Business & Econ   cofc.edu   BS,MS
Dept Phone: 953-7835   66 George Street
Homepage: cofc.edu/~acctls

Pitts, Robert E.	Dean	953-5627	pittsr	Mktg	PHD	77	S Carol		2004
Koprowski, William R.	C-Ac	953-0849	koprowskiw	NO	PHD	87	Temple		2005
Arsenault, Steve	Assoc	953-7990	arsenaults	XL	LLM	94	Florida		1999
Bradley-McKee, Linda J.	Assoc	953-8039	bradleyl	XFH	PHD	93.	North Tx		&1993
Daniels, Roger B.	Assoc	953-8041	danielsr	FHT	PHD	91.	Miss		&1992
Elshazly, Talaat A.	Assoc	953-8104	elshazlyt	CM	MSA	64	Illinois	*	&1979
Yost, Jeffrey A.	Assoc	953-8056	yostj	MVY	PHD	89.	Ohio St		&2000
Cipriano, Michael C.	Asst	953-7166	ciprianom	AFJ	PHD	06.	S Carol		2006
DeLaurell, Roxane	Asst	953-5358	delaurellr	IL	PHD	00	Tx-Dallas		2000
Trinkle, Bradley S.	Asst	953-6669	trindleb	DQS	PHD	06.	Alabama		8-06

Cheyney University   Cheyney, PA   19319   (610) Fax=399-2197
Accounting Faculty - Box 175   Business Adm Department   cheyney.edu   BS
Dept Phone: 399-2133   Cheyney & Creek Roads   Idella Q. Byers
Homepage: www.cheyney.edu

Carter, Bernadette	Dean$								
Burks, Ernestine P.	C-Ac	399-2301	eburks	Mgt	MS	76	N Car Cen		1976
Adighibe, Michael E.	Assoc	399-2362	madighibe	PTLX	ABD		Drexel		1988

University of Chicago   Chicago, IL   60637   (773) Fax=702-2225   (2) 1916
Accounting Faculty   Graduate School of Bus   chicagogsb.edu   MBA,PHD
Dept Phone: 702-7743   5807 South Woodlawn Ave   Karen Johnson

Snyder, Edward A.	Dean	792-1680	tsnyder	Econ	PHD	84	Chicago		2001
Ball, Raymond J.	Prof	834-5941	ray.ball	F	PHD	72.	Chicago		&2000
Sidney Davidson Professor of Accounting									
Berger, Philip G.	Prof	834-8687	pberger	F	PHD	92.	Chicago		2002
Davidson, Sidney	Emer	702-7136		1999	PHD	50.	Michigan		&1958
Erickson, Merle M.	Prof	834-0716	merle.erickson	FX	PHD	96.	Arizona		& 9-96
Leftwich, Richard W.	Prof	702-7266	richard.leftwich	F	PHD	80.	Rochester		&1979
Fuji Bank and Heller Professor of Accounting and Finance									
Leuz, Christian	Prof	834-1996	leuz	M	PHD	96	Goethe		
Skinner, Douglas J.	Prof		douglas.skinner	F	PHD	89.	Rochester		2005
Smith, Abbie J.	Prof	702-7295	abbie.smith	F	PHD	81.	Cornell		1980
Boris and Irene Stern Professor of Accounting									
Weil, Roman L.	Prof	702-7261	roman.weil	FM	PHD	66.	Car Mellon	*	&1965
V. Duane Rath Professor of Accounting									
Zmijewski, Mark E.	Prof	464-8757	mark.zmijewski	FDP	PHD	83.	SUNY-Buf		1984
Leon Carroll Marshall Prof of Atg; Deputy Dean Part-Time MBA Prog; 312 area									
Engel, Ellen	Assoc	834-0966	ellen.engel	F	PHD	97.	Stanford		&1996
Hayes, Rachel M.	Assoc	834-4489	rachel.hayes	FM	PHD	96.	Stanford		9-00
Piotroski, Joseph D.	Assoc	834-4199	joseph.piotroski	F	PHD	99.	Michigan		1999

Name	Rank	Phone	Email		Degree	Yr	School	Year
Roulstone, Darren T.	Assoc	834-5966	darren.roulstone	F	PHD	00.	Michigan	2000
Sapra, Haresh	Assoc	834-5951	hsapra	FMT	PHD	00	Minnesota	2000
Dey, Aiyesha	Asst		adey	F	PHD	05.	Nrthwstrn	2005
Ray, Korok	Asst	834-1709	krayu	CMTY	PHD	04	Stanford	2004
Rogers, Jonathan L.	Asst	834-0161	jrogers2	FM	PHD	05.	Penn	2004
Srinivasan, Suraj	Asst	834-1720	ssriniva	FIKM	DBA	04.	Harvard	2004
VanBuskirk, Andrew	Asst	834-1712	avanbusk	F	PHD	05.	Penn	2004
Weiss, Ira S.	VAsst	854-9158	piweiss	FX	PHD	01.	Chicago	&

Chicago State University
Dept of Accounting & Finance
Dept Phone: 995-3979
Homepage: www.csu.edu

Chicago, IL 60628-1598
College of Business
9501 S. King Drive

(773) Fax=995-2256
csu.edu

BS
Anne Outerbridge

Name	Rank	Phone	Email		Degree	Yr	School	Year
Simyar, Farhad	Dean	995-3976	simyar	EIM	DBA	75	S Calif	&2005
Tolia, Bijesh J.	C-Ac	995-3950	btolia	Fnce	PHD	97	Wi-Milwa	1997
Carter, Tollie L.	Assoc	995-3803	t-carter	FCVA	MBA	85	Illinois	&1986
Grange, Janet	Assoc	995-3967	j-grange	PMLX	JD	83	Illinois	&1989
Hunt, Atha	Assoc	995-3948	a-hunt	XJL	JD	78	DePaul	1975
Osaghae, Vincent	Assoc	995-3940	v-osaghae	MSVT	MBA	86	Gov St	&1989
Smith, Lute	Assoc	995-3968	l-smith1	LJ	JD	62	J Marshal	1978
Vaughn, Thomas E.	Assoc	995-3956	t-vaughn	LJPX	JD	78	Kansas	&1982
Arredondo, Richard	Asst	995-3943	r-arredondo	NACF	MBA	91	DePaul	* &1994
Bryant, Linnae W.	Asst	995-3950	lw-bryant	LPNA	JD		DePaul	&1992
Roper, Barbara E.	Asst	995-3956	b-roper	PMXF	MST	82	DePaul	&1988

Christian Brothers Univ
Department of Accounting
Dept Phone: 321-3315

Memphis, TN 38104-5581
School of Business
650 East Parkway S.

(901) Fax=321-3566
cbu.edu

BS,MBA

Name	Rank	Phone	Email		Degree	Yr	School	Year
Ryan, Michael R.	Dean	321-3316	ryan	Mktg	PHD	73	Miss	2004
Nash, Claire Y.	C-Ac	321-3023	cnash	XMF	PHD	99.	Miss	&1998
Ramage, Judy Anne	Prof	321-3320	jramage	FM	DBA	95	Nova SE	&1992
Tansey, James N.	Prof	321-3313	jtansey	AC	MBA	69	Memphis	&1977
Eaton, Ronald H.	Assoc	321-3322	reaton	SA	PHD	73	Arkansas	&2002

Christopher Newport Univ
Dept Atg, Economics & Fnce
Dept Phone: 594-7068

Newport NewsVA 23606-2988
School of Business
1 University Place

(757) Fax=594-7808
cnu.edu

2004,2004
BS,BA
Mrs. Lee Ann Wise

Name	Rank	Phone	Email		Degree	Yr	School	Year
Mottilla, Donna T.	Dean	594-7184	mottilla	Mgt	DBA	83	Kent St	1999
Jordan, Leland G.	C-Ac	594-7270	ljordan	MS	DBA	85.	Geo Wash	1999
Cohen, Ronnie	Prof	594-7075	rcohen	LX	LLM	88	Wm&Mary	1983
Frucot, Veronique G.	Assoc	594-7146	vfrucot	FI	PHD	87.	Tx A&M	1998
Hicks, Donald W.	Assoc	594-7263	dhicks	FTW	PHD	78.	Mich St	&1990
Riley, Donald B.	Emer	594-7068		1992	MBA	63	N Carol	&1963
Schell, Wayne M.	Assoc	594-7238	wschell	X	PHD	84.	Va Tech	&1976
Dawson, John W.	Emer	594-7068		1999	MBA	78	Va Comm	&1979
Fellowes, Robert E.	Emer	594-7068		1995	MS	57	MIT	&1979
Lingenfilter, Gabriele	Inst	594-7142	gabriele	PA	MBA	92	NW Mo St	&2004

University of Cincinnati
Department of Accounting
Dept Phone: 556-7040
Homepage: http://www.cba.uc.edu

Cincinnati, OH 45221-0211
College of Business
Lindner Hall

(513) Fax=556-6278
uc.edu

β 1919,1966
BA,MACC,MAT,PHD
Barbara Metzger

Name	Rank	Phone	Email		Degree	Yr	School	Year
McIntosh, Will	Dean	556-7001	will.mcintosh	Fnce	PHD		North Tx	
Sale, J. Timothy	C-Pr	556-7062	tim.sale	MQIS	PHD	70.	Cincinnati	&1964
Burns, David C.	Prof	556-7059	david.burns	FA	DBA	71.	Indiana	&1976
Ernst & Young Professor								
Sen, Pradyot K.	Prof	556-7033	pk.sen	M	PHD	85.	Columbia	2000
Ricketts, Jeri B.	Assoc	556-7046	jeri.ricketts	F	PHD	86.	Cincinnati	&1982
Stephan, Jens A.	Assoc	556-7055	jens.stephan	F	PHD	85.	Cornell	1989
Wood, Wallace R.	Assoc	556-7060	wallace.r.wood	SM	DBA	80	Tennessee	&1980
Adut, Davit	Asst	556-4891	davit.adut	F	PHD	03.	Tx A&M	
Booker, Donna M.	Asst	556-7057	donna.booker	BM	PHD	00.	Mich St	&2000
Jiang, Xiaowen	Asst	556-6278	xiaowen.jiang	F	DBA	05.	Boston U	9-05
Reed, Margaret P.	Asst	556-7054	margaret.reed	X	PHD	97.	Kansas	& 8-97
Zhang, Liping	Asst	556-4891	liping.zhang		PHD	06.	Geo Wash	
Clark, Virginia	Inst	556-7064	virginia.clark	F	MBA	80	Cincinnati	&1986

The Citadel
Accounting Faculty
Dept Phone: 953-5056

Charleston, SC 29409-0215
School of Business Adm
171 Moultrie St

(843) Fax=953-6764
citadel.edu

1996,1996
BSBA

Name	Rank	Phone	Email		Degree	Yr	School	Year
Walker, W. Earl	Dean	953-5056	earl.walker		PHD	80	MIT	8-02
Foster, Sheila D.	D-Pr	953-7468	fosters	FIMP	PHD	94.	Va Tech	& 8-92
Bolt-Lee, Cynthia E.	Assoc	953-6973	boltc	PAX	MTX	88	S Carol	& 8-90
Moody, Janette W.	Assoc	953-6947	moodyj	SPE	PHD	93	S Fla	& 1-93
Washington-Arnold, Liz	Asst	953-5168	lwarnold	FEPA	PHD	06	Rutgers	8-05

CUNY-Baruch College New York, NY 10010-5585 (646) Fax=312-3161 ß (123) 1933,1981
Stan Ross Dept Atcy B12-225 Zicklin Sch of Business baruch.cuny.edu BS,MBA,MS,PHD
Dept Phone: 312-3160 17 Lexington Avenue Barbara Olney/Shirley Curtis
Homepage: http://zicklin.baruch.cuny.edu/faculty/accountancy

Name	Rank	Phone	Email	Field	Degree	Yr	School	
Elliott, John A.	Dean	312-3030	john_elliott	XAF	PHD	82	Cornell	& 9-02
Darrough, Masako N.	C-Pr	312-3183	masako_darr+	MY	PHD	75	Brit Colum	9-98
Carmichael, Douglas R.	Prof	312-3197		A	PHD	68.	Illinois	&1983
Wollman Distinguished Professor of Accountancy								
Davis, Harry Zvi	Prof	312-3194	harry_davis	FATH	PHD	78.	Columbia	1974
Ghosh, Aloke	Prof	312-3184	aloke_ghosh	FV	PHD	93.	Tulane	9-93
Gorenberg, Hyman	Prof	312-3225		X	LLM	60	NYU	&1960
Green, David O.	Emer	312-3202	david_green	1999	PHD	56.	Chicago	& 9-78
Lilien, Steven B.	Prof	312-3163	steven_lilien	CF	PHD	76	NYU	&1972
Irving Weinstein Professor of Accountancy								
Lustgarten, Steven	Prof	312-3191	steven_lustg	F	PHD	71	UCLA	1988
Neimark, Marilyn D.	Prof	312-3190	marilyn_neimar	PS	PHD	83	NYU	1983
Nurnberg, Hugo	Prof	312-3196	hugo_nurnberg	FMT	PHD	68.	Columbia	&1980
Ruland, William J.	Prof	312-3188	william_ruland	F	PHD	76.	SUNY-Buf	9-81
Tinker, Tony	Prof	312-3175	tony_tinker	PWMB	PHD	75	Manchest	&1983
Weintrop, Joseph	Prof	312-3185	joseph_weintrop	F	PHD	84.	Oregon	& 9-93
Stan Ross Professorship in Accountancy								
Byard, Donal A.	Assoc	312-3187	donal_byard	F	PHD	98.	Maryland	9-02
Davis-Friday, Paquita Y.	Assoc	312-3385	paquita_friday	F	PHD	96.	Michigan	& 2-06
Dutta, Saurav K.	Assoc	312-3210	saurav_dutta	S	PHD	91.	Kansas	* 9-06
visiting from SUNY-Albany								
Joos, Peter R.	Assoc	312-3238	peter_joos	F	PHD	97.	Stanford	2-05
Kerstein, Joseph	Assoc	312-3160	joseph_kerstein	FC	PHD	90	Penn	1989
Claire & Eli Mason Scholar in Accountancy								
Marquardt, Carol A.	Assoc	312-3241	carol_marquardt	F	PHD	97.	Cornell	9-06
Melnik, Steven Y.	Assoc	312-3227	steven_melnik	X	LLM	00	NYU	2000
Sarath, Bharat	Assoc	312-3170	bharat_sarath	M	PHD	88.	Stanford	9-97
Vaysman, Igor	Assoc	321-3207	igor_vaysman	M	PHD	93.	Stanford	2-07
visiting from INSEAD								
Ye, Jianming	Assoc	312-3193	jimmy_ye	F	PHD	92	Chicago	2001
Young, Susan M.	Assoc		susan_young	F	PHD	00.	S Calif	9-05
Cenedella, David	Asst	312-3172	david_cenedella	T	LLM	97	NYU	9-06
Deng, Zhen	Asst	312-3203	zhen_deng	F	PHD	00.	NYU	1999
Huang, Rong	Asst	312-3204	rong_huang	M	PHD	06	Tx-Dallas	9-06
Lee, Jaywon	Asst	312-3237	jaywon_lee	F	ABD		Columbia	9-06
Ozbilgin, Mehmet	Asst	312-3233	mehmet_ozbilgin	M	PHD	02.	Purdue	9-02
Shon, John J.	Asst	312-3230	john_shon	F	PHD	04.	Chicago	9-03
Tan, Christine E. L.	Asst	312-3206	christine_tan	FA	PHD	00	Melbourne	1999
Strauss, Norman	SInst	312-3174	norman_strauss	A	MA	69	Baruch	9-01
Cherry, Julius	Lect	312-3235	julius_cherry	F	PHD	82	NYU	9-03

CUNY-Brooklyn College Brooklyn, NY 11210-2889 (718) Fax=951-4867
Accounting Faculty Department of Economics brooklyn.cuny.edu BS,MA
Dept Phone: 951-5317 2900 Bedford Ave Patricia Peter
Homepage: www.brooklyn.cuny.edu

Name	Rank	Phone	Email	Field	Degree	Yr	School	
Giladi, Kreindel	C-Ac	951-5568	kgiladi	PCFM	MA	81	CUNY-Brk	& 2-97
Solomon, Howard B.	Prof	951-5266	alicesolomon@a	LX	LLM	67	NYU	9-74
Davidoff, Howard	Assoc	951-5037	davidoff	LXP	LLM	87	NYU	& 9-86
McTague, Edward P.	Assoc	951-5037	emctague	PNFR	MBA	81	Fairl Dick	& 9-82
Testa, Gary J.	Assoc	951-5686	gtest	TXP	MBA	78	St Johns	& 9-79
Widman, Robert A.	Assoc	951-5266	rwidman	FPX	MBA	73	Rutgers	& 9-78
Zelcer, Moishe	Assoc	951-5245	mzelcer	DMF	PHD	91.	Baruch	& 2-77
Kass-Schraibman, Frimette	Asst	951-5568	frimette	APF	MA			& 9-05

CUNY-Lehman College Bronx, NY 10468-1589 (718) Fax=960-1173
Dept of Econ & Accounting College of Business lehman.cuny.edu
Dept Phone: 960-8297 250 Bedford Park Blvd W Kim Pierce
Homepage: www.lehman.cuny.edu

Name	Rank	Phone	Email	Field	Degree	Yr	School	
Tramontano, William A.	Dean							
Shreiber, Chanoch	C-Pr	960-8297	chanoch.schre+		PHD	73	Columbia	
Honig, Susan	Asst	960-8389	susan.honig	XCDS	MS		Pace	&1990
Kamen-Friedman, Michelle	Asst	960-8384	michelle.kamen	XPRA	MBA		St Johns	&1985
Murrell, F. Anthony	Lect	960-8388	anthony.murrell					&1994
Rodriguez, Ada	Lect	960-8159	ada.rodriguez		MBA		Columbia	1994
Ross, Marshall	Lect	960-8296	marshall.ross					
Tauber, Linda	Lect	960-8389	linda.tauber		MBA			&1990

CUNY-Hunter College New York, NY 10021 (212) Fax=772-5398
Department of Economics School of Arts & Sci hunter.cuny.edu BS
Dept Phone: 772-5401 695 Park Avenue Janet Tyson
Homepage: www.hunter.cuny.edu
  Did Not Respond--2005-2006 Listing

Name	Rank	Phone	Email	Field	Degree	Yr	School	
Friedlander, Judith	Dean	772-5121			PHD			

Honig, Marjorie	C-Pr	772-5401	mhonig		PHD	71	Columbia	9-81
Liveson, Avi O.	Prof	772-5394	aliveson	LX	LLM	75	NYU	9-86
Director of Accounting Program								
Kim, John J.	Assoc	772-5409	okim	F	PHD	93.	Memphis	1994
Cebenoyan, Fatma	Asst	772-5393	fatma.cebenoyan	FPX	PHD	98.	Maryland	1999
Mitsudome, Toshiaki	Asst	772-5430	toshiaki.mits+		PHD	01.	Baruch	9-00
Schleifer, Michael	Lect	772-5395	mschleif	AF	MBA	84	Pace	9-98

CUNY-Queens College
Dept Acctg & Info Sys PH 215
Dept Phone: 997-5070

Flushing, NY 11367-1597				(718) Fax=997-5079				
65-30 Kissena Blvd				qc.cuny.edu				BA,MS
65-30 Kissena Boulevard								Kerry Piorkowski
Blumenfrucht, Israel	C-Pr	997-5071	israel.blumen+	XV	PHD	81	NYU	& 9-81
Adelberg, Arthur H.	Prof	997-5074	arthur.adelberg	MBQ	PHD	77.	Baruch	& 7-73
Hitzig, Neal B.	Prof	997-5087	neal.hitzig	AQ	PHD	85.	Baruch	& 9-00
Levine, Marc H.	Prof	997-5084	marc.levine	AF	PHD	83	Yeshiva	& 2-75
Siegel, Joel G.	Prof	997-5083	joel.siegel	FM	PHD	78.	Baruch	& 9-74
Simon, Abraham J.	Prof	997-5078	abraham.simon	FTGN	PHD	71	Penn	& 9-75
Walker, John P.	Prof	997-5090	john.walker	AG	PHD	76.	Cincinnati	& 9-98
Leibowicz, Barry	Assoc	997-5081	barry.leibowicz	XL	LLM	73	NYU	9-74
Milich, Marvin M.	Assoc	997-5076	marvin.milich	LR	JD	71	NYU	& 9-87
Stevens, Michael	Assoc	997-5070	michael.stevens		LLM		NYU	& 9-82
Erlach, David	Asst	997-5086	david.erlach	TC	PHD	95	SW Jose	2-78
Mintz, Seymour	Asst	997-5096			JD		Touro	&
Silliman, Benjamin	Asst	997-5094	benjamin.sillman	TF	EDD	04	NYU	& 9-04
Dauber, Nicky	Lect	997-5089	nicky.dauber	A	MS	80	Long Isl	& 2-76
David, Amy	Lect	997-5069	amy.david		MS	06	Queens	&
Davidovits, Murray	Lect	997-5083	murray.david+	LR	JD	83	NY Law	2-98
Hornung, David	Lect	997-5073	david.hornung	F	MBA	75	Baruch	6-77

CUNY-Col of Staten Island
Accounting Faculty
Dept Phone: 982-2920

Staten Isl, NY 10314				(718) Fax=982-2965				
Department of Business				postbox.csi.cuny.edu				BS
2800 Victory Blvd								Loretta Brausewetter
Soto, Francisco	Dean	982-2315	soto	Span	PHD			
Nowak, Laura S.	C-Pr	982-2934	nowak	Fnce	PHD	78	CUNY	1986
Gottlieb, Max M.	Prof	982-2957	gottlieb	SD	PHD		Gdansk	& 9-87
Weiss, Aron	Assoc	982-2935	weiss	ASF	MBA	63	CUNY	&1971
Brickman, Deborah	Asst	982-2962	brickman	DA	MBA	85	CUNY-Brk	&1979
Englard, Baruch	Asst	982-2928	englard	CF	MBA	74	Long Isl	&1972
Martin, Barry	Asst	982-2961	martin	TX	MS	72	Long Isl	&1978
Sandler, John	Asst	982-2921	sandler	TX	JD	96	Lgls-Post	&1998
Scarinci, Cynthia	Asst	982-2954	scarinci	S	MBA	88	Pace	&2001

CUNY-York College
Accounting Faculty
Dept Phone: 262-2500

Jamaica, NY 11451				(718) Fax=				
Accounting & Business				york.cuny.edu				
94-20 Guy R. Brewer Blvd								
Althaus, Paul	C-Ac	262-2508	althaus					
Gellis, Harold C.	Prof	262-2523	gellis		MBA		Baruch	&1981
Bartman, Richard J.	Assoc	262-2519	bartman					
Kranacher, Mary-jo	Assoc	262-2517	kranacher					
Ruiz, Rosemarie	Assoc	262-2512	ruiz					
Clovey, Robert	Asst		rclovey					
Stern, Lorraine	Asst	262-2516	lstern					

Claremont McKenna College
Accounting Program
Dept Phone: 607-3041

Claremont, CA 91711-6400				(909) Fax=621-8249				2004
Department of Economics				claremontmckenna.edu				BA
500 E. 9th Street								Mrs. N. Faust
Hess, Gregory D.	Dean	621-8117	greg.hess	Econ	PHD	90	J Hopkins	2002
Massoud, Marcos F. (Marc)	D-Pr	607-3203	marc.massoud	FTI	PHD	73	NYU	* 1980
Robert A. Day Distinguished Professor of Accounting								
Ferris, Kenneth R.	Prof			FI	PHD	74.	Ohio St	2006
Ganguly, Ananda R.	Assoc			FM	PHD	95.	Pittsburgh	2007
Rosett, Joshua G.	Assoc	607-3625	jrosett	FTV	PHD	89	Princeton	2003
Wallace, James S.	Assoc	607-6063	james.wallace	FM	PHD	96.	U Wash	
Taylor, James D.	SLect	607-3455	james.taylor	XLPR	JD	74	Wayne St	&1989
Weis, Frederick	Exec		fweis	FAQ	ABD		Claremont	2003

Clarion University
Department of Accountancy
Dept Phone: 393-2628

Clarion, PA 16214-1232				(814) Fax=393-1910				1998,1998
College of Business				clarion.edu				BS,MBA
Wood Street								Vickie Persic
Pesek, James G.	Dean$	393-2600	jpesek	Mgt	PHD	84	Pittsburgh	8-80
Oliver, Thomas W.	C-Pr	393-2628	toliver	FT	PHD	83.	Mass	8-92
Danvers, Kreag	Prof	393-2628	kdanvers	CMS	PHD	99.	Kent St	* & 8-05
Grenci, Anthony	Prof	393-2608	agrence	XM	PHD	03	Pittsburgh	# * & 8-03
Otte, Randon C.	Asst	393-2606	rotte	ANP	MBA	74	Clarion St	& 8-76

Clark University　　Worcester, MA　　01610-1477　　(508) Fax=793-8822　　　1986,1986
Accounting Faculty　　Grad School of Mgt　　clarku.edu　　　　　MBA,MSF
Dept Phone: 793-7670　　950 Main Street　　　　Laurie Kennedy Yvanauskas
Homepage: www.clarku.edu

Ottensmeyer, Edward J.	Dean$	793-7670	eottensmeyer	Pol	PHD	83	Indiana	1986
Dhavale, Dileep G.	Prof	793-7781	ddhavale	FM	PHD	75	Penn St	&9-87
Seol, Inshik	Asst	793-7748	iseol	FM	PHD	96	Conn	2001

Clark Atlanta University　　Atlanta, GA　　30314-4391　　(404) Fax=880-8458　　1974,1974
Department of Accounting　　School of Business Adm　　cau.edu　　　　BA,MA
Dept Phone: 880-8480　　Brawley Dr at Fair St SW

Jefferson, Jonathan	Dean				MS		Cornell	2004
Friar, Shirley A.	C-Ac	880-8855		MF	PHD	86.	Tx-Austin	
Gokarn, Rajul Y.	Assoc	880-8145	rgokarn	FIMT	PHD	84.	Geo St	1994
Carr, Virgil A.	Asst	880-8143	vcarr	AFN	MBA	72	Atlanta	&1988
Rubenfield, Allen J.	Asst	880-8786	arubenfield	EFJX	JD	76	Pittsburgh	&1998

Clarkson University　　Potsdam, NY　　13699-5790　　(315) Fax=268-3810　　1977,1982
Accounting Area　　School of Business　　clarkson.edu　　　　BS
Dept Phone: 268-2300　　　　　　Susan Wood 268-2300

Sugrue, Timothy F.	Dean	268-2300	tsugrue	Fnce	PHD	85	Mass	2000
Brown, Clifford D.	Prof	268-6434	cbrown	AGVX	PHD	68.	Mich St	* 2005

Clayton State University　　Morrow, GA　　30260-0285　　(678) Fax=466-4599　　2006
Accounting Dept　　School of Business　　mail.clayton.edu　　　BBA,BS
Dept Phone: 466-4500　　2000 Clayton State Blvd　　Mary Alice Gladin 961-3410
Homepage: http://business.clayton.edu

Miller, Ernest M.	Dean	466-4523	ernestmiller		MBA	70	Harvard	N-97
Bullen, Maria Lombardi	Assoc	466-4516	mbullen	BAF	PHD	82.	UCLA	&2006
Butterfield, Scott	Assoc	466-4506	sbutterfield	CX	PHD	02.	Geo St	8-06
Kordecki, Gregory S.	Assoc	466-4507	gregkordecki	AFBI	MPA	76	Geo St	&1976
Novin, Adel M.	Asst	466-4508	adelnovin	SCMG	PHD	82.	Georgia	8-01
Ogden, Judith	Asst	466-4509	jogden	X	JD	79	Duquesne	8-04

Clemson University　　Clemson, SC　　29634-1303　　(864) Fax=656-4892　　ß (13) 1977,1983
Sch Acctncy & Legal Studies　　Col Bus & Soc Science　　clemson.edu　　BS,MPACC
Dept Phone: 656-3265　　301 Sirrine Hall　　　　Linda Sears
Homepage: http://business.clemson.edu/account/index.htm

Grigsby, David W.	Dean$	656-3177	grigsby	Mgt	PHD	80	N Carol	1982
Welton, Ralph E.	D-Pr	656-4881	edwlsur	FTJ	PHD	82.	LSU	1983
Cash, L. Stephen	Prof	656-1019	cl	X	LLM	72	Wash U	&1982
Dickens, Thomas L.	Prof	656-4890	dickent	XF	PHD	83.	Tx A&M	* &1984
University Alumni Professor								
Guffey, Daryl M.	Prof	656-3999	dguffey	FJ	PHD	89.	S Carol	# * &9-99
McMillan, Jeffrey J.	Prof	656-4880	mjeffre	FABO	PHD	90.	S Carol	1990
Winters, Alan J.	Prof	656-3245	awinter	AP	PHD	74.	Tx Tech	&1994
Clark, Lawrence S.	Assoc	656-4887	clawren	FV	MA	70	Georgia	* &1977
Dull, Richard B.	Assoc	656-0610	rdull	S	PHD	97.	Va Tech	&2001
Kennedy, Frances A.	Assoc	656-4712	fkenned	CM	PHD	02.	North Tx	&2001
Schleifer, Lydia L.	Assoc	656-4710	schleif	FA	PHD	88.	Georgia	1985
Hollingsworth, Carl W.	Asst	656-4883		A	PHD	07	Tennessee	&2007
Mowrey, Megan E.	Asst	656-4879	mmowrey		PHD			
Owens, Lisa A.	Asst	656-4888	lisao	FM	PHD	01.	Okla St	&2004
Stanley, Jonathan D.	Asst	656-4882		AF	PHD	07	Alabama	&2007
Madray, J. Russell	SLect	656-3745	mj	PF	MPAC	88	Clemson	# * & 8-94
Prater, Mary Ann M.	SLect	656-3774	maryann	FMP	MS	83	Clemson	&1985

Cleveland State University　　Cleveland, OH　　44114　　(216) Fax=687-9212　　ß (13) 1974,1978
Department Accounting　　College of Business Adm　　csuohio.edu　　BA,MACC
Dept Phone: 687-4720　　1860 E. 18 St - Su 512　　Reina Ruano
Homepage: www.cba.csuohio.edu

Scherer, Robert F.	Dean	687-2130	r.scherer	Mgt	PHD	87	Miss	2002
Gaffney, Dennis J.	C-Pr	687-4723	dennis.gaffney	XF	PHD	73.	Illinois	&2004
Fuglister, Jayne	Prof	687-4773	j.fuglister	F	DBA	85.	Geo Wash	&1986
Kreiser, Lawrence A.	Emer	687-3670	l.kreiser	2005	PHD	75.	Cincinnati	# &1976
McClain, Bruce W.	Assoc	687-3652	b.mcclain	XL	JD	82	Case Wes	& 6-87
Meier, Heidi H.	Assoc	687-3671	h.meier	AFO	DBA	87.	Kent St	&1986
Poznanski, Peter John	Assoc	687-4764	p.poznanski	BCM	PHD	91.	Tx Tech	* &1991
Rozen, Etzmun S.	Assoc	687-4727	e.rozen	F	PHD	86.	NYU	1981
Spero, Abba V.	Assoc	687-4725	a.spero	F	PHD	76.	NYU	&1973
Yetmar, Scott A.	Asst	687-3999	s.yetmar	BDJX	PHD	95.	Okla St	* &2002
Cipriano, Angela	VInst	687-3672	a.cipriano	FM	MACC	04	Clev St	2006
Kaminsky, Daniel	VInst	687-2081	d.a.kaminsky	AF	MSA	78	Cen Fla	&2006
Lee, P.	VInst	687-4729	p.lee	FIC	PHD	01	Kyung-He	&2001
Thornton, Phillip W.	VInst	687-3658	pthor71945@y	FM	PHD	93.	North Tx	2004

Coastal Carolina University
Actg, Fin & Eco POBox 261954
Dept Phone: 349-2574

Conway, SC	29528-6054			(843) Fax=349-2455				1999
Wall College of Bus				coastal.edu				BS,MBA
119 Chanticleer Dr; Wall Bld								Pat Silva
Lowenstein, Henry	Dean	349-2640		Mgt	PHD	84	Illinois	7-07
Henderson, Linda R.	C-Ac	349-2649	henderso	FXIV	DBA	89.	La Tech	&1986
Krippel, Gregory L.	Assoc	349-2643	krippel	AFS	PHD	91.	Fla St	1994
Maguire, Karen A.	Asst	349-4163	kmaguire	FM	PHD	04.	Alabama	2004
Mortimer, John W.	Asst	349-2609	jmortim	SFMT	PHD	01.	Fla Atl	2002
Smith, Tracy L.	Asst	349-6443	smith	FI	PHD	01.	Alabama	&2006

The Colorado College
Accounting Faculty
Dept Phone: 389-6407

Colorado Spr, CO 80903-3298				(719) Fax=389-6927				
Dept Econ & Business				coloradocollege.edu				
14 East Cache La Poudre								Nancy Heinecke
Stimpert, Larry	C-Pr	389-6418	lstimpert	FM	PHD	92	Illinois	1996
Chesley, Julie	Prof	389-6407	jchesley		PHD	96	Colorado	2007
Laux, Judith A.	Prof	389-6414	jlaux	FM	PHD	90	Colorado	1979

Univ of Colorado at Boulder
Accounting & Business Law
Dept Phone: 492-4271

Boulder, CO	80309-0419			(303) Fax=492-5962				ß 1938,1967
Leeds School of Bus				colorado.edu				BS,MBA,MS,PHD
								Ms. Connie Blazon
Ahlburg, Dennis	Dean	492-1809	dennis.ahlburg		PHD	79	Penn	2005
Solto, Frank H.	O-Pr	492-1549	frank.selto	M	PHD	77.	U Wash	1985
Jackson, Betty R.	Prof	492-6621	betty.jackson	X	PHD	82.	Tx-Austin	&1983
Tracy, John A.	Emer	492-7217	john.tracy	2000	PHD	61.	Wisconsin	&1965
Buchman, Thomas A.	Assoc	492-8350	thomas.buchman	F	PHD	76.	Illinois	&1974
Frederick, David M.	Assoc	492-8372	david.frederick	BAF	PHD	86.	Michigan	&1986
Gazur, Wayne M.	Assoc	492-7013	wayne.gazur	XL	LLM	84	Denver	&1986
Jacob, John	Assoc	735-6335	john.jacob	FM	PHD	95.	Nrthwstrn	2000
Rock, Steven K.	Assoc	735-5009	steven.rock	F	PHD	96.	Penn St	# * 8-98
Shane, Philip B.	Assoc	492-4271	phil.shane	F	PHD	82.	Oregon	& 8-97
Soderstrom, Naomi S.	Assoc	735-6620	naomi.soderst+	SM	PHD	90.	Nrthwstrn	2000
Gunny, Katherine	Asst	492-4272	katherine.gunny	F	PHD	05	Berkeley	2005
Burns, Cathleen S.	Inst	492-4076	cathleen.burns	CM	PHD	95	N Mex St	&2002
MacFee, Raymond D.	Inst	492-3969	raymond.macfee	FAN	MBA	70	Penn St	&1987
Morley, Susan	Inst	492-4312	susan.morley	XL	JD	00	Colorado	2004
Stec-Helstad, Nancy	Inst	492-0141	nancy.stec-hel+	X	MS	96	Colorado	2002

U of Colorado at Co Springs
Accounting & Finance Dept
Dept Phone: 262-3113

Colorado Spr, CO 80933-7150				(719) Fax=262-3494				1991,1991
College of Bus & Adm				uccs.edu				BS,BA,MBA
1420 Austin Bluffs Parkway								Sandy Loux
Reddy, Venkat	Dean	262-3113	vreddy	Fnce	PHD	92	Penn St	8-91
Zwirlein, Thomas J.	C-Pr	262-3241	tzwirlei	Fnce	PHD	85	Oregon	1984
Claiborne, M. Cathy	Prof			FGM	PHD	94.	Tennessee	* &2007
Miller, Paul B. W.	Prof	262-3590	pmiller	FJ	PHD	71.	Tx-Austin	&1988
Wilcox, Kirkland A.	Assoc	262-3413	kwilcox	FA	PHD	72.	Tx-Austin	&1972
McAllister, Brian P.	Asst			FA	PHD	05.	Nebraska	&2007
Trumpfheller, Sheri L.	Inst	262-3754	strumpfh	FM	MBA	00	Colo Spr	&2000

Univ of Colorado at Denver
Accounting Program
Dept Phone: 556-5803

Denver, CO	80217-3364			(303) Fax=556-5899				ß (123) 1986,1986
Col Bus & Adm Box173364				cudenver.edu				BS,MS-ACCT
Camput Box 165								
Ambron, Sueann	Dean	556-5801	sueann.ambron		EDD	73	Stanford	2000
Neumann, Bruce R.	D-Pr	556-5884	bruce.neumann	MNCB	PHD	75.	Illinois	1984
Murray, Dennis F.	Prof	556-5891	dennis.murray	FB	PHD	81.	Mass	&1983
Colbert, Gary J.	Assoc	556-5844	gary.colbert	FAM	PHD	91.	Oregon	& 9-93
Martin, L. Ann	Assoc	556-5827	louisa.martin	FMIZ	PHD	93.	Minnesota	& 9-94
Roberts, Michael L.	Assoc	556-6518	michael.roberts	XAB	PHD	88.	Geo St	&2004
Dee, Carol Callaway	Asst			FM	PHD	99.	LSU	& 8-06
Klersey, George F.	Asst	556-5801	george.klersey	MS	PHD	90.	S Calif	&2007
Nieschwietz, Robert J.	Asst	556-5805	robert.niesch+	FA	PHD	01.	Ariz St	& 8-01
Conner, Elizabeth C.	SInst	556-5882	elizabeth.connor	FTX	MS	79	Colo St	& 9-89
Fischer, Cindy Ogden	Inst	556-6618	cindy.fischer	FSG	MBA	80	Colorado	&1983
Hockenbury, Robert D.	SInst	556-5862	robert.hocken+	FMTX	MTX	84	Houston	& 6-87

Colorado State University
Department of Accounting
Dept Phone: 491-5102
  email @1=lamar.colostate.edu

Fort Collins, CO	80523-1271			(970) Fax=491-2676				ß 1970,1976
College of Business				business.colostate.edu				BS,MBA,MACC
								Laura L. McGrath
Menon, Ajay	Dean	491-6471	ajay.menon	Mktg	PHD	93	North Tx	1991
Lewis, Barry L.	C-Pr	491-2977	barry.lewis		PHD	78.	Penn St	4-04
Mister, William G.	Prof	491-6256	bmister@1	CMFV	PHD	73.	Berkeley	1989
Casterella, Jeffrey R.	Assoc	491-5242	jeff.casterella	F	PHD	95.	Colorado	&2000

| Johnson, Laurence E. | Assoc | 491-6126 | laurence.john+ | GAF | PHD | 91. Tx Tech | &1990 |
| Lenk, Margarita M. | Assoc | 491-4983 | margarita.lenk | MSBC | PHD | 91. S Carol | * 1991 |
| joint appointment with Computer Info System |
Rankin, Frederick W.	Assoc	491-2422	bill.rankin	M	PHD	99. Tx A&M	2005
Samelson, Donald P.	Assoc	491-6420	don.samelson	AX	PHD	92. Va Tech	&1998
Johnston, Derek	Asst	491-6443	derek.johnston	F	PHD	01. Colorado	&2002
Lowensohn, Suzanne H.	Asst	491-7481	suzanne.lowen+	ABGM	PHD	96. U Miami	&2002

Colorado State Univ-Pueblo — Pueblo, CO 81001-4901 — (719) Fax=549-2909 — 2003,2003
Dept of Business Adm — Hasan School Business — colostate-pueblo.edu — BSBA/MBA
Dept Phone: 549-2142 — 2200 Bonforte Blvd — Emily Forsyth

Hanks, Sue	Dean$	549-2882	sue.hanks	Mgt	EDD	83 Arkansas	1992
Eriksen, Scott	Asst	549-2142	scott.eriksen	MC	PHD	87. North Tx	* &2005
Todd, Christine	Lect	549-2142	christine.todd	FP	MS	98 Co-Denve	2005
Wink, Geri B.	Lect	549-2030	geri.wink	FP	MBA	78 Sam Hous	&2004

Columbia University — New York, NY 10027 — (212) Fax=316-9219 — 1916
Accounting Faculty — Graduate School of Bus — columbia.edu — MBA,PHD
Dept Phone: 854-3162 — Uris Hall, 3022 Broadway — Jeffrey Jullich

Hubbard, R. Glen	Dean	854-6083	rgh1	Econ	PHD	83 Harvard	1988
Nissim, Doron	C-Ac	854-4249	dn75	F	PHD	98. Berkeley	1997
Melumad, Nahum D.	Prof	854-2475	ndm4	MAF	PHD	85. Berkeley	&1993
James L. Dohr Professor of Accounting & Business Law
Penman, Stephen H.	Prof	854-9151	shp38	F	PHD	78. Chicago	&1999
George O. May Professor of Accounting
Baldenius, Tim	Assoc	854-8659	tb171	M	PHD	98 Vienna	1998
Jorgensen, Bjorn N.	Assoc	854-9220	bnj2101	MF	PHD	98. Nrthwstrn	2002
Mohanram, Partha S.	Assoc	854-2561	pm2128	F	PHD	98. Harvard	2003
Balachandran, Sudhakar	Asst	854-4582	svb34	MF	PHD	01. Harvard	2000
Sadka, Gil	Asst	854-5391	gs2235	FIL	PHD	05 Chicago	2005
Schmidt, Andrew P.	Asst	854-0768	aps2113	FX	PHD	04. Ariz St	&2004
Yee, Kenton K.	Asst	854-4495	kky2001	FLT	PHD	01. Stanford	2001
Yeo, Julian J. L.	Asst	854-6172	jy2176	F	PHD	03 Melbourne	2004
Zhang, Yuan	Asst	854-0159	yz2113	F	PHD	03. S Calif	2003

Columbus State University — Columbus, GA 31907-5645 — (706) Fax=568-2184 — 2004,2004
Dept of Accounting & Finance — Turner College of Bus — colstate.edu — BBA
Dept Phone: 568-2044 — 4225 University Avenue
Homepage: www.colstate.edu

Hadley, Linda U.	Dean	568-2044	hadley_linda	Fnce	PHD	92 Auburn	1992
Langston, Vicky	C-Ac	562-1663	langston_vicky	Econ	PHD	83 Tx-Austin	2003
Kettering, Ronald C.	Prof	562-1660	kettering_ron	MFCP	DBA	77 La Tech	# * &1986
Carter, Fonda Long	Assoc	568-2152	carter_fonda	FPA	DBA	98. Miss St	&1988
Jones, Rita C.	Assoc	562-1661	jones_rita	FMT	DBA	94. Miss St	* 2003
Lang, Teresa	Asst	562-1671	lang_teresa	SXP	PHD	04 Auburn	&2004

Concordia College — Moorhead, MN 56562 — (218) Fax=299-4277
Accounting Faculty — Dept Bus, Atg & Econ — cord.edu — BA
Dept Phone: 299-4411 — 901 South Eighth Street — Jessi Mithun
Homepage: www.cord.edu/dept/busecon

Stradley, Scot A.	C-Pr	299-3115	stradley	Econ	PHD	77 Utah	2001
Specht, James	Assoc	299-4538	specht	AC	PHD	88. Geo St	&2000
Foss, Robert K.	Asst	299-3486	bfoss	FP	MACC	N Dakota	& 8-90
Twedt, Ronald G.	Asst	299-3484	twedt	XT	MTAX	Minnesota	&1991

University of Connecticut — Storrs, CT 06269-1041 — (860) Fax=486-4838 — ß (12) 1958,1971
Dept Accounting Unit 1041A — School of Business — business.uconn.edu — BS,MBA,MS,PHD
Dept Phone: 486-3018 — 2100 Hillside Road — Linda Petrofsky/Leanne Bruder
Homepage: http://www.business.uconn.edu/accounting

| Hussein, Mohamed E. A. | H-Pr | 486-3087 | mo | MF | PHD | 77 Pittsburgh | 9-78 |
| Biggs, Stanley F. | Prof | 486-2374 | stan | BFA | PHD | 78. Minnesota | 9-84 |
| KPMG Professor of Accounting |
| Kochanek, Richard Frank | Prof | 486-2864 | dickk | FPV | PHD | 72. Missouri | 9-72 |
| Willenborg, Michael | Prof | 486-3020 | mikew | AF | PHD | 96. Penn St | & 9-96 |
| Ackerman Scholar |
Dunbar, Amy E.	Assoc	486-5138	amy.dunbar	X	PHD	89. Tx-Austin	& 1-99
Hoskin, Robert E.	Assoc	486-4071	robh	MF	PHD	81. Cornell	9-86
Hurley, Richard E.	Assoc	257-8466	rhurley	FXM	PHD	94. Conn	& 9-99
Phillips, John D.	Assoc	486-2789	jphillips	X	PHD	99. Iowa	1-99
Plesko, George A.	Assoc	486-3018	gplesko	XM	PHD	85 Wisconsin	2005
Rosman, Andrew J.	Assoc	486-5891	andy	BFV	PHD	89. N Carol	& 1-89
Director, MS in Accounting
Seow, Gim S.	Assoc	486-3019	gim	FT	PHD	85. Oregon	9-91
Gramling, Lawrence J.	Asst	486-2892	larry	AFM	DBA	82. Maryland	& 9-80

Liu, Zhu (Alfred)	Asst	486-3847	aliu	FV	PHD	06.	Ca-Irvine	2006
Nelson, Clifford	Asst	486-4510	cliff	MS	DBA	63	Illinois	8-97
Rice, Sarah	Asst	486-1928	srice	ASB	PHD	06	Ohio St	2006
Weber, David P.	Asst	486-3018	dweber	FX	PHD	05.	Colorado	&2005
Redemske, Mike	Inst	486-4413	mredemske	X	MS		DePaul	2001

Cornell University   Ithaca, NY   14853-6201   (607) Fax = 254-4590   1950,1950
Accounting Faculty   Johnson Grad Sch of Mgt   cornell.edu   MBA,PHD
Dept Phone: 255-9431   Sage Hall   Fran Ormsbee
Homepage: www.johnson.cornell.edu

Swieringa, Robert J.	Dean	255-6418	rjs22	FB	PHD	69	Illinois	7-97
The Anne and Elmer Lindseth Dean								
Libby, Robert	C-Pr	255-3348	rl54	FBA	PHD	74.	Illinois	& 7-89
David A. Thomas Professor of Management								
Bloomfield, Robert J.	Prof	255-9407	rjb9	MTFB	PHD	92	Michigan	& 9-91
Nicholas H. Noyes Professor of Management; Director of Graduate Studies								
Dyckman, Thomas R.	Emer	255-3491	trd2	2007	PHD	62	Michigan	9-64
Ann Whitney Olin Professor of Accounting								
Hilton, Ronald W.	Prof	255-4851	rwh5	MQC	PHD	77.	Ohio St	9-77
Lee, Charles M. C.	Prof	255-6255	cl86	FB	PHD	90.	Cornell	& 8-96
Henrietta Johnson Louis Professor of Management								
Nelson, Mark W.	Prof	255-6323	mwn2	FBA	PHD	90.	Ohio St	& 7-90
Eleanora and Goorge Landow Profcooor of Management								
Bhojraj, Sanjeev	Assoc	255-4069	sb235	F	PHD	00.	Florida	& 8-99
D'Souza, Julia M.	Assoc	255-2349	jd48	F	PHD	95.	Nrthwstrn	9-94
Nichols, D. Craig	Asst	255-0053	dcnb	F	PHD	05.	Indiana	2005
Yehuda, Nir	Asst		ny35		PHD	05.	Columbia	2005

Cornell Univ-Hotel School   Ithaca, NY   14853-6902   (607) Fax = 255-1277   2004,2004
Finance, Atg & Real Estate   School of Hotel Adm   cornell.edu   BA,MMH,MS,PHD
Dept Phone: 255-5263   435 Statler Hall   Sue Foote

Johnson, Michael D.	Dean	255-5106	mdj27		PHD		Chicago	2006
Dittman, David A.	Prof	255-6697	dad19	MCU	PHD	73.	Ohio St	7-90
The Hubert E. Westfall Professor of Accounting								
Eyster, James	Emer	255-5269	jje5	2000	PHD	77	Cornell	1972
Geller, A. Neal	Prof	255-0335	ang5	MA	PHD	77.	Syracuse	&1976
Robert H. Beck Professor of Hospitality Financial Management								
Canina, Linda	Assoc	255-8051	lc29	F	PHD	90	NYU	1994
Carvell, Steven	Assoc	255-8369	sac20	F	PHD	84	SUNY-Bin	1986
deRoos, Jan A.	Assoc	255-8716	jad10	Fnce	PHD	94	Cornell	1988
Potter, Gordon S.	Assoc	255-8061	gsp6	FM	PHD	86.	Wisconsin	&1994
Quan, Daniel	Assoc	255-6404	dq22	F	PHD	90	Berkeley	1999
Chang, Charles	Asst	255-9882	cc378	F	PHD	03	Berkeley	2003
Hesford, James W.	Asst	255-9003	jh383	B	PHD	98.	S Calif	2004
Ma, Qing Zhong	Asst	255-8140	qm26	F	PHD	06	S Calif	2006

Cornerstone University   Grand Rapids, MI 49525-5897   (616) Fax =
Accounting Faculty   Division of Business   cornerstone.edu   BA
Dept Phone: 222-1551   1001 E. Beltline, NE

Stamm, Brad K.	C	254-1630	brad_stamm		PHD	97	Fordham	8-99
Bos, Lawrence J.	Assoc	949-5300	lawrence_j_bos	PCM	MBA	74	Mich St	1-76
Riter, William R.	Assoc	222-1551	willian_r_riter	ASVX	MS	71	Illinois	& 8-85

Creighton University   Omaha, NE   68178-0308   (402) Fax = 280-5565   ß (1) 1949,1981
Department of Accounting   College of Business Adm   creighton.edu   BSBA
Dept Phone: 280-2602   2500 California Plaza   Mary Pojar
Homepage: http://business.creighton.edu/departments/accounting.html

Hendrickson, Anthony	Dean	280-2852		Sys	PHD	91	Arkansas	2005
Lewis, Thomas D.	C-Ac	280-2181	tlewis	FM	PHD	79.	Nebraska	* & 9-81
Krogstad, Jack L.	Prof	280-2620	jkrogstad	A	PHD	75.	Nebraska	& 9-80
Union Pacific Professor of Accountancy								
Raval, Vasant H.	Prof	280-5518	vraval	SMIC	DBA	76.	Indiana	9-80
Flinn, Ronald E.	Assoc	280-2063	rflinn	CFXZ	DBA	89.	Kentucky	* & 9-86
Purcell, Thomas J. III	Assoc	280-2062	tpurcell	XLI	PHD	88.	Nebraska	& 9-79
Shimerda, Thomas A.	Assoc	280-2615	tshimerda	CMS	PHD	78.	Nebraska	* & 9-80
Taylor, Mark H.	Assoc	280-2441	mhtaylor	ABMS	PHD	94.	Arizona	& 9-02
Begley Endowed Chair in Accounting								

Univ of the Cumberlands   Williamsburg, KY 40769-7984   (606) Fax = 539-4449
Accounting Faculty Box 7984   Dept of Business & Econ   ucumberlands.edu   BS
Dept Phone: 539-4254   820 Walnut Street   Agnes Brown

Combs, Margaret D.	C-Ac	539-4254	mcombs	FAC	DBA	04	Sarasota	&2005
Hubbard, Harold F.	Prof	539-4254	hhubbard	FD	MBA	60	Kentucky	& 7-60
Bailey, Micaiah	Assoc	539-4272	mibailey	PX	MBA	72	Murray St	* & 8-73
LaGrone, R. Michael	Assoc	539-4254	mlagrone	FMC	PHD	90.	S Carol	* & 8-98

Daemen College
Accounting Department
Dept Phone: 839-8329

	Amherst, NY	14226-3592		(716) Fax=839-8261				
	Div of Business & Comm			daemen.edu				BS,MS
	4380 Main Street							
Kuechler, Linda J.	C-Ac	839-8398	lkuechle	CSFI	PHD	96	SUNY-Buf	* &1984
Tschopp, Daniel J.	Assoc	839-8239	dtschopp	FACX	MBA	96	SUNY-Buf	2000

University of Dallas
Accounting Faculty
Dept Phone: 721-5277
Homepage: thedallasmba.com/ac/

	Irving, TX	75062-4736		(972) Fax=721-4007				
	College of Business			gsm.udallas.edu				BA,MS,MBA,MM
	1845 East Northgate Drive							Sue Stevens
Whittington, J. Lee	Dean	721-5276	jlee		PHD	97	Tx-Arlin	
Scofield, Barbara W.	Assoc	721-5034	scofield	VFDS	PHD	89.	Tx-Austin	&2004
Walsh, Robert J.	Assoc	721-5361	rwalsh	XF	PHD	95	Notre Dm	&2006
Shoemaker, Bill	Asst	721-5256	shoe	XAM	MBA	73	Golden Gt	&

Dallas Baptist University
Accounting Faculty
Dept Phone: 333-5244

	Dallas, TX	75211-9211		(214) Fax=333-6823				
	College of Business			dbu.edu				BBA,MBA
	3000 Mountain Creek Parkway							Shirley Mitchell
Conner, Charlene	Dean	333-5239	charlene		DBA	04	Argosy	
Martindale, Bobbie C.	Prof	333-5268	bobbie	XM	PHD	89.	North Tx	&1993
Moore, Debra	Asst	333-5263	debram	FS	PHD	07	Touro	&2001

Dartmouth College
Accounting Faculty
Dept Phone:

	Hanover, NH	03755-9000		(603) Fax=646-1308				1916
	Amos Tuck Sch of Bus Ad			dartmouth.edu				MBA
	100 Tuck Hall							
Danos, Paul	Dean	646-2460	paul.danos	F	PHD	74	Tx-Austin	& 6-95
Laurence F. Whittemore Professor of Business Administration								
Govindarajan, Vijay	Prof	646-2156	vijay.govind+	M	DBA	78.	Harvard	1985
Daum Professor of International Management								
Howell, Robert A.	VProf	646-0780	robert.a.howell	FM	DBA	66.	Harvard	&2000
Sansing, Richard C.	Prof	646-0392	richard.c.san+	XMT	PHD	90.	Tx-Austin	1998
Stickney, Clyde P.	Emer	646-2640	clyde.p.stickney	2004	DBA	70.	Fla St	&1977
Ormond Beach, FL; 386-677-9712								
Stocken, Phillip C.	Assoc	646-2843	phillip.c.sto+	F	PHD	98.	Penn St	2003
Robinson, Leslie A.	Asst	646-4018	leslie.a.rob+	XF	PHD	06.	N Carol	&2006

University of Dayton
Department of Accounting
Dept Phone: 229-2429
Homepage: www.sba.udayton.edu/acc/

	Dayton, OH	45469-2242		(937) Fax=229-2270	ß (1)			1983,1988
	School of Business Adm			notes.udayton.edu				BS,MBA
	300 College Park				Teresa Wehmeyer			229-2429
Meyers, Patricia W.	Dean	229-3731	pat.meyers	Mktg	PHD	83	Syracuse	2003
Burrows, Ron J.	C-Ac	229-2429	ron.burrows	FI	PHD	80.	Penn St	8-81
Castellano, Joseph F.	Prof	229-4605	joseph.castel+	GMF	PHD	71.	St Louis	1999
Roehm, Harper A.	Emer	229-2429	harper.roehm	2001	DBA	72.	Fla St	&1992
Street, Donna L.	Prof	229-2461	donna.street	FIT	PHD	87.	Tennessee	2002
Mahrt Chair in Accounting								
Brady, Thomas J.	Assoc	229-2437	thomas.brady	FS	PHD	82.	St Louis	1981
Clark, Willard C. Jr.	Emer	229-2429	williard.clark	2001	MBA	60	Miami U	& 9-63
Eley, Marion J.	Emer	229-2429		1996	MBA	64	Xavier	&1961
Geary, K. Michael (Mike)	Assoc	229-4625	mike.geary	AEF	PHD	82.	Cincinnati	& 9-76
Greenlee, Janet S.	Assoc	229-4790	janet.greenlee	NFSP	PHD	93.	Kentucky	&1999
Larson, Robert K.	Assoc	229-2497	robert.larson	IFMV	PHD	93.	Utah	* &2001
Rosenzweig, Kenneth Y.	Emer	229-2429	ken.rosenzweig	2001	PHD	77.	Mich St	# * &1981
Randolph, David W.	Asst	229-4069	david.randolph	XF	PHD	00.	Indiana	&2003
Carlson, Carolyn	Lect	229-2429	carolyn.carlson	MP	MBA	81	Dayton	&2007
Shankar, Geeta R.	Lect	229-4572	geeta.shankar	P	MBA	01	Dayton	&2001
Shishoff, John W.	Lect	229-4173	john.shishoff	MP	ABD		Penn St	&1999
Director, SBA Undergraduate Programs								

University of Delaware
Dept of Accounting & MIS
Dept Phone: 831-2961

	Newark, DE	19716-2715		(302) Fax=831-4676	ß (13)			1966,1982
	Lerner Col Bus & Econ			lerner.udel.edu				BS,MS
	South College Avenue							Nina Warren
Gempesaw, Conrado M.	Dean	831-1221	gempesaw		PHD	85	Penn St	2006
Gillespie, Jackson F.	C-Ac	831-1790	gillespj	MC	PHD	78.	Va Tech	* 9-77
Baroudi, Jack	Prof		baroudi	SB	PHD	84	NYU	2002
Buckmaster, Dale A.	Prof	831-2962	buckmasd	FH	PHD	73.	Penn St	& 9-70
Debessay, Araya	Prof	831-6890	debessaa	AFMI	PHD	79.	Syracuse	# * & 9-78
Jones, Scott K.	Prof	831-6515	joness	MC	PHD	88.	Drexel	1988
Kane, Gregory D.	Prof	831-6826	kaneg	FS	PHD	92.	Va Tech	& 2-93
Pollack, Sheldon D.	Prof	831-1803	pollacks	XL	PHD	79	Cornell	1994
St. Pierre, E. Kent	Prof	831-1793	stpierrk	FTE	PHD	81.	Wash U	& 7-93
White, Clinton E. Jr. (Skip)	Prof	831-6902	whitec	SA	DBA	81.	Indiana	9-87

Geerts, Guido L.	Assoc	831-6413	geertsg	S	PHD	93	Free U	9-00
Paretta, Robert L.	Assoc	831-1802	parettar	F	PHD	73.	Syracuse	& 9-72
Velury, Uma K.	Assoc	831-1764	veluryu	F	PHD	99.	S Carol	9-99
Wragge, John H.	Assoc	831-1807	wraggej	AS	PHD	75.	Houston	&1981
Blue, Jon	Asst		bluej	S	PHD	06	Va Comm	2006
Cao, Jin Wei	Asst	831-1796		S	PHD	95	Arizona	9-05
DeLuca, Dorrie	Asst	831-4226	delucad	S	PHD	02	Temple	9-02
Everard, Andrea	Asst	831-4677		S	PHD	93	Pittsburgh	9-03
Jenkins, David S.	Asst	831-6823	jenkinsd	AF	PHD	02.	Maryland	9-02
Serva, Mark A.	Asst	831-1795	servam	S	PHD	94	Tx-Austin	9-99
Wang, Jiannan	Asst		wangh	S	PHD	06	Arizona	2006
Brady, Joseph A.	Inst	831-1765	bradyj	S	MBA	77	Drexel	9-90
Davidson, Spring	Inst		davidso	S	MBA	03	Delaware	1996
Kingery, Rita	Inst	831-4675	kingeryr	FM	MS	78	CS-Sacra	&1980
Monk, Ellen	Inst	831-1794	monke	S	MBA	87	Delaware	1989
VanLeer, Michael	Inst	831-4673	vanleerm	FM	MBA	78	Drexel	& 9-86
Wright, Diane	Inst		wrightd	S	MS	94	Delaware	2001

Delaware State University — Dover, DE   19901-2277   (302) Fax=857-6924   2006

Dept of Accounting & Finance	School of Management			desu.edu				BS
Dept Phone: 857-6911	1200 North DuPont Highway							Mrs. Raquel Lang
Minter, Robert L.	Dean	857-6902	minter	Mgt	PHD	69	Purdue	2007
Kwak, Young-Sik	C-Ac	857-6913	ykwak	Fnce	PHD		Miss	
Ruf, Bernadette M.	Prof	857-6915	bruf	DS	PHD	90.	Va Tech	&2004
Williamson, Joan W.	Assoc	857-6910	jwwillia	FACN	PHD	97	Delaware	&1976
Anakwe, Bridget	Asst	857-6915	banakwe	FM	PHD	03.	Rutgers	2004

Delta State University — Cleveland, MS   38733-3222   (662) Fax=846-4429

Div Acctncy, CIS & Fnce 3222	College of Business			deltastate.edu				BBA,MBA,MPA
Dept Phone: 846-4180								Susan McCreary
Moore, Billy C.	Dean	846-4200	bmoore	Fnce	PHD	96	Miss	1986
Morehead, William	C-As	846-4183	wmorehed	GIJN	ABD		S Miss	&2007
Ford, Sharon K.	Assoc	846-4218	shford	XM	PHD	96.	Miss	& 8-01
Barfitt, Laurie	Asst	846-4224	lbarfitt	PCG	PHD	06.	Miss	* &1998
Wilson, W. Tony	Asst	846-4184	twilson	FXVM	MBA	79	Delta St	# * &1981
Blount, Jimmie	Inst	846-4217	jblount	M	MPA		Delta St	&2004
Sandifer, Lisa	Inst	846-4182	lsandifr	SPAF	MBA	90	Miss	&1998

University of Denver — Denver, CO   80208-3337   (303) Fax=871-2016   ß (123) 1923,1966

School of Accountancy	Daniels College of Bus			du.edu				BS,MBA,MACC,MAT
Dept Phone: 871-3337	2101 S. University Blvd #355							Paula Martin
Homepage: http://www.daniels.du.edu/accountancy/								
Newman, Karen L.	Dean	871-2249	kanewman	Mgt	PHD	78	Chicago	2005
Kucic, A. Ronald	D-Ac	871-2017	rkucic	MSC	PHD	77.	NYU	* 1976
Bazley, John D.	Prof	871-2023	jbazley	F	PHD	72.	Minnesota	&1976
Firmin, Peter A.	Emer	871-2293	pfirmin	6-96	PHD	57.	Michigan	& 7-74
Grove, Hugh D.	Prof	871-2026	hgrove	FMZ	DBA	75.	S Calif	& 9-75
Hanbery, Glyn W.	Prof	871-2019	ghanbery	FA	PHD	71.	Ariz St	&1973
Associate Dean								
Sorensen, James E.	Prof	871-2028	jsorense	MCG	PHD	65.	Ohio St	&1965
Tripp, John C.	Prof	871-2029	jtripp	X	PHD	80.	Houston	&1979
White, John H.	ClPr	871-2031	johwhite	DSF	PHD	96	Co Mines	2000
Zimmer, Robert K.	Emer	871-3337	rzimmer	2000	PHD	64.	Ohio St	1983
Battaglia, Samuel T.	Emer	871-3337	sbattagl	2002	PHD	68.	SUNY-Buf	1969
Frakes, Joyce E.	Assoc	871-2025	jfrakes	F	PHD	71	Stanford	&1977
Leaman, Richard S.	Assoc	871-2079	rleaman	X	JD	79	Chicago	& 9-91
Vogel, Mark A.	Assoc	871-6241	mvogel	X	LLM	76	Denver	&1976
Davisson, Kathleen E.	Lect	871-4104	kdavisso	MS	MACC	91	Denver	2003
Goodyear, Alice	Lect	871-3479	lgoodyea	F	MACC	76	Denver	1978
Honodel, David	Lect	871-7484	dhonodel	FMC	MT	89	Denver	&1990
Nee, Laura M.	Lect	871-3965	lnee	FM	MACC	01	Denver	&2007

DePaul University — Chicago, IL   60604-2287   (312) Fax=362-6208   ß (123) 1957,1963

School of Accountancy & MIS	College of Commerce			depaul.edu				BS,MA,MB,MS,MST
Dept Phone: 362-8770	1 East Jackson Blvd							Sarah Musto 362-5207
Homepage: http://accountancy/depaul.edu								
Whittington, O. Ray	Dean	362-6783	rwhittin	AF	PHD	78	Houston	# * &1997
Stevens, Kevin T.	D-Pr	362-6989	kstevens	TVX	DBA	89.	Kentucky	&1989
Ledger & Quill Director								
Cohen, Edwin	Prof	362-8775	ecohen	FTV	PHD	60.	Mich St	&1981
Frigo, Mark L.	Prof	362-8784	mfrigo	MR	PHD	81	N Illinois	* & 9-80
Ledger & Quill Distinguished Professor of Accounting								
Hill, Nancy Thorley	Prof	362-8815	nhill	MC	PHD	90.	Wisconsin	* &1990

McEnroe, John E.	Prof	362-8748	jmcenroe	FTA	DBA	77.	Kentucky	&1981
Deloitte Distinguished Professor								
Needles, Belverd E. Jr.	Prof	362-5130	bneedles	AFI	PHD	69.	Illinois	* &1978
Ernst & Young Alumni Distinguished Professor								
Shannon, Donald S.	Prof	362-8358	dshannon	FT	PHD	72	N Carol	&1981
Ahern, John T.	Assoc	362-8770	jahern	FAV	DBA	76.	Kentucky	&1973
Alford, R. Mark	VAsoc		ralford	FM	PHD	78.	Tx A&M	&2004
visiting from University of Texas-San Antonio								
Dekleva, Sasha	Assoc	362-6789	sdekleva	S	PHD	87	Belgrade	1986
Foth, Edward C.	Assoc	362-6900	efoth	X	PHD	71.	Mich St	&1975
Grant, Delvin	Assoc	362-6635	dgrant	S	PHD	91	SUNY-Bin	2000
Kanter, Howard A.	Assoc	362-8449	hkanter	SE	EDD	84	N Illinois	&1979
Murphy, Elizabeth A.	Assoc	362-5023	emurphy	FTVR	PHD	95.	Kentucky	&1994
Nitterhouse, Denise	Assoc	362-8752	dnitterh	SBN	DBA	81.	Harvard	1985
Roberts, David J.	Assoc	362-8388	droberts	XR	JD	82	DePaul	&1977
Shelton, Sandra W.	Assoc	362-8098	sshelton	AB	PHD	94.	Wisconsin	& 8-94
Sullivan, Mark J.	Assoc	362-5707	msulliva	XF	PHD	79.	Wisconsin	&1976
Du, Ning	Asst	362-8308	ndu1		PHD	05.	Illinois	2005
Heltzer, Wendy	Asst	362-8473	wheltzer	FPQ	PHD	06	Chicago	2007
Hwang, Yujong	Asst	362-5487	yhwang	S	PHD	03	S Carol	2003
McCarthy, Mark	Asst	362-6901	mmccarth	XMFR	JD	85	Illinois	* &1979
Pope, Kelly R.	Asst	362-5821	kpope2	BCJM	PHD	01	Va Tech	2006
Arakawa, Randy	Inst	362-5378	rarakawa	SF	MBA		DePaul	2002
Kohlmeier, John M.	Visit	362-5601	jkohlmei	S	DBA	64	Harvard	1995
Lueders, Susan	Inst	362-5600	slueders	PFGQ	MSA	90	Illinois	&2001
Smith, Patricia	Inst	362-8798	psmith14	AFP	MBA	92	DePaul	&1995
Tower, Margaret	Inst	362-5049	mtower	FMP	MBA	94	DePaul	&2003
Wendorf, Michelene D.	Inst	362-6299	mwendorf	FCP	MSED	76	Wisconsin	&1997

DePauw University
Accounting Faculty
Dept Phone: 658-4878
Greencastle, IN 46135-0037
Dept of Econ & Mgt
Locust Street
(765) Fax=658-4764
depauw.edu

Jayne Williams

Dixon, Mary P.	C-Pr	658-6562	mdixon	Econ	PHD	89	So Meth	1988
Musser, Thomas H.	Prof	658-6695	musserth	FM	MA	80	Arizona	&2001

University of Detroit Mercy
Department of Accounting
Dept Phone: 993-3327
Detroit, MI 48219-0900
Col Bus Adm POBox 19900
4001 West McNichols Road
(313) Fax=993-1673
udmercy.edu

ß 1949,1963
BSBA,MBA
Mary Hassett

Nivi, Hossein	Dean	993-1204	hossein.nivi		PHD	75	London	2006
Wirtz, Patrick T.	C-Ac	993-3327	wirtzpt	FMA	MBA	74	Detroit	&1985
David, Jeanne M.	Assoc	993-3325	davidjm	FMV	PHD	88.	Tx A&M	* &1988
Zorski, Christopher	Assoc	993-1161	zorskic	FM	PHD	74	Warsaw	&1985

Dickinson State University
Dept of Business & Mgt
Dept Phone: 483-2333
Homepage: www.dicksonstate.com
Dickinson, ND 58601-4896
Col Ed, Bus & App Sci
291 Campus Drive
(701) Fax=
dickinsonstate.edu

BS,BA
Twila Petersen

LaPlante, Doug	Dean	483-2151		Ed	PHD	84	Iowa St	7-91
email: doug.laplante@dsu.nodak.edu								
Kilwein, Roger	C-Ac	483-2118	roger.kilwein	Edd	MS	68	N Dakota	9-69
Ballard, Deborah	Asst	483-2143	deborah.ballard	FGNX	MBA	95	Plymouth	& 8-03
Hanson, Scott	Asst	483-2319	scott.hanson	ACFM	MACC	85	Georgia	& 8-02

Dillard University
Accounting Faculty
Dept Phone: 816-4698
New Orleans, LA 70122
Division of Business
2601 Gentilly Blvd
(504) Fax=816-4851
dillard.edu

Helen Bougere

Fugar, Christian V.	Dean	816-4697	cfugar	Fnce	PHD	89	Howard	
Baucum, Richard P.	Assoc	816-4698	rbaucum		MA		Loyola	&
Washington, Kimberly	Asst	816-4200			MA		Southern	

Univ of District of Columbia
Dept Atg, Fnce & Econ MB52
Dept Phone: 274-7002
Homepage: www.udc.edu
Washington, DC 20008
Sch of Bus & Public Adm
4340 Connecticut Ave NW
(202) Fax=
udc.edu

AAS,BBA,MBA
Ms. Sarah G. Hardeman

Anderson, Melanie A.	Dean$	274-7000	manderson		PHD	86	Maryland	1976
Goyal, Tarsiam L.	C-Pr	274-7002	tgoyal	Fnce	DSC	70	Geo Wash	1971
Chatman, Emanuel D.	Prof	274-7059	echatman	GF	EDD	80	S Calif	&1974
Green, Eva S.	Assoc	274-7056	egreen	XFM	MBA	63	Cincinnati	&1969
Ramsey, Donald D.	Assoc	274-7054	ramsey	EPS	MBA	69	American	&1972
Green, Darien	Asst	274-7065	dgreen	F	MBA	72	American	&1980
Martin, Peter	Asst	274-7052	pmartin	VX	MBA	71	American	&1972
Salmon, Errol D.	Asst	274-7058	esalmon	RDA	MBA	71	American	&1975

Doane College
Accounting Faculty
Dept Phone: 826-8231

	Crete, NE	68333		(402) Fax=826-8600				
	Business			doane.edu				
	1014 Boswell Avenue							
Moorman, Amy H.	C-Ac	824-8240	amy.moorman			JD		
Bale, Jill M.	Prof	826-8212	jill.bale	FMC	PHD	93	Nebraska	1993
Springer, Kathleen A.	Assoc	826-8633	kathleen.spr+	TVX	ABD		Missouri	1998

Dominician University
Accounting Faculty
Dept Phone: 524-6810

	River Forest, IL	60305		(708) Fax=524-6939			
	Brennan Sch of Business			dom.edu			
	7900 W. Divison St.						
Burke, Molly	Dean	524-6826	burkemg	Mgt	PHD		Nrthwstrn
Drougas, Anne	C-Ac	524-6938	drougasa	Econ	PHD		Il-Chicago
Harrington, Stephen	Assoc	524-6773	sharring	F	JD	86	Notre Dm
Pollastrini, Raymond	Asst	524-6763	poliraym		ABD		Nrthwstrn

Drake University
School of Accounting
Dept Phone: 271-2007
Homepage: www.drake.edu/cbpa/acctg/

	Des Moines, IA	50311-4505		(515) Fax=271-4518			ß (1) 1949,1973	
	Col of Bus & Pub Adm			drake.edu			BS,MBA,MACC	
	25th & University Ave							
Edwards, Charles C.	Dean	271-3565	charles.edwards		BA	69	Colorado	2003
Simpson, LouAnn	D-Pr	271-2007	louann.simpson	L	JD	68	Drake	1974
Dodd, Jamoo L.	Prof	271-2829	jim.dodd	PMT	PHD	92.	Georgia	&1992
Aliber Professor of Accounting								
Heaston, Patrick H.	Prof	271-3565	pat.heaston	FVT	PHD	82.	Nebraska	&1983
Aliber Professor of Accounting								
Hillman, A. Douglas	Prof	271-2720	doug.hillman	PSM	PHD	70.	Missouri	* 1970
Aliber Professor of Accounting								
Gara, Stephen C.	Assoc	271-2871	steve.gara	X	PHD	98.	Memphis	&2005
Terlouw, Charles D.	Assoc	271-3106	chuck.terlouw	PA	BS	71	Drake	&2004
Njoroge, Joyce	Asst	271-3287	joyce.njoroge	FM	PHD	01.	Wash St	2000
Walker, Sara K.	Asst	271-4159	sara.walker	P	JD	83	Drake	&1992

Drexel University
Department of Accounting
Dept Phone: 895-2116
Homepage: www.lebow.drexel.edu/accounting

	Philadelphia, PA	19104-2875		(215) Fax=895-6279			ß 1967,1978	
	LeBow Col of Business			drexel.edu			BS,MBA,PHD	
	3141 Chestnut Street						Michele Sykes	
Tsetsekos, George P.	Dean	895-2111	tsetsekos	Fnce	PHD	86	Tennessee	1988
Campbell, David R.	C-Pr	895-0222	davidcampbell		PHD	75.	Georgia	&2004
Curatola, Anthony P. (Tony)	Prof	895-1453	curatola	XB	PHD	81.	Tx A&M	9-89
Joseph F. Ford Professor of Accounting								
Ndubizu, Gordian A.	Prof	895-2120	ndubizga	FI	PHD	85.	Temple	1-87
Agoglia, Christopher P.	Assoc	895-6007	cpa22	ACB	PHD	99.	Mass	4-98
Chandar, Nandini	Asst	895-6982	chandar	FMH	PHD	97.	Case Wes	&2004
Cianci, Anna M.	Asst	895-2116	amc66	AF	PHD	00.	Duke	&2005
Grein, Barbara Murray	Asst	895-1454	bmg33	F	PHD	02.	N Carol	2004
Tsakumis, George T.	Asst	895-2115	gtt22	ACB	PHD	03.	S Carol	2003
Werner, Edward M.	Asst	895-4984	emw38	FX	PHD	05.	Ariz St	2005
Wesnerll, Edward M.	Asst	895-2116			PHD	05	Ariz St	2005
Kaplan, Jane E.	Inst	895-1455	kaplanje	F	MSA	85	Drexel	&1994
Kline, Stacey	Inst	895-6983	klinesa	FMX	MBA	98	Temple	1997
Welker, Michael G.	Inst	895-6978	welkermg	AFM	MBA	73	Drexel	* &1988
Wright, Jennifer J.	Inst	895-6983	wrightjj	FX	MST	94	Villanova	&1995

Drury University
Accounting Faculty
Dept Phone: 873-7508
Homepage: breech.drury.edu

	Springfield, MO	65802		(417) Fax=873-7537				
	Breech Sch of Bus Adm			drury.edu			BA,MBA	
	900 North Benton Avenue						Jan Wiggins	
Wyatt, Robert L.	Dir	873-7241	rwyatt	C	PHD	93	Memphis	# * &1996
Clayton, Penny R.	Prof	873-7396	pclayton	FG	PHD	90.	Okla St	&1990
Oglesby, Rodney A.	Prof	873-7806	roglesby	CGS	PHD	91	Missouri	* 2002
Still, Kelley	Assoc	873-7383	kstill	CT	PHD	97	Oklahoma	&1995

Duke University
Accounting Faculty
Dept Phone: 660-7841

	Durham, NC	27708-0120		(919) Fax=660-7971			1979	
	Fuqua School of Bus			duke.edu			MBA,PHD	
	One Towerview Drive						Mia Ketchum 660-7752	
Sheppard, Blair	Dean	660-7725	bsheppar	Mgt	PHD	80	Illinois	1981
Schipper, Katherine	C-Pr	660-1947	schipper	F	PHD	77.	Chicago	2006
Thomas F. Keller Professor Business Administration								
Ashton, Robert H.	Prof	660-7842	rha2	MAB	PHD	73.	Minnesota	&1986
L. Palmer Fox Professor of Business Administration								
Francis, Jennifer	Prof	660-7817	jfrancis	F	PHD	87.	Cornell	& 7-99
Douglas & Josie Breeden Doctoral Professor of Accounting & Senior Assoc Dean								

Keller, Thomas F.	Emer	660-8045	tfk1	F	PHD	60.	Michigan	& 9-59
R. J. Reynolds Professor of Business Administration								
Ashton, Alison Hubbard	Assoc	660-7852	aha1	FAB	PHD	79.	Tx-Austin	1986
Chen, Qi	Assoc	660-7753	qc2	FM	PHD	00	Chicago	7-00
Nanda, Dhananjay (DJ)	Assoc	660-7966	djnanda	M	PHD	97	Rochester	7-02
Olsson, Per M.	Assoc	660-7835	pol	F	PHD	98	Stockholm	7-01
Venkatachalam, Mohan	Assoc	660-7859	vmohan	F	PHD	96.	Iowa	7-02
Wilson, Peter R.	Assoc	660-7755	prw	F	PHD	84.	N Carol	9-91
Dikolli, Shane S.	Asst	660-1949	dikolli	M	PHD	98	Waterloo	&2006
Ecker, Frank	Asst	660-2934	fecker	F	PHD	05	Trier	2007
Ertimur, Yonca	Asst	660-7765	yertimur	F	PHD	03.	NYU	2006
Kim, Irene	Asst	660-2932	irenekim	F	PHD	04.	Michigan	& 7-04
Mayew, William J.	Asst	660-7781	wmayew	F	PHD	06.	Tx-Austin	& 7-06
Zhang, Yun (Clement)	Asst	660-7778	czhang1	M	PHD	04	Yale	2003

Duquesne University Pittsburgh, PA 15282-0104 (412) Fax=396-4764 ß 1961,1963
Accounting Faculty Palumbo Sch of Bus Adm duq.edu BS,MBA,MACC
Dept Phone: 396-5832 600 Forbes Avenue Debbie Kennedy
Homepage: www.bus.duq.edu/accounting

Miciak, Alan	Dean	396-1848	miciaka	Mktg	PHD	93	Kent St	2005
Rau, Stephen E.	C-Ac	396-6265	rau	AFMS	PHD	97	Pittsburgh	1999
Frandk & Ann Cahouet Professor								
Sisaye, Seleshi	Prof	396-6274	sisaye	BCM	PHD	88.	Pittsburgh	1985
Bodnar, George H.	Assoc	396-6260	bodnar	SC	PHD	75	Penn	1980
Green, Sharon L.	Assoc	396-5474	green	BCM	PHD	89.	Pittsburgh	1993
Nagle, Brian M.	Assoc	396-6240	nagle	AFN	PHD	94.	St Louis	&1993
Austin, Pricilla M.	Asst	396-5150	austin	AFE	MBA	77	Duquesne	&1982
Kollar, Robert	Asst	396-5832	kollar	AFV	MBA	94	Duquesne	2003
Trott-Williams, Valerie C.	Asst	396-5700	trott	AMS	MBA	94	Pittsburgh	* &2001

East Carolina University Greenville, NC 27858-4353 (252) Fax=328-4091 ß 1967,1976
Department of Accounting College of Business mail.ecu.edu BSBA,MSA
Dept Phone: 328-6055 East Fifth Street Shelly Spear
Homepage: http://www.business.ecu.edu/depts/acct

Niswander, Frederick D.	Dean	328-6966	niswanderf	FI	PHD	93	Tx A&M	&1993
Schisler, Dan L.	C-Pr	328-6622	schislerd	XF	PHD	92.	Memphis	&1992
McCarthy, Mark G.	Prof	328-6623	mccarthym	FM	PHD	92.	S Carol	& 8-91
Schneider, Douglas K.	Prof	328-6161	schneiderd	FTC	PHD	89.	Georgia	&1991
Doty, Edwin A.	Assoc	328-6626	dotye	SACM	PHD	81.	Mass	&1988
Hagan, Joseph M.	Assoc	328-6635	haganj	XM	PHD	90.	Geo St	&1995
O'Doherty, Brian A.	Assoc	328-6585	odohertyb	M	PHD	78.	Florida	1984
Reisch, John T.	Assoc	328-6619	reischj	ABC	PHD	97.	S Carol	& 8-99
Austen, Lizabeth A.	Asst	328-6055	austenl	SMC	PHD	97.	Florida	* &2003
Christian, Cal	Asst	328-6633	christianj	FA	PHD	00.	Fla St	& 8-00
Dickins, Denise E.	Asst	737-1544	dickinsd		PHD	06.	Fla Atl	& 8-06
Kohlmeyer, James M. III	Asst	328-6592	kohlmeyerj	MBC	PHD	01.	S Fla	&2002
Rieman, Mark	Asst	328-6055	riemanm	MSU	PHD	03.	Wash St	2003
Seese, Larry P.	Asst	328-6568	seesel	ICFB	PHD	00.	S Carol	& 8-00
Fritz, Patricia	Lect	328-6588	fritzp	FM	MSA	97	E Carol	2007
McCarthy, Ann	Lect	328-6630	mccarthya	F	MBA	85	Winthrop	&1993
Reisch, Michele	Lect	737-1435	reischm	FM	MBA	99	Fla Atl	2002
Schisler, Debra	Lect	737-1543	schislerd	FG	MAC	89	Auburn	2006
Workman, Jan	Lect	328-6609	workmanj	FM	MBA	90	E Carol	1995

East Central University Ada, OK 74820-6899 (580) Fax=421-9801
Accounting Faculty Sch Bus & Prof Studies ecok.edu BS
Dept Phone: 310-5527 1100 E. 14th Street Mary Tilley

Hall, Delma	Dean$	Ext 274	dhall	Comm	PHD	02	Oklahoma	1986
Holmes, Sarah A.	C-Pr	310-5271	sholmes	F	PHD	84.	North Tx	& 1-06
Harjo, Yvette	Prof	Ext 268	yharjo	CLP	JD	84	Oklahoma	& 9-84
Ashcroft, Paul A.	Asst	310-5272	pashcroft	AF	PHD	99.	Tx A&M	& 8-02

East Tennessee State Univ Johnson City, TN 37614-1710 (423) Fax=439-5274 ß (13) 1987,1987
Department of Accountancy College of Business etsu.edu BBA,MACC
Dept Phone: 439-4432 P.O. Box 70710 Ms. Valerie Swartz
Homepage: http://business.etsu.edu/acc/index.htm

Garceau, Linda R.	Dean	439-5489	garceaul	SDAP	DBA	86	Boston U	&2000
Burkette, Gary D.	C-Ac	439-5327	burkette	A	PHD	94.	Va Tech	&1992
Anthony, Murray S.	Prof	439-5302	anthonym	MF	PHD	75.	Missouri	&1972
McKee, Thomas E.	Prof	439-5326	temckee	TAOE	PHD	75.	Geo St	# * &1976
Morgan, Robert G.	Prof	439-5298	morgan	FXM	PHD	74.	Georgia	* &1985
Schneider, Kent N.	Prof	439-5335	kent	XDE	JD	78	Missouri	&1984
Berg, Gary G.	Assoc	439-5336	bergg	FCM	PHD	87.	Tx A&M	&1987
Pointer, Martha M.	Assoc	439-5334	pointer	FMI	PHD	92.	S Carol	& 9-91
Steadman, Mark E.	Assoc	439-5322	steadman	FEJW	PHD	90.	Tennessee	* &1989
Becker, Lana	Lect	439-8592	becker	P	MBA	90	E Tn St	&1997
Sparks, Shelby	Lect	439-8657	sparkss	P	MACC	98	E Tn St	&1998

Eastern Conn State Univ
Dept of Business Adm
Dept Phone: 465-5265

Willimantic, CT   06226-2295
Sch of Profess Studies
83 Windham Street

(860) Fax = 465-4469
easternct.edu   BS,MS
Jean Stencel/Carla Sheldon

Name	Rank	Phone	Email		Degree	Yr	School	Date
Kleine, Patricia A.	Dean	465-5293	kleinep	Ed	EDD	90	Maine	1998
Rujoub, Mohamad A.	C-Pr	465-5284	rujoubm	CFIS	PHD	88.	Arkansas	8-99
Lim, Kwang Soo	Assoc	465-4678	liuw		PHD	94.	Purdue	
Silkoff, Richard	Assoc	465-5326	silkoffr	FX	SCD	02	NewHaven	&
Ryack, Kenneth N.	Asst	465-0249	ryackk	F	ABD		Mass	&

Eastern Illinois Univ
School of Business
Dept Phone: 581-2627
Homepage: www.eiu.edu/~buslum/

Charleston, IL   61920-3099
Lumpkin Cl Bus & App Sc
600 Lincoln Avenue

(217) Fax = 581-6642   ß (1) 1993,1993
eiu.edu   BS,MBA
Judy Lang

Name	Rank	Phone	Email		Degree	Yr	School	Date
Hoadley, Diane	Dean	581-3526	dhoadley	L	JD	82	Illinois	2002
Monippallil, Matthew M.	D-Pr	581-6111	mmonippallil	XL	JD	84	S Illinois	&1986
Davis, Henry H. (Hank)	Prof	581-6938	hhdavis	FMTS	PHD	84.	N Carol	1991
Kopel, Roann R.	Prof	581-6045	rrkopel	FE	PHD	86.	N Carol	1991
Laribee, Stephen F.	Prof	581-2527	sflaribee	PABI	DBA	74.	Kent St	&1989
Mills, Timothy H.	Prof	581-6202	thmills	FG	DBA	89.	La Tech	&1989
Palmer, Richard J.	Prof	581-8308	rjpalmer	MSC	DBA	90.	S Illinois	&2000
Lumpkin Distinguished Professor of Business								
Wootton, Charles W. (Bill)	Prof	581-6929	cwwootton	FHV	DBA	82.	Mioo St	1988
Joyoc, William D.	Assoc	581-6919	wbjoyce	CTFB	PHD	97	Nebraska	&1999
Moncada, Thomas P.	Assoc	581-6112	tpmoncada	XEM	JD	75	IIT Kent	&1980

Eastern Kentucky University
Dept of Acc, Fnce & Info Sys
Dept Phone: 622-1087

Richmond, KY   40475-3102
Col of Business & Tech
Combs 320

(859) Fax = 622-8071   2003,2003
eku.edu   BA,MBA
Mary Swelnis

Name	Rank	Phone	Email		Degree	Yr	School		Date
Rogow, Robert B.	Dean	622-1409	robert.rogow	GFA	PHD	76	Arkansas		&1998
Feltus, Oliver L.	C-As$	622-4977	oliver.feltus	GMS	PHD	86.	Alabama		&1991
Colbert, Janet L.	Prof	622-8881	jan.colbert	A	PHD	84.	Georgia	#	&2006
Fern, Richard H.	Prof	622-4979	richard.fern	F	DBA	86.	Kentucky		&1986
Chen, C. Richard	Assoc	622-1094	richard.chen	SF	PHD	80.	Tx-Austin		&1989
Fenton, Edmund D. Jr.	Assoc	622-1119	ed.fenton	X	DBA	86.	Kentucky		&2000
Frazier, Jessica J.	Assoc	622-1087	jessica.frazier	MX	DBA	90.	Kentucky		1986
Thorne, Daniel T.	Assoc	622-1092	dan.thorne	F	DBA	86.	Kentucky		&1986
Jones, Pam	Asst	622-1093	pamela.jones	FM	ABD				2005

Eastern Michigan University
Dept of Accounting & Finance
Dept Phone: 487-3320
Homepage: www.accfin.emich.edu

Ypsilanti, MI   48197
College of Business
406 Owen

(734) Fax = 482-0806   ß 1973,1982
emich.edu   BBA,MSA
Lisa Golub

Name	Rank	Phone	Email		Degree	Yr	School		Date
Mielke, David E.	Dean	487-4140	david.mielke	FI	PHD	81	Wisconsin		7-04
Kattelus, Susan C.	H-Pr	487-3305	susan.kattelus	XGNF	PHD	90.	Mich St		&1990
Bunsis, Howard	Prof	487-2519	howard.bunsis	FGN	PHD	93.	Chicago		& 5-98
Burilovich, Linda	Prof	487-3304	linda.burilovich	XF	PHD	90	Michigan		& 1-91
Khan, Zafar U.	Prof	487-1261	zafar.khan	MFCS	PHD	87.	LSU	# *	1989
Okopny, D. Robert	Prof	487-0246	robert.okopny	IAO	PHD	85.	Tx A&M	# *	1988
Ross, Barbara W.	Prof	487-2349	bwadding	ESA	PHD	97.	Mich St		&2003
Snyir, Andrew G. (Drew)	Prof	487-1016	andrew.snyir	MCFS	PHD	81.	Purdue		6-84
Brickner, Daniel R.	Assoc	487-0075	daniel.brickner	FAM	PHD	02.	Kent St		&2000
Etter, Edwin N.	Assoc	487-6819	ed.etter	FV	PHD	92.	Ohio St		&2002
Hwang, Angela L. J.	Assoc	487-6818	angela.hwang	EFTV	PHD	97.	Houston		2002
Mahoney, Lois S.	Assoc	487-0157	lois.mahoney	FMCW	PHD	97.	Cen Fla	*	& 8-04
McCombs, Gary B.	Assoc	487-0109	gary.mccombs	DEFS	MBA	68	Michigan		&1982
Keener, Mary	Asst	487-1350	mary.keener	FEX	PHD	07.	Kent St		2005
LaGore, William	Asst	487-4339	bill.lagore	FGN	ABD		Fla St		2006
Lewis, Philip	Asst	487-6817	phil.lewis	IBF	PHD	01.	Cincinnati		&2005
Cooper, Rolland	Lect	487-1007	rolland.cooper	CFA	MBA	84	E Mich		&1980

Eastern New Mexico Univ
Dept of Atg, Fnce & Info Sys
Dept Phone: 562-2365
Homepage: www.enmu.edu

Portales, NM   88130
College of Business
Station 49

(505) Fax = 562-2252
enmu.edu   BBA

Name	Rank	Phone	Email		Degree	Yr	School	Date
Grossbeck, John	Dean	562-2343	john.grossbeck	Econ	PHD		Utah St	2006
Smith, Gene	C-As	562-2816	gene.smith	A	PHD	05	N Cen Un	2002
Bourret, Ralph	Asst	562-2672	ralph.borret	A	PHD	05.	Miss St	2005
Frashier, Ira Kaye	Asst	562-2366	ira.kaye.fras +	A	MS	80	Miss	2006

Eastern Washington Univ
Atg & Info Sys Dept MS-3
Dept Phone: 358-2234

Spokane, WA   99202-1660
Col of Bus & Public Adm
668 N. Riverpoint, Suite A

(509) Fax = 358-2267   ß 1975,1981
mailserver.ewu.edu   BA,MSA
Susan Lopez

Name	Rank	Phone	Email		Degree	Yr	School	Date
Fuller, Rex D.	Dean	358-2237	rex.fuller	Econ	PHD	82	Utah	8-06
Birch, Nancy	C-Pr	259-2234		Mgt	PHD	88	Ariz St	

Cameron, Alex B.	Prof	358-2260	alex.cameron	ASM	PHD	82.	Utah	* &1981
Megaard, Susan L.	Prof	358-2282	susan.megaard	XL	LLM	82	Geotown	1984
Stephens, Lynn	Prof	358-2235	lynn.stephens	FTN	PHD	83.	Nebraska	&1981
Dowd, Joe E.	Assoc	358-2280	joe.dowd	C	PHD	97.	Tx-Austin	&1999
McGonigle, William	Assoc	358-2260	william.mcgon+	FXL	JD	76	Gonzaga	&1978
Ekins, Gayle	Lect	358-2236	gayle.ekins	F	MA	04	E Wash	&2006
McNellis, Casey	Lect	358-2249	casey.mcnellis	FM	MA	03	Gonzaga	&2004

Edgewood College — Madison, WI 53711-1977 — (608) Fax=663-3445
Accounting Faculty — School of Business — edgewood.edu — BS,MBA,MS
Dept Phone: 663-3457 — 1000 Edgewood College Drive — Lisa Goldthorpe
Homepage: business.edgewood.edu

Taylor, Chuck	Dean	663-3374	ctaylor	Ed	PHD	88	Wisconsin	2007
Macur, Kenneth M.	C-Pr	663-4216	kmacur	STFC	PHD	88.	Illinois	&2003
Talarczyk, Alan B.	Prof	663-2251	atalarczyk	X	JD	78	Wisconsin	&1979
Roberts, Bruce J.	Asst	663-6761	broberts	AUF	MBA	64	Wisconsin	&1997
Dragoo, Amie	Inst	663-2323	adragoo	PM	MBA	91	Michigan	&1998
Saxunova, Darina		663-4216	dsaxunova	AFJ	PHD	07	Comenius	2007

Edinboro University of PA — Edinboro, PA 16444 — (814) Fax=732-1610
Dept of Bus Adm & Econ — Science, Mgt & Tech — edinboro.edu — BS
Dept Phone: 732-2407 — — Ms. Kathleen Schruers
Homepage: www.edinboro.edu

Randall, Eric	Dean	732-2400	erandall	Bio	PHD			
Hannan, Michael J.	C-Pr	732-2407	hannan	Econ	PHD	88	W Virginia	1988
Stamm, Janis	Prof	732-1525	jstamm	X	JD	71	Ohio No	1988
Carnes, Gerald	Asst	732-2616	carnes	FX	MBA	74	Gannon	&1976
Lisowski, Paul	Asst	732-2571	plisowski	FV	MBA	75	Pittsburgh	1975
Farlik, Terry E.		732-2403	tfarlik		DSC	06	Rbt Morr	&2003

Elizabeth City State Univ — Elizabeth Cty NC 27909 — (252) Fax=335-3491
Accounting Faculty — School of Bus & Econ — mail.ecsu.edu — BS
Dept Phone: 335-3311 — 1704 Weeksville Road — Selma Davis
Homepage: www.ecsu.edu

McBride, Freda D.	Dean	335-3488	fdmcbride	FB	PHD	98	Va Tech	&2002
Jackson, George S.	Prof	335-3310	gsjackson	XL	LLM	91	Geotown	&1998
Mitchell, E. Carla	Asst	335-3488	ecmitchell	FC	PHD	03	Old Dom	&2003
Worthington, Michael	Lect	335-3313	mworthington	AF	MBA		E Carol	&1983

Elizabethtown College — Elizabethtown PA 17022-2298 — (717) Fax=361-1487
Accounting Faculty — Department of Business — etown.edu — BS
Dept Phone: 361-1270 — One Alpha Drive — Eunice Ginder
Homepage: www.etown.edu — business

Melvin, Sean P.	C-As	361-1280	melvins	BLaw	JD		Rutgers	
Riportella, Terrie L.	Inst	361-3753	riportellat	AFM	MBA		St Joe	&2002
Molony, Jospeh T.	Lect	361-1281	molonyj	MF	MS		American	2001

Elmhurst College — Elmhurst, IL 60126-3296 — (630) Fax=617-6497
Accounting Faculty — Center for Bus & Econ — elmhurst.edu
Dept Phone: 617-3099 — 190 Prospect Ave — Janet Nichols
Homepage: cbe.elmhurst.edu

Wilson, Gary S.	D-Pr	617-3785	garyw	Ltm	PHD	93	Il-Chicago	2001
Simmons, Bonnie A.	Assoc	617-3113	bsimmons	FM	MBA	82	Ill Tech	&2002
White, John J.	Assoc	617-3117	jwhite	F	PHD	99.	Arkansas	8-00
Jacobs, Paul	Asst	617-3121	paulj	FX	MS	95	DePaul	&2001

Elon University — Elon, NC 27244-2020 — (336) Fax=278-5952 — 2004,2003
Dept of Accounting & Finance — Love School of Business — elon.edu — BS,MBA
Dept Phone: 278-5951 — Haggard Avenue — Ms. Mary Kaczor
Homepage: www.elon.edu/users/o/acct/

Gowan, Mary A.	Dean	278-6000		Mgt	PHD		Georgia	2007
Cassill, Arthur D.	C-Pr	278-5921	acassill	X	PHD	86.	Tennessee	&2002
Helms, Glenn L.	Prof	278-5939	ghelms	AF	PHD	84.	Houston	# &2006
McGregor, Calvert C. (Buck)	Assoc	278-5924	mcgregor	FM	PHD	87.	Va Tech	&1990
Poulson, Linda L.	Assoc	278-5923	poulson	FX	PHD	99.	St Louis	& 1-98
Cox, Patty J.	Asst	278-5925	coxpat	FA	MS	87	NC-Green	&1987
Cardwell, Paula M.	Inst	278-5922	weller	F	MACC			&2000

Embry-Riddle Aeronautical U — Daytona Bch, FL 32114-3900 — (386) Fax=226-6696
Accounting Faculty — College of Business — erau.edu
Dept Phone: 226-6694 — 600 S. Clyde Morris Blvd — Judy Williams

Petree, Daniel L.	Dean	226-6293	daniel.petree	Mgt	PHD	93	Kansas	2001
Williams, Michael	C-Pr	226-6777	williams	DT	PHD	00	Nova SE	1986
Ledgerwood, John	Asst	226-4965	ledgerwj	FMPT	MACC			2006
Zarb, Bert	Asst	226-7942	zarbb	FMPI	DBA	04	Argosy	&1998

Emory University
Accounting Area
Dept Phone: 727-6271

	Atlanta, GA	30322-2710	(404) Fax=727-6313				ß 1949,1963
	Goizueta Bus School		bus.emory.edu				BBA,MBA,PHD
	1300 Clifton Road						Michelle Kirkland
Benveniste, Lawrence M.	Dean	727-7603	larry_benveniste	Fnce	PHD	75 Berkeley	7-05
Candler Professor of Finance							
Kertz, Connie	C-Pr	727-6642	consuelo_kertz	XL	JD	75 Emory	1980
Benston, George J.	Prof	727-7831	george_benston	FM	PHD	63. Chicago	& 9-87
Cooper, Robin	Prof	727-6679	robin_cooper	M	DBA	82. Harvard	& 8-98
Hartgraves, Al L.	Prof	727-6641	al_hartgraves	FM	PHD	75. Geo St	* &1980
Pownall, Grace	Prof	727-0775	grace_pownall	FI	PHD	85. Chicago	8-93
Waymire, Gregory B.	Prof	727-6271	gregory_waymire	F	PHD	84. Chicago	8-99
Candler Professor							
Barton, Jan J.	Assoc	727-6398	jan_barton	F	PHD	98. Alabama	& 8-98
Kadous, Kathryn	Assoc	727-4967	kathryn_kadous	AF	PHD	96. Illinois	& 8-03
Brown, Stephen	Asst	727-1634	stephen_brown	F	PHD	01. Nrthwstrn	& 9-00
Butler, Marcus B.	Asst	727-5133	marty_butler	FKX	PHD	03. Chicago	&2004
Hecht, Gary W.	Asst	727-5178	gary_hecht	MB	PHD	05. Illinois	& 9-04
Markov, Stanimir	Asst	727-5329	stanimir_markov	F	PHD	02. Rochester	2001
Towry, Kristy L.	Asst	727-4895	kristy_towry	MB	PHD	02. Tx-Austin	9-02
Wang, Xue	Asst	727-7538	xue_wang	F	PHD	05 Chicago	8-05

Emory and Henry College
Department of Business Adm
Dept Phone: 944-0190

	Emory, VA	24327-0947	(276) Fax=944-6695				
	Div of Social Sciences		ehc.edu				BS
Cumbo, L. James Jr.	H-Pr	944-6196	ljcumbo	Mgt	PHD	81 Va Tech	1975
Stanley, A. Denise	Assoc	944-6187	dstanley	FALV	PHD	Regent	& 8-92
Macione, Kyle	Inst	944-6131	kmacione	FALV	JD	Miss	2007
White, Laura	Inst		lwhite	FALV	MS	Webster	2003

Emporia State University
Dept of Atg & Info Systems
Dept Phone: 341-5346

	Emporia, KS	66801-5087	(620) Fax=341-6346				2002,2002
	School of Business		emporia.edu				BS,MBA
	1200 Commercial Street						Barbara Givens
Hite, Robert E.	Dean	341-5274	rhite	Mktg	PHD	82 Arkansas	7-03
Waegelein, James F.	C-Pr	341-5680	jwaegele	AS	PHD	82. Penn St	&2006
Down, Alexis	Assoc	343-6931	adowns	X	PHD	98 LSU	2005
Durler, M. George	Assoc	341-5346	mdurler	AFS	PHD	97. LSU	& 8-00
Edmiston, G. Dean	Assoc	341-5376	gedmisto	FMC	MS	67 EmporiaSt	& 8-78
Falcetto, Larry R.	Assoc	341-5284	lfalcett	FP	MBA	76 Pittsburgh	* & 8-76
Kennett, Danny L.	Assoc	341-5088	dkennett	MP	DBA	83. Miss St	1988
Rich, John C.	Assoc	341-5225	jrich	FP	PHD	85. North Tx	& 9-68
Associate Dean							
Swanson, Zane L.	Assoc	341-5087	zswanson	FTV	PHD	91. Oklahoma	&1997

University of Evansville
Dept of Accounting & Bus Adm
Dept Phone: 479-2851
Homepage: http://business.evansville.edu
  1-800-423-8633 Ext 2851

	Evansville, IN	47722	(812) Fax=479-2872				2006,2006
	School of Business Adm		evansville.edu				BS
	1800 Lincoln Avenue						Sherry Hawkins
Clark, Robert A.	Dean	479-2851	rc60	Fnce	PHD	89 Purdue	2003
Blalock, M. Gale	C-Pr	479-2868	gb3	Econ	PHD	80 Okla St	1977
Schaefer, James C.	Prof	479-2859	js2	AGN	DBA	90. S Illinois	&1990
McKeag, Christine L.	Asst	479-2856	cm2	FS	MBA	75 Pittsburgh	&1981

Fairfield University
Accounting Faculty
Dept Phone: 254-4070
  phone 254-4000 Ext 2290

	Fairfield, CT	06824-7524	(203) Fax=254-4105				1997,1997
	School of Business		mail.fairfield.edu				BS,MBA,MSA,MST
	1073 North Benson Road						Barbara Dusenbery
Solomon, Norman A.	Dean	Ext 4070	nsolomon	Mgt	PHD	80 Wisconsin	2001
Massey, Dawn W.	C-Ac	Ext 2844	dmassey	FJBV	PHD	98. Conn	&1997
Bradford, Bruce M.	Assoc	Ext 2825	bbradford	FMT	DBA	89. Memphis	&1994
Caster, Paul	Assoc	Ext 2057	pcaster	AFB	PHD	87. North Tx	&1994
Poli, Patricia M.	Assoc	Ext 2882	ppoli	FI	PHD	94 NYU	&1996
VanHise, Joan	Assoc	Ext 3015	jvanhise	PFJV	PHD	97 NYU	&1998
Kravet, Robert W.	Asst	Ext 2827	kravet	PM	MS	69 Mass	&1978
McDevitt, Roselie E.	Asst	Ext 2829	rmcdevitt	MFJ	SCD	01 NewHaven	&1984
Peck, Milo W. Jr.	Asst	Ext 2896	mpeck	GFXR	LLM	80 Boston U	&1990
Weiden, Kathleen	Asst	Ext 2160	kweiden	FX	PHD	01. Baruch	&2002

Fairleigh Dickinson Univ
Dept Accounting, Tax, & Law
Dept Phone: 443-8810
Homepage: www.fdu.edu

	Madison, NJ	07940	(973) Fax=443-8377				2001,2001
	Silberman Col of Bus Ad		fdu.edu				BS,MS
	285 Madison Avenue						Terry Tomeo
Chaplin, J. Richard	C-Pr	443-8813	chaplin	CAS	ABD	69 Rutgers	* &1970
DeFilippis, Robert A.	D-Ac	443-8768	defilippis	FA	MBA	73 Rutgers	&1974
Skarbnik, John H.	Asst	443-8810	john_skarbnik	X	LLM	87 NYU	&1988
West, Ron	Asst	443-8869	west_	X	LLM	92 NYU	&1997

Fairleigh Dickinson Univ
Atg, Econ, Fnce & Intl Bus
Dept Phone: 692-7215
Homepage: www.fdu.edu

Teaneck, NJ   07666
College of Business Adm
1000 River Road

(201) Fax=692-7219
fdu.edu

Eileen Kerrigan

Greenfield, Robert	Dean$				PHD		Rutgers		
DeFilippis, Robert A.	C-Ac	692-7220	defilippis	FA	MBA	73	Rutgers		&1974
Brunetti, Frank L.	Prof	692-7215	frank_l_brunetti	X	LLM		NYU		9-80
Schiff, Jonathan B.	Prof	692-7259		CMF	PHD	84	NYU	# *	9-86
Stiner, Frederic M. Jr.	Prof			FSV	PHD	76.	Nebraska		&
Calderisi, Matthew C.	Assoc	692-7251	matthew_c_cal+	AIFM	MBA	75	Iona		9-76
David, Theodore M.	Assoc	692-7256		X	LLM		NYU		1982
Fuentes, Henry L.	Assoc	692-7203		AF	MBA	74	Seton Hall		& 9-76
Gillies, Kenneth R.	Assoc	692-7257		CMI	MBA	66	Rutgers		& 9-74

   email: kgilliescpa@yahoo.com

Fairmont State University
Accounting Department
Dept Phone: 367-4261

Fairmont, WV   26554-2470
School of Business
1201 Locust Ave.

(304) Fax=367-4613
fairmontstate.edu

BS
Trucilla Harton

Harvey, Richard	Dean	367-4261	rharvey	Law	JD	94	W Virginia	1988
Bennett, Gary K.	H-Ac	367-4183	gbennett	ACFX	MBA	75	W Virginia	&1980
Lawrence, Joan	Assoc	367-4732	jlawrence	FGNV	MBA	73	W Virginia	&1973
Burnell, Mary A.	Asst	367-4189	mburnell	DFMS	MPA	85	W Virginia	&1989

Fayetteville State Univ
Department of Accounting
Dept Phone: 486-1591

Fayetteville, NC   28301-4298
Sch of Business & Econ
1200 Murchison Road

(910) Fax=672-1591
uncfsu.edu

2006
Vivian Humphrey

Prabhaker, Paul R.	Dean	672-1267	pprabhaker	Mgt	PHD	84	Rochester	
Taylor, Ulysses	C-Pr	672-1998	utaylor	XL	JD	92	N Car Cen	1992
Balogun, Jacob O.	Prof	672-1997	jbalogun	GCL	PHD	80.	LSU	&1985
Yallapragada, RamMohan R.	Assoc	672-1980	ryallapragada		PHD	82.	Houston	&
Berry, Delano Howard	Asst	672-1985	dberry	GMF	PHD	91.	Kentucky	* 8-05
Cezair, Joan A.	Asst	672-1009	jcezair		PHD			
Davis, Garistine	Asst	672-1764	gmdavis		JD			
Garlick, John R. Sr.	Asst	672-1028	jgarlick	MX	PHD	89.	S Carol	
Souissi, Mottsen	Asst	672-1362	msouissi		PHD			

Ferris State University
Dept Atg, Fnce & Info Sys
Dept Phone: 591-2434
Homepage: ferris.edu/htmls/colleges/business/cfm/dept_accounting.cfm

Big Rapids, MI   49307-2284
College of Business
119 South Street

(231) Fax=591-3521
ferris.edu

BS
Darlene Waring

Nicol, David M.	Dean	591-2422	nicold	Mgt	PHD	94	Houston	2001
Woolen, James R.	H-Pr	591-2434	woolenj		DBA		Nova SE	2002
Jakubowski, Stephen T.	Prof	591-2576	jakubows	GFAM	PHD	88.	Kent St	&2001
McNabb, Patrick J.	Prof	591-2445	patrick_j_mcn+	XFP	MBA	78	Geo Wash	&1981
Wolgamott, Charles W.	Prof	591-2417	charles_w_w+	CGRN	PHD	87	Michigan	# * &1978
Cook, Teresa	Inst	591-2475			PHD		Capella	2002

University of Findlay
Accounting Faculty
Dept Phone: 434-4539
Homepage: www.findlay.edu

Findlay, OH   45840-3695
College of Business
1000 North Main Street

(419) Fax=434-6781
findlay.edu

BS,MBA
Ms. Natalie Scaife-Fittro

Sears, Paul A.	Dean	434-4439	sears	Econ	PHD	90	Case Wes	2006
Asbury, Douglas	C-As	434-4646	asbury	FC	MBA	86	Xavier	1986
Cummings, Lu Ann	Assoc	434-6698	cummings	MA	EDM		Case Wes	2000
El-Zayaty, Ahmed I.	Assoc	434-4897	el-zayaty	FGN	PHD	86.	Baruch	1993
Abels, Patricia B.	Asst	434-4461	abels	P	PHD	06	Sarasota	2006

Fisk University
Department of Accounting
Dept Phone: 329-8570
Homepage: www.fisk.edu

Nashville, TN   37208-3051
Div of Business Adm
1000 17th Ave N. Box 21

(615) Fax=329-8758
fisk.edu

BA,BS
Duanechei Harris

Cambronero, Alfredo	D-Ac$	329-8570	acambron	Econ	PHD	92	Vanderbilt	1992
Holman, Vinita R.	Asst	329-8662	vholman	ATR	MBA	78	Berkeley	&1987

Fitchburg State College
Accounting Faculty
Dept Phone: 665-3378

Fitchburg, MA   01420-2697
School of Business
160 Pearl Street

(978) Fax=665-3081
fsc.edu

Anne L. Burrill

McAloon, Joseph E.	C-Ac	665-3745	jmcaloon	Mktg	MBA	84	S Dakota	1984
Schonbeck, Harold	Assoc	665-3526	hschonbeck		MBA		Clark	&
Hollingsworth, Beverley A.	Asst	685-3567	bholling					
Vostok, Gary J.	Asst	665-3307	gvostok		MBA		Babson	* &1979

Flagler College
Accounting Faculty
Dept Phone:

St Augustine, FL   32085-1027
Business Administration
P.O. Box 1027

(904) Fax=
flagler.edu

Kelly, Yvan J.	C-Ac				MA		Auburn	
Chester, Michael C.	Assoc			FT	PHD	91.	Va Comm	&
Levelle, Michael J.	Assoc				MBA		Dayton	&
Makowski, James S.	Asst				MBA		Notre Dm	&

University of Florida
Fisher School of Accounting
Dept Phone: 273-0200
Homepage: www.cba.ufl.edu/fsoa

Gainesville, FL   32611-7166
Warrington Col of Bus
210 Gerson Hall

(352) Fax=392-7962
cba.ufl.edu

ß (13) 1929,1963
BSA,MBA,MAC,PHD
Sandra Subach

Kraft, John	Dean	392-2397	john.kraft	Econ	PHD	71	Pittsburgh	1990
McGill, Gary A.	D-Ac	273-0219	gary.mcgill	XI	PHD	88.	Tx Tech	& 8-86
PricewaterhouseCoopers Professor of Accounting								
Ajinkya, Bipin B.	Prof	273-0208	bipin.ajinkya	FM	PHD	76.	Minnesota	3-75
Demski, Joel S.	Prof	273-0200	joel.demski	TMF	PHD	67.	Chicago	7-94
Frederick E. Fisher Eminent Scholar								
Knechel, W. Robert	Prof	273-0215	w.knechel	FA	PHD	81.	N Carol	& 8-81
Ernst & Young Professor of Accounting								
Kramer, John L.	Prof	273-0216	john.kramer	X	PHD	75.	Michigan	9-79
on leave								
Schaefer, Hadley P.	Prof	273-0220	hadley.schaefer	MCU	PHD	63.	Michigan	8-80
Snowball, Doug	Prof	273-0222	doug.snowball	MFB	PHD	75.	U Wash	& 3-75
J. Michael Cook/Deloitte & Touche Professor of Accounting								
Asare, Stephen K.	Assoc	273-0209	stephen.asare	ABF	PHD	89.	Arizona	1-89
Boyles, Jesse V.	Assoc	273-0210	jesse.boyles	X	PHD	75.	Florida	& 9-74
Kramer, Sandra S.	Assoc	273-0217	sandra.kramer	X	PHD	79.	Tx-Austin	9-79
Dickinson, Victoria	Asst	273-0235	victoria.dick+		PHD	05.	Wisconsin	& 8-06
Lin, Haijin	Asst	273-0211	haijin.lin		PHD	04.	Car Mellon	8-04
Grant Thornton Term Professor								
Tinaikar, Surjit	Asst	273-0211	surjit.tinaikar		PHD	07	Toronto	8-06
Tucker, Jennifer W. (Jenny)	Asst	273-0214	jenny.tucker	F	PHD	04.	NYU	& 8-04
Prida Term Professor								
DeSantiago, Dominique	Lect	273-0200	dom.desantiago	F	MACC	89	Florida	& 5-94
Garvin, Deborah R.	Lect	273-0213	debbie.garvin	X	JD	78	N Carol	& 8-83
McDonald, Charles L.	Lect	273-0218	charles.mcd+	F	PHD	72.	Mich St	& 5-01
Tucker, Robert R.	Adj	273-0226	robert.tucker	A	PHD	87.	Fla St #	& 8-05

Florida A&M University
Accounting Faculty
Dept Phone: 599-3565
Homepage: www.famu.edu/sbi

Tallahassee, FL   32307-5200
Sch of Bus & Industry
One SBI Plaza

(850) Fax=599-3533
famu.edu

BS,MBA
Sylvia Petties

McKinley-Floyd, Lydia A.	Dean			Mktg	PHD	90	Emory	2006
Thompson, Forrest	C-Ac	599-8331	forrest.thompson	FAGV	PHD	78.	Tx A&M	# * &1989
Drumming, Saundra T.	Assoc	412-7729	saundra.drum+	FT	PHD	82.	Wisconsin	&1983
Smith, Wilbur I.	Assoc	412-7728	wilbur.smith	MC	PHD	84.	Wisconsin	1984
Bates, Ira W.	Asst	599-8337	ira.bates	FT	PHD	00.	Arkansas	2001
Hill, Aretha Y.	Asst	599-8352	aretha.hill	OAFB	PHD	01.	Tx A&M	&2002
Holloman, Derek	Asst	599-8341	derek.holloman	F	ABD		Grenoble	2006
Musazi, Buagu	Asst	599-8344	buagu.musazi	X	PHD	97	Wayne St	&2006
Selby, Daniel	Asst	599-8347	daniel.selby	FM	ABD		Fla St	2007
Swirsky, Steve	Asst	412-7749	steven.swirsky	MCS	PHD	04.	Fla St	2002
Johnson, Johnny	Inst	599-3790	johnny.johnson	FM	MBA	95	Fla A&M	2000
Reeder, Craig	Inst		craig.reeder	FM	MBA			

Florida Atlantic Univ
School of Accounting
Dept Phone: 297-3636
Homepage: www.soa.fau.edu
  236 & 762 phone numbers have a 954 area code

Boca Raton, FL   33431-0991
Barry Kaye Col of Bus
777 Glades Road

(561) Fax=297-7023
fau.edu

ß 1977,1977
BS,MTX,MACC,PHD
Trisha Dewey

Coates, J. Dennis	Dean	297-3635	coates	F	PHD	89	LSU	& 8-89
Bhattacharya, Somnath	D-Ac	297-3638	sbhatt	SMA	PHD	94.	S Fla	1999
Friedberg, Alan H.	Prof	297-3647	friedber	SCO	PHD	83.	Florida	&1989
Hooks, Karen L.	Prof	762-5690	khooks	AB	PHD	81.	Geo St	&1996
Hopwood, William S.	Prof	762-5237	hopwood	SC	PHD	78.	Florida	8-92
Means, Kathryn M.	Prof	297-2667	meansk	F	PHD	79.	Geo St	&1985
Orbach, Kenneth N.	Prof	297-2779	orbach	X	PHD	78.	Tx A&M	&1990
Borgia, Carl R.	Assoc	297-3638	borgiac	VFI	PHD	74	Mass	&1987
Higgs, Julia L.	Assoc	297-3663	jhiggs		PHD	98.	S Carol	1-98
Skantz, Terrance R.	Assoc	762-5217	skantz	MC	PHD	79.	Okla St	* 1992
Young, George R.	Assoc	762-5610	gyoung	ABFX	PHD	96.	Tx-Arlin	&1996
Cao, Jian	Asst	297-3636			PHD	07	Kent St	8-07
Coyner, Randolph S.	Asst	362-5411	coyner	CMS	MBA	68	U Miami	* &1975

Dunn, Kimberly A.	Asst	297-3643	kdunn	AF	PHD	97	Geo St		2001
Kang, Tony	Asst	297-3636			PHD	03.	Illinois		& 8-07
Kohlbeck, Mark J.	Asst	297-1363	mkohlbec	F	PHD	99.	Tx-Austin		&2005
Mailibayeva, Zhanel D.	Asst	297-3636			PHD	07	Purdue		8-07
Radtke, Robin R.	Asst	297-3636		BCJ	PHD	92.	Florida		8-07
Urquhart, William	Inst	297-2836	urquhart		MPA	79	Tx-Austin		8-98

Florida Gulf Coast Univ Fort Myers, FL 33965-6565 (239) Fax=590-7367 2003,2003
Dept of Atg, Tax & Bus Law College of Business fgcu.edu BS,MS
Dept Phone: 590-7300 10501 FGCU Blvd South Sigrid Davidson 590-7314
Homepage: http://www.fgcu.edu/cob/acg/

Pegnetter, Richard	Dean	590-7300	rpegnett	IndR	PHD	71	Cornell		1995
Volkan, Ara G.	C-Pr	590-7380	avolkan	FINT	PHD	79.	Alabama		& 8-04
Moorings Park Chair in Managerial Accounting									
Pacini, Carl J.	Prof	590-7344	cpacini	AFI	PHD	97.	Fla St		&2000
Marguerite and Guy Howard Professorship in Business									
Rue, Joseph C.	Prof	590-7345	jrue	F	PHD	79.	Penn St		&1997
Burgess, Deanna O.	Assoc	590-7341	dburgess	F	PHD	91.	Cen Fla		&1997
Cecil, H. Wayne	Assoc		wcecil	X	PHD	96.	Kentucky	*	&2007
Andrews, Christine P.	Asst	590-7342	candrews	SM	DBA	98.	Clev St		&1999
Placid, Raymond	Asst	590-7380	rplacid	X	JD	90	U Miami		&2002

Florida Institute of Tech Melbourne, FL 32901-6975 (321) Fax=674-8896
Accounting Faculty College of Business fit.edu
Dept Phone: 674-7327 150 W. University Blvd Mrs. Jean Grunke
Homepage: http://www.cob.fit.edu
  phone 674-7327

Bean, LuAnn G.	Prof	674-7374	lbean	PAFM	PHD	89	Arkansas	#	& 8-02
Pierce, Barbara Gugliotta	Assoc	674-7392	bpierce	FV	PHD	92.	Indiana		& 8-99
Associate Dean									
Szendi, Joseph Z.	Asst	674-8781	jszendi	GFVX	PHD	88.	La Tech		8-06

Florida International Univ Miami, FL 33199-0001 (305) Fax=348-2914 β (13) 1983,1986
School of Accounting College of Business Adm fiu.edu BAC,MAC,MST,PHD
Dept Phone: 348-2582 11200 S.W. 8 St, RBB 246 Ana Estevill
Homepage: business.fiu.edu

Elam, Joyce J.	Dean	348-2751	elam	Sys	PHD	77	Tx-Austin		1997
Lassar, Sharon S.	D-Ac	348-3265	lassars	X	PHD	88.	S Calif		2006
Davidson, Lewis F.	Prof	348-3563	davidson	FA	PHD	74.	Penn St		1984
Hennig, Cherie J.	Prof	348-3266	hennigc	X	PHD	80.	Colorado		&2005
Raghunandan, K.	Prof	348-2582	raghu	FA	PHD	90.	Iowa	*	2003
Rama, Dasaratha V.	Prof	348-2582	dasaratha.rama	S	PHD	90	Iowa	*	2003
Sharma, Vineeta	VProf	348-2582	sharmav	F	PHD	06	UAUS		2007
Lin, Stephen W.	Assoc	348-3253	lin2	IF	PHD	99	Manchest		2005
Sharma, Divesh S.	Assoc	348-2582	sharma	FA	PHD	99	Griffith		2007
Surysekar, Krishnamurthy	Assoc	348-3259	suryseka	FM	PHD	94.	Maryland		2001
Wheatley, Clark M.	Assoc	348-4209	wheatley	F	PHD	94.	Va Tech		& 8-94
Barua, Abhijit	Asst	348-3404	baruaa	F	PHD	06.	LSU		2006
Chen, Yunhao	Asst	348-2582	yunhao.chen	FM	PHD	07	Minnesota		2007
Desai, Renu V.	Asst	348-2582	desari	FM	PHD	07	Cen Fla		2007
Lynch, Antoinette L.	Asst	348-4207	antoinette.lynch		PHD	04.	S Fla		8-06
Maiga, Adam S.	Asst	348-2582	maiga	FM	PHD	98.	Memphis		2007
Sbaraglea, Andrew	Asst	348-7287	andrew.sbaraglea		PHD		Penn St		2006
Dieguez, Manuel	Lect	348-3263	dieguezm	FM	MSM	76	Fla Intl		&1976
Associate Director									
Gelman, Wendy	Lect	919-5870	gelmanw	X	LLM	93	U Miami		2001
Gray, C. Delano	Lect	348-4208	graycd	AIS	MS	92	NYU		1999
Henry, Kenneth	VLect	348-4210	henryk	AFGS	MA	94	Fla Intl		&2000

Florida Southern College Lakeland, FL 33801-5698 (863) Fax=680-4355
Accounting Faculty Dept of Business & Econ flsouthern.edu BS,MBA
Dept Phone: 680-4269 111 Lake Hollingsworth Dr Sarah Salamin 680-4280
Homepage: www.flsouthern.edu

Brown, Carl C.	C-Pr	680-4280	cbrown	Econ	PHD	79	Okla St		1980
William F. Chatlos Professorship in Business & Economics									
Buccino, Joan G.	C-Pr	680-4280	cbuccino	Econ	PHD	94	S Fla		1980
Clements, Lynn H.	Prof	680-4288	lclements	PTVG	DBA	02	Nova SE	*	&1990
Stancil, John L.	Assoc	680-4286	jstancil	ACPX	DBA	89.	Memphis	# *	&1998
Sutton, Bernice R.	Asst	680-4974	bsutton	ABDP	MBA	88	Fla So		2001

Florida State University Tallahassee, FL   32306-1110   (850) Fax = 644-8234   ß (13) 1962,1964
Department of Accounting College of Business   cob.fsu.edu   BS,MA,PHD
Dept Phone: 644-2771 Academic Way P.O. Box 306110   Donna Arnold
Homepage: www.fsu.edu

Name	Rank	Phone	Email					
Beck-Dudley, Caryn L.	Dean	644-3090	cbeckdudley	Law	JD	83	Idaho	3-06
Fennema, Martin G. (Bud)	C-Ac	644-8231	bfennema	MB	PHD	93.	Illinois	* & 8-93
Ernst & Young Professor of Accounting								
Hillison, William A.	Prof	644-7872	bhillis	AS	PHD	77.	Florida	* & 1-77
Andersen Professor of Accounting								
Icerman, Rhoda C.	Prof	644-7874	ricerma	GA	DBA	83.	Fla St	& 1-83
Bathke, Allen W. Jr.	Assoc	644-7888	abathke	F	DBA	82.	Fla St	8-84
Billings, Bruce K.	Assoc	644-7889	bbilling	F	PHD	96.	Penn St	8-96
KPMG Fellow								
Bowen, Paul L.	Assoc	644-4224	pbowen	SA	PHD	92.	Tennessee	& 1-06
Dusenbury, Richard B.	Assoc	644-7856	rdusenb	MB	PHD	89.	Florida	& 1-90
Gerard, Gregory J.	Assoc	644-9115	ggerard	S	PHD	98.	Mich St	& 8-98
Heflin, Frank L.	Assoc	644-7862	fheflin	F	PHD	92.	Purdue	8-05
Icerman, Joe D.	Assoc	644-3070	jicerma	F	PHD	77.	N Carol	& 9-77
Associate Dean								
Morton, Richard M.	Assoc	644-7877	rmorton	F	PHD	94.	Penn St	& 8-94
Deloitte Professor of Accounting								
Paterson, Jeffrey S.	Assoc	644-7887	jpaterso	XF	PHD	95.	Georgia	8-95
Andersen Professor								
Stevens, Douglas E.	Assoc	644-7055	dstevens	FMB	PHD	96.	Indiana	8-05
Baik, Bok	Asst	644-9847	bbaik	F	PHD	03.	Berkeley	8-03
Blay, Allen D.	Asst	644-2771	ablay	AF	PHD	00.	Florida	& 8-07
Hobson, Jessen	Asst	644-9933	jhobson		PHD	06.	Tx-Austin	8-06
Huston, Ryan	Asst	644-2771	rhuston	X	PHD	07	Tx A&M	& 8-07
Lulseged, Ayalew Ali	Asst	644-6554	alulsege	CMF	PHD	99.	LSU	8-02
Falk, Christopher W.	Lect			F	MACC	96	Miami U	& 8-06
Greenberg, Rochelle	Lect	644-7866	rgreenbe	FM	MBA	77	Ohio St	8-04
Pierno, Ronald J.	Lect	644-7886	rpierno	FC	JD	81	Fla St	& 8-94
Sudano, Holly A.	Lect	644-6693	hsudano	M	MACC	98	Fla St	& 8-01

Fontbonne University St. Louis, MO   63105-3098   (314) Fax = 719-3633
Accounting Faculty Dept of Business Adm   fontbonne.edu   BS,MS,MSTX
Dept Phone: 889-4518 6800 Wydown Boulevard   Julie Factor
Homepage: www.fontbonne.edu

Name	Rank	Phone	Email					
Maurer, Linda	C-As	889-1423	lmaurer	CDMX	JD	83	St Louis	&1999
Carver, M. Robert Jr.	Prof	889-4521	rcarver	AEFR	PHD	80.	Missouri	&2002

Fordham University New York, NY   10023-7484   (212) Fax = 765-5573   ß 1939,1982
Accounting Area School of Business Adm   fordham.edu   BS,MBA,MST
Dept Phone: 636-6127 113 West 60th Street   Ms. Naomi Robinson

Name	Rank	Phone	Email					
Tuckman, Howard P.	Dean	636-6311		Econ	PHD	70	Wisconsin	2006
O'Connor, Walter F.	C-Pr	636-6122	woconnor	XI	PHD	76.	Baruch	& 9-87
Schiff, Allen I.	Prof	636-6177	schiff	FPC	PHD	73	NYU	1976
Kushel, Paul S.	Assoc	636-6125	kushel	X	PHD	81.	Tx-Austin	&1988
Mozes, Haim A.	Assoc	636-6124	mozes	FPQV	PHD	89.	NYU	1989
Newman, Harry A.	Assoc	636-6209	hnewman	CM	PHD	84.	Nrthwstrn	1995
Rapaccioli, Donna	Assoc	636-6205	dmr1255@a	V	PHD	88.	NYU	&1986
Williams, Patricia A.	Assoc	636-6759	profpatw@a		DBA	92.	Boston U	1992
Bochner, Paul	Asst	636-6761	bochner	XF	LLM	80	NYU	1997
Peng, Yan (Emma)	Asst		ypeng	F	PHD	05.	Oregon	8-05

Fort Hays State University Hays, KS   67601-4099   (785) Fax = 628-5398
Dept Accounting & Info Sys Col of Bus & Leadership   fhsu.edu   BBA,MBA
Dept Phone: 628-4121 600 Park Street   Conni Dreher
Homepage: www.fhsu.edu/ais/

Name	Rank	Phone	Email					
Williams, Steve	Dean	628-5339	swilliams	Mgt	PHD	90	Nebraska	2003
Rucker, Jim D.	C-Pr	628-4121	jrucker	Ed	EDD	83	Nebraska	1982
Peters, Richard M.	Prof	628-5683	rpeters	FMT	PHD	76.	Penn St	&1994
Gnizak, Charles J.	Asst	628-4328	cjgnizak	XF	PHD	93.	Kent St	&2001
Jordan, Win G.	Asst	628-4016	wjordan	MS	PHD	96	Mich St	1998
Rumpel, Joan H.	Asst	628-4179	jrumpel	PMC	MBA	77	Ft Hays	&1977
Young, Arthur E.	Asst	628-5682	aeyoung	AXF	PHD	02.	Tx Tech	&2006

Fort Lewis College Durango, CO   81301-3999   (970) Fax = 247-7623   ß 1974
Department of Accounting School of Business Adm   fortlewis.edu   BA
Dept Phone: 247-7543 1000 Rim Drive   Jean Walter

Name	Rank	Phone	Email					
Harrington, Thomas C.	Dean	247-7294	harrington_t	Mgt	PHD	79	N Carol	2004
McGurr, Paul T.	C-As	247-7543	mcgur_p	AMS	PHD	96	Purdue	&2004
Gore, Richard A.	Assoc	247-7603	gore_r	FX	PHD	98.	Wash St	&2006
email: rick.gore@gmail.com								
Herz, Paul J.	Assoc	247-7591	herz_p	EFV	PHD	94.	Utah	&2004
Crowley, Steve M.	Asst		crowley_s	CMS	PHD	03.	Utah	* &2007
Lyon, Chris S.	Inst	247-7236	lyon_c	FX	MS	90	Colorado	&2002

Fort Valley State University   Fort Valley, GA   31030-4313   (478) Fax=825-6062
Dept of Business Adm & Econ   Col of Arts & Sciences   fvsu.edu   BBA
Dept Phone: 825-6270   1005 State University Drive   Mrs. Shuri Rand
   Did Not Respond--2005-2006 Listing
Scipio, Julius   Dean   825-6000   scipioj

Framingham State College   Framingham, MA   01701-9101   (508) Fax=626-4040
Accounting Faculty   Econ & Bus Adm Dept   frc.mass.edu   BA,BS
Dept Phone: 626-4851   100 State Street   Ms. Dori Pedroli

Name	Rank	Phone	email		Field	Deg	Yr	School	Yr
Wallace, Robert B.	C-Pr	626-4888	bwallac		Econ	PHD	72	Nrthwstrn	1978
Farina, Louis J.	Asst	626-4885	lfarina		ACTV	MS	80	DePaul	&1991
Soriano, Beverly A.	Asst	626-4856	bsorian		CFM	MS	80	Bentley	&1984

Francis Marion University   Florence, SC   29506-0547   (843) Fax=661-1432   1995,1995
Business Adm & Economics   School of Business   fmarion.edu   BBA,MBA
Dept Phone: 661-1419   4822 E. Palmetto Street   JoAnn Mack
   Homepage: www.fmarion.edu

Name	Rank	Phone	email		Field	Deg	Yr	School		Yr
O'Brien, M. Barry	Dean	661-4664	bobrien		Econ	PHD	86	S Carol		8-88
Johnson, Brad R.	C-Ac	661-1427	bjohnson		XLF	PHD	93.	Houston		& 8-03
Holland, Rodger G.	Prof	661-1428	rholland		MC	PHD	81.	Ohio St		&2007
Paquette, Laurence R.	Prof	661-1419	lpaquette		CSQ	PHD	85.	Mass	*	2006
Carpenter, Charles G.	Assoc	661-1419	ccarpenter		F	PHD	69.	Illinois		& 8-05
David, Betty P.	Asst	661-1659	bdavid		FMS	MBA	88	S Carol		8-00

Franklin University   Columbus, OH   43215-5399   (614) Fax=255-9479
Accounting Program   Div Atg, Fnce & IntlBus   franklin.edu   BS
Dept Phone: 947-6103   201 South Grant Avenue

Name	Rank	Phone	email		Field	Deg	Yr	School		Yr
Hrubec, Thomas	C-Pr	947-6100	hrubect		BCGM	EDD	04	Illin St	*	&2005
Seiler, Thomas G.	Prof	947-6103	seilert		FAHO	JD	98	Capital		&2002
Welch, David	Prof	947-6101	weschd		FMXJ	MBA	86	E Tn St		&2007

Franklin and Marshall Coll   Lancaster, PA   17604-3003   (717) Fax=358-4568
Accounting Faculty   Dept Bus, Org & Society   fandm.edu   AB
Dept Phone: 291-4069   501 Harrisburg Pike   Deb Miller
   Homepage: www.fandm.edu/business.xml

Name	Rank	Phone	email		Field	Deg	Yr	School	Yr
Glazer, Alan S.	C-Pr	291-3921	alan.glazer		AFT	PHD	78	Penn	&1975
Stager Professor of Business									
Nelson, Martha K.	Assoc	291-3937	martha.nelson		MBCF	PHD	90.	Pittsburgh	& 1-91

Freed Hardeman University   Henderson, TN   38340-2399   (731) Fax=989-6737
Accounting Faculty   School of Business   fhu.edu   BBA,MBA
Dept Phone: 989-6091   158 East Main Street   Pam Carverll
   Homepage: we.fhu.edu/academics/business

Name	Rank	Phone	email		Field	Deg	Yr	School	Yr
Eldridge, C. Ray	Dean	989-6093	redlridge		Mgt	DBA	01	Sarasota	8-00
DeBerry, Thomas W.	Prof	989-6659	tdeberry		PA	PHD	94	Tx Tech	& 8-06
Smith, Keith	Prof	989-6053	ksmith		PSGN	PHD	88.	Miss	& 8-00
Brashier, April	Asst	983-3570	abrashier		PC	ABD		Alabama	8-05
McKenzie, Judy	Asst	989-6097	jmckenzie		PXV	MS	90	Memphis	& 8-87

Friends University   Wichita, KS   67213-3397   (316) Fax=295-5042
Accounting Faculty   Business   friends.edu   BS
Dept Phone: 295-5526   2100 W. University St

Name	Rank	Phone	email		Field	Deg	Yr	School		Yr
Howdeshell, Wayne	Dean		wayneh			PHD		Okla St		1967
Honts, Arlen K.	C		ahonts		Mgt	PHD	97	Vanderbilt		2005
Reding, Kurt F.	Prof	295-5878	reding		OAF	PHD	88.	Tennessee	# * &	1-07
Pendleton, Nichole	Asst	295-5414	pendleton		X	MACC	01	Kansas St		N-04

Frostburg State University   Frostburg, MD   21532-1099   (301) Fax=687-4380   2006,2006
Department of Accounting   College of Business   frostburg.edu   BS,BA,MBA
Dept Phone: 687-4297   101 Braddock Road   Carolyn Wolfe
   Homepage: www.frostburg.edu/dept/acct

Name	Rank	Phone	email		Field	Deg	Yr	School		Yr
Arnold, Danny R.	Dean	687-4019	darnold		Mktg	DBA	76	La Tech		7-03
Robinson, Sharon L.	C-Pr	687-4388	srobinson		AP	MPA	70	Tx Chr		& 9-72
Bandura, Randall P.	Prof	687-4182	rbandura		VFP	MS	76	Penn St		& 9-83
Johnson, Richard A.	Prof	687-4452	rjohnson		PFS	PHD	89.	Georgia		& 9-87
Middleton, Joyce M.	Prof	687-4154	jmiddleton		XPF	PHD	92.	Georgia		& 1-90
Shaffer, Kathie J.	Prof	687-4793	kshaffer		C	MBA	85	Frostburg	*	1-86
Simmons, Donald C.	Prof	687-4124	dsimmons		CPF	MBA	77	Jms Mad		& 9-78
Ross, Ronald L.	Assoc	687-3086	rross		MF	MBA	81	Frostburg		& 8-82
Bao, Yan	Asst	687-4272	ybao		PFI	PHD	04.	Kent St		& 8-02
Gilmore, Joseph	Inst	739-8128	jgilmore		VAFN	ABD		Pace		& 9-91

Furman University
Accounting Faculty
Dept Phone: 294-2132

Greenville, SC 29613-1150
Dept Bus & Accounting
3300 Poinsett Highway

(864) Fax=294-2990
furman.edu

BA
Brenda Chandler

Karwan, Kirk R.	C-Pr	294-2285	kirk. karwan	Mgt	PHD	79	Car Mellon	2005
Chen, Sean	Assoc	294-3554	sean.chen	FS	PHD	92	Pittsburgh	2006
Roberson, Sandy	Assoc	294-2225	sandy.roberson	AF	MPA	81	W Virginia	& 1-99
Summers, Suzanne B.	Assoc	294-3313	suzy.summers	CMX	PHD	92.	Georgia	9-99

Gallaudet University
Accounting Faculty
Dept Phone: 651-5312

Washington, DC 20002-3695
Grad Sch & Prof Program
800 Florida Avenue NE

(202) Fax=651-5516
gallaudet.edu

Georgette Lopes

Allen, Thomas E.	Dean	651-5576	thomas.allen	EdPs	PHD	78	Minnesota	1972
Agboola, Isaac	C-Pr	651-5312	isaac.agboola	Cpt	PHD		Maryland	
Chukwuma, Emilia	Assoc	651-5312	emilia.chukwuma	CFPT	MS	87	Baltimore	&1988
Sloboda, William P.	Assoc	651-5312	william.sloboda	AFNS	MBA	72	Geo Wash	&1969
Wilk, Edward F.	Assoc	651-5312	edward.wilk	FPTV	MBA	85	Gallaudet	&1985
Brown, Bernard P.	Asst	651-5312	bernard.brown		MBA		Gallaudet	

Gannon University
Department of Accounting
Dept Phone: 871-7571

Erie, PA 16541-0001
Dahlkemper Sch Bus Adm
109 University Square

(814) Fax=871-7210
gannon.edu

BS,MBA

Millor, James C.	D-As	871-7571	miller005	FMAX	DBA	96	Gannon	&1997
O'Neill, Michael J.	C-As$	871-7339	oneill001	MXJL	JD	83	Syracuse	* 1991
Dean, Graduate Studies; Director School of Business								
Miller, Scott E.	Asst	871-7397	miller032	FXLP	JD	97	Pittsburgh	&1998

Gardner-Webb University
Accounting Faculty
Dept Phone: 406-4375
Homepage: http://business.gardner-webb.edu

Boiling Spr, NC 28017
Broyhill Sch of Mgt
110 S. Main Street

(704) Fax=406-4738
gardner-webb.edu

BS,MBA,MACC
Janie McClain

Negbenebor, Anthony I.	Dean	406-4382	anegbenebor	Mgt	PHD	88	Miss St	1989
Godfrey, Earl	C-Ac	406-4381	egodfrey	ACF	DBA		Nova SE	& 8-92
Schumacher, Michael G.	Assoc	406-4389	mschumacher	CM	PHD	03.	Miss	* 2006
Foss, Emily W.	Asst	406-3911	efoss	FP	MBA	94	W Carol	1994

Geneva College
Accounting Faculty
Dept Phone: 847-6615
Homepage: www.geneva.edu

Beaver Falls, PA 15010-3599
Dept of Bus, Atg & Mgt
3200 College Avenue

(724) Fax=847-6686
geneva.edu

BSBA,MBA
Pam Watterson

Nutter, J. Randall	C-Pr	847-6613	jrn	Mgt	DBA	91	Nova SE	1992
Adels, Christen	Assoc	847-6619	csadels	ALX	JD	01	Pittsburgh	&2003
Raver, Daniel H.	Assoc	847-6618	dhraver	PFM	MBA	85	Pittsburgh	&1980

George Mason University
Accounting Faculty
Dept Phone: 993-4199
Homepage: www.gmu.edu

Fairfax, VA 22030-4444
School of Mgt, MSN 5F4
4400 University Drive

(703) Fax=993-1809
gmu.edu

ß (12) 1989,1989
BS
Kathleen Powell

Klimoski, Richard J.	Dean	993-1828	rklimosk	Mgt	PHD	70	Purdue	9-95
Nutter, Sarah E.	C-Ac	993-1860	snutter	FMX	PHD	93.	Mich St	1995
Heller, Kenneth H.	Prof	993-1765	kheller	FX	PHD	77.	Tx-Austin	& 7-87
on sabbatical 2007-2008 then retiring								
Buchanan, Phillip G.	Assoc	993-1129	buchanan	FV	PHD	83.	Temple	&1981
Director, MBA Program								
Krishnan, Gopal V.	Assoc	993-1966	gkrishn1	FS	PHD	86.	North Tx	& 1-04
VSCPA Nova Chapter Professorship in Accounting								
Sengupta, Partha	Assoc	993-4991	psengupt	FM	PHD	95.	Florida	&
Yahya-Zadeh, Massood	Assoc	993-2142	mzaheh	FM	PHD	92.	Syracuse	&
Douthett, Edward B. Jr.	Asst	993-4234	edouthet	AMI	PHD	95.	Georgia	&2002
Harr, David J.	Asst	993-1760	dharr	FMN	PHD	78.	Wisconsin	&1997
Associate Dean								
Jones, Keith	Asst	993-4819	kjonesm	AU	PHD	04.	Arizona	8-04
Parsons, Linda M.	Asst	993-1755	lparsons	SGN	PHD	01.	Houston	&2001
Phillips, Samuel H.	Asst	993-4199	sphillah	AFNS	PHD	91.	Houston	&
Shen, Min	Asst	993-189	mshen3	F	PHD	05.	Mich St	2005
Visvanathan, Gnanakumar	Asst	993-4236	gvisvana	F	PHD	96.	NYU	&2002
Zhang, Suning	Asst	993-1804	szhang4		PHD		Minnesota	
Hylton, Connie	Inst	993-1753	chylton	FM	MBA	81	Ariz St	&2000
Moraglio, Joseph	Inst	993-1763	jmoragli	FM	BS	57	Holy Cr	&2000

George Washington Univ Department of Accountancy Dept Phone: 994-6825 Homepage: www.sbpm.gwu.edu/depts/accy	Washington, DC 20052 Sch Business & Pub Mgt 710 21st St NW Suite 401	(202) Fax=994-5164 gwu.edu	ß (123) 1977,1982 BA,MAC,PHD Louba Hatoum

Smith, Keith E.	C-Ac	994-7461	kes	XF	LLM	78 Florida	&1984
Baber, William R.	Prof	994-5089	baber	FMG	PHD	80. N Carol	& 1-91
Benjamin Franklin Professor of Accountancy; Assoc Dean, Doctoral Programs							
Kang, Sok-Hyon	Prof	994-6058	sokkang	FMY	PHD	88. MIT	2000
Kumar, Krishna R.	Prof	994-5976	kkumar	FT	PHD	88. Columbia	1992
Paik, Chei-Min	Prof	994-6735	cpaik	CUM	DBA	63. Harvard	1964
Sheldon, Debra R.	Prof	994-8217	sheldon	FG	DBA	80. Geo Wash	& 9-80
Lindahl, Frederick W.	Assoc	994-5639	lindahl	MCI	PHD	85. Chicago	& 9-93
Moersen, Leo C.	Assoc	994-3955	moersen	LIJK	JD	81 Wm&Mary	&1984
Singleton, Lawrence G.	Assoc	994-4987	lgs	FMI	PHD	85. LSU	&1984
Tarpley, Robin L.	Assoc	994-8349	rtarpley	F	PHD	00. Cornell	2000
Gore, Angela K.	Asst		agore	AFG	PHD	00. SUNY-Buf	&2007
Hansen, Stephen C.	Asst	994-7335	shansen	M	PHD	88. Car Mellon	2002
Jones, Christopher L.	Asst	994-3529	jonesc	FM	PHD	98 Stanford	8-97
Kulp, Susan Cohen	Asst		skulp	M	PHD	00 Stanford	2007
Li, Ying	Asst	994-1268	yingli	F	PHD	02. MIT	2007
Liang, Lihong	Asst	994-8346	lihong	F	PHD	02. Penn St	2002
Sullivan, Mary	Asst	994-5189	msull	M	PHD	Chicago	2004

Georgetown University Accounting Faculty Dept Phone: 687-4112 email @1=msb.edu	Washington, DC 20057 McDonough Sch of Bus 37th and O Streets NW	(202) Fax=687-4031 georgetown.edu	1983,1988 BSBA,MBA Emma Thompson

Daly, George	Dean	687-3883	dalyg	Econ	PHD	67 Nrthwstrn	2006
Jain, Prem C.	C-Pr	687-2260	pcj3	F	PHD	84. Florida	&2000
Fairfield, Patricia M.	Assoc	687-4583	fairfiep	F	PHD	86. Columbia	1989
Mayer-Sommer, Alan P.	Assoc	687-3792	mayersom	FJH	PHD	76. Geo St	* &1981
Weiss, Lawrence A.	Assoc	687-3802	law62	FM	DBA	89. Harvard	&2006
Anderson, Kirsten L.	Asst	687-3798	kla2	F	PHD	97. Ohio St	2000
Cooke, Thomas B.	Asst	687-3210	cooket	LX	MLT	85 Geotown	1975
Distinguished Teaching Professor							
Ramnath, Sundaresh	Asst	687-3812	sr66	F	PHD	96. Penn St	2001
Sankaraguruswamy, Srini	Asst	687-6977	sankaras@1	FM	PHD	96. Purdue	1996
Tang, Vicki	Asst	687-4112		F	PHD	05. Michigan	2005
Taranto, Karen A.	Asst	687-3737	kat32	FM	ABD	Geo Wash	2004

University of Georgia Tull School of Accounting Dept Phone: 542-1616 Homepage: www.terry.uga.edu	Athens, GA 30602-6252 Terry Coll Business Adm 255 Brooks Hall	(706) Fax=542-3630 terry.uga.edu	ß (123) 1926,1964 BA,MBA,MA,PHD Marsha Dickerson

Sumichrast, Robert T.	Dean	542-8100		Mgt	PHD	84 Clemson	7-07
Ayers, Benjamin C.	D-Ac	542-3772	bayers	X	PHD	96. Tx-Austin	&1996
Baginski, Stephen P.	Prof	542-3612	sbaginski	FM	PHD	86. Illinois	& 8-02
Herbert E. Miller Chair in Financial Accounting							
Bamber, E. Michael	Prof	542-3601	mbamber	AB	PHD	80. Ohio St	1990
Harold M. Heckman Professor of Accounting							
Bamber, Linda S.	Prof	542-3501	lbamber	CMF	PHD	83. Ohio St	&1990
J.M. Tull Professor of Accounting							
Beresford, Dennis R.	Exec	542-3502	dberesford	FTI	BS	61 S Calif	* & 6-97
Ernst & Young Executive Professor							
Edwards, James Don	Emer	583-0222		1999	PHD	53. Tx-Austin	&1972
Gaver, Jennifer J.	Prof	542-3699	jgaver	F	PHD	86. Arizona	&1990
James Don Edwards Chair in Corporate Accounting Policy							
Smith, E. Daniel	Prof	542-3625	dsmith	FEY	PHD	74. Ohio St	1991
Streer, Paul J.	Prof	542-3596	pstreer	X	PHD	78. Illinois	&1978
Dawkins, Mark C.	Assoc	542-3602	mdawkins	F	PHD	94. Fla St	* & 8-94
Harvey, David W.	Assoc	542-3617	dharvey	FMTV	PHD	72. Minnesota	* & 8-03
Klassen, Kenneth J.	Assoc	542-3602	kklassen	XF	PHD	95. Stanford	&2006
Basu, Progyan	Asst	542-4672	pbasu	FSM	PHD	92. Nebraska	2001
on leave to University of Maryland							
Call, Andrew C.	Asst	542-1616		F	PHD	07 U Wash	8-07
Carpenter, Tina D.	Asst	542-3619	tcarpenter		PHD	04. Fla St	& 8-04
Hammersley, Jacqueline S.	Asst	542-3500	jhammers	AB	PHD	03. Illinois	& 8-03
Laplante, Stacie O. Kelley	Asst	542-3620	slaplante	XF	PHD	05. U Wash	2005
Ramalingegowda, Santhosh	Asst	542-3612	smr	FM	PHD	06. Penn St	8-06
Wieland, Matthew	Asst	542-1616	mwieland	FX	PHD	05. Indiana	2005
Yeung, Ping Eric	Asst	542-3615	yeung	FS	PHD	03. Oregon	8-03

Georgia College & State Univ Milledgeville GA 31061-0490 (478) Fax=445-3199 1997,1997
Department of Accounting Bunting School of Bus gcsu.edu BBA,MAAC
Dept Phone: 445-4023 231 W. Hancock Street Susan Kukua

Name	Rank	Phone	Email		Deg	Yr	School	Year
Gilbert, Faye W.	Dean		faye.gilbert	Mktg	PHD	88	North Tx	
Samprone, Joe	C	445-6054	joe.samprone	Econ	PHD		Ca-SnBarb	
Yakhou, Mehenna	Prof	445-2580	mehenna.yakhou	MI	PHD	85	Ca-Irvine	1994
Moore, Tom C.	Assoc	445-2583	tom.moore	LXP	PHD	84	Georgia	1987
Whelan, Catherine	Asst	445-2482	catherine.whelan	F	PHD	04	Bond	2003
Collier, Karen	Inst	445-4023	karen.collier					

Georgia Institute Tech Atlanta, GA 30308-0520 (404) Fax=894-6030 1969,1969
Accounting Faculty College of Management mgt.gatech.edu BS,MBA,PHD
Dept Phone: 894-4907 800 W. Peachtree St
Homepage: mgt.gatech.edu

Name	Rank	Phone	Email		Deg	Yr	School	Year
Salbu, Steve R.	Dean	894-2600	steve.salbu	Law	PHD	90	Penn	7-06
Schneider, Arnold	C-Pr	894-4907	arnold.schneider	AMBO	PHD	82.	Ohio St	& 1-82
Church, Bryan K.	Prof	894-3907	bryan.church	ABF	PHD	86.	Florida	& 9-96
Comiskey, Eugene E.	Prof	894-4394	eugene.comiskey	FMIT	PHD	65.	Mich St	* &1980
Callaway Professor; Associate Dean of Faculty and Research								
Mulford, Charles W.	Prof	894-4395	charles.mulford	F	DBA	83.	Fla St	& 1-83
Invesco Chair								
Turner, Deborah H.	Assoc	894-4900	deborah.turner	FXMI	PHD	05.	Geo St	& 1-85
Kuang, Jason Xi	Asst	894-1555	jason.kuang	BJM	PHD	05	Pittsburgh	8-05
Turner, James M.	Lect		james.turner	FMX	PHD	96.	Geo St	& 8-07

Georgia Southern University Statesboro, GA 30460-8141 (912) Fax=681-0105 ß (123) 1977,1982
School of Accountancy College of Business Adm georgiasouthern.edu BBA,MBA,MACC
Dept Phone: 681-5678 Forest Drive, PO Box 8141 Cynthia Parrish/Zandra Brasington
Homepage: coba.georgiasouthern.edu/depts/acc

Name	Rank	Phone	Email		Deg	Yr	School	Year
Shiffler, Ronald E.	Dean	681-5106	shiffler	Mgt	PHD	80	Florida	
Harter, Charles I.	D-Pr	681-0103	charter	FPT	PHD	91.	Nebraska	&2006
Fletcher, Leslie B.	Prof	681-0104	lfletcher	FMI	PHD	93.	LSU	& 9-93
Lockwood, M. Jill	Prof	681-5670	mjl	XL	LLM	79	Emory	&1984
Mooney, J. Lowell	Prof	681-5217	lmooney	SMC	PHD	89.	Georgia	* &1989
Buckhoff, Thomas A.	Assoc	486-7142	tbuckhoff	PCJ	PHD	95.	Kentucky	&2004
Higgins, Leslee N.	Assoc	681-5688	higginsl	SAF	PHD	97	Cincinnati	1998
Noland, Thomas G.	Assoc	486-7562	tgnoland	A	PHD	00.	Miss	* &2002
Cairney, Timothy D.	Asst	486-7157	tcairney	MS	PHD	95.	Va Tech	&2003
Jackson, Robert E.	Asst	681-0759	rjackson	FGNP	PHD	01	Kansas St	2005
McKay, Britton A.	Asst			PI	ABD		S Illinois	2007
Metrejean, Cheryl T.	Asst	681-5274	cmetrejean	XS	PHD	97.	Tx A&M	&2005
Metrejean, P. Eddie	Asst	486-7139	emetrejean	AS	PHD	04.	Miss	&2005
Parham, Abbie Gail	Asst	681-5037	aparham	PC	MBA	88	Ga Srthrn	* &1990
Sinclair, Debra T.	Asst	681-0379	dsinclair	P	PHD	05.	Temple	* 2004
Sneathen, L. Dwight Jr.	Asst	681-0167	dsneathen	FV	PHD	01.	Arizona	2005
Berecz, Don L.	Clln		berecz	PJ	MBA	81	W Illinois	2007
Kelly, J. Ann	Inst	681-0513	annkelly	P	MBA	02	Ga Srthrn	2002
Moore, William T..	Inst	871-1961	wtmoore	FMP	MBA	84	Auburn	# 1993
Olliff, Edie A.	Inst	871-1839	eolliff	P	MBA	98	Ga Srthrn	&1999
Stone1 Olivia J.	Inst	681-0736	omeeks	P	MACC	02	Ga Srthrn	2002
Stuart, Gloria J.	Inst	486-7141	gstuart	P	MACC	99	Ga Srthrn	2004
Tatum, Cheryl L.	Inst		ctatum	P	MACC	06	Ga Srthrn	2007

Georgia Southwestern St Univ Americus, GA 31709-4379 (229) Fax=931-2092
Accounting Faculty School of Business Adm canes.gsw.edu BBA,MBA
Dept Phone: 931-2090 800 Wheatly Street Martha Crimes
Homepage: http://www.business.gsw.edu/

Name	Rank	Phone	Email		Deg	Yr	School	Year
Kooti, John G.	Dean	931-2090	jgk		PHD	80	Mich St	7-98
Talukdar, Mohammed Yusuf	Assoc	931-5130	myt	AIFS	PHD	79	City-UK	& 7-02
Howell, Curtis C.	Asst	931-2125	chowell	CX	EDD	96	N Illinois	* & 7-01

Georgia State University Atlanta, GA 30302-4050 (404) Fax=651-1033 ß (123) 1960,1963
School of Accountancy J. Mack Robinson Cl Bus gsu.edu BBA,MPA,MTX,PHD
Dept Phone: 651-2611 35 Broad St 5th Fl POBox4050 Mignon Jackson-Jones
Homepage: http://www-cba.gsu.edu/~wwwacc/
  email @1=langate.gsu.edu

Name	Rank	Phone	Email		Deg	Yr	School	Year
Huss, H. Fenwick	Dean	651-2604	hfhuss	FA	DBA	82.	Tennessee	& 6-89
Sevcik, Galen R.	D-Pr	651-4477	gsevcik	M	PHD	91.	Minnesota	* & 6-97
Borthick, A. Faye	Prof	651-4472	borthick	S	DBA	82.	Tennessee	* & 9-94
Brown, Lawrence D.	Prof	651-0545	ldb	FM	PHD	75	Rochester	9-97
J. Mack Robinson Professor								
Larkins, Ernest R.	Prof	651-4469	elarkins	X	PHD	82.	Va Tech	1-82
School of Accountancy Alumni Professor								

Mutchler, Jane F.	Dean	463-9334	jmutchler	A	PHD	83	Illinois	& 7-99
J. W. Holloway/Ernst & Young Professor; Associate Dean								
Messier, William F. Jr.	Prof	651-2611	bmessier	AFB	DBA	79.	Indiana	& 1-98
Deloitte & Touche LLP Professor								
Sriram, Ram S.	Prof	651-4464	accrss@1	S	PHD	87.	North Tx	& 9-95
Controllers Roundtable Professor of Information Systems								
Hannan, R. Lynn	Assoc	651-2616	rhannan	M	PHD	00.	Pittsburgh	& 8-00
Joe, Jennifer R.	Assoc	651-4483	jjoe	A	PHD	99.	Pittsburgh	& 8-00
Nathan, Siva	Assoc	651-4455	snathan	FT	PHD	88.	SUNY-Buf	9-93
Chen, Lei (Tony)	Asst	651-4486	acclcc@1	M	PHD	04	Tx-Dallas	2005
Hugon, J. Artur	Asst	651-2738	jhugon	F	PHD	04.	S Calif	2004
Lee, Yen-Jung	Asst	463-4813	ylee		PHD	05.	Mich St	2005
Pinello, Arianna S.	Asst	463-4183	apinello	F	PHD	04.	Fla St	8-04
Ransopher, Tad D.	Asst	651-4467	acctdr@1	X	JD		Geo St	9-94
Director Master of Taxation Program								
Clark, Kris	Inst	651-4496	kjclark	F	MAC	01	Arizona	& 8-02
Fenn, Christopher J.	Inst	651-4493	acccjf@1	X	MTX		Geo St	& 9-94
Richards, Robert W.	Inst	651-4468	brichards	X	MTX	81	Geo St	& 8-84
Springer, Carol W.	Inst	651-2611	cspringer	FM	MS	82	Virginia	& 6-98

Georgian Court College
Accounting Faculty
Dept Phone: 987-2724
Homepage: www.georgian.edu

Lakewood, NJ   08701-2697
School of Business
900 Lakewood Ave

(732) Fax=987-2024
georgian.edu

BS,MBA
Ms. Susan Hoven

Shojai, Siamack	Dean	987-2724	shojais	Econ	PHD	89	Fordham	2004
Okpokwasili, Bertram	C-As	987-2722	okpokwasilib	Mgt	PHD	84	Columbia	1998
Carroll, James J.	Prof	987-2664	carrollj	CAVU	DBA	87	Nova SE	* &1991
Fosbre, Anne	Prof	987-2725	fosbre	PFM	PHD	84	NYU	&1993
Flynn, Robert	Assoc	987-2721	flynn	TVXR	MBA	74	Pace	&1984

Gettysburg College
Accounting Faculty
Dept Phone: 337-6646

Gettysburg, PA   17325-1486
Dept of Management
Constitution Ave

(717) Fax=337-6488
gettysburg.edu

Rosalyn Sterner

Frey, Karen	Assoc	337-6650	kfrey	CFM	PHD	94	Maryland	&1993
Walton, H. Charles	Assoc	337-6988	cwalton	SF	PHD	81	Fla St	&1989

Golden Gate University
Accounting Faculty
Dept Phone: 442-6528

San FranciscoCA 94105-2968
Ageno School of Bus
536 Mission Street

(415) Fax=442-6579
ggu.edu

BS,MBA,MACC
Yvonne Hynes

Did Not Respond--2005-2006 Listing; 961 exchange has 650 area code

Connelly, Terrence	Dean	442-6514	tconnelly		JD	68	NYU	2004
Schwartz, James	C-As	442-6593	jschwartz	FIV	MS	75	Wisconsin	&1996
Hoppe, Paul P.	Assoc	442-7035	phoppe	FMQ	PHD	93.	NYU	& 1-97
Jordan, Dan	Asst			FA	MBA	76	Berkeley	&2000

Golden Gate University
Tax Faculty
Dept Phone: 442-7880
Homepage: www.ggu.edu

San Francisco CA 94105-2968
School of Taxation
536 Mission Street

(415) Fax=543-2607
ggu.edu

MS
Kimberly Chun

752- has 949 area code; 622- has 206 area code

Canning, Mary	Dean	442-7885	mcanning		LLM	82	Golden Gt	1988
Walsh, Joseph G.	Prof	442-7881	jwalsh	X	LLM	78	NYU	&1984
Henderson, James	Assoc	442-7884	jhenderson	XL	JD	81	San Fran	&1988
Neslund, Kristofer	Assoc	442-7883	kneslund	XKF	LLM	85	NYU	&2005
Vinson, Michael	Asst	442-5328	mvinson	X	LLM	86	NYU	&2006

Goldey-Beacom College
Accounting Faculty
Dept Phone: 998-8814

Wilmington, DE   19808
Atg/Cpt Info Sys Dept
4701 Limestone Road

(302) Fax=998-8631
gbc.edu

BS,MBA

Ilyas, Mohammad	Pres	Ext 234	ilyasm	F	PHD		Conn	9-75
Burkey, Julie L.	C-Ac	Ext 221	burkeyj	FA	DBA	02	Sarasota	& 9-94
Leitsch, Deborah	Assoc	Ext 239	leitschd	FM	DBA	03	Sarasota	2-95
Murray-Jackson, Lynda H.	Assoc	Ext 341	murrayl	FX	PHD	97.	Temple	& 8-02

Gonzaga University
Dept of Accounting
Dept Phone: 323-5502
Homepage: www.jepson.gonzaga.edu/accounting

Spokane, WA   99258-0009
School of Business Adm
East 502 Boone Avenue

(509) Fax=323-5811
jepson.gonzaga.edu

ß 1990,1990
BBA,MACC
Dorothy Greenamyer

Barnes, Clarence H.	Dean	323-5502	barnes	Econ	PHD	73	Tennessee	9-73
Carnes, Kay C.	D-Pr	323-3420	carnes	AN	PHD	90.	St Louis	# &1979
Birrer, G. Eddy	Prof	323-3435	birrer	F	PHD	81	N Dakota	&1984

Teets, Walter R.	Assoc	323-3416	teets	F	PHD	89.	Chicago	&1994
Weber, Gary J.	Assoc	323-3427	weber	X	PHD	97.	Ariz St	1995
Associate Academic Vice President								
Barrone, Gerhard	Asst	323-7032	barrone	FS	PHD	02	Wisconsin	2006
Law, Daniel	Asst	323-5502	law	CF	PHD	03.	Wash St	&2002
Melendy, Sara R.	Asst		melendy	FA	PHD	05.	SUNY-Buf	&2005

Goshen College Goshen, IN 46526 (574) Fax=535-7293 BA
Accounting Faculty Business Department goshen.edu Linda Rouch
Dept Phone: 535-7450 1700 South Main Street

Stalter, Anita	Dean	535-7503	dean		PHD	96	Mich St	7-01
Weldy, Alan L.	C				JD	86	Notre Dm	1998
Horning, Michele Y.	Assoc	535-7453	michelleeh	CPMX	MS	95	Drexel	& 7-98
Rupp, Russ	Assoc	535-7455	russjr	FAD	MBA	84	Notre Dm	& 9-95

Governors State University Univ Park, IL 60466-0975 (708) Fax=534-6981 BS,MS,MBA
Div Accounting, Finance, MIS College Bus & Pub Adm govst.edu Olivia Cooper, Lynn Ware
Dept Phone: 534-4930 One University Parkway
Homepage: www.govst.edu/users/gcbpa

Nowlin, William A.	Dean	534-4932	w-nowlin	Ed	PHD	86	SUNY-Buf	8-97
Finkley, Richard H.	C-Pr	534-4960	r-finkley	BLaw	PHD	75	Tx-Austin	1979
Grivette, Denise	Prof	534-5629	d-grivette		JD		DePaul	
Shekib, Aida A. H.	Prof	534-4969	a-shekib	AMC	PHD	70	Illinois	* &1973
Washington, Mary T.	Prof	534-4964	m-washington	FPMX	PHD	87.	S Calif	&1993

Graceland University Lamoni, IA 50140 (641) Fax=784-5410 BA
Accounting Faculty Division of Business graceland.edu
Dept Phone: 784-5170 1 University Place
Homepage: www.graceland.edu

Lindgren, Richard K.	D-Ac	784-5172	rlindgre	CJ	MBA	80	Michigan	* &2002
DeBarthe, Linda M.	C-Pr	784-5177	lindad	PX	PHD	97	Iowa	&1990
Pitt, Max	Asst	784-5348	maxpitt	AJM	MBA	93	Tx-Brown	2004

Grambling State University Grambling, LA 71245 (318) Fax=274-3201 2000,2000
Dept Accounting POBox 4197 College of Business gram.edu BS
Dept Phone: 274-2404 403 Main Street Mrs. Rita Hood-Simmons
Homepage: www.gram.edu

Nelson, Anthony C.	Dean$	274-2275	nelsonac	Cis	PHD	91	Pittsburgh	2001
Kedia, Sushila	Asst	274-3848	skedia	PMS	MBA	88	La Tech	&1991
Witherspoon, Aaron	Asst	274-2741	aaron_spoon@y	F	ABD		JacksonSt	& 8-88

Grand Valley State Univ Grand Rapids, MI 49504-6431 (616) Fax=331-7445 (1) 1997,1997
Dept Accounting & Taxation Seidman Sch Bus & Adm gvsu.edu BBA,MBA,MSA,MST
Dept Phone: 331-7414 401 W. Fulton, 4th Floor Kathy Goralski

Williams, H. James	Dean	331-7385	williahj	AFIX	PHD	82	Georgia	* & 7-04
Goldberg, Stephen R.	C-Pr	331-7410	goldbers	AIF	PHD	88.	Wisconsin	&1996
Godwin, Joseph H.	Prof	331-7413	godwinj	FI	PHD	88.	Wisconsin	&1995
Associate Vice President of Academic Affairs								
Harris, Richard W.	Prof	331-7399	harrisr	X	LLM	90	Geotown	&1995
L. William Seidman Professor of Accounting								
Lindquist, Stanton C.	Prof	331-7404	lindquis	AP	PHD	72.	Missouri	&1974
Sopariwala, Parvez R.	Prof	331-7406	sopariwp	M	PHD	85.	Mich St	& 8-92
Yuhas, Michael A.	Prof	331-7398	yuhasm	X	LLM	80	Geotown	&1985
de la Rosa, Denise M.	Assoc	331-7411	delarosd	FI	PHD	96.	North Tx	8-03
DeBruine, Marinus	Assoc	331-7407	debruinm	FT	PHD	91.	Ohio St	& 9-91
Dunn, Cheryl L.	Assoc	331-7379	dunnc	SD	PHD	94.	Mich St	& 8-05
Fanning, Kurt	Assoc	331-7402	fanningk	S	PHD	94.	Kansas	* & 8-00
Grant, Rita H.	Assoc	331-7409	grantr	TF	MBA	82	Mich St	&1980
Veazey, Richard E.	Assoc	331-7408	veazeyr	MC	PHD	81.	St Louis	& 9-79
Cannon, David M.	Asst	331-7396	cannond	S	PHD	02.	Kent St	& 8-00
Kessler, Lara	Asst	331-7190	kessllar	LMP	JD	95	Vanderbilt	8-07
Ratliff-Miller, Paulette A.	Asst	331-7190	ratlifp	CFM	PHD	01.	Oklahoma	8-07
Danko, Dori	Inst	331-7397	dankod	FM	MBA	91	Gr Valley	& 8-98
Stovall, Dennis	Inst	331-7405	stovalld	FM	MBA	97	Gr Valley	8-05

Grand View College Des Moines, IA 50316-1599 (515) Fax=263-6190 BA
Accounting Faculty Dept of Business gvc.edu
Dept Phone: 263-2934 1200 Grandview Avenue

Rinke, Patricia	C-Ac	263-6135	prinke	LQS	JD		Iowa	* &
Hollensbe, Ronda L.	Prof	263-2932	rhollensbe	CFRX	MBA	88	Drake	* &
VanRoekel, Arlan W.	Prof	263-2933	avanroekel	FPTV	MBA		Iowa	&

Greensboro College
Department of Accounting
Dept Phone: 272-7102
  phone 272-7102

Greensboro, NC   27401-1875
Div of Bus Adm & Econ
815 West Market Street

(336) Fax=271-6634
gborocollege.edu

BA,BS

Schraeder, Donald P.	C-Pr	Ext 291	schraederd	PFSV	ABD		Mich St	&1989
Tharrington, Angel	Asst	Ext 369	atharrington	PFAX	MS		NC-Green	&1999

Grove City College
Accounting Faculty
Dept Phone: 458-2000
Homepage: www.gcc.edu/academics/artsletters/business

Grove City, PA   16127-2104
Dept Bus Adm, Econ & IM
100 Campus Drive

(724) Fax=458-3852
gcc.edu

BA

Sparks, John A.	Dean	458-2056	jasparks	BLaw	JD	69	Michigan	1976
Baglia, David S.	C-Ac	458-3361	dsbaglia	AF	DBA	99.	Clev St	&1995
Patterson, Jeffrey L.	Prof	458-3861	jlpatterson	FGHX	PHD	83.	Penn St	&1995
McFesters, M.	Asst	458-2009	mrmcfesters	CF	MS	98	Grove Cy	2007

Guilford College
Department of Accounting
Dept Phone: 316-2240

Greensboro, NC   27410
College of Business
5800 West Friendly Ave

(336) Fax=316-2949
guilford.edu

BS

Johnson, Raymond E.	C-Ac	316-2177	rjohnson	XF	MBA	73	E Carol		&1988
Grubbs, William A.	Prof	316-2240	bgrubbs	RFC	MBA	65	N Carol		&1967
Sulon Bibb Stedman Professor of Accounting									
Granger, H. Garland III	Assoc	316-2283	ggranger	AF	MA	71	Appalach	#	&1983
Boyett, Arthur S.	Visit	316-2870	aboyett	FAT	PHD	80.	Tx Tech		&2005

Gustavus Adolphus College
Accounting Faculty
Dept Phone: 933-7414

Saint Peter, MN   56082-1498
Econ & Management Dept
800 West College Avenue

(507) Fax=933-6032
gustavus.edu

BA
Connie Baum

Johnson, Bruce H.	C-Ac	933-7011	bruce	Mgt	PHD	79	Houston	1986
Barnette, Glenn	Asst	933-6120	gbarnett	FCMV	PHD	98	Rensselaer	1997
Klimesh, Michael	Asst	933-7476	mklimesh	C	MBA			2002
Peterson, Timothy	Asst	933-7410	tpeterso	FXM	MBA	76	Wisconsin	&1997

Hampton University
Dep of Banking, Fnce & Atg
Dept Phone: 727-5205
Homepage: http://www.hamptonu.edu

Hampton, VA   23668
School of Business
Buckman Hall

(757) Fax=727-5048
hamptonu.edu

BS,MBA
Ms. JoAnn Debro

Credle, Sid Howard	Dean	727-5361	sid.credle	FSH	PHD	89	Tx-Austin	& 9-99
Pyatt, Edward J.	C-Pr	727-5205	edward.pyatt	Fnce	PHD	85	Temple	1984
Adeyiga, Janet A.	Assoc	727-5862	janet.adeyiga	FT	PHD	80.	Missouri	1991
Angima, Jacob M.	Asst	727-5360	jacob.angima	FV	PHD	93	UCLA	&2000
LeBow, Marc I.	Asst	727-5360	marc.lebow	ADX	PHD	91	Va Comm	&2004
McClain, Michael	Lect	727-5505	michael.mcclain	FT	PHD	98	Nova SE	1998

Hannibal-LaGrange College
Accounting Faculty
Dept Phone: 221-3675
  phone 221-3675

Hannibal, MO   63401-1999
Department of Business
2800 Palmyra Road

(573) Fax=221-6594
hlg.edu

BA,BS

Snider, Lois A.	C-As	Ext 267	lsnider	FPM	MA	85	NE Mo St		1982
Schafer, John	Prof	Ext 263	jschafer	TE	PHD	91	Missouri		&1987
Johnson-Dennis, Margaret	Asst	Ext 351	mjohnson	CVAX	MACC	88	W Illinois	*	&1997

Hardin-Simmons University
Dept Accounting, Fnce & Econ
Dept Phone: 670-1363
Homepage: www.hsutx.edu

Abilene, TX   79698-6220
Sch of Bus-PO Box 16220
2200 Hickory Street

(325) Fax=670-1523
hsutx.edu

BBA
Mrs. Clara Stovall

Monhollon, Michael L.	Dean	670-5870	mmonholl	Law	JD	84	Virginia	1998
Lemler, Bradley K.	Assoc	670-1524	blemler	FMXA	PHD	90.	Indiana	&2006
Burling, Shaylee	Asst	670-1360	sburling		MBA	99	HardSimm	2004
Walts, Charles	Asst	670-1293	cwalts		MPA	73	Tx-Austin	&1968

Harding University
Accounting Program
Dept Phone: 279-4301
Homepage: www.harding.edu/accounting

Searcy, AR   72149-0001
Sch of Bus Box 10774
Center Street & Blakely Ave

(501) Fax=279-4665
harding.edu

BBA

Burks, Bryan	Dean	279-4317	bburks	SFPC	DBA	06	Nova SE	&1995
Brown, Philip A.	C-Ac	279-4301	pbrown	FTBR	PHD	99.	Miss	&1987
Allen, David L.	Assoc	279-4458	allen	XF	MBA	81	Cen Ark	&1987
Churchman, Robert J.	Asst	279-4267	bchurchman	FBR	MBA	03	Cen Ark	&2004
Emerson, Mike	Asst	279-4571	memerson	ATF	MS	89	Harding	&1985
Ross, Gary	Asst	279-8901	gross	FMVP	MBA	94	Tx Tech	2000

University of Hartford   W Hartford, CT   06117-1599   (860) Fax=768-4398   2001,2004
Dept Accounting & Taxation   Barney Sch of Business   hartford.edu   BS,MBA,MS
Dept Phone: 768-4576   200 Bloomfield Avenue   Beverly Collins
Homepage: http://barney.hartford.edu

Name	Rank	Phone	Email	Area	Deg	Yr	School	
Fairfield-Sonn, James P.	Dean$	768-4187	fairfield	Mgt	PHD	85	Yale	1982
Bannister, James W.	C-Ac	768-5301	bannister	FI	PHD	88.	N Carol	1994
Broden, Barry C.	Prof	768-4271	broden	X	DBA	77.	Maryland	&1983
Nodoushani, Patricia	Prof	768-4346	nodoushan	X	PHD	87.	Houston	&1995
Lamberton, Barbara A.	Assoc	768-5810	lamberton	MC	PHD	98	Mich St	&1999
Mihalek, Paul H.	Assoc	768-4363	mihalek	FMA	PHD	86	Conn	&1986
Smith, Carl S.	Assoc	768-4343	casmith	CS	PHD	88	Conn	* & 9-81
Gantt, Karen	Asst	768-5809	gantt	XL	LLM	96	Baltimore	9-02
Generas, George P. Jr.	Asst	768-4578	generas	FL	JD	90	Conn	&1979
Machuga, Susan	Asst	768-4184	machuga	FA	PHD	96.	Mass	& 9-06
Kulesza, Marie G.	Lect	768-4394	kulesza	FMA	MS	99	Hartford	& 9-05
Thompson, Steven W.	Lect	768-4577	sthompson	MS	MS	05	Hartford	& 9-06

Hartwick College   Oneonta, NY   13820   (607) Fax=431-4953
Accounting Faculty   Dept Bus Adm & Atg   hartwick.edu   BS,BA
Dept Phone: 431-4863   Elizabeth Maldohado

Name	Rank	Phone	Email	Area	Deg	Yr	School	
Dalrymple, Scott	C	431-4863						
Kolenda, Stephen A.	Prof	431-4951	kolendao	FIJ	MBA	83	Conn	&1983
Sears, Thomas G.	Prof	431-4947	searst	MXQ	MBA	87	Syracuse	&1978
Wightman, Priscella Z.	Asst	431-4338	wightmanp	AFC	MS	90	SUNY-Alb	&1985

Harvard University   Boston, MA   02163   (617) Fax=496-7387   1916
Accounting & Control Area   Grad School of Bus Adm   hbs.edu   MBA,DBA,PHD
Dept Phone: 495-8017   Soldiers Field Road   Alison D'Elia
Homepage: www.hbs.edu/units/ac/

Name	Rank	Phone	Email	Area	Deg	Yr	School	
Clark, Kim B.	Dean	495-6550	kclark	Mgt	DBA	78	Harvard	1978
Dean of Faculty								
Healy, Paul M.	C-Pr	495-1283	phealy	FM	PHD	83.	Rochester	&1997
MBA Class '49 Professor of Business Administration								
Anthony, Robert N.	Emer	495-6504		1984	DCS	52.	Harvard	1940
email: rnanthony@valley.net								
Christenson, Charles J.	Emer	495-6668		1996	DBA	61	Harvard	1957
Royal Little Professor of Business Administration								
Datar, Srikant M.	Prof	495-6543	sdatar	FMA	PHD	85.	Stanford	* &1996
Arthur Lowes Dickenson Professor of Accounting								
Hawkins, David F.	Prof	495-6793	dhawkins	F	DBA	62.	Harvard	1960
Lovett-Learned Professor of Business Administration								
Kaplan, Robert S.	Prof	495-6150	rkaplan	MC	PHD	68.	Cornell	1983
Marvin Bower Professor of Leadership Development								
Narayanan, V. G.	Prof	495-6359	vnarayanan	MF	PHD	96.	Stanford	1994
Palepu, Krishna G.	Prof	495-6759	kpalepu	FM	PHD	83.	MIT	1983
Ross Graham Walker Professor; Senior Associate Dean; Director Research								
Piper, Thomas R.	Prof	495-6370	tpiper	FJ	DBA	70	Harvard	1970
Industrial Bank of Japan Professor								
Simons, Robert L.	Prof	495-6757	rsimons	MBU	PHD	84	McGill	&1984
Charles M. Williams Professor of Business Administration								
Bradshaw, Mark T.	Assoc	495-6956	mbradshaw	F	PHD	00.	Michigan	2000
Kimbrough, Michael D.	Assoc	495-6222	mkimbrough		PHD	02.	Indiana	8-02
Miller, Gregory S.	Assoc	495-8014	gmiller	F	PHD	98.	Michigan	1998
Riedl, Edward J.	Assoc	495-6368	eriedl	F	PHD	02.	Penn St	2002
Autrey, Romana L.	Asst	495-5057	rautrey	FY	PHD	05.	Tx-Austin	* & 8-05
Campbell, Dennis	Asst		dcampbell		DBA	04.	Harvard	2004
Ferri, Fabrizio	Asst		fferri	FM	PHD	04.	NYU	2004
Katz, Sharon P.	Asst	495-5395	skatz		PHD	06.	Columbia	7-06
Martinez-Jerez, Francisco	Asst	495-6844	amartinezjerez	FM	PHD	02.	Harvard	2002
Shanthikumar, Devin M.	Asst	495-6856	dshanthikumar	FM	PHD	04	Stanford	7-04

University of Hawaii at Hilo   Hilo, HI   96720-4091   (808) Fax=974-7685   2004,2004
Business Administration   Col of Bus & Economics   hawaii.edu   BBA
Dept Phone: 974-7400   200 W. Kawili Street   Mitzi Hennessey

Name	Rank	Phone	Email	Area	Deg	Yr	School	
Sakai, Marcia	Dean	974-7400	marcias	Econ	PHD	85	Hi-Manoa	1991
Hennessey, Harry W.	C-Pr	974-7400	harryh	Mgt	PHD	80	Georgia	8-90
Leonard, Barbara Brockie	Assoc	974-7457	leonardb	PFTI	PHD	91.	Okla St	* 2002
Jones, Roberta A.	Asst	974-7593	rajones	SAF	PHD	96.	Illinois	&2006

Univ of Hawaii at Manoa   Honolulu, HI   96822   (808) Fax=956-9888   ß 1967,1972
School of Accountancy   Shilder Col Business   hawaii.edu   BBA,MAC,MBA,PHD
Dept Phone: 956-7332   2404 Maile Way, C-306   Pauline Abe 956-7332
Homepage: www.hawaii.edu/soa

Name	Rank	Phone	Email	Area	Deg	Yr	School	
Roley, V. Vance	Dean	956-8377	vroley	Econ	PHD	77	Harvard	1-05
Teruya, Jenny N.	D-Ac	956-7118	jteruya	CFM	PHD	98.	Arizona	& 8-97

Daniel, Shirley J.	Prof	956-3249	sdaniel	AM	PHD	85.	Okla St	& 1-86
Henry A. Walker Jr. Professor of Business Enterprise								
Debreceny, Roger S.	Prof	956-8545	rogersd	AFS	PHD	98	Australia	&2004
Shidler College Distinguished Professor								
Pearson, Thomas C.	Prof	956-7591	tpearson	XJK	LLM	05	NYU	& 1-89
Pourjalali, Hamid	Prof	956-5578	hamid	CMFI	PHD	92.	Okla St	8-96
Wendell, John P.	Prof	956-6694	cbaajwe	SA	PHD	89.	Union-NY	& 8-89
Yang, David C.	Prof	956-6975	yangd	FI	PHD	85.	Columbia	* 1-85
Guan, Liming	Assoc	956-7002	lguan	SF	PHD	01.	Okla St	8-01
Jung, Boo Chun	Asst			FI	PHD	07	Colorado	8-07
Mescall, Devan	Asst				PHD	07	Waterloo	8-07
Sun, Jialin (Kevin)	Asst	956-8063	sunj	IF	PHD	05.	Colorado	8-05
Hatanaka, Robert K.	Inst	956-7028	rhatanak	FA	MACC	83	Hawaii	& 8-04
Kaiama, Cathy M.	Inst	956-7300	manu.kaiama	F	MACC	88	Hawaii	& 8-91
Woollen, Mary	Inst	956-6678	woollen	FM	MACC	97	Hawaii	& 8-02

Univ of Hawaii - West Oahu
Accounting Faculty
Dept Phone: 454-4735

Pearl City, HI   96782
Business Administration
96-129 Ala Ike

(808) Fax = 453-6176
hawaii.edu

BA

Aono, June Y.	C-Ac	454-4735	jaono	AFM	PHD	81	UCLA	&1999

Hawaii Pacific University
Accounting Faculty
Dept Phone: 544-0283
Homepage: www.hpu.edu

Honolulu, HI   96813
College of Business Adm
1188 Fort Street Mall

(808) Fax = 566-2403
hpu.edu

BS,MBA

Kearns, John	Dean	566-2440	jkearns	Clas	PHD	82	UCLA	8-97
Karbens, John P.	Assoc	544-1156	jkarbens	FPER	EDD	83	Hawaii	# * & 8-90
Kelly, Lauren	Assoc	544-0871	lkelly	MF	PHD	76.	Alabama	8-02
Wee, Warren Y. F.	Assoc	544-9325	wwee	AN	PHD	82.	U Wash	& 8-88
Associate Dean								
Kam, Thomas	Asst	544-9348	tkam	MPE	MBA	78	Hawaii	* & 8-86
Waddington, James	Asst	566-2415	jwaddington	FPG	MBA	82	Hawaii	& 8-86

Heidelberg College
Accounting Faculty
Dept Phone: 448-2280
Homepage: www.heidelberg.edu

Tiffin, OH   44883-2462
Dept Bus Adm, Atg & Eco
310 East Market Street

(419) Fax = 448-2236
heidelberg.edu

BA,BS
Mary Puffenberger

Tucker, Barbara L.	Prof	448-2307	btucker	TADR	MSA	83	Jms Mad	&1989
Cook, John P. Jr.	Asst	448-2205	jcook	F	PHD	94	Kentucky	&1995
Stine, Linda	Inst	448-2326	lstine		MBA		Heidelbg	2004

Henderson State University
Accounting Faculty
Dept Phone: 230-5377
Homepage: www.hsu.edu/dept/schoolofbusiness

Arkadelphia, AR   71999-0001
School of Business
1100 Henderson Street

(870) Fax = 230-5286
hsu.edu

1998,1998
BBA
Nancy Holland/Betty Magnini

Huo, Y. Paul	Dean	230-5377	huop	Mgt	PHD	87	Berkeley	2005
Hoskins, Margaret A.	Prof	230-5302	hoskins	FTAJ	PHD	92.	Miss	&1991
Don Dodson Professor								
Linn, Gary	Prof	230-5300	linng	FBX	DBA	97.	La Tech	&1995
Cecil Cupp Chair								
Robertson, Paul J. (Jep)	Prof	230-5482	robertp	FCN	DBA	88.	Miss St	&2004
Watters, Michael Paul	Prof	230-5345	watterm	FTA	DBA	89.	Miss St	&1996
Louis Dawkins Professor								

Hendrix College
Accounting Faculty
Dept Phone: 329-6811

Conway, AR   72032-3080
Dept of Econ & Business
1600 Washington Ave

(501) Fax = 450-1200
hendrix.edu

BA,MA

Scott, Ralph D. Jr.	C-Pr	450-1306	scott	Econ	PHD	83	Tulane	1979
Kerr, Stephen W.	Prof	450-1305	kerr	XF	MBA	77	So Meth	&1979
Rupert, Lyle M.	Prof	450-1237	rupert	DSM	MBA	85	Chicago	&1987
Oxner, Karen	Asst	450-1259	oxner	AF	DBA	94.	S Illinois	&1997

High Point University
Accounting, Fnce & Econ
Dept Phone: 841-4521

High Point, NC   27262-3598
Earl Phillips Sch Bus
833 Montlieu Avenue

(336) Fax = 841-4599
highpoint.edu

BS,MBA
Anne Grube

Wehrley, James	Dean	841-4521	jwehrley		PHD		Va Tech	1994
Noxon, George	C-As	841-9233	gnoxon	ACFJ	MBA		Tulane	&1993
King, Arthur Edward	Assoc	841-9203	aking	AFM	MBA		W Virginia	&1989
Davis, Scott	Asst	841-9033	sdavis	CMXJ	MSA		NC-Green	&1996
Lavery, Kenneth A.	Asst	841-4597	klavery	FXM	ABD		La Tech	&1997

Hillsdale College

Accounting Faculty
Dept Phone:
Homepage: www.hillsdale.edu

Hillsdale, MI	49242-1298				(517) Fax=437-3923			
Dept of Econ, Bus & Atg					hillsdale.edu			
33 E. College Street								Carol Kratzer
Paas, David	C-Pr	437-7341	david.paas	BLaw	PHD	82	Nebraska	1993
Ikawa, Bruce E.	Assoc	437-7341	bruce.ikawa	FMX	PHD	88.	Michigan	&1999

Brouwer D. & Jane E. McIntyre Chair in Business Administration

Sweeney, Michael P.	Assoc	452-8494	michael.sweeney	FXM	PHD	95.	Kentucky	&1996

Evert McCabe/UPS Professor

Hofstra University

Dept Atg/Taxation/Legal Stud
Dept Phone: 463-5684

Hempstead, NY	11549				(516) Fax=463-4834		ß (123) 1968,1982	
Zarb School of Business					hofstra.edu		BBA,MBA,MS	
134 Hofstra Univ							Joan Tsapelas	
Sedano, Salvatore	Dean	463-5676	salvatore.sedano		MBA	83	Hofstra	2006
Warner, Paul D.	C-Pr	463-6994	paul.d.warner	ADOS	PHD	81.	NYU	&1991
Fonfeder, Robert	Prof	463-6988	robert.fonfeder	PM	PHD	80.	Baruch	* &1980
Katz, Robert	Prof	463-5682	robert.katz	X	LLM	71	NYU	1975
Lehman, Cheryl R.	Prof	463-6986	cheryl.r.lehman	BHW	PHD	85	NYU	1979
Polimeni, Ralph S.	Prof	463-5685	ralph.polimeni	C	PHD	73.	Arkansas	& 9-73

Provost

Slavin, Nathan S.	Prof	463-5690	nathan.s.slavin	F	PHD	80.	Baruch	& 9-74
Burke, Jacqueline A.	Assoc	463-6987	jacqueline.a.b+	P	PHD	00	NYU	& 8-93
Jones, Richard C.	Assoc	463-6990	richard.c.jones	CP	PHD	01.	Rutgers	& 8-97
Maccarrone, Eugene T.	Assoc	463-6991	eugene.t.macc+	A	MBA	81	Hofstra	& 5-80
Petra, Steven	Assoc	463-5684	steven.petra	CFMX	PHD	02.	Rutgers	&2002
Venuti, Elizabeth K.	Assoc	463-5359	elizabeth.venuti	TV	PHD	97.	Columbia	&1999
Basile, Anthony	Asst	463-5349	anthony.basile	APX	PHD	01	NYU	&1993
Marsicovetere, Dominic A.	Asst	463-6993	dominic.a.mar+	PF	MBA	73	Pace	&1978
Schain, Linda J.	Asst	463-5692	linda.j.schain	PV	MBA	78	Iona	&1984

College of the Holy Cross

Accounting Faculty
Dept Phone: 793-3362

Worcester, MA	01610-2395				(508) Fax=793-3708			
Dept of Economics					holycross.edu			AB
1 College Street							Beverly Bylund	
Baldiga, Nancy R.	C-Ac	793-2684	nbaldiga	FA	MST	92	Bentley	& 9-91
Chu, David	Assoc	793-2206	dchu	FCN	PHD	85	Indiana	9-91
O'Connell, John D.	Assoc	793-3875		FVX	MBA	58	Boston U	& 9-57
Sandstrom, Scott	Assoc	793-2677	ssandstr	FLX	JD	83	Suffolk	& 9-83
O'Connor, Debra	Asst	793-2681	doconnor	FX	PHD	06	Mass	8-06
Teitel, Karen	Asst	793-2679	kteitel	FM	PHD	02.	Mass	& 8-04

Hope College

Accounting Faculty Box 9000
Dept Phone: 395-7580

Holland, MI	49422-9000				(616) Fax=395-7490			
Econ, Mgt & Accounting					hope.edu			BA
41 Graves Place							Joy Forgwe Ortiz	
Lunn, John E.	C-Pr	395-7931	lunn	Econ	PHD	80	UCLA	1992
Hendrix, Lynne	Assoc	395-7575	hendrix	A	MBA		Gr Valley	&1985
Martin, Herbert	Assoc	395-7578	martin	XS	MA	79	Arkansas	& 8-82
Ritsema, Christina M.	Asst	395-7580	ritsemac	X	PHD	01.	Arkansas	&2001

University of Houston

Dept of Accountancy & Tax
Dept Phone: 743-4820
Homepage: www.bauer.uh.edu

Houston, TX	77204-6283				(713) Fax=743-4828		ß (123) 1964,1967	
C.T. Bauer Col of Bus					uh.edu		BBA,MBA,MAC,PHD	
4800 Calhoun							Linda Guerrero	
Warga, Arthur D.	Dean	743-4779	warga	Fnce	PHD	77	Michigan	1997

Judge James A. Elkins Professor of Banking and Finance

Lobo, Gerald J.	C-Pr	743-4838	gjlobo	F	PHD	82.	Michigan	2004

Arthur Andersen Chair

Francia, Arthur J.	Prof	743-4826	afrancia	M	PHD	69.	Minnesota	1974

KPMG Peat Marwick Professor

Gamble, George O.	Prof	743-4824	ggamble	FM	PHD	80.	Penn St	1978

Robert Grinaker Professor

Hemmer, Thomas	Prof		themmer	M	PHD	90	Odense	9-05

Charles McMahen Chair

Newberry, Kaye J.	Prof		knewberry	X	PHD	94.	Ariz St	& 9-05

C. T. Bauer Professor

Pratt, James W.	Prof	743-4842	jwpratt	X	DBA	72.	S Calif	&1972

PricewaterhouseCoopers Professor

Rees, Lynn L.	Prof		lrees	FI	PHD	94.	Ariz St	9-05

C. T. Bauer Professor

Sivaramakrishnan, K. (Shiva)	Prof	743-4630	ksivaram	FM	PHD	88.	Nrthwstrn	1-03

C.T. Bauer Endowed Chair

Alciatore, Mimi L.	Assoc	743-4848	malciatore	FVZ	PHD	89.	Tx-Austin	&2001
Khumawala, Saleha B.	Assoc	743-4829	saleha	FGI	PHD	78.	N Carol	&1978
Meade, Janet A.	Assoc	743-4841	jmeade	X	PHD	87.	Ariz St	&1988

Noland, Thomas R.	Assoc	743-4819	tnoland	F	PHD	92.	Illinois	& 9-92
Schugart, Gary L.	Assoc	743-4820	gschugart	FZI	PHD	74	Kansas	1989
Whisenant, J. Scott	Assoc	743-4852	scottwhisenant	FAT	PHD	97	Oklahoma	* & 9-01
Drymiotes, George C.	Asst	743-4853	gdrymiotes	M	PHD	04.	Florida	9-04
Lazer, Ron	Asst	743-4847	rlazer	F	PHD	04.	NYU	9-04
Lu, Tong	Asst	743-0448	tlu4	F	PHD	04	Minnesota	9-04
Milbrath, Robert S.	VAsst	743-4854	milbrath	FM	PHD	86	Michigan	1993
Nathan, Edward C.	VAsst	743-4827	enathan	FB	PHD	81.	Tx-Austin	&1980
Newman, Michael Program Director	VAsst	743-4857	michaeln	FMX	MBA	00	Houston	9-06
Stinson, James B.	VAsst	743-4898	jbstinson	FMS	PHD	00	Houston	5-02
Yampuler, Michael E.	Asst	743-4027	myampuler	F	PHD	04	Harvard	9-04
Weber, Catherine K.	Lect	743-4820			PHD	06.	Tx A&M	

Univ of Houston-Clear Lake Houston, TX 77058-1098 (281) Fax = 283-3951 ß (13) 1981,1986
Accounting Faculty School of Business uhcl.edu BS,MS
Dept Phone: 283-3155 2700 Bay Area Blvd Renee Sweeney
Homepage: ptrl.uhcl.edu/portal/page page = 416,725537& dad = portal&

Cummings, William T.	Dean	283-3102	cummings	Mktg	PHD	78	Ariz St	9-98
Marks, Barry R.	C-Pr	283-3214	marks	FGX	PHD	75	Purdue	9-84
Bruno, Joan D.	Prof	283-3111	bruno	FT	PHD	69.	LSU	& 9-75
Heagy, Cynthia D.	Prof	283-3164	heagy	MS	DBA	87.	Memphis	* & 9-90
Kyle, Donald L.	Prof	283-3176	kyle	CM	PHD	69.	Arkansas	& 6-74
Porter, Mattie C.	Prof	283-3163	porter	AFM	PHD	79.	Tx A&M	&1986
Rusth, Douglas B.	Assoc	283-3165	rusth	VIJE	PHD	91.	Houston	& 9-91
Du, Hui	Asst	283-3155		AFS	PHD	02.	Rutgers	9-07
Lacina, Michael J.	Asst	283-3171	laciha	CFM	PHD	98.	Purdue	& 9-05
Lehmann, Constance M.	Asst	283-3157	lehmann	ABFS	PHD	01.	Tx A&M	9-01
Shin, Haeyoung	Asst	283-3155		F	PHD	07	Tx-Dallas	9-07
Sorensen, Susan M.	Asst	283-3160	sorensen	FXI	PHD	03	Minnesota	& 1-03
Xu, Zhaohui	Asst	383-3155		AF	PHD	07	Alabama	9-07
Isleib, R. Bruce	Lect	283-3162	isleib	FV	PHD	95.	Houston	& 9-93

Univ of Houston-Downtown Houston, TX 77002-1001 (713) Fax = 226-5238 1994
Finance, Atg & CIS Dept College of Business uhd.edu BBA
Dept Phone: 221-8017 One Main Street Rosa Bermudez
Homepage: www.dt.uh.edu

Bates, Donald L.	Dean	221-8179	batesdon	Mgt	PHD	73	Arkansas	2005
Omer, Khursheed	C-Pr	221-8630	omerk	MCS	DBA	90.	Memphis	&1991
Duangploy, Orapin S.	Prof	221-8596	duangployo	F	PHD	77.	Missouri	&1987
Wadhwa, Darshan L. (Dash)	Prof	221-8517	wadhwad	X	DBA	88.	La Tech	&1984
Pence, Diana Kay	Assoc	221-8456	pencee	F	PHD	96.	North Tx	2006
Serrett, Randall K.	Assoc	221-8578	serrettr	G	PHD	86.	Houston	&2000
Shelton, Margaret L.	Assoc	221-8963	sheltonm	F	PHD	86.	Houston	&1989
Williams, Marvin	Assoc	221-8918	williamsm	X	JD	86	Houston	* &1988
Bressler, Linda	Asst	221-8490	bresslerl	S	DBA	00	Sarasota	2001
Manrique-Gutierrez, Justo	Asst	221-8209	manriquej	M	PHD	91	Iowa St	2002

Univ of Houston-Victoria Victoria, TX 77901-5731 (361) Fax = 570-4229 2004,2004
Accounting Faculty School of Business uhv.edu
Dept Phone: 570-4231 3007 N. Ben Wilson Jolynn Young
Homepage: www.uhv.edu
  275- phones have 281 area code

Bullock, Charles	Dean	570-4231	bullockc	X	LLM	84	Denver	9-96
Satava, David R.	Assoc	570-4236	satavad	AFP	DBA	94.	Miss St	& 8-95
Du, Jianjun	Asst	570-4231	duj	F	PHD	02	St Louis	8-01
Lee, Yong-Gyo	Asst	275-3381	leey	FM	PHD	93.	Geo St	9-01

Houston Baptist University Houston, TX 77074-3298 (281) Fax = 649-3436
Accounting Area College of Bus & Econ hbu.edu BS,BA,BBA,MACCT
Dept Phone: 649-3325 7502 Fondren Road Mary Weber

Tauer, Ritamarie C.	Dean$	649-3325	rtauer	FCMP	MACC	85	Hou Bapt	&1986
Serrato, Darlene Bohac	C-Ac	649-3457	dserrato	MCFP	PHD	87.	Houston	* 1987
Wescott, Shari H.	Prof	649-3437	swescott	SFV	PHD	82.	S Carol	1990
Kuruvilla, Mohan	Assoc	649-3014	mkuruvilla	AIP	PHD	96.	Houston	* & 9-03

Howard University Washington, DC 20059 (202) Fax = 986-4160 ß (12) 1976,1980
Department of Accounting School of Business howard.edu BA,MBA
Dept Phone: 806-1565 2600 Sixth St NW Suite 340
Homepage: www.bschool.howard.edu
  email @1 = fac.howard.edu

Harvey, Barron H.	Dean	806-1508	bharvey	FC	PHD	77	Nebraska	&1982

Glover, Hubert D.	C-Ac	806-1566	hglover	AF	PHD	92. Tx A&M	# *	&2004
Cheng, Kang	Assoc	806-1587	kcheng	F	PHD	98. Geo Wash		&2006
Fritsche, Steven R.	Assoc	806-1857	sfritsche	EFIT	PHD	91. Alabama		&2004
Hicks, Margaret	Assoc	806-1565	mhicks@1	CF	DBA	82. Maryland		&1987
Blue, Eugene R.	Asst	806-1528	eblue	FMB	PHD	97. Mich St		2000
Henry, Byron K.	Asst	806-1581	bhenry	FMG	PHD	99. Tx A&M		&1997
Hill, Alphonse G.	Asst	806-1582	alhillcpa98@y	F	PHD	80 Union-NY		&1992
Warsame, Mohamed	Asst	806-1525	mwarsame	F	PHD	06 MorganSt		&2006
Wells-Jessup, Jean	Asst	806-1856	jwellsjessup	JD		98 Geo Wash		2002
Gagne, Bridgett	Lect	806-1564	bgagne6@y		MBA	88 Texas		&2006
Harvey, Samuel	Lect	806-1693	hrrdluc@a		JD	83 Geotown		2002
Ross, Frank	Visit	806-1637		A	MBA	68 Long Isl		&2003
email fross10130@earthlink.net								

University of Idaho Moscow, ID 83844-3161 (208) Fax=885-6296 ß (13) 1993
Department of Accounting College of Bus & Econ uidaho.edu BS,MACC
Dept Phone: 885-6453 P.O. Box 443161 Amber Gray
Homepage: www.uidaho.edu/cbe/depts/accounting

Morris, John S.	Dean	885-7024	jmorris	Mgt	PHD	88 Oklahoma	2006
Kraut, Marla Myers	H-Ac	885-7116	marlam	AFX	PHD	92. Arizona	&1991
Gordon, Teresa P.	Assoc	885-8960	tgordon	NMF	PHD	86. Houston	&1986
Harkins, Jeffrey L.	Assoc	885-7602	jeffh	FT	PHD	80. U Wash	&1983
Utzman, Glen G.	Assoc	885-7800	utz	X	LLM	94 NYU	&1973
Porter, Jason	Asst	885-7153	jporter	F	PHD	06. Georgia	2006
Woolley, Darryl J.	Asst	885-7300	dwoolley	FS	PHD	02. Utah	&2007
Hatheway-Dial, K. D.	Inst	885-6311	kddial	AFM	MACC	Idaho	2003

Idaho State University Pocatello, ID 83209-8020 (208) Fax=282-4367 ß (12) 1975,1980
Department of Accounting College of Business isu.edu BA,MBA
Dept Phone: 282-3585 741 S. 7th St Karma Morrison
Homepage: www.isu.edu

Stratton, William E.	Dean	282-3585	strabill	Mgt	PHD	74 Case Wes	1973
Picard, Robert R.	C-Pr	282-4067	picarobe	MVS	PHD	94. Kentucky	&1994
Boes, Richard F.	Prof	282-2422	boesrich	XMF	PHD	78. Mich St	& 1-77
Frischmann, Peter J.	Prof	282-3501	frispete	XM	PHD	92. Ariz St	&2000
Plewa, Franklin J.	Prof	282-3550	plewfran	VF	PHD	83. LSU	1984
Smith, Kenneth A.	Prof	282-2975	smithken	ARM	PHD	71. Tx-Austin	&1970
Associate Dean							
Reis, Priscilla R.	Assoc	282-3638	reispris	MS	PHD	91 Rensselaer	* &1994
Bezik, Mark H.	Asst	282-4769	bezimark	PF	MBA	78 Case Wes	&1999
Smith, Jill M.	Asst	282-3025	smitjill	PF	MBA	75 Idaho St	&1986

University of Illinois Champaign, IL 61820 (217) Fax=244-0902 ß (13) 1924,1963
Department of Accountancy Com & Bus Adm 1206 Sixt uiuc.edu BS,MS,PHD
Dept Phone: 333-0857 1206 S. Sixth Street Sharon McLeod
Homepage: www.cba.uiuc.edu

Ghosh, Avijit	Dean	333-2747	ghosha	Mktg	PHD	79 Iowa	2001
Solomon, Ira	H-Pr	333-3808	isolomon	AB	PHD	79. Tx-Austin	& 8-83
RC Evans Endowed Chair in Business							
Abdel-khalik, A. Rashad	Prof	265-0539	rashad	FU	PHD	72. Illinois	6-00
Director, Center for International Education and Research in Accounting							
Bailey, Andrew D. Jr.	Emer	333-7612	jabaile	2003	PHD	71. Ohio St	# * &1994
Securities and Exchange Commission							
Beck, Paul J.	Prof	333-4563	p-beck2	AX	PHD	77. Tx-Austin	8-83
Irwin Jecha Professor							
Brighton, Gerald D.	Emer	333-4540		1989	PHD	53. Illinois	&1954
Brown, Clifton E.	Prof	333-2849	ce-brown	BCM	PHD	78. Florida	8-78
H. T. Scovill Professor							
Holzer, H. Peter	Emer	333-4545		1992	DBA	51 Vienna	&1954
The University of Economics							
Neumann, Frederick L.	Emer	333-0857	fneumann	2002	PHD	67. Chicago	# &1965
Peecher, Mark E.	Prof	333-4542	peecher	BAF	PHD	94. Illinois	6-98
Schoenfeld, Hanns-Martin	Emer	333-4530	hschoenfeld	1994	PHD	54 Hamburg	6-62
Sougiannis, Theodore	Prof	244-0555	sougiani	F	PHD	90. Berkeley	1990
KPMG Distinguished Professor							
Trotman, Ken T.	Prof	333-0857		AB	PHD	84 NS Wales	& 8-05
visiting from Univ of New South Wales							
Willis, Eugene	Emer	333-4527	e-willis	2003	PHD	75. Cincinnati	& 9-75
Wyatt, Arthur R.	Emer	244-7568			PHD	53. Illinois	&1993
Chandler, John S.	Assoc	333-4539	chandlej	UMS	PHD	77 Ohio St	8-78
Molloy, Karen H.	Assoc	333-1389	kmolloy	X	PHD	80. Va Tech	& 1-81
Schwartz, Rachel	Assoc	333-0975	rschwart	A	PHD	94. Nrthwstrn	2003
Silhan, Peter A.	Assoc	333-8815	p-silhan	SMI	DBA	80. Tennessee	* 8-79
Ziegler, Richard E.	Emer	333-4343	rziegler	2002	PHD	73. N Carol	& 9-72

Name	Rank	Phone	Email		Degree	Yr	School	
Chen, Clarra	Asst	244-3953	cxchen	FM	PHD	06	UCLA	8-06
Doogar, Rajib K.	Asst	224-8083	doogar	FMT	PHD	94.	Penn St	8-98
Elliott, W. Brooke	Asst	333-9247	wbe	F	PHD	03.	U Wash	6-03
Farrell, Anne M.	Asst	244-3307	amf	M	PHD	02.	Mich St	& 6-02
Gong, James	Asst	333-8878	gong	FM	PHD	05	S Calif	8-05
Ibrahim, Adel	VAsst	333-0857		F	PHD	03.	Illinois	8-05
Jackson, Kevin E.	Asst	244-0532	kjack	F	PHD	04.	Tx-Austin	& 8-04
Koga, Kentaro	Asst	244-8790	kkoga	M	DBA	99.	Harvard	1-02
Krische, Susan D.	Asst	265-5496	krische	FB	PHD	02.	Cornell	8-01
Li, Laura	Asst	265-5086	liyue	FM	PHD	06	Tulane	8-06
Li, Siyi	Asst	244-9213	siyili	F	PHD	03.	Columbia	8-03
McHugh, Marion	VAsst	244-2365	mmchugh	A	PHD	05.	Arkansas	1-07
Mosebach, Janet	VAsst	333-4381	jmosebac	X	PHD	06	Arkansas	& 8-06
Mosebach, Michael	VAsst	244-8546	mosebach	F	PHD	96.	Oklahoma	& 8-06
Narayanamoorthy, Ganapathi	Asst	244-6707	gnarayan	F	PHD	02.	Rochester	1-07
Pike, Joel E.	Asst	244-8993	joelpike	FM	PHD	03.	Wisconsin	8-03
Shin, Jae Yong	Asst	244-5759	jyshin	FM	PHD	06	Wisconsin	8-06
Smith, Steven D.	Asst	265-6770	smithsd	F	PHD	05.	Cornell	8-04
Wright, William F.	VAsst	265-0361	wrightwf	M	PHD	75.	Berkeley	8-05
Wu, Martin G. H.	Asst	333-0857	martinwu	FM	PHD	95	Brit Colum	08-0
Xie, Hong	Asst	333-0857	hongxie	FM	PHD	98.	Iowa	7-01
Curtis, Susan M.	Lect	333-4529	smcurtis	BA	PHD	00.	Illinois	8-00
Engle, Howard	AdjLe		h-engle		MS	75	DePaul	1988
Feller, Anita L.	Lect	333-6673	a-feller	EPX	PHD	89	Illinois	&1990
Finnegan, Thomas R.	Lect	244-7783	tfinnegn	MFX	PHD	93.	Illinois	1993
Nekrasz, Frank Jr.	Lect	333-4521	nfrank	A	PHD	93.	Illinois	& 8-99
Perkins, Jon D.	Lect			ABXM	PHD	03.	Illinois	* & 8-07
Sandretto, Michael J.	Lect	244-6410	sandrett	FM	PHD	79.	Illinois	& 8-98
Shapland, Julie	Lect	333-1366	jshaplan	X	MS	97	Illinois	& 8-99
Showalter, Scott	VLect	244-8790						
Slutsky, Joanne	Lect	333-4567	slutsky		MBA	94	Tulane	8-97
Sternburg, Thomas J.	Lect	244-0199	t-stern	X	PHD	93.	Ariz St	& 5-93
Turner, Cynthia Williams	Lect	333-4538	cwillims	F	PHD	95.	Ohio St	& 8-95
Zhou, Flora	Lect	333-3937	hzh	FM	PHD	07	Cornell	8-06
Holder, Dan	AdjLe	244-3341	dholder	X	JD	79	Loyola	8-06

Univ of Illinois at Chicago Chicago, IL 60607-7123 (312) Fax=996-4520 ß (123) 1971,1981
Dept of Accounting College Bus Adm M/C006 uic.edu BS,MBA,MBA/MSA
Dept Phone: 996-2650 601 S. Morgan Edita Wingert Asst to Head
Homepage: http://accounting.cba.uic.edu/

Name	Rank	Phone	Email		Degree	Yr	School	
Lenway, Stefanie	Dean	996-2671	slenway		PHD	82	Berkeley	8-05
Ramakrishnan, Ram T. S.	H-Pr	996-3270	rramakri	FMT	PHD	81.	Nrthwstrn	1994
Ernst & Young Professor of Accounting								
Chalos, Peter	Prof	996-2869	pchalos	M	PHD	82.	Illinois	1985
Chan, James L.	Prof	996-2529	jimchan	GN	PHD	76.	Illinois	1981
Das, Somnath	Prof	996-4482	sdas	NFIM	PHD	88	Car Mellon	1996
Picur, Ronald D.	Prof	996-5216	rpicur	GFTN	PHD	73.	Nrthwstrn	&1978
Roe, George	ClAc	996-3391	groe	JL	JD	80	DePaul	1977
Soffer, Leonard C.	Assoc	996-2284	soffer	PERF	PHD	91.	Berkeley	&2000
Chen, Xiaolin (Clara)	Asst	244-3893	cxcgeb		PHD	06.	S Calif	2006
Hansen, James	Asst	996-4284	jh56	F	PHD	04.	Georgia	2004
Hong, Keejae P.	Asst	996-0671	keejae	FX	PHD	06.	Illinois	2006
Kim, Kyonghee	Asst	996-4438	kyonghee	FM	PHD	05.	Pittsburgh	2005
Weber, Margaret (Peggy)	Asst	996-0727	pegweg	F	PHD	04.	Tx-Austin	8-04
Galvan, Abel	Lect	413-8965	galvan	ARFM	MBA	96	Il-Chicago	1997
Leventhal, Brian	Lect	996-4827	brianlev	FM	MBA	87	N Illinois	&1993
Popowits, Michael T.	Lect	413-0998	popowits	DSJ	MSA	83	Illinois	&1988
Roe, Helen	Lect	413-2854	helenroe	XL	JD	72	DePaul	1989
Salama, Yehia A.	Lect	413-1532	ysalama	CFIM	PHD	83.	Alabama	2002

Univ Illinois at Springfield Springfield, IL 62703-5407 (217) Fax=206-7543 2007
Dept of Accountancy College of Bus & Mgt uis.edu BA,MA
Dept Phone: 206-6541 One University Plaza Ruth Mullenix
Homepage: www.uis.edu/accountancy

Name	Rank	Phone	Email		Degree	Yr	School	
McNeil, Ronald D.	Dean	206-6533	rmcne1	Mgt	PHD	82	Memphis	2002
Branson, Leonard L.	C-Ac	206-6299	lbran1	BSMF	PHD	90.	St Louis	* &1987
Crain, Gilbert W.	Assoc			GF	PHD	78.	Illinois	2007
Decker, Jeffrey	Assoc	206-7293	jdeck3	FMS	PHD	01.	Arizona	* &2005
Sage, Judith A.	Assoc	206-8273	jsage3	XF	PHD	87.	Okla St	&2005
Clausen, Thomas S.	Asst			S	PHD	02	Conn	2007
Cronin, William	Asst	206-7909	wcron2	TL	LLM		Wash U	&2005
Jessup, Carol	Asst	206-7923	cjess1	GSF	PHD	98	St Louis	&1998
Leraghan, Rosemary	Asst	206-7294	rleraols	F	PHD	06	UIS	2006

Illinois Institute of Tech
Accounting Faculty
Dept Phone: 906-6500
Homepage: www.stuart.iit.edu

	Chicago, IL	60661-3691		(312) Fax=906-6549			1999
	Stuart Grad School Bus			stuart.iit.edu			MBA
	565 W. Adams Street						Jurline Pullen
Kahalas, Harvey	Dean	906-6596		Mgt	PHD	71 Mass	2006
Bariff, Martin L.	Assoc	906-6522	bariff	AS	PHD	73. Illinois	&1983
Hamilton, Charles T.	Assoc	906-6528	hamilton	AMF	PHD	87. Illinois	&1991

Illinois State University
Department of Accounting
Dept Phone: 438-7651
Homepage: www.acc.ilstu.edu

	Normal, IL	61790-5520		(309) Fax=438-8431		(13) 1981,1986	
	College of Business			ilstu.edu		BS,MSA,MPA	
	University Ave.					Nancy Scherer	
McGuire, Charles	Dean$	438-2253	crmcquire	BLaw	JD	71 Illinois	1980
McKean, Gerald W.	C	438-7779		S	PHD	85 Illin St	1974
Craig, Caroline K.	Prof	438-7147	ckcraig	X	PHD	87. Illinois	&1987
Craig, Thomas R.	Prof	438-7908	trcraig	AT	PHD	84. Illinois	&1981
Leinicke, Linda M.	Prof	438-7149	lmleini	F	PHD	87. Miss	&1984
Moon, James E.	Prof	438-7651	jemoon	2006	PHD	70. Alabama	& 8-94
Associate Dean							
Ostrosky, Joyce A.	Prof	438-2396	jaostro	FCE	PHD	87. Miss	* & 9-74
Patten, Dennis M.	Prof	438-7857	dmpatte	MGW	PHD	87. Nebraska	&1985
Razaki, Khalid A.	Prof	438-5861	karazaki	M	PHD	86. Illinois	1980
Jones, Keith T.	Assoc	438-2473	kjones	MAF	PHD	01. Kentucky	& 8 06
Lindberg, Deborah L.	Assoc	438-7166	dllindb	AF	DBA	97. Boston U	&1997
McClure, Malcolm M.	Assoc	438-5771	mmmcclu	FI	PHD	83. Illinois	&1982
Rich, Jay S.	Assoc	438-7040	jsrich	ABF	PHD	97. Illinois	&2004
Brown, Darryl L.	Asst	438-7588	dbrown2	X	PHD	06. Arizona	2005
Seifert, Deborah	Asst	438-7651		FCG	PHD	06. Wash St	&2007
Borders, Barbara	Lect	438-5259	bjborde	MF	MS	Illinois	&2005
Dawson, Marie	Lect	438-7186	madawso	MF	MS	80 Illin St	&2005
Fuller, Harlan	Lect	438-5192	hjfulle	GMA	MS	79 Illin St	* &1982
Thomas, Charles	Lect	438-7208	cethoma	M	MS	97 Illin St	&1998

Illinois Wesleyan University
Accounting Faculty
Dept Phone: 556-3171
Homepage: http://titan.iwu.edu/~business/

	Bloomington, IL	61702-2900		(309) Fax=556-3719			
	Dept of Business Adm			titan.iwu.edu			BA,BS
	205 E. Beecher						Sue Virtue
Kearney, Robert A.	C-Ac	556-3570	rkearneyu		JD	94 Notre Dm	9-02
Olson, Gerald A.	Prof	556-3170	golson	AFVR	MS	86 Illin St	& 9-86
Willis, David M.	Assoc	556-3660	dwillis	ACFV	PHD	92. Cincinnati	& 9-95

Immaculata University
Accounting Faculty
Dept Phone:
Homepage: www.immaculata.edu
  phone: 647-4400

	Immaculata, PA	19345-0724		(610) Fax=251-1668			
	Dept of Econ, Atg & Bus			immaculata.edu			BS
	King Road						
Fitzwater, Charlene	C						

Univ of the Incarnate Word
Accounting Faculty
Dept Phone: 829-3191

	San Antonio, TX	78209-6397		(210) Fax=829-3169			
	HEB Sch Business & Adm			universe.uiwtx.edu			BBA,MS
	4301 Broadway						
Ryan, Robert	Dean	829-6000	ryan	Quan	PHD	Tx-Austin	
Elrod, Henry	C-As	829-3184	elrod	AJFM	MBA	69 Tx Chr	& 8-00
Tiggeman, Theresa	Prof	283-3986	tiggeman	FMPX	MBA	87 Incarnate	& 4-87
Green, Richard	Assoc	829-6000	greenr	FCX	PHD	99. St Louis	& 8-01

Indiana University
Department of Atg & Info Sys
Dept Phone: 855-8966
Homepage: http://www.indiana.edu/~aisdept/

	Bloomington, IN	47405-1701		(812) Fax=855-4985		β (13) 1921,1963	
	School of Business			indiana.edu		BS,MBA,PHD	
	1309 E. 10th Street					Eve Sparks	
Smith, Daniel C.	Dean$	885-8489	dansmith	Mktg	PHD	88 Pittsburgh	1996
Fisher, Joseph G.	C-Pr	855-3705	jofisher	FM	PHD	87. Ohio St	&1993
Fed Ex Faculty Fellow							
Beneish, Messod D. (Daniel)	Prof	855-2628	dbeneish	FJI	PHD	87. Chicago	1996
Sam Frumer Professor of Accounting							
Greene, David	ClPr	855-3513	dagreene	FM	JD	73 Indiana	&1997
Groomer, S. Michael	Prof	855-4026	groomer	AS	PHD	75. Missouri	&1974
Heitger, Lester E.	Prof	855-2606	heitger	M	PHD	72. Mich St	&1972
Hill, John W.	Prof	855-8924	hillj	MCFA	PHD	86. Iowa	1985
Arthur Weimer Faculty Chair							
Hite, Peggy A.	Prof	855-2649	hitep	XBE	PHD	86. Colorado	&1988
Maines, Laureen A.	Prof	855-2611	lmaines	FM	PHD	90. Chicago	&1997
PricewaterhouseCoopers Faculty Felllow							

Parry, Robert W. Jr. (Rob)	Prof	855-2629	parry	FNEG	PHD	79.	Lehigh	1979
Pratt, Jamie H.	Prof	855-2657	jpratt	BAEI	DBA	77.	Indiana	&1990
KPMG Professor of Accounting								
Salamon, Gerald L.	Prof	855-2612	salamon	FM	PHD	71.	Ohio St	&1986
Prickett Professor of Accounting								
Stern, Jerrold J.	Prof	855-2648	stern	X	PHD	79.	Tx A&M	1979
Wahlen, James M.	Prof	855-2658	jwahlen	FM	PHD	91.	Michigan	1997
Ford Motor Company Teaching Fellow								
Blacconiere, Walter G.	Assoc	855-2653	wblaccon	F	PHD	88.	U Wash	&1994
Ernst & Young Faculty Fellow								
Grandorf, James	ClAso	855-2868	jgrandor	F	MBA	64	Indiana	&1998
Hopkins, Patrick E.	Assoc	855-2617	peh	ABFV	PHD	95.	Tx-Austin	&1995
Deloitte Faculty Fellowship								
Kennedy, Tom	ClAc	855-8925	tokenned	X	JD	71	Indiana	&2002
Sprinkle, Geoffrey B.	Assoc	855-3514	sprinkle	M	PHD	96.	Iowa	&1999
Deere & Company Faculty Fellow								
Tiller, Mikel G.	Assoc	855-2619	tiller	FMBE	DBA	80.	Indiana	1985
Yohn, Teri Lombardi	Assoc	855-8966		F	PHD	91.	Indiana	&2007
Hewitt, Max	Asst	855-8966	hewittmr	F	PHD	07	U Wash	&2007
Hodder, Leslie D.	Asst	855-9951	lhodder	F	PHD	01.	Tx-Austin	&2003
McLelland, Malcolm J.	ClAs	855-8966	mjmclell	F	PHD	99.	Mich St	&2007
Oler, Derek K.	Asst	855-2381	doler	F	PHD	04.	Cornell	& 7-04
Picconi, Marc P.	Asst	856-1592	mpicconi	F	PHD	04.	Cornell	7-04
Glass, Kathrine	VLect	855-4175	kglass	F	MBA	84	Indiana	2006
Head, Julie	Lect	855-4782	jhead	F	BS	82	Indiana	& 9-92
Keenan, Sue	Lect	855-4175	skeenan	F	BA	82	Dartmouth	1997
Rearick, Thomas R.	Lect	855-0664	trearick	F	BA	87	Indiana	2002
Schrimper, Richard	Lect	855-7795	rschrimpe	F	MBA	85	Indiana	&1984

Indiana U at Indianapolis
Accounting Faculty
Dept Phone: 274-0893
Homepage: www.kelley.iupui.edu

Indianapolis, IN 46202-5151
Kelley Sch of Business
801 W. Michigan Street

(317) Fax=274-3312
iupui.edu

(13) 1921 1963
BS,MBA,MPA
Sherri Hendricks

Schmenner, Roger W.	AcDn	274-2481	rschmenn		PHD	73	Yale	1986
Hassell, John M.	Prof	274-4805	jhassell	FBE	PHD	83.	Indiana	& 8-96
OneAmerica Chair								
Jamison, Robert W.	Prof	274-4936	rjamison	X	PHD	80.	Tx-Austin	& 8-98
Johnson, Eric N.	Assoc	274-5695	erijohns	ABS	PHD	89.	Ariz St	* &1999
Kulsrud, William N.	Assoc	274-3422	wkulsrud	X	PHD	80.	Tx-Austin	&1979
Patterson, Evelyn R.	Assoc	278-7843	evpatter	AF	PHD	87.	Tx-Austin	& 8-05
Rogers, Richard L.	Assoc	274-3506	rrogers	FA	PHD	81.	Penn St	&1981
Smith, J. Reed	Assoc	274-0867	jrsmith2	SM	PHD	89.	Ohio St	8-02
Birr, Martin	SLect	274-0873	mbirr	FVN	MBA	87	Indiana	* & 1-89
Keller, J. Howard	SLect	274-4855	jkeller	FM	MBA	78	Indiana	&1981
Lambert, Jane	SLect	278-1118	jlambert	FM	MBA	84	Indiana	&1998

Indiana Univ - Purdue Univ
Dept of Accounting & Finance
Dept Phone: 481-6471
Homepage: www.ipfw.edu/bms/

Fort Wayne, IN 46805-1499
School of Bus & Mgt Sci
2101 Coliseum Boulevard

(260) Fax=481-6879
ipfw.edu

1987,1987
BS
Jane Hirschbiel

Wellington, John	Dean	481-6061	wellingj	Mgt	PHD	77	SUNY-Buf	2000
Pollock, Kathy S.	C-Ac	481-5751	pollockk	A	PHD	98.	Kentucky	& 8-96
Davis, Stanley W.	Prof	481-6477	davissw	MTAJ	PHD	84.	Penn St	&2000
Papiernik, Janet C.	Assoc	481-6477	papiernj	FT	DBA	97.	Clev St	& 8-99
Slaubaugh, Michael D.	Assoc	481-6465	slaubau	MFNG	PHD	92.	Indiana	& 8-95
Keller, Carl E.	Asst	481-6856	kellerce	CX	PHD	97.	Tennessee	& 8-02
Minke, Susan	Lect	481-4115	minke	FMP	MBA	88	W Mich	9-98

Indiana University East
Accounting
Dept Phone: 973-8343

Richmond, IN 47374-1289
Business
2325 Chester Blvd

(765) Fax=973-8220
indiana.edu

BS
Sandy Baldwin

Frantz, David W.	C-Ac	973-8337	dfrantz	Mgt	DMN	80	Chicago	2004
Englert, Lawrence R.	Emer	973-8340	englertl	D-05				
Kunskek, Rudy	Asst							2007

Indiana University Kokomo
Accounting Faculty
Dept Phone: 455-9275
Homepage: www.iuk.edu/academics/business/

Kokomo, IN 46904-9003
School of Business
2300 South Washington St

(765) Fax=455-9348
iuk.edu

2001,2001
BS
Terri Butler

Pati, Niranjan	Dean	455-9275	npati	Mgt	PHD	90	Nrthwstrn	2001
Kintzele, Marilyn R.	Prof	455-9318	mkintzel	FAM	MBA	77	Indiana	&1977

Indiana Univ South Bend

Accounting Faculty	South Bend, IN	46634-7111		(574) Fax=520-4866				1989,1989
	Sch of Business & Econ			iusb.edu				BS,MSA
Dept Phone: 520-4346 | 1700 Mishawaka Avenue | | | | | | | Pat Agbetsiafa |
Ducoffe, Robert | Dean | 520-4228 | rducoffe | Mktg | PHD | 89 | Mich St | 2005 |
Aghimien, Peter A. | C-Pr | 520-4476 | paghimie | AFIM | DBA | 86. | La Tech | &1988 |
Anderson, Tracey A. | Prof | 520-4364 | tanderso | X | LLM | 85 | Florida | &1988 |
Espahbodi, Reza | Prof | 520-5563 | respahbo | AFM | PHD | 81. | Alabama | & 8-98 |
Fred, J. David | Assoc | 520-4246 | dfred | CFV | MS | 75 | Purdue | &1978 |
Kern, Beth B. | Assoc | 520-4352 | bkern | FX | PHD | 86. | Indiana | &1995 |
Saksena, Pankaj | Assoc | 520-4456 | psaksena | AEIM | PHD | 97 | Geo St | &1995 |

Indiana Univ Northwest

Accounting Faculty	Gary, IN	46408-1197		(219) Fax=980-6916				2004,2001
	Sch of Business & Econ			iun.edu				BS,MBA
Dept Phone: 980-6633 | 3400 Broadway | | | | | | | Karen Peterson |
Homepage: www.iun.edu~busnw/ | | | | | | | | |
Rominger, Anna S. | Dean | 980-6633 | arominge | Law | JD | 72 | Boston U | 1992 |
Keinath, Annemarie K. | Assoc | 980-7769 | akeinath | AF | PHD | 89. | Mich St | & 8-92 |
Linton, Sara M. | Assoc | 980-6878 | smlinton | LCSX | PHD | 92. | Houston | 8-04 |
Strupeck, C. David | Assoc | 980-7762 | strupeck | FDM | PHD | 81 | S Illinois | & 8-93 |
Vasquez, Marilyn | Assoc | 980-6633 | mvasquez | XL | JD | 88 | Valparaiso | &1979 |
  Vice Chancellor | | | | | | | | |
Thomas, James | Lect | 980-6909 | jamthoma | BUXE | MBA | 77 | N Illinois | 8-00 |

Indiana Univ Southeast

Accounting Faculty	New Albany, IN	47150-6405		(812) Fax=941-2672				1990,1990
	School of Business			ius.edu				BS,MBA,MSSF
Dept Phone: 941-2362 | 4201 Grant Line Rd | | | | | | | Ms. Diane Fuchs |
White, Jay | Dean | 944-2362 | jwhite | | PHD | | Miss | |
French, G. Richard | C-Pr | 941-2429 | gfrench | MXE | PHD | 90. | Miss | &1990 |
Barney, Douglas K. | Prof | 941-2532 | dbarney | FX | PHD | 93. | Miss | * & 8-93 |
Meredith, Vicki Banet | Prof | 941-2268 | vmeredit | FES | DBA | 85. | Kentucky | * &1983 |
Tipgos, Manuel A. | Prof | 941-2644 | mtipgos | FIAB | PHD | 74. | LSU | & 8-90 |
Bjornson, Chris E. | Assoc | 941-2694 | cbjornso | FX | PHD | 93. | Illinois | & 8-92 |
Christiansen, Linda | Assoc | 941-2519 | lchristi | FLJ | JD | 87 | Indiana | & 8-98 |

Indiana U of Pennsylvania

Department of Accounting	Indiana, PA	15705-1087		(724) Fax=357-3776				2001,2001
	Eberly Col Bus & Info T			iup.edu				BS,MBA
Dept Phone: 357-2686 | 421 Eberly Bldg 664 Prett Dr | | | | | | | Stacy L. Stewart |
Homepage: www.eberly.iup.edu/ag | | | | | | | | |
Camp, Robert C. | Dean | 357-4783 | bobcamp | Econ | PHD | 75 | Miss | 1988 |
Kline, Germain P. | C-Ac | 357-5750 | gpkline | GNP | PHD | 00 | Walden | &1989 |
Ghobashy, Mohamed E. | Prof | 357-5754 | ghobashy | CF | PHD | 63 | Intl Com | &1976 |
Rahman, Monsurur | Prof | 357-5742 | mrahman | FC | DBA | 92. | S Illinois | |
Anderson, Kim L. | Assoc | 357-4059 | kanderso | BA | PHD | 94. | Pittsburgh | & 9-91 |
Bradwick, Faye | Assoc | 357-5753 | bradwick | X | LLM | 88 | Geotown | &1991 |
Joseph, Jerry A. | Assoc | 357-5741 | jjoseph | FT | PHD | 93. | Pittsburgh | * &1990 |
Tickell, Geoff | Assoc | 357-2753 | geoffrey.tickell | F | GRAD | | Vic | |
Woan, Ronald J. | Assoc | 357-2686 | ronwoan | FS | PHD | 88. | Fla St | 1991 |
Ponko, Duane M. | Asst | 357-4585 | dponko | VAF | MS | 75 | Duquesne | &1978 |

Indiana State University

Accounting Program	Terre Haute, IN	47809-5402		(812) Fax=237-8129				ß 1980,1983
	College of Business			isugw.indstate.edu				BS
Dept Phone: 237-2112 | 9th & Sycamore East Tower | | | | | | | |
Homepage: www.indstate.edu/acct/ | | | | | | | | |
Green, Ronald F. | Dean | 237-2000 | green | Mgt | PHD | 86 | Clemson | 7-02 |
Sanders, Joseph C. | C-Pr | 237-2015 | jsando | RPFV | PHD | 92. | Kentucky | & 9-92 |
Moncada, Susan M. | Prof | 237-4137 | s-moncada | FGSR | PHD | 90 | Illinois | & 8-90 |
Czyzewski, Alan B. | Assoc | 237-2010 | a-czyzewski | PCR | PHD | 85. | S Calif | & 9-92 |
Harmon, Michael R. | Assoc | 237-2007 | m-harmon | LXR | JD | 77 | Indiana | & 7-86 |
Harris, Thomas D. | Asst | 237-2005 | t-harris | TFXP | PHD | 89. | S Carol | & 7-88 |
Svihla, William H. | Asst | 237-2009 | w-svihla | APR | PHD | 02. | Miss St | & 8-96 |

Indiana Wesleyan

Division of Business	Marion, IN	46953		(765) Fax=677-2524				
	College of Arts & Sci			indwes.edu				
Dept Phone: 677-2289 | 4201 S. Washington St | | | | | | | Susi Stephenson |
Lightfoot, Connie D. | Dean | | connie.lightfoot | | | | | |
Rogas, Harriet L. | C | | | | | | | |
Hamill, Robert P. | Prof | 677-2356 | bob.hamill | PL | PHD | 03 | Ind St | & |
Showalter, Jerry E. | Assoc | 677-2303 | jerry.showalter | XP | MA | 67 | Ball St | &1966 |
Williams, Kent | Asst | 677-2304 | kent.williams | ACJM | MBA | 02 | Ball St | & |

University of Indianapolis

Department of Accounting	Indianapolis, IN	46227-3697		(317) Fax=788-3300				
	School of Business			uindy.edu				BS,MACC
Dept Phone: 788-3378 | 1400 East Hanna Avenue | | | | | | | Debby McGary |
Shapiro, Mitch | Dean | 788-3340 | mshapiro | Mgt | PHD | | Ohio St | |
Balcom, N. Jean | Assoc | 788-3374 | jbalcom | ACPX | PHD | 91. | Arkansas | &1992 |

International College

International College	Naples, FL	34119		(239) Fax=513-9108				
Accounting Program	Johnson Sch Business			internationalcollege.edu				BS
Dept Phone: 513-1122	2655 Northbrooke Drive						Kimberly Van Housen	
Homepage: www.internationalcollege.edu								
Nerone, Frederick	Dean	774-4700	fnerone	M	PHD	97	Union-NY	1992
Nohl, Thomas	C-As	447-7400	tnohl	POA	MS	89	Wisconsin	&1996
Chaney, Melinda	Prof				PHD			&
Baker, Denton	Inst		hbaker		MBA			
D'Amore, Anthony	Inst	482-0019	adamore	XF	MBA	55	NYU	&1995
Sterling, Genevieve	Inst		groyes-sterling		MS			
Yurkovac, William	Inst		wyurkovac		MS			

Iona College

Iona College	New Rochelle NY 10801-1890			(914) Fax=633-2012				1999,1999
Accounting	Hagan School of Bus			iona.edu				BBA
Dept Phone: 633-2267	715 North Avenue							
Homepage: http://www.iona.edu/academic/hagan/pages/dpt_act.htm								
Calluzzo, Vincent J.	Dean	633-2256	vcalluzzo	Mis	PHD	86	Polytech	9-80
Strittmatter, Robert G.	C-Ac	633-2616	rstrittmatter	PC	MBA	71	NYU	& 9-71
Bean, David F.	Prof	633-2677	dbean	PV	PHD	94.	Temple	& 9-98
Ryan, Huldah A.	Prof	633-2527	hryan	PI	PHD	90.	Houston	9-96
Bottiglieri, William A.	Assoc	633-2655	wbottiglieri	PX	JD	79	NYU Law	& 9-85
D'Aquila, Jill M.	Assoc	633-2273	jdaquila	PA	PHD	97	NYU	& 9-96
Haber, Jeffry R.	Assoc	633-2244	jhaber	PN	PHD	94	Rensselaer	& 9-00
Mitchell, LeRoy W.	Assoc	633-2178	lmitchell	PG	DPA	85	NYU	& 9-72

University of Iowa

University of Iowa	Iowa City, IA	52242-1000		(319) Fax=335-1956		ß (1)	1923,1963	
Department of Accounting	College of Business Adm			uiowa.edu			BBA,MAC,PHD	
Dept Phone: 335-0910							Kay Wheeler 335-0910	
Hunter, W. Curt	Dean	335-0866	curt-hunter	Fnce	PHD	78	Nrthwstrn	7-06
Johnson, W. Bruce	H-Pr	335-1048	bruce-johnson	F	PHD	75.	Ohio St	6-88
Arthur Andersen Professor of Accounting								
Balakrishnan, Ramji	Prof	335-0958	ramji-balakri+	MY	PHD	86.	Columbia	* 8-86
Ernst & Young Research Professor								
Collins, Daniel W.	Prof	335-0912	daniel-collins	TF	PHD	73.	Iowa	9-77
Henry B. Tippie Research Chair in Accounting								
DeJong, Douglas V.	Prof	335-0919	douglas-dejong	AFQ	PHD	80.	Michigan	& 9-80
John F. Murray Professor of Accounting								
Hribar, S. Paul	Prof	335-1085	paul-hribar	F	PHD	00.	Iowa	
Lloyd J. & Tholma W. Palmer Research Fellow								
Penno, Mark C.	Prof	335-1409	mark-penno	FM	PHD	83.	Nrthwstrn	&2004
Soumyo Sarkar Fellow in Accounting								
Berg, Joyce E.	Assoc	335-0840	joyce-berg	MF	PHD	88.	Minnesota	&1992
Pioneer Hi-Bred Fellow								
Rego, Sonja Olhoft	Assoc	335-0910	sonja-olhoft	FX	PHD	99.	Michigan	& 8-99
Lloyd J. and Thelma W. Palmer Research Fellow								
Tubbs, Richard M.	Emer	335-0848	richard-tubbs	2006	PHD	88.	Florida	& 8-88
Gleason, Cristi A.	Asst	335-1505	cristi-gleason	F	PHD	98.	Cornell	2004
Li, Haidan	Asst	335-0910	haidan-li	F	PHD	02.	Tx-Austin	8-02
Pringle, Lynn M.	ClAs	335-0910	lynn-pringle	AM	PHD	87.	Colorado	& 9-98
Director, Master of Accountancy Program								
An, Amy	Lect	335-0910	amy-an	X	MA	82	Iowa	& 8-87
Carroll, Thomas J.	Lect	335-2727	thomas-carroll	F	PHD	88.	Michigan	& 1-89
Hartman, Robert J.	Lect	335-0910	robert-hartman	F	MAC	98	Iowa	& 8-99

Iowa State University

Iowa State University	Ames, IA	50011-1350		(515) Fax=294-3525		ß (1)	1991,1991	
Department of Accounting	College of Business			iastate.edu			BS,MS,MBA,MACC	
Dept Phone: 294-8106	2330 Gerdin Business Bldg						Pat Wagaman	
Homepage: www.bus.iastate.edu/accounting/								
Hira, Labh S.	Dean	294-2422	lhira	FX	PHD	75	Missouri	&1982
Bouillon, Marvin L.	C-Ac	294-9276	bouillon	CM	PHD	86.	Kansas	& 7-86
Ravenscroft, Sue P.	Prof	294-3574	sueraven	MFBE	PHD	89.	Mich St	& 8-98
Dilla, William N.	Assoc	294-1685	wdilla	AFB	PHD	87.	Tx-Austin	& 8-98
Doran, B. Michael	Assoc	294-9448	bdoran	FE	PHD	84.	Iowa	& 1-84
Jeffrey, Cynthia G.	Assoc	294-9427	cjeffrey	FJIT	PHD	89.	Minnesota	&1988
Kurtenbach, James M.	Assoc	294-9994	jmk	FG	PHD	92.	Missouri	8-91
Gary, Robert F.	Asst	294-8106	rgary	XF	PHD	05.	Arizona	&2005
Janvrin, Diane J.	Asst	294-9450	djanvrin	S	PHD	01.	Iowa	&2000
Terando, William D.	Asst	294-8462	bterando	XF	PHD	93.	Illinois	& 8-01
Wilkinson, Christine A.	Asst	294-7721	daw	M	PHD	06.	Iowa	&2006
Clem, Anne M.	Lect	294-9408	aclem	F	PHD	97.	Tx-Austin	& 8-95
Curtis, Larry R.	Adj	294-1078	lrcmayor	P	JD	73	Iowa	1973
Duffy, Jan	Adj	294-1481	jduffy	FM	MS	80	Penn St	&1985
Mazzitelli, James R.	Adj	294-5200	mazz	FC	MBA	71	Drake	&1971

Ithaca College

Department of Accounting
Dept Phone: 274-3117

Ithaca, NY 14850-7170
School of Business
953 Danby Road

(607) Fax=274-1152
ithaca.edu

2004,2004
BS,MBA
Shyrlee Gardner

Name	Rank	Phone	Email	Area	Degree	Yr	School	
Engelkemeyer, Susan West	Dean	274-3341	sengelkemeyer		PHD	91	Clemson	1-05
Lewis, Eric E.	C-Ac	274-1279	elewis	AV	PHD	95.	Union-NY	8-02
Burress, Joanne	Assoc	274-5796	jburress	FM	PHD	94	SUNY-Buf	8-04
Cohen, Alan H.	Assoc	274-3949	acohen	FCMX	MS		SUNY-Bin	& 8-76
Libby, Patricia A.	Assoc	274-1314	libby	FETN	PHD	84	Michigan	& 8-89
Lippitt, Jeffrey W.	Assoc	274-3118	jlippitt	CFM	PHD	82.	Penn St	8-02
Schlesinger, Warren	Assoc	274-3951	warren	FCMT	MBA		Cornell	& 8-82

Jackson State University

Department of Accounting
Dept Phone: 979-2414

Jackson, MS 39217-0670
College of Business
1400 John R. Lynch Street

(601) Fax=979-2690
jsums.edu

1995,1995
BBA,MPA,PHD
Ms. Monica Williams

Name	Rank	Phone	Email	Area	Degree	Yr	School	
Glover, Glenda B.	Dean	979-2411	glenda.glover	FS	PHD	90	Geo Wash	&1994
Booker, Quinton	C-Pr	979-2704	qbooker	FGN	DBA	84.	Miss St	&1981
Gupta, Rameshwar D.	Assoc	979-2676	rdgupta	GFN	PHD	84.	Arkansas	1967
Daniels, Bobbie W.	Asst	979-2708	bobbie.daniels	GF	PHD	05.	JacksonSt	&2005
Grayson, Michael M.	Asst	979-2331	michael.m.gra+	AM	DBA	01.	La Tech	&2001
Hill, Cecil L.	Asst	979-2414	cecil.hill@1	FS	PHD	02.	JacksonSt	&1995
Russell, Richard	Asst	979-2414	rlrussel@1	X	JD	97	Iowa	& 1-97
Turner, Marvel A.	Asst	979-2706	marvel.a.turner	AF	PHD	04	JacksonSt	&2004
Nabulsi, Mahmound	Inst	979-2699	mnabulsi	GM	MPA	86	JacksonSt	&2004

Jacksonville University

Accounting Faculty
Dept Phone: 256-7432

Jacksonville, FL 32211-3394
Davis College of Bus
2800 University Blvd N

(904) Fax=256-7467
ju.edu

BS,BA
Ms. Patty West

Name	Rank	Phone	Email	Area	Degree	Yr	School	
Duggar, Jan W.	Dean	256-7431	jduggar	Fnce	PHD	67	Fla St	1-05
Boylan, Robert L.	D-As	256-7496	rboylan	CEFX	PHD	90	Duke	&2003
O'Keefe, Ruth R.	Prof	256-7449	rokeefe	LX	JD	79	SUNY-Buf	&1982
Ratliff, Dennis J.	Assoc	256-7445	dratlif	CFXV	MBA	76	Wright St	&1978
Capriotti, Kim	Asst	256-7443	kcaprio	AFS	PHD	92.	Fla St	& 8-01

Jacksonville State Univ

Dept Fnce, Econ & Accounting
Dept Phone: 782-5776
Homepage: jsucc.jsu.edu.depart.ccba

Jacksonville, AL 36265-1602
College Comm & Bus Adm
700 Pelham Road North

(256) Fax=782-8346
jsu.edu

1998,1998
BS,MBA
Pam Pope

Name	Rank	Phone	Email	Area	Degree	Yr	School		
Fielding, William T.	Dean	782-5508	fielding	Econ	PHD	76	S Carol		1968
Scroggins, William A.	H-Pr	782-5380	scroggin	Fnce	DBA	85	Miss St		8-79
Sandberg, Angela H.	Assoc	782-5348	asand	CFAP	DBA	90.	Miss St	# *	& 9-82
Sneed, Cynthia Smith	Assoc	782-5792	csneed	M	PHD	94.	Alabama		8-01
Sneed, John E.	Assoc	782-5772	jsneed	F	PHD	94.	Alabama		& 9-01
Zanzig, Jeffrey S.	Asst	782-5776	jzanzig	S	PHD	98.	Miss	# *	& 8-00
Collum, Taleah	Inst	782-8418	tcollum	FM	MACC	04	Fla St		&

James Madison University

Sch of Accounting MSC 0203
Dept Phone: 568-3071
Homepage: http://cob.jmu.edu/accounting

Harrisonburg, VA 22807
College of Business
MSC 0203

(540) Fax=568-3017
jmu.edu

ß (13) 1982,1985
BBA,MS
Ms. Mitzie Preston

Name	Rank	Phone	Email	Area	Degree	Yr	School		
Reid, Robert D.	Dean	568-3252	reidrd	Mktg	EDD	85	Va Tech		9-86
Copley, Paul A.	D-Pr	568-3081	copleypa	AGV	PHD	88.	Alabama		& 7-04
Hantzmon, Wiebel & Company Faculty Fellow									
Baril, Charles P.	Prof	568-3092	barilcp	F	PHD	87.	Florida		& 1-89
Frank & Co. Faculty Fellow									
Fordham, David R.	Prof	568-3024	fordhadr	SD	PHD	92.	Fla St	*	& 9-92
PBGH Faculty Fellow									
Gabbin, Alexander L.	Prof	568-3093	gabbinal	F	PHD	86.	Temple		& 9-85
KPMG Professor									
Louwers, Timothy J.	Prof	568-3071	louwertj	ASD	PHD	93.	Fla St	#	& 9-05
Jackson E. Ramsey Centennial Professor									
Riordan, Diane A.	Prof	568-3208	riordada	XI	PHD	88.	Va Tech		& 9-89
Journal of Accounting Education Research Professor									
Riordan, Michael P.	Prof	568-3209	riordamp	FM	PHD	89.	Va Tech		& 9-89
Cherry, Bekaert & Holland Faculty Fellow									
Roof, Bradley M.	Prof	568-3087	roofbm	A	PHD	85	Virginia	*	& 9-77
Nichols, Nancy B.	Assoc	568-8778	nicholnb	X	PHD	97.	North Tx		& 9-97
Deloitte & Touche Faculty Fellow									
Richardson, Robert C.	Assoc	568-3084	richarrc	AP	PHD	98.	Va Tech		& 9-01
Briggs, John W.	Asst	568-3084	briggsjw	SPD	PHD	04.	Va Tech		9-02
Cole, Elizabeth T.	Asst	568-3084	coleet	FCA	PHD	99.	Kent St		& 9-02
Hayes, David C.	Asst		hayesdc	BS	PHD	02.	S Fla		& 8-07
VanDenburgh, William M.	Asst	568-3026	vandenwm	XGF	PHD	04.	LSU		& 8-06
Brown, Molly G.	Inst	568-1697	brownmg	FGN	MSA	99	Jms Mad		& 8-02
Foreman, Kimberley A.	Inst	568-3090	foremaka	PCM	MSA	96	Jms Mad		& 9-96
Manktelow, Loretta M.	Inst	568-3091	manktemi	FPM	MBA	87	U Miami		& 8-05
Scott, Irana J.	Inst	568-7310	scottij	FPM	MACC	01	E Tn St		& 8-05
Shifflett, Eileen M.	Inst	568-3088	shifflem	FCM	MBA	98	Jms Mad		& 1-02

Jamestown College Jamestown, ND   58405   (701) Fax=253-4318
Accounting Faculty Box 6026 Dept of Bus, Atg & Econ jc.edu   BS,BA
Dept Phone: 252-3467 6000 College Lane
Homepage: www.jc.edu
  phone 252-3467 ext 2549

Name	Rank	Ext	Email					
Gash, Dennis N.	Dean	Ext 2481	gash	Econ	ABD	78	Nrthwstrn	1993
Greshik, Vicki	Asst	Ext 5549	greshik	FTVX	MBA	92	Moorhead	&1989
Weispfenning, William W.	Inst	Ext 5474	wweispfe	AFG				&2006

John Carroll University Cleveland, OH   44118   (216) Fax=397-3063   (123) 1988,1988
Department of Accountancy Boler Sch of Business jcu.edu   BS,MBA,MS
Dept Phone: 397-4393 20700 North Park Blvd   Ms. Cathy Kraynak
Homepage: http://bsob.jcu.edu/accountancy/accountancy.htm

Name	Rank	Phone	Email					
Calingo, Luis Ma. R.	Dean	397-4391	lcalingo	Mgt	PHD	84	Pittsburgh	2006
Weinstein, Gerald P.	C-Ac	397-4609	weinstein	FXE	PHD	90.	Kent St	&1988
Bloom, Robert	Prof	397-4471	rbloom	FIT	PHD	76.	NYU	1986
Cenker, William J.	Prof	397-4299	wcenker	AFX	PHD	89.	Kent St	&1987
Madison, Roland L.	Prof	397-4404	rmadison	CFU	PHD	78.	Nebraska	&1983
Nagy, Albert L.	Assoc	397-4454	alnagy	APF	PHD	99.	Tennessee	& 8-99
Schuele, Karen	Assoc	397-4606	kschuele	PFS	PHD	91.	Kent St	&1989
KPMG Associate Professor of Accounting								

Johnson & Wales University Providence, RI   02903   (401) Fax=598-2228
Department of Accountancy Business jwu.edu   BS,MBA
Dept Phone: 598-1052 8 Abbott Park Place

Name	Rank	Phone	Email					
Mitchell, David	Dean	598-4645	dmitchell		PHD	01	Salve Rg	1999
Poirier, Kevin W.	C-Ac	598-1052	kpoirier	ADS	ABD	97	Salve Rg	* 1990
Davis, Helen E.	Assoc	598-1020	hdavis	MC	MBA	85	Bryant	* 1987
Degnan, Donna M.	Assoc	598-1952	ddegnan	P	MS	95	John&Wal	1987
DerManelian, Guenther	Assoc	598-1859	gdermanelian	P	MBA	85	Bryant	&1986
Doonan, Deborah A.	Assoc	598-1065	ddoonan	P	MST	95	Bryant	&1990
Higgins, Marie L.	Assoc	598-1008	mhiggins	PXL	JD	99	N Eng Cl	&2000
Robinson, Patricia A.	Assoc	598-4774	probinson	P	MSA	94	Bentley	1994
Cannata, Elizabeth A.	Asst	598-1077	ecannata	FP	MBA	96	Providen	&2005
Etzold, Michele	Asst	598-1951	metzold	F	MBA	95	Bryant	&2002
Martino, Peter A. III	Asst	598-1859	pmartino	PGN	MBA	96	Bryant	&2002
Norris, Barbara	Asst	598-4789	bnorris	DP	MBA	88	Bryant	2001
Ragsdale, Robert W.	Asst	598-1079	rragsdale	IXF	MBA	79	Fairl Dick	&1994
Turchetta, Alexander	Asst	598-1079	aturchetta	P	MS	95	John&Wal	2001
Ciccio, Star	Inst		sciccio	MP	MBA	05	John&Wal	2005
Viens, Donna J.	Inst		dviens	CMX	MBA	96	John&Wal	2005

University of Kansas Lawrence, KS   66045-7585   (785) Fax=864-5328   (13) 1925,1970
Accounting & Info Sys School of Business ku.edu   BS,MACC,PHD
Dept Phone: 864-4500 1300 Sunnyside Ave
Homepage: www.business.ku.edu

Name	Rank	Phone	Email					
Fuerst, William L.	Dean	864-7575	bfuerst	S	PHD	79	Tx Tech	2000 '
Heintz, James A.	D-Pr	864-4568	jheintz	AF	DBA	72.	Wash U	&1998
Deloitte & Touche Faculty Fellow								
Ettredge, Michael L.	Prof	864-7537	mettredge	FT	PHD	82.	Tx-Austin	1993
Crown/Sheff Professor								
Ford, N. Allen	Prof	864-7523	aford	X	PHD	70.	Arkansas	1976
Larry D. Horner/KPMG Peat Marwick Distinguished Professor								
Shaftel, Timothy L.	Prof	864-7534	tshaftel	SQFM	PHD	72	Car Mellon	1988
Jordan Haines Distinguished Professor								
Srivastava, Rajendra P.	Prof	864-7590	rsrivastava	MA	PHD	82.	Oklahoma	1982
Ernst & Young Distinguished Prof & Dir. of Center Audit Res. & Adv Tech								
Marakas, George	Assoc	864-7527	gmarakas	S	PHD	95	Fla Intl	8-05
Scholz, Susan	Assoc	864-7554	sscholz	FAV	PHD	97.	S Calif	1997
Harper Faculty Fellow								
Alexander, Raquel Meyer	Asst	864-7318	raquela	X	PHD	01.	Tx-Austin	& 8-05
Chen, Andrew N. K.	Asst	864-7529	achen	S	PHD	99	Conn	2006
Ilie, Virginia	Asst	864-7594	vilie	S	PHD	05	Cen Fla	2005
Karuga, Gilbert	Asst	864-7512	gkaruga	S	PHD	02	Conn	8-02
Lee, Younghwa (Gabe)	Asst	864-7559	gabelee	S	PHD	05	Colorado	2005
O'Donnell, Edward F.	Asst	864-7505	eod	A	PHD	95.	North Tx	&2006
Ottinger, Lisa L.	Asst	864-7572	lottinger	S	PHD	94	Tx A&M	&2000
Smith, Kevin R.	Asst	864-7555	krsmith		PHD	05.	Arizona	8-05
Boone, Ted	Lect	864-1851	tedboone	S	MS	00	Penn St	2005
Feiden, Marci	Lect	864-3733	mfeiden	M	MBA	95	DePaul	1998
Freix, Greg	Lect	864-7544	gfreix	S	MBA	99	Kansas	1998
Mason, Paul T.	Lect	864-4516	pmason	FAVM	MBA	76	Conn	# * &1998
Phillips, ALee	Lect	864-3948	aphillips	FM	MAIS	98	Kansas	2001

Kansas State University

Manhattan, KS 66506-0502 (785) Fax=532-5959 ß (13) 1973,1980
Department of Accounting — College of Business — ksu.edu — BS,MAC
Dept Phone: 532-6184 — 109 Calvin Hall — Diane Landoll
Homepage: www.cba.ksu.edu/cba/depart/account/

Name	Rank	Phone	email		Degree	Yr	School	
Ebadi, Yar M.	Dean	532-7227	ebadi	Mgt	DBA	77	Indiana	1-83
Ott, Richard L.	H-Ac	532-6184	rlo	XFB	PHD	86.	Tx Tech	& 6-86
Grant Thornton Faculty Fellow								
Deines, Dan S.	Prof	532-6038	ddeines	F	PHD	85.	Nebraska	& 9-82
Ralph Crouch - KPMG Professor of Accounting								
Fisher, Dann G.	Assoc	532-6037	dfisher	XFJ	PHD	92.	Missouri	& 6-91
Deloitte & Touche Faculty Fellow								
Kovar, Stacy E.	Assoc	532-6083	skovar	MS	PHD	95.	Okla St	& 8-97
PricewaterhouseCoopers Faculty Fellow								
Thomas, Lynn R.	Assoc	532-5672	lynnthom	F	PHD	80.	Kansas	& 1-86
Vruwink, David R.	Assoc	532-5897	dvruwink	F	PHD	82.	Arkansas	9-82
Linville, Mark E.	Asst	532-6381	linville	AF	PHD	95.	U Wash	& 8-02
BKD Faculty Fellow								
Olibe, Kingsley	Asst			F	PHD	99.	Tx A&M	8-07
Valentine, Erick G.	Asst	532-6380	valenti	M	PHD	03.	Memphis	& 8-02
Charland, Kimberly	Inst	532-6967	charland	AFMN	MACC	85	Kansas St	& 8-96
Ernst & Young Teaching Fellow								
Lyle, Johanna D.	Inst	532-7752	jlyle	FLG	MACC	83	Kansas St	& 9-83
Ernst & Young Teaching Fellow								
Smith, Fred W.	Inst	532-6763	fwscpa	FM	MACC	88	Kansas St	& 8-94
Ernst & Young Teaching Fellow								
Vogt, Rodney L.	Inst	532-6091	rlvogt	FATM	MACC	91	Kansas St	& 8-01
Ernst & Young Teaching Fellow								
Woods, Monica	Inst	532-6621	mwoods	FM	MACC	00	Kansas St	8-05

Kean University

Union, NJ 07083-7131 (908) Fax=737-4105
Department of Accounting — Sch of Bus & Public Adm — kean.edu — BS,MS
Dept Phone: 737-4100 — 1000 Morris Ave, 203 Willis — Cynthia Mosejchuk
Homepage: www.kean.edu

Name	Rank	Phone	email		Degree	Yr	School	
Ntoko, Alfred N.	Dean	737-4120	anotoko	Econ	PHD	86	SUNY-Bin	2005
Capone, James J. Jr.	C-Pr	737-4110	jcapone	PLMC	JD	68	Rutgers	1975
Carlsen, Eric	Prof	737-4104	ecarlsen	VCNG	PHD	69	Cornell	&1976
Comerford, Ellen	Prof	737-4108	ecomerfo	XADF	MBA	79	Seton Hall	&1988
Wailoo, Bert A.	Prof	737-4109	kean203@a	CMTF	MBA	79	Pace	* &1985
Schader, Gary	Assoc	737-4111	gschader	MXPD	MBA	73	Penn	&1980
Stewart, Louis J.	Assoc	737-4102	lstewart	ACN	PHD	98	Wisconsin	&2005
Bornstein, Samuel	Asst	737-4106	bornsteinsong@a	PXFM	MBA	76	NYU	&1978

Keene State College

Keene, NH 03435-2101 (603) Fax=358-2612
Accounting Faculty — Dept of Management — keene.edu — BS
Dept Phone: 358-2603 — 229 Main Street — Kerri Atherton

Name	Rank	Phone	email		Degree	Yr	School	
Charkey, Barbara	C-Pr	358-2621	bcharkey	VCFM	MS	85	Mass	&1987
Brown, Elizabeth	Assoc	358-2618	bbrown	CDFM	EDD	93	Mass	1987
Hadden, Linda	Asst	358-2601	lhadden	ACFM	PHD	02	Nova SE	2002

Kennesaw State University

Kennesaw, GA 30144-5591 (770) Fax=499-3420 ß (13) 1994,1994
Dept of Accounting — Michael J. Coles Cl Bus — kennesaw.edu — BBA,MBA,MACC
Dept Phone: 423-6084 — 1000 Chastin Road
Homepage: http://coles.kennesaw.edu/acc

Name	Rank	Phone	email		Degree	Yr	School		
Mescon, Timothy S.	Dean	423-6342	tim_mescon	Mgt	PHD	79	Georgia		1990
Harmon, W. Ken	C-Pr			SA	DBA	82.	Tennessee		&
Alsup, Rodney G.	Prof	423-6578	rodney_alsup	CSM	DBA	84.	Kentucky		&1991
Senior Associate Dean - Executive Programs									
Campbell, Jane E.	Prof	423-6080	jane_campbell	FEBT	DBA	81.	Tennessee		& 9-92
Hermanson, Dana R.	Prof	423-6077	dana_hermanson	AOME	PHD	93.	Wisconsin		1993
Dinos Eminent Scholar Chair of Private Enterprise									
Hill, Mary Callahan	Prof	499-3487	mary_hill	SAB	PHD	93.	Georgia		1997
Manners, George E.	Prof	499-3663	george_manners	M	PHD		Geo St		1996
Clements, A. Bruce	Assoc	423-6518	bruce_clements	XCF	PHD	89.	Florida		&1992
Gramling, Audrey A.	Assoc	423-6495	agraml1	PA	PHD	95.	Arizona	#	& 8-05
Greenwell, Gregory A.	Assoc	423-6084	greg_greenwell	XF	JD	93	Marshall		&1978
Morris, Paula H.	Assoc	423-6095	paula_morris	FA	MPA	79	Geo St		&1981
Schulzke, Kurt S.	Assoc	423-6084	kurt_schulzke	XIPM	JD	98	Geo St		& 9-90
Schwaig, Kathy S.	Assoc	423-6323	kathy_schwaig	S	PHD	96	S Carol		2002
Smalt, Steven W.	Assoc	423-6386	steve_smalt	FA	PHD	99	Union-NY		&1988
Capozzoli, Ernst	Asst	423-6309	ecopozzo		PHD		Miss		
Cleaveland, M. Catherine	Asst	423-6375		T	PHD	06.	Geo St		8-06
Clune, Richard R.	Asst	423-6084	richard_clune	AFM	EDM	05	Case Wes		&2002
Epps, Kathryn K.	Asst	423-6085	karthyrn_epps	FA	PHD	01.	Geo St		2004
Malgeri, Linda M.	Asst	423-6479	linda_malgeri	FVE	MBA	77	Stetson		&1989

Kent State University

Kent State University		Kent, OH	44242-0001		(330) Fax=672-2548			ß 1964,1965	
Department of Accounting		College of Business Adm			bsa3.kent.edu			BBA,MS,PHD	
Dept Phone: 672-2545								Diane Fields	
Homepage: www.kent.edu									
Stevens, George E.	Dean	672-2772	gstevens	Mgt	DBA	79	Kent St	8-95	
Brown, Richard E.	C-Pr	672-1113	dbrown	GMNO	DPA	68	Harvard	8-84	
Alam, Pervaiz	Prof	672-1121	palam	FA	PHD	84.	Houston	& 6-85	
Barniv, Ran	Prof	672-1112	rbarniv	FI	PHD	83	Ohio St	8-90	
Meonske, Norman R.	Prof	672-1120	nmeonske	FM	PHD	72.	Missouri	&1972	
Pearson, Michael A.	Prof	672-1123	mpearson	AJ	DBA	79.	Kent St	* & 6-83	
Altieri, Mark P.	Assoc	672-1114	maltieri	X	LLM	82	NYU	* & 1-92	
Zucca, Linda J.	Assoc	672-1117	lzucca	F	PHD	89.	Case Wes	& 8-88	
Dow, Kevin E.	Asst	672-2545	kdow	S	PHD	00.	S Carol	8-02	
Laksmana, Indrarini (Rini)	Asst	672-1119	ilaksman	CM	PHD	04.	Geo St	& 8-04	
Li, Wei	Asst	672-1125		F	PHD	06.	Wash St	& 8-06	
McFall, Donald	Lect	672-1128	dmcfall	F	MS	91	Kent St	& 8-00	
Tietz, Wendy	Lect	672-1111	wtietz	M	PHD	07	Kent St	* & 8-00	

University of Kentucky

University of Kentucky		Lexington, KY	40506-0034		(859) Fax=257-3654			ß (13) 1926,1963	
Von Allmen Sch Accountancy		Gatton Cl of Bus & Econ			uky.edu			BS,MS,PHD	
Dept Phone: 257-1876								Sarah Wells	
Homepage: http://gallon.gws.uky.edu/acc/sch_acc.htm									
Sudharshan, D.	Dean	257-8939	sudharshan	Mktg	PHD	82	Pittsburgh	2003	
Ziebart, David A.	D-Pr	257-1876	ziebart	NFT	PHD	83.	Mich St	& 8-05	
Knoblett, James A.	Emer	257-1763	knoblett	2000	PHD	63.	U Wash	* &1968	
Madden, Donald L.	Emer	257-1878	dmadden	2000	PHD	67.	Tx-Austin	* &1968	
McDaniel, Linda S.	Prof	257-2018	tarcat	AB	PHD	88.	Michigan	&2002	
Von Allmen Chair of Accountancy									
Stone, Dan N.	Prof	257-3043	dstone	BEMS	PHD	87.	Tx-Austin	&2000	
Gatton Chair of Accounting									
Tearney, Michael G.	Emer	257-3592	tearney	2005	PHD	71.	Missouri	&1983	
Clark, Myrtle W.	Assoc	257-3851	cmyrtle	FM	PHD	78.	S Carol	* 1977	
Cooper, Jean C.	Assoc	257-1807	acc224	MB	PHD	85.	N Carol	&1990	
Holmes, James R.	Assoc	257-1947	acc101	CSM	PHD	77.	Missouri	&1975	
Hulse, David S.	Assoc	257-3276	dshuls00	X	PHD	93.	Penn St	1993	
Deloitte and Touche Professor of Accountancy									
Payne, Jeff L.	Assoc	257-1435	jeff.payne	AFS	PHD	95.	Florida	&2004	
Peffer, Sean A.	Assoc	257-3149	speffer	CMF	PHD	96.	Indiana	&1997	
Chelgren Professor of Accounting									
Pope, Thomas R.	Assoc	257-4794	tpope	X	DBA	76.	Kentucky	&1984	
Ernst & Young Professor of Accounting									
Ramsay, Robert J.	Assoc	257-3702	rjrams2	AB	PHD	91.	Indiana	&1995	
Arthur Andersen & Co. Professor of Accounting									
Vines, Cynthia C.	Assoc	257-4675	cvines	X	PHD	92.	S Calif	& 8-98	
Wells, Jane B.	Assoc	257-4223	jbwell01	F	MS	86	Kentucky	&1987	
Chambers, Dennis J.	Asst	257-3031	dennis.chambers	F	PHD	96.	Tx-Austin	2003	
Goldman, Arthur H.	Lect	257-4648	art.goldman	P	MBA	88	Wi-LaCros	&2003	

Kentucky State University

Kentucky State University		Frankfort, KY	40601		(502) Fax=597-6404				
Accounting Faculty		School of Business			gwmail.kysu.edu			BA	
Dept Phone: 597-6708		East Main Street						Pamela Black	
Lake, Gashaw W.	Dean	597-6105	glake	FG	PHD		Oklahoma		
Parrish, Sharon R.	Assoc	597-6910	sparrish	FG	DBA	86.	Kentucky	&1985	
Rich, Dave	Asst	597-6912	drich	MS	MBA		W Virginia	1985	
Sipes, Kimberly A.	Asst	597-6423	ksipes	FM	MSA	82	Kentucky	&2000	
Wilhelm, Jana	VAsst			PMA	MBA		Wayne St		

Kentucky Wesleyan College

Kentucky Wesleyan College		Owensboro, KY	42302-1039		(270) Fax=852-3197				
Accounting Faculty		Business Department			kwc.edu			BA,BS	
Dept Phone: 926-3111		3000 Frederica St							
Welch, James E.	H-Pr	926-3111	jimwe	Mgt	EDD	96	Vanderbilt	1989	
Chenna, S. Raju	Assoc	926-3111	rajuch	AFGX	MBA	81	W NewMex	&1988	
Hunter, Debra R.	Assoc	926-3111		CEFI	PHD	04.	La Tech	&2005	

Kettering University

Kettering University		Flint, MI	48504-4898		(810) Fax=762-9944				
Accounting Faculty		Dept Business & Ind Mgt			kettering.edu			BS	
Dept Phone: 762-7959		1700 West Third Avenue						Tyana Allen 762-7959	
Homepage: www.kettering.edu									
Did Not Respond--2005-2006 Listing									
White, Charles W.	H-Ac	762-7956	cwhite	Sys	PHD	71	Tx A&M	1989	
McCarthy, Neil T.	Assoc	762-7970	nmccarth	F	PHD	77	Rensselaer	1973	

King's College
Department of Accounting
Dept Phone: 208-5900
Homepage: www.kings.edu
  phone 208-5900 Ext 5699

Wilkes-Barre, PA   18711
McGowan School of Bus
133 North River Street

(570) Fax=208-5989
kings.edu

2003
BS
Deborah Shaw

Ryan, John J.	D-Ac	Ext5932j	jryan	Cpt	PHD	98	Temple		
Williams, Barry H.	C-Ac	Ext 5699	bhwillia	XVP	JD	95	Widener	& 9-89	
Boscia, Marian Larson	Assoc	Ext 5780	jlboscia	CMX	PHD	93.	Colorado	& 9-97	
McGowan, John J.	Assoc	Ext 5788	jjmcgowan	ACP	MBA	66	Scranton	* & 9-70	
Mercincavage, Janet	Assoc	Ext 5878	jemercin	FPR	MBA	84	Temple	& 9-80	
Vice President									
Kociolik, Rev. Charles	Asst	Ext 5912		P	MBA		Notre Dm	9-81	
Shawver, Tara J.	Asst	Ext 5455	tjshawve	FPV	DBA	02	Nova SE	1-03	

Kutztown Univ of Penn
Dept Accounting & Finance
Dept Phone: 683-4580

Kutztown, PA   19530-0730
College of Business

(610) Fax=683-1514
kutztown.edu

BS
Donna DeLong

Ikem, Fidelis M.	Dean$	683-4575	ikem					
Grant, Thomas J.	C-Ac	683-4581	grant	CPM	MBA		Drexel	* 1987
Dinger, Mark	Assoc	683-4578	dinger	PSD	MBA		Lehigh	1980
Wagaman, David	Assoc	683-4705	dwagaman	PXT	MS		Drexel	&1984
Kruglinski, John	Asst	683-4588	kruglins	FSX	MBA	05	NYU	&2005
Patrick, Patricia	Asst	683-1372	ppatrick	ANO	PHD	06	Penn St	&
Sigmond, Norman C.	Asst	683-4702	sigmond	APX	MST	99	Temple	&1995

Lafayette College
Accounting Faculty
Dept Phone: 330-5306

Easton, PA   18042-1776
Dept of Econ & Business

(610) Fax=330-5715
lafayette.edu

Bukics, Rose Marie L.	C-Pr	330-5306	bukicsr	TFIK	MBA	80	Lehigh	&1980
Thomas Roy and Lura Forrest Jones Professor								
Handy, Sheila	Asst	330-5306	handys	PEX	PHD	01	NYU	&1996

LaGrange College
Accountancy
Dept Phone: 880-8317

LaGrange, GA   30240-2999
Prof Programs Division
601 Broad Street

(706) Fax=880-8019
lagrange.edu

BS
Brenda Riley

Rosencrants, Lydia	C-Ac	880-8302	lrosencrants	FMP	PHD	99	Mich St	* & 6-99
Boatwright Professor of Accounting								
Bearden, Cindi S.	Assoc	880-8187	cbearden	FPS	MACC	90	Alabama	& 8-01
Hampton, Jenny	Asst	880-8743	jhampton	ALV	JD	93	Chicago	&2000

Lake Superior State Univ
Accounting Faculty
Dept Phone: 635-2426
Homepage: www.lssu.edu

Sault S Marie MI 49783-1626
Sch of Bus, Econ & LS
650 W. Easterday Ave

(906) Fax=635-2821
lssu.edu

BS
Ms. Katherine Danielkiewicz

Harger, Bruce T.	Prov	635-7560	bharger	Econ	PHD	91	Mich St	9-67
Schmitigal, Linda S.	C-Ac	635-2195	lschmitigal		MBA	93	Cen Mich	
Beckon, Susan	Asst	786-5802		ACSU	MBA	96	Mich St	9-96
email: beckons@baydenoc.cc.mi.us								
Suneson, Scott	Asst	635-2426	ssuneson	ACSX	MBA	93	Lake Sup	9-96
Poliski, Mindy	Inst		mpoliski	ACPX	MBA	05	Lawrence	9-07

Lamar University
Dept Atg & Bus LawPOBox10069
Dept Phone: 880-8610

Beaumont, TX   77710
College of Business
4400 Martin Luther King Pkwy

(409) Fax=880-8611
hal.lamar.edu

ß 1980,1986
BBA,MBA
Phyllis Johnson

Lynch, Howell J.	C-Pr	880-8609	lynchhj	XJ	PHD	91	Tx A&M	& 1-97
Veuleman, Malcolm W.	Prof	880-8618	veulemanmw	FCP	PHD	71.	Arkansas	&1970
Moss, Gisele J.	Assoc	880-8616	mossgj	PMV	PHD	95.	LSU	&2000
Varick, Celia B.	Assoc	880-8324	varickcb	FGP	PHD	95.	Arkansas	&1995

Lander University
Accounting Faculty
Dept Phone: 388-8232

Greenwood, SC   29649
School of Business Adm
Stanley Avenue

(864) Fax=388-8020
lander.edu

2003
BS
Joyce Shelton

Caines, W. Royce	Dean	388-8232	rcaines	Econ	PHD	88	Clemson	2004
Benton, James E.	Asst	388-8302	jbenton	XLJR	JD	00	Geo St	1-01
Wood, Carol	Asst	388-8136	cwood		MS		S Carol	

La Salle University
Dept of Accounting Box 332
Dept Phone: 951-1008
Homepage: www.lasalle.edu/schools/sb/accounting

Philadelphia, PA 19141-1199
School of Business
1900 W. Olney Avenue

(215) Fax=951-1886
lasalle.edu

1995,1995
BS,MBA
La Toya Williams

Welsh, Mary Jeanne	C-Pr	951-1883	welsh	FTB	PHD	87	LSU	& 9-91
Borkowski, Susan C.	Prof	951-1491	borkowsk	ICBS	PHD	88.	Temple	9-89

Stickel, Scott E.	Prof	951-1439	stickel	MF	PHD	85	Chicago	& 7-92
Joseph Markmann Accounting Alumni Professor								
Leauby, Bruce A.	Assoc	951-1490	leauby	FGAH	PHD	90.	Drexel	* & 9-89
Ugras, Yusuf Joseph	Assoc	951-1027	ugras	FCM	PHD	91.	Temple	* 9-84
Wentzel, Kristin	Assoc	951-5176	wentzel	MB	PHD	98.	Temple	9-00
Brazina, Paul R.	Asst	951-1623	brazina	FAM	MBA	72	Penn St	# * & 9-73
Fitzgerald, Gerald	Asst	951-1856	fitzgera	FP	MA	76	Villanova	9-95
Massimini, Al	Asst	951-1026	massimin	FV	MBA		Drexel	& 9-81
Zook, John	Asst	951-1626	zook	FX	MBA		Drexel	& 1-79

La Sierra University Riverside, CA   92515-8247   (951) Fax = 785-2700
Accounting Department Sch of Business & Mgt   lasierra.edu   BS,BA
Dept Phone: 785-2464 4500 Riverwalk Pkwy   Cheryl Bauman/VernellKaufholtz
Homepage: lasierra.edu/sbm/index.html

Thomas, Johnny	Dean	785-2064	jthomas	QFI	PHD	02	Claremont	1994
Zurek, Danette	Assoc	785-2184	dzurek	AXON	MBA	98	Andrews	&2006
Webster-Poole, Kristine	Asst	785-2405	kwebster	XCR	MBA	91	LomaLinda	&2006

Lehigh University Bethlehem, PA   18015-3117   (610) Fax = 758-6429   ß (1) 1938,1963
Department of Business College of Bus & Econ   lehigh.edu   BS,MBA
Dept Phone: 758-3451 621 Taylor Street   Kathleen Smith
Homepage: http://www.lehigh.edu

Brown, Paul R.	Dean	758-6725		FA	PHD	79	Tx-Austin	&2007
Sinclair, Kenneth P.	C-Pr	758-3431	kps1	M	PHD	72.	Mass	9-72
Largay, James A. III	Prof	758-3429	jal3	FVX	PHD	71.	Cornell	&1980
Paul, John W.	Prof	758-4452	jwp1	AM	PHD	78.	Lehigh	& 9-74
Sami, Heibatollah	Prof	758-3451	vmsami	F	PHD	84.	LSU	2005
Mercy Professor								
Collins, Karen M.	Assoc	758-3458	kmc0	FB	PHD	88.	Va Tech	&1990
Gupta, Parveen P.	Assoc	758-3443	ppg0	FAIO	PHD	87.	Penn St	1987
Hall, James A.	Assoc	758-4446	jah0	DS	PHD	80.	Okla St	1979
Moore, Erin A.	Asst	758-3451	eam205	F	PHD	06.	Mass	2005
Zhang, Sanjian (William)	Asst				PHD	06.	Ca-Irvine	

LeMoyne College Syracuse, NY   13214-1399   (315) Fax = 445-4540
Accounting Faculty Dept of Accounting   lemoyne.edu   BS,MBA
Dept Phone: 445-4348 1419 Salt Springs Road
Homepage: www.lemoyne.edu

Ammar, Salwa	Dean	445-4280	ommar	Mgt	PHD	86	Florida	1987
Crawford, Dean	C-Ac	445-4348	crawford	XFR	PHD	87.	Rochester	& 9-06
Collins, Mary K.	Assoc	445-4280	collinsmk	FABC	PHD	91.	Syracuse	& 9-84
Krause, Michael J.	Assoc	445-4426	krausemj	PFCA	MS		Syracuse	& 9-82
Myers, Joan K.	Assoc	445-4387	myersjk	CFMP	PHD	93.	Syracuse	& 9-89
Havranek, Susan F.	Asst	445-4430	havransf	F	PHD	07	Ariz St	9-06

Lenoir-Rhyne College Hickory, NC   28603   (828) Fax = 328-7368
Accounting Faculty School of Business   lrc.edu   BA,MBA
Dept Phone: 328-7198 7th Ave & 8th St, NE   Ms. Pam Deal
Homepage: www.lrc.edu

| Wallace, Sarah R. | Prof | 328-7202 | wallace s | P | MA | 66 | Appalach | |
| Reingold, Theodore | Assoc | 328-7045 | reingoldt | F | DBA | 95 | Golden Gt | &1998 |

Liberty University Lynchburg, VA   24502   (434) Fax = 582-2366
Department of Accounting School of Bus & Gov   liberty.edu   BS
Dept Phone: 1971 University Blvd   Verdie Waldron 582-2481
Homepage: www.liberty.edu/academics/busgov/index.html
  Did Not Respond--2005-2006 Listing

Bell, Bruce K.	Dean	582-2480	bkbell	Mktg	PHD	00	Walden	1996
Sullivan, Gene	C-Ac	582-2913	gsacct	FPJ	PHD	04	Regent	&1987
Shelton, James B.	Prof	582-2501	jbshelto	PCA	PHD	93.	Va Comm	&1995
Gilmore, Philip N.	Assoc	582-7429	pngilmor	P	DBA	02	Nova SE	* &1980
Gilmore, JoAnn W.	Asst	582-2470	jwgilmor	PX	MBA	91	Liberty	&1995

Lincoln University Jefferson Cty MO 65102-0029   (573) Fax = 681-6085
Dept of Business & Econ Col of Bus & Prof Stds   lincolnu.edu   BS,MBA
Dept Phone: 681-5487 820 Chestnut Street   Sheila Moallister

Edoho, Felix M.	Dean	681-5489	ehohof		PHD			7-06
Anunoby, Ogugua	H-Ac	681-5487	anunobyo		PHD			1991
Headrick, Marilyn	Asst	681-6089	headrick	X	JD		Tx Tech	& 8-98
Koechling, Sherrie	Asst	681-6083	koechling	M	PHD		Webster	8-89
Rankin, Debbie	Asst	681-6086	rankind	F	MS		Missouri	& 8-86

Lindenwood University
Accounting Faculty
Dept Phone: 949-4840

St. Charles, MO   63301-1695
Division of Management
209 S. Kingshighway

(636) Fax=949-4834
lindenwood.edu

BS,MS,MBA

Name	Rank	Phone	Email		Field	Degree		School	Year
Morris, Edward L.	Dean	949-4832	emorris			PHD		St Louis	2002
White, Scott	Assoc	949-4829	swhite	CMFX	MACC		Missouri	&2002
Ammann, Elizabeth	Asst	949-4811	ammann	FMP	MBA		S Il-Edw	1983
Brickler, Kim	Asst	949-4672	kbricker	AFPS	MBA		St Louis	&2003
Waring, Glen	Asst	949-4835	gwaring	FMP	MBA		Lindenwo	&1999

Lindsey Wilson College
Accounting Faculty
Dept Phone: 384-8061
  Did Not Respond--2005-2006 Listing

Columbia, KY   42728
Division of Bus & CIS
210 Lindsey Wilson St

(270) Fax=
lindsey.edu

BA

Name	Rank	Phone	Email		Field	Degree		School	Year
Green, Wes	C-Ac	384-8061	greeng		DBA		Nova SE	
Gibson, Gary	Assoc	384-8478	gibsong	FX	MAC	92	Tennessee	&2004
Crowe, Lisa	Inst			FA	MPA	96	Wstrn Ky	2001

Linfield College
Accounting Faculty
Dept Phone: 883-2405

McMinnville, OR   97128-6894
Department of Business
900 SE Baker

(503) Fax=883-2370
linfield.edu

BA,BS

Name	Rank	Phone	Email		Field	Degree		School	Year
Nelson, Michelle	C-Ac	883-2404	mnelson	Mktg	PHD	00	Wash St	2000
Emery, Richard F.	Prof	883-2298	rfemery	XPT	MBA	71	E New Mex	& 8-86
Greenlees, E. Malcolm	Prof	883-2403	mgreen	ACGR	PHD	72.	U Wash	&1984
Glenn L. & Helen S. Jackson Professor of Business								
Jones, Michael A.	Prof	883-2251	mjones	TFV	MBA	74	Oregon	&1977

Lipscomb University
Department of Accounting
Dept Phone: 966-5950

Nashville, TN   37204-3951
College of Business
3901 Granny White Pike

(615) Fax=966-1818
lipscomb.edu

BS,BA,MACC,MBA
Nane Roberts 966-5950

Name	Rank	Phone	Email		Field	Degree		School	Year
Carnes, Gregory A.	Dean	966-6606	greg.carnes	X	PHD	91	Geo St	& 1-06
Frasier, Charles E.	C-Ac	966-5738	charles.frasier	PXFM	MA	67	Alabama	* & 9-71
Galbreath, Susan Coomer	Prof	966-5952	susan.galbreath	SAFP	PHD	93.	Tennessee	&2001
Moore, Perry G.	Prof	966-5795	perry.moore	OAVP	PHD	92.	Georgia	# & 8-82
Mankin, Jeff A.	Asst	966-5742	jeff.mankin	MPCX	PHD	00.	Miss	* & 1-91

Lock Haven University
Accounting Faculty
Dept Phone: 484-2492

Lock Haven, PA   17745
Dept Bus Adm, Cpt & Inf

(570) Fax=484-6279
lhup.edu

BS
Beth Lawless

Name	Rank	Phone	Email		Field	Degree		School	Year
Strayer, Susan H.	C-Pr	484-2494						
Berry, Nancy W.	Assoc	893-2492	nberry	FAX	MBA	78	Penn St	* & 9-84
Lloyd, William H.	Asst	484-2273			MBA			&
Shawver, Todd	Asst							

Long Isl U, Brooklyn Campus
Dept of Acctg, Tax, & Law
Dept Phone: 780-4062
Homepage: www.brooklyn.liu.edu/cwis/bklyn/sbpais/busmain/business.htlm

Brooklyn, NY   11201-5372
Sch of Bus Adm & Info S
Flatbush & DeKalb Ave H-700

(718) Fax=488-1125
liu.edu

BS,MS,BS/MS
Ms. Francine Sparks

Name	Rank	Phone	Email		Field	Degree		School	Year
Ghriga, Mohammed	Dean$	488-1130	mohammed.ghriga		PHD			
Fischman, Myrna L.	C-Pr$	488-1071	myrna.fischman	JMGA	PHD	76	NYU	&1968
Dworetsky, Ephraim D.	Emer	488-1070		1990	MBA	49	CCNY	&1946
Lee, Ben B.	Emer	488-1070	ben.lee	2003	PHD	65	NYU	&1965
Rochlin, Robert E.	Emer	488-1070	robert.rochlin	2002	MBA	65	NYU	* &1964
Wolitzer, Philip	Emer	488-1070	philip.wolitzer	2001	MBA	61	NYU	&1965
Scerbinski, Vincent	Assoc	488-1146	vincent.scer+	X	MBA		St Johns	&1990
Owsen, Dwight M.	Inst	246-6464	dwight.owsen	SFAM	ABD		U Portsm	8-03

Long Island U.-C.W. Post
School of Prof Accountancy
Dept Phone: 299-2364
Homepage: www.liu.edu/msacc

Brookville, NY   11548-0570
College of Management
720 Northern Blvd

(516) Fax=299-2297
liu.edu

2001,2001
BS,MS,MST
Frances Orlando/Vinnie Simon

Name	Rank	Phone	Email		Field	Degree		School	Year
Cordaro, Matthew C.	Dean$	299-3017	matthew.cordaro		PHD		Cooper	
Barragato, Charles A.	D-Pr	299-3279	cbarraga	XFVN	PHD	02.	Baruch	&1986
Abatemarco, Michael J.	Prof	299-3271	mabatema	LX	LLM		NYU	&1985
Bertucelli, Robert E.	Prof	299-2380	rbertuce	XF	MSTX	73	Long Isl	&1974
Comunale, Christie L.	Assoc	299-2366	comunale	PF	PHD	99.	S Fla	&1999
Persoff, Ilene L.	Assoc	299-2091	ipersoff	VF	MS	78	Lgls-Post	&1984
Rosner, Rebecca L.	Assoc	299-2094	rrosner	AS	PHD	99.	Baruch	&1999
Markelevich, Ariel	Asst	299-2085	ariel.markele+	CFP	PHD	04.	Baruch	2003

Long Isl Univ-Southampton
Accounting Faculty
Dept Phone: 287-8284
  Did Not Respond--2005-2006 Listing

Southampton, NY 11968-4198
Sch of Bus & Public Adm
239 Montauk Hwy

(631) Fax=287-8441
southampton.liunet.edu

BS,BS-MS,MS
Helene Camara

Name	Rank	Phone	Email		Field	Degree		School	Year
Drexel, Michael	D-As	287-8286	cddrexel	Fnce	PHD	98	Union-NY	9-99

Longwood University
Accounting Faculty
Dept Phone: 395-2042
Homepage: www.longwood.edu/business/

Farmville, VA 23909-1899
College of Bus & Econ
201 High Street

(434) Fax=395-2203
longwood.edu

1998
BSBA
Mrs. Kathy Dunnavant

Name		Phone	email		Degree	Year	School	
Cross, James S.	Dean	395-2137	crossjs		PHD			2006
Brown, William P.	C-Ac	395-2365	brownwp	XS	PHD	85.	N Carol	& 8-87
Carr, John E. III	Emer	395-2362		1989	MBA	60	Syracuse	1966
Flanigan, Mary A.	Prof	395-2364	flaniganma	CFI	PHD	95.	Va Comm	&1989
Hume, Evelyn C.	Prof	395-2037	humeec	XJ	PHD	88.	LSU	2004
Gilfillan, Sally W.	Assoc	395-2363	gilfillansw	VNI	MS	90	Virginia	&1986
Cochran, Robert J.	Asst	395-2361	cochranrj	FM	PHD	01.	Va Comm	&2003
Fowlkes, Melinda I.	Asst	395-2379	fowlkesmi	P	MBA	94	Va Comm	&1996

Loras College
Accounting Faculty
Dept Phone: 588-7695

Dubuque, IA 52004-0178
Div of Business Adm
1450 Alta Vista

(563) Fax=588-7339
loras.edu

BA
Becky Frommelt

Name		Phone	email		Degree	Year	School	
Collins, Thomas S.	C-Pr	588-7725	tcollins	AL	MA	85	Iowa	&1988
Pauly, Deborah M.	Prof	588-7609	dpauly	CM	MBA	92	N Iowa	* &1983
Sturm, Karen K.	Prof	588-7405	ksturm	AS	MA	81	Iowa	&1982
Schleicher, Debra	Assoc	588-7404	dschleic	XL	MACC	87	S Illinois	&2000

U of Louisiana at Lafayette
Dept of Accounting
Dept Phone: 482-6218
Homepage: http://cobweb.louisiana.edu/departments/accounting

Lafayette, LA 70504-3450
Col of Bus Adm Box43450
214 Hebrand Blvd

(337) Fax=482-5906
louisiana.edu

1996,1996
BS,MBA
Debra Broussard

Name		Phone	email		Degree	Year	School	
John, Joby	Dean	482-6493		Mktg	PHD	87	Okla St	
Cook, Ellen D.	H-Pr	482-6212	edcook	XFE	MS	75	LSU	&1977
Ward, Dan R.	Prof	482-5381	dward	XFE	DBA	79.	La Tech	1981
Ward, Suzanne Pinac	Prof	482-6085	spward	FTE	PHD	87.	LSU	&1979
Wilson, Thomas E. Jr.	Prof	482-6388	tw	AFEG	PHD	91.	LSU	& 8-90
Bundy, Tracy L.	Asst	482-6228	tbundy	FX	ABD		La Tech	8-06
LaGroue, Harold	VAsst	482-5384	hjl5830	FS	PHD	06	LSU	& 8-06
Sonnier, Blaise M.	VAsst	482-5383		F	PHD	07	Grenoble	2007
email: blaisesennier@allengooch.com								
Meyer, Pamela	Inst	482-6083	pam0202	FMS	MBA	98	USL	& 8-98
Scheuermann, Sandra	Inst	482-5388	sbs2948	F	MBA	84	Nicholls	&1985

Univ of Louisiana at Monroe
Department of Accounting
Dept Phone: 342-1108
Homepage: ele.ulm.edu/accounting/acct.html

Monroe, LA 71209-0110
College of Business Adm
700 University Avenue

(318) Fax=342-1191
ulm.edu

ß (1) 1972,1977
BBA
Ms. Louise Till

Name		Phone	email		Degree	Year	School		
Berry, Ronald L.	Dean	342-1100	rberry	Cis	DBA	90	Miss St		1990
McEacharn, E. Michelle	H-Pr	342-1108	mceacharn	GNAF	DBA	94.	La Tech	#	&1989
Hood/DeFatta Professor of Accounting									
Davis, Dorothy A. (Dot)	Assoc	342-1119	davis	SV	DBA	88.	Miss St		&1989
George T. Walker Professor of Entrepreneurship									
Hodge, Thomas G.	Assoc	342-1116	hodge	FXJ	PHD	91.	Miss	# *	&1990
John L. Luffey, Sr. Professor of Accounting									
Guidry, Ronald P.	Asst	342-1112	guidry	F	PHD	04.	Miss St		&2003
Hibbets, Aleecia R.	Asst	342-1115	hibbets	AM	PHD	06.	Alabama		&2003
Roshto, Patricia G.	Inst	342-1118	roshto	P	MBA	80	La-Monroe		&1986

Louisiana State University
Department of Accounting
Dept Phone: 578-6202
Homepage: www.bus.lsu.edu/accounting/

Baton Rouge, LA 70803-6304
E. J. Ourso Col Bus
3101 CEBA Building

(225) Fax=578-6201
lsu.edu

ß 1931,1963
BA,MS,PHD
Debby Arledge

Name		Phone	email		Degree	Year	School	
Apostolou, Barbara A.	C-Pr	578-6222	acapos	A	PHD	88	LSU	& 8-88
E&Y Alumni Distinguished Professor								
Apostolou, Nicholas G.	Prof	578-6211	acnicha	FG	DBA	82.	Tennessee	& 8-85
U. J. LeGrange Endowed Professor								
Cheng, C.S. Agnes	Prof	578-6202		F	PHD	83.	Illinois	8-07
Ourso Distinguished Chair								
Christie, Andrew A.	Prof	578-6226	achrist	FCTM	PHD	81.	Stanford	1995
Crumbley, D. Larry	Prof	578-6231	dcrumbl	XAZ	PHD	67.	LSU	& 8-96
KPMG LLP Endowed Professor								
Sumners, Glenn E.	Prof	578-6210	gsumner	O	DBA	81.	Tennessee	& 1-80
U.J. LeGrange Endowed Prof; Director, Center for Internal Auditing								
Hughes, K. E. II (Skip)	Assoc	578-6216	khughe2	FM	PHD	96.	Georgia	8-97
LeGrange Professor; Associate Dean								
Legoria, Joseph	Assoc	578-6225	jlegoria	F	PHD	97.	Arkansas	& 8-01
Moffitt, Jackie S.	Assoc	578-6219	jsmoff22	F	PHD	01.	Fla St	8-01
Tiras, Samuel L.	Assoc	578-6202		F	PHD	94.	Ohio St	& 8-07
KPMG Endowed Professor								

Diaz, Michelle C.	Asst	578-6216	michelle	S	PHD	06.	Tx A&M		& 8-06
Liu, Cathy Zishang	VAsst	578-6202			PHF	07	Houston		8-07
Melendrez, Kevin D.	Asst	578-6925	kdm	FM	PHD	04.	Arizona		7-07
KPMG LLP Developing Scholar									
Rakow, K. C.	Asst	578-6214	kcrakow	FM	PHD	05.	Georgia		& 8-05
Reichelt, Kenneth	Asst	578-6233	hykenreichelt@h	FM	PHD	05	Missouri		& 8-05
Wilson, George R.	Asst	578-6218	gwilson	FM	PHD	06.	Georgia		8-06
Woodland, Angela M.	Asst	578-6229	woodland	SAF	PHD	01.	Missouri		& 8-04
Anderson, David M.	Inst	578-6542	dmander	FXZ	MBA	81	LSU		& 8-81
Armentor, Jesse J.	Inst	578-6542	jarmen2	F	MBA	75	SanDgoSt		& 8-86
Blue, Michael A.	Inst	578-7057	mblue	FCM	MS	91	LSU		& 8-95
Chenier, Julie C.	Inst	578-9056	bachen	FM	MBA	79	Tulane	#	&1983
DeLaune, Laura D.	Inst	578-7466	delaune	FS	PHD	04	LSU		& 8-96
Denstel, Chris	Inst	578-9059	lcdenst1	FM	MS	02	LSU		& 1-03
Holmes, Janice R.	Inst	578-7367	jholme4	FM	MS	98	LSU		& 8-98
Lafleur, Lydia M.	Inst	578-6282	llafle2	FO	MBA	00	LSU		& 6-00
Lowe-Ardoin, Letti	Inst	578-6282	llowea1	FX	MS	83	LSU		& 8-98
Rakow, Jessica	Inst	578-6227	jsrakow	FM	MS	00	Miss		& 8-07
Torres, Donna K.	Inst	578-1623	dtorres		MS	97	LSU		& 8-97

Louisiana St in Shreveport   Shreveport, LA   71115-2399   (318) Fax = 797-5253   1992,1992
Dep of Accounting & Bus Law   College of Business   lsus.edu   D3
Dept Phone. 797-5241   One University Place   Charles Boyd
Homepage: www.lsus.edu/acctblaw/

Jones, Charlotte A.	Dean	797-5383	cjones	Stat	DBA	84	La Tech	8-84
Bible, Douglas S.	C-Pr	797-5241	dbible	F	PHD	77	Ohio St	8-85
Oscar Cloyd Professorship								
Parker, Frederick R. Jr.	Assoc	797-5109	rparker	JLX	LLM	88	NYU	& 8-98
Smolinski, H. Carl	Assoc	797-5014	csmolins	FCT	DBA	87.	La Tech	& 8-87
Wampler, Bruce M.	Assoc	797-5240	bwampler	AFP	DBA	94.	La Tech	& 1-03
Hays, Stanley W.	Asst	797-5118	shays	GPVX	DBA	00.	La Tech	& 8-02

Louisiana Tech University   Ruston, LA   71272-0001   (318) Fax = 257-4253   ß (123) 1955,1979
School of Accountancy   College of Business   cab.latech.edu   BS,MBA,MPA,DBA
Dept Phone: 257-2822   Pam Meyer

Lumpkin, James R.	Dean	257-4526	jlumpkin	Mktg	PHD	80	Arkansas	2007
Phillips, Thomas J. Jr.	D-Pr	257-2822	phillips	FBTJ	PHD	84.	Geo St	&1987
KPMG Endowed Professor								
Englebrecht, Ted D.	Prof	257-3552	tenglebr	XF	PHD	76.	S Carol	2001
Smolinski Eminent Scholar Endowed Chair of Accounting								
Johnson, Gene H.	Prof	257-3984	johnson	BMI	PHD	86.	Tx Tech	# * & 9-90
Drake, Andrea R.	Assoc	257-4378	adrake	BMF	PHD	99.	Mich St	2007
Luehlfing, Michael S.	Assoc	257-3490	luehlfing	FTA	PHD	90.	Georgia	* &1998
Max P. Watson, Jr. Endowed Professor								
Stammerjohan, William W.	Assoc	257-3828	wstammer	MC	PHD	95.	Wash St	&2004
George E. Breazel Family Endowed Professor								
Park, Jinyonng (Jeanne)	Asst	257-3948	jpark	FM	PHD	05.	Purdue	& 9-05
Aldredge, Melissa M.	Inst	257-3599	aldredge	FMX	MBA	90	La Tech	&2003
McCallister Endowed Teaching Professor								
Shaver, Carol G.	Inst	257-3984	cshaver	FM	MBA	85	La-Monroe	# &2002
McCallister Endowed Teaching Professor								

University of Louisville   Louisville, KY   40292-0001   (502) Fax = 852-6072   ß (1) 1982,1987
School of Accountancy   Col of Bus & Public Adm   louisville.edu   BS,MAC
Dept Phone: 852-5847   Denise McKnight

Moyer, R. Charles	Dean	852-6440	charlie.moyer	Fnce	PHD	71	Pittsburgh	1-05
Stout, William D.	D-Ac	852-4830	william.stout	FN	PHD	97.	S Fla	& 8-96
Attaway, Alan N.	Prof	852-4812	a.attaway	XS	PHD	83.	Cincinnati	1977
Baxendale, Sidney J.	Prof	852-4813	baxendale	MC	DBA	78.	Indiana	* &1984
Brown, Betty C.	Prof	852-4889	betty.brown	AF	PHD	85.	Va Tech	# * &1983
Coppage, Richard E. (Rick)	Prof	852-4817	coppage	FVT	DBA	86.	Kentucky	* &1979
Levitan, Alan S.	Prof	852-4822	levitan	MS	DBA	83.	Kentucky	&1979
Walter, Richard M.	Prof	852-4835	richard.walter	X	PHD	88.	Tennessee	& 8-93
Faircloth, Archie W.	Assoc	852-4818	archie.faircloth	FNH	DBA	77.	Kentucky	& 9-72
Foster, Benjamin P.	Assoc	852-4826	ben.foster	MCF	PHD	91.	Tennessee	* & 8-94
Karcher, Julia N.	Assoc	852-4821	julia.karcher	FEJ	PHD	92.	Fla St	* 8-91
McDowell, Wyatt	Assoc	852-4827	wyatt.mcdowell	XL	LLM	89	Capital	8-91
Shastri, Trimbak	Asst	852-4816	t0shas01	AS	PHD	92.	Oklahoma	# * & 8-01
Blum, Lisa M.	Inst	852-4823	lmivan01	PLX	LLM	03	NYU	&1995
Burge, Christy A.	Inst	852-4816	christy.burge	PS	MBA	87	Bowl Gr	7-00
Johnston, Sheila A.	Inst	852-4820	sheila.johnston	PF	MST	92	Cincinnati	* & 1-91
Smith, Mark E.	Inst	852-4834	mesmit01	PL	JD	82	Louisville	&1984

Loyola College in Maryland

Department of Accounting
Dept Phone: 617-2474
Homepage: www.loyola.edu/sellinger/accounting

Baltimore, MD 21210-2699
Sellinger Sch Bus & Mgt
4501 N. Charles St, SH318

(410) Fax=617-2006 ß (12) 1988,1988
loyola.edu BBA,MBA
Josephine Munoz

Name	Rank	Phone	Email					
Dahringer, Lee D.	Dean	617-2301	ldahringer	Mktg	DBA	75	Colorado	
Michenzi, Alfred R.	C-Ac	617-2386	amichenzi	AFS	PHD	74	Case Wes	&1989
Blouch, William E.	Prof	617-2598	wblouch	FM	DBA	87.	Kent St	1984
Soroosh, Jalal	Prof	617-2543	jsoroosh	FM	PHD	81.	Miss	* 1983
KPMG LLP Faculty Fellow								
Keeling, Kermit O.	Assoc	617-2752	kkeeling	XP	LLM	87	Houston	&1987
Sedaghat, Ali M.	Assoc	617 2843	asedaghat	CFM	DBA	86.	Geo Wash	* 1986
Maas, Jayne D.	Asst	617-5416	jmaas	FM	EDD	02	Nova SE	&2002
Rice, E. Barry	Emer	617-2478	rice	2003	MBA	75	Maryland	&1975
Zhu, Hong	Asst	617-2597	hzhu1	FM	PHD	05.	Missouri	2003
Langmead, Joseph	Exec	617-2474	jmlandmead	FJKU	MBA	73	Loyola	1-04

Loyola University Chicago

Department of Accounting
Dept Phone: 915-7111
Homepage: gsb.luc.edu/depts/accounting/

Chicago, IL 60611-2196
School of Business Adm
820 North Michigan Avenue

(312) Fax=915-7224 ß (123) 1955,1980
luc.edu BBA,MBA,MSA

Name	Rank	Phone	Email					
Abolhassan, Juliiuand	Dean	915-7054		Fnce	PHD	81	N Carol	2005
Stanko, Brian B.	C-Pr	915-7106	bstanko	FTBR	PHD	92.	Kentucky	& 9-91
Janiga, John M.	Prof	915-7104	jjaniga	RX	LLM	91	DePaul	& 9-88
Metzger, Lawrence M.	Prof	915-7107	lmetzge	MN	PHD	87	Il-Chicago	* 9-85
Zeller, Thomas L.	Prof	915-7626	tzeller	CMS	PHD	91.	Kent St	& 9-91
Kostolansky, John W.	Assoc	915-7103	jkostol	FT	PHD	75	Columbia	& 9-72
Landgraf, Ellen L.	Assoc	915-7105	elandgr	APRF	PHD	91	Il-Chicago	& 9-89
Werner, Charles A.	Assoc	915-7102	cwerner	ADR	JD	61	Chicago	& 9-82
Gillespie, Lisa	Lect	915-6278	lgilles	FM	ABD	97	Notre Dm	9-03

Loyola Univ New Orleans

Department of Accounting
Dept Phone: 864-7977

New Orleans, LA 70118
College of Business Adm
6363 Saint Charles Avenue

(504) Fax=864-7970 ß 1950,1974
loyno.edu BACC

Name	Rank	Phone	Email					
Dauterive, Jerry	Dean$	864-7945	dauteriv	Econ	PHD	76	Tx Tech	7-79
Baskett, James	Assoc	864-7953	jbaskett	MFX	PHD	76	Arizona	* &1982
Dozier, Donald D.	Assoc	864-7963	dozier	SFA	PHD	81.	Missouri	& 9-85
Lynch, Patrick M.	VAsst	864-7974	pmlynch		MS		N Orleans	
Polledo, Donna	VAsst	864-7956	dpolledo		ABD		Miss St	
Schorg, Chandra A.	Asst	864-7022	caschorg	FM	MBA	86	Tx Woman	& 8-02

Loyola Marymount Univ

Department of Accounting
Dept Phone: 338-2946

Los Angeles, CA 90045-2659
College of Business Adm
One LMU Drive MS 8385

(310) Fax=338-2843 1981,1987
lmu.edu BS

Name	Rank	Phone	Email					
Wholihan, John T.	Dean	338-7504	jwholiha	Mgt	PHD	73	American	1984
Cherry, Alan A.	C-Pr	338-4541	acherry	FW	PHD	78.	UCLA	1983
Bengel, Ross	Prof	338-3036	rbengel	X	JD	75	S Carol	&1984
Daroca, Frank P.	Prof	338-7660	fdaroca	AMG	PHD	81.	Illinois	&1986
Dasaro, George A.	Prof	338-7656	gdasaro	FVX	MS	66	CS-L Ang	&1977
Falcon, Alan H.	Prof	338-7502	afalcon	FME	MAC	73	Arizona	# * &1979
Kalbers, Lawrence P.	Prof		lkalbers	JFAS	PHD	89.	Penn St	&2005
R. Chad Dreier Chair in Accounting Ethics								
Nourayi, Mahmoud M.	Prof	338-2946	mnourayi	MCQ	PHD	89.	S Calif	* & 9-87
Douglas, Patricia C.	Assoc	338-2945	pdouglas	MFIJ	PHD	95.	Va Comm	* 1995

Luther College

Accounting Faculty
Dept Phone: 387-1340
Homepage: http://luther.edu/learning/dept/business.html

Decorah, IA 52101-1045
Dept of Econ & Business
700 College Drive

(563) Fax=387-1088
luther.edu BA
Dodi Bernatz

Name	Rank	Phone	Email					
Craft, William	Dean	387-1005						
Christianson, Charles	H-Pr	387-1340	christch	FMX	MBA	75	S Dakota	&1988
Nelson, Ramona F.	Prof	387-1569	nelsonra	AFX	MBT	85	Minnesota	& 9-90
Rudolf, Uwe J.	Prof	387-1295	rudolfuw	FVI	ABD		Cincinnati	&1971
Rabe, Craig	Asst	387-1035	rabecr01	FMC	MBA	04	Minnesota	&2004

Lycoming College

Department of Accounting
Dept Phone:

Williamsport, PA 17701
Business Faculty
700 College Place

(570) Fax=321-4337
lycoming.edu BA
Mary Ann Holenbach

Name	Rank	Phone	Email					
Kuhns, Eldon F. II	Assoc	321-4172	kuhns	FXG	MAC	75	Oklahoma	&1979
Kremer, Larvi	Asst	321-4381		A	MBA		Wilkes	2006
Wienecke, Richard E.	Asst	321-4174	wienecke	AX	MBA	79	Lgls-Post	&1982

Lynchburg College
Accounting Faculty
Dept Phone: 544-8417
Homepage: www.lynchburg.edu

Lynchburg, VA	24501-3199		(434) Fax=544-8639					
Sch of Business & Econ			lynchburg.edu					BA
1501 Lakeside Drive					Virginia Kern, Janice Quattlebaum			
Seldon, Sally	Dean			Mgt	DPA	01	Virginia	2001
Murphy, David S.	C-Ac	544-8387	murphy.d	AFGI	PHD	89.	Wash St	& 8-02
Schneider, Nancy W.	Prof	544-8259	schneider	ACFT	MPA	78	Geo St	* & 7-90
Rosson, Gerald W.	Assoc	544-8263	rosson	ACEX	MAC	72	Va Tech	&1980

Lyndon State College
Accounting Faculty
Dept Phone: 626-6200

Lyndonville, VT	05851		(802) Fax=626-9770					
Business Adm Department			lsc.vsc.edu					BS,BA
Bradley, David B.	Prof	626-6482	david.bradley	MAX	MBA	82	Plymouth	# * 9-81
Siegel, Rachel S.	Prof	626-6207	rachel.siegel	QF	MBA	89	Yale	9-90

Lyon College
Accounting Faculty
Dept Phone: 698-4258

Batesville, AR	72501-2317		(870) Fax=698-4622					
Div of Business & Econ			lyon.edu					BS
2300 Highland Drive					Peggy Weaver			
Creighton, Cassie F.	C-Ac	698-4325	ccreighton	FLXP	MBA	83	Ark St	&1984
Peek, John	Dean$	698-4202	johnpeek	PolS	PHD		Kansas	1999
McNamee, Alan H.	Prof	698-4209	amcnamee	RCMS	PHD	88.	N Carol	&1994

Frank & Marion Bradley Lyon Professor of Accounting

Macon State College
Accounting Faculty
Dept Phone: 471-2724
Homepage: www.maconstate.edu

Macon, GA	31206-5145		(478) Fax=471-2802					
Business & Economics			mail.maconstate.edu					BS
100 College Station Drive					Pat Fountain			
Wolfenbarger, J. Larry	C-Pr	471-2724	lwolfenb	Econ	PHD	74	Tennessee	2000
McAlum, Harry G.	Prof	471-2724	hmcalum	APS	DBA	83.	La Tech	&2001
Ford, Wilhelmina H. (Mimi)	Assoc	471-2724	wford	FLPX	JD	95	Mercer	&2000
Ryerson, Frank E. III	Assoc	471-2724	fryerson	ACFV	PHD	83.	Alabama	2005
Seay, Sharon S.	Assoc	471-2724	sseay	ACFV	PHD	92.	Georgia	2005
Woods, Janet	Assoc	471-2724	jwoods	CFM	MBA	79	Georgia	&1989

Madonna University
Dept of Accounting & Bus
Dept Phone: 432-5367

Livonia, MI	48150-1173		(734) Fax=432-5364					
School of Business			madonna.edu					BS
36600 Schoolcraft Road								
Arends, Stuart R.	Dean	432-5366	sarends	M	PHD		Walden	1978
McMillan, William	C	432-5367	wmcmillan		PHD	96	Wayne St	1976
Stahl, Charles E. III	Prof	432-5368	cstahl	XLF	LLM	91	Wayne St	&1991
Critchett, John D.	Assoc	432-5349	jcritchett	BWM	PHD	97.	Kentucky	&1994

University of Maine
Accounting Faculty
Dept Phone: 581-1968

Orono, ME	04469-5723		(207) Fax=581-1956					1974,1982
Cl Bus Adm, Pub Pl & Hl			maine.edu					BS
Mahon, John F.	Dean$	581-1968	jmahon	Mgt	DBA	82	Boston U	
Colburn, Steven C.	C-Ac	581-1982	colburn	XF	PHD	89.	Georgia	& 9-92
Vollmers, Gloria Lucey	Assoc	581-1979	vollmers	CFM	PHD	94.	North Tx	&1992
Barrett, David J.	Asst	581-1978	david.barrett	F	PHD	04	Indiana	2004
Siagian, Ferdinand	Asst			AF	PHD	02.	Oregon	2007

Manchester College
Dept of Accounting & Bus
Dept Phone: 982-5300

No Manchester IN	46962-1276		(219) Fax=982-5043					
Education/Prof Prog Div			manchester.edu					BS,BA
604 East College Avenue								
Fahs, Janis K.	H-Ac	982-5300	jkfahs	FRS	MIM	86	AGSIM	&1996
Lutz, Jennifer L.	Assoc	982-5372	jllutz	DMP	MAS	96	Illinois	1999
Olive, Franklin T.	Assoc	982-5304	ftolive	FGNP	MBA	80	Maryland	&1999
Pyrah, Bradan D.	Assoc	982-5303	bdpyrah	LPX	JD	86	Brighm Yg	&1995
Twomey, Heather C.	Assoc	982-5373	hctwomey	DPS	MA	97	Manchest	&2000

Manhattan College
Accounting, Law & Info Sys
Dept Phone: 862-7117

Riverdale, NY	10471		(718) Fax=862-8032					2003
School of Business			manhattan.edu					BS
Suarez, James M.	Dean	862-7440	james.suarez		PHD	72	Columbia	1984
Michel, Mary	C-As	862-7467	mary.michel	FM	PHD	97.	Columbia	1998
Baggett, Walter O.	Assoc	862-7223	walter.baggett	ASP	PHD	73	N Carol	&1983
Basoglu, Besalet	Assoc	862-7465	besalet.basoglu	CFM	DBA	79.	Fla St	1984
Goma, Ahmed Tawfik	Assoc	862-7117	ahmed.goma	FM	PHD	85.	Baruch	1987

Marian College
Accounting & Finance Dept
Dept Phone: 955-6765

Indianapolis, IN	46222-1997			(317) Fax=955-6030				
Business				marian.edu				BS,AS
3200 Cold Spring Road								Kpuce Harting
Truesdell, Marie K.	Dean	955-6035	mtrue	Econ	PHD	99	Georgia	2000
Akin, Timothy R.	Prof	955-6062	tra	FJPX	MBA	73	Xavier	&1975
Huston, Kevin E.	Assoc	955-6061	kevinhus	FXAC	JD	80	Duke	&1989

Marietta College
Accounting Faculty
Dept Phone: 376-4633
Homepage: marietta.edu/~ema

Marietta, OH	45750-4029			(740) Fax=376-7501				
Dept of Econ, Mgt & Atg				marietta.edu				BA
215 Fifth Street								Paula Lewis
Osborne, Edward H.	C-Pr	376-4632	osbornee	AFX	MBA	65	Indiana	&1971
McCoy Professor								
Johnson, Grace F.	Prof	376-4631	johnsong	FST	MA	88	S Fla	* &1989
McCoy Professor								

Marist College
Dept of Atg, Econ/Finance
Dept Phone: 575-3225
Homepage: www.marist.edu/management

Poughkeepsie NY 12601-1387				(845) Fax=575-3640				2001,2001
School of Management				marist.edu				BS
3399 North Road								Robin Will
Alexander, Elmore R.	Dean	575-3225	elmore.alexander	Mgt	PHD	77	Georgia	
Kobos, Chester	C-Ac	575-3000	chet.kobos	Fnce	PHD	72	Fordham	1982
Gagne, Margaret L.	Assoc	575-3000	margaret.gagne	CMQ	PHD	89.	Indiana	2000
Tully, Gregory J.	Assoc	575-3000	gregory.tully	FMC	PHD	83.	Berkeley	1996
Williams, Satina	Asst	575-3000	satina.williams	FA	PHD	03.	Va Comm	&

Marquette University
Dept of Accounting & Finance
Dept Phone: 288-7340
Homepage: http://www.busadm.mu.edu/accounting

Milwaukee, WI	53201-1881			(414) Fax=288-5755		ß (1)	1928,1963
Straz College of Bus Ad				marquette.edu				BS,MSA
1217 West Wisconsin Ave								Amanda Ames
Shrock, David L.	Dean	288-7141	david.shrock	Tran	DBA	74	Indiana	1999
Akers, Michael D.	C-Pr	288-1453	michael.akers	AFS	PHD	88.	Miss	# &1987
Charles T. Horngren Professor of Accounting								
Giacomino, Don E.	Prof	288-5669	don.giacomino	FA	DBA	78.	Kentucky	&1977
Donald F. & Beverly L. Flynn Chair in Accounting								
Naples, Gregory J.	Assoc	288-7331	gregory.naples	XLI	LLM	83	DePaul	1984
Trebby, James P.	Assoc	288-7344	james.trebby	X	DBA	81.	Kentucky	&1983
Yahr, Robert B.	Assoc	288-1459	robert.yahr	FGVT	PHD	79.	Nebraska	& 9-77
Ling, Qianhua	Asst		qianhua.ling	C	PHD	07	Okla St	8-07
Mascha, Maureen F.	Asst	288-0668	maureen.mascha	ASM	PHD	98.	Kentucky	&2003
Gruber, Cindy	VInst	288-7340	cindy.gruber	FM	MBA	98	Wi-Milwa	&2000
Kren, Barbara	Inst	288-3549	barbara.kren	FM	MS	85	Wi-Milwa	&1999
Dole, Michael	Adj	288-6587	michael.dole	FMC	MS	81	Wi-Milwa	&1987

Mars Hill College
Dept of Business Adm
Dept Phone: 689-1160

Mars Hill, NC	28754-0370			(828) Fax=689-1309				
Div Bus & Social/Beh				mhc.edu				
124 Cascade Street								Peggy Fender
Caudle, G. Grainger	Dean	689-1127	gcaudle	Econ	PHD	93	Colorado	1991
Blair, Joe S.	Prof	689-1160	jblair	AMPF	MACC	73	S Carol	&1979

Marshall University
Div Accountancy & Legal Envi
Dept Phone: 696-2310

Huntington, WV	25755-2310			(304) Fax=696-2652				1996,1996
Lewis Col of Business				marshall.edu				BBA,MBA
400 Hal Greer Blvd								Suzann Workman
Uselding, Paul J.	Dean	696-3319	uselding	Econ	PHD	70	Nrthwstrn	2005
Wenzel, Loren A.	H-Pr	696-2260	wenzel	PFGV	DBA	90.	Memphis	2000
Maheshwari, Suneel	Prof	696-6492	maheshwari	CMP	PHD	98.	Fla Atl	1999
Saunders, Gary J.	Prof	696-2654	saunderg	PMCT	DBA	77.	Kentucky	&1990
Archambault, Jeffrey J.	Assoc	696-2656	archambault	FMAS	PHD	92.	Mich St	* &2001
Archambault, Marie E.	Assoc	696-2653	archambaultm	FGPV	PHD	92.	Mich St	* &2001
Conrad, Bruce	Assoc	696-1957	bconrad	PF	MBA	73	SUNY-Buf	&
Forget, Robert Sr.	Assoc	696-1965	bforget	P	MBA	89	NewHamp	
Price, Jean B.	Assoc	696-2657	price91	PFVE	PHD	92.	Indiana	2002
Lockridge, T. Maurice	Asst	698-2659	lockrighet	FMPU	PHD	04.	Memphis	&2006
Stivason, Charles T.	Asst	696-6492	stivason	SAMO	PHD	98.	Va Tech	&

University of Mary
Accounting Faculty
Dept Phone: 255-7500
phone 255-7500

Bismarck, ND	58504-9652			(701) Fax=255-7687				
Division of Business				umary.edu				BA,BS
7500 University Drive								Marvin Borgelt
Borgelt, Marvin	C-Ac	Ext 439	mborgelt	Mgt	MBA	82	Maryland	9-82
Sipes, Daniel E. Sr.	Assoc	Ext 342	dsipes	PFVT	MS	71	N Dakota	& 9-73
Cuperus, Susann	Asst	Ext 391	cuperus	ARX	MS	00	Mary	9-98

Mary Baldwin College
Accounting Faculty
Dept Phone: 887-7055
Homepage: www.mbc.edu

	Staunton, VA	24401		(540) Fax=887-7040				
	Business Administration			mbc.edu				BA,BS
	Frederick & New Streets							
Kent, Claire	H-Ac	961-5433	ckent	Mgt	MBA		Jms Mad	1991
Ewing, Janet S.	Assoc	887-7055	jewing	PFD	ABD		Va Comm	1977
Pond, Lallon	Assoc	887-7274	lpond	PF	ABD		Fla St	1992

Univ of Mary Hardin-Baylor
Accounting Faculty
Dept Phone: 295-4644

	Belton, TX	76513-2599		(254) Fax=295-4651				
	School of Business			umhb.edu				BBA,MBA
	900 College St							Suzanne Fiala
King, James R.	Dean	294-4544	jking		PHD	88	Tx-Arlin	1993
Bolick, Bruce A.	C-Ac	295-4652	bbolick	FXR	MS	77	Tx Tech	&1987
Davis, Jenny R.	Asst	295-4105	jenny.davis	FCQ	MBA	99	AngeloSt	&2005
Mitchell, Tiffany	Asst	295-4656	tiffany.mitchell	AFM	MBA	03	MryHrd-B	2005

Univ of Mary Washington
Accounting Faculty
Dept Phone: 654-1019

	FredericksburgVA	22401-5358		(540) Fax=654-1462				
	Dept of Business Adm			umw.edu				BS
	1301 College Avenue							Lucy S. Quann
DeGraff, Galen f.	C-Pr	654-148g	degraff	Fnce	PHD	91	Geo Wash	8-94
Frackelton, R. Leigh	Prof	654-1452	rfrackel	XL	JD	77	Richmond	&9-86
Hubbard, Daniel J.	Assoc	654-1451	dhubbard	M	PHD	92	Va Tech	8-99
Machande, Kenneth D.	Asst	654-1457	kmachand	FP	MBA	98	Albany St	1-03

University of Maryland
Accounting & Info Assurance
Dept Phone: 405-4072
Homepage: www.rhsmith.umd.edu/accounting

	College Park, MD	20742-1815		(301) Fax=314-9414				ß 1940,1964
	Robert H. Smith Sch Bus			rhsmith.umd.edu				BS,MBA,PHD
	VanMunching Hall							Diane Hall
Frank, Howard	Dean	405-2308	hfrank	Sys	PHD	65	Nrthwstrn	1997
Loeb, Martin P.	C-Pr	405-2209	mloeb	M	PHD	75	Nrthwstrn	8-82
Deloitte & Touche Faculty Fellow								
Bedingfield, James P.	Emer	405-2138	jbedingfield	MA	DBA	71.	Maryland	&1967
Gordon, Lawrence A.	Prof	405-2255	lgordon	M	PHD	73.	Rensselaer	1980
Ernst & Young Alumni Professor of Managerial Accounting								
Kim, Oliver	Prof	405-2243	okim	FM	PHD	90.	Penn	9-95
Ernst & Young Professor of Accounting								
Loeb, Stephen E.	Prof	405-2207	sloeb	JAG	PHD	70.	Wisconsin	&1970
Ernst & Young Alumni Professor of Accounting & Business Ethics								
Basu, Progyan	VAsst			FSM	PHD	92.	Nebraska	2007
Bulmash, Gary F.	VAsst	405-8928	gbulmash	FMA	DBA	74.	Maryland	&2005
Cowling, John F.	VAsst	405-0570	jcowling	FM	PHD	89.	Indiana	2007
Finch, Michael L.	Asst	405-0563	mfinch	AJV	PHD	94.	Tennessee	& 9-00
Linsley, Colin A.	VAsst			FM	PHD	86	Exxes	2007
McKinney, James J.	VAsst			SABH	PHD	02.	Maryland	2007

Univ of Maryland Univ Coll
Dept of Accounting & Finance
Dept Phone: 582-2810
Did Not Respond--2005-2006 Listing

	College Park, MD	20742-1660		(240) Fax=582-2993				
	Business Adm			umuc.edu				BS,MS
	Univ Blvd at Adelphi Rd							Ms. Paula Adeline
Whelan, Joseph M.	C-Ac	582-2810	jwhelan	FIV	MS	88	Geo Wash	&1993
Loughlin, Brian	Assoc	582-2810	bloughlin	AOF	MBA	88	Maryland	# * &1999
Director, Undergraduate Accounting Programs								
Lubich, Bruce H.	Assoc	985-7226	blubich	XFJ	PHD	91.	Penn St	& 7-03
Director, Graduate Accounting Programs								
Michel, Kevin A.	Assoc	582-2810	kmichel	NG	EDD	99	Nova SE	&1998

U of Maryland Eastern Shore
Dept of Business, Mgt & Atg
Dept Phone: 651-6523
Homepage: www.umes.edu

	Princess Anne MD			21853		(410) Fax=651-6529		
	School of Bus & Tech			mail.umes.edu				
	Backbone Road							Mrs. Marian Birkhead
Alade, Ayodele J.	Dean$	651-6532	ajalade	Econ	PHD	81	Utah	
Jin, Jong-Dae	Prof	651-6884	jjin	FMCX	PHD	89.	Arizona	8-92
Burza, Vernon	Assoc	651-7884	vrburza	FMX	JD	76	Loyl-Chgo	9-03
Elsayed-Ahmed, Sameh M.	Assoc	651-6213	selsayed-ahmed	VCFI	PHD	86.	North Tx	8094
Mattison, Dorothy M.	Assoc	651-6522	dmmattison	FMNP	PHD	90.	Geo Wash	8-93
Hummer, William R.	Lect	651-7719	wrhummer	FMX	MBA	77	Montana	1-01

Marymount University
Dept of Acct, Econ & Fnce
Dept Phone: 284-5976
Homepage: www.marymount.edu

	Arlington, VA	22207-4299		(703) Fax=527-3830				
	School of Business Adm			marymount.edu				BBA,MBA
	2807 North Glebe Road							
Ryerson, James	Dean$	384-5965	james.ryerson	Mktg	MBA		Clarkson	1983
Marshall, Louise	C-Pr$	284-5932	louise.marshall	Econ	PHD	89	Maryland	1976
Quigley, Behnaz Z.	Prof	284-5939	behnaz.quigley		PHD	87	Maryland	2002

Marymount Manhattan Coll
Accounting Faculty
Dept Phone: 517-0631
Homepage: www.mmm.edu

	New York, NY	10021-4597		(212) Fax=517-0638					
	Div of Atg & Bus Mgt			mmm.edu					BS
	221 East 71 Street								Carmen Torres
Tynan, Eileen A.	C	517-0631			PHD				
Crawford, Corinne L.	Asst	517-0623	ccrawford		MBA	84	Pace		&2005
Wachtel, Rosina	Asst	517-0632	rwachtel	XFL	LLM	78	NYU		& 9-81

Maryville Univ St. Louis
Accounting Faculty
Dept Phone: 529-9418

	St. Louis, MO	63141-7299		(314) Fax=529-9975					
	J.E. Simon School Bus			maryville.edu					BS,MBA
	650 Maryville University Dr								Alma Johnson
Horwitz, Pamela S.	Dean	529-9572	horwitz		PHD	87	St Louis		1980
Roman, Mark A.	Assoc	529-9571	mroman	FV	MS	87	Truman St		&1999
Tabak, Karen G.	Assoc	529-9678	tabak	CMS	PHD	97.	St Louis		&1996
Temme, Kim	Assoc	529-9639	temme	AX	MBA	92	Notre Dm		&1993

Marywood University
Accounting Faculty
Dept Phone: 348-6274
Homepage: www.marywood.edu

	Scranton, PA	18509-1598		(570) Fax=961-4762					
	Bus & Mgr Science Prog			es.marywood.edu					BBA,MBA,MS/MIS
	2300 Adams Avenue								Marie Griffin/Susan Koche
Namm, Devorah	Dean	340-6000	namm		PHD				2003
Comstock, Art	C	348-6274	comstock	Fnce	PHD	00	Lehigh		2000
Smetana, Joan G.	Assoc	348-6274	smetana	PM	EDD		Temple		
Marcinek, George	Asst	348-6274	marcinek	CV	MBA	81	Scranton		&1986

University of Massachusetts
Dept Accounting & Info Sys
Dept Phone: 545-5645
Homepage: http://www.umass.edu/acctg/
email @1=acctg.umass.edu

	Amherst, MA	01003-4915		(413) Fax=545-3858			ß (123) 1958,1963		
	Isenberg Sch Management			som.umass.edu			BBA,MS,PHD		
							Deborah Puchalski		
Bisgaard, Soren	Dean	545-5581	bigaard		PHD	85	Wisconsin		2002
Mannino, Ronald C.	C-Ac	545-5625	rcm	MN	DBA	77.	Colorado		&1974
Elgers, Pieter T.	Prof	545-5648	elgers@1	FM	DBA	78.	Maryland		&1979
Kida, Thomas E.	Prof	545-5650	tkida	BF	PHD	78.	Mass		1982
Krzystofik, Anthony T.	Emer	545-5645		1992	MA	61	Conn		&1958
Sardinas, Joseph L. Jr.	Emer	545-5645		2004	PHD	75.	Penn St		9-75
Asebrook, Richard J.	Assoc	545-5651	asebrook	AF	PHD	74.	Wisconsin		9-77
Gal, Graham	Assoc	545-5649	gfgal	SD	PHD	85.	Mich St		1985
O'Connell, James P.	Emer	545-5645		1994	JD	73	W New Eng		& 9-65
Pfeiffer, Ray J.	Assoc	545-5653	pfeiffer@1	F	PHD	94.	N Carol		1994
Porter, Susan L.	Assoc	545-5582	porter@1	FX	PHD	94.	U Wash		& 9-98
Simpson, Richard H.	Assoc	545-5657	rsimpson	F	PHD	67.	N Carol		&1967
Smith, James F.	Assoc	545-5661	jfs	BMF	PHD	80.	U Wash		& 1-87
Stone, Donald E.	Emer	545-5685		1996	PHD	65.	Wisconsin		&1970
Whiteman, Michael J.	VAsoc	545-5660	whiteman@1	X	LLM	75	Boston U		9-81
Piercey, David	Asst	545-5585	piercey	AF	PHD	06.	Illinois		2006
Pion, Nelson E.	Emer	545-5645		1997	EDD	83	Mass		1964
Schmerling, Shirley	Lect	547-0917	sshmerling@y	SD	PHD	94	Mass		2005
Sorcinelli, Gino	Lect	545-5636	gino	S	MS	75	Mass		1994
Trafford, Pam	Lect	545-5645	trafford	F	ABD		Mass		1997
West, Cathy	Lect	577-2409	chwest	F	MBA	01	Mass		2006

U Massachusetts Boston
Dept of Accounting & Finance
Dept Phone: 287-7671

	Boston, MA	02125-3393		(617) Fax=287-7725			2001,2001		
	College of Management			umb.edu			BS,MBA		
	100 Morrissey Boulevard					Denise Radko, Leona Thomas			
Quaglieri, Phillip	Dean	287-7707	phillip.quagl+	Mgt	PHD	82	St Stevens		1983
Bandopadhyaya, Arindam	C-Ac	287-7854	arindam.band+	Fnce	PHD	91	Indiana		1991
Wright, Sally	Prof	287-7682	sally.wright	MAB	DBA	93.	Boston U		&1991
Hogan, Thomas J.	Assoc	287-7689	thomas.hogan	FA	PHD	86.	Mass		&1992
Verma, Kiran	Assoc	287-7681	kiran.verma	M	PHD	87.	Mich St		1992
Brennan, Julia M.	Asst	287-7687	julia.brennan	X	PHD	03.	Kentucky		8-03
Connors, Elizabeth	Asst	287-7768	elizabeth.con+	SMB	PHD	04.	Mich St		
Johnston, Holly H.	Asst	287-7768	holly.johnston	CMU	PHD	90	Car Mellon		
Jones, Anne L.	Asst	287-7683	anne.jones	F	DBA	03.	Boston U		2002
Vogel, Alan	Lect	287-3902	alan.vogel	FT	MBA	84	Bryant		&1999

U Massachusetts-Dartmouth
Dept of Accounting & Finance
Dept Phone: 999-8423

	N Dartmouth MA	02747-2300		(508) Fax=999-8776			2000,2000		
	College of Business			umassd.edu			BS,MBA		
	285 Old Westport Road								
Peacock, Eileen	Dean	999-8432	epeacock	CM	PHD	74	Birminghm		* & 8-04
Puri, Trib	C-Pr	999=8759	tpuri	Fnce	PHD	86	Tennessee		9-98
Jones, Frederick L.	Prof	999-8261	fjones	FA	DBA	91.	Boston U		& 9-82

Logan, Lawrence B.	Assoc	999-8311	llogan	FA	PHD	83	Wisconsin		1994
Shangguan, Zhaoyun	Assoc	999-8887	zshangguan		PHD	05.	Conn		2004
Akindayomi, Aksuloye	Asst	910-6969	aakindayomi	FX	PHD	06	Calgary		2006
Hostak, Peter	Asst	999-8748	phostak	F	PHD	05.	Nrthwstrn		2005
Prentice, Deborah	Asst	999-8261	dprentice	FA	PHD	99	Alabama		&2001
Wu, Jia	Asst	999-8428	jwu	F	PHD	06	Rutgers		2005
Griffin, Michael	Lect	999-6642	mgriffin	M	MBA	81	Bryant	*	1986
Assistant Dean									

U of Massachusetts-Lowell
Department of Accounting
Dept Phone: 934-2820

Lowell, MA   01854-2881
College of Management
1 University Avenue

(978) Fax = 934-3035
uml.edu

1987,1987
BS,MBA

Verreault, Kathryn M.	Dean	934-2741	kathryn_verr+	FM	PHD	82	Tx A&M		1986
Collins, J. Stephen	C-Ac	934-2829	jstephen_collins	FMGN	PHD	75	Boston C		& 9-86
Carter, Clairmont P. (Monty)	Prof	934-2826	clairmont_carter	FV	DBA	71.	Kent St		1982
Feeney, Charles F.	Prof	934-2827	charles_feeney	FMX	MBA	70	Northeas		&1968
Hamer, John G.	Assoc	934-2822	john_hamer	FM	PHD	84.	Tx A&M		1982
Nogler, George E.	Assoc	934-2844	george_nogler	AF	DBA	87.	Boston U		&2001
Strickland, Sherre	Assoc	934-2828	sherre_strick+	AS	PHD	81.	Tx A&M		&1991
Thompson, Charles F.	Assoc	934-2831	c+_thomp+1	NFGS	MBA	69	Northeas		&1969
Casello-Bouges, Janie C.	Asst	934-2808	janie_casello+	FX	PHD	05	Mass		&2005
Joseph, George	Asst	934-2842	george_joseph	CM	PHD	97	Templo		&2005

Mass College of Liberal Arts
Accounting Faculty
Dept Phone: 662-5311
    phone (413) 662-5311

North Adams, MA 01247-4100
Business Adm/Econ Dept
375 Church Street

(413) Fax = 662-5173
mcla.edu

Barbara P. Sunskis

Ovitsky, Nancy L.	C-Pr	662-5311	novitsky	Mktg	PHD	82	Illinois		8-84
Miano, Edward	Prof	Ext 5329	emiano	M	MBA	78	Pace		1985
Moriarity, James	Assoc	Ext 5313	jmoriart		MBA	80	Am Intl		1980
Casey-Baker, Donna	Asst	Ext 5343	dcaseyba		MBA	02	SUNY-Alb		2004

Massachusetts Inst of Tech
Accounting Faculty
Dept Phone: 253-6130
Homepage: http://web.mit.edu/sloan-accounting/

Cambridge, MA   02142-1347
Sloan School of Mgt
50 Memorial Drive, E52-325

(617) Fax = 253-0603
mit.edu

1957,1963
MS,PHD
Jeff Werner

Schmalensee, Richard L.	Dean	253-7150	rschmal	E	PHD	70	MIT		1970
Kothari, S. P.	C-Pr	253-0994	kothari	F	PHD	86.	Iowa		1999
Asquith, Paul	Prof	253-7177	pasquith	F	PHD	80	Chicago		7-90
Watts, Ross L.	Prof	253-2668	rwatts	FHT	PHD	71.	Chicago		&2006
Keating, A. Scott	VAsoc			FM	DBA	95.	Harvard		2007
Weber, Joseph P.	Assoc	253-4310	jpweber	FM	PHD	00.	Penn St		&2000
Wysocki, Peter D.	Assoc	253-6623	wysockip	F	PHD	99.	Rochester		2001
Khan, Mozaffav	Asst	252-1131	mkhan	FM	PHD	05	Toronto		2005
LaFond, Ryan Z.	Asst		rzlafond	F	PHD	05.	Wisconsin		2005
on leave									
Roychowdhury, Sugata	Asst	253-4903	sugatarc	F	PHD	03	Rochester		2003
Sletten, Ewa	Asst			F	PHD	07	Nrthwstrn		2007
Verdi, Rodrigo	Asst	253-2956	rverdi	F	PHD	06.	Penn		2006
Yu, Jeff Jiewei	Asst			F	PHD	07	Ohio St		2007

McMurry University
Accounting Faculty
Dept Phone: 793-3851

Abilene, TX   79697
School of Business
Box 398 McM Station

(325) Fax = 793-3849
mcmurryadm.mcm.edu

BBA,BS
Larue Williams

Long, K. O.	Dean	793-3850	longk	Law	JD		Tx-Austin		2002
Richardson, Clara L.	Assoc	793-3858	richardc	FMA	PHD	85.	Tx A&M		&1998
Starbuck, George	Inst	793-4950	starbug	PX	MBA		Tx Chr		&1995

McNeese State University
Dept Atg,Fnce & Econ 91415
Dept Phone: 475-5522
Homepage: www.mcneese.edu

Lake Charles, LA 70609-1415
College of Business
4205 Ryan St. BBC 145

(337) Fax = 475-5010
mcneese.edu

ß 1989,1989
BS
Mary Bertrand

Adrian, Mitchell	Dean	475-5514	madrian	Mgt	DBA	96	Miss St		
Kurth, Michael M.	H-Pr	475-5522	mmkurth@a	Econ	PHD	82	Va Tech		1984
Burckel, Daryl V.	Prof	475-5522	dburckel	FX	DBA	86.	Miss St		&1992
Swindle, C. Bruce	Prof	475-5576	bswindle	F	PHD	79.	LSU		&1980
Bandua, Frank	Asst	475-5558	fbandua	FAN	ABD		Rutgers		2004
Walker, Edward R.	Asst	475-5568	ewalker	FAN	PHD	96.	Houston		&2003
Watts, James C.	Asst	475-5571	jwatts	MC	MS	68	LSU		&1968
Watts, Olga	Inst	475-5564	owatts	FO	MBA	93	McNeese	#	&1999

University of Memphis

School of Accountancy — Memphis, TN 38152-6312 — Fogelman Col Bus & Econ
Dept Phone: 678-4569 — 200 Fogelman College Adm Blg
Homepage: www.people.memphis.edu/~dspice/accountancy/html

(901) Fax=678-4282 — memphis.edu — ß (13) 1970,1971 — BBA,MBA,MS,PHD — Martha Miller

Name	Rank	Phone	Email					
Pepin, John J.	Dean	678-2432	jjpepin	Mktg	PHD	69	Miss	1965
Lambert, Kenneth R.	D-Pr	678-4569	klambert	FN	PHD	76.	Arkansas	1982
Agrawal, Surendra P.	Emer	678-2446	sagrawal	M	PHD	73.	Florida	&1982
Bailey, Charles D.	Prof	678-5614	cbailey2	MBCJ	PHD	81.	Geo St	* 8-03
Arthur Andersen Chair of Excellence								
Langstraat, Craig J.	Prof	678-4577	cjlngstr	X	LLM	82	SanDiego	&1987
Malloy, John M.	Prof	678-5326	jmalloy	X	PHD	70.	LSU	& 1-88
McMickle, Peter L.	Prof	678-4567	mcmickle	DS	PHD	77.	Alabama	&1978
Minmier, George S.	Prof	678-3551	gminmier	F	PHD	74.	Arkansas	* &1976
Rezaee, Zabihollah	Prof	678-4652	zrezaee	MA	PHD	85.	Miss	# * &2001
Thompson-Hill Chair of Excellance								
Spiceland, J. David	Prof	678-2441	dspice	F	PHD	76.	Arkansas	&1981
Abbott, Lawrence J.	Assoc	678-4576	ljabbott	S	PHD	98.	Oregon	8-98
Collins, Denton L.	Assoc	678-4327	dlcollin	FM	PHD	95.	Colorado	8-03
Lukawitz, James M.	Assoc	678-3040	jlukawtz	F	PHD	89.	Fla St	& 1-89
Turner, Jerry L.	Assoc	678-2536	jturner1	MSA	PHD	94.	Tx A&M	& 8-99
Hossain, Mahmud	Asst	678-4422	mhossain	M	PHD	04.	Baruch	&2006
Collins, Allison B.	Inst	678-4578	acollins1	FM	PHD	87.	Houston	& 8-03
Morgret, Andrew J.	Inst	678-2972	amorgret	F	MBA	86	Memphis	&1997

Mercer University-Atlanta

Accounting Faculty — Atlanta, GA 30341-4155 — Stetson Sch Bus & Econ
Dept Phone: 547-6199 — 3001 Mercer University Drive

(678) Fax=547-6337 — mercer.edu — 2004,2004 — BBA,MBA — Joyce Hyche

Name	Rank	Phone	Email					
Mounts, Wm. Stewart Jr.	Dean	547-6438	mounts_ws	Econ	PHD	77	Georgia	1978
Weisel, James A.	Assoc	678-6117	weisel_ja	CEMU	DBA	91.	Kentucky	&2000
Pinson, Kathleen	VAsst	547-6179	pinson_kb	PVX	MBA	82	Mercer	&2005

Mercer University-Macon

Accounting Faculty — Macon, GA 31207-0001 — Stetson Sch Bus & Econ
Dept Phone: 301-2832 — 1400 Coleman Avenue
Homepage: www.mercer.edu/ssbe

(478) Fax=301-2635 — mercer.edu — 2004,2004 — BBA — Mamye Rogers

Name	Rank	Phone	Email					
Mounts, Wm. Stewart Jr.	Dean		mounts_ws	Econ	PHD	77	Georgia	1978
Austin, Walter W.	Prof	301-2861	austin_ww	FMEP	PHD	88.	Georgia	&1990
McIntyre, D. David	Asst	301-5541	mcintyre_dd	F	PHD	01.	Kentucky	&2004
Morris, Stephanie	Lect	301-2063	morris_sb	F	MACC	01	Georgia	&2006

Mercy College

Accounting Program, SWA 28 — Dobbs Ferry, NY 10522 — Liberal Arts
Dept Phone: 674-7490 — 555 Broadway

(914) Fax=674-7493 — mercy.edu — AS,BS,MS

Name	Rank	Phone	Email					
Mann, Lucretia S.	D-Ac	Ext 7492	lmann	FAVT	MBA	78	Iona	& 9-82
Shook, Charles H.	Prof	Ext 7490	cshook	GCNR	PHD	79.	Okla St	& 9-80
Baccari, Richard	Assoc	Ext 7490	rbaccari	DX	MBA	96	Long Isl	& 9-00
Blacker, Kelly	Asst	Ext 7490	kblacker	FMAV	MBA	87	Baruch	& 9-98
Stefano, Denise	Asst	Ext 749	dftefano	CDNU	MBA	02	Iona	& 9-06

Meredith College

Accounting Faculty — Raleigh, NC 27607-5298 — School of Business
Dept Phone: 760-8471 — 3800 Hillsborough Street

(919) Fax=760-8470 — meredith.edu — BS,MBA — Ms. Martha Yates

Name	Rank	Phone	Email					
Rotondo, Denise M.	Dean	760-8471	rotondo	Mgt	PHD	95	Fla St	2006
Wessels, Susan B.	H-Pr	760-8475	wesselss	AMCV	PHD	05	Sarasota	&1978
Oatsvall, Rebecca J.	Prof	760-8484	oatsvallr	XFP	PHD	78.	S Carol	1984
Lenard, Mary Jane	Assoc	760-8488	lenardmj	ACNS	PHD	95	Kent St	* 8-05

Merrimack College

Dept of Accounting & Finance — No Andover, MA 01845 — Girard Sch Bus & Intl C
Dept Phone: Ext 4413 — 315 Turnpike Road
Homepage: www.merrimack.edu
phone: 837-5000

(978) Fax=837-5013 — merrimack.edu — BS — Sharon LaRoche

Name	Rank	Phone	Email					
Cuomo, Robert	Dean	837-5402	cuomor		PHD	77	Boston C	2004
Hanson, Donald T.	C-Ac	Ext 4418	hansond	JFCR	MBA	70	Northeas	&1970
DelGaudio, Richard	Prof	837-5402	delgaudior	FAV	MBA	66	Northeas	&1972
Morton, Jane E.	Assoc	Ext 4421	mortonj	ACFJ	PHD	93.	Arizona	&2001
Nelson, Donald A.	Assoc	Ext 4423	nelsond	KM	MS	71	Mass	&1975
Puretz, Elliott H.	Assoc	837-5416	puretze	FXTR	MBA	74	Boston U	&1974
Wiest, David N.	Asst	Ext 4117	wiestd	F	PHD	92.	N Carol	2006

Mesa State College   Gr Junction, CO   81501-3122   (970) Fax=248-1730
Accounting Faculty   Business   mesastate.edu   BS
Dept Phone: 248-1087   1100 North Ave   Ellin Alstatt
Homepage: www.mesastate.edu/schools/sbps/acct/index.htm

Bridge, Morgan	H-Ac	248-1168	mbridge		PHD	Wyoming	1995
Rogers, David E.	Prof	248-1720	drogers	MC	MBA	72 Golden Gt	&1975
Gurka, Geoffrey J.	Assoc	248-1230	ggurka	XP	PHD	92. Mich St	&2001
Fossett, G. Craig	Asst	248-1727	cfossett	PMGV	MBA	89 Wstrn St	# * &2004

Methodist University   Fayetteville, NC   28311-1420   (910) Fax=630-7221
Accounting Faculty   Reeves School of Bus   methodist.edu   BA,BS
Dept Phone: 630-7047   5400 Ramsey Street   Victoria Wood

Zimmerman, Jeffrey	Daen	630-7320	jazimm		PHD	91 Purdue	1994
Kirchner, Mary	C-Pr	630-7048	mkirchner	FPVJ	PHD	98 Tennessee	&1996
Clark, Theresa	Prof	630-7171	tclark	LX	JM	71 N Carol	1992
Cooper, Robert	Prof	630-7063	rcooper	VCXI	DBA	97 Nova SE	* &1989
Hartman, Randall	Prof	630-7062	rhartman	AFGS	JD	93 Widener	&1997
Strickland, Pamela	Asst	630-7064	pstrickland	FPM	MBA	02 Phoenix	&2002

Metropolitan St Coll Denver   Denver, CO   80217-3362   (303) Fax=556-5120
Dept Accounting Box 173362   Business PO Box 173362   mscd.edu   D3
Dept Phone: 556-3181   1006 11th Street   Grace Reed
Homepage: www.mscd.edu/~acc

Cochran, John P.	Dean	556-3235	cochranj	Econ	PHD	85 Colorado	1984
Parker, M. Virginia	C-Pr$	556-3181		FV	PHD	82. Colorado	& 9-87
Crosser, Rick L.	Prof	556-4694	crosserr	XJ	PHD	87. Okla St	& 8-95
Laufer, Doug	Prof	556-2948	lauferd	PAFJ	PHD	85. Okla St	& 8-95
Uliss, Barbara Turk	Prof	556-3413	uliss	FSAH	PHD	91. Case Wes	& 8-96
Abbasi, Nishat	Assoc	556-3499	abbasin	ASM	PHD	87. Colorado	8-96
Holt, Andrew	Assoc	556-4428	aholt7		PHD		
Lombard, J. Larry	Assoc	556-4697	lombardl	PFAG	PHD	71. Arkansas	9-80
Murphy, Ann B.	Assoc	556-2947	murphann	CM	PHD	96. Arkansas	* 1-02
Ryu, Tae Ghil	Assoc	556-3002	ryut	FMT	PHD	93. Rutgers	& 8-93
Clifton, Gregory	Asst	556-3183	gclifto4		LLM		
Hathorn, John M.	Asst	556-3001	hathornj	FC	PHD	00. Kent St	& 8-04
Rosenbaum, Allen S.	Asst	556-4420	arosenba		PHD	68. Illinois	
Skougstad, David	Asst	556-8580	skougsta	CMP	MS	73 Colo St	3-76
Holland, Alexander	Inst	556-4692	hollanal	P	MS	77 Colorado	& 8-04
Kulkarni, Joyce	Inst	556-3183	kulkarnj	P	MBA	87 UCA	1-90

Metropolitan State Univ-MN   Minneapolis, MN   55403-1897   (612) Fax=659-7268
Department of Accounting   College of Management   metrostate.edu   BS,MBA
Dept Phone: 659-7295   1500 Hennepin Avenue

Seiler, Gary	Dean$	659-7256	gary.seiler	Mgt	PHD	89 Minnesota	
Daly, Dennis C.	C-Ac	659-7295	dennis.daly	MC	MBA	62 Detroit	* 1993
Cleveland, Grover A.	Prof	659-7297	grover.cleveland	XF	DBA	73. Indiana	&1995
Slaymaker, Adrianne E.	Assoc	659-7261	adrianne slay+		DBA	84. Kentucky	&
Dosch, Jennifer	Asst	659-7249	jennifer.dosch	M	MBA	92 St Thom	* 2005
Wilson, Michael	Asst	659-7263	michael.wilson	F	MBA	94 Minnesota	&2001

University of Miami   Coral Gables, FL   33146-6531   (305) Fax=284-5737   ß (123) 1957,1963
Dept of Accounting   School of Business Adm   miami.edu   BA,MST
Dept Phone: 284-5428   5250 University Dr, KE301   Willie Risby-Hannah
Homepage: http://www.bus.miami.edu/acc/

Sugrue, Paul K.	Dean	284-4643	psugrue	Mas	PHD	77 Mass	1977
Tatum, Kay W.	C-Ac$	284-6903	ktatum	A	PHD	86. Tx Tech	&1986
Phillips, Lawrence C.	Prof	284-6669	lphillip	X	PHD	66. Ohio St	&1985
Dennis-Escoffier, Shirley	Assoc	284-5577	sdennis	X	PHD	81 U Miami	&1983
Friedman, Mark E.	Assoc	284-6296	markfriedman	CDS	PHD	77 NYU	&1977
Holzmann, Oscar J.	Assoc	284-6342	holzmann	IFV	PHD	74. Penn St	1980
Quintana, Olga	Assoc	284-4613	oquintan	MNG	DBA	75. Geo Wash	&1979
Rushinek, Avi	Assoc	284-6350	arush	SM	PHD	79 Tx-Austin	1980
Burnett, Royce D.	Asst	284-5428	rburnett	M	PHD	03. Okla St	* 2003
Falsetta, Diana	Asst	284-8642	falsetta	X	PHD	02. S Carol	&2006
Henry, Elaine R.	Asst	284-4821	ehenry777@a	F	PHD	05. Rutgers	2005
Yang, Ya-wen	Asst	284-1745	yyang	F	PHD	03. Tennessee	&2004
Collins, Jacklyn	Lect	284-9902	jcollins		MPRA	03 U Miami	2006
Levine, Seth	Lect	234-4927	slevine	PM	MBA	89 U Miami	&2001
Perez, Mario	Lect	284-6668	mperez		MST	Fla Intl	2006
Rodriguez, Juan M.	Lect	284-5812	jrodrigu	PXI	MPA	03 U Miami	&1991
Werner, Michael L.	Lect	284-6507	mwerner	PFM	MPA	83 U Miami	&1984

Miami University Oxford, OH 45056-3628 (513) Fax=529-4740 ß (13) 1932,1963
Department of Accountancy R.T. Farmer Sch Bus Adm muohio.edu BS,MACC
Dept Phone: 529-6200 310 Laws Hall Susan Asher
Homepage: http://www.sba.muohio.edu/acc/

Jenkins, Roger L.	Dean	529-3631	jenkinrl	Mktg	PHD	76	Ohio St	7-02
Rubin, Marc A.	C-Pr	529-3381	rubinma	FG	PHD	85.	Tx-Austin	&1990
PricewaterhouseCoopers Professor of Accountancy								
Arlinghaus, Barry P.	Prof	529-6216	arlingbp	X	PHD	79.	Cincinnati	&1983
Deloitte & Touche Professor of Accountancy								
Ballou, Brian	Prof	529-6213	balloubj	AM	PHD	96.	Mich St	& 8-03
Campbell, Robert J.	Prof	529-6200	campberj	M	DBA	76.	Indiana	* 1-77
Cashell, James D.	Prof	529-6204	casheljd	SA	PHD	84.	Cincinnati	&1986
C. Rolin Niswonger Professor of Accounting								
Cottell, Philip G. Jr.	Prof	529-6214	cottelpg	FE	DBA	82.	Kentucky	1982
Cumming, John	Emer	529-6212	cumminj	FGN	PHD	73.	Illinois	& 8-77
Hock, Clayton A.	Prof	529-6246	hockca	IF	PHD	74.	Penn St	& 1-74
Porcano, Thomas M.	Prof	529-6221	porcantm	XI	DBA	76.	Indiana	& 1-77
Arthur Andersen & Co. Alumni Professor of Accounting								
Salzarulo, W. Peter	Prof	529-6245	salzarwp	X	PHD	73.	Colorado	& 9-73
Ernst & Young Professor of Accountancy								
Brewer, Peter C.	Assoc	529-6271	brewerpc	M	PHD	94.	Tennessee	1994
Eaton, Tim V.	Assoc	529-2132	eatont	F	PHD	96.	Tennessee	& 8-05
Heitger, Dan L.	Assoc	529-6208	heitgedl	M	PHD	00.	Mich St	8-04
Rankin, Larry J.	Assoc	529-6217	rankinlj	AE	PHD	82.	Mich St	&1980
Presutti, Anthony H. Jr.	Asst	529-6202	presutah	SMC	PHD	88.	Cincinnati	&1989
Schultz, Thomas D.	Asst	529-4127	schulttd	XF	PHD	04.	Ariz St	& 8-06
Ames, Roger	Inst	529-8145	amesrd	P	MBA	82	St Fran	& 1-01
Bentley, Kathleen	Inst	785-3200	bentlek2	P	MBA	04	Franciscan	& 8-06
Collins, Ronald	Inst	529-6212	collinrg	P	MS	77	Missouri	& 8-05
Himes, Ella R.	Inst	529-1869	himesr	P	MBA	79	Wright St	& 8-06
Kennedy, Kathryn	Inst	529-6200	kennedkl	P	MBA	82	Miami U	& 8-05
Metcalf, Christopher C.	Inst	727-3200	metcalcc	P	MBA	74	Indiana	8-00
Eighme, Jan E.	Lect	529-6244	eighmeje	S	PHD	01.	Fla St	8-00
Wiegand, Daniel G.	Lect	529-6207	wiegandg	P	MBA	76	Miami U	2003

University of Michigan Ann Arbor, MI 48109-1234 (734) Fax=647-2871 ß 1919,1963
Department of Accounting Stephen M. Ross Sch Bus umich.edu BBA,MAC,MBA,PHD
Dept Phone: 647-4911 701 Tappan Street Pam Russell
Homepage: webuser.bus.umich.edu/departments/accounting

Dolan, Robert J.	Dean	764-1361	rjdolan	Mktg	PHD	77	Rochester	2001
Lundholm, Russell J.	C-Pr	763-5934	lundholm	F	PHD	87.	Iowa	1993
Arthur Andersen Professor of Accounting								
Griffin, Carleton H.	Emer	764-0217	carl.griffin	1996	JD	53	Michigan	&1985
Assistant Director, Paton Accounting Center								
Imhoff, Eugene A. Jr. (Gene)	Prof	763-1192	imhoff	FI	PHD	73.	Mich St	& 8-77
Ernst & Young Professor of Accounting								
Indjejikian, Raffi J.	Prof	936-1460	raffii	MC	PHD	89.	Penn	& 8-96
Robert L. Dixon Collegiate Professor of Accounting								
Lanen, William N.	Prof	763-0487	lanen	MC	PHD	83.	Penn	1990
Michael and Joan Sakkinen Accounting Scholar								
Dichev, Ilia D.	Assoc	763-9780	dichev	F	PHD	95.	U Wash	8-96
Michael and Joan Sakkinen Accounting Scholar								
Hanlon, Michelle	Assoc	647-4954	mhanlon	FX	PHD	03.	U Wash	2002
Wright, David W.	Assoc	763-1292	dwwright	AF	PHD	86.	Mich St	&1984
Director of MAcc Program								
Cheng, Shijun	Asst	763-6822	chengsj	M	PHD	01.	Pittsburgh	2001
Hooper, Cameron G.	Asst	615-4178	chooper	AF	PHD	03	NS Wales	2001
Lehavy, Reuven	Asst	763-1508	rlehavy	F	PHD	97.	Nrthwstrn	2002
Bank One Corporation Assistant Professor in Business Administration								
Li, Feng	Asst	936-2771	feng		PHD	05.	Chicago	
Matejka, Michal	Asst	764-3175	matejka	M	PHD	02	Tilburg	2004
Nagar, Venkatesh (Venky)	Asst	647-3292	venky	M	PHD	99	Penn	1998
Auerbach Faculty Fellow								
Shakespeare, Catherine M.	Asst	647-6984	shakespe	F	PHD	02.	Illinois	2001
Bird, Karen S.	Lect	763-0214	birdk	F	MBA	88	Michigan	1988
DeSimpelare, James M.	Lect	764-2552	desimpel	FX	MBA	92	Indiana	&1993
Dungan, Kelli	Lect	647-7926	kdungan	F	MACC	93	Michigan	1998
Klemstine, Charles F.	Lect	764-0122	cfk	AM	PHD	91	Michigan	1987
Williams, Jefferson	Lect	763-5933	williamj	FX	MA	96	Michigan	6-96

Univ of Michigan-Dearborn Dearborn, MI 48126-2638 (313) Fax=271-9837 1997,1997
Dept of Accounting & Finance School of Management umd.umich.edu BBA,MBA,MSA,MSF
Dept Phone: 593-5230 19000 Hubbard Drive Victoria Hage
Homepage: www.umd.umich.edu

Harkness, Michael D.	C-Ac	593-5247	mharknes	SX	PHD	99	S Fla	& 8-97

Bayou, Mohamed E.	Prof	593-9962	mbayou	MF	PHD	83. Cincinnati	1990
Bublitz, Bruce O.	Prof	593-5248	bbublitz	F	PHD	82. Illinois	& 8-05
Special Assistant to the Provost							
Foran, Michael F.	Prof	593-5286	mforan	TFE	PHD	72. U Wash	# * & 8-01
Green, Brian Patrick	Prof	593-5301	bpgreen	ANS	PHD	91. Kent St	& 5-92
Martin, Susan W.	Prof	593-5030	swmartin	NGX	PHD	88. Mich St	# * &
Blatz, Robert E. Jr.	Assoc		blatzr	LX	LLM	91 NYU	9-05
Philipich, Kirk L.	Asst		klpdba	FAV	DBA	84. Indiana	9-05
Baker, Susan	Lect		skbaker	FM	MA	95 Michigan	9-05

Univ of Michigan-Flint — Flint, MI 48502-1950 — (810) Fax=762-3282 — ß 1982,1986
Accounting Faculty — School of Management — umflint.edu — BBA,MBA
Dept Phone: 237-6589 — 303 East Kearsley St. — Sharon Seames
Homepage: umflint.edu/departments/som

Helmuth, John A.	Dean			FIX	PHD	81 S Carol	7-07
Fortner, Richard W.	Emer	237-6589	rwfortner	1999	DBA	64. Indiana	& 9-80
Moreland, Keith A.	Prof	762-3264	moreland	AFE	PHD	92. Cincinnati	* &1994
Chen, Clement C.	Assoc	762-3267	clementc	MBCE	PHD	01. Kentucky	2001
Arya, Avinash C.	Asst	762-3160	aarya	F	PHD	99. SUNY-Buf	9-05
Peng, Jacob	Asst	762-3160	jcpeng	S	PHD	05. Tx Tech	9-05

Michigan State University — East Lansing, MI 48824-1122 — (517) Fax=432-1101 — ß (13) 1953,1963
Dept Accounting & Info Sys — Eli Broad Grad Sch Mgt — msu.edu — BA,MS,PHD
Dept Phone: 355-7486 — N270 North Business Complex — Patty Geller
Homepage: www.bus.msu.edu/acc

Duncan, Robert B.	Dean	355-8378	duncan	Mgt	PHD	71 Yale	1-02
Petroni, Kathy R.	C-Pr$	432-2924	petroni	FA	PHD	90. Michigan	& 9-90
Deloitte/Michael Licata Professor of Accounting							
Arens, Alvin A.	Emer	432-2918	arens	2006	PHD	70. Minnesota	& 9-68
Dilley, Steven C.	Prof	432-2926	dilleys	X	PHD	72. Wisconsin	& 9-72
Haka, Susan F.	Prof	432-2920	suehaka	MBI	PHD	83. Kansas	& 9-82
Ernst & Young Professor of Accounting							
Luft, Joan L.	Prof	432-2917	luftj	MB	PHD	92. Cornell	1992
Eli Broad Professor of Accounting							
McCarthy, William E.	Prof	432-2913	mccarth4	S	PHD	78. Mass	1-78
Outslay, Edmund	Prof	432-2912	outslay	XI	PHD	81. Michigan	& 1-81
Deloitte/Michael Licata Teaching Fellow							
Pentland, Brian T.	Prof	432-2927	pentlan2	S	PHD	91 MIT	2000
Ramesh, Krishnamoorthy	Prof	432-8350	rameshk	FK	PHD	91. Mich St	8-03
Plante & Moran Teaching Fellow							
Sambamurthy, V.	Prof	432-2916	smurthy	S	PHD	89 Minnesota	8-02
Eli Broad Professor of Information Technology							
Shields, Michael D.	Prof	432-2915	shields	M	PHD	78. Pittsburgh	1997
Schaberg Endowed Chair in Accounting							
Sollenberger, Harold M.	Prof	432-2914	hsolly	MI	DBA	67. Indiana	&1967
Speier, Cheri	Prof	355-7448	cspeier	S	PHD	96. Indiana	8-98
Ward, D. Dewey	Emer	432-2919	wardddd	2006	PHD	79. Tx-Austin	9-78
Anderson, Matthew J.	Assoc	432-2910	ander130	FB	PHD	82. Mich St	1988
Anthony, Joseph H.	Assoc	432-2921	anthony	FT	PHD	84. Ohio St	&1983
Grabski, Severin V.	Assoc	432-2922	grabski	SD	PHD	83. Ariz St	* &1983
Hogan, Chris E.	Assoc	353-8647	hogan@bus.	AF	PHD	94. Ohio St	&2006
Jacobs, Fred H.	Assoc	432-2911	jacobs	MQ	PHD	77. Illinois	& 3-76
Johnson, Marilyn F.	Assoc	432-0152	john1614	F	PHD	92. U Wash	&2000
Krishnan, Ranjani	Assoc	353-4687	krishn15	M	PHD	98. Pittsburgh	8-98
Marshall, Ronald M.	Emer	432-4407	marsha21	2003	PHD	69. Ohio St	&1969
Sedatole, Karen L.	Assoc	432-2919	sedatole	M	PHD	00. Michigan	&2006
Weber, Richard P.	Assoc	432-2925	weberr	X	PHD	75. Michigan	& 9-82
Bronson, Scott N.	Asst	432-0615	bronso15	A	PHD	06. Tennessee	&2006
Jiang, John	Asst	432-3031	jiangj	F	PHD	05. Georgia	2005
Lankton, Nancy	Asst	432-3229	lankton	S	PHD	00 Ariz St	1-01
McKnight, D. Harrison	Asst	432-2929	mcknig26	S	PHD	97 Minnesota	2001
Wang, Isabel	Asst	432-2923	wang	F	PHD	05. Georgia	2005
Bettinghaus, Bruce	Lect	432-2909	betting3	F	PHD	00. Penn St	1-02
Bokemeier, L. Charles	Lect	432-9849	bokemei3	FG	DBA	83. Kentucky	&2000

Michigan Technological Univ — Houghton, MI 49931-1295 — (906) Fax=487-1963 — 2001,2001
Accounting Faculty — School of Bus & Econ — mtu.edu — BA,BS
Dept Phone: 487-2669 — 1400 Townsend Drive — Judy Chapman
Homepage: sbea.mtu.edu/rrtidd/accounting/

Walck, Christa L.	Dean		cwalck	Mgt	PHD	80 Harvard	1986
Davis, Larry R.	Assoc	487-3081	lrdavis	AFV	PHD	86. Indiana	& 9-93
Buche, Mari W.	Asst	487-3440	mwbache	S	PHD	03. Kansas	
Johnson, Randy	Lect		rdjohnson	X	MS	85 Clarkson	1995
Tuoriniemi, Joel C.	Lect	487-1877	jctuorin	XL	JD	87 Detroit	2001
Warrington, Ann	Lect	487-2669	acwarrin	CFM	MS	La Tech	&1999

MidAmerica Nazarene Univ   Olathe, KS   66062-1899   (913) Fax=791-3409
Accounting Faculty   Div of Business Adm   mnu.edu   BA
Dept Phone: 791-3440   2030 E. College Way   Leanna Higgins

Moore, Frank	Dean	Ext 210	fmoore	J	PHD		Vanderbilt	1985
Ford, Mark	C-Pr	Ext 173	mford	Law	JD	90	Missouri	1991
Myrtle, Jamie	Assoc	Ext 174	jmyrtle	U	MBA		Kansas	&2001

Middle Tennessee State Univ   Murfreesboro, TN 37132   (615) Fax=898-5839   ß (1) 1977,1983
Dept of Accounting PO Box 50   College of Business   mtsu.edu   BBA,MBA,MS
Dept Phone: 898-2558   1301 East Main Street   Violet Rigsby, Melanie Nicholas
Homepage: http://www.mtsu.edu/~business/accounting/index.html

Name	Rank	Phone	Email					
Burton, E. James	Dean	898-2764	eburton	BFMC	PHD	76	Illinois	&1990
Thomas, Paula B.	C-Pr	898-5655	pbthomas	FT	DBA	87.	Miss St	* &1989
Advisory Board Distinguished Professor of Accounting								
Colvard, Robert G.	Prof	898-2353	rcolvard	ATF	PHD	81.	Georgia	& 1-78
Farmer, Larry E.	Prof	898-2356	lfarmer	AFTG	DBA	75.	La Tech	# * &1980
Ward, Terry J.	Prof	898-2644	tward	F	PHD	91.	Tennessee	&1994
Wilson, Harold O.	Prof	898-2367	hwilson	FMAQ	PHD	68.	Alabama	&1983
Bush, James L. Jr.	Assoc	898-2102	jlbush	CM	PHD	77.	Arkansas	&1985
Harper, Betty S.	Assoc	898-2619	bharper	P	EDD	76	Miss St	&1982
Harper, Phil	Assoc	898-2625	pharper	XF	JD	70	Nashvil	&1966
Harrington, Jeannie D.	Assoc	898-2038	jdjohnson	FM	PHD	95.	Kentucky	* &1988
Koski, Timothy R.	Assoc	898-2558	tkoski	X	PHD	98.	Missouri	&2002
Smith, G. Robert Jr.	Assoc	898-2345	smitty	GF	PHD	95.	Tx Tech	& 8-99
Bahmanziari, Tammy E.	Asst	898-2367	tbahmanz	SM	PHD	06.	S Illinois	2006
Cox, Carol	Asst	898-5139	ccox		PHD	03	Va Comm	&2006
James, Kevin L.	Asst	898-2558	kjames	FA	PHD	00.	Tennessee	&2000
Kile, Charles O.	Asst	898-2354	ckile	FP	PHD	93.	Wash U	2003
McSwain, Dwayne N.	Asst	898-2347	smcswain		PHD	02.	Tx-Arlin	&2003
Phillips, Mary E.	Asst	898-2372	mephilli	F	PHD	04.	Kentucky	&2004
Wermert, John G.	Asst	898-2558	jwermert	SA	PHD	95	Indiana	* &2002

Midwestern State University   Wichita Falls TX   76308-2099   (940) Fax=397-4280
Department of Accounting   Dillard Col Bus Adm   mwsu.edu   BBA,MBA
Dept Phone: 397-4364   3410 Taft Boulevard   Shauna Blackman

Name	Rank	Phone	Email					
Chelte, Anthony F.	Dean	397-4088	tony.chelte		PHD	83	Mass	2005
Fritzsch, Ralph B.	C-Ac	397-4364	ralph.fritzsch	SCM	DBA	72	Geo Wash	& 9-84
Gooch, Roxanne L.	Assoc	397-6206	roxanne.gooch	FM	PHD	05.	Oklahoma	& 9-06
Bauer, Kathleen	Asst	397-4716	kathleen.bauer	VPX	MA	72	Alabama	& 9-81

Millersville Univ of PA   Millersville, PA   17551-0302   (717) Fax=871-2464
Dept of Business Adm   Sch Humanities & Soc Sc   millersville.edu   BS
Dept Phone: 872-3566   North George Street
Homepage: www.muweb.millersville.edu/

Name	Rank	Phone	Email					
Short, John N.	Dean	872-3553	john.short					2002
Blazer, Eric L.	C-Ac	871-2273	eric.blazer		PHD	96	Va Tech	1996
Bhatia, Ramesh C.	Prof	872-3642	ramesh.bhatia	M	PHD	78	W Virginia	* 1978
Frazer, J. Douglas	Prof	872-3566	doug.frazer	MSTV	PHD	87.	Temple	&1979
Galante, Joseph	Assoc	872-3749	joseph.galante	X	JD	92	Cooley	1998

Millikin University   Decatur, IL   62522-2084   (217) Fax=424-6286
Accounting Faculty   Tabor School Business   mail.millikin.edu   BS
Dept Phone: 424-6284   1184 West Main Street

Name	Rank	Phone	Email					
Dahl, James G.	Dean	424-6285	jdahl	Mgt	PHD	91	Mo-StLou	1990
Brown, Michael H.	C-As	424-6381	mbrown	FXV	PHD	94.	Miss	&2002
Smith, Charles R.	Assoc	424-6288	crsmith	FMO	PHD		Amer-Lond	&1992

Millsaps College   Jackson, MS   39210-0001   (601) Fax=974-1260   ß 1990,1990
Accountancy Program   Else School of Mgt   millsaps.edu   BBA,MBA,MACC
Dept Phone: 974-1250   1701 North State Street   Martha Lee

Name	Rank	Phone	Email					
McMillan, Howard L.	Dean	974-1250	howard.mcmillan		BBA	60	Miss	2006
Burke, Kimberly G.	D-Pr	974-1280	burkekg	ASFB	PHD	95.	Okla St	&1995
Kelly Gene Cook Chair of Business Administration								
Beeler, Jesse D.	Prof	974-1269	beelejd	FTPB	PHD	94.	Tx-Arlin	&1994
H.F. McCarty Chair in Business Administration								
Culpepper, David H.	Prof	974-1272	culpedh	PFXI	PHD	91.	Alabama	&1984
Kelly Gene Cook Chair of Business Administration								
Collins, Jane	Inst			XFG	LLM	05	U Miami	2005
Warren, Sanford D.	Inst	974-1252	warresd	GFPX	MBA	65	S Miss	&1994

University of Minnesota Minneapolis, MN 55455-0413   (612) Fax=626-1335   ß (1) 1920,1963
Department of Accounting Carlson School of Mgt   csom.umn.edu   BS,MBCC,MBT,PHD
Dept Phone: 624-6506   321 19th Avenue South   Lisa Bell
Homepage: www.csom.edu/WWWPages/Depts/Acct/

Rayburn, Judy D.	C-Pr	624-3840	jrayburn	F	PHD	85 Iowa	&1985
Dickhaut, John W.	Prof	624-9891	jdickhaut	B	PHD	70. Ohio St	1976
Curtis Carlson Professor							
Joyce, Edward J.	Prof	624-5753	ejoyce	BM	PHD	76. Illinois	1981
Associate Dean							
Kanodia, Chandra	Prof	624-6880	ckanodia	M	PHD	78. Car Mellon	1981
Arthur Andersen-Duane Kullberg Land Grant Chair							
Duke, Gordon Leon	Assoc	624-4853	gduke	ASI	PHD	80. Georgia	& 9-81
Gigler, Frank B.	Assoc	624-7641	fgigler	B	PHD	92. Minnesota	2002
Shroff, Pervin K.	Assoc	626-1570	pshroff	FA	PHD	92. Columbia	1998
Issaevitch, Thomas	Asst	626-3277	tissaevitch		PHD	06. Columbia	2006
Venkataraman, Ram	Asst	625-7584	rvenkataraman	F	PHD	01. Penn St	&2001
Zhang, Ivy Xiying	Asst	626-3118	izhang	IF	PHD	06. Rochester	2005
Beil, Frank	SLect	624-7390	fbeil	F	MS	77 N Dakota	&
Biondich, Nick	SLect	624-7055	nbiondich	FA	MS	79 N Dakota	&1990
Caliendo, Charles	SLect	625-6877	ccaliendo	FX	MBA	93 Minnesota	&1995
Gutterman, Paul	SLect	624-8515	pgutterman	X	LLM	88 NYU	&1992
Kallio, Larry	SLect	624-9818	lkallio	A	MBA	Minn-Dul	
Tranter, Terry	SLect	624-5246	ttranter	F	PHD	70. U Wash	&1979
Sellner, Mark	Lect		msellner				
White, Paul	Lect	626-9156	pwhite	M	ABD	Minnesota	

U of Minnesota Duluth   Duluth, MN   55812-3029   (218) Fax=726-8510   2000,2000
Department of Accounting Labovitz Sch Bus & Econ d.umn.edu   BAC
Dept Phone: 726-7966   412 Library Drive   Kora G. Cavanaugh
Homepage: http://www.d.umn.edu/sbe/departments/accounting

Knudsen, Kjell R.	Dean	726-7288	kkundsen	Mgt	PHD	73 Minnesota	1979
Roline, Alan C.	C-Ac	726-8550	aroline	JKL	JD	87 Minnesota	1993
Brannan, Rodger L.	Assoc	726-8566	rbrannan	GNEC	PHD	89. Nebraska	& 8-89
Lin, Jerry W.	Assoc	726-7972	jlin	FASB	PHD	94. North Tx	1999
Kang, Gerui	Asst				ABD	North Tx	2007
Skalberg, Randall	Asst	726-7150	rskalber	JLX	LLM	96 Case Wes	2001
Yang, Joon S.	Asst	736-7454	jyang1	FMS	PHD	02. Temple	2002
Salmela, Karen E.	Inst	726-8541	ksalmela	M	MBA	91 Minnesota	1989

Minnesota St Univ Mankato   Mankato, MN   56001   (507) Fax=389-5497   1999
Accounting Department College of Business mnsu.edu   BS
Dept Phone: 389-2965   Dianna Brandenburg
Homepage: www.business.mankato.msus.edu/dept/acct

Johnson, Scott	Dean	389-5420		Mktg	PHD	90 Mich St	2002
Rolfes, Mary S.	C-Ac	389-5427	mary.rolfes	CFQ	MAS	71 Illinois	1979
Habib, Abo-El-Yazeed	Prof	389-5408	abo-el-yazeed.+	FTV	PHD	83. North Tx	1988
Schwinghammer, Paul H.	Prof	389-6440	paul.schwing+	F	PHD	86. Arkansas	&1986
Woehrle, Stephen L.	Prof	389-5407	stephen.woehrle	MCG	PHD	78 Nebraska	1976
Baird, Jane E.	Assoc	389-2314	jane.baird	AP	PHD	94. Cincinnati	&1993
Okleshen, Marilyn	Assoc	389-5411	marilyn.okleshen	CMP	PHD	91. Nebraska	&1983
Zelin, Robert C. II	Assoc	389-5412	robert.zelin	MD	PHD	91. Indiana	* &1993
Brennan, Paul J.	Asst	389-5415	paul.brennan	X	PHD	99. S Illinois	2002
Hwang, Iny	Asst	389-5413	iny.hwang	C	PHD	05 Tx-Dallas	2005
Olach, Thomas J.	Asst	389-5410	thomas.olach	AP	PHD	05. Miss St	2005

Minnesota State U Moorhead   Moorhead, MN   56563   (218) Fax=477-2238
School of Business   College Bus & Industry mnstate.edu   BS
Dept Phone: 477-4646   1104 7th Avenue South   Mary Jane Langseth
Homepage: www.mnstate.edu

Crockett, David J.	Dean	477-2076	crockett	Fnce	PHD	76 Iowa	6-93
Phillips, Cynthia					JD	76 N Dakota	1979
Dexter, Lee	C-Pr	477-4071	dexter	EVF	PHD	86. Nebraska	* &1988
Bader, Mary	Prof	477-4069	bader	LX	LLM	91 Wm Mitch	&2000
Sanderson, George C.	Prof	477-2268	sanderg	NFM	PHD	85. Nebraska	&1976
Sliwoski, Leonard J.	Prof	477-2666	sliwoski	F	PHD	88 N Dakota	* &1982
Violet, William	Prof	477-4074	violetbi	LI	JD	97 N Dakota	# * &1981
Hansen, James D.	Assoc	477-2594	hansenjd	AP	PHD	93. Nebraska	&2002
Segovia, Joann R.	Assoc	477-4067	segovia	SVPB	PHD	03. Tx Tech	&2002
Erickson, Sheri	Asst	477-4073	sherieri	ACP	PHD	06 N Dak St	&1998

Minot State University   Minot, ND   58707-5002   (701) Fax=858-3127
Dept of Accounting & Finance College of Business minotstateu.edu   BS
Dept Phone: 858-3089   500 University Ave West   Deanna Head
Homepage: http://www.misu.nodak.edu/

Linrud, JoAnn	Dean	858-3113	joann.linrud	Mktg	PHD	84 Arkansas	2006
Wahlund, Jay L.	C-As	858-3207	jay.wahlund	FPNG	MPA	94 Nebraska	&1990

Caborle, Carla	Asst	858-3824	carla.caborle	FXUP	MS	96	Colo St		&2004
Fedje, Patti A.	Asst	858-3293	patti.fedje	MPFD	MACC	87	N Dakota		&1987
Houston, Joan E.	Asst	858-3290	joan.houston	PAC	MS	81	N Dakota	*	&1984
Walz, Karen S.	Asst	858-3292	karen.walz	FPV	MS	80	N Dakota		&1980

Mississippi College — Clinton, MS 39058 — (601) Fax = 925-3954 — mc.edu — BSBA,MBA — Shea Elkins
Accounting Faculty — School of Business
Dept Phone: 925-3214 — 200 South Capital Street

Eduardo, Marcelo	Dean	925-3419	eduardo	Fnce	PHD	95	Miss		1997
Jones, Jacqueline	Assoc	925-3415	jones03	FRVG	ABD	71	Miss St		&1971
Corkern, Sheree M.	Asst	925-3422	corkern	AFPS	PHD	04.	JacksonSt		1985
Morgan, Mark	Asst	925-3214	morg	PAFM	PHD	07	JacksonSt		2006
Nix, Wayne E.	Asst	925-3214	wnix	AFPS	DBA	95.	Miss St		&2004
Parks, Sandra	Asst	925-3417	parks	PAFM	MBA	76	Miss Col		&1976

University of Mississippi — University, MS 38677-1848 — (662) Fax = 915-7483 — ß (13) 1944,1972 — olemiss.edu — BA,MACC,MTX,PHD — Heather Chance
Accounting Faculty — Patterson Sch Accntcy
Dept Phone: 915-7468 — 200 Conner Hall
Homepage: www.olemiss.edu/depts/accountancy

Wilder, W. Mark	Dean$	915-5756	acwilder	FGN	PHD	94	Fla St		& 8-93
Davis, James W.	Prof	915-7468	acdavis	VH	PHD	72.	Miss		&1965
Peery Chair of Accountancy									
Elam, Rick	Prof	915-5281	relam	CS	PHD	73.	Missouri		& 8-99
Reynolds Distinguished Professor									
Flesher, Dale L.	Prof	915-7623	acdlf	FHMO	PHD	75.	Cincinnati	# *	& 9-77
Arthur Andersen Alumni Professer; Associate Dean									
Flesher, Tonya K.	Prof	915-5731	actonya	XH	PHD	79.	Miss		&1979
Arthur Andersen Alumni Professor									
Lawrence, Howard J.	ClPr			FM	PHD	72.	Miss	*	&2005
Stocks, Morris H.	Prof	915-5773	acstocks	FCB	PHD	91.	S Carol		& 8-91
Senior Vice Chancellor									
Cassidy, Judith H.	Assoc	915-5445	jcassidy	MSI	PHD	86.	Tx Tech	*	& 1-89
Nichols, Dave Leroy	Assoc	915-5237	acdln	FA	PHD	92.	Okla St		& 1-91
Bizarro, Pascal A.	Asst	915-5755	pbizarro	S	PHD	03.	Alabama		2003
Morf, Duffy A.	ClAs	915-5266	mgmorf	CFGH	PHD	00.	Miss		& 8-00
Payne, Elizabeth A.	Asst		lizpayne	AF	PHD	02.	Kentucky		&2005
Rhodes, William R.	ClAs	915-5449	wrhodes	LX	JD	82	Miss		& 1-97
Shaw, J. Riley	Asst	915-5446	jrshaw	FX	PHD	02.	Okla St		& 8-02
Wang, Karl J.	Asst	915-3980	karlwang	AB	PHD	03.	S Carol		&2003
McCaffrey, Suzanne	Inst	915-5999	suzannem	P	MACC	97	Miss		& 8-00

Mississippi Univ for Women — Columbus, MS 39701 — (662) Fax = 329-7458 — muw.edu — BS — Mary Brook
Dept Accounting & MIS W-940 — Div of Business & Comm
Dept Phone: 329-7152

Balazs, Anne L.	Dean$	329-7153	abalazs	Mktg	PHD		Mass		
McClintock, Margareat E.	C	329-7257	maggiem	Cis	PHD		Ohio U		
Bruington, Rex G.	Asst	329-7165	rbruing	A	MS		Miss St		&1994
Russell, Louisa L.	Inst	329-7156	llr1	FP	MPA	02	Miss St		2004

Mississippi State Univ — Miss St, MS 39762-5661 — (662) Fax = 325-1646 — ß (13) 1960,1964 — cobilan.msstate.edu — BAC,MPA,MTX,PHD — Margaret Cordell
Sch of Accountancy Box EF — College Bus & Industry
Dept Phone: 325-3710 — Darden Avenue
Homepage: http://www.cbi.msstate.edu/cobi/sac/
email @1 = msstate.edu

Hollingsworth, Danny P.	Dean	325-2580	dhollingsworth	FX	DBA	88	Memphis		& 7-00
H. Devon Graham, Jr. Professorship in Accounting									
Herring, Clyde E.	D-Ac$	325-7451	ceh4@1	FT	PHD	88.	Alabama		&1986
Bill Simmons Teaching Fellow									
McNair, Frances E.	Prof	325-1636	fmcnair	XMP	PHD	87.	Miss		&1987
KPMG Peat Marwick Professorship in Accounting									
Addy, Noel D.	Assoc	325-1644	naddy	F	PHD	85.	Florida		&1991
Lehman, Mark W.	Assoc	325-1641	mlehman	AS	PHD	95.	Miss		&1984
Tenneco Professorship in Accounting									
Rigsby, John T.	Assoc	325-1640	jrigsby	FA	DBA	86.	Memphis		&1989
McWhorter, Laurie B.	Asst	325-1637	lmcwhorter	M	PHD	01.	Kentucky	*	&2004
Weidenmier, Marcia L.	Asst	325-1638	mweidenmier	S	PHD	00.	Tx-Austin		2004
Yoder, Timothy R.	Asst	325-1634	try11@1	X	PHD	06.	Penn St		8-06

Miss State Univ Meridian — Meridian, MS 39307-5799 — (601) Fax = 484-0495 — meridian.msstate.edu — BS — Ms. Stacey Parkes
Accounting Faculty — Div Business & Industry
Dept Phone: 484-0152 — 1000 Highway 19 North
Homepage: msuinfo.ur.msstae.edu/meridian/

Nichols, Harold J.	Dean	484-0221	hnichols		PHD	71	Indiana		2002
Tucci, Jack	C-Pr	484-0151	jtucci		PHD	96	North Tx		2003
Allen, Paul W.	Prof	484-0157	pallen	FM	DBA	94.	Miss St		&1986
Ennis, Kevin L.	Asst	484-0161	kennis	AX	PHD	05.	JacksonSt	# *	& 8-95

Mississippi Valley St Univ
Accounting Faculty Box 7252
Dept Phone: 254-3600

Itta Bena, MS   38941-1400
Department of Business
14000 Highway 82 West

(601) Fax = 254-6704
mvsu.edu

Mrs. Mary Carter

Lee, Dae Sung	Dean	254-3801	dslee	Econ	PHD	69	Mass	1999
Brookhart, Jess	Assoc	254-3600	jmbrookhart	AC	PHD		Alabama	2002
Ahuja, Mulak	Asst	254-3602	mahuja	AC	MBA		Delta St	1982
Simms, Walter	Inst	254-3712	wsimms		MPA		Delta St	8-98

U of Missouri - Columbia
School of Accountancy
Dept Phone: 882-4463
Homepage: business.missouri.edu

Columbia, MO   65211
College of Business
303 Cornell Hall

(573) Fax = 882-2437
missouri.edu

ß (13) 1926,1964
BSA,MACC,PHD
Mary Meyer

Walker, Bruce J.	Dean	882-6688	walkerb	Mktg	DBA	71	Colorado	6-90
Howard, Thomas P.	D-Pr	882-3225	howardtho	AE	PHD	78.	Ariz St	& 8-04
Joseph A. Silvoso Director								
Arunachalam, Vairam	Prof	882-1935	arunachalamv	SB	PHD	91.	Illinois	* 1991
PricewaterhouseCoopers/Joseph A. Silvoso Professor								
Francis, Jere R.	Prof	882-5156	francisjr	FA	PHD	82	N Eng-Au	&1994
KPMG/Joseph A. Silvoso Distinguished Research Professor								
Khurana, Inder K.	Prof	882-3474	khuranai	F	PHD	89.	Ariz St	&1989
Deloitte Professor								
Nikolai, Loren A.	Prof	882-2869	nikolail	F	PHD	73	Minnesota	&1976
Ernst & Young Professor								
Mauldin, Elaine G.	Assoc	882-2474	mauldine	SA	PHD	97.	Nebraska	&1997
BKD Professor								
Pereira, Raynolde	Assoc	882-6253	pereirar	X	PHD	01.	Arizona	2000
Andersen/Joseph A. Silvoso Professor								
Prather-Kinsey, Jenice J.	Assoc	882-3671	pratherj	CHI	PHD	85.	Alabama	&1984
Shaw, Kenneth W.	Assoc	882-5939	shawke	F	PHD	95.	Wisconsin	&2002
CBIZ/MHM Scholar								
Farber, David B.	Asst	882-6867	farberd	AF	PHD	02.	Cornell	&2006
Moser, William J.	Asst	882-4463	moserw	X	PHD	05.	Arizona	&2005
Wheeler, Patrick R.	Asst	882-6056	wheelerp	S	PHD	99.	Geo St	&2002
Zhang, May H.	Asst	882-4463	zhangm	F	PHD	05.	Tx-Austin	2005
Cunningham, Billie M.	AcTch	882-5665	cunninghambm	P	PHD	80.	North Tx	1994
Hockman, Kristen	AsTch	882-1071	hockmank	GA	MACC	00	Missouri	2004
Kleen, Penny L.	AsTch	882-1050	kleenp	F	PHD	96.	Missouri	&2007
Prestigiacomo, Chris	AsTch	882-7227	prestigiacomoc	FM	PHD	96	Missouri	* 2004

U Missouri - Kansas City
Department of Accountancy
Dept Phone: 235-2218
Homepage: http://www.umkc.edu/bloch/accountancy

Kansas City, MO 64110-2499
Bloch School of Bus
5100 Rockhill Road

(816) Fax = 235-6560
umkc.edu

ß 1969,1971
BS,MS
Arden Philips

Erekson, O. Homer	Dean	235-2204	ereksono	Econ	PHD	80	N Carol	2002
Donnelly, David P.	C-Pr	235-1333	donnellyd	AB	PHD	83.	Illinois	& 7-04
Garrison, Larry R.	Prof	235-2340	garrisonl	X	PHD	86.	Nebraska	&1986
Solomon, Lanny M.	Prof	235-2304	solomonl	CM	PHD	74.	Case Wes	* 8-98
Associate Dean								
Cornell, David W.	Assoc	235-2306	cornelld	F	PHD	88.	LSU	* &1989
Gardner, J. Randall	Assoc	235-2303	gardnerjr	X	LLM	86	Mo-Ks Cty	&1983
Krueger, Lavern E.	Assoc	235-2307	kruegerl	FT	DBA	74.	Colorado	&1970
Weatherholt, Nancy D.	Assoc	235-2301	weatherholtn	FPA	PHD	88	Kansas	&1991
Smedley, Georgia A.	Asst		smedleyg	S	PHD	01.	Okla St	2007

Univ of Missouri - Rolla
Department of Business Adm
Dept Phone: 341-4184

Rolla, MO   65409
Sch Mgt & Info Systems
1870 Minor Circle

(573) Fax = 341-4812
business.unr.edu

BS
Sherri Light

Fisher, Caroline	Dean	341-7262	cfisher		PHD	75	Bowl Gr	2005
Bradley, Joseph	Asst	341-7261	josephb	FMA	PHD	04	Claremont	2006
Lea, Bih-Ru	Asst	341-6436	leabi		PHD	98	Clemson	2003
Chiu, Yu-Hsien	Inst	341-6907	chiuy		MS	91	Wi-Milwa	2007

Univ of Missouri - St. Louis
Accounting Area
Dept Phone: 516-6138
Homepage: www.umsl.edu/business/accounting/acctg.html

St. Louis, MO   63121-4499
College of Business Adm
8001 Natural Bridge Road

(314) Fax = 516-6420
umsl.edu

ß (13) 1970,1973
BS,MBA,MAC
Jennifer Dennis

Womer, N. Keith	Dean	516-6109	womerk	Econ	PHD	70	Penn St	2004
Mohrman, Mary Beth	C-Ac	516-5524	mohrman	F	PHD	91.	Wash U	1990
Farmer, Timothy A.	Assoc	516-6137	farmert	MB	PHD	84.	Ohio St	& 9-87
Geisler, Gregory G.	Assoc	516-6135	geisler	X	PHD	95.	N Carol	&2002
Moehrle, Stephen R.	Assoc	516-6142	moehrle	F	PHD	97.	Indiana	&1999
Reynolds-Moehrle, Jennifer	Assoc	516-6764	jreynolds.mo +	F	PHD	97.	Indiana	&1999
Her, Young-Won	Asst	516-4605	hery	MB	PHD	06.	S Carol	2006

Krueger, James M. Vice Chancellor	Asst	516-6539		FG	DBA	76.	Indiana	&1975
Mintchik, Natalia	Asst	516-6686	mintchikn		PHD	05.	North Tx	2005
Stuerke, Pamela S.	Asst	516-6132	stuerkep	F	PHD	98.	Indiana	&
Brown, Michael	Lect	516-6264	michaelbrown	FM	MS	78	Walsh	&2001
Link, William R.	Lect	516-6124	link	FM	MBA	67	Missouri	&1981
Tiburzi, D. James	Lect	516-6147	tiburzid	FX	JD	74	Illinois	&2002

Missouri Baptist University — St. Louis, MO 63141-8698 — (314) Fax= — mobap.edu — BS,BA
Accounting Faculty — Business Division
Dept Phone: 744-5351 — One College Park Dr.

Bradford, Brenda D.	C	392-2339	bradfbd		MA	90	Wash U	
Thompson, Mary S.	Prof	341-3941	thompson	FP	DMGT	03	Webster	
Felty, William M.	Asst	744-5311	feltywm	AFMP	MBA	91	SE Mo St	* &
Kannenberg, Karen	Asst	392-2337	kannen	FM	DMGT	99	Webster	
Moore, Sandra A.	Asst	392-2288	moore	FMP	MBA	81	Wash U	

Missouri Southern St Univ — Joplin, MO 64801-1595 — (417) Fax=625-9604 — mssu.edu — BSBA — Elaine Sandtorf
Accounting Faculty — School of Business Adm
Dept Phone: 625-9617 — 3950 E. Newman Road
Homepage: www.mssc.edu/business/accounting

Kleindl, Brad	Dean	625-9319	kleindl-b	Mktg	PHD	95	Okla St	1986
Smith, David M.	C-Ac	625-3012	smith-d	FCSM	PHD	97.	North Tx	&1995
Comstock, S. Mark	Prof	625-3122	comstock-m	AFM	PHD	91.	Oklahoma	&1993
Huffman, William E.	Assoc	625-9778	huffman-w	AEPG	PHD	98.	North Tx	&2000
Cossey, Tiffany J.	Asst	625-9514	cossey-t	PXV	LLM	02	Mo-Ks Cty	&2005
Smith, Jill A.	Asst	625-9593	smith-j	PAF	MBA	87	Minnesota	&1986

Missouri State University — Springfield, MO 65897-0094 — (417) Fax=836-5164 — ß (13) 1992,1992 — missouristate.edu — BS,MACC — Cora Besabe
School of Accountancy — College of Business
Dept Phone: 836-5414 — 901 S National Av Glass Hall
Homepage: missouristate.edu/accounting

Bottin, Ronald R.	Dean	836-5646	ronaldbottin	FSM	PHD	74	Missouri		8-90
Williams, J. Richard (Dick)	D-Ac	836-5415	johnwilliams	FI	PHD	93.	Miss		& 8-90
Bunn, Radie G.	Prof	836-5678	radiebunn	X	JD	77	Wm Mitch		8-84
Byrd, David B.	Prof	836-4183	davidbyrd	FER	PHD	79.	Arkansas		& 8-84
Byrd, Sandra D.	Prof	836-4181	sandrabyrd	FTPE	PHD	79.	Arkansas		& 8-84
Cerullo, M. Virginia	Prof	836-6353	margaretcerullo	FSO	PHD	90.	LSU	#	& 8-88
Cerullo, Michael J.	Prof	836-5337	mcerullo	S	PHD	71.	LSU		& 8-88
Ewer, Sid R.	Prof	836-6354	srewer	GMIO	PHD	89.	Miss	# *	& 8-88
Greer, Olen L.	Prof	836-4184	olengreer	MB	PHD	86.	Colorado		8-79
McDuffie, R. Steve	Prof	836-4186	robertmcduffie	ASG	DBA	90.	La Tech		& 8-88
Oden, Debra H.	Prof	836-4185	debraoden	X	LLM	81	Mo-Ks Cty		& 8-89
Olson, Stevan K.	Prof	836-5697	stevanolson	FMBN	PHD	74.	Wisconsin		& 8-87
Chaloupecky, Kurt E.	Assoc	836-5027	kurtchaloupecky	FA	PHD	77.	Missouri		& 8-73
Harsha, Phillip D.	Assoc	836-5646	philharsha	MCSO	PHD	83	Geo St	#	8-89
Lampe, James C.	Assoc	836-5068	jlampe	ASJO	PHD	70.	Michigan		& 8-06
Margavio, Geanie W.	Assoc	836-4724	geaniemargavio	FX	PHD	90	Alabama		& 8-90
Schmelzle, George D.	Assoc	836-5041	gschmelzle	MS	PHD	92.	Miss		& 8-06
Keller, A. Craig	Asst	836-8470	craigkeller	M	PHD	00.	Tx A&M		8-01
Hammond, Michael	Inst	836-5061	mrhammond	M	MACC	02	Mo St		8-02
Smillie, Donald	Inst	836-6914	smillie	F	MACC	01	Mo St		8-02

Missouri Western St Univ — Saint Joseph, MO 64507-2294 — (816) Fax=271-4508 — missouriwestern.edu — BSBA — Cherie Gemmell
Department of Business — Col of Prof Studies
Dept Phone: 271-4338 — 4525 Downs Drive

Estes, Steve	Dean	271-4207	estess		PHD	90	Ohio St	2007
Roever, Carol	C-Ac	271-5827	roeverc		MS	86	Wi-White	1986
Fowler, M. Lou	Asst	271-4338	fowler	G	MS	86	NE Mo St	&1991
Gunderson, Konrad E.	Asst	271-4338	gunder	F	PHD	92.	Nebraska	&2000

Monmouth College IL — Monmouth, IL 61462-1998 — (309) Fax=457-2310 — monm.edu — BA — Janet Hull
Accounting Faculty — Accounting Department
Dept Phone: 457-2160 — 700 East Broadway
Homepage: http://department.monm.edu/accounting/

Peterson, Judy	C-Ac	457-2365	jpeterso	FMXV	MBA	80	Mankato	&1998
Gersich, Frank III	Prof	457-2119	fgersich	ACSV	EDD	93	N Illinois	&1998

Monmouth University — W Lg Branch NJ 07764-1898 — (732) Fax=263-5515 — monmouth.edu — 1999,1999 — BS,MBA — Kathleen Hardaker
Dept of Accounting & Bus Law — School of Business Adm
Dept Phone: 571-7535 — 400 Cedar Avenue

Kelly, Frederick J.	Dean	571-3423	fkelly	Fnce	PHD	74	Columbia	2001
Agacer, Gilda M.	C-Ac	263-5549	gagacer	MGI	PHD	87.	S Carol	&1998

Savoth, Paul	Assoc	571-3648	psavoth	XL	LLM	84	Villanova	&1986
Flaming, Linda J.	Asst	571-3657	flaming	FA	PHD	02	Oklahoma	2003
He, Yi-Hong (Daniel)	Asst	571-3663	dhe	FI	DBA	02.	Clev St	* &2002
Uddin, Nancy	Asst	571-5537	nuddin	AS	PHD	00.	Rutgers	1999
Zhao, Ronald	Asst	571-3629	rzhao	FMI	PHD	94.	Tx Tech	* &2002
Stives, Douglas	Spec	263-5894	dstives	X	MBA	69	Lehigh	&2006

University of Montana　　Missoula, MT　　59812-6808　　(406) Fax=243-2086　　ß (13) 1949,1982
Dept of Accounting & Finance　School of Business Adm　business.umt.edu　　BS,MBA,MACC
Dept Phone: 243-2233　　Gallagher Business Bldg　　Gail Greymorning, Adm Asst
Homepage: www.business.umt.edu

Gianchetta, Larry D.	Dean	243-6195	larry.gianchetta	Mgt	PHD	75	Tx A&M	1969
Herron, Terri L.	C-Pr	243-5878	terri.herron	AS	PHD	96.	Tx-Arlin	&1996
Beed, Teresa K.	Prof	243-4983	teresa.beed	FT	PHD	81.	Colorado	&1980
Regel, Roy W.	Prof	243-5203	roy.regel	MC	PHD	85.	Colorado	* & 9-85
Reider, Barbara P.	Prof	243-5145	barbara.reider	FM	PHD	91.	Kent St	# * &2001
Weber, Joseph A.	Prof	243-4182	joseph.weber	XFP	PHD	84.	Minnesota	&1983
Chaney, Barbara A.	Assoc	243-5954	barbara.chaney	GPF	PHD	97.	Georgia	&2003
Herbold, Joshua	Asst	243-2724	joshua.herbold	FAP	PHD	05.	Illinois	&2004

Montana State University　　Bozeman, MT　　59717 3040　　(400) Fax=994-6206　　ß 1981,1981
Department of Accounting　College of Business　montana.edu　　BS,MPAC
Dept Phone: 994-4423　　449 Reid Hall　　Halina Rickman
Homepage: www.montana.edu/cob/

Semenik, Richard J.	Dean	994-4423	semenik	Mktg	PHD	76	Ohio St	7-00
Christensen, Anne L.	C-Pr	994-2043	annec	X	PHD	89.	Utah	8-02
Kramer, Bonita K. Peterson	Prof	994-4620	bonitap	AFR	PHD	94.	Wash St	# * & 8-94
Schmidt, Dennis R.	Prof	994-2653	dschmidt	XS	PHD	85.	Nebraska	& 8-05
Johnson, Christie W.	Assoc	994-2041	christie	FVP	MBA	77	Wyoming	& 9-80
Giullian, Marc A.	Asst	994-1965	mgiullian	FP	PHD	96.	Illinois	& 8-01
Solheim, Perry	Asst			F	PHD	07.	Utah	8-07
Wisner, Priscilla S.	Asst	994-2773	pwisner	M	PHD	97.	Tennessee	8-05
Munro, Michelle C.	Inst	994-6198	mmunro	FPM	MPAC	96	Mont St	& 8-05

Montana State Univ-Billings　　Billings, MT　　59101-0298　　(406) Fax=657-2327
Business Adm Programs　College of Business　msubillings.edu　　BSBA
Dept Phone: 657-2296　　1500 University Drive　　Suzie Thomas
Homepage: www.msubillings.edu

Young, Gary F.	Dean	657-2326	njbyoung@y	Econ	PHD	77	La Tech	2006
Campbell, Michael C.	C-Pr	657-1651	mcampbell	DNGS	MS	75	Colo St	&1978
Brown, Douglas S.	Prof	657-2135	dsbrown	FAOL	MBA	79	Colorado	&1988
Johnson, Debra	Asst	657-1606	djohnson	X	JD			2003
Kaminski, Kathleen A.	Asst	657-2273	kkaminski	FST	PHD	02.	Okla St	& 8-05
Wheeling, Barbara M.	Asst	657-1756	bwheeling	FP	PHD	99	Alberta	& 8-04

Montclair State University　　Montclair, NJ　　07043　　(973) Fax=655-7968　　2000,2000
Dept of Acct, Law & Taxation　School of Business　mail.montclair.edu　　BS,MBA,MS
Dept Phone: 655-4174　　1 Normal Avenue　　Gail Smyth
Homepage: www.montclair/edu/pages/accounting/index.htm

Oppenheim, Alan J.	Dean	655-4304	oppenheima	Stat	PHD	73	NYU	1973
Aquilino, Frank	C-Ac	655-4174	aquilinof	AXFP	MBA	74	St Johns	&1978
Douma, Irene K.	Prof	655-5166	doumai	AFTV	PHD	82.	Baruch	&1973
George, Nashwa E.	Prof	655-4123	georgen	FMIC	PHD	88	Baruch	* 1999
Yang, James G. S.	Prof	655-4174	yangg	XVFM	ABD		NYU	* &1982
Chang, Chiaho	Assoc	655-7458	changch	FMPC	PHD	97	NYU	2001
Narasimhan, Ramesh	Assoc	655-7456	narasimhanr	ABIO	PHD	88.	Va Tech	# * & 8-98
Pinto, JoAnn	Assoc	655-4282	pintoj	FMIC	PHD	99.	Rutgers	9-99
Poon, Wing W.	Assoc	655-7454	poonw	FMIC	PHD	96.	LSU	1997
Hughes, Peggy Ann	Asst	655-7457	hughesp	BIM	PHD	99.	Rutgers	9-05
Jeffers, Agatha E.	Asst	655-7451	jeffersa	ACMO	PHD	00.	Rutgers	&2004
Lauriclla, Leonard	Asst	655-4174	lauricellal	FX	LLM	86	NYU Law	2002
Lin, Beixin	Asst	655-7401	linb	FM	PHD	04.	Rutgers	2003
LiPari, Joseph	Asst	655-4123	liparij	PTF	MBA	81	Fairl Dick	&1989

Monterey Inst Intl Studies　　Monterey, CA　　93940　　(831) Fax=647-6506　　2003
Accounting Faculty　Fisher Grad Sch Intl Bs　miis.edu　　MBA
Dept Phone: 647-4140　　460 Pierce Street　　Tasha Tolbert
Homepage: www.miis.edu/fgsib-about-dean.html

Scalberg, Ernest J.	Dean	647-4140	escalberg	Mgt	PHD	78	UCLA	2001
Landry, Steven P.	Prof	647-6407	steve.landry	MIGB	PHD	92.	Colorado	* &2000
Chan, Canri	Assoc	647-6501	canri.chan	FIB	PHD	01	Flinders	&2001

University of Montevallo
Accounting Faculty
Dept Phone: 665-6540

	Montevallo, AL	35115-6000		(205) Fax=665-6560			1987	
	Stephens Col of Bus			montevallo.edu				BBA
							Loretta Trussel	
Rupp, William T.	Dean	665-6540	ruppwt	Mgt	PHD	74	Georgia	6-03
Martin, Jimmy W.	Prof	665-6531	martinj	FAK	PHD	78.	Alabama	&1984
Narz, Marvin J.	Assoc	665-6539	narz	XLF	LLM	89	Alabama	&1978
Rovelstad, Richard G.	Assoc	665-6538	rovelsta	FNH	PHD	86.	Alabama	&1982

Moravian Col & Theological S
Accounting Faculty
Dept Phone: 861-1591

	Bethlehem, PA	18018-6650		(610) Fax=625-7919				
	Economics & Bus Dept			moravian.edu				BA,MBA
	1200 Main Street						Mrs. Michelle Matuczinski	
Marabella, Santo D.	C-Ac	625-7093		Mgt	DSW	91	Penn	
Rossi, John D. III	Assoc	861-1380	mejdr01	CFNP	MBA	97	Moravian	* &5-96
Vinciguerra, Barbara M.	Asst	861-1377	bvinciguerra	ABCP	PHD	01	Drexel	&9-05

Morehead State University
Dept of Atg, Econ & Finance
Dept Phone: 783-2152

	Morehead, KY	40351-1689		(606) Fax=783-5025			2004,2004	
	College of Business			morehead-st.edu				BBA
	University Boulevard						Mary Howard	
Albert, Robert L. Jr.	Dean	783-5219	r.albert	Fnce	PHD	92	Cincinnati	1995
Grace, Bruce K.	C-Ac	783-2357	b.grace	Fnce	PHD	95	LSU	1999
Williams, L. K.	Prof	783-2911	l.willia	FMR	DBA	87.	Kentucky	&1988
Elliott, Terry G.	Assoc	783-2901	t.elliott	CA	MSA	87	Morehead	&1989
Walters, Sharon T.	Assoc	783-2725	s.walters	RX	MBA	74	Morehead	&1989
Criscione, Eugene Richard	Asst	783-2723	r.criscione	CJO	ABD		Miss	&2005
Meisel, Scott T.	Asst	783-2152	s.meisel	FLM	PHD	01.	Kent St	&2002
Madden, Deborah	Inst	783-2389	d.madden	CA	MBA	98	Kentucky	&1999

Morehouse College
Accounting Area
Dept Phone: 215-2618

	Atlanta, GA	30314-3773		(404) Fax=215-2719			1999	
	Div of Bus Adm & Econ			morehouse.edu				BA
	830 Westview Drive SW						Patricia Allen-Jackson	
Williams, John E.	Dean	215-2618		Fnce	PHD	86	Geo St	1976
Mills B. Lane Professor of Banking and Finance								
Stivers, Bonnie P.	Prof	215-2618	bstivers	MCB	PHD	83.	Geo St	&
Allen, Cheryl L.	Assoc	215-2618	callen	MABF	PHD	98.	Georgia	&1998
Onifade, Emmanuel O.	Assoc	215-2618	eonifade	MCBF	PHD	93.	S Carol	&1994
Ellis, Yvonne	Asst	215-2618		MFBV	PHD	05.	JacksonSt	2005

Morgan State University
Dept of Accounting & Finance
Dept Phone: 885-3445
Homepage: www.morgan.edu
   email @1=jewel.morgan.edu

	Baltimore, MD	21251-001		(443) Fax=885-8251		(1)	1996,1996	
	Graves Sch of Bus & Mgt			moac.morgan.edu				BS,PHD
	Cold Spring Lane & Hillen Rd						Linda D. Clark	
Thomas, Otis A.	Dean	885-3160	othomas	QMth	PHD	71	American	1972
Finney, Sharon G.	C-Ac	885-3445	sfinney	FEJ	PHD	89.	Geo St	&1999
Sun, Huey-Lian	Prof	885-3971	hsun@1	FM	PHD	91.	Houston	* &1990
Makkawi, Bilal	Assoc	885-4459	bmakkawi@y	FA	PHD	98	Fla Intl	&1998
Rao, Arundhati S. (Aru)	Assoc	885-1693	arao	FS	PHD	96.	Cincinnati	2001
Yaari, Varda	Assoc	885-3971	alexgum21@h	T	PHD	89.	NYU	
Ibrahim, Salma	Asst	885-3881	sibrahim	FS	PHD	05.	Maryland	2006
Xu, Li	Asst	885-1698	lxu@1	F	PHD	06.	Duke	2006

Morningside College
Accounting Faculty
Dept Phone: 274-5131

	Sioux City, IA	51106-1751		(712) Fax=274-5439				
	Div Bus, Econ, Com & So			morningside.edu				BS
	1501 Morningside Avenue						Ms. Pam Anderson	
Deeds, William C.	Dean		deeds		PHD	79	Kansas St	
Clovis, Samuel	C-Pr	274-5437						
Hopkins, James M.	Prof	274-5173	hopkins	AXDS	MA	73	Nebraska	&1986
Livermore, Douglas	Prof	274-5284	livermore	B	EDD	86	N Colo	1980
Daniels, Deanna	Assoc	274-5290	daniels	PCNG	PHD	85.	S Calif	&1991

Mount Olive College
Dept of CIS and Accounting
Dept Phone: Ext 3120
Homepage: www.moc.edu
   phone: 658-2502

	Mount Olive, NC	28365		(919) Fax=658-7179				
	School of Business			moc.edu				BSBA
	634 Henderson Street							
Best, Kathy T.	Dean	Ext 3090	kbest	ACPX	PHD		N Car St	&1981
Reimers, Karl	C-Ac	658-7865	kreimers					2003
Day, Henry J. II	Assoc	Ext 3038	hday	CFSX	PHD	97.	Va Tech	1995
McDevitt, Rosalie								2007

Mount St. Mary's College
Accounting Faculty
Dept Phone: 954-4155
Alhanati, Mark S.
Rigone, Anne

	Los Angeles, CA 90049-1599		(310) Fax=954-4159			
	Business		msmc.la.edu			
	12001 Chalon Road					Olga Medina
	C-As 954-4153	malhanati		MBA	Loyl Mrm	
	Inst			MS	S Calif	&

Mount St. Mary's Univ-MD
Accounting Faculty
Dept Phone: 447-5396
Forgang, William G.
Balch, John W.
Butt, Don
Speciale, Raymond

	Emmitsburg, MD 21727		(301) Fax=447-5335			
	Dept of Bus, Atg & Econ		msmary.edu			
	C	forgang	Econ	PHD	Lehigh	
	447-6122	balch		MS	Geotown	&
	447-5396	butt		MBA	Geo Wash	1996
	447-5396	speciale		MBA	Maryland	&1996

Mount Union College
Accounting Faculty
Dept Phone: 823-3253
  phone 821-5320
Myler, Michael R.
Strefeler, John M.
Zoky, David C.
Pogacnik, Ruth C.

	Alliance, OH 44601-3993		(330) Fax=823-3248			
	Dept Econ, Atg & Bus Ad		muc.edu			BA
	1972 Clark Avenue					
	C-Pr 823-3255	mylermr	Econ	PHD	83 Mich St	1983
	Prof 823-3086	strefejo	XVP	PHD	77. Arizona	* &1997
	Prof 823-3263	zokydc	ACFP	MBA	79 Youngstwn	&1979
	Asst 823-3253	pogachrc	MC	MBA	97 Youngstwn	2007

Muhlenberg College
Accounting Faculty
Dept Phone: 664-3058
Raymond, Arthur J.
Irwin, Paula L.
Doran, Jamie T.
Knox, Trevor

	Allentown, PA 18104-5586		(484) Fax=664-3536			
	Dept Bus & Accounting		muhlenberg.edu			AB
	2400 Chew Street					Justine Frantz
	C-Pr 664-3288	raymond	Fnce	PHD	90 Tufts	1991
	C-Ac 664-3286	irwin	JEBD	MBA	77 Lehigh	& 9-91
	Assoc 664-3289	doran	MDSE	MS	71 Duquesne	& 9-92
	Assoc 664-3287	tknox	BMX	PHD	00 Conn	& 9-00

Murray State University
Department of Accounting
Dept Phone: 809-4193
Todd, Timothy
Chamberlain, Don H.
Carpenter, Floyd W.
Miller, Thomas I. (Tim)
Seay, Robert A.
Stambaugh, Clyde T.
Thompson, John A.
Rudolph, Holly R.
Johnson, Leigh
Tervo, Wayne
Driver, Betty A.

	Murray, KY 42071-0009		(270) Fax=809-3922			ß 1976,1981
	Coll Bus & Public Affrs		murraystate.edu			BA,BS,MBA,MPAC
	351 Business Bldg					Nikki Faulkner
	Dean$ 809-4181	timothy.todd		PHD	N Carol	2006
	C-Ac 809-6215	don.chamberlain	GSF	DBA	90. Kentucky	1986
	Prof 809-4321	floyd.carpenter	FX	PHD	84. Miss	&1987
	Prof 809-4195	tim.miller	F	PHD	73. Arkansas	&1967
	Prof 762-4297	rob.seay	A	DBA	86. Miss St	&1985
	Prof 809-3169	tommy.stam+	AS	DBA	81. Kentucky	&1986
	Prof 809-3248	john.thompson	FA	PHD	74. Arkansas	& 8-66
	Assoc 809-4296	holly.rudolph	F	DBA	94. S Illinois	&1980
	Asst 809-7014	leigh.johnson	J	JD	02 Kentucky	2006
	Asst 809-7013	wayne.tervo	CM	PHD	06 Tx-SanAnt	&2006
	Inst 809-4281	betty.driver	F	MBA	83 Murray St	1983

Myers Universiy
Accounting Faculty
Dept Phone: 432-8966
Banjac, Joyce
Smigla, John E.
Mahsua, Amos
Broers, Larry

	Cleveland, OH 44144		(216) Fax=426-9296			
	McDonald Sch of Bus		myers.edu			
	3921 Chester Avenue					
	Dean 432-8966	jbanjac		PHD		
	C-Ac 432-8982	jsmigla	FM	MS	78 Kent St	&2005
	Prof 432-8976	amahsua	FMX	MBA	76 Gannon	&1977
	Assoc 432-8981	lbroers	MA	MBA	87 Bald-Wal	&1988

Naval Postgraduate School
Accounting Faculty
Dept Phone: 656-2471
Homepage: http://www.nps.navy.mil/gsbpp/
Beck, Robert N.
Moses, O. Douglas
Euske, Kenneth J.
Liao, Shu S.
San Miguel, Joseph G.
Thibodeau, Nicole.
Troy, Carmelita

	Monterey, CA 93943-5104		(831) Fax=656-3407			2000
	Grad Sch Bus & Pub Plcy		nps.edu			MBA
	555 Dyer Road				Mary Lou Vossen 656-2471	
	Dean 656-2161	nrbeck	Mgt	MS	68 SanDgoSt	2005
	D-Ac 656-3218	dmoses	FM	PHD	83. UCLA	1985
	Prof 656-2860	0123p	MB	PHD	78. Ariz St	1978
	Emer 656-2505	liao	2004	PHD	71. Illinois	1977
	Prof 656-2187	jsanmiguel	BCMU	PHD	73. Tx-Austin	&1982
	Asst 421-2833	nthibode	MFGN	PHD	03 Pittsburgh	2005
	Asst 656-2646	cjtroy	FM	PHD	03. Maryland	2003

University of Nebraska
School of Accountancy
Dept Phone: 472-2337
Homepage: www.cba.unl.edu/dept/accounting
Milligan, Cynthia H.
Shoemaker, Paul A.
  Nebraska CPAs Distinguished Professor

	Lincoln, NE 68588-0488		(402) Fax=472-4100			ß (13) 1916,1963
	College of Business Adm		unl.edu			BS,MPA,PHD
	12th & R Streets					
	Dean 472-9500	cmilligan		JD	70 Geo Wash	7-98
	D-Ac 472-2328	pshoemaker1	FXH	PHD	89. Penn St	&1989

Brown, James F. Jr.	Prof	472-2320	jbrown2	CM	DBA	81. Tennessee	*	1980
Chen, Kung H.	Prof	472-3360	kchen1	UMBC	PHD	74. Tx-Austin		1973
Steinhart Foundation Professor								
Smith, David B.	Prof	472-2927	dsmith19	F	PHD	79. Illinois		&2005
Raymond C. Dein Professor & Deloitte & Touche Scholar								
Allen, Arthur C.	Assoc	472-3275	aallen1	F	PHD	89. Alabama		6-89
Lawrence, Janice E.	Assoc	472-5152	jlawrence1	PEJI	PHD	92. Tx A&M		&1992
Ruchala, Linda V.	Assoc	472-8812	lruchala1	MBCN	PHD	91. Indiana		1991
Crabtree, Aaron D.	Asst	472-1753	acrabtree2	XF	PHD	04. Va Tech		2004
Gao, Lei	Asst	472-2902	lgao3	A	PHD	05. Kansas		2005
Price, Renee A.	Asst	472-0530	rprice1	FM	PHD	93. Tx A&M		&2000
Wang, Dechun	Asst	472-6055	dwang2	FA	PHD	04. Missouri		2004
Cosgrove, Debra	Lect	472-0525	dcosgrove2	S	MPA	89 Nebraska		2001

Univ of Nebraska at Kearney Kearney, NE 68849-4420 (308) Fax=865-8310 2006
Dept of Accounting & Finance Coll of Business & Tech unk.edu BS,MBA
Dept Phone: 865-8112 West Center E 200 Christine Rumery
Homepage: www.unk.edu/acad/acct_fin

| Forster, Bruce A. | Dean | 865-8342 | | Econ | PHD | 74 Australi | 7-05 |
| Hall, Steven C. | C-Ac | 865-8124 | hallsc | CPM | PHD | 90 Utah | & 8-01 |

Univ of Nebraska at Omaha Omaha, NE 68182-0048 (402) Fax=554-3747 ß 1965,1981
Dept of Accounting College of Business Adm unomaha.edu BSBA,MACC
Dept Phone: 554-3650 60th & Dodge Streets
Homepage: cba.unohama.edu/acct
  email @1=mail.unomaha.edu

Pol, Louis	Dean	554-2599	lpol@1	Mktg	PHD	78 Fla St		1990
Armitage, Jack L.	C-Pr	554-2912	jarmitage	AF	PHD	87. Nebraska		& 8-83
Spencer Professor								
File, Richard G.	Prof	554-2913	rfile	FTYZ	PHD	81. Tx-Austin		&1988
Union Pacific Professor								
Kwak, Wikil	Prof	554-2821	wkwak	CM	PHD	90. Nebraska		1989
Distinguished Alumni Professor								
Ortman, Richard F.	Prof	554-2822	rortman	MCU	PHD	71. Wisconsin	*	& 8-79
Hockett Professor								
Copple, Scott E.	Assoc	554-2566	scopple	X	LLM	82 Denver		&1990
Watanabe, Judith E.	Assoc	554-2744	jwatanabe	FX	PHD	85. Nebraska		&1983
Blaskovich, Jennifer L.	Asst	554-3984	jblaskovich	BCF	PHD	05. Nebraska		&2005
Eldridge, Susan	Asst	554-2504	seldridge@1	FP	PHD	97. N Carol		&2002
Kealey, Burch T.	Asst	554-3571	bkealey@1	F	PHD	96. Oklahoma		2001
Bauers, Ron	Inst	554-3139	rbauers	FSCA	MPA	89 Ne-Omaha	# *	&1995
Ilcisin, Laura	Inst	554-2633	lilcisin	FM	MBA	80 Ne-Omaha		&1996
Simonsen, Lori	Inst	554-2608	lsimonsen	FM	MACC	06 Ne-Omaha		2006
Windler, John	Inst	554-2643	jwindler	FM	MBA	89 Ne-Omaha		&1999

Nebraska Wesleyan Univ Lincoln, NE 68504-2796 (402) Fax=465-2179
Accounting Faculty Business Adm/Econ Dept nebrwesleyan.edu
Dept Phone: 465-2213 5000 Saint Paul Avenue Rhoda Lakey

Patrick, Richard	C-Ac	465-2201	rrp	Mgt	PHD	97 Nebraska		1995
Baillie, Courtney	Assoc	465-2207	ccb	FS	PHD	03 Nebraska		1999
Olds, Nanne	Asst	465-2206	nko	PXM	MPA		*	&1999
Swift, Christopher	Asst	465-2202	cfs	ACP	MPA	Nebraska		&2001

Univ of Nevada, Las Vegas Las Vegas, NV 89154-6003 (702) Fax=895-4306 ß (123) 1991,1991
Department of Accounting College of Business unlv.edu BS,MS,MBA
Dept Phone: 895-1559 4505 Maryland Parkway Sonja Longoria, Maria Cortes
Homepage: business.unlv.edu/accounting/

Tandy, Paulette R.	C-Ac	895-1559	paulette.tandy	AOF	PHD	87 Tx A&M	& 8-89
Messier, William F. Jr.	Prof	895-1559	bill.messier	AFB	DBA	79. Indiana	& 1-08
Kenneth & Tracy Knauss Endowed Chair of Accounting							
Moores, C. Tommy	Prof	895-3991	tommy.moores	FET	PHD	82. LSU	&1989
Charron, Kimberly F.	Assoc	895-3975	kim.charron	FNV	PHD	97. Arizona	1997
Cocco, Anthony F.	Assoc	895-4658	anthony.cocco	F	PHD	91. Fla St	& 1-92
McCaslin, Thomas E.	Assoc	895-1326	tom.mccaslin	FAS	DBA	82. Tennessee	&1988
Swayze, James P.	Assoc	895-3992	jim.swayze	XF	PHD	92. Houston	1991
Vent, Glenn A.	Assoc	895-3386	glenn.vent	CF	PHD	83. Arizona	&1982
Zimmerman, John C.	Assoc	895-1335	john.zimmerman	XF	JD	89 Southwes	&1989
Beck, Grant M.	Asst	895-3768	grant.beck	S	PHD	04. Missouri	2004
Koo, Meihua	Asst	895-4659	meihua.koo	IF	PHD	01. Okla St	2001
Raschke, Robyn L.	Asst	895-1559	robyn.raschke	S	PHD	07 Ariz St	&2007
France, Jim	Inst	895-3236	jim.france	M	MS	03 Nev-L Vg	2004
Sevalstad, Suzanne	Inst	895-3990	suzanne.sev+	F	MS	72 Mont St	&1979

University of Nevada, Reno
Dept of Accounting & IS
Dept Phone: 784-4028
Homepage: http://www.cis.unr.edu/accindex.htm

Reno, NV 89557-0205
Col of Bus Adm Mail0026
1664 N. Virginia Street

(775) Fax=784-8044
unr.edu

ß (1) 1961,1971
BS,MBA,MA
Marianne Fuller

Name		Rank	Phone	email		Fld	Deg	Yr	School	Yr
Edberg, Dana		C	784-4912	dte		Sys	PHD	99	Claremont	1984
Carslaw, Charles A.P.N.		Assoc	784-6549	carslaw		VFI	MA	71	Oxford	&1990
Mills, John R.		Prof	784-6884	mills		F	PHD	79.	Colorado	&1982
Vreeland, Jannet M.		Assoc	784-1740	vreeland		CFGM	PHD	92.	Tx A&M	1-91
Yamamura, Jeanne H.		Assoc	784-4823	yamamura		AS	PHD	95.	Wash St	&1993
Mason, Richard		Asst	784-6886	mason		X	PHD	01	Conn	2000
Pippin, Sonja		Asst	784-1337	sonjap		X	PHD	06	Tx Tech	2006
Purvis, S. E. C.		Asst	784-6108	secp		F	PHD	85.	Columbia	&2006
Wong, Jeffrey		Asst	784-4825	jawong		M	PHD	99.	Oregon	2006
Birk, Cynthia		Lect	784-6428	cbirk		F	MA	86	Iowa	&1989
Cossitt, Betty		Lect	784-6456	cossitt		M	MBA	91	Nev-Reno	&2000

University of New Hampshire
Dept of Accounting & Finance
Dept Phone: 862-3380
Homepage: www.unh.edu/wsbe
email @1=christa.unh.edu @2=alberti.unh.edu @3=hopper.unh.edu

Durham, NH 03824-3593
Whittemore Sch Bus & Ec
15 College Rd, Mclonnell Hl

(603) Fax=862-4468
unh.edu

1994,1994
BA,MBA,MS
Ginette Couture

Name	Rank	Phone	email	Fld	Deg	Yr	School	Yr
Innis, Daniel A.	Dean	862-1983		Mktg	PHD	91	Ohio St	2007
Etebari, Ahmad	C-Pr	862-3359	ahmad.etebari	MZE	PHD	79	North Tx	1980
Plante, Catherine A.	Assoc	862-3384	catherine.plante	FG	PHD	91.	Ohio St	&1991
Irani, Afshad J.	Asst	862-3342	aji@1	F	PHD	98.	Penn St	1998
Tate, Stefanie	Asst	862-3391	sltate	AF	PHD	01.	Mich St	2001
Xu, Le (Emily)	Asst		emily.xu	F	PHD	03.	Mass	2003
Colliander, John	Inst	433-2111		X	JD	71	Boston U	1990
Knowles, William	Inst	862-2864	bilknow	F	MS		Mass	* &1993
Nelson, Edwin R.	Inst	862-4959	ernelson@2	AFM	ABD		Boston U	# * &1994

University of New Haven
Department of Accounting
Dept Phone: 932-7109
Homepage: www.newhaven.edu

West Haven, CT 06516-1999
College of Business
300 Boston Post Road

(203) Fax=931-6016
newhaven.edu

BS,MBA,MST
Betty Miller

Name	Rank	Phone	email	Fld	Deg	Yr	School	Yr
Boronico, Jess S.	Dean			Mgt	PHD		Penn	7-05
Wnek, Robert	C-Pr	932-7111	rwnek	XL	LLM		Boston U	& 9-78
McDonald, Robert	Assoc	932-7127	rmcdonald	MCF	MBA		NYU	# * & 9-84
Rolleri, Michael	Assoc	932-7092	mrolleri	F	MBA		Conn	& 9-80
Daneshfar, Alizera	Asst	931-6038	adanesh	FMT	PHD	01	Concordia	1-01
Goldberg, Martin	Asst	932-7110	mgoldberg	BL	LLM	79	NYU	9-01
Lane, Scott J.	Asst	932-7091	slane	MFU	PHD	99.	Kentucky	9-99
Miller, Macy J.	Inst	479-4556	mjmiller	F	MBA	06	NewHamp	9-05

The College of New Jersey
Accountancy
Dept Phone: 771-2566
Homepage: www.tcnj.edu/%7ebusiness/accountancy/index.html

Ewing, NJ 08628-0718
School of Business
P.O. Box 7718

(609) Fax=637-5129
tcnj.edu

1998
BS
Mrs. Joyce Jammer

Name	Rank	Phone	email	Fld	Deg	Yr	School	Yr
Kirnan, Jack	Dean$	771-3345	kirnan	Econ	PHD	84	Fordham	2007
Nouri, Hossein	C-Pr	771-2176	hnouri	ABF	PHD	92.	Temple	1992
Chiang, Bih-Horng (Bea)	Assoc	771-3056	bchiang	CM	PHD	99.	Drexel	1998
Miller, Gerald J.	Assoc	771-2250	millerge	FGV	PHD	94.	Kentucky	&1995
Shahid, Abdus	Assoc	771-3468	shahid	F	PHD	92.	Temple	1990
Ahlawat, Sunita S.	Asst	731-3044	ahlawat	SM	PHD	93.	Penn St	2002

New Jersey City University
Accounting Faculty
Dept Phone: 200-3353
Bloomberg, Sandra

Jersey City, NJ 07305-1597
Dept of Business Adm
2039 Kennedy Boulevard

(201) Fax=200-3242
njcu.edu

BS,MS
Mohammed Kaifa

Name	Rank	Phone	email	Fld	Deg	Yr	School	Yr
Bloomberg, Sandra	Dean	200-3321	sbloomberg		PHD	84	Utah	1998
Ettinger, Marilyn J.	C-Ac	200-3353	mettinger	Fnce	MBA	88	NYU	1988
Craven, William	Assoc	200-3353	wcraven	FGX	MBA	70	NYU	* &1989
Matthews, Robert J.	Assoc	200-3353	rmatthews	ACFV	MBA	84	Pace	&1988
Ramos-Alexander, Jeannette	Assoc	200-3353	jalexander	ACDF	MBA	79	Fairl Dick	* &1989
Shalaby, Afaf A.	Assoc	200-3353	ashalaby	DFV	PHD	96.	Rutgers	1992

New Jersey Ins of Technology
Accounting Faculty
Dept Phone: 596-3248
Homepage: www.njit.edu

Newark, NJ 07102-1982
Sch of Industrial Mgt
323 Martin Luther King Blvd

(973) Fax=596-3074
njit.edu

1997,1997
BSM,MS
Kasheema Akbar

Name	Rank	Phone	email	Fld	Deg	Yr	School	Yr
Hawk, David	Dean	596-3019	david.hawk		PHD		Penn	
Anandarajan, Asokan A.	Prof	596-8568	asokan.anand+		PHD	95.	Drexel	1994

University of New Mexico   Albuquerque, NM 87131-1221   (505) Fax=277-7108   ß (123) 1975,1975
Department of Accounting   R O Anderson Sch of Mgt   mgt.unm.edu   BBA,MBA,MACC
Dept Phone: 277-6471   1924 Las Lomas Blvd
Homepage: http://accounting.mgt.unm.edu

Wohlert, Amy	Dean$	277-6148	wohlert				
Hamill, James R.	C-Pr	277-8890	hamill	X	PHD	87. Ariz St	&1993
KPMG Professor of Accounting							
Preston, Alistair M.	Prof	277-0335	alistair	MBS	PHD	82 Bath	1992
Grant Thornton Professor of Accounting							
Togo, Dennis F.	Prof	277-7106	togo	CMS	PHD	86. Ariz St	* & 8-87
Young, Joni J.	Prof	277-0334	young	FH	PHD	91. Illinois	&1992
REDW Lecturer							
Bougen, Philip D.	Assoc	277-8776	bougen	FI	PHD	87 LondonSE	1995
Brody, Richard G.	Assoc	277-7258	brody	ABO	PHD	93. Ariz St	&
Chwastiak, Michele E.	Assoc	277-8810	chwastiak	MC	PHD	91. Pittsburgh	1999
Oakes, Leslie S.	Assoc	277-8442	oakes	FHN	PHD	88. Wisconsin	1995
White, Craig G.	Assoc	277-8777	white	X	PHD	98. Tx Tech	1998
Brooks, Ann	Lect	277-6471	brooks	F	MBA	New Mex	2002
Colter, Norman	Lect	277-7081	colter	F	MBA	New Mex	&2001
Tepper, Robert	Lect	277-6471	rjtepper	FL	JD	83 New Mex	2004

New Mexico Highlands Univ   Las Vegas, NM 87701-4211   (505) Fax=454-3354
Accounting Faculty   School of Business   nmhu.edu   BA,MBA
Dept Phone: 454-3522   University Avenue   Gloria Brown-Lopez
 phone 454-3115

Taylor, William	Dean	454-3344	btaylor	Econ			
Bost, Patricia J.	C-Ac	994-0219	pjbost	MCGN	PHD	92 Geo Wash	* 1998
Romero, Mary	Visit	Ext 3580	mbromero	DPMG	MBA	91 Nw Mx Hi	&2001

New Mexico State Univ   Las Cruces, NM 88003-8001   (505) Fax=646-1552   ß (13) 1973,1981
Accounting & BI MSC 3DH   College Bus Adm & Econ   nmsu.edu   BA,MA
Dept Phone: 646-4901   University Ave at Solano Dr   Leona Silva
Homepage: http://busines.nmsu.edu/~is/

Carruthers, Garrey E.	Dean	646-4083	garreyc	Econ	PHD	68 Iowa St	7-03
Tunnell, P. Larry	H-Ac	646-4904	ltunnell	X	PHD	90. Okla St	& 8-94
Mills, Sherry K.	Prof	646-5681	smills	BM	PHD	88. Tx Tech	& 8-88
Scribner, Edmund A.	Prof	646-5163	escribne	STJ	PHD	85. Okla St	& 8-83
Billiot, Mary Jo	Assoc	646-3184	mbilliot	FM	DBA	97. Miss St	& 8-01
Calk, Russell	Assoc	646-4901	rcalk	M	PHD	97. Okla St	& 8-01
Seipel, Cindy L.	Assoc	646-5206	cseipel	AF	PHD	90. Okla St	& 8-90
McNelis, L. Kevin	Asst	646-2485	kmcnelis	FMS	PHD	97. Tx-Arlin	& 8-97
Schoener, Robert B.	Asst	646-1520	schoener	FM	MBA	69 Penn	& 1-04
Smith, William L.	Asst	646-1422	smith	F	PHD	04 N Mex St	& 1-05

University of New Orleans   New Orleans, LA 70148-1530   (504) Fax=280-6426   ß (13) 1969,1975
Department of Accounting   College of Business Adm   uno.edu   BS,MS,MS-TX
Dept Phone: 280-6245   Lake Front   Angie Webster

Logan, James W.	Dean	280-6954	jlogan	Mgt	PHD	90 LSU	1988
Harmelink, Philip J.	C-Pr	280-6427	pharmeli	X	PHD	72. Iowa	&1979
Ernst & Young Professor of Accounting							
Gardner, John C.	Prof	280-6245	jcgard	FTM	PHD	83. Mich St	8-04
KPMG Professor of Accounting							
Hosch, Gordon A.	Emer	280-6438	gahosch	2004	PHD	72. LSU	&1967
Graduate Coordinator							
Lambert, Joyce C.	Prof	280-6429	jlambert	AFJ	PHD	73. LSU	# & 8-84
Arthur Andersen Professor of Accounting							
Lambert, S. Joseph III	Prof	280-6425	sjlamber	CAFS	PHD	73. LSU	& 8-84
Oil & Gas Professor of Accounting							
Manry, David	Assoc	280-6432	dmanry	FTKV	PHD	92. Tx-Austin	2001
Energy Accounting Conference Professsor							
Parker, Robert J.	Assoc	280-6433	rjparker	CM	PHD	92. Temple	&2002
Reid, Mark E.	Assoc	280-6428	mreid	X	PHD	98. Geo St	&1997
Young, Ronald M.	Assoc	280-6436	rmyoung	S	PHD	92. Tx Tech	&1991
Energy Accounting and Tax Conference Profesor							
Beams, Joseph D.	Asst	280-6431	jbeams	MS	PHD	03. Va Tech	& 8-03
Wandler, Scott A.	Asst	280-6430	swandler	FM	PHD	07 LSU	&2006
Haydel, Jennifer A.	Inst	280-6246	jahaydel		MS	03 N Orleans	&2005

New York University   New York, NY 10012-1118   (212) Fax=995-4004   ß 1916,1916
Dept Atg, Tax & BL, 44 W 4th   Stern School of Bus   stern.nyu.edu   BS,MBA,MS,PHD
Dept Phone: 998-0010   44 West 4th St, Suite 10-180   Bebi Karimbaksh/Shevon Estwick
Homepage: www.stern.nyu.edu/acc/

Cooley, Thomas F.	Dean	998-0909	tcooley	Econ	PHD	71 Penn	1999
Paganelli-Bull Professor of Economics							
Choi, Frederick D. S.	C-Pr	998-0047	fchoi	IFM	PHD	72. U Wash	1981

Balachandran, K. R.	Prof	998-0029	kbalacha	MYQC	PHD	68	Berkeley	*	1979
Bartov, Eli	Prof	998-0016	ebartov	F	PHD	89.	Berkeley		1992
Bildersee, John S.	Prof	998-0027	jbilders	F	PHD	72	Chicago		1978
Hipscher, Aaron	ClPr	998-0011	ahispche	F	MBA	66	Rutgers	&2000	
Jones, Seymour	ClPr	998-0067	sjones	FA	MBA		NYU		1993
Lev, Baruch	Prof	998-0028	blev	F	PHD	68.	Chicago	&1995	

Phillip Bardes Chair in Accounting & Finance

Livnat, Joshua	Prof	998-0022	jlivnat	FM	PHD	87	NYU	&1987	
Ronen, Joshua	Prof	998-4144	jronen	TABX	PHD	70.	Stanford	&1973	
Dontoh, Alex	Assoc	998-0064	adontoh	M	PHD	84	NYU		1988

Deputy Chair

Fried, Haim Dov	Assoc	998-0005	hfried	MF	PHD	77	NYU		1979
John, Teresa A.	Assoc	998-0025	tjohn	F	PHD	86.	NYU		1987
Klein, April	Assoc	998-0014	aklein	F	PHD	83	Chicago		1987
Maindiratta, Ajay	Assoc	998-0066	amaindir	MCYN	PHD	84	Car Mellon		1985
Ryan, Stephen G.	Assoc	998-0020	sryan	F	PHD	88.	Stanford		1990
Zarowin, Paul A.	Assoc	998-0015	pzarowin	F	PHD	85.	Chicago		1984
Billings, Mary	Asst	998-0119	mbilling		PHD	07	Indiana		2007
Cohen, Daniel A.	Asst	998-0267	dcohen	F	PHD	04.	Nrthwstrn		2005
Gode, Dhananjay K.	Asst	998-0021	dgode	FM	PHD	94.	Car Mellon		1998
McVay, Sarah E.	Asst	998-0040	smcvay		PHD	04.	Michigan		2004
Petrovits, Christine M.	Asst	998-0988	cpetrovi	F	PHD	05.	N Carol	&2005	

New York Institute of Tech Old Westbury, NY 11568-8000   (516) Fax=686-7425
Accounting Faculty School of Management nyit.edu   BS,MBA
Dept Phone: 686-7423 Northern Blvd   Constance Canning
Homepage: www.nyit.edu
Did Not Respond Again; all 261- phones have 212 area code (Manhattan campus)

Decker, David R.	Dean	686-7423	ddecker	Intl	PHD	77	Kansas		2000
Harris, Peter	Assoc	686-7554	pharris	X	MBA		Columbia	&	
Hayes, Nancy T.	Assoc	686-7554	nhayes	M	MBA		Long Isl	&	

Niagara University Niagara Univ, NY 14109-2201   (716) Fax=286-8206   2001,2001
Department of Accounting College of Business niagara.edu   BAA,MBA
Dept Phone: 286-8160   Melissa Heidt

Oddo, Alfonso R.	C-Pr	286-8158	aroddo	F	MBA		SUNY-Buf	&1973	
Jain, Jagat P.	Prof	286-8159	jjain	ICFG	PHD	85	Patna		1979
Ho, Kathy S.	Assoc	286-8164	kh	MF	PHD	88.	Syracuse	9-96	
Desir, Rosemond	Asst	286-8160		FM	PHD	07	Mass		2007
O'Donnell, Joseph B.	Asst	286-8160		AS	PHD	02	SUNY-Buf		2007

Nicholls State University Thibodaux, LA 70310   (985) Fax=448-4922   ß(1) 1983,1989
Dept Atg & Info Sys Box 2015 College of Business nicholls.edu   BS
Dept Phone: 448-4173 Highway 1   Gina LaGrange
Homepage: www.nicholls.edu/accounting

| Mauldin, D. Shawn | Dean | 448-4170 | shawn.mauldin | BFVX | PHD | 97 | Miss | * & 6-00 | |

Betsy Ayo Endowed Professorship

| Chiasson, Michael A. | C-Ac$ | 448-4173 | michael.chiasson | FMX | DBA | 94. | La Tech | 8-94 | |

John C. Daigle Free Enterprise Endowed Professorship

Zachry, Benny R.	Prof	448-4186	benny.zachry	AFMS	DBA	85.	La Tech	& 8-93	
Gaharan, Catherine	Assoc	448-4213	kitty.gaharan	CF	PHD	88.	LSU	& 8-90	
Breaux, Kevin	Asst	448-4218	kevin.breaux	CFM	PHD	04.	LSU	8-03	
Guidry, Michele D.	Inst	448-4212	michele.guidry	FLM	MBA	89	Nicholls	& 8-89	

Nichols College Dudley, MA 01571-5000   (508) Fax=213-2225
Accounting & Finance Program Business Faculty nichols.edu   BSBA
Dept Phone: 213-2124 Center Road

Reinhardt, Alan J.	Dean	213-2201	alan.reinhardt	Engr	PHD	83	Ind-Penn	9-98	
Armstrong, John A.	C-Ac	213-2124	john.armstrong	AFCP	MBA	76	Pace	&1986	
Behrens, Marcia	Asst	213-2166	marcia.behrens		MBA	89	Nichols	8-05	
Cote, Sean	Asst	213-2236	sean.cote		MBA	99	Nichols	8-05	

Norfolk State University Norfolk, VA 23504-8060   (757) Fax=823-2506   1990
Dept Atg, Fnce & Info Mgt School of Business nsu.edu   BS
Dept Phone: 823-8870 700 Park Avenue   Ms. Sylvia D. Brooks

Whaley, Gary L.	Dean$	823-8009	glwhaley	Mgt	PHD	83	SUNY-Buf	7-84	
Chen, Jim	C-Ac	823-2564	jchen	Mgt	PHD	82	North Tx	7-84	
Banatte, Jean-Marie	Prof	823-2483	jbanatte	XF	PHD	77.	Missouri	& 7-83	
Damtew, Desta	Prof	823-2486	ddamtew	CMI	DBA	79.	Kentucky	9-84	
Mapp, Johnnie A.	Prof	823-8217	jamapp	FI	PHD	81.	Georgia	9-83	

University of North Alabama   Florence, AL   35632-0001   (256) Fax = 765-4811
Dept of Accounting & Bus Law   College of Business   una.edu   BBA,MBA
Dept Phone: 765-4400   One Harrison Plaza   Ms. Jennifer Tittle
Homepage: www2.una.edu/business

Name	Rank	Phone	Email		Degree	Yr	School	
Gatlin, Kerry P.	Dean	765-4261	kpgatlin	Mgt	PHD	82	Oklahoma	1987
Campbell, Sharon N.	C-Pr	765-4544	sncampbell	FEP	DBA	95.	La Tech	&1996
Campbell, Walter M.	Prof	765-4421	wmcampbell	AFTE	PHD	82.	North Tx	&1994
Lawrence, Mark L.	Prof	765-4332	mlawrence	SXVT	DBA	01	Nova SE	* &2004
Sellers, Keith F.	Prof	765-4769	kfsellers	XF	DBA	89.	Memphis	&2006
LaGrange Eminent Scholar of Business Valuations & Director, Center Bus Val								
Ferry, Jerry W.	Assoc	765-4887	jwferry	MC	PHD	86.	Arkansas	9-91
Glasscock, Lorraine	Assoc	765-4423	lgglasscock	FPC	MBA	77	N Alab	* 1979
Holley, Paul	Asst	765-4577	pjholley	MP	MBA	69	Memphis	&1981
Mosakowski, Joe	Asst	765-4245	jjmosakowski	MP	ABD		Miss	1972

North Carolina at Asheville   Asheville, NC   28804-8507   (828) Fax = 251-6857   2004
Accounting Faculty   Dept Mgt & Accountancy   unca.edu   BS
Dept Phone: 251-6554   One University Heights   Cindy Reagan

Name	Rank	Phone	Email		Degree	Yr	School	
McKenzie, Claudel B.	C-Ac	251-6842	cmckenzie	FJTP	MBA	80	W Carol	* & 8-81
Nelms, Linda L.	Prof	251-6851	lnelms	CSMP	MBA	78	N Carol	* & 8-78
Bushong, J. Gregory	Assoc	251-6852	gbushong	FGNV	PHD	89.	LSU	* & 8-00
Mayes, Sarah E.	Lect	251-6846	bmayes	FPX	MBA	82	W Carol	* & 8-86
Parks, Charles	Lect	251-6856	cparks	AS	MS		NC-Green	

University of North Carolina   Chapel Hill, NC   27599-3490   (919) Fax = 962-4727   ß 1923,1963
Accounting Faculty - CB3490   Kenan-Flagler Bus Sch   unc.edu   MBA,MAC,PHD
Dept Phone: 962-9668   Cathy Bordeaux 962-9668
email @1 = kenan-flagler.unc.edu

Name	Rank	Phone	Email		Degree	Yr	School	
Jones, W. Steve	Dean			Mgt	MBA		Harvard	7-03
Bushman, Robert M.	C-Pr	962-9809	bushmanr	FM	PHD	89.	Minnesota	& 7-99
The Forensic Accounting Distinguished Professor								
Blocher, Edward J.	Prof	962-3200	blochere	MAS	PHD	74.	Tx-Austin	* &1976
Hand, John R. M.	Prof	962-3173	handj	F	PHD	87.	Chicago	9-93
The H. Allen Andrew Distinguished Professor of Entrepreneurial Education								
Landsman, Wayne R.	Prof	962-3221	wayne_landsman	F	PHD	84.	Stanford	9-90
KPMG Professor of Accounting								
Lang, Mark H.	Prof	962-1644	mark_lang	FI	PHD	90.	Chicago	& 9-94
Thomas W. Hudson Jr./Deloitte & Toughe LLP Distinguished Professor								
Maydew, Edward L.	Prof	843-9356	edward_maydew	X	PHD	94.	Iowa	& 7-99
David E. Hoffman Distinguished Professor								
Shackelford, Douglas A.	Prof	962-3197	doug_shack	X	PHD	90.	Michigan	& 7-90
Meade H. Willis Professor of Accounting								
Abarbanell, Jeffery S.	Assoc	962-0698	jeffery_abar+@1	F	PHD	89.	Penn	& 7-97
Bylinski, Joseph H.	Assoc	962-3201	joseph_byl+@1	M	PHD	80.	Ohio St	& 1-80
Raedy, Jana Smith	Assoc	962-7475	jana_raedy	F	PHD	98.	Penn St	& 7-97
Jaffer, Ashraf	Asst	962-3273	ashraf_jaffer	FMT	PHD	07	LondonSE	2006
Stubben, Stephan	Asst	962-9835	stubbens@1	F	PHD	06.	Stanford	2006
Bowen, Linda C.	Adj	962-3175	bowenl	F	PHD	72.	Geo St	& 9-74
Edwards, Courtney H.	Adj	962-3560	courtneyedwards	X	PHD	06.	N Carol	&2004
Raedy, Kevin M.	Adj	962-0284	kevin_raedy	AF	PHD	98.	Penn St	&2002
Skender, C. J.	Adj	962-3143	cj_skender	FM	MBA	81	Duke	# * &1999

North Carolina at Charlotte   Charlotte, NC   28223-0001   (704) Fax = 687-6938   ß (123) 1983,1985
Department of Accounting   Belk Col of Business   uncc.edu   BS,MACC
Dept Phone: 687-2445   9201 University City Blvd   Ms. Elizabeth Brown

Name	Rank	Phone	Email		Degree	Yr	School	
Lilly, Claude C. III	Dean	687-2165	cclilly	Insu	PHD	73	Geo St	8-97
Wiggins, Casper E. Jr.	C-Pr	687-3620	cwiggins	ADS	DBA	82.	Tennessee	& 8-99
Godfrey, L. Howard	Prof	687-4478	hgodfrey	X	PHD	75.	Alabama	&1974
Schroeder, Richard G.	Prof	687-2446	rgschroe	BFT	PHD	74.	Ariz St	&1991
Turner, Thomas C.	Emer	687-2445		1993	MBA	55	N Carol	& 8-61
Bhamornsiri, Surasakdi	Assoc	687-4403	sbhamorn	FM	DBA	79.	Tennessee	&1978
Blankley, Alan I.	Assoc	687-4970	aiblankl	FS	PHD	92.	Tx A&M	1-04
Burton, Hughlene A.	Assoc	687-2117	haburton	X	PHD	94.	Alabama	&1996
Cathey, Jack M.	Assoc	687-4408	jmcathey	CFS	PHD	89.	Va Tech	&1988
Elias, Nabil S.	Assoc	687-6466	nelias	FM	PHD	70.	Minnesota	* 2001
Guinn, Robert E.	Assoc	687-4407	reguinn	AFR	PHD	73.	Alabama	&1976
Kerr, David S.	Assoc	687-4875	dkerr	AS	PHD	89.	Mich St	2005
Malmgren, Edward G.	Assoc	687-4404	egmalmgr	MQ	PHD	72	Iowa	&1972
Matherly, C. Michele	Asst	687-4434	matherly	S	PHD	94.	Alabama	&2001
Carlini, Jeffrey	Lect	687-2043	jcarlini	FM	MS	02	Lehigh	2005
Yarbrough, Kathryn	Lect	687-3036	skyarbro	F	MBA	83	Winthrop	2003
Sevin, Suzanne K.	Clin	687-4434	ssevin	F	PHD	02.	Georgia	2001

North Carolina at Greensboro

Department of Accounting
Dept Phone: 334-5647
Homepage: http://www.uncg.edu/bae/acc

Greensboro, NC 27402-6165
Bryan Sch of Bus & Econ
P.O. Box 26165

(336) Fax=334-4706
uncg.edu

ß (123) 1982,1982
BS,MSA
Portia Moffitt

Weeks, James K.	Dean	334-5338	weeksjk	OpM	PHD	74	S Carol	1976
Winkler, Daniel T.	H-Pr	334-5647	dtwinkler	Fnce	PHD	86	S Carol	8-86
Arrington, C. Edward	Prof	256-0116	cearring	HMT	DBA	80.	Fla St	& 8-98
Harden, J. William	Assoc	256-0188	bill_harden	FX	PHD	97.	Kentucky	& 8-88
Iyer, Venkataraman M.	Asst	256-0187	vmiyer	AS	PHD	94.	Georgia	& 8-99
Livingstone, Jane R.	Asst	256-0128	jrlivin2	XF	PHD	98.	Penn St	2004
Shough, Evan	Asst		emshough	FM	PHD	05.	Oklahoma	8-05
Upton, David R.	Asst	256-0186	drupton	BC	PHD	06.	Indiana	8-05
Watkins, Ann L.	Asst	256-0189	alwatki2	AFI	PHD	95.	LSU	& 8-04
Hershberger, Melissa	Lect	334-5658	mjhershb	F	MBA	05	Duke	8-05
Khanlarian, Cynthia J.	Lect	256-0126	cjkhanla	PF	MSA	95	NC-Green	& 8-97

North Carolina Wilmington

Dept of Accountancy & B Law
Dept Phone: 962-3509
Homepage: csb.uncwil.edu/depts/abl/

Wilmington, NC 28403-5901
Cameron Sch of Business
601 South College Road

(910) Fax=962-3663
uncw.edu

ß 1993,1993
BS,MSA
Gloria Sasser

Clark, Lawrence S.	Dean	395-7301	clarkl	Law	LLM	78	DePaul	2001
Hanson, Randall K.	C-Pr	962-3801	hansonr	JL	LLM	87	So Meth	1990
Ivancevich, Daniel M.	Prof	962-7681	ivancevichd	FS	PHD	91.	Tx A&M	2000
Rockness, Howard O.	Prof	962-3508	rocknessh	MCU	PHD	73.	U Wash	8-93
Rockness, Joanne W.	Prof	962-3776	rocknessj	FJV	PHD	80.	N Carol	&1993
Cameron Professor								
Elikai, Fara M. H.	Assoc	962-3614	elikai	MC	PHD	83.	Oklahoma	1986
Evers, Pamela	Assoc	962-7709	eversp	JL	LLM	99	Lewis&Cl	2001
Ivancevich, Susan H.	Assoc	962-3969	ivancevichs	GFA	PHD	94.	Tx A&M	&2000
Mautz, R. David Jr.	Assoc	962-3505	mautzd	AF	PHD	87.	Tennessee	&2007
Earney, Charles L.	Asst	962-3505	earneyc	GF	MBA	70	Wisconsin	&1982
Evans, Allison L.	Asst	962-7142	evansal	X	PHD	06.	N Carol	2006
Kerler, William A.	Asst	962-7632	kerler	FA	PHD	05.	Va Tech	2005
Roscher, Richard A.	Asst	962-3507	roscher	AFM	MBA	72	Denver	&1982
Sawyer, Rebecca S.	Asst	962-3506	sawyer	SMF	MBA	75	Duquesne	&1978
Schaupp, L. Christian	Asst	962-4259	schauppl	S	PHD	05.	Va Tech	2005
Walberg, Glenn	Asst	962-7152	walbergg	LX	LLM	04	Geotown	2001

North Carolina at Pembroke

Dept of Business Adm
Dept Phone: 521-6214

Pembroke, NC 28372-1510
School of Business
One University Drive

(910) Fax=521-6750
uncp.edu

BS
Thelma Colon

Dent, Eric B.	Dean	521-6214	eric.dent	Mgt	PHD	97	Geo Wash	2003
Shoulders, Craig D.	Prof	521-6463	craig.shoulders	FG	PHD	82.	Tx Tech	&2004
Bukowy, Stephen J.	Assoc	521-6668	stephen.bukowy	MNCS	PHD	93.	Georgia	& 8-94
Bell, Sharon	Asst	521-6214	sharon.bell	P	MBA		Campbell	* &1989
Bishop, Ollie	Asst	521-6214	ollie.bishop	FD	MBA		N Carol	&1979

North Carolina A&T State Un

Department of Accounting
Dept Phone: Ext 6001
phone 334-7581

Greensboro, NC 27411
School Business & Econ
1601 East Market Street

(336) Fax=256-2274
ncat.edu

ß (1) 1979
BS
Mary Hastye

Craig, Quiester	Dean	334-7632	craigq	FC	PHD	71	Missouri	& 8-72
Robinson-Backmon, Ida B.	C-Ac	Ext 2006	irobinso	CM	PHD	93.	Okla St	&2005
Cooper, William D.	Prof	Ext 6005	cooperw	FAHV	PHD	80.	Arkansas	& 5-85
Anderson, Susan E.	Assoc			XF	PHD	91.	Tx-Arlin	&2006
Highsmith-Quick, Gwendolyn	Assoc	Ext 6016	highsmig	SEIR	PHD	88.	Houston	&1980
Kiel, Mark	Assoc	Ext 2007	kielm	FGN	PHD	78.	Georgia	&1980
Malone, Charles F.	Assoc	Ext 6007	malonec	AF	PHD	92.	Missouri	&1982
McFadden, Gwendolyn	Assoc	Ext 6006	mcfaddeg	XP	LLM	90	Florida	&1990
Thorne, Jerry	Assoc	Ext 6010	jethorne	CM	PHD	98.	Tx A&M	&1980
Campbell, Ronald L.	Asst	Ext 6011	camber	FN	PHD	89.	Tx A&M	&1993
Robinson, Diana W.	Asst	Ext 6009	drobins	FM	PHD	02.	Okla St	&1989
McBrayer, Phillip D.	Inst	Ext 6013	pdmcbray	XP	MBA		NC-Green	# * &2003

North Carolina Central Univ

Accounting Discipline
Dept Phone: 530-6405
Homepage: www.nccu.edu

Durham, NC 27707
School of Business
1801 Fayetteville St

(919) Fax=530-6163
nccu.edu

2006
Sonya Scott

Sahoo, Bijoy	Dean	530-6178	bsahoo	Fnce	PHD	95	S Carol	2006
Moffie, Robert P.	L-Ac	530-7377	bmoffie	AXFH	PHD	78.	N Carol	&1987
Newhouse, Benjamin	Prof	530-7512	bnewhouse	AF	PHD	82.	Michigan	&2004
Phillips, Mary	Prof	530-6120	mphillips	CFJ	PHD	83.	N Carol	1983
Associate Dean								
Iyengar, Raghavan J.	Assoc	530-7387	riyengar	FP	PHD	95.	Maryland	&2001
Chiang, Catherine	Asst	530-6123	cchiang	FGPS	PHD	01	CUNY	&2001
Land, Judy K.	Asst	530-7161	jland	F	PHD	05.	N Carol	2005

North Carolina State Univ

Raleigh, NC 27695-8113 (919) Fax=515-4446 2000,2000
Department of Accounting College of Management ncsu.edu BS,MAC
Dept Phone: 515-2256 Hillsborough Street Ginger Howell

Name	Rank	Phone	email	code	degree	year	school	extra
Weiss, Ira R.	Dean	515-5560	ira_weiss	SDMA	PHD	76	UCLA	D-04
Buckless, Frank A.	H-Ac	515-4442	frank_buckless	AF	PHD	89.	Mich St	&1988
KPMG Professor								
Bartley, Jon W.	Prof	515-5560	jon_bartley	FT	PHD	78.	N Carol	& 8-87
Beasley, Mark S.	Prof	515-6064	mark_beasley	AF	PHD	94.	Mich St	&1994
Chen, Al Y. S.	Prof	515-4437	al_chen	MS	PHD	88.	Ga Tech	1988
Krawczyk, Katherine A.	Prof	515-4439	katherine_kra+	BXF	PHD	92.	Tx-Austin	& 8-92
Director, Masters of Accounting Program								
Peace, Robert L.	Prof	515-4434	robert_peace	XL	JD	74	NYU	1982
Sawyers, Roby B.	Prof	515-4443	roby_sawyers	MXB	PHD	90.	Ariz St	&1989
Williams, Paul F.	Prof	515-4436	paul_williams	MFT	PHD	77.	N Carol	1985
Zuckerman, Gilroy J.	Prof	515-0316	gilroy_zucker+	CQ	PHD	74	N Car St	1979
Branson, Bruce C.	Assoc	515-4435	bruce_branson	FV	PHD	92.	Fla St	8-92
Pagach, Donald P.	Assoc	515-4447	don	FT	PHD	92.	Fla St	8-94
Wright, Lorraine W.	Assoc	515-4440	lorraine_wright	BXM	PHD	92.	Va Tech	1992
Bradford, Marianne	Asst	515-2256	marianne_brad+	S	PHD	01.	Tennessee	&2003
Brazel, Joseph F.	Asst	515-2256	joe_brazel	AF	PHD	04.	Drexel	2003
Nunez, Karen R.	Asst	513-0526	karen_nunez	CFM	PHD	02.	Oklahoma	* 2001
Pennington, Robin R.	Asst			BS	PHD	02.	S Carol	8-07
Taylor, Eileen	Asst	513-2476	eileen_taylor	ABS	PHD	06.	S Fla	2006
Carraway, Ernest R.	Lect	515-4510	ernest_carraway	LXR	JD	77	N Carol	&1985
Giles, John	Lect	515-4449	john_giles	MF	MS	84	N Car St	&1991
Griffin, Hariette	Lect	515-1008	hariette_griffin	FS	ME	78	N Car St	&1978
Thomas, Robin	Lect	515-6150	robin.thomas	FM	MS	89	N Carol	1991

University of North Dakota

Grand Forks, ND 58202-8097 (701) Fax=777-6183 ß 1984,1990
Department of Accountancy Business & Public Plcy und.nodak.edu BBA,BACC,MBA
Dept Phone: 777-2921 293 Centennial Dr, Stop 8097 Marsha Oss
Homepage: www.und.nodak.edu/dept/acct/
  email @1=mail.business.und.edu

Name	Rank	Phone	email	code	degree	year	school	extra
Elbert, Dennis J.	Dean	777-2135	dennis_elbert	Mktg	PHD	76	Missouri	8-80
Wilde, Harold H.	C-Ac	777-4679	harold_wilde	AFG	PHD	81.	Nebraska	& 8-82
Hansen, Kenneth A.	Prof	777-4685	kenneth_hansen	LX	LLM	89	DePaul	& 9-91
Campbell, Katherine	Assoc	777-6309	kate.campbell	F	PHD	96.	U Wash	& 8-03
Carlson, Steven J.	Assoc	777-4737	steve.carlson@1	FS	PHD	91.	Arkansas	& 7-94
Dosch, Robert J.	Assoc	777-4686	robert_dosch	A	PHD	96.	Iowa	& 8-00
Ellingson, Dee Ann	Assoc	777-4682	deeann_ellingson	CMP	PHD	96.	Va Tech	&1993
Loyland, Mary J.	Assoc	777-4680	mary_loyland	AF	PHD	89.	Nebraska	& 1-87
deMagalhaes, Roberto	Asst	777-4692	roberto_demag+	A	PHD	98.	Miss	& 8-05
Altepeter, Donna J.	Lect	777-2923	donna_altepeter	FD	MACC	86	N Dakota	& 9-86

North Dakota State Univ

Fargo, ND 58105-5075 (701) Fax=231-6545 2001,2001
Dept of Accounting & Info Sy College of Business Adm ndsu.edu BS,MBA
Dept Phone: 231-5845 Minard Hall #403 Jill Blazek

Name	Rank	Phone	email	code	degree	year	school	extra
Johnson, Ronald D.	Dean	231-7577			DBA	70	Indiana	2005
Bowlin, William F.	H-Pr	231-8970	bud.bowlin	CMNG	PHD	84.	Tx-Austin	2007
Klamm, Bonnie K.	Assoc	231-8813	bonnie.klamm	DSF	PHD	99.	Va Comm	&2000
Snyder, Herbert	Assoc	231-8512	herbert.snyder	AJS	PHD	94	Syracuse	2003
Dietz, Donna K.	Asst	231-8653	donna.dietz	CMU	PHD	89	N Dakota	* &2000
Dowdell, Thomas D.	Asst	231-5876	thomas.dowdell	AF	PHD	04.	Temple	* &2003
Clifton, James W.	SLect	231-7504	james.clifton	NFXG	MS	88	N Dakota	&1998
Glatt, Janice	SLect	231-8820	janice.glatt	PF	MBA	85	N Dak St	&1985
Jorgenson, Maggie D.	Lect	231-7649	maggie.jorge+	MS	MS	80	N Dakota	* &2004

University of North Florida

Jacksonville, FL 32224-2675 (904) Fax=620-3861 (123) 1976,1981
Dept Accounting & Finance Coggin Col of Business unf.edu BS,MBA,MAC
Dept Phone: 620-2630 4567 St. Johns Bluff Rd.,S Alice Davies/Gloria Meehan

Name	Rank	Phone	email	code	degree	year	school	extra
McAllister, John P.	Dean	629-2590	jmcallis	FAI	PHD	80	Penn St	& 7-05
Calhoun, Charles H. III	C-Pr	620-2630	ccalhoun	FXI	DBA	73.	Fla St	&1995
Barton, Thomas L.	Prof	620-2630	tbarton	FMT	PHD	84.	Florida	&1982
Bates, Homer L.	Prof	620-2630	hbates	MFC	PHD	77.	Illinois	&1984
MacArthur, John B.	Prof	620-2630	jmacarth	MUCI	PHD	85	Wales	&1994
McEldowney, John E.	Assoc	620-2630	jmceldow	FAO	DBA	84.	Miss St	# * &1980
Michelman, Jeffrey E.	Assoc	620-2630	jmichelm	FSNM	PHD	87.	Wisconsin	* &1990
Waldrup, Bobby E.	Assoc	720-2630	bwaldrup	SFJ	PHD	97.	Miss	&2003
Adams, Bettie M.	Asst	620-2589	badams	FOV	MA	65	Fla St	# &1977
Jaeger, David G.	Asst	620-2630	djaeger	XL	JD	79	Cincinnati	1996
Jones, Lynn C.	Asst	620-2630	lcjones	FX	PHD	03.	Geo St	& 8-03
Gill, Hubert W.	Inst	620-2630	hgill	FM	MACC	90	N Fla	&1992
Tanner, Diane L.	Inst	620-2630	dtanner	FP	MACC	80	N Fla	&1984

North Georgia Col & St Univ Dahlonega, GA 30597 (706) Fax=864-1607 2007
Accounting Faculty Sch of Business & Gov ngcsu.edu BBA
Dept Phone: 864-1610 Christie Waters
Homepage: http://www.ngc.peachnet.edu/Academic/Bus_Gov/BADM/badm.htm

Skelly, Gerald U.	Dean	864-1609	gskelly	Mktg	DBA	78	Fla St	1993
Grant, Clayton	H-Pr	864-1620	cgant	Econ	PHD	72	Clemson	1985
Morris, David E.	Assoc	864-1611	dmorris	CX	PHD	93	American	&1983
Poff, J. Kent	Assoc	864-1679	kpoff	X	PHD	91.	Va Tech	&1995
Merritt, Martha E.	Asst	864-1481	mmerritt	AF	MACC	84	S Carol	&1988

University of North Texas Denton, TX 76203-5219 (940) Fax=565-3803 ß (13) 1961,1966
Dept Accounting Box 305219 College of Business Adm unt.edu BS,MS,MBA,PHD
Dept Phone: 565-3080 1167 Union Circle Ivy Naude
Homepage: www.coba.unt.edu/acct

Cooper, Kathleen	Dean	565-3037	cooperk	Econ	PHD	80	Colorado	2005
Merino, Barbara D.	C-Pr	565-3097	merino	FHT	PHD	75.	Alabama	&1983
Horace Brock Chair & Regents Professor of Accounting								
Clay, Raymond J. Jr.	Prof	565-3093	clay	AFO	DBA	74.	Kentucky	&1983
Institute of Internal Auditors Professor								
Conover, Teresa L.	Prof	565-3867	conovert	FI	PHD	88.	Tx A&M	&1989
Paden Neeley Professor of Accounting								
Frost, Carol A.	Prof	565-3080	frostc	F	PHD	89.	Michigan	2007
Bonard A. Coda Chair of Accounting								
Graves, O. Finley	Prof	565-3076	gravesf	FIW	PHD	85.	Alabama	& 8-02
Associate Dean								
Klammer, Thomas P.	Prof	565-3099	klammer	MF	PHD	71.	Wisconsin	& 9-70
Regents Professor of Accounting								
Mayper, Alan G.	Prof	565-3100	mayper	FTAB	PHD	81.	Florida	&1987
Price, John E.	Prof	780-3601	price@scd.unt.ed	X	PHD	81.	North Tx	&1987
Vice Provost, UNT at Dallas; area code (972)								
Raman, K. K.	Prof	565-3089	raman	FGN	PHD	79.	Indiana	&1981
O. J. Curry Professor								
Curtis, Mary B.	Assoc	565-4366	curtism	ASDB	PHD	95.	Kentucky	& 8-98
Hutchison, Paul D.	Assoc	565-3083	hutchp	FWBS	PHD	97.	Tx Tech	8-98
Plummer, C. Elizabeth	Assoc	565-3069	plummere	X	PHD	94.	Tx-Austin	& 8-03
KPMG Faculty Fellow								
Wilner, Neil A.	Assoc	565-3102	wilner	FMB	PHD	80.	Ohio St	&1987
Atwood, T. J.	Asst	565-3077	atwoodt	X	PHD	95.	Illinois	&2006
Reed, Anita	Asst	565-3090	reeda	ASM	PHD	07	S Fla	2006
Cutler, Ross	Inst	565-3098	cutlerr	F	MA	75	Brighm Yg	& 8-04
Elam, Dennis	Inst	780-3007		FMA	PHD	03	Tx-Austin	&2006
email=delam@scd.unt.edu; area code (972)								
Zimmermann, Harvey	Inst	565-2096	zimmerh	AFO	MBA	72	North Tx	& 8-02

Northeastern University Boston, MA 02115-5000 (617) Fax=373-8814 ß 1962,1974
Accounting Group College of Business Adm neu.edu BS,MS/MBA,MST
Dept Phone: 373-3240 360 Huntington Ave Linda Costa
Homepage: www.cba.neu.edu/acc

Moore, Thomas E.	Dean				PHD		Boston C	8-04
Platt, Marjorie B.	H-Pr	373-4647	m.platt	BCEM	PHD	77	Michigan	* 1982
Bruns, Sharon M.	Prof	373-4648	s.bruns	FM	PHD	81.	Geo St	9-80
Sherman, H. David	Prof	373-4640	h.sherman	MU	DBA	81.	Harvard	& 9-85
Wright, Arnold M.	Prof			ABIE	PHD	79.	S Calif	& 9-07
Joseph M. Golemme Research Professor of Accounting								
Hertenstein, Julie H.	Assoc	373-4711	j.hertenstein	FMB	DBA	84.	Harvard	9-92
Jackson, Cynthia M.	Assoc	373-4643	c.jackson	FS	PHD	92.	S Carol	& 7-98
Krishnamoorthy, Ganesh	Assoc	373-4644	g.krishnamoorthy	ABFS	PHD	94.	S Calif	& 9-00
Maletta, Mario J.	Assoc	373-8397	m.maletta	FB	PHD	89.	Mass	9-97
Cowan Research Professor of Accounting								
Maroney, James J.	Assoc	373-5976	j.maroney	F	PHD	94.	Conn	& 9-93
Rupert, Timothy J.	Assoc	373-5165	t.rupert	BX	PHD	94.	Penn St	9-92
Joseph M. Golemme Professor of Accounting								
Bame-Aldred, Charles	Asst			AFB	PHD	04.	Mass	9-07
Moreno, Kimberly K.	Asst			AF	PHD	98.	Mass	9-07
Zhang, Yue (May)	Asst	373-3357	yu.zhang	MB	PHD	06.	Pittsburgh	9-06
Crossland, Hugh J.	Lect	373-5022	h.crossland	X	LLM	74	Boston U	9-94
Bruns, William J. Jr.	Lect	373-8374	w.bruns	FM	PHD	63.	Berkeley	2001
Cottrill, Michael D.	Lect	373-4639	m.cottrill	FVA	MAC	75	Va Tech	* & 9-85
Marples, Lynn W.	Lect	373-4642	l.marples	MF	MBA		Stanford	* 6-90
O'Kelly, Peggy	Lect	373-5270	p.okelly	AFV	MS	74	Northeas	& 9-81

Northeastern Illinois Univ

Dept Atg, Bus Law, & Finance
Dept Phone: 442-6140
Homepage: www.neiu.edu
Did Not Respond--2005-2006 Listing

Chicago, IL 60625-4699
College Business & Mgt
5500 North St. Louis Ave

(773) Fax=442-4900
neiu.edu

BS,MBA
Debra Pfeiffer

Name	Rank	Phone	Email	Field	Degree	Yr	School	
Titus, Varkey K.	Dean	442-6100	v-titus	Econ	PHD	80	Wash St	7-02
Chen, Chong-Tong	C-Pr	442-6150	c-chen3	MCS	PHD	72	Illinois	* & 9-85
Maksy, Mostafa M.	Prof	442-6155	m-maksy	FM	PHD	83.	Baruch	& 9-89
Alkafaji, Yass A.	Assoc	442-6167	y-alkafaji	FIA	DBA	83.	Miss St	& 9-87
Geren, Donald	Assoc	442-6151	d-geren	P	MBA	69	DePaul	& 9-78
Goran, Ruth	Assoc	442-6152	r-goran	X	MSA	76	Roosevelt	& 1-80
Kinkle, Charas	Assoc	442-6153	c-kinkle	XL	JD	77	Howard	9-84
Yoon, Myung Ho	Assoc	442-6164	m-yoon	CMQS	PHD	88.	Houston	1-89
Chen, Andy H.	Asst	442-6148	h-chen	S	PHD	90	Tennessee	& 9-90
Chen, Ring D.	Asst	442-6149	r-chen	VF	PHD	85.	Florida	& 9-87
Krissek, Thomas J.	Asst	442-6154	tj-krissek	CMQV	MBA	82	Loyola	& 9-83
Neal, Philip G.	Asst	442-6156	p-neal	XL	JD	78	S Illinois	& 9-89
Nyadroh, Emmanuel M. K.	Asst	442-6157	e-nyadro	FM	PHD	81.	Nrthwstrn	9-87
Zheng, Lin (Sandy)	Asst	442-6172	l-zheng	FA	PHD	04.	Alabama	9-04

Northeastern State Univ

Dept of Accounting & Finance
Dept Phone: 449-6521
Homepage: www.cbt.nsuok.edu

Tahlequah, OK 74464-2304
Col of Bus & Technology
700 North Grand

(918) Fax=449-6561
nsuok.edu

BBA,MS

Name	Rank	Phone	Email	Field	Degree	Yr	School	
Schleede, John M.	Dean	454-2959	schleede	Mktg	PHD	78	Mich St	2006
Collier, Roger E.	C-Ac	449-6521	colliere	Fnce	PHD	93	Okla St	2000
Freeman, Gary R.	Assoc	449-6524	freemadg	FM	PHD	88.	Geo St	2004
Jackson, Gary Todd	Assoc	449-6525	jacksongt	FAM	PHD	94.	Arkansas	* &2002
Slusarz, George	Asst	444-2905	slusarz	AL	JD	00	Memphis	&2005
Yeutter, John P.	Asst	444-2968	yeutter	XFJC	PHD	96.	Oklahoma	&1995
Gorden, Paula	Inst	449-6506	walteusg	AX	MBA	98	NE Ok St	&2002
Lee, Deborah	Inst	444-2934	leedl	FS	MS	00	Okla St	&2000
Rabe, Elizabeth	Inst	449-6560	rabeec	FS	MS	01	SMSU	&2006
Trammell, Vicki	Inst	444-2902	trammell	MS	MBA	97	NE St	&2000

Northern Arizona University

Department of Accounting
Dept Phone: 523-3657
Homepage: www.cba.nau.edu

Flagstaff, AZ 86011-5066
College of Business Adm
70 McConnell Drive

(928) Fax=523-7331
nau.edu

ß 1969,1977
BS,MBA

Name	Rank	Phone	Email	Field	Degree	Yr	School	
Gerety, Mason S.	Dean	523-2345	mason.gerety	Fnce	PHD	86	U Wash	8-93
Kilpatrick, Bob G.	C-Pr	523-7399	bob.kilpatrick	XFM	PHD	84.	Okla St	& 1-88
Amer, Tarek S.	Prof	523-7370	tsamer	SMC	PHD	89.	Ohio St	&1994
Bain, Craig E.	Prof	523-7383	craig.bain	FCP	PHD	87.	Tx A&M	&1991
Lorek, Kenneth S.	Prof	523-7406	ken.lorek	FMC	PHD	75.	Illinois	& 8-96
Ralph M. Bilby Endowed Professor								
Mohrweis, Lawrence C.	Prof	523-9580	lawrence.mo +	AFPE	PHD	86.	Wisconsin	& 8-92
Savage, Kathryn S.	Prof	523-7397	kathryn.savage	CM	PHD	93.	Penn St	& 1-91
Watkins, Larry E.	Prof	523-7368	larry.watkins	FTP	PHD	84.	Okla St	&1985
Wilburn, Nancy L.	Prof	523-7395	nancy.wilburn	FPEV	PHD	87.	Tx A&M	& 1-88
Pitt, Kay C.	SLect	523-7402	kay.pitt	PFGM	MS	73	Okla St	&1981
Fox, Wayne	Lect	523-7340	wayne.fox	AMP	MS	71	UCLA	&1983
Director, Bank One Center for Business Outreach								

Univ of Northern Colorado

Sch Accounting & Cpt Info Sy
Dept Phone: 351-2855
Homepage: http://mcb.unco.edu/

Greeley, CO 80639
Monfort College Bus
501 W. 20th Street

(970) Fax=351-1078
unco.edu

ß (1) 1992
BS
Audrey Litfin

Name	Rank	Phone	Email	Field	Degree	Yr	School	
Jares, Timothy	Dean$	351-2347	tim.jares	Fnce	PHD	98	Nebraska	2001
Newmark, Richard I.	D-Ac	351-1213	richard.newmark	PXSE	PHD	96.	U Miami	&2001
McConnell, Allen W.	Prof	351-2856	allen.mcconnell	FVP	MS	66	N Dakota	&1968
Reed, Ronald O.	Prof	351-1252	ronald.reed	APFJ	PHD	81.	Tx Tech	&1988
Turner, Karen F.	Asst	351-1216	karen.turner	FTJD	PHD	95.	Tx-Arlin	&2005
Milam, Lorie	Inst	351-1211	lorie.milam	CFGX	MPA	95	Tx-Austin	&2005
Parish, Beth	Exec	351-1215	beth.parish	FMP	MS	85	Colo St	2006

Northern Illinois Univ

Department of Accountancy
Dept Phone: 753-1637
Homepage: http://www.cob.niu.edu/accy

DeKalb, IL 60115-2854
College of Business
Barsema Hall

(815) Fax=753-8515
niu.edu

ß (13) 1969,1977
BS,MAS,MST
Margaret Berg 753-6095

Name	Rank	Phone	Email	Field	Degree	Yr	School	
Schoenbachler, Denise D.	Dean	753-6225	denises	Mktg	PHD	92	Kentucky	1992
Young, James C.	C-Pr	753-1250	jyoung	X	PHD	88.	Mich St	& 8-00
Crowe Chizek Professor of Accountancy								
Baker, Richard E.	Emer	753-1637	rbaker	2005	PHD	74.	Wisconsin	& 6-79
Bolling, Rodger A.	Emer	753-1637	rbolling	2001	LLM	81	Florida	8-87

Clinton, B. Douglas	Prof	753-1637	clinton	CMU	PHD	94.	Tx-Arlin	* & 8-01
Alta Via Consuiltng Professor of Management Accounting								
Engstrom, John H.	Emer	753-6222	jengstrom	2004	DBA	77.	Indiana	& 6-82
Kieso, Donald E.	Emer	753-1637		1993	PHD	63.	Illinois	&1963
Norton, Curtis L.	Emer	753-6204	nortonc	2005	PHD	76.	Ariz St	9-76
Simon, John R.	Emer	753-6203	jsimon	2001	PHD	74.	Illinois	& 9-73
Smith, Pamela A.	Prof	753-8673	pamsmith	FIJ	PHD	93.	North Tx	& 1-94
KPMG LLP Professor of Accountancy								
Tidrick, Donald E.	Prof	753-1637	dtidrick	AM	PHD	87.	Ohio St	# * & 8-00
Deloitte Professor of Accountancy								
Churyk, Natalie T.	Assoc	753-6210	nchuryk	F	PHD	01.	S Carol	& 8-01
Catearpillar Professor of Accountancy								
Cummings, C. William	Assoc	753-6098	cummings	SDM	PHD	86.	Missouri	& 8-84
Mantzke, Katrina L.	Assoc	753-1637	kmantzke	X	PHD	01.	Wisconsin	& 8-01
Kieso Professor of Accountancy								
Sinason, David H.	Assoc	753-6501	dsinason	SA	PHD	96.	Fla St	# & 8-96
PricewaterhouseCoopers Professor of Accountancy								
Webber, Sally A.	Assoc	753-6212	swebber	SME	PHD	94.	Tx-Arlin	& 8-99
HSBC Professor of Accountancy								
Cripe, Bradrick L.	Asst	753-6206	bcripe	X	PHD	06.	Nebraska	&2006
Lee, Chih-Chen	Asst	753-1637	cclee	S	PHD	00.	S Illinois	& 8-05
Matuszewski, Linda J.	Asst	753-6379	imatus	F	PHD	07	Cincinnati	&2006
Riley, Mark E.	Asst	753-1637		FX	PHD	07	Tx Tech	&2007
Shortridge, Rebecca T.	Asst	753-1637	shortridge	F	PHD	99.	Mich St	& 8-05
Yu, Carol Shaokun	Asst	753-1637		FA	PHD	07.	Houston	&2007
Blanc, Steven D.	Inst	753-6382	sblanc	X	JD	86	San Fran	&2006
Devona, Sandra J.	Inst	753-6206	sdevona	F	MAS	94	N Illinois	& 8-94
Gilbert, Julitta	Inst	753-6369	jgilbert	MX	MAS	90	N Illinois	& 8-00
Madlinger, Lisa L.	Inst	753-6194	madlinger	F	MBA	00	N Illinois	& 6-01
Phelan, Tamara	Inst	753-6208	tphelan	FMS	MM	86	Nrthwstrn	1-02
Youngberg, Suzanne	Inst	753-6099	youngberg	FX	MST	91	DePaul	& 8-00
Hopkins, Debra R.	Fac	753-6207	dhopkins	AR	MAS	87	N Illinois	# &1987
Linden, Rowene F.	Fac	753-6200	rlinden	E	MS	95	N Illinois	7-98

University of Northern Iowa
Department of Accounting
Dept Phone: 273-2394
Homepage: http://www.cba.uni.edu/accounting/

Cedar Falls, IA 50614-0127
College of Business Adm
1227 West 27th Street

(319) Fax=273-2922
uni.edu

1993,1993
BA,MACC,MBA
Katrinka Smith

Moussavi, Farzad	Dean	273-6240	farzad.moussavi		PHD	85	Arkansas	1985
Wartick, Martha L.	H-Ac$	273-7754	marty.wartick	XF	PHD	91.	Penn St	1998
Smith, Gerald	Prof	273-6345	gerald.smith	AF	PHD	74.	Oklahoma	# &1989
Bauman, Christine C.	Assoc	273-2968	christine.bauman	XF	PHD	97.	Wisconsin	&2005
Bauman, Mark P.	Assoc	273-4323	mark.bauman	F	PHD	97.	Wisconsin	2005
Christ, Leroy F. (Rick)	Assoc		rick.christ	XF	PHD	91.	Tx-Austin	&2007
Christ, Mary York	Assoc		mary.christ	FAO	PHD	88.	Tx-Austin	&2007
Lindquist, Timothy M.	Assoc	273-2975	timothy.lind+	BFM	PHD	91.	Colorado	1991
Abraham, Ronald J.	Asst	273-2402	ronald.abraham	AS	MBA	71	Wisconsin	&1974
Francis, Rick N.	Asst	273-3965	rick.francis	F	PHD	03.	Oklahoma	& 1-06
Harrast, Steven A.	Asst	273-8380	steven.harrast	S	PHD	99	Memphis	&2003
Coarts, Darlene G.	Inst	273-3091	darlene.coarts	CM	MBA	76	Maryland	&2006

Northern Kentucky Univ
Department of Accountancy
Dept Phone: 572-6526
Homepage: www.nku.edu/~accountancy/

Highland Hght KY 41099
College of Business
Nunn Drive

(859) Fax=572-6177
nku.edu

1996,1996
BS,MACC
Ann Peelman

Carrell, Michael R.	Dean	572-5165	carrellm	Mgt	DBA	76	Kentucky	7-98
Turner, Leslie D.	C-Pr	572-6381	turnerl	SM	DBA	88.	Kentucky	* 8-88
Marquis, Linda M.	Prof	572-6331	marquis	MC	DBA	78.	Kentucky	* & 7-86
Owhoso, Vincent E.	Assoc	572-7548	owhosv1	AF	PHD	98.	Florida	1-06
Theuri, Peter M.	Assoc	572-5734	theuri	F	DBA	99.	Miss St	& 8-99
Barty, Scottie	Asst	572-6319	bartyg	MF	MBA	78	Cincinnati	& 8-82
Russ, Robert W.	Asst	572-6526	russr	F	PHD	05.	Va Comm	& 8-05
Weickgenannt, Andrea	Asst	572-5499	weickgenannt	FA	MBA	94	Maryland	& 8-00
Ruh, Lorraine	Inst	572-5911	ruhl	PM	MBA	75	Kentucky	8-96
Salyer, Robert	Inst	572-5164	salyerb	X	MS	84	Cincinnati	& 8-01
Director, Graduate Programs								

Northern Michigan Univ
Accounting Faculty
Dept Phone: 227-2900
Homepage: www.nmu.edu

Marquette, MI 49855-5359
Walker Cisler Col Bus
1401 Presque Isle

(906) Fax=227-2930
nmu.edu

2002
BS
Annette Brown

Sanyal, Rajib	Dean	227-2947	rsanyal	Mgt	PHD	87	Geo St	2006
Graci, Samuel P.	Prof	227-2604	sgraci	MFT	PHD	82.	Arkansas	&1980
Janson, Kenneth R.	Prof	227-2682	kjanson	ACM	PHD	79.	Wisconsin	&2001
Thompson, Joel E.	Prof	227-1803	jothomps	FQHT	PHD	82.	Mich St	&1988
Fleming, Robert J.	Assoc	227-1810	rfleming	MFT	PHD	82.	Miss	* &1977
Foulks, Steve	Assoc	227-1805	sfoulks	AX	MBA	72	Chicago	&1975

Northern State University   Aberdeen, SD   57401-7198   (605) Fax=626-2980
Accounting Faculty   School of Business   northern.edu   BS
Dept Phone: 626-2401   1200 South Jay Street   Nancy Naughten

Name	Rank	Phone	email		Degree		School	
Paranto, Sharon	Dean$	626-2402	parantos	Mis	PHD			
Peterson, Scott	C-As	626-2304	petersos	FS	MPA	87	S Dakota	&1987
Kennedy, James Kevin	Assoc	626-7718	kennedyj	GCFI	DBA	94.	S Illinois	1999
Eischen, Erick	Asst	626-3003	emeischen					8-06
Everson, Paul	Asst	626-2469	poe	FMTV	MBA	78	S Dakota	&1977

Northwest Missouri St Univ   Maryville, MO   64468-6001   (660) Fax=562-1750
Dept of Atg, Econ & Finance   Booth Cl Bus & Prof St   nwmissouri.edu   BS,MBA
Dept Phone: 562-1835   800 University Drive   Alisa Meyer
Homepage: www.nwmissouri.edu

Name	Rank	Phone	email		Degree		School	
Billesbach, Thomas	Dean	562-1227	tombill	Mgt	PHD	93	Nebraska	1994
McLaughlin, J. Patrick	C-Ac	562-1280	jpat	L	JD	78	Mo-Ks Cty	1978
Baker, John	Assoc	562-1699	jbaker	JKXL	LLM	77	Mo-Ks Cty	1977
Wood, Rahnl A.	Assoc	562-1759	wood	CMP	PHD	93.	St Louis	&1993
Ludwig, Stephen E.	Asst	562-1835	sludwig	AS	PHD	99.	Arkansas	&2001
Woods, Roger	Asst	562-1752	rwoods	CPFV	MBA	81	NW Mo St	* &1981
Fry, Dovi	Inst	562-1063	dfry	FCP	MBA	94	NW Mo St	&2000
Nance, Michelle	Inst	562-1755	mnance	FP	MBA	03	NW Mo St	2004
Northup, Michael	Inst	562-1891	northup	FP	MS	88	Mo-Ks Cty	&1999

Northwestern University   Evanston, IL   60208-2002   (847) Fax=467-1202   1916
Accounting Info & Mgt   Kellogg School of Mgt   kellogg.northwestern.edu
Dept Phone: 491-3427   2001 Sheridan Road   Bonnie Lee

Name	Rank	Phone	email		Degree		School	
Jain, Dipak C.	Dean	491-3300	d-jain	Mktg	PHD	87	Tx-Dallas	1986
Dye, Ronald A.	C-Pr	491-2663	rdye	FM	PHD	80	Car Mellon	1986
Leonard Spacek Professor of Accounting Information & Management								
Balachandran, Bala V.	Prof	491-2678	b-bala	AMS	PHD	73	Car Mellon	# * &1973
J.L. Kellogg Distinguished Professor; Dir Atg Research Center								
Drebin, Allan R.	Prof	491-2668	ard	FG	PHD	62	Michigan	&1969
Lys, Thomas Z.	Prof	491-2673	tlys	FM	PHD	82.	Rochester	1981
Eric L. Kohler Chair in Accounting								
Magee, Robert P.	Prof	491-2676	r-magee	MQ	PHD	74.	Cornell	1976
Keith I. DeLashmutt Professor of Accounting; Associate Dean								
Prince, Thomas R.	Prof	491-2669	t-prince	MSF	PHD	62.	Illinois	&1962
Revsine, Lawrence	Prof	491-3427	l-revsine	FTI	PHD	68.	Nrthwstrn	&1971
John & Norma Darling Distinguished Professor of Financial Accounting								
Sridhar, Sri S.	Prof	491-8807	s-sridharan	FM	PHD	90.	Pittsburgh	&1990
John L. and Helen Kellog Distinguished Professor of Accounting Info & Mgt								
Vincent, Linda	Assoc	491-2659	l-vincent	F	PHD	95.	Nrthwstrn	1999
Walther, Beverly R.	Assoc	467-1595	bwalther	FM	PHD	95.	Chicago	* &1995
Cadman, Brian	Asst		b-cadman	F	PHD	05.	Oregon	2005
Finn, Mark W.	Asst	467-1635	m-finn	FM	PHD	95.	Cornell	1996
Lansford, Benjamin N.	Asst		b-lansford		PHD	05.	Penn St	8-05
Sunder, Jayanthi	Asst	491-2672	j-sunder	F	PHD	02	NYU	2003
Sunder, Shyam V.	Asst	491-3427	shyam-sunder	F	PHD	02	NYU	2002
Rusticus, Tjomme O.	SLect		t-rusticus	MC	PHD	06.	Penn	2006

Northwestern State U of LA   Natchitoches, LA   71497   (318) Fax=357-5990   1996
Accounting Faculty   College of Business   nsula.edu   BS
Dept Phone: 357-5161   Beth Carter

Name	Rank	Phone	email		Degree		School	
Elliott, Stephen	Dean	357-5161	elliott	Insu	PHD	83	La Tech	
Kilpatrick Insurance Endowed Professor of Insurance								
Briscoe, Nat R.	Prof	357-5709	briscoe	CFMG	PHD	88.	Fla St	&1997
Poindexter Fund Professor of Accounting								
Bechtel, Terence W.	Assoc	357-4233	bechtelt	FMX	PHD	96.	Oklahoma	&1994
Cooley, Glen	Assoc	357-5058	cooleyg	EJPX	PHD		North Tx	& 8-81
Vienne, Margaret W.	Inst	357-6987	woodsb	P	MBA		La Tech	& 1-07

Northwood University   Midland, MI   48640-2398   (989) Fax=837-4331
Accounting Department   College of Business   northwood.edu   BBA
Dept Phone: 837-4834   4000 Whiting Drive   Stacey Thurston 837-4218

Name	Rank	Phone	email		Degree		School	
Grether, John	Dean	832-4371		Econ	JD	05	Mich St	1994
Minbiole, Elizabeth	C-Ac	837-4834	eaminbio	PFCM	MBA	84	Cen Mich	&1982
Bennett, Jeffrey A.	Emer	837-4290	bennett	5-04	MBA	65	Cen Mich	1965
Sumi, Barbara E.	Prof	837-4832	sumi	PFMS	MS	80	Cen Mich	1980
Hunkins, Brett C.	Assoc	837-4289	bhunkins	AFMP	MBA	03	Cen Mich	&1999
Tofteland, Elmer H.	Assoc	837-4833	toftelan	PFGN	MBA	78	Cen Mich	&1982
Dexter, John E.	Asst	837-4250	dexter	FMVX	MA	86	Webster	&1999

Norwich University
Accounting Faculty
Dept Phone: 485-2210

Northfield, VT 05663-1035
Div of Business & Mgt

(802) Fax=485-2087
norwich.edu

BS
Sandra Kingsley

Name	Rank	Phone	Email		Degree	Year	School	
Rotondi, Robert T.	C-Pr	485-2221	rrotondi	FX	MBA	71	Fordham	& 9-77
Yandow, Thomas H.	Asst	485-2222	tomy	ACF	MBA	98	Lincoln	&2000

University of Notre Dame
Department of Accountancy
Dept Phone: 631-7324
Homepage: http://www.nd.edu/~acctdept/

Notre Dame, IN 46556-5646
Mendoza Col of Business
102 Mendoza Col of Business

(574) Fax=631-5255
nd.edu

ß (13) 1962,1972
BBA,MBA,MSA
Dena M. Leinen

Name	Rank	Phone	Email		Degree	Year	School	
Woo, Carolyn Y.	Dean	631-7992	woo.5	Mgt	PHD	79	Purdue	1997
Mittelstaedt, H. Fred	C-Pr	631-5087	mittelstaedt.1	F	PHD	87.	Illinois	&1992
PricewaterhouseCoopers Faculty Fellow								
Easton, Peter	Prof	631-6096	easton.5	F	PHD	84.	Berkeley	&2003
Alumni/Andersen Chair								
Frecka, Thomas J.	Prof	631-8395	frecka.1	FM	PHD	78.	Syracuse	& 7-90
Vincent and Rose Lizzadro Chair								
Milani, Kenneth W.	Prof	631-5296	milani.1	XMN	PHD	72.	Iowa	& 1-72
Morris, Michael H.	Prof	631-5077	morris.2	MCQ	PHD	80.	Cincinnati	* & 9-79
Nichols, William D.	Prof	631-5245	nichols.1	F	DBA	78.	Fla St	& 9-77
Associate Dean								
Ramanan, Ramachandran	Prof	631-8670	ramanan.1	FM	PHD	86.	Nrthwstrn	1991
Ricchiute, David N.	Prof	631-5276	ricchiute.1	A	DBA	77.	Kentucky	& 9-77
Deloitte Chair								
Schaefer, Thomas F.	Prof	631-9095	schaefer.12	F	PHD	83.	Illinois	& 8-98
KPMG Chair								
Wittenbach, James L.	Prof	631-5147	wittenbach.1	X	DBA	71.	Oklahoma	& 5-72
Liu, Chao-Shin	Assoc	631-6029	liu.17	FM	PHD	92.	Illinois	1992
Deloitte Faculty Fellow								
Miller, Jeffrey S.	Assoc	631-2324	miller.294	F	PHD	00.	Tx-Austin	&2000
Misiewicz, Kevin M.	Assoc	631-7314	misiewicz.1	XJ	PHD	74.	Mich St	& 9-78
Rivera, Juan M.	Assoc	631-5195	rivera.1	FI	PHD	75.	Illinois	& 9-83
Seida, Jim A.	Assoc	631-7324	seida.1	FX	PHD	97.	Tx A&M	& 8-01
Ernst & Young Faculty Fellow								
Stober, Thomas L.	Assoc	631-7614	stober.1	F	PHD	83.	Chicago	&1995
Vera-Munoz, Sandra C.	Assoc	631-9041	vera-munoz.1	BM	PHD	94.	Tx-Austin	&1994
KPMG Faculty Fellow								
Shackell-Dowell, Margaret B.	Asst	631-3299	shackell.2	M	PHD	99.	Michigan	2000
Fuehrmeyer, James	Spec	631-7324	fuehrmeyer.3	FA	MBA	80	Chicago	&2007
Hums, Edward F.	Spec		hums.2	FM	MBA	89	Ind-S Bn	&1992
O'Tousa, Janet L.	Spec	631-9090	otousa.6	FM	MBA	88	Notre Dm	2001
Schmuhl, William	Spec	631-6280	schmuhl.7	FM	MBA	72	Chicago	&2006

Nova Southeastern University
Department of Accounting
Dept Phone: 262-5195
Homepage: www.huizenga.nova.edu

Ft.Lauderdale FL 33314-7796
Huizenga Sch Bus & Entr
3301 College Ave

(954) Fax=262-3849
huizenga.nova.edu

MAC,MBA,MTX,DBA
Aimee Fernandez

Name	Rank	Phone	Email		Degree	Year	School	
Pohlman, Randolph A.	Dean	262-5001	pohlman	Fnce	PHD	76	Okla St	5-96
Moore, Walter B.	D-Ac	262-5101	walter	AMF	PHD	89.	Nebraska	&1996
Hoffman, Michael J. R.	Prof	262-5154	hoffmanm	X	DBA	83.	Indiana	2007
McKenzie, Karen S.	Prof	262-5145	karenmck	MG	PHD	89.	LSU	&2007
Sennetti, John T.	Prof	262-5112	sennetti	TAS	PHD	73	Va Tech	&1996
Harris, Judith A.	Assoc	262-8120	harrisj	FMC	DBA	88.	Boston U	*
Kim, Joung	Assoc	262-5110	joung	FA	PHD	99	S Carol	2007
Landau, Barbara	Asst	262-5133	landau	XL	LLM	86	NYU	2003
Rentfro, Randy W.	Asst	262-5279	rentfro	SFCE	PHD	00.	Fla Atl	* &2006

Oakland University
Dept of Accounting & Finance
Dept Phone: 370-4288

Rochester, MI 48309-4401
School of Bus Adm

(248) Fax=370-4275
oakland.edu

ß (1) 1988,1988
BS,MA
Sally Galloway

Name	Rank	Phone	Email		Degree	Year	School	
Silberman, Jonathan	Dean	370-3286	silberma	Econ	PHD	73	Fla St	2006
Parkash, Mohinder	C-Ac	370-4361	parkash	FT	PHD	87.	Arizona	&1991
Bazaz, M. Sadegh	Prof	370-4286	bazaz	FI	PHD	85.	Oklahoma	1987
Callaghan, Joseph H.	Prof	370-3538	callagha	FMS	PHD	92.	Illinois	&1989
Dillon, Gadis J. (Buck)	Prof	370-4289	dillon	FT	PHD	77.	Michigan	&1987
Pelfrey, Sandra H.	Assoc	370-3276	pelfrey	NOG	MBA	74	Wright St	&1986
Cho, Seong-Yeon	Asst			FMS	PHD	01.	SUNY-Buf	2007
Hutchinson, Robert	Asst			MC	PHD	07	Ohio No	2007
Liu, Min-Hsin (Carol)	Asst		liu2	FM	PHD	05.	SUNY-Buf	8-05
Nehmer, Robert A.	Asst		nehmer	FMS	PHD	88.	Illinois	2005
Serocki, James	Asst	370-2842	serocki	LX	LLM		Wayne St	2005

Oglethorpe University Atlanta, GA 30319-2797 (404) Fax=364-8500
Accounting Program Econ & Business Adm oglethorpe.edu BS
Dept Phone: 364-8530 4484 Peachtree Road NE
Hetherington, Bruce W. C-Pr 364-8348 bhetherington Econ PHD 80 Va Tech 8-80
Benton, Christian Y. D-As 364-8346 cbenton AFM MA 84 Webster &1999
Herring, Nancy A. Assoc 364-8349 nherring F PHD 83. Geo St &2006
Turner, James M. Assoc 364-8530 jturner FMX PHD 96. Geo St &1995

Ohio University Athens, OH 45701-2979 (740) Fax=593-2412 ß (1) 1950,1969
School of Accountancy College of Business ohio.edu BA,MBA
Dept Phone: 593-2020 Copeland Hall 409 Rochelle Lawless
Homepage: www.cob.ohiou.edu/~accounting
Corlett, Glenn E. Dean 593-2001 corlett JD 68 Ohio St 1997
Stephens, Ray G. D-Pr 597-1805 stepher1 KFAV DBA 78. Harvard * & 8-99
  James E. Daley Professor of Accounting
Gist, Willie E. Prof 593-2014 gist FTA PHD 88. Tx A&M &2003
  O'Bleness Professor of Accounting
Hoshower, Leon B. Prof 593-2011 hoshower MC PHD 83. Mich St & 9-88
Kirch, David P. Prof 593-9321 kirch F PHD 90. Penn St & 8-94
Meddaugh, E. James Emer 593-2020 meddaugh 2006 PHD 74. Penn St & 9-87
Reininga, Warren H. Emer 593-2020 1988 MS 47 Indiana &1950
Sharp, Florence C. Emer 593-2020 sharpf 2003 PHD 82. Illinois & 9-88
Voss, William M. Emer 593-2020 1995 PHD 67. Chicago 1971
Cox, James S. Emer 593-2023 cox 1999 PHD 74. Pittsburgh &1964
Esmond-Kiger, Connie L. Assoc 593-1988 kiger FAGN PHD 95. Indiana & 9-99
  Richard P. & Joan S. Fox Professor in Business
Sarikas, Robert H. S. (Zeke) Assoc 593-2080 sarikas FI PHD 92. Illinois &2002
Senteney, David L. Assoc 593-2129 senteney PMI PHD 87. Illinois & 9-94
Sharp, Robert F. Emer 593-2020 1999 PHD 78. Tx-Austin & 9-88
Stephenson, C. B. Emer 593-2020 1988 MBA 59 Geo Wash &1964
Stock, Toby Assoc 593-2016 stockt XF PHD 95. Indiana & 9-01
  Robert H. Freeman Professor of Accounting
Stuchell, Donald V. Emer 593-2020 stuchell 1995 MAS 61 Illinois &1969
Gabriel, E. Ann Asst 593-2019 gabriele MUF PHD 93. Ohio St & 9-01
Meyer, Michael J. Asst 593-2179 meyerm1 M DBA 97. Miss St & 1-05
Bagwell, Jennifer Inst 597-3049 bagwell M MST Alabama & 9-03
Freeland, Susanne Inst 597-1508 freeland F MST 88 Capital & 9-01
Hollingsworth, Mont C. Exec 593-2078 hollingm MS MS 73 Kent St * & 1-06
Werner, R. Budd Exec 593-9324 wernerb & 7-98
  Executive in Residence

Ohio Northern University Ada, OH 45810 (419) Fax=772-1498 2003
Accounting Faculty College of Business Adm onu.edu BSBA
Dept Phone: 772-2070 525 S. Main Street Diane Thede 772-2082
Fenton, James W. Jr. Dean 772-2070 j-fenton Mgt PHD 81 Iowa 2005
Christopher, Jill R. Prof 772-2071 j-christopher PD DBA 99. Clev St &1988
Woods, Dexter R. Prof 772-2075 d-woods LXPR LLM 84 Florida &1987
Zekany, Kay E. Asst 772-2074 k-zekany FCMP PHD 94. S Carol * 1998

Ohio State University Columbus, OH 43210-1144 (614) Fax=292-2118 ß (12) 1916,1963
Dept of Accounting & MIS Fisher College of Bus osu.edu BS,MACC,MBA,PHD
Dept Phone: 292-9368 2100 Neil Avenue Barbara Shoemaker
Homepage: http://www.cob.ohio.state.edu/~acctmis/acctmis.html
Alutto, Joseph A. Dean 292-2666 alutto.1 Org PHD 68 Cornell 1990
Dietrich, J. Richard C-Pr 292-2082 dietrich.59 F PHD 81. Car Mellon 2000
Arya, Anil Prof 292-2221 arya.4 T PHD 91 Iowa 1991
  John J. Gerlach Chair in Accounting
Beatty, Anne L. Prof 292-5418 beatty.86 F PHD 92. MIT &2004
  Deloitte & Touche Chair in Accounting
Bentz, William F. Emer 292-9368 bentz.1 FUMC PHD 69. Ohio St &1988
Fellingham, John C. Prof 292-2488 fellingham.1 FM PHD 75. UCLA 1995
  H.P. Wolfe Chair in Accounting
Jensen, Daniel L. Emer 292-2529 jensen.7 2004 PHD 70. Ohio St & 6-80
Tomassini, Lawrence A. Prof 688-3773 tomassini.1 FM PHD 74. UCLA & 8-93
Young, Richard A. Prof 292-0889 young.53 BCMY PHD 84. Ohio St 1990
  Director of PhD Program
Chu, Pai-Cheng Assoc 292-2451 chu.4 S PHD 87 Tx-Austin 1987
Kinard, James C. Assoc 292-2328 kinard.1 SMCY PHD 69. Stanford &1972
Krasniewski, Raymond J. Emer 292-1822 krasniewski.1 XMN PHD 72 Purdue &1970
Muhanna, Waleed A. Assoc 292-3808 muhanna.1 S PHD 87 Wisconsin 1987
Murdock, Richard J. Assoc 292-1720 murdock.3 FK PHD 77. Cornell &1974
Schroeder, Douglas A. Assoc 292-6427 schroeder.9 FM PHD 81. Kansas 1986
Spires, Eric E. Assoc 292-4422 spires.1 ABF PHD 87. Illinois &1985
Wallin, David E. Assoc 292-3291 wallin.1 ABFM PHD 90. Arizona &1989

Williams, David D.	Assoc	292-8566	williams.77	A	PHD	84.	Penn St	&1984
Altamuro, Jennifer L. M.	Asst	688-8679	altamuro_1		PHD	05.	Penn St	8-06
Johnston, Ricky M.	Asst	688-5791	johnston.365	F	PHD	04.	Penn	2004
Pandit, Shailendra	VAsst	292-4101	pandit.7	F	PHD	06.	Rochester	2006
Zhang, Helen	Asst	292-6547	zhang_614	F	PHD		Minnesota	2006
Mulchandani, Prakash	SLect	247-6267	mulchandani.3	CM	MACC	01	Ohio St	2001
Raabe, William A.	SLect	292-4023	raabe.12	XIE	PHD	79.	Illinois	&2003
Turner, Patrick	SLect	292-2966	turnerp	AFJK	BS	76	Ohio St	2002
Ziegler, Teresa	SLect	292-5316	ziegler.44	F	MBA	88	Ohio St	&1998

Ohio Wesleyan University   Delaware, OH   43015-2370   (740) Fax = 368-3551
Accounting Faculty   Department of Economics   owu.edu   BA
Dept Phone: 368-3535   S. Sandusky St   Patti Krebehene
Homepage: http://www.owu.edu/~econweb

MacLeod, Barbara	C-Ac	368-3547	bamacleo	FJV	MBA	86	Nrthwstrn	1999
John J. Joseph Professor of Economics								
Boos, John D.	Prof	368-3546	jdboos	VFMA	JD	66	Geo Wash	1983
Harvey, Joann P.	Prof	368-3541	jpharvey	XFV	MBA	82	Ohio St	&1981
Tecklenburg, Donald	Asst	368-3539		VFMA	MBA	78	Virginia	2007

University of Oklahoma   Norman, OK   73019-4004   (405) Fax = 325-7348   ß (13) 1926,1963
Steed School of Accounting   Price Col of Business   ou.edu   BAC,BBA,MAC,PHD
Dept Phone: 325-4221   307 W. Brooks #200   Linda D. Moore
Homepage: http://www.ou.edu/business/accounting/price/

Evans, Kenneth	Dean							
Ayres, Frances L.	D-Pr	325-5768	fayres	FX	PHD	82.	Iowa	&1982
John W. Jr. and Barbara J. Branch Professor								
Ghosh, Dipankar	Prof	325-5777	dghosh	MBC	PHD	91.	Penn St	1-91
Knapp, Michael C.	Prof	325-5784	mknapp	ACF	PHD	83.	Oklahoma	* &1988
McLaughlin Chair in Business Ethics								
Lipe, Marlys Gascho	Prof	325-2293	mlipe	MB	PHD	85.	Chicago	* & 8-97
Rath Chair in Accounting								
Willinger, G. Lee	Prof	325-5780	lwilling	FTV	DBA	82.	Fla St	& 1-83
John F. Y. Stambaugh Centennial Professor								
Crain, Terry L.	Assoc	325-5759	tcrain	XZ	PHD	89.	Tx Tech	& 9-89
Dale Looper Chair in Accounting								
Cuccia, Andrew D.	Assoc	325-5796	cuccia	X	PHD	90.	Florida	&1999
Grant Thornton Faculty Fellow								
Jensen, Kevan L.	Assoc	325-5763	kjensen	A	PHD	00.	Florida	1999
Lipe, Robert C.	Assoc	325-2401	rlipe	F	PHD	85.	Chicago	& 1-98
KPMG Centennial Professor								
Thomas, Wayne B.	Assoc	325-5789	wthomas	FI	PHD	95.	Okla St	&2000
John T. Steed Chair								
Knapp, Carol A.	Asst	325-5809	cknapp	MF	PHD	95.	Oklahoma	2001
Price, Renee A.	Asst	325-4221		FM	PHD	93.	Tx A&M	&2007
visiting from University of Nebraska								
Yi, Han S.	Asst	325-5792	han.yi	F	PHD	06.	Mich St	2006
Cuccia, Cynthia	Lect	325-4224	ccuccia		PHD	91.	Florida	&2006

Oklahoma Baptist University   Shawnee, OK   74804-2590   (405) Fax = 878-3253
Accounting Faculty   Dickinson Sch of Bus   okbu.edu   BBA
Dept Phone: 878-3254   500 West University   Peggy Herron

Rudebock, Rich	Dean	878-3283	rich.rudebock	Mgt	EDD		Okla St	
Flint, Roger D.	Assoc	878-3272	roger.flint	BPTV	MBA	80	SW Mo St	& 8-80

Oklahoma Christian Univ   Oklahoma Cy OK 73136-1100   (405) Fax = 425-5574
Accounting Faculty   College of Business   oc.edu   BBA,MBA
Dept Phone: 425-5560   2501 East Memorial   Cynthia Helmuth

Lewis, Phillip V.	Dean	425-5567		Mgt	EDD	70	Houston	8-99
Cowan, Mickey W.	Assoc	425-5562		VPX	MS	70	Okla St	& 9-00
Kelly, Elaine D.	Assoc	425-5564		AT	MBA	89	Cen Okla	& 8-92
Johnson, Kenneth D.	Asst	475-5568		OX	MBA	98	Cen Okla	& 7-02

Oklahoma City University   Oklahoma Cy OK 73106-1493   (405) Fax = 208-5098
Department of Accounting   Meinders School of Bus   okcu.edu   BS,MSA
Dept Phone: 208-5276   2501 North Blackwelder   Jean Kobs

Orza, Vince	Dean	208-5276	vorza		PHD		Oklahoma	2005
Rodgers, Jacci L.	C-Ac	208-5824	jrodgers	CME	PHD	88.	Oklahoma	* & 8-92
Thompson, James H.	Prof	208-5486	jht	FVT	PHD	82.	Oklahoma	& 8-91
Ward, Bart H.	Prof	208-6048	bward	A	PHD	73.	Nrthwstrn	& 1-00
Austin, Jane S.	Assoc	208-5278	jaustin	EGM	EDD	99	Okla St	& 8-82
Stetson, T. Beth	Asst	208-5517	tstetson	X	PHD	06.	Oklahoma	8-05

Oklahoma State University Stillwater, OK 74078-0555 (405) Fax=744-1680 ß (13) 1958,1964
School of Accounting Spears School of Bus okstate.edu BS,MS,PHD
Dept Phone: 744-5123 401 Business Bldg Sherry Roberts
Homepage: http://spears.okstate.edu.accounting/

Freedman, Sara M.	Dean	744-5075	sara.freedman	Mgt	PHD	76	N Carol	2006
Hansen, Don R.	H-Pr	744-8626	don.hansen	CM	PHD	77.	Arizona	* 1989
Kerr-McGee Professor								
Chasteen, Lanny G.	Prof	744-5357	lanny.chasteen	EF	PHD	70.	Arkansas	&1969
Kerr McGee Professor								
Dorr, Patrick B.	Prof	744-6349	patrick.dorr	XS	PHD	79.	North Tx	& 9-77
Haskell Cudd Professor								
Meek, Gary K.	Prof	744-5100	gary.meek	IF	PHD	80.	U Wash	&1980
Oscar S. Gellein/Deloitte & Touche Professor								
Wetzel, T. Sterling (Tom)	Prof	744-8610	thomas.s.wetzel	A	PHD	80.	Okla St	1986
Wilguess, John H.	Prof	744-5124	wil	X	PHD	79.	Arkansas	&1979
Wright, Charlotte J.	Prof	744-8611	charlotte.wright	MCB	PHD	82.	North Tx	&1982
Wilton T. Anderson Professor of Accounting								
Herrmann, Donald R.	Assoc	744-5123	don.herrmann	AF	PHD	95.	Okla St	& 7-05
Johnson, Carol B.	Assoc	744-7627	carol.johnson	FI	PHD	93.	Ariz St	&1992
Lacy, Bud	Assoc	744-6994	bud.lacy	X	PHD	83.	Colorado	&1981
Mowen, Maryanne M.	Assoc	744-5139	mmowen	MCB	PHD	79	Ariz St	* 1980
Murphy, Kevin E.	Assoc	744-8607	kevin.murphy	X	PHD	83.	Wisconsin	&1981
Ransom, Charles R. (Chuck)	Assoc	744-8608	c.ransom	FIT	PHD	83.	Wisconsin	&1981
Church, Kimberly	Asst	744-5123	kimberly.church		PHD	07.	Arkansas	2007
Cornell, Robert M.	Asst	744-6377	robert.cornell	BCUM	PHD	06.	Utah	2006
Eng, Li Li	Asst	744-5123	engli	F	PHD	95.	Michigan	& 8-02
Fisher, Lance M.	Asst	744-5123	lance.fisher		PHD	07.	Arizona	2007
Nabar, Sandeep M.	Asst	744-5123	sandeep.nabar	FM	PHD	97.	Tx-Austin	8-02
Spencer, Angela W.	Asst	744-2863	angela.spencer	F	PHD	06.	Arkansas	2006

Old Dominion University Norfolk, VA 23529-0229 (757) Fax=683-3258 ß (13) 1974,1980
Department of Accounting Col Business & Pub Adm odu.edu BSBA,MSA
Dept Phone: 683-3529 Constant Hall, Room 2157 Frenchon Nixon
Homepage: bpa.odu.edu/accounting/

Bagranoff, Nancy A.	Dean	683-3520	nbagranoff	SM	DBA	86	Geo Wash	&2003
Ziegenfuss, Douglas E.	C-Ac	683-3514	dziegenf	AOJS	PHD	89.	Va Comm	# * &1988
Martinson, Otto B.	Prof	683-3505	obmartin	CJM	DBA	70.	Geo Wash	* &1989
Henry, Laurie J.	Assoc	683-4720	lhenry	SFBG	PHD	93.	Miss	&1993
Kim, Francis C.	Assoc	683-3662	ckim	F	PHD	94	Baruch	2006
McKee, Tim C.	Assoc	683-3577	tmckee	XLJP	LLM	81	DePaul	& 1-85
Stein, Michael T.	Assoc	683-5495	mtstein	AF	PHD	88,	Brit Colum	2006
Pinsker, Robert	Asst	683-6553	rpinsker	MF	PHD	02.	S Fla	& 8-02
Xu, Yin	Asst	683-3554	yxu	BMF	PHD	01.	S Carol	2001
Berry, Walter W.	SLect	683-4716	wberry	PXC	MBA	77	Old Dom	&1977
Doherty, Patricia M.	SLect	683-3550	pdoherty	PF	MBA	91	Golden Gt	&1985
Kubican, Terry R.	SLect	683-4346	tkubicha	PSAC	MSA	95	Old Dom	* &1995
Spurrier, Randall R.	SLect	683-6312	rspurrie	PFAS	MBA	68	Hawaii	&1999

Oral Roberts University Tulsa, OK 74171 (918) Fax=495-6500
Accounting Faculty School of Business oru.edu BS
Dept Phone: 495-6555 7777 South Lewis Avenue Sylvia Johnson

Lewandowski, Mark	Dean		mlewandowski	Mgt	PHD	95	Walden	
Russell, James	C-Pr	495-6551	jrussell	Mktg	PHD	81	Va Tech	2000
Gregg, M. Ray	Assoc	495-6561	raygregg	PX	MBA	71	Tx Tech	& 8-73
Unruh, Terry M.	Asst	495-7781	tunruh	VFC	MBA	80	Oral Rob	& 8-80

University of Oregon Eugene, OR 97403-1208 (541) Fax=346-3341 ß (13) 1923,1963
Department of Accounting Lundquist Coll of Bus uoregon.edu BS,BA,MACC,PHD
Dept Phone: 346-1461 1208 University of Oregon
Homepage: lcb.uoregon.edu/Departments/Actg/

Bean, James C.	Dean	346-3300		OprR	PHD	80	Stanford	7-04
Gernon, Helen	C-Pr	346-5127	heleng	FXI	PHD	78.	Penn St	&1978
Lundquist Professor of Accounting (1994-2006); Associate Dean								
Guenther, David A.	H-Pr	346-1461	guenther	FX	PHD	90.	U Wash	2005
Scharpf Professor of Accounting								
King, Raymond D.	Prof	346-3357	rking	F	PHD	80.	Oregon	&1982
Rippey Professor of Accounting								
Morse, Dale C.	Prof	346-3342	dmorse	FM	PHD	78.	Stanford	1991
Charles E. Johnson Memorial Professor of Accounting								
O'Keefe, Terrence B.	Prof	346-3317	tokeefe	AF	PHD	70	Purdue	1980
also Professor at University of Queensland								
Matsunaga, Steven R.	Assoc	346-3340	stevem	FX	PHD	92.	U Wash	&1992
Bryant-Kutcher, Lisa L.	Asst	346-3252	lbryant	F	PHD	99.	Colorado	&2003
Davis, Angela K.	Asst	346-3210	davisan	F	PHD	01.	U Wash	&2006

Hu, Xuesong	Asst	346-3968	xuesong	F	PHD	05.	S Calif	2006
Williams, Michael G.	Asst	346-3622	mwilliam	TXF	PHD	92	Princeton	2004
Clement, Robin P.	Inst		rclement	F	PHD	94.	Mich St	&2003
Henney, Michele C.	Inst	346-3281	mhenney	AFX	PHD	94.	Oregon	&2004
Sneed, Joel	Inst	346-3417	sneed	FX	PHD	01.	Arizona	&2000
Tomcal, Michael P.	Inst	346-1626	mpt	FCX	MACC	05	Oregon	2005

Oregon Institute of Tech   Klamath Falls OR   97601-8801   (541) Fax=885-1687
Management   Engr, Tech & Management   oit.edu
Dept Phone: 885-1408   3201 Campus Drive

Jones, Charles	C	885-1377	jonesch		PHD	02	Utah St	1997
Bailey, Richard L.	Prof	885-1964	baileyr	XMF	MACC	85	Utah St	&1991
Morgan, Carmen	Assoc	885-1502	morganc	FVA	MBA	91	Port St	* &1989
Wolverton, Janet Bear	Assoc	885-1505	wolvertj	DSM	MS	89	Colorado	&1994

Oregon State University   Corvallis, OR   97331-2603   (541) Fax=737-4890   ß (1) 1960,1970
Department of Accounting   Col Bus,Bexell Hall 200   bus.oregonstate.edu   BS
Dept Phone: 737-4028

Kleinsorge, Ilene K.	Dean	737-6024	Ilene	MC	PHD	87	Kansas	&1987
Graham, Roger C.	H-Pr	737-4028	roger.graham	XF	PHD	90.	Oregon	&1991
Brown, Carol E.	Assoc	737-3309	carol.brown	MS	PHD	89	Oregon St	&1978
Coakley, James R.	Assoc	737-4118	coakley	G	PHD	82.	Utah	1990
Associate Dean of Academic and Student Services								
Banyi, Monica L.	Asst	737-4102	monica.banyi	F	PHD	04.	Arizona	&2004
Caplan, Dennis H.	Asst	737-2727	dennis.caplan	ATM	PHD	94.	Berkeley	* &2004
Marshall, Byron	Asst	737-6054	byron.marshall	S	PHD	05	Arizona	2005
Moore, Jared A.	Asst	737-1517	jared.moore	XF	PHD	06.	Ariz St	&2006
Bourne, Amy	Inst	737-6064	amy.bourne	F	MS	96	Tx Tech	&2006
Brown, Larry	Inst	737-3226	larry.brown	AF	BS	73	Oregon St	&2005

Otterbein College   Westerville, OH   43081   (614) Fax=823-1014
Accounting Faculty   Dept of Bus, Atg & Econ   otterbein.edu   BA,BS,MBA
Dept Phone: 823-1310   Park & Grove   Teresa Piper

Volkman, John A.	C-Ac$	823-1332	jvolkmar	Mgt	PHD		Temple	
Dennis, David K.	Prof	823-1461	ddennis	FSB	PHD	75.	Cincinnati	&1990
Huber, Marsha M.	Assoc	823-1758	mhuber	ANFX	PHD	03	Ohio St	&1986
Smith, Henry C. III	Assoc	823-1298	hcsmith	MC	PHD	94.	Va Comm	* 2001

Ouachita Baptist University   Arkadelphia, AR   71998-0001   (870) Fax=245-5061   2001
Dept of Accounting Box 3689   Hickingbotham Sch Bus   obu.edu   BA
Dept Phone: 245-5254   410 Ouachita St

Rice, Philip F.	Dean	245-5253	ricep		PHD	68	Clemson	1993
Webster, Robert L.	C-Ac	245-5254	websterb	CFN	DBA	93.	La Tech	1993
George Young Chair of Business								
Curry, Jeanie	Asst	245-5248	curryj	TF	ABD		Miss	&1988
Files, James A.	Asst	245-5202	filesj	FS	PHD	05.	Miss St	2005
Rothwell, James C.	Asst	245-5205	rothwellj	FA	MBA	79	La Tech	&1981

Pace University   New York, NY   10038-1502   (212) Fax=618-6410   ß 1996,1996
Department of Accounting   Lubin School of Bus   pace.edu   BBA,MBA,MS,DPS
Dept Phone: 618-6420   1 Pace Plaza   Margaret Duval
   phones with 773- at Westchester with 914 area code

Baczko, Joseph	Dean	618-6600	jbaczko		MBA		Harvard	2005
Jacob, Rudolph A.	C-Pr	618-6425	rjacob		PHD	87.	NYU	1973
Berman, Arnold L.	Prof	773-3494	aberman	FX	LLM	76	NYU	&1974
Cable, Roberta J.	Prof	773-3688	rcable	CM	PHD	81	Columbia	* 1989
Chan, Kam C.	Prof	773-3912	kchan	FP	PHD	91.	S Carol	1997
Chung, Kwang-Hyun	Prof	618-6422	kchung	DFTQ	PHD	90.	Baruch	1990
DiBenedetto, Joseph C.	Prof	618-6417	jdibenedetto	RJMC	JD	75	Brooklyn	* &1971
El-Gazzar, Samir M.	Prof	618-6423	selgazzar	F	PHD	84.	Baruch	1992
KPMG Peat Marwick Professor of Accounting								
Lee, John Y.	Prof	773-3443	jylee	CM	PHD	79.	LSU	1992
Schaeberle Professor of Accounting								
Newman, Bernard H.	Prof	618-6426	bnewman	AVGN	PHD	66	NYU	&1975
Rabinowitz, Allan M.	Prof	618-6415	arabinowitz	FOUB	MBA	62	NYU	&1962
Russo, Joseph A. Jr.	Prof	618-6433	jrusso	AB	PHD	94.	Rutgers	&1968
Schier, Lewis	Prof	618-6431	lschier	F	PHD	71	NYU	1965
Tinkelman, Daniel P.	Prof	618-6414	dtinkelman	FA	PHD	97.	NYU	&1996
Donabedian, Bairj	Assoc	773-3421	bdonabedian	PM	PHD	89.	Columbia	1994
Finn, Philip M.	Assoc	773-3516	pfinn	VPI	PHD	90.	Baruch	&1983
Healy, Patricia	Assoc	773-3661	phealy	VC	MBA	75	NYU	* &1977
Lee, Picheng	Assoc	618-6424	plee	FM	PHD	00.	Rutgers	2000

O'Callaghan, Susanne	Assoc	618-6427	socallaghan	AVGN	PHD	94.	Cincinnati	& 9-94
Sen, Kaustav	Assoc	618-6413	ksen	FM	PHD	94.	Rutgers	1996
Tang, Charles Y.	Assoc	618-6430	ytang	FMA	PHD	94	Baruch	1997
Anabila, Andrew A.	Asst	618-6421	aanabila	FM	PHD	02.	Columbia	2003
Farrell, Barbara	Asst	773-3489	bfarrell	DFRS	EDD	93	Columbia	&1993
Li, Chunyan	Asst	773-3794	cli2	FM	PHD	01.	Rutgers	2001
Reisig, Raymond	Asst	773-3489	rreisig	AF	MBA	76	Pace	&1979
Tagliaferri, Lee	Asst	618-6429	ltagliaferri	M	MBA	58	Chicago	1975
Ulinski, Michael	Asst	773-3914	mulinski	CM	PHD	87	NYU	&1984
Zwicker, Robert P.	Asst	773-3914	rzwicker	FRV	EDD	91	Bridgepr	&1983

University of the Pacific Stockton, CA 95211 (209) Fax=946-2586 ß 1983,1983
Accounting Faculty Eberhardt School of Bus pacific.edu BS
Dept Phone: 946-2476 3601 Pacific Avenue Stephanie Fong
Homepage: www.pacific.edu/esb

Williams, Charles R.	Dean	946-7710	cwilliams	Mgt	PHD	90	Mich St	8-06
Vargo, Richard J.	Prof	946-2644	rvargo	FCIM	PHD	69.	U Wash	1981
Wheeler, Stephen W.	Prof	946-2630	swheeler	FAMV	PHD	88.	Ariz St	& 6-94
Neven C. Hulsey Chair in Business Excellence								
Eakin, Cynthia F.	Assoc	946-2476	ceakin	FXM	PHD	93.	Fla St	&1996
Typpo, Eric W.	Asst	946-2260	etyppo	AFS	PHD	94.	Fla St	& 8-98

Pacific Lutheran University Tacoma, WA 98447-0001 (253) Fax=535-8723 ß (1) 1971.1976
Department of Accounting School of Business Adm plu.edu BBA
Dept Phone: 535-7224 12180 Park Ave S Rebecca Torgerson

Turner, Andrew	Dean	536-7445	aturner	Fnce	PHD	81	Penn	6-06
Ramaglia, Judith A.	D-Pr	535-7224	ramaglja	FI	PHD	88.	U Wash	&1982
Myers, Gerald M.	Prof	535-7304	myersgm	MC	PHD	84.	Iowa	1982
VanWyhe, Glenn	Assoc	535-7305	vanwyhga	FA	PHD	91	U Wash	&1979
Zabriskie, Fern	Asst	535-8130	zabrisfh	MF	PHD	02.	U Wash	* &2001

Pacific Union College Angwin, CA 94508-9797 (707) Fax=965-6237
Accounting Faculty Dept of Bus Adm & Econ puc.edu BBA
Dept Phone: 965-6238 Angwin Avenue

Voth, Richard	C-Pr	965-6525	rvoth	FM	PHD	74	Ariz St	1968
Hardcastle, Rodney	Prof	965-6530	rhardcastle	OFAX	MBA	89	Golden Gt	&1989
Kopitzke, Henry	Prof	965-6526	hkopitzke	FLXV	JD	80	Idaho	&1973
Lighthouse, Wally D.	Assoc		wlighthouse	FLX	JD	91		2007
Taylor, Lary	Assoc	965-6528	ljtaylor	FMP	MBA	76	Maryland	1978
Toledo, Marcia L.	Assoc	965-6531	mtoledo	FMP	MED	89	Boston U	1984
Madrid, Daniel G.	Asst	963-6524	dmadrid	CIFN	ABD		Golden Gt	1991

University of Pennsylvania Philadelphia, PA 19104-6365 (215) Fax=573-2054 ß 1916,1963
Accounting Department Wharton Sch 2400 SH-DH wharton.upenn.edu BSE,MBA,PHD
Dept Phone: 898-7772 3620 Locust Walk Mary Lou Day

Holthausen, Robert W.	C-Pr	898-1290	holthausen	F	PHD	80	Rochester	&1989
Nomura Securities Company Professor								
Baiman, Stanley	Prof	898-6782	baiman	F	PHD	74.	Stanford	1991
Ernst & Young Professor of Accounting								
Core, John E.	Prof	898-4821	jcore	M	PHD	95.	Penn	1996
Gonedes, Nicholas J.	Prof	898-7054	gonedes	C	PHD	69.	Tx-Austin	1978
Ittner, Christopher D.	Prof	898-7786	ittnerc	M	PHD	92.	Harvard	1991
Lambert, Richard A.	Prof	898-7782	lambert	FM	PHD	82.	Stanford	1999
Miller-Sherrerd Professor								
Verrecchia, Robert E.	Prof	898-6976	verrecchia	F	PHD	76	Stanford	1983
Elizabeth F. Putzel Professor								
Bushee, Brian J.	Assoc	898-4872	bushee	F	PHD	97.	Michigan	2000
Guay, Wayne R.	Assoc	898-7775	guay	F	PHD	98.	Rochester	1997
Schrand, Catherine M.	Assoc	898-6798	schrand	F	PHD	94.	Chicago	1994
Blouin, Jennifer	Asst	898-1266	blouin	F	PHD	04.	N Carol	2003
Carter, Mary Ellen	Asst	898-7125	carterme	F	PHD	98.	MIT	2002
Cassar, Gavin	Asst	898-2023	cassar	MC	PHDM	05	Berkeley	2005
Hail, Luzi	Asst	898-8205	lhail	F	PHD	96	Zurich	2005
Tuna, Irem	Asst	898-2063	tunaai	F	PHD	03.	Michigan	2002
on leave 2007-08								
Wittenberg Moerman, Regina	Asst	898-2610	rwittenb	F	PHD	06	Chicago	2006
Defeo, Victor J.	Lect	898-4985	defeo	FM	PHD	83.	Illinois	1999
Lane, Marguerite Bishop	Adj	898-8601	pbishop	F	PHD	95.	Nrthwstrn	1997

Penn State University

Penn State University	Univ Park, PA	16802-1912		(814) Fax=863-8393			ß (123) 1957,1963	
Department of Accounting	Smeal College of Bus			psu.edu			BS,MBA,MS,PHD	
Dept Phone: 865-1809	354 Business Bldg						Tammy Snook	
Homepage: http://www.smeal.psu.edu/acctg								
Thomas, James B.	Dean	863-0448	jthomas	Sys	PHD	88	Tx-Austin	1987
Givoly, Dan	C-Pr	865-0041	dgivoly	F	PHD	75.	NYU	& 8-02
Ernst & Young Professor of Accounting								
Dirsmith, Mark W.	Prof	865-3901	eu3	AB	PHD	75.	Nrthwstrn	& 9-75
Deloitte Touche Professor of Accounting								
Fischer, Paul E.	Prof	863-3569	pef5	F	PHD	89	Rochester	& 8-99
Huddart, Steven J.	Prof	865-3271	huddart	MXY	PHD	91	Yale	& 8-99
KPMG Professor of Accounting								
McKeown, James C.	Prof	865-1471	jcm12	FST	PHD	69.	Mich St	8-89
Mary Jean & Frank P. Smeal Professor of Accounting								
Smith, Charles H.	Emer	865-0374	chs2	F	PHD	68.	Penn St	& 1-87
KPMG Professor Emeritus of Accounting								
Barron, Orie E.	Assoc	863-3230	oeb1	AFST	PHD	93.	Oregon	& 8-97
Crum, Robert P.	Assoc	863-4001	rpc1	MX	DBA	83.	Kentucky	& 9-83
Enis, Charles R.	Assoc	865-1149	c3e	X	DBA	81.	Maryland	& 9-81
Jablonsky, Stephen F.	Emer	865-6473	jir	2007	PHD	74.	Illinois	& 9-75
Ke, Bin	Assoc	865-0572	bxk127	X	PHD	99.	Mich St	& 8-99
Ketz, J. Edward	Assoc	865-1361	edketz	FJ	PHD	77.	Va Tech	9-81
Leone, Andrew J.	Assoc	863-5469	ajl14	FMT	PHD	97.	Pittsburgh	* & 9-05
Muller, Karl A. III	Assoc	865-0202	kam23	FI	PHD	97.	Illinois	8-02
Gong, Guojin	Asst	863-7055	gug3	F	PHD	05.	Iowa	7-05
Liu, Michelle	Asst	863-9321	mxl60	F	PHD	06.	MIT	7-06
Louis, Henock	Asst	865-4160	hul4	F	PHD	01.	Ohio St	8-01
Sun, Amy Xue	Asst	863-7071	aus17	F	PHD	05.	Car Mellon	7-05
Licastro, Ralph D.	SLect	865-9252	rdl2	AX	MS	71	Penn St	& 9-72
McClure, Nancy L.	Inst	863-4004	nlm1	FM	MS	87	Penn St	8-94
Pasch, Kenneth W.	Inst	863-3838	kwp2	M	MBA	82	N Colo	1-98
Samuel, Sajay	Clin	865-0054	sajay	AB	PHD	95.	Penn St	8-03
Wright, Suzanne A.	Inst	863-4003	sma118	F	MBA	92	Penn St	& 8-96

Penn St Sch Hospitality Mgt

Penn St Sch Hospitality Mgt	Univ Park, PA	16802-1307		(814) Fax=863-4257				
Hotel Restaurant & Inst Mgt	Health & Human Dev			psu.edu				
Dept Phone: 863-0009	201 Mateer Bldg						Dawn Driver	
Homepage: www.hrrm.psu.edu								
VanHoof, Hubert B.	D-Pr	863-0009	hbv7	MI	PHD	96	Ariz St	8-04
Andrew, William P.	Assoc	863-0272	wpa	FIMQ	PHD	88	Penn St	6-78
Mount, Dan	Assoc	863-2675	djm24	FIQM	PHD	94	US Intl	8-95
Upneja, Arun U.	Assoc	863-7442	aupneja	CFIM	PHD	96.	Houston	8-96
Verbeeten, Marja J.	Asst	863-9775	mjv13	MI	EDD	04	NAU	1-05

Penn State Univ-Erie

Penn State Univ-Erie	Erie, PA	16563-1400		(814) Fax=898-6223			2003,2003	
Department of Accounting	Black Sch of Business			psu.edu			BS,MBA	
Dept Phone: 898-6107	1501 Jordan Road							
Homepage: www.pserie.psu.edu/academic/business/index.htm								
Magenau, John M.	D-Ac	898-6173	owc	Mgt	PHD	88	SUNY-Buf	1985
Voss, James A.	C-In	898-6437	jav7	ABXF	ABD		Pittsburgh	&1984
Deshmukh, Ashutosh	Prof	898-6438	avd1	SA	PHD	93.	Memphis	* &1993
Doran, David T.	Assoc	898-6429	dtd1	FMIN	PHD	85.	Pittsburgh	&1989
Brown, Charles	Asst	898-6432	cab51	PM	PHD	02.	Kent St	& 8-01
Patterson, Robert D.	Inst	898-6418	rdp4	PCFQ	MBA	88	Penn St	&1988

Penn State U Great Valley

Penn State U Great Valley	Malvern, PA	19355-1443		(610) Fax=725-5224			2006	
Management	Grad Prof Studies			psu.edu			MBA	
Dept Phone: 648-3229	30 East Swedesford Rd							
Pak, Simon J.	H-Ac	725-5343	sjp14	Fnce	PHD	80	Berkeley	1-02
Felo, Andrew J.	Asst	648-3380	ajf14	MFC	PHD	99.	SUNY-Bin	* 2001

Penn State Univ-Harrisburg

Penn State Univ-Harrisburg	Middletown, PA	17057-4898		(717) Fax=948-6456			1998,1998	
Department of Accounting	School of Business Adm			psu.edu			BS,MBA	
Dept Phone: 948-6139	777 West Harrisburg Pike						Kathy Schweitzer	
Homepage: www.hbg.psu.edu/sbus/								
Buttross, Thomas E.	C-Ac	948-6145	teb11	CM	PHD	91	Miss	* & 8-00
Schappe, Stephen	D-Ac	948-6141		Mgt	PHD			
Harris, Jean E.	Assoc	948-6157	jeh6	GXHW	PHD	90.	Va Tech	&1990
Trussel, John M.	Assoc	948-6171	jmt12	FAN	PHD	93.	Geo Wash	&1998
Amlie, Thomas T.	Asst	948-6141	tta2	MFG	PHD	96.	Maryland	* 2005
Griffin, Nancy	Inst	948-6149	nag11	SP	BS	81	Penn St	&2006
Schieb, Richard	Inst	948-6161	rgs12	LPX	LLM	93	Geotown	2006

Pepperdine Un-Los Angeles　Los Angeles, CA　90045　(310) Fax = 568-5778　2000,2000
Accounting & Finance　School of Bus & Mgt　pepperdine.edu　BS,MBA
Dept Phone: 258-2827　6100 Center Drive　Doris Jones
　258 numbers have (310) area code

Livingstone, Linda A.	Dean	568-5500	linda.livings +	Mgt	PHD	92	Okla St	2002
Powell, Richard W.	C-Ac	506-4874	rpowell	XF	PHD	97.	Arkansas	&1996
Petro, Fred A.	Prof	258-2827	fpetro	IFME	PHD	73.	Arkansas	* 1980
Samuelson, Bruce A.	Prof	831-9116	bsamuels	FMS	PHD	78.	S Calif	& 9-83
Briginshaw, John	Asst	568-5551	john.briginshaw	FM	PHD	03	Berkeley	2004
McPeak, Charles	Lect	568-5500	cmcpeak	FM	MBA	66	S Calif	&1990

Pepperdine Univ-Malibu　Malibu, CA　90263-4237　(310) Fax = 506-4696　2000,2000
Business Adm Division　Seaver College　pepperdine.edu　BS
Dept Phone: 506-4237　24255 Pacific Coast Highway
Homepage: server.pepperdine.edu/business

Baird, W. David	Dean	506-4280	dbaird	Hst	PHD	69	Oklahoma	1988
Whitney, L. Keith	C-Ac	506-4237	kwhitney	Law	JD	77	Tx Tech	1990
Gean, G. Farrell	Assoc	506-4539	fgean	F	PHD	81.	Geo St	* &1981
Misch, Marilyn B.	Assoc	506-7562	mmisch	Fl	PHD	99.	Ariz St	&1997
Culpepper, Anthony	Asst	506-6811	anthony.culp +	CM	EDD	05	Pepperdi	* &2005
Galantine, Carolyn A.	Asst	506-7469	carolyn.gall +	TF	PHD	94.	S Calif	&2003

Pfeiffer University　Misenheimer, NC　28109-0960　(704) Fax = 463-1363
Department of Accounting　School of Business　pfeiffer.edu　BS,MBA
Dept Phone: 463-1360
Homepage: www.pfeiffer.edu

Booth, W. Scott III	C-Pr	463-1360	sbooth	ACXG	MA	71	Appalach	& 8-82
Preslar, Tina	Asst	463-1360	tpreslar	AFPM	MA	00	NC-Charl	8-01

Philadelphia University　Philadelphia, PA　19144-5497　(215) Fax = 951-2652
Accounting Faculty　School of Business Adm　philau.edu　BS,MBA,MSTX
Dept Phone: 951-2827　School House Ln & Henry Ave
Homepage: philau.edu/sba/

Poteau, Raymond	Prof	951-2811	poteaur	AEFG	MBA	73	Geo Wash	&1984
Borowsky, Stuart	Assoc	951-2817	borowskys	FPXM	MBA	67	Drexel	&1967
Solano, James	Assoc	951-2826	solanoj	XFMP	MS	67	Temple	&1977
Lafond, C. Andrew	Asst	951-5328	lafonda	XMPE	PHD		Sarasota	&2001

Piedmont College　Demorest, GA　30535-0010　(706) Fax = 776-0315
Dept of Atg, CIS & Dec Sci　Walker Sch of Business　piedmont.edu
Dept Phone: 778-8500　P.O. Box 10 / 165 Central Av　Ms. Joyce M. Webb
Homepage: www.piedmont.edu

Piper, William E.	Dean	Ext 1349	bpiper	Econ	PHD	93	Am London	1997
Nelms, Keith R.	C-Pr	Ext 1289	knelms		PHD		Geo St	
Forney, Janet A.	Assoc	Ext 1258	jforney	CF	DBA	94	Nova SE	8-01
Miller, J. Glenn	Assoc	Ext 1326	gmiller	QM	PHD	02	Ga Tech	&2002
Kreiner, Raymond F.	Asst	Ext 1317	rkreiner		MS	91	Ball St	8-04

Pikeville College　Pikeville, KY　41502-1194　(606) Fax = 218-5031
Accounting Faculty　Business & Economics　pc.edu　BBA
Dept Phone: 218-5020　147 Sycamore Street　Cathy Maynard
Homepage: www.pc.edu

Roberts, Howard V.	C-Ac	218-5019	hroberts	FCRV	MBA	78	Marshall	1984

Pine Manor College　Chestnut Hill MA　02467　(617) Fax = 731-7199
Accounting Faculty　Business Administration　pmc.edu　BA
Dept Phone: 731-7050　400 Heath Street

Chester, Nia	Dean				PHD		Boston U	1983
Bergman, Ruthann	C-Ac	731-7050	bergmanr	DFN	MBA		Penn	1983

Pittsburg State University　Pittsburg, KS　66762-7500　(620) Fax = 235-4558　1999,1999
Department of Accounting　G.A. Kelce Col of Bus　pittstate.edu　BBA,MBA
Dept Phone: 235-4561　1701 South Broadway　Mary Scimeca
Homepage: www.pittstate.edu/acctg

Dearth, Richard C.	Dean$	235-4590	rdearth	BLaw	JD	69	Washburn	1993
Casey, Rebecca	C-In	235-4561	rcasey	F	MBA	95	Pitt St	&2002
Fay, Jack R.	Prof	235-4567	jfay	XF	PHD	75.	Arkansas	&1996
O'Bryan, David W.	Prof	235-4566	obryan	FU	PHD	92.	Missouri	* &1992
Roush, Melvin L.	Assoc	235-6196	mroush	CM	PHD	03	Victoria	&2005
Rupp, Galen L.	Assoc	235-4563	grupp	CMF	PHD	82.	Okla St	* 1985
Heath, Rebekah A.	Asst	235-6197	rheath	FM	PHD	99.	Nebraska	# &2005
Hines, Christopher	Inst	235-6509	chines	FA	MBA	01	Mo St	* &2006

University of Pittsburgh   Pittsburgh, PA   15260   (412) Fax = 648-1693   1979,1916
Accounting Faculty   Katz Grad School of Bus   katz.pitt.edu   BSBA,MBA,PHD
Dept Phone:

Name	Rank	Phone	Email					
Delaney, John T.	Dean	648-1500	jtdelaney	IndR	PHD	83	Illinois	1983
Hoffman, Vicky B.	C-Ac	648-1627	vickyh	BAF	PHD	88.	Michigan	&1988
Birnberg, Jacob G.	Emer	648-1719	birnberg	6-06	PHD	62.	Minnesota	1964
Evans, John H. III (Harry)	Prof	648-1714	jhe	MTN	PHD	80.	Car Mellon	1978
Alumni Professor of Accounting								
Moser, Donald V.	Prof	648-1726	dmoser	FBM	PHD	86.	Wisconsin	& 9-86
Nagarajan, Nandu J.	Prof	648-1675	nagaraja	CMY	PHD	84.	Nrthwstrn	* 1-84
Prakash, Prem	Prof	648-1671	ppr	FM	PHD	71	MIT	1977
Carlin, Madeleine J.	Assoc	648-1679	mjcarlin	FX	MBA	78	Temple	&1991
Shastri, Karen A.	Assoc	648-1533	kshastri	FNM	PHD	90.	Pittsburgh	&1998
Feng, Mei	Asst	624-1347	mfeng	F	PHD	05.	Michigan	2004
Srinivasan, Dhinu	Asst	648-1513	dhinus	M	PHD	97	Minnesota	1996

U of Pittsburgh at Johnstown   Johnstown, PA   15904   (814) Fax = 269-7255
Dept of Business   Social Sciences Div   upj.pitt.edu   BA
Dept Phone: 269-2990   450 Schoolhouse Rd   Sharon Wilson

Name	Rank	Phone	Email					
Thompson, Ray	Assoc	269-2970		MS	DBA	84	Nova SE	* 1980
Zakrzwski-Smiach, Deborah	Assoc	269-2969	smiachzk	FADN	MBA	89	Pittsburgh	&1986
Rummell, Janice	Asst	269-2968	jrummell		MA		StFran-NY	1998
Yorop, Stanley J.	Asst	269-2904	sjy4	FAM	MED	72	Ind-Penn	&2004

Plymouth State College   Plymouth, NH   03264-1600   (603) Fax = 535-2611
Accounting Faculty   Department of Business   mail.plymouth.edu   BS,MBA
Dept Phone: 535-2610   Highland Street   Diane Winsor

Name	Rank	Phone	Email					
Buck, Paul M.	C-Pr	535-2208	pbuck	FXAM	MS	68	Northeas	& 9-72
Canlar, Mehmet	Prof	535-2408	mcanlar	FMV	PHD	77	Hacettep	9-88
Babin, Roger O.	Assoc	535-2261	rbabin	FXL	JD	77·	Boston C	9-79
Kopczynski, Frank J.	Assoc	535-2318	frankk	MCSJ	PHD	93	Union-NY	& 9-90

University of Portland   Portland, OR   97203-5798   (503) Fax = 943-8041   1977,1981
Accounting Faculty   Pamplin Sch of Bus Adm   up.edu   BBA
Dept Phone: 943-7224   5000 N. Willamette Blvd   Christine Naylor

Name	Rank	Phone	Email					
Anderson, Robin D.	Dean	943-7155	anderson		EDD	84	Nebraska	
Lewis, Lawrence D.	Prof	943-7224	lewis	CM	PHD	84.	Nebraska	* 2001
Jurinski, James J.	Assoc	943-7426	jurinski	LX	JD	80	Lewis&Cl	&1987
Lippman, Ellen	Assoc	943-7268	lippman	BF	PHD	91.	Oregon	&1983
Lin, Cecila H.	Asst	943-7195	lin	AFS	PHD	00.	North Tx	&2006

Portland State University   Portland, OR   97207-0751   (503) Fax = 725-5850   ß (3) 1970,1982
Actg Faculty PO Box 751   School of Business Adm   sba.pdx.edu   BS,BA,MSFA
Dept Phone: 725-3721   631 SW Harrison Rm 560   Kathy Grove 725-3791
Homepage: http://www.sba.pdx.edu

Name	Rank	Phone	Email					
Dawson, Scott	Dean	725-3757	scottd	Mktg	PHD	84	Arizona	1985
Brown, Darrell L.	D-Ac	725-3096	darrellb	SBM	PHD	94.	Utah	1994
Les Fahey/KPMG Accounting Fellow								
Dillard, Jesse F.	Prof	725-2278	jessed	MBW	PHD	76.	S Carol	8-03
Retzlaff Chair								
Johnson, H. Thomas	Prof	725-4771	tomj	HM	PHD	69	Wisconsin	& 7-88
Johnson, Raymond N.	Prof	725-5354	rayj	AEF	PHD	81.	Oregon	&1980
Kenny, William J.	Prof	725-3747	billk	XL	JD	73	Gonzaga	&1985
Philbrick, Donna R.	Prof	725-3725	donnap	F	PHD	84.	Cornell	&1989
Visse, Richard H.	Emer	725-3716	dickv	2003	PHD	74.	Ariz St	&1976
Watne, Donald A.	Emer	725-3726	donw	2001	PHD	77	Berkeley	&1976
Almer, Elizabeth Dreike	Assoc	725-3729	elizabetha	A	PHD	96.	Ariz St	&2001
Meadows Faculty Fellow								
Yuthas, Kristi	Assoc	725-3784	kristiy	MSWJ	PHD	91.	Utah	1999
Swigert Professor Information Systems								
Rupley, Kathleen Hertz	Asst	725-3133	rupleyk	F	PHD	06.	U Wash	9-06
Carr, Tyee	Inst			FX	MBA		Oregon	2004
Chope, Roger A.	Inst	725-3791	rogerc	FM	PHD	81.	Oregon	2002
Francisco, Cherie	Inst	725-3783	cherief	FM	MBA	95	Bowl Gr	&2001
Henton, Michael C.	Inst	725-3720	mikeh	FP	MBA	73	Oregon	&1979
Schuster, Michael	Inst	725-8701	michaels	M	MBA		City U	

Post University   Waterbury, CT   06723-2540   (203) Fax = 575-9691
Accounting Faculty   Division Business Adm   post.edu   AS,BS
Dept Phone: 596-4657   800 Country Club Road   Mellssah Kochera
  Did Not Respond--2005-2006 Listing

Name	Rank	Phone	Email					
Huxley, Sharon J.	C-Ac	596-4657	shuxley	M	MBA	76	Hartford	1978
Sanders, Patricia	VP	596-8590	psanders	Mgt	PHD	80	Conn	2001

Prairie View A&M University
Dept of Atg, Fnce & Inf Sys
Dept Phone: 261-9275
Homepage: www.pvamu.edu

Prairie View, TX   77446-0638
College of Business
Universtiy Drive

(936) Fax=261-4273
pvamu.edu

2006
BBA,MBA,MSA
Theresa Harris

Quddus, Munir	Dean	261-9200	muquddus	Econ	PHD	85	Vanderbilt	2001
Khan, M. Moosa	H-Ac	261-9244	mmkhan	Fnce	PHD	86	Simon Fr	1989
Chong, H. Gin	Assoc	261-9250	hgchong	AMSJ	PHD	99	Sheffield	2005
Lee, Brian	Assoc	261-9258	brlee	MTV	PHD	94	Temple	2005
Desselle, Bettye	Asst	261-9251	brdesselle	NFA	MBA		Wisconsin	&2001
Feucht, Fred	Asst	261-9253	fjfeucht	FXP	PHD	04	Tx A&M	2004
Dobiyanski, Alfreda	Inst	261-9252	ardobiyanski	ACM	MS	84	Sam Hous	* &1992
Till, Ada	Inst	261-9264	altill	FCJ	MS	87	Tx A&M	2005

Providence College
Department of Accountancy
Dept Phone: 865-2790

Providence, RI   02918-0001
Accounting
Eaton Street & River Avenue

(401) Fax=865-2978
providence.edu

BS

Kelly, Patrick T.	C-As	865-1266	pkelly	CMF	PHD	04	Conn	2001
Bongiorni, Peter J.	Asst	865-2653	pjbnjrni	FX	MS	56	Columbia	&1972
Hartley, Carol A.	Asst	865-2154	chartley	AFT	MBA		Rhode Isl	&1980
Kelley, Ann G.	Asst	865-2656	akelley	FPVX	MBA		Northeas	&1986
Morse, Judith M.	Asst	865-2721	jmorse	MCXF	MST		Bryant	&1989
Rambo, Robert G.	Asst	865-2485	rrambo	FV	PHD	94.	Fla St	&2006
Ruggieri, Margaret	Asst	865-2654	rugieri		MST		Bryant	1995
Walsh, Cassandra	Asst	865-2069	cwalsh		ABD		Conn	2004

Purdue University
Accounting Faculty
Dept Phone: 494-4469
Homepage: http://www.mgmt.purdue.edu/academics/accounting/home.asp

W Lafayette, IN   47907-2056
Krannert School of Mgt
1310 Krannert Building

(765) Fax=494-9658
purdue.edu

ß 1967,1969
BS,MS,PHD
Ms. Sue Stone

Cosier, Richard A.	Dean	494-4366	rcosier	Mgt	PHD	76	Iowa	1999
Leeds Professor of Management								
Bagnoli, Mark	C-Pr	494-4484	mbagnoli	FTX	PHD	85	Princeton	8-99
Eskew, Robert K.	Prof	494-4475	eskew	AFEK	PHD	73.	Purdue	1976
Kross, William J.	Prof	494-5907	kross	F	PHD	75.	Iowa	&1978
Lawrence, Charles	Emer	494-4473	lawrence	1986	PHD	52.	Illinois	&1967
Ro, Byung T.	Prof	494-4494	btro	F	PHD	76.	Mich St	1976
Tritschler, Charles A.	Emer	494-4512	trit	1999	PHD	67.	Stanford	&1967
Kirschenheiter, Michael T.	Assoc	496-2862	mkirsche	FMT	PHD	95.	Nrthwstrn	&2004
Watts, Susan G.	Assoc	494-4504	swatts	FMT	PHD	91.	Iowa	&1997
Anilowski, Carol L.	Asst	494-0735	canilows	F	PHD	06.	Michigan	2006
Hatcher, John W.	Asst	494-4478	jack	XFR	MBA	62	Chicago	&1982
Li, Ying-Hua	Asst	496-3510	yli		PHD	05	Brit Colum	2005
Thoman, Lynda	Asst	494-4489	thoman	M	PHD	84	Stanford	1986
Greig, Anthony C.	ClLe	494-4394	greig	F	PHD	92.	Rochester	2002

Purdue University Calumet
Accounting Faculty
Dept Phone: 989-2388

Hammond, IN   46323-2094
School of Management
173rd & Woodmar Avenue

(219) Fax=989-2750
calumet.purdue.edu

BS,MACC

Duchatelet, Martine	Dean	989-2595	duchatel	Econ	PHD	77	Stanford	2006
Chen, Kuan-Chou	H-Ac$	989-2336	kchen	InfS	PHD	95	Mich St	1990
Daryseh, Musa M.	Prof	989-2776	aldara	FCM	PHD	90.	Nebraska	1990
Rinke, Dolores F.	Prof	989-2605	dfrinke	FIAK	EDD	90	N Illinois	&1987
Empey, Philip H.	Assoc	989-2389	empey	FMAS	PHD	72	Purdue	&1970
Waples, Elaine	Assoc	989-2791	waples	XMCF	MST	88	Iowa	&1991
Khaledi, Naser	Asst		khaledin		PHD		Temple	2005
Pollack, Robert C.	VAsst	989-2440	pollock	LFN	JD		Valparaiso	
Pogach, Kenneth S.	VInst	989-2135	pogach	FM	MBA		Chicago	

Queens Univ of Charlotte
Accounting Faculty
Dept Phone: 337-2210

Charlotte, NC   28274
McColl Sch of Business
1900 Selwyn Ave

(704) Fax=337-2521
queens.edu

2007

Lisa Newman

Broderick, Terry	Dean	688-2701	broderit					
Henderson, Michele C.	C-As	337-2210	hendersm	ABM	PHD	98.	Georgia	&2002
Eason, Catherine	Inst	337-2236	easonc		MS	00	Charlest	&2002

Quincy University
Accounting Faculty
Dept Phone: 228-5385
Homepage: www.quincy.edu

Quincy, IL   62301-2699
School of Business
1800 College Avenue

(217) Fax=228-5651
quincy.edu

BS,MBA
Judy Janes

Griswold, Melissa	Dean	228-5653	griswme	F	PHD	96	Nebraska	1998
Ellison, Mitchell	Prof	228-5386	ellismi	CFMP	PHD	93	St Louis	* &1993
Eidson, Vicky	Assoc	228-5385	eidsovi	APV	DMGT	98	Webster	&2004
Singer, Robert	Assoc	228-5652	singero	FI	PHD	96	St Louis	&1998

Quinnipiac University
Department of Accounting
Dept Phone: 582-8787

Hamden, CT   06518-1908
School of Business
275 Mount Carmel Avenue

(203) Fax=582-8664
quinnipiac.edu

2000,2000
BS,MBA,MS

Thompson, Mark	Dean	582-8914	mark.thompson	Econ	PHD	94	Geo St	1998
Ammons, Janice L.	C-Pr	582-8310	janice.ammons	FM	PHD	94.	Michigan	&1997
Gosman, Martin L.	Prof	582-8755	martin.gosman	F	PHD	71.	Wisconsin	&1996
Tucker, Michael J.	Prof	582-3470	michael.tucker	XL	PHD	80.	Houston	&1993
Sheikh, Aamer	Asst	582-8261	aamer.skiekh	FA	PHD	01.	Georgia	2006
Simione, Kathleen	Asst	582-8519	kathleen.simione	CP	MBA	80	Bentley	&1989

Radford University
Accounting & Finance Dept
Dept Phone: 831-5668

Radford, VA   24142
College of Bus & Econ

(540) Fax=831-6626
radford.edu

1992,1992
BBA
Ms. Mildred Ritter

Dempsey, William A.	Dean	831-5300	wdempsey	Mktg	DBA	73	Maryland	1999
Davidson, Daniel V.	C-Pr	831-6240	ddavidson	BLaw	PHD		Indiana	1986
Amenkhienan, Felix E.	Prof	831-5669	famenkhi	CMUI	PHD	84.	Miss	* 1985
Chase, Bruce W.	Prof	831-5744	bchase	FNG	PHD	91.	Va Comm	&1992
Saubert, Lynn K.	Prof	831-5076	lsaubert	FCT	PHD	77.	Wisconsin	* &1985
Saubert, R. Wayne	Prof	831-5491	wsaubert	XLP	JD		Drake	1985
Chatham, Michael D.	Asst	831-5604	mchatham	PMC	PHD	04.	Okla St	&2004
Roybark, Helen M.	Asst	831-5106	hmroybark	AMS	PHD	03.	Va Comm	2002

Ramapo College-New Jersey
Department of Accounting
Dept Phone: 684-7378

Mahwah, NJ   07430-1680
Anisfield Sch of Bus
505 Ramapo Valley Road

(201) Fax=684-7957
ramapo.edu

BS,MBA

Charkin, Lewis	Dean	684-7377	lcharkin	Fnce	PHD		NYU	2006
Crawford, Constance	C-Ac	684-7396	crawfor	AFT	MBA	86	Iona	1992
Harvey, Maryellen	Assoc	684-6736	mogrady	CIT	PHD	01	Nova SE	1993
Rigoli, Raymond C.	Assoc	684-7372	rrigoli	AFT	MBA	83	Fairl Dick	&1983
Stellenwerf, Anita L.	Assoc	684-7394	astellen	CDX	MBA	78	Rutgers	&1984
Yeaton, Kathryn G.	Asst	684-7392	kyeaton	FM	PHD	94.	S Fla	&2003

University of Redlands
Dept of Bus Adm & Accounting
Dept Phone: 793-2121

Redlands, CA   92373-0999
College of Business
1200 East Colton Avenue

(909) Fax=748-8015
335-5130.edu

BS

Welborn, Stephen I.	Prof	748-8501	stephen.welborn	M	MPA	68	Miss St	&1981
Bergevin, Peter M.	Assoc	748-8764	peter.bergevin	FM	PHD	85.	Ariz St	2005
Mitchell, Laurel B.	Assoc	748-8500	laurie.mitchell	FAS	PHD	97.	Columbia	&2003
Frazin, Alex	Lect	748-3930	alexander.frazin	FLX	BS	78	CS-Pomon	&2002

Regent University
Accounting Faculty
Dept Phone: 226-4351
Homepage: www.regent

Virginia Bch, VA   23464-9850
Grad School of Business
1000 Regent Univ Drive

(757) Fax=226-4369
regent.edu

MA,MBA
Rose Gilliana

Winston, Bruce E.	Dean	226-4354	bwinston	Mgt	PHD	98	Va Comm	
Redmer, Timothy A. O.	Prof	226-4360	timored	MFN	PHD	88.	Va Comm	* 5-91

Rensselaer Poly Institute
Accounging Faculty
Dept Phone: 276-6802

Troy, NY   12180-3590
Lally Sch Mgt & Tech
110 8th Street

(518) Fax=276-8661
rpi.edu

1977,1983

Gautschi, David A.	Dean	276-6802	lally-dean-l	Mktg	PHD	79	Berkeley	
Park, Jong Chool	Asst	276-2342	parkj	F	PHD	06.	Car Mellon	2006
Shin, Yong-Chul	Asst	276-4414	shiny2	F	PHD	00.	MIT	2004
St. John, William C.	SLect	276-6587		FSPC	PHD	89	Rensselaer	1-90

University of Rhode Island
Accounting Faculty
Dept Phone: 874-2073

Kingston, RI   02881-0802
College of Business Adm
7 Lippitt Road

(401) Fax=874-4312   ß (13) 1969,1973
uri.edu

BS,MBA,MS
Kay Guilbert

Higgins, Mark M.	Dean	874-4346	markhiggins	FX	PHD	89	Tennessee	&1988
Graham, Allan W.	C-Ac	874-4333	grahamaw	MS	PHD	00.	Va Tech	2000
Hazera, Alejandro	Prof	874-4332	hazera	FIV	DBA	89.	Kentucky	&1989
Martin, Spencer J.	Prof	874-4335	smartin	FT	PHD	70.	Illinois	& 9-70
Matoney, Joseph P.	Prof	874-4380	taxman	FX	PHD	73.	Penn St	&1973
Schwarzbach, Henry R.	Prof	874-4327	henrys	MQS	DBA	76.	Colorado	&1976
Vangermeersch, Richard G.	Emer	874-4338	rvang	2004	PHD	70.	Florida	* & 9-71
Beckman, Judy K.	Assoc	874-4321	beckman	FIT	PHD	91.	Tx Tech	&1992
Boyle, Edmund J.	Assoc	874-4199	eboyle	AO	PHD	90.	Penn St	&1988
Blanthorne, Cynthia	Asst			FX	PHD	00.	Ariz St	&2007
Jelinek, Kate	Asst	874-7470	kjelinek	FA	PHD	05	Conn	&2005
Jervis, Kathryn J.	Asst			FG	PHD	97.	Conn	&2007

Rhode Island College
Accounting & CIS Dept
Dept Phone: 456-8036
Homepage: ric.edu/acctcis

Providence RI   02908-1991
School of Management
600 Mt. Pleasant Avenue

(401) Fax=456-8379
ric.edu   BS,MPAC
Pamala Santos

Name		Phone	email					
Schweikart, James A.	Dir	456-8009	jschweikart	MCI	PHD	84	Indiana	& 9-98
Filipek, David	C-As	456-9535	dfilipek	FMPV	MBA	76	Babson	& 7-90
Church, Lisa	Assoc	456-8036	lchurch	LXF	JD	92	NE Law	& 9-00
Przybyla, Jane	Assoc	456-9546	jprzybyla	AEFS	MBA	73	Rutgers	& 9-85
Snow, Charles G. Jr.	Assoc	456-9528	csnow	FCM	PHD	93.	Drexel	* & 9-92
Sylvestre, Marilyn S.	Assoc	456-8412	msylvestre	IXF	MS	75	Rhode Isl	* & 9-76

Rhodes College
Accounting Faculty
Dept Phone: 843-3863
Homepage: www.rhodes.edu/academics/3375.asp

Memphis, TN   38112-1690
Dept of Econ & Business
2000 North Parkway

(901) Fax=843-3736
rhodes.edu   MS
Linda Gibson

Name		Phone	email					
Church, Pamela H.	C-Ac	843-3920	church	M	PHD	86	Houston	&1988
Thompson, Ferron	Inst	843-3567	thompsonf	F	MBA	75	Memphis	&2001

Rice University
Accounting Faculty
Dept Phone: 348-5396
Homepage: http://ww.ruf.rice.edu/~jgs/

Houston, TX   77252-2932
Jones Grad Sch of Mgt
6100 South Main Street

(713) Fax=348-5251   1998
rice.edu   MBA
Suzanna Vazquez

Name		Phone	email					
Glick, William H.	Dean	348-5928		Mgt	PHD	81	Berkeley	
Dharan, Bala G.	Prof	348-5382	bala	FMT	PHD	81.	Car Mellon	&1982
J. Howard Creekmore Professor of Accounting								
Epstein, Marc J.	VProf	348-6140	epstein	FM	PHD	73.	Oregon	1998
Research Professor of Management								
Uecker, Wilfred C.	Prof	348-4869	uecker	BMC	PHD	73.	Tx-Austin	&1984
Harmon Whittington Professor of Management; Assoc Dean for Executive Ed								
Zeff, Stephen A.	Prof	348-6066	sazeff	FHT	PHD	62.	Michigan	1978
Herbert S. Autrey Professor								
Anderson, Shannon W.	Assoc	348-5393	swa	M	PHD	93.	Harvard	2001
Nelson, Karen K.	Assoc	348-5388	nelsonk	F	PHD	96.	Michigan	2003
Price, Richard A. III	Asst	348-6303	richardp	FD	PHD	05.	Stanford	2005
Rountree, Brian R.	Asst	348-5328	rountree	M	PHD	03.	N Carol	2003
Widener, Sally K.	Asst	348-5396	widener	FM	PHD	99.	Colorado #	&2001
Mandel, James P.	Lect	348-4893		FMT	PHD	73.	Illinois	&1988
Viebig, V. Richard Jr.	Lect	529-9949	viebig	XAPZ	MAC	77	Rice	&1969

University of Richmond
Department of Accounting
Dept Phone: 289-8581

Richmond, VA   23173
E. C. Robins Sch of Bus
1 Gateway Rd

(804) Fax=289-8878   (1) 1965,1981
richmond.edu   BS
Ayana Nicholson

Name		Phone	email					
Haddock, Jorge	Dean	289-8550	jhaddock	Mgt	PHD	81	Purdue	2005
Slaughter, Raymond L.	C-Ac	289-8596	rslaught	XLP	LLM	91	Wm&Mary	&1977
Geiger, Marshall A.	Prof	289-8813	mgeiger	AJST	PHD	88.	Penn St	&2000
Clikeman, Paul M.	Assoc	287-6575	pclikema	AFM	PHD	95.	Wisconsin #	&1995
Hoyle, Joe B.	Assoc	289-8594	jhoyle	FV	MBA	72	Appalach	&1979
Lawrence, Carol M.	Assoc	289-8598	clawrenc	CGMN	PHD	89.	Indiana	1996
Sanborn, Robert H.	Assoc	289-8573	rsanborn	FTPK	PHD	82.	Georgia	1988
Vendrzyk, Valaria P.	Assoc	287-1832	vvendrzy	AM	PHD	93.	Tx A&M	&2003
Walden, W. Darrell	Assoc	289-8577	dwalden	FMS	PHD	94.	Va Comm	&1994
Middleton, Mary A.	VAsst	287-1937	mmiddlet	FM	PHD	88.	Georgia	&2000

Rider University
Department of Accounting
Dept Phone: 896-5032
Homepage: http://www.rider.edu/academics/depts.htm

Lawrenceville NJ 08648-3099
College of Business Adm
2083 Lawrenceville Road

(609) Fax=896-5304 (13) 1993,1993
rider.edu   BSBA,MACC
Sallie Gordon

Name		Phone	email					
Newman, Larry M.	Dean	895-5152	newman	Mktg	PHD	81	Penn St	1984
O'Reilly-Allen, Margaret	C-Ac	895-5505	oreillyallen	F	PHD	97.	Drexel	&1997
Dunne, Kathleen M.	Assoc	895-5540	dunne	VI	PHD	88.	Temple	1989
McMullen, Dorothy A.	Assoc	895-5518	mcmullen	AT	PHD	93.	Drexel	&1991
Persons, Obeau S.	Assoc	895-5475	persons	F	PHD	91.	Tx-Austin	&1991
Prober, Larry M.	Assoc	895-5524	prober	F	PHD	85.	Temple	* &1987
Sumutka, Alan R.	Assoc	896-5193	sumutka	XA	MBA	77	Seton Hall	&1977
Wygal, Donald E.	Assoc	895-5543	wygal	FMEI	PHD	77.	Pittsburgh	1984
Haywood-Sullivan, Betsy	Asst	895-5544	msullivan	MS	PHD	01.	Georgia	* &2001
Li, Fang Sherry	Asst	895-7731	fanli	F	ABD		Mass	2007
McDowell, Evelyn	Asst	895-5712	emcdowell	F	PHD	06	Case Wes	8-05
Sanchez, Maria H.	Asst	895-5582	msanchez	AT	PHD	03.	Drexel	&2002

University of Rio Grande
Accounting Faculty
Dept Phone: 245-7267
Homepage: www.rio.edu

Rio Grande, OH 45674
School of Business
East College Avenue

(740) Fax=245-7123
rio.edu   BS
Brenda Loucks

Name		Phone	email					
Kool, Krishna L.	Dean	245-7268	kkool	Econ	PHD	76	Tennessee	1978
Higgins, Larry	Prof	245-7283	lhiggins	AFS	MBA	75	Marshall	& 9-85
Campbell, Richard J.	Asst	245-7288	campbell	MSC	MBA	81	Gannon	* & 8-93

Roanoke College	Salem, VA	24153-3794	(540) Fax=375-2577				
Accounting Faculty	Dept of Bus Adm & Econ		roanoke.edu				BBA,BS,BA
Dept Phone: 375-2413	221 College Lane						Dreama Poore
Lynch, Larry A.	C-Pr	375-2413	llynch	Fnce	PHD	87 Va Tech	1978
Clifton, Norma	Asst	375-2491	clifton	FPX	MBA	00 Radford	1-01
Gibbs, Sharon	Asst	375-2429	sgibbs	FAO	MA	95 Va Tech	8-02
Hagadorn, Michelle	Asst	375-2501	hagadorn	FMN	MA	92 Va Tech	8-04
Shaff, Greg	Asst	375-4909	shaff	APU	MA	84 Jms Mad	8-04

Robert Morris University	Moon Township PA		15108-1189	(412) Fax=262-8672			
Dept Accounting & Taxation	School of Business		rmu.edu				BSBA,MST
Dept Phone: 262-8433	6001 University Blvd						Patty Miller
Homepage: www.rmu.edu							
Jacobs, Derya A.	Dean	262-8452	jacobs	Engr	PHD	Mo-Rolla	
Bryan, Lois D.	H-Ac	262-8427	bryan	FX	DSC	06 Rbt Morr	& 9-82
Kleinman, Gary	Prof			ABF	PHD	92. Rutgers	2007
Rebele, James E.	Prof	269-4894	rebele	AFS	PHD	84. Indiana	1-04
Berenbaum, Gerald J.	Assoc	227-6893	berenbaum	FCRM	MBA	68 Mass	& 9-71
Hanwell, Jerry W.	Assoc	227-6888	hanwell	GX	JD	90 Duquesne	# * & 9-82
Rubenfield, Ronald R.	Assoc	262-8301	rubenfield	FMC	MBA	Shippensb	* & 9-87
Boyas, Elise A.	Asst	262-8476	boyas	F	PHD	91. Rutgers	* & 8-05
Brucker, William	Asst	227-6876	brucker	X	JD	Duquesne	& 9-82
Fratto, Victoria A.	Asst	262-8488	fratto	CNM	MS	Rbt Morr	9-05
Hess, David	Asst	227-6887	hess	FXRA	MBA	Ohio St	& 9-84
Lee, Tanya M.	Asst	397-4263	leeta	MS	PHD	99. Ariz St	8-06
Raghavan, Kamala	Asst	269-3970	raghavan	CF	DBA	04 Clev St	8-04

Roberts Wesleyan College	Rochester, NY	14624-1997	(585) Fax=594-6316				
Accounting Faculty	Div of Business & Mgt		roberts.edu				BS
Dept Phone: 594-6571	2301 Westside Drive						Susan Carl
Bovee, Steven L.	Dean	594-6763	bovees	Econ	PHD	88 Okla St	1997
Starr, Ervin J.	D-Ac	594-6937	starr_ervin	Mgt	PHD	SUNY-Alb	7-01
Barlow, Daniel W.	Prof	594-6571	barlowd	LPX	JD	87 Colorado	&1989
O'Brien, Marcia L.	Asst	594-6571	obrien_marcia	MPJ	MBA	90 Rochester	2002

University of Rochester	Rochester, NY	14627	(585) Fax=442-8195				1964
Accounting Faculty	Simon Grad Sch of BusAd		simon.rochester.edu				MBA,PHD
Dept Phone: 275-3211	Wilson Boulevard						Kathleen Jones
Zupan, Mark	Dean	275-3316	mark.zupan	Econ	PHD	87 MIT	1-04
Wasley, Charles E.	C-Ac	275-3362	chales.wasley	FT	PHD	87. Iowa	1999
Zimmerman, Jerold L.	Prof	275-3397	jerry.zimmerman	FTM	PHD	74. Berkeley	1974
Ronald L. Bittner Professor of Business Administration							
Wu, Joanna S.	Assoc	275-5468	wujo	FT	PHD	99. Tulane	1999
Heitzman, Shane M.	Asst	275-1079	shane.heitzman	FX	PHD	06. Arizona	&2006
Zang, Amy	Asst	275-3491	amy.zang	F	PHD	06. Duke	2006
Tribunella, Heidi	SLect	275-3757	heidi.tribunella	A	MS	03 SUNY-IT	&2005
Wojdat, Kurt V.	SLect	275-4230	wojdatku	F	PHD	99. SUNY-Buf	2000

Rochester Inst of Technology	Rochester, NY	14623-5608	(585) Fax=475-6920				1988,1988
Accounting and Finance	College of Business		cob.rit.edu				BS,MBA
Dept Phone: 475-6063	105 Lomb Memorial Drive						Jennifer Fedele
Homepage: cob.rit.edu							
Rao, Ashok	Dean	475-7181	arao	Engr	PHD	68 Iowa	2007
Gold, Steven C.	C-Pr	475-2318	scgbbu	Fnce	PHD	79 SUNY-Bin	9-90
Morse, Wayne J.	Prof	475-4746	wmorse	CMS	PHD	71. Mich St	& 7-01
Associate Dean							
Oliver, Bruce L.	Prof	475-6668	boliver	FJV	PHD	69. U Wash	9-85
Karim, Khondkar E.	Assoc	475-5268	kkarim	FCM	DBA	95. Miss St	& 9-01
Kearns, Francis E.	Asst	475-6781	fkearns	FA	PHD	86. SUNY-Buf	& 9-86
Tessoni, Daniel D.	Asst	475-6054	dtessoni	FT	PHD	86. Syracuse	& 9-77
Evans, William	Lect	475-6337	wevans	M	MBA	84 Rochester	9-04
Klein, Roberta	Lect	475-6838	rklein	FMX	MBA	79 Roch Tech	& 9-95

Rockford College	Rockford, IL	61108-2393	(815) Fax=394-5171				
Dept Econ, Business & Acct	Div Soc & Beh Sci & Edu		rockford.edu				BA,BS
Dept Phone: 226-4175	5050 East State Street						
Espensen, Henry J.	C-Pr	226-4095	hespensen	FRTX	MA	Iowa	* &1986
Evans, Robert	C-Ac	226-4175	revans	Econ	MA	N Illinois	1976
Lewis, William	Assoc	226-4014	wlewis	CP	MBA	Illinois	&1992

Rockhurst University
Div of Decision Sciences
Dept Phone: 501-4200
Homepage: www.rockhurst.edu

Kansas City, MO 64110-2561
Helzberg School of Mgt
1100 Rockhurst Road

(816) Fax=501-4650
rockhurst.edu

2006
BSBA,MBA
Crystal Goodman, Lynn Ross

Daley, James M.	Dean	501-4200	james.daley	Mktg	PHD	77	Arkansas	7-02
Hoover, Gail A.	C-Ac	501-4147	gail.hoover	SIME	EDD	95	N Illinois	& 8-95
Tocco, Anthony L.	Prof	501-4083	anthony.tocco	MF	PHD	86.	St Louis	1969
McConnell, Cheryl A.	Assoc	501-4155	cheryl.mcconnell	XAF	MPA	84	Wichita St	&1988
Vicknair, David B.	Assoc	501-4089	david.vicknair	FTV	DBA	83.	Tennessee	&1993

Roger Williams University
Accounting
Dept Phone: 254-3401

Bristol, RI 02809-2921
Gabelli Sch of Bus
One Old Ferry Road

(401) Fax=254-3545
rwu.edu

2006,2006
BS
Sue Proto

Ebrahimpour, Maling	Dean	254-3444	bizdean	OPS	PHD	86	Nebraska	2002
Bernardi, Richard A.	C-Pr	254-3672	rbernardi	FBJ	PHD	92.	Union-NY	& 9-99
Sim, Khim Ling	Assoc	254-3401	ksim	MC	PHD	96.	Drexel	8-05
Ruggieri, Lynn	Asst		lruggier	XAF	MS	91	Bryant	& 9-04

Rollins College
Accounting Faculty
Dept Phone: 646-1520
Homepage: www.crummer.rollins.edu

Winter Park, FL 32789-4499
Crummer Grad Sch of Bus
1000 Holt Avenue-2722

(407) Fax=646-1550
rollins.edu

1985
MBA
Pam Clark

McAllaster, Craig M.	Dean	646-2249	cmcallaster	Ed	EDD	87	Columbia	2000
Brandon, Charles H.	Prof	646-2483	cbrandon	CM	PHD	72.	Georgia	&1982
Drtina, Ralph E.	Prof	646-2344	rdrtina	CMU	PHD	80	Ohio St	&1984
Reimers, Jane L.	Prof	646-2499	jreimers	MB	PHD	86.	Michigan	& 8-03

Roosevelt University
School of Accounting
Dept Phone: 281-3293
Homepage: www.roosevelt.edu
  phones with 619- have 847 area code

Chicago, IL 60605-1394
Heller College Bus Adm
430 South Michigan Ave

(312) Fax=281-3290
roosevelt.edu

BS,MBA,MSA
Mary Denwiddie

Patzer, Gordon L.	Dean	281-3342	gpatzer	Mktg	PHD	80	Va Tech	2003
Pavelka, Deborah D.	D-Pr	281-3265	dpavelka	FT	PHD	85.	Missouri	&1989
Ament, Joseph D.	Prof	281-3257	jament	XP	JD	62	J Marshal	&1966

  The Samuel Specthire Professor of Accounting; jament@muchlaw.com

Groner, Michael I.	Assoc	619-4861	mgroner	CF	PHD	77.	Illinois	&1981
Holtzblatt, Mark A.	Assoc	281-3277	mholtzbl	IF	PHD	84.	Arkansas	&1981
Hoppa, Donald A.	Asst	281-3266	dhoppa	FC	MSA	85	Roosevelt	&1985
Ruby, Richard	Asst	281-3261	rruby		JD	78	J Marshal	1980
Stinnette, Undine M.	Asst	281-3264	ustinnet	FC	MSA	76	Roosevelt	&1978

Rowan University
Dept of Accounting & Finance
Dept Phone: 256-4028
Homepage: www.rowan.edu/business/af
  phone 256-4028

Glassboro, NJ 08028-1701
Rohrer College of Bus
201 Mullica Hill Road

(856) Fax=256-4439
rowan.edu

2003,2003
BS,MBA
Ginny Bardsley

Schoen, Ted	Dean	256-4025	schoen		JD	68	Geotown		1999
Welsh, Carol N.	C-As	256-4039	welsh	VF	EDD	07	Delaware	#	&1983
Bao, Da-Hsien	Prof	Ext 3031	bao	MF	PHD	81.	S Calif		1995
Kyj, Larissa S.	Prof	Ext 3479	kyj	CM	PHD	85	Columbia	*	&1992
Romeo, George C.	Prof	256-4384	romeo	F	PHD	91.	Drexel	# *	&1979
Chung, Shifei	Assoc	Ext 3032	chung	FA	PHD	95.	Memphis		&1997
Hughes, Diane Y.	Assoc	256-4064	hughes	LF	JD	87	Rutgers	*	&1983
Marmon, Richard	Assoc	Ext 3474	marmon	FXR	JD	90	Widener	*	&1985
Weidman, Stephanie M.	Assoc	Ext 3475	weidman	BMSJ	PHD	02.	Drexel	*	1995

Rutgers University-Camden
Accounting Faculty
Dept Phone: 225-6216
Homepage: http://camden-sbc.rutgers.edu

Camden, NJ 08102
School of Business
227 Penn St

(856) Fax=225-6231
crab.rutgers.edu

1995,1995
BS,MBA,MACC
MaryAnn D'Orazio

Koza, Mitchell P.	Dean	225-6217	mitchell.koza	Mgt	PHD	85	Chicago	2006
Kenis, Izzet	H-Ac	225-6711	kenis	BCFM	PHD	74	NYU	9-72
Kahya, Emel	Assoc	225-6218	kahya	F	PHD	91.	Rice	1991
Kim, Sung-soo	Assoc	225-6584	sungsoo	FVT	PHD	93.	Baruch	1998
Han, Jongsoo	Asst	225-6723	jhan	BAS	PHD	01.	Pittsburgh	2000
Janes, Troy D.	Asst	225-6216	janeses	FA	PHD	05.	Michigan	&2007
Jansen, Ivo Ph.	Asst	225-6216	jansen	FM	PHD	01.	Indiana	2007
Miller, Allie F.	Asst	225-6652	milleraf	FM	PHD	86.	Ariz St	&
Vance, David	Asst	225-6921	dvance	LF	JD	87	Rutgers	2003

Rutgers University-Newark

Newark, NJ 07102-1897
Accounting & Info Sys Dept — Rutgers Business School
Dept Phone: 353-1644 — 180 University Avenue
Homepage: accounting.rutgers.edu/raw/accounting/
email @1=business.rutgers.edu @2=rci.rutgers.edu @3=rbsmail.rutgers.edu
(973) Fax=353-1283 (23) 1983,1941
andromeda.rutgers.edu BS,MBA,PHD
Jacqueline Adams, Terry Cumiskey

Name	Rank	Phone	Email		Deg		Univ	
Cooper, Michael R.	Dean	353-5126		Mgt	PHD	72	Ohio St	6-07
Palmon, Dan	C-Pr	353-5472	dpalmon	F	PHD	74.	NYU	1980
Kogan, Alexander	Prof	353-1064	kogan		PHD	88	USSR Acad	1993
Miranti, Paul J. Jr.	Prof	353-5221	miranti@1	AFH	PHD	85	J Hopkins	&1982
Associate Dean for Faculty								
Shafer, Glenn	Prof	353-1604	gshafer	SAQ	PHD	73	Princeton	9-93
Soled, Jay A.	Prof	353-1727	jaysoled	X	LLM	89	NYU	1-95
Sudit, Ephraim F.	Prof	353-5241	sudit	F	PHD	73	NYU	1976
Vasarhelyi, Miklos A.	Prof	353-5002	miklosv	FSA	PHD	73	UCLA	1989
Alles, Michael G.	Assoc	353-5352	alles@1	MCT	PHD	91.	Stanford	8-98
Govindaraj, Suresh	Assoc	353-1017	sureshg	CFM	PHD	90.	Columbia	2000
Sannella, Alexander J.	Assoc	353-5680	sannella@2	ACFV	PHD	84	NYU	& 9-87
Dimitrov, Vaneltin	Asst	353-1131	vdimitr		PHD	03	Tulane	2003
Sun, Lili	Asst	353-5762	sunlili@3	A	PHD	04.	Kansas	

Rutgers Un-New Brunswick

Piscataway, NJ 08854-8054
Dept Accounting & Info Sys — Rutgers Business Sch
Dept Phone. 445-3540 — 94 Rookafollor Road
Homepage: accounting.rutgers.edu/raw/accounting/
@1=andromeda.rutgers.edu @2=rci.rutgers.edu
(732) Fax=445-3201 ß 1983 1941
business.rutgers.edu BS,MBA,MACC,PHD
Ms Terri Cumiskey

Name	Rank	Phone	Email		Deg		Univ	
Oppenheim, Rosa	Dean$	353-5128	roppenhe@1		PHD	73	Polytech	7-73
Palmon, Dan	C-Pr	353-5472	dpalmon@1	F	PHD	74.	NYU	1980
Goodman, Leonard	Prof	445-4396	goodman	GXH	PHD	82	NYU	&1976
Jaggi, Bikki L.	Prof	445-3539	jaggi	FM	PHD	68	Free U	7-82
Mensah, Yaw M.	Prof	445-4369	mensah	FM	PHD	79.	Illinois	* 1984
Gillett, Peter R.	Assoc	445-4765	gillett	SDAB	PHD	96.	Kansas	& 9-96
Schoderbek, Michael P.	Assoc	445-4438	schoderb	FH	PHD	92.	Indiana	1991
Werner, Robert H.	Assoc	445-4441	werner	GA	PHD	89	NYU	&1977
Zaumeyer, David J.	Assoc	445-5311	dzaumeye	A	PHD	79	Columbia	&1982
Beniluz, Yoel	Asst	445-5107	yoel	FM	PHD	06.	Chicago	9-04
Yuschak, Marjorie E.	Inst	445-4364	yuschak	FM	MBA	84	Fairl Dick	* 2002

Sacred Heart University

Fairfield, CT 06432-1000
Accounting Faculty — Fin Studies, Gov & Law
Dept Phone: 371-7953 — 5151 Park Avenue
(203) Fax=365-7538 2006
sacredheart.edu BS,BA
Madeline Sanfilipgo

Name	Rank	Phone	Email		Deg		Univ	
Brown, Stephen M.	Dean		browns		EDD			
Boyer, Benoit	C-Pr	396-8084	boyerb	F	PHD	87.	UCLA	&1997
Cascini, Karen T.	Prof	371-7874	cascini	IFJ	PHD	88	Conn	&1992
Pannese, Danny A.	Assoc	371-7953	pannesed	XAF	MST	84	NewHaven	&1985
Shim, E. Daniel	Assoc	371-7853	shime	FM	PHD	93.	Rutgers	1997
Scarpati, Stephen	Asst	396-8270	scarpats	FJPU	MBA	77	Fordham	
Tarasovich, Barbara	Asst	416-3513	tarasovichb	FMUS	MBA	82	Sacred H	&2006

Saginaw Valley State Univ

Univ Center, MI 48710
Department of Accounting — College of Bus & Mgt
Dept Phone: 964-4338 — 7400 Bay Road
(989) Fax=964-4699 2003,2003
svsu.edu BBA,MBA,PBA
Donna Helmreich-Lopez

Name	Rank	Phone	Email		Deg		Univ	
Wafa, Marwan A.	Dean	964-4064		Oper	DBA	86	Clemson	2005
Kickham, Lawrence J.	C-Pr	964-4338	lkickham	AM	MS	72	Northeas	&1974
McCartney, Mark W.	Prof	964-4301	mwmccar	FA	PHD	95.	Memphis	& 8-99
Jacoby, Louis R.	Asst	964-4171	ljacoby	SN	PHD	71	Michigan	&1980
Knight, Marilyn Y.	Asst	964-4017	myk	FXEM	MT	88	Walsh	&1984

St. Ambrose University

Davenport, IA 52803
Accounting Department — College of Business
Dept Phone: 333-6155 — 518 West Locust Street
Homepage: www.sau.edu
(563) Fax=333-6268
sau.edu BA,MACC

Name	Rank	Phone	Email		Deg		Univ	
Dienesch, Richard M.	Dean	333-6447	dieneschrichardm	OBeh	PHD	87	G a	
Tech								2001
Marx, Lewis	C-As	333-6186	marxlewisd	ASGM	MA	86	W Illinois	&1989
Faulkner, Robert	Assoc	333-6168	faulknerrobert	DGVF	DBA	61	Heed	1976
Pogue, Elizabeth	Asst	333-6158	pogueelizabeth	AOPC	MA	04	St Ambro	* &2004
Wellman, Delores	Asst	333-6177	wellmandeloresm	VFXP	MS		Drake	&1984

Saint Bonaventure Univ

S BonaventureNY 14778
Department of Accounting — School of Business
Dept Phone: — Route 417
(716) Fax=375-2191 2004,2004
sbu.edu BBA,MBA

Name	Rank	Phone	Email		Deg		Univ	
Watson, John G.	Dean$	375-2200	jwatson	Mgt	PHD	74	St Louis	1975
Coate, Charles Joseph	C-Ac	375-2277	ccoate	AMJ	PHD	92.	Maryland	&2000

Anders, Susan B.	Prof	375-2063	sanders	XIF	PHD	98.	Tx Tech		&1998
Fischer, Carol M.	Prof	375-2021	cfischer	FTXB	PHD	93.	Penn St		&1985
Fischer, Michael J. Provost	Prof	375-2200	mfischer	FTA	PHD	93.	Penn St		&1985
King, Darwin L.	Prof	375-2138	dking	XSHA	MBA	71	Mich St		&1983
McAllister, Brian C.	Asst	375-2193	bmac	FDMV	MBA	81	St Bonav		&1977
Kasperski, Michael D.	Lect	375-2634	mkaspers	CFMV	MBA	83	St Bonav		& 8-03

St. Cloud State University Saint Cloud, MN 56301-4498 (320) Fax=308-6074 (12) 1976,1982
Department of Accounting Heberger College of Bus stcloudstate.edu BS,MBA
Dept Phone: 308-3038 720 Fourth Avenue South Vi Dinndorf
Homepage: //cob.stcloudstate.edu/acctweb/

Busta, Bruce	C-Pr	308-3967	harv	FS	PHD	90	Nebraska		&1988
Carlson, Ronald E.	Prof	308-3281	rcarlson	FV	PHD	73.	Wisconsin		&1972
Gaumnitz, Bruce R.	Prof	308-2268	bgaumnitz	F	PHD	82.	Wisconsin	# *	&1996
Gaumnitz, Carol B.	Prof	308-6135	cgaumnitz	FT	PHD	85.	Wisconsin		&2001
Johnson, Scott	Prof	308-3214	sjohnson	FPX	LLM	82	Boston U		&1987
Lere, John C.	Prof	308-3287	johnlere	MC	PHD	76.	Wisconsin		&1983
Mooney, Kate	Prof	308-4987	kate	FS	PHD	89.	Tx A&M		&1986
Schwieger, Bradley J.	Prof	308-2081	brads	AFOP	DBA	70.	Indiana		&1976
Wells, Wayne R.	Prof	308-2211	wwells	XL	LLM	81	Pacific		1983
Portz, Kristin	Assoc	308-3279	kportz	FS	PHD	00.	Nebraska		&2000
Smith, James A.	Assoc	308-4942	jasmith	PGI	DBA	94.	La Tech		&1994
Strong, Joel M.	Assoc	308-3277	jmstrong	FS	PHD	99.	Nebraska		&1999
Zupanc, Thomas	Assoc	308-6678	tzupanc	XL	LLM	82	Geo Wash		2000
Olsberg, Michael D.	Asst	308-3241	molsberg	P	MS	67	N Dakota		&1967
Lewis, Roger	Inst	308-4950	rplewis	P	MAC	88	Arizona		&2001

St. Edward's University Austin, TX 78704-6489 (512) Fax=416-5819
Accounting Faculty School of Business Adm admin.stedwards.edu BBA,MBA
Dept Phone: 448-8696 3001 South Congress Ave Donna Goodner
Homepage: http://www.stedwards.edu/badm/business.htm

Kelliher, Marsha	Dean	448-8696	marshak	Law	LLM	87	South Tx		1986
Guess, A. Kay	C-Ac	448-8562	aundreag	AFXB	PHD	93.	North Tx		& 8-98
Harris, Michael	Prof	448-8644	mikeh	FMS	PHD	98	Tx-Austin		&1997
Conn, Carolyn T.	Asst		caroltc	MCN	PHD	78.	Arkansas		&2007
Single, Louise E.	Asst		louises	XF	PHD	95.	Florida		&2007

St. Francis College Brooklyn Hght NY 11201-4398 (718) Fax=522-1274
Department of Accounting Business stfranciscollege.edu BS,MS
Dept Phone: 489-5283 180 Remsen Street
 phone 489-5283

Horlick, Geoffrey R.	C-Pr	Ext 5283	ghorlick	PF	PHD	78	Tx A&M		&1980
Yellin, William	Prof	Ext 5380	wyellin	FXAC	MBA	61	NYU		&1972
Nogara, Carmine	Asst	Ext 5301	cnogara	FGSV	MBA	93	St Johns		&2002

Univ of St. Francis-IL Joliet, IL 60435 (815) Fax=774-2920
Accounting Faculty Dept of Business Adm stfrancis.edu BBA
Dept Phone: 740-3360 500 Wilcox Street
Homepage: stfrancis.edu/ba/

LaRocco, Michael	Dean								
Zordan, Anthony	Prof	740-3608	azordan	PAFX	DBA	98	Nova SE	*	&1983
Leone, Sara	Asst	740-3808	sleone	CVFX	MS	87	N Illinois		&1992

Saint Francis College Loretto, PA 15940-0600 (814) Fax=472-3044
Accounting Faculty Dept of Business Adm francis.edu BS,MBA
Dept Phone: 472-3087 Roxane Hogue, Nicole Bauman
 Did Not Respond--2005-2006 Listing

DeConcillis, Father Anthony	Dean	472-3004							
Frye, Randy L.	C-As	472-3087	rfrye	PFC	EDD	97	Pittsburgh	*	1980
Logue, James	Asst	472-3046	jlogue		MS		Widener		1995
Rager, Larry	Asst	472-3074	lrager		DBA	04	Nova SE		1999

St. John Fisher College Rochester, NY 14618 (585) Fax=385-8094 2003,2003
Dept of Accounting & Fnce Division of Business sjfc.edu BS,MBA
Dept Phone: 3690 East Avenue

Ilter, Selim	Dean$	385-8079	silter	Mgt	PHD		Geo St		
Tyson, Thomas N.	C-Pr	385-8431	ttyson	CHJM	PHD	87.	Geo St	*	9-90
Fedoryshyn, Michael W.	Assoc	385-8091	mfedorysh	ARPC	MBA	75	Rochester	*	&1989
Hintz, Arthur F.	Assoc	385-8248	ahintz	VQF	MBA	76	Indiana		&1979

Saint John's University-MN
Accounting Faculty
Dept Phone: 363-3516
Homepage: www.csbjsu.edu
  shares same faculty with College of Saint Benedict, Saint Joseph, MN 56374

Collegeville, MN   56321-2000
Dept of Accounting
csbjsu.edu

(323) Fax=363-3298
csbsju.edu

BS,BA
Sue Zimmer

Jepperson, Mary	C-As	363-2031	mjepperson	AFPM	MBA	04	St Cloud	2003
Gerber, Quentin N.	Prof	363-3483	qgerber	MNFV	PHD	77.	Minnesota	&2000
O'Meara, James W.	Prof	363-3522	jomeara	CMXF	MS	71	Minnesota	&1974
Pladson, Paul R.	Prof	363-3521	ppladson	PMFX	MBA	71	St Cloud	&1975
Ochu, Jean M.	Assoc	363-5403	jochu	PMF	MBA	74	St Cloud	&1982
Bostrom, Warren	Asst	363-3301	wbostrom	NSPM	MBT	04	Minnesota	2004

St. John's University
Dept Accounting & Taxation
Dept Phone: 990-6460
  Department Phone 990-6461; X have phone 390-4545 (Staten Island)

Jamaica, NY   11439
Peter J. Tobin Col Bus
8000 Utopia Parkway

(718) Fax=990-1868   ß (123) 1968,1982
stjohns.edu   BS,MS,MBA
                            Ms. Susan Adamski

Highfield, Richard A.	Dean	990-6477	highfier		PHD	87	Chicago	2003
Shoaf, Victoria	C-Ac	Ext 6460	shoafv	FE	PHD	97.	Baruch	1997
Badawi, Ibrahim M.	Prof	Ext 7346	badawii	FMC	PHD	77	NYU	& 9-77
Boyd, Thomas	Prof	Ext 7341	boydt	XP	MBA	62	NYU	&1975
Casabona, Patrick A.	Prof	Ext 7344	casabonp	CP	PHD	79	Baruch	1982
Fitzsimons, Adrian P.	Prof	Ext 7306	fitzsima	AFK	PHD	84	New Sch	* &1990
McCarthy, Irene N.	Prof	390-3079	mccarthi	EJFV	PHD	03	NYU	&1975
Thompson, James W.	Prof	990-7379	thompsoj	TNF	EDD	81	Columbia	&1980
Aquilio, Mark	Assoc	Ext 7361	aquiliom	X	LLM	84	NYU	&1989
Choi, Yeong Chan	Assoc	390-4545	choiyc	CF	PHD	89.	Drexel	&1989
Colabella, Patrick R.	Assoc	390-7412	collabep	MX	MBA	80	Pace	&1987
Danile, Teresa M.	Assoc	Ext 4537	danilet	PMA	EDD	06	St Johns	&1981
Elifoglu, Ibrahim H.	Assoc	Ext 6461	elifogli	MSA	PHD	76	New Sch	1999
Gornik-Tomaszewski, Sylwia	Assoc	Ext 2499	gornikts	IFV	DBA	96.	Clev St	* F-00
Grego, Michael J.	Assoc	Ext 7342	gregom	ADC	MBA	71	St Johns	&1979
Lai, Richard T.	Assoc	Ext 7355	lair	X	LLM	83	NYU	&1987
Lange, Gerard A.	Assoc	Ext 7360	langeg	PA	EDD	07	St Johns	&1985
Latshaw, Craig A.	Assoc	390-4316	latshawc	CF	PHD	00.	Drexel	&1999
Zollo, Raynard	Assoc	390-4409	zollor	FAS	MBA	82	St Johns	& 9-82
Dorata, Nina	Asst	Ext 7329	doratan	FV	PHD	03.	Rutgers	&2006
Mannino, Laura Lee	Asst	Ex 7315	manninol	X	LLM	01	NYU	2002

Saint Joseph College
Accounting Faculty
Dept Phone: 231-5288

West Hartfort CT   06117-2791
Dept of Business Adm
1678 Asylum Avenue

(860) Fax=233-5695
sjc.edu

FMAC MPA

Jarett, Steven B.	C-Ac	231-5288	sjarett	FMAC	MPA	77	Tx-Austin	&1984

Saint Joseph's College
Accounting Faculty
Dept Phone: 893-7917

Standish, ME   04084-5263
Dept of Business Adm
278 Whites Bridge Road

(207) Fax=893-7866
sjcme.edu

BS

Zenillo, John	C	893-7917						
Bond, Christopher	Asst	893-7917	cbond	JLMR	JD		Maine	&2005
Girlando, Anthony	Asst	893-7986	agirland	JMF	DBA		Nova SE	1998

Saint Joseph's University
Department of Accounting
Dept Phone: 660-1650
Homepage: www.sju.edu/www/accounting

Philadelphia, PA   19131-1395
Erivan K. Haub Sch Bus
5600 City Avenue

(610) Fax=660-1126   (1) 2000,2000
sju.edu   BS,MBA
                            Peggy Spaoss

DiAngelo, Joseph A. Jr.	Dean	660-1645	jodiange	HRel	EDD	87	Temple	2000
Ragan, Joseph M.	C-Ac	660-1654	jragan	MVSU	MBA	75	Penn	* &1977
Sherman, W. Richard	Prof	660-1662	rsherman	XFI	LLM	91	Villanova	&1989
Stagliano, A. J.	Prof	660-1652	astaglia	XN	PHD	77.	Illinois	1985
Ghani, Waqar I.	Assoc	660-1661	wghani	FM	PHD	94.	Drexel	&1990
Haverty, John L.	Assoc	660-1656	jhaverty	FMU	PHD	86	Temple	&1976
Larkin, Joseph M.	Assoc	660-1658	jlarkin	FA	PHD	88.	Temple	# * &1984
Lin, Jean	Asst	660-3246		FM	PHD	07	Tennessee	2007
McDougal, Karen	Asst	660-1653		CB	ABD		Temple	8-06
Sullivan, Stephen	Lect			FM	MBA		Temple	&2002
Teti, Robert	Lect			XFM	MBA	72	Drexel	&2001

Saint Leo University
Department of Accounting
Dept Phone: 588-8599
Homepage: www.saintleo.edu

St. Leo, FL   33574-6665
Sch of Business MC2067
33701 Highway 52 W.

(352) Fax=588-8912
saintleo.edu

BA,MBA
Josephine Passand

Nastanski, Michael	Dean	588-8406		Mktg	DBA		Sarasota	
Bal, Balbin	C		balbinbal	Cis	PHD		Aston	
Cobb, Laurel G.	Assoc	588-8469	laurel.cobb	FAEJ	PHD	93.	S Fla	&1986
Foley, William T.	Assoc	588-8313	bill.foley	XCVS	MBA		S Fla	* & 1-83
Tollett, Annette	Asst	766-1814	annette.tollett		MBA		W Fla	& 8-88

Saint Louis University
Department of Accounting
Dept Phone: 977-3828
Homepage: sluacc.slu.edu

St. Louis, MO 63108-3397
John Cook School of Bus
3674 Lindell Blvd

(314) Fax=977-1473
slu.edu

ß 1948,1978
BS,MACC
Patricia Galati

Name	Rank	Phone	Email	Area	Deg	Yr	School	Year
Harshman, Ellen M.	Dean	977-3833	harshman	Mgt	PHD	78	St Louis	1972
Seetharaman, Ananth	C-Ac	977-3828	acas	XMI	PHD	91.	Geo St	& 1-92
Jennings, James P.	Prof	977-3811	jenninpp	FK	PHD	70.	Missouri	* &1976
Keithley, John P.	Prof	977-3856	keithley	MVTW	PHD	72.	Missouri	&1968
Guithues-Amrhein, Denise M.	Assoc	977-3832	amrheidm	FQT	PHD	83.	St Louis	&1997
Kissinger, John N.	Assoc	977-3862	kissingerjn	FTS	PHD	74.	Mich St	&1985
McGowan, John R.	Assoc	977-2473	mcgowanjr	XFI	PHD	88	S Illinois	&1987
Wang, Weimin	Asst	977-3861	wwang4	F	PHD	00.	Wash U	2006
Barbeau, Debra	Inst	977-3895	barbeaud	F	MA	85	S Illinois	&1997
Pike, Debra	Inst	977-3562	dpike	FA	MBA	92	St Louis	&2006

Saint Martin's University
Department of Accounting
Dept Phone: 438-4512
Homepage: stmartin.edu/business/busadmin.htm

Lacey, WA 98503-1297
Business & Econ Div
5300 Pacific Avenue SE

(360) Fax=438-4522
stmartin.edu

BA
Sharon Sullivan

Name	Rank	Phone	Email	Area	Deg	Yr	School	Year
Wilson, Haldon D. Jr.	Dean	438-4326	hwilson	Mgt	MBA		Citadel	1989
Gideon, Michael C.	C-Ac	438-4361	mgideon	AU	MBA	74	U Wash	&1990
Rasmussen, David J.	Assoc	438-4331	davidr	MP	MBA	73	Utah	&1993

Saint Mary's Col of Calif
Dept of Accounting Box 4230
Dept Phone: 631-4082

Moraga, CA 94575-4230
Sch of Econ & Bus Adm
1928 St. Mary's Road

(925) Fax=376-5625
stmarys-ca.edu

BS
Lucia Minor

Name	Rank	Phone	Email	Area	Deg	Yr	School	Year
Allen, Roy E.	Dean	631-4604	rallen	Econ	PHD	83	Berkeley	1985
Smith, Virginia G.	C-Le	631-4598	vsmith	PMX	MBA		CS-Haywa	&1985
Anderson, Fred E. Jr.	Emer	631-4580		1997	MBA	78	Golden Gt	& 9-78
Udpa, Suneel C.	Prof	631-4752	sudpa	FM	PHD	90.	Wash U	8-93
White, Stanford W.	Emer	631-4610		1996	MBA	72	Golden Gt	&1963
Lupino, Joseph F.	Assoc	631-4594	jlupino	ADGP	MBA	69	Armstron	&1977
Smith, Anne	Asst				EDD		N Illinois	* 2006
Bichsel, Mark	Lect	631-8185	mbichsel		MBA			1999

Saint Marys College
Accounting Faculty
Dept Phone: 284-4501

Notre Dame, IN 46556-5001
Dept of Bus Adm & Econ

(574) Fax=284-4566
saintmarys.edu

BBA
Vivian Vargo, Adm Asst

Name	Rank	Phone	Email	Area	Deg	Yr	School	Year
Merryman, Maryann	C-Pr	284-4501	merryman	AFN	MSA	80	Notre Dm	& 8-83
Renshaw, Claude D.	Prof	284-4750	crenshaw	XIP	MBA	70	Mich St	& 1-77
Vance, Susan M.	Prof	284-4507	svance	LC	JD	77	Cooley	& 9-81
Hicks, Joyce A.	Assoc	284-4526	jhicks	VFX	MBA	90	Notre Dm	& 1-91

St. Mary's University
Department of Accounting
Dept Phone: 436-3705

San Antonio, TX 78228-8607
School of Bus & Adm
One Camino Santa Maria

(210) Fax=431-2115
stmarytx.edu

1999,1999
BBA,MBA
Lisa Garcia Guajando

Name	Rank	Phone	Email	Area	Deg	Yr	School	Year
Russell, Keith A.	Dean	436-3712	krussell	ICPF	PHD	80	Arkansas	* 1-05
Madison, Thomas F.	C-Ac	431-4393	tmadison	FBCM	PHD	99.	Tx Tech	* & 8-98
Cory, Suzanne N.	Prof	431-2040	scory	FB	PHD	88.	Maryland	& 8-91
Persellin, Mark B.	Prof	431-2038	busmark	X	PHD	87.	Houston	& 8-91
Royalty, Kent W.	Prof	431-2037	buskent	XL	LLM	94	Houston	& 8-86
Sedki, S. Sam	Prof	431-2023	ssedki	FM	PHD	73	N Colo	* & 8-81
Oliva, Suzanne	Inst	431-8091	solival	PXL	JD	96	St MryTX	& 9-05
Pickard, Andrew	Inst	431-6700	apickard	FC	MACC	93	St MryTX	& 9-94

Saint Michael's College
Accounting Faculty
Dept Phone:

Colchester, VT 05439
Business Administration

(802) Fax=
smcvt.edu

Name	Rank	Phone	Email	Area	Deg	Yr	School	Year
Letovsky, Robert	C-Ac	654-2477	rletovsky		PHD		Concordia	
Kenny, Robert	Prof	654-2247	rkenny		MBA		Vermont	&
Benson, M. Birger	Assoc	654-2467	bbenson		MBA		Harvard	
Kuklis, Richard	Assoc	654-2639	rkuklis		PHD		Syracuse	
Voigt, Dennis	Assoc	654-2255	dvoigt	FMS	MBA		Vermont	1990
Walker, Norman	Assoc	654-2459	nwalker	FMC	MBA		NYU	&1984
Nigrini, Mark J.	Asst	654-2894	mnigrini	CX	PHD	93.	Cincinnati	&

St. Norbert College
Dept of Business Adm
Dept Phone: 403-3113
Homepage: www.snc.edu/busadmin

DePere, WI 54115-2099
Social Sciences
100 Grant Street

(920) Fax=403-4098
snc.edu

BBA
Cindy Rentmeester

Name	Rank	Phone	Email	Area	Deg	Yr	School	Year
Jenkel, Iris A.	C-Ac	403-3083	iris.jenkel	CGMN	PHD	90	Wisconsin	&1999
Ritter, Jeffrey D.	Assoc	403-3234	jeff.ritter	AFRV	MBA	74	Miami U	&1983
Vandenberg, Amy T.	Asst	403-3047	amy.vandenberg	FVX	MST	92	Wi-Milwa	&1992

St. Olaf College
Accounting Faculty
Dept Phone: 646-3149

Northfield, MN   55057-1098
Dept of Economics
1520 St. Olaf Avenue

(507) Fax=646-3523
stolaf.edu

Goedde, Richard	D-Ac	646-3126	goedde	M	MBA	78	Wisconsin	* &1988
Emery, Mary Ann	Assoc	646-3155	emerym	PFM	MA	65	Minnesota	&1969

Saint Peter's College
Department of Accountancy
Dept Phone: 761-6215

Jersey City, NJ   07306
College of Business
2641 Kennedy Boulevard

(201) Fax=451-0036
spc.edu

BS,MS
Margaret Greenwood

Leeds, Kevin A.	C-Pr	761-6215	kleeds	FX	MBA		Fairl Dick	&1981
DelVacchio, James E.	Prof	761-6214	jdelvacchio	FX	MBA		Seton Hall	&1976
Zagier, Allen F.V.	Prof	761-6212	azagier	C	MBA		Geo Wash	&1978
Brough, Kathleen	Assoc	761-6216	kbrough	FCMX	MBA		Rutgers	&1981
Harrison, James J.	Assoc	761-6219	jharrison	IJL	JD		Seton Hall	1976
Koch, Robert F.	Assoc	761-6217	rkoch	X	MBA		Fairl Dick	&1976
Pogogeff, Andrew D.	Assoc	761-6218	apogogeff	AF	MBA		Fairl Dick	&1978

College of Saint Rose
Accounting Faculty
Dept Phone: 454-5272

Albany, NY   12203
School of Business
432 Western Ave

(518) Fax=458-5449
strose.edu

BS,MS,MBA
Maria Freund

Carlson, Severin C.	Dean	454-2122	carlsons	Fnce	DBA	79	Indiana	1999
Amyot, Thomas G.	C-Ac	454-2005	amyott	PSAN	MS		St Rose	& 9-96
Dean, Donald C.	Prof	454-5202	deand	FCVA	PHD	91	Rensselaer	* &1979
Hughes, Barry J.	Assoc	458-5466	hughesb	XVP	MAS	90	St Rose	&1985
Katagiri, Catherine M.	Assoc	458-5473	katagirc	PFCA	MS		SUNY	* & 9-80

College of St. Scholastica
Accounting Faculty
Dept Phone: 723-6470

Duluth, MN   55811-4199
Dept of Management
1200 Kenwood Avenue

(218) Fax=723-6150
css.edu

BA
Mary E. Lee

Hartl, Robert J.	C-Ac	723-6651	rhartl	BM	MA	90	St Schol	8-01
Khoury, Paul	Asst	723-6470	pkhoury	MANS	MBA	92	Wright St	& 8-96
Revoir, Richard L.	Asst	723-6424	rrevoir	PFSX	MBA	96	Ariz St	8-04

St. Thomas University-FL
Accounting Faculty
Dept Phone: 628-6627
Homepage: www.stu.edu/busadm

Miami, FL   33054
Dept of Business Adm
16400 N.W. 32nd Ave

(305) Fax=628-6504
stu.edu

BBA,MBA,MAC
Mercedes Rodriguez, 628-6627

Mitchell, Lloyd A.	C-As	628-6622	lmitchel	FCA	MBA	81	U Miami	&1984
Kulzick, Raymond S.	Prof	628-6624	rkulzick	DMSU	DBA	90	Nova SE	1997
Reese, Craig E.	Prof	628-6623	creese	XGAT	PHD	79.	Tx-Austin	8-92
Kelsey, Richard L.	Assoc	628-6631	rkelsey	FCA	PHD	79.	U Wash	&2005
Gariboldi, Nicole	Asst	628-6598	ngariboldi	FI	DBA	99	Nova SE	&2002
Ogazon, Agueda	Asst	474-6812	aogazon	BEMN	EDD	96	Fla Intl	2002

University of St. Thomas-MN
Department of Accounting
Dept Phone: 962-5549
Homepage: www.stthomas.edu/cob
1-800-328-6819

St. Paul, MN   55105-1096
Col Business MCN 6014
2115 Summit Ave.

(651) Fax=962-5093
stthomas.edu

BA,MBA,MS

Puto, Christopher P.	Dean	962-4201		Mktg	PHD	84	Duke	
Saly, P. Jane	C-Ac	962-4254	pjsaly	FM	PHD	91	Brit Colum	9-99
Polejewski, Shirley A.	Prof	962-5112	sapolejewski	ICMU	PHD	83	Minnesota	9-76
Coglitore, Frank J.	Assoc	962-5542	fjcoglitore	AF	MBA	65	Scranton	& 9-82
Gelardi, Alexander M. G.	Assoc	962-4402	amgelardi	MX	PHD	91.	Ariz St	& 9-04
Matson, Diane M.	Assoc	962-5149	dmmatson	ABF	PHD	97	Minnesota	* & 9-01
Raffield, Janice M.	Assoc	962-5113	jmraffield	FAE	MPAC	91	Clemson	& 9-92
Sathe, Richard	Assoc	962-5115	rssathe	JEFH	EDD	00	StThomMN	& 9-90
Shapiro, Brian P.	Assoc	962-5086	bpshapiro	FWSH	PHD	90.	Minnesota	1-04
Anctil, Regina M.	Asst	962-4237	rmanctil	CFM	PHD	93	Minnesota	9-05
Asdemir, Özer	Asst	962-5549	oasdemir	F	PHD	05	Tx-Dallas	9-06
Pitre, Terence J.	Asst			BF	PHD	04.	Mich St	9-07
Weiss, Renee E.	Asst			AK	PHD	06.	Baruch	9-07
Yu, Wen	Asst			KFE	PHD	07.	Case Wes	9-07
Felton, Mark	Inst	962-5246	mafelton		MBA	90	Minnesota	& 9-06

University of St. Thomas-TX
Accounting Department
Dept Phone: 525-2106
Homepage: www.stthom.edu/bschool

Houston, TX   77006-4696
Cameron School of Bus
3800 Montrose Blvd

(713) Fax=525-2110
stthom.edu

BBA,MBA,MS
Christina Mucha

Mishab, Bahman	Dean	522-7911			PHD		Wayne St	8-06
Leavins, John R.	C-Pr	942-3479	leavinj	AS	PHD	87.	Houston	& 8-03

Carl, Lee	Assoc	525-2108	carl	FP	MBA	74	N Illinois	& 8-74
Hebble, Annette	Assoc	525-2107	hebble	MXI	PHD	89.	Houston	* & 8-91
Ramaswamy, Vinita M.	Assoc	525-6913	vinitar	FVT	PHD	94.	Houston	8-95
Fernandez, Ramon	Asst	525-2103	ramonf	XGMR	MBA	83	Houston	# * & 8-83
Simms, Jack	Asst	525-3446	simmsj	M	PHD	06.	Houston	9-06

Saint Vincent College
Accounting Faculty
Dept Phone: 537-4597
  email @1=stvincent.edu

Latrobe, PA   15650-2690
McKenna Sch Bus/Ec/Gov
300 Fraser Purchase Rd

(724) Fax=537-4599
stvincent.edu

BS,MS
Eva Kunkel

Quinlivan, Gary M.	Dean	537-4597	gq@1	Econ	PHD	83	SUNY-Alb	1981
DePasquale, Robert J.	Prof	537-4589	rob.depasquale	CMR	PHD	92	Pittsburgh	* &1978
Fazzi, Charles	Prof	539-9761	charles.fazzi	JNI	PHD	83.	Penn St	2002
Holowaty, Thomas C.	Assoc	539-9761	tholowaty@1	AXC	MBA	72	Duquesne	&1972
Director of Graduate Studies								

Saint Xavier University
Accounting Faculty
Dept Phone: 298-3600

Chicago, IL   60655-3000
Graham School of Mgt
3825 West 103rd Street

(773) Fax=298-3610
sxu.edu

BS
Carol Evans

Eber, John E.	Dean	298-3601	eber		EDD	83	N Illinois	
Cyze, Donald A.	D-Ac	298-3600	cyze	TLXP	LLM		Valparaiso	&1985
Schwer, Pamela	Assoc	298-3600	schwer	PTCV	MBA			* 1983
Kresse, William J.	Asst	298-3600	kresse	AL	JD			&1996
Mohammadi, Hamid Reza	Asst	298-3600	mohammadi	CQPD	PHD	90	Ill Tech	&1989

Salem State College
Dept of Accounting & Finance
Dept Phone: 542-6608
  phone 542-6608 or 542-7314

Salem, MA   01970-4589
School of Business
352 Lafayette Street

(978) Fax=542-6027
salemstate.edu

BS,MBA
Lesia DeJesus, Debra Fabrizio

Doran, E. Brewton	Dean		kathleen.doran					
McGee, Paul F.	C-Pr	542-6647	paul.mcgee	AT	MS	76	Bentley	&1984
Jacobsen, David M.	Prof	542-6664	david.jacobson	IM	JD	69	Boston U	1978
Lannan, John	Prof	542-6641	john.lannan	CX	MBA	76	Suffolk	&1979
Larson, Douglas A.	Prof	542-6633	douglas.larson	VA	MBA	77	Conn	# * &1979
Dow, Kathy J.	Assoc	542-6627	kathy.dow	F	DBA	89.	Boston U	1994
Main, Daphne	Assoc		daphne.main	FAB	PHD	90.	Ohio St	& 8-06
Purisky, John C.	Assoc	542-6621	john.purisky	MN	MBA	89	Rider	* & 9-90

Salisbury University
Department of Accounting
Dept Phone: 543-6315

Salisbury, MD   21801-6860
Franklin Perdue Sch Bus
1101 Camden Avenue

(410) Fax=546-6208
salisbury.edu

ß 1994,1994
BS,MBA

Moore, William M.	Dean	543-6315	wmmoore	Mgt	PHD	87	Ohio St	7-02
Smith, Kenneth J.	C-Pr	548-5563	kjsmith	FMT	DBA	86.	Geo Wash	# * & 8-92
Trice, Geary, & Myers Professor of Accounting								
DeRidder, Jerome J.	Prof	543-6326	jjderidder	FH	PHD	81.	Nebraska	1985
Dombrowski, Robert F.	Prof	543-6325	rfdombrowski	AMI	DBA	75.	La Tech	&1989
Garner, R. Michael	Prof	543-6351	rmgarner	VGI	PHD	86.	Arkansas	&1990
Marshall, P. Douglas	Prof	548-5554	pdmarshall	CMP	PHD	96	Maryland	&1976
Derrick, Patricia L.	Asst	543-6507	plderrick	FXT	PHD	05.	Geo Wash	&2005
Summers, George F.	Asst	543-3885	gfsummers		PHD	03.	Houston	

Salve Regina University
Accounting Faculty
Dept Phone:

Newport, RI   02840-4192
Business Adm
100 Ochre Port Ave.

(401) Fax=
salve.edu

BS

Atkins, Ronald	C-Ac	847-3286	atkinsr	Mgt	PHD		Salve Rg	1985
McQuilkin, John	Asst	847-3123	john.mcquilkin	A	JD		Lewis&Cl	&2004
Arruda, Lucia M.	Lect	847-3122	arrudal	FPX	MSA	86	Rhode Isl	&
McKillop, Paul	Lect	847-2170	mckillop	PSF	MS		Salve Rg	

Sam Houston State Univ
Department of Accounting
Dept Phone: 294-1258

Huntsville, TX   77341-2056
College of Business
1821 Avenue I #302 Box 2056

(936) Fax=294-1982
shsu.edu

1996,1996
BBA,MBA
Mandy Carrell

Lewis, R. Dean	Dean	294-1981	bed_rdl	Mktg	PHD	72	Arkansas	1980
Morris, Philip W.	C-As	294-1259	aac¯pwm	MF	PHD	03.	Tx Tech	&2000
Gaertner, James F.	Prof	294-1012	gaertner	FI	PHD	77.	Tx A&M	&2002
University President								
Hawkins, Ennis M.	Prof	294-1127	aac_emh	MC	DBA	74.	Tx Tech	# * &1966
Ketchand, Alice A.	Prof	294-1284	aac¯aak	BFI	PHD	94.	Houston	&1992
Quarles, N. Ross	Prof	294-1258	rquarles	SAM	PHD	88.	North Tx	&1994
Ameen, Elsie C.	Assoc	294-1280	aac_eca	FA	PHD	89.	S Carol	&1995
Brewer, Carl W.	Assoc	294-1830	aac¯cwb	TM	PHD	81.	Houston	& 9-88
Duvall, Linda G.	Assoc	294-1292	aac¯lgd	FI	PHD	93.	Maryland	&1994

Klett, Taylor	Assoc	294-1260	klett	XL	JD	88	Houston		&1999
Strawser, Jeffrey W.	Assoc	294-1280	aac_jws	MS	PHD	97.	Tx A&M		1998
Daigle, Ronald J.	Asst	294-1479	rjd005	S	PHD	02.	Tx Tech		& 8-06
Green, Diane J.	Asst	294-1262	aac_djg	AX	MS	71	LSU		&1978
Harwell, Jeff L.	Asst	294-1257	aac‾jlh	FGVE	MBA	77	Tx A&M		& 9-81
Sale, Martha L.	Asst	294-1258	msale	CM	DBA	99.	La Tech		&2005

Samford University — Birmingham, AL　35229-2306　(205) Fax=726-2464　1999 1999
Accounting Faculty — School of Business — samford.edu — BS,MACC,MBA
Dept Phone: 726-2547 — 800 Lakeshore Dr — Jackie McMurry
Homepage: www.samford.edu/schools/business

Taylor, Beck A.	Dean	726-2364	btaylor	Econ	PHD	97	Purdue		2005
Reburn, James P.	D-Pr	726-2067	jpreburn	FNS	DBA	88.	La Tech		&1996
Associate Dean									
Lohrke, Cynthia A.	Assoc	726-2682	cflohrke	S	PHD	94.	Drexel		&2000
Minter, Frank C.	Exec	726-2546	fcminter	T	MBA	67	Memphis		& 9-88
Belski, William H.	Asst	727-2182	whbelski	FV	PHD	04.	Va Tech		& 8-04
Jackson, Sharon S.	Asst	726-2761	ssjackso	FM	MBA	84	Aub-Mont		& 8-97
Price, Dennis W.	Asst	726-2446	dwprice	X	JD	88	Alabama		&2003
Smith, Douglas L.	Asst	726-4014	dusmith	AM	PHD	01	Al-Birm	# *	&2000

University of San Diego — San Diego, CA　92110-2492　(619) Fax=260-7725　ß (13) 1980,1981
Accounting Faculty — School of Business Adm — sandiego.edu — BA,MAFM,MTAX
Dept Phone: 260-2975 — 5998 Alcala Park — JoAnne Lavin
Homepage: http://www.sandiego.edu/business

Allen, Andrew T.	Dean$	260-4886	andrewt	Econ	PHD	83	Illinois		1984
Pattison, Diane D.	D-Pr	260-4850	pattison	CJM	PHD	81.	U Wash		1986
Cook, N. Ellen	Prof	260-4845	e_cook	MI	PHD	78.	UCLA		1975
Dalton, Thomas M.	Prof	260-2328	dalton	FX	PHD	92.	Houston		& 1-92
Kelley, Timothy	Prof	260-4846	tkelley	F	PHD	84.	Houston		&1983
Margheim, Loren L.	Prof	260-4834	margheim	F	PHD	84.	Ariz St		&1984
Hora, Judith A.	Assoc	260-4220	jhora	FV	PHD	99.	Va Comm		&1998
Smith, James K.	Assoc	260-2975	smithj	X	PHD	95.	Arizona		&2001
Lougee, Barbara A.	Asst			F	PHD	99.	Cornell		2007
Ayers, Susan	Lect	260-7560	sayers	SA	PHD	95.	Ariz St		&2000
Judd, Mark	Lect	260-2258	mjudd	FMA	IMBA	94	SanDiego		&1997
Morris, Janice T.	Lect	260-7674	jmorris	EFS	MBA	88	Hou-ClLk		&2003

San Diego State University — San Diego, CA　92182-8221　(619) Fax=594-3675　ß (13) 1959,1963
School of Accountancy — College of Business Adm — mail.sdsu.edu — BS,MS
Dept Phone: 594-5070 — 5500 Campanile Drive — Debra Woodman
Homepage: ~cba/acct/index.html

Naughton, Gail K.	Dean	594-5259	gnaughton		PHD	81	NYU		2002
Lightner, Sharon Douglas	D-Ac	594-3735	slightne	F	PHD	77.	Oregon		& 9-77
Anderson, John C..	Prof	594-8954	janders	SAB	PHD	87.	Tennessee		8-01
Barnett, Andrew H.	Emer	594-6273	abarnett	AF	PHD	76.	Tx Tech		&1983
Capettini, Robert J.	Prof	594-4307	rcapetti	MCE	PHD	75.	Illinois		&1985
Chang, C. Janie	Prof	594-8383	jchang	SFMA	PHD	95.	Ca-Irvine		2006
Vern Odmark Professor of Accountancy									
Chow, Chee W.	Emer	594-5331	chow	MC	PHD	81.	Oregon		1984
Grudnitski, Gary M.	Prof	594-6713	grudnits	S	PHD	75.	Mass		1988
Lightner, Kevin M.	Emer	594-3736	klightne	F	PHD	70.	UCLA		1968
Oestreich, Nathan	Prof	594-2478	drno	X	PHD	81.	Houston		&1985
Toole, Howard R.	Emer	594-5328	htoole	SMC	PHD	76.	Iowa		&1972
Venable, Carol F.	Prof	594-2662	venable	BJE	PHD	88.	Arizona		&1988
Williamson, James E.	Prof	594-6021	william6	MX	PHD	68.	Minnesota		&1968
Doran, Martha S.	Assoc	594-6841	doran1	AF	PHD	94	Ariz St		&1996
Joh, Gun-Ho	Assoc	594-2716	gun.joh	F	PHD	88.	Penn		1988
Krivogorsky, Victoria	Assoc	594-7189	vkrivogo	AF	PHD	99.	Wisconsin		2005
DeBoskey, David	Asst	594-2376	debocpafa2005@a	F	PHD	06	Rutgers		&2006
Fleming, Damon M.	Asst	594-6347	dfleming	BFM	PHD	06.	Va Tech	*	1-07
Snyder, Willard S. Jr.	Lect	594-2476	snyder1	XF	MBA	76	S Calif		&1990

University of San Francisco — San FranciscoCA　94117-1080　(415) Fax=422-2502　ß 1953,1982
Accounting Faculty — School Business & Mgt — usfca.edu — BS
Dept Phone: 422-2526 — 2130 Fulton Street
Homepage: www.usfca.edu

Duffy, Michael L.	Dean	422-2508	mike.duffy	X	JD	83	Berkeley		8-07
Roberts, Diane H.	C-Pr	422-6380	droberts	AFM	PHD	95.	Ca-Irvine	*	& 9-94
Neilson, Denis P.	Prof	422-2526	neilsond	SM	PHD	74.	Berkeley		& 9-80
Weiner, David P.	Prof	422-6685	weiner	AFM	PHD	72.	Michigan		& 9-70
Graham, Carol	Assoc	422-5647	graham	FM	PHD	95	Strathcl		9-98
Koeplin, John P. S.J.	Assoc	422-2563	koeplin	FM	PHD	98.	North Tx		& 9-98
Sayre, Todd L.	Assoc	422-6990	sayre	SM	PHD	94.	Arizona		& 9-98

San Francisco State Univ

San Francisco State Univ		San FranciscoCA 94132-4171		(415) Fax=338-0596					ß 1963,1975	
Department of Accounting		College of Business		sfsu.edu					BS,MBA,MSBA	
Dept Phone: 338-1147		1600 Holloway Avenue							Pat Cierra	
Homepage: sfsu.edu/~acctg/										
Hayes, K. Nancy	Dean	338-2670	nkhayes	Mktg	MBA	80	Chicago		2005	
Huang, Jiunn C.	C-Pr	338-2473	jchuang	CFMI	PHD	80.	North Tx	*	1986	
Choo, Freddie	Prof	338-1332	fchoo	A	PHD	89	NS Wales		&1990	
Daniels, Robert H.	Prof	338-7476	rdaniels	XL	JD	72	Harvard		1983	
partial retirement										
Danko, Kenneth L.	Prof	338-1959	kdanko	BMCQ	DBA	82.	Indiana	*	1986	
Duke, Joanne C.	Prof	338-1127	jduke	VFT	PHD	87.	Penn St	*	1987	
Frankel, George	Prof	338-7483	grf100@a	X	LLM	89	NYU		&1991	
Franz, David P.	Prof	338-1688	dfranz	MC	PHD	86.	Penn St	*	1987	
Hsieh, Su-Jane	Prof	338-2738	sjhsieh	F	PHD	85.	Purdue		1992	
Jerris, Scott I.	Prof	338-6713	sjerris	FE	PHD	87.	Purdue		1997	
Kang, Jai S.	Prof	338-6362	jkang	CSI	PHD	77.	Tx A&M		&1983	
McWilliams, John	Prof	338-6345	jmcwill	XL	JD	72	Duke		&1976	
partial retirement										
Naser-Tavakolian, Mohsen	Prof	338-6391	mntavako	FMS	PHD	80.	Missouri	*	1978	
O'Shaughnessy, John	Prof	338-6285	joshaun	AFO	PHD	90	Golden Gt	#	&1982	
Yuen, Alexander E. C.	Prof	338-7478	ayuen	AGNI	PHD	89	Golden Gt	&	9-80	
Schaze, Vincent J.	Emer	338-1176	vschaze	2004	MS	56	SanFranSt		1956	
Wagner, Robin M.	Assoc	338-1524	rwagner	FT	PHD	82.	Berkeley		1986	
Braswell, Michael	Asst	305-2735	braswell	FA	PHD	07.	Missouri		2007	
Chang, Chun-Chia	Asst	405-0963	amychang	F	PHD	06.	Houston		2006	
Landis, Mark	Asst	405-0960	landism	MS	PHD	06.	Missouri		2006	

San Jose State University

San Jose State University		San Jose, CA 95192-0066		(408) Fax=924-3463					ß 1967,1973	
Accounting and Finance		College of Business		cob.sjsu.edu					BS,MST,MBA,MSA	
Dept Phone: 924-3460		One Washington Square							Julie Ryan 924-3465	
Homepage: www.cob.sjsu.edu/dept/acct&fin										
Magid, Bruce	Dean	924-3461	magid_b	Econ	PHD	77	Tufts		2005	
Zaima, Janis K.	C-Pr	924-3490	zaima_j	Fnce	PHD	80	U Wash		1986	
Black, Thomas G.	Prof	924-3467	black_t	SMC	PHD	79.	Missouri	*	&1979	
Donnelly, William J.	Prof	924-3493	donnelly_b	FA	PHD	87	Golden Gt		&1975	
Grace, Elizabeth V.	Prof	924-3474	grace_e	F	PHD	84	Penn		1986	
Jenkins, Elizabeth K.	Prof	924-3483	jenkins_e	FBE	PHD	86.	Houston		&1985	
Karlinsky, Stewart S.	Prof	924-3482	karlinsky_s	X	PHD	81.	NYU	&	8-88	
Nellen, Annette	Prof	924-3508	nellen_a	XP	JD	87	Loyola	&	5-90	
Turetsky, Howard	Prof	924-3460	turetsky_h	FM	PHD	97.	Va Comm		&2000	
Ingraham, Laura R.	Assoc		ingraham_l	SMF	PHD	95.	Ariz St		&2003	
Calegari, Mary F.	Asst	924-3487	calegari_m	P	PHD	01.	Georgia	*	2003	
Brubeck, Helen	Lect	924-3591	brubeck_h		ABD		Berkeley		1999	
Buck, Carroll	Lect	924-3494	buck_c	FM	MBA	82	Maine		2002	
Chang, Chi	Lect	924-3459			MBA		CS-Fresno			
DeVincenzi, Bill	Lect	924-3488	devincenzi_b		MBA		Berkeley		1995	
Fowler, Kenneth	Lect	924-3473	fowler_k	PX	PHD	97	Miss	# *	&2000	
Lam, Edmund	Lect	924-3495	lam_e		MBA		Wyoming		1999	
Maxson, Lisa	Lect	924-3464	maxson_l	SMF	MBA	82	Pepperdi		2000	
McWilliams, Mallory L.	Lect	924-3469	mcwilliams_m	FM	MBA	78	San Jose		&1980	
Moschetti, Tom	Lect	924-3492	moschetti_t	X	MST		San Jose		1989	
O'Brien, William	Lect	924-3468	obrien_w	FM	MBA	79	Pepperdi		&1993	

Santa Clara University

Santa Clara University		Santa Clara, CA 95053-0380		(408) Fax=554-5193				(1) 1953,1963	
Department of Accounting		Leavey School Bus & Adm		scu.edu				BSC	
Dept Phone: 554-4578		500 El Camino Real						Remy Herandez	
Homepage: business.scu.edu/actg/									
Posner, Barry Z.	Dean	554-4523	bposner	Mgt	PHD	76	Mass		1976
Calegari, Michael J.	C-Ac	551-1964	mcalegari	FX	PHD	96.	Arizona		&2001
Eames, Michael J.	Assoc	554-4896	meames	FM	PHD	95.	U Wash		&1996
Luttman, Suzanne M.	Assoc	554-4897	sluttman	XF	PHD	88.	Illinois		1991
Ou, Jane A.	Assoc	554-4085	jou	FV	PHD	84.	Berkeley		1984
Parker, Susan	Assoc	554-4899	sparker	AF	PHD	98.	Oregon		1998
Sepe, James F.	Assoc	554-4036	jsepe	F	PHD	80.	U Wash		&1979
Ushman, Neal L.	Assoc	554-4560	nushman	F	PHD	83.	Cornell		&1982
Kim, Yongtae	Asst	554-4667	y1kim	F	PHD	01.	SUNY-Buf		2001
Donohoe, Wendy	Lect	551-1731	wdonohoe	FMX	MS	88	Golden Gt		&1998
Hasseini, Ahmad	Lect	554-4899		FM	PHD	81	Missouri		&2007
Johnston-Blair, Donna	Lect	554-4893	djohnstonblair	M	MBA	76	Toronto		&2001
Kaschmitter, Ursula	Lect	554-4893	ukaschmitter	FX	MBA	83	Golden Gt		&1987
O'Brien, William	Lect	554-5463	wobrien	FM	MBA	79	Pepperdi		&1992
Paisley, Christopher B.	Exec	551-5458	cpaisley	F	MBA	77	UCLA		2001
Wade, Steven	Exec	551-5458	swade	FM	MBA	73	W Ontario		&1994

Savannah State University Savannah, GA 31404 (912) Fax=356-2803 2004
Accounting Faculty College of Business Adm savstate.edu BBA
Dept Phone: 356-2335 P.O. Box 20359 Ms. Zelda James
Did Not Respond Again--2003-2004 Listing
Sarhan, Mostafa H. Dean 356-2335 sarhanm MCU PHD 83 Arkansas * 1-99
Crump, Zelma Asst 356-2851 crumpz AFI ABD JacksonSt & 8-03
Whatley, Maliece Asst 356-2841 whatleym FM MS 83 Georgia & 8-03

University of Scranton Scranton, PA 18510-4602 (570) Fax=941-4826 1996,1996
Department of Accounting Arthur J. Kania Sch Mgt scranton.edu BS,MBA
Dept Phone: 941-4047 Ms. Nancy Gownleyni
Homepage: http://matrix.scranton.edu/academics/ac_factsheet_accounting
Mensah, Michael O. Dean 941-7569 mom352 FTS PHD 89 Houston 1987
  Alperin Teaching Fellow
Lawrence, Robyn C-Ac 941-7786 lawrencer1 CMIF PHD 88. Houston * 1993
Carpenter, Brian W. Prof 941-7632 bwc352 FBHM PHD 87. Penn St * 1987
  Alperin Teaching Fellow
Mahoney, Daniel P. Prof 941-4188 mahoneyd1 FVG PHD 90 Syracuse &1989
  Alperin Teaching Fellow
Grambo, Ronald J. Assoc 941-7762 rjg352 AMCD PHD 81. Penn St 1977
Johnson, Roxanne T. Assoc 941-6179 johnsonr1 IMF PHD 87. Penn St &1993

Seattle University Seattle, WA 98122-1090 (206) Fax=296-2464 ß 1965,1980
Accounting Department Albers Sch Bus & Econ seattleu.edu BA,MBA,MPAC
Dept Phone: 296-5690 901 12th Ave Nadeje Alexandre
Homepage: www.seattleu.edu/asbe/accounting
Phillips, Joseph M. Dean 296-5700 phillipsj Econ PHD 82 Notre Dm 2001
Weihrich, Susan G. C-Ac 296-5874 weihrich XF PHD 86. Houston &1989
Tinius, David E. Prof 296-5692 dtinius MBC PHD 77 U Wash &1971
Awasthi, Vidya N. Assoc 296-5628 vawasthi MBC PHD 88. U Wash # * &1996
Chipalkatti, Niranjan Assoc 296-5764 chipalka FI PHD 93. Mass &2004
Koch, Bruce S. VAsoc 296-5815 kochb MFB PHD 77. Ohio St &2002
Mello-e-Souza, Carlos A. Asst 296-5739 carlosms FI PHD 89. Cornell 2002
Bee, Sarah Inst 296-5788 bees SP MBA 93 Seattle 1999
Kelley, Thomas Inst 296-5799 tjkelley ACFP MBA 72 NewHamp &2002

Seattle Pacific University Seattle, WA 98119-1950 (206) Fax=281-2733 2000,2000
Accounting Faculty School of Bus & Econ spu.edu BA,MBA
Dept Phone: 281-2992 3307 Third Ave W Lindsey Peterson 281-2992
Homepage: www.spu.edu/depts/sbe
VanDuzer, Jeffrey B. Dean 281-2087 vandj Law JD 79 Yale 9-98
Stewart, Ross E. C-Pr 281-2900 rstewart THFM PHD 87 Glasgow 1986
Sawers, Kimberly M. Asst 281-2221 ksawers BMN PHD 02. U Wash 9-06
Kauppila, William Clin 281-2397 kauppw AFPX MBA 70 W Mich & 9-06

Seton Hall University South Orange NJ 07079-2692 (973) Fax=761-9217 ß 1978,1984
Dept of Acct & Taxation Stillman Sch Business shu.edu BS,MBA,MST,MSAC
Dept Phone: 761-9235 400 South Orange Avenue Christine Digirolomo
Boroff, Karen E. Dean$ 761-9013 boroffka Mgt PHD 91 Columbia 9-91
Gelb, David S. C-Ac 761-9235 gelbdavi FAS PHD 97. NYU & 9-96
Abdallah, Wagdy M. Prof 761-9246 abdallwa MIC PHD 82. North Tx * 9-84
Easton, Reed W. Assoc 761-9264 eastonre XKLO LLM 82 NYU & 9-89
Greenstein, Brian R. Assoc 761-9428 greensbr X PHD 87. Houston 9-93
  Director, Graduate Tax Program
Murtuza, M. Athar (Art) Assoc 761-9233 murtuzat BCEH PHD 77 Wash St * 1988
Shapiro, Robert E. Assoc 761-9264 shapirro X LLM 61 NYU &1981
Strawser, Joyce A. Assoc 761-9225 strawsjo FM PHD 89. LSU 9-95
  Associate Dean
Henry, Theresa Asst 761-9642 henrythe FP PHD 03. NYU & 1-03
Holtzman, Mark P. Asst 761-9133 holtzmma MPF PHD 97. Tx-Austin & 9-03
Mest, David P. Asst 769-2961 mestdave FKST PHD 95. Tx-Austin & 9-03

Shenandoah University Winchester, VA 22601-5195 (540) Fax=665-5437 2007
Accounting Faculty Byrd School of Business su.edu BBA,MBA
Dept Phone: 665-4572 1460 University Drive Emily Tremoulis
Boxx, W. Randy Dean 665-4572 boxx Mgt PHD 71 Arkansas 8-04
Pineno, Charles J. Prof 665-4615 cpineno CM PHD 79 Penn St 2004
Tyree, L. Mark Prof 665-4616 mtyree PXMV EDD 84 Wm&Mary &1987
  Yount, Hyde and Barbour Professor of Accounting

Shepherd University
Department of Accounting
Dept Phone: 876-5241
phone 876-5000 or 876-5241

			ShepherdstwnWV 25443-3210	(304) Fax=876-5193				
			Sch Bus Adm & Soc Sci	shepherd.edu				BS
			King Street					Sharon Earl
Brown, V. J. Jr.	Dean	876-5241	vbrown	Soc	PHD	77	S Dak St	1971
Hamood, Roger B.	C-Ac	Ext 5339	rhammood	CXVP	MBA	72	Marshall	&1978
Thatcher, Joseph W.	Assoc	Ext 5433	jthatche	FGP	MBA	80	SF Austin	&1983
Williams, Dan	Assoc	Ext 5338	dwilliam	ADP	MSA	91	Ferris	&2000

Shippensburg University
Accounting & MIS Deptartment
Dept Phone: 477-1436

			Shippensburg PA 17257-2299	(717) Fax=477-4073				1981
			John L. Grove Col Bus	ship.edu				BSBA,MBA
			1871 Old Main Drive					Ms. Christina Hall
Holoviak, Stephen J.	Dean	477-1435	sjholo	Mgt	PHD	80	W Virginia	1980
Myers, Mary D.	C-Pr	477-1436	mdmyer	CFMV	PHD	88.	Maryland	&1985
Bitner, Larry N.	Prof	477-1702	lnbitn	MC	PHD	85.	Geo Wash	* 1998
Cairns, Scott N.	Prof	477-1641	sncair	FX	PHD	83.	Illinois	&1990
Bardo, Frederic S.	Assoc	477-1607	fsbard	AMPI	PHD	88	Stirling	& 1-85
Mackie, James J. (Jay)	Assoc	477-1675	jjmack	CFM	PHD	86.	Tx A&M	2003
Hocking, Deborah E.	Asst	477-1425	destur	CFMA	MBA	98	Frostburg	&2004

Siena College
Accounting & Business Law
Dept Phone: 783-2321

			Loundonville, NY 12211-1462	(518) Fax=786-5040				2006
			School of Business	siena.edu				BBA
			515 Loudon Road					
Nolan, James R.	Dean	783-2321	jnolan	Stat	PHD	87	SUNY-Alb	
Stokes, Leonard E.	Prof	786-5926	stokes	FMPV	PHD	97.	Union-NY	& 9-86
Carmody, Robert	Assoc	783-2300	carmody	FA	MBA		Siena	& 9-79
Hotaling, Andrea	Assoc	783-2300	hotaling	FX	MS		SUNY-Alb	& 9-80
Silvester, Katherine J.	Assoc	783-2321	ksilvester	CM	PHD	92.	Maryland	2003
Garnsey, Margaret R.	Asst	783-2397	garnsey	SVM	PHD	01	SUNY-Alb	1997
Marcuccio, Elizabeth	Asst	783-2321	emancuccio	FL	JD		AlbanyLw	2004
Raux, Donald	Asst	783-4124	raux	FGN	PHD	02	SUNY-Alb	&
Smith, Walter P.	Asst	783-2321	wsmith	CM	PHD	98.	Ohio St	* 2004

Siena Heights University
Accounting Faculty
Dept Phone: 264-7620

			Adrian, MI 49221-1796	(517) Fax=264-7704				
			Div of Business & Mgt	sienahts.edu				BA
			1247 East Siena Heights Dr					Donna Harowelli
Baker, Donna	C-Ac	264-7628	dbaker	AS	MBA	86	Mich St	&1990
Campbell, Linda M.	Assoc	264-7625	lcampbel	APCV	MBA	87	Toledo	&2000
Bearden, Laura	Asst	264-7689	lbearden	F	MBA	94	Toledo	&2006

Simmons College
Accounting Faculty
Dept Phone: 521-2400

			Boston, MA 02115-5898	(617) Fax=521-3138				
			Dept of Management	simmons.edu				BA,MBA
			300 The Fenway					
Merrill-Sands, Deborah	Dean$	521-3800	deborah.merrill+		PHD		Cornell	* 1995
Senge, Stephen V.	D-Pr	521-2395	stephen.senge	MGN	DBA	85.	Kent St	* 2000
Nitkin, Mindell	Asst	521-2391	mindell.nitkin	F	DBA	06.	Boston U	9-06

Simpson College
Accounting Faculty
Dept Phone: 961-1652

			Indianola, IA 50125	(515) Fax=961-1498				
			Dept of Mgt, Atg & Econ	storm.simpson.edu				
			701 North C					Cindy Hamilton
Schmidt, Tom	C-As	961-1491	schmidt	Quan	PHD	01	St Louis	1999
Juffernbruch, Mark	Assoc	961-1880	juffernb	ACGX	JD		Iowa	1999
Shafer, Steve	Asst	961-1216	steve.shafer	ACGT				2004

Skidmore College
Accounting Faculty
Dept Phone: 580-5100
Homepage: www.skidmore.edu/academic/business/index.htm

			Saratoga SprgNY 12866-1632	(518) Fax=580-5118				
			Dept Management & Bus	skidmore.edu				BS
			815 North Broadway					Nancy Walker
Balevic, Betty V.	C-Ac	580-5104	bbalevic	Mgt	MS		SUNY-Alb	9-69
Canavan, Martin J.	Assoc	584-5103	mcanavan	PFWE	MS	75	SUNY-Alb	&1979
Marcinko, David J.	Assoc	580-5228	dmarcink	M	PHD	73	Boston C	2007
Chiarella, Carol L.	Lect	580-5112	cchiavel		MS	85	SUNY-Alb	& 8-04

Slippery Rock University
School of Business
Dept Phone: 738-4865
Homepage: www.sru.edu/depts/cisba/acct/account.htm

			Slippery Rock PA 16057-1326	(724) Fax=738-2959				
			Col Bus, Info & Soc Sci	sru.edu				BSBA
			110 Eisenberg Classroom Bldg					Cathy Howryla 738-4865
Russell, Bruce	Dean	738-2008						
Culp, David B.	C-Ac	738-2971	david.culp	Econ	PHD	96	S Illinois	1978
Chan, Hong Tak (Andy)	Assoc				PHD	94	Purdue	2000
Lusher, Anna	Assoc		anna.lusher		EDD		Marshall	&2006
Nugent, David A.	Assoc				PHD	92.	Pittsburgh	&2007
Tallapally, Pavani	Assoc				ABD		La Tech	2007

Sonoma State University

Accounting Faculty		Rohnert Park, CA 94928-3609		(707) Fax=664-4009			2007
Dept Phone: 664-2377		School Business & Econ		sonoma.edu			BA,MBA
Homepage: www.sonoma.edu		1801 East Cotati Avenue					Lorraine Tang
Robertson, James W.	Dean	664-2220			PHD	63 U Wash	2004
Stanny, Elizabeth	C-Pr	664-4287	elizabeth.stanny	FM	PHD	96. Chicago	&1998
Anderson, Sherri C.	Prof	664-2684	sherri.anderson	SD	MBA	83 SanFranSt	&1980
Lease, Terry M.	Prof	664-3074	terry.lease	PX	PHD	96. S Calif	&2002
Richman, Vincent	Prof	664-2025	vincent.richman	CM	PHD	97. Columbia	* 2002
Ely, Kirsten M.	Assoc	664-2185	kirsten.ely	SA	PHD	88. Chicago	2005
Taylor, Henry	Inst	664-2685	henry.taylor	CF	MBA	79 Santa Cl	&1982

University of South Alabama

Department of Accounting		Mobile, AL 36688-0002		(251) Fax=460-6529			ß 1976,1980
Dept Phone: 460-6144		Mitchell College of Bus		usouthal.edu			BS,MACC
Homepage: bms.usouthal.edu/accounting/index.html		307 University Blvd					Jane Sawyer
Moore, Carl C.	Dean	460-6418	cmoore	Mgt	PHD	70 Alabama	1971
Hardin, J. Russell	C-Pr	460-6144	jhardin	XF	PHD	95. Miss	&2007
Segal, Mark A.	Prof	460-6144	msegal	X	MLT	82 Emory	&1986
Sylvestre, A. Jeannette	Prof	460-6144	jsylvest	FV	PHD	79. Georgia	1-77
Urbancic, Frank R.	Prof	460-6144	furbanci	F	DBA	77. Kent St	&1990
Ernest G. Cleverdon Professor of Business							
Hsu, Ko-Cheng	Assoc	460-6144	khsu	SA	PHD	93. Memphis	&1993
Parker, Diane	Asst	460-6144	pparker	AP	PHD	04. Miss St	&2003
Suberly, Lynn A.	Asst	460-6144	lsuberly	CGM	PHD	02. Fla St	* & 8-06
Prescott, Gregory L.	Inst	460-6144	gprescot	P	MACC	93 S Alabama	&1994

Univ So Carolina at Aiken

Accounting Faculty		Aiken, SC 29801		(803) Fax=641-3445			2000
Dept Phone:		School Bus Adm & Econ		usca.edu			BS
Homepage: www.usca.sc.edu		171 University Parkway					Gina Buckley
phone 648-6851							
Byington, J. Ralph	Dean	641-3340	ralphb	FV	PHD	85 Arkansas	& 7-03
Harrison, David S.	Assoc	Ext 3376	davidh	PFC	PHD	98. Va Tech	8-97
Adebayo, Arinola O.	Asst	641-3316	arinolaa	FC	PHD	04. Va Comm	&2004
Wates, Kathleen W.	SInst	Ext 3350	kittyw	PFCV	MACC	91 S Carol	* &1991

Univ of South Carolina

School of Accounting		Columbia, SC 29208		(803) Fax=777-0712			ß (13) 1962,1964
Dept Phone: 777-7440		Moore School Business		moore.sc.edu			BS,MAC,PHD
Smith, Joel A. III	Dean	1705 College Street		Bank	BA	67 South	Cindy Parker
							F-00
Doupnik, Timothy S.	D-Pr	777-7450	doupnik	FI	PHD	83. Illinois	&1982
Cramer Fellow of International Accounting							
Edwards, James B.	Prof	777-6497	edwardsj	2005	PHD	71. Georgia	# * &1971
Harrell, Adrian M.	Emer	777-6034	harrell	2005	PHD	75. Tx-Austin	&1980
Leitch, Robert Alan	Prof	777-6418	leitch	SMQ	PHD	73 Tennessee	&1989
Wilbur S. Smith Distinguished Foundation Fellow							
Spiller, Earl A. Jr.	Emer	777-4405	spillere	1999	PHD	60. Michigan	& 9-89
Strobel, Caroline D.	Prof	777-2713	strobel	XM	PHD	78. Georgia	* &1981
Tuttle, Brad M.	Prof	777-6639	tuttle	SMA	PHD	91. Ariz St	& 1-92
Cramer Fellow of Accounting Information Systems							
White, Richard A.	Prof	777-4374	whiter	X	PHD	81. Ariz St	&1985
Moore Faculty Fellow							
Lopez, Thomas J.	Assoc	777-4387	tom.lopez	F	PHD	98. Ariz St	* &2004
Bailey, Wendy J.	Asst	777-3058	wendy.bailey	F	PHD	00. Pittsburgh	&2005
Caylor, Marcus L.	Asst	777-6041	marcus.caylor	F	PHD	06. Geo St	8-06
Cecchini, Mark	Asst	777-6643	cecchini	S	PHD	05 Florida	2005
Jackson, Scott B.	Asst	777-6145	scott.jackson	FM	PHD	97. Nebraska	&2002
Rodgers, Theodore C.	Asst	777-2641	ted.rodgers	AFM	PHD	06. Arizona	&2006
Vandervelde, Scott D.	Asst	777-6075	vandervelde	ASFC	PHD	02. Iowa	&2002
Lynch, Mariah	Inst	777-6202	mariah.lynch	FM	MACC	03 NC-Wilm	2005
Burkett, Jimmy	Lect	777-6412	burkett	MX	MX	95 S Carol	&1995
Fergusson, Janice	Lect	777-4903	fergusson	FMS	MACC	01 S Carol	&2004
Kerr, Rebecca A.	Lect	777-6440	bkerr	F	MACC	91 S Carol	&1999

U South Carolina Upstate

Accounting Faculty		Spartanburg, SC 29303		(864) Fax=503-5583			1999
Dept Phone: 503-5581		School of Bus Adm & Eco		uscupstate.edu			BSBA
Homepage: www.uscupstate.edu/academics/business/business.asp		800 University Way					Janet Searcey
Parker, Darrell F.	Dean	503-5580	dparker	Econ	PHD	84 Purdue	2006
Bennett, Jerome V.	Prof	503-5593	jbennett	CS	PHD	76. S Carol	* 1986
Wilson, Sonja B.	Asst	503-5582	swilson	X	JD	98 S Carol	2000
Shough, J. Stuart	Inst	503-5589	sshough	FC	MACC	86 S Carol	&1986

South Carolina St University Orangeburg, SC 29117-0001 (803) Fax=536-8726 2001,2001
Dept of Atg, Agribus & Econ Sch Business POBox 7234 scsu.edu BS
Dept Phone: 531-7956 300 College Avenue Helen Zimbro
Did Not Respond Again--2003-2004 Listing

Spann, Ora	Dean$	536-8980	ospann	Mgt	PHD	91	Ohio St	3-00
Sykes, Viceola D.	C-Ac$	536-8215	vsykes	FX	PHD	89.	Florida	&1997
Adams, Barbara L.	Prof	536-8980	badams	FAJ	PHD	81.	Tx A&M	&1990
Agrawal, Om P.	Prof	536-8440	agrawal	FM	PHD	71	Jiwasi	# * & 8-74
Onyeocha, Joseph	Asst	536-8457	jonyeocha	FA	MBA	81	Wright St	&1987

University of South Dakota Vermillion, SD 57069-2390 (605) Fax=677-5427 ß 1949,1965
Accounting Faculty Beacom Sch of Business usd.edu BBA,MPA
Dept Phone: 677-5455 414 East Clark St Borert Noonan

Keller, Michael J.	Dean	677-5455	mjkeller		JD	74	S Dakota	2002
Davies, Thomas L.	C-Pr	677-5230	tdavies	XF	LLM	92	Mo-Ks Cty	&1987
Associate Dean								
Carpenter, Jon R.	Prof	677-5556	jcarpent	FTC	PHD	81.	Va Tech	1989
Director of Atg Internships; Coord of Masters of Prof Accountancy								
Ragothaman, Srinivasan C.	Prof	677-6430	sragotha	ASF	PHD	91.	Kansas	&1991
Rosacker, Robert E.	Prof	677-5374	rrosacke	FS	PHD	89.	Nebraska	&1992
Korte, Leon	Assoc	677-5495	lkorte	CMGN	PHD	92.	Nebraska	* &1992
Rosacker, Kirsten	Asst	677-5205	krosacke	PS	PHD	05	Nebraska	* 2005
Dickey, Ellen M.	Inst	677-5201	edickey	MP	MA	99	Oklahoma	* &2004
Epping, Lori L.	Inst	677-5499	lepping	P	MBA	99	S Dakota	&2000
on leave University Mississippi doctoral program								
Olson, Angela	Inst	677-5499	aolson01	F	MPA	02	S Dakota	&2004

University of South Florida Tampa, FL 33620-5500 (813) Fax=974-6528 ß (13) 1969,1980
School of Accountancy College of Business Adm coba.usf.edu BA,MACC,PHD
Dept Phone: 974-4186 4202 E. Fowler Ave. BSN 3403 Donna Pontonero
Homepage: http://coba.usf.edu/accounting/accounting.html
359 have 941 area code

Forsythe, Robert	Dean	974-3229	rforsyth	Econ	PHD	75	Car Mellon	2006
Bryant, Stephanie M.	D-Ac	974-6550	sbryant	S	PHD	96.	LSU	& 8-91
Dan R. and Tina P. Johnson Distinguished Professor of Accounting								
Engle, Terry J.	Prof	974-6561	tengle	AS	PHD	83.	Missouri	&1983
Advisory Council Professor								
Murthy, Uday S.	Prof	974-6523	umurthy	ASD	PHD	89.	Indiana	& 8-02
Jim and Leacy Quinn Eminent Scholar Chair								
Laursen, Gary A. H.	Assoc	974-6565	glaursen	XL	LLM	72	U Miami	& 8-80
Parrott, William H.	Assoc	974-6736	wparrott	F	PHD	71.	Illinois	1-77
Reck, Jacqueline L.	Assoc	974-6721	jreck	GMF	PHD	96.	Missouri	& 8-96
James E. Rooks Distinguished Professor								
Albring, Susan M.	Asst	974-6562	salbring	FX	PHD	02.	Arizona	2004
Butler, Maureen	Asst	974-6597	mbutler	F	PHD	06.	Arkansas	8-06
Caban-Garcia, Maria T.	Asst			PM	PHD	04.	Missouri	& 8-04
email caban@banshee.sar.usf.edu								
Dong, Bei	Asst	974-4186	bdong	F	PHD	07	Mich St	8-07
Gaynor, Lisa M.	Asst	974-6566	lgaynor	A	PHD	00.	Tx-Austin	&2006
Kahle, Jennifer B.	Asst	974-6519	jkahle	FX	PHD	03.	S Carol	& 8-03
Kelton, Andrea	Asst	974-6507	akelton	S	PHD	06.	Tennessee	8-06
Robinson, Dahlia	Asst	974-4186		F	PHD	00.	Georgia	5-07
Schafer, Brad A.	Asst	974-6534	bschafer	S	PHD	03.	Utah	8-03
Stuart, Nathan V.	Asst		nstuart	M	PHD	01.	Indiana	8-05
Cainas, Jennifer	Inst	677-7008		F	MACC		S Fla	8-05
eamil: jcainas@lakeland.usf.edu; area code 863								
Cockrum, Robert B.	Inst	359-4575		F	JD	74	Indiana	& 8-02
email cockrum@banshee.sar.usf.edu								
Jozsi, Celina L.	Inst	974-6574	cjozsi	F	MACC	77	S Fla	& 6-76
Price, Theresa	Inst	974-6578	tprice	AP	MACC	92	Florida	& 8-92
Quilliam, William C.	Inst	359-4359		AB	PHD	91.	Florida	# & 8-92
email quilliam @banshee.sar.usf.edu								
Mastracchio, Nicholas J.	Lect	974-6744	nmastrac	FA	PHD	93.	Union-NY	& 8-06

U of South Fla St Petersburg St Petersburg FL 33701-5016 (727) Fax=553-4192 (12) 2004,2004
Program of Accountancy College of Business stpt.usf.edu BA,BS,MBA
Dept Phone: 553-4998 140 Seventh Ave S COB 348
Homepage: www.stpt.usf.edu/cob/program 0f accountancy/academic_areas.h

Walker, David F.	D $	873-4998	dfwalker	AK	MBA	80	Chicago	&D-02
Fellows, James A.	Prof	873-1587	fellows	CXM	PHD	77	LSU	&1982
Lander, Gerald H.	Prof	873-1185	lander	MAF	DBA	80.	Kentucky	& 8-81
Barker, Katherine J.	Assoc	873-4154		AFC	PHD	99.	Arkansas	& 8-07
Kearns, Grover S.	Asst	873-4085	gkearns	S	PHD	97	Kentucky	& 8-01
Mulig, Elizabeth	Asst	873-4321	mulig	PF	DBA	96.	La Tech	& 7-05

Danese, Stephen P.	Inst	873-1027	danese	F	PHD	80.	Georgia	& 8-01
Gaukel, Patricia	Inst	873-4122	5pgaukel	PC	MA	83	Florida	& 8-04
Jewell, John	Inst	873-4550	jewell	LX	LLM	93	Florida	& 1-01
Strachan, James L.	Inst	873-4024	jstrach2	PNG	PHD	76	Tx-Austin	* 8-03
email jstrach@gte.net								

Southeast Missouri St Univ — C Girardeau, MO 63701-4799 — (573) Fax=651-2992 — 1996,1996
Dept Accounting & MIS — Harrison Col of Bus — semo.edu — BSBA,MBA
Dept Phone: 651-2121 — One University Plaza — Judy Beussink
Homepage: www6.semo.edu/acct&mis

McDougall, Gerald S.	Dean	651-2112	gmcdougall	Econ	PHD	74	Claremont	1993
Wen, H. Joseph	C-Ac	651-2121	hjwen	Mis	PHD	93	Va Comm	2004
Johnson, Gary G.	Prof	651-2324	ggjohnson	ANXS	PHD	89.	Arkansas	* &1982
Beard, Deborah F.	Assoc	651-2118	dfbeard	PFIE	PHD	87.	Arkansas	* 1976
Henry, Eleanor G.	Assoc	651-5124	ehenry	CFMV	PHD	94.	St Louis	2002
Varnon, Anthony N.	Assoc	651-2098	avarnon	STIX	DBA	91.	Miss St	&1979
Humphrey, Roberta L.	Inst	986-4916	rhumphrey	PS	ABD		Miss	2006
Lohmann, Rebecca	Inst	651-2898	rlohmann	P	MS	03	S Illinois	2005

Southeastern University — Washington, DC 20024-2788 — (202) Fax=488-8093
Dept of Accounting & Tax — School of Business — seu.edu — BS,MS,MBA
Dept Phone: 488-8162 — 501 I Street SW — Lawanda Pelote
Homepage: www.southeastern.edu

Peters, David H.	C-Ac			MS	82	American	&
Geriesh, Lotfi H.	Asst			DBA	02	Nova SE	2000
McRae, Issac	Asst			MST	86	Southeas	
Miller, Jerome	Asst			MBA	89	Southeas	
Tisone, A. Anthony Jr.	Asst			MBA	76	Geo Wash	&

Southeastern Louisiana Univ — Hammond, LA 70402 — (985) Fax=549-2891 — ß (12) 1987,1987
Dept Accounting SLU Box10468 — College of Business — selu.edu — BS,MBA
Dept Phone: 549-2052 — 610 Western Ave/Garrett Hall — Anita Farkas
Homepage: www.selu.edu/acad_research/depts;/acct/index.htlm

Settoon, Randall P.	Dean	549-2250	rsettoon	BusA	PHD	96	LSU	8-94
Simpson, Rick	H-Ac	549-2052	rsimpson	FX	PHD	96.	Houston	& 8-96
Carruth, Paul J.	Prof	549-3598	pcarruth	FMC	PHD	79.	LSU	& 8-79
Braun, Robert L.	Assoc	549-3599	bbraun	AF	PHD	94.	LSU	# 8-96
Davis, Harold E.	Assoc	549-3101	hdavis	SDF	DBA	02.	La Tech	&1998
DiGregorio, Dean M.	Assoc	549-2182	ddigregorio	FGN	PHD	98.	Houston	& 8-99
Morris, Joseph L.	Assoc	549-3100	jmorris	FT	PHD	86.	Miss	& 8-84
Titard, Pierre L.	Assoc	549-3535	ptitard	FMC	PHD	70.	LSU	& 1-00
Pollado, Donna S.	Asst	549-3086	donna.pollado	F	MBA	02	N Orleans	& 8-07
DeFranceschi, James	Inst	549-3597	jdefranceschi	FM	MS	94	LSU	& 8-96
Harper, Ashley B.	Inst	549-3j08	5aharper	FM	MS	01	LSU	& 8-02
Helluin, Stella B.	Inst	893-6251	shelluin	FM	MBA	90	Houston	& 8-93
Jones, Kris Tina	Inst	549-3102	kjones	FZ	MPA	85	Miss	& 8-87

Southeastern Oklahoma St — Durant, OK 74701-0609 — (580) Fax=745-7485
Department of Accounting — School of Business — sosu.edu — BBA
Dept Phone: 745-2328 — 5th and Montgomery — Lisa Guyer
Homepage: www.sosu.edu/academics/degrees/accounting

Gaster, W. Buddy	Dean$	745-2030	bgaster	Mktg	DBA	82	La Tech	2000
Hrncir, Theresa	C-Ac	745-2570	thrncir	AFJO	PHD	94	Oklahoma	&1996
Smith, G. Stevenson	Prof	745-2490	sgsmith	CM	PHD	78.	Arkansas	* &2006
Benco, Daniel C.	Assoc	745-2498	dbenco	SGFM	PHD	04.	Tx-Arlin	&2002
Hobbs, Ed	Asst	745-2578	ehobbs	DXF	MT	90	Denver	&1993

Southern Adventist Univ — Collegedale, TN 37315-0370 — (423) Fax=236-1527
Accounting Faculty — Sch of Bus & Management — southern.edu — BBA,MBA,MFS
Dept Phone: 236-2527 — Taylor Circle — Linda Wilhelm/Lisa Kuhlman
Homepage: http://business.southern.edu

VanOrnam, Don	Dean	236-2750	vanornam	MP	PHD	95	Claremont	&1997
Gadd, H. Robert	Prof	236-2697	bobgadd	FIT	PHD	00.	Tx-Arlin	2000
Wentworth, Jon	Assoc	236-2698	jwentwor	MX	MTX	79	Tennessee	&1996
Hyde, Julie	Asst	236-2756	jhyde	AF	MA	04	Tennessee	2006
Steele, Dennis	Asst	236-2756	steele	PS	MBA	98	Kennesaw	1999

Southern University — Baton Rouge, LA 70813-9723 — (225) Fax=771-5262 — 1998,1998
School of Accountancy — College of Business — subr.edu — BS
Dept Phone: 771-5642 — A. Holmes
Homepage: www.subr.edu

Andrews, Donald R.	Dean	771-5641		Econ	PHD	80	Tx A&M	1995
Darby, Mary Alice G.	D-As$	771-5642	magdarby@y	FLX	JD	90	Southern	& 8-71
Toerner, Michael C.	Prof	771-5642	drmike749@a	FEOT	PHD	90.	LSU	& 8-90
Vessel, Herbert	Prof	771-5642	hvessel@y	FAT	PHD	86.	Missouri	& 8-93
Omonuk, Joseph Ben	Asst	771-5642	omonuk@y		ABD		LSU	

Southern Univ at New Orleans   New Orleans, LA   70126-0002   (504) Fax=286-5131
Department of Accounting   College of Business   suno.edu   BS
Dept Phone: 286-5301   6400 Press Drive   Deborah Bevins
Homepage: www.suno.edu
   Did Not Respond--2005-2006 Listing

Name	Rank	Phone	Email		Degree		School	Year
Martin, Frank	Dean$	286-5028	fmartin	Econ	PHD	84	Tulane	1984
James, Tyronne	C-As	286-5349	tjames3025@a	FACV	MACC	83	Florida	&1983
Rahman, Sheikh F.	Asst	286-5305	srahman	PFXG	MBA	69	Tx So	&1969
Berry, G.	Adj	286-5330		TF	MS	99	N Orleans	&1998
Mitchell, T.	Adj	286-5330		FA	MBA	99	N Orleans	&1999

Southern Arkansas Univ   Magnolia, AR   71754-9410   (870) Fax=235-4800   2004
Dept of Atg, Fnce & Econ   College of Business   saumag.edu   BBA
Dept Phone: 235-4304   100 East University   Angela McLaughlin
Homepage: www.saumag.edu/business/

Name	Rank	Phone	Email		Degree		School	Year
Stennis, Earl A.	Dean$	1		AgEc	PHD		Miss St	&
Ashby, J. David	C	235-4304	jdashby	FJV	PHD	96	La Tech	
Riner, Sam	Assoc	235-4318	hsriner	AMSG	DBA	97.	La Tech	&1999
Stinson, Terrye A.	Assoc	235-4300	tastinson	FPR	DBA	89.	La Tech	&1980
Ford, Tim	Asst	235-4309	tcford					2006
Logan, Jennifer	Asst	235-4310			PHD		Oklahoma	2007
Zhao, Limount	Asst	235-5055	lxzhao		PHD		Miss St	2002
Coleman, Fred	Inst	235-5054	flcoleman	SE	MBA	03	Hend St	
Warrick, Shane	Inst	235-5162	cswarrick	PJV	MBA	99	Ark-LtlR	2002

Univ of Southern California   Los Angeles, CA   90089-0441   (213) Fax=747-2815   ß (1) 1922,1963
Accounting Faculty   Leventhal Sch of Acct   marshall.usc.edu   BS,MBT,MACC,PHD
Dept Phone: 740-4838   3660 Trousdale Parkway   Candi Spencer
Homepage: www.marshall.usc.edu/lsoa

Name	Rank	Phone	Email		Degree		School	Year
Beatty, Randolph P.	Dean	740-4841	rbeatty	F	PHD	82	Illinois	2001
Alan Casden Dean's Chair								
Arnold, Jerry L.	Prof	740-4860	jarnold	F	PHD	75.	Michigan	&1979
Bonner, Sarah E.	Prof	740-5025	sbonner	BFA	PHD	88.	Michigan	& 7-92
USC Accounting Associates Professor								
DeFond, Mark L.	Prof	740-5016	mdefond	FAI	PHD	87.	U Wash	&1987
Joseph A. DeBell Professor of Business Administration								
Diamond, Michael A.	Prof	740-2101		FI	PHD	78.	UCLA	&1985
email mdiamond@usc.edu; Executive Vice Provost								
Holder, William W.	Prof	740-4855	wholder	NGFA	DBA	74.	Oklahoma	&1979
Ernst & Young Professor								
Larsen, E. John	Prof	740-4858	jlarsen	KVFJ	DBA	67	S Calif	& 6-63
Lin, Thomas W.	Prof	740-4851	wtlin	MIA	PHD	75.	Ohio St	* 1975
Accounting Circle Professor								
Merchant, Kenneth A.	Prof	821-5920	kmerchant	MB	PHD	78.	Berkeley	&1990
Deloitte & Touche LLP Chair of Accountancy								
Mock, Theodore J.	Prof	740-4861	mock	ABS	PHD	69.	Berkeley	1973
Arthur Andersen Alumni Professor of Accounting								
O'Leary, Daniel E.	Prof	740-4856	oleary	S	PHD	86.	Case Wes	# * &9-85
Elaine and Kenneth Leventhal Research Fellow								
Palmrose, Zoe-Vonna	Prof	740-5019	zpalmrose	AF	PHD	82.	U Wash	&1989
PricewaterhouseCoopers Auditing Professor; on leave SEC								
Swenson, Charles W.	Prof	740-4854	cswenson	X	PHD	84.	S Calif	&1987
Elaine & Kenneth Leventhal Research Fellow								
Young, S. Mark	Prof	740-4848	markyoun	BCM	PHD	83.	Pittsburgh	7-92
KPMG Foundation Professor								
Barcal, John J.	Assoc	740-4874	jack.barcal	X	JD	68	Stanford	&1975
Manegold, James G.	Assoc	740-4850	jmanegold	F	PHD	78.	Stanford	1982
Associate Dean								
Subramanyam, K. R.	Assoc	740-5017	krs	CFQ	PHD	93.	Wisconsin	1993
Trezevant, Robert H.	Assoc	740-5013	trezeva	X	PHD	89.	Arizona	8-90
Elaine & Kenneth Leventhal Research Fellow								
Wang, Shiing-Wu	Assoc	740-5012	swang	X	PHD	88.	Michigan	1996
Brown, Nerissa C.	Asst	740-1345	nerissab	M	PHD	05.	Maryland	2005
Cohen, Daniel A.	Asst	821-4408	daniel.cohen	F	PHD	04.	Nrthwstrn	2004
on leave to New York University								
Hann, Rebecca N.	Asst	740-6939	rhann	F	PHD	00.	Penn	2002
Karaoglu, N. Emre	Asst	821-5979	karaoglu		PHD	02.	Nrthwstrn	&2004
Lu, Yvonne	Asst	821-6478	yvonne.lu		PHD	04.	Stanford	2003
Sandino, Tatiana	Asst	740-4842	sandino	M	PHD	04.	Harvard	2004
Zhang, Jieying	Asst	740-8705	jieying	F	PHD	05.	MIT	2005
Davila, Ruben A.	Clin	740-5005	rdavila	FM	JD	00	Loyola	&1984
Freed, Chrislynn	Clin	740-4867	cfreed	FAE	MBA	92	S Calif	&1991
Hopkins, Merle W.	Clin	740-4879	mwh	F	PHD	82.	Mich St	&1995
Jackson, Cecil W.	Clin	740-5020	ceciljac	M	DCOM	93	Rhodes	1987
Layton, Rose	Clin	740-5022	rlayton	PAF	MACC	83	DePaul	&1993

Mills, Patricia	Clin	740-5007	pmills		LLM	86	SanDiego	2002
Porter, Leslie R.	Clin	740-5004	lporter	DS	PHD	80	UCLA	1994
Roussey, Robert S.	Clin	740-5009	roussey	FAI	BS	57	Fordham	&1992
Scharlach, Robert A.	Clin	740-8510	scharlac	X	BS	61	Illinois	&1994
Simmonds, Kendall L.	Clin	740-5014	simmonds	AFPX	MBA	77	Berkeley	1992

Southern Connecticut St Un
New Haven, CT 06515 — (203) Fax = 392-5863
Department of Accounting — School of Business — southernct.edu — BSBA,MBA
Dept Phone: 392-5691 — 501 Crescent Street — Joan DeMorro demorrojl

Hein, Henry	Dean$	392-5631	heinh1		EDD			
Emenyonu, Emmanuel N.	C-Pr	392-6148	emenyonue1	VPT	PHD	93	Glasgow	&2000
Abdelsayed, Wafeek H.	Prof	392-5690	abdelsayedw1	FPVG	PHD	96.	Conn	# * &1984
Kirsch, Robert J.	Prof	392-5697	kirschr1	FI	PHD	86.	S Carol	&1993
Phillips, Janet F.	Prof	392-5698	phillipsj1	FGNM	SCD	97	NewHaven	&1991
Horn, Betty C.	Assoc	392-5671	hornb1	AS	PHD	87.	Geo St	&1995
Narumanchi, Radha R. M.	Assoc	392-5673	narumanchir1	CAFT	MBA	74	CUNY	* &1977

Southern Illinois Univ
Carbondale, IL 62901-4631 — (618) Fax = 453-1411 — ß (13) 1962,1972
School of Accountancy — College of Bus & Adm — cba.siu.edu — BS,MBA,MACC,PHD
Dept Phone: 453-2289 — 1025 Lincoln Drive — Jeri Novara
Homepage: http://www.cba.siu.edu/acct

Cradit, J. Dennis	Dean			Mktg	PHD	84	Iowa	8-06
Odom, Marcus Dean	D-Ac	453-1408	modom	ABOS	PHD	93.	Okla St	& 5-98
Deloitte & Touche Faculty Fellow								
Basi, Bart A.	Emer	453-2289	basi	1996	DBA	71.	Indiana	&1978
Karnes, Allan L.	Prof	453-2289	karnes	X	JD	86	S Illinois	&1981
KPMG Tax Research Professor								
Rivers, Richard A.	Prof	453-1412	rrivers	MFS	DBA	76.	Kent St	& 6-78
Associate Dean								
Tucker, Marvin W.	Emer	453-1406		1996	PHD	66.	Alabama	7-66
Welker, Robert B.	Prof	453-2289	welker	FMTB	PHD	77.	Ariz St	1987
Hahn, Randall L.	Assoc	453-1498	hahn	XA	DBA	84.	Kentucky	&1984
Masoner, Michael M.	Assoc	453-1405	mmasoner	SM	PHD	75	Minnesota	&1978
Rose, Jacob M.	Assoc	453-1490	jakerose	SB	PHD	98.	Tx A&M	1-06
Sobery, Julie S.	Assoc	453-2289	sobery	FT	PHD	82.	St Louis	&1985
Wacker, Raymond F.	Assoc	453-2289	wacker	XJ	PHD	89.	Houston	& 9-89
Groennert/Emerson Electric Teaching Excellence Professor								
Rose, Ania M.	Asst	453-1497	aniarose	ATF	PHD	98.	Tx A&M	8-05
Lumbattis, Catherine E.	Inst	453-2289	clumbatt	F	MBA	75	S Illinois	&1981
Treece, Darla	Inst	453-2289	treece	F	MACC	00	S Illinois	& 8-00

So Illinois, Edwardsville
Edwardsville, IL 62026-1104 — (618) Fax = 650-5230 — (13) 1975,1980
Department of Accounting — School of Business — siue.edu — BS,MS,MBA
Dept Phone: 650-2633 — Campus Box 1104 — Karen York

Schoenecker, Tim	Dean$	650-3823	tchoen		PHD	94	Purdue	1994
Costigan, Michael L.	C-Pr	650-2657	mcostig	MF	PHD	85.	St Louis	9-91
King, Thomas E.	Emer	650-2635	tking	2005	PHD	73.	UCLA	&1977
Lovata, Linda M.	Prof	650-2623	llovata	MS	PHD	83.	Indiana	&1989
Ortegren, Alan K.	Prof	650-2658	aortegr	FT	PHD	82.	Arkansas	&1982
Boldt, Margaret N.	Assoc	650-2655	mboldt	MF	PHD	97.	Oklahoma	2006
Reed, Bradford J.	Assoc	650-2656	brreed	FA	PHD	95.	Arizona	&1995
Hunt, Allen K.	650-2	692allhu	ntlenhunt	FT	PHD	01.	LSU	2006
Rose-Green, Ena	Asst	650-2107	erosegr	FT	PHD	94.	Fla St	2004
Brant, Steve	Inst	650-2624	sbrant	FM	MS	79	Illin St	1999
Dixon, James	Inst	650-2622	jadixon	FX	LLM	91	Wash U	1999

Univ of Southern Indiana
Evansvillle, IN 47712-3597 — (812) Fax = 465-1044 — (12) 1999,1999
Dept Accounting & Bus Law — School of Business — usi.edu — BS,MBA,MACC
Dept Phone: 464-1718 — 8600 University Blvd — Arlene R. Campbell
Homepage: //business.usi.edu/dept_acct_law.htm

Khayum, Mohammed F.	Dean	465-1681	mkhayum	Econ	PHD	90	Temple	1991
McGuire, Brian L.	C-Pr	465-7031	bmcguire	CMS	PHD	96.	Cen Fla	* &1995
Ehlen, Craig R.	Prof	464-1785	cehlen	PAB	DBA	94.	S Illinois	&1991
Kocakulah, Mehmet C.	Prof	464-1730	mkocakul	PMC	PHD	82	Istanbul	1987
Wade, Daniel E.	Prof	464-1796	dwade	XF	DBA	81.	Kentucky	&1986
Long, Brett J.	Assoc	465-7146	blong	XL	LLM	93	Missouri	&1993
Khallaf, Ashraf	Asst	464-1718	akhallaf	FS	PHD	04.	Fla Atl	2003
Shanklin, Stephen B.	Asst	461-5398	sbshanklin	FP	PHD	99.	St Louis	&2007
Hanley, Philip M.	Inst	464-1983	phanley	FP	MSA	69	Illinois	&2005
Maier-Lytle, Jeannette	Inst	464-1915	jmaier	PFM	MBA	97	S Indiana	&1995

Univ of Southern Maine

Accounting Faculty
Dept Phone: 780-4020
Portland, ME 04104-9400
School of Business
96 Falmouth Street
(207) Fax=780-4662
usm.maine.edu
1999,1999
BS

Name	Rank	Phone	Email		Degree	Yr	School	Yr
Shaffer, James	Dean	780-4020	jshaffer		MBA			1999
Gold, Joel I.	C-Pr	780-4301	jgold	Fnce	PHD	90	Fla St	1973
Gramlich, Jeffrey D.	Prof	780-4020	gramlich	XF	PHD	88.	Missouri	&2003
L.L. Bean Endowed Chair								
Gutmann, Jean	Prof	780-4183	gutmann	DPS	MBA	74	Maine	1977
Potts, Andrew J.	Prof	780-4305	apotts	FM	EDD	77	Geo Wash	&1985
Violette, George R.	Prof	780-4405	violette	XBF	PHD	87.	Ariz St	&1988
Pryor, Charlotte A.	Assoc	780-4020	cpryor	MSGN	PHD	96.	Penn St	&1999
Sanders, John	Assoc	780-4310	jsanders	PF	MBA	77	S Maine	* &1982
Shields, Jeffrey F.	Assoc	780-4020	jshields	CM	PHD	91.	Pittsburgh	2001
Chene, Douglas	Asst	780-4328	dgchene		PHD	95	Illinois	2007

Southern Methodist Univ

Department of Accounting
Dept Phone: 768-3170
Homepage: http://www.cox.smu.edu
Dallas, TX 75275-0333
Cox School of Business
6212 Bishop Blvd
(214) Fax=768-4099
mail.cox.smu.edu
ß 1925,1979
BA,MBA,MSA
Ginny Shearin

Name	Rank	Phone	Email		Degree	Yr	School	Yr
Niemi, Albert W. Jr.	Dean	768-3012	amiemi	Econ	PHD	69	Conn	8-97
Magliolo, Joseph III	C-Pr	768-1678	jmagliol	F	PHD	86.	Stanford	9-93
Distinguished Professor of Accounting								
Desai, Hemang A.	Prof	768-3185	hdesai		PHD	97.	Tulane	8-98
Shaw, Wayne H.	Prof	768-3053	wshaw	XF	PHD	85.	Tx-Austin	& 8-95
Robert B. Cullum Distinguished Professor								
Greynolds, Elbert B.	Assoc	768-3168	egreynol	CSD	PHD	71.	Geo St	&1974
Hanna, J. Douglas	Assoc	768-2234	dhanna	FKQ	PHD	91.	Cornell	* &2004
VanBreda, Michael F.	Assoc	768-3178	mvanbred	FMT	PHD	79.	Stanford	1981
Bhattacharya, Nilabhra	Asst	768-3082	neilb	F	PHD	98.	Georgia	2004
Li, Zining	Asst				PHD		Minnesota	
Pizzini, Mina J.	Asst		mpizzini	MC	PHD	02.	Penn	& 8-05
Sommers, Gregory A.	Asst	768-1188	gsommers		PHD	02.	Ohio St	8-02
Venkataraman, Ramgopal	Asst				PHD			
Wilson, Wendy M.	Asst		wwilson	FI	PHD	05.	N Carol	& 8-05
Riffe, Susan M.	SLect	768-3176	sriffe	F	PHD	92.	S Calif	1992
Austin, Jeffrey R.	Lect	768-3630	jraustin	X	PHD	95.	Georgia	& 8-00

U of Southern Mississippi

Sch Accountancy & Info Sys
Dept Phone: 266-4641
Hattiesburg, MS 39406-5178
College of Business Adm
118 College Dr. #5178
(601) Fax=266-4642
cba.usm.edu
ß (12) 1976,1980
BS,MPA
Kerry Duke

Name	Rank	Phone	Email		Degree	Yr	School	Yr
Doty, D. Harold	Dean	266-4660	harold.doty	Mgt	PHD	90	Tx-Austin	2003
Lewis, Stanley X.	D-Pr	266-4641	s.lewis	S	DBA	75.	Miss St	&1980
Clark, Stanley J.	Prof	266-4725	stanley.clark	FTV	PHD	91.	Kentucky	&1990
DePree, Chauncey M. Jr.	Prof	266-4515	m.depree	M	DBA	87.	Kentucky	1988
Jordan, Charles E.	Prof	266-4843	charles.jordan	FC	DBA	86.	La Tech	&1988
Posey, Roderick B.	Prof	266-4322	roderick.posey	MGN	PHD	80.	Okla St	& 9-79
Jerold J. Morgan Professor								
Albin, Marvin J.	Assoc	266-5920	m.albin	AF	PHD	87.	Houston	&1987
Henderson, James R.	Assoc	266-6964	james.henderson	FC	PHD	80.	Tx A&M	&1988
Jackson, Steven R.	Assoc	266-5789	steven.r.jackson	AM	PHD	93.	Ariz St	&2006
Pate, Gwen R.	Assoc	266-5574	gwen.pate	FMV	PHD	91.	Tennessee	&1990
Smith, W. Robert	Assoc	266-5928	bob.smith	XFM	PHD	88.	LSU	&1995
Anderson, Mary M.	Asst	266-4405	mary.anderson	XF	DBA	05.	La Tech	&2005
Brown, John A.	Inst	865-4558	john.a.brown	FM	MPA	75	S Miss	& 8-01
Munn, Patricia P.	Inst	266-4647	patricia.polk	FM	MPA	86	S Miss	&1986

Southern Nazarene Univ

Department of Accounting
Dept Phone: 491-6359
Bethany, OK 73008
School of Business
6729 NW 39th Expressway
(405) Fax=491-6384
snu.edu
BS
Sandie Goddard

Name	Rank	Phone	Email		Degree	Yr	School	Yr
Herskowitz, Thomas K.	C	491-6359	therskowitz		JD	85	Loyola	2005
Garrett, Randall	Asst	491-6675	rgarrett	PATJ	MSA	78	Okla Cty	&1976
Harris, Iris	Asst	491-6672	iharris	PCMJ	MBA	92	Cen Okla	&1982
Powell, Cindy	Asst	491-6677	cpowell	PXFJ	MBA	91	Cen Okla	&1985

Southern New Hampshire Un

Accounting Faculty
Dept Phone: 668-2211
Homepage: www.snhu.edu
Manchester, NH 03106-1045
School of Business
2500 North River Road
(603) Fax=645-9603
snhu.edu
BS,MBA,MS
Patricia Spirou

Name	Rank	Phone	Email		Degree	Yr	School	Yr
Bradley, Martin	Dean	644-3153	m.bradley	Mgt	EDD	94	Vanderbilt	9-81
Caruso, Karin	C-Ac	668-2211	k.caruso	PFMC	MBA		NewHamp	9-77
Pelletier, Laurence	C-Pr	668-2211	l.pelletier	FPMN	EDD		Nova SE	9-88
Dupuis, Euclid A.	Prof	668-2211	e.dupuis	XC	MS	77	Bentley	* 9-84
Hanson, Richard O.	Prof	668-2211	r.hanson	FUM	PHD		Nova SE	* 9-83
VanSantvoord, John C.	Prof	668-2211	j.vansantvoord	MFCX	MBA	75	NewHamp	& 9-80
Lanzillotti, Louis	Assoc	668-2211	l.lanzillotti	FMNC	MBA		Northeas	& 9-75
Doyon, David	Asst	668-2211	d.dayon	FMI	MBA		S NwHamp	9-01

Southern Oregon University Ashland, OR   97520-5045   (541) Fax=482-6715
Department of Accounting   School of Business   sou.edu   BS,BA
Dept Phone: 552-6484   1250 Siskiyou Boulevard   Mrs. Kathy Mattson
Homepage: www.sou.edu/business/

Harris, David J.	Dean	552-6718	harris da	Law	JD	86	Willamette		
Case, Al	H-Ac	552-6556	casea	FX	MACC	93	Brighm Yg	&2001
Cain, Susan	Asst	552-6717	cains	APV				&2004
Slattery, Dennis	Asst	552-6491	slatterd	CMN	MBA	97	S Oregon	&2004

Southern Utah University Cedar City, UT   84720   (435) Fax=586-5493   2006
Accounting Program   Department of Business   suu.edu   BS,BA,MACC
Dept Phone: 586-5405   351 West Couter Street

Templin, Carl	Dean	586-5401	templin		PHD		Arizona	1996
Christensen, David S.	C-Pr	865-8058	christensend	MCJ	PHD	87.	Nebraska	* & 8-98
Rees, David A.	Prof	586-5416	rees	FGT	PHD	82.	Tx Tech	&1985
Barnes, Jeffrey N.	Assoc	586-5406	barnes	AS	MACC	84	Brighm Yg	&1986
Lewis, Timothy B.	Assoc	586-5443	lewis t	XL	JD	79	Brighm Yg	1985
Merrill, Joseph S.	Assoc	586-5405	merrill	VTFM	PHD	67.	Wisconsin	& 1-94
Boneck, Robin	Asst	586-7773	boneck	XL	JD	86	Brighm Yg	&2005

Southwest Baptist Univ Bolivar, MO   65613-2496   (417) Fax=328-1887
Department of Accounting   Col of Bus & Cpt Sci   sbuniv.edu   BS
Dept Phone: 328-1951   1600 University Ave
Homepage: www.sbuniv.edu/academics/accounting

Whitlock, David W.	Dean	328-1759	dwhitloc	Mgt	PHD	95	Oklahoma	1999
Clark, Wayne	C-As	328-1951	wclark	FPAX	MBA		Mo St	&1991
Bailey, Sharla S.	Asst	328-1754	sbailey	MZPG	MBA		Okla St	* &1994
Walker, J. C.	Inst		jwalker	SM				2006

Southwest Minnesota St Univ Marshall, MN   56258-1598   (507) Fax=537-7179
Accounting Faculty   Col Bus, Ed & Public Af   southwestmsu.edu   BS
Dept Phone: 537-6114   1501 State Street   Jan Christenson
Homepage: www.southwestmsu.edu
  Did Not Respond--2005-2006 Listing

Mitchell, George	Dean	537-6218		Mgt	MBA		Nebraska	1981
Toland, Gerald	C-Pr	532-6260	toland	Econ	PHD		Mich St	1990
Boedigheimer, Michael	Prof	537-7394	boedie	SDG	MBA	68	St Cloud	* &1968
Bayerkohler, Glenn M.	Assoc	537-7393	bayer	VXPD	JD	79	Wm Mitch	&1988
Douglas, Ronald D.	Asst	537-7392	douglasr	ACP	MS	70	SUNY	2000
Patterson, David W.	Asst	537-7372	patterson	CFMP	PHD	01	Nev-L Vg	* &2005

Southwestern University Georgetown, TX   78627-0770   (512) Fax=863-1535
Dept of Econ & Business   Brown Col Arts & Sci   southwestern.edu   BA
Dept Phone: 863-1588   University at Maple
Homepage: http://www.southwestern.edu/~econbus/

Hunt, James W.	Dean	863-1567	huntj	Ed	EDD	88	NW St La	1988
Delaney, John E.	C-Ac	863-1588	delaneyj	FACP	PHD	89.	Tx-Austin	& 8-88
Sellers, Fred E.	Assoc	863-1574	sellersf	FGTV	PHD	84.	Kansas	&1987

Southwestern Oklahoma St U Weatherford, OK   73096-3098   (580) Fax=774-7067
Accounting Faculty   School of Business   swosu.edu   BBA,MBA
Dept Phone: 774-3282   100 Campus Drive   Erin Hawkins
Homepage: www.swosu.edu

May, John M.	C-In	774-3081	john.may	PF	MBA	75	Okla Cty	&2002
Ashenfelter, Melody	Prof	774-3747	melody.ashen+	ANFP	EDD	86	Okla St	&1987
Penner, Nancy	Assoc	774-3746	nancy.penner	P	PHD	99	North Tx	1986
Hays, Rita	Inst	774-7020	rita.hays	XFP	MACC	88	Oklahoma	&2004
Tinsley, Steve	Inst	774-3061	steve.tinsley					

Stanford University Stanford, CA   94305-5015   (650) Fax=725-0468   1926
Accounting Faculty   Graduate School of Bus   gsb.stanford.edu   MBA,PHD
Dept Phone: 723-3424   518 Memorial Way   Joyce Maroon

Joss, Robert L.	Dean	723-3951	joss_robert	Fnce	PHD	70	Stanford	1999
Philip H. Knight Professor								
Rajan, Madhav V.	C-Pr	724-1546	rajan_madhav	M	PHD	90.	Car Mellon	2001
Barth, Mary E.	Prof	723-8536	barth_mary	F	PHD	89.	Stanford	&1995
Atholl McBean Professor of Accounting; Assoc Dean for Academic Affairs								
Beaver, William H.	Emer	723-4409	beaver_william	F	PHD	65.	Chicago	&1969
Joan E. Horngren Professor of Accounting, Emeritus								
Foster, George	Prof	723-2821	foster_george	MFC	PHD	75.	Stanford	1978
Paul L. and Phyllis Wattis Professor of Management								

Horngren, Charles T.	Emer	723-2764	horngren_charles	1995	PHD	55.	Chicago	&1965
Edmund W. Littlefield Professor of Accounting, Emeritus								
Larcker, David F.	Prof	725-6159	larcker_david	M	PHD	78.	Kansas	2005
McNichols, Maureen F.	Prof	723-0833	mcnichols_mau+	FN	PHD	84.	UCLA	& 1-84
Marriner S. Eccles Professor of Public and Private Management								
Patell, James M.	Prof	723-2765	patell_james	FMC	PHD	77.	Car Mellon	9-75
Herbert Hoover Professor of Public & Private Management								
Reichelstein, Stefan	Prof	736-1129	reichelstein_s+	MF	PHD	84	Nrthwstrn	2001
William R. Timken Professor of Accounting								
Wolfson, Mark A.	Consu	723-0311	wolfson_mark	FX	PHD	77.	Tx-Austin	&1977
Kasznik, Ron	Assoc	725-9740	kasznik_ron	F	PHD	95.	Berkeley	1995
Beyer, Anne	Asst	736-0605	beyer_anne	F	PHD	06.	Nrthwstrn	2006
Guttman, Ilan	Asst	723-0825	guttman_ilan		PHD	04	Hebrew	2004
Jagolinzer, Alan	Asst	725-2741	jogolinzer_alan		PHD	04.	Penn St	8-04

Fredonia State University Fredonia, NY 14063-1198 (716) Fax=673-3332
Business Adm & Accounting Dept of Business Adm fredonia.edu BSBA,BS
Dept Phone: 673-3505 E336 Thompson Hall Bobbi Tabak
Homepage: www.fredonia.edu/business/

Seyedian, Mojtaba	C	673-3505	mojtaba.seyedian		PHD	85	SUNY-Bin	2001
Hall, Linda A.	Asst	673-3402	linda.hall	FITV	PHD	99	SUNY-Buf	&2001
Olsavsky, John	Asst	673-4691	john.olsavsky	CDEF	MS	82	Rbt Morr	&1982
Plucinski, Kenneth J.	Asst	673-4602	kenneth.pluc+	AFM	MBA	79	Pittsburgh	&1984

SUNY Brockport Brockport, NY 14420-2965 (585) Fax=395-2542 2003,2003
Accounting Faculty Dept of Bus Adm & Econ brockport.edu BS
Dept Phone: 395-2623 350 New Campus Drive Mary Derleth
Homepage: brockport.edu/bus-econ

Murray, Christine	Dean	395-2510	cmurray	Ed	PHD	90	Syracuse	1985
Dresnack, William H.	C-Ac	395-5532	wdresnac	EFTX	JD	97	SUNY-Buf	&1989
Briggs, Gary P.	Assoc	395-5526	gbriggs	CEFN	MBA	76	Indiana	&1979
Kent, D. Donald	Assoc	395-5521	dkent	ABES	PHD	96.	Union-NY	&1994
Romal, Jane B.	Assoc	395-5056	jromal	MCV	DBA	00.	Clev St	* &2000
Eramus, Edward W.	Asst	395-5525		JLXY	JD	73	Case Wes	1977
Yang, Rong	Asst		ryang	FIKT	PHD	04.	Rutgers	&2004

State Un College at Geneseo Geneseo, NY 14454-1401 (585) Fax=245-5467 2002
Department of Accounting Jones Sch of Business geneseo.edu BA,BS
Dept Phone: 245-5367 1 College Circle Kathy Ackerman
Homepage: http://www.bus.geneseo.edu/index.html

Zuckerman, Mary Ellen	Dean	245-5367	waller	Mktg	PHD	86	Columbia	9-85
Howe, Harry	C-Ac	245-5465	howeh	FSG	PHD	95.	Union-NY	& 9-95
Mitschow, Mark C.	Prof	245-5427	mitschow	FJV	PHD	94.	Maryland	9-94
Bossung, Sharon	Assoc	245-5424	bossung	AJX	MBA		Arkansas	& 9-88
Gifford, Richard H.	Assoc		gifford	AF	PHD	02.	Temple	& 9-01
Schiffel, Lee	Asst		schiffel	S	PHD	03.	Missouri	9-05

SUNY at Old Westbury Old Westbury NY 11568-0210 (516) Fax=876-3360
Accounting Faculty D 300 School of Business oldwestbury.edu BS,MS
Dept Phone: 876-3331 223 Storehill Road Laura Gallagher
Homepage: www.oldwestbury.edu

Delener, N. J.	Dean	876-3292	delenern					
Biondo, John	C-Ac	876-3331	biondoj	FVXT	MBA	86	Hofstra	&1985
Buttermilch, Rita	Assoc	876-3331	buttermilchr	GFPE	MS	79	Lgls-Post	&1984
Fornaro, James M.	Asst	876-2883	fornargoj	FIPT	DPS	03	Pace	* &2003
Glodstein, David	VAsst	876-3331	glodsteind	AFP	MS	89	Lgls-Post	&1999
Herbold, Marita I.	VAsst	876-3313	herboldm	VCPD	JD	98	Touro	&1995
Jiang, Wei	Asst	876-3488	jiangw	FPS	PHD	05.	Rutgers	&2003
Lucido, Peter	Asst	876-4245	lucidop					
Winkelman, Kenneth	Asst	876-4245	winkelmank	CLMT	LLM	04	NYU	2004

SUNY College at Oneonta Oneonta, NY 13820-4015 (607) Fax=436-2543
Div of Economics & Business Behavioral & Applied Sc oneonta.edu
Dept Phone: 436-3458 226 Netzer Adm Building Ms. Dawn Tompkins
Homepage: http://www.oneonta.edu/econbus

Thomas, Wade L.	Dean	436-3458	thomaswl	Econ	PHD	82	Nebraska	1989
O'Dea, William P.	C-Pr	436-3458	odeawp	Econ	PHD	88	SUNY-Alb	1999
Buchan, Howard	Asst	436-3553	buchyanhf	JBX	PHD	04.	SUNY-Bin	& 8-02
Flynn, Lisa	Asst	436-3195	flynnlm	JB	PHD	01.	SUNY-Bin	8-00
Trippeer, Donald R.	Asst	436-3509	trippear	MX	PHD	93.	S Carol	&
Potter, Thomas	Lect	436-2448	pottertc	GNX	BS	69	SUNY-Alb	&1978

SUNY College at Oswego
Accounting, Fnce & Law Dept
Dept Phone: 312-2272

	Oswego, NY	13126		(315) Fax=312-5440			2003,2003	
	School of Business			oswego.edu			BS,MBA	
	Rich Hall						Melody Scott	
Karns, Lanny	Dean	312-3168	karns	MgtS	PHD	78	Syracuse	1976
Skolnik, Richard	C-Ac	312-2539	skolnik	Fnce	PHD	85	Rensselaer	1998
Spector, Charles A.	Prof	312-2613	spector	FPTE	MS	74	Clarkson	&1974
Carroll, Joan M.	Assoc	312-2864	carroll	FEPW	MS	76	Clarkson	&1980
Kirk, Florence R.	Assoc	312-2934	fkirk	FT	PHD	88.	Cornell	9-93
Lundy, William T.	Assoc	312-2533	lundy	FTR	MS	84	SUNY-Bin	&1978
Tribunella, Thomas	Assoc	312-2544	tribunel	SC	PHD	98	SUNY-Alb	&2006
Rao, Hema	Asst	312-2522	hrao	AFGN	DBA	90.	Miss St	&2000
Hollenbeck, R.		312-2532	rhollenb	VX	MS	95	SUNY-Osw	2005

Stony Brook University
Accounting Faculty
Dept Phone: 632-7491

	Stony Brook, NY	11794-3775		(631) Fax=632-9412				
	College of Business			stonybrook.edu			BS,MS	
							Ronee Baldwin	
Turner, William H.	Dean	632-1321	william.h.t+		MBA	66	NYU	2004
Allocca, Carl	Inst	632-7191	carl.allocca		MST			&1992

SUNY at Albany
Department of Accounting
Dept Phone: 442-4978
Homepage: http://www.albany.edu/acc

	Albany, NY	12222		(518) Fax=442-3045		ß (13)	1974,1974	
	School of Business			albany.edu			BS,MS,PHD	
	1400 Washington Avenue						Lisa Scholz	
Leonard, Paul A.	Dean$	442-4910	p.leonard	Fnce	PHD	80	Oregon	1987
Gangolly, Jagdish S.	C-Ac	442-4949	j.gangolly	ASF	PHD	77.	Pittsburgh	# 1990
Srinidhi, Bin N.	Prof	442-4930	bsrinidhi	FMA	PHD	84.	Columbia	2005
Chandra, Uday	Assoc			FVM	PHD	92.	Purdue	8-05
Dutta, Saurav K.	Assoc	442-4426	s.dutta	MA	PHD	91.	Kansas	* 1998
Zhang, Wei	Assoc			FM	PHD	00.	Nebraska	2007
Fernando, Guy	Asst			FM	ABD		Syracuse	2007
Fisher, Ingrid	Asst	442-4937	i.fisher	AS	PHD	02	SUNY-Alb	&1994
Tam, Kinsum	Asst	442-4950	tam	FS	PHD	99.	Conn	1999
Tripathy, Arindam	Asst			FAS	PHD	06	Tx-Dallas	2007
Zhang, Yifeng	Asst			FS	ABD		Tx-Dallas	2007
Collura, Thomas	Lect	442-4528		X	JD	88	AlbanyLw	2001
Moshier, Michelle R.	Lect	442-3788		X	MSA	87	Hartford	1998

SUNY at Binghamton
Accounting Faculty
Dept Phone:

	Binghamton, NY	13902-6015		(607) Fax=777-4422		ß 1991,1991		
	School of Management			binghamton.edu			BS,MS	
Dhillon, Upinder S.	Dean	777-4381	dhillon	Fnce	PHD	86	LSU	1987
Reiter, Sara A.	C-Ac	777-6174	sreiter	F	PHD	85.	Missouri	&1990
Braiotta, Louis Jr.	Assoc	777-6859	braiott	AF	MBA	75	Iona	&1981
Schwartz, Steven T.	Assoc	777-2102	sschwart	FMA	PHD	97.	Ohio St	&1998
Zhou, Nan	Assoc	777-2401	nzhou	F	PHD	00	Minnesota	1999
Ciftci, Mustafa	Asst			F	PHD	06	Tx-Dallas	2007
Duellman, Scott	Asst	777-2544	duellman	F	PHD	06.	Syracuse	8-06
Zhang, Yan	Asst	777-6195	yzhang	F	PHD	04.	LSU	2004
Zhou, Jian	Asst	777-6638	jzhou	F	PHD	00.	Syracuse	&2001
Kamlet, Elliot	Lect	777-6062	ekamlet	F	MS	77	SUNY-Bin	&1982

SUNY at Buffalo
Dept of Accounting & Law
Dept Phone: 645-3290

	Buffalo, NY	14260-4000		(716) Fax=645-3823		ß (12)	1930,1972	
	School of Management			buffalo.edu			BS,MBA,MS,PHD	
	Jacobs Management Center						Janet Kiefer 645-3290	
Thomas, John M.	Dean	645-3221	jmthomas	Intl	PHD	68	MIT	9-68
Hamlen, Susan S.	C-Ac	645-3288	hamlen	FMYV	PHD	73.	Purdue	* 1973
Huefner, Ronald J.	Prof	645-3276	rhuefner	FMV	PHD	68.	Cornell	* &1968
Distinguished Teaching Professor								
Ampadu, Alex B.	VAsoc	645-3265	ampadu	FASM	MBA	76	Roch Tech	# * &1986
Cohen, Ann Burstein	VAsoc	645-3269	abc	XF	MBA	82	SUNY-Buf	&1986
Gu, Feng	Asst	645-3273	fgu	FI	PHD	97	Wash U	2005
Kim, Myung-Sun	Asst	645-7900	mk88	F	PHD	95.	Purdue	
Pacharn, Parunchana	Asst	645-3277	ppacharn	FM	PHD	02.	Car Mellon	2002
Xu, Weihong	Asst	645-5434	wxu4	F	PHD	00.	Wash U	2004

SUNY at New Paltz
Accounting Faculty
Dept Phone: 257-2930
Homepage: www.newpaltz.edu/schoolofbusiness/

	New Paltz, NY	12561-2499		(845) Fax=257-3737				
	School of Business			newpaltz.edu			BS,MBA	
	1 Hawk Drive						Toni Rizzo	
Salavitabar, Hadi	Dean	257-2930	salavith	Fnce	PHD	82	SUNY-Bin	1982
Schultz, Sally M.	Assoc	257-2941	schultzs	FTH	PHD	87.	Penn St	1984
Ebrahim, Ahmed	Asst	257-3988	ebrahima	CM	PHD	04.	Rutgers	1994
Hollister, Joan	Asst	257-2937	hollistj	FM	PHD	98.	Union-NY	* 2006
Forehand, Thomas	Lect	257-2672	forehant	FX	MBA		Michigan	&1993
Kanan, Rief	Lect	257-2936	kananr	FM	MS	76	Syracuse	&1998

SUNY at Plattsburgh Plattsburgh, NY 12901-2681 (518) Fax=564-4215 (1) 2001
Department of Accounting School of Bus & Econ plattsburgh.edu BS
Dept Phone: 564-4185 101 Broad Street Connie Nephew
Homepage: http://www.plattsburgh.edu/buseco/

Read, Colin	Dean	564-4185	colin.read	Econ	PHD	88	Queen's	6-05
Gaber, Mohamed K.	C-Pr	564-4198	mohamed.gaber	FMI	PHD	85.	Baruch	1985
Coffey, James J.	Prof	564-4213	james.coffey	XL	JD	74	Suffolk	1981
Lusk, Edward J.	Prof	564-4190	luskej	AMSG	PHD	72.	Nrthwstrn	& 8-06
Kandiel, El-Sayed H. A.	Asst	564-4199	ehk26@a	CFMV	PHD	85.	Baruch	1989
Lee, Chuo-Hsuan (Jason)	Asst	564-4211	leeca	FMP	PHD	03.	Kent St	* 8-06
Kaiser, Mark	Lect	564-4206	mark.kaiser	AFX	MBA	80	Clarkson	&1986

SUNY Inst Tech @ Utica/Rome Utica, NY 13504-3050 (315) Fax=792-7138
Department of Accounting School of Business sunyit.edu BS,BBA,MS,MBA
Dept Phone: 792-7429 P.O. Box 3050 Carol Gargash
Homepage: www.sunyit.edu

Havlovic, Stephen	Dean	792-7429	havlovs	Mgt	PHD	87	Ohio St	
Karl, Peter A. III	Prof	792-7120	pak3rd	XL	JD	78	AlbanyLw	&1981
Wallis, Kenneth	Assoc	792-7124	fkrw	XM	MS	78	Akron	* &1978
Francis-Gladney, Laura E.	Asst	792-7126	francil		PHD	04.	S Illinois	
Lee, Hoseoup	Asst	792-7130	leeh	AF	PHD	00	Conn	&1996
Smith-Gaffney, Maureen H.	Asst	792-7439	maureen.smith+		PHD	79.	Ohio St	

Stephen F. Austin St Univ Nacogdoches, TX 75962-3005 (936) Fax=468-1482 ß 1976,1982
Department of Accounting College of Business sfasu.edu BBA,MPA,MPAC
Dept Phone: 468-3105 1936 North Street Earline Barrow
Homepage: www.cob.sfasu.edu/acc/

Rogers, Violet C.	Dean	468-3101	vrogers	FBA	PHD	93	North Tx	&1991
Marsh, Treba A.	C-Ac	468-3105	tmarsh	FGN	DBA	97.	La Tech	&1996
Ethridge, Jack R.	Prof	468-3105	jethridge	FTA	PHD	86.	Arkansas	&1983
Ormsby, Susan Young	Prof	468-3105	sormsby	CEMQ	PHD	82.	Arkansas	&1981
Smith, Aileen	Prof	468-3105	asmith	BFIJ	PHD	92.	LSU	&1993
Clark, Wilbur Rhea	Assoc	468-3105	rclark	NAM	PHD	80.	Missouri	&1984
Graves, Sharron Marlow	Asst	468-3105	sgraves	SF	MBED	75	SF Austin	&1975
Hunt, George L.	Asst	468-3105	huntgl	XO	PHD	06.	Tx Tech	* &1984

Stetson University Deland, FL 32723 (386) Fax=822-7426 (3) 1996,1996
Rinker Institute Sch Bus Adm Unit 8398 stetson.edu BBA,MACC
Dept Phone: 822-7415 421 N. Woodland Blvd. Linda Bateman

Scheiner, James H.	Dean	822-7405	james.scheiner	AS	PHD	75	Ohio St	& 7-04
Stryker, Judson P.	C-Pr	822-7418	judson.stryker	XF	DBA	81.	Miss St	&1976
Eugene M. Lynn Professor								
Bitter, Michael E.	Prof	822-7422	michael.bitter	AFEF	PHD	94.	Miss	& 8-96
Brenner, Vincent C.	Prof	822-7439	vbrenner	FZT	PHD	69.	Penn St	& 8-98
David M. Beights Professor of Accountancy								
Dascher, Paul E.	Prof	822-7404	paul.dascher	C	PHD	69.	Penn St	1993
M. E. Rinker Professor								
Ferrara, William L.	Emer	822-7421	william.ferrara	1999	PHD	59.	Mich St	&1989
Jens, William G.	Prof	822-7363	william.jens	FMA	PHD	92	Cen Fla	&1987
Lindback Professor								
Copeland, Richard W.	Assoc	822-7417	rcopelan	XL	LLM	72	U Miami	1976
Taft, Harry J.	Asst	822-7420	harry.taft	FX	MBA	72	Stetson	&1975
Jeancola, Monica	Inst	822-8898	mjeancol	FSM	MBA	00	Stetson	&1998

Richard Stockton College Pomona, NJ 08240-0195 (609) Fax=652-4858
Accounting Faculty Prof Studies Division stockton.edu BA,BS,MBS
Dept Phone: 652-4869 Jimmie Leed Rd Lynn Berkowitz

Chhatwal, Gurprit S.	Assoc	652-4615	iaprod561	FV	PHD	80	Kansas St	1992
Fink, Gregory	Assoc	652-4410		FT	MBA		Rutgers	&
email: glfink@mindspring.com								
Thomas, Frank	Assoc	652-4253	iaprod546	FXS	MBA	79	St Johns	&1979
Kachur, Robert L.	Asst	652-4471	robert.kachur	CSUM	ABD		Capella	2004
McEnerney, JoAnn	Asst	652-4623		ARV	MBA	82	NYU	&1982
Tyska, Claudia R.	Asst	626-6053	claudia.tyska	ACMV	PHD	00.	Rutgers	&2004
Vito, Marilyn	Asst	652-4273	mev	AFT	MBA	85	Monmouth	&1994

Stonehill College Easton, MA 02357-1135 (508) Fax=565-1444
Accounting Faculty Business Adm Department stonehill.edu BSBA,MSA
Dept Phone: 565-1463 320 Washington Street Julie Pick

Salvucci, Debra M.	C-Ac	565-1314	dsalvucci	XCFM	MS	79	Bentley	& 9-84
Schatzel, John A.	Prof	565-1376	jschatzel	VFS	DBA	88.	Boston U	& 9-93
Anderson, J. Richard	Assoc	565-1224	jranderson	FB	MS	77	Northeas	* & 9-79
Ilacqua, Glen	Asst	565-1240	gilacqua	AFXN	MST	87	Bentley	& 9-05

Suffolk University
Department of Accounting
Dept Phone: 573-8652
Homepage: www.sawyer.suffolk.edu/faculty/acct/htm

Boston, MA   02108-2770
Sawyer School of Mgt
8 Ashburton Place

(617) Fax = 994-4260   ß (123) 1989,1989
suffolk.edu   BSBA,MSA,MST
Denise Rodriguez-Malvo

Name	Rank	Phone	Email	Fields	Deg	Yr	School	
O'Neill, William J.	Dean	573-8665	woneill		JD	74	Suffolk	2001
Fuerman, Ross D.	C-Ac	573-8615	rfuerman	FM	PHD	96.	Cincinnati	&1997
McEwen, Ruth Ann	Prof	573-8511	rmcewen	F	PHD	86.	Ga Tech	&1998
Associate Dean								
McInnes, Morris	Prof	573-8339	mmcinnes	FMB	DBA	69.	Harvard	1987
Associate Dean								
Pant, Laurie W.	Prof	573-8394	lpant	MCJ	DBA	86.	Boston U	* 1991
Rahman, Mawdudur	Prof	573-8372	mrahman	FCBS	PHD	76	Manchest	1981
Wojdak, Joseph F.	Exec	994-4276	jwojdak	AF	PHD	68.	LSU	2006
Angelini, James P.	Assoc	573-8361	jangelin	X	PHD	86.	Houston	&1993
Sergenian, Gail K.	Assoc	573-8757	gsergeni	FAB	PHD	94.	Conn	& 1-93
Shaw, Lewis	Assoc	573-8205	lshaw	SF	PHD	02	Durham	* 1996
Cataldo, James	Asst	305-1798		F	PHD	86	Columbia	2006
Gomaa, Mohamed	Asst	884-0710	mgomaa		PHD	05	Maastrich	2007
Kraten, Michael	Asst	973-5388	mkraten	FMB	PHD	04.	Conn	&2005
Li, John Q.	Asst	305-1704	jli	FI	PHD	00.	Wash U	2003
Mistry, Jamshed J.	Asst	484-6064		FM	DBA	99.	Boston U	2007
email: jamshed.mistry@verizon.net								
Muehlmann, Brigitte	Asst				PHD	95	Vienna	
Whalen, Tom	CLAs	305-1703	twhalen	FM	MS	01	Boston C	2001
Yen, Alex C.	Asst	973-5387	ayen	AFB	PHD	04.	Tx-Austin	&2005
May, D.	Inst	375-4083	dmay	ACFX	MS	94	Bentley	&2004
Pelletier, Mary-Joan	Lect	573-8740	mpelleti	ACFK	MSA	04	Suffolk	&2005

Susquehanna University
Acct & Info Systems Dept
Dept Phone: 372-4454
Homepage: www.susqu.edu/accounting

Selinsgrove, PA   17870-1001
Sigmund Weis Sch Bus
514 University Avenue

(570) Fax = 372-4491   1993
susqu.edu   BS
Cindy Inkrote

Name	Rank	Phone	Email	Fields	Deg	Yr	School	
Jackson, Alicia J.	Dean	372-4455	jackson	FM	PHD	97	Tx-Austin	* 9-07
Habegger, Jerrell W.	C-Ac	372-4461	habegger	AFV	PHD	88.	Va Tech	& 9-89
Tressler Chair of Accounting								
Davis, Richard O.	Prof	372-4460	rdavis	XFL	LLM	92	Geotown	& 9-92
McElroy, Barbara W.	Assoc	372-4454	mcelroyb	MF	PHD	97.	Penn St	& 9-02

Syracuse University
Lubin School of Accounting
Dept Phone: 443-1040

Syracuse, NY   13244-2130
Whitman School of Mgt
721 University Ave

(315) Fax = 443-1761   ß 1920,1963
syr.edu   BS,MBA,MS,PHD

Name	Rank	Phone	Email	Fields	Deg	Yr	School	
Stith, Melvin T.	Dean	443-3751	mtstith	Mktg	PHD	77	Syracuse	1-05
Elder, Randal J.	C-Pr	443-3359	rjelder	AG	PHD	93.	Mich St	&1992
Ismail, Badr E.	Prof	443-3598	bismail	CM	PHD	74.	Illinois	1979
Harris, David G.	Assoc	443-3362	dgharris	X	PHD	94.	Michigan	& 8-99
Thevaranjan, Alex	Assoc	443-3355	athevara	M	PHD	93.	Minnesota	1993
Brown, William D.	Asst	443-3884	wdbrow01	F	PHD	01.	Mass	&2003
Hanouille, Leon J.	Asst	443-3356	ljhanoui	FAS	PHD	83	Syracuse	& 9-78
Okyere, Kofi Appiah	Asst		kaokyere	F	PHD	05.	Wisconsin	2005
Franklin, Mitchell	Inst	448-9641	mifrankl	FM	MS	00	Syracuse	&2004
Walsh, William	Inst	443-3359	wiwalsh	FMAX	MBA	90	Syracuse	1997

University of Tampa
Department of Accounting
Dept Phone: 253-6221
Homepage: www.utampa.edu/acad/cob/accindex69.htm
phone 253-3333

Tampa, FL   33606-1490
John H. Sykes Col Bus
401 West Kennedy Blvd

(813) Fax = 258-7408   1999,1999
ut.edu   BS,MBA,MSACC
Joyce Keller

Name	Rank	Phone	Email	Fields	Deg	Yr	School	
McCann, Joseph E. III	Dean	253-6221	jmccann	Mgt	PHD	80	Penn	2000
Krause, James D.	C-Ac	Ext 3602	jkrause	FMCU	DBA	97	Nova SE	&1985
Joseph, Gilbert W. (Joe)	Prof	Ext 3586	gjoseph	FGIS	PHD	92.	S Fla	&1986
Dana Professor								
Platau, Steven M.	Prof	Ext 3583	platau	FXL	JD	84	Cincinnati	&1984
Nelsestuen, Linda B.	Assoc	Ext 1790		XCM	PHD	96.	S Fla	* & 8-06
Squires, Karen D.	Assoc	Ext 3667	ksquires	FMCT	MBA	76	Alabama	&1978
Verreault, Daniel A.	Assoc	Ext 3824	dverreault	MJO	PHD	84.	Tx A&M	&2004
Walters, L. Melissa	Assoc	Ext 1789		SMB	PHD	93.	Cen Fla	
Bostick, Lisa N.	Asst	Ext 3251	lbostick	FA	DBA	01.	La Tech	&2001
Lippincott, Barbara J.	Asst	Ext 3857	blippincott	FG	PHD	98.	Missouri	&2004
Pergola, Teresa M.	Inst	Ext 3298	tpergola	FM	ABD		Nova SE	&2002
Pike, Gene E.	Inst	Ext 3531	gpike	FM	MBA	77	Tampa	* &2001

Tarleton State University
Dept Atg, Fnce & EcBoxT-0920
Dept Phone: 968-9331

Stephenville, TX   76402
College of Business Adm
1257 West Washington

(254) Fax = 968-9665
tarleton.edu
BBA,BS,MBA
Pam Hecox

Name	Rank	Phone	Email	Fields	Deg	Yr	School	
Barker, Ruby F.	Dean	968-9350	rbarker	AdmS	PHD	82	North Tx	1972

Cullers, Sue	H-Ac	968-9913	cullers	MPV	PHD	89.	North Tx	&1985
Collier, Boyd D.	Prof	968-9908	collier	FV	PHD	70	Tx-Austin	&1983
Sundarrajan, Sankar	Prof	968-9916	sundar	FP	PHD	94	Alabama	1992
Liu, Chao M.	Assoc	968-9907	liu	XV	PHD	82.	North Tx	&1984
Cadle, Judith	Asst	968-9940	jcadle	PSD	MBA	91	Tarleton	1993
Varnell, Karen D.	Asst	968-9915	varnell	ACJP	MBA	98	Tarleton	1998
Wade, Linda G.	Asst	968-9914	lwade	FCP	MBA	82	Tarleton	&1982
Foster, Christi	Inst	968-9917	cfoster	FP	MBA	00	Tarleton	8-04

Taylor University Upland, IN 46989-1001 (765) Fax=998-4853
Accounting Faculty Division of Business taylor.edu BS,BA
Dept Phone: 998-5135 236 West Reade Ave Nancy Gillespie
Homepage: www.taylor.edu/academics/acaddepts/business/

Adams, Scott A.	Dean	998-5135	scadams	Fnce	DBA	05	Anderson	2000
Tapp, Marvin L.	Asst	998-5138	mrtapp	PFJ	MBA	88	St Fran	&2001

Temple University Philadelphia, PA 19122 (215) Fax=204-5587 ß 1934,1973
Department of Accounting Fox School of Bus & Mgt temple.edu BBA,MBA,MS,PHD
Dept Phone: 204-8110 13th & Montgomery Streets Gwen Bond
Homepage: www.sbm.temple.edu/~acctdept

Porat, Moshe	Dean	204-7676	porat	Risk	PHD	81	Temple	1981
Press, Eric G.	C-Ac	204-8127	eric.press	F	PHD	88.	Oregon	&1992
Balsam, Steven	Prof	204-5574	drb	FX	PHD	91.	Baruch	&1991
Merves Research Fellow								
Banker, Rajiv D.	Prof	204-2029	banker	MSCQ	DBA	80.	Harvard	* &2005
Merves Chair in Accounting and Information Systems								
Lipka, Roland	Prof	204-8125	rlipka	XF	PHD	76	Rutgers	&1983
Reeb, David	Prof	204-6117	dreeb	M	PHD	96	S Carol	2006
Basu, Sudipta	Assoc			F	PHD	95.	Rochester	2007
Fogg, Stephen L.	Assoc	204-1915	sfogg	SA	PHD	78	NYU	&1976
Gaffney, Mary Anne	Assoc	204-8129	gaffney	NFM	PHD	84.	Maryland	1983
Gordon, Elizabeth A.	Assoc			FI	PHD	98.	Columbia	&2007
Greenberg, Ralph H.	Assoc	204-6830	greenber	MSB	PHD	81.	Ohio St	& 9-88
Krishnan, Jagan (Krish)	Assoc	204-8126	krish	AF	PHD	91.	Ohio St	&1991
Merves Research Fellow								
Ryan, David H.	Assoc	204-8131	ryan	XF	PHD	89.	S Carol	&1989
Krishnan, Jayanthi	Asst	204-3085	jaykrish	AFM	PHD	90	Ohio St	9-00
Malandra, Marco	Inst	204-8124	marco.malandra	FX	MTAX	83	Golden Gt	&1992
Moughan, Michael	Inst	204-8149	moughan	F	PHD	98	Delaware	2006
Wurst, Christian	Inst	204-8461	cwurst	FMX	MBA	96	Rutgers	1998

University of Tennessee Knoxville, TN 37996-0560 (865) Fax=974-4631 ß (13) 1941,1971
Dept Accounting & Info Mgt College of Business Adm utk.edu BS,MBA,MACC,PHD
Dept Phone: 974-2551 916 Volunteer Blvd
Homepage: http://acct.bus.utk.edu/

Williams, Jan R.	Dean	974-5061	jwilli13	FTE	PHD	70	Arkansas	& 7-77
Pilot Chair of Excellance								
Murphy, Daniel P.	H-Pr	974-1752	dmurphy	X	PHD	90.	N Carol	& 8-90
Deloitte & Touche Professor								
Anderson, Kenneth E.	Prof	974-1753	kea	X	PHD	83.	Indiana	& 1-84
Pugh & Company Professor of Accounting								
Behn, Bruce K.	Prof	974-1760	bbehn	F	PHD	94.	Ariz St	& 8-94
Ergen Professor of Business								
Carcello, Joseph V.	Prof	974-1757	jcarcell	AF	PHD	90.	Geo St	# * & 8-93
Ernst & Young Professor								
Kiger, Jack E.	Prof	974-1748	jkiger	AF	PHD	71.	Missouri	& 6-76
Warren L. Slagle Professor of Accounting								
Roth, Harold P.	Prof	974-1756	hroth	M	PHD	80.	Va Tech	* & 1-81
Stanga, Keith G.	Prof	974-1758	kstanga	F	PHD	74.	LSU	& 7-77
Andersen Professor of Accounting								
Neal, Terry L.	Assoc	974-2551	tneal3	A	PHD	98.	Tennessee	& 8-03
William & Sara Clark Professor								
Townsend, Richard L.	Assoc	974-1750	rtownsen	F	PHD	72.	Tx-Austin	& 9-69
Accounting Excellence Teaching Scholar								
Woodroof, Jonathan B.	Assoc	974-1762	jwoodroof	S	PHD	94	Tx Tech	& 8-99
Bradley, Randy	Asst	974-1761	rbradley	S	PHD	06	Auburn	8-06
Fuller, Robert	Asst	974-1749	rmfuller	S	PHD	03	Indiana	8-06
Luna, LeAnn	Asst	974-2551	lluna	FC	PHD	00.	Tennessee	& 6-05
Anderson, Ellen B.	Lect	974-2660	eanders2	FC	MACC	85	Tennessee	& 9-86
Hollander, Anita Sawyer	Lect	974-1754	ahollan5	S	PHD	87.	Tennessee	8-02
College of Business Reagan Scholar								
Hughes, Harry N.	Lect	974-1680	hhughes2	F	BS	75	Tennessee	& 4-76
Mayfield, Vicki	Lect	974-1755	vmayfiel	XL	JD		Tennessee	8-07
Valades, Karyn	Lect	974-1355	kvalades	F	MACC	02	Tennessee	8-02
West, Alice	Lect			S	MACC	86	Tennessee	8-07

Tennessee at Chattanooga   Chattanooga, TN 37403-2598   (423) Fax=425-4162   ß (13) 1982,1988
Department of Accounting   College of Business Adm   utc.edu   BS,MBA,MACC
Dept Phone: 425-2112   615 McCallie Ave Dept 6206   Christi Underwood
Homepage: www.utc.edu/academic/business

Name	Rank	Phone	Email		Degree	Year	School	
Casavant, A. Richard	Dean	425-4333	richard-casavant	Mktg	PHD	76	Geo St	9-77
Sheridan, Kaye F.	H-Ac	425-4770	kaye-sheridan	X	DBA	98.	Miss St	& 8-02
Fulmer, John G. Jr.	Prof	425-4101	john-fulmer	F	PHD	70	Alabama	9-77
Vieth Professor; Associate Dean								
Gavin, Thomas A.	Prof	425-4638	tom-gavin	FAO	DBA	82.	Tennessee	& 9-71
Joseph Decosimo Professor of Accounting								
Scheidt, Marsha A.	Prof	425-5337	marsha-scheidt	MCS	DBA	91.	Miss St	* 9-90
UC Foundation Professor								
Thibadoux, Gregory M.	Prof	425-4408	greg-thibadoux	MC	PHD	84.	Houston	9-86
Davis, Stanley B.	Assoc	425-4152	stan-davis	M	PHD	00.	Alabama	* & 7-06
McCoskey, Melanie G.	Assoc	425-5253	melanie-mc+	XF	PHD	96.	Georgia	& 8-98
Brice L. Holland Associate Professor of Taxation								
Sompayrac, Joanie	Assoc	425-4428	joanie-sompa+	FLPX	JD	91	Cincinnati	& 8-98
UC Foundation Associate Professor of Accounting								
Turpin, Richard A. (Rick)	Assoc	425-4664	rick-turpin	FM	PHD	94.	Alabama	& 8-93
UC Foundation Associate Professor of Accounting								
Willis, Marilyn	Assoc	425-4179	marilyn-willis	F	EDD	76	Kentucky	& 9-76
Archambeault, Deborah S.	Asst		debbie-archam+	FAH	PHD	00.	Alabama	&2004
Long, Kathleen G.	Asst	425 5372	kathleen-long	P	MBA	98	La-Lafay	& 1-00
Turner, Kim A.	Asst	425-2326	kim-turner	F	MBA		Tn-Chatt	8-98

Univ of Tennessee at Martin   Martin, TN   38238-5015   (731) Fax=881-7241   1995,1995
Dept Atg, Econ, Fnce & InBus   Col of Bus & Public Aff   utm.edu   BS,MAC
Dept Phone: 881-7226   111 Business Adm Building   Mary Prather
Homepage: http://www.utm.edu/departments/cbpa/aefib

Name	Rank	Phone	Email		Degree	Year	School	
Moser, Ernest C.	Dean	881-7225	emoser	Econ	PHD	73	Tx A&M	8-01
Griffin, Richard B.	Prof	881-7308	rgriffin	FVSM	PHD	79.	Miss	* 8-88
Kilgore, Ronald W.	Prof	881-7240	rkilgore	FX	PHD	74.	Miss	9-75
Putman, Robert L.	Prof	881-7305	bputman	GFC	DBA	88.	Memphis	& 8-90
Williams, P. Richard	Assoc		rwilliams	FGM	PHD	95.	Arkansas	& 8-01
VanVuren, Kenneth W.	Asst	881-7397	vanvuren	C	PHD	03.	Miss	8-03
Green, James S.	Inst	881-7333	jgreen	P	MBA	68	Arkansas	* & 9-98
Hearn, Paula S.	Inst	881-1202	phearn	XL	MAC	03	Tennessee	8-04

Tennessee State University   Nashville, TN   37203-3401   (615) Fax=963-7177   1994,1994
Dept Accounting & Bus Law   College of Business   tnstate.edu   BBA,MBA
Dept Phone: 963-7162   330 Tenth Ave North, Box 137   Catherine Willis 963-7162
Homepage: www.tnstate.edu/acbl/

Name	Rank	Phone	Email		Degree	Year	School	
Curry, Tilden J.	Dean	963-7124	tcurry	Plan	PHD	78	Fla St	1976
Jermakowicz, Eva K.	H-Pr	963-7052	ejermakowicz	FIV	PHD	82	Warsaw	&2007
Hayes, Robert D.	Prof	963-7164	rhayes	FM	PHD	86.	Arkansas	* &1990
Laska, Lewis L.	Prof	963-7166	llaska	FL	PHD	78	Peabody	&1973
Lea, Kenneth R.	Prof	963-7166	klea	AMNO	DBA	80.	La Tech	&1975
Porter, Grover L.	Prof	963-5996	gporter	FM	PHD	73.	LSU	&2001
Reynolds, Ruthie G.	Prof	963-7168	rreynolds	CFLX	PHD	81.	Geo St	&1998
Banham, Richard L.	Assoc	963-7163	rbanham	DISX	PHD	84.	Tx-Austin	1993

Tennessee Technological Un   Cookeville, TN   38505-0001   (931) Fax=372-6249   ß (12) 1978,1981
Dept Atg & Bus Law Box 5024   College of Business Adm   tntech.edu   BS,MBA
Dept Phone: 372-3358   1105 N. Peachtree Street   Ms. Gwen Paul
Homepage: www.tntech.edu/accounting

Name	Rank	Phone	Email		Degree	Year	School	
Niebuhr, Robert E.	Dean	372-3372	niebuhr	Mgt	PHD	77	Ohio St	2001
Fesler, Robert D.	C-Pr$	372-3685	dfesler	AFM	DBA	86.	Miss St	# * &1986
Booker, Jon A.	Prof	372-3885	jonbooker	FAS	PHD	71.	North Tx	# &1984
Caldwell, Charles W.	Prof	372-3358	ccaldwell	MF	DBA	79.	Fla St	* 8-91
Elmore, Robert C.	Prof	372-3359	relmore	CMX	PHD	86.	Miss	&1988
Maples, Larry	Prof	372-3887	lmaples	X	DBA	76.	Miss St	&1985
Foundation Professor of Accounting								
Swanson, G. A.	Prof	372-3883	gaswanson	FMT	PHD	82.	Geo St	&1982
Earles, Melanie James	Assoc	372-6537	mearles	XC	DBA	97.	Miss St	& 8-98
Rand, Richard S. Jr.	Assoc	372-6121	richardrand	AFO	PHD	89.	S Carol	&1989

U of Texas at Arlington   Arlington, TX   76019-0468   (817) Fax=272-5793   ß (123) 1969,1973
Dept of Accounting Box 19468   College of Business Adm   uta.edu   BBA,MST,MPA,PHD
Dept Phone: 272-3481   701 S. West Street
Homepage: www2.uta.edu/accounting

Name	Rank	Phone	Email		Degree	Year	School	
Himarios, Daniel	Dean	272-2881	himarios	Econ	PHD	84	Va Tech	1983
Walther, Larry M.	C-Ac	272-3050	lwalther	F	PHD	80.	Okla St	* &1980
Hall, Thomas W.	Prof	272-3087	tom.hall	AFB	PHD	80.	Okla St	&1981
Public Accounting Professor								

Taylor, Martin E.	Prof	272-3030	mtaylor	AF	PHD	74.	Tx-Austin	& 6-88
Ho, Li-Chin Jennifer	Assoc	272-3058	lichinho	FM	PHD	90.	Tx-Austin	1-90
Mark, Richard S.	Assoc	272-3059	richmark	XLZ	LLM	81	Denver	&1981
McConnell, Donald K. Jr.	Assoc	272-3057	mcconnell	AF	PHD	81.	North Tx	&1978
Pierce, Bethane Jo (Becky)	Assoc	272-3080	bpierce	X	PHD	87.	North Tx	&1985
Subramaniam, Chandra	Assoc	272-3142	subramaniam	F	PHD	93.	Minnesota	* & 6-03
Tsay, Jeffrey J.	Assoc	272-3048	jefftsay	SM	PHD	73.	Missouri	* &1974
Efendi, Jap	Asst	272-7029		FA	PHD	04.	Tx A&M	8-07
Wintgerbotham, Glyn J.	Asst	272-7029		FA	ABD		Oklahoma	& 8-07
Andrews, Carly	Lect	272-7326	candrews	F	MSA		Tx-Arlin	6-04
Bitenc, Sandra	Lect	272-1115	bitenc	FM	MS	82	Wi-White	& 8-05
Brown, Terra	Lect	272-0710	tcbrown	FM	MPA	05	Tx-Arlin	& 1-07
Hagan, Dan	Lect	272-3031	dhagan	FM	MPA	85	Tx-Arlin	&2002
Lee, Patsy L.	Adj	272-3047	plee	F	PHD	83.	North Tx	&1997
Prachyl, Cheryl L.	Adj	272-3065	cprachyl	S	PHD	96.	Tx-Arlin	& 6-03

Univ of Texas at Austin Austin, TX 78712-0211 (512) Fax = 471-3904 ß (123) 1916,1963
Department of Accounting McCombs School of Bus mccombs.utexas.edu BBA,MBA,MPA,PHD
Dept Phone: 471-5215 2100 Speedway 1 Univ B6400 Mary Ann Fair maryann.fair
Homepage: http://www.mccombs.utexas.edu/dept/accounting/

Gau, George W.	Dean	471-5058	george.gau	REst	PHD	75	Illinois	9-88
George S. Watson Centennial Professor in Real Estate								
Anderson, Urton L.	Prof	471-5339	urton.anderson	AMO	PHD	85.	Minnesota	# 9-84
Clark W. Thompson, Jr. Profesorship in Accounting Education								
Atiase, Rowland K.	Prof	471-5841	rowland.atiase	FM	PHD	80.	Berkeley	& 7-87
Ernst & Young Faculty Fellowship in Teaching Excellence								
Cooper, William W.	Emer	471-1822	william.cooper	1994	DSC	70	Ohio St	1980
Foster Parker Centennial Professor Emeritus of Finance and Management								
Deitrick, James W.	Prof	471-7602	james.deitrick	FEV	DBA	77.	Tennessee	6-77
KPMG Peat Marwich Centennial Fellow in Accounting								
Freeman, Robert N.	Prof	471-5332	robert.freeman	F	PHD	77.	Tx-Austin	& 6-88
Arthur Andersen & Co. Alumni Centennial Professorship in Accounting								
Granof, Michael H.	Prof	471-4678	michael.granof	FG	PHD	72.	Michigan	& 1-72
Ernst & Young Distinguished Centennial Professor of Accounting								
Hirst, D. Eric	Prof	471-5565	eric.hirst	BF	PHD	92.	Minnesota	9-91
Ernst & Young Faculty Fellowship in Accounting								
Jennings, Ross G.	Prof	471-1251	ross.jennings	F	PHD	87.	Berkeley	1-87
PricewaterhouseCoopers Centennial Fellowship								
Kachelmeier, Steven J.	Prof	471-3517	steve.kach +	AVFB	PHD	88.	Florida	& 1-88
Charles T. Zlatkovich Centennial Professorship in Accounting								
Kinney, William R. Jr.	Prof	471-3632	william.kinney	A	PHD	68.	Mich St	&1987
Charles & Elizabeth Prothro Regents Chair/PricewaterhouseCoopers Fel in Audit								
Koonce, Lisa	Prof	471-5576	lisa.koonce	BF	PHD	90.	Illinois	* & 1-90
Deloitte & Touche Professor of Accounting								
Larson, Kermit D.	Emer	482-8515		1994	DBA	66.	Colorado	&1966
Arthur Andersen and Co. Alumni Centennial Emeritus Professor of Accounting								
Limberg, Stephen T.	Prof	471-5347	stephen.limberg	X	PHD	82.	Ariz St	9-82
PricewaterhouseCoopers Centennial Professor of Accountng; MPA/PPA Director								
May, Robert G.	Prof	471-5155	bob.may	FM	PHD	70.	Mich St	6-79
KPMG Centennial Professor of Accounting								
Newman, D. Paul	Prof	471-9474	paul.newman	FT	PHD	77.	Tx-Austin	9-77
Clark W. Thompson Jr., Chair of Accounting Education								
Robinson, John R.	Prof	471-5315	john.robinson	XV	PHD	81.	Michigan	& 9-85
C. Aubrey Smith Professor of Accounting								
Clement, Michael B.	Assoc	471-5619	michael.clement	F	PHD	97.	Stanford	& 1-97
KPMG Faculty Fellowship in Accounting Education								
Mills, Lillian F.	Assoc	471-4607	lillian.mills	X	PHD	96.	Michigan	&2006
Corona, Carlos	Asst	471-1427	carlos.corona	TMFA	PHD	06.	Stanford	& 7-06
Hales, Jeffrey W.	Asst	471-2163	jeffrey.hales	BF	PHD	03.	Cornell	9-02
Krull, Linda K.	Asst	232-7729	linda.krull	FX	PHD	01.	Arizona	&2001
Laux, Volker	Asst	471-6569	volker.laux		PHD	03	Frankfurt	7-06
Williamson, Michael G.	Asst	471-5215	michael.will +	M	PHD	05.	Indiana	7-05
Xue, Yanfeng	Asst	471-5328	yanfeng.xue	F	PHD	04.	MIT	8-04
Yang, Sunny	Asst	471-5619	sunny.yang	F	PHD	06.	Colorado	& 7-06
Yu, Yong	Asst	471-6714	yong.yu	F	PHD	06.	Penn St	8-06
Platt, David E.	SLect	471-3518	david.platt	CM	PHD	97.	Cornell	& 9-96
Atiase, Florence J. A.	Lect	471-5329	florence.atiase	FM	MACC	83	Florida	& 1-93
Charrier, Gretchen B.	Lect	471-6379	gretchen.char +	FMX	MPA	96	Tx-Austin	& 6-97
deVidal, Douglas	Lect	471-7893	doug.devidal	FX	PHD	91.	Tx-Austin	9-92
Gillespie, Janet D.	Lect	471-5327	jan.gillespie	FSG	MBA	82	W Wash	& 9-88
Kamas, J. William	Lect	232-9158	j.kamas		MBA	91	Chicago	&2002
Verduzco, David	Lect	471-7873	david.verduzco	F	MPA	93	Tx-Austin	& 9-00
Zvinakis, Kristina	Lect	471-5215	kristina.zvin +	X	PHD	99.	Tx-Austin	& 9-05

Univ Texas at Brownsville

Accounting Department — Brownsville, TX 78520 — (956) Fax=882-3897
Dept Phone: 882-3837 — School of Business — utb.edu — BBA,MBA
80 Ft. Brown — Patricia Vela

Name	Rank	Phone	Email					
Shane, Martin	Dean	882-5800	hugh.m.shane	Mgt	PHD		Iowa	2006
Collinsworth, Carol	C-As	882-8863	carol.collins+		MBA	83	Tx-PanAm	&1982
Sauceda, Mary Jane	Assoc	882-7135	mjsauceda		PHD	01.	Tx A&M	&1992
Elshafie, Essam A.	Asst	882-5811	essam.elshafie		PHD	05.	Kent St	2005
Ortiz, Dennis S.	Asst	882-7208	dennis.ortiz		PHD	00.	North Tx	1998
Schmid, Lauran	Lect	882-7207	lauran.schmnidt		MBA	88	Tx-PanAm	&2004

Univ of Texas at Dallas

Accounting & Info Mgt — Richardson, TX 75083-0688 — (972) Fax=883-6811 — (123) 2002,2002
Dept Phone: 883-2564 — School of Management — utdallas.edu — BS,MS,PHD
2601 North Floyd Road — G. Thompson, S. Tran, N. Hamilton
Homepage: http://som.utdallas.edu/aim

Name	Rank	Phone	Email					
Pirkul, Hasan	Dean	883-4080	hpirkul	SQ	PHD	83	Rochester	1996
Cready, William M.	D-Pr	883-2564	cready	CFM	PHD	85.	Ohio St	2004
Ali, Ashiq	Prof	883-6360	ashiq.ali	F	PHD	88.	Columbia	2004
Charles and Nancy Davidson Distinguished Professor								
Enthoven, Adolf J. H.	Prof	883-2320	enthoven	IMT	PHD	60	Netherl	&1975
Konstans, Constantine	Prof	883-6345	konstans	MSX	PHD	66.	Mich St	# * &1993
Radhakrishnan, Suresh	Prof	883-4438	sradhakr	FCMA	PHD	92.	NYU	&1999
Anderson, Mark C.	Assoc	883-2056	andersmc	FTYX	PHD	95.	Florida	&1995
Janakiraman, Surya N.	Assoc	883-6370	suryaj	MCS	PHD	94.	Penn	1998
Natarajan, Ram	Assoc	883-2739	nataraj	MCS	PHD	92.	Penn	1998
Bardhan, Indranil R.	Asst	883-2736	bardhan	SQM	PHD	95	Tx-Austin	2001
Dai, Zhonglan	Asst	883-6337	zdai	XYM	PHD	05.	N Carol	2005
Franzen, Laurel	Asst	883-6396	laurelf	FX	PHD	00.	U Wash	2000
Gurun, Umit G.	Asst	883-5719	umit.gurun	F	PHD	04	Mich St	2004
Li, Xu	Asst	883-2564	xu.li	FX	PHD	04.	MIT	2004
Liu, Xiaohui Gloria	Asst	883-4187	xiaohui.liu	F	PHD	04.	Nrthwstrn	2004
Mishra, Birendra K. (Barry)	Asst	883-6385	bmishra	SM	PHD	96.	Tx-Austin	2000
on leave at University of California, Riverside								
Muslu, Volkan	Asst	883-2492	vmuslu	FI	PHD	05.	MIT	2005
Vargus, Mark E.	Asst	883-4772	vargus	FM	PHD	96.	Penn	2002
Zhou, Yibin	Asst	883-4426	yibin.zhou	FMY	PHD	06	Toronto	2006
Agulnek, Arthur	SLect	883-4773	axa022000	XL	BS	67	CUNY	&2002
Blair, Ronald J.	SLect	883-4430	rblair	X	MBA	73	Oklahoma	&1999
Bortz, Tiffany A.	SLect	883-4774	tabortz	FPA	MSA	95	Tx A&M	&2001
Goodrich, Mary Beth W.	SLect	883-4775	goodrich	SA	MBA	94	LSU	# &2002
Salamasick, Mark L.	SLect	883-4729	mark.salamasick	ADOF	MBA	76	Cen Mich	# 2003
Solcher, Charles J.	SLect	883-6347	solcher	LX	JD	71	S Tx Law	&1995
Troutman, Amy	SLect	883-6719	amybass	FPA	MPA	97	Tx-Austin	2001
Bardin, John P.	Lect	883-4434	john.bardin	AEJ	MBA	98	Manhatten	&2006

Univ of Texas at El Paso

Department of Accounting — El Paso, TX 79968-0542 — (915) Fax=747-8618 — ß (123) 1989,1989
Dept Phone: 747-5192 — College of Business Adm — utep.edu — BBA,MBA,MACC
Martha Escontrias
Homepage: //academics.utep.edu/default.aspx — alias=academics.utep.edu

Name	Rank	Phone	Email					
Zimmermann, Raymond A.	C-Ac$	747-7738	rzimmer	LX	PHD	91	Tx Tech	9-92
Eason, Patricia L.	Asst	747-5192	peason	X	PHD	94.	Tx Tech	& 9-95
Associate Dean								
Mann, Gary J.	Emer	747-5241	gmann	2006	PHD	86.	Tx Tech	& 1-86
Salter, Stephen B.	Prof	747-5192		IF	PHD	91.	S Carol	9-07
Austin, Walter G.	Emer	747-5192		1995	PHD	64.	Tx-Austin	& 7-79
Braun, Gary P.	Assoc	747-7742	gbraun	ABFI	PHD	95.	Arizona	9-94
Putnam, Karl B.	Assoc	747-7740	kputnam	FMGR	PHD	80.	Okla St	6-86
Glandon, Sid	Asst	747-7759	sglandon	FAB	DBA	97.	La Tech	& 9-00
Glandon, Terry Ann	Asst	747-8681	tglandon	SCB	PHD	00.	Tx-Arlin	& 9-00
Howell, Sharon K.	Asst	747-5192	skhowell	AF	PHD	05.	Cen Fla	& 9-05
Huerta, Esperanza E.	Asst	747-5192		MSB	PHD	03	Claremont	9-07
Leahey, Anne L.	Asst	747-7734	aleahey	FV	MBA	70	Hawaii	& 9-76
Mayne, Frank A.	Asst	747-7737	fmayne	CFMX	PHD	82	Arizona	& 9-78
Otero, Kathy F.	Lect	747-7764	kotero	FM	MACC	95	Tx-ElPaso	* 9-95
Stevens, Mary	Lect	747-7739	mstevens	FX	MACC	87	Tx-ElPaso	& 8-88

Univ of Texas-Pan American

Dept of Accounting & Bus Law — Edinburg, TX 78541-2999 — (956) Fax=381-2407 — 1979,1985
Dept Phone: 381-2406 — College of Business Adm — utpa.edu — BBA,MACC,MSA
1201 West University Drive — Mrs. Emma Leal
Homepage: w3.panam.edu/accounting/

Name	Rank	Phone	Email					
Ozuna, Teofilo	Dean	384-5087	ozuna	Fnce	PHD	89	Tx A&M	9-00
Lantz, Keith W.	C-Pr	381-3384	kwlantz	FMT	PHD	75.	Iowa	2006
Ganguli, Gouranga	Prof	381-3399	ganguli	FCI	PHD	83.	Miss	# * & 8-90
Atamian, Rubik	Assoc	381-3387	atamian	SM	PHD	84.	Tx-Austin	9-86
Garverick, James E.	Assoc	292-1327		X	MS	64	Kent St	&2007

McKee, A. James	Assoc	381-2831		ACM	PHD	82.	Okla St	* &2007
Moyes, Glen D.	Assoc	381-2406	glenmoyes	AS	DBA	91	US Intl	9-01
Owusu-Ansah, Stephen	Assoc	381-3385	stephen	FIQ	PHD	98	Middlesex	9-01
Smolarski, John	Assoc			CFM	PHD	96.	North Tx	&2007
VanZante, Neal R.	Assoc			CFMG	PHD	76.	Okla St	* &2007
Darcy, John W.	Asst	292-7316	johndarcy	XIJL	PHD	02.	Oklahoma	& 9-02
Zhou, Haiyan	Asst	381-3334	zhaiyan	FA	PHD	03.	Temple	9-03
Ayala, Marion	Lect	316-7936		FM	MS	06	Tx-PanAm	2007
Sanchez, Della	Lect	316-2831		FM	MS	06	Tx-PanAm	2007

U of Texas of Permian Basin — Odessa, TX 79762-0001 (432) Fax=552-2174 2006,2006
Accounting Faculty — School of Business — utpb.edu — BBA,MBA,MPA
Dept Phone: 552-2170 — 4901 East University — Carolyn Jennings 552-2170

Gaulden, Corbett	Dean$	552-2170	gaulden_c	Mktg	PHD	80	LSU	7-83
Dye, Wilma R.	Assoc	552-2177	dye_w	XF	PHD	98.	Tx Tech	& 9-92
Counts, R. Wayne	Asst	552-2180	counts_w	XC	PHD	05.	Tx Tech	2004
Davenport, Shirley	Asst	552-2176	davenport_s	AM	PHD	02	Tx Tech	9-02
Greenfield, Chad	Inst	552-2170	greenfield_c	PMV	ABD		Va Comm	9-05

Un of Texas at San Antonio — San Antonio, TX 78249-0632 (210) Fax=458-4322 ß (123) 1980,1980
Department of Accounting — College of Business — utsa.edu — BBA,MSA,PHD
Dept Phone: 458-4320 — One UTSA Circle — Cheri McMaster
Homepage: business.utsa.edu/departments/acc

de la Vina, Lynda Y.	Dean	458-4313	lynda.delavina	Econ	PHD	82	Rice	2004
Groff, James E.	C-Pr	458-5239	james.groff	MSG	PHD	84.	Iowa	* 1988
Briner, Russell F.	Prof	458-5320	russell.briner	AMF	PHD	76.	Okla St	&1988
Forgione, Dana A.	Prof	458-6319	dana.forgione	NCM	PHD	87.	Mass	* & 8-06
Janey S. Briscoe Endowed Chair in the Business of Health								
Welch, Sandra T.	Prof	458-5242	sandra.welch	AFHO	PHD	91.	Tx A&M	&1991
Associate Provost								
Asthana, Sharad C.	Assoc	458-5232	sharad.asthana	FS	PHD	95.	Tx-Austin	8-06
Boone, Jeff P.	Assoc	458-4320	jeff.boone	F	PHD	94.	North Tx	&2005
Fasci, Martha A.	Assoc	458-2510	martha.fasci	FM	PHD	77	Tx-Austin	&1977
Linthicum, Cheryl L.	Assoc	458-5785	cherly.linthicum	FIS	PHD	93.	Okla St	&1993
Nwaeze, Emeka T.	Assoc	458-7462	emeka.nwaeze	CMF	PHD	92.	Conn	8-06
Pitman, Marshall K.	Assoc	458-5238	marshall.pitman	AFM	PHD	83.	Miss	* &1984
Sanders, D. Elaine	Assoc	458-5787	elaine.sanders	CMB	PHD	95.	Oklahoma	8-94
Skekel, Ted D.	Assoc	458-5240	ted.skekel	FTVE	PHD	77.	Oregon	&1986
Lopez, Dennis	Asst	458-5249	dennis.lopez	MA	PHD	07.	Arkansas	& 8-06
Smith, Pamela C.	Asst	458-5235	pamela.smith	X	PHD	01.	Va Tech	9-01
Willis, Veronda	Asst	458-4320	veronda.willis	F	PHD	05.	Colorado	&2005
Yin, Qin Jennifer	Asst	458-4320	jennifer.yin	FM	PHD	99.	Houston	&2005
Bridges, Gary	SLect	458-4323	gary.bridges	FM	PHD	99	Co-Denve	& 8-04
Vaello, Linda	Lect		linda.vaello	MFX	MBA	80	Tx-SanAnt	&2001

Univ of Texas at Tyler — Tyler, TX 75799 (903) Fax=566-7372 1999,1999
Department of Business Adm — College of Bus & Tech — mail.uttyl.edu — BBA,MBA
Dept Phone: 566-7365 — 3900 University Blvd — Amy Weakley

Tarter, Jim L.	Dean	566-7360	jtarter	Mgt	PHD	72	Mich St	N-95
Odom, Oris L.	C-Pr	566-7240	oodom	Fnce	DBA	70	Oklahoma	9-83
Fischer, Mary L.	Prof	566-7433	mfischer	GFV	PHD	83	Conn	9-90
Gates, Sandra	Asst				PHD		Ariz St	&
Runyan, Bruce W.	Asst	565-5660	brunyan	FMI	PHD	05.	Tx A&M	* & 9-05
Zhong, Ke	Asst				PHD	05.	S Illinois	2004
Washburn, Mark	Lect	565-5833	mwashburn	XFS	MS	97	Tx-Arlin	& 9-04

Texas A&M University — Coll Station, TX 77843-4353 (979) Fax=845-0028 ß (13) 1972,1972
Department of Accounting — Mays Business School — tamu.edu — BBA,MS,PHD
Dept Phone: 845-5014 — 401 Wehner Building — Jenny Green
Homepage: http://acct.tamu.edu

Strawser, Jerry R.	Dean	845-4711	jstrawser	AF	PHD	85	Tx A&M	& 7-01
Leland/Weinke Chair								
Benjamin, James J.	H-Pr	845-0356	j-benjamin	F	DBA	72.	Indiana	& 6-74
Andersen Professor								
Bravenec, Lorence L.	Prof	845-4384	l-bravenec	X	LLM	66	NYU	& 8-71
Daily, R. Austin	ClPr	862-1944	rad	F	PHD	70.	N Carol	& 9-92
Deloitte & Touche Professional Program Director's Professor								
Giroux, Gary A.	Prof	845-2375	g-giroux	GFN	PHD	79.	Tx Tech	& 9-78
Shelton Professor								
Kratchman, Stanley H.	Prof	845-3175	s-kratchman	VFJ	PHD	73.	Penn St	9-77
Lassila, Dennis R.	Prof	845-4584	d-lassila	X	PHD	81.	Minnesota	& 7-83
Shelton Tax Professor								
Nixon, Clair J.	Prof	845-3875	c-nixon	X	PHD	80	Tx A&M	& 9-80
PricewaterhouseCoopers Professor								

Omer, Thomas C.	Prof	845-5014	tomer	X	PHD	86.	Iowa	8-05
Ernst & Young Professor								
Shaub, Michael K.	ClPr	458-1375	mshaub	A	PHD	89.	Tx Tech	& 6-06
Shearon, Winston T. Jr.	Prof	845-1607	w-shearon	MS	DBA	74	Virginia	8-75
Ernst & Young Professor								
Smith, L. Murphy	Prof	845-3108	lmsmith	JISA	DBA	83.	La Tech	& 6-84
Strawser, Robert H.	Prof	845-4575	rhstrawser	PTBA	DBA	69.	Maryland	& 7-73
Andersen Chair								
Swanson, Edward P.	Prof	845-8970	e-swanson	FTYI	PHD	77.	Wisconsin	& 5-82
Nelson Durst Chair								
Tse, Senyo Y.	Prof	845-3784	stse	FM	PHD	83.	Berkeley	&2004
KPMG Professor								
Wolfe, Christopher J.	Prof	845-0964	cjwolfe	S	DBA	84.	Kent St	& 1-85
KPMG Faculty Fellowship								
Ahmed, Anwer S.	Assoc	845-5014	aahmed	F	PHD	92.	Rochester	7-05
Mays Faculty Fellow								
Fiechtner, Susan B.	ClAc	845-9974	sfiechtner		PHD	82	Oklahoma	1-99
Flagg, James C.	Assoc	845-7607	j-flagg	AFKO	PHD	88.	Tx A&M	& 9-87
Grossman, Steven D.	Assoc	845-4507	s-grossman	F	PHD	72	Tufts	6-76
Kinney, Michael R.	Assoc	862-2078	kinneym	ICMX	PHD	90.	Arizona	8-89
KPMG Faculty Fellowship								
Loudder, Martha L.	Assoc	845-1807	m-loudder	F	PHD	90.	Ariz St	9-89
PricewaterhouseCoopers Fellowship								
McAnally, Mary Lea	Assoc	845-7585	mmcanally	F	PHD	94.	Stanford	# & 9-02
May Faculty Fellowship								
McGowan, Annie S.	Assoc	845-2055	al-mcgowan	M	PHD	94.	North Tx	9-93
Carroll Phillips Fellowship								
Myers, James N.	Assoc	845-5014	jmyers	F	PHD	97.	Michigan	8-05
Shelley, Marjorie K.	Assoc	845-5014	mshelley	BM	PHD	89.	Tx-Austin	* & 8-05
Weaver, Connie D.	Assoc	845-7934	cweaver	X	PHD	97	Ariz St	& 7-06
Wilkins, Michael S.	Assoc	845-4375	mswilkins	F	PHD	94.	Arizona	9-94
PricewaterhouseCoopers Fellowship								
Myers, Linda A.	Asst	845-7935	lmyers	AF	PHD	01.	Michigan	8-05
PricewaterhouseCoopers Faculty Fellow								
Allen, Natalie L.	SLect	845-0655	n-allen	FM	MS	88	Tx A&M	& 1-89
Myers, Adam	SLect			PX	JD	85	Harvard	9-07
Perry, Linda	SLect	845-9695	lsperry	F	MS	71	Illinois	& 6-87
Thornton, Lanie	SLect	845-4075	l-thornton	FP	MS	89	Tx A&M	& 9-89
Barrett, Jeannie A.	Lect	845-7585	jbarrett	F	MBA	02	Sam Hous	1-03
Phinney, Theresa	Lect	845-5014	tphinney	S	MS	84	Tx A&M	9-05
Sanders, Joan	Lect	845-4884	jsanders	S	MS	90	Tx A&M	& 9-00
Stasny, Mary	Lect	862-2725	mstasny	FP	MBA	83	Tx A&M	9-99

Texas A&M Univ-Commerce Commerce, TX 75429-3011 (903) Fax=468-3216 ß 1975,1982
Department of Accounting Col of Business & Tech tamu-commerce.edu BBA,BPA,MBA
Dept Phone: 886-5659 2600 Neal Street Sheri Humphries
Homepage: http://www.tamu-commerce.edu/accounting/

Langford, Harold P.	Dean	886-5189	hal_langford	Mgt	PHD	86	Geo St	2001
Edwards, Wendell E.	H-Pr	886-5657	wendell_edwards	MCE	PHD	73.	North Tx	&1969
Carmichael, Bobby J.	Prof	886-5658	bobby_carmi+	XRFD	EDD	79	Florida	&1980
Heslop, Gordon B.	Asst	886-5259	gordon_heslop	CM	DBA	86.	Miss St	*
Fullwood, Virginia	Inst	886-5454	virginia_full+	FDEP	MBA	89	Tx A&M-C	&2002

Texas A&M - Corpus Christi Corp Christi, TX 78412 (361) Fax=825-5609 1999,1999
Dept of Accounting & Law College of Business Adm cob.tamucc.edu BBA,MACC
Dept Phone: 825-2385 6300 Ocean Drive Ms. Shay Lee
Homepage: www.cob.tamucc.edu

Abdelsamad, Moustafa H.	Dean	825-2655	moustafa	Fnce	DBA	70	Geo Wash	7-91
Tillinger, Janet W.	C-Pr	825-2385	jtillinger	XF	PHD	89.	Houston	& 9-95
Deis, Donald R. Jr.	Prof	825-2351	ddeis	AG	PHD	88.	Tx A&M	& 9-04
Ennis & Virginia Joslin Endowed Chair of Accounting								
Hall, Steven D.	Prof	825-2357	shall	FNGT	EDD	82	N Illinois	& 9-81
Zebda, Awni M.	Prof	825-6029	azebda	BCM	PHD	82.	Va Tech	9-94
Cameron, Paul A. Jr.	Assoc	825-2493	pcameron	FM	MS	65	Air Force	& 9-78
Chambers, Valrie	Assoc	825-6012	vchambers	XFM	PHD	00.	Houston	& 9-00
Slater, Robert D.	Asst	825-3256	rslater	FS	PHD	07.	S Fla	& 9-05

Texas A&M Univ-Kingsville Kingsville, TX 78363-8202 (361) Fax=593-3912
Dept of Accounting & CIS Cl Business Adm MSC 184 tamuk.edu BBA,MPA
Dept Phone: 593-2501 1115 University Blvd Mrs. Helen McCreight

Diersing, Robert J.	Dean	593-3801	r-diersing	D	PHD	91	Tx A&M	1990
Aukerman, Richard	C-Ac	593-3940	richard.auker+	D	PHD	75	N Dakota	2002
Holt, Paul E.	Prof	593-3927	p-holt4625	FIVP	PHD	92.	Okla St	&1990
Huff, Kendra	Assoc	593-3929	k-huff581	PDF	PHD		Tx-PanAm	&1989
Rivera, Gonzalo Jr.	Assoc	593-3941	g-rivera137	ILPX	JD	88	Baylor	&1989
Nikias, Anthony D.	Asst	593-3986	kfadn01	MPS	PHD	02.	Ohio St	2005

Texas A&M International Univ
Dept Accounting & Info Sys
Dept Phone: 326-2490

Laredo, TX 78041-1900
College of Business Adm
5201 University Blvd

(956) Fax=326-2494
tamiu.edu

2002,2002
BBA,MBA,MPACC
Gabby Gamez

So, Jacky C.	Dean	326-2480	jso	Fnce	PHD	83	Ohio St	7-04
Rodriguez, Antonio J.	C-Pr	326-2517	rodriguez	Fnce	PHD	85	Alabama	8-93
Cargill, Willie N.	Prof	326-2501	cargill	ASX	PHD	86.	Missouri	& 9-89
Collins, Frank	Prof	326-2493	fcollins	MB	PHD	74.	Houston	& 6-04

  Radcliffe Killam Distinguished Professor of Accounting

Texas Christian University
Department of Accounting
Dept Phone: 257-7223
Homepage: www.neeley.tcu.edu

Fort Worth, TX 76129
MJ Neeley School of Bus
2900 Lubbock Street

(817) Fax=257-7227
tcu.edu

ß (13) 1963,1966
BS,MBA,MAC
Debra Proctor

Short, Daniel G.	Dean	257-7526	d.short	F	PHD	77	Michigan	& 8-04
Vigeland, Robert L.	C-Pr	257-7215	b.vigeland	F	PHD	77.	Columbia	& 8-89
Bryan, Barry J.	Prof	257-7551	b.bryan	AJS	PHD	94.	Tx A&M	&
Haw, In-Mu G.	Prof	257-7563	i.haw	FM	PHD	83.	Alabama	1990
Nichols, Donald R.	Prof	257-7552	d.nichols	AF	PHD	70.	Oklahoma	&1984
Stanford, Mary Harris	Prof	257-7483	m.stanford	F	PHD	94.	Michigan	&2002
Barkman, Arnold I.	Assoc	257-7553	a.barkman	SM	PHD	74.	Houston	* &1974
Callaghan, Sandra Renfro	Assoc	257-7191	s.callaghan	FX	PHD	98.	Mich St	& 8-98
Lim, Steve C.	Assoc	257-7536	s.lim	F	PHD	89.	Penn	1999
Fu, Huijing	Asst	257-7148	h.fu	F	PHD	05	Minnesota	
Lanier, Danny	Asst	257-7567	d.lanier	F	PHD	03.	Georgia	& 8-03
Schneible, Richard A. Jr.	Asst	257-7150	r.schneible	M	PHD	03.	Syracuse	8-03
Wempe, William F.	Asst	257-7614	w.wempe	M	PHD	98.	Tx A&M	&2001
Cobb, Janice	Inst	257-7367	j.brightwell	F	MBA	86	Tx Chr	&1997

Texas Lutheran University
Dept of Business Adm
Dept Phone: 372-6051

Seguin, TX 78155-5999
College of Prof Studies
1000 W. Court Street

(830) Fax=372-6065
tlu.edu

BBA,BS
Marie Paiz

Lockard, Nick A.	Dean	372-6050	nlockard	BuAd	EDD	00	Baylor	1980
Huntsman, Ronald O.	C-Ac	372-6053	rhuntsman	AGMF	MBA		Mich St	# &1986

  Elton Bohmann Professorship in Accounting

Cook, Sally V.	Assoc	372-6057	scook	LTXP	JD		Tx-Austin	&1997
Thompson, Melanie	Asst	372-6096	mthompson	JRSV	MBA		Tx A&M-C	&2003

Texas Southern University
Department of Accounting
Dept Phone: 313-7910

Houston, TX 77004
Jones Sch of Business
3100 Cleburne Avenue

(713) Fax=313-7722
tsu.edu

ß 2001,2001
BBA,MBA
Doris Samuels

Boyd, Joseph L.	Dean	313-7215	boyd_jl	X	PHD	77	S Carol	&2001
Iqbal, Zahid	C-Ac	313-7737	iqbal_zx	Fnce	PHD	88	North Tx	1988
Hyman, Ladelle M.	Prof	313-7715	hyman_lm	FM	PHD	75.	North Tx	&1981
Malone, Fannie L.	Prof	313-7718	malone_fl	ASEM	PHD	84.	Tx A&M	& 1-85
Pitre, Richard	Prof	313-7717	pitre_rx	EF	PHD	78.	Houston	&1991
Chau, Chak-Tong	Assoc	313-7714	chau_c	FA	PHD	92.	Fla St	&2004
O, Sewon	Asst	313-7719	sewono	FM	PHD	01.	Miss St	& 1-05
Perkins, Carlton	Asst	313-7187	perkins_cl	FLX	JD	78	Houston	&1982
Wang, Kun	Asst	313-7710	wangk_	FCG	PHD	05.	Tx A&M	2005

Texas State U - San Marcos
Department of Accounting
Dept Phone: 245-2566
Homepage: http://www.business.txstate.edu/dept/acct

San Marcos, TX 78666-4616
McCoy Col Business Adm
601 University Drive

(512) Fax=245-7973
txstate.edu

1997,1997
BBA,MACY,SAIT
Angela Hernandez

Smart, Denise T.	Dean	245-2311	ds37	Mktg	PHD	84	Tx A&M	2000
Morris, Roselyn E.	C-Pr	245-2311	rm13	AFX	PHD	93.	Houston	&1993
Eikner, A. Elaine	Prof	245-3688	ee02	FPV	PHD	94.	Arkansas	& 9-92
Humphrey, Joseph L.	Prof	245-3305	jh13	FM	PHD	71.	Tx Tech	&1972
Meixner, Wilda F.	Prof	245-3295	wm05	BF	PHD	85.	Tx A&M	&1986
Montondon, Lucille M.	Prof	245-3540	lm03	GFNO	PHD	90.	Houston	1989
Raiborn, Cecily A.	Prof	245-3878	cr37	FCJM	PHD	75.	LSU	* &2006
McCoy Professor of Accounting								
Rutledge, Robert W.	Prof	245-3301	rr28	FMBJ	PHD	89.	S Carol	& 1-01
Thompson, Steven C.	Prof	245-3302	st18	X	PHD	84.	Houston	& 8-04
McCoy Professor								
Turner, Mark A.	Assoc	245-3900	mt25	XM	DBA	87.	Memphis	* &2006
Butler, Janet B.	Asst	245-3315	jb73	SCM	PHD	92.	Georgia	&2003
Pier, Charles A.	Asst	245-3182	cp27	FX	PHD	04.	Tx-Arlin	2006
Ellison, Robert	Lect	245-3307	re13	CFM	MACY	01	SW Tx St	2003
Ross, Sherry K.	Lect	245-3227	sr19	PFM	MBA	87	SW Tx St	& 1-00
Severance, Robert L.	Lect	245-3296	rs27	PFM	MBA	00	SW Tx St	# &2001
Thoede, Steven W.	Lect	245-3227	st13	P	MBA	81	SW Tx St	* &1993

Texas Tech University Lubbock, TX 79409-2101 (806) Fax=742-3182 ß (13) 1958,1981
Area of Accounting Rawls Col of Business ba.ttu.edu BA,MSA,PHD
Dept Phone: 742-3181 15th & Flint Michelle Crosby
Homepage: accounting.ba.ttu.edu
  email @1=ttu.edu; @2=coba.ttu.edu

McInnes, Allen	Dean	742-0632			PHD	66	Tx-Austin	2001
Nichols, Linda M.	D-Pr	742-1541	linda.nichols@1	FZA	PHD	89.	LSU	& 7-89
Anderson, Lane K.	Emer	742-2047	landerson	2007	PHD	70.	Wisconsin	* &1978
Ernst & Young Professor								
Clancy, Donald K.	Prof	742-3183	don.clancy@1	CM	PHD	76.	Penn St	1982
Associate Dean								
Dowell, C. Dwayne	Prof	742-2090	ddowell	FTV	PHD	74.	Mich St	& 9-91
PricewaterhouseCoopers Professor								
Freeman, Robert J.	Prof	742-2098	rjfreeman	GN	PHD	66.	Arkansas	&1979
Distinguished Professor								
Mann, M. Herschel	Prof	742-2037	h+.mann@1	TF	PHD	71.	Alabama	&1972
KPMG Professor								
Pasewark, William R.	Prof	742-2038	pasewark	MF	PHD	86.	Tx A&M	& 9-00
Ricketts, Robert C.	Prof	742-3180	rricketts	X	PHD	88.	North Tx	&1988
Frank Burke Chair in Taxation								
Viator, Ralph E.	Prof	742-1444	rviator	S	PHD	86.	Tx A&M	& 9-00
Buchheit, Steve	Assoc	742-1542	buchheit	CH	PHD	97.	Tx-Austin	9-01
Rawls Professor								
Malone, J. David	Assoc	742-1545	malone	FIS	PHD	87.	Arkansas	1997
Masselli, John J.	Assoc	742-2392	jmasselli	X	PHD	98.	Geo St	& 9-98
Haskell Taylor Professor								
Lightner, Teresa A.	Asst	742-2039	tlightner	FX	PHD	01.	Oklahoma	9-02
Roman, Francisco J.	Asst			M	PHD	03.	Arizona	2007
Romanus, Robin	Asst			F	PHD	07	Va Tech	2007
Allen, Roberta S.	Lect	742-2032	rallen	F	MSA	96	Tx Tech	& 9-99
Kelley, Dawn	Lect	742-3250	dawn	F	MBA	87	Tx Tech	1988
Lynn, Quepha	Lect	742-2035	qlynn	FCH	MSA	88	North Tx	& 9-91

Texas Wesleyan University Fort Worth, TX 76105-1536 (817) Fax=531-6585
Department of Accounting School of Business txwes.edu BBA,MBA
Dept Phone: 531-4840 1201 Wesleyan JoAnn Moore

Quintanilla, Hector	Dean$	531-4840	hquintanilla	BFX	PHD	96	Tx-Arlin	&1995
Tolleson, Thomas D.	Assoc	531-4297	ttolleson	ACM	PHD	96.	North Tx	&1996
Webb, Kim	Visit		kwebb	ASV	MA	96	Tx-Arlin	&2002

Texas Woman's University Denton, TX 76204-5738 (940) Fax=898-2120
Accounting Faculty School of Management twu.edu BBA,MBA
Dept Phone: 898-2111 1322 Oakland Avenue

Hughes, Paula Ann	D-Pr	898-2106	pahughes	Mgt	PHD	78	North Tx	2002
Rezac, Reg N.	Prof	898-2114	rrezac	XTV	PHD	74	N Colo	1983
Baker, Pamela S.	Asst	898-2108	pbakerll	STV	PHD	96.	North Tx	2002

Thomas More College Crestview Hl, KY 41017 (859) Fax=
Department of Accountancy Business thomasmore.edu BA
Dept Phone: 344-3316

Flynn, R. Steven	C-Pr	344-3316	steven.flynn	MNAS	PHD	87	Cincinnati	1997
Gilday, Thomas J.	Assoc	344-3405	thomas.gilday	FXP	MBA	93	Xavier	1979
Mitchell, Maria	Asst	344-3657	maria.mitchell	FVCM	MBA	95	Xavier	2003

Thunderbird Sch Global Mgt Glendale, AZ 85306-6010 (602) Fax=843-6143 1994
Accounting Faculty Garvin Sch Intl Mgt thunderbird.edu MBA,EMBA
Dept Phone: 978-7150 15249 N. 59th Avenue

Cabrera, Angel	Pres	978-7200	angel.cabrera		PHD		Ga Tech	8-04
Rankine, Graeme W.	C-Ac	978-7299	graeme.rankine	FI	PHD	87.	U Wash	1995
Davison, Dale L.	ClPr	978-7150	dale.davison	FX	PHD	73.	Georgia	&1990

Tiffin University Tiffin, OH 44883 (419) Fax=
Accounting School of Business tiffin.edu BSBA
Dept Phone: 448-3371 155 Miami St. Chari Mullen

Daly, Shawn	Dean	448-3404		Mktg				
Schultz, Tim	Prof	448-3320	tschultz	PC	MBA		Wash U	
Burkett, Teresa	Assoc	448-3448	tburkett	PQ	MAC	85	Bowl Gr	&
Turner, Martha J.	Assoc	448-3297	turnerm	CM	PHD	91.	Cornell	

University of Toledo   Toledo, OH   43606-3390   (419) Fax=530-5516   ß 1955,1963
Department of Accounting   College of Business Adm   utoledo.edu   BBA,MS
Dept Phone: 530-2270   2801 West Bancroft   Susan Welch
Homepage: http://www.accounting.utoldeo.edu

Gutteridge, Thomas G.	Dean	530-2285	thomas.gutt+	Mgt	PHD	71	Purdue	2003
Franz, Diana R.	C-Ac	530-4264	diana.franz	AF	PHD	92.	Tx Tech	&1992
Fink, Philip R.	Prof	530-2281	philip.fink	XFM	JD	74	Ohio No	&1975
Laverty, Brian L.	Prof	530-4261	brian.laverty	FXV	PHD	84.	Mich St	&1990
Raghunathan, Bhanu	Prof	530-2340	bhanu.raghuna+	MC	PHD	86.	Pittsburgh	&1985
Saftner, Donald V.	Prof	530-2327	donald.saftner	SF	PHD	80.	Penn St	1987
Schroeder, Nicholas W.	Prof	530-2343	nick.schroeder	MCF	DBA	84.	Colorado	&1985
Wolfe, Glenn	Assoc	530-2196	glenn.wolfe	S	PHD	84	Va Tech	1989
HassabElnaby, Hassan R.	Asst	530-2780	hassan.hassab+	FI	PHD	98	Cairo U	&2003
Said, Amal A.	Asst	530-2197	amal.said	MI	PHD	03.	Va Comm	2003
Latimar, Amy	VInst	530-2560	amy.latimer	P	MBA	07	Toledo	2005
Snow, Nancy	Inst	530-2374	nancy.snow	P	MS	95	Toledo	&1998

Touro College   New York, NY   10010-4202   (212) Fax=627-9144
Accounting Faculty   Business & Economics   academic.touro.edu   BS,MS,MBA
Dept Phone: Ext 425   27-33 West 23rd Street   Pearl Newman Ext 263
Homepage: www.touro.edu
phone 252-7800

Bressler, Barry	Dean	Ext 235			PHD		NYU	
Snow, Charles J.	Dean			AFVX	PHD	80.	NYU	* 9-04
Sklar, Albert	C-Pr	Ext 425	asklar	PANV	ABD		NYU	& 9-71
Cohn, Gordon M.	Assoc	Ext 244	moshegc	ACP	PHD	97	Baruch	7-98
Barcuh, D.	Asst			ACLP	JD		NYU	& 2-91
Isaac, Klepfish	Asst				JD		NYU	9-85
Privo, A.	Asst			PMF	PHD			2-87
Schneck, W.	Asst			ACPX	MBA		Pace	& 8-84
Bienenstoch, S.	Inst			AXP	MBA			& 3-85
Erlich, L.	Inst			PT	BS			& 1-97
Langer, B.	Inst			NAVG	MBA		Brooklyn	& 9-01
Pfeiffer, F.	Inst			ACB	MS			& 2-93
Tagerstein, D.	Inst			AV	JD		Brkyn-Law	& 9-01
Abraham, O.	Lect			NPC	JD			& 9-03
Berkowitz, C. S.	Lect			XP	MS			& 2-01
Garris, Henry	Lect			CFMX	MS		Pace	& 9-05
Jenner, Paul	Lect			CFPX	MS		Baruch	& 9-05
Saltz, S.	Lect			CVT	BS			& 2-84

Towson University   Towson, MD   21252-0001   (410) Fax=704-3641   ß (13) 1992
Department of Accounting   College of Bus & Econ   towson.edu   BS,MS
Dept Phone: 704-2227   8000 York Road   Paulette Pearson
Homepage: www.towson.edu/cbe/department/accounting

Kaynama, Shohreh A.	Dean		skaynama	Mktg	PHD	91	Geo Wash	1984
Freedman, Martin	Prof	704-4143	mfreedman	TBWF	PHD	75.	Illinois	2000
Holter, Norma C.	Prof	704-4093	nholter	NAMB	PHD	92	Geo Wash #	&1985
Maloo, Man Chand	Prof	704-3231	mmaloo	CFM	DBA	77.	Fla St	1988
Martin, Charles L. Jr.	Prof	704-2064	chmartin	FTAE	DBA	81.	Geo Wash	&1988
Rosenberg, Donald L.	Prof	704-3726	drosenberg	FMXL	JD		Baltimore	* &1984
Schiff, Andrew	Prof	704-3227	aschiff	SMB	PHD	93.	Rutgers	&2000
Steedle, Lamont F.	Prof	704-3226	lsteedle	CFMT	PHD	78.	Penn St	* 1990
Stewart, Barbara R.	Prof	704-2676	bstewart	VFBE	PHD	69	Columbia	&1988
Hammer, Seth	Assoc	704-3083	shammer	FCXB	PHD	93	Pittsburgh	* &1993
Buchoff, Barry S.	Asst	704-3228	bbuchoff	CFMT	MBA		Loyola	&1972
Cong, Yu	Asst	704-3704	ycong	SMAD	PHD	04.	Rutgers	2005

Transylvania University   Lexington, KY   40508-1797   (859) Fax=233-8749
Accounting Faculty   Div of Business & Econ   transy.edu   BA
Dept Phone: 233-8104   300 North Broadway   Tammy Jennings

Fulks, Daniel L.	D-Ac	233-8184	dfulks	XF	PHD	80	Geo St	&1997
Jones, Judy L.	C-Pr	233-8247	jjones	CAG	ABD		Anderson	&1980
Baldwin, William T. Jr.	Prof	233-8175	wbaldwin	F	PHD	75	Kentucky	1988

Tri-State University   Angola, IN   46703-0307   (260) Fax=665-4309
Accounting Faculty   Ketner School of Bus   tristate.edu   BSBA
Dept Phone: 665-4177   1 University Avenue   Judy Miller

Sherlock, Jeffrey F.	Dean	665-4193	sherlockj		EDD	Ball St	
Miller, Kim	Asst	665-4184	millerk		MBA	Indiana	&

Trinity University
Accounting Program
Dept Phone: 999-7296
Homepage: www.trinity.edu

San Antonio, TX   78212-7200
Dept of Business Adm
One Trinity Place

(210) Fax=999-8134
trinity.edu

1996,1996
BS,BA,MS
Debbie Bowling

Name	Rank	Phone	Email					
Walz, Daniel T.	Dean	999-7289	dwalz	Fnce	PHD	82	Wash U	8-82
Sandlin, Petrea K.	D-Ac	999-7296	psandlin	FBE	PHD	87.	Tx-Austin	8-88
Rice, John D.	Assoc	999-7689	jrice	XP	JD	79	Tx Tech	& 1-84
Specht, Linda B.	Assoc	999-7348	lspecht	AFEJ	JD	85	St Marys	& 8-88
Venkateswar, Sankaran	Assoc	999-7288	svenkate	FNIC	PHD	89.	Georgia	8-89
Lopez, Kathrine J.	Asst	999-7347	kathrinelopez	BJTE	MS	01	Trinity	& 8-07

Troy University
Dept of Accounting & Finance
Dept Phone: 670-3137
Homepage: www.troy.edu/divisions/html/business/acct.html

Troy, AL   36082
Sorrell College of Bus
University Avenue

(334) Fax=670-3592
troy.edu

BS,MBA

Name	Rank	Phone	Email					
Hines, Donald C.	Dean			Econ	PHD	73	Kansas St	1993
Burks, Eddy J.	Assoc		eburks	X	DBA	88.	La Tech	&2006
Magrath, Lorraine K.	Assoc	670-3299	lmagrath	MS	PHD	99.	Alabama	&1998
Daniel, C. Lee	Asst	670-3158	ldaniel	P	MBA	76	Tx Tech	&1985
Moten, Sebrena	Asst	670-3709	smoten	LR	JD	80	Alabama	1994
Paul, Amanda	Asst		apaul	F	MBA	00	Troy	2007
Moody, Ray	Lect	670 5764	rmoody	F	MBA	68	Fla St	1-01

Troy University Dothan
Dept of Accounting & Bus Law
Dept Phone: Ext 269
Homepage: www.dothan.troy.edu
phone 983-6556

Dothan, AL   36304-0368
School of Business
500 University Drive

(334) Fax=983-6322
dothan.troy.edu

BS,MBA
Beth Livingston

Name	Rank	Phone	Email					
Gilbert, Adair	Dean	Ext 265	agilbert	QM	PHD	76	Alabama	1982
Bilbeisi, Khamis	C-Ac	Ext 269	kbilbeisi	AGM	PHD	89.	Miss	1986
Schreiner, Paul W.	Prof	Ext 306	pschreiner	MS	PHD	76.	Illinois	&1993
Cluskey, G. Robert Jr.	Assoc	Ext 266	gcluskey	ACFM	DBA	94.	S Illinois	&2006
Gaddis, Marcus D.	Assoc	Ext 271	mgaddis	C	PHD	93.	Kentucky	2002
Lewis, Johnston C.	Assoc	Ext 264		X	MACC	82	Alabama	&2001
Teed, Dan	Asst	Ext 268	dteed		MPA	73	Tx-Austin	&2006

Troy University, Montgomery
Accounting Program
Dept Phone: 241-9703

Montgomery, AL   36103-4419
Business PO Box 4419
231 Montgomery Street

(334) Fax=241-9734
troyst.edu

BSA,MBA
Cecelia Womack

Name	Rank	Phone	Email					
Rhee, Anthony	Dean	241-9703		Mgt	PHD	79	Kent St	
Simpson, Jimmy C.	C-Ac	241-9711	jsimpson	Mgt				
Lee, Sangsoo	Prof				PHD	86.	Tx-Austin	
Strachan, Beverly	Prof	241-9735			MBA	93	Aub-Mont	

Truman State University
Accounting Unit
Dept Phone: 785-4346
Homepage: business.truman.edu

Kirksville, MO   63501-4221
School of Business
100 East Normal

(660) Fax=785-7471
truman.edu

(13) 1999,1999
BS,MA
Lana Dowell

Name	Rank	Phone	Email					
Wachter, Renee M.	Dean	785-4346	rwachter	S	PHD	93	Indiana	2006
Fouch, Scott R.	C-Pr	785 4371	bu58	XP	PHD	90.	Okla St	&1985
Fleak, Sandra K.	Prof	785-4359	sfleak	FTP	PHD	88.	Missouri	&1984
Kerby, Debra K.	Prof	785-4363	dkerby	FMP	PHD	89.	Nebraska	* &1982
Romine, Jeffrey M.	Prof	785-4378	jromine	AS	PHD	92.	Memphis	&1976
Weber, Sandra L.	Prof	785-4362	bu25	MRFP	PHD	90.	Missouri	* &1976
Davis, Alan B.	Assoc	785-5550	abdavis	XP	JD	92	Geo St	&2004
Harrison, Keith E.	Assoc	785-4375	kharriso	APS	PHD	99.	Kansas	&1987
Turner, James R.	Assoc	785-4348	jturner	LP	JD	81	Missouri	&1982
Turner, Laurie M.	Asst	785-4369	lturner	FGP	MS	75	Missouri	&1983

Tulane University
Area of Accounting
Dept Phone: 865-5680

New Orleans, LA   70118-5669
Freeman Sch of Business
#7 McAlister Place

(504) Fax=865-6751
tulane.edu

β 1981,1916
BSM,MAC,MBA,PHD
Clara A. Brickley, Prog Coord

Name	Rank	Phone	Email					
DeNisi, Angelo S.	Dean	865-5407	adenisi	Mgt	PHD	77	Purdue	7-05
Cowen, Scott S.	Prof	865-5201		MU	DBA	75.	Geo Wash	* 1998
President of the University								
Kemsley, Deen	Prof	865-5324	dkemsley	TX	PHD	95.	N Carol	&2004
Lee, Chi-Wen Jevons	Prof	865-5467	jevons.lee	FMAI	PHD	77	Rochester	* &1988
Lesmond, David A.	Assoc	865-5665	dlesmond	FMS	PHD	94.	SUNY-Buf	1997
Page, John R.	Assoc	865-5475	johnpage	FMS	PHD	75	Tulane	&1984
Soliman, Soliman Y.	Assoc	865-5460	soliman	CMFS	PHD	79.	Georgia	* &1979
Xie, Yuan	VAsst	865-5037	yxie		PHD	06.	Utah	
Zhou, Ling	Asst	865-5435	lzhou	FM	PHD	04	Yale	2004
Parent, Beauregard J. Jr.	Inst	865-5490	bparent	FASC	ABD		LSU	&1977
Foust, Karen M.	ClPr	865-5548	kfoust	FMPT	PHD	94.	Tulane	&2003
Riess, F. Kelleher	ClPr	865-5401	friess	X	LLM	72	Boston U	&1974
Shaw, Pamela E.	ClPr	865-5033	pshaw	FA	PHD	89.	Florida	&2000

University of Tulsa
School of Accounting
Dept Phone: 631-2217
Homepage: http://www.cba.utulsa.edu

Tulsa, OK   74104-3194
College of Business Adm
600 South College Avenue

(918) Fax=631-2164
utulsa.edu

ß 1949,1972
BS,MBA,MTX
Jennie Dugger

Sullenberger, A. Gale	Dean	631-3184	gale-sullenbe+	Engr	PHD	71	Oklahoma	6-99
Cravens, Karen S.	D-Pr	631-2790	karen-cravens	C	PHD	92.	Tx A&M	* & 9-92
Chapman Professor of Accounting								
Hennessee, Patrick A.	Prof	631-2794	patrick-henn+	XPE	PHD	77.	North Tx	& 7-81
Bradley, Wray E.	Assoc	631-2792	wray-bradley	BXE	PHD	99.	Arkansas	* & 8-98
Hudson, Dennis H.	Assoc	631-2791	dennis-hudson	FP	PHD	86.	Arkansas	9-82
Manly, Tracy S.	Assoc	631-2789	tracy-manly	XF	PHD	00.	Arkansas	& 7-01
A. Charles Funai Faculty Fellow								
Rockwell, Stephen R.	Assoc	631-2938	steve-rockwell	AS	PHD	93.	Mich St	8-98
McColl, Anna	Visit	631-2789	anna-mccoll	XFP	MAC	98	Tx-Dallas	& 8-00
McCrary, J. Michael	App	631-2793	michael-mccrary	AF	MAC	74	Okla St	& 8-96

Tuskegee University
Department of Accounting
Dept Phone: 727-8116

Tuskegee, AL   36088
School of Business
Chambliss Business House

(334) Fax=727-8604
tuskegee.edu

1998

Delores Harkless

Gulley, Lawrence	Prof	727-8018	gulleyl	PFTC	PHD	86	Tx A&M	*
Guttikonda, Rama R.	Assoc	727-4651	rguttikonda	F	PHD	84.	Arkansas	1-03

Union College-KY
Accounting Faculty
Dept Phone: 546-1323

Barbourville, KY   40906-1499
Department of Business
310 College Street

(606) Fax=546-1688
unionky.edu

BS

Hensley, Ella K.	C-Pr	546-1323	ehensley					
Stewart, Cheryl	Asst	546-1329	cstewart	F	MBA	89	Kentucky	* 2000
Payne, Carolyn	Inst	546-1304	cpayne	ST	MBA	02	Morehead	&2001

Union Graduate College
Accounting Faculty
Dept Phone: 388-6302

Schenectady, NY 12308-3151
School of Management
807 Union Street

(518) Fax=388-6861
union.edu

2001
MBA
Marcia Catrambone

Chudzik, Mel	Dean	388-6447	chudzikm	Mgt	MS	70	Long Isl	2003
Arnold, Donald F.	D-Pr	388-6302	arnoldd	AFG	PHD	72.	SUNY-Buf	9-82
Neidermeyer, Presha E.	Assoc	388-6598	neidermp	ABI	PHD	97	Va Comm	& 9-96

Union University
Accounting Faculty
Dept Phone: 661-5360

Jackson, TN   38305-3697
McAfee Sch of Bus Adm
1050 Union University Dr

(731) Fax=661-5366
uu.edu

Judy Leforgee

Absher, R. Keith	Dean	661-5367	kabsher	Mktg	PHD	85	Arkansas	2004
Proctor, Thomas	C-Pr	661-5361	tproctor	X	PHD	00	Memphis	1996
Miller, Karen C.	Asst	661-5056	kcmiller		PHD	06.	Miss	1998
Newell, Deborah	Asst	661-5486	dnewell		MBA	81	Murray St	1988

U.S. Air Force Academy
Accounting Faculty
Dept Phone: 333-4130

Colorado Spr, CO 80840
Dept of Management
2354 Fairchild Dr. Ste 6H94

(719) Fax=333-9715
usafa.af.mil

2001
BS

Jordan, Rita A.	H-Pr	333-4131	rita.jordan	Mgt	PHD	93	Colorado	
Green, Steve G.	Prof	333-4130	steve.green	CN	DBA	87	US Intl	6-88
Cycyota, Cynthia	Assoc	333-4130			PHD	03	Tx-Austin	& 6-02
Ferrante, Claudia	Assoc	333-4130			PHD	03	Car Mellon	& 6-02
Jennings, William W.	Assoc	333-4130	william.jennings	FN	PHD	98	Michigan	& 6-98

Ursinus College
Accounting Faculty
Dept Phone: 409-3583
  phone: 409-3000

Collegeville, PA   19426-2020
Dept of Econ & Bus Adm
PO Box 1000, Main Street

(610) Fax=489-0627
acad.ursinus.edu

Cathy Bogusky

Economopoulos, Andrew J.	C	409-3583	aeconomopoulos	Econ	PHD	85	Va Tech	
Harris, Cindy K.	Assoc	Ext 2417	charris	FMAP	MBA		Penn	&1984

University of Utah
School of Accounting
Dept Phone: 581-7798
Homepage: http://www.business.utah.edu/accounting/

Salt Lake Cy, UT 84112
David Eccles Sch of Bus
1645 E Campus Center Rm 108

(801) Fax=581-3581
business.utah.edu

ß (13) 1936,1963
BS,MACC,PHD
Andi Shields

Brittain, Jack W.	Dean	481-7347	mgtjwb	Mgt	PHD	89	Berkeley	1999
Allen, Robert D.	C-Ac	581-7798	bob.allen	AF	PHD	92.	Mich St	& 9-91
C. Roland Christensen Faculty Fellow								
Eining, Martha M.	Prof	581-7673	actme	SA	PHD	87.	Okla St	&1987
Associate Dean for Information Technology								
Plumlee, R. David	Prof	585-9466	actdp	SA	PHD	82.	Florida	&1997

Botosan, Christine A.	Assoc	581-8695	actcb	F	PHD	95.	Michigan	& 7-99
C. Roland Christensen Faculty Fellow								
Harline, N. Lavar	Assoc	581-3120	actnlh	X	PHD	82.	Nebraska	&1982
Lechner, Thomas A.	Asst	581-4998	tom.lechner	AEFM	PHD	98.	SUNY-Buf	&2005
Magilke, Matthew J.	Asst	585-6947	actmm	F	PHD	04.	Wisconsin	8-04
Plumlee, Marlene A.	Asst	581-3397	actmp	FI	PHD	97.	Michigan	&1997
Randall, Taylor R.	Asst	581-3074	acttr	M	PHD	99	Penn	1999
Elderedge, Tom	Adj	232-2218	actte	FS	MBA	94	Utah	&2002

Utah State University
School of Accountancy
Dept Phone: 797-2330
Homepage: www.usu.edu/cob/acct/

Logan, UT   84322-3540
College of Business
3540 Old Main Hill

(435) Fax=797-1475   ß (123) 1972,1981
business.usu.edu   BS,BA,MBA,MAC
Mary Ann Clark

Anderson, Douglas D.	Dean	797-2272		Mgt	PHD		Harvard	2006
Jenson, Richard L.	H-Pr	797-2335	richard.jenson	S	PHD	88.	Utah	&1987
ATK Thiokol Professor								
Johnson, I. Richard	Prof	797-2337	richard.johnson	FVT	PHD	84	Wisconsin	&1985
Larzette G. Hale Professor								
Price, Jay H. Jr.	Prof	797-2993	jay.price	FTVG	DACC	93	Utah St	& 9-88
Arthur Andersen Executive Professor								
Skousen, Clifford R.	Prof	797-2331	clifford.skousen	MI	PHD	70	Golden Gt	* & 9-78
Ernst & Young Professor								
Doyle, Jeffrey T.	Assoc	797-2882	jeffrey.doyle	F	PHD	03.	Michigan	&2003
George S. Eccles Chair in Capital Markets Research								
Durtschi, Cindy	Assoc	797-2330	cindy.durtschi	FV	PHD	98.	Arizona	2003
Fullerton, Rosemary R.	Assoc	797-2332	rosemary.full+	MF	PHD	98.	Utah	&1999
Grange, E. Vance	Assoc	797-2702	vance.grange	XE	PHD	87.	Tx-Austin	&1978
Nelson, Irvin T.	Assoc	797-2543	irv.nelson	CEFT	PHD	92.	Nebraska	&1992
Novack, Garth	Asst	797-8204	garth.novack	XF	PHD	03.	Arizona	8-03
Skousen, Chris	Asst		chris.skousen	S	PHD	04.	Okla St	2007
Shuman, Franklin	SLect	797-2339	frank.shuman	FMCR	MACC	89	Utah St	# * &1992
Larkin, Ryan E.	Lect	797-3958	ryan.larkin	FX	MPRA	02	Utah	&2006

Utah Valley State College
Accounting Faculty
Dept Phone: 863-8526

Orem, UT   84058-5999
Business
800 West University Pkwy

(801) Fax=863-8060   2006
uvsc.edu   AA,AS,BA
Paula V. Poulson

Jenne, Stanley Earl	Dean	863-8239	jennest	FA	PHD	82	Illinois	&2006
Johnson, Steven D.	C-Ac	863-7186	johnsosd	MCB	PHD	91.	Va Tech	&2000
Bean, Benjamin W.	Prof	863-8469	beanbe	FMH	MBA	71	Utah	&1976
Black, Katherine D.	Prof	863-6419	blackka	X	LLM	89	Ca-Davis	&2005
Smith, Sheldon R.	Prof	863-6153	smithsh	MFVE	PHD	93.	Mich St	# * &2001
Stemkoski, Michael J.	Prof	863-8221	stemkomi	IMFC	MACC	72	Utah St	1992
Teeter, Steven C.	Prof	863-8121	teeterst	FMSC	MBA	87	Phoenix	1987
Balden, John A.	Assoc	863-8202	baldenjo	X	MACC	80	Brighm Yg	&1996
Henage, Richard T.	Assoc	863-6151	henageri	FS	PHD	95.	Utah	&2001
Helquist, Joel H.	Asst		helquijo	SF	PHD	07	Arizona	&2007
Schmidt, Bunney L.	Asst	863-8381	schmidbu	AMCF	DBA	06	Nova SE	* &1998

Utica College
Accounting Faculty
Dept Phone: 792-3055
Homepage: www.utica.edu

Utica, NY   13502-4892
Div Social Sci & Mgt
1600 Burrstone Road

(315) Fax=792-3173
utica.edu   BS
Susan Cox

Johnson, John H.	Dean	792-3055	jjohnson	Anth	PHD	80	SUNY-Buf	1977
Heian, James B.	Assoc		jheian	AFS	PHD	85.	Utah	&2003
Basu, Atasi	Asst	792-3167	abasu	AFMQ	PHD	05	Syracuse	2005

Valdosta State University
Dept Accounting & Finance
Dept Phone: 333-5967
Homepage: www.valdosta.edu/accfin/

Valdosta, GA   31698
Langdale Col of Bus
1500 North Patterson Street

(229) Fax=249-2706   1990,1990
valdosta.edu   BBA
Becky Tracey

Allen, Ralph C.	Dean	245-2243	rcallen	Econ	PHD	81	Geo St	1982
Weld, Leonard G.	H-Pr	333-5967	lweld	FX	PHD	89.	Tx A&M	7-02
Caster, A. Bruce	Prof	245-3809	bcaster	FM	PHD	88.	Georgia	&1985
Holland, Michael L.	Prof	245-3811	mholland	XF	PHD	78.	Georgia	&1987
Marshall, Leisa G.	Prof	245-3815	lmarshal	FES	DBA	93.	Miss St	* & 9-93
Seat, Donald L.	Prof	245-3813	donseat	XF	DBA	80.	Kentucky	&1985
Gupta, Sanjay.	Assoc	293-6061	sgupta	FM	PHD	97.	Cen Fla	* & 8-97
Elson, Raymond J.	Asst	333=5961	relson	A	PHD	01	Sarasota	& 8-03
Swanson, Nancy J.	Asst	333-5967		F	ABD		Miss St	& 8-07
Causseaux, Wanda	Inst	245-4344	wcaussaux	F	MBA		Valdosta	& 8-06

Valparaiso University
Accounting Area
Dept Phone: 464-5035
Homepage: www.valpo.edu/cba/

Valparaiso, IN   46383-6493
College of Business Adm

(219) Fax = 464-5789
valpo.edu

1993
BSA,BSBA,MBA

Boyt, Thomas E.	Dean	464-5040	tom.boyt	Mktg	PHD	94	Oklahoma		7-04
Reichardt, Karl E.	Assoc	464-5043	karl.reichardt	CSME	PHD	71.	Missouri	*	1988
LeClere, Marc J.	Asst		marc.leclere	FX	PHD	89	Penn St		&2007
Guydan, Donna	Lect	464-5066	donna.guydan	FXM	LLM	98	DePaul		&1987
Kirkland, Charles	Lect	464-7958	charles.kirkland	FGMS	MBA	80	Augusta	*	&2002

Vanderbilt University
Accounting Faculty
Dept Phone:

Nashville, TN   37203
Owen Grad School of Mgt
401 21st Avenue South

(615) Fax = 343-7177
owen.vanderbilt.edu

1979
MBA,PHD

Bradford, Jim	Dean$	343-5705	jim.bradford	Stra	JD	73	Vanderbilt		9-02
Boer, Germain B.	Prof	322-2059	germain.boer	M	PHD	64.	LSU		& 9-77
Chaney, Paul K.	Prof	322-2685	paul.chaney	F	PHD	83.	Indiana	*	& 1-84
Hackenbrack, Karl E.	Assoc	322-3641	karl.hackenbrack	A	PHD	88.	Ohio St		&2004
Jeter, Debra C.	Assoc	322-3638	debra.jeter	F	PHD	90.	Vanderbilt		& 9-93
Willis, Richard H.	Assoc	343-1050	richard.willis	MF	PHD	98.	Chicago		&2006
Chen, Hui	Asst	343-7177	hui.chen	F	PHD	05.	Tennessee		2005

University of Vermont
Accounting Faculty
Dept Phone: 656-3175
Homepage: http://www.bsad.uvm.edu

Burlington, VT   05405-0157
School of Business Adm
55 Colchester Ave Kalkin Hl

(802) Fax = 656-8279
bsad.uvm.edu

1986,1986
BS,MBA
Meghan Oliver

DeWitt, Rocki-Lee	Dean	656-3177	dewitt	Mgt	PHD	91	Columbia		1-02
Dempsey, Stephen J.	Assoc	656-8322	dempsey	FM	PHD	86.	Va Tech		1987
Hughes, Susan B.	Assoc	656-0504	shughes	FMA	PHD	90.	Cincinnati		&2006
Arel, Barbara M.	Asst	656-5478	barel	AS	PHD	06.	Ariz St		2006
Hodgdon, Christopher D.	Asst	656-5774	chodgdon	FM	PHD	04.	Va Comm		2005
Woodman, Martha (Marti)	Lect	656-0512	woodman	MCF	MBA	78	Mo-Ks Cty	*	1984

Villanova University
Department of Accountancy
Dept Phone: 519-4340
Homepage: //www.villanova.edu/business/academics/undergrad/programs/

Villanova, PA   19085-1678
School of Business
800 Lancaster Avenue

(610) Fax = 519-5204
villanova.edu

(123) 1975,1985
BS,MT,MACC
Nancy Carpenter

Danko, James	Dean	519-4331	james.danko	Mgt	MBA		Michigan		2005
Bremser, Wayne G.	C-Pr	519-4314	wayne.bremser	BKEM	PHD	74.	Penn		&1974
Derstine, Robert P.	Prof	519-4318	robert.derstine	AF	PHD	73.	SUNY-Buf		&1972
Monahan, Thomas F. (Tim)	Prof	519-4354	thomas.monahan	FTM	PHD	81.	Temple		&1981
Ward, Burke T.	Prof	519-4375	burke.ward	JLWX	LLM	78	NYU		1977
Barsky, Noah P.	Assoc	519-6272	noah.barsky	MU	PHD	98.	Conn	*	&1998
Bierstaker, James L.	Assoc	519-6101	james.bierstaker	ABEM	PHD	95.	Conn		2004
Borden, James P.	Assoc	519-4227	james.borden	MSCD	PHD	87.	Drexel		&1986
Catanach, Anthony H. Jr.	Assoc	519-4825	anthony.cata+	FM	PHD	94.	Ariz St	*	&1998
Emig, James M.	Assoc	519-4344	james.emig	CFME	PHD	87.	Tx A&M		&1983
Hiltebeitel, Kenneth M.	Assoc	519-7994	kenneth.hilte+	AEFJ	PHD	85.	Drexel		&1986
Licata, Michael P.	Assoc	519-7996	michael.licata	AFMS	PHD	84.	Tx A&M		1983
O'Mara, Daniel J.	Assoc	519-4342	daniel.omara	TF	MBA	71	Fordham		&1976
Rhoades-Catanach, Shelley C.	Assoc	519-4356	shelley.rhoades	XM	PHD	95.	Tx-Austin		&1998
Lee, Johnny	Asst	519-3299	johnny.lee	MS	PHD	06.	Utah		2006
Peters, Michael F.	Asst	519-4048	michael.peters	FB	PHD	96.	Indiana		&2004
West, Robert N.	Asst	519-4359	robert.west	SAMF	PHD	88.	S Calif		&1994
Pelesh, Jeffrey N.	Inst	519-7995	jeffrey.pelesh	AF	MBA	88	Villanova		&1991

University of Virginia
Accounting Area
Dept Phone: 924-0893
Homepage: http://www.commerce.virginia.edu/

Charlottesvil VA   22903-2493
McIntire School Comm
Monroe Hall

(434) Fax = 924-7074
virginia.edu

β (13) 1925,1981
BS,MS
Saundra Mason

Zeithaml, Carl P.	Dean	924-3176	czeithaml	Mgt	PHD	80	Maryland		7-97
F.S. Cornell Professor of Free Enterprise									
Williams, Susan Perry	C-Pr	924-3988	sep4v	FMV	PHD	90.	Wisconsin	*	& 9-90
KPMG Professor									
Broome, O. Whitfield	Prof	924-6866	owb	FIV	PHD	71.	Illinois		& 9-67
Frank Kaulback Jr. Professor									
Maloney, David M.	Prof	924-3668	dmm9s	X	PHD	84.	Illinois		& 1-84
Carmen Blough Professor									
Carter, William K.	Assoc	924-3261	wkc2z	CM	PHD	78.	Okla St		& 1-78
LaRue, David W.	Assoc	924-3235	dwl2c	X	PHD	84.	Houston		8-83
Lathan, Malcolm H. (Mac)	Assoc	924-0873	mhl	FA	PHD	82.	N Carol		& 8-83
Martin, Roger D.	Assoc	982-2182	rdm3h	FA	PHD	96.	Tx-Austin	*	& 9-03
Walker, Paul L.	Assoc	924-0887	pw4g	FAS	PHD	94.	Colorado		& 9-94
Wilkie, Patrick J.	Assoc	982-4504	pjw6n	FX	PHD	84.	Michigan		9-02
Lefanowicz, Craig E.	Asst	924-6356	cef5f	FM	PHD	90.	Tx-Austin		& 9-04

University of Virginia-Grad Charlottesvil VA   22906-6550   (434) Fax=243-5021   1971
Dept of Accounting Box 6550   Darden Grad Sch Bus Adm   darden.virginia.edu   MBA,PHD
Dept Phone: 924-7357   100 Darden Boulevard   Liz Tallon

Name	Rank	Phone	Email	Field	Degree	Yr	School	
Bruner, Robert F.	Dean	924-7481	brunerr	Fnce	PHD	82	Harvard	1982
Brownlee, E. Richard II	H-Pr	924-4800	brownleer	FMIT	PHD	75.	Geo St	& 8-75
Allen, Brandt R.	Prof	924-4842	allenb	FMIT	DBA	67.	Harvard	1970

James C. Wheat, Jr. Professor of Business Administration

Name	Rank	Phone	Email	Field	Degree	Yr	School	
Haskins, Mark E.	Prof	924-4826	haskinsm	IFMB	PHD	84.	Penn St	&1984
Sack, Robert J.	Emer	924-4814	sackr	2001	BS	56	Miami U	&1987
Lynch, Luann J.	Assoc	924-4721	lynchl	FMU	PHD	98.	N Carol	1998

Robert F. Vandell Research Chair; Assoc Dean for Intellectual Capital

Name	Rank	Phone	Email	Field	Degree	Yr	School	
Simko, Paul J.	Assoc	924-1391	simkop	FMTX	PHD	96.	Tx-Austin	&2002
Frank, Mary M.	Asst	924-4432	frankm	XFI	PHD	99.	N Carol	&2002

Virginia Commonwealth Univ   Richmond, VA   23284-4000   (804) Fax=828-8884   ß (13) 1975,1981
Department of Accounting   School of Business   vcu.edu   BS,MACC,MAT,PHD
Dept Phone: 828-1608   1015 Floyd Avenue   Ms. Dvora Baldwin
Homepage: bus.vcu.edu/accounting

Name	Rank	Phone	Email	Field	Degree	Yr	School	
Sesnowitz, Michael L.	Dean	827-0072	msesnowi	Econ	PHD	71	Pittsburgh	2000
Coffman, Edward N.	C-Pr	828-7193	encoffma	FT	DBA	73.	Geo Wash	1966
Epps, Ruth W.	Prof	828-7137	rwepps	MGN	PHD	87.	Va Comm	&1987
Everett, John O.	Prof	028-3163	joeveret	X	PHD	78.	Okla St	&1982
Tondkar, Rasoul H.	Prof	828-7156	rhtondka	FIH	PHD	80.	North Tx	8-80
Wier, Benson	Prof	828-7162	bwier	MB	PHD	92.	Tx Tech	&1992
Edmunds, Wayne L.	Assoc	828-7115	wledmund	X	MLT	84	Wm&Mary	&1984
Norman, Carolyn Strand	Assoc	828-3160	castrand	SM	PHD	98.	Tx A&M	&2002
Olds, Philip R.	Assoc	828-7120	prolds	F	PHD	82.	Geo St	&1981
Spede, Edward C.	Assoc	828-7117	ecspede	F	PHD	82.	Va Tech	&1981
Spindle, Roxanne M.	Assoc	828-7113	rmspindl	XJ	PHD	90.	Colorado	& 1-90
Vijayakumar, Jayaraman	Assoc	828-7157	jvijayak	MGN	PHD	90.	Pittsburgh	1997
Park, Myung S.	Asst	828-3161	mpark	FS	PHD	99.	Purdue	2004
Wasan, Sonia	Asst	828-7558	swasan	F	PHD	06.	LSU	2006

Virginia Military Institute   Lexington, VA   24450-0304   (540) Fax=464-7005
Accounting Faculty   Dept of Econ & Business   mail.vmi.edu
Dept Phone: 464-7234   Letcher Avenue   Mrs. Donna Potter

Name	Rank	Phone	Email	Field	Degree	Yr	School	
Duncan, Floyd H.	H-Pr	464-7237	duncan fh	Econ	PHD	72	S Carol	1978
Bush, H. Francis	Prof	464-7632	bushhf	AFMS	PHD	89.	Florida	&1994

Virginia Poly Inst & St Un   Blacksburg, VA   24061   (540) Fax=231-2511   ß (13) 1966,1971
Dept Acct & Info Sys (0101)   Pamplin Col of Business   vt.edu   BS,MACIS,PHD
Dept Phone: 231-6591   Phyllis Neece
Homepage: http://www.acis.pamplin.vt.edu/
538- N Va Grad Ctr, Falls Church VA 22043; fax 703-538-8415

Name	Rank	Phone	Email	Field	Degree	Yr	School	
Sorensen, Richard E.	Dean	231-6601	sorensen	Mgt	PHD	73	NYU	1982
Brown, Robert M.	H-Pr	231-6591	moren	SM	PHD	77.	Geo St	1977

R. B. Pamplin Professor of Accounting and Information Systems

Name	Rank	Phone	Email	Field	Degree	Yr	School	
Cloyd, C. Bryan	Prof	231-3181	bcloyd	X	PHD	92.	Indiana	& 8-05

John E. Peterson, Jr. Professor of Accounting and Information Systems

Name	Rank	Phone	Email	Field	Degree	Yr	School	
Hicks, James O. Jr.	Prof	231-5881	jhicks	SDCM	PHD	76.	Geo St	* 1-76
Killough, Larry N.	Prof	231-6542	larry	CMB	PHD	69.	Missouri	&1969

KPMG Professor of Accounting and Information Systems

Name	Rank	Phone	Email	Field	Degree	Yr	School	
Maher, John J.	Prof	231-4505	jmaher	SF	PHD	85.	Penn St	1989

L. Mahlon Harrel Research Fellow

Name	Rank	Phone	Email	Field	Degree	Yr	School	
Richardson, Frederick M.	Prof	231-7745	frich	FMT	PHD	80.	N Carol	1980
Seago, W. Eugene	Prof	231-6564	seago	X	PHD	70.	Georgia	&1970

R. B. Pamplin Professor of Accounting and Information Systems

Name	Rank	Phone	Email	Field	Degree	Yr	School	
Sen, Tarun K.	Prof	231-6152	tksen	S	PHD	85	Iowa	1985
Barkhi, Reza	Assoc	231-5869	reza	S	PHD	95	Ohio St	8-97

Alumni Research Fellow

Name	Rank	Phone	Email	Field	Degree	Yr	School	
Belanger, France	Assoc	231-6720	belanger	S	PHD	97	S Fla	8-97

Alumni Research Fellow

Name	Rank	Phone	Email	Field	Degree	Yr	School	
Brozovsky, John A.	Assoc	231-5971	jbrozovs	BFMX	PHD	90.	Colorado	&1989

William S. Gay Research Fellow

Name	Rank	Phone	Email	Field	Degree	Yr	School	
Fan, Weiguo (Patrick)	Assoc	231-6588	wfan	S	PHD	02	Michigan	2002
Hicks, Samuel A.	Assoc	231-6577	shicks	XS	PHD	76.	Wisconsin	&1979
Jenkins, J. Gregory	Assoc	231-2527	greg.jenkins	ABF	PHD	98.	Va Tech	& 8-05
Salbador, Debra A.	Assoc	231-8163	salbador	X	PHD	93.	S Carol	& 8-94
Sheetz, Steven D.	Assoc	231-6096	sheetz	S	PHD	96	Colorado	8-96
Tegarden, David P.	Assoc	231-6099	david.tegarden	S	PHD	91	Colorado	8-94
Wallace, Linda G.	Assoc	231-6328	wallacel	S	PHD	99	Geo St	2000
Yardley, James A.	Assoc	231-7352	jyardley	AF	PHD	86.	Illinois	&1986
Bhattacharjee, Sudip	Asst	231-8422	sudipb	ABM	PHD	97.	Mass	2001
Oler, Mitchell J.	Asst				PHD	06.	U Wash	2007

Song, Chang Joon	Asst	231-7155	sjsong	F	PHD	04. Mich St	1-07
Wood, Lynette I.	Asst	231-6103	lynwood	B	PHD	03. Indiana	&2004
Easterwood, Cintia M.	Inst	231-7920	cmeast	FS	PHD	93. Houston	8-92
Griffin, Marilyn T.	Inst	231-7436	marilyn.griffin	S	MA	01 Va Tech	2001
Lacoste, Jean M.	Inst	231-9642	lacoste	S	MA	Va Tech	1997
Lobingier, Patricia G.	Inst	231-5504	plobingi	F	PHD	97. Va Tech	8-05

Virginia State University
Dept of Accounting Box 9047
Dept Phone: 524-5842

Petersburg, VA   23806-9047
School of Business
1 Hayden Drive

(804) Fax=524-5400
vsu.edu

2006
BS
Mrs. Donna Hayes

Bejou, David	Dean	524-5166	dbejou	Mktg	PHD	94 Memphis	8-03
Wright, Carl N.	C-Ac	524-5841	cwright	AM	PHD	03. JacksonSt	& 9-76
Mitchem, Cheryl E.	Assoc	524-5831	cmitchem	FCI	PHD	90. Va Comm	* & 8-91
Moore, John W.	Assoc	524-6778	jmoore	FS	PHD	92. Va Comm	& 1-91
Sharma, Hari	Assoc	524-5324	hsharma	F	PHD	89 Agra Un	2003
Smith, Joyce van der laan	Asst	524-6995	jsmith	FIW	PHD	05 Va Comm	8-05

Virginia Union University
Accounting Dept Box 424
Dept Phone: 257-5710

Richmond, VA   23220
S. Lewis School of Bus
1500 North Lombardy Street

(804) Fax=257-5844
vuu.edu

BS
Ms. Diane Williams

Seshie, Godwin O.	C-Ac	257-5704	gseshie	PFT	PHD	88 Geo St	8-97
Umansky, Philip H.	Assoc	257-5714	pumansky	VFGA	PHD	94. Va Comm	& 1-89
Reese, Sara F.	Asst	257-5696	sreese	SCM	MACC	80 Miss	& 8-87

Wagner College
Accounting Faculty
Dept Phone: 390-3447
Homepage: www.wagner.edu

Staten Island,NY   10301
Business Administration
One Campus Road

(718) Fax=420-4274
wagner.edu

BS,MS
Arleen Wilk

Goodman, Robert	C-Pr	390-3182	robert.goodman	Mgt	PHD	Minnesota	
Horan, Margaret H.	Assoc	390-3437	phoran	PV	MBA	84 Wagner	&
Olson, William C.	Assoc	390-3439	wolson	CMQ	MBA	73 Pace	& 9-85
Buddensick, Janice	Asst	390-3429	jbuddens	PAQ	MBA	85 Pace	&

Wake Forest University
Accountancy
Dept Phone: 758-5305

Winston-SalemNC 27109-7285
Calloway S Bus & Acctcy
1834 Wake Forest Road

(336) Fax=758-6133
wfu.edu

(13) 1985
BS,MS
Patty Lanier

| Wilkerson, Jack E. Jr. | Dean | 758-5027 | jwilker | PVN | PHD | 84 Tx-Austin | & 9-89 |
| Knight, Lee G. | D-Pr | 758-4714 | knightlg | PTFX | PHD | 81. Alabama | 9-00 |
| Hylton Professor of Accountancy |
| Beets, S. Douglas | Prof | 758-5905 | beets | PA | PHD | 87. Va Tech | & 1-87 |
| Martin, Dale R. | Prof | 758-5784 | martin | FTI | DBA | 76. Kentucky | 9-82 |
| The Wayne Calloway Professor of Accountancy |
| Tower, Ralph B. | Prof | 758-5735 | tower | PX | PHD | 78. N Carol | & 9-80 |
| The Wayne Calloway Professor of Taxation |
| Aldhizer, George R. III | Assoc | 758-5778 | aldhizgr | PAS | PHD | 94. Tx Tech | # & 9-01 |
| PricewaterhouseCoopers Faculty Fellow |
| Baker, Terry A. | Assoc | 758-4323 | bakert | PFT | PHD | 98. Kentucky | & 9-98 |
| PricewaterhouseCoopers Professor of Accountancy |
| Duchac, Jonathan E. | Assoc | 758-4458 | duchacje | PF | PHD | 93. Georgia | & 9-93 |
| Merrill Lynch Professor of Accountancy |
| Hinson, Yvonne L. | Assoc | 758-5113 | hinsonyl | PX | PHD | 97. Tennessee | & 9-97 |
| PricewaterhouseCoopers Faculty Fellow; Director of Graduate Studies |
| Juras, Paul E. | Assoc | 758-4836 | juras | PCM | PHD | 91. Syracuse | * & 9-91 |

Wake Forest University-MBA
Accounting Faculty
Dept Phone: 758-5418

Winston-SalemNC 27109-7659
Babcock Grad Sch of Mgt
2601 Wake Forest Road

(336) Fax=758-4514
mba.wfu.edu

1985
MBA,MA
Ms. Judy Sowers

Patel, Ajay	Dean	758-5575	ajay.patel	Fnce	PHD	87 Georgia	7-93
Beatty, Bernard L.	Assoc	758-5049	bern.beatty	ACM	DBA	72. Harvard	# * &1974
Bryan, Stephen H.	Assoc	758-4492	stephen.byran	F	PHD	94. NYU	8-99
Middaugh, J. Kendall II	Assoc	758-5047	ken.middaugh	MU	PHD	81. Ohio St	7-87
Director, Full-Time MBA Program & Associate Dean

Warner Southern College
Accounting Faculty
Dept Phone: 638-7117
Homepage: www.warner.edu

Lake Wales, FL   33859
School of Business
13895 Highway 27

(863) Fax=638-4907
warner.edu

BA
Mrs. Danielle Richardson

| Robinson, Cynthia Welch | Dean | Ext 7120 | robinsoncw | | EDD | Tennessee | |
| Zapalski, Christopher | Asst | | zapalskic | | JD | 02 Nova SE | 2002 |

Wartburg College
Accounting Faculty POBox1003
Dept Phone: 352-8415
Homepage: www.wartburg.edu/bus

Waverly, IA 50677-0903
Dept of Bus Adm & Econ
100 Wartburg Blvd

(319) Fax=352-8581
wartburg.edu

BA
Ann Killion

Campbell, Gloria L.	C-Ac	352-8229	gloria.campbell	L	MBA	84	N Iowa	1979
Magnall, Paul	Assoc	352-8428	paul.magnall	DSXF	MBA	82	N Iowa	&1983
Haugen, John D.	Asst	352-8419	john.haugen	AFG	MS	73	N Dakota	&1979

Washburn University
Department of Accounting
Dept Phone: 670-1308
Homepage: www.washburn.edu/sobu

Topeka, KS 66621
School of Business
1700 College Avenue

(785) Fax=231-1063
washburn.edu

2006
BBA

Sollars, David L.	Dean	670-1308	david.sollars	Econ	PHD	91	Fla St	2003
Moellenberndt, Richard A.	Prof	670-2052	richard.moell+	F	PHD	73.	Nebraska	& 8-76
Clevenger, Novella Noland	Assoc	670-1595	novella.clev+	X	LLM	87	Wm&Mary	& 8-88
Clevenger, Thomas B.	Assoc	670-2051	thomas.clev+	AM	DBA	87.	Memphis	& 8-88
Mazachek, JuliAnn	Assoc	670-1020		M	PHD	93.	Kansas	* 8-92
on leave; email: jmazachek@wea.org								
Ockree, Kanalis A.	Assoc	670-1589	kanalis.ockree	FTSM	PHD	93.	Kansas	* & 8-85
Martin, Jim	Lect	670-1588	jim.martin	XF	MTX	83	Tx-Austin	8-04

University of Washington
Dept Accounting Box 353200
Dept Phone: 543-4368
Homepage: http://depts.washington.edu/bschool/

Seattle, WA 98195-3200
UW Business School
231 Mackenzie Hall

(206) Fax=685-9875
u.washington.edu

ß (13) 1921,1963
BA,MBA,MPA,PHD
Cynthia Silvernale

Jiambalvo, James J.	Dean	543-9132	jjiambal	MA	PHD	77	Ohio St	&1977
PricewaterhouseCoopers and Alumni Professor								
Shevlin, Terry	C-Pr	543-7223	shevlin	FX	PHD	86.	Stanford	1-86
Piggot-PACCAR Professor								
Berg, Kenneth B.	Emer	543-4368		1983	PHD	52.	Illinois	&1950
Bowen, Robert M.	Prof	543-4569	rbowen	MF	PHD	78.	Stanford	9-78
Burgstahler, David C.	Prof	221-5749	dburg	FMA	PHD	81.	Iowa	&1980
Dukes, Roland E. (Pete)	Prof	543-7742	rdukes	FTI	PHD	74.	Stanford	1979
Associate Dean								
Heath, Loyd C.	Emer	543-4368	lheath	1998	PHD	65.	Berkeley	1962
Kennedy, S. Jane	Prof	543-6405	jkennedy	BF	PHD	92.	Duke	* 1-92
Mueller, Gerhard G.	Emer	543-4368		1996	PHD	62.	Berkeley	&1960
Noreen, Eric W.	Emer	543-4368	enoreen	2005	PHD	77.	Stanford	1976
Rajgopal, Shivaran	Prof	543-7913	rajgopal	F	PHD	98.	Iowa	2003
Ramanathan, K. V.	Emer	543-4378	kramnath	CMU	PHD	70.	Nrthwstrn	&1971
Sefcik, Stephan E.	Prof	543-5679	sefcik	FWP	PHD	83.	Illinois	&1986
Sundem, Gary L.	Prof	543-9390	glsundem	CM	PHD	71.	Stanford	1971
Julius A. Roller Professor								
Hodge, Frank D.	Assoc	616-8598	fhodge	F	PHD	00.	Indiana	2000
Matsumoto, Dawn A.	Assoc	543-4454	damatsu	FM	PHD	98.	U Wash	2000
Shores, D.	Assoc	543-5605	shores	F	PHD	86.	Stanford	1986
Soliman, Mark T.	Assoc			FB	PHD	03.	Michigan	& 6-07
Chen, Shuping (Michelle)	Asst	543-3021	shupingc	F	PHD	02.	S Calif	2002
Ge, Weili	Asst	221-4835	geweili	F	PHD	06.	Michigan	7-06
Sedor, Lisa M.	Asst			AF	PHD	01.	U Wash	& 7-07
Gillick, J.	SLect	543-4578	click	AFS	BBA	57	Manhatten	1986
Medlar, Deborah	SLect	616-8394	medlard@a	X	LLM	84	NYU	&2000
Resler, William M.	SLect	685-8043	resler	X	LLM	73	NYU	1982
Rice, Steven J.	SLect	543-4567	ricesj	X	PHD	74.	Tx-Austin	&1985
Wells, William L.	SLect	543-7694	wellsbil	F	MPAC	89	U Wash	1988
Adams, Helen D.	Lect	685-9867	hda	MCS	PHD	86.	U Wash	1991
DuCharme, Larry L.	Lect	543-8194	lducharm	DFMS	PHD	94.	U Wash	1972
Widdison, Elizabeth	Lect	543-7742	widdison	FM	BS	92	City U	1999

Univ of Washington, Tacoma
Accounting Area
Dept Phone: 692-5630

Tacoma, WA 98402-3100
Milgard School Business
1900 Commerce St

(253) Fax=692-4523
u.washington.edu

BABA,MBA
Julia S.

Saudagaran, Shahrokh M.	Dean	692-4580	shahrokh	FIG	PHD	86	U Wash	&2004
Feroz, Ehsan H.	Prof	692-4728	ehf2	FKIG	PHD	82	Chicago	# &2005
Bryan, Daniel M.	Asst	692-5630		FSM	PHD	02.	Oregon	&2007
Cao, Zhiyan	Asst	692-5630	zycao	FM	PHD	06	Yale	2007
Kimbro, Marinilka B.	Asst	692-4773	mkimbro	FI	PHD	99.	Maryland	2005
Parker, Dorothy J.	SLect	692-5682	djparker	MXFS	PHD	92.	Arkansas	&1997

Washington University
Accounting Faculty
Dept Phone:

St. Louis, MO 63130-4899
Olin School of Bus/1133
One Brookings Drive

(314) Fax=935-6359
wustl.edu

1921,1963
BSBA,MSBA,PHD

Gupta, Mahendra	Dean	935-6344	guptam	MC	PHD	90	Stanford	1990

Dopuch, Nicholas	Emer	935-4564	dopuch	MA	PHD	61. Illinois	&1983
Herbert C. & Dorothy R. Moog Professor of Accounting							
King, Ronald R.	Prof	935-6385	rking	FA	PHD	86. Arizona	&1986
Myron Northrop Professor of Accounting							
Jayaraman, Sudarshan	Asst			F	PHD	07 N Carol	2007
Martin, Xiumin	Asst			F	PHD	07 Missouri	2007
Mashruwala, Raj	Asst	935-5924	mashruwala	M	PHD	02 Tx-Dallas	2001
Shalev, Ron	Asst			F	PHD	07 Columbia	2007
Zach, Tzachi	Asst	935-4528	zach	F	PHD	04. Rochester	2002
Fields, Thomas D.	Lect	935-6113	tfields	F	PHD	04. Nrthwstrn	2006
Soczek, Mark E.	Lect	935-7442	soczek	FT	ABD	Nrthwstrn	1997

Washington & Jefferson Col Washington, PA 15301-4801 (724) Fax=223-5271
Accounting Faculty Dept of Economics & Bus washjeff.edu
Dept Phone: 223-6150 60 South Lincoln Street
Homepage: www.washjeff.edu/users/jgroegor/economics/detault.htm

Gregor, John J.	C-Pr	223-6150	jgregor	Econ	PHD	76 Penn St	1989
Robison, K. Wayne	Prof	223-6153	wrobison	AFTX	MBA	79 Ohio St	&1979
Galley, Lori J.	Assoc		lgalley	CFI	DBA	04 Nova SE	*
Kuhn, Stephen D.	Assoc	223-6542	skuhn	CDIN	MAC	Bowl Gr	&1987
Kinder, Richard	Asst		rkinder	FMP	MBA	Penn	2003

Washington and Lee Univ Lexington, VA 24450-0303 (540) Fax=458-8639 1927
Department of Accounting Williams Sch Comm, Econ wlu.edu BS
Dept Phone: 458-8637 Lynda Bassett-deMaria
Homepage: http://www.wlu.edu/~cschool/acct.html

Peppers, Larry C.	Dean	458-8602	peppersl	Econ	PHD	70 Vanderbilt	1986
Oliver, Elizabeth G.	H-Pr	458-8637	olivere	F	PHD	92. Tx A&M	&1991
King, J. William (Bill)	Prof	458-8611	kingw	MCI	PHD	86. Fla St	1989
Wheeler, Lyn F.	Prof	458-8608	wheelerl	FXM	DBA	74. Geo Wash	&1983
Boylan, Scott J.	Assoc	458-8585	boylans	F	PHD	95. Ohio St	&1999
Fafatas, Stephan A.	Asst	458-8222	sfafatas	FA	PHD	06. Colorado	2006
Weiss, Jane M.	Asst	458-8407	weissj	FM	PHD	01. Wisconsin	2006

Washington State University Pullman, WA 99164-4729 (509) Fax=335-4275 ß (13) 1960,1965
Department of Accounting Coll of Business & Econ wsu.edu BA,MAC,PHD
Dept Phone: 335-8541 Lorie Mochel
Homepage: www.cbe.wsu.edu/acctg/
  email @1=vancouver.wsu.edu area code 360; @2=tricity.wsu.edu

Spangenberg, Eric	Dean	335-3596	ers	Mktg	PHD	90 U Wash	1990
Sweeney, John T.	C-Pr	335-8543	jtsweeney	FBJ	PHD	92. Missouri	&1998
Greenberg, Robert R.	Prof	335-2410	greenberg	MCS	PHD	81. Ariz St	1983
Sanders, Debra L.	Prof	335-4473	dsanders	XB	PHD	86. Ariz St	&1985
Toolson, Richard B.	Prof	335-2121	toolson	XI	PHD	87. Ariz St	&1987
Wong-On-Wing, Bernard	Prof	335-4434	wow	SBCM	PHD	86. Ariz St	1986
Cote, Jane M.	Assoc	546-9756	cotej@1	MCNB	PHD	94. Wash St	1-93
Gill, Susan	Assoc	335-5633	gills	FMC	PHD	94. Mich St	&1994
Latham, Claire K.	Assoc	546-9757	latham@1	FAS	PHD	94. Geo St	&1994
Nunamaker, Thomas R.	Assoc	335-4472	nunamaker	FN	PHD	83. Wisconsin	&1982
Chan, Siew H.	Asst	335-5723	siewchan	SM	PHD	01. Utah	2006
Thornburg, Steven W.	Asst	335-4446	sthornburg	CM	PHD	05. Cen Fla	2005
Thornton, John M.	Asst	372-7246	jthornt@2	FMJ	PHD	96. Wash St	&2000
Zuber, Jill	Asst	335-5358	jmzuber	M	ABD	Arkansas	2006

Wayne State College Wayne, NE 68787 (402) Fax=375-7434
Accounting Faculty Division of Business wsc.edu BS,BA
Dept Phone: 375-7245 1111 Main St
Homepage: http://www.wsc.edu/academic/business

Benson, Vaughn L.	Dean	375-7245	vabenso1	FG	PHD	85 Nebraska	&1974
Volk, Gary A.	H-Ac	375-7021	gavolk1	FTM	PHD	86. Nebraska	1992
Bondhus, JoAnn	Prof	375-7412	jobondh1	XL	LLM	83 Denver	1979
Garvin, Sharon	Asst	375-7516	shgarvi1	SFPA	EDD	05 S Dakota	&1982
Ras, Gerard	Inter	375-7464	geras1	APG	MBA	03 Wayne Co	&2005

Wayne State University Detroit, MI 48202-3930 (313) Fax=577-2000 ß 1976,1982
Department of Accounting School of Business Adm wayne.edu BS,BA,MSA,MST
Dept Phone: 577-4530 5229 Cass Ave, 100 Rands Geraldine White

Paschke, Randolph C.	C-Le	577-6032	ao0994	XI	BBA	71 Michigan	& 8-02
Billings, B. Anthony	Prof	577-4214	aa4816	XI	PHD	86. Tx A&M	1989
Reinstein, Alan	Prof	577-4486	aa1692	AF	DBA	80. Kentucky	&1987
George R. Husband Professor of Accounting							
Volz, William H.	Prof	577-4694	ab9241	JLX	JD	75 Wayne St	1978

Miller, Cathleen L.	Assoc	577-6256	dt9403	MBAB	PHD	98.	Kentucky		& 1-07
Mitra, Santanu	Assoc	577-9908	ce5511	FM	PHD	02.	LSU		1-07
Spalding, Albert D. Jr.	Assoc	577-4469	ab1186	JLX	JD	79	Geo Wash		&1983
Stern, Myles S.	Assoc	577-4489	ac8360	MS	PHD	74.	Mich St	*	1971
Andrews, Angela	Asst	577-4528	angela.andrews	F	PHD	04.	Mich St		8-04
Jones, Deborah K.	SLect	577-4455	aa4946	FX	PHD	96.	Kent St		1994
Lamarra, Frank	Lect	577-4560	af5956	M	MBA	99	Wayne St		8-02
Weimer, Daniel	Lect	577-8635	aay6233	F	MACC	05	Michigan	*	8-05
Welden, Mary Ann	Lect	577-7835	ax7811	M	MBA	78	Notre Dm		8-05

Webber International Univ
Department of Accounting
Dept Phone: 638-2927
Homepage: www.webber.edu
Babson Park, FL 33827-0096
Business PO Box 96
1201 Scenic Hwy. N.

(863) Fax=638-2823
webber.edu

BSBA,MBA
Tonya White

Wade, H. Keith	Dean	638-2971		Mgt	DBA	04	Argosy	2004
email keithwade@usa.net								
Logsdon, John J.	Assoc	638-2972	jjlogs@y	AGMS	MS	88	Cen Fla	&1986
Nagoda, Robert J.	Assoc	638-2973	nagodar@h	XFJS	PHD	82.	Arizona	1997

Weber State University
School of Accountancy
Dept Phone: 626-6072
Ogden, UT 84408-3803
College of Bus & Econ
3750 Harrison Boulevard

(801) Fax=626-7423
weber.edu

ß (13) 1992,1992
BA,BS,MPACC
Jaimee Bailey

Gale, Lewis R.	Dean	626-6063	lewisgale	Econ	PHD	94	Ariz St		7-05
Mano, Ronald M.	C-Pr	626-6730	rmano	FA	PHD	78.	Nebraska		&1985
Willard Eccles Research Fellow									
Deppe, E. Devon	Prof	626-6768	ddeppe	X	JD	77	Brighm Yg		&1978
McDermott, Richard E.	Prof	626-6418	rmcdermott	CM	PHD	84.	Okla St		1989
Simkins, Allen F.	Prof	626-6003	asimkins	MCQF	PHD	76.	Ariz St		&1976
Swearingen, James G.	Prof	626-6897	jswearingen	AF	PHD	82.	U Wash		&1985
Davis, Jefferson T.	Assoc	626-6064	jtdavis	SAF	PHD	93.	Tennessee		1998
Deppe, Larry A.	Assoc	626-7838	ldeppe1	FA	PHD	88.	Utah	*	&1996
Durkee, David A.	Assoc	626-6085	ddurkee	FSI	PHD	87.	Okla St		&1991
Coordinator of Graduate Program									
Mouritsen, Matthew L.	Assoc	626-8151	mmouritsen	FS	PHD	97	Utah St		&2001
Allen, Tom	Asst	626-8593	tallen	AG	BS	71	Weber St		2005
Pace, Ryan	Asst	626-7562	rpace	X	JD	92	Washburn		2004
Swearingen, Sandy	Asst	626-7653	sswearingen	FT	MPAC	86	Weber St		&1988
Kattelman, Lorsanne	Inst	626-7702	lkattelman	FT	MS	90	Weber St		1998

Webster University
Department of Business
Dept Phone: 968-7021
Homepage: www.webster.edu/depts/business
St. Louis, MO 63119-3194
Sch of Business & Tech
470 East Lockwood Avenue

(314) Fax=968-7077
webster.edu

BS
Debbie Ray

Akande, Benjamin Ola	Dean	968-5950	akandeb	Econ	PHD	95	Oklahoma		2000
Scott, Bradford C.	C-Ac		bradford	Fnce	PHD	98	St Louis		1998
Luh, Troy V.	Assoc	968-2660	tluh	FA	PHD	03	St Louis		&2002
Ulmer, Donna K.	Assoc	961-2660	dulmer	MD	PHD	99	St Louis		&2005
Viele, Daniel F.	Assoc	968-2660	vieleda	CMS	MS	79	Colo St	*	&1998

Wesley College
Department of Accounting
Dept Phone: 736-2582
Dover, DE 19901-3875
School of Prof Studies
120 North State Street

(302) Fax=736-2301
mail.wesley.edu

BS,MBA
Lisa Patterson

Johnson, Marilyn	C-Ac	736-2463	johnsoma	FTV	MBA	96	Drexel	1982

Wesleyan College
Accounting Program
Dept Phone: 757-5185
Homepage: www.wesleyan.college.edu
Macon, GA 31210-4462
Dept of Bus & Economics
4760 Forsyth Road

(478) Fax=757-5183
wesleyancollege.edu

AB,BSBA
Sandra Baskin

Crisp, Delmas	Dean	757-5229	dcrisp	E	PHD	79	S Miss	2001
Taylor, Philip	C-Pr	757-5184	ptaylor	F	PHD	89	Va Tech	2000
Eyler, Kel-Ann S.	Assoc	757-5132	keyler	AM	PHD	90.	Geo St	&2006

University of West Alabama
Accounting & Bus Adm
Dept Phone: 652-3444
Homepage: www.uwa.edu
Livingston, AL 35470
Col of Bus Station 21
Highway 11

(205) Fax=652-3516
uwa.edu

BBA
Sieglinde Fleming

Carr, Linda A.	Dean$	652-3476		Econ	EDD	68	Alabama	1965
Green, Mitzi C.	Prof	652-3777	mgreen	ARPV	DBA	83.	Miss St	&2005
Kent, Martha	VAsst	652-3215	mkent	PC	MBA	79	Auburn	&1979
Stipe, Sharon	Asst	652-3444	sstipe	PLX	LLM		NYU	1965

West Chester University
Department of Accounting
Dept Phone: 436-2236

West Chester, PA 19383-2210			(610) Fax=436-3458					2006
Sch of Bus & Public Afr			wcupa.edu					BS,MBA
Anderson Hall, Room 309A								Mrs. Zellman
Fiorentino, Christopher M.	Dean	436-2930	cfiorentino	Econ	PHD	89	Temple	9-85
Galbraith, Clyde J.	C-Ac	436-2236	cgalbraith	AFM	MBA	71	Drexel	& 9-74
Naggar, Ali K.	Prof	436-3324	anaggar	XC	PHD	75.	Oklahoma	9-77
Flynn, Kevin E.	Assoc	436-3324	kflynn	XNF	PHD	03.	Drexel	9-97
LaSalle, Randall E.	Assoc	436-6998	rlasalle	CFA	PHD	91.	Drexel	&1998
Oehlers, Peter F.	Asst	738-0562	poehlers	SMPE	DBA	03.	La Tech	* & 9-04
Rolland, Beatrice	Asst	738-0451	brolland	FAVC	MBA	95	Temple	& 9-94

University of West Florida
Dept of Accounting & Finance
Dept Phone: 474-2717

Pensacola, FL 32514-5752			(850) Fax=473-7060					1994,1994
College of Business			uwf.edu					BSBA,MACC
11000 University Parkway								Sheila A. Etheredge
Ranelli, Edward	Dean	474-2348	eranelli	Econ	PHD	69	Alabama	2000
King, Chula G.	C-Pr	474-2738	cking	F	PHD	83.	LSU	&1981
Calvasina, Richard V.	Prof	474-2737	rcalvasi	CM	PHD	73.	Miss	* &1980
Donelan, Joseph G.	Prof	863-6591	jdonelan	CPME	PHD	89.	St Louis	* &1999
Fahnestock, Robert T.	Prof	474-2728	rfahnest	TFMX	PHD	84.	Miss	&1974
Gray, O. Ronald	Prof	474-2734	rgray	AFHV	PHD	80.	Arkansas	# * &1982
Hasselback, James R.	Prof	473-7100	jhasselback	X	PHD	76.	Mich St	8-06
Mary Ball Washington Eminent Scholar								
O'Keefe, W. Timothy	Prof	494-2654	tokeefe	CM	DBA	78.	Fla St	&1998
Associate Dean								
Usry, Milton F.	Emer	474-2916	musry	D-05	PHD	64.	Tx-Austin	&1986
Yost, Gregory C.	Prof	474-2736	gyost	A	EDD	85	Fla St	&1977
Gilbert, Arthur H. Jr.	Assoc	474-2992	agilbertjr	MSU	DBA	95.	La Tech	&2004
Guyette, Roger W.	Asst	474-2729	rguyette	X	LLM	77	Florida	&1980
Moussalli, Stephanie D.	Asst	863-6586	smoussalli	AF	PHD	05.	Miss	& 8-06
Frank, Allen J.	Inst	474-2993	afrank	FJ	MACC	88	W Fla	1988
Frank, Sarah L.	Inst	474-2931	sfrank	SDP	EDD	99	W Fla	& 8-84

University of West Georgia
Dept Accounting & Finance
Dept Phone: 839-6469
Homepage: http://www.westga.edu/~accfin/

Carrollton, GA 30118-4150			(678) Fax=839-5041				(13)	1984,1990
Richards College of Bus			westga.edu					BBA,MPACC
								Becky Cole
McIntyre, Faye	Dean	839-6467	fmcintyr	Mktg	PHD	89	Georgia	9-98
Colley, J. Ronald	C-Pr	839-4811	rcolley	MSP	PHD	86.	Geo St	& 9-89
Bird, Bruce M.	Prof	839-4813	bbird	XP	JD	84	Cincinnati	& 9-91
Haynes, Christine M.	Prof	839-4814	chaynes	AFMP	PHD	93.	Tx-Austin	8-06
McCraw, J. Harrison	Prof	839-4817	jmccraw	CMP	PHD	87.	Georgia	9-85
Moffeit, Katherine S.	Prof	839-4818	kmoffeit	AFGN	PHD	85.	North Tx	& 8-01
Colquitt, Denise	Lect	839-4815	dcolquit	P	MPAC	96	W Geo	8-06
Smith, Sondra	Lect	839-4819	sondras	P	MPAC	96	W Geo	& 9-03

West Liberty State College
Dept of Financial Systems
Dept Phone: 336-8053
Homepage: www.wlscu.wvnet.edu

West Liberty, PA 26074-0295			(304) Fax=336-8418					
School of Business Adm			westliberty.edu					
								Ms. Eleanor Coen
Robinson, Elizabeth	Dean$	336-8152	robinsea	Mgt	MBA	83	W Virginia	1979
Turrentine, S. Michael	C-As	336-8164	mturrent	BLaw	JD	96	Duquesne	1999
Hypes, Gary	Asst	336-8054		CP	JD	03	W Virginia	&2004
Mudrinich, Andrew K.	Asst	336-8165	amudrinich	PR	JD	96	Akron	&2006
Blackwell, Michael T.	Inst	336-8166	mblackwell	AMPX	MBA	00	Wheeling	&2004

West Texas A&M University
Dept of Atg, Econ & Finance
Dept Phone: 651-2525

Canyon, TX 79016-0001			(806) Fax=651-2514					
College of Business			mail.wtamu.edu					BBA,MPA
2501-4th Ave.								Betsey Tonne
Terry, Neil W.	Dean	651-2512	nterry	Econ	PHD	97	Tx Tech	1997
Owens, James K.	H-Pr	651-2616	jowens	Fnce	PHD	71	Harvard	1971
Hiner, Ronald R.	Prof	651-2517	rhiner	FM	EDD	73	Okla St	& 9-84
Smith, Darlene A.	Prof	651-2521	dasmith	XF	PHD	87.	North Tx	& 8-97
Thomas, Bob D.	Asst	651-2509	bthomas	AGS	PHD	07	Tx Tech	2007

West Virginia University
Division of Accounting
Dept Phone: 293-7840
Homepage: www.be.wvu.edu/

Morgantown, WV 26506-6025			(304) Fax=293-0635		ß (13)			1954,1963
Coll of Business & Econ			mail.wvu.edu					BS,MPA
University Avenue						Karen R. Smith	293-7840	
Sears, R. Stephen	Dean	293-7800	steve.sears	Fnce	PHD	80	N Carol	2005
Pearson, Timothy A.	D-Ac	293-7847	timothy.pearson	FAS	PHD	90.	Wisconsin	& 7-91
Brooks, Richard C.	Prof	293-7843	richard.brooks	FGN	PHD	91.	LSU	8-91
Maust, Robert S.	Prof	293-7842	rsmaust	FT	ABD		Michigan	&1959
Louis F. Tanner Distinguished Professor of Public Accounting								

Neidermeyer, Adolph A. (Ade)	Prof	293-7841	ade.neidermeyer	FX	PHD	74. Iowa		1971
Pariser, David B.	Prof	293-7844	david.pariser	FGNI	PHD	70 S Illinois	*	&1989
Pushkin, Ann B.	Prof	293-7845	ann.pushkin	ADOS	PHD	78. Va Tech		&1981
Shaw, Gail Allan	Emer	293-4092	gail.shaw	2002	PHD	71. Missouri		&1973
Morris, Bonnie W.	Assoc	293-7851	bonnie.morris	SOA	PHD	92. Pittsburgh		& 1-90
Riley, Richard A.	Assoc	293-7849	richard.riley	FTU	PHD	98. Tennessee		& 8-98
Louis F. Tanner Distinguished Professor of Public Accounting								
Fleming, A. Scott	Asst	293-7896	scott.fleming	MFS	PHD	05. Va Tech		&2005
Lynch, Nancy Pennoyer	Lect	293-7853	nancy.lynch	PA	MS	86 Colorado	*	& 8-91
Ruhe, Nancy C.	Lect	293-7846	nancy.ruhe	FP	MPA	82 W Virginia		&1987

West Virginia Univ Inst Tech — Montgomery, WV 25136-2436 — (304) Fax=442-3810 — wvutech.edu — BS,BS/MBA — Sandra Stephenson
Dept of Accounting & Finance — Col of Bus, Hum & Sci
Dept Phone: 442-3483 — 405 Fayette Pike

Brown, Stephen W.	Dean	442-3105	sbrown	Hist				
Sarin, Madhuri	C-Ac	442-3484	msarin	FPXM	MBA		*	1988
Amin, Md Nurul	Assoc	442-3206	mamin	FMPC	MBA			&1997
Melton, Paul D.	Assoc	442-3034	pmelton	CGPA	MBA			&
Perry, Jacqueline A.	Assoc	442-3227	jperry	EPV	PHD			&1999

West Virginia State Univ — Institute, WV 25112-1000 — (304) Fax=766 3080 — wvstateu.edu — BSBA — Sandi Thompson
Accounting Faculty — Dept of Business Adm
Dept Phone: 766-3129 — 112 Hill Hall

Shafer, Patricia M.	Dean$	766-3063	shaferpm	CFGT	MBA	75 WVCOGS		&1980
Hodges, John P.	Asst	766-3099	jhodges304@a	FCPA	MPA	81 W Virginia		&1984
Pauley, C. Edman	Asst	766-3091	epauley	FPTX	MBA	74 W Virginia		&1982
email epauley@citynet.net								
Williams, Deborah	Asst	766-3097		FMPT	MPA	82 W Virginia		&2005
email: mdmswilliams@verizon.net								

Western Carolina University — Cullowhee, NC 28723-9033 — (828) Fax=227-7414 — wcu.edu — 1983,1984 — BSBA,MAC — Dona R. Potts
Dept Accountancy, Fnce & Ent — College of Business
Dept Phone: 227-7404

Lirely, Roger L.	H-Ac	227-7404	lirely	X	DBA	96 S Illinois		1996
Coffee, C. David	Prof	227-3415	coffee	FT	DBA	83. Kentucky		&1988
Little, Philip L.	Prof	227-3498	plittle	FT	DBA	86. La Tech		&1993
Jones, Elizabeth H.	Assoc	227-3465	bjones	SFP	PHD	88 Indiana		&1994
Kauffman, N. Leroy	Assoc	227-3480	kauffman	CMPU	PHD	88. Ohio St		&1994
Swanger, Susan L.	Assoc	227-3525	swanger	ABJK	PHD	98. S Carol		&1997
Liu, Jiangxia Renee	Asst	227-3711	jliu	FPT	PHD	06 Tx-Dallas		2006
Roig, Reed	Asst	227-7189	rroig	MS	ABD	Case Wes		1-06

Western Conn State Univ — Danbury, CT 06810 — (203) Fax=837-8527 — wcsu.edu — BBA — Sandra Santa Maria
Accounting Department — Ancell School of Bus
Dept Phone: 837-8741 — 181 White Street
Homepage: www.wcsu.ctstateu.edu

Morton, Allen D.	Dean	837-9600	morton	Fnce	DPS	93 Pace		1986
Frizzell, Monica	C-Ac	837-8745	frizzelm	MFMP	MSA	82 W Conn	*	1981
Moser, Duane	Prof	837-8746	moserd		PHD	84. Ohio St		&1990
Proctor, Richard J.	Prof	837-8744	proctorr	AUVX	MBA	70 Columbia		&1983
Donegan, James J.	Assoc	837-9035	doneganj	F	PHD	95. Arizona		&1999
Monks, Thomas	Assoc		monkste	LX	LLM	92 Quinnipi		2004
Ganon, Michelle W.	Asst	837-8742	ganonm	X	PHD	96. Arizona		&1991

Western Illinois University — Macomb, IL 61455-1390 — (309) Fax=298-2952 — ß (123) 1978,1983 — wiu.edu — BB,MAC — Shirley Stolp
Accountancy — College of Bus & Tech
Dept Phone: 298-1152 — 1 University Circle
Homepage: www.wiu.edu/users/miactg/wiu/

Erekson, Tom	Dean	298-2442	tl-erekson	Tech	EDD		Illinois		6-06
ElFrink, John A.	C-Pr	298-1152	ja-elfrink	F	PHD	87. St Louis			& 8-06
Espahbodi, Hassanali	Prof	298-1455	h-espahbodi	FM	PHD	81. Alabama			& 9-90
Espahbodi, Pouran T.	Prof	298-1454	p-espahbodi	FM	PHD	81. Alabama			& 9-90
Lucas, Marcia J.	Prof	298-2129	mj-lucas	FEP	PHD	91. St Louis			& 9-79
Peek, George S.	Prof	298-1390	g-peek	MS	PHD	90. Georgia	*		& 9-87
Peek, Lucia E.	Prof	298-1398	l-peek	AM	PHD	87. Georgia			& 9-87
Coe, Martin	Assoc	762-3999	mj-coe	SV	MBA	92 St Ambro	# *		& 9-94
Falgiani, A. Anthony	Assoc	762-3999	aa-falgiani	XML	JD	81 S Texas	*		9-89
Hunt, Steven C.	Assoc	762-3999	sc-hunt	AFB	PHD	91. Florida			& 9-98
Woodruff, Gregg S.	Assoc	298-1022	gs-woodruff	X	PHD	03 Memphis			& 9-01
Ford, Amy	Inst	298-1152	am-ford	P	MACC	02 W Illinois			& 8-06
Foster, Cynthia	Inst	298-1152	c-foster	P	MACC	05 St Ambro			& 8-06
Pendergast, Susanna D.	Inst	298-1033	sd-pendergast	P	MACC	95 W Illinois			& 9-94
Westen, Cheryl	Inst	298-1152	ca-westen	P	MBA	00 W Illinois			& 9-01

Western Kentucky University Bowling GreenKY 42101-1061 (270) Fax=745-5953 ß 1982,1982
Department of Accounting Gordon Ford Col of Bus wku.edu BS,MBA
Dept Phone: 745-3895 1906 Col Heights Blvd #11061 Ruthene Glass
Homepage: www.wku.edu/gfcb/accounting/index.htm

Tallon, William J.	Dean	745-6311	william.tallon	Mgt	PHD	87	Iowa	2006
Aldridge, Charles Richard	H-Pr	745-3099	richard.aldridge	CVMP	DBA	84.	Kentucky	&1978
Chen, Yining	Prof	745-2982	yining.chen	SA	PHD	93.	S Carol	2005
Mary R. Nixon Professor of Accounting								
Hall, Jack O.	Prof	745-3896	jack.hall	TRF	PHD	73.	Missouri	&1968
Hays, Charles T.	Prof	745-2093	charles.hays	XF	PHD	68.	Missouri	&1963
Magner, Nace Richard	Prof	745-2998	nace.magner	MCB	DBA	90.	S Illinois	* 1989
J. C. Holland Professor of Accounting								
Kinnersley, Randall L.	Assoc	745-7054	randall.kinne+	PNG	PHD	97.	Tx Tech	& 1-03
Lee, Minwoo	Assoc	745-5001	minwoo.lee	MV	PHD	93.	Pittsburgh	1993
Little, Harold T. Jr.	Assoc	745-6978	harold.little	CFMP	PHD	99.	S Illinois	# * &1993
Ross, Mark T.	Asst	745-2964	mark.ross	PF	PHD	96.	Arizona	&1994
Wade, Stacy R.	Asst	745-6189	stacy.wade	FX	PHD	03.	Kentucky	&2003
Henson, Sheri	Inst	745-5382	sheri.henson	PC	MPA	98	Wstrn Ky	& 8-01

Western Michigan University Kalamazoo, MI 49008-3899 (269) Fax=387-5710 ß (13) 1970,1981
Department of Accountancy Haworth College of Bus wmich.edu BBA,MSA
Dept Phone: 387-5210 Mrs. Luann Bigelow
Homepage: http://www.hcob.wmu.edu

Shields, P. David	Dean	387-5050	david.shields	FM	PHD	80	Michigan	&2006
Gribbin, Donald W.	C-Pr	387-5209	donald.gribbin	CM	PHD	89.	Okla St	&2006
Dykxhoorn, Hans J.	Prof	387-5264	hans.dykxhoorn	AFO	PHD	78.	Mich St	&1979
Kreuze, Jerry G.	Prof	387-5266	jerry.kreuze	FT	PHD	83.	Missouri	&1983
Langsam, Sheldon A.	Prof	387-5289	sheldon.langsam	AFG	PHD	89.	Arkansas	&1989
Ruhl, Jack M.	Prof	387-5523	jack.ruhl	M	PHD	91.	Case Wes	1993
Sinning, Kathleen E.	Prof	387-5259	kathleen.sinning	XI	PHD	78.	Mich St	8-79
Tang, Roger Y. W.	Prof	387-5247	roger.tang	MI	PHD	77.	Nebraska	# * 1988
Upjohn Chair of Business Administration								
Forrest, J. Patrick	Assoc	387-5269	pat.forrest	S	DBA	87.	Kentucky	&1982
Hines, Charles E. (Chip)	Assoc	387-5263	charles.hines	F	PHD	79.	Mich St	&1976
Hodges, Richard L.	Assoc	387-5423	richard.hodges	NM	PHD	79.	Nebraska	&1985
Rozelle, David L.	Assoc	387-5265	david.rozelle	XP	MS	70	W Mich	* &1974
Smith, Ola	Asst	387-5307	ola.smith	M	PHD	02.	Mich St	&2000
Hays, Laurie	Inst	387-5749	laurie.hays	P	MSA	84	W Mich	&1995

Western New England Coll Springfield, MA 01119-2684 (413) Fax=796-2068 2003,2003
Dept Accounting & Finance School of Business wnec.edu BSBA,MBA,MSAC
Dept Phone: 782-1506 1215 Wilbraham Road Dawn Rock

Siciliano, Julie	Dean	782-1224	jsicilia	Mgt	PHD	90	Mass	1984
Vogel, Thomas J.	C-Ac	782-1501	tvogel	FMVT	PHD	93	Penn St	&1998
Coulter, John M.	Prof	782-1720	jcoulter	ABES	PHD	94.	Mass	&1997
Lo, May Hwa	Prof	782-1369	mlo	FVM	PHD	92.	Drexel	1993
Carlson, R. Loring	Assoc	782-1572	lcarlson	PXTF	JD	72	Conn	&1984
Solomon, Paul E.	Assoc	782-1708	psolomon	FTME	PHD	81.	Minnesota	2006
Lee, Sang-Kyu	Asst	796-2305	slee2	MC	DBA	05.	Boston U	8-04

Western New Mexico Univ Silver City, NM 88062-0680 (505) Fax=538-6264
Accounting Faculty Box 680 Dept of Business Adm wnmu.edu BBA,MBA
Dept Phone: 538-6321 12th Street, Phelps Dodge Bd Adele Springer
Homepage: wnmu.edu/academic/business/businessf.htm

Baldwin, Linda	C	538-6329	baldwinl	Mgt	PHD	02	N Mex St	1981
McGee, Linda	Assoc	538-6442		XPJF	MBA	72	W NewMex	1980
Meares, Irene	Asst	538-6331	mearesi	APRX	DBA	02	Sarasota	2002

Western State College of CO Gunnison, CO 81231-7042 (970) Fax=943-7042
Accounting Faculty Dept of Bus, Atcg & Eco western.edu BA
Dept Phone: 943-2019 Liz Fuller

Newman, Monica D.	C-Pr	943-2183	mnewman	XPCT	PHD	88	Tx-Austin	&1990
Hahn, F. James	Prof	943-3110	jhahn	PLJ	JD	66	Wisconsin	1969
Newman, Scott G.	Prof	943-2116	snewman	PFVR	PHD	86.	Tx-Austin	&1989
Hudson, Mary	Lect	943-3017	mhudson	APM	MHCA	81	Minnesota	&2004

Western Washington Univ Bellingham, WA 98225-9071 (360) Fax=650-4844 ß 1990,1990
Accounting Department College of Bus & Econ wwu.edu BA,MBA
Dept Phone: 650-3202 Parks Hall 451 Marty Hitchcock
Homepage: http://www.cbe.wwu.edu/acct

Murphy, Dennis R.	Dean	650-3896	dennis.murphy	Econ	PHD	74	Indiana	1979
Lockhart, Julie A.	C-Pr	650-4891	julie.lockhart	M	MS	82	Illinois	* &1982

Hutton, Marguerite R. (Zite)	Prof	650-4889	zite.hutton	X	PHD	85.	Houston	&1989
Sanders, George D.	Prof	650-4811	george.sanders	FGN	PHD	89.	Alabama	&1995
Singleton, W. Ron	Prof	650-4895	ron.singleton	XFI	PHD	83	Hawaii	& 1-76
Gilbertson, David L.	Assoc	650-4986	david.gilbertson	AF	PHD	97.	Utah	* &1998
Reynolds, Mary Ann	Assoc	650-4892	maryann.rey+	FWJ	PHD	88	Utah	1995
Sailors, William M. (Skip)	Assoc	650-4893	skip.sailors	FS	MBA	71	S Calif	&1974
Etheridge, Harlan L.	Asst	650-3202	harlan.ethridge	AMS	PHD	91.	LSU	&2007
Hsu, H. Y. Kathy	Asst	650-3202	kathy.hsu	FMI	PHD	94.	Houston	2007
Smith, Steven H.	Asst	650-2010	steven.smith	MX	PHD	00.	Ariz St	&2000
Taylor, Audrey G.	Asst	650-2204	audrey.taylor	MC	PHD	02	Wayne St	&2002

Westfield State College Westfield, MA   01086-1630   (413) Fax=572-5617
Accounting Faculty Dept of Econ & Mgt   wsc.ma.edu   BS
Dept Phone: 572-5590 577 Western Ave.   Carmen Diaz
Homepage: wwwbus.wsc

Merlo, Gary E.	C-As	572-5694	gmerlo	Mktg	MBA		W New Eng	1983
Irujo, Christine	Asst	572-5314	cirujo	PM	MS	85	Mass	
Maggio, Michele	Asst	572-5591	m.maggio					

Westminster College Salt Lake Cy, UT 84105-3697   (801) Fax=832-3106
Accounting Program Gore Sch of Business   westminstercollege.edu   BA,BS,MBA
Dept Phone: 832-2600 1840 South 1300 East
Homepage: www.westminstercollege.edu/catalog/

Van Os, Jerry A.	D-Pr	832-2651	jvanos	MSD	PHD	90	Brighm Yg	* &1988
Rogers, Alan	Prof	832-2619	arogers	PF	MBA	77	Utah	&1979
Bunker, Gaylen	Assoc	832-2616	gbunker	FMNU	MBA		Utah	&1989
Hoffa, Dara A.	Asst	832-2617	dhoffa	PCMS	MACC	87	Utah St	&1990

Westmont College Santa Barbara CA 93108-1099   (805) Fax=565-6255
Accounting Faculty Economics & Business   westmont.edu   BA
Dept Phone: 565-6156 955 La Paz Road
Homepage: www.westmont.edu

Noell, Edd S.	C-Pr			Econ	PHD	LSU	1986

Wichita State University Wichita, KS   67260-0087   (316) Fax=978-3660   ß (1) 1968,1974
School of Accountancy Barton School of Bus   wichita.edu   BBA,MACC
Dept Phone: 978-3215 1845 Fairmount   Danna Sprankle
Homepage: webs.wichita.edu/accountancy

Beehler, John M.	Dean	978-3200	john.beehler	X	PHD	85	Indiana	& 8-00
Bryant, Jeffrey J.	D-Ac	978-6261	jeffrey.bryant	X	PHD	93.	Tx Tech	&1993
BKD Faculty Fellow								
Harrison, Paul D.	Prof	978-6254	paul.harrison	CM	PHD	82.	Ariz St	2000
H. Dene Heskett Chair in Accounting								
Jarnagin, Bill D.	Prof	978-6262	bill.jarnagin	F	PHD	76.	Arkansas	&1987
Allen, Gibbs & Houlik Faculty Fellow								
Quirin, Jeffrey J.	Assoc	978-6258	jeffrey.quirin	CMF	PHD	98.	Nebraska	2000
W. Frank Barton Distinguished Chair in Business								
Flores, Michael B.	Asst	978-3724	michael.flores	BM	ABD		Tx Tech	&1998
Assistant Director								
Hamburg, Jared M.	Asst	973-3215		F	ABD		Wash St	2007
Kearney, Linwood W.	Asst	978-3215		F	ABD		Fla St	2007
Rai, Atul	Asst	978-3215		F	PHD	96.	NYU	2007
Sisneros, Craig	Asst	978-3215		F	PHD	06.	Ariz St	2007
Jones, Roger G.	Inst	978-6263	roger.jones	DS	MPA	92	Wichita St	1993

Widener University Chester, PA   19013-5792   (610) Fax=499-4614   1999,1999
Dept of Atg & Taxation School of Business Adm   widener.edu   BS,MSTAX,IS
Dept Phone: 499-4511 One University Place   Gina J. Newman
Homepage: http://sba.widener.edu/home4.html
  email @1=mail.widener.edu

Ozatalay, Savas	Dean	499-4310	sozatalay	Mgt	PHD	74	Nrthwstrn	1978
Hargadon, Joseph M.	H-Ac	499-4280	joseph.m.har+	VITF	PHD	93.	Drexel	* &1981
Miller, Sandra K.	Prof	499-4313	sandra.k.miller	XLF	LLM	90	Villanova	&1991
Tacchino, Kenn B.	Prof	499-4328	kenn.b.tacchino	XL	LLM	94	Widener	1990
Cermignano, Gregory P.	Assoc	499-4311	gregory.p.cer+	VLE	JD	84	Widener	* 1979
Greenberg, Penelope Sue	Assoc	499-4475	penelope.s+	ASMU	PHD	82.	Ohio St	* &1995
Lordi, Frank C.	Assoc	499-4308	frank.c.lordi	FMEH	MBA	70	Penn St	# * &1976
Tucker, James J. III	Assoc	499-4611	james.j.tucker	TFMH	PHD	85.	Penn St	&1990
Fuller, Lori R.	Asst		lori.fuller	AS	PHD	96.	Ariz St	&2002
Santomero, Nicole G.	Inst	499-1144	ngs0300@1		MST	97	Widener	&2004

Wilkes University
Business Division
Dept Phone: 408-4725
Browne, Paul
Rexer, Marianne M.
Chisarick, Cynthia J.
Das, Nandita

Wilkes-Barre, PA 18766
Sidhu Sch Bus & Leaders
170 South Franklin Street
Dean 408-4700 browne
C-Pr 408-4716 rexer
Assoc 408-4708 chisaric
Assoc 408-4700 das

(570) Fax=408-7874
wilkes.edu

							BS,MBA	
							Ms. Annet Kaminski	
			Bus	PHD	81	Harvard	2-04
			AS	PHD	97.	Drexel	& 8-90
			XF	MBA	84	Scranton	& 8-81
			F	PHD	04	Lehigh	8-05

Willamette University
Accounting Faculty
Dept Phone: 370-6440
Ringold, Debra
Smith, Ken A.

Salem, OR 97301-3931
Atkinson Grad Sch Mgt
900 State Street
Dean 370-6440 dringold
Asst 375-5302 smithk

(503) Fax=370-3011
willamette.edu

				1996	
				MBA	
			Mary Stout	
Mktg	PHD	86	Maryland	1994
MGN	PHD	01.	Missouri	&2004

College of William & Mary
Accounting Prog 328 Blow Hl
Dept Phone: 221-2046
Homepage: business.wm.edu/mac
Pulley, Lawrence B.
Smith, Kimberly J.
  Assistant Dean
Dafashy, Wagih G.
Smith, James E.
  John S. Quinn Professor of Accounting
White, Godwin T. (Tom)
Geary, William T.
Dey, Mithu R.
Irving, James H.
Jones, Denise A.
Lindsey, Bradley
Martin, Harold
Morris, Susan B.
Ramamurthy, Rama
Busbee, Howard

Williamsburg, VA 23187-8795
Mason School Business
PO Box 8795

Dean 221-2890 lawrence.pulley
Assoc 221-2867 kim.smith

Prof 221-2863 wagih.dafashy
Prof 221-2883 james.smith

Prof 221-2887 tom.white
Assoc 221-2888 william.geary
Asst 221-2696 mithu.dey
Asst 221-2657 james.irving
Asst 221-2876 denise.jones
Asst 221-7548 bradley.lindsay
Asst 273-6240 harold.martin
Asst 221-7833 susan.morris
Asst 221-2849 rama.ramamurthy
Adj 221-2641 howard.busbee

(757) Fax=221-2937
business.wm.edu

(123) 1972,1974				
BBA,MBA,MAC				
Priscilla Case, Martha Howard				
Econ	PHD	80	Virginia	1985
MFU	PHD	89.	Maryland	&1988
FM	PHD	66.	Arkansas	1965
X	PHD	72.	Arizona	&1970
FA	PHD	84.	Va Tech	&1983
FM	PHD	76.	Nrthwstrn	&1978
FM	PHD	05.	Geo Wash	&2006
FA	PHD	06.	N Carol	&2006
F	PHD	00.	Colorado	2000
FX	PHD	06.	N Carol	&2006
XFG	MBA	95	Old Dom	&
CFM	MAS	91	Illinois	2006
X	JD	67	Wm&Mary	& 1-02

William Carey College
Accounting Faculty
Dept Phone: 318-6199
Dale, Cheryl D.
Keasler, Hubert L. Jr.
Lewis, Eddie M. Jr.
Schamber, Sharon B.

Hattiesburg, MS 39401-5461
School of Business
498 Tuscan Avenue
Dean 318-6204 cheryl.dale
Assoc 318-6449 hurbert.keasler
Assoc 318-6537 eddie.lewis
Inst 318-6198 sharon.schamber

(601) Fax=318-6281
wmcarey.edu

				BS,MBA	
				Sandra Meeler	
	PHD	98	Alabama	1997
CMGN	DBA	91.	Miss St	*	1999
FIM	DBA	74.	Miss St	2003
AFVX	MPA	80	S Miss	2004

William Jewell College
Accounting Faculty
Dept Phone: Ext 5701
  phone 781-7700 Ext 5701
Hawkins, Jean L. G.
Bell, Linda Joyce

Liberty, MO 64068-1896
Business Department
500 College Hill

C-Pr Ext 5701 hawkinsj
Prof Ext 5700 belll

(816) Fax=415-5027
william.jewell.edu

				BS	
CTNM	MA	70	Cen Mo St	* & 9-76
AFSX	MBA	83	Missouri	& 9-85

William Paterson University
Dept of Accounting & Law
Dept Phone: 720-2435
Basu, Sam N.
Xu, Lianzan
Grippo, Frank
Medinets, Ann F.
Mwaura, Muroki
Nassiripour, Sia
Nyaboga, Andrew
Rudnick, Martin
Ekmekjian, Elizabeth
Xu, Wei

Wayne, NJ 07470
Cotsakos College of Bus
1600 Valley Rd
Dean 720-2964 basus
C-Pr 720-2963 xul
Assoc 720-3118 grippof
Assoc 720-3744 medinetsa
Assoc 720-2953 mwaruam
Assoc 720-2241 nassiripours
Assoc 720-2403 nyabogaa
Assoc 720-2628 rudnickm
Asst 720-3851 ekmekjiane
Asst 720-3618 xuw

(973) Fax=
upunj.edu

			2004,2004	
Fnce	PHD	75	Houston	2006
FVM	PHD	96.	Kentucky	1996
AF	MBA	77	Fairl Dick	&1979
ACM	PHD	04.	Rutgers	2006
FM	PHD	94	Illinois	1994
CF	PHD	93.	Wash St	&2001
SFM	PHD	00	Stevens	1996
FVM	MS	73	Alabama	&1978
XL	LLM	98	NYU Law	1999
FTM	PHD	07	Rutgers	2004

Wilmington College Delaware
Accounting Faculty
Dept Phone: 356-6785
Edelson, Robert E.
Stokes, Sally

New Castle, DE 19720-6491
Business
320 DuPont Highway
Dean 328-9401 robert.e.edelson
Asst 856-5780 sstok

(302) Fax=322-7021
wilmcoll.edu

			Barbara Quattro	
BMQ	PHD	00	Claremont	2005
EFPX	MS	97	WilminDE	&1995

Wingate University
Accounting
Dept Phone: 233-8147

Wingate, NC 28174
School of Business

(704) Fax=233-8146
wingate.edu

						Mary Maye
Graham, Joseph M.	Dean	233-8147	graham		MBA	Winthrop	&
Morrison, Theodore D. III	Assoc	233-8140	tmorriso	FVAM	DBA	92. Miss St	&

Winona State University
Department of Accounting
Dept Phone: 457-5860
Homepage: www.winona.edu/accounting

Winona, MN 55987-5838
College of Business
Johnson and Sanborn Streets

(507) Fax=457-2967
winona.edu

BS

Manrique, Gabriel	Dean$	457-5014	gmanrique	Econ	PHD	82 Notre Dm	1989
Ihrke, Frederic	C-Pr	457-5185	fihrke	XGFL	JD	79 Wm Mitch	&1981
Bergin, J. Lawrence	Prof	457-5174	lbergin	FCM	ABD	Kent St	1981
Sallee, Larry	Prof	285-7132	lsallee	FX	DBA	91 US Intl	* &1985
Schneider, Richard	Prof	457-5187	rschneider	FSX	MS	71 Ariz St	&1981
Hurley, James F.	Assoc	457-5172	jhurley	FIPT	PHD	83. Nebraska	&1983
McVay, Gloria	Assoc	457-5860	gmcvay	FMP	PHD	01. Kentucky	2000
Morgan, John D.	Assoc	457-2573	jmorgan	FS	PHD	92. Nebraska	* &2006
Ortega, William R.	Assoc	457-5180	wortega	MAC	PHD	95. Fla St	* 2003
Yoon, SungWook	Asst	457-5184	syoon	FV	PHD	04. Colorado	2004

Winston-Salem State Univ
Department of Accounting
Dept Phone: 750-2280
Homepage: wssu.edu/sbe/acc.page/acc.asp

Winston-Slm NC 27110
School of Bus & Econ
601 Martin Luther King Dr

(336) Fax=750-2335
wssu.edu

2000
BS
Jacqueline Hicks

Bailey, Jessica M.	Dean	750-2330	baileyjm	Mktg	PHD	83 Missouri	8-06
Morton, Russell S.	C	750-2359	mortonr	Mis	PHD	96 Kentucky	8-97
Weisenfeld, Leslie W.	Prof	750-2336	weisenfeldl	FABE	PHD	87. Va Tech	* 8-93
Sara Lee Professor							
Clark, Gloria	Assoc	750-2347	clarkg	XFM	EDD	87 Atlanta	& 8-95
Johnson, George A.	Assoc	750-2349	johnsong	FMVP	PHD	90. Va Tech	7-99

Winthrop University
Dept of Atg, Fnce & Econ
Dept Phone: 323-2186

Rock Hill, SC 29733
College of Business Adm
209 Thurmond Building

(803) Fax=323-3960
winthrop.edu

1979,1983
BS,MBA

Weikle, Roger D.	Dean	323-2185	weikler	Mgt	PHD	85 S Carol	9-74
Letourneau, Angela	C-Ac	323-2679	letourneaua	CMX	DBA	87. La Tech	& 9-88
Breakfield, Robert H.	Prof	323-2685	breakfieldr	XL	LLM	75 Boston U	9-76
Coleman, Clarence Jr.	Prof	323-2673	colemanc	AFC	PHD	90. S Carol	& 9-02
Meeting, David T.	Prof	323-2162	meetingd		DBA	86. Kent St	&
Alvis, Charles E.	Assoc	323-2695	alvisc	PFX	MBA	81 Winthrop	& 6-86
Cornick, Michael F.	Assoc	323-4264	cornickm	DM	PHD	80. N Carol	& 9-02
Grigsby, William W.	Assoc	323-4622	grigsbyw	GNFV	DBA	73. Oklahoma	& 9-87
Manasa, Harold J.	Assoc	323-2467	manasah	PX	MA	85 Oklahoma	# &

U of Wisconsin-Eau Claire
Dept of Accounting & Finance
Dept Phone: 836-2184

Eau Claire, WI 54702-4004
College of Business
105 Garfield Avenue

(715) Fax=836-3582
uwec.edu

ß 1991,1991
BBA,MBA
Gail Nelson

Dock, V. Thomas	Dean	836-5509	dockv	Mis	PHD	70 N Colo	7-92
Becker, D'Arcy A.	C-Pr	836-6028	dbecker	AF	PHD	92. Wisconsin	& 8-95
Holmen, Jay S.	Prof	836-2101	holmenjs	SM	PHD	81. Minnesota	* & 6-84
Selin, J. Roger	Prof	836-3738	selinj	FP	PHD	74 Minnesota	& 1-66
Devine, Margaret D.	Assoc	836-2710	dwyermm	DF	PHD	92. Wisconsin	& 8-82
Sheikholeslami, Mehdi	Assoc	836-3158	msheikho	FMI	PHD	86 Tx-Dallas	* 8-88
Orchard, Lou X.	Asst			FM	PHD	98. Arizona	& 8-07
Rundall, James	Inst	836-3207	rundaljd	F	MS	74 Illin St	& 8-82
Ulstad, Ingrid	Inst	836-2990	ulstadic	P	MBA	79 Minnesota	& 1-98

Un of Wisconsin-Green Bay
Department of Accounting
Dept Phone: 465-2051

Green Bay, WI 54311-7001
Pro Programs Business
2420 Nicolet Drive

(920) Fax=465-2660
uwgb.edu

BS
Kelly Anklam

Erickson, Fritz	Dean	465-2050	ericksof		EDD	87 N Colo	2003
Zehms, Karl M.	C-Ac	465-2553	zehmsk	FG	PHD	70. Wisconsin	& 9-70
Doering, James A.	Assoc	465-2347	doeringj	LX	LLM	88 NYU	&1991
Sagrillo, Marilyn	Assoc	465-2762	sagrillm	SAM	PHD	95. Wisconsin	& 8-94
Muzatko, Steven R.	Asst	465-2578	muzatkom	FA	PHD	00. Wisconsin	8-99
Fischer, James H.	Lect	465-2353	fischerj	FMX	PHD	71. Wisconsin	* 8-03
Selk, Ann	Lect	465-2756	selka	FMNG	MBA	83 Wi-Milwa	& 8-83

U of Wisconsin-La Crosse
Department of Accountancy
Dept Phone: 785-8093
Homepage: www.uwlax.edu/ba/acc/

La Crosse, WI   54601
College of Business Adm
1725 State Street

(608) Fax = 785-8549
uwlax.edu

1982,1987
BS,MBA
Lori Komarek

Name	Rank	Phone	Email	Area	Deg	Yr	School	Notes
May, Bruce E.	Dean$	785-8095	mary.bruc	Law	DBA		US Intl	8-02
Eide, Barbara J.	C-Pr	785-6827	eide.barb	CM	PHD	98.	Va Comm	& 8-98
Gardner, John C..	Prof	785-6829	gardner.john	XPJE	PHD	74	LSU	& 8-85
Burrowes, Ashley W.	Assoc	785-6825	burrowes.ashl	AOST	PHD	86.	Nebraska	* & 8-02
Kastantin, Joseph T.	Assoc	785-6832	kastanti.jose	VGPI	MBA	79	Butler	* & 1-84
Winter, Kenneth M.	Assoc	785-6830	winter.kenn	FPH	PHD	88.	Wisconsin	* & 8-88
Hendricks, Ann	Asst	785-6833	hendricks.ann	AF	PHD	99.	Nebraska	# * & 8-02
Bice, Phillip	Inst	785-6835	bice.phil	FMA	MS	75	Wi-White	& 8-81
Lyons, Kimberly	Inst	785-6836	lyons.kimb	PX	MS	94	Illinois	& 1-97

Univ of Wisconsin-Madison
Dept Accounting & Info Sys
Dept Phone: 262-1693

Madison, WI   53706-1323
School of Business
975 University Avenue

(608) Fax = 263-0477   ß (12) 1916,1963
bus.wisc.edu   BBA,MAC,PHD
Judy Schaeffer, Dept Admin

Name	Rank	Phone	Email	Area	Deg	Yr	School	Notes
Knetter, Michael M.	Dean	265-4937	mknetter	Fnce	PHD	88	Stanford	2002
Davis, Jon S.	C-Pr	263-4264	jdavis	XB	PHD	87.	Arizona	&2000
Covaleski, Mark A.	Prof	262-4239	mcovaleski	N	PHD	79.	Penn St	& 1-79
Robert Beyer Professor of Managerial Accounting and Control								
Eichenseher, John W.	Prof	262-1539	jeichen	FIA	PHD	80.	Michigan	& 8-83
Nair, R. D.	Prof	262-3819	rnair	F	PHD	77.	Michigan	& 1-78
PricewaterhouseCoopers Professor of Accounting								
Rittenberg, Larry E.	Prof	262-2267	lrittenberg	AO	PHD	75.	Minnesota	# &1976
Ernst & Young Professor of Accounting								
Weygandt, Jerry J.	Prof	262-1891	jweygandt	F	PHD	68.	Illinois	&1968
Arthur Andersen & Co. Alumni Chair in Accounting								
Wild, John J.	Prof	262-8122	jwild	FT	PHD	83.	Wisconsin	1989
Robert and Monica Beyer Professor of Accounting								
Ashbaugh-Skaife, Hollis	Assoc	263-7979	hashbaugh	F	PHD	97.	Iowa	* &1997
Skaife, Hollis - 2007								
Johnstone, Karla M.	Assoc	262-3544	kjohnstone	AB	PHD	97.	Conn	&1997
Matsumura, Ella Mae	Assoc	262-9731	ematsumura	MAT	PHD	84	Brit Colum	9-85
Mayhew, Brian W.	Assoc	262-2714	bmayhew	A	PHD	97.	Arizona	&1999
Skaife, Hollis	Assoc	263-7979	hashbaugh	F	PHD	97.	Iowa	* &1997
Warfield, Terry D.	Assoc	262-1028	twarfield	FT	PHD	89.	Iowa	1989
Holder-Webb, Lori L.	Asst	263-4386	lholder	F	PHD	02.	Tx A&M	2002
Boucher, Joseph W.	SLect	262-1892	jboucher	XL	JD	77	Wisconsin	1980
Harms, Bruce L.	SLect	262-3873	bharms	LX	JD	75	Wisconsin	&1975
Mucklow, Belinda	Lect	265-5275	bmucklow	F	PHD	90.	Cornell	1990
O'Brien, Ann D.	Lect	262-5852	aobrien	FX	MBA	85	Tx-Austin	&1999
Schroeder, Roger G.	Lect	265-1133		X	BBA	64	Wisconsin	&2000
Tierney, Thomas G.	Lect	262-1943	ttierney	X	BBA	72	Wisconsin	&1991

Un of Wisconsin-Milwaukee
Accounting Faculty Box 742
Dept Phone: 229-4545

Milwaukee, WI   53201
School of Business Adm
3202 N. Maryland

(414) Fax = 229-6957   ß 1970,1971
uwm.edu   BBA,MS,MAT

Name	Rank	Phone	Email	Area	Deg	Yr	School	Notes
Prasad, V. Kanti	Dean	229-4235	vkp	Mktg	PHD	70	Mich St	1971
Fischer, Paul M.	C-Pr	229-4545	pfischer	FC	PHD	69.	Wisconsin	&1969
J. A. Leer Professor of Accounting								
Cheng, Rita H.	Prof	229-5165	rcheng	GFN	PHD	88.	Temple	&1988
A. O. Smith Teaching Professor								
Arnold, Patricia J.	Assoc	229-3837	arnold	FMN	PHD	87.	Wisconsin	&1989
Kimmel, Paul D.	Assoc	229-4249	pkimmel	FA	PHD	89.	Wisconsin	&1989
Kozub, Robert M.	Assoc	229-4649	kozub	XF	DBA	83.	Kentucky	&1983
Kren, Leslie	Assoc	229-6075	lkren	CM	PHD	88.	Houston	&1991
Pillsbury, Ceil M.	Assoc	229-4164	ceil	SA	PHD	84.	Okla St	&1984
Saemann, Georgia C.	Assoc	229-6292	gsaemann	BFA	PHD	87.	Mich St	&1991
Schadewald, Michael S.	Assoc	229-5005	schade	X	PHD	88.	Minnesota	&1992
Daugherty, Brian E.	Asst	229-5737	daught	FA	PHD	06.	Tx-SanAnt	&2006
Healy, John C.	Lect	229-2262	jhealy	X	MS	92	Wi-Milwa	&1977
Konkol, Charles A.	Lect	229-3825	konkol	XFAM	MS	81	Wi-Milwa	&1983
Viet, Sheila	Lect	229-3874	viet	FM	MS	79	Wi-Milwa	&2006

Univ of Wisconsin-Oshkosh
Department of Accounting
Dept Phone: 424-3027

Oshkosh, WI   54901-8676
College of Business Adm
800 Algoma Boulevard

(920) Fax = 424-7413   ß 1970,1978
uwosh.edu   BBA,MBA
Donna Molus 424-3027

Name	Rank	Phone	Email	Area	Deg	Yr	School	Notes
Hartman, E. Alan	Dean	424-1424	hartman	Mgt	PHD	72	Mich St	1976
Simons, Donald R.	C-Pr	424-3472	simons	NMG	PHD	72.	Wisconsin	&1985
Cross, Joann Noe	Prof	424-1311	crossj	FHN	PHD	81.	Illinois	* &1980
Tatikonda, Lakshmi U.	Prof	424-7188	tatikond	CMOQ	PHD	66	Tx-Austin	# * &1978
Makar, Stephen D.	Assoc	424-0158	makar	FMC	PHD	94.	Kent St	&1994
Westort, Peter J.	Assoc	424-3124	westort	FX	PHD	90.	Oregon	&2003
Hyatt, Troy A.	Asst	424-1090	hyatt	AS	PHD	95.	Arizona	&2003
Pofahl, James W.	Inst	424-2091	pofahl	F	MBA	66	Chicago	&1998
Potratz, Wendy K.	Inst	424-2091	potratzw	FM	MBA	88	Wi-Oshko	* &2007

Univ of Wisconsin-Parkside Kenosha, WI 53141-2000 (262) Fax=595-2680 1996,1996
Department of Business School Business & Tech uwp.edu BS,MBA
Dept Phone: 595-2280 900 Wood Road Debra Dawdy, Bradley Piazza
Homepage: http://uwp.edu/academic/business/

Ebeid, Fred J.	Dean	595-2243	ebeid	Fnce	PHD	74	Illinois	7-06
Baldwin, Dirk S.	C-Ac	595-2449	dirk.baldwin	Mis	PHD	89	Tx Tech	8-96
Wang, Zhemin M. (Jamie)	Prof	595-2436	zhemin.wang	FV	PHD	91.	Wisconsin	8-98
Zammeeruddin, Rizvanna	Asst	595-2280	rizvanna.zamm+	LX	JD	01	DePaul	8-03
Cholak, Michael	Lect	595-2648	michael.cholak	FM	MBA	98	Marquette	8-03
Determan, Thomas	Lect	595-2476	determan	PM	MS	05	Card Str	8-06

U of Wisconsin-Platteville Platteville, WI 53818-3099 (608) Fax=342-1466
Dept Business & Accounting Col Bus,Ind,LifeSci&Ag uwplatt.edu BS
Dept Phone: 342-1660 One University Plaza LaVon Blum
Homepage: uwplatt.edu/~busacctng

Ford, Duane M.	Dean	342-1547	fordd		PHD	84	Iowa St	8-99
Kleisath, Steven	C-Pr	342-1660	kleisath	Mgt	DBA	93	Nova SE	1980
Borke, John	Prof	342-1337	borkej	FPV	MAS	79	N Illinois	& 8-81
Conway, Robert	Prof	342-1749	conway	PTM	PHD	92.	Wisconsin	8-90
Moiz, Syed	Asst	342-1336	moizs		MBA	94	Minn St	8-06
Montgomery, Patrick	Asst	342-1464	montgomeryp		MAS	02	St Ambro	8-06

U of Wisconsin-River Falls River Falls, WI 54022-5001 (715) Fax=425-0707 2007
Dept of Business Adm Col of Business & Econ uwrf.edu BA,BS
Dept Phone: 425-3337 410 South 3rd Street Pat Lofgren

Nemecek, Barbara H.	Dean	425-3335	barbara.nemecek	Mktg	PHD	87	Minnesota	2001
Rahgozar, Reza	C-Pr	425-3335	reza.rahgozar	Fnce	PHD	85	Claremont	9-87
Hukai, Dawn	Assoc	425-3337	dawn.hukai		PHD	98	Minnesota	1998
Popelka, Carl B.	Assoc	425-3335	carl.b.popelka	FCS	MBA		Roosevelt	* &1981
Tichich, Mary C.	Assoc	425-3337	mary.c.tichich	CFMV	PHD	89.	Tx A&M	&2000
Li, June F.	Asst	425-3337	june.li	EFPV	PHD	92.	Kentucky	&2006

U Wisconsin-Stevens Point Stevens Point WI 54481-3897 (715) Fax=346-4215
Division of Business & Econ Col of Letters & Sci uwsp.edu BS,BA
Dept Phone: 346-2728 Erika Staven
Homepage: www.uwsp.edu/business

Mullins, Gary	C-As	346-2728		Mgt	PHD	94	Wash U	8-94
Love, William H.	Assoc	346-3871	wlove	FA	PHD	86.	Arkansas	# * & 8-82
Maas, William	Asst	346-2728	wmaas	FM	JD	92	N Illinois	&2002

Univ of Wisconsin-Superior Superior, WI 54880-4500 (715) Fax=394-8180
Accounting Faculty Dept Business & Econ uwsuper.edu BS
Dept Phone: 394-8206 Belkanp and Catlin, POBox200
Homepage: www.uwsuper.edu

Trudeau, Gregory P.	C-Pr	394-8209	gtrudeau	FCMA	EDD	01	Minnesota	# * &1988
Reichert, Charles J.	Prof	394-8291	creicher	FX	MST	77	Colo St	# &1977

U of Wisconsin-Whitewater Whitewater, WI 53190-1790 (262) Fax=472-5499 β 1974,1980
Accounting Department College of Bus & Econ uww.edu BBA,MBA,MPA
Dept Phone: 472-1344 800 West Main Street Marlene Denson

Clements, Christine	Dean	472-1343	clementc	Mgt	PHD	90	Arkansas	1990
Gruber, Robert A.	C-Pr	472-9463	gruberr	EGI	PHD	90.	Wisconsin	# * &1986
C.A. Black Professor of Accounting								
Barton, Peter	Prof	472-5454	bartonp	XM	JD	88	Wisconsin	&1983
Weatherwax, Roy C.	Prof	472-1029	weatherr	FC	PHD	74.	Wisconsin	&1976
Arora, Alka	Assoc	472-5452	aroraa	FT	PHD	95.	Kent St	&1996
Holmes, Linda	Assoc	472-5451	holmesl	GFN	PHD	97.	Okla St	* 2000
Normand, Carol J.	Assoc	472-5453	normandcj	MS	EDD	98	N Illinois	&2002
Sager, Clayton R.	Assoc	472-1229	sagerc	FM	PHD	81.	Iowa	1983
Cummings, Richard	Asst	472-3936	cummingsr	FX	PHD	95	Kansas St	&2002
Czaja, Rita J.	Asst	472-1639	czajar	EF	PHD	95.	Nrthwstrn	&2005
Gerard, Joseph	Lect	472-5450	gerardj	BCE	MS	96	Wi-Milwa	&2007
Hafemeister, Lynn	Lect	472-5464	hafemeil	FP	MS	82	Wi-White	&2002
MacDonald, Michael	Lect	472-1639	macdonam	CFX	MS	76	Wi-White	&1997
Packee, Jennifer	Lect	472-3925	packeej	FM	MS	02	Marquette	&2007
Tatman, William	Lect	472-1707	tatmanw	AF	MS	05	Wi-Milwa	&2005

Wittenberg University Springfield, OH 45501-0720 (937) Fax=327-6143
Accounting Faculty Dept of Management wittenberg.edu BA
Dept Phone: 327-7902 200 West Ward Street Sarah Dundon
Homepage: www.wittenberg.edu

Gradwohl, Wendy C.	C							
Stockstill, Lowell E.	Prof	327-7908	lstockstill	FL	JD	82	Toledo	9-81
Fenimore, John R.	Assoc	327-7931	jfenimore	FMA	MACC	73	Bowl Gr	& 8-01
Maurer, Wayne O.	Assoc	327-7909	wmaurer	VCM	MBA	74	Wright St	* 9-74

Wofford College
Accounting Faculty
Dept Phone: 597-4530

Spartanburg, SC	29303-3663		(864) Fax=597-4549					
Dept Accounting & Fnce			wofford.edu					BA,BS
429 North Church Street								
Richardson, Wm. Eddie	C-Ac	597-4532	richardsonwe	DF	PHD	92	Tennessee	9-02
Keenan, Philip S.	Assoc	597-4588	keenanps	XFC	MBA	78	Michigan	& 9-81
Gonzalez, Lillian	Asst	597-4515	gonzalezle	CA	MPA	95	Clemson	& 9-01

Woodbury University
Accounting Faculty
Dept Phone: 252-5133
Homepage: www.woodbury.edu

Burbank, CA	91510-7846		(818) Fax=767-0032					
Sch of Business & Mgt			woodbury.edu					BS
7500 Glenoaks Boulevard								Lori McCall
van Niekerk, Andre B.	Dean	252-5284	andre.vannickerk		PHD	85	Mich St	7-05
Myers, Jon W.	C-Ac	767-0888	jon.myers	ACFP	MBA	60	Berkeley	& 3-83

Worcester Polytechnic Inst
Accounting Faculty
Dept Phone: 831-5218
Homepage: mgt.wpi.edu

Worcester, MA	01609-2280		(508) Fax=831-5720					2003,2003
Dept of Management			wpi.edu					BS,MBA,MS
100 Institute Road								M. Kwederis, R. Cane
Banks, McRae C.	H-Pr	831-5218	macb	Mgt	PHD	87	Va Tech	1995
Harry G. Stoddard Professor								
O'Connor, John T.	Prof	831-5452	joconnor	FM	PHD	70	Notre Dm	1986
Higgins, Huong Ngo	Asst	831-5626	hhiggins	FM	PHD	98.	Geo St	1998

Worcester State College
Accounting Faculty
Dept Phone: 929-8091

Worcester, MA	01602-2597		(508) Fax=929-8048					
Dept of Bus Adm & Econ			worcester.edu					BBA,BS
486 Chandler Street								Mrs. Denise Lovely
Jain, Renuka	C-Pr	929-8091	rjain	Econ	PHD	85	McGill	1985
Moore, Dennis P.	Prof	929-8094	dmoore	CVXP	MST		Bentley	9-83
Stefanini, Maureen C.	Prof	929-8094	mstefanini	PMF	EDD		Boston U	7-93
Swanson, James J.	Assoc	929-8092	jswanson	PAMX	MST		Bryant	1984
Dahlin, Laurie	Asst	929-8094	ldahlin	PAJM	DBA		Nova SE	* 5-01

Wright State University
Department of Accountancy
Dept Phone: 775-2377
Homepage: wright.edu/coba/acc/

Dayton, OH	45435-0001		(937) Fax=775-2310		ß (123)	1974,1979		
Raj Soin College of Bus			wright.edu					BS,MACC
3640 Colonel Glenn Highway								Ms. Sharon Sexton
Farmer, Berkwood M.	Dean	775-2377	berkwood.farmer	Econ	PHD	70	N Car St	7-01
Greenspan, James W.	C-Pr	775-2377	james.greenspan	AFMV	PHD	86.	Tx A&M	1-03
Lightle, Susan S.	Prof	775-4169	susan.lightle	A	PHD	91.	Cincinnati	# & 9-91
Sprohge, Hans Dieter	Prof	775-2365	hans.sprohge	FM	PHD	74	SUNY-Buf	& 9-88
Talbott, John C.	Prof	775-2720	john.talbott	MX	DBA	74.	Kentucky	* 9-75
Bukovinsky, David M.	Assoc	775-3643	david.bukovinsky	MCPG	PHD	93.	Kentucky	& 9-99
Hartwell, Carolyn L.	Assoc	775-2377	carolyn.hartwell	FTS	PHD	93.	Cincinnati	& 9-01
Lin, Pao-Chuan (Paul)	Assoc	775-3480	pao-chuan.lin	S	PHD	88.	LSU	9-00
Brown, Kevin F.	Asst	775-3138	kevin.brown	AFT	PHD	01.	Case Wes	& 9-04
Cook, John K.	Asst	775-3483	john.cook	X	LLM	96	Florida	9-04
Houston, Margaret A.	Lect	775-2390	maggie.houston	SM	MBA	85	Wright St	* & 9-88
Terzian, Susan E.	Lect	775-3644	sue.terzian	F	MBA	79	Cincinnati	* & 9-98

University of Wyoming
Department of Accounting
Dept Phone: 766-3136
Homepage: //business.uwyo.edu

Laramie, WY	82071-3275		(307) Fax=766-4028		ß 1956,1982			
College of Business			uwyo.edu					BS,MS
Dept 3275, 1000 E Univ Ave								Ema Shenefelt
Hathaway, Brent A.	Dean	766-4194	bhathawa	Mktg	PHD	97	Illinois	7-01
Ainsworth, Penne L.	C-Pr	766-3167	penne	MCP	PHD	88.	Nebraska	# * &1997
Walker, Kenton B.	Prof	766-3154	kbwalk	SMV	PHD	86.	Tx A&M	1985
Webster, Stuart K.	Prof	766-3801	swebster	F	PHD	75.	Iowa	&1994
Elmendorf, Richard G.	Assoc	766-3962	elmendor	FN	DBA	87.	Boston U	1989
Director, MS Accounting Program								
Fleischman, Gary M.	Assoc	766-3136	gflash	X	PHD	95.	Tx Tech	* &2000
Kidwell, Linda A.	Assoc	766-3136	lkidwell	AJB	PHD	93.	LSU	8-05
Stephenson, Teresa M.	Asst	766-3136	teresas	TM	PHD	05.	Kentucky	2005
Benson, Janice	Lect	766-2048	jabenson	FM	MBA	93	Kansas St	&1999
Doherty, Michael	Lect	766-2114	mdoherty	S	MBA	00	Wyoming	&2000
Pedersen, Ronald	Lect	766-4919	pointy	PM	MS	02	Wyoming	&2003

Xavier University
Department of Accountancy
Dept Phone: 745-3236
Homepage: xu.edu/colleges/cba/acct/account.html

Cincinnati, OH	45207-5161		(513) Fax=745-4383					1994,1994
College of Business			xavier.edu					BSBA,MBA
3800 Victory Parkway								Shirlee James
Malekzadeh, Ali R.	Dean	745-3528	malekzadeh	Mgt	PHD	82	Utah	2003

Name	Rank	Phone	Email		Deg	Yr	School	
Richtermeyer, Sandra B.	C-Ac	745-3654	richtermeyer	FMN	PHD	97.	Colorado	* &2004
IMA Professor in Residence								
Devine, Kevin M.	Prof	745-2045	devine	BMU	PHD	90.	Nebraska	1989
O'Clock, Priscilla M.	Prof	745-4245	oclock	BMX	PHD	91.	Nebraska	&1992
Surdick, John J.	Prof	745-3493	surdick	VFMN	PHD	88.	Wisconsin	&1986
VanDerbeck, Edward J.	Prof	745-3633	vanderbeck	CM	MS	68	SUNY-Alb	&1976
Allen, Joyce S.	Assoc	745-3471	allenj	FP	MBA	71	Cincinnati	&1979
Tracey, Ann marie	Asst	745-3129	tracey	LR	JD	75	Cincinnati	2003

Xavier Univ of Louisiana New Orleans, LA 70125-1098 (504) Fax=520-7900
Department of Business Coll of Arts & Sciences xula.edu
Dept Phone: 520-7505 1 Drexel Drive Ms. Veronica J. Davis

Vincent, Harold	Dean		hvincent	Phys	PHD			
Kukreja, Anil	C-Ac	520-7505	akukreja	Mgt	PHD		Alabama	
Wright, Clifford S.	Prof		cwright	FAXL	MBA		Loyola	&
Meyer, Jean A.	Inst		jameyer	FMGV	MBA		LSU	&

Yale University New Haven, CT 06520-8200 (203) Fax=432-5092 1991
PO Box 208200 School of Management yale.edu MBA,PHD
Dept Phone: 432-6035 PO Box 208200 Sheril Frano

Podolny, Joel M.	Dean	432-6035	joel.podolny	Mgt	PHD	91	Harvard	2005
Antle, Rick	Prof	402-0048	rick.antle	AMFT	PHD	81.	Stanford	1985
William S. Beinecke Professor of Accounting								
Garstka, Stanley J.	Prof	432-6042	stanley.garstka	FMT	PHD	70	Car Mellon	1978
Deputy Dean								
Sunder, Shyam	Prof	432-6160	shyam.sunder	FTM	PHD	73.	Car Mellon	1999
James L. Frank Professor of Accounting, Economics and Finance								
Thomas, Jacob K.	Prof	432-5977	jacob.thomas	FC	PHD	84.	Michigan	* 7-03
Ernst & Young Professor of Accounting & Finance								
Mittendorf, Brian	Assoc	432-3245	brian.mittendorf	AMFT	PHD	02.	Ohio St	7-02
Ederhof, Merle	Asst			MT	PHD	07	Stanford	7-07
Zhang, Frank X.	Asst	432-7938	frank.zhang	XT	PHD	06	Chicago	7-05

Yeshiva University New York, NY 10033-3201 (212) Fax=960-0824
Accounting Faculty Sy Syms School of Bus ymail.yu.edu BS
Dept Phone: 960-0845 500 West 185th Street Mrs. Natalie Goldman

Hochman, Joel A.	Dean$	960-0845	hochman	MF	JD	82	Pace	& 9-94
Philip H. Cohen Chair in Accounting								
Pava, Moses L.	Prof	960-0844	mpava	MF	PHD	90.	NYU	9-87
Alvin H. Einbender Chair in Business Ethics								
Leibowitz, Martin A.	Asst	960-0001		MF	PHD	96.	Columbia	& 9-95
Kirzner Chair; leibowitz613@juno.edu								
Kahn, David C.	Inst	960-0853		F	BS	73	Lng Isl	& 2-02

York College of Pennsylvania York, PA 17405-7199 (717) Fax=849-1653
Accounting Faculty Dept of Business Adm ycp.edu BS,MBA
Dept Phone: 815-1423 Country Club Road Julie Sterner E-Mail jsterner

Meisenhelter, Mary C.	C-Pr	815-1277	mmeisenh	Mgt	PHD		Geo Wash	1985
Smith, Becky L.	C-As	815-1571	blsmith		PHD	94	US Intl	& 9-97
Azad, Hamid R.	Asst	815-1493	hazad	FMQ	PHD		Utah St	& 9-88
Barbor, John F.	Asst	815-1924	jbarbor	CDFV	MBA		Shippensb	& 9-73
Leinheiser, Frederick D.	Asst	815-1387	fleinhei	AF	MBA		Shippensb	& 9-80

Youngstown State University Youngstown, OH 44555-0001 (330) Fax=941-1459 2000,2000
Accounting & Finance Dept Williamson Col Bus Adm cc.ysu.edu BS,MBA
Dept Phone: 941-3084 One University Plaza Becky Ifft
Homepage: www.ysu.edu

Licata, Betty Jo	Dean	941-3062	bjlicata	Mgt	PHD	82	Rensselaer	1995
Woodlock, Peter D.	C-Pr	941-1483	p_woodlock@y	CF	PHD	90.	Ohio St	& 9-95
Antenucci, Joseph W.	Prof	941-3590	jwantenu	F	PHD	93.	Va Tech	9-93
Claypool, Gregory A.	Prof	941-1877	gregclaypool@y	FAEJ	PHD	88.	Kent St	9-86
Law, David B.	Prof	941-1881	dblaw	F	DBA	95.	Clev St	& 1-94
Parsegian, Elsa V.	Prof	941-3087		FMI	PHD	85.	Pittsburgh	* & 9-98
email: evparsegian@cs.com								
Shaffer, Raymond J.	Prof	941-3196	rjshaffer	FXG	PHD	90.	Kentucky	& 9-90
Stout, David E.	Prof	941-3509	destout	MCE	PHD	82.	Pittsburgh	9-03
Tackett, James A.	Prof	941-3083	jatacket	F	PHD	83.	Ohio St	& 9-84

CANADIAN SCHOOLS

Acadia University
Faculty of Prof Studies
Dept Phone: 585-1216
Homepage: //business/acadiau.ca
Did Not Respond--2005-2006 Listing

Wolfville Canada   B4P 2R6
Manning Sch of Bus Adm
21 University Ave.

(902) Fax=585-1085
acadiau.ca   BBA
                        Kerrianne Stewart

Name	Rank	Phone	Email					
McLeod, Bill	Dean							
Knowles, David	Prof	585-1216	david.knowles	FV	MBA	95	Queen's	
Hutchinson, Ian R.	Assoc	585-1216	ian.hutchinson	IA	PHD	00	Queen's	&
Corkum, Patricia E.	Asst	585-1216	pat.corkum	FX	MBA		Dalhousie	&
Feltmate, Ian	Asst	585-1216	ian.feltnate	FV	MBA		Dalhousie	7-91

University of Alberta
Dept of Accounting & MIS
Dept Phone: 492-3053

EdmontonCanada AB T6G 2R6
School of Business

(780) Fax=492-3325   1968,1973
business.ualberta.ca   BCOM,MBA,PHD
                        Debbie Picken

Name	Rank	Phone	Email					
Tiessen, Peter	C-Pr	492-2808	ptiessen	MF	PHD	75	Minnesota	&1975
Cooper, David J.	Prof	492-5413	dcooper	WGH	PHD	79	Manchest	1989
Certified General Accountants Professor of Accounting								
Gaa, James C.	Prof	492-5388	jgaa	BJTW	PHD	82.	Illinois	1995
Gibbins, Michael	Prof	492-2718	mgibbins	FAB	PHD	76.	Cornell	&1984
Winspear Foundation Distinguished Chair in Professional Accounting								
Jamal, Karim	Prof	492-5829	kjamal	ABJK	PHD	91.	Minnesota	&1989
Chartered Accountants Chair								
Kao, Jennifer L.	Prof	492-7972	jkao	F	PHD	91	Brit Colum	&1998
Scott, Thomas W.	Prof	492-2350	twscott	FM	PHD	88	Queens	1985
Lee, Jason	Assoc	492-4839	jasonlee	FI	PHD	91	Alberta	1998
Wier, Heather A.	Assoc	492-5752	wierh	CF	PHD	94.	Cornell	&1992
Amerongen, Loretta	VAsst	492-2225	lamerong	FVX	PHD	96	Alberta	&1996
Choy, Amy	Asst	492-2585	ac31	AF	PHD	05	U Wash	2005
Gao, Yanmin	Asst	492-9547	yanmin	FTY	PHD	06	Brit Colum	2006
Hilton, Andrew (Sandy)	Asst	492-6205	hilton	FI	PHD	03	Waterloo	&2002
Matthews, Thomas	Asst	492-9064	tm9	XFIM	PHD	02	Waterloo	2001
Sabac, Florin	Asst	492-8791	fsabac	MTY	PHD	01	Brit Colum	2000
Tian, Joyce	Asst	492-8471	jiejoyce	AMTY	PHD	06.	Florida	2006

Athabasca University
Centre for Accounting & Tax
Dept Phone: 675-6328
Homepage: http://business.athabascau.ca

Alberta, Canada   AB T9S 3A3
School of Business
1 University Drive

(780) Fax=675-6338
athabascau.ca   BADM,BGS,BCOMM
                        Linda Doroshenko

Name	Rank	Phone	Email					
Annand, David	D-Pr	675-6193	davida		EDD	98	Alberta	1989
Quon, Pamela	C-As	675-6298	pamelaq		BCOM		Alberta	2001
Byrd, Clarence	Prof	827-3000	clarence		MBA		Michigan	2000
Elloumi, Fathi	Assoc	795-1741	fathie		PHD		Montreal	2000
Wong, Betty	Asst	482-2882	bettyw		BCOM		Alberta	1991
Gillard, Concetta			concetta		CA			
Jensen, Tilly			tillyl		BCOM			*

Bishop's University
Accounting Faculty
Dept Phone: 822-9620
Did Not Respond--2005-2006 Listing

Lennoxvil Canada   PQ J1M 1Z7
Business Division

(819) Fax=822-9720
ubishops.ca   BBA,BABUS
                        Mrs. Marilyn Turner

Name	Rank	Phone	Email					
Robson, William J.	Dean	822-9622	brobson	Mgt	MBA		McMaster	1983
Cunningham, Peter G.	Assoc	822-9600	pcunning	F	MBA		McGill	&
Schenk, Robert B.	Assoc	822-9600	rschenk	M	MBA		SUNY	* & 6-78
Lessard, Camille	Asst	822-9600	clessard	F	MA		Sherbrooke	&

Univ of British Columbia
Division of Accounting
Dept Phone: 822-8502
Homepage: sauder.ubc.ca/faculty/divisions/accounting.cfm

Vancouver Cnda   BC V6T 1Z2
Sauder Sch of Business
2053 Main Mall

(604) Fax=822-9470   (12) 2003,2003
sauder.ubc.ca   BCO,MBA,MSC,PHD
                        Debra Harris

Name	Rank	Phone	Email					
Muzyka, Daniel	Dean	822-8555	dan.muzyka	Pol	PHD	89	Harvard	1999
Simunic, Dan A.	C-Pr	822-8530	dan.simunic	AFMI	PHD	79.	Chicago	&1979
Certified General Accountants Professor								
Feltham, Gerald A.	Emer	822-8397	jerry.feltham	2003	PHD	67.	Berkeley	&1971
Deloitte and Touche Emeritus Professor of Accounting								
Mattessich, Richard V.	Emer	822-8419	richard.matte+	1988	DRP	45	Vienna	&1967
Begley, Joy	Assoc	822-8527	joy.begley	F	PHD	91.	Rochester	1989
Ronald L. Cliff Professor in Accounting								
Chamberlain, Sandra L.	Assoc	822-8531	sandra.chambe+	FM	PHD	91.	Chicago	2001
Deloitte and Touche Chair in Accounting								
Lo, Kin	Assoc	822-8430	kin.lo	FQK	PHD	99.	Nrthwstrn	& 7-99
CA Professorship in Accounting								

Chen, Xia	Asst	822-8528	xia.chen	F	PHD	04	Chicago		2003
Cheng, Qiang	Asst	827-5156	qiang.cheng	F	PHD	02.	Wisconsin		2003
Alisharan, Steve S.	Inst	822-8532	steve.alisharan	FMX	BA	71	Brit Colum	*	&1981
Kroeker, Jeff	Lect	822-8438	jeff.kroeker	FM	MBA	90	Queens	*	1998
Lockwood, Donald	Lect	822-8428	don.lockwood	F	MBA	76	Chicago		&1976
Sinclair, Scott	Lect	827-4413	scott.sinclair	AF	BCO	79	Brit Colum		&2006

Brock University — St CatharinesCda ON L2S 3A1 — (905) Fax=688-9779 — 2003,2003
Department of Accounting — Faculty of Business — brocku.ca — BBA,BACC,MACC
Dept Phone: Ext 3918 — 500 Glenridge Avenue — Marisa Battista
Homepage: www.bus.brocku.ca
phone 688-5550

Kusy, Martin I.	Dean	Ext 4006	mkusy	Mgt	PHD	78	Brit Colum		1998
Young, Allister	C-Ac	Ext 3432	ayoung	X	LLM	01	Toronto	*	1982
Roubi, Raafat R.	Prof	Ext 4186	rroubi	CFUV	PHD	85.	North Tx	*	1-91
Adamson, Ian L.	Assoc	Ext 3911	iadamson	SF	PHD	93	Waterloo		&1987
Bay, Darlene D.	Assoc	Ext 4524	darlene.bay	FM	PHD	97.	Wash St		&2004
Cook, Gail L.	Assoc	Ext 3919	gail.cook	MCSE	PHD	90.	Utah		&2000
Culumovic, Louis	Assoc	Ext 3907	louis.culumovic	ADES	PHD	89	W Ontario		& 7-90
Donnelly, Maureen E.	Assoc	Ext 3914	mdonnelly	ELX	LLM	93	Toronto		&1984
Dunn, Paul	Assoc	Ext 4185	pdunn	FAJ	DBA	99.	Boston U		&1998
Elayan, Fayez	Assoc	Ext 4160	felayan						
Felton, Sandra	Assoc	Ext 3452	sfelton	EFH	PHD	88.	SUNY-Buf		&1976
Herath, Hemantha	Assoc	Ext 3519	hherath		PHD		Auburn		
Myers, Patricia M.	Assoc	Ext 5016	pmyers	AOSE	PHD	95.	Arizona		&2003
Sainty, Barbara J.	Assoc	Ext 3182	bsainty	MF	PHD	95.	Ohio St	*	&1999
Associate Dean									
Scarbrough, D. Paul	Assoc	Ext 3915	paul.scarbrough	M	PHD	87.	Va Tech		1995
Shome, Anamitra	Assoc	Ext 4540	ashome	MS	PHD	98	Concordia		1997
Stillabower, Linda M.	Assoc	Ext 3910	linda	X	PHD	82.	Case Wes		& 7-93
Brown, H. Donald	Asst	Ext 3912	brown	EM	MSC	85	Saskatch	*	& 7-85
Li, Jennifer	Asst	Ext 4238	jennifer.li	FT	PHD	03	Massey		2003
Nikitkov, Alexia	Asst	Ext 3271	alex.nikitkov	SM	PHD	04.	Missouri		8-04
Trabelsi, Samir	Asst	Ext 4463	samir.trabelsi	FT	PHD	05	HEC-Mont		2004

University of Calgary — Calgary, Canada AB T2N 1N4 — (403) Fax=210-2217 — 1985,1985
Accounting Area — Haskayne School of Bus — haskayne.ucalgary.ca — BCOMM,MBA,PHD
Dept Phone: 220-3812 — 2500 University Drive, NW — Ms. Sylvia Fuchek
Homepage: www.haskayne.ucalgary.ca/programs/undergrad/bcomm/acct

Jones, Vern	Dean$	220-5689	vern.jones	SGMA	PHD	75	Brit Colum		1978
Beaulieu, Philip R.	C-Ac	220-7304	philip.beaulieu	FMBA	PHD	91.	U Wash		1991
Green, Duncan L.	C-Ac	220-7171	duncan.green	FM	MSC	89	Saskatch		&1989
Neu, Dean	Prof	220-4836	dean.neu	B	PHD	89	Queen's		&1989
Future Fund Professor of Accounting; Director, Centre for Public Interest Atg									
Herremans, Irene M.	Assoc	220-8320	irene.herremans	BIJM	PHD	89.	Kent St		& 9-89
Jones, Stuart H.	Assoc	220-3341	stuart.jones	FM	PHD	70	Wales		&1978
Rahaman, Abu Shiraz	Assoc	220-8538	abu_shiraz.rah+	SB	PHD	98	Waikato		&2002
Simmons, Cynthia V.	Assoc	220-3807	cynthia.simmons	BMW	PHD	89.	Houston		1988
Warsame, Hussein	Assoc	220-7169	hussein.warsame	X	PHD	95	Calgary		2000
Wright, Michael E.	Assoc	220-7838	mighael.wright	FIZW	PHD	89	Queen's		1989
Everett, Jeffery	Asst	220-3812	jeff.everett	AEG	PHD	01	Calgary		2003
Irvine, Wayne	Inst	220-7171	wayne.irvine	AF	BCOM	80	Calgary		&1992
Larka, Anita	Inst	220-9171	anita.lakra	C	BCOM	87	Calgary		&1995

Carleton University — Ottawa, Canada ON K1S 5B6 — (613) Fax=520-4427
Accounting Faculty — School of Business — carleton.ca
Dept Phone: 520-2388 — 1125 Colonel By Drive — Anne Irvin
Homepage: http://www.business.carleton.ca
Did Not Respond--2005-2006 Listing; phone 520-2600

Cray, David	C-Ac	520-2395	david_cray	Mgt	PHD		Wisconsin		
Brouard, Francois	Asst	Ext 2213	francois_brouard	BEFX	DBA	04			&1999
Pollanen, Raili M.	Asst	Ext 2376	raili_pollanen	MU	PHD	97	Lancaster		2000
Soukhovtseva, Olga	Asst	Ext 2370	olga_soukhou+	A	PHD	79	Moscow St		2004
Becker, Hilary	Inst	Ext 3717	hilary_becker	F	MBA	90	Windsor		1996
Clarke-Okah, Ann	Inst	Ext 2374	ann_clarke-okah	F	BA	73	Simon Fr		&1983
Herauf, Darrell	Inst	Ext 2371	darrell_herauf	F	BCOM	76	Alberta		&1985
Maurice, Jacques	Inst	Ext 2393	jacques_maurice	FC	MBA	99	McGill	*	&1988

Concordia University — Montreal, Canada PQ H3G 1M8 — (514) Fax=848-4518 — (1) 1997,1997
Department of Accountancy — John Molson Sch of Bus — jmsb.concordia.ca — BCOM,MBA,MS,PHD
Dept Phone: 848-2424 — 1455 de Maisonneuve Blvd — Mary Mullins
Did Not Respond--2005-2006 Listing;email @1=vax2.concordia.ca; phone 848-2424

Magnan, Michel L.	Prof	Ext 4145	mmagnan	FMES	PHD	89	U Wash		&2000
Associate Dean, External Affairs & Executive Programs									

Aly, Ibrahim M.	Assoc		ialy	FMBQ	PHD	86.	North Tx		1989
Dauderis, Henry J.	Assoc	Ext 2759	dauderi	ASFI	MBA	72	McGill		&1967
on sabbitical 2005-2006									
Draimin, K. Charles	Assoc	Ext 2795	draimin@1	TWN	PHD	82	Concordia		&1973
Gheyara, Kelly F.	Assoc	Ext 2757	kellyd@1	MS	PHD	79.	Okla St		&1986
Kanaan, George K.	Assoc	Ext 2720	georgek@1	FMEV	PHD	84.	Wisconsin		1987
Associate Dean Academic & Student Affairs, Undergraduate Programs									
Kapoor, M. Rai	Assoc		rkapoor	FM	PHD	86	Toronto	*	1980
sabbatical 2005-2006									
Peltier-Rivest, Dominic	Assoc	Ext 2778	drivest	F	PHD	96.	Fla St		2000
Segovia, Juan J.	Assoc	Ext 2761	jjsegovia	FM	PHD	79	Paris		1983
Boulianne, Emilio	Asst	Ext 2754	emilio	MS	PHD	00	Montreal		1999
Cho, Charles	Asst			F	PHD	07.	Cen Fla		2007
Ho, Sandra W.	Asst	Ext 2747	sho	AFM	PHD	00	HK Poly		&2004
Islam, Majidul	Asst	Ext 2768	mislam	FMA	PHD	78	Moscow		2000
Lara, Rafael M.	Asst	Ext 4143	rlara	FM	PHD	03.	Colorado		2003
Lowenfeld, George	Asst	Ext 2745	glowe	XA	ABD		Toronto		&1976
Markarian, Garen	Asst	Ext 2749	gmarkarian	MF	PHD	04.	Case Wes		2004
Mustafa, Sameer	Asst	Ext 2765	smustafa	AM	PHD	03	Clev St		2001
Delaney, Patrick	Lect	Ext 2751	pdelaney	AF	BCOM	81	Concordia		&1997
Fayerman, G.	Lect	Ext 7343	gfay	F	MBA	89	McGill		&1984
Ramsaran, Tara	Lect	Ext 2756	ramsaran	T	MBA	00	Concordia		&2001
Robinson, Sandra	Lect	Ext 2748	srobinson	AF	MBA	76	NYU		&1980
Director, Accountancy Co-op									
Roscoe, W.	Lect	Ext 2774	wroscoe	AF	BCOM	79	Concordia		&1986
Director, D. Acco. Programme									

Dalhousie University
Department of Accounting
Dept Phone: 494-7080
Homepage: www.mgmt.dal.ca
Did Not Respond--2005-2006 Listing

Halifax, Canada NS B3H 3J5
School of Business Adm
6152 Coburg Road

(902) Fax = 494-1107
dal.ca

2003,2003
BCOM,MBA
Susan DeYoung, Viola Caume

Klapstein, Raymond	D-Ac	494-7080	r.e.klapstein	Bus	MBA	75	Dalhousie		1977
Conrod, Joan E. D.	Prof	494-1797	j.conrad	FT	MBA	86	Toronto		&1989
Oppong, Andrews	Prof	494-1809	andrews.oppong	MT	PHD	76.	Iowa		1978
Carroll, Ray F.	Assoc	494-1799	r.carroll	FV	PHD	96	Dalhousie		&1987
Cherry, Donald C.	Assoc	494-1823	d.cherry	FEPU	MBA	73	McMaster	*	1978
Dirksen, Charles J.	Assoc	494-1839	c.j.dirksen	MS	DBA	73.	Oregon		1979
Baird, Michael	Asst	494-2419	m.baird		MBA	98	Bowl Gr		1997
MacLean, Bruce W.	Asst	494-1819	b.w.mclean	SA	MBA	72	Dalhousie		&1977

HEC Montreal
Accounting Faculty
Dept Phone: 340-6510
Homepage: www.hec.ca/sco/
Did Not Respond--2005-2006 Listing

Montreal Canada PQ H3T 2A7
School of Business
3000 Chmin d la Cote-Sainte

(514) Fax = 340-5633
hec.ca

2003,2003
BAA,MSC,MBA,PHD

Martel, Louise	C-Pr	340-6785	louise.martel	ADFJ	MSC	81	HEC-Mont		9-78
Boisvert, Hugues	Prof	340-6521	hugues.boisvert	BCMU	PHD	77	Stanford	*	6-86
Drew, James	Prof	340-6513	james.drew	X	LSCC	72	HEC-Mont		&6-75
Fortin, Jacques	Prof	340-6048	jacques.fortin	FLUV	MBA	77	HEC-Mont		&9-74
Gagne, Gilles	Prof	340-6523	gilles.gagne	X	LSCC	61	HEC-Mont		&9-80
Guindon, Michel	Prof	340-6511	michel.guindon	BIMT	PHD	92	Montreal		6-78
Labelle, Real	Prof	340-6374	real.labelle	DLMT	DSC	84	Grenoble		&7-96
Laurin, Claude	Prof	340-6536	claude.laurin	FMG	PHD	96	Brit Colum	*	D-99
Peres, Andre	Prof	340-6522	andre.peres	DOSV	LSCC	73	HEC-Mont		&O-75
Vezina, Michel	Prof	340-6514	michel.vezina	MSU	DSC	95	Montpell		&9-85
Andre, Paul E.	Assoc	340-6528	paul.andre	FM	PHD	96	Waterloo		&8-97
Bergeron, Jacques	Assoc	340-6563	jacques.bergeron	DS	MBA	03	HEC-Mont		&6-04
Chevalier, Gilles	Assoc	340-7016	gilles.chevalier	LJ	PHD	75.	Illinois		&7-02
Cote, Louise	Assoc	340-7022	louise.cote	JMV	PHD	95	Quebec		&8-01
Girard, Aline C.	Assoc	340-6502	aline.girard	BFIN	PHD	90.	Tennessee		&6-89
LaFortune, Andree	Assoc	340-6529	andree.lafortune	BFMS	MBA	86	Laval		&9-82
Laroche, D.-Claude	Assoc	340-6525	claude.laroche	AFO	MBA	80	HEC-Mont		&8-78
Maher, Michel	Assoc	340-6564	michel.2.maher	X	LLD	03	Ottawa		6-04
Mersereau, Alexander	Assoc	340-5643	alexander.mer+	CMU	PHD	99	Paris	*	D-96
Morin, Danielle	Assoc	340-6787	danielle.morin	AMUY	PHD	99	ENAP		&8-99
Naud, Marjolaine	Assoc	340-6786	marjolaine.naud	FXW	MFIS	90	Sherbrooke		&6-92
Paul, Diane	Assoc	340-5610	diane.paul	AJMT	MSC	93	HEC-Mont		&9-86
Prieur, Nicole	Assoc	340-6519	nicole.prieur	X	LLM	00	HEC-Mont		6-99
Turbide, Johanne	Assoc	340-6555	johanne.turbide	FMNU	PHD	97	Warwick		&6-95
Van The, Nhut	Assoc	340-6534	nhut.van-the	BFM	PHD	82.	Illinois		&8-76
Vidal, Jean-Pierre	Assoc	340-6514	jean-pierre.v+	GX	PHD	90	Montreal		&6-02
Bozec, Yves	Asst	340-6560	yves.bozec	FM	PHD	04	HEC-Mont	*	1-04
Francoeur, Claude	Asst	340-6847	claude.francoeur	FM	PHD	03	Quebec		6-03
Morissette, Raymond	Asst	340-6517	raymond.moris+	AMU	PHD	97	Waterloo	* &	4-04
Rakotonjanahary, Philemon	Asst	340-6517	philemon.rak+	ABFI	PHD	99	HEC-Mont		6-01
Schiehll, Eduardo	Asst	340-6516	eduardo.schiehll	FM	PHD	02	HEC-Mont		6-01

Lakehead University
Accounting Faculty
Dept Phone: 343-8386

Thunder Bay, Can ON P7B 5E1
Faculty of Business Adm
955 Oliver Road

(807) Fax = 343-8443
lakeheadu.ca

BADMIN,HBCOM
Arlene / Morna

Dadgostar, Bahram	Dean	343-8400	bahram.dad +	Mgt	PHD	77	Iowa St	1983
Thatcher, Jan C.	C-Ac	343-8534	jan.thatcher	FVA	MSC	88	Saskatch	&1983
Sayed, Naqi	Asst	343-8385	naqi.sayed	FM	PHD	02	Wollong	2002

Laurentian University
Accounting Faculty
Dept Phone: 673-1151

Sudbury, Canada ON P3E 2C6
Sch of Commerce & Adm
Ramsey Lake Road

(705) Fax = 673-6518
laurentian.ca

BCOM,MBA
Diane Daigle Ext 2153

Ganjavi, Ozhand	D-Pr	675-1151	oganjavi	Mgt	PHD	84	W Ontario	7-75
Blanco, Huguette	Prof	675-1151	hblanco	FITY	PHD	94	Lancaster	7-84
Leonard, Valorie	Prof	675-1151	vleonard		MBA	87	Laurentian	& 7-83
Zanibbi, Louis	Prof	675-1151	lzanibbi	BCMU	PHD	89	Bradford	* 7-77
Robichaud, Yves	Assoc	675-1151	robichau		PHD	01	Aixlmars	7-90
Davey, Austin	Asst	675-1151	jadavey		BA	68	W Ontario	& 7-75
McGillis, Sheila	Asst	675-1151	mcgillis		MBA	87	Laurentian	* 7-85
Steinke, Greg L.	Asst	675-1151	gsteinke		MBA	86	Laurentian	& 8-82

Universite Laval
Dept of Accounting Sciences
Dept Phone: 650-0207

Quebec   PQ G1K 7P4
Faculte Science Adm

(418) Fax = 656-2624
ctb.ulaval.ca

2004,2004
DCOM,MBA,PHD

Mantha, Robert W.	Dean$							
Bedard, Jean	Prof	656-2894	jean.bedard	AS	PHD	86.	S Calif	&1985
Coulombe, Daniel	Prof	656-2827	daniel.coulo +	FT	PHD	87,	Brit Colum	&1985
Paquette, Suzanne M.	Prof	656-2796	suzanne.paq +	TY	PHD	94	Waterloo	&1994

Universite Laval
School of Accounting
Dept Phone: 656-2131
   phone 656-2131 #5158

Quebec   PQ G1K 7P4
Faculte des sci de adm

(418) Fax = 656-7746
fsa.ulaval.ca

BCOM,MBA,PHD
Caroline Demers

Gosselin, Maurice	D-Pr	656-5158	maurice.goss +	MB	DBA	95	Boston U	* &1988
Carpentier, Cecile	Prof	Ext 6385	cecile.carpen +		PHD	98	Lille II	1999
Cormier, Elise	Prof	Ext 3784	elise.cormier		PHD	96	Laval	1999
Desfleurs, Aurelie	Prof	Ext 3167	aurelie.defleurs		PHD	04	Laval	2004
Gendeon, Yves	Prof	656-2431			PHD	97	Laval	2006
Gvenin-Paracini, Henri	Prof	656-3936			ABD			2006
Henri, Jean-Francois	Prof	656-7737	jean-f +.henri		PHD	03	HEC-Mont	1999
Pare, Paul-Victor	Prof	656-7302	paul-victor.pare	FM	PHD	83.	Michigan	1981

University of Lethbridge
Accounting Faculty
Dept Phone: 329-2633
Homepage: http://home.uleth.ca/man/

Lethbridge Canad AB T1K 3M4
Faculty of Management
4401 University Drive

(403) Fax = 329-2038
uleth.ca

BMGT
Corie Slauenwhite

Lindsay, R. Murray	Dean	329-2633	m.lindsay	BMST	PHD	88	Lancaster	* 2005
Downey, Angela	C-Ac	329-2019	angela.downy	MQUB	PHD	00	W Ontario	* 1996
Nelson, Toni L.	Assoc	329-2594	melson	EFMQ	PHD	92.	Oregon	&1990
Thomas, Stuart	Assoc	329-2067	stuart.thomas	BM	PHD	98	Fla Intl	7-98
Carnaghan, Carla	Asst	329-2351	carla.carnaghan	BFS	PHD	99	Alberta	2006
Kopp, Lori S.	Asst	329-5197	lori.kopp	ABME	PHD	00.	Alabama	& 7-02
Baker, Glen	Lect	329-2115	glen.baker	F	BCOM	77	Calgary	* 7-02
Jarvie, Deborah	Lect	329-2151	jarvdl	X	MSC	02	Lethbridge	7-00

University of Manitoba
Dept of Accounting & Finance
Dept Phone: 474-9362
Homepage: www.umanitoba.ca/management
   email @1 = cc.umanitoba.ca

Winnipeg Canada MB R3T 5V4
Asper Sch of Business
181 Freedman Crescent

(204) Fax = 474-7545
umanitoba.ca

1999,1999
BCOM,MBA
Colleen Loewen

Feltham, Glenn D.	Dean	747-8434		X	PHD	95	Waterloo	2004
Stangeland, David	H-Pr	474-9362	d_strangeland	Fnce	PHD	94	Alberta	1991
Morrill, Cameron K. J.	Assoc	474-8435	cameron_morrill	FM	PHD	91	Alberta	1997
Biscontri, Robert G.	Asst	474-6255	biscontr@1	MQ	PHD	02	Macquarie	2004
Morrill, Janet	Asst	474-6854	janet_morrill	AF	PHD	94	Alberta	1997

Mc Gill University
Accounting Area
Dept Phone: 398-4057

Montreal, Canada PQ H3A 1G5
Faculty of Management
1001 Sherbrooke St West

(514) Fax = 398-3876
management.mcgill.ca

BCOM,MBA,PHD
Karen Robertson

Drury, Donald H.	C-Pr	398-4057	drury	MS	PHD	76	Nrthwstrn	* 1976
Fortin, Steve	Asst	398-4021	fortin	F	PHD	01	Waterloo	&2001
Tsang, Desmond	Asst	398-5417	tsang	F	PHD	06	Berkeley	2006
Zhou, Lei	Asst	398-6228	zhou	M	PHD	02.	Maryland	2004

Cecere, Ralph	Lect	398-4000	cecere	F	BCOM	88	McGill	&1993
Eley, Robin	Lect	398-6161	robin	FT	MBA	83	McGill	&1989
Goldsman, Larry	Lect	398-1262	goldsman	F	BCOM	77	Concordia	&1997
Levy, Philippe	Lect	398-4064	levy	FM	MBA	90	McGill	&1990
Valliant, Bill	Lect	398-4000	valliant	F	BSC	69	Holy Cr	&1994

McMaster University — Hamilton, Canada ON L8S 4M4 — (905) Fax=521-8995 — 2006

Accounting & Fin Mgt Srvs Ar — DeGroote Sch Business — mcmaster.ca — BCOM,HONBCO,MBA

Dept Phone: Ext24630 — 1280 Main Street, West — Alicja Siek

phone 525-9140 Ext 24630

Bates, Paul	Dean	Ext24431	batesp					7-04
Shehata, Mohamed	C-Pr	Ext27030	shehata	FM	PHD	88.	Florida	7-87
Amershi, Amin H.	Prof	Ext23969	amershi	MF	PHD	79	Brit Colum	7-04
AIC Chair in Valuation and Portfolio Management								
Nainar, S. M. Khalid	Prof	Ext23990	nainar	FZJI	PHD	89	Florida	7-88
Chan, Y. C. Lilian	Assoc	Ext23974	ylchan	CFM	PHD	85.	Va Tech	* & 1-86
Kanagaretnam, Kiridaran	Assoc	Extw7857	giri	FM	PHD	00.	Syracuse	7-02
Lrang, Xinghua	Asst	Ext23992	xliang	F	PHD	07	Toronto	7-06
Mohammed, Emad	Asst	Ext27432	mohde	F	PHD	03	Geo St	7-04
Seaman, Alfred E.	Asst	Ext23991	seaman	MA	PHD	95	Queens	* 7-01
Siam, J.	Asst	Ext27028	siamj	F	PHD	01	Concordia	7-02
Hao, H. T.	Lect	Ext23984	haohorn	FM	ABD		SUNY-Buf	7-99

Memorial U of Newfoundland — St.John's Canada NL A1B 3X5 — (709) Fax=737-7680 — 2002,2002

Accounting Faculty — Faculty of Business Adm — morgan.ucs.mun.ca — BCOM,BBA,MBA

Dept Phone: 737-8854

Homepage: www.busi.mun.ca

Gorman, Gary	Dean	737-8851	ggorman	Entr	PHD	01	Stirling	1984
Cumby, Judy	Assoc	737-4006	jcumby	F	MBA	94	Memorial	&1994
Downer, Pauline	Assoc	737-8510	pdowner	F	MBA	98	Memorial	&1998
King, Wayne	Assoc	737-7937	wking	F	MBA	69	McMaster	&1991
Pittman, Jeffrey A.	Assoc	737-8510	jpittman	F	PHD	00	Waterloo	* &2000
Wong, Shu-Lun	Assoc	737-8510	swong	MFEC	MSC	74	Durham	* 1985

Mount Allison University — Sackville Canada NB E4L 1A7 — (506) Fax=364-2625

Accounting Faculty — Commerce Department — mta.ca

Dept Phone: 364-2326 — 144 Main Street — Darlene Estabrooks

Homepage: http://www.mta.ca/faculty/socsci/commerce/index.htm

Hudson, Richard	H-Ac	364-2332	rhudson	JCQ	PHD	84	Ottawa	* 7-85
Berry, Paul	Assoc	364-2330	pberry	FQM	MBA	82	Queens	* 7-82
Farooqi, Nauman	Assoc	364-2281	nfaroogi	FM	PHD	93	St Louis	7-00

Mount Saint Vincent Univ — Nova Scotia Can NS B3M 2J6 — (902) Fax=445-2582

Accounting Faculty — Dept of Business Adm — msvu.ca — BBA

Dept Phone: 457-6175 — 166 Bedford Highway — Miriam Gallant

Lyon, Mary	Dean	457-6124	mary.lyon					
Young, Jeff	C-Pr	457-6361	jeff.young	Mgt	PHD	94	Dalhousie	9-87
Doyle, Wendy	Prof	457-6506	wendy.doyle	VFGN	MBA	80	Dalhousie	& 7-74
Tilley, J. Rod	Assoc	457-6392	rod.tilley	FIMP	MBA	87	Dalhousie	& 7-83
Hicks, Elizabeth	Asst	457-6366	elizabeth.hicks	FXWJ	MBA	94	StMry-Cd	& 9-85

University of New Brunswick — Fredericton, Can NB E3B 5A3 — (506) Fax=453-3561

Accounting Faculty POBox4400 — Faculty Adminstration — unb.ca — BBA,MBA

Dept Phone: 453-4869 — Anna Ward

Homepage: www.business.unbf.ca

Coleman, Daniel F.	Dean	453-4869	dan	Mgt	PHD		SUNY-Buf	1986
Abekah, Joseph Yaw	Prof	453-4869	abekah	FIM	PHD	91.	Nebraska	1991
Maher, Elin	Prof	453-4869	mahere	CMI	MBA	93	Maine	&1988
Maher, Robert	Prof	453-4869	maherr	IVF	MBA	75	McGill	&1988
Ritchie, Pamela C.	Prof	453-4869	pr	HFTY	PHD	89	Lancaster	1984
Trenholm, Barbara A.	Prof	453-4869	trenholb	AF	MBA	85	Maine	&1980
Betts, Norman M.	Assoc	453-4869	betts	FTY	PHD	92	Queen's	&1992
Leonard, Glenn	Inst	453-4869	rleonard		MA		New Bruns	2006
Hinton, Joanne	SrTch	453-4869	jhinton		BSC		Guelph	2005

Univ New Brunswick-St John — Saint John, Can NB E2L 4L5 — (506) Fax=648-5574

Accounting Faculty — Faculty of Business — unbsj.ca — BBA,MBA

Dept Phone: 648-5571 — P.O. Box 5050 — Melody McElman

Homepage: www.business.unbsj.ca

Did Not Respond--2005-2006 Listing

Rinehart, Shelley M.	Dean	648-5677	rinehart	Mktg	PHD	98	Oklahoma	1988
Hurley, Catherine	Prof	648-5820	churley	MCFD	MBA		N Brunswk	&1997
Mellon, Mark J.	Prof	648-5852	mmellon		MBA		StMry-Cd	
Dunstan, Judith	Inst	648-5740	dunstan		LLB	95	Toronto	&1999
Keeping, David	Inst	648-5572	dkeeping		MBA	03	St Marys	&2003

University of Ottawa — Ottawa, Canada ON K1N 6N5 — (613) Fax=562-5164 — 2003,2003
Accounting/Finance/Info Sys — School of Mgt CANADA — management.uottawa.ca — BCOMM
Dept Phone: 562-5800 — 55 Laurier Ave East
Homepage: www.management.uottawa.ca
phone 613-562-5800 Ext 4757

Name	Rank	Ext	Email		Degree	Yr	School		
Kelly, Michael	Dean	Ext 5815	kelly		PHD	86	Carleton		
Bujaki, Merridee L.	C-Ac	Ext 4757	bujaki	FA	PHD	96	Queen's		&1995
Adjaoud, Fodil	Prof	Ext 4767	adjaoud	FM	PHD	82	Laval	*	1981
Zeghal, Daniel	Prof	Ext 4769	zeghal	FM	PHD	79	Laval		1977
Bozec, Richard	Assoc	Ext 4739	bozec	FG	PHD	01	Quebec		1997
Durocher, Sylvain	Assoc	Ext 4734	durocher	FIN	PHD	03	Quebec		&2006
Eden, Ronald	Assoc	Ext 4770	eden	MGN	PHD	94	SUNY		1988
Maingot, Michael	Assoc	Ext 4918	maingot	FA	PHD	81	Belfast		&1981
Yaansah, Robert A.	Assoc	Ext 4909	yaansah	FM	PHD	90	Lancaster		&2001
Ben Amar, Walid	Asst	Ext 4723	benamar	FM	PHD	03	HEC-Mont		2004
Kalyta, Pavlo	Asst	Ext 4702	kalyta	FMC	PHD	07	Concordia		2006
Pedwell, Kathryn	Asst	Ext 4766	pedwell	X	PHD	00	Calgary		1996
Pyper, Rhonda	Asst	Ext 4790	pyper	MB	MBA	03	Laurentian	*	2006
Collier, Robert	TchAc	Ext 4741	collier	CF	BAH	71	Carleton	*	2003
Conheady, Brian	TchAc	Ext 4758	conheady	CM	MBA	77	McGill	*	&2006

Univ du Quebec en Outaouais — Gatineau Canada PQ J8X 3X7 — (819) Fax=773-1760
Accounting Department — Dept des Sci Comptables — uqo.ca — BAAS,DESS,MBA
Dept Phone: Ext 1755 — 101, Rue St-Jean-Bosco — Carmen Gagne
Homepage: www.uqo.ca/secteors/sciences-comptable
phone: 595-3900

Name	Rank	Ext	Email		Degree	School		
Poirier, Gilles	H	Ext 1765	gilles.poirier	CEMJ	PHD		*	
Beauregard, Claude		Ext 1751	claude.beaur+	X	MSC			&
Bigras, Diane		Ext 1767	diane.bigras	FG	MSC			
Blanchette, Michel		Ext 1752	michel.blan+	FTVY	MBA		*	&
Briand, Louise		Ext 1668	louise.briand	AJU	PHD			&
Charron, Pierre		Ext 1634	pierre.charron	CMF	MBA			&
Fontaine, Marie		Ext 1739	marie.fontaine		PHD			
Labelle, Andre		Ext 1761	andre.labelle	X	MFIS			&
LeRoux, Emile		Ext 1753	emile.leroux	F	BCOM			&
Lussier, Madeleine		Ext 1766	madeleine.lu+	ACM	BCOM			&

Univ du Quebec a Montreal — Montreal Canada PQ H3C 3P8 — (514) Fax=987-6629
Accounting Department — School of Mgt POBox8888 — uqam.ca — BBA,MSC,MBA,PHD
Dept Phone: 987-3000 — 315 rue Ste-Catherine Est — Helene Harnois
Homepage: http://www.er.uqam.ca/nobel/dsc
phone 987-3000 Ext 4124

Name	Rank	Ext	Email		Degree	Yr	School		
LeDoux, Marie-Josee	D								
Naciri, M. Ahmed	C-Pr	Ext 7765	naciri.ahmed	M	PHD		Laval		8-82
Belzile, Rejean	Prof	Ext 7732	belzile.rejean	M	PHD		Montreal		& 7-81
Bernard, Michel	Prof	Ext 4217	bernard.michel	F	MBA		Montreal	*	8-73
Bilodeau, Julien	Prof	Ext 4211	bilodeau.julien	F	PHD		W Ontario		& 6-87
Breton, Gaetan	Prof	Ext 4774	breton.gaetan	F	PHD		London		& 6-90
Callimaci, Antonello	Prof	Ext 8938	callimaci.an+	FT	PHD	97.	Florida		& 6-91
Caron, Marie-Andree	Prof	Ext 2094			PHD		HEC-Mont	*	
Chabot, Marc	Prof	Ext 4892	chabot.marc	M	PHD		Montreal		& 7-80
Chlala, Nadi	Prof	Ext 4426	chlala.nadi	F	MSC		Saskatch	*	& 1-78
Clapin-Pepin, Daniel	Prof	Ext 4212	clapin-p+.d+	A	PHD		Quebec		& 7-80
Cormier, Denis	Prof	Ext 8358	cormier.denis	FT	DSC		Mons	# *	& 6-84
Cucumel, Guy	Prof	Ext 4701	cucumel.guy	M	DSC		Paris		6-91
Fontaine, Richard	Prof	Ext 2480			PHD		Quebec		
Fortin, Anne	Prof	Ext 3987	fortin.anne	F	PHD	86.	Illinois		6-83
Gagnon-Valotaire, Danielle	Prof	Ext 4222	gagon-valota+	F	MBA		Montreal		& 8-79
Gelinas, Francine	Prof	Ext 4206	gelinas.franc+	M	BAA		Sherbrook		& 8-79
Giguere, Pierre	Prof	Ext 4210	giguere.pierre	M	LIC		Montreal		& 8-80
Heroux, Sylvie	Prof	Ext 0274			PHD		Quebec		
Houle, Sylvain	Prof	Ext 4775			PHD		Laval		
Laferriere, Claude	Prof	Ext 4218	laferriere.cla+	X	MFIS		Sherbrook		& 8-80
Lafond-LaVallee, Carole	Prof	Ext 8331	lafond-lavalle+	F	MA		Montreal		& 6-78
Lanoue, Nicole	Prof	Ext 8557	lanoue.nicole	F	PHD	93	Laval		& 7-79
Lanthier, Denise	Prof	Ext 4208	lanthier.denise	F	MBA		McGill		& 9-80
Lauly, Jean-Paul	Prof	Ext 3408			MBA		Paris		
Lauzon, Leo-Paul	Prof	Ext 3954	lauzon.leo-paul	M	DSG		Grenoble	*	6-73
Ledoux, Marie-Josee	Prof	Ext 0287	ledoux.marie_+	M	PHD		Waterloo	*	& 7-94
McDonough, Helen L.	Prof	Ext 3139	mc_donoug_	M	MBA		Concordia	*	6-85
Menard, Louis	Prof	Ext 4209	meñard.louis	F	MBA		Montreal		& 8-82
Montreuil, Francis	Prof	Ext 4865	montreuil.fr+	X	MFIS		Sherbrook		& 1-84
Pilote, Claude	Prof	Ext 7944	pilote.claude	S	PHD	90.	S Calif		& 7-94
Rassi, Faouzi	Prof	Ext 3746	rassi@1	M	DSCE		Geneva		6-83
Renault, Micheline	Prof	Ext 6508	renault.miche+	M	DSC		Mons		& 6-89

Saremejeanne, Jacques	Prof	Ext 6564			PHD	Quebec	
Veronneau, Pierre	Prof	Ext 7999	veronneau.pi+	F	PHD	Montreal	& 7-81
Viger, Chantal	Prof	Ext 6986	viger.chantal	F	PHD	96. Drexel	& 6-89
Villeneuve, Guy	Prof	Ext 4459	villeneuve.guy	S	PHD	Laval	& 7-80

Queen's University — Kingston Canada ON K7L 3N6 (613) Fax=533-2013 1999,1999
Accounting Faculty — Queen's Sch of Business business.queensu.ca BCO,MBA,MSC,PHD
Dept Phone: 533-2305 — 143 Union St Goodes Hall Maureen Boisvert

Saunders, David M.	Dean	533-2305	dsaunders	Mgt	PHD	84	W Ontario	2003
Salterio, Steven E.	Prof	533-2035	ssalterio	AF	PHD	93.	Michigan	&2003
Thornton, Daniel B.	Prof	533-6194	dthornton	F	PHD	78	York	&1993
Anger, T. G.	Assoc	533-2311	tanger	F	MBA	82	Queen's	1982
Shearer, Teri L.	Assoc	533-2318	ts16	WTM	PHD	96.	Iowa	&1997
Welker, Michael	Assoc	533-2317	mw18	FT	PHD	93.	Iowa	&1996
Free, Clinton	Asst	533-3255	cfree	FI	PHD	04	Oxford	2004
Moore, John C.	Asst	533-2331	moorejc	BCME	MBA	76	Queen's	* 1980
Murphy, Pam	Asst	533-2305	pmurphy	AF	PHD	07	Wisconsin	2007
Pae, Jinhan	Asst		jpae		PHD	99	Brit Colum	2002

University of Regina — Regina, Canada SK S4S OA2 (306) Fax=585-4805
Accounting Faculty — Faculty of Bus Adm uregina.ca DIPBA,BBA
Dept Phone: 585-4724 — 3737 Wascana Parkway Ms. Sheila Potts, Adm Asst

Garven, Garnet	Dean	585-4162	garnet.garven		MBA	80	Saskatch	1996
Anderson, Robert	Prof	585-4728	robert.anderson		PHD	97	Saskatch	2001
Austin, Bryan J.	Prof	585-4783	bryan.austin	F	MSC	80	Oregon	&1975
Rennie, Morina D.	Prof	585-4715	morina.rennie	ABEF	PHD	89	Alberta	* &1982
Associate Dean								
Senkow, David W.	Prof	585-4719	david.senkow	CFM	PHD	92.	Minnesota	1992
Baker, Ronald	Asst	337-2382	ronald.bake		MBA	98	Athabasc	2003
Bonner, Bill	Asst	585-4794	bill.bonner		PHD	02	Calgary	&2003
Sylvestre, Glenys	Inst	585-4964	glenys.sylves+		BADM	94	Saskatch	2000

St. Francis Xavier Univ — Antigonish NS B2G 2W5 (902) Fax=867-5385
Dept of Business Adm — Gerald Schwartz Sch Bus stfx.ca BBA,BIS
Dept Phone: 867-2167 — West Street Anne Marie Durant

Stuart, F. Ian	D	867-2167						
Gallant, Leo T.	Prof	863-3300	lgallant	FMH	FCA	71	Queens	&1973
Madden, Robert F.	Prof	863-3300	rmadden	MF	FCA	71	Queens	&1971
MacAulay, Ken	Assoc	863-3300	kmacaula	FTW	PHD	97	Queen's	&1992
Oxner, Mary	Asst	863-3300	mmoxner	FC	PHD	06	Alberta	&2000

Saint Mary's University — Halifax, Canada NS B3H 3C3 (902) Fax=420-5011 2004,2004
Department of Accounting — Faculty of Commerce smu.ca BCOM,MBA,MBA-CM
Dept Phone: 420-5617 — 903 Robie Street Cathy Golden
Homepage: http://stmarys.ca/academic/commerce/accounting/index.htm

Secord, Peter C.	C-Ac	420-5462	peter.secord	FVIH	PHD	03	Reading	# * 1989
Cheng, Thomas T.	Prof	420-5800	thomas.cheng	MFA	PHD	81.	Missouri	# * &1992
Chesley, G. Richard	Emer	420-5624	d.chesley	MFT	PHD	73.	Ohio St	&1989
Gorman, F. Barry	Prof	420-5619	barry.gorman	X	PHD	91	Bath	&1979
Song, Xiaofei	Prof	420-5683	xiaofei.song	F	PHD	99	Baruch	1998
Young, Nicola	Prof	420-5108	nicola.young	FVP	MBA	82	Dalhousie	&1993
Bateman, David H.	Assoc	420-5623	david.bateman	DSPE	MBA	83	Dalhousie	& 9-80
Ansong, Granville	Asst	420-5618	granville.ansong	FTMY	PHD	88	Queens	1990
Lightstone, Karen	Asst	420-5625	karen.lightstone	FEU	PHD		Portsmouth	&1999
Power, Jeffrey	Asst	420-5621	jeff.power	MCE	PHD	91.	Purdue	* 1995

Univ of Saskatchewan — Saskatoon Cnda SK S7N 5A7 (306) Fax=966-2514
Department of Accounting — College of Commerce commerce.usask.ca BCOM,MSC,MPACC
Dept Phone: 966-8395 — 25 Campus Drive Mrs. Christine Hillis

Vaidyanathan, Ganesh	C-Ac	966-8416	vaidyanathan	BCDS	PHD	91	Waterloo	* 2001
Lindsay, W. Daryl	Prof	966-8399	dlindsay	AF	PHD	80.	Minnesota	&1971
Buhr, Nola	Assoc	966-4788	buhr	FHW	PHD	94	W Ontario	&2000
Entwistle, Gary M.	Assoc	966-8403	entwistle	FAIW	PHD	97	W Ontario	&1990
Kalagnanam, Suresh S.	Assoc	966-8404	kalagnamam	CMB	PHD	97.	Wisconsin	* 1996
Kim, Soon Nam	Assoc	966-1642	kim	FMW	PHD	01	Wollong	2005
Phillips, Fred	Assoc	966-8401	phillips	AFB	PHD	96.	Tx-Austin	&1996
Sheehan, Norman T.	Assoc	966-4801	sheehan	MUB	PHD	02	Norwegia	* 2002
Fox, Ken	Asst	966-7729	fox	FO	MPAC	01	Saskatch	2006
Johnstone, Nathalie	Asst	966-6478	johnstone	FX	MPAC	00	Saskatch	&2005
Kalesnikoff, Doug	Asst	966-1471	kalesnikoff	AFO	BCOM	77	Saskatch	&2004
Klassen, Mark	Asst	966-1300	klassen	MS	MBA	94	Saskatch	* 2004
Mackintosh, Brandy	Asst	966-7749	mackinstosh	FA	BCOM	97	Saskatch	2006

Universite de Sherbrooke
Dept of Accounting & Tax — Sherbrooke Cnda QC J1K 2R1 — Faculte d'admin — (819) Fax=821-8010 — adm.usherb.ca — BBA,MS,MBA,DBA
Dept Phone: 821-8000
Did Not Respond Again--2003-2004 Listing: phone 821-8000 Ext 2368

Name	Rank	Phone	Email		Degree	Yr	School	
Noel, Roger	Dean	Ext 2312		FR	MS	70	Sherbrook	&
Allard, Marie-Pier	Prof	Ext 2348	mpallard	X	MFIS	01	Sherbrook	2001
Beauchesne, Alain	Prof	Ext 2322		FT	LCOM	69	Laval	&1972
Beaulieu, Suzanne	Prof	Ext 2309	sbeaulieu	S	MS	92	HEC-Mont	&1986
Bedard, Gerald	Prof		gbedard	X	MFIS	84	Sherbrook	2001
Blanchette, Danielle	Prof	Ext 2326	dblanchette	CFB	PHD	01	UQVAM	&1996
Comtois, Jean	Prof	Ext 2357		F	MCOM	67	Sherbrook	&1968
Godbout, Luc	Prof		lgodbout	X	MRIS	95	Sherbrook	2002
Goulet, Bernard	Prof	Ext 2355	bgoulet	X	MFIS	85	Sherbrook	1986
Lemieux, Pierre A.	Prof	Ext 2320		FRV	MBA	67	Sherbrook	* &1970
Morin, Robert J.	Prof	Ext 2340	rmorin	X	MFIS	78	Sherbrook	&1982
Robert, Anne-Marie	Prof	Ext 2375	amrobert	MNS	PHD	91	Laval	&1985
Roy, Chantale	Prof	821-8000	croy	CMT	DSC	94	Montpell	&1986
Turmel, Francine	Prof	Ext 2360	fturmel	FT	PHD	91	Laval	&1990
Vice Dean								
Vaillement, Benoit	Prof	Ext 2351	bvaillancout	X	MRIS	00	Sherbrook	2001
Bedard, Gaston	Assoc	Ext 2344	gbedard	X	MBA	57	McGill	&1989
Jacques, Marie	Assoc	Ext 2333	mjacques	X	MFIS	86	Sherbrook	1988
Gaudreau, Lucie	Asst	23511	gaudreau	X	MFIS	02	Sherbrook	2002
Conture, Lyne	Lect			F	MS	85	Sherbrook	2002
Cote, Marle	Lect	Ext 3308		CMT	MS	95	Sherbrook	1995
Huamon, Remi	Lect	Ext 3308		F	MS	85	Sherbrook	
Lessard, Nathalie	Lect	Ext 3304	stebonin.login	AR	MS	91	Sherbrook	1985

Simon Fraser University
Accounting Faculty — Burnaby, Canada BC V5A 1S6 — Faculty of Business Adm — (604) Fax=291-4920 — sfu.ca — 2006,2006 — BA,MBA,PHD
Dept Phone: 291-3708

Name	Rank	Phone	Email		Degree	Yr	School	
Smart, Carolyne	Dean	291-5227	smart	Plcy	PHD	80	Brit Colum	9-81
Emby, Craig	Prof	291-3140	emby	AB	PHD	89	Alberta	& 1-87
Gordon, Irene M.	Prof	291-4226	gordon	FT	PHD	81,	Simon Fr	& 9-81
Chung, Dennis Y.	Assoc			AFT	PHD	91	Alberta	* & 9-05
Chen, Yasheng	Asst	291-4485	yashengc	MI	PHD	05	W Ontario	2-05
Favere-Marchesi, Michael	Asst	291-4745	favere	ABI	PHD	95.	S Calif	# & 7-00
Jermias, Johnny	Asst	291-6257	jjermias	M	PHD	96	Waterloo	9-01
Duncan, Alain C. B.	SLect	291-3637	duncan	FM	MBA	75	York	& 9-95
Hsieh, James	SLect	291-3308	hsieh	F	MBA	74	Oregon	& 1-85
Macdonald, Anne	SLect	291-4225	amacdond	FM	MACC	98	Monash	& 9-98
Fizzell, Maureen R.	Lect	291-3700	fizzell	FM	MS	86	Saskatch	* 9-93
Hrazdil, Karel	Lect		khrazdil	F				7-07
Specdtor, Stephen	Lect	291-3637		FMA	ANA	82	Simon Fr	9-06

Thompson Rivers University
Dept Management PO Box 3010 — Kamloops Canada — School of Bus & Econ — BC V2C 5N3 — tru.ca — (250) Fax=828-5051 — BBA
Dept Phone: 828-5211 — 900 McGill Road — Diane Cottell
Homepage: http://www.tru.ca/psd/bus/accounti/acchome.htm

Name	Rank	Phone	Email		Degree	Yr	School	
Williams, Heather	C-In	371-5903	hwilliams	AM	MBA	04	Athabasc	* &
Collins, Roger	Assoc	371-5560	rcollins	FPTS	MSC	81	LondonEc	* 1992
Thompson, Dan	Asst	828-5078	dthompson	PFMV	MBA		Queens	* 1988
Bell, Tony	Inst	828-5612	tbell	PFMA	MBA		Thom River	2006
Breitkreitz, Duane	Inst	371-5890	breikreitz		MBA		City	1979
Desjardins, Ivan	Inst	828-5233	idesjardins	FPXV	MS		Sherbrook	* &1993
Kirkey, Bernie	Inst	371-5763	bkirkey	DP	MBA		W Ontario	1992
Sigloch, Berndt A.	Inst	828-5231	sigloch	PMQ	MBA		Brit Colum	1980

University of Toronto
Accounting Area — Toronto, Canada ON M5S 3E6 — Joseph Rotman Sch Mgt — (416) Fax=971-3048 — rotman.utoronto.ca — 1999,1999 — BCOM,MBA,MMPA
Dept Phone: 978-2480 — 105 St. George St. — Mrs. Gilda Serrao

Name	Rank	Phone	Email		Degree	Yr	School	
Martin, Roger	Dean	978-3422	martin	Mgt	MBA	81	Harvard	1998
Richardson, Gordon D.	C-Pr	946-8601	gordon.richard+	F	PHD	83.	Cornell	&2002
Amernic, Joel H.	Prof	978-3796	amernic	FM	MBA	71	Toronto	&1973
Brooks, Leonard J.	Prof	978-4457	brooks	MWJ	MBA	67	Toronto	&1974
Callen, Jeffrey L.	Prof	946-5641	callen	FM	PHD	76	Toronto	2000
Rotman Chair in Accounting								
Mintz, Jack	Prof	978-3985	mintz	X	PHD	80	Essex	1989
Rotenberg, Wendy D.	Prof	978-2664	rotenber	FI	PHD	87	Toronto	1990
Smieliauskas, Wally	Prof	978-1454	smieli	A	PHD	80.	Wisconsin	&1979
Elitzur, R. Ramy	Assoc	978-3827	elitzu	AF	PHD	88.	NYU	* &1988
Wensley, Anthony K. P.	Assoc	978-4418	wensle	S	PHD	89	Waterloo	&1988
Wong, M. H. Franco	Assoc	946-0729		F	PHD	97.	Penn	2006
Yue, Li	Assoc	978-0857	yueli	FM	PHD	95	Queen's	1994

Name	Rank	Phone	Email		Degree	Yr	School		
Zhang, Ping	Assoc	946-5655	pzhang	A	PHD	94	Waterloo		&2000
DeFranco, Gaetano	Asst				PHD	04.	Penn		
Hope, Ole-Kristian	Asst	946-3610	okhope	F	PHD	01.	Nrthwstrn		&2001
Lu, Hai	Asst	946-0677	hai.lu	FM	PHD	04.	S Calif		2004
McCracken, Susan A.	Asst	978-3386	mccracken	AM	PHD	98,	Waterloo		&1998
Segal, Dan	Asst	946-5648	dsegal	F	PHD	00.	NYU		&2000
Kitunen, Joan	SLect	978-3108	kitunen	X	BBM	77	Ryerson		&1990
Losell, Donna	SLect	978-2544	losell	FA	MBA	78	Toronto		&1981
Reed, Connie	SLect	978-3108	rotman	FM	MBA	96	Leicester	*	1989
Schneider, Manfred	Tut	978-4418	schnei	FA	MBA	86	York		&1985
Wiecek, Irene	Tut	978-0857	wiecek	FPBV	BCOM	79	Toronto		& 7-91
Zuliani, Elisa	Tut	946-7529	ezuliani	FM	BBA	87	Ryerson		1991

University of Victoria
Faculty of Human & Soc Dev
Dept Phone: 721-8055

Victoria, Canada BC V8W 2Y2
School of Public Adm

(250) Fax = 721-8849
uvic.ca

MPA
Belle Young

Name	Rank	Phone	Email		Degree	Yr	School		
Dastmalchian, Ali	Dean	492-4614			PHD	81	Cardiff		7-02
Lindquist, Evert A.	D-Ac	721-8054	evert		PHD		Berkeley		
Gagne, Lynda	Prof	721-8063	lgagne		PHD	02	Brit Colum		2001
Will, Hartmut J.	Prof	721-8069	hwill		PHD	69.	Illinois	*	1979

University of Waterloo
School of Accountancy
Dept Phone: Ext36536
Homepage: http://accounting.uwaterloo.ca/index.html
  phone 888-4567 Ext 36536

Waterloo, Canada ON N2L 3G1
Faculty of Arts

(519) Fax = 888-7562
uwaterloo.ca

BA,MACC,MTX,PHD
Donna Sutherland

Name	Rank	Phone	Email		Degree	Yr	School		
Barnett, James J.	D-Le	Ext35143	jbarnett	X	BCOM	75	Queens		&1990
Armitage, Howard M.	Prof	Ext35776	howard	IMC	PHD	83.	Mich St	*	1981
Gordon H. Cowperthwaite Professor of Accounting									
Atkinson, Anthony A.	Prof	Ext36514	aatkinson	M	PHD	77.	Car Mellon	*	1992
Boritz, J. Efrim	Prof	Ext35774	jeboritz	SJAB	PHD	83.	Minnesota		&1983
Chartered Accountants Chair of Ontario									
Gunz, Sally P.	Prof	Ext36524	sgunz	ALJ	LLB	75	Sydney		1981
Laiken, Stanley N.	Prof	Ext36507	snlaiken	X	PHD	72	W Ontario		1981
Deloitte Professor of Taxation									
O'Brien, Patricia C.	Prof	Ext35423	pobrien	FIK	PHD	85.	Chicago		&2000
Ernst & Young Professor									
Bandyopadhyay, Sati P.	Assoc	Ext32533	bandy	FAIZ	PHD	89.	Iowa		1989
Douglas, Alan V. S.	Assoc	Ext35945	adouglas	FMTY	PHD	94	Queens		1995
Kennedy, Duane B.	Assoc	888-4752	dkennedy	MF	PHD	87.	Cornell	*	7-87
Macnaughton, Alan	Assoc	Ext35423	amacnaughton	X	PHD	83	Brit Colum		1985
KPMG Professor in Accounting									
Russell, Grant W.	Assoc	Ext36516	russell	M	MBA	70	McMaster	*	1974
Wiedman, Christine I.	Assoc	Ext33732	cwiedman	FP	PHD	94.	Cornell		&2006
Chen, Changling	Asst	Ext35731	clchen	F	PHD	04.	Wisconsin		2004
Kotchetova, Natalia V.	Asst	Ext37027	nkotchet	A	PHD	02.	Geo St	*	2002
Lim, Jee-Hae	Asst	Ext35702	jh2lim	S	PHD	06.	Kansas		2006
Panukcu, Omer	Asst	Ext37119	pamukcu	F	BSC	98	Car Mellon		2003
Stratopoulos, Theophanis	Asst	Ext35943	tstralop	FS	PHD	94	NewHamp		2006
Webb, Alan	Asst	Ext36548	a2webb	BM	PHD	01	Alberta		&2000
PricewaterhouseCoopers Fellow									
Charters, Darren	Lect	Ext32570	dcharters	ALJ	MBA	00	Wilfr Lau		2002
Clements, Lori	Lect		l3clemen	X	MTAX	99	Waterloo		&2007
Robinson, Linda	Lect	Ext36995	lrobins	A	BCOM	82	Manitoba		&2003
Robson, Julie	Lect	Ext35385	jrobson	X	MACC	92	Waterloo		&2001
Spoule, Robert	Lect	Ext35602	bsproule	M	MBA	78	Calgary	*	2003
Vander Bosch, Nancy	Lect	Ext37026	nvanderb	AF	MACC	86	Waterloo	*	&2002
Vert, David	Lect	Ext 3801	2dvert	EFLQ	HBBA	83	Wilfr Lau		&2006

Univ of Western Ontario
Mgr Accounting & Cntr Area
Dept Phone: 661-3260

London, Canada ON N6A 3K7
Richard Ivey Sch of Bus
1151 Richmond Street North

(519) Fax = 661-3485
ivey.uwo.ca

HBA,MBA,PHD

Name	Rank	Phone	Email		Degree	Yr	School		
				Mgt			Toronto		6-03
Stephenson, Carol	Dean	661-3278		AOPS	PHD	95	Alberta		2003
Radcliffe, Vaughan S.	C-Ac	661-4170	vradcliffe	M	PHD	83.	Cincinnati		&1980
Bryant, Murray J.	Assoc	661-4188	mbryant	XFMT	PHD	87,	W Ontario		&1985
Robertson, Darroch A.	Assoc	661-3216	rrobertson	IMJE	PHD	87	MIT		8-92
Sharp, David J.	Assoc	661-3945	dsharp	IFMV	ABD		Concordia		7-07
Shi, Yari	Asst			F	MBA	02	W Ontario		& 7-90
Heisz, Mary A.	Lect	661-4277	mheisz	F	MBA				
Sturby, Chris	Lect	661-4146							

Wilfrid Laurier University

Accounting Area
Dept Phone: 884-0710
 phone 884-1970 ext 2062

Waterloo, Canada ON N2L 3C5
School of Bus & Econ
75 University Ave. West

(519) Fax=884-0201
wlu.ca

2003,2003
BBA,MBA,AD
Sandra Castellanos

Name	Title	Ext	Email		Degree	Yr	School	
Dybenko, Ginny	Dean	Ext 2671	dybenko	Plcy	MMTH	72	Waterloo	2006
Banks, William	C-Ac	Ext 2774	wbanks	FS	PHD	92	McMaster	&1988
Libby, Theresa	Assoc	Ext 2301	tlibby	MB	PHD	96	Waterloo	&1996
MacDonald, Laura D.	Assoc	Ext 2815	lmacdona	MH	PHD	99	Queen's	* 1998
Mathieu, Robert	Assoc	Ext 3124	rmathieu	F	PHD	95	Waterloo	&1998
McConomy, Bruce J.	Assoc	Ext 2890	bmcconom	FTA	PHD	96	Queen's	&1999
McCutcheon, John	Assoc	Ext 2582	jcmccutc	FMV	ABD		Manchest	* 1980
Salatka, William K.	Assoc	Ext 2912	wsalatka	FTV	PHD	84.	Iowa	&1993
Zeng, Tao	Assoc	Ext 2562	tzeng	XF	PHD	00	Queen's	1998
Berberich, Greg	Asst	Ext 2660	gberberi	AEJ	PHD	05	Waterloo	2002
Chu, Ling	Asst	Ext 2422	lchu	XF				
Kozloski, Thomas M.	Asst	Ext 2679	tkozloski	AB	PHD	02.	Drexel	&2003
Niu, Flora	Asst	Ext 3293	fniu	F	PHD	04	Waterloo	2003
Xu, Bixia	Asst	Ext 2659	bxu		PHD	03	Concordia	2002
Clark, Greg	Lect	Ext 2383	gclark	FM	CMA	90	McMaster	2001
Foerster, Al	Lect	Ext 2365	afoerster					
Mbagwu, Chima	Lect	Ext 2803	cmbagwu	F	MSC	03	Saskatch	2006
Scallen, David	Lect	Ext 2880	dscallen	FM	MBA	99	Wilfr Lau	1999

University of Windsor

Accounting Area
Dept Phone: 253-3000

Windsor, Canada ON N9B 3P4
Odette School of Bus

(519) Fax=973-7073
uwindsor.ca

BCOM,MBA
Stephanie Miller

Name	Title	Ext	Email		Degree	Yr	School	
Conway, Allan	Dean	Ext 3091	aconway		DBA	83	Harvard	2005
Lan, George P. W.	C-Ac	Ext 3482	glan	F	PHD	91	Queens	1988
Freeman, Jack L.	Prof	Ext 3116	freeman	FM	PHD	81.	Mich St	1972
Kantor, Jeffrey	Prof	Ext 3142	kantor	CM	PHD	84	Bradford	&1983
Lam, Wai P.	Emer	Ext 3109	lamd	2002	PHD	74.	Mich St	&1973
Al-Hayale, Talal	Asst	Ext 3120	talal	MFV	PHD	90	Wales	2001
Gowing, Maureen	Asst	Ext 4252	mgowing	A	PHD	96	Queen's	2005
Ong, Audra	Asst	Ext 3155	aong	FM	PHD	00	W England	2000
Pathak, Jagdish	Asst	Ext 3131	jagdis	AS	PHD	95	Goa	2002
Dunning, Greg	LT	Ext 3154	profgrd	A	MBA	75	E Mich	2002
Horniachek, Dale	LT		dale	FM	MBA	84	York	2003
Jones, Don	LT	Ext 3139	djones	A	MBA	76		2004
Stevens, R. Jim	LT	Ext 3114	stevens	FS	BCOM	75	Windsor	2003
Arya, Seema	Sess	Ext 3120	sarya	A	PHD			2006
Petro, Louis W.	Sess	Ext 3457	petro	ASMF	PHD	74.	Michigan	# * &1998

York University

Accounting Area
Dept Phone: 736-5062

Toronto, Canada ON M3J 1P3
Schulich Sch of Bus
4700 Keele Street

(416) Fax=736-5687
schulich.yorku.ca

BBA,MBA,MPA,PHD
Teresa Colavecchia

Name	Title	Phone	Email		Degree	Yr	School	
Horvath, Dezso J.	Dean	736-5070	dhorvath	Mgt	PHD		UMEA	1979
Richardson, Alan J.	C-Pr	736-5062	arichardson	BHM	PHD	85	Queen's	&2003
Beechy, Thomas H.	Emer	736-5097	tbeechy	2000	DBA	71.	Wash U	&1971
Dermer, Jerry D.	Prof	736-5087	jdermer	MS	PHD	69.	Illinois	1980
Rosen, L. S. (Al)	Emer	736-5062		2001	PHD	66.	U Wash	&1972
Annisette, Marcia A.	Assoc	736-5066	mannisette	FMI	PHD	96	Manchest	2005
Bewley, Kathryn	Assoc	736-5066	kbewley	AFST	PHD	98,	Waterloo	&2002
Chung, Janne O. Y.	Assoc	736-5062	jchung	ABEO	PHD	98	E Cowan	2000
Dewhirst, John F.	Emer	736-5066		1977	PHD	68	Michigan	1966
Mawani, Amin	Assoc	736-5062	amawani	TM	PHD	95	Waterloo	* 2000
Roy, S. Paul	Assoc	736-5066	proy	M	PHD	79.	Iowa	&1986
Thorne, Linda	Assoc	736-5062	lthorne	ABIJ	PHD	97	McGill	& 1-97
Trivedi, Viswanath U.	Assoc	736-5066	strivedi	ABSX	PHD	97.	Ariz St	&2002
Graham, Cameron	Asst	736-5063	cgraham	WGHT	PHD	05	Calgary	2005
Hsu, Sylvia H.	Asst	736-5063	shsu	CM	PHD	06	Wisconsin	2006
Qu, Sandy Q.	Asst	736-5066	squ	FM	PHD	06	Alberta	2006

York Univ-Atkinson College

Accounting Area
Dept Phone: 736-5210
Homepage: www.atkinson.yorku.ca/frschoolms.htm
 Did Not Respond--2005-2006 Listing

No York, Canada ON M3J 1P3
Sch Administrative Stde
4700 Keele Street

(416) Fax=736-5963
yorku.ca

BAS
Ms. Vita Lobo

Name	Title	Phone	Email		Degree	Yr	School	
Lenton, Rhonda	Dean	736-5220	akdean					
Gaber, Brian G.	Dir	736-5210	bgaber	ABFS	PHD	83.	Wisconsin	&1993
Cavanagh, W. Forbes	Assoc	736-5210	forbesc	MC	PHD	85.	SUNY-Buf	&1976
Macintosh, John C. C.	Assoc	736-5210	johnmac	VFTN	PHD	84	S Africa	& 7-90
Parkinson, John M.	Assoc	736-5210	johnmp	CIM	PHD	84	Bradford	* &1984
Spraakman, Gary P.	Assoc	736-5210	garys	AMN	PHD	96,	Concordia	* 1991
Hayes, Louise	Asst	736-5210	lhayes	AFS	MBA	74	Brit Colum	&2000
Ohta, Yasuhiro	Asst	736-5210	yohta	F	PHD	03.	SUNY-Buf	2002
Splettstoesser, Ingrid	Asst	736-5210	ingrids	ADS	PHD	96	Waterloo	&1991

OTHER FOREIGN SCHOOLS

RWTH Aachen University
Accounting Faculty
Dept Phone: 8096164
Homepage: www.uf.rwth-aachen.de

Aachen 52056   Germany
School of Econ & Bus Ad
Templergraben 64

49241 Fax=8092167
wiwi.rwth-aachen.de   DIPL,MBA,MA,PHD
Gisela Hilgers

Moeller, Hans Peter	C-Pr	Ext96164	moeller	FCIA	PHD	72	Cologne	1990
Hoemberg, Reinhold	Prof	Ext96147	hoemberg	AXQ	PHD	73	Muenster	1994
Huefner, Bernd	Asst	Ext96169	huefner	FCM	PHD	00	Aachen	1994
Kavermann, Markus	Asst	Ext96168	kavermann	FCM	MA	99	Aachen	1999
Ketteriss, Holger	Asst	Ext96166	ketteriss	FCM	MA	99	Aachen	2000
Willms, Matthias	Asst	Ext96167	willms	FCM	MA	05	Aachen	2005

University of Aberdeen
Dept of Accountancy & Fnce
Dept Phone: 272205
Homepage: http://www.abdn.ac.uk/business/
  phone: 1224 272205 Fax: 1224 272214

AberdeenAB24 3QY
Busines School
Dunbar Street

Scotland   01144 Fax=272214
abdn.ac.uk   MA,MSC,PHD
Teri Pascoe

Molyneaux, David	SLect	272208	d.molyneaux	NAJ	PHD	01	Edinburgh	2001
Black, Angela	Prof	272204	a.black	FQ	PHD	95	Dundee	1999
Buckland, Roger	Prof	272206	r.buckland	FGI	MPHL	85	York	1993
Fraser, Patricia	Prof	272210	prof.p.fraser	FQ	PHD	89	City Bus	1995
Roberts, Clare	Prof	273395	c.roberts	FIW	PHD	88	Glasgow	1997
Arthur, Alex	SLect	272211	a.arthur	ABDM	MLIT	87	Aberdeen	&1990
Alawattage, Chanzdana	Lect	272209	c.g.alawattage	BGWT	PHD	05	Keele	2005
How, Shimin	Lect	272207	sh.h.min	C	MSC	02	Manchester	2006
Tee, Kai-Hong	Lect	272212	k.h.tee	FQ	MBA	06	Heriot W	2004
Wang, Shiyun	Lect		s.wang	FQ	PHD	02	Cambridge	2007
Whittington, Mark	Lect	274360	m.whittington	ME	MBA	94	Open	2006

University of Adelaide
Accounting Faculty
Dept Phone: 83034755
Homepage: www.commerce.adelaide.edu.au
  Did Not Respond--2005-2006 Listing

Adelaide 5005   Australia
School of Commerce
233 North Terrace

61-8 Fax=83034368
commerce.adelaide.edu.auBCO,MCO,PHD
Mary-Rose Alfonsi

Bloch, Fred A.	H	83035529	fred.bloch	F	PHD	72	Adelaide	1969
Parker, Lee D.	Prof	83034236	lee.parker	MGHJ	PHD	83	Monash	&1997
Taylor, Dennis W.	Prof	83035527	dennis.taylor	FGIM	PHD		HongKong	&2003
Carbone, Domenic	LectB	83034759	domenic.car+	X	LLB		Adelaide	1992
Gerrard, Michael J.	LectC	83034509	michael.gerr+	D	PHD	76	London	1990
Gould, Graham P.	LectB	83034508	graham.gould	F	MCOM	97	Adelaide	1997
Harris, Cathryn A.	LectB	83035532	kate.harris	F	DAC		Flinders	1988
Langton, Robert J.	LectC	83034758	robert.langton	JL	PHD		Massey	1991
Lightbody, Margaret	LectB	83033104	margaret.ligh+	CMFA	PHD	00	S Austrl	&1997
McKee, Stephen K.	LectC	83034757	steve.mckee	D	PHD		Flinders	1991
McMurtrie, Anthony J. E.	LectB	83034515	tony.amcmur+	MF	MCOM	99	Flinders	1997
Ritson, Philip A.	LectA	83034754	philip.ritson	MF	BCOM	89	Flinders	1997

Ajou University
Accounting Faculty
Dept Phone: 219-2702
  Did Not Respond Again--1998-99 Listing

Suwon, Korea   442-749
College of Business Adm
5 Wongchun-Dong, Paldal-Gu

82331 Fax=219-1616
mandang.ajou.ac.kr   BBA,MS,PHD

Dokko, Yoon	Dean	219-2700	sbadean	Fnce	PHD	84	Penn	1994
Kim, Kwang-Yoon	Prof	219-2716	kimkyn	FX	PHD	90	Korea	&1983
Sohn, Min	Prof	219-2715	sonmin	AFMX	PHD	86	Hong-Ik	&1984
Suh, Yoon S.	Prof	219-2726	yoonsuh	MFT	PHD	85.	Tx-Austin	&1995
Han, Bong-Heui	Assoc	219-2727	bhhan	FM	PHD	91.	Tx-Austin	&1995

American Univ of Kuwait
Accounting Faculty Box 3323
Dept Phone:
Homepage: www.auk.edu.kw
  Did Not Respond--2005-2006 Listing

Safat, 13034   Kuwait
Sch of Mgt & Bus Adm

(965) Fax=574-9303
auk.edu.kw

Ross-Black, Carol	Dean							
Cripps, Jeremy G. A.	Prof	802040	jcripps	ACIN	PHD	92	Union-NY	&2004

American Univ of Sharjah
Dept of Accounting & Finance
Dept Phone: 65152320
  Did Not Respond--2005-2006 Listing

Sharjah United   Arab Emira
School of Bus & Mgt

(971) Fax=65585065
ausharjah.edu   BSBA,MBA
Karen Leschke

Atiyah, Wadiah	Dean	515 2304	watiyah	F	PHD	97	American	&1997
Zeidan, Rabih	Asst				PHD	07.	Houston	8-07
Al Khazli, Osamah	C-Ac	515 2320	kazali	Fnce	PHD	97	Memphis	1997

Zoubi, Taisier A.	Prof	515 2367	tzoubi	FMIZ	PHD	92. North Tx		2004
Boyd, Sanithia	Assoc	515 2329	sboyd	FAO	DED	96 Grambling	*	&2004
Redding, Rodney J.	Assoc	515 2534	rredding	FPT	PHD	79. Penn St		&2003
McCallum, Brent	Asst	515 2311	bmccallum	FPCX	MS	93 American	*	&1999
Williams, Ron	Inst	515 2330	rwilliams	FCX	MBA	98 Lincoln	#	&2001

University of Amsterdam
Dept Accountancy & Info Mgt
Dept Phone: 525-4170
  Did Not Respond Again--2001-2002 Listing

Amsterdam 1018WB   Netherland   3120   Fax=525-5281
Faculty of Economics   fee.uva.nl
Roetersstraat 11

Hoogendoorn, Martin	Prof	Ext 4142		AFIP	PHD	82 Rotterdam	1991
Langendijk, Henk P. A. J.	Prof	Ext 4260	lang	A	PHD	94 Leiden	1980
Leenaars, Hans	Prof	Ext 4170			PHD	93 Amsterdm	1994
Schilder, Arnold	Prof	Ext 4178		AJDR	PHD	94 Groningn	1991
Wallage, Philip	Prof	Ext 4178	wallage	AIR	PHD	91 Amsterdm	1982
Goot, T van der	Asst	Ext 4171	tjalling	FGKY	PHD	97 Amsterdm	1990
Majoor, Barbara	Asst	Ext 4178		A	PHD	97 Amsterdm	1991
Offeren, Dick H. van	Asst	Ext 4259	dick	INPT	MBA	78 Amsterdm	1979

Athens Univ of Econ & Bus
Accounting & Finance
Dept Phone: 8203302
Homepage: www.aueb.gr
  Did Not Respond Again 2002 2003 Listing

Athens, 104-34   Greece   3010   Fax=8228816
Dept of Actg & Finance   aueb.gr   BS,MBA
76 Patission Street   Vassilios Assimakopoulos

Ghicas, Dimitrios C.	Prof	8203175	gikas	FM	PHD	85 Florida	1994
Kavussanos, Emmanuel	Prof	8203167	mkavus	FQ	PHD	93 City-UK	2001
Tzavalis, Elias	Prof	8203334t	zavalis	FQ	PHD	93 London	2001
Venieris, George	Prof	8203229	venieris	MS	PHD	75 Birminghm	1977
Georgoutsos, Dimitris	Asst	8203441	d.georgoutsos	F	PHD	89 Essex	2002
Hevas, Dimosthenis	Asst	8203463	hevas	FT	PHD	85 Wales	1987
Koen, Sandra	Asst	8214903	scohen	C	PHD	01 Athens	2002
Papadaki, Aphroditi	Asst	8203571	afroditi.papad +	FT	PHD	97 Athens	1998
Leledakis, George	Lect		g.leledakis	F	PHD	99 Warwick	2002
Sprou, Spyros	Lect	8203169	sis@hol.gr	F	PHD	97 Brunel	2001
Staikouras, Christos	Lect		cstaikouras	F	PHD	01 City-UK	2002

University of Auckland
Dept of Accounting & Finance
Dept Phone: 373-7599
  phone: 373-7599

Auckland   NewZealand   64-9   Fax=373-7406   2004,2004
Sch of Business & Econ   auckland.ac.nz   BCOM,MCOM,PHD
18 Symonds St   Herena Newall

Spicer, Barry H.	Dean	Ext87629	b.spicer	MA	PHD	76 U Wash		1989
Wong, Jilnaught	H-Pr	Ext88528	j.wong	FA	PHD	87 Auckland		&1992
Bowman, Robert G. (Jerry)	Prof	Ext87618	j.bowman	F	PHD	78. Stanford		&1987
Cahan, Steven F.	Prof	Ext87175	s.cahan	FA	PHD	88. Colorado		&2004
Emanuel, David M.	Prof	Ext87658	d.emanuel	FA	PHD	84 Auckland		&1975
How, Janice C. Y.	Prof	Ext84861	j.how	F	PHD	94 W Austrl		2004
Hay, David C.	Assoc	Ext84878	d.hay	FA	PHD	99 Auckland	#	&2000
Marsden, Alastair	Assoc	Ext88564	a.marsden	F	PHD	97 Auckland		1991
Rouse, Paul A.	Assoc	Ext87192	p.rouse	MA	PHD	96 Auckland		&1987
Wong, Norman	Assoc	Ext87098	n.wong	FA	PHD	00 Auckland		1992
Austin, Lloyd M.	SLect	Ext87425	l.austin	FA	MCOM	73 Auckland		1989
Cheung, Joe	SLect	Ext85176	j.cheung	F	MSC	88 Wash		2000
Cliffe, Cheryl	SLect	Ext87171	c.cliffe	F	PHD	03 Auckland		1987
Keenan, Michael G.	SLect	Ext87191	m.keenan	FA	PHD	77 St Andre		1984
Kober, Ralph	SLect	Ext87174	r.kober	MA	PHD	06 Queensld		2005
Poskitt, Russell	SLect	Ext85908	r.poskitt	F	PHD	01 Auckland		2002
Wilton, Robert	SLect	Ext87170	r.wilton	F	MCOM	78 Auckland		1996
Zilca, Shlomi	SLect	Ext87190	s.zilca	F	PHD	03 Tel Aviv		2002
Akroyd, Chris	Lect	Ext87194	c.akroyd	MA	ABD	Auckland		2000
Askarany, Davood	Lect	Ext85785	d.askarany	MA	PHD	03 S Austral		2005
Chan, Kam Fong	Lect	Ext85172	k.chan	F	PHD	06 Queenslnd		2005
Kerr, Jennifer	Lect	Ext87292	j.kerr	MA	MCOM	88 Auckland		1997
O'Grady, Winnie	Lect	Ext87196	w.ogrady	BMS	MBS	93 Massey		2000
Speer, Derek M.	Lect	Ext87290	d.speer	MA	MCOM	81 Auckland		&1984
Truong, Cameron	Lect	Ext85171	c.truong	F	PHD	07 Auckland		2006
Verhoeven, Peter	SLect	Ext89431	p.verhoeven	F	PHD	04 W Austr		2004
Alexander, Deborah	STut	Ext89415	d.alexander	MA	BCOM	96 Auckland		2002
Caird, Kathryn G.	STut	Ext88936	k.caird	MA	BCOM	78 Auckland		1979
Camp, Graeme	STut	Ext87321	g.camp	F	PHD	00 Auckland		1995
Chow, Charles	STut	Ext84690	c.chow	FA	BCOM	85 Auckland		2007
Clarke, Christine	STut	Ext88444	c.clarke	F	BCOM	82 Auckland		2002
Davy, Anne R.	STut	Ext85906	a.davy	FA	MCOM	91 Auckland		&1989
Grobbelaar, Johan	STut	Ext84838	j.grobbelaar	MA	BCOM	76 S Africia		2004
Lane, Susan	STut	Ext87151	s.lane	FA	BA	85 Nottinghm		2007
Liew, Angela	STut	Ext85800	a.liew	MA	MCOM	03 Auckland		2007
Rechtschaffen, Glenn	STut	Ext87180	g.rechtschaffen	FA	JD	82 UCLA		2001
Wilberfoss, Caroline	STut	Ext84895	c.wilberfoss	FA	BSC	81 Leichest		2002

Australian Grad Sch Mgt Sydney NSW 2052 Australia (029) Fax=93137279 2003
Accounting Faculty Business agsm.edu.au MBA,PHD
Dept Phone: 99319200 Gate 11 Botany St, Randwick Diana Ramsay
  Did Not Respond Again--2000-2001 Listing

Name	Rank	Phone	Email		Deg	Yr	School	Yr
Clinch, Gregory J.	Prof	99329363	gregc	F	PHD	88	Stanford	1991
Hirst, Mark K.	Prof	99319313	m.hirst	M	PHD	87	NS Wales	1992
Lyon, John D.	Prof	99319570	johnl	AFS	PHD	91.	Ohio St	&1999
Whittred, Gregory P.	Prof	99319251	gregw	F	PHD	86	NS Wales	&1990
Sidhu, Baljit K.	SLect	99319511	baljits	FI	PHD	93	Sydney	& 1-99

Australian National Univ Canberra Act0200 Australia 61 2 Fax=61255005
Fac of Economics & Commerce Sch of Bus & Info Mgt anu.edu.au BCOM,MCOMM,PHD
Dept Phone: 61254310 Hanna Neumann Bldg Kingsley Ms. Dora Gava
  Did Not Respond--2005-2006 Listing

Name	Rank	Phone	Email		Deg	Yr	School	Yr
Houghton, Keith A.	Dean	61253596	dean.ecocomm	FA	PHD	84	W Austrl	&
Gregor, Shirley	C-Pr	61253749	shirley.gregor	DS	PHD		Queenslnd	2001
Barton, Allan D.	Prof	61258462	allan.barton	GPI	PHD	61	Cambridge	&1996
Monroe, Gary S.	Prof	61255906	gary.monroe	ABEJ	PHD	78.	Mass	2002
Burritt, Roger L.	Assoc	61253670	roger.burritt	MNTI	MPHL	75	Oxon	&1989
Freeman, Colin	Assoc	61255460	colin.freeman	DS	MSC	71	Sheffield	2001
Hart, Dennis	Assoc	61253588	dennis.hart	DS	PHD			2001
Shailer, Gregory E. P.	Assoc	61254333	greg.shailer	ABQT	PHD	96	Adelaide	&1990
Tran, Alfred V. H.	Assoc	61255118	alfred.tran	FITX	PHD	97	Austr Natl	&1991
Birt, Jacqueline L.	Asst	61254857	jacqueline.birt	EF	MBUS	98	RMIT	2000
Fraser, Steven G.	Asst	61255453	steven.fraser	MS	PHD	02	Melbourne	2003
Goode, Sigi	Asst	61255048	ligi.goods	DS	GRAD	97	Austr Natl	2000
Ikin, Catherine	Asst	61259774	catherine.ikin	FX	BEC	74	Tasmania	2003
Ikin, Chris	Asst	61255048	chris.ikin	AFT	MCOM	01	Melbourne	&2003
Johns, Leanne	Asst	61254626	leanne.johns	EHM	MPHL	01	Austr Natl	2002
Kend, Michael	Asst	61253586	michael.kend	AFT	PHD	02	Melbourne	2003
Lee, Janet	Asst	61254336	janet.lee	EFG	PHD	01	N Eng-Au	2001
Lodhia, Sumit K.	Asst	61258460	sumit.lodhia	CDS	MA	99	USP	2001
Osman, Adam	Asst	61255478	adam.osman	FG	MPHL	02	Austr Natl	2003
Radoll, Peter	Asst	61259793	peter.radoll	S	MIT	03	Canberra	2003
Richardson, Alex	Asst	61259807	alex.richardson	S	BIT	99	C Queensln	2003
Tan, Rebecca	Asst	61254336	rebecca.tan	FTW	PHD	03	Murdoch	2003
Teh, Seng Thiam	Asst	61253316	seng.teh	AEFT	BCOM	91	W Austrl	2003

University of Bath ClavertonDown EngBA2 7AY 01225 Fax=386473
Accounting Faculty School of Management bath.ac.uk
Dept Phone:
  Did Not Respond--2005-2006 Listing

Name	Rank	Phone	Email		Deg	Yr	School	Yr
Pettigrew, Andrew	Dean	383052	a.m.pettigrew	Mgt	PHD			
Vass, Peter	Assoc	826826	p.vass	FGU	MSC	70	London	1990
Birts, Anthony N.	SLect	383675	a.n.birts	F	MBA	76	Manchest	1988

Bond University Gold Coast 4229 Australia (07) Fax=55951160
Accounting Faculty Faculty of Business bond.edu.au BCO,MCO,MAC,PHD
Dept Phone: 55951111 University Drive, Robina
  Did Not Respond--2005-2006 Listing

Name	Rank	Phone	Email		Deg	Yr	School	Yr
Marchant, Garry	Dean	55952074	gmarchan	MCU	PHD	87	Michigan	&O-04
Iselin, Errol R.	H-Pr	55952230	eiselin	BCM	PHD	82	Queensld	&2004
Moores, Kenneth J.	Prof	55952252	kmoores	MBE	PHD	82	Birminghm	* &1988
Duncan, Keith R.	Assoc	55952238	keith duncan	FTY	PHD	93	Bond	&1989
McNamara, Raymond P.	Assoc	55952219	mcnamara	ABFS	PHD	91	Queensld	* &1989
Bloore, Ross	Asst	55952232	bloorer	ABFS	PHD	98	Bond	1992
Routledge, James	Asst	55952077	james.routledge	FT	PHD	00	UNI Sun	& 9-03
Anderson, Sharlene	Fell	55951695	shanders	MA	BBSU	98	Griffith	&O-00
Gunther, Christopher	Fell	55952099	cgunther	M	BBUS	95	Capetown	& 5-02

Bournemouth University Dorset BH12 5BB England 01202 Fax=965261
Accounting & Finance Business School bournemouth.ac.uk BA,MA,MSC
Dept Phone: 965187

Name	Rank	Phone	Email		Deg		School	Yr
McElroy, Trefor	H-Ple	96 5190	tmcelroy	FPM	MSC			4-89
Ball, Frazer	SLect	96 5032	fball	MS	BA			9-95
Day, Robert	SLect	96 5359	rday	FGHT	MSC			9-88
Hosking, Malcolm	SLect	96 5209	mhosking	M	BA			8-01
Marshall, David	SLect	96 5541	dmarshall	CDFP	MBA			& 9-90
Miller, Angharad	SLect	96 5205	amiller	X	MSC			1-96
Stonelake, Bernadette	SLect	96 5187	bstonela	AFM	MA			9-02
Tauringana, Vern	SLect	96 5187	vtauring	FA	PHD			9-02
Allerston, Anne	PLect	96 5113	aallerst	FPM	MSC			9-89
Willcocks, Geoff	PLect	96 5189	gwillcocks	FXQ	PHD			7-88

University of Bristol

Accounting Faculty — Bristol BS81TN England — 0117 Fax=928-8577
Dept Phone: 928-8415 — Sch of Econ, Fnce & Mgt — bristol.ac.uk — **BSC,MSC,PHD**
8, Woodland Rd — Kate Steele
Homepage: www.efm.bris.ac.uk/finance

Name	Rank	Phone	Email					
Ashton, David J.	C-Pr	928-8423	david.ashton	QT	PHD	79	Warwick	9-89
Acker, Daniella E.	Prof	928-8438	daniella.acker	FQ	PHD	96	Bristol	&1992
Dugdale, David	Prof	928-9049	david.dugdale	CM	PHD	71	Hull	2003
Ellwood, Sheila	Prof	928-9847	sheila.ellwood	ACFG	PHD	95	Aston	2006
Lyne, Stephen R.	SLect	928-8408	stephen.lyne	CUBM	PHD			& 8-79

University of Canterbury

Dept Acctcy, Fnce & Inf Sys — Christchurch1 NZ NewZealand — (03) Fax=364-2727
Dept Phone: 364-2604 — Faculty of Commerce — canterbury.ac.nz — **BCO,MCO,MBA,PHD**
phone: 364-2604 — Ilam Road — Tineke Patterson

Name	Rank	Ext	Email					
Shanahan, Yvonne	H-Ac	Ext 6619	yvonne.shanahan	CFMN	PHD	02	Syracuse	1991
Ball, Amanda	Prof	Ext 6614	amanda.ball	JNW	BA	85	CNAA	2006
Clarke, Bevan J.	Prof	Ext 6611	bevan.clarke	DSFT	PHD	75	Brit Colum	&1963
Milne, Markus J.	Prof	Ext 6624	markus.milne	JW	MA	88	Lancaster	2006
Chetwin, Maree C.	Assoc	Ext 6616	maree.chetwin	LX	LLB	74	Canterbu	1979
Hampton, Lindsay F.	SLect	Ext 6637	lindsay.hampton	GJL	SJD	95	Wisconsin	1968
Sawyer, Adrian J.	Assoc	Ext 6617	adrian.sawyer	FLX	MCOM	93	Canterbu	1991
Dixon, Keith	SLect	Ext 3681	keith.dixon	BGHM	PHD	96	Massey	2007
Fisher, Richard T	SLect	Ext 6621	richard.fisher	ABFS	MCM	05	Lincoln	&2004
Lord, Beverley R.	SLect	Ext 6622	beverley.lord	FMQ	PHD	01	Waikato	1991
Maples, Andrew J.	SLect	Ext 6636	andrew.maples	LX	LLM	95	Canterbu	1998
Mills, Annette J.	SLect	Ext 6625	annette.mills	SDM	PHD	96	Waikato	1998
Todorova, Nelly	SLect	Ext 6628	nelly.todorova	DMQS	MSC	94	Sunderla	1998
Vargo, John J.	SLect	Ext 6627	john.vargo	DMS	PHD	01	Canterbu	&1981
Anderson, Warwick	Lect	Ext 6626	warwick.and+	BFQY	MCOM	97	Canterbu	2002
Crombie, Neil	Lect	Ext 7359	neil.crombie	CMU	MCOM	02	Canterbu	2004
Jackman, Susan	Lect	Ext 7625	sue.jackman	CEFM	MCOM	99	Canterbu	2005
Lewis, Karen	Lect	Ext 7268	karen.lewis	FHW	PHD	03	Canterbu	2004
Suraweera, Theek	Lect	Ext 7386	theek.suraweera	SDM	MBA	91	Sri Jayewa	2002
Mortensen, Tony	ALect	Ext 7637	tony.mortensen	BFP	BCOM	93	Lincoln	2005

Cardiff University

Accounting Section — Cardiff CF10 3EU U Kingdom — 44029 Fax=20874419
Dept Phone: 20874271 — Cardiff Business School — cardiff.ac.uk
Colum Drive — Sue O'Brien/Penny Smith
Homepage: http://www.cardiff.ac.uk/carbs/accfin/index.html

Name	Rank	Phone	Email					
Mellett, Howard J.	H-Pr	20875704	mellett	GNH	MSC	84	Cardiff	&1974
Chandler, Roy A.	Prof	20876018	chandler	AFHI	BSC	77	Cardiff	&1980
Edwards, John Richard	Prof	20876658	edwardsjr	FH	MSC	75	Cardiff	&1971
Ezzamel, Mahmoud A.	Prof	20874277	ezzamel	BHMW	PHD	75	Southampt	1975
Jones, Mike	Prof	20874959	jonesm12	FHIW	MA	75	Oxford	&1979
Marginson, David E. W.	Prof	20876954	marginsonde	M	PHD	97	Lancaster	2005
Peel, Michael J.	Prof	20876839	peel	AF	MBA	87	Bradford	* 1987
Pendlebury, Maurice	Prof	20874833	pendlebury	NGE	PHD	86	Cardiff	&1977
Robson, Keith	Prof	20875515	robsonk	MFAB	PHD	88	Manchest	2005
Taylor, Nicholas	ResFl	20876736	taylorn	MQ	PHD		London	2000
Walker, Stephen P.	Prof	2077628	walkers2	HF	PHD			&2003
Xiao, Jason Zezhong	Prof	20875374	xiao	I	PHD	95	Napier	1987
Xu, Gary	Prof	20875481	xug	Q	PHD	93	Lancaster	2005
Karbhari, Yusuf	Read	20876057	karbhari	AGMN	PHD	97	Cardiff	1990
Tolikas, Kostus	Asst	20876652	tolikask	MQ	PHD	05		2006
Anderson, Malcolm	Lect	20875764	andersonm3	HAE	MPHL	94	Cardiff	* 1991
Clatworthy, Mark A.	Lect	20875847	clatworthyma	FI	BSC	96	Cardiff	1996
Dhanani, Alpa	Lect	20876952	dhananiav	IM	PHD	98	Cardiff	1998
Evans, Kevin	Lect	20874558	evansk1	Q	MSC	99	Warwick	2005
Norton, Simon	Lect	20876675	nortonsd	AFI	PHD		Cardiff	1996
Roberts, Roydon A.	Lect	20875130	robertsra	AH	BSC	72	Cardiff	&1976
Sian, Suki	Lect	20870040	sians	H	PHD	06		2004
Solomon, Jill	Lect	20875722	solomonjf	FIJW	PHD	96	Manchest	2000
Taylor, Suetlana	Lect	20876439	miras	MQ	PHD	06	Cardiff	2006
Bartlett, Sue	Tutor	20875193	bartlett	DFM	PHD	96	Cardiff	1990
Edgley, Carla	Tutor	20876567	edgleycr	FX	MA	85	Oxford	&1998
Morse, Barry	Tutor	20875742	morserb	FMP	MA	71	Oxford	&1997
Thomas, Gwen	Tutor	20875849	thomasg4	FX	MA	80	Oxford	&2000
Macniven, Louise	ResAc	20875715	macnivenj1	F	BSC	01	Cardiff	2001

Chinese Univ of Hong Kong

School of Accountancy — Shatin, NT Hong Kong — (852) Fax=26035114 — (13) 1999,1999
Dept Phone: 26097744 — Faculty of Business Adm — baf.msmail.cuhk.edu.hk — **BBA,MAC,MPH,PHD**
Alan Wong
Homepage: http://www.cuhk.edu.hk/acy/index.html

Name	Rank	Phone	Email					
Wong, Tak Jun	C-Pr	26097750	tjwong	F	PHD	90	UCLA	2004
Xie, Jia-Zheng James	D-Pr	26097901	xie	AFMT	PHD	91	Brit Colum	1999

Fan, Joseph P. H.	Prof	26097839	pjfan	F	PHD	96	Pittsburgh	2004
Wu, Woody	Prof	26097834	woody	FM	PHD	92.	NYU	1995
Ferguson, Michael J.	Assoc	26097646	ferguson	BEF	PHD	97	Minnesota	1997
Hung, Mingyi	Assoc	26098604	mhung	FI	PHD	99.	MIT	2006
Jiang, Zhaodong	Assoc	26097751	jiang	LX	SJD	92	Michigan	1995
Lam, Kevin	Assoc	26097894	kevin	IMS	PHD	97	Toronto	* &1998
Rui, Oliver M.	Assoc	26097838	oliver	F	PHD	97.	Houston	2003
Tong Wu, Marian	Assoc	26097833	marian	AEF	MPA	77	Tx-Austin	1989
Young, Danqing	Assoc	26097892	dyoung	BCM	PHD ·	98.	Conn	1998
Lee, Hua	Asst	26097742	leehua	ACF	PHD	01	Ntl Taiwan	2004
Wang, Xin	Asst	26097836	wangx	F	PHD	06.	Duke	2006
Yang, Yong	Asst	26097838	yyong	F	PHD	05.	Nrthwstrn	2005
Zhang, Yinglei	Asst	26097838	yzhang	F	PHD	05.	Ohio St	2005
Zhuang, Zili	Asst	26097776	ziliz	FM	PHD	01	Car Mellon	2006
Cheng, Alan	Inst	26097841	achengwl	F	MA	97	Charles S	&2007
Kan, Shirley	Inst	26098557	skan	FVX	MA	91	Lancaster	&1999
Li, Karen	Inst	26097467	karenli	AFD	MBA	90	SanFranSt	&1999
Wong, Edmund	Inst	26097822	kwong	AS	MBA	97	HKUST	&2001
Wong, Raymond	Inst	26098552	raykwong	AF	MSC	04	HKU	2007
Kwong, K. S.	TFell	26097837	kskwong	EM	MBA	81	ChinesHK	&1986
Leung, Victor	TFell	26097835	victor	CMBA	PHD	91	Arkansas	1980
Ng, Andy	TFell	26097770	andy	AF	MBA	82	Ottawa	&1991

Chosun University
Department of Accounting
Dept Phone: 230-6848
Did Not Respond Again--1998-99 Listing

Kwangju, Korea 501-759
College of Business Adm
375 Seosuk-dong Donggu

82-62 Fax = 232-8834
chosun.ac.kr

BBA,MBA,PHD
Min-Gyun Kim

Chi, Kwang Soo	Dean	230-6817	ksji	Econ	PHD	90	Junnam	1989
Kim, Seung Yong	C-Ac	230-6843	snckim	BCMP	PHD	90	Junnam	1989
Kim, An-Gyu	Prof	230-6837	agkim	ANPS	PHD	96	Seogang	1979
Kim, Ki-Pyung	Prof	230-6812	gpkim	EPRX	PHD	91	Hanyang	1979
Lee, Chun-Eui	Prof	230-6836	celee	BFHW	PHD	92	Sejong	1980
Jo, Seung Je	Assoc	230-6842	sjjo	CIJM	PHD	96	Sejong	1984
Park, Gil-Young	Asst	230-6837	kypark	GNPR	ME	82	Chosun	1979

Chulalongkorn University
Department of Accountancy
Dept Phone: 22185799
Homepage: account.acc.chula.ac.th

Bangkok 10330 Thailand
Faculty of Comm & Accty
Room 206 Building 3

(662) Fax = 22185798
acc.chula.ac.th

BAC,BBA,MAC,PHD
Chatchanee Krabeethong

Kunpanitchakit, Danuja	Dean	22185781	fcomdku	CM	PHD	83	Wisconsin	1976
Soongswang, Oranuj	H-As	22185800	fcomoso	DS	DBA		Miss St	1975
Tanlamai, Uthai	Prof	22185826	fcomutc	DS	PHD	83	Illinois	1995
Boonmak, Supattra	Assoc	22185833		DMS	MA	81	Detroit #	1984
Hirunrusme, Tharee	Assoc	22185814	fcomthi	EFS	MS	72	Radford	1973
Komaratat, Duangmanee	Assoc	22185813	fcomdko	CDMU	MACC	73	Chulalong	1971
Boonyanet, Wachira	Asst	22185818	fcomwby	AFR	PHD	02	Southhamp	&1995
Chalermkanjana, Kotchakorn	Asst	22185816	fcomkch	CM	MACC	82	Chulalong	1976
Chatraphorn, Pongprot	Asst	22185806	fcompct	F	PHD	01.	Va Tech	1995
Cheniam, Supapon	Asst	22185814	fcomsie	DFMS	DBA	94	Miss St	1978
Chookhiatti, Sarun	Asst	22185797	fcomscc	ACDR	MACC	95	Chulalong	&1995
Hawat, Prachit	Asst	22185802	fcompha	ADQS	PHD	98	Calgary	&1986
Keerasuntonpong, Prae	Asst	22185796	fcomprae	CM	MBA	92	SASIN	1995
Orapin, Duangsamorn	Asst	22185797	fcomdor	F	MS	77	S Illinois	1978
Peeyawan, Polpadhoo	Asst	22185814	fcomppe	S	MBA	86	Arizona	1981
Rodwanna, Pannipa	Asst	22185817	fcomprw	ABFS	PHD	96	Chulalong	&1996
Sribunnak, Visarut	Asst	22185796	fcomvsb	F	PHD	04	Berkeley	1994
Tunlayadechanont, Suchitra	Asst	22185801	fcomsvc	FM	PHD	91.	Geo Wash	&1981
Vimuktanandana, Boonserm	Asst	22185815	fcombvi	FIMP	MBA	83	Ariz St	1970
Wongwanich, Suree	Asst	22185833	suree	CFMU	MACC	84	Arkansas	1971
Audsabumrungrat, Juthathip	Lect	22185815	fcomjad	AF	MBA	97	Seattle	&2004
Bidaya, Nantaporn	Lect	22185892	fcomnpi	CM	MAS	71	Illinois	1968
Boonlert-U-Thai, Kriengkrai	Lect	22185743	fcomkbl	F	PHD	04.	Okla St	1995
Chiwamit, Palida	Lect	22185798		FM	MS	03	Warwick	&2007
Jaikengkit, Aim-orn	Lect	22185811	fcomajk	F	PHD	03	Case Wes	1995
Kiattikulwattana, Prapaporn	Lect	22185798	fcompki	F	MACC	00	Chulalong	&2001
Komutphong, Thitiphol	Lect	22185798	fcomtkm	F	MSPA	01	Mich St	&1998
Maneeroj, Parinda	Lect	22185798	fcompmn	F	MSA	97	Illinois	&1995
Manowan, Pavinee	Lect	22885798	fcompma	F	MSPA	02	Mich St	2002
Peetathawatchai, Pimpana	Lect	22185810	fcompss	FI	DBA	96	Boston U	1996
Pongpun, Jirada	Lect	22195798		FM	MSPA	03	Mich St	&2007
Pornupatham, Sompong	Lect	22185819	fcomspu	AFSX	PHD	06	Cardiff	&2000
Shutibhinyo, Wasatorn	Lect	22185182	fcomwsu	ACM	MACC	04	Chulalong	&2004
Soncharoen, Sonthilaksn	Lect	22185837	fcomsso	FMP	MBA	81	Wisconsin	1970
Tachamontrikul, Suphamit	Lect	22185801	fcomstc	AIO	DBA	97	Chulalong	&1988
Tepalagul, Nopmanee	Lect	22185811	fcomntp	F	MBA	03	Imperial	&2005
Toommanon, Vorasak	Lect	22185820	fcomvto	F	PHD	92.	Okla St	1983
Vichitsarawong, Thanyaluk	Lect	22185798	fcomtvc	F	MBA	01	Illinois	&1997

Chung-Ang University
Department of Accounting
Dept Phone: 820-5535
Homepage: www.cau.ac.kr
Did Not Respond Again--2003-2004 Listing

Seoul, Korea   156-756
College of Business Adm
221 Hukseuk-Dong

822 Fax=813-8910
chungang.edu   BBA,MBA,PHD

Jang, Jee In	Dean	820-5564	jjang	FI	PHD	89	SUNY-Buf	1990
Cheon, Youngsoon Susan	C-Ac	820-5572	yscheon	FIV	PHD	94.	Georgia	&2000
Kim, Kil-Cho	Prof	820-5561	kekim	AS	PHD	80	Korea	1980
Koh, Sung Sam	Prof	820-5563	sskoh	AX	PHD	99	Inha	&1978
Hwang, In-Tae	Assoc	820-5571	ihwang	FI	PHD	94.	SUNY-Buf	&1995
Choe, Kukhyun	Asst	820-5577	kukchoe	FTA	PHD	99	Geo Wash	&2002
Hong, Cheolkyu	Asst	820-5575	ckhong04	CMQT	PHD	98	London SE	2002

Chung-Ang University
Department of Accounting
Dept Phone: 670-3197
Did Not Respond Again--2001-2002 Listing

Ansung-Shi Korea 456-756
School of Business
40-1 Nae-Ri, Daeduk-Myun

8231 Fax=675-1384
cau.ac.kr   BBA,MBA,PHD

Kim, Changsoo	C-Ac	670-3225	kimc	AFS	PHD	93	Fla Intl	1994
Choi, Jung Ho	Prof	670-3222		FPQ	PHD	87.	Houston	1988
Huh, Youngpin	Prof	670-3221	yphuh	CMI	PHD	86	Korea	1984
Lee, Yang Hyun	Prof	670-3220		FX	PHD	85	Chung-Ang	1985
Lim, Changwoo P.	Assoc	670-3223		CMY	PHD	89.	Purdue	1989
Na, Young	Assoc	670-3224	nayoung	CPQT	PHD	93.	Rutgers	1993

City Univ of Hong Kong
Department of Accountancy
Dept Phone: 27887932
Homepage: http://www.cityu.edu.hk/ac/

Kowloon Tong   Hong Kong
Faculty of Business
83 Tat Chee Avenue

(852) Fax=27887944   2004,2004
cityu.edu.hk   BA,MA,MPHL,PHD
                            Ms. Winnie Chung

Chen, Charles J. P.	H-Ac	27887909	achead	FM	PHD	95	Houston	9-95
Courtis, John K.	Prof	27887945	acapjajc	VTH	PHD	74.	Minnesota	&1992
Hui, W. F.	Assoc	27887908	acwf	V	MBA	89	Brunel	& 7-84
Kim, Francis C.	Assoc	27887912	acckim	FM	PHD	94	Baruch	2004
Leung, Sidney C. M.	Assoc	27887924	acsleung	FYA	PHD	97	NS Wales	&1997
Low, Pek Yee	VFell	27887946	aclow	IV	PHD	96.	Nebraska	&1996
Lynn, Stephen G.	Assoc	27888546	acsgl	IMV	PHD	97	NYU	1997
Poon, Margaret C. C.	Assoc	27888486	acmp	EMB	PHD	96	Bradford	9-87
Su, Xijia	Assoc	27887995	acsu	AFIT	PHD	96	Concordia	9-96
Yip, David S. O.	VAsoc	27888548	acdy	CMT	MSC	87	LondonEc	9-89
Chen, Zhihong	Asst	27887912	chenzhh	F	PHD	05	HKUST	2006
Dithipyangkul, Pattarin	Asst	27887919	padithip	MTO	PHD	05	Brit Colum	2005
Fidow, Margarret A.	Asst	27887906	acmf	MSJ	MCOM	80	Auckland	* 8-89
Guan, Yu Yan	Asst	27887136	yyguan	F	PHD	06	Toronto	2006
Leung, Olivia S. L.	Asst	27887928	olivia	FMC	PHD	04	CityU HK	&2004
Leung, Tak Yan	Asst	27844763	acyleung	AF	PHD	04	PolyU HK	&2005
Ma, Alfred K. W.	Asst	27887917	acma	MF	MBA	86	ChinesHK	9-89
Poh, Paul P. H.	Asst	27888488	acpp	M	MBA	89	Henley	2-90
Richardson, Grant	Asst	27887923	acgrant	X	PHD	02	Monash	&2003
Shieh, Tony	Asst	27887910	acts	IF	PHD	99.	NYU	1999
Sohn, B. Charlie	Asst	27888964	bcohn	AFT	PHD	06	Seoul Ntl	2006
Wa, Jeanette H. S.	Asst	27887907	acjw	A	MBA	94	Henley	9-86
Yang, Zhi Feng	Asst	27844013	zhifeng	F	PHD	06	Alberta	8-06
Yim, Andrew T. L.	Asst	27888544	acatyim	AMT	PHD	95	Yale	2001
Zhang, Tianyu	Asst	27888043	tyzhang	F	PHD	05	HKUST	2005
Chai, Deborah H. S.	Inst	27887902	acchai	CMTJ	MSCA	99	UMIST	# 2004
Chan, Yvonne	Inst	27887469	yvonnec	A	MBA	03	HKUST	O-06
Lai, David T. W.	Inst	27887843	acdavid	FXL	MTAX	04	Sydney	* &2005
Lai, Min Mei	Inst	27887153	aclai	F	MBA	83	Ohio U	4-97
Mak, Kelvin P. L.	Inst	27888545	ackm	X	MAIA	98	CityUnHK	N-00
Mok, Annie Y. N.	Inst	27887414	acannie	FMAX	MBA		CityU HK	
Ong, April W. Y.	Inst	27887935	april.wong	FX	MA	03	CityU HK	&2005
Wong, Jenny S. F.	Inst	27888547	ac.jenny	F	MA	98	HKUST	1-07
Wong, Sai On	TFell	27888484	acso	FM	MBA	83	Alberta	* 2002
Wong, Sunny T. M.	TFell	27887855	actm	VM	MBA	92	Heriot-W	* 1998

Univ Nacional de Cordoba
Accounting Faculty
Dept Phone:
Did Not Respond Again--1998-99 Listing

Cordoba CP 5000 Argentina
Grupo de Investigacion
Av Valparaiso S/N

Fax=
eco.uncor.edu   BA,BB,MBA,PHD

de Roitter, Hebe G.	Dean						
Garcia, Norberto	D		ngarcia		PHD		DeCordoba
Porporato, Marcela	Prof		porpomar		MS		Suffolk
Sandin, Ariel	Prof		asandin		ABD		DeCordoba

Coventry University
Accounting Division
Dept Phone: 888410
Homepage: www.stile.coventry.ac.uk
Did Not Respond Again--2001-2002 Listing

Coventry CV1 5FB
Coventry Bus School

England   0247   Fax=888400
coventry.ac.uk   BS,MBA
Mrs. G. Child

Morris, D.	Dean	888412	d.morris	VSF	MSOC	80	Birminghm	& 4-74
Sara, Graham L.	H-Pl	888449	g.sara	VBM	MSC	85	Warwick	& 9-80
Horsman, Simon J.	SLect	888462	s.lorsman	FM	MA	69	Manchest	9-71
Hughes, Steward	SLect	888410	s.hughes	AFX	BSC	84	Exeter	&N-94
Maynard, Jennifer	SLect	888410	j.maynard	VM	MSC	71	Warwick	9-73
Panther, John H.	PLect	888456	j.panther	P	MPHL	75	Warwick	9-72
Redhead, Keith J.	PLect	888473	k.redhead	M	MBA	90	Warwick	9-98
Proctor, Raymond	SLect	888423	r.proctor	DQ	MSC			9-71
Blight, David	PLect	888468	d.blight					

University of Cyprus
Dept of Bus Adm
Dept Phone: 22892461
Did Not Respond Again--2003-2004 Listing

Nicosia, Cyprus   CY 1678
Div Accounting & Fnce
Kallipoleos 75, PO Box 20537

(357) Fax=22892460
ucy.ac.cy   BSC,MSC,PHD
Myna Fourri, Eugenia Tsinti

Leonidou, Leonidas	Dean	22892461			PHD	87	Bath	1992
Charitou, Andreas	C-Ac	22892469	charitou	FMI	PHD	86.	Penn St	* &1992
Charalambous, Chris	Prof	22892461	bacchris	Q	PHD	71	McMaster	1993
Trigeorgis, Lenos	Prof	22892461	lenos	F	PHD	86	Harvard	1993
Zenios, Stavros A.	Prof	22892461	zenioss	F	PHD	86	Princeton	1993
Vafeas, Nikos	Assoc	22892461	bafeas	FMI	PHD	94.	Kansas	&1994
Diold, Christioua	Asst	22892462			BS	97	Oxford	&2002
Karamanou, Irene	Asst	22892461		FMI	PHD	00.	Penn St	2000
Kassinis, George	Asst	22892461		FMW	PHD	97	Princeton	1997
Martzoukos, Spyros	Asst	22892461		FQT	PHD	95	Geo Wash	1998
Nisiotis, George	VAsst	22892461		FQ	PHD	99	Nrthwstrn	2001
Pierides, Yiannis	Asst	22892461	bayianni	F	PHD	94	MIT	1994
Tsaggari, Harithini	VAsst	22892461		QF	PHD	00	Penn St	2000
Timinis, Loizos	Inst	22892461		FMA	BS	87	LondonEc	&1994
Mavrides, Costas	Lect	22892461		F	PHD	95.	Houston	1995

Deakin Univ at Burwood
Sch of Accounting & Finance
Dept Phone: 92446626
Did Not Respond Again--2003-2004 Listing

Burwood Victoria   Australia
Faculty Bus & Law   3125

(613) Fax=92517243
deakin.edu.au   BCOM,MCOM,PHD

Jackling, Beverley	H-SL$	92446180	bevjackl	ME	PHD	01	Melbourne	&1991
Batten, Jonathan	Prof	92446560	jabatten	F	PHD	96	Sydney	2000
Hutchinson, Marion	SLect	92446913	hutch	MQY	PHD	01	Deakin	&1998
McDonald, Thomas	SLect	92446359	tomxx	DF	MCOM	91	Deakin	1978
McGinley, Leslie	SLect	92446577	lessmcg	F	MEC	78	Monash	1988
Donald, John	Lect	92446466	johnd	FM	MBA	86	Monash	1987
Ekanayake, Samson	Lect	92446563	samson	FM	MA	82	Lancaster	1992
Johnson, Rodney	Lect	92446227	rodj	FA	MEC	93	N Eng-Au	1978
Nagy, Judy	Lect	92446178	jnagy	M	BCOM	80	Melbourne	&1998
Purnell, Allan	Lect	92446267	allanp	F	BBUS	76	VColl	&1984
Raar, Jean	Lect	92446470	raar	EM	PHD	99	RMIT	&1993
Thomson, Dianne	Lect	92446173	dithom	F	BCOM	88	LaTrobe	2002
VanEekelen, Antonie	Lect	92446174	tveek	EF	BED	85	VColl	1989
Viney, Christopher W.	Lect	92446906	cviney	F	MBAS	96	Monash	1999
Vinning, Russell	Lect	92446535	rvinn	F	MBA	91	Monash	&1988

Deakin University-Geelong
Sch of Accounting & Finance
Dept Phone: 52271287
Homepage: http://www.deakin.edu.au/fac-buslaw/acc-fin/
Did Not Respond Again--2003-2004 Listing

Geelong Victoria   Australia
Faculty Bus & Law 3217

(613) Fax=52271255
deakin.edu.au   BCOM,MCOM,PHD

Clarke, Philip H.	Dean	52272748	deanbuslaw		LLM		Auckland	
Carnegie, Garry D.	Prof	52272566	carnegie	FH	PHD	94	Flinders	&1988
O'Connell, Brendan T.	Assoc	52271287	boconnel	F	PHD	99	Monash	&2002
Clayton, Bruce M.	SLect	52271420	bc	CM	DCOM	84	Potchef	1982
Kelly, Chris F.	SLect	52272562	cfk	AF	MEC	81	N Eng-Au	&1977
Norris, Gweneth	SLect	52272568	gweneth	BCM	MCOM	93	Deakin	&1983
Dimovski, William	Lect	52272560	wd	F	MBA	79	GSU	&1985
Kelly, Andrea	Lect	52272132	andreak	F	BCOM	93	Deakin	1994
Kerry, Mike	Lect	52272467	mk	F	MCOM	92	Melbourne	&2002
Margret, Julie	Lect	52272131	jemz	FM	MCOM	94	Deakin	1992
Williams, Sarah	Lect	52272567	sarahw	F	MCOM	96	Deakin	&1983
Yee, Helen	Lect	52272732	helenyee	F	MA	84	Dundee	1992

Deakin Univ - Warrnambool   Warrnambool 3280   Australia   (613) Fax=55633320
Sch of Accounting & Finance   Faculty of Bus & Law   deakin.edu.au   BCOM,MCOM,PHD
Dept Phone: 55633510   Denise Patterson
Homepage: http://www.deakin.edu.au/fac_buslaw/acc-fin

Name	Rank	Phone	Email					
Wines, Graeme	Assoc	55633271	winesg	AFT	MEC	92	N Eng-Au	&1984
Betts, Jenny	Lect	55633254	bettsj	FE	MBA	89	Monash	&1986
Williams, Brian G.	Lect	55633230	brianw	FHE	GDAC	80	Deakin	&1988

Dongguk University   Seoul 100-715   Korea   02822 Fax=22603684
Department of Accounting   College of Bus & Econ   cakra.dongguk.ac.kr   BS,MS,PHD
Dept Phone: 22603518   3-Ga, Pil-Dong, Chung-Gu
    Did Not Respond--2005-2006 Listing; phone 2260-3518

Name	Rank	Phone	Email					
Chung, Yong-Keun	C-Pr	Ext 3291	ykchung	FPV	PHD	86	Korea	3-80
Han, Jin-Soo	Prof	Ext 3294	jshan	SF	PHD	86.	Indiana	9-86
Kim, Dong C.	Prof	Ext 3295	dckim	BCM	PHD	89.	Iowa	9-91
Kim, Jin-Sun	Assoc	Ext 3719	jsnk	FPT	PHD	90.	Tx-Austin	9-95
Park, Jaewan	Assoc	Ext 3819	jwpark	ACM	PHD	95.	Tx-Austin	9-96
Kim, Kap-Soon	Asst	Ext 3293	kks	XF	PHD	98	Seoul Ntl	3-02
Lee, Sang-Chul	Asst	Ext 3899	sclee68	CM	PHD	02	Yonsei	9-04

University College Dublin   Belfield Dublin4   Ireland   353 1 Fax=716 4707   2003,2003
Department of Accountancy   Quinn Sch of Business   ucd.ie   BCOM,MACC,PHD
Dept Phone: 716-4700   Catherine Allen, Erin Finnerty
Homepage: www.ucdie/~commere/accounting/accountinghome.htm

Name	Rank	Phone	Email					
Begley, Tom	Dean			Bus	PHD		Cornell	
Clarke, Peter J.	H-Pr	716-4711	peter.clarke	EMH	PHD	84	Dublin	&1980
Brennan, Niamh	Prof	716-4707	niamh.brennan	FIY	PHD	95	Warwick	&1980
Walsh, Eamonn J.	Prof	716-8090	eamonn.walsh	FIP	PHD	83	Glasgow	1999
Brabazon, Anthony	SLect	716-4705	tony.brabaon	CDM	MS	95	Kingston	* &1992
Pierce, Aileen	SLect	716-4745	aileen.pierce	FIP	PHD	75	Dublin	&1979
Doyle, Gerardine	Lect	716-4717	gerardine.doyle	FIMN	BSC	85	Dublin	&1992
Drechsler, Christoph	Lect	716-4772	christoph-dre+		PHD	02	Paris	2002
Harrigan, Fiona	Lect	716-4724	fiona.m.harrigan					2001
Kenny, Mark	Lect	716-4829	mark.kenny	FIP	ACA			2004
Lee, Linden	Lect	716-8996	linden.lee	D				&1992
McCallig, John	Lect	716-4730	john.mccallig	DMF	PHDM	03	Lancaster	* &1993
O'Dea, William A.	Lect	716-4741	tony.odea	CM	MCOM	80	Dublin	* 1991
Tagoe, Noel	Lect	716-4755	noel.tagoe	M	PHD		Dundee	2001

Dublin City University   Dublin 9   Ireland   353 1 Fax=700 5446
Accounting Group   Business School   dcu.ie   BAAF,PDA,MBS,PH
Dept Phone: 700 5681   Clare Balfe
    Did Not Respond--2005-2006 Listing

Name	Rank	Phone	Email					
Pierce, Bernard	Dean$	700 5450	bernard.pierce	JM	PHD	93	Lancaster	&1982
Willis, Pauline	C-Le$	700 5451	pauline.willis	EFX	BCOM	82	NUI	&1987
Byrne, Marann	SLect	700 5166	marann.byrne	EFT	PHD	92	Dublin Cty	&1982
Canning, Mary	SLect	700 5679	mary.canning	AF	PHD	97	Wales	&1992
O hOgartaigh, Ciaran	SLect	700 5637	ciaran.ohogar+	BFHI	PHD	97	Leeds	&1992
Flood, Barbara	Lect	700 5684	barbard.flood	EM	PHD	04	Loughbor	&1995
Mattimoe, Ruth	Lect	700 5171	ruth.mattimoe	M	PHD	03	Manchest	&1986
McCluskey, Tom	Lect	700 5167	thomas.mcclu+	FX	BCOM	77	NUI	&1982
Murphy, Brid	Lect	700 5685	brid.murphy	AEM	MACC	95	NUI	&2002
Smith, Barry	Lect	700 5441	barry.smith	DFS	MECO	01	NUI	&2001
Townsend, Eileen	Lect	700 5852	eileen.townsend	AF	MBS	95	Dublin Cty	&2001

University of Dundee   Dundee, DD1 4HN   Scotland   01382 Fax=388421
Dept Accounting & Finance   Arts & Social Sciences   dundee.ac.uk   BACC,MA,PHD
Dept Phone: 384193   Perth Road   Alison Anderson, Audrey Stewart
Homepage: www.dundee.ac.uk

Name	Rank	Phone	Email					
Burns, John E.	Dean	384769	j.e.burns	MTUS	PHD	96	Manchest	2004
Gallhofer, Sonja	Prof	386706	s.hallhofer	EHIT	PHD	84	Austria	2005
Haslam, James	Prof	384857	j.a.haslam	HGTW	PHD	92	Essex	&2004
Helliar, Christine V.	Prof	384198	c.v.helliar	ACFK	PHD	99	Dundee	&1990
Nixon, Bill	Prof	384200	w.a.nixon	MBSC	PHD	95	Dundee	&1982
Power, David M.	Prof	384854	d.m.power	FQTI	PHD	92	Dundee	1987
Brown, Richard A.	SLect	385879	r.a.brown	DQS	PHD	70	Newcastle	2001
Burton, Bruce M.	SLect	384199	b.m.burton	FJMT	PHD	98	Dundee	1999
Collison, David J.	SLect	384192	d.j.collison	FMTA	MACC	93	Dundee	&1989
Lyon, Robert A.	SLect	384195	r.a.lyon	IMVZ	MA	69	Dundee	* &1976
Stevenson, Lorna A.	SLect	384196	l.a.stevenson	EFJW	BA	89	Strathcl	&2000
Tooze, Michael J.	SLect	388250	m.j.tooze	MBT	MA	66	St Andrew	1966
Baldvinsdottir, Gudrun	Lect							2005
Cobb, Ian	Lect	387941	i.cobb	CDMS	PHD	97	Dundee	* 1989

Crawford, Louise	Lect	386803	l.crawford	AESN	PHD	90	Edinburgh	2006
Dey, Colin	Lect	385838	c.r.dey	WJDM	PHD		Edinburgh	1997
Dunne, Theresa	Lect	85174	t.m.dunne	BEFI	PHD	03	Dundee	2003
Ferguson, John	Lect	84941	j.x.ferguson	ETWJ	MACC	02	Dundee	2005
Fifield, Suzanne	Lect	385148	s.g.m.fifield	FITZ	PHD	99	Dundee	2000
Fox, Alison	Lect	384873	a.m.fox	FX	BA	89	Dundee	&2000
Hannah, Gwen	Lect	85147	g.m.hannah	INLX	PHD	04	Dundee	2003
Kamia, Rania	Lect	386804	r.kamia	IJTW	PHD	05	Edinburgh	2006
Michaelson, Rosa	Fello	384858	r.michaelson	DQSE	MSC	83	Heriot W	1990
Monk, Lissa	Fello	384789	l.a.monk	DQSE	BA	87	Liverpool	1997

University of East Anglia Norwich, NR4 7TJ England 01603 Fax=593715
Faculty Accountancy & Fnce School of Management uea.ac.uk
Dept Phone: 592316

Williams, Bernard C.	H-SL	592310	b.williams	SAD	PHD			&
Kaye, R.	Prof	591463	t.kaye	SCM	MSC		Sheffield	
Dewing, I. P.	SLect	592316	i.dewing	FG	BA			&
Russell, P. O.	SLect	593256	p.o.russell	AGN	MA		Manchest	&1981
Greenhalgh, Robert	Lect	591286	robert.greenh+	CM	BA	82	Wales	&
Guven, P.	Lect	591179	p.guven	BCM	PHD		E Anglia	
Lovatt, D. A.	Lect	592316	d.lovatt	FM	PHD		Cambridge	

University of East London Dagenham Essex England (081) Fax=849-3529
Accounting & Finance Group Business RM8 2AS BA,MBA,MA,DBA
Dept Phone: Ext 2135 Longbridge Road
Did Not Respond Again--2003-2004 Listing; school phone: 081-590-7722

Bashir, Tariq H.	SLect	Ext 2301	F	BA	1991
Clingan, J. A. P.	SLect	Ext 6222	FM	BA	1978
Cooper, R. J.	SLect	Ext 2180	FM	MSC	1984
Everitt, Mary	SLect	Ext 2186	FT	BA	1985
Lawrence, S. C.	SLect	Ext 2188	FMI	MSC	&1984
Malinowski, Carolyn	SLect	Ext 2179	F	BA	1987
O'Connor, W.	SLect	Ext 2295	F	MSC	1986
Stirk, Christina	SLect	Ext 2709	X	BA	1990
Tobbell, Graham	SLect	Ext 2218	FM	BSC	1991

University of Essex Colchester England 01206 Fax=873429
Dept of Atg, Fnce & Mgt Business Faculty C043SQ uk.ac.essex BSC,MA,MSC,PHD
Dept Phone: 872546 Mrs. Joanna Partner
Did Not Respond Again--2003-2004 Listing

Sikka, Prem N.	H-Pr	873773	prems	AEFW	PHD	91	Sheffield	&1996
Arnold, Tony J.	Prof	872730	arna	FHT	PHD	95	LondonEc	&1985
Coakley, Jerry	Prof	872455	jcoakley	FQ	PHD	92	Open	2001
McSweeney, Brendan M.	Prof	873973	bmcs	AFBM	PHD	95	LondonEc	1999
Seal, William	Prof	873492	wdseal	FM	PHD	91	Sheffield	1998
Sherer, Michael J.	Prof	872762	mikes	AFMN	MA	72	Manchest	&1984
Wearing, Robert T.	Assoc	872750	wear	FGNI	PHD	91	Essex	&1980
Abdala, Khaled	Asst	872465	khala	DSQ	PHD	98	Birminghm	2000
Abdel-Kader, Magdy	Asst	872375	mabdel	FM	PHD	97	Bristol	2000
Brewis, Joanna	Asst	873813	jbrewis	BM	PHD	96	Manchest	1999
Collins, David	Asst	873491	dscollin	BM	MSC	89	Strathcl	1999
Dale, Karen	Asst	874156	kdale	BM				2002
Haven, Emmanuel	Asst	873768	ehaven	PQ	PHD	01	Montreal	1999
Kellard, Neil	Asst	874153	nkellard	F	PHD	00	Nottingh	2002
King, Ian	Asst	872637	kingi	BM	PHD	90	Liverpool	1990
Ma, Chenghu	Asst	874670	cma	FQ	PHD	92	Montreal	1999
Manson, Stuart	Asst	872063	manss	AFT ·	MA	79	Strathcl	&1988
McCartney, Sean	Asst	872373	mccas	AFTX	MSC	90	LondonEc	&1991
Milanova, Elena	Asst	873371	emilan	BMI	DIP	92	HIE	2000
Stittle, John	Asst	874860	jstittle	AFW	MSC	88	London	2001
Thomas, Hardy M.	Asst	873432	hardt	DFMQ	PHD	94	Ulster	1991
Uddin, Shahzad	Asst	874150	snuddin	AEFW	PHD	97	Manchest	2002
Watkins, Ceri	Asst	874877	cwatki	MI	MA			2002
Wood, Andrew	Asst	872402	wooda	FI	PHD	00	London	2001

University of Exeter Exeter EX4 4PU England 01392 Fax=263210
Accounting Faculty Sch of Business & Econ exeter.ac.uk BA,MPHIL,PHD
Dept Phone: 263201 Rennes Drive Mrs. C. I. Downs
Did Not Respond Again--2002-2003 Listing

Cooke, Terence E.	H-Pr	263239	t.e.cooke	FI	PHD	89	Exeter	&1980
Parker, Robert H.	Prof	263209	r.h.parker	FHI	BSC	54	London	&1976
Tippett, Mark J.	Prof	264484	m.tippett	CMQ	PHD	79	Edinburgh	&1997
Collier, Paul A.	Lect	263238	p.a.collier	DX	PHD	94	Exeter	&1984

Haniffa, Roszaini M.	Lect	263234	r.mohamad-han+	FI	PHD	99	Exeter	1999
McMeeking, Kevin P.	Lect	263206	k.p.mcmeeking	A	PHD	00	Lancaster	1999
Shah, Syed Zultiqar Ali	Lect	263216	sza_shah	CF	MBA	97	Peshawap	2001
Wright, Brian	Lect	264480	b.wright	CF	MSC	98	Aberyst	2001
Lim, Chen	Tutor	264523	c.v.lim	CF	MSC	00	Lancaster	2001

Flinders U of S Australia GPOBox 2100 5001   Australia   61-08 Fax=82012644
School of Commerce   Faculty of Soc Sciences   afm1.law.flinders.edu. BCOM,MCOM,PHD
Dept Phone: 82012226   Ms. Mary Bywater 82012226
  Did Not Respond Again--2000-2001 Listing

McMahon, Richard G. P.	H-Pr	82012840	mcmahon	IF	PHD	98	N Eng-Au	& 1-78
Bohn, Helmut	LectA	82013898	bohn	AY	BEC	96	Flinders	2-98
Demosthendus, Maz	LectA	82013896	demosthe	TP	DIP	97	S Austr	2-98
Kandunias, Chris	LectA	82013893	kandunia	DTQ	BCOM	92	Adelaide	1-93
Larkin, Jim	LectA	82013300	larkin	QAT	BA	91	SAIT	1-96
Brand, Vivienne	LectB	82012729	brand	LWEJ	LLM	92	London	2-95
Jones, Jane	LectB	82012707	jones	BM	MCOM	96	NS Wales	7-97
Kenny, Paul	LectB	82012102	kenny	XTI	MTAX	98	Deakin	2-95
Petrone, Franca	LectB	82012013	petrone	IJLM	MBA	98	Adelaide	1-93
Stanger, Anthony M. J.	LectB	82012764	stanger	AFQ	MCOM	98	N Eng-Au	2-89
Superina, Susan C.	LectB	82012766	superina	FDS	MBA	95	Adelaide	2-88
Xydias, Maria	LectB	82013891	xydias	3CM	MCOM	97	Adelaide	1-93
Forsaith, David M.	LectC	82012344	forsaith	FI	MSC	75	London	7-90
Gerhardy, Peter G.	LectC	82012397	gerhardy	AT	MEC	86	N Eng-Au	1-86
Symes, Christopher	LectC	82013890	symes	IJL	LLM	96	Adelaide	1-93
Tilt, Carol A.	LectC	82013892	tilt	CDW	PHD	98	Flinders	1-93

University of Glamorgan Treforest, Wales   U Kingdom   1443 Fax=482711
Accounting Faculty   Sch of Atg & Math   glam.ac.uk   BA,MSC,MPHL,PHD
Dept Phone: 482251
Homepage: http://www.maths.glam.ac.uk
  Did Not Respond Again--1999-2000 Listing

Ryley, Alan R.	C-Pr	482250	aryley	Math	PHD	81	Salford	1-89
Coombs, Hugh M.	PLect	482392	hmcoombs	NMI	PHD	98	Glamorgan	& 1-87
Davies, Jeff R.	PLect	482594	jrdavies	SM	MA	69	Wansea	* 4-75
Davies, Marlene	PLect	482364	mdavies7	AN	BSC	74	Wales	& 6-89
Grant Thornton Research Fellow								
Jenkins, D. Ellis	PLect	482585	ejenkins	NM	MSOC	79	Birmingh	& 1-79
Brown, Nigel	SLect	482471	nbrown1	BF	BA	79	Kent	& 9-98
Christopher, Jeff	SLect	482321	jchristo	FS	MA	78	Manchest	* & 9-78
Gracia, Louise	SLect	482592	lgracia	FX	BA	93	Glamorgan	7-93
Hobbs, Dave	SLect	482349	dhobbs	CM	MBA	94	Strathcl	* 1-91
James, Lisa E.	SLect	482346	ljames	NA	BA	87	Glamorgan	& 1-95
Lane, Alison J.	SLect	482592	alane	NM	BA	86	Lancaster	&O-94
Marriot, Pru	SLect	482592	pmarriot	FS	BA	89	Glamorgan	& 9-91
McCarthy, Simon D. I.	SLect	482471	smccarth	FS	BSC	90	Cardiff	&O-94
Porch, Mike G.	SLect	482392	mporch	XFM	BSC	86	Wansea	& 1-96
Shellard, Elaine	SLect	482346	eshellar	MG	CPFA	77		& 9-91
Williams, Hywel D.	SLect	482471	hwilliam	XMF	BA	77	Glamorgan	& 9-86
Williams, Mel C.	SLect	482349	mcwillia	BF	MSC	79	Bath	* & 9-89

University of Glasgow Glasgow G12 8QQ   Scotland 44141 Fax=330-4442   2006
Dept of Accounting & Finance Glasgow Business School   accfin.gla.ac.uk   BACC,MACC,PHD
Dept Phone: 339-8855   W Quadrangle, Main Bldg Univ   Mrs. Veda Smillie
Homepage: http://www.accfin.gla.ac.uk/accfin/
  area code (011-44)

Opong, Kwaku K.	H-Pr	339-8855	k.opong	F	PHD	89	Glasgow	2002
Beattie, Vivien A.	Prof	339-8855	v.beattie	AFE	PHD	94	Southampt	&2004
Danbolt, Jo	Prof	339-8855	j.danbolt	F	PHD	97	Heriot-Wat	1998
Emmanuel, Clive R.	Prof	339-8855	c.emmanuel	FMS	PHD	72	Lancaster	1987
Holland, John B.	Prof	339-8855	j.holland	IM	PHD	78	CNAA	1979
McPhail, Kenneth J.	Prof	339-8855	k.mcphail	JEN	PHD	97	Dundee	1997
Aleksanyan, Mark	Asst	339-8855	m.aleksanyan	F	PHD	04	Glasgow	2004
Jetty, Juliana	Asst	339-8855	j.jetty	DF	PHD	03	Dundee	2002
Kininmonth, Kirsten	Asst	339-8855	k.kininmonth	HM	BACC	98	Paisley	2002
Kominis, George	Asst	339-8855	g.kominis	MB	PHD	02	Glasgow	2002
Kreander, Niklas	Asst	339-8855	n.kreander	FW	PHD	03	Glasgow	2002
McKernan, John F.	Asst	339-8855	j.f.mckernan	F	PHD	01	Glasgow	1990
Milner, Margaret M.	Asst	339-8855	m.m.milner	QS	MACC	87	Glasgow	1986
Siganos, Antonios	Asst	339-8855	a.siganos	F	MA	01	Exeter	2004
Stoner, Gregory N.	Asst	339-8855	g.n.stoner	MS	BSC	78	Lancaster	&1984

University of Graz	A-8010 Graz	Austria		0316	Fax=380-9565			
Accounting Faculty	Fac Comm & Social Sci			uni-graz.at			BS,MBA,DR,PHD	
Dept Phone: 380-3500	Universitaetsstrasse 15						Marika Adam	
Mandl, Gerwald	Prof	380-3470	gerwald.mandl	AF	PHD	77	Vienna	1978
Niemann, Ranier	Prof	380-6444	ranier.niemann	FX	PHD	04	Tuebingen	2004
Wagenhofer, Alfred	Prof	380-3500	alfred.wagenh+	YIMF	PHD	90	Vienna	1991
Klonigsmaier, Heinz	Asst	380-3471	heinz.koenigs+	AFI	PHD	04	U Graz	1988

Griffith University	Nathan, Brisbane	Australia		61-07	Fax=38757760			
Sch of Atg, Banking & Fnce	Faculty of Comm & Mgt			mailbox.gu.edu.au			BCOM,MCOM,PHD	
Dept Phone: 38757705							Ms. Preethi Weerasinghe	
Homepage: http://www.cad.gu.edu.au/abf/								
Did Not Respond Again--2003-2004 Listing								
Ng, Chew	C-Pr	33821361	c.ng	BFT	PHD	93	Melbourne	&1995
Hodgson, Allan	Prof	38757668	allan.hodgson	FQT	PHD	95	Austr Natl	&1996
Ma, Ronald	Prof	38757761	r-ma	FI	MBA	64	Brit Colum	&1990
Stevenson-Clarke, Peta	Lect	33821064	peta.stevenson	FIQ	PHD	02	Griffith	1999
Auyeung, Pak K.	SLect	38757448	p.auyeung	FM	PHD	01	Griffith	1990
Dagwell, Ron	SLect	38757557	r.dagwell	FV	MFM	80	Queensld	&1981
Huang, Allen R.	SLect	38757278	a.huang	IB	PHD	91	Griffith	1990
Lambert, Cecilia	SLect	38753837	c.lambert	FT	PHD	99	N Eng-Au	&1988
Roca, Eduardo	SLect	38757583	e.roca	FIQ	PHD	99	Griffith	1999
Tahir, Mohammad I.	SLect	38757767	m.tahird.t+	FQT	PHD	01	N Eng-Au	&1999
Windsor, Carolyn A.	SLect	38757598	c.windsor	ABJT	PHD	95	Queensln	1990
Brimble, Mark	Lect	33821355	m.brimble	FQ	BCOM	98	Griffith	2000
Lyons, Lyndon	Lect	38757644	l.lyons	FQ	MCOM	79	NS Wales	1989
Sands, John Stephen	Lect	33821195	j.sands	ABEI	MCOM	89	GCUCGU	1990
Dixon, Glen	ALect	38757609	g.dixon	FQZ	BSC	98	Queenslnd	2001
Hooi, George	ALect	38757776	g.hooi	FQT	BCOM	01	Griffith	2001
Nanayakkara, Gemunu	ALect	38755243	g.nanayakkara	CMN	MBA	99	USQ	2001

Griffith Univ-Gold Coast	Gold Coast GLD	Australia		61-07	Fax=55528068			
School of Accounting & Fnce	Faculty Bus & Hotel Mgt			gu.edu.au			BACC,MACC,PHD	
Dept Phone: 55528539	Parklands Dr, Queensland						Ms. Jo Burling	
Homepage: www.gu.edu.au/school/acf/								
Mia, Lokman	Prof	55528540	l.mia	M	PHD	85	Queensld	&1994
Guilding, Chris	AProf	55528790	c.guilding	MW	PHD	91	Bradford	* 1996
Smith, Christine	AProf	38757670	christine.smith					
Lamminmake, Dawne	ALect	55528791	d.lamminmaki	M	MBA	92	England	* 1996
Alagiah, Ratnam	Lect	55528765	r.alagiah	HIJT	PHD	97	Wollong	1998
McManus, Lisa	Lect	55528022	l.mcmanus	A	BBUS	97	Griffith	1993
Subramaniam, Nava	Lect	55528769	n.subramaniam	M	PHD		Griffith	&1990
Cameron, Robyn	ALect	55528522	r.cameron	FT	BBUS	98	Griffith	1999
Vecchio, Nerina	ALect	55528284	n.vecchio	W	MECO	96	Queenslnd	1998

University of Guam	Mangilao, Guam	96923		(671)	Fax=734-5362			
Accounting Faculty	Sch Bus & Pub Adm			uog9.uog.edu			BBA	
Dept Phone: 735-2501	UOG Station						Ms. Ferna Duplito-Davis	
Homepage: http://www.uog.edu/cbpa								
Williams, Anita B.	Dean	735-2550	awilliam	Mktg	DBA	95	US Intl	1996
Cantoria, Filomena M.	C-Pr	735-2503		AFRM	DBA	84	Phillipe	&1991
Phillips, John M.	Assoc	735-250w	erensiag@y	JVC	MBA	83	Guam	&1981
Crisostomo, Doreen	Inst	735-2529		GFMS	MA	04	Phoenix	2005
Johnson, John	Inst	735-2506		FM	MBA	06	Am InterCo	2007

HEC School of Mgt Paris	Jouy-en-Josas	France		331	Fax=39677086			2001
Dept of Atg & Controll 78351	HEC School of Mgt			hec.fr			MBA,MSCM,PHD	
Dept Phone: 39677293	1, rue de la Liberation						Marie-Helene Chaix	
Homepage: www.hec.fr								
Malleret, Veronique	Dean$	39677264	malleret	CUMN	PHD	93	Paris IX	1987
Chiapello, Eve	H-Ac	39673441	chiapello	BMTW	PHD	89	Paris IX	1989
Cauvin, Christian	Prof	39677289	cauvin	ACFM	HECD	69	HEC Paris	&1970
Fiol, Michel	Prof	39677281	fiol	BEMU	PHD	91	Paris IX	1985
Jordan, Hugues	Prof	39677293	jordan	CUM	HECD	69	HEC Paris	1970
Pham, H. Dang	Prof	39677282	phamhuy	FTIE	HECD	67	HEC Paris	1968
Sole, Andreu	Prof	39677250	sole	MJSW	PHD	81	Nancy II	1979
Stolowy, Herve	Prof	39679442	stolowy	FIVA	PHD	90	Paris I	&1994
Kalfon, Charles	Assoc	39679218	kalfon	FLNP	HECD	65	HEC Paris	1990
Loning, Helene	Assoc	39677263	loning	MBCI	PHD	94	HEC Paris	1989
Capkun, Vedran	Asst	39679611	capkun	FIAV	PHD	06	HEC Lausa	2006
Dambrin, Claire	Asst	39677294	dambrin	UMCB	PHD	05	Paris IX	2004
Jeanjean, Thomas	Asst	39677286	jeanjean	FAIV	PHD	02	Paris IX	2003
Lambert, Caroline	Asst	39679565	lambert	UMBC	PHD	05	Paris IX	2004
Lesage, Cedric	Attac	39679572	lesage	FABV	PHD	99	Rennes 1	2006
Messner, Martin	Asst	39677477	messner	UCMB	PHD	06	Innsbruck	2006
Ranirez, Carlos	Asst	39677221	ramirezc	AHIJ	PHD	03	EHESS Pari	2002

Hebrew Univ of Jerusalem — Mount Scopus   Israel   972-2 Fax=5881341
Department of Accounting   School of Bus Adm 91905   mscc.huji.ac.il   BA,MBA,PHD
Dept Phone: 5883235
  Did Not Respond Again--2003-2004 Listing

Name	Rank	Phone	Email		Deg	Yr	School	Year
Kornbluth, Jonathan	Dean		mskorn		PHD	70	Imperial	1972
Bar-Yosef, Sasson	C-Pr	588-3104	mssasson	FM	PHD	73	Aston	1978
Julius Fienstein Chair in Accounting								
Barlev, Benzion	Prof	588-3103	bbarlev	F	PHD	70	NYU	&1972
Chaired Professorship								
Peles, Yoram C.	Prof	588-3215	mspeles	M	PHD	69	Chicago	1971
Ophir, Tsvi	Assoc	588-3112	msophir	F	PHD	60.	MIT	1966

Helsinki Sch of Economics — Helsinki Finland   FIN-001000   358-9 Fax=43138678
Dept of Accounting & Finance   Business   hkkk.fi   BS,MS,PHD
Dept Phone: 43138473   Runeberginkatu 14-16   Leena Kallonen
Homepage: www.hkkk.fi/laskenta
  Did Not Respond Again--2003-2004 Listing

Name	Rank	Phone	Email		Deg	Yr	School	Year
Virtanen, Kalervo	C-Pr	43138465	virtanen	CMU	PHD	80	Helsinki	&1965
Artto, Eero	Emer	43138973	artto	FIT	PHD	62	Helsinki	1956
Ikaheimo, Seppo	Prof	43138474	ikaheimo	BF	PHD	96	Turku	1999
Kinnunen, Juha	Prof	43138466	jkinnune	F	PHD	88	Helsinki	1978
Kylakoski, Kalevi	Prof	43138472	kylakosk	CM	PHD	81	Helsinki	1970
Leppiniemi, Jarmo	Prof	43138459	thp@dlc.fi	PFTX	PHD	85	Helsinki	1972
Malmi, Teemu	Prof	43138471	malmi	CM	PHD	97	Helsinki	1990
Troberg, Pontus	Prof	43138634	ptroberg	AFI	PHD	82.	Oklahoma	2000
Seppanen, Harri J.	Asst	43138677	hseppane	FI	PHD	99	Helsinki	1987
Vaivio, Juhani	Asst	43138460	vaivio	CMU	PHD	01	Helsinki	1989
Virtanen, Tuija	Asst	43138476	tvirtane	CM	MS	95	Helsinki	1990
Juurmaa, Risto	Res	43138487	juurmaa	FM	MS	92	Helsinki	1992
Lehtonen, Taru	Res	43138469	tlehton	CGMN	MS	95	Helsinki	1995
Niemi, Lasse	Res	43138733	lniemi	A	MS	96	Helsinki	1996
Sandelin, Mikko	Res	43138457	sandelin	CMU	MS	02	Helsinki	2003
Walden, Risto	Res	43138488	walden	X	MS	93	Helsinki	1997
Koivistoinen, Kari	Lect	43138470	kkoivist	CM	MS	82	Helsinki	1983
Kykkanen, Tapani	Lect	43138461	kykkanen	FM	MS	90	Helsinki	1983
Toiviainen, Kari	Lect	43138468	toiviain	ADFC	MS	83	Helsinki	1983
Riistama, Veijo	Adj	43138462	riistama	AFI	PHD	78	Helsinki	&1963

Hitotsubashi University — Kunitachi, Tokyo   Japan 8601   042   Fax=580-8747
Accounting Area   Faculty of Commerce   srv.cc.hit-u.ac.jp   BA,MA,DBA
Dept Phone: 580-8561   2-1 Naka Kunutachi-Shi
Homepage: http://www.hit-u.ac.jp/commerce/

Name	Rank	Phone	Email		Deg	Yr	School	Year
Obata, Hiroshi	C-Pr	580-8834	cc00065	CM	DBA		Hitotsub	1987
Hiki, Fumiko	Prof	580-8484	cc00384	MC	DBA	07	Hitotsub	1998
Hiromoto, Toshiro	Prof	580-8287		MC	DBA	93	Hitotsub	1981
Itami, Hiroyuki	Prof	580-8950		MY	PHD	73.	Car Mellon	1973
Ito, Kunio	Prof	580-8266		FK	DBA	96	Hitotsub	1980
Mandai, Katsunobu	Prof	580-8273	cc00273	FH	DBA		Hitotsub	1996
Nitta, Tadachika	Prof	580-8880		FA	DBA	87	Hitotsub	1994
Sasaki, Takashi	Prof	580-8685		FA	DBA		Hitotsub	1997
Fukukawa, Hironori	Assoc	580-8468		FA	DBA	02	Hitotsub	2007
Kagaya, Tetsuyuki	Assoc	580-8482	t.kagaya	FA	DBA		Hitotsub	2000

University of Hong Kong — Hong Kong   Hong Kong   (852) Fax=28585614
Faculty of Business & Econ   School of Business   business.hku.hk   BBA,MBA,MFN,PHD
Dept Phone: 28591000   Pokfulam Road   Mrs. Henrietta Yim
  email @1 = hku.hk

Name	Rank	Phone	Email		Deg	Yr	School	Year
Chang, Eric C.	D-Pr	28578347	ecchang	Fnce	PHD	82	Purdue	1997
Lau, Amy Hing-Ling	C-Pr	28578369	ahlau	CMIF	PHD	82.	Wash U	& 6-03
Chan, Chris W. H.	Assoc	28591082	chrischan	MBI	PHD	93.	Missouri	* 1999
Chan, Derek K. W.	Assoc	28578357	dereckchan	F	PHD	95	Brit Colum	2001
O'Connor, Neale G.	Assoc	22415664	oconnor	CM	PHD	96	Griffith	2006
Chan, Lilian Him-Lai	Asst			F	PHD	07	Tx-Dallas	2007
Chiu, Edward K. C.	Asst	28591005	edcchiu@1	FP	BEC	71	Monash	& 9-79
Guan, Yanling	Asst	28578346	ylguan	FM	PHD	06	London	2006
Han, Jun	Asst			FMB	PHD	05	NTU	2005
Lu, Zemin	VAsst	28591026	zmlu	IF	PHD	98.	Tulane	2006
Mao, Chunlin	Asst	28578345	clmao	F	PHD	06.	Penn St	8-06
Wong, David W. S.	Asst	28591006	dwongws	CM	MBA	82	York	9-76
Zhang, Huai	Asst	28591026	hzhang	FI	PHD	00.	Columbia	2003
on leave Nanyang Tech								
Zheng, Liu	Asst	28578349	lzheng	FM	PHD	03	S Calif	2003
Wong, Raymond M. K.	TCons	28591123	raymond	AF	PHD	05	Poly U	2005
Petty, Richard M.	TFell	28591004	rmpetty	AFT	MCOM	96	NS Wales	* &1998

Hong Kong Polytechnic Univ
School of Accounting & Fnce
Dept Phone: 27667038
Homepage: www.af.polyu.edu.hk

Hunghom, Kowloon
Faculty of Business

Hong Kong   (852) Fax=27749364
inet.polyu.edu.hk   BA,MSC,MPHL,PHD

Name	Rank	Phone	Email	Area	Degree	Yr	School	Yr
Tsui, Judy S. L.	Dean	27665093	j.tsui	AJIE	PHD	94	Chinese U	&2002
Chair Professor								
Gul, Ferdinand A.	H-Pr	27667771	afgul	A	PHD	83	N Eng-Au	&2004
Kim, Jeong-Bon	Prof	27667046	afjbkim	FIM	PHD	86.	Temple	&1995
Associate Dean								
Bao, Ben-Hsien	Assoc	27667078	afbhbao	FIT	PHD	84.	Missouri	1996
Chan, Samuel	Assoc	27667050	afschan	XCJ	PHD	01	RMIT	1984
Chen, Shimin	Assoc	27667028	afschen	FM	PHD	92.	Georgia	2005
Cheng, Peter	Assoc	27664582	afpsch	FMT	PHD	82.	Mich St	2001
Cheung, Daniel	Assoc	27667060	afdaniel	X	PHD	04	Chinese U	1984
Cho, Stella	Assoc	27667071	afstella	X	PHD	99	HongKong	&1983
Yu, Wayne	Assoc	27667970	afwyu	F	PHD	97	Alberta	1999
Yuen, Susana	Assoc	27667059	afsyuen	CMU	PHD	98	Bond	&1997
Bliss, Mark	Asst	27667058	afmbliss	AF	PHD	06	City U	2004
Chau, Gerald K.	Asst	27667061	afgerald	A	PHD	00	Warwick	1984
Cheng, June	Asst	27664084	afzcheng	AIS	PHD	05	Ohio St	2005
Fung, Yu Kit Simon	Asst	27664246	afsf	AF	PHD	06	City U	2004
Huang, Yuan	Asst	27667953	afyhuang	AF	PHD	06	HKUST	
Lau, Thomas	Asst	27664396	afthomas	AF	PHD	99	Chinese	2000
Leung, Patrick W. Y.	Asst	27667031	afpleung	AM	PHD	02	NS Wales	&1995
Poon, Pak-lok	Asst	27667072	afplpoon	DS	PHD	00	Melbourne	1999
Su, Lixin (Nancy)	Asst	2766-703	3afnancy		PHD	05	Tx-Dallas	2005
Wu, Donghui	Asst	27667068	afdwu	AFI	PHD	03	CUHK	2005
Yi, Cheong H.	Asst	27667083	afchyi	VF	PHD	97	UCLA	1997
Chan, Philip	Lect	27664160	afphilip	FT	MPHL	93	Wales	2004
Cheng, Sarah	Lect	27667027	afsarah	FJ	MBA	98	Chinese U	2000
Fung, Teresa	Lect	27667107	aftfund	CMX	MBUS	02	Monash	2005
Ho, Mabel	Lect	27664068	afmhho	F	MTAX	02	NS Wales	&2004
Lam, Francis	Lect	27667084	afflam	FT	MBA	92	Warwick	1987
Lee, Heather	Lect	27664015	afmflee	FM	MBA	96	York	2004
Lee, William	Lect	27667035	afwylee	FJ	MBT	87	S Calif	&1997
Li, David	Lect	27664996	afdavidl	FS	MBA	88	Iowa	&2000
Liu, Ou	VLect	27664071	afouliu	DS	PHD	06	City U	2006
Pheny, Monica	VLect	27667079	afmpheny	JX	MTAX	02	NS Wales	&2005
Tsui, Christina	Lect	27667053	aftsui	VF	MBA	95	Brunel	1974
Wong, Jody	Lect	27664074	afjody	X	MSC	00	HK Poly	2001
Wong, Percy	Lect	27667036	afpercy	X	MBA	98	City U	2000
Wong, Rita	Lect	27664159	afrita	AF	MSC	95	London	&2001
Yuen, Kam-por	Lect	27667030	afkpyuen	FT	MBA	91	Sheffield	2000
Ho, Chi-Kun	VFell	27664539	afckho	AIJX	DBA	01	HK Poly	2002

Hong Kong Univ Sci & Tech
Department of Accounting
Dept Phone: 23587552
Homepage: www.bm.ust.hk/~acct/

CWaterB Kowloon Hong Kong
Sch of Business & Mgt

(852) Fax=23581693   (1) 1999,1999
ust.hk   BBA,MBA,EMB,PHD
Swallow Wei Shau-Yen

Name	Rank	Phone	Email	Area	Degree	Yr	School	Yr
Chan, K. C.	Dean	23587549	kcchan	Fnce	PHD	85	Chicago	1994
Biddle, Gary C.	H-Pr	23587552	biddle	FIAM	PHD	80.	Chicago	&1996
Synergis-Geoffrey YEH Chair Professor of Accounting								
Chen, Kevin C. W.	Prof	23587585	acchen	FI	PHD	85.	Illinois	&1996
Chair Professor								
Zhang, Guochang	Prof	23587569	acgzhang	FMT	PHD	92	Brit Colum	1993
Chen, Peter F.	Assoc	23587572	acpchen	F	PHD	98	Alberta	1998
Harvey, Patrick J.	AdjAc	23587561	acharvey	BAX	PHD	94.	S Calif	&2000
Hilary, Gilles	Assoc	23587579	acgh	FI	PHD	02	Chicago	2002
Kwan, Sabrina Y. S.	AdjAc	23587566	acskwan	FIX	PHD	96	London	&1996
Lennox, Clive S.	Assoc	23587571	accl	AFM	PHD	98	Oxford	2001
Ramaswamy, K. P.	AdjAc	23587556	acramasw	CFM	PHD	93.	Kansas	1994
Chen, Chih-Ying	Asst	23587567	accychen	F	PHD	97.	Berkeley	&2000
Chen, Tai Yuan	Asst	23587575	acty	F	PHD	06	Tx-Dallas	2006
Hsu, Charles	Asst	23587568	achsu	FIM	PHD	04.	Purdue	2004
Hui, Kai Wai	Asst	23587563	ackw	FIM	PHD	04.	Oregon	8-04
Liu, Xiaohong	Asst	23587558	acliu	AFMT	PHD	02	Brit Colum	2002
Wu, Min	Asst	23587559	acwu	IF	PHD	02.	NYU	2002
Zhang, Mingshan	Asst	23587584	acms	F	PHD	05.	UCLA	2005
Zhang, Yong	Asst	23587574	acyz	F	PHD	06.	Rochester	2005

University of Hull
Accounting & Finance
Dept Phone: 465710

E Riding Yorkshr England
Hull Univ Business Sch
Cottingham Road

01482 Fax=466377
uk.ac.hull   BS,MBA,PHD
Carol Dean

Name	Rank	Phone	Email	Area	Degree	Yr	School	Yr
Simon, J. B.	H-Lec	465710	jbsimon	EF	MBA	88	Cardiff	9-89
Ozkan, A.	Prof	463789	aozkan	F	PHD	96	York	2-07

Tayles, M. E.	Prof	466617	metayleses	M	PHD	00	Bradford	*	O-03
Wang, Peijie J.	Read	465663	pwang	F	PHD	02	Manchest		O-04
Benson, A.	Lect	466333	abenson	M	PHD	05	Hull		9-93
Boczko, T.	Lect	466206	tboczko	IFST	MA	95	Humbersi		9-01
Fewson, V. R.	Lect	466384	vfewson	X	BSC	88	Hull		9-94
Han, L.	Lect	465021	lhan	F	PHD	05	Warwick		8-04
Mould, P.	Lect	466206	pmould	XF	MSC	04	Humbersi		O-01
Reid, Graeme C.	Lect	466333	gcreid	FD	BSC	82	Hull		9-92
Scanlan, D. M. S.	Lect	466394	dmscanlan	M	BSC	66	Leeds		9-90
Vosseberg, G.	Lect	466302	gmvosseberg	F	MBA	93	Hull		9-93

Intl Inst for Mgt Dev–IMD   Lausanne CH-1001   Switzerlan   41-21 Fax=618-0707 2003
Accounting Faculty   Box 915   imd.ch   MBA
Dept Phone: Chemin de Bellerive 23
  Did Not Respond Again--1999-2000 Listing; phone 618-0111

Lorange, Peter	Pres	618-0200	lorange	IM	DBA	72	Harvard		1993
Ellert, James C.	Prof	618-0242	ellert		PHD	75	Chicago		1981
Hamilton, Stewart	Prof	618-0319	hamilton	IMF	MA	66	Edinburgh		&1985
Schaer, Kurt	Prof	618-0273	schaer		DBA	76	Harvard		1973
Sjoblom, Leif M.	Prof	618-0305	sjoblom	MUFI	PHD	93	Stanford	*	1993

INSEAD   Fontainebleau   France   33-1 Fax=60729253   2003
Accounting & Control Area   Business 77305   insead.edu   MBA
Dept Phone: 60729204   Boulevard de Constance   Isabelle Seyrig
  phone (33) 1-6072 9238

Morris, Deigan	C-Pr	Ext 9238	deigan.morris	M	PHD	72	Warwick		1972
Young, S. David	Prof	Ext 9257	david.young	F	PHD	85	Virginia		&1989
Vaysman, Igor	Assoc	Ext 9248	igor.vaysman	M	PHD	93	Stanford		2001
on leave to CUNY-Baruch									
Demers, Elizabeth A.	Asst	Ext 9206	liz.demers	F	PHD	99	Stanford		2006
Hillegeist, Stephen A.	Asst	Ext 9208	stephen.hill+	M	PHD	98	Berkeley		2005
Monahan, Steven J.	Asst	Ext 9214	steven.monahan	F	PHD	99	N Carol		2003
Segal, Benjamin	Asst	Ext 9245	benjamin.segal	F	PHD	03	NYU		2006
Cohen, Jacob	Affil	Ext 9207	jake.cohen	F					2003

King Fahd Un of Petro & Mn   Dhahran 31261   Saudi Arab   966-3 Fax=860-3489   2003,2003
Dept of Accounting & MIS   College Industrial Mgt   dpc.kfupm.edu.sa   BSC,MACC
Dept Phone: 860-2656   Julian M. Fernandez Jr.
Homepage: http://www.kfupm.edu.sa
  Did Not Respond Again--2003-2004 Listing

Al-Ashban, Aref Abdullah	Dean			Mktg	PHD	95	Houston		
Al-Rumaihi, Jassim S.	C-As	860-1290	jrumaihi		PHD	97	Dundee		2000
Al-Abdul-Gader, Abdulla H.	Prof	860-2144	agader	S	PHD	88	Colorado		1988
Azad, Ali N.	Prof	860-1459	alinazad	AEF	PHD	88	North Tx		&2001
Zaid, Omar A.	Prof	860-1714	omarzaid	HAE	PHD	78	CS-Humbo		2002
Al-Jabri, Ibrahim	Assoc	860-2821	imjabri	S	PHD	92	Ill Tech		1992
Mirghani, Mohamed Ali	Assoc	860-2377	mirghani	MS	DBA	79.	Indiana		1983
Abu-Musa, Ahmad A.	Asst	860-1420	abumusa	FIM	PHD	01	Aberdeen		2002
Ahmed, Mirghani	Asst	860-2656	mnahmed	MF	PHD	90	Manchest		1998
Al-Hazmi, Mohammed H.	Asst	860-4741	mhazmi	MA	PHD	96	Manchest		1996
Al-Khaldi, Muhammad A.M.	Asst	860-2696	makhaldi	MSD	PHD	91	Okla St		1991
Fraihat, Haidar M.	Asst	860-4217	haidarfr	S	PHD	92	Illinois		2002
Madani, Haider H.	Asst	860-2508	madani	FA	PHD	96	Henley		1996
Nehari-Talet, Amine	Asst	860-3450	nehari	MIS	PHD	02	Tlemcen		2001
Khan, Israr	Inst	860-3964	iskhan	S	PHD	85	Kanpur		1992
Menon, Gopenathan	Inst	860-2740	gmenon	S	MS	90	Monash		1992
Ilyas, Irfan A.	Lect	860-4041	irfan	S	MS	99	King Fahd		2000
Islam, Muhammad S.	Lect	860-2734	msislam	FS	MS	86	Boston U		1990
Raza, Syed A.	Lect	860-3427	saraza	MIS	MS	00	King Fahd		2001

King Saud University   Riyadh 11451   Saudia Ara   966-1 Fax=467-4283
Department of Accounting   College of Adm Sciences   ksu.edu.sa   BAS,MS
Dept Phone: 467-4295   P.O. Box 2459
  Did Not Respond Again--1999-2000 Listing

Al-Rwita, Saad S.	H-Ac	467-4297	srwita	FM	PHD	93	Colorado		1993
AbouMundour, Ahmed	Prof	467-4266		FM	PHD	74	Alexandria		1975
Al-Sultan, Sultan	Prof	467-4295		XG	PHD	80	Missouri		1980
Alhumaid, Abdulrhman I.	Prof	467-4235		FA	PHD	81.	LSU		1981
Alwabil, Wabil Ali	Prof	467-4245		FM	PHD	83.	Missouri		1983
Gomaa, Ismail I.	Prof	467-4237	igomma	FM	PHD	82.	Florida		1996
Al-Amari, Saleh	Assoc	467-4242		F	PHD	89	Glasgow		1990
Al-Amin, Mohamed Badr	Assoc	467-4282		M	PHD	88	Zkzk		1995
Eid, Saleh	Assoc	467-4279	seid	FX	PHD	87	Cairo		1997

Tahoun, Mohamed	Assoc	462-3530		F	PHD	92	Alexandria	1997
Al Deeb, Awad	Asst	467-4261		FA	PHD	93	Alexandria	1996
Al-Heizan, Osama	Asst	467-4246		FM	PHD	96	Syracuse	1996
Al-Meghames, Ahmad	Asst	467-4267	ameghame	AF	DBA	97	Miss St	1997
Al-Tassan, Mohammed S.	Asst	467-4295		MF	PHD	83.	Missouri	1984
Alaraini, Sulaiman	Asst	467-4241	salaraim	FS	PHD	98	KSU	1998
Basyouni, Mohamed	Asst	467-4270		M	PHD	93	Alexandria	1996
Karim Eldin, Ahmed	Asst	467-4240		F	PHD	85	Birminghm	1989
Malik, Mohamed	Asst			F	PHD	83	Reading	1991
Miro, Abdelradi	Asst	467-4238		FX	PHD	84	Birminghm	1987

Kookmin University   Seoul, Korea   136-702   (822) Fax=910-4519
Dept Accounting & Info Sys   Col of Bus Adm & Econ   kookmin.ac.kr   BBA,MBA,MA,PHD
Dept Phone: 910-4556   861-1 Jeungneung Dong
  Did Not Respond Again--2002-2003 Listing

Kim, Byoung Ho	C-Ac	910-4556	bkim	CFMQ	PHD	91	Nrthwstrn	&1992
Hong, Changmok	Prof	910-4555	cmhong	AMTY	PHD	90.	Tx-Austin	1991
Park, Changgil	Prof	910-4551	cgpark	FHJP	PHD	84	Seoul Ntl	&1982
Suh, Chung Woo	Prof	910-4553	cwsuh	FNT	PHD	88.	Illinois	&1988
Yi, Jaekyung	Assoc	910-4554	jkyi	FKPV	PHD	92.	Tx-Austin	8-93
Lee, Tae Hee	Asst	910-4557	thlee	FQS	PHD	94.	Illinois	1994
Nam, Young Ho	Asst	910-4558	yhnam	CMNU	PHD	90.	Mich St	1996

Korea University   Seoul 136-701   Korea   82-2 Fax=39227220   2005,2005
Accounting Faculty   School of Business Adm   kuccma.korea.ac.ku   BBA,MBA,PHD
Dept Phone: 39201171   1 Anam-dong 5 ka   Jaeyeol Kim
  Did Not Respond Again--2003-2004 Listing

Kim, Dong-Ki	Dean							
Cho, Seong Ha	Prof	32901915		F	MBA	70	Houston	3-71
Kwon, Soo Young	Prof	32901937	sykwon	FV	PHD	92.	Wash U	3-93
Lee, Manwoo	Prof	32901927	leemm	AFVX	PHD	87.	Georgia	& 3-88
Shin, Joon Y.	Prof	32901923	jyshin	MY	PHD	83.	Minnesota	3-85
Yoo, Kwan H.	Prof	32901935	khyoo	MC	PHD	85.	Indiana	3-95
Bae, Gil Soo	Assoc	32901951	gilbae	FM	PHD	94.	Minnesota	& 3-98
Jeong, Seok Woo	Assoc	32901946	jeong	FA	PHD	96.	SUNY-Buf	3-97
Kim, Jinbae	Asst	32901958	jinbae	MC	PHD	97.	Car Mellon	9-00

Korea Adv Inst of Sci & Tech   Seoul, Korea   130-012   (02) Fax=958-3604   2004,2004
Accounting Faculty   Graduate Sch of Mgt   kgsm.kaist.ac.kr   BS,MS,MBA,PHD
Dept Phone: 958-3601   207-43 Cheongryangri-dong
Homepage: kgsm.kaist.ac.kr
  Did Not Respond--2005-2006 Listing

Park, Sungjoo	Dean	958-3011	sjpark	Mis	PHD	78	Mich St	8-80
Jung, Kooyul	H-Pr	958-3062	kyjung	FM	PHD	87.	Florida	&2002
Han, Ingoo	Prof	958-3613	ighan	SMF	PHD	90.	Illinois	* &1992
Yu, Seongjae	Prof	958-3525	yu	CFM	PHD	72.	Minnesota	9-02

Kuwait University   Kuwait 13055   Fax=4837596   2004,2004
Department of Accounting   College of Business Adm   cba.edu.kw
Dept Phone: 4831059
  Did Not Respond--2005-2006 Listing

Al Hussainan, Adel	Dean			OR	PHD	94	Calif	1987
Al-Bassam, Sadik M.	H-Ac	Ext 8510	albassam	F	PHD	80.	Tx-Austin	1980
Abdulraheem, Ali	Prof	Ext 8487	arahim	CM	PHD	66	Manchest	1972
Al Rashed, Waeel	Prof	Ext 8518	alrashed	XS	PHD	89	Hull	1992
El-Adly, Yousef A.	Prof	Ext 8500	eladly	FM	PHD	70.	Illinois	9-95
El-Azma, Mohammed A.	Prof	Ext 8527	elazma	FVI	PHD	76	Manchest	1978
Al-Mudaf, Jassim	Assoc	Ex 8505	icc	F	PHD	84	Birminghm	1984
El-Rajabi, Mohamed	Assoc	Ext 8515	elrajabi	CF	PHD	86	Wisconsin	2001
El-Shamy, Mostafa	Assoc	Ext 8486	elshamy	FI	PHD	89	NYU	1993
Wahba, Sami	Assoc	Ext 8502	sam	F	PHD	80	Sterling	1998
Al-Hemaldi, Saud	Asst	Ext 8529	humaidi	GF	PHD	88	Leeds	1995
Al-Qenae, Rashid	Asst	Ext 8512	rashid	F	PHD	00	Essex	2000
Alhusaini, Walid	Asst	Ext 8514	walidh	AF	PHD	00	Sheffield	2000
Ben-Daihan, Meshari	Asst	Ext 8510	meshari	F	PHD	03	Arkansas	2003
El-Bahr, Hussa	Asst	Ext 8522	hussaha	GS	PHD	85	Ain Shams	1985
Kayed, Metwally	Asst	Ext 8504	kayed	IF	PHD	90	Hull	1993
AlBarak, Mahdy	Lect			F	PHD	95	Glasgow	1996
Mostafa, Ghaleb	Lect			PC	PHD	90	Kent	1993

Kyungpook National Univ Taegu 702-701   Korea   (53) Fax=950-6247
Accounting Faculty   School of Business Adm   knu.ac.kr   BBA,MBA,PHD
Dept Phone: 950-5439   1370 Sankyuk-dong, Bukgoo
  Did Not Respond Again--2003-2004 Listing

Cho, Seong-Pyo	H-Pr	950-5446	spcho	F	PHD	90	Yonsei	&1986
Bae, Byung-Han	Prof	950-5879	bhbae	M	PHD	89	Keimyung	1981
Choe, Jong-Min	Prof	950-5445	choejj	MS	PHD	93	KAIST	&1987
Kang, Ho-Young	Prof	950-5443	hykang	C	PHD	91	Pusan	1983
Kown, Soon-Chul	Prof	950-5442	sckwon	X	PHD	85	Hanyang	1981
Kwon, Chan-Tae	Prof	950-5441	ctkwon	FA	PHD	85	Pusan	&1980
Kwon, Sun-Kook	Assoc	950-5447	skwon	FA	PHD	89.	Oklahoma	* & 7-95

University of Lancaster   LancasterLA1 4YX England   01524 Fax=847321
Dept of Accounting & Finance Business   lancaster.ac.uk   BA,MA,PHD
Dept Phone: 593632
  area code (01524) - school phone 594024

Cox, Sue	Dean		s.cox	Mgt	MPHL	88	Nottingh	2001
O'Hanlon, John F.	H-Pr	59 3631	j.ohanlon	F	MA	84	Lancaster	&1984
Otley, David T.	Prof	59 3636	d.otley	MB	PHD	76	Manchest	1972
Peasnell, Kenneth V.	Prof	59 3977	k.peasnell	F	PHD	75	Lancaster	&1970
Pope, Peter F.	Prof	59 3978	p.pope	FM	MA	77	Lancaster	1977
Young, Steven	SLect	59 4242	s.young	FM	PHD	95	Lancaster	2000
Beekes, Wendy	Lect	59 0020	w.beekes	FM	PI ID	00	Wales	2000
Choi, Young-Soo	Lect	59 4738	y.choi	FQ	PHD	03	Lancaster	2005
Gore, J. P. O.	Lect	59 3627	p.gore	FA	PHD	89	Lancaster	1991
Lubberink, Martien	Lect	59 3637	m.lubberink	F	MSC	92	Groningn	2000
Lui, Daphne	Lect	50 3638d	d.lui	F	PHD	05	London	2005
Talib, Sayjda	Lect	59 3626	s.talib	F	PHD	06	Lancaster	2006
Taylor, Paul A.	Lect	59 3621	p.a.taylor	FVQ	MA	77	Lancaster	&1978

LaTrobe University   Bundoora3086 Vic   Australia   61-3 Fax=94792368
Department of Accounting   Faculty of Law & Mgt   latrobe.edu.au   BCOM,MCOM,PHD
Dept Phone: 94792909
Homepage: http://www.business.latrobe.edu.au

Ahmed, Kamran	C-Pr	94791125	k.ahmed	FIM	PHD	94	Austr Natl	1999
Adams, Carol	Prof	94792680	c.adams		PHD			2006
Hoque, Zahirul	Prof	94793433	z.hoque	BGMN	PHD	93	Manchest	*
Hill, Glenn	SLect	94791225	g.hill	F	BBUS		Swinburn	&1990
Ji, Xu-Dong	SLect	94793061	x.ji	IHF	PHD		LaTrobe	1996
Yapa, Premasiri	SLect	94791642	p.yapa	AEJ	PHD	02	RMIT	2003
Langa, Leo	Lect	94792711	l.langa	FT	MEC		LaTrobe	1993
Leveson, Lynne	Lect	94791718	l.leveson	BEMC	MED		LaTrobe	1990
Lim, Selena	Lect	94791413	s.lim	MDS	BEC		RMIT	1984
Lye, Joanne M.	Lect	94791773	j.lye	FM	MBS	96	Massey	2001
Salmon, Suzanne	Lect	94791221	s.salmon	M	BEC		LaTrobe	&1991
Khan, Radib	AsLec	94792713	r.khan					2006
Louie, Judy	AsLec	94792713	j.louis					2005

University of Leeds   Leeds, LS2 9JT   England   44113 Fax=343-4459
Accounting Division   Leeds Univ Business Sch   lubs.leeds.ac.uk   BA,BSC,MA,PHD
Dept Phone: 343-4499   The Maurice Keyworth Bldg   Michelle Dickson
Homepage: www.leeds.ac.uk/lubs/

Baker-Collins, Mae	H-SLe	3432644	mb	FNH	PHD	94	Leeds	9-94
Collins, Mike	Prof	3434493	mc	FNH	PHD	72	LondonSE	9-74
Gerrand, W.	Prof	3434458	wjg	FQ	PHD	95	York	9-95
Hillier, David	Prof	3434509	dhi	FMQ	PHD	00	Strathcl	1-05
Keasey, Kevin	Prof	3432618	kk	FBMQ	PHD	81	Newcastle	9-90
Moizer, Peter	Prof	3434499	pm	ABJ	PHD	93	Manchest	4-89
Schenk-Hoppe, K.	Prof	3434509	krs	VFQB	PHD	96	Bremen	1-05
Wilson, Nicholas	Prof	3434472	nw	MQ	PHD		Nottingh	7-98
Duxbury, Darren	SLect	3434508	dd	BMQ	PHD	96	Leeds	9-94
Hudson, Robert	SLect	3431677	rsh	MQ	PHD	06	Leeds	9-02
Robinson, Andrew	SLect	3434907	amr	MQ	PHD	98	Bradford	D-00
Short, Helen	SLect	3431679	hs	BMQ	PHD	96	Leeds	9-90
Clark, Julie	Lect	3434480j	jc	FX	BA	88	Manchest	9-97
Hagendorff, Jeus	Lect	343483	juh	FMQ	MA	04	Leeds	9-06
Hill, Paula	Lect	3434463	ph	FI	PHD	02	Leeds	D-00
Summers, Barbara	Lect	3434473	bs	MQ	PHD	02	Bradford	7-98
Gallagher, Denise	STcFl	3432628	dg	DEF	MSC	02	Huddersf	7-02
Molyneux, Steve	STcFl	3434486	sm	CFMQ	MBA	98	Leicester	8-02

Lincoln University-NZ
Commerce Division
Dept Phone: 325-2811
Homepage: www.lincoln.ac.nz/comm/story2297.html

Canterbury, NZ   NewZealand
PO Box 84
Corner Springs & Ellesmere

(03) Fax = 325-3847
lincoln.ac.nz

MCOM,MCM,PHD
Robyn Valentine

Name	Rank	Phone	Email	Fields	Degree	Yr	School	Year
Aldwell, Patrick	Dir	325-3860	aldwellp		PHD	88	U Wash	1988
Wright, Chris	Prof	325-3627	wright	GST	PHD	92	Simon Fr	* 2006
Weil, Sidney H.	Assoc	325-3627	weils	EF	PHD	89	WestnCape	&1995
Clark, Murray B.	SLect	325-3627	clarkm	EFHP	MCOM	70	Canterbu	&1978
Radford, Jack J.	SLect	325-3627	radford	BCMW	BCOM	74	Otago	&1987
Roudaki, Jamal	SLect	325-3627	roudakij	EJP	PHD		Wollong	2007
DeSilva, Tracy-Anne	Lect	325-3627	desilvat	BE	BCOM		Lincoln	2004
Habib, Ahsan	Lect	325-3627	habiba	AG	PHD		Hitotsub	2005
McGuigan, Craig	Lect	325-3627	mcguigac		BCM		Canterbu	2006
Trent, Miles	Lect	325-3627	trentm	D	BCOM		Canterbu	1997

Lingnan University
Department of Accountancy
Dept Phone: 26168171
Homepage: www.ln.edu.hk/acct

Fu Tei, Tuen Mun Hong Kong
Business
1/F Business Building

(852) Fax = 24664751
ln.edu.hk

BBA

Name	Rank	Phone	Email	Fields	Degree	Yr	School	Year
Chan, K. Hung J.K. Lee Chair Professor	D-Pr	26168171	khchan	AIMX	PHD	74	Penn St	* &2000
Mo, Phyllis Lai Lan	H-Pr	26168160	llmo	AXY	PHD	99	HongKong C	2006
Lin, Kenny Z. P.	Assoc	26168162	klin	AXF	PHD	96	Glasgow	2000
Shafer, William E.	Assoc	26168165	weshafer	AJW	PHD	94.	Houston	* &2003
Lee, Meina Grace	Asst	26168164	gracelee	FIJ	PHD	97	Utah	2003
Lo, Agnes W. Y.	Asst	26188163	wylo	IX	PHD	04	Lingnan	2004
Simmons, Richard S.	Asst	26168175	simmons	AX	PHD	02	London	&1991
Wong, Brossa	Asst	26168181	byhwong	XE	PHD	00	Xiamen	2002
Luo, Rebecca K. W.	SLect	26168174	kimwan	XFL	MBA	94	Toronto	2002
Lee, Kent O. K.	VTcFl	26168187	ok2lee	AEG	MBA	05	HongKong U	2006
Li, Melody M. W.	TchFl	26168177	melody	AF	MA	05	City U	2006

Liverpool John Moores Univ
Atg & Financial Mgt Group
Dept Phone: 231-3269
Homepage: http://www.livjm.ac.uk/bus
   school phone: 44-51 231-2121

Liverpool L3 5UZ   England
Liverpool Business Sch
98 Mount Pleasant

44-51 Fax = 707-0423
livjm.ac.uk

BA,MSC

Name	Rank	Phone	Email	Fields	Degree			Year
Sargant, C.	D-PLe	Ext 3641	c.m.sargant	FG	MA			
Pyke, C. J.	H-PLe	Ext 3269	c.j.pyke	FG	MPHL			1995
Pegum, R. H.	PLect	Ext 3849	r.h.pegum	AFM	FCCA			
Cook, A. M.	SLect	Ext 3812	a.m.cook	FM	FCA			
Evans, M.	SLect	Ext 3416	j.m.evans	MF	MA			1992
Foster, G.	SLect	Ext 3819	g.foster	FG	CPFA			
Gordon, L.	SLect	Ext 3413	l.gordon	FD	ICAE			1999
McMahon, C.	SLect	Ext 3810	c.mcmahon	FP	MA			1993
Quirke, B.	SLect	Ext 3833	b.j.quirke	F	MPHL			1992
Shoesmith, D. E.	SLect	Ext 3834	d.e.shoesmith	FT	MA			
Bowdery, A.	PLect	Ext 3821	a.bowdery	MF	ACA			1996
Dodd, P.	SLect	Ext 3673	p.dodd	F	FCMA			2006
Fisher, I.	SLect	Ext 3412	i.fisher	M	FCMA			1997
Fraser, J.	SLect	Ext 3408	j.fraser	SG	CPFA			2002
Mooncroft, D.	SLect	Ext 3673	d.v.moorcroft	M	CPFA			2006

London Business School
Inst of Finance & Accounting
Dept Phone: 70008100
Homepage: www.london.edu/accounting
   phone number: 44(0) 207262-5050

London, NW1 4SA
Grad Sch of Bus Studies
Sussex Place, Regent's Park

England   44020 Fax = 70008101 2001
london.edu   MBA,PHD
Bernadette Salas, Debbie Hughes

Name	Rank	Phone	Email	Fields	Degree	Yr	School	Year
Buchanan, Robin	Dean	Ext 6060	rbuchanan	Mgt	MBA		Harvard	7-07
Amir, Eli	C-Pr	Ext 8121	eamir	F	PHD	91.	Berkeley	&2003
Likierman, Sir Andrew	VProf	Ext 8114	alikierman	MGJ	MA	65	Oxford	&1979
Talmor, Eli	Prof	Ext 8116	etalmor	F	PHD	81	N Carol	2000
Higson, Christopher	Assoc	Ext 8116	chigson	FMT	PHD	93	London	&1986
Kraft, Arthur G.	Asst	Ext 8112	akraft	F	PHD	01	Chicago	2001
Oswald, Dennis R.	Asst	Ext 8113	doswald	M	PHD	00	Chicago	1999
Shivakumar, Lakshmanan	Asst	Ext 8115	lshivakumar	F	PHD	96	Vanderbilt	* 1996
Tamayo, Ane	Asst	Ext 8118	atamayo	F	PHD	01	Rochester	2001

London Guildhall University
Dept of Atg & Financial Ser
Dept Phone: 320-1538
   phone 020-7320-1000

EC2M 6SQ   England
Faculty of Business
84 Moorgate

0171- Fax = 320-1557
londonmet.ac.uk   BA, MSC
A. Kynaston, C. Richardson

Name	Rank	Phone	Email		Degree			Year
Dawes, N. Academic Leader North Campus	Lead	71333053	n.dawnes		MA			1992

Akinwande, B.	SLect	71333003	b.akinwande	FM	PHD			2001
Balachandran, I.	SLect	73201603	l.balachandran	CM	MBA			1998
Bruce, E.	SLect	71333042	e.bruce	AFX	BSC			2002
Cleary, T.	SLect	73201622	t.cleary	DS	MSC			1999
Coshell, J.	SLect	71333027	j.coshall	Q	PHD			1989
DeJonge, A.	SLect	71333214	a.dejonge	F	MBA			1999
Essien, C.	SLect	71333321	c.essien	FI	MSC			2001
Idowu, S.	SLect	73201549	s.idowu	FM	MSC			2002
Menyah, Kojo	SLect	73201535	k.menyah	M	PHD			1990
Monk, D.	SLect	73201622	d.monk	DFS	BSC			1999
Musa, G.	SLect	71333080	g.musa	D	MA			1989
Odedra, S.	SLect	71333321	s.odedra	F	MSC			
Preston, R.	SLect	73201580	r.preston	X				&
Shaw, H.	SLect	71333323	h.shaw	FM	PHD			1999
Tejura, C.	SLect	71333003	c.tejura	M	MSC			2001
Ukaegbu, B.	SLect	71333012	u.ukaegbu		PHD			
Alderman, R.	PLect	73201549	r.alderman	AF				&
Lyons, J.	PLect	73201550	jon.lyons	FMNE	MBA			1990
Natan, R.	Lect	73201530	r.natan	FM	BA			2001
Rees, D.	Lect	73201540	d.rees	DS	MSC			2001
Sale, C.	PLect	73201339	c.sale	FMN	MSC			&1991
Thompson, T.	PLect	73201425	t.thompson	CDE				&
Trodden, D.	PLect	73201645	d.trodden	MN	MSC			&1990
Reid, K.	PLect	71000042	k.reid	ΓA	MBA			1989
Topple, M.	PLect	71333070	m.topple	QMD	MSC			1983
Kelly, J.								

London School Economics London WC2A 2AE England 44207 Fax=955-7420
Dept of Accounting & Finance Business lse.ac.uk BSC,MSC,D
Dept Phone: 955-7736 Houghton Street Osmana Raie

Miller, Peter B.	C-Pr	955-7231	p.b.miller	MW	PHD	83	London	1987
Bhimani, Alnoor	Prof	955-7329	a.bhimani	BIM	PHD	92	London	* 1988
Bromwich, Michael	Prof	955-7323	m.bromwich	FMT	BSC	65	London	* 1985

Chartered Inst of Mgt Accountants Professor of Accounting & Financial Mgt

Macve, Richard H.	Prof	955-6138	r.macve	FHP	MSC	76	London	&1996
Power, Michael K.	Prof	955-7228	m.k.power	AFTO	PHD	84	Cambridge	&1987
Van der Stede, Wim A.	Prof	955-6695	w.van-der-stede	BM	PHD	97	Ghent	2006
Kurunmaki, Liisa	Read	955-6394	l.kurunmaki	BNM	PHD	00	Jyvaskyla	1999
Noke, Christopher	SLect	955-7317	c.noke	FH	MSC	78	London	&1976
Beccalli, Elena	Lect	849-4633	e.beccalli	FI	PHD	00	Milan	2000
Frantz, Pascal	Lect	955-7233	p.frantz	AFY	PHD	94	London	1993
Goh, Lisa	Lect	955-6211	l.goh	FQ	PHD			2007
Hall, Matthew	Lect	849-4633	m.v.hall	BM	PHD			2006
Horton, Joanne	Lect	955-6210	j.horton	FT	PHD	94	Aberystwyt	1997
Labro, Eva	Lect	849-4632	e.labro	MS	PHD	01	Leuven	2000
McMillan, Keith P.	Lect	955-7315	k.p.mcmillan	HJW	PHD	98	London	&2000
Mennicken, Andrea	Lect		a.m.mennicken	AGPI	PHD	00	London	2006
Simpson, Aua	Lect	955-7232	a.simpson	FIQ	PHD	06	London	2006
Soonawalla, Kazbi	Lect	955-7671	k.kothavala	FIQ	PHD	02.	Stanford	2002
Samiolo, Riva	JLect	955-7932	r.samiolo	ACPI	MSC			2000

Loughborough University Loughborough UK LE 11 3TU 509 Fax=223961
Accounting Faculty Business School lboro.ac.uk BSC,MBA,MPL,PHD
Dept Phone: 223139 Ashby Road Brian Pile
Wish to be eliminated; area code 44 1 phone extension: 1509 2231

Wilson, Richard M. S.	H-Pr	223120	r.m.wilson	EM	MSC	69	Bradford	* &1995
Belk, Penelope A.	Lect	263116	p.a.belk	IF	MA	75	Lancaster	1987
Higson, Andrew W.	Lect	263104	a.w.higson	MA	PHD	87	Bradford	&1986
King, Ruth M.	Lect	263127	r.m.king	FE	BSC	77	Nottingh	&1989
McAuley, Laurie	Lect	262341	l.mcauley	MD	PHD	93	Loughbor	* 1997
O'Sullivan, Noel	Lect	263394	c.n.o'sullivan	FK	PHD	00	Nottingh	1994
Whittaker, John	Lect	263107	j.whittaker	FN	MA	80	Manchest	&1976

Univeresiteit Maastricht Maastricht6200MD Netherland 31-43 Fax=388-4876 2002,2002
Dept Atg & Inf Mgt, Box 616 Faculty Econ & Bus Adm aim.unimaas.nl
Dept Phone: 388-3755 Tongersestraat 53 M. Scheepers, Konings
Homepage: www.fdewb.unimaas.nl/marc/

Meuwissen, Roger H. G.	H-Pr	388-3754	r.meuwissen	A	PHD	99	Maastricht	&1992
Hassink, Harold	Prof	388-3672	h.hassink	AFOU	PHD	01	Maastricht	&1990
Moers, Frank	Prof	388-3753	f.moers	M	PHD	01	Maastricht	6-97
Vaassen, Eddy	Prof	388-3655	e.vaassen	AMOS	PHD	94	Maastricht	&1994
Vergoossen, Ruud G. A.	Prof	388-3762	r.vergoossen	FI	PHD	94	Vrije	&1999
Bollen, Laury	Assoc	388-3634	l.bollen	FM	PHD	96	Maastricht	1985
Peek, Erik	Assoc	338-3669	e.peek	F	PHD	01	Vrije	1999

Vanstraelen, Ann	Assoc	388-4923	a.vanstraelen	FA	PHD	00	Antwerp	1999
Vergauwen, Philip	Assoc	388-3681	p.vergauwen	M	PHD	98	Leuven	6-97
Walczuch, R.	Assoc	388-3724	r.walczuch	S	PHD	94	Georgia	1996
Adelaar, Thomas	Asst	388-3552	t.adelaar	S	PHD	05	Michigan	2005
Bruggen, Alexander	Asst	388-4924	a.bruggen	M	PHD	05	Maastricht	2001
Deumes, R.	Asst	388-3720	r.deumes	FM	PHD	05	Maastricht	1998
Renders, Annelies	Asst	388-3674	a.renders	F	PHD	06	Leuven	2006
Schelleman, C.	Asst	388-3682	c.schelleman	AFOS	PHD	03	Maastricht	1997
Vluggen, Mark	Asst	388-3684	m.vluggen	SM	PHD	06	Maastricht	6-97
Volmer, Frans G.	Asst	388-3718	f.volmer	FH	PHD	92	Rotterdam	&1986

Macquarie University   NSW 2109   Australia   61-2 Fax=98508497
Dept of Accounting & Finance   Div of Econ & Fin Stds   efs.mq.edu.au   BCOM,MACC,PHD
Dept Phone: 98508511   NSW, 2109   Jan Fourro, Iris Chung
Homepage: www.accg.mq.edu.au
   department phone 61-2 9850-8535

Patel, Chris	H-Pr	Ext 7825	cpatel	FI	PHD	99	Macquarie	* &1995
Cummings, Lorne S.	Prof	Ext 8531	lcumming	JTW	PHD	02	Macquarie	&1996
Eddey, Peter H.	Prof	Ext 8523	peddey	F	MCOM	75	NS Wales	&1977
Fargher, Neil L.	Prof	Ext 9281	nfargher	FA	PHD	93.	Arizona	&2004
Harrison, Graeme L.	Prof	Ext 8515	gharriso	MI	PHD	90	Macquarie	&1974
Loudon, Geoffrey F.	Prof	Ext 8536	gloudon	F	PHD	96	AGSM	&1985
Okunev, John	Prof	Ext 9282	jokunev	F	PHD	89	Aust Natl	&2005
Perera, Sujatha	Prof	Ext 8525	sperera	M	PHD	00	Macquarie	* 1991
Radich, Renee	Prof	Ext 8534	rradich	A	PHD	02	Bond	&1999
McKinnon, Jill L.	Asst	Ext 8519	jmckinno	FI	PHD	84	Macquarie	&1979
Baird, Kevin M.	SLect	Ext 8532	kbaird	M	PHD	04	Macquarie	&1998
Blair, Bill	SLect	Ext 6873	bblair	S	MEC	00	N Eng-Au	2000
Boyce, Gordon	SLect	Ext 8530	gboyce	SA	BCOM	94	Deakin	1997
Dale, Mary L.	SLect	Ext 8538	mdale	F	MEC	84	Macquarie	&1991
Davids, Cindy	SLect	Ext 8478	cdavids	LJ	PHD	05	NS Wales	2003
Dyball, Maria Cadiz	SLect	Ext 9176	mdyball	HEFS	PHD	03	NS Wales	2004
Evans, Elaine	SLect	Ext 6477	eevans	HE	PHD	03	NS Wales	&2001
Haswell, Stephen	SLect	Ext 8542	shaswell	F	MEC	90	ANU	&2001
Hobbes, Garry	SLect	Ext 8510	ghobbes	FQ	PHD	99	UTS	1994
Kilgore, Alan	SLect	Ext 8564	akilgore	IF	MEC	89	Macquarie	&2001
Sin, Samantha	SLect	Ext 8529	ssin	E	MCOM	92	Macquarie	1990
Watts, Edward J.	SLect	Ext 8533	ewatts	F	PHD	88	N Eng-Au	1988
Wright, Susan J.	SLect	Ext 8521	swright	F	PHD	97	Macquarie	1985
Baker, Pam P.	Lect	Ext 8518	pbaker	M	MEC	95	Macquarie	1988
Baumann, Chris	Lect	Ext 8551	cbaumann	IM	MBA	00	Simon Fr	2004
Blount, Yvette	Lect	Ext 8514	yblount	SM	MBA	00	N Eng-Au	&2005
Boon, Kym	Lect	Ext 8451	kboon	A	BCOM	02	Macquarie	2003
Cable, Dawn	Lect	Ext 8540	dcable	M	BCOM	75	Queensld	&1992
Chand, Parmod	Lect	Ext 6137	pchand	IFA	MA	03	S Pacific	2004
Considine, Brett A.	Lect	Ext 8522	bconsidi	S	BCOM	99	Melbourne	
Greer, Susan	Lect	Ext 8520	sgreer	FW	PHD	06	Macquarie	1993
Hazelton, James C. P.	Lect	Ext 8486	jhazelto	F	BEC	93	Macquarie	&1993
Jebeile, Sam	Lect	Ext 8572	sjebeile	SM	MED	02	Macquarie	&2001
Kalotay, Egon A.	Lect	Ext 8490	ekalotay	F	PHD	02	AUSM	1991
Lavermicocca, Catriona	Lect	Ext 8528	clavermi	XL	MLAW	92	NS Wales	, &1995
Millanta, Brian	Lect	Ext 8547	bmillant	F	MEC	87	Macquarie	&1993
Narayan, Venkat	Lect	Ext 9175	vnarayan	MUF	BCOM	02	Macquarie	2003
Nevicky, Barbara	Lect	Ext 9192	bnevicky	MFS	BCOM	02	Macquarie	2003
Perera, Ryle	Lect	Ext 8578	rperera	FQ	PHD	02	NS Wales	2002
Sadeghi, Mehdi	Lect	Ext 8527	msadeghi	F	PHD	82	Kentucky	2001
Searchfield, Chris	Lect	Ext 8462	csearchf	SM	MCOM	98	Macquarie	&2001
Sinnadurai, Philip T.	Lect	Ext 7101	psinnad	F	PHD	04	Sydney	1993
Truuvert, Toomas	Lect	Ext 8524	ttruuver	F	MCOM	92	NS Wales	2001
Aoun, Chadi	ALect	Ext 9178						
Chen, Charlene	ALect	Ext 9285	cchen	F	BCOM	01	Macquarie	2001
Chen, Jessica	ALect	Ext 4839						
Cheung, Esther	ALect	Ext 4773	echeung					
Cui, Tracey	ALect							
DiLernia, Cary	ALect	Ext 6479	cdilerni					
Guo, Feng	ALect		guof					
Lau, James	ALect	Ext 9284	jlau					
Lim, Roslinda	ALect	Ext 9173	rlim	FM	MFIN	00	UWA	2004
Misic, Milica	ALect	Ext 7848	mmisic	FA	BCOM	99	Macquarie	2002
Murir, Rahat	ALect	Ext 4765	rmurir					
Proimos, Alex	ALect	Ext 9179	aproimos	FM	BAF	03	Macquarie	2004
Ryker, Kirsty	ALect	3xt 9177	kryken	AS	BBA	03	Macquarie	2005
Siu, David	ALect	Ext 9193	dsiu					
Soh, Joseph	ALect	Ext 4760	jsoh					
Wu, Steven	ALect	Ext 7295	swu					
Young, Raymond	ALect	Ext 4850	ryoung					
Yu, Lichen	ALect							

University of Manchester ManchesterM156PB England UK (061) Fax=275-4023 2003
Sch of Accounting & Finance Manchester Business Sch man.ac.uk
Dept Phone: 275-4010 Booth Street East Hilary Garraway
  Did Not Respond Again--2001-2002 Listing

Name	Rank	Phone	email				School	
Humphrey, Christopher G.	H-Pr	275-4010	chris.humphrey	ABCF	PHD		Manchest	&2001
Arnold, John A.	Prof	275-6333	j.arnold	A	MSC	69	Manchest	&1994
Garrett, Ian	Prof	275-4958	ian.garrett	FQTY	PHD		Brunel	1993
Hopper, Trevor M.	Prof	275-4014	trevor.hopper	BCH	MPHL	78	Aston	1983
O'Leary, Ted	Prof	274-4011	ted.oleary	BCH	PHD	83	Warwick	2001
Ogden, Stuart G.	Prof	200 3458	stuart.ogden	MN	MA	71	Warwick	9-00
Scapens, Robert W.	Prof	275-4020	robert.scapens	BCIM	PHD		Manchest	&1970
Stark, Andrew W.	Prof	275-6333	a.stark	F	PHD	83	Manchest	1995
Strong, Norman C.	Prof	275-4006	norman.strong	FQTY	MA		Newcastle	1989
Turley, W. Stuart	Prof	275-4015	stuart.turley	AFI	MA		Manchest	&1978
Walker, Martin	Prof	275-4008	martin.walker	FQY	PHD	80	Newcastle	1989
Williams, Karel	Prof	275-4016	karel.williams	HIMW	BSC		LondonEc	1993
Newman, Michael	Read	275-4003	mike.newman	DMS	PHD		Bcolom	1981
Edwards, Pamela	SLect	200 3454	pam.edwards	FIMW	MSC	93	Manchest	9-90
Froud, Julie	SLect	275-4018	julie.froud	GNWF	PHD		Manchest	1996
Saadouni, Brahim	SLect	200 8792	brahim.saadouni	FIM	MSC	84	Glasgow	1-00
Shaoul, Jean E.	SLect	275-4027	jean.shaoul	HIGW	PHD		Salford	1983
Westrup, Chris	SLect	275-4007	chris.westrup	BDW	PHD	96	UMIST	1993
Collett, Nick J.	Lect	275-6333	n.collett	F	PHD	94	Manchest	1986
Domuta, Daniela	Loot	200 3162	daniola.domuta	FIMT	PHD	01	Manchost	0 01
Erturk, Ismail	Lect	275-6333	i.erturk	F	MA	85	NYU	1987
Espenlaub, Susanne	Lect	275-4026	susanne.esp+	FQTY	PHD		Oxford	1992
Goergen, Marc	Lect	200 3456	marc.g.goergen	FIY	PHD	97	Oxford	1-99
Howell, Syd D.	Lect	275-6333	s.howell	Q	PHD	76	Manchest	1978
Hyde, Stuart J.	Lect	275-4017	stuart.j.hyde	FQTY	PHD		Newcastle	2000
Khurshed, Arif	Lect	275-4475	arif.khurshed	FQTY	PHD		Reading	1999
Liu, Weimin	Lect	275-3854	weimin.liu	FQTY	PHD		Manchest	2000
Nasralla, Ali	Lect	275-6333	a.nasralla	M	BA	72	Baghdad	&1985
Newton, David	Lect	275-6333	d.newton	F	PHD	79	Salford	1990
Nicholson, Brian	Lect	275-4024	brian.nicholson	BDW	PHD		Salford	1999
Paxson, Dean A.	Lect	275-6333	d.paxson	Z	DBA	70	Harvard	1974
Schleicher, Thomas	Lect	275-4022	t.schliecher	FQ	MPHL		Manchest	1996
Zaman, Mahbub	Lect			FA	MA	95	Essex	&
Jones, Julian W.	Fell	275-6383	j.w.jones	M	MSC	96	Cardiff	1996
Poon, Ser-Huang				FQ	PHD	91	Lancaster	
Stapleton, Richard C.				FQ	PHD	72	Sheffield	

Massey University Palmerston 30974 NewZealand 64-06 Fax=350 5617
School of Accountancy College of Business Std massey.ac.nz BBS,MBS,PHD
Dept Phone: 350-9099 Tennant Drive
Homepage: www-accountancy.massey.ac.nz
  phone 64-06-356-9099

Name	Rank	Phone	email				School	
Laswad, Fawzi	H-Pr	Ext 2860	f.laswad	FIV	PHD	88	Sydney	&1989
Tooley, S.	Assoc	Ext 2173	s.tooley	WGEF	MBS	91	Massey	1990
Tan, Lin Mei	Sen	Ext 2172	l.m.tan	CEFX	MA		Lancaster	&1987
Botica, Redmayne N.	Lect	Ext 2148	r.n.botica	FQAV	MSC		Zagreb	1992
Chan, C.	Lect	Ext 2151	c.p.chan-f	EXJP	MBS		Massey	&1988
Chua, Francis C. K.	Lect	Ext 2152	f.c.chua	HEFT	MBS		Massey	1987
Hawkes, L. C.	Lect	Ext 2157	l.c.hawkes	JMW	MBS		Massey	1987
Kirk, N.	Lect	Ext 2170	n.e.kirk	AFW	BBS		Massey	1998
Momin, M.	Lect	Ext 2181	m.momin		PHD		Glasgow	2005
Nath, N.	Lect	Ext 2154	n.nath		MA			2003
Robertson, J. S.	Lect	Ext 2168	j.s.robertson	AH	MBS		Massey	&1987
Tozer, L. E.	Lect	Ext 2174	l.tozer	JOPA	MBS		Massey	&1997
Woon, P. P.	Tutor	Ext 2160	p.woon					

Massey Univ - Albany Campus Palmerston 30974 NewZealand 64-09 Fax=441-8133
School of Accountancy College of Business Std massey.ac.nz
Dept Phone: 414-0800
Homepage: www-accounting.massey.ac.nz
  phone 64-09-443-9700

Name	Rank	Phone	email				School	
Bradbury, Michael E.	Prof	Ext 9415	m.e.bradbury	FYI	PHD	90	Auckland	&2006
Rahman, Asheq Razaur	Prof	Ext 9587	a.r.rahman	F	PHD	88	Sydney	2006
Van Staden, C.	Sen	Ext 9849	c.van-staden	FW	DM		Pract SA	&1999
Bishop, Helen E.	Lect	Ext 9294	h.e.bishop	FY	MACC	96	Victoria	1999
Hooks, Jill J.	Lect	Ext 9458	j.j.hooks	FW	PHD	00	Waikato	1997
Sleenkamp, N.	Lect	Ext 0434	n.sleenkamp		PHD			2006
Stent, W. J.	Lect	Ext 0542	w.j.stent		BCOM		Rhodes	2005
Yammeesri, J.	Lect	Ext 9459	j.yammeersi		PHD		Wollong	2004
Perreau, D.	Tutor	Ext 9598	d.c.perreau		BBS			

Massey University-Wellington　Palmerston 30974　NewZealand　64-04 Fax=801-2885
School of Accountancy　　　　　College of Business　　　　　　massey.ac.nz
Dept Phone: 801-5799
Homepage: www-accounting.massey.ac.nc

Dunmore, Paul V.	Prof	Ext 6898	p.v.dunmore	AFMQ	PHD	75	McMaster	2004
Arcus, J.	Sen	Ext 6887	j.d.arcus	ACFN	BCA		Victoria	1999
Heslop, J.	Sen	Ext 6880	j.d.heslop	NMWF	MBS		Massey	1999
Islam, A.	Lect	Ext 6879	a.islam		PHD		Wellingt	2003
Pinny, J.	STuto	Ext 6802	j.a.pinny		BCA		Wellingt	2005

University of Melbourne　　Victoria 3010　　Australia　61-3　Fax=93492397
Dept of Atg & Bus Info Sys　　Faculty of Econ & Comm　unimelb.edu.au　　BCO,MCO,MAC,PHD
Dept Phone: 83445475　　　　　　　　　　　　　　　　　　　　　　　　Ms. Leanne M. Clark
Homepage: www.ecom.unimelb.edu.au/accwww/
　Did Not Respond--2005-2006 Listing

Abernethy, Margaret A.	Dean	83445311	m.abernethy	M	PHD	89	LaTrobe	1990
Spear, Nasser A.	H-Pr	83447498	nasser	FI	PHD	92.	North Tx	1996
G. L. Wood Professor of Accounting								
Ferguson, Colin B.	Prof	83444482	colinf	ASY	PHD	94	Deakin	&2004
Professor of Accounting and Business Information Systems								
Leech, Stewart A.	Prof	83445314	saleech	S	MEC	76	Tasmania	&2000
Professor of Accounting and Business Information Systems								
Burrows, Geoffrey H.	PFell	83445716	gbh	M	MCOM		Melbourne	&1971
Collier, Philip A.	AProf	83445716	pcollier	S	MSC	79	Essex	2001
Davern, Michael J.	AProf	83445475	m.davern	BDMS	PHD	98	Minnesota	2003
Lillis, Anne M.	AProf	83445351	alillis	M	PHD	98	Melbourne	1997
Schulz, Axel K-D.	AProf	83447665	axels	MB	PHD	98	NS Wales	1999
Cobbin, Phillip E.	SLect	83444039	pecobbin	FA	MCOM	02	Melbourne	&1989
Coram, Paul	SLect	83447023	pcoram	ABE	MACC		W Aust	2004
Pinnuck, Matthew L.	SLect	83447539	mpinnuck	FA	PHD	03	Melbourne	1997
Potter, Bradley N.	SLect	83444989	bnpotter	F	PHD	03	Deakin	2003
Smith, David	SLect	83445338	dsmi	BCMQ	PHD		Monash	2003
Wise, Trevor D.	SLect	83445309	trevordw	FA	PHD	02	Melbourne	* &1988
Grafton, Jennifer	Lect	83447662	j.grafton	MN	PHD	02	Melbourne	2002
Ho, Susanna	Lect	83448897	suho	DGI	PHD		Hong Kong	2004
Hronsky, Jane J. F.	Lect	83445301	janejfh	FA	MCOM	93	Melbourne	&1997
Lee, Michael T.	Lect	83443677	mlee1	DS	MCOM	98	Monash	2002
Lee, Richard E.	Lect	83446237	renlee	FY	BEC	74	Monash	&1992
Lim, Nena	Lect	83445305	limn	BDJS	PHD	03	QueensInd	2005
Pan, Gary	Lect	83443466	gpan	MSI	PHD	04	Manchest	2005
Parkes, Alison	Lect	83446772	aparkes	S	MBS	01	Massey	2001
Taylor, Sarah J.	Lect	34443414	sjt2	F	BCOM	99	Sydney	2003
Thomson, Genevieve	Lect	34443836	g.thomson	BCM	PHD	98	Melbourne	2003
Wilkin, Carla	Lect	83445275	cwilkin	DS	PHD	01	Deakin	2003
Comerford, Richard	STut	83447024	rctcome		BCOM		Melbourne	1999
Dowling, Carlin	STut	83443415	carlin	ABES	BCOM	99	Tasmania	2003
Stamatelatos, Anna	STut	34447537	astama	M	BBUS	95	Monash	2003
Boys, Noel	Teach	83443416	nboys	BEFY	BBUS	83	RMIT	2002
Leahy, Alison	Teach	83443465	leahya	M	BCOM	03	Melbourne	2004

Monash University　　　　　Clayton　　　Australia　　61-03 Fax=99055475
Dept of Accounting & Finance　Faculty Business & Econ　buseco.monash.edu.au　　BAC,MCO,MBA,PHD
Dept Phone: 99052353　　　　Dandenong Road　　　　　　　　　　　　　　　Miss Tanya Pelle
Homepage: http://www.buseco.monash.edu/au/depts/aaf/
　DNR; 9903 Caulfield　9905 Clayton　9902 Churchill　9904 Frankston

Godfrey, Jayne M.	H-Pr	99032152	jayne.godfrey	FTIU	PHD	91	Queensl	&2002
Ariff, Mohamed	Prof	99031809	mohamed.ariff	IFYX	PHD	97	Queensl	1997
Chenhall, Robert H.	Prof	99052355	robert.chenhall	MBS	PHD	81	Macquarie	&1989
Farley, Alan A.	Prof	99052356	alan.farley	DMQE	PHD	86	Monash	&1976
Associate Dean								
Langfield-Smith, Kim	Prof	99058403	kim.langfield-s+	MCB	PHD	92	Monash	&2002
Peirson, C. Graham	Emer	99052324	graham.peirson	2002	MEC			&1963
Ratnatunga, Janek	Prof	99032508	janek.ratnatunga	MC	PHD	90		&1990
Schelluch, Peter	Prof	99055182	peter.schelluch	BAFO	MCOM	78	NS Wales	&1989
Skully, Michael	Prof	99032407	michael.skully	FI	GRAD			&1992
Gay, Grant E.	Assoc	99052392	grant.gay	A	MEC			&1986
Mather, Paul	Assoc	99055427	paul.mather	F	PHD			&1991
Nethercott, Leslie J.	Assoc	99052380	les.nerthercott	FX	MEC			&1970
Ramsay, Alan L.	Assoc	99052440	alan.ramsay	EF	MEC			1981
Beaman, Ian	SLect	99032027	ian.beaman	QD	PHD	77	Newcastle	1985
Carey, Peter	SLect	99032110	peter.cary	AJO	MBA	93	Monash	&1990
DeLange, Paul	SLect	99044361	paul.delange	FTVE	PHD		LaTrobe	1988
Lu, Wei	SLect	99032972	wei.lu	IH	PHD	99	LaTrobe	1994
Mudalige, Nihal	SLect	99032259	nihal.mudalige	MC	MBA	86	Monash	* &1988
Rice, John F.	SLect	99032182	john.rice	EPF	MEC	77	Monash	&1988

Tanewski, George	SLect	99032388	george.tane+	QBMW	PHD	95			1995
Tant, Kevin	SLect	99032386	kevin.tant	FIJ	MBA	96	S Cross		&1990
Vincent, Michael	SLect	99032390	michael.vincent	FMSW	MEI	92		*	1990
Waldman, Erwin	SLect	99044626	erwin.waldman	ECM	PHD	00	Monash	*	&1989
Webb, Laurie	SLect	99032026	laurie.webb	T	MADM				&1980
Wyatt, Kim	SLect	99044628	kim.wyatt	EFX	MTAX	92	Melbourne		&1989
Bir, Poonam	Lect	99055847	poonam.bir	FAJO	MPHI	83	Delhi		&1996
Clarke, Brian	Lect	99032024	brian.clarke	MCAB	MBA	89	Monash		&1989
Cochrane, Dorothy	Lect	99031107	dot.cochrane	FT	PHD	96	Waikato		&2000
Goyal, Mahendra K.	Lect	99026626	mahendra.go+	MF	PHD	84	Rajasthn		&1996
Halabi, Abdel K.	Lect	99026646	abdel.halabi	FE	MACC				1990
Krueger, Peter	Lect	99044363	peter.krueger	SD	GRAD				&1984
Langfield-Smith, Ian A.	Lect	99052701	ian.langefie+	FTV	LLB				&1999
Raven, John	Lect	99052374	john.raven	EF	MBA				1995
Richardson, William M.	Lect	99032032	bill.richard+	CEM	MEC	84	Monash	*	1987
Sharp, Kevin	Lect	99026645	kevin.sharp	BMN	MEC				&1988
Wickramanayake, J.	Lect	99032403	j.wickraman+	F	PHD				&1990
Dyt, Robyn	ALect	99026715	robyn.dyt	AF	BA				2001
Hardy, Leslie	ALect	99026652	les.hardy	IFE	GRAD				1995
Jackson, Janet	ALect	99026650	janet.jackson	OA	BBUS				1995
Maxfield, Jodie	ALect	99026715	jodie.maxfield	DF	GRAD				&1993
Phillips, Jon	ALect	99044174	jon.phillips	FCM	BBUS				2001
Samy, Martin	ALect	99047138	martin.samy	F	MED		Monash		2000
Serry, Alan J.	ALect	99051500	alan.serry	FD	BEC				&1991
Webster, Carly	ALect	99052322	carly.webster	MA	BBUS				2001

Murdoch University		Murdoch 6150	W Australi	61-09 Fax=93605004					
Commerce Programme		School of Business		murdoch.edu.au		BCO,MPH,MBA,PHD			
Dept Phone: 93602705									Emma Bertram
Did Not Respond Again--2003-2004 Listing									
Avenell, Simon	H		avenell						
Griffiths, Marion D.	Lect	93606024	marion.griffiths	FX	MACC		W Austrl		1988
Holloway, David A.	Lect	93602704	d.holloway	FG	MBA		W Austrl		1988
Kestel, Joanne	Lect	93606041	j.kestel	FM	MACC		Australia		1990
Marshall, Rex L.	Lect	93606043	r.marshall	X	BEC		W Austrl		1989
Richards, James D.	Lect	93602706	j.richards	FM	BCOM		W Austrl		1986

Nanyang Technological Univ		Nanyang Av639798	Singapore	(65) Fax=67937956		(1)	2004,2004		
Accounting		Nanyang Business School		ntu.edu.sg		BA,MA,MBA,PHD			
Dept Phone: 67904902									Adeline Tang
Hong, Hai	Dean	67905692	ahhong		PHD	76	Car Mellon		2002
Tan, Mui Siang Patricia	H-Ac	67904902	amstan	FQ	PHD	94	Brit Colum		&1987
Tan, Hun-Tong	Prof	67904819	ahttan	ABF	PHD	92	Michigan		&1987
Yeo, Gillian H. H.	Prof	67905622	ahhyeo	FT	PHD	90.	Illinois		&1984
Executive Associate Dean									
Boo, Hian Youn El'Fred	Assoc	67906146	ahyboo	AF	PHD	01	Nanyang		&1993
Choo, Teck Min	Assoc	67905685	atmchoo	AF	PHD	93.	Pittsburgh		&1987
Chung, Lai Hong	Assoc	67904655	alhchung	CM	PHD	92.	Pittsburgh		&1987
Foo, See Liang	Assoc	67905722	aslfoo	AF	PHD	88	Hull		&1984
Goh, Chye Tee	Assoc	67905742	actgoh	CM	MCOM	79	NS Wales		&1980
Hossain, Mahmud.	Assoc	67905560	amhossain	F	PHD	98	Massey		1998
Lee, Foong Tow Marina	Assoc	67905717	amlee	FM	MBA	80	Melbourne		&1985
Lee, Lip Nyean	Assoc	67905710	alnlee	AF	MBA	79	Strathcl	*	&1987
Ng, Bu Peow	Assoc	67906144	abpng	AB	PHD	03	Nanyang		&1993
Ng, Eng Juan	Assoc	67905716	aejng	CM	MBA	78	S Calif		&1987
Seow, Jean Lin	Assoc	67906147	ajlseow	AF	MSC	96	Manchest		&1993
Shankar, Premila G.	Assoc	67906403	apmaha	AB	PHD	03	Nanyang		&1994
Tan, Kai Guan Clement	Assoc	67905737	akgtan	DS	MSC	90	London		&1989
Zhang, Huai	Assoc	67904097	huaizhang	F	PHD	00.	Columbia		2006
Geisler, Charlene	Asst	67906222	acsgeisler	ABF	PHD	04.	Tx-Austin		&1997
Jian, Ming	Asst	67906051	amjian	FT	PHD	03	HKUST		2003
Kelly, Khim	Asst	67904805	alkong	MB	PHD	03	S Calif		&1997
Lee, Kin Wai	Asst	67904663	skwlee	AF	PHD	04	Nanyang		&2000
Lim, Chee Yeow	Asst	67904098	slimch	F	PHD	00	Nanyang		2000
Low, Bernardine	Asst	67906255	amflow	ABF	PHD	04.	Cornell		1997
Low, Kin-Yew	Asst	67904903	alimcy	AB	PHD	01.	Illinois		&1993
Mak, Wai Yeong	Asst	67904656	wymak	M	PHD	03	Nanyang		&2006
Tan, Seet Koh	Asst	67905656	asktan	ABDO	MSC	99	NUS		&1999
Tong, Yen Hee	Asst	67905743	ayhtong	F	PHD	05	U Wash		1999
Chan-Ng, Ai Lin	Lect	67904632	aing		MBA	99	Nanyang		2006
Chong, Eng Heng	Lect	67904650	mehchong		MSC	97	Nanyang		&2001
Hu, Kin Hoi Billy	Lect	67906129	akhhu	FM	MSC	96	Manchest		&1995
Lau, Chew King	Lect	67906182	cklau		MIB	98	Monash		2005

Napier University Edinburgh Scotland 44-31 Fax=455-3575
Dept of Accounting & Finance Business Sch EH11 4BN napier.ac.uk BA(HONS),MSC
Dept Phone: 455-3356 Eileen
Did Not Respond Again--2003-2004 Listing

McKay, Tim	H-Le	455 3551		XF	BSC	&1989
Gao, Simon	Prof	455-3351			PHD	1999
Bate, J. Benedict	SLect	455 3433		M	MA	* 9-85
Gardner, Penelope J.	SLect	455 3367		F	BSC	& 9-87
Sievewright, Douglas J. A.	SLect	455 3380		AF	FCCA	& 3-80
Wright, Iain A.	SLect	455 3399		FA	MACC	& 2-75
Brown, James	Lect	455-3355			MSC	1999
Deacon, James	Lect	455 3331		X	BCOM	& F-85
FitzGerald, Adrian A.	Lect	455-3547		FM	BCOM	1998
Fotheringham, Alun	Lect	455-3481			BA	1999
Handley-Schachler, Ian Morri	Lect	455-3355			DPHL	1999
MacAskill, Donald	Lect	455 3385		M	BA	* 4-87
MacKenzie, John	Lect	455-3391		M	CIMA	* 1991
Moffat, Andrew	Lect	455-3461		MF	BA	&1991
Newman, Leslie	Lect	455 3377		M	BSC	* 3-81
Owen, Heather	Lect	455 3329		M	BSC	* 1991
Perman, James	Lect	455 3347		X	BSC	&1989
Soutar, Louise	Lect	455 3325		A	BCOM	&1991
Steven, Graham J.	Lect	455 3331			BA	* 1992
Watson, Robert.	Lect	455-3578			ACII	1999
Windram, Brian	Lect	455-3572		A	BCOM	&1991

National Univ of Singapore Singapore 117591 1 Bus Link (65) Fax=67792083 2004,2004
Dept of Finance & Accounting School of Business nus.edu.sg MSC,PHD
Dept Phone: 68743066 Jyoti Karuppiah
Did Not Respond Again--2002-2003 Listing

Mak, Yuen Teen	C-Ac	68743032	bizmakyt	FM	PHD	94	Victoria	&1996
Chong, Y. S. Sebastian	Assoc	68743009	bizsc	FM	MECO	83	Sydney	&1980
Loh, Lye Chye Alfred	Assoc	68746205	bizlohlc	FMI	PHD	89	W Austrl	&1981
Shih, S. H. Michael	Assoc	68743087	bizshihm	M	PHD	88.	Minnesota	&1996
Wilkins, Trevor A.	Assoc	68743162	biztw	FIM	PHD	89	Queensla	1989
Cheng, Nam Sang	Asst	68744675	bizcns	AM	PHD	97	Bradford	&1999
Ho, Yew Kee	Asst	68743024	bizhoyk	F	PHD	98.	Car Mellon	&1998
Talib, Ameen A.	Asst		biztaas	FM	MSC	85	London	&1981
Zubaidah, Ismail	Asst	68747947	bizzbi	AF	PHD	93	NS Wales	&1994
Ching, Chee Kiong	Fell	B8743082	bizcck	FM	PHD	00	Queensla	&2000

National Chengchi Univ 11623 Taipei ROC Taiwan 886-2 Fax=29387113 2006
Department of Accounting College of Commerce nccu.edu.tw BS,MS,EMBA,PHD
Dept Phone: 29387112 No. 64 Sec.2, Chih-Nan Road Yu-chi Lin
Homepage: http://acct.nccu.edu.tw
Did Not Respond Again--2001-2002 Listing

Su, Robert K.	C-Pr	29398039	robert	FTMI	PHD	87	LSU	1992
Cheng, Ting-Wong	Prof	29398068	dwjeng	FV	PHD	74.	Missouri	&1975
Chou, Ling-Tai Lynette	Prof	29397326	chou	AFNO	PHD	85.	Houston	&1990
Kuo, Horng-Ching	Prof	29387346	hckuo	CFM	PHD	84.	Miss	1992
Lin, Mei-Hwa	Prof	29397112	mwlin	FTV	PHD	87.	Drexel	* &1989
Ma, Sheree Shiow-Ru	Prof	29387458	sma	AMOV	PHD	89.	Alabama	&1989
Wang, Yang-Ruoh	Prof	29387640	yrwang	ACF	MC	77	Chengchi	1977
Wu, Anne	Prof	29387128	anwu	MFQ	PHD	90.	Geo Wash	* &1990
Wu, Se-Hwa	Prof	29390529	sehwa		PHD	84	Chungchi	1983
Chen, Jiin-Feng	Assoc	29387696	jfchen	ADFS	PHD	91.	Wisconsin	&1991
Chen, Ming-Chin	Assoc	29387128	mingchin	FPX	PHD	97.	Ariz St	&1997
Hsu, Chung-Yuan	Assoc	29387112	cyhsu	PTX	PHD	96.	Memphis	&1986
Kang, Jungpao	Assoc	29387339	kang	FQT	PHD	91	NYU	1991
Lin, Wan-Yin	Assoc	29387112	wanying	PCT	DBA	99.	Boston U	1986
Yu, Hung-Chao	Assoc	29387693	hjyu	ACFM	PHD	96.	Wisconsin	1996
Chang, Chinfu	Asst	29387112	ctchang3	FPQ	PHD	99.	Rutgers	2000
Liang, Jia-Wen	Asst				PHD	02.	Oregon	2003
Wang, Wen-Ying	Asst	29387112	wywang1	CIM	PHD	98	Hitotsub	&1999
Lin, Liang-Feng	Lect	29388163	ducer	PCF	MC	94	Temple	1984

National Chung Cheng Univ Min-HsiungChia-Y Taiwan 621 886-5 Fax=2721197
Dept Accounting & Info Tech Management ccu.edu.tw
Dept Phone: 2720411 168 University Blvd Min-Hsiu
Homepage: www.ait.ccu.edu.tw
phone 2720411 email@1=mis.ccu.edu.tw

Huang, Shi-Ming	C-Pr$	Ext16810	smhuang@1	ADMS	PHD	94	Sunderland	1999
Ou, Chin-Shyh	Prof	Ext34566	actcso	CMS	PHD	93.	Minnesota	# * &1998
Hung, Yu-Chung	Assoc	Ext34517	actych	DFMS	PHD	95	Mo-Rolla	2005

Lee, Chia-Ling	Assoc	Ext34502	actcll	CM	PHD	98	Sun Yat-se	1999
Chang, She-I	Asst	Ext34510	actsic	DS	PHD	03	Queensland	2003
Hsieh, Pei-Gin	Asst	Ext34511	actpgh	FQM	PHD	05.	Case Wes	2004
Lee, Chao-Hsiung	Asst	Ext34501	actchl	BCM	PHD	02	Tsukuba	2002
Lin, Ting-Ting	Asst	Ext34509	actttl	CM	DBA	04.	Boston U	2004
Lin, Y. C. George	Asst	Ext34505	actycl	BFQT	PHD	98	Syracuse	1999
Tsai, Chih-Fong	Asst	Ext34519	actcft	DS	PHD	05	Sunderla	2005
Yu, Sui-Hua	Asst	Ext34507	actshy	CFM	PHD	03	Chengchi	2003
Chou, Shu-Chen	Lect	Ext34508	actscc	FT	MA	96	Chengchi	2002

National Economics Univ Hanoi Vietnam 84-4 Fax=8691862
Accounting Faculty Management Training Ctr netnam.org.vn BA,PHD
Dept Phone: 8691067 Giai Phong Street
  Did Not Respond Again--1999-2000 Listing

Quynh, Nguyen Quang	Dean	8691792		AOFM	PHD	82	Karel Mark	1968
Cong, Nguyen Van	Lect	8694589		FMCV	PHD	95	Natl Econ	1986
Dong, Nguyen Thi	Lect	8691825		FMCV	PHD	91	Natl Econ	1976
Gai, Pham Thi	Lect	8691869		FMCV	PHD	88	Natl Econ	1976
Vice-Dean								
Loan, Dang Thi	Lect	8691887		FMCV	PHD	91	Kiev	1976
Loi, Nguyen	Lect	6640113		FCT	PHD	96	Natl Econ	1997
Phuong, Nguyen Minh	Lect	5141697		FMCV	PHD	91	Natl Econ	1976
Thanh, Chu	Lect	8631623		AOFM	MS	94	Illinois	1988
Chi, Pham Bich	Asst	8609084		FM	MBA	97	Boise St	1989
Dinh, Nguyen Van	Asst	8694197		FTMC	MBA	96	Boise St	1989
Hien, Vu Dinh	Asst	8694197		FMCS	MBA	95	Boise St	1990
Hoa, Nguyen Thi Phoung	Asst	8573429		FAOM	MSC	98	London	1996
Ngoc, Le Thi Bich	Asst	8694197		FPTM	MBA	95	Boise St	1988
Trung, Pham Quang	Asst	8694197		FTMP	MBA	95	Boise St	1988
Tue, Ngo Tri	Asst	7330583		FAOM	PHD	96	Acad Sci	1997

National Taiwan University Taipei 10020 ROC Taiwan 106 886-2 Fax=23638038
Department of Accounting College of Management ccms.ntu.edu.tw BBA,MBA,PHD
Dept Phone: 23623857 No. 1, Sec. 4, Roosevelt Rd Ms. Sandy Chen
Homepage: www.acc.ntu.edu.tw
  Did Not Respond--2003-2004 Listing; 886-2-2363-0231 email @1=mba.ntu.edu.tw

Ko, Chen-en	Dean	Ext 2958	chenenko	ASM	PHD	87	Minnesota	# *	& 8-88
Lin, Chan-Jane	C-Pr	Ext 2954	cjlin	FIA	PHD	89.	Maryland		&D-90
Duh, Rong-Ruey	Prof	Ext 2977	rrduh@1	ABCM	PHD	86.	Minnesota		8-88
Li, Shu-Hsing	Prof	Ext 2997	shuhsingli@y	FM	PHD	90.	NYU		8-93
Liu, Chi-Chun	Prof	Ext 2948	ccliu@1	FM	PHD	94	NYU		8-97
Tsai, Yann-Ching	Prof	Ext 2982	yanntsai	FKP	PHD	89.	UCLA		2-90
Tsay, Jimmy Yang-Tzong	Prof	Ext 2863	yttsay@1	FMS	PHD	88.	Maryland	#	&1988
Wang, Tay-Chang	Prof	Ext 2960	tcwang	FT	PHD	88	Penn	#	& 2-88
Wu, Chung-Fern (Rebecca)	Prof	Ext 2962	rwu@1	ADMS	PHD	87	UCLA		& 1-90
Chen, Kuo-Tay	Assoc	Ext 2972	ktchen@1	SMF	PHD	92	Tx-Austin		8-93
Lin, Hwey-Jane	Assoc	Ext 2955	hweyjane@1	CFME	MA	80	Penn		& 8-84
Lin, Suming (Tim)	Assoc	Ext 2991	suming@1	XF	PHD	93.	Ariz St		& 8-93
Liu, Shuen-Zen	Assoc	Ext 2961	sliu@1	PFN	PHD	93.	Pittsburgh		8-94
Yeh, Shu	Assoc	Ext 2862	shuyeh@1	FM	PHD	90.	UCLA		2-93
Liao, Pei-Cheng	Asst	Ext 2999	pcliao	FIT	PHD	02	U Wash		& 2-03
Liu, Chiawen	Asst	Ext 2974	acliu	AFT	PHD	97	Natl Taiw		& 2-02

University of Navarra Barcelona, Spain 08034 3493 Fax=253 4343
Accounting & Control IESE Business School iese.edu MBA,PHD
Dept Phone: 253 4200 Avda. Pearson, 21
Homepage: www.iese.edu

Grandes, Maria J.	H-Pr	253 4200	grandes	FM	DOCT		UPC	N-84
Ocariz, Jose	Emer	253 4200	ocariz	2004	DOCT		ETSIN	9-63
Pereira, Fernando	Emer	253 4200	pereira	2004	DOCT		ETSIC	9-58
Rosanes, M. Josep	Prof	253 4200	jrosanes	JM	PHD	77.	Nrthwstrn	7-71
Sutton, Timothy G.	VProf	253 4200	sutton	F	PHD	80.	U Wash	
Vazquez-Dodero, Juan-Carlos	Prof	253 4200	vazquezd	JM	DOCT		IESE	8-69
Velilla, Manuel	Prof	253 4200	velilla	JMS	DOCT		IESE	7-71
Davila, Antonio	Assoc	253 4200	adavila	SM	DBA	98.	Harvard	9-04
Weber, Eric C.	Assoc	253 4200	eweber	M	PHD	98.	Nrthwstrn	6-87
Fernandez, Albert	Asst	253 4200	afernandez	SM	DBA	02.	Boston U	6-91
Palencia, Luis Enrique	Asst	253 4200	palencia	MF	PHD	99.	Berkeley	9-92
Penalva, Fernando	Asst	253 4200	penalva	F	PHD	98.	Berkeley	9-98
Urrutia, Ingacio	Asst	253-4200	iurrutia	SM	DOC	99	UC Madrid	1-04

University of New England

Accounting Faculty — Sch Atg, Fnce, & Entpre — Armidale 2351NSW — Australia　61-2　Fax=67733148
Dept Phone: 67732201 — North Hill — metz.une.edu.au　MACC,MBA,PHD
Homepage: http://www.une.edu.au/febl/safe/index.htm — Carole Mtichell
Did Not Respond Again--2003-2004 Listing

Name	Rank	Phone	Email		Degree		School	Year
Piggott, R.	Dean	67732990	rpiggott		PHD		Cornell	2003
Eddie, Ian	C-Ac	67733403	ieddie	I	PHD		N Eng-Au	&1982
Hutchinson, Patrick J.	Prof	67733902	phutchin	F	PHD		Bath	&1979
Shamsuddin, Abdul	Assoc	67732558	ashamsul	Q	PHD		Simon Fr	1998
Kotey, Bernice	SLect	67732830	bkotey	M	PHD		N Eng-Au	2000
Saravanamuthu, Kala	SLect	67733276	ksaravan	M	PHD		SA	2002
Shannon, Robert P.	SLect	67733617	rshannon	A	MEC	85	N Eng-Au	&1993
Warwick, David	SLect	67732838	dwarwick	M	MSC		Bath	&1973
Adams, A.	Lect	67733057	aadams	S	MEC		N Eng-Au	&1986
Geddes, S.	Lect	67732434	sgeddes	P	MEC		N Eng-Au	&1988
Gerk, J.	Lect	67732474	jgerk	D	HONS		Cologne	2001
Hillier, J.	Lect	67732604	jhillier	F	PHD	99	Otago	1999
Whitman, J.	Lect	67732711	jwhitman	F	MA		Canterbu	2002
Spizewski, A.	ALect	67732608	aspizews	D	BFIN		N Eng-Au	2001

Univ of New South Wales

Accounting Faculty — Faculty of Business — Sydney 2052　NSW Austra — 61-02　Fax=93855925
Dept Phone: 93855829 — ANZAC PDE, Sydney — unsw.edu.au　BCOM,MCOM,PHD
— Colin C. Withers, Adm Officer

Name	Rank	Phone	Email		Degree		School	Year
Simnett, Roger	H-Pr	93855825	r.simnett	AB	PHD	92	NS Wales	&1987
Brown, Philip R.	Prof	93856109	philip.brown	F	PHD	68.	Chicago	&
Chua, Wai Fong	Prof	93855828	wf.chua	MH	PHD	83	Sheffield	&1985
Senior Associate Dean								
Taylor, Stephen L.	Prof	93855837	s.taylor	FA	PHD	91	NS Wales	&
Trotman, Ken T.	Prof	93855831	k.trotman	AB	PHD	84	NS Wales	&1974
Luckett, Peter F.	Assoc	93855912	p.luckett	MB	PHD	84	Sydney	&1983
Miller, Malcolm C.	Assoc	93855820	m.miller	FI	MCOM	73	NS Wales	&1964
Briers, Michael L.	SLect	92369117	m.briers	MB	PHD	97	NS Wales	1988
Morris, Richard D.	SLect	93855818	richard.morris	FH	PHD	88	NS Wales	&1974
Cheng, Mandy M.	SLect	93856343	m.cheng	M	MCOM	00	NS Wales	1998
Ferguson, Andrew	SLect	93856443	a.ferguson	AFOQ	PHD		Tech-Sydn	
Gallery, Gerry	SLect	83855813	g.gallery	FTLY	PHD	01	Queensl	
Green, Wendy J.	SLect	93855805	w.green	AB	PHD	00	NS Wales	&1985
Harding, Noel	SLect		n.harding	A	MCOM	95	NS Wales	1994
Roebuck, Peter J.	SLect	93855845	p.roebuck	AB	MCOM	88	NS Wales	&1985
Andon, Paul	Lect	93855821	p.andon	M	MCOM		NS Wales	2000
Ang, N.	Lect	93855832	n.ang		MA	01	Stanford	
Balatbat, Maria	Lect	93855808	m.balatbat	FA	PHD	98	Sydney	
Boedker, C.	Lect	93855839	c.boedker		MCOM		NS Wales	
Carson, Elizabeth	Lect	93855822	e.carson	F	MCOM	99	NS Wales	1998
Chong, Kar Ming	Lect	93855916	km.chong	F	PHD		E Cowan	2000
Coulton, Jeffery J.	Lect	93855811	j.coulton	FAY	LLB	94	Sydney	
Coyte, Rodney	Lect	93855810	r.coyte	MB	MCOM	88	NS Wales	&1992
Curtis, A.	Lect	93855814	a.curtis	F	MCOM		NS Wales	
Czernkowski, Robert M.	Lect	93855807	r.czernkowski	FQ	BCOM	88	Tasmania	&1989
Gormly, C.	Lect	93855812	c.gormly		MEC	92	Sydney	
Humphreys, K.	Lect	93855833	k.humphreys		BCOM		NS Wales	
Kang, Helen	Lect	93855824	helen.kang	MF	MCOM	00	NS Wales	1999
Lam, Peter	Lect	93856081	p.lam	F	MBA		Chicago	
Mahama, Habib	Lect	93855843	h.mahama	M	PHD		NS Wales	2001
Martinov, Nonna	Lect	93855940	n.martinov	AB	PHD		NS Wales	&1990
Mayorga, Diane	Lect	93855814	d.mayorga		MCOM		NS Wales	
Pflugrath, G.	Lect	93855802	g.pflugrath		MBA		Melbourne	
Ruddock, C.	Lect	93855806	c.ruddock		LLB		UTS	
Taylor, Stuart D.	Lect	93855826	stuart.taylor	F	MCOM		Melbourne	
Chang, Linda	AsLec	93855817	linda.change	M	MCOM	00	NS Wales	1998
Chugh, S.	ALect	93855823	s.chugh		MBA		Ntl Sch	

University of Newcastle

Displine of Atg & Finance — Newcastle Business Sch — N So Wales 2308　Australia — 61-49　Fax=216911
Dept Phone: 216642 — University Drive, Callaghan — newcastle.edu.au　BCOM,MBA,MS,DTX
— Carmel O'Regan

Name	Rank	Phone	Email		Degree		School	Year
Stanton, Patricia A.	H-SLe	215043	cmpas	FET	PHD	95	Newcastle	1989
Easton, Steve	Prof	215040	cmse	F	PHD	93	Monash	1991
Psaros, Jim	Prof	215048	cmjp	A	PHD	97	NS Wales	&1982
Winsen, Joseph K.	Prof	215045	cmjkw	F	PHD	73.	Ohio St	&1977
Motyka, Wolodymyr	SLect	215047	cmwm	DHIM	PHD	94	NS Wales	1988
Hartnett, Neil A.	Lect	215039	cmnah	CFM	MCOM	91	Newcastle	&1986
Naidoo, Krish	Lect	212033	krish.naidoo		BCOM	84	S Africa	2004
Seamer, Michael	Lect	215992	michael.seamer		BCOM	99	Newcastle	1998
Yap, Christine L.	STut	215036	cmcly	CFP	MCOM	99	Newcastle	&1989

Norwegian Sch Ec & Bus Adm
Inst Atg, Auditing & Law
Dept Phone: 95 90 00
Homepage: nhh.no/rrr
DNR; phone +4755 959324 or +4755 959322; Telefax +4755 959320

Bergen-Sandviken Norway
N-5045
Helleveien 30

47-55 Fax=95 93 20
nhh.no
BS,MS,PHD
Elizabeth Stiegler/Turid Roraas

Name	Rank	Ext	Email					
Gjesdal, Froystein	C-Pr	Ext59316	froystein.gje+	VT	PHD	79	Stanford	
Bjornenak, Trond	Prof	Ext59317	trond.bjorne+	M	DOEC			
Eilifsen, K. Aasmund	Prof	Ext59323	aasmund.eili+	A	DOEC			
Fallan, Lars	Prll			X	DOEC			
email lars.fallan@aoa.hist.no								
Johnsen, Atle	Prof	Ext59299	atle.johnsen	PF	LIC		Norwegia	
Kinserdal, Arne	Emer	Ext59251	arne.kinserdal	2003				
Langholm, Odd	Emer	Ext59318	odd.langholm	1999	DOEC			
Norstrom, Carl J.	Emer	Ext59312	carl.norstrom	2004	DOEC			
Olson, Olov	Prll		olov.olson	MG	DREK		Gothenbu	
visiting from School of Economics & Comm Law, Gothenburg Univ								
Syversen, Jan	Prll			X				
Bjorndal, Endre	Assoc	Ext59375	endre.bjorndal	Q	DOEC		Norwegia	
Brudvik, Arthur	Assoc	Ext59395	arthur.brudvik	X				
Fjell, Kenneth	Assoc	Ext59687	kenneth.fjell	MQ	DOEC			
Hamberg, Mattias	Acll	Ext59619	mattias.hamberg	F	DREK	00	Uppsala	
Hope, Ole-Kristian	Acll			F	PHD	01.	Nrthwstrn	&
visiting from University of Toronto								
Knivsfla, Kjell Henry	Assoc	Ext59550	kjell.knivsfla	F	DOEC		Norwegia	
Monsen, Norvald	Assoc	Ext59314	norvald.mon+	G	DOEC			
Ostergren, Katarina	Assoc	Ext59637		B	PHD			
Stemsrudhagen, Jan-Ivar	Assoc	Ext59319	jan.stemsrud+	M	DOEC		Norwegia	
Dahl, Gunnar A.	SLect		gunnar.dahl	F				
Fladstad, Harald	SLect			P				
Hartz-Hanssen, Petter	SLect			X				
Nagell, Terje	SLect			A				
Elling, Jens O.	Prll				PHD		Copenhag	1989
visiting from Copenhagen School of Economics								
McKee, Thomas E.	Prll			TA	PHD	75.	Geo St	* &1990
visiting from East Tenn State Univ								
Messier, William F. Jr.	Prll			AFB	DBA	79.	Indiana	&1992
visiting from Georgia State University								
Romney, Marshall B.	Prll			SA	PHD	77.	Tx-Austin	&1998
visiting from Brigham Young University								

Norwegian Sch of Management
Accounting Faculty
Dept Phone: 06600
Homepage: www.bi.no

N-0442 Olso
Accounting, Aud & Law
Nydalsveier 37

Norway
bi.no
47 Fax=23264793
BA,MBA,MSC
Anne Christine Thestrup

Name	Rank	Phone	Email					
Brathen, Tore	H-Pr	46410415	tore.brathen	LX	DJUR	98	Oslo	1990
Gjems-Onstad, Ole	Prof	46410419	ole.g.onstad	X	DRJU	84	Oslo	1985
Langli, John Christian	Prof	46410429	john.c.langli	FI	DREC	93	NHH Berg	8-93
Nobes, Christopher W.	Prll			FI	PHD	83	Exeter	2003
Roberts, Hanno	Prll	46410434	hanno.roberts	M	PHD	93	Maastricht	O-96
Schwencke, Hans Robert	Prof	46410436	hans.r.schwe+	TFI	DJUR	02	Oslo	&1990
Berthling-Hansen, Pal	Assoc	46410412	pal.berthling+	CM	PHD	93	Southmptn	1994
Kvaal, Erlend	Assoc	46410426	erlend.kvaal	TFI	CAND	94	Oslo	1991
Skalpe, Ole	Assoc	46410439	ole.skalpe	FM	DOEC	96	NHH Berg	2003
Vyrtveit, Ingunn	Assoc		ingunn.myrtveit	CDMQ	DREC	95	NHH Berg	8-87
Rasmussen, Janicke	SLect	46410433	janicke.rasm+	FM	CPA	90	NHH Berg	2000
Skaldehaug, Espen	SLect	46410438	espen.skalde+	CM	MSCR	83	Linkoping	1989
Tangenes, Tor	SLect	46410442	tor.tangenes	CM	ABD		NHH Berg	1999
Blattner, Emanuel	Lect	46410414	emanuel.blat+	FM	MBUS	81	Friboug	1991
Kristensen, Roy	Lect	46410684	roy.kristensen	FX	ABD	94	Oslo	2007
Strand, Rolf Gunnar	Lect	46410441	rolf.g.strand	FM	ABD	74	NHH Berg	1992
Dyrnes, Sverre	IndPr	46410417	sverre.dyrnes	CFM	MBUS	78	NHH Berg	&2001
Gjonnes, Svein	Doct	46410420	svein.h.gjonnes	FM	MBA	92	NHH Berg	2004
Gulden, Bror Petter	IndPr	46410422	bror.p.gulden	A	MBUS	78	NHH Berg	& 8-83
Kildal, Tor S.	IndPr	46410425	tor.a.kildal	X	MBUS	90	NHH Berg	&1993
Loken, Svein A.	IndPr	46410430	sal	ADO	MBUS	70	NHH Berg	1985

University of Nottingham
Accounting Faculty
Dept Phone: 84-66602
Homepage: http://www.nottingham.ac.uk/unbs/
Did Not Respond Again--2003-2004 Listing

Nottingham Engla NG8 1BB
Business School
Jubilee Campus, Wollaton Rd

0115 Fax=84-66667
nottingham.ac.uk
BA,MA,MBA,PHD
Janet Cooke

Name	Rank	Phone	Email					
Hodges, Ron	H-Re	951-5487	ron.hodges	FGN	MBA	91	Nottingh	&1992
Berry, R. H.	Prof	951-5256	robert.berry	HQ	PHD	87	Warwick	1994
Ebrahim, M. Shahid	Read	846-7654	m.shadid.ebr+	FQ	DBA	95	S Illinois	2003
Klumpes, Paul J. M.	Prof	846-7414	paul.klumpes	FMN	PHD	96	NS Wales	&

Toms, Steven	Prof	951-5276	steve.toms	FH	PHD	96	Nottingh	&1994
Wright, Mike	Prof	951-5257	mike.wright	FU	PHD	86	Nottingh	1978
Goddard, Scott	SLect	951-5488	scott.goddard	F	MCOM	72	Birminghm	1990
Hasseldine, D. John	SLect	951-5279	john.hasseld+	XB	PHD	97.	Indiana	&1997
Woods, Margaret M.	SLect	846-6692	margaret.woods	M	MSC	80	London	&2001
Grubnic, Suzana	Lect	951-5258	suzana.grubnic	M	PHD	00	Derby	2001
Henderson, Brian	Lect	951-5258	brian.henderson	F	BA	97	Derby	2001
Reber, Beat	Lect	846-6970	beat.reber	M	PHD	00	Nottingh	2001
McLintock, Alyson J.	Teach	846-6971	alyson.mclintock	M	BCOM	73	Edinburgh	2000

University of Otago
Dept Accountancy & Bus Law
Dept Phone: 479-8192
Homepage: http://divcom.otago.ac.nz/actg/

Dunedin Box 56   NewZealand
School of Business
Corner Union & Clyde Streets

64-03 Fax = 479-8450   2006
commerce.otago.ac.nBCO,MCO,MBA,PHD
                                Shelley West

Wynn-Williams, Kate	H-SLe	Ext 8151	kwynnwms	NME	PHD	99	Otago	1994
Adler, Ralph W.	Prof	Ext 8192	radler	BEM	PHD	91	SUNY-Alb	1-91
Burke, John L.	Assoc	Ext 8071	jburke	FQT	PHD	72	Toronto	1998
Liyanarachchi, Gregory	SLect	Ext 8070	gliyanarachchi	FMA	PHD	04	Otago	1994
Lont, David	SLect	Ext 8119	dlont	DEQF	PHD	01	Otago	1-89
Stringer, Carolyn	SLect	Ext 5299	cstringer	BM	PHD	06	Otago	1998
Whiting, Ros	SLect	Ext 8109	rwhiting	FES	PHD	07	Otago	1993
Gardner, Clare	Lect	Ext 9071	cgardner	JESM	MCOM	96	Otago	1994
Harold, Linda	Lect	Ext 7047	lharold	EFW	MMS		Waikato	2006
Poletti, Elena	Lect	Ext 8108	epoletti	FM	PHD	87	Otago	1988
Seng, Dyna	Lect	Ext 9072	dseng	FI	MCOM	96	Otago	1994
Theivananthampillai, Paul	Lect	Ext 8117	priyan	FMVQ	PHD	96	Otago	1989

University of Oxford
Accounting Faculty
Dept Phone: 288800
Homepage: www.sbs.ox.ac.uk

Oxford OX1 1HP   U Kingdom
Said Business School
Park End Street

1865 Fax = 288805
sbs.ox.ac.uk

Chapman, Christopher S.	Read	288908	chris.chapman	MS	PHD	95	LondonSE	1996
Hopwood, Anthony G.	Prof	422562	anthony.hopw+	MB	PHD	71	Chicago	1995
Dechow, Niels	Lect	288503	niels.dechow	MS	PHD	01	Copenhag	2004
Quattrone, Paolo	Lect	278808	paulo.quattrone	MS	PHD	96	Catania	2003
Suzuki, Tomo	Lect	288942	tomo.suzuki	FIS	PHD	01	Oxford	2002

ESCP-EAP
Department of CPO
Dept Phone: 49232171
Homepage: www.escp-eap.net

75543 Paris Cede France
Business 70511
79 avenue de la Re'publique

33-1 Fax = 49232049
escp-eap.net   BA,MA,MBA
                                Sophie Compte

Saulpic, Olivier	H-Pr	Ext 2615	saulpic	BMSU	PHD	00	Ecole Pl	1997
Mendoza, Carla	Prof	Ext 2052	mendoza	BCMU	PHD	91	HEC	1987
Naulleau, Gerard	Prof	Ext 2275	gnaulleau	CEMU	PHD	90	EHESS	1986
Dobler, Philippe	Assoc	Ext 2017	dobler	CM	MS	71	Paris-I	1979
Giraud, Françoise	Assoc	Ext 2050	giraud	BCMU	PHD	00	ESC Bord	1991
Le Vourc'h, Joelle	Assoc	Ext 2057	levourch	IFAC	MBA	73	ESCP	1985
Fourcade, Francois	Asst	Ext 2630	ffourcade	CEMU	PHD	04	Ecole Pl	2004
Zrihen, Robert	Asst	Ext 2056	rzrihen	BCMU	PHD	02	Paris Daup	1996

Group ESCP de Paris
Department of CPO
Dept Phone: 49232049
   Did Not Respond Again--2002-2003 Listing

Paris Cedex 11   France
Business 70511
79 Av de la Republique

33-1 Fax = 49232039
escp.fr   BA,MA,MBA
                        Mayte Ponce, Natasha Boyer

Eglem, Jean-Yves	H-Pr	Ext 2058	eglem	FIMU	PHD	80	Paris I	1971
Causse, Genevieve	Prof	Ext 2047	causse	CFUN	PHD	82	Paris I	1971
Mikol, Alain	Prof	Ext 2045	mikol	AHJ	PHD	89	Paris I	1982
Simon, Claude	Prof	Ext 2236	csimon	TM	PHD	92	CPA	1990
Bonnier, Carole	Assoc	Ext 2053	bonnier	CFMU	PHD	01	CNAT	1992
Delvaille, Pascale	Assoc	Ext 2051	delvaill	AFI	PHD	01	Paris IX	1984
Kennedy, John	Assoc	Ext 2054	kennedy	AGI	MBA	66	Carleton	1988
Mailett, Catherine	Assoc	Ext 2113	mailllet	AFX	PHD	87	Paris IX	1985
Hossfeld, C.	Asst	Ext 2646	chossfeld	AFI	PHD	96	Saar Bruck	2000

Universitat Pompeu Fabra
Accounting Faculty
Dept Phone: 542 1766
Homepage: www.econ.upf.es

Barcelona 08005   Spain
Dept of Econ & Business
Ramon Trias Fargas 25

(93) Fax = 542 1746
upf.edu   LIC,MSC,PHD
                                     Ana Mas

Freixas, Xavier	Dean	542-2726	xavier.freixas	F	PHD	78	Toulouse	
Amat, Oriol	Prof	542-1655	oriol.amat	F	PHD	90	Barcelona	1993
Kim, Moshe	Prof	542-2771	moshe.kim			82	Toronto	
Marin, Jose	Prof	542-2727	jose.marin	F	PHD	94	Penn	

Rubio, Gonzalo	Prof	542-2727	gonzalo.rubio			85	UCB
Cunat, Vicente	Assoc	542-2578	vicente.cunat	PHD		01	London SE
Oliveras, Esster	Assoc	542-1673	ester.oliveras	PHD		99	Lancashire
Alemany, Fina	Asst	542-2737	fina.alemany			06	UPC
Bagur, Llorenc	Asst	542-2693	llorenc.bagur			05	UB
Boned, Josep Lluis	Asst	542-2971	josep.boned			05	UB
DeFalguera, Jordi	Asst	542-2405	jordi.falguera			02	UPF
Monllau, Teresa	Asst	542-2405	teresa.monllau			98	UPC
Penaranda, Francisco	Asst	542-2638	francisco.pen+			03	CEMFI
Puig, Xavier	Asst	542-2535	xavier.puig			02	UPF

University of Portsmith — Portsmouth PO1 3DE — 02392 Fax=844319
Dept of Accounting & Law — Portsmouth Business Sch — port.ac.uk — BA,MSC,PHD
Dept Phone: 844095 — Portland Street — Martine McGilligan
Homepage: www/[bs/[prt/ac/uk/departments/academic/acclaw

Ridley, Ann	Dean	84 4057	ann.ridley		LLM		
Callaghan, Clare	H-SLe	84 4157	clare.callaghan	NIG	MSC		1992
Fearnley, Stella	Prof	84 4234	stella.fearnley	A	BA		1994
Page, Michael J.	Prof	84 4148	mike.page	AFT	PHD		1990
Bevington, Alexandra	Lect	84 4142	alexandra.bev+		BA		2003
Brandon-Pollard, Sonia	Lect	84 4722	sonia.brandon-p+			MSC	2004
Davey-Evans, Sue	Lect	84 4784	sue.davey-evans				2006
Daynes, Arief	Lect	84 4182	arief.daynes	IF	PHD		1994
Dockery, Everton	Lect	84 4065	everton.dockery		PHD		2005
Gillies, Annette	Lect	84 4239	annette.gillies		MBA		2003
Graham, Alan	Lect	84 4795	alan.graham		MA		2005
Hicks, James R.	Lect	84 4154	james.hicks	EA	DPH		1989
Major, Robert	Lect	84 4165	robert.major	EI	BSC		1994
McBride, Karen	Lect	84 4282	karen.mcbride	MBF	BSC		1997
Pagas, Paraskevas	Lect	84 4721	paraskevas.p+		MSC		2004
Toon, Ian	Lect	84 4720	ian.toon		BSC		2005
Yarr, Margaret	Lect	84 4160	margaret.yarr		MSC		2003
Andrew, Peter	PLect	84 4093	peter.andrew		PHD		2001
Bowhill, Bruce	PLect	84 4222	bruce.bowhill	M	BSC		1984
Conrad, Lynne	PLect		lynne.conrad	BCM	PHD	Essex	&
Gladstone-Millar, Charlotte	PLect	84 4175	charlotte.gla+	E	BA		1988
Hines, Tony	PLect	84 4156	tony.hines	FN	MSC		1986
Tonge, Richard	PLect	84 4161	richard.tonge	MGN	MA		1989
Willett, Caroline	PLect	84 4195	caroline.willett	FAJ	BA		1990

Univ of Puerto Rico-Mayaguez — Mayaguez, PR 00681-9009 — (809) Fax=832-5320
Accounting Faculty — College of Business Adm — uprm.edu — BS,MBA
Dept Phone: 265-3800 — Mrs. Irma Perez
   Did Not Respond Again--2003-2004 Listing; phone 265-3801

Perez, Candido	C-Pr	Ext 2075		ADFS	MSA	85	Mass	# * & 6-83
Almodovar, Luis R.	Prof	Ext 3483		CFP	MBA	78	P Rico	& 1-76
Jetter, Ina	Prof	Ext 3475		EFPT	MACC	80	Va Tech	& 1-78
Ortiz, Eulalio	Prof	Ext 3483		CFMX	MBA	76	Syracuse	& 8-73
Hernandez, Digna	Assoc	Ext 3615		CEMP	MBA	78	Florida	1-76
Quinones, Eva Z.	Assoc	265-3801		CFPR	MPA	88	Tx-Austin	& 1-90
Rios, Arcadio	Assoc	Ext 2075		FPRV	MS	82	Mass	& 1-82
Oltikar, Pratima	Asst	Ext 3615		PCM	MBA	91	P Rico	& 1-91

University of Puerto Rico — San Juan, PR 00931-3326 — (787) Fax=Ext 3995
Accounting Department — Faculty of Business Adm — rrpac.upr.clu.edu — BBA,MBA
Dept Phone: Ext 3326 — Myriam Maldonado
Homepage: rrpac.upr.clu.edu:9090/~contrrp/index.htm
   Did Not Respond Again--2003-2004 Listing; phone 764-0000

Alicea, Juan Carlos	Dean$	Ext 3903	jalicea	BMT	MBA	91	P Rico	&1992
Mattei-Ballester, Wanda M.	D-Ac	Ext 3330	wmattei	FIE	PHD	02.	Tx A&M	&1995
Calaf, Jorge E.	Prof	Ext 3326	jcalaf	CSQ	MAS	75	Duke	* &1982
Gonzalez Tobaoada, Jose A.	Prof	Ext 3326	jgonzalez	TFQ	DBA	81	Kent St	# * &1994
Gutierrez, Elsa	Prof	Ext 3326		EFV	MBA	79	P Rico	&1985
Huertas, Yvonne	Prof	Ext 3326	yhuerta	CMS	MBA	72	P Rico	&1976
Martinez Colon, Juan L.	Prof	Ext 3326		IRX	ABD		NYU	# * &1976
Rodriguez de Marrero, Aurea	Prof	Ext 3326		FP	JSD	01	Compluten	1986
Roman, Damian	Prof	Ext 3326	droman	T	MBA	63	NYU	1960
Garcia, Merced Juan	Assoc	Ext 3326		AR	MBA	85	Wisconsin	&1982
Prado, Edwin	Assoc	Ext 3326		X	LLM	91	NYU	&1991
Fernandez, Leticia	Asst	Ext 3326		TF	MBA	80	Geo Wash	&1982
Betancourt, Wanda	Inst	Ext 3326		A	MBA			&2001
Maldonado, Edwin	Inst	Ext 3326		X	LLM	02	Geotown	&2000
Marrero, Rafael	Inst	Ext 3326		EFP	MBA	91	P Rico	&1995

University of Queensland Brisbane, Qld Australia 64-07 Fax=33656788 2003,2003
UQ Busness School Faculty Bus, Econ & Law business.uq.edu.au BCO,MCOM,PHD
Dept Phone: 33656283 Blair Drive Bld T. Smith/C. A. Cochrane
Homepage: www.business.uq.edu.au
Did Not Respond Again--2003-2004 Listing

Brailsford, Timothy J.	H-Pr	33656225	t.brailsford	F	PHD	94	Monash	&2002
Clarkson, Peter M.	Prof	33656259	p.clarkson	A	PHD	86	Brit Colum	2002
Craswell, Allen T.	Prof	33656267	a.craswell	A	PHD	84	Sydney	&2001
Finn, Frank J.	Prof	33656591	f.finn	F	PHD	81	Queensl	&1969
Gray, Stephen F.	Prof	33656586	s.gray	F	PHD	95	Stanford	1997
O'Keefe, Terrence B.	Prof	33656267	t.okeefe	FA	PHD	70	Purdue	1980
Weber, Ron A.	Prof	33656585	r.weber	SA	PHD	77	Minnesota	&1979
Gray, Phil	Assoc	33656992	p.gray	F	PHD	00	NS Wales	1999
Green, Peter	Assoc	33811029	p.green	DS	PHD	97	Queensl	&1999
Avkiran, Necmi	SLect	33811216	n.avkiran	MFDQ	PHD	95	VUT-Melb	2000
Gaunt, Clive	SLect	33656580	c.gaunt	F	PHD	99	Queensld	2001
Kavanagh, M.	SLect	33811003	m.kavanagh	FM	PHD	01	Queensl	2000
Kent, Pamela F.	SLect	33656611	p.kent	A	PHD	91	N Eng-Au	&1987
Rohde, Fiona H.	SLect	33656530	f.rohde	FM	PHD	00	Queensl	1990
Walker, Julie	SLect	33656588	j.walker	FM	PHD	94	Queensl	1990
Alpert, Karen	Lect	33656261	k.alpert	FX	MTAX	86	S Calif	2001
Benson, Karen	Lect	33654348	k.benson	F	MCOM	95	Jms Cook	2002
Clutterbuck, Peter	Lect	33811035	p.clutterbuck	S	MSC	95	Queenl Tc	
Crockcroft, Sophie	Lect	33656272	s.crockcroft	S	PHD	99	Otago	2000
Elijido-Ten, Evangeline	Lect	33811031	e.elijido-ten	A	MBA	91	St Thomas	2002
Hall, Jason	Lect	33469421	j.hall	F	BCOM	96	Queenslnd	1999
Heales, Jon	Lect	33656433	j.heales	ADOS	PHD	98	Queensln	&1998
Herbohn, Kathleen	Lect	33656581	k.herbohn	FB	BCOM	93	Jms Cook	2001
Koh, Ping Sheng	Lect	33656249	p.koh	FTY	PHD	01	Tasmania	2001
Lamb, James	Lect	33811414	j.lamb	DS	BBUS	87	Deakin	1998
Lim, Nena	Lect	33651334	n.lim	DS	MSC	95	Geo St	1999
Manning, Chris	Lect	33811226	c.manning	A	BSC	90	Tasmania	2001
Monem, Reza	Lect	33656422	r.monem	A	PHD	00	Queenslnd	2000
O'Brien, Paul	Lect	33811217	p.obrien	S	BSC	90	Queenslnd	2000
Ragunthan, Vanitha	Lect	33658204	v.ragunthan	QI	PHD	99	RMIT	1999
Robb, Alastair	Lect	33811219	a.robb	DS	BBUS	97	Queenslnd	1994
Rowlands, Terrence	Lect	33811218	t.rowlands	S	PHD	97	NS Wales	2000
Simmons, Sharelle	Lect	33654346	s.simmons	A	MCOM	91	NS Wales	2000
Tutticci, Irene	Lect	33656587	i.tutticci	F	PHD	01	Queenslnd	1996
Wallace, Sandra	Lect	33656630	s.wallace	CM	MFM	96	Queensland	1999

Queensland Univ of Tech Brisbane Q 4001 Australia (07) Fax=38641812 (X) 2005,2005
School of Accountancy Business Box 2434 qut.edu.au MACC,MBA,PHD
Dept Phone: 38642058 2 George Street K. Pollard
Did Not Respond Again--2003-2004 Listing

Little, Peter C.	Dean	38642881	pl.little	Law	PHD	97	Bond	
McGregor-Lowndes, M.	Prof	38642936	m.megregor	F	PHD		Madmin Qld	1984
Willett, Roger J.	Prof	38642856	r.willett	AFM	PHD	86	Aberdeen	&1996
Best, Peter J.	Assoc	38642739	p.best	AD	PHD	78	Newcastle	& 4-88
Gallagher, Lynn	SLect	38644317	l.gallagher	F	MFM			&1982
Katter, Norm	SLect	38641017	n.katter	F	PHD		Queensld	1987
Mirza, Malik	SLect	38642061	m.mizra	F	MCOM	76	Queensld	& 7-90
Percy, Majella	SLect	38642880	m.percy	F	MFM	90	Queensld	& 4-88
Ryan, Christine	SLect	38644320	cm.ryan	F	MFM	80	Queensld	& 7-76
Sweeting, J.	SLect	38642534	j.sweeting	F	MEC	84	N Eng-Au	& 9-87
Buckby, Sherrena	Lect	38644324	s.buckby	A	MBUS	81	Queensl	& 1-90
Craig, Robert	Lect	38645198	r.craig	F	MBA		Queensld	1995
Hocken, Mike	Lect	38644236	m.hocken	F	LLM	94	Queensld	1987
Kent, Ros	Lect	38642403	r.kent	F	MFM	78	Queensld	& 1-76
Marsden, Stephen	Lect	38642018	s.marsden	F	MBUS	94	Queensld	& 1-92
Munro, Lois	Lect	38641450	l.munro	F	MFM	93	Queensld	& 1-89
O'Leary, Connor	Lect	38641019	c.oleary	AO	MBUS	93	Queensld	& 6-89
Scheiwe, Dan J.	Lect	38641155	d.scheiwe	AF	MACC	93	N Eng-Au	& 7-93
Stanley, Trevor	Lect	38645291	t.stanley	FE	MSC	85	Griffith	& 1-79
Taylor, Sue	Lect	38642514	sm.taylor	F	MBUS	93	Queensld	& 1-87
Vincent, Carolyn	ALect	38642850	c.vincent	X	BCOM	89	Queensld	1994

University of St. Andrews St Andrews Fife Scotland 1334 Fax=462812
Accounting Faculty School of Management st-andrews.ac.uk BA,MLITT,PHD
Dept Phone: 462800 Gateway Bldg, North Haugh Latie M. Allen

McKiernan, Peter	H	462871	peter		PHD			
Bebbington, Jan	Prof	462348	kjb10	WETJ	PHD	99	Dundee	&2004
Gray, Robert H.	Prof	462799	rhg1	WETJ	PHD	03	Glasgow	&2004
Mueller, Frank	Prof	462798	fum	WTI	PHD	91	Oxford	2004
Carter, Chris	Read	462820	cc67	WTI	PHD	01	Aston	2002
Wilson, John	Read	462803	jsw7	QF	PHD	99	Wales	2000
Fearfull, Anne	Lect	462875	af22	WT	PHD	94	UMIST	2002

Seoul National University
Accounting Faculty
Dept Phone: 880-6857

Seoul, Korea 151-742				(02) Fax=872-6900			2004,2004	
College of Business Adm				snu.ac.kr			BBA,MBA,PHD	
San 56-1, Shinlim-dong							Jong-In Jung	
Choi, Jong-Hag	C-Pr	880-6873	acchoi	AFIQ	PHD	00	Illinois	2006
Ahn, Tae-Sik	Prof	880-8260	ahnts	CMSN	PHD	87.	Tx-Austin	1997
Hwang, Lee-Seok	Prof	880-5075	lshwang	FIQ	PHD	94.	NYU	2003
Jung, Woon-Oh	Prof	880-5764	wjung	FQTX	PHD	86.	UCLA	1998
Kim, Song-Ki	Prof	880-6932	songkim	FCMV	PHD	79.	Tx-Austin	&1983
Kwak, Su-Keun	Prof	880-6949	sukeun	FMCW	PHD	87.	N Carol	1988
Lee, Chang-Woo	Prof	880-6852	changwoo	FIAX	PHD	87.	Berkeley	&1992
Nam, Sang-Oh	Prof	880-6936	sonam	FMA	PHD	81	Seoul Natl	&1974

University of Sharjah
Department of Accounting
Dept Phone: 505-0653
Homepage: www.sharjah.ac.ae

Sharjah UAE				9716 Fax=505-0513				
College of Bus & Mgt				sharjah.ac.ae				
							AlJaber Reem	
Ibrahim, Mohamed E.	Dean	505-0540	acebrahim	FAB	PHD	85	North Tx	&2000
Velayutham, Sivakumar	H-Ac	505-0533	sivav	FMHT	PHD	97	Massey	&2000
Abdel Maksoud, Ahmed	Asst	505-3559	aabdelmaksoud	M	PHD	03	Bristol	2004
AlSegini, Sabri	Asst		ssegini	SM	PHD	93	Warwick	2001

Southern Cross University
Division of Business
Dept Phone: 20 3835
Homepage: http://www.scu.edu.au/schools/comm

Lismore NSW 2480				Australia		61 66 Fax=22 1724		
Sch of Commerce & Mgt				scu.edu.au			BBUS,MBUS,MAS	
Military Road, East Lismore							Jaki Martin	
Kelly, Stephen	H							
Alizadeh, Youness	SLect	20 3811	yalizade	M	DBA		N Eng-Au	&1989
Arnull, Robert John	Lect	20 3082	barnull	M	DBA		N Eng-Au	&1986
Bakker, Patricia	Lect	20 3982	pbakker	XF	MBUS	94	So Cross	&1991
Hudson, Christopher	Lect	20 3841	chudson	SF	MBAM	95	So Cross	&1989
Lamberton, Geoff	Lect	20 3846	glambert	MF	MBUS	94	So Cross	&1991
Phillips, Jillian	Lect	20 3093	jphillip	FE	DIP	90	Victoria	&1981
Rowe, Stephen	Lect	20 3047	srowe	AFE	MA	92	So Austrl	&1986

Univ of Southern Denmark
Dept Business & Economics
Dept Phone: 65503233
Homepage: www.sam.sdv.dk/e/depts/virkl/index.shtml

DK-5230 Odense M				Denmark		(45) Fax=65503237		
Sch of Bus & Economics				sam.sdu.dk			BCOM,MSC,PHD	
Campusvej 55							Mona Andersen	
Petersen, Niels Chr.	C	65503233						
Christensen, John	Prof	65503244	jcn	TMF	PHD	79.	Stanford	1973
Frimor, Hans	Prof	65503245	haf	TMF	PHD	96	Odense	1992
Larsen, Jytte G.	Assoc	65503195	jyt	M	PHD	94	Odense	1992
Nielsen, Mogens	Assoc	65503252	mni	TF	PHD	86	Odense	1983
Friis, Ole	Asst	65503391	ofr	ATF	PHD	04	Odense	1999

Univ of Southern Queensland
Accounting Faculty 4350
Dept Phone: 46312863
Homepage: www.usq.edu/faculty/commerce/
  Did Not Respond Again--2001-2002 Listing

Toowoomba Qld Australia				61-7 Fax=46312625				
Faculty of Commerce				usq.edu.au			BCOM,MCOM,MPA	
West Street								
Harvey, David	H-Pr	46312408	harveyd	AFMP	PHD	88	Bath	&2000
Brown, Noel	SLect	46312616	brownn	DSXF	MEC	96	N Eng-Au	&1986
Cotter, Julie	SLect	46312916	cotter	FTY	PHD	98	Queensld	1991
Delany, Tom	SLect	46312903	delany	FXDE	MTAX	95	NS Wales	&1993
Johnson, Ronald	SLect	46312404	johnson	FD	MACC	90	N Eng-Au	&1977
Pragasam, John	SLect	46312902	pragasam	AIB	MSC	80	Hull	&1992
Stower, Alwyn E.	SLect	46312617	stower	CM	MACC	93	N Eng-Au	&1989
Jenner, Maurice	Lect	46312865	jenner	EFTY	MFM	86	Queensld	1991
Maloney, Suzanne	Lect	46312790	maloneys	AM	MPHL	96	Griffith	&1991
Rankin, Michaela	Lect	46312860	rankinm	TFW	MEC	97	N Eng-Au	1994
McComiskey, Terese	AcLec	46311486	mccomisk	W	BCOM	94	Griffith	1997
Silvester, Mark	AcLec	46312896	silvestm	ADFQ	BBUS	93	S Queens	1996
Vallely, Mark	AcLec	46312639	vallely	FTI	BBUS	84	S Queens	&1990
Hopley, Brian	AcLec	46312968	hopley	MX	MFM	96	UCQ	1999
Keene, David	AsLec	46311573	keene	ATW	MBS	97	Massey	1999

University of Stirling
Dept of Acounting & Finance
Dept Phone: 86467280
Homepage: www.accountingandfinance.stir.ac.uk
  phone for all 441 78643171

Stirling FK9 4LA Scotland				44-17 Fax=86467308				
Business				stirling.ac.uk			BACC,MS,MBA,PHD	
Goodacre, Alan	H-Pr	Ext 7291	alan.goodacre	AFQ	PHD	81	Exeter	&1981

Evans, Lisa	Prof	Ext 7288	lisa.evans	FHI	PHD	00	Reading		&2006
Fraser, Ian A. M.	Prof	Ext 7307	i.a.m.fraser	AF	MA	74	Glasgow		&2004
McInnes, William M.	Prof	Ext 7280	w.m.mcinnes	AFET	PHD	87	Glasgow		&1994
Stopforth, David P.	Prof	Ext 7298	d.p.stopforth	X	PHD	89	Glasgow	*	&1980
Collins, William	Assoc	Ext 7290	bill.collins	M	MBA	82	Glasgow		1979
Davie, Elizabeth	Asst	Ext 7300	e.s.davie	DEQ	PHD	71	Edinburgh		1991
Li, Yong	Asst	Ext 7306	yong.li	AF	MSC	01	Stirling		2004
Masocha, Walter	Asst	Ext 7286	walter.masocha	AFO	PHD	00	Strathcl		&2001
Stevenson, Joanna	Asst	Ext-7299	j.e.stevenson	AI	MA	84	Edinburgh		&1995

Stockholm School of Econ Stockholm S-113 83 Sweden 46-8 Fax = 32 01 09
Accounting & Finance Box 6501 hhs.se MA,PHD
Dept Phone: 736 9000 Sveavagen 65 Karin Albinson

Wiman, Bertil	H-Pr							
Johansson, Sven-Erik	Emer	736-9301	sven-erik.joh +	1995	ED	61	Stockholm	1953
Ostman, Lars	Prof	736-9302	lars.ostman	T	ED	73	Stockholm	1968
Skogsvik, Kenth	Prof	736-9307	kenth.skogsvik	P	ED	94	Stockholm	1977
KPMG Professor of Business Administration								
Charpentier, Claes	Asst	736-9315	claes.charpe +	M	ED	92	Stockholm	1983
Lind, Johnny	Asst	736-9317	johnny.lind	M	ED	96	Uppsala	2000
Schuster, Walter	Asst	736-9306	walter.schuster	P	ED	89	Stockholm	1981
Glader, Mats		736-9308	mats.glader	D	EL	71	Umea	1985
Hellman, Niclas		736-9312	niclas.hellman	V	CE	90	Sundsvall	1990
Hellstrom, Katerina		736-9313	katerina.hell +	F	CE	97	Stockholm	1997
Hjelstrom, Tomas		736-9313	tomas.hjelst +	F	CE	95	Stockholm	1994
Lindlolm, Gunnar		736-9310	gunnar.lindholm	M	CE	68	Stockholm	1994
Portnoff, Linda		736-9389	linda.portnoff	M	CE	00	Goteborg	1994
Skogsvik, Stina		736-9320	stina.skogsvik	F	CE	90	Stockholm	1990

University of Strathclyde Glasgow G4 OLN Scotland 44-41 Fax = 552-3547 2003,2003
Dept of Accounting & Finance Strathclyde Bus School strath.ac.uk BA,BS,MBA,MS,D
Dept Phone: 548-3683 100 Cathedral Street Ms. Susanne Robertson
Did Not Respond Again--1999-2000 Listing; +44 0 141 548-3688 Ext 3688

Capstaff, John	H-SLe	548-3890	j.capstaff	FM	MSC	83	Strathcl	1983
Yadav, Pradeep K.	Prof	548-3939	p.k.yadav	F	PHD	92	Strathcl	1988
Ciancanelli, Penelope L.	SLect	548-3896	p.ciancanelli	WIT	PHD	83	New Sch	1996
Cooper, Christine	SLect	548-3231	c.cooper	F	MSC	84	LondonEc	1988
Davies, J. R.	SLect	548-3710	j.r.davies	F	BSC	64	LondonEc	1976
Coulson, Andrea	Lect	548-3179	a.b.coulson	FN	PHD		Durham	1999
Dunn, John	Lect	548-3893	a.dunn	AF	MACC	88	Glasgow	&1991
Grey, Richard	Lect	548-3935	r.grey	MW	BA	77	Manchest	1996
Hillier, David .	Lect	548-3889	k.j.hillier	F	BSC	92	Paisley	1998
Koch, Barry W.	Lect	548-3888	barry.koch	F	MBL		SA	&1977
Marshall, Andrew P.	Lect	548-3894	a.marshall	F	MPHL	95	Strathcl	1992
Thomson, Ian	Lect	548-3229	i.h.thomson	PN	BAW	83	Hentwatt	1997
Unni, Sanjay	Lect	548-3892	s.unni	F	PHD	94	So Meth	1994
Wilson, R. Alan	Lect	548-3873	r.a.wilson	MD	MS	80	Durham	&1981

Sultan Qaboos University Al-Khod Oman PC123 Fax = 514043
Accounting Faculty Col of Commerce & Econ squ.edu.om BS
Dept Phone: 515837 PO Box 20, AL - Khod
Did Not Respond Again--2000-2001 Listing

Oleyere, Peter	H-As	petro		PHD		Queen's	
Hasson, Naim	Assoc	naim	M	PHD		Birminghm	1999
Seetharaman, A.	Asst		FM	PHD	00	Madris	1987
Siva, Velayutham	Asst	sivav	FM	PHD	96	Massey	1998
Ehab, Mohammed	Lect		FA	PHD	97	City-UK	1998
Hussein, Mostaque	Lect		M	PHD	00	VASA	2000

University of Sydney Sydney NSW 2006 Australia 61-2 Fax = 93516638 (13) 2004,2004
Discipline of Accounting Faculty of Econ & Bus econ.usyd.edu.au BEC,BCO,MEC,PHD
Dept Phone: 93513901 Codrington Street Kate Wade
Did Not Respond--2005-2006 Listing; phone 61 2 93513552

Wolnizer, Peter W.	Dean	Ext13084	p.wolnizer	AFHI	PHD	86	Sydney	&1999
Gray, Sidney J.	H-Pr	Ext13552	s.gray	IFT	PHD	76	Lancaster	& 7-03
Dean, Graeme W.	Prof	Ext13107	g.dean	FHTA	MEC	76	Sydney	&1974
Jones, Stewart	Prof	Ext17755	s.jones	FTI	PHD	91	Wellingt	&2001
Walker, Robert G.	Prof	Ext69529	r.walker	FGHP	PHD	77	Sydney	&2004
Baxter, Jane A.	AProf	Ext17093	j.baxter	NNW	PHD	95	NS Wales	&2003
Newberry, Susan	AProf	Ext65473	s.newberry	FG	PHD	02	Canterbu	2005
Poullaos, Chris	AProf	Ext69056	c.poullaos	FHW	PHD	93	NS Wales	&2004
Arthur, Neal A.	SLect	Ext16624	n.arthur	FM	PHD	97	Sydney	&1988
Emsley, David	SLect	Ext67084	d.emsley	MWS	PHD	96	Macquarie	&2005

English, Linda M.	SLect	Ext13900	l.english	EGF	BCOM	83	Monash	&1990
Frost, Geoff	SLect	Ext13778	g.frost	FW	PHD	00	N Eng-Au	2000
Gallery, Natalie	SLect	Ext16590	n.gallery	FT	PHD	99	Griffith	&2001
Lee, Philip J.	SLect	Ext13067	p.lee	FS	PHD	03	Sydney	&1990
Loftus, Janice A.	SLect	Ext69061	j.loftus	FTI	MCOM	91	NS Wales	2002
Mladenovic, Rosina	SLect	Ext16691	r.mladenovic	FEW	PHD	01	NS Wales	&2002
Trowell, John R.	SLect	Ext69421	j.trowell	FM	MEC	78	N Eng-Au	&2003
Bugeja, Martin	Lect	Ext13079	m.bugeja	FY	PHD	04	Sydney	&1997
Edwards, Peter	Lect	Ext13899	p.edwards	BCDM	BEC	92	Macquarie	&1994
Gordon, Isabel	Lect	Ext17013	I.gordon	AFHI	MCOM	95	NS Wales	&1995
Pickering, Joanne	Lect	Ext14875	j.pickering	FI	MSC	92	Saskatch	* &1992
Razeed, Abdul J.	Lect	Ext66237	a.razeed	FWS	BCOM	98	Murdoch	&2005
Silowati, Isabelly	Lect	Ext69435	i.susilowati	FIM	BCOM	03	NS Wales	2004
Van der Laan, Joyce	Lect	Ext16431	s.vanderlaan	FWA	MCOM	00	Wollong	&2001
Hardy, Martine	ALect	Ext69060	m.hardy	BFJT	BCOM	98	Newcastle	2002
Hor, Jamal	ALect	Ext66041	j.hor	FI	BCOM	03	W Sydney	2004
Preda, Paul	ALect	Ext12263	p.preda	FMT	BBUS	97	UTS	&2001

University of Tasmania Sandy Bay Tsmn Australia 61 3 Fax=62267845
School Accounting & Finance Faculty Commerce utas.edu.au BCOM,MCOM,PHD
Dept Phone: 62262266 French Street 7005 Suellen Lampkin
Homepage: http://www.utas.edu.au/accfin/
DNR; area code: within Australia (03); outside Australia (61 3)

O'Donovan, Gary	C-Ac	62262278	gary.odonovan		PHD		Victoria	&2003
Wilmshurst, Trevor	SLect	63243570	trevor.wilmhurst		MED		N Eng-Au	2003
Collett, Peter H.	Lect	62262277	peter.collett	FT	MA	88	Tasmania	1990
Hrasky, Sue L.	Lect	62262280	sue.hrasky	FA	MSOC	95	Tasmania	1987
Moore, David	Lect	63243558	david.moore	F	MBUS	02	RMIT	2004
Chaplin, Sally	AcLec	63243697	sally.chaplin		BIS	01	Tasmania	2002
Mitewa, Helen	AcLec	62267800	helen.mitewa		MBUS	02	Victoria	2003
Shimeld, Sonia	AcLec	62267586	sonia.shimeld	F	MCOM	02	Newcastle	2003
Smith, Bernandette	AcLec	62262282	b.n.smith	F	BCOM	03	Tasmania	2002
Tng, Cheong	AcLec	63243068	cheong.tng	F	MFIN	01	Queenslnd	2004
Williams, Belinda	AcLec	63243661	belinda.williams	FX	BCOM	91	Tasmania	2002

Univ of Technology, Sydney Sydney NSW 2007 Austrialia 61-2 Fax=9514360006
Sch of Accounting Box 123 Faculty of Business uts.edu.au
Dept Phone: 95143562 Broadway Ms. Judy Dousha

Matolcsy, Zoltan P.	Prof	Ext 3564	zoltan.matol+	F	PHD	83	NS Wales	1982
Stokes, Donald J.	Prof	Ext 3743	donald.stokes	FA	PHD	90	NS Wales	&1997
Tyler, Jonathan	Assoc	Ext 5326	jon.tyler	AJX	MCOM	87	NS Wales	1985
Wells, Peter	Assoc	Ext 5295	peter.wells	F	PHD	01	Sydney	1992
Wieder, Bernhard	Assoc	Ext 3569	bernhard.wie+	DMSU	PHD	98	Vienna	1998
Wyatt, Anne	Asst	Ext 3582	anne.wyatt	F	PHD	02	Tech-Sydn	* 2007
Brown, David	SLect	Ext 3773	david.brown	BCM	PHD	00	Tech-Sydn	2000
Farrell, Brian	SLect	Ext 5226	brian.farrell	DT	PHD	97	Tech-Sydn	1992
Lanis, Roman	SLect	Ext 3081	roman.lanis	FA	PHD	01	Newcastle	2004
Lim, Stephen	SLect	Ext 3588	stephen.lim	FTY	PHD	96	Tech-Sydn	1992
Pazmandy, Greg	SLect	Ext 3585	greg.pazma+	CDFS	MBUS	93	Tech-Sydn	1990
Topple, Stephen	SLect	Ext 3566	stephen.topple	AFT	PHD	02	Sydney	1980
Wright, Anna	SLect	Ext 3592	anna.wright		PHD	05	Tech-Sydn	2000
Befford, David	Lect	Ext 3638	david.bedford	M	BBUS	04	Tech-Sydn	2005
Bond, David	Lect	Ext 3034	david.bond	FA	BBUS	02	Tech-Sydn	2003
Bridges, Alan	Lect	Ext 5417	alan.bridges	BCEG	MA	81	Macquarie	1975
Brown, Paul J.	Lect	Ext 3436	paul.j.bond	FA	MBA	04	Tech-Sydn	2005
Chan, Kelly	Lect	Ext 3586	kelly.chan	FT	MCOM	95	NS Wales	1997
Giacobbe, Francesco	Lect	Ext 3568	francesco.gia+	M	PHD	94	Tech-Sydn	1992
Gillam, Helen	Lect	Ext 3567	helen.gillam	FNW	MBUS	92	Tech-Sydn	1991
Petty, John	Lect	Ext 3591	john.petty	CMU	MBUS	97	Tech-Sydn	1993
Portelli, Frank	Lect	Ext 3570	frank.portelli	FIMS	MCOM	79	NS Wales	1975
Sivabalan, Prabhu	Lect	Ext 3627	prabhu.siv+	CSI	BBUS	90	Tech-Sydn	2001
White, Amanda	Lect	Ext 3736	amanda-white-1	CSI	BBUS	90	Tech-Sydn	2002
Thiagarajah, Tirukumar	ALect	Ext 3033	tirukumar.thia+		BBUS	02	Tech-Sydn	2003

Tel Aviv University Tel Aviv 69978 Israel 972-3 Fax=640-7738 2003,2003
Department of Accounting Faculty of Management post.tau.ac.il BA,MBA,PHD
Dept Phone: 640-9901 Ms. Malka Moshe
Homepage: recanati.tau.ac.il

Dotan, Amihud	C-Ac	640-6001	adotan	FM	PHD	77	Cornell	1978
Aharony, Joseph	Prof		aharoni	FM	PHD	74	Nrthwstrn	1980
Swary, Itzhak	Prof		swary	F	PHD	79	Rochester	&1989
Einhorn, Ester	Asst	640-8506	einhorn	F	PHD	03	Tel Aviv	2003
Kama, Itay	Asst		kamaitay	F	PHD	05	Tel Aviv	2006
Weiss, Dan	Asst	640-6303	weissd	M	PHD	01	Tel Aviv	2003
Peretz, Moshe	Lect		moshep	F	MA		Tel Aviv	&1998

Tilburg University 5000 LE Tilburg   Netherland   31-13 Fax=466-2611   2002,2002
Dept Atg, Accountancy & CER   Faculty of Economics   kub.nl
Dept Phone: 466-3422   PO Box 90153   Mrs. Loes Lavrijsen
   Did Not Respond Again--2001-2002 Listing

Name	Rank	Phone	Email		Deg	Yr	School	Year
Bac, Aad D.	C-Pr	466-8305	a.d.bac	AG	MBA	71	Rotterdam	&1974
Blommaert, Jos	Prof	466-3187	j.m.j.blommaert	FE	PHD	95	Maastricht	&1997
Buijink, Willem F. J.	Prof	466-8288	w.buijink	FE	PHD	77	Antwerp	&2001
Moonen, Hans	Prof	466-3422		AD				&1986
Van der Zanden, Peter	Prof	466-3422	p.m.vderzanden	AFM	MBA	84	Tilburg	1993
VanHelleman, Johan	Prof	466-3407	j.vhelleman	FIK	PHD	77	Rotterdam	&1996
VanKessel, Paul	Prof	466-3422		AD	MBA	85	Tilburg	&1991
VanKollenburg, John	Prof	466-3422	j.c.e.vkollenb+	A	MBA	80	Tilburg	&1985
VanLent, Laurence	Prof	466-3403	l.a.g.m.vlent	FM	PHD	99	Tilburg	1993
VanSchaik, Frans	Prof	466-3422		AD	MBA	82	Groningen	&1999
Vlotman, Fred	Prof	466-3320	f.w.vlotman	CMU	PHD	81	Amsterdm	&1993
DeWaegenaere, Anja	Assoc	466-2913	a.m.b.b.dew+	M	PHD	93	Antwerp	1996
Suijs, Jeroen	Assoc	466-3334	j.p.m.suijs	FM	PHD	98	Tilburg	1998
Wijn, Martin	Assoc	466-2406	wijn	CMU	PHD	88	Tilburg	&1978
Burm, Karel	Asst	466-3077	k.t.a.l.burm	FT	MBA	96	Tilburg	1998
Dahlmans, Hanneke	Asst	466-3422	j.a.j.a.m.dahl+	A	MBA	89	Maastricht	&1993
Hameleers, Michel	Asst	466-3422	m.v.c.h.hame+	F	MBA	86	Tilburg	&1993
Hop, Gerrold	Asst	466-3422	g.w.hop	F	MBA	90	Tilburg	&1993
Kamp-Roelands, Nancy	Asst	466-3422	a.e.m.roelands	A	MBA	86	Rotterdam	&1993
Van den Brand, Bob	Asst	466-3339	b.r.c.j.vdnbrand	BE	MBA	96	Tilburg	1996
Van Es, Wim	Asst	466-3422	w.a.m.vanes	M				&1993
Van Veen-Dirks, Paula	Asst	466-3406	p.m.g.dirks	BC	MBA	91	Eindhoven	1993
VanVlodrop, Jacques	Asst	466-3422	j.m.j.vanvlodr+	M				1993
Vousten-Sweere, Annemarie	Asst	466-8207	a.m.j.sweere	CD	MBA	94	Rotterdam	1997
Wielhouwer, Jacco L.	Asst	466-3102	j.l.wielhouwer					

University of Tsukuba   Tsukuba Ibaraki   Japan   (029) Fax=853-5070
Quantitative Finance & Mgt   Inst of Policy & Plan S   tsukuba.ac.jp   PHD
Dept Phone: 853-5182
Homepage: http://www.tsukuba.ac.jp/
   Did Not Respond Again--2003-2004 Listing

Name	Rank	Phone		Deg	Yr	School	Year
Monden, Yasuhiro	H-Pr	853-5182	CMQ	PHD	90	Tsukuba	3-83

Universite de Tunis III   Tunis 2080   Tunisia   2161 Fax=701270
Accounting Department   ISCAE   iscae.rmu.tn   BA,MS
Dept Phone: 701018   Zi Aeroport
   Did Not Respond Again--2000-2001 Listing

Name	Rank	Phone	Email		Deg	Yr	School	Year
Alouane, Youssef	D-Pr	701018		Mgt	DOC	81	Dauphine	1995
Zarrouk, Ridha	H-As	799243		SAV	DOC	90	IGR France	&1994
Baccouche, Chedli	Assoc	771899	chedi.bacco+	FHIT	DBA	88.	Kentucky	* &1991
Baazaoui, Hedi	Asst			F	DEA	97	ISCAE	1997
Bakini, Olfa	Asst			F	DEA	98	ISCAE	1998
BenSaoud, Nejib	Asst	798147		AO	EXPC		IHEC	
Besbes, Hichem	Asst	844910		AR	EXPC		IHEC	
Bouattour, Mohamed	Asst	753-620		F	EXPC	91	IHEC	1995
Boumedienne, Emma	Asst	886626		F	DEA	93	ISC	1993
Bourouni, Mounira	Asst	734147		M	DEA	98	ISCAE	1998
El Fquir, Bayrem	Asst	02682443		F	DEA	99	ISCAE	1999
ElEuch, Sarra	Asst			CM	DEA	97	ISCAE	1997
Ennouri, Imed	Asst	752611		AFK	EXPC	91	IHEC	1992
Gabsi, Abedrrazak	Asst	849922		VR	EXPC		IHEC	
Hajji, Nourredine	Asst	788306		AO	EXPC		IHEC	
Hechmi, Abdelwahed	Asst	844910		RAV	EXPC		IHEC	
Khelifi, Ali	Asst			F	DEA	96	ISCAE	&1996
Ktat, Sara	Asst	926660		F	DEA	99	ISCAE	1999
Marita, Riadh	Asst	396072		F	DEA	99	ISCAE	1999
Mejri, Malek	Asst	801713		F	DEA	97	ISCAE	1997
Moalla, Hannene	Asst			F	DEA	97	ISCAE	1997
Nefzaoui, Ali	Asst	554473		VR	EXPC		IHEC	
Agoun, Abderahmen	Inst	861100		F	EXPC	98	ISCAE	1999
Bejaoui, Raoudha	Inst	873954		F	EXPC	99	ISCAE	1999
Boubaker, Souheil	Inst			F	ECM	92	ISCAE	1998
Dammak, Lotfi	Inst	791432		F	EXPC			
Elloumi, Iyadh	Inst	843171		RAV	EXPC	98	ISCAE	1999
Gamra, Houcine	Inst	361524		F	EXPC	99	ISCAE	1999
Ghamni, Chiheb	Inst	04990887		F	EXPC	99	ISCAE	1999
Ghedamsi, Mohamed N.	Inst	584848		F	ECM	97	ISCAE	1998
Moalla, Mohamed	Inst	832224		F	EXPC	99	ISCAE	1999
Nedri, Bechir	Inst	801713		F	EXPC	97	ISCAE	1999
Nehdi, Bechir	Inst	750948		C	EXPC			
Zahi, Lotfi	Inst	797606		FG	ECM	97	ISCAE	1999
Zaziri, Lassaad	Inst	792922		F	EXPC	99	ISCAE	1999

Univ Ulster at Jordanstown

Sch of Accounting BT37 0QB	Co Antrim N	Ireland	4428 Fax=6852				
Dept Phone: 68384	Faculty of Bus & Mgt		ulster.ac.uk			BSC,BA,MSC,PHD	
						Hazel Boyd	
Hutchinson, R.	Dean	Ext66130	g.webb	F	MA		4-90
Greenan, K.	H-Pr	Ext68384	ka.greenan	E	MBA		0-04
Glass, C.	Prof	Ext27431	jc.glass	F	MSC		8-87
Kirk, R. S.	Prof	Ext68384	rs.kirk	FMI	BSC		& 1-92
Ward, J.	Prof	Ext75332	jd.ward	FXT	BA		& 1-84
Gilligan, C.	Assoc	Ext68384	cp.gilligan	FX	MSC		& 9-03
Kelly, M. B.	Assoc	Ext68384	mb.kelly	AF	BA		&O-03
McStraw, T.	Assoc	Ext68384	t.mcstraw	FM	BA		& 9-03
Murphy, K.	Assoc	Ext68384	kd.murphy	XF	MBA		& 1-04
Telford, C.	Assoc	Ext68384	c.telford	F	MSC		N-04
Green, J. Peter	SLect	Ext68384	jp.green	FQT	DPHL		1-86
Patton, R.	SLect	Ext68384	r.patton	J	MBA		1-04
Rankin, D. C.	SLect	Ext68384	d.rankin	FX	FCA		& 1-72
Scharf, W. F.	SLect	Ext24554	f.scharf	I	BSC		1981
Acheson, G. G.	Lect	Ext23054	g.acheson	F	BSC		1-07
Boyle, MT	Lect	Ext24731	mt.boyle	F	BSC		2-90
Bradely, EM	Lect	Ext24731	e.bradley	F	PHD		9-02
Bryne, G.	Lect	Ext24711	gm.byrne	B	BSC		1994
Coulter, D.	Lect	Ext68384	ddj.coulter	AD	BSC	*	D-03
Devlin, R.	Lect	Ext24731	rh.devlin	FM	DA	*	1-85
Dyson, K.	Lect	Ext24731	ka.dyson	F	MSC		9-92
Fee, H. M.	Lect	Ext68716	hm.fee	CFI	BSC		1-06
Foster, H.	Lect	Ext68384	h.foster	FNX	BA		& 9-02
Grant, J. L.	Lect	Ext68384	l.grant	FD	MSC	*	1-84
Hunter, R.	Lect	Ext24437	l.hunter	M	BA		1990
Kelly, M.	Lect	Ext68384	m.kelly	FM	MBA		&O-03
Martin, G.	Lect	Ext68384	g.martin	BJ	BSC		9-02
McAree, D.	Lect	Ext24731	d.mcaree	F	BA		2-95
McCann, C.	Lect	Ext24731	c.badger	F	MSC		9-98
McGrath, G.	Lect	Ext68384	j.mcgrath	FM	MSC		1-91
McLean, C. W. S.	Lect	Ext24434	c.mclean	B	BA		1990
McWall, D. M.	Lect	Ext66466	dm.mcwall	AOJ	BSC		1-06
Pogue, M. A.	Lect	Ext68384	m.pogue	FM	MBA		O-04
Rasaratnam, S.	Lect	Ext24731	s.rasaratnam	F	MSC		4-98
Smyth, M. J.	Lect	Ext68384	m.smyth2	FI	BSC		& 1-78
Thompson, M.	Lect	Ext27431	rm.thompson	FD	MSC		& 9-88
Wall, T.	Lect	Ext68384	ap.wall	FNM	BA		1-99
Wilson, A. W.	Lect	Ext68384	a.wilson	FX	BSC		& 1-81

University of Umea

Accounting Faculty	Umea S-901 87	Sweden	46-90 Fax=786-7764					
Dept Phone: 786-5255	Umea Sch of Bus & Econ		usbe.umu.se			BA,MA,MBA,PHD		
Homepage: http://www.usbe.umu.se						Katarina Pousette		
Hassel, Lars G.	C-Pr	786-7132	lars.hassel	BCMI	PHD	92	Abo	7-98
Cornelius, Barbara H.	Prof	786-6497	barbara.corn+	F	PHD	94	N Eng-Au	1-05
Cunningham, Gary M.	Prof	786-5775	gary.cunningham	FIM	PHD	76.	Tx-Austin	& 9-06
Sundgren, Stefan	Prof	786-5255	stefan.sundgren	AFIT	PHD	95	Swedish	7-04
Larsson, Claes-Goran	Assoc	786-9552	claes-goran.l+	FTA	PHD	75	Umea	8-94
Nilsson, Stellan	Assoc	786-5160	stellan.nilsson	AF	LIPH	95	Umea	9-90
Andersson, Hakan	Asst	786-6155	hakan.anders+	TM	MSC	72	Umea	9-88
Carlsson, Torbjorn	Asst	786-5718	torbjorn.carl+	F	BSC	00	Umea	1-00
Haggqvist, Ann-Christin	Asst	786-6164	ann-christin.h+	F	MSC	82	Umea	7-88
Isaksson, Anders	Asst	786-6162	anders.isaks+	SBYA	BSC	93	Umea	
Lindberg, Erik	Asst	786-6496	erik.lindberg	MA	LIPH	98	Lulea	8-98
Lindbergh, Lars	Asst	786-5520	lars.lindberg	F	PHD	03	Umea	8-92
Nilsson, Henrik	Asst	786-5166	henrik.nilsson	FT	PHD	03	Umea	8-95
Olsson, Rickard	Asst	786-6812	rickard.olsson	FT	MSC	95	Umea	8-95
Soderstrom, Gosta	Asst	786-6163	gosta.soders+	FT	BSC	84	Umea	8-85
Svanstrom, Tobias	Asst	786-5526	tobias.svan+	AMU	MSC	00	Umea	1-02
Thorsell, Anna	Asst	786-9213	anna.thorsell	FU	MSC	05	Umea	1-05
Wahlstrom, Fedrick	Asst	786-5384	fredrik.wahls+	CM	MSC	95	Stockholm	9-96

Victoria Univ of Wellington

Sch Accounting & Comm Law	Wellington	NewZealand	64-4 Fax=463-5076					
Dept Phone: 463-5365	Fac of Commerce & Adm		vuw.ac.nz			BCA,MCA,BCA		
Homepage: http://www.vuw.ac.nz/sacl/	Rutherford House					M. Lotz		
Thirkell, Peter	Dean$	463-5822	peter.thirkell		PHD			
Dunstan, Keitha	H-Pr	463-6957	keitha.dunstan	FGMT	PHD	98	Queenlsd	&2000
Ball, Ian	Prof	463-5775	ian.ball	FGMN	PHD	76	Birminghm	1995
Brown, Judy A.	Prof	643-7054	judy.a.brown	FTW	PHD	95	Victoria	1988
Holmes, Kevin J.	Prof		kevin.holmes	FTPX	MCOM	77	Auckland	
Porter, Brenda	Prof	463-5724	brenda.porter	AFM	PHD	90	Victoria	2003

Name	Rank	Phone	Email		Degree	Yr	School		Yr
van Zijl, Tony	Prof	463-5329	tony.vanzijl	FPT	PHD	86	Victoria		&1978
Morley, Rachel	Assoc	463-6474	rachel.morley		PHD		Otago		&
OhOgartaigh, Ciaran	Assoc	463-9651	ciaran.ohogar+		PHD		NUI		2006
Smith, Andrew M. C.	Assoc	463-6707	andrew.smith	FX	MCA	84	Victoria		1982
Van Roy, Yvonne	Assoc	463-5762	yvonne.vanroy	GL	LLB	84	Victoria		1980
White, David	Assoc	463-5705	david.white	ILX	PHD	97	Sydney		2000
Dunbar, David	SLect	463-7422	david.dunbar	FILX	LLM	79	Victoria		1995
Fairhall, Tim	SLect	463-6709	tim.fairhall	AJS	BCA	73	Victoria		2002
Fowler, Carolyn	SLect	463-6506	carolyn.fowler	MSHG	MCOM	95	Canterbu		2002
Hunt, Chris	SLect	463-6921	chris.hunt	F	PHD		Queenslnd		&2006
Khanna, Bhagwan S.	SLect	463-5843	bhagwan.kha+	BCEF	PHD	92	Victoria	*	1986
Bradshaw, John H.	Lect	463-5779	john.bradshaw	CEM	MCOM	90	Port Eliz		1998
Carter, David	Lect	463-7009	david.carter		LLB				
Colquhoun, Philip	Lect	463-5776	philip.colquh+	FGWH	PHD		Canterbu		1992
Fraser, Michael	Lect	Ext 8093	michael.fraser	WMG	BCA	02	Victoria		2003
Karim, A.K.M. Waresul	Lect	Ext 8547	wares.karim	FMIW	PHD	95	Leeds		1997
Molisa, Pala	Lect	463-6154	pala.molisa	BCA					
Cordery, Carolyn	ALect	463-5761	carolyn.cordery		MCOM			*	&
Macdonald, David	Adj	463-5938	david.macdonald	AGFI	BCOM	63	NZealand		2002
Alves, Jenny	ALect	463-5233	jenny.alves		MCA				2006
Marriott, Lisa	ALect	463-6107	lisa.marriott		MBA				2006
McLeod, Rose Anne	SenFl	463-5044	roseanne.macl+		MBA		Massey		2006
Simpkins, Kevin	SenFl	463-9651	kevin.simpkins		BCOM				2007
Truong, Thu Phyong	ALect	463-5233	thuphuoug.truong				BCOM		2006
Turner, Martin	SenFl	463-6591	martin.turner		MBA		AGSM		2006

Univ of the Virgin Islands St. Thomas, VI 00802-9990 (340) Fax=693-1311
Accounting Faculty Business Adm Division uvi.edu BA,MBA
Dept Phone: 693-1300 #2 Brewer's Bay Ms. Mercedes Donastorg
 Did Not Respond Again--2002-2003 Listing

Name	Rank	Phone	Email		Degree	Yr	School		Yr
Esdaille, Eustace	C-Ac	693-1300	eesdail	CFM	PHD	95	U Wash		1999
Depusoir, Francisco	Assoc	692-4113	fdepuso	AFGH	MBA	78	Missouri		&1989
Washington, Aubrey	Asst	692-4151	awashin	CDFX	MBA	83	Michigan		&1989

Vrije Universteit Amsterdam Amsterdam1081 HV Netherland 31-20 Fax=598-9870
Department of Accounting Faculty Econ, Bus Adm feweb.vu.nl MS,PHD
Dept Phone: 598-6040 1105 De Boelelaan Laura Dessens
Homepage: http://www.feweb.vu.nl/

Name	Rank	Phone	Email		Degree	Yr	School		Yr
Groot, Tom L. C. M.	C-Pr$	598-6040	tgroot	BCM	PHD	88	Groningn		1995
Camfferman, C. (Kees)	Prof	598-6076	ccamfferman	FHP	PHD	96	Vrije		1989
Huizink, J. B.	Prof	598-6153	jhuizink	LX	PHD	89	Groningen		2000
Dekker, Henri C.	Assoc	598-6066	hdekker	CM	PHD	03	Vrije		1997
Vernooij, A. T. J. (Fons)	Assoc	598-6076	fvernooij	EMF	PHD	93	Erasmus		2002
Hengel, H. G. (Hugo)	Asst	598-6078	hhengel	BGN	MS				2005
Budding, G. T. (Tjerk)	Inst	598-6073	gbudding	BGN	MS	97	Vrije		2001
Bavelaar, Anja	Lect	598-6076	abavelaar	FP	MS	95	Christian		2003
Boone, Pieter W.	Lect	598-6104	pboone	FM	MS	76	Vrije		1976
Boterenbrood, D. Rob	Lect	598-6071	dboterenbrood	FP	MS	02	Vrije		2004
Broeze, G. B. (Ed)	Lect	598-6129	ebroeze	A	PHD		Amsterdam		2005
Claes, Paul C. M.	Lect	598-6068	pclaes	EFIM	MS	94	Maastricht		1999
Ding, Rong	Lect	598-6073	rding	MI	BA	98	JiaoJong		2003
Duimstra, Frits	Lect	598-6104	fduimstra	FM	MS				1988
Guldemond, A. C.	Lect	598-6078	aguldemond	UM	MS	99	Erasmus		2001
Jansen, Nico A.	Lect	598-6153	njansen	LX	MS	87	Utrecht		2002
Nieuw Ammerongen, Niels van	Lect	598-6129	camerongen	AB	MS	95	Vrije		2000
Quadackers, Luc L. M.	Lect	598-6129	lquadackers	AB	MS	92	Maastricht		2004
Sasovova, Zuzana	Lect	598-6061	zsasovova	MB	MS	99	Comenius		1999
Schoute, Martin	Lect	598-6068	m.schoute	QMB	MS	97	Vrije		1998
Turkenburg, Dirk	Lect	598-6104	dturkenburg	FM	MS	77	Vrije		2001
Veldman, J. F. (Hanne)	Lect	598-6073	jfveldman	AJEF	MS	97	Vrije		1999
Vooren, Wim M. van der	Lect	598-6104	wvooren	FM	MS	66	Vrije		1966
Wiersma, Eelke	Lect	598-6066	ewiersma	BM	PHD	03	Groningn		1997
Withsde, Elbert	Lect	598-6071	ewith	MFIU	MS	79	Erasmus		1982

University of Wales Aberystwyth UK SY23 3DD 44970 Fax=622409
School of Mgt & Business United Kingdom aber.ac.uk BSC,MSC,MBA,PHD
Dept Phone: 622202 Cledwyn Building Julie Miles, Janet Sutton
Homepage: www.aber.ac.uk/

Name	Rank	Phone	Email		Degree	Yr	School		Yr
Ap Gwilym, Owain	Prof	621834	oma	FM	PHD	93	Swansea	#	2003
Lane, Jennifer	Lect	622206	jel	FM	BSC	85	Aberystw		&2002
Soobaroyen, Teeroven	Lect	622211	t.soobaroyen	FM	MB	96	Lancaster		2004
Varas, J.	Lect	622520	jmr						2006
Williams, Megan	Lect	622207	rww	FM	BSC	87	Aberystw		&2000

Univ of Wales, Bangor

Bangor, Gwynedd Wales UK
Div of Financial Studies — Sch Bus & Rgionalal Dev
Dept Phone: 382194 — College Road
01248 Fax=383228
bangor.ac.uk
BA,MA,MBA,PHD
Mrs. Debbie Mitchell
Homepage: www.bangor.ac.uk/sbard/
Did Not Respond Again--2003-2004 Listing

Name	Rank	Phone	Email					
Gardener, Edward	Dir	382168	abs022	FM	PHD	79	Bangor	9-75
McLeay, Stuart	Prof	382180	s.j.mcleay	F	PHD	88	Lancaster	& 1-88
Molyneux, Philip	Prof	382170	abs005	FQ	PHD	96	Bangor	9-98
Ayling, David E.	Lect	382174	d.ayling	F	PHD	82	Aston	9-82
Altunbas, Yener	Lect	382191	abs011	FQ	PHD	02	Bangor	2001
James, David	Lect	383227	tcs016	F	BA	75	Manchest	9-92
Neal, David	Lect	382120	d.neal	BIF	BA	80	Leeds	9-94
Williams, Jonathan	Lect	382642	abs056	FQ	PHD	02	Bangor	D-92

University of Warwick

CoventryCV4 7AL Un Kingdom
Accounting & Finance — Warwick Business Sch
Dept Phone: 524507
02476 Fax=523719
wbs.warwick.ac.uk
1999,1999
Did Not Respond Again--2003-2004 Listing

Name	Rank	Phone						
Thomas, Howard	Dean		Mgt	PHD	70	Edinburgh		
Bryer, Robert A.	Prof	Ext22450	FHIT	PHD	77	Warwick		
Hodges, Stewart D.	Prof	Ext23606	QMF	PHD	71	London		
Gsmee Fairbairn Professor of Accounting								
Hooklin, Keith W.	Prof	Ext21681	HTEM	PHD	73	Penn		
Steele, Anthony	Prof	Ext22955	AQ	MA	79	Lancaster		
Tyson, Thomas N.	Prof	Ext28955	CHJM	PHD	87.	Geo St	*	2003
Fitzgerald, Lin	SLect	Ext22173	CM	BA	71	Essex		
Lamb, Margaret	SLect	Ext24542	XFH	PHD	01	Reading		
Anderson-Gough, Fiona	Lect	Ext28226		BA	89	Leeds		
Bates, Kenneth	Lect	Ext22174	FMSE	BA	76	Nottingh	&	
Oates, Lynn	Lect	Ext22393		PHD	00	W Austrl		
Pierce-Brown, Rhoda	Lect	Ext24503		PHD	00	Warwick		
Pitts, Marianne	Lect	Ext28229	H	BA	63	Oxford		

Univ of The West Indies

Bridgetown   Barbados
Dept of Management Studies — Faculty of Social Sci
Dept Phone:
(809) Fax=425-1327
425-1310 Barbados, 927-1661 Jamaica, 663-1364 Trinidad; Did Not Respond Again

Name	Rank	Phone			
Chaderton, Robertine	H-Lec	425-1310	AI	PHD	Manchest
Williams, Randolph	Prof	927-1661	X	PHD	Colorado
Bakre, Owalabi M.	Lect	927-1661	M	MCOM	Rajastha
Dick-Forde, Emily	Lect	425-1310	F	MPHL	Cambridge
Layne, Armand W.	Lect	425-1310	MT	PHD	Birminghm
Mendes, Margaret	Lect	927-1661	AE	MA	W Indies
Raghurandam, Moolchand	Lect	663-1364	C	MSC	W Indies
Williams, Michael	Lect	927-1661	C	MSC	W Indies
Carrington, Donley	ALect	425-1310	MT	MSC	Iowa St

Univ of Western Australia

Nedlands 6009   WAustralia
Sch of Accounting & Finance — Faculty of Econ & Comm
Dept Phone: 93802917
618   Fax=93801047
ecel.uwa.edu.au
BCOM,MCOM,PHD
Ms. Taylor
Homepage: af.ecel.uwa.edu.au/accfin/
Did Not Respond Again--2003-2004 Listing

Name	Rank	Phone	Email					
Eggleton, Ian R. C.	Prof	93802903	ieggleto	BGM	PHD	79	Chicago	1984
Watson, John	Assoc	93802876	jwatson	F	PHD	96	W Austrl	1976
DaSilva Rosa, Raymond	Asst	93802974	vdsilvaa	B	PHD	95	W Austrl	2001
Lau, Chong Man	Asst	93802910	clau	M	PHD	98	W Austrl	&2000
Maller, Ross	Asst	93803906	rmailer	Q	PHD	76	W Austrl	1999
Woodliff, David R.	Asst	93802911	dwoodlif	F	PHD	96	W Austrl	1991
Chong, Vincent K.	SLect	93802914	vchong	M	PHD	99	W Austrl	&2000
Clarke, Alex	SLect	93802902	aclarke	F	MCOM	91	W Austrl	1983
Gilders, Frank	SLect	93802916	fgilders	X	DIPE	88	Monash	1988
Johnson, Jaqueline	SLect	93802444	jjohnson	S	MCOM	90	W Austrl	1985
Moore, Mark	SLect	93807224	mmoore	Q	PHD	00	Rutgers	&2001
Ng, Hock Guan	SLect	93802971	hgng	Q	PHD		Stanford	1999
Ng, Juliana	SLect	93802627	jng	AM	PHD	95	W Austrl	&1996
Watson, Iain D.	SLect	93802925	iwatson	F	PHD	96	Ulster	1998
Chang, Millicent	Lect	93801808	mchang	F	BCOM	90	W Austrl	1992
Durand, Robert	Lect	93803764	rdurand	F	MBA	97	Edinburgh	1998
Holub, Mark	Lect	93802647	mholub	F	BCOM	88	W Austrl	1991
Lloyd, Paul	Lect	93802099	plloyd	FC	BCOM	91	W Austrl	1994
Newby, Rick	Lect	93802798	rnewby	F	MPHL	96	Murdoch	2001
Robinson, Peter	Lect	93803867	probinso	F	MED	80	W Austrl	1990
Szimayer, Alex	Lect	93801759	aszimaye	Q	PHD	99	Bonn	2003
Tarca, Ann	Lect	93803868	atarca	FI	MACC	97	W Austrl	1998

Wee, Marvin Ge Way	Lect	93801821	mwee	F	MFIN	99	W Austrl	1999
Boujos, Jocelyne	ALect	93802633	jboujos	T	LLB	90	W Austrl	1987
Goh, Alicia	ALect	93802464	agoh	F	BCOM	99	W Austrl	2000
Gould, John	ALect	93802633	jgould	Q	BCOM	01	W Austrl	2001
Johnson, Darren	ALect	93801727	djohnson	M	BBUS	97	E Cowan	&2001
Leong, Michele	ALect	93803406	mleong	F	MEC	95	Macquarie	&2001
Smith, Gary	ALect	93803855	gsmith	F	BCOM	96	Curtin	1998
Vander Vyver, Mark	ALect	93802510	mvyer	FQ	BCOM	91	UTS	1996

Univ Western Sydney   Penrith DC 1797   Australia   61 2   Fax=96859339
School of Accounting   College of Law & Bus   uws.edu.au   BCO,MCO,MPA,PHD
Dept Phone: 96859210   Locked Bag 1797   Ms. Lorraine Starr
   Did Not Respond--2005-2006 Listing

Tibbits, Garry E.	C-Pr	96854182	g.tibbits	MJTU	MCOM	70	Auckland	&
Ryan, John B.	Assoc	46203358	john.ryan	TFH	PHDM	02	Wollong	* &1990
Mitchell, Graeme	SLect	98524195	g.mitchell	BCEJ	GDIP	94	NS Wales	
O'Neill, Sharron	SLect	98529213	s.oneill	BFJM	MCOM	02	NS Wales	&1996
Ross, Phillip	SLect	96859451	p.ross	AU	PHDM	94	UTS	
Tang, Qingliang	SLect	96859465	q.tang	AFI	PHD	93	Glasgow	&1999
Taylor, Sharon	SLect	98524190	sharon.taylor	F	MCOM	82	NS Wales	
Wheldon, Brett	SLect	98524196	b.wheldon	CEFP	MCOM	94	W Sydney	
Bubalo, Nigel	Lect	96859226	n.bubalo	CFJX	MCOM	96	W Sydney	1998
Cowen, Janet	Lect	98524178	j.cowen	EFJ	MEC	99	N Eng-Au	
Davis, Glenda	Lect	46203212	g.davis	CDSX	BCOM	00	W Sydney	
Diggins, Bruce	Lect	46203401	b.diggins	FAMC	MACC	90	Wollong	
Endrawes, Medhat	Lect	46204174	m.endrawes	AF	MCOM		NS Wales	
McCartney, Jean	Lect	96859219	j.mccartney	EF	BCOM	76	Witwaters	&1989
Miah, Zaman	Lect	96859215	z.miah	CFGI	MEC	85	Sydney	1989
Micet, Paul	Lect	96859114	p.micet	ADES	MCOM	02	W Sydney	1998
Puttee, Colleen	Lect	46203477	c.puttee	ABEF	MCOM	94	Wollong	
Tibbits, Hendrika	Lect	98524191	r.tibbits	DEFS	MBA	95	Wollong	
Wood, Dorothy	Lect	98524328	d.wood	BFW	PHD	02	W Sydney	
Yeung, Daniel	Lect	96859221	d.yeung	SEMB	MCOM	96	Wollong	1997
Borovnjak, Juny	ALect	46203483	j.borovnjak	AFIF	MCOM	03	W Sydney	
Cowgill, Kim	ALect	98524202	k.cowgill	FJRX	BCOM	91	W Sydney	
Cull, Michele	ALect	46203519	m.cull	CFMX	BCOM	96	W Sydney	
Ferlauto, Kimberly	ALect	46203420	k.ferlauto	AFST	MCOM	05	W Sydney	
Gleeson, Derek	ALect	47360808	d.gleeson	CMT	MEC			
Humphreys, Peter	ALect	46203210	p.humphreys	FINP	MCOM	04	N Eng-Au	
James, Stanley	ALect	98524179	s.james	MEOL	PHD	01	MSU	
Lenthen, Simon	ALect	47200310	s.lenthen	DNST	BCOM	02	W Sydney	
Wilson, Kerrie	ALect	46203551	k.a.wilson	AFOJ	BECO	98	Macquarie	
Zakrzewski, Dorothea	ALect	46203478	d.zakrzewski	EIMF	MINT	02	Bond	

University of Wollongong   Wollongong 2522   Australia   61-02   Fax=42214297
Sch of Accounting & Finance   New South Wales   uow.edu.au   BCO,MCO,MPA,PHD
Dept Phone: 42213718   Northfields Avenue   2522   Cynthia Nicholson
Homepage: www.uow.edu.au/commerce/accy

Leitch, Shirley	C-Pr	42213665	sleitch					2006
Kaidonis, Mary A.	H-Ac	42213681	kaidonis	BTW	PHD	96	Wollong	&1989
Funnell, Warwick N.	Prof	42213739	wfunnell	MGH	PHD	94	Wollong	&1981
Gaffikin, Michael J. R.	Emer	42213718	gaffikin	FHTW	PHD	86	Sydney	&1988
Tian, Gary	Assoc	42214301	gtian	FIU	PHD	94	Macquarie	2007
Abraham, Anne	SLect	42213738	a.abraham	MN	PHD	99	Wollong	&1993
Cooper, Kathleen Anne	SLect	42213392	k.cooper	HFLW	PHD	94	Wollong	1985
Deo, Hemant	SLect	42214006	hemant	VW	PHD	99	Wollong	&1995
Irvin, Helen	SLect	42215919	hirvine	FN	PHD		Wollong	&2003
Mickhail, George M. E.	SLect	42214619	mickhail	DSA	MIS	90	LondonEc	1994
Smark, Ciorstan	SLect	42215222	csmark	JNE	PHD		Wollong	&2004
Watts, Ted	SLect	42214005	tedw	CMUP	PHD		UTS	&2004
Andrew, Jane	Lect	42214009	jane_andrew	FJT	PHD	99	Wollong	1999
Bhati, Shyam	Lect	42214006	shyam_bhafi	FI	PHD	94	Punjab	&1998
Bowrey, Graham	Lect	42213858	gbowrey	FTM	MCOM	05	Wollong	&2006
Chapple, Sandra	Lect	42214006	schapple	F	MCOM		Wollong	&2003
Cortese, Corinne	Lect	42213097	corrinne	FIP	PHD			2006
DeZoysa, Anura	Lect	42215328	anura	FEM	PHD	03	Wollong	&2002
Koplin, Mara	Lect	42213680	mara_koplin	FQ	MEC	93	N Eng-Au	&1998
Kurtovich, Annamaria	Lect	42214004	kurtovic	AO	PHD		Wollong	&2004
McCombie, Kellie	Lect	42214003	k.romic	TW	MCOM	96	Wollong	1996
Moerman, Lee	Lect	42215575	lee_moerman	FT	MCOM	00	Wollong	2001
Murphy, Brian	Lect	42215510	bmurphy	OU	MCOM		CSU	&2004
Perrin, Ronald W.	Lect	42214118	perrin	FTW	MCOM	91	Wollong	&1991
Rudkin, Kathy	Lect	42214003	k.rudkin	PTW	PHD	02	Wollong	&1996
Silaen, Parulian	Lect	422-3696	parulian	CMU	MCOM		Wollong	2004
Spasich, Connie	Lect	42213655	spasich	FTW	MCOM	95	Wollong	&1992
Tan, Andrew	Lect	42215301	atan					2007
Jun, Aelee	AcLec	42215007	ajun		PHD		Sydney	2007

Yarmouk University   Irbid   Jordan   962 2 Fax=274 725
Department of Accounting   Faculty Econ & Adm Sci   yu.edu.jo   BS
Dept Phone: Ext 2281
  Did Not Respond--2005-2006 Listing; phone 271 100

Al Salih, Subhi	Assoc	Ext 2384		FM	PHD	·85	Pittsburgh	1992
Al-Hmoud, Turki	Assoc			AD	PHD	87	Wales	1987
on leave								
Qagish, Mahmoud	Assoc			CM	PHD	87	Rensselaer	1987
on leave								
Al Khilani, Safa	Asst	Ext 3084		DFMA	PHD	91	WU	1992
Al Momani, Munther T.	Asst	Ext 3549		FD	PHD	93	UST	1993
Al omari, Ahmad	Asst	Ext 2386		FM	PHD	94	Manchest	1994
Khasharmeh, Hussein	Asst	Ext 2380		FM	PHD	95	Middlesex	1987
Al Khoury, Abeer	Inst	Ext 2388		FM	MS	94	Manchest	1995
Alshaerairi, Malek Amhad	Inst	27211111	m.alsharairi	PFTI	MSC	05	Yarmouk	2005
Assaf, Asma Sh.	Inst	27211111	assaf	ABOC	PHD	06	Amman Arab	1999
Baddour, Jamal	Inst	Ext 3089		FGND	MS	93	Illinois	1993

Yonsei University   Seoul, Korea   120-749   (02) Fax=21235331
Department of Business Adm   Coll of Business & Econ   yonsei.ac.kr   BBA,MBA,PHD
Dept Phone: 21232495   134 Shinchong-dong
Homepage: base.yonsei.ackr
  Did Not Respond Again--2000-2001 Listing

Chung, Chong A.	Dean	21232502	cca609	FA	PHD	84	Yonsei	&1978
Joo, In Ki	Prof	21232509	ijoo	FIA	PHD	86.	NYU	&1987
Kim, Jeehong	Prof	21232517	jeehong	FI	PHD	87.	Berkeley	1989
Kim, Joon Seuk	Prof	21232510	jskim	MSBC	DBA	82.	Indiana	1982
Lee, Kyung Tae	Assoc	21232527	kyungtae	MYCT	PHD	92.	UCLA	1994
Sohn, Sungkyu	Assoc	21232525	sksohn	FA	PHD	92.	Nrthwstrn	&1993
Kwak, Byungjin	Asst				PHD	04.	Purdue	

University of Zimbabwe   Harare Zimbabwe   2634 Fax=335407
Department of Accountancy   Faculty of Commerce   zimbix.uz.zw
Dept Phone: Ext 1198   Mount Pleasant
  Did Not Respond Again--1999-2000 Listing; phone 263-4 303211 ext 1198

Chikondo, J. T. M.	H-Le	Ext 1686	M	MACC		&
Hove, Mfandaidza R.	SLect			MA		&
Chamisa, Edward E.	Lect	Ext 1290	V	PHD		
Mareeta, F.	Lect	Ext 1530		MBA		
Masasi, M.	Lect	Ext 1849	F	MBL		
Mazhandu, STSM	Lect	Ext 1667		BACC		&
Mgwenya, J.	Lect			MBA		
on study leave						
Ndlovu, S.	Lect	Ext 1630	C	MBL		
Paradza, P.	Lect	Ext 1870	T	MSC		
Ruzengwe, C. M.	Lect	Ext 1685	A	BSC		&
Sithole, J. S.	Lect	Ext 1372	X	MSC		

ALPHABETICAL BY INDIVIDUAL

NAME	RANK	SCHOOL	AREA	DEGREE			START
Aabel, Don C.	Retir	Wis-Rvr Fall	1995	MBE		Colorado	&1964
Abarbanell, Jeffery S.	Assoc	No Carolina	F	PHD	89.	Penn	& 7-97
Abatemarco, Michael J.	Prof	Lg Isl-Post	LX	LLM		NYU	&1985
Abbasi, Nishat	Assoc	Metro State	ASM	PHD	87.	Colorado	8-96
Abbe, Suzanne C.	Lect	Baylor	P	MBA		Baylor	1987
Abbott, H. Don		Texarkana TX	1988	PHD	86.	Arkansas	
Abbott, Lawrence J.	Assoc	Memphis	S	PHD	98.	Oregon	8-98
Abdala, Khaled	Asst	Univ Essex	DSQ	PHD	98	Birminghm	2000
Abdallah, Wagdy M.	Prof	Seton Hall	MIC	PHD	82.	North Tx	* 9-84
Abdeen, Adnan M.	Prof	CS-L Angeles	MCI	DBA	74.	Miss St	&9-86
Abdel Maksoud, Ahmed	Asst	Univ Sharjah	M	PHD	03	Bristol	2004
Abdel-Fattah, Zakariah			FM	PHD	83.	Arkansas	
Abdel-Kader, Magdy	Asst	Univ Essex	FM	PHD	97	Bristol	2000
Abdel-khalik, A. Rashad	Prof	Illinois	FU	PHD	72.	Illinois	6-00
Director, Center for International Education and Research in Accounting							
Abdel-khalik, Ahmed F.		Egypt		PHD	71.	Missouri	
Abdel-Magid, Moustafa F.	Retir	Simon Fraser	2002	PHD	72.	Illinois	9-80
Abdel-Moneim, Mahmoud		Saudi Arabia	1992	PHD	58.	Illinois	
PO Box 12190; Jeddah 21473 Saudi Arabia							
Abdelsayed, Wafeek H.	Prof	So Conn St	FPVG	PHD	96.	Conn	# * &1984
Abdoelkadir, Kajep K.		Indonesia Un	1996	PHD	82.	Tx A&M	
Wisma Baja 7th Fl; Gatot Subroto 54; Jakarta 12790 Indonesia							
Abdolmohammadi, Mohammad	Prof	Bentley	AMST	DBA	82.	Indiana	&1988
John E. Rhodes Chair in Accountancy							
Abdul Ramim, Hassan		Bahrain		PHD	93.	North Tx	
Abdul-Kader, Abdullah A.		Saudi Pharam	1992	DBA	79.	Fla St	
Saudi Pharmaceutical Ind Corp; PO Box 20001; Riyadh 11455 Saudia Arabia							
Abdulla, Khalid Amin		U Jordan		PHD	72.	Georgia	
Abdulraheem, Ali	Prof	Kuwait Univ	CM	PHD	66	Manchest	1972
Abe, Donald Kazuhito		Playa CA		PHD	63.	Berkeley	
Abekah, Joseph Yaw	Prof	New Brunswic	FIM	PHD	91.	Nebraska	1991
Abel, Rein		Cost Acc Std	1994	PHD	67.	Columbia	&
725 17th St NW; Rm 9001; Washington DC 20503; 202-395-3254							
Abels, Patricia B.	Asst	Findlay	P	PHD	06	Sarasota	2006
Abendroth, Charlene	Lect	CS-East Bay	FT	MS	72	Brigham Yg	&9-76
Abernethy, Margaret A.	Dean	U Melbourne	M	PHD	89	LaTrobe	1990
Abeysekera, Indra	Lect	Sydney U	BJI	PHD	04	Macquarie	&2003
Aboody, David	Assoc	UCLA	F	PHD	95.	Berkeley	1995
Abouelezz, Mohamed		Zagazip U		PHD	84.	Minnesota	
AbouMundour, Ahmed	Prof	King Saud U	FM	PHD	74	Alexandria	1975
Abraham, Anne	SLect	U Wollongong	MN	PHD	99	Wollong	&1993
Abraham, O.	Lect	Touro	NPC	JD			&9-03
Abraham, Ronald J.	Asst	No Iowa	AS	MBA	71	Wisconsin	&1974
Abraham, Stanley C.		CS-Pomona		PHD	76.	UCLA	
Management Dept; Calif State Univ-Pomona							
Abramowicz, Kenneth F.	Assoc	Alaska-Fairb	XF	PHD	91.	Missouri	&1994
Abu-Abbas, Bassam				PHD	02.	Kent St	
Abu-Musa, Ahmad A.	Asst	King Fahd Un	FIM	PHD	01	Aberdeen	2002
Abu-Romman, Mohamed Abd-Alaz		Al-Azhar U		PHD	74.		
Wisconsin							
Abuwakid, Ibrahim				PHD	98.	Nebraska	
Accola, Wilton L.	Deces	Memphis St	2-94	PHD	91.	Kentucky	&1990
Acheson, G. G.	Lect	Univ Ulster	F	BSC			1-07
Acker, Daniella E.	Prof	Univ Bristol	FQ	PHD	96	Bristol	&1992
Ackerson, Jim	Retir	MidAmer Naz	1996	MS		Virginia	1994
Acklin, James F.	Retir	Duquesne	1988	MBA	60	Duquesne	* &1956
Acland, C. Derek	Retir	Concordia U	2001	PHD	73.	N Carol	&6-83
Acton, Daniel D.	Retir	Alfred	6-07	DBA	86.	Kent St	&1986
Adair, Lorinda P. (Lyn)	Deces	Saginaw Vall	3-04	PHD	98.	Indiana	&2000
Adams, A.	Lect	N Eng-Austr	S	MEC		N Eng-Au	&1986
Adams, Barbara L.	Prof	So Carol St	FAJ	PHD	81.	Tx A&M	&1990
Adams, Bettie M.	Asst	North Fla	FOV	MA	65	Fla St	# &1977
Adams, Carol	Prof	LaTrobe Univ		PHD			2006
Adams, Erma L.	Deces	Antioch Col		PHD	68.	N Carol	
Adams, Helen D.	Lect	U Washington	MCS	PHD	86.	U Wash	1991
Adams, Hobart W.	Retir	Akron	1993	DBA	67	Indiana	9-69
Adams, Richard D.	Retir	Baltimore	2003	MS	90	N Carol	# &9-92
Adams, Steven J.	Prof	CS-Chico	SMU	PHD	81.	Cincinnati	* &9-82
Adamson, Ian L.	Assoc	Brock Univ	SF	PHD	93	Waterloo	&1987
Adamson, Willie D.	Prof	CS-Pomona	XFC	EDD	84	Pepperdi	1973
Addy, Noel D.	Assoc	Miss State	F	PHD	85.	Florida	&1991
Adebayo, Arinola O.	Asst	So Car-Aiken	FC	PHD	04.	Va Comm	&2004
Adelaar, Thomas	Asst	Maastricht	S	PHD	05	Michigan	2005

Adelberg, Arthur H.	Prof	CUNY-Queens	MBQ	PHD	77.	Baruch	&7-73
Adels, Christen	Assoc	Geneva	ALX	JD	01	Pittsburgh	&2003
Aderemi, Oluyemisi S.		U Lagos Nige	1992	PHD	85.	Geo St	
Dept of Acctg; Faculty of Bus Adm; Unin of Lagos; Lagos Nigeria							
Adeyiga, Janet A.	Assoc	Hampton	FT	PHD	80.	Missouri	1991
Adhikari, Ajay	Assoc	American U	I	PHD	91.	Va Comm	9-91
Adiel, Ron			FM	PHD	94.	Penn	
Adighibe, Michael E.	Assoc	Cheyney	PTLX	ABD		Drexel	1988
Adjaoud, Fodil	Prof	Univ Ottawa	FM	PHD	82	Laval	* 1981
Adkins, Neal G.	Retir	Marshall	2000	MA	68	Marshall	&9-69
Adkins, Nell	Assoc	Alabama-Birm	X	PHD	95.	Fla St	&1-99
Adler, Hirschel (Hank)	Asst	Chapman	FX	MBA	69	UCLA	9-04
Adler, Jabob	Retir	Hawaii	1977	PHD	59.	Columbia	&9-48
Adler, James R.		Checkers Sim	1998	PHD	72	NYU	&1979
American Express; One South Wacker Dr; Chicago IL 60606; 312-917-0625							
Adler, Ralph W.	Prof	Univ Otago	BEM	PHD	91	SUNY-Alb	1-91
Adut, Davit	Asst	Cincinnati	F	PHD	03.	Tx A&M	
Agacer, Gilda M.	C-Ac	Monmouth	MGI	PHD	87.	S Carol	&1998
Agami, Abdel M.	Retir	Old Dominion	5-05	PHD	70.	Illinois	&1978
Aghimien, Peter A.	C-Pr	Ind-So Bend	AFIM	DBA	86.	La Tech	&1988
Agoglia, Christopher P.	Assoc	Drexel	ACB	PHD	99.	Mass	4-98
Agoun, Abderahmen	Inst	Univ Tunis	F	EXPC	98	ISCAE	1999
Agrawal, Om P.	Prof	So Carol St	FM	PHD	71	Jiwasi	# * &8-74
Agrawal, Surendra Γ.	Emer	Memphis	M	ΓI ID	73.	Florida	&1982
Agudelo, Jaime	Deces	Pacific	1994	PHD	80.	Okla St	&1983
Agulnek, Arthur	SLect	Texas-Dallas	XL	BS	67	CUNY	&2002
Ahadiat, Nasrollah	Prof	CS-Pomona	CFM	PHD	83.	Arkansas	# * 1991
Aharony, Joseph	Prof	Tel Aviv	FM	PHD	74	Nrthwstrn	1980
Ahern, Cornilius	Retir	CUNY-Baruch		MS	38	Columbia	1939
Ahern, John T.	Assoc	DePaul	FAV	DBA	76.	Kentucky	&1973
Ahiarah, Sol	C-Ac	Buffalo St	FMGI	PHD	85	Pittsburgh	&8-90
Ahlawat, Sunita S.	Asst	C New Jersey	SM	PHD	93.	Penn St	2002
Ahmed, Anwer S.	Assoc	Texas A&M	F	PHD	92.	Rochester	7-05
Mays Faculty Fellow							
Ahmed, Kamran	C-Pr	LaTrobe Univ	FIM	PHD	94	Austr Natl	1999
Ahmed, Mirghani	Asst	King Fahd Un	MF	PHD	90	Manchest	1998
Ahmed, Sania				PHD	83.	Arkansas	
Ahn, Tae-Sik	Prof	Seoul Natl	CMSN	PHD	87.	Tx-Austin	1997
Ahuja, Mulak	Asst	Miss Vall St	AC	MBA		Delta St	1982
Ainsworth, Penne L.	C-Pr	Wyoming	MCP	PHD	88.	Nebraska	# * &1997
Ajinkya, Bipin B.	Prof	Florida	FM	PHD	76.	Minnesota	3-75
Akathaporn, Parporn			F	DBA	88.	Kent St	
Akers, Michael D.	C-Pr	Marquette	AFS	PHD	88.	Miss	# &1987
Charles T. Horngren Professor of Accounting							
Akin, Timothy R.	Prof	Marian	FJPX	MBA	73	Xavier	&1975
Akindayomi, Aksuloye	Asst	Mass-Dartmou	FX	PHD	06	Calgary	2006
Akinwande, B.	SLect	London Metro	FM	PHD			2001
Akpa, Bimaje		Ahmadu Bel U	1992	PHD	84.	S Calif	
Ahmadu Bello Univ, PM 1013/Dept of Atg, Zaria Nigeria							
Akpori, Mary O.				PHD	84.	S Calif	
Akroyd, Chris	Lect	U Auckland	MA	ABD		Auckland	2000
Aksu, Celal			MCQF	PHD	87.	Syracuse	
Aksu, Mine H.			FP	PHD	93.	Syracuse	
Al Bastake, Hassan		Bahrain		PHD	93.	North Tx	
Al Deeb, Awad	Asst	King Saud U	FA	PHD	93	Alexandria	1996
Al Hussainan, Adel	Dean	Kuwait Univ	OR	PHD	94	Calif	1987
Al Khilani, Safa	Asst	Yarmouk Univ	DFMA	PHD	91	WU	1992
Al Khoury, Abeer	Inst	Yarmouk Univ	FM	MS	94	Manchest	1995
Al Momani, Munther T.	Asst	Yarmouk Univ	FD	PHD	93	UST	1993
Al Rai, Ziad K.	Asst	Sky Inst	CF	PHD	83	NYU	1977
Al Rashed, Waeel	Prof	Kuwait Univ	XS	PHD	89	Hull	1992
Al Salih, Subhi	Assoc	Yarmouk Univ	FM	PHD	85	Pittsburgh	1992
Al Shabani, Waleed		Saudia Arabi		PHD	01.	North Tx	
Al-Abdul-Gader, Abdulla H.	Prof	King Fahd Un	S	PHD	88	Colorado	1988
Al-Amari, Saleh	Assoc	King Saud U	F	PHD	89	Glasgow	1990
Al-Amin, Mohamed Badr	Assoc	King Saud U	M	PHD	88	Zkzk	1995
Al-Bassam, Sadik M.	H-Ac	Kuwait Univ	F	PHD	80.	Tx-Austin	1980
Al-bukhayyet, Salah				PHD	98.	Geo Wash	
Al-Eranai, Sulaiman				PHD	98.	Kent St	
Al-Eryani, Mohamed				DBA	87.	Kent St	
Al-Ghamdi, Saad A.		Saudia Arabi	1992	PHD	80.	Okla St	
PO Box 86434; Riyadh 11622 Saudi-Arabia							
Al-Harbi, Abdullah				PHD	03.	Fla Atl	
Al-Harshani, Meshari		Kuwait		PHD	03.	Arkansas	
Al-Hayale, Talal	Asst	Univ Windsor	MFV	PHD	90	Wales	2001
Al-Hazmi, Mohammed H.	Asst	King Fahd Un	MA	PHD	96	Manchest	1996
Al-Heizan, Osama	Asst	King Saud U	FM	PHD	96	Syracuse	1996

Al-Hemaldi, Saud	Asst	Kuwait Univ	GF	PHD	88	Leeds	1995
Al-Hmoud, Turki	Assoc	Yarmouk Univ	AD	PHD	87	Wales	1987
Al-Jabri, Ibrahim	Assoc	King Fahd Un	S	PHD	92	Ill Tech	1992
Al-Khaldi, Muhammad A.M.	Asst	King Fahd Un	MSD	PHD	91	Okla St	1991
Al-Meghames, Ahmad	Asst	King Saud U	AF	DBA	97	Miss St	1997
Al-Moshaigeh, Abdulla				PHD	06.	Fla Atl	
Al-Mudaf, Jassim	Assoc	Kuwait Univ	F	PHD	84	Birminghm	1984
Al-Narsullah, Abdulaziz		Saudia Arabi	1991	DBA	86.	Geo Wash	
PO Box 7183; Riyadh 11462 Saudi Arabia							
Al-Qenae, Rashid	Asst	Kuwait Univ	F	PHD	00	Essex	2000
Al-Rai, Ziad K.	Asst	Jordan	F	PHD	83.	NYU	1981
email sky@go.com.jo; 962-6-535-9218							
Al-Rumaihi, Jassim S.	C-As	King Fahd Un		PHD	97	Dundee	2000
Al-Rwita, Saad S.	H-Ac	King Saud U	FM	PHD	93	Colorado	1993
Al-Salmen, Ahmad				PHD	03.	Fla Atl	
Al-Shinafi, Saleh				PHD	02.	Fla Atl	
Al-Shuaib, Shaib A.		Kuwait U		PHD	74.	Missouri	
Al-Sudairy, Salman A.				PHD	91.	Tx-Austin	
Al-Sultan, Sultan	Prof	King Saud U	XG	PHD	80	Missouri	1980
Al-Tassan, Mohammed S.	Asst	King Saud U	MF	PHD	83.	Missouri	1984
Al-Tuwaijri, Sulaiman A.			CFM	PHD	98.	Case Wes	
Al-Yamani, Abullah Gassim		King Adbul U	1992	DBA	80.	Colorado	
King Abdulaziz Univ; Col of Eco/Dept of Atg; Jeddah Saudia Arabia							
Al_omari, Ahmad	Asst	Yarmouk Univ	FM	PHD	94	Manchest	1994
Alāgiah, Ratnam	Lect	Griffith-GC	HIJT	PHD	97	Wollong	1998
Alali, Fatima A.	Assoc	CS-Fullerton	AF	PHD	05	Rutgers	2007
Alam, Pervaiz	Prof	Kent State	FA	PHD	84.	Houston	& 6-85
Alaraini, Sulaiman	Asst	King Saud U	FS	PHD	98	KSU	1998
Alawattage, Chanzdana	Lect	Aberdeen	BGWT	PHD	05	Keele	2005
AlBarak, Mahdy	Lect	Kuwait Univ	F	PHD	95	Glasgow	1996
Alberni, Carl W.	Retir	Manhattan	1997	PHD	76.	Missouri	* &1984
Albers, Ursel	Retir	New Mex High	2001	MA	52	Mich St	* &1985
Albin, Marvin J.	Assoc	So Miss	AF	PHD	87.	Houston	&1987
Albrecht, Conan C.	Asst	Brigham Yg	S	PHD	00	Arizona	1-01
Albrecht, W. David	Assoc	Bowling Gr	FKA	PHD	91.	Va Tech	&1990
Albrecht, W. Steve	Prof	Brigham Yg	FA	PHD	75.	Wisconsin	# & 6-77
Arthur Andersen Professor							
Albright, Thomas L.	Prof	Alabama	M	PHD	90.	Tennessee	&1990
J. Reese Phifer Faculty Fellow							
Albring, Susan M.	Asst	South Fla	FX	PHD	02.	Arizona	2004
Albuloushi, Saad				PHD	00.	Kent St	
Albuquerque, Ana Maria	Asst	Boston Univ	FM	PHD	06.	Rochester	9-05
Alciatore, Mimi L.	Assoc	Houston	FVZ	PHD	89.	Tx-Austin	&2001
Alcorn, John M.	Retir	Morehead St	2002	MBA	75	Geo St	1966
Alderman, C. Wayne	Prof	Auburn	FA	DBA	77.	Tennessee	# & 4-77
Alderman, R.	PLect	London Metro	AF				&
Aldhizer, George R. III	Assoc	Wake Forest	PAS	PHD	94.	Tx Tech	# & 9-01
PricewaterhouseCoopers Faculty Fellow							
AlDiab, Taisier F.			MTSF	PHD	92.	North Tx	
Aldina, Mohamed				PHD	84.	Temple	
Aldredge, Melissa M.	Inst	Louisiana Te	FMX	MBA	90	La Tech	&2003
McCallister Endowed Teaching Professor							
Aldridge, Charles Richard	H-Pr	W Kentucky	CVMP	DBA	84.	Kentucky	&1978
Aleksanyan, Mark	Asst	Univ Glasgow	F	PHD	04	Glasgow	2004
Alemany, Fina	Asst	Pompeu Fabra			06	UPC	
Alexander, Deborah	STut	U Auckland	MA	BCOM	96	Auckland	2002
Alexander, Raquel Meyer	Asst	Kansas	X	PHD	01.	Tx-Austin	& 8-05
Alexander, Robin A.	Retir	Wis-La Cross	2002	PHD	81.	Nrthwstrn	8-83
Alexander, Sherman	Assoc	Ark Tech	CFM	PHD	95.	Kentucky	&1993
Alford, Andrew W.		Pennsylvania	FK	PHD	90.	Chicago	
Finance Dept; University of Pennsylvania							
Alford, R. Mark	VAsoc	DePaul	FM	PHD	78.	Tx A&M	&2004
visiting from University of Texas-San Antonio							
Alhanati, Mark S.	C-As	Mt St Mary's		MBA		Loyl Mrm	
AlHashim, Dhia D.	Emer	CS-Northrdge	IT	PHD	71.	Missouri	1974
Alhumaid, Abdulrhman I.	Prof	King Saud U	FA	PHD	81.	LSU	1981
Alhusaini, Walid	Asst	Kuwait Univ	AF	PHD	00	Sheffield	2000
Ali, Ashiq	Prof	Texas-Dallas	F	PHD	88.	Columbia	2004
Charles and Nancy Davidson Distinguished Professor							
Alicea, Juan Carlos	Dean$	Puerto Rico	BMT	MBA	91	P Rico	&1992
Alino, Nelson	Inst	Benedict Col	IF	MBA	98	Nigeria	&2002
Alisharan, Steve S.	Inst	British Colu	FMX	BA	71	Brit Colum	* &1981
Alizadeh, Youness	SLect	So Cross Un	M	DBA		N Eng-Au	&1989
Alkafaji, Yass A.	Assoc	NE Illinois	FIA	DBA	83.	Miss St	& 9-87
Alkire, Durwood L.	Retir	U Washington	1987	BA	35	U Wash	&1972
Allard, Marie-Pier	Prof	Sherbrooke	X	MFIS	01	Sherbrook	2001
Allen, Arthur C.	Assoc	Nebraska	F	PHD	89.	Alabama	6-89

Allen, Brandt R.	Prof	Virg-Grad	FMIT	DBA	67. Harvard	1970
James C. Wheat, Jr. Professor of Business Administration						
Allen, Cheryl L.	Assoc	Morehouse	MABF	PHD	98. Georgia	&1998
Allen, Darryl E.	Lect	Cen Florida	M	PHD	03. Geo Wash	&
Allen, David L.	Assoc	Harding	XF	MBA	81 Cen Ark	&1987
Allen, G. Louis	Retir			PHD	85. North Tx	&
Allen, Joyce S.	Assoc	Xavier	FP	MBA	71 Cincinnati	&1979
Allen, Mary F.	Retir	Boise State	SF	PHD	00. Wash St	& 9-01
Allen, Natalie L.	SLect	Texas A&M	FM	MS	88 Tx A&M	& 1-89
Allen, Paul W.	Prof	Miss St-Mer	FM	DBA	94. Miss St	&1986
Allen, Robert D.	C-Ac	Utah	AF	PHD	92. Mich St	& 9-91
C. Roland Christensen Faculty Fellow						
Allen, Roberta S.	Lect	Texas Tech	F	MSA	96 Tx Tech	& 9-99
Allen, Steven A.			FS	PHD	82. SUNY-Buf	
Allen, Tom	Asst	Weber State	AG	BS	71 Weber St	2005
Allerston, Anne	PLect	Bournemouth	FPM	MSC		9-89
Alles, Michael G.	Assoc	Rutgers-Newk	MCT	PHD	91. Stanford	8-98
Alley, Sheryl J.	Inst	Ball State	FM	MA	79 Ball St	& 9-79
Allocca, Carl	Inst	SUNY-Stony B		MST		&1992
Allport, Christopher D.	Asst	Alabama-Hunt	FMA	PHD	05. Va Tech	2005
Alltizer, Richard L.	Asst	Central Okla	XF	PHD	94. Oklahoma	& 8-07
Alm, Ingvald W.	Deces			PHD	36. Minnesota	
Almer, Elizabeth Dreike	Assoc	Portland St	A	PHD	96. Ariz St	&2001
Meadows Faculty Fellow						
Almodovar, Luis R.	Prof	Puerto RicoM	CFP	MBA	78 P Rico	& 1-76
Almutairi, Ali				PHD	06. Fla Atl	
Alpert, Irving	Retir	Seton Hall	1984	PHD	73. NYU	&1948
Alpert, Karen	Lect	U Queensland	FX	MTAX	86 S Calif	2001
Alread, Burvin C.		Hendrix Col		PHD	61. Missouri	
AlSegini, Sabri	Asst	Univ Sharjah	SM	PHD	93 Warwick	2001
Alshaerairi, Malek Amhad	Inst	Yarmouk Univ	PFTI	MSC	05 Yarmouk	2005
Alsultan, Sultan M.				PHD	80. Missouri	
Alsup, Rodney G.	Prof	Kennesaw St	CSM	DBA	84. Kentucky	&1991
Altamuro, Jennifer L. M.	Asst	Ohio State		PHD	05. Penn St	8-06
Altepeter, Donna J.	Lect	North Dakota	FD	MACC	86 N Dakota	& 9-86
Althaus, M. Clinton	Deces	Sam Houston	1988	PHD	75. North Tx	* &1980
Altieri, Mark P.	Assoc	Kent State	X	LLM	82 NYU	* & 1-92
Altunbas, Yener	Lect	Wales-Bangor	FQ	PHD	02 Bangor	2001
Alvarez, Francisco E.	Retir	Puerto Rico	1992	MBA	62 NYU	&1975
Alves, Jenny	ALect	Victoria NZ		MCA		2006
Alvin, Gerald	Retir	Wayne State	1995	JD	64 Wayne St	&1958
Alvis, Charles E.	Assoc	Winthrop	PFX	MBA	81 Winthrop	& 6-86
Alvis, John M.	Retir	Tenn-Chattan	FM	PHD	82. Arkansas	& 9-84
Alwabil, Wabil Ali	Prof	King Saud U	FM	PHD	83. Missouri	1983
Alworth, Charles H.	Retir	Tx A&M-Kings	2004	DBA	79. Miss St	&1989
				PHD	53. Wisconsin	
Aly, Ibrahim M.	Assoc	Concordia U	FMBQ	PHD	86. North Tx	1989
Alyousef, Husain		Kuwait		PHD	06. Tx-Arlin	
Amat, Oriol	Prof	Pompeu Fabra	F	PHD	90 Barcelona	1993
Ameen, Elsie C.	Assoc	Sam Houston	FA	PHD	89. S Carol	&1995
Ameiss, Albert P.	Retir	Mo-St Louis	1991	PHD	68. St Louis	1962
Amenkhienan, Felix E.	Prof	Radford	CMUI	PHD	84. Miss	* 1985
Ament, Joseph D.	Prof	Roosevelt	XP	JD	62 J Marshal	&1966
The Samuel Specthire Professor of Accounting; jament@muchlaw.com						
Amer, Metwalli B.	Retir	CS-Sacrament	2002	PHD	66. Illinois	&1969
Amer, Tarek S.	Prof	No Arizona	SMC	PHD	89. Ohio St	&1994
Amernic, Joel H.	Prof	Univ Toronto	FM	MBA	71 Toronto	&1973
Amerongen, Loretta	VAsst	Univ Alberta	FVX	PHD	96 Alberta	&1996
Amershi, Amin H.	Prof	McMaster Un	MF	PHD	79 Brit Colum	7-04
AIC Chair in Valuation and Portfolio Management						
Ames, Gary Adna			SCJ	PHD	88. Georgia	&
Ames, Roger	Inst	Miami U-Ohio	P	MBA	82 St Fran	& 1-01
Amey, Lloyd R.	Retir	McGill Univ	1993	PHD	55 Nott	& 8-69
Amin, Md Nurul	Assoc	W Virg Tech	FMPC	MBA		&1997
Amir, Eli	C-Pr	London Bus	F	PHD	91. Berkeley	&2003
Amlie, Thomas T.	Asst	Penn St-Harr	MFG	PHD	96. Maryland	* 2005
Ammann, Elizabeth	Asst	Lindenwood	FMP	MBA	S Il-Edw	1983
Ammons, Hubert L.	Retir	Clark Atlant	1997	MBA	92 Clark Atl	&1992
Ammons, Janice L.	C-Pr	Quinnipiac	FM	PHD	94. Michigan	&1997
Amobi, Emmanuel N.			FST	PHD	87. Alabama	
Amoruso, Anthony J.			FA	PHD	99. Georgia	&
Ampadu, Alex B.	VAsoc	SUNY-Buffalo	FASM	MBA	76 Roch Tech	# * &1986
Amry, Mohamed Y.		King Adbul U		PHD	76. Arizona	
Amyot, Thomas G.	C-Ac	St Rose	PSAN	MS	St Rose	& 9-96
An, Amy	Lect	Iowa	X	MA	82 Iowa	& 8-87
Anabila, Andrew A.	Asst	Pace	FM	PHD	02. Columbia	2003
Anakwe, Bridget	Asst	Delaware St	FM	PHD	03. Rutgers	2004

Name	Rank	School	Code	Degree	Yr./University	
Anandarajan, Asokan A.	Prof	NJ Inst Tech		PHD	95. Drexel	1994
Anantharaman, Sekhar	C-Ac	Alabama A&M	FSVP	PHD	96. Cen Fla	8-96
Ancier, Sherman M.	Retir	Rider	1991	MBA	56 Rutgers	&1957
Anctil, Regina M.	Asst	St Thomas-MN	CFM	PHD	93 Minnesota	9-05
Andbo, Kare Jarl	Retir	Norwegian U	2003	HRE	Norwegia	&
Anderman, Steven G.		Price Waterh	1994	PHD	81. Nebraska	&
1251 Avenue of the Americans; 36th Fl; New York NY 10020						
Anders, Susan B.	Prof	St Bonaventu	XIF	PHD	98. Tx Tech	&1998
Andersen, Anker V.	Retir	Bridgeport	1992	PHD	64. Minnesota	1972
Anderson, Bonnie B.	Asst	Brigham Yg	S	PHD	01. Car Mellon	9-01
Anderson, Brenda H.			FA	PHD	89. Mass	&
Anderson, Carl A.	Retir	Florida	6-78	MBA	50. Florida	&1947
Anderson, Clayton W.				PHD	69. Nrthwstrn	
Anderson, David A.	Inst	Louisiana St	FXZ	MBA	81 LSU	&8-81
Anderson, Donald L.	Deces	CS-Northrdge		PHD	64. Minnesota	1969
Anderson, Donald T.	Deces	So Illinois	1987	PHD	80. Tx A&M	9-79
Anderson, Earl H.			SM	PHD	78. Nebraska	&
Anderson, Ellen B.	Lect	Tennessee	FC	MACC	85 Tennessee	&9-86
Anderson, Fred E. Jr.	Emer	St Marys-Cal	1997	MBA	78 Golden Gt	&9-78
Anderson, H. Kyle	Prof	Anderson Col	CPVX	MPA	84 Clemson	* &1997
Anderson, Harry	Asst	Cedarville	AMVS	MACC	69 Ohio St	2003
Anderson, Henry R. (Hank)	Retir	Cen Florida	1999	PHD	71. Missouri	* &8-83
Anderson, Hershel M.	Retir	North Texas	1988	PHD	61. Illinois	&1962
Anderson, J. Richard	Assoc	Stonehill	FB	MS	77 Northeas	* &9-79
Anderson, James A.	Retir	Cal Poly-SLO	FM	PHD	73. Wash U	3-87
Anderson, John C.	Retir	Syracuse	2000	PHD	78. Syracuse	&1987
Anderson, John C..	Prof	San Diego St	SAB	PHD	87. Tennessee	8-01
Anderson, John J.	Retir	Mo-St Louis	2004	PHD	67. Wisconsin	* &8-74
Anderson, John W.	Retir	Massachusett	1980	MBA	53. Indiana	&1955
Anderson, Kenneth E.	Prof	Tennessee	X	PHD	83. Indiana	& 1-84
Pugh & Company Professor of Accounting						
Anderson, Kim L.	Assoc	Indiana U-PA	BA	PHD	94. Pittsburgh	&9-91
Anderson, Kirsten L.	Asst	Georgetown	F	PHD	97. Ohio St	2000
Anderson, Lane K.	Emer	Texas Tech	2007	PHD	70. Wisconsin	* &1978
Ernst & Young Professor						
Anderson, Malcolm	Lect	Cardiff U	HAE	MPHL	94 Cardiff	* 1991
Anderson, Mark C.	Assoc	Texas-Dallas	FTYX	PHD	95. Florida	&1995
Anderson, Mary M.	Asst	So Miss	XF	DBA	05. La Tech	&2005
Anderson, Matthew J.	Assoc	Michigan St	FB	PHD	82. Mich St	1988
Anderson, O. J.	Retir	Nebraska	1989	JD	56 Nebraska	&1948
Anderson, Paul S.		Fed Res-Bost		PHD	57. Minnesota	
Anderson, Paul V.	Asst	Azusa Pacif		MBA	75 UCLA	8-04
Anderson, Philip N.	Retir	East Wash	1999	PHD	85. S Carol	&1965
Anderson, Robert	Prof	Univ Regina		PHD	97 Saskatch	2001
Anderson, Robert W.	Lect	Cal-Santa Br		MAC	92 Ca-SnBarb	2004
Anderson, Shannon W.	Assoc	Rice	M	PHD	93. Harvard	2001
Anderson, Sharlene	Fell	Bond Univ	MA	BBSU	98 Griffith	&O-00
Anderson, Sherri C.	Prof	Sonoma State	SD	MBA	83 SanFranSt	&1980
Anderson, Susan E.	Assoc	N Carol A&T	XF	PHD	91. Tx-Arlin	&2006
Anderson, Thomas N. Jr.		Delta Group		PHD	80. Va Tech	
Delta Group; Norfolk VA						
Anderson, Tracey A.	Prof	Ind-So Bend	X	LLM	85 Florida	&1988
Anderson, Urton L.	Prof	Texas-Austin	AMO	PHD	85. Minnesota	# 9-84
Clark W. Thompson, Jr. Profesorship in Accounting Education						
Anderson, Warwick	Lect	Canterbury	BFQY	MCOM	97 Canterbu	2002
Anderson, William Hart	Retir	Auburn-Montg	1982	PHD	64. Florida	1980
Anderson, William T.	Retir	Grove City	5-03	PHD	84. Va Tech	&1992
Anderson, Wilton T.	Retir	Okla State	1982	EDD	53. Colorado	&
60 Yellow Brick Road; Stillwater OK 74074						
Anderson-Gough, Fiona	Lect	Un Warwick		BA	89 Leeds	
Anderson-Roberts, Ellen G.			FT	PHD	89. Okla St	&
Andersson, Hakan	Asst	Univ of Umea	TM	MSC	72 Umea	9-88
Ando, Hideyoshi	Retir	Hitotsubashi	FA	DBA	85 Hitotsub	1974
Andon, Paul	Lect	New So Wales	M	MCOM	NS Wales	2000
Andrade, Louis E.		Normal, IL		PHD	65. Nebraska	
Andre, Paul E.	Assoc	HEC-Montreal	FM	PHD	96 Waterloo	&8-97
Andreessen, LaVerne W.	Retir	No Iowa	RF	MA	65 N Iowa	&1979
Andrew, Jane	Lect	U Wollongong	FJT	PHD	99 Wollong	1999
Andrew, Peter	PLect	U Portsmith		PHD		2001
Andrew, William P.	Assoc	Penn St-Hotl	FIMQ	PHD	88 Penn St	6-78
Andrews, Angela	Asst	Wayne State	F	PHD	04. Mich St	8-04
Andrews, Carly	Lect	Tx-Arlington	F	MSA	Tx-Arlin	6-04
Andrews, Charles T.	Retir	Cal Poly-SLO	1996	DBA	68. Indiana	&9-72
Andrews, Christine P.	Asst	Fl GulfCoast	SM	DBA	98. Clev St	&1999
Andrews, Edna M.	Retir	CS-L Angeles	1982	MBA	67 CS-LgBch	&1967
Andrews, Wesley T. Jr.	Deces	St Marys-Tx	4-99	PHD	76. N Carol	&8-93
Andrus, Jon M.			AS	PHD	96. Arizona	&

Name	Rank	School	Flags	Deg	Yr	Univ	
Ang, N.	Lect	New So Wales		MA	01	Stanford	
Angel, Jack	Asst	Adelphi	X	MS	78	Lgls-Post	&1981
Angelini, James P.	Assoc	Suffolk	X	PHD	86.	Houston	&1993
Anger, T. G.	Assoc	Queen's Univ	F	MBA	82	Queen's	1982
Angima, Jacob M.	Asst	Hampton	FV	PHD	93	UCLA	&2000
Anilowski, Carol L.	Asst	Purdue	F	PHD	06.	Michigan	2006
Annand, David	D-Pr	Athabasca Un		EDD	98	Alberta	1989
Annisette, Marcia A.	Assoc	York Univ	FMI	PHD	96	Manchest	2005
Ansari, Shahid L.	Prof	Babson	BM	PHD	73.	Columbia	2005
Ansong, Granville	Asst	St Marys-Cdn	FTMY	PHD	88	Queens	1990
Antenucci, Joseph W.	Prof	Youngstown	F	PHD	93.	Va Tech	9-93
Anthony, Joseph H.	Assoc	Michigan St	FT	PHD	84.	Ohio St	&1983
Anthony, Murray S.	Prof	East Tenn St	MF	PHD	75.	Missouri	&1972
Anthony, Robert L.	Retir	Cen Michigan	1985	MBA	41	Michigan	&1970
Anthony, Robert N.	Emer	Harvard	1984	DCS	52.	Harvard	1940
Antle, Rick	Prof	Yale	AMFT	PHD	81.	Stanford	1985
William S. Beinecke Professor of Accounting							
Anton, Hector R.	Retir	New York U	1989	PHD	53.	Minnesota	&1981
Antonio, James F.	Chrm	Gov Atg Stds		PHD	67.	Illinois	&1984
Antrosiglio, Victor	Deces	Jersey City	1991	MBA	71	Penn	&1980
Anyane-Ntow, Kwabena	Deces	N Carol Cen	2001	PHD	82.	Georgia	&1983
Anyanwu, Casimir I.	Retir	Howard	FGIN	PHD	77.	Missouri	&1996
Anzalotti, Salvatore	Retir	American Int	2003	MBA	63	Am Intl	&1963
Aono, June Y	C-Ac	Hawaii-WOahu	AFM	PHD	81	UCLA	&1999
Aoun, Chadi	ALect	Macquarie Un					
Ap Gwilym, Owain	Prof	Univ Wales	FM	PHD	93	Swansea	# 2003
Apostolou, Barbara A.	C-Pr	Louisiana St	A	PHD	88.	LSU	& 8-88
E&Y Alumni Distinguished Professor							
Apostolou, Nicholas G.	Prof	Louisiana St	FG	DBA	82.	Tennessee	& 8-85
U. J. LeGrange Endowed Professor							
Apple, Jerome E.	Inst	Akron	XF	JD	70	Clev St	& 9-96
Appleton, Robert W.	Retir	N Car-Wilmin	2002	ABD		Geo St	&1967
Applewhite, George	Retir	CUNY-Stn Isl	1993	PHD	77.	NYU	1971
Appleyard, William T.	Retir	Salem State	2000	LLM	69	Boston U	&1969
Aquilino, Frank	C-Ac	Montclair St	AXFP	MBA	74	St Johns	&1978
Aquilio, Mark	Assoc	St John's	X	LLM	84	NYU	&1989
Arafa, Said Mohmound				PHD	70.	Berkeley	
Arakawa, Randy	Inst	DePaul	SF	MBA		DePaul	2002
Aranowski, Erwin C.	Retir	Notre Dame	1984	BSC	42	Notre Dm	&1955
Arbaugh, Lawrence G.	Retir	W Carolina	1981	MCS	50	Ben Frnk	& 9-63
Arbesfeld, Shirley M.	Prof	Berkeley Col	2003	PHD	69.	NYU	&
205 West End Avenue - 22C; New York NY 10023-4813; 212-787-0950							
Arcadi, Antony	Deces	CUNY-Brookly	CDMS	MA	82	CUNY-Brk	& 9-88
Archambault, Jeffrey J.	Assoc	Marshall	FMAS	PHD	92.	Mich St	&2001
Archambault, Marie E.	Assoc	Marshall	FGPV	PHD	92.	Mich St	* &2001
Archambeault, Deborah S.	Asst	Tenn-Chattan	FAH	PHD	00.	Alabama	&2004
Archibald, T. Ross	Retir	West Ontario	2001	PHD	69.	Chicago	&1966
Arcus, Albert L.		US Dept Def		PHD	63.	Berkeley	
Arcus, J.	Sen	Massey-Welli	ACFN	BCA		Victoria	1999
Ardoin, Jean-Loup	Retir	HEC Paris	2001	PHD	74.	Minnesota	1974
Arel, Barbara M.	Asst	Vermont	AS	PHD	06.	Ariz St	2006
Arens, Alvin A.	Emer	Michigan St	2006	PHD	70.	Minnesota	& 9-68
Ariff, Mohamed	Prof	Monash Univ	IFYX	PHD	97	Queensl	1997
Aris, E. Maynard		Albion MI	1988	PHD	66.	Michigan	
Ariyo, Ademola		U Ibadan Nig	1988	PHD	82.	Arizona	
Arlinghaus, Barry P.	Prof	Miami U-Ohio	X	PHD	79.	Cincinnati	&1983
Deloitte & Touche Professor of Accountancy							
Armentor, Jesse J.	Inst	Louisiana St	F	MBA	75	SanDgoSt	& 8-86
Armitage, Howard M.	Prof	Un Waterloo	IMC	PHD	83.	Mich St	* 1981
Gordon H. Cowperthwaite Professor of Accounting							
Armitage, Jack L.	C-Pr	Neb-Omaha	AF	PHD	87.	Nebraska	& 8-83
Spencer Professor							
Armstrong, Dale Ellsworth			AXN	PHD	66.	Tx-Austin	&
Armstrong, Deborah J.				PHD	01.	Kansas	
Armstrong, John A.	C-Ac	Nichols Col	AFCP	MBA	76	Pace	&1986
Armstrong, Mary Beth	Retir	Cal Poly-SLO	2005	PHD	84.	S Calif	& 9-84
Arndt, Terry L.	Prof	Cen Michigan	FP	PHD	73	Arkansas	&1993
Arnett, Harold E.	Retir	Michigan	1996	PHD	63.	Illinois	* &1962
Arnold, Boyd E.	Retir	York-Penn	2001	PHD	74	Penn St	9-65
Arnold, Donald F.	D-Pr	Union	AFG	PHD	72.	SUNY-Buf	9-82
Arnold, Jerry L.	Prof	So Calif	F	PHD	75.	Michigan	&1979
Arnold, John A.	Prof	U Manchester	A	MSC	69	Manchest	&1994
Arnold, Patricia J.	Assoc	Wis-Milwauke	FMN	PHD	87.	Wisconsin	&1989
Arnold, Robert H.				PHD	70.	Nrthwstrn	
Arnold, Tony J.	Prof	Univ Essex	FHT	PHD	95	LondonEc	&1985
Arnold, Vicky	Prof	Cen Florida	MAS	PHD	89.	Arkansas	& 8-05
Ernst & Young Professor							

Arnull, Robert John	Lect	So Cross Un	M	DBA		N Eng-Au		&1986
Arora, Alka	Assoc	Wis-Whitewat	FT	PHD	95.	Kent St		&1996
Arredondo, Richard	Asst	Chicago St	NACF	MBA	91	DePaul	*	&1994
Arrington, C. Edward	Prof	N Car-Greens	HMT	DBA	80.	Fla St		& 8-98
Arruda, Lucia M.	Lect	Salve Regina	FPX	MSA	86	Rhode Isl		&
Arsan, Noyan	Retir	West Georgia	2000	PHD	73	Syracuse	*	9-84
Arsenault, Steve	Assoc	Charleston	XL	LLM	94	Florida		1999
Arthur, Alex	SLect	Aberdeen	ABDM	MLIT	87	Aberdeen		&1990
Arthur, Neal A.	SLect	Univ Sydney	FM	PHD	97	Sydney		&1988
Artto, Eero	Emer	Helsinki Sch	FIT	PHD	62	Helsinki		1956
Arunachalam, Vairam	Prof	Missouri	SB	PHD	91.	Illinois	*	1991
PricewaterhouseCoopers/Joseph A. Silvoso Professor								
Arvey, Richard E.			FMB	PHD	83.	U Wash		
Arya, Anil	Prof	Ohio State	T	PHD	91	Iowa		1991
John J. Gerlach Chair in Accounting								
Arya, Avinash C.	Asst	Mich-Flint	F	PHD	99.	SUNY-Buf		9-05
Arya, Seema	Sess	Univ Windsor	A	PHD				2006
Asare, Stephen K.	Assoc	Florida	ABF	PHD	89.	Arizona		1-89
Asbury, Douglas	C-As	Findlay	FC	MBA	86	Xavier		1986
Aschbacher, Bernard F.	Retir	CS-Northrdge	F	PHD	58.	Illinois		&
Asdemir, Ozer	Asst	St Thomas-MN	F	PHD	05	Tx-Dallas		9-06
Asebrook, Richard J.	Assoc	Massachusett	AF	PHD	74.	Wisconsin		9-77
Asechemie, Daniel P. S.		U Port Harco	1992	PHD	87.	Illinois		
Dept of Atg; Univ of Port Harcourt; 5323 Port Harcourt Nigeria								
Ash, Ehiel	Retir	Iona	1994	PHD	64	Moscow		1980
Ashad, Younis				PHD	81.	Missouri		
Ashburne, Jim G.	Deces	Texas	1996	PHD	53.	Tx-Austin		&1949
Ashby, J. David	C	Southern Ark	FJV	DBA	96	La Tech		
Ashcroft, Paul A.	Asst	East Central	AF	PHD	99.	Tx A&M		& 8-02
Ashenfelter, Melody	Prof	SW Okla St	ANFP	EDD	86	Okla St		&1987
Ashorn, Leroy W. Jr.		Sam Houston		PHD	74.	Arkansas		
Dept of Finance; Sam Houston University								
Ashton, Alison Hubbard	Assoc	Duke	FAB	PHD	79.	Tx-Austin		1986
Ashton, David J.	C-Pr	Univ Bristol	QT	PHD	79	Warwick		9-89
Ashton, Robert H.	Prof	Duke	MAB	PHD	73.	Minnesota		&1986
L. Palmer Fox Professor of Business Administration								
Askarany, Davood	Lect	U Auckland	MA	PHD	03	S Austral		2005
Asman, Mark F.	Retir	Bowling Gr	1998	PHD	72.	Missouri		&1966
Asquith, Paul	Prof	MIT	F	PHD	80	Chicago		7-90
Assaf, Asma Sh.	Inst	Yarmouk Univ	ABOC	PHD	06	Amman Arab		1999
Assumpta, Sister Virginia	Retir	Immaculata	5-07	MA		Catholic		9-68
Asthana, Sharad C.	Assoc	Tx-S Antonio	FS	PHD	95.	Tx-Austin		8-06
Atamian, Rubik	Assoc	Tx-Pan Amer	SM	PHD	84.	Tx-Austin		9-86
Atamna, Said		Israel		PHD	74.	Missouri		1977
Athreya, Mrityuniav B.				DBA	67.	Harvard		
Atiase, Florence J. A.	Lect	Texas-Austin	FM	MACC	83	Florida		& 1-93
Atiase, Rowland K.	Prof	Texas-Austin	FM	PHD	80.	Berkeley		& 7-87
Ernst & Young Faculty Fellowship in Teaching Excellence								
Atieh, Sulayman H.			FGIA	PHD	75.	Arizona		
Atiyah, Wadiah	Dean	Am U Sharjah	F	PHD	97	American		&1997
Atkinson, Anthony A.	Prof	Un Waterloo	M	PHD	77.	Car Mellon	*	1992
Atkinson, Keith E.	Prof	Cen Arkansas	AM	PHD	96.	Miss		& 7-01
Atkinson, MaryAnne	Asst	Central Wash	AS	PHD	90.	Drexel		1997
Attaway, Alan N.	Prof	Louisville	XS	PHD	83.	Cincinnati		1977
Atwood, K. Edward			FX	PHD	83.	Wisconsin		&
Atwood, T. J.	Asst	North Texas	X	PHD	95.	Illinois		&2006
Aubert, Joseph D.	Retir	Bemidji St	PA	MA		SanFranSt	*	&1975
Audsabumrungrat, Juthathip	Lect	Chulalongkor	AF	MBA	97	Seattle		&2004
Auerbach, Melvin P.	Assoc	CS-Dominguez	AF	MS	75	CS-Nrthr		&1977
Austen, Lizabeth A.	Asst	East Carol	SMC	PHD	97.	Florida	*	&2003
Auster, Rolf	Retir	Fla Internat	2004	PHD	71	Nrthwstrn	# *	&1980
Austin, Bryan J.	Prof	Univ Regina	F	MSC	80	Oregon		&1975
Austin, Jane S.	Assoc	Okla City	EGM	EDD	99	Okla St		& 8-82
Austin, Jeffrey R.	Lect	So Methodist	X	PHD	95.	Georgia		& 8-00
Austin, Kenneth R.	Deces	Memphis	1997	DBA	79.	Kentucky		&1988
Austin, Lloyd M.	SLect	U Auckland	FA	MCOM	73	Auckland		1989
Austin, Pricilla M.	Asst	Duquesne	AFE	MBA	77	Duquesne		&1982
Austin, Walter G.	Emer	Txs-El Paso	1995	PHD	64.	Tx-Austin		& 7-79
Austin, Walter W.	Prof	Mercer-Macon	FMEP	PHD	88.	Georgia		&1990
Autrey, Romana L.	Asst	Harvard	FY	PHD	05.	Tx-Austin	*	& 8-05
Auyeung, Pak K.	SLect	Griffith Un	FM	PHD	01	Griffith		1990
Avary, Jan M.	Retir	Angelo State	1991	MBA	46	Tx-Austin		1979
Avery, Clarence G.	Retir	Cen Florida	1990	PHD	59.	Illinois		&1975
Avkiran, Necmi	SLect	U Queensland	MFDQ	PHD	95	VUT-Melb		2000
Avritch, Richard T.	Retir	Central Conn	1996	MED	56	Boston U		9-66
Awad, Saber A.		U Cairo	1995	PHD	70.	Mich St		
Univ of Cairo; Khartum Brach; Cario, Egypt								

Awasthi, Vidya N.	Assoc	Seattle	MBC	PHD	88.	U Wash	# * &1996
Ayala, Marion	Lect	Tx-Pan Amer	FM	MS	06	Tx-PanAm	2007
Ayers, Benjamin C.	D-Ac	Georgia	X	PHD	96.	Tx-Austin	&1996
Ayers, Susan	Lect	San Diego	SA	PHD	95.	Ariz St	&2000
Ayling, David E.	Lect	Wales-Bangor	F	PHD	82	Aston	9-82
Ayres, Frances L.	D-Pr	Oklahoma	FX	PHD	82.	Iowa	&1982
John W. Jr. and Barbara J. Branch Professor							
Azad, Ali N.	Prof	King Fahd Un	AEF	PHD	88	North Tx	&2001
Azad, Hamid R.	Asst	York-Penn	FMQ	PHD		Utah St	& 9-88
Azzeh, Jawad J.		Industry Sau		PHD	75.	Nebraska	1990
Arab Jordan Investment Bank, Jordan							
Baazaoui, Hedi	Asst	Univ Tunis	F	DEA	97	ISCAE	1997
Baber, William R.	Prof	George Wash	FMG	PHD	80.	N Carol	& 1-91
Benjamin Franklin Professor of Accountancy; Assoc Dean, Doctoral Programs							
Babin, Roger O.	Assoc	Plymouth St	FXL	JD	77	Boston C	9-79
Bac, Aad D.	C-Pr	Tilburg Univ	AG	MBA	71	Rotterdam	&1974
Baccari, Richard	Assoc	Mercy-NY	DX	MBA	96	Long Isl	& 9-00
Baccouche, Chedli	Assoc	Univ Tunis	FHIT	DBA	88.	Kentucky	* &1991
Bachar, Joseph			FM	PHD	87.	Berkeley	&
Bachman, Joseph W.	Retir	Colorado	1975	PHD	56	Illinois	&1954
Bachman, Virginia A.	Retir	Ark Tech	PM	MSA	76	Arkansas	&1981
Backer, Morton	Retir	Massachusett	1986	PHD	59.	Pittsburgh	&1966
Bacon, Leonard A.	Prof	CS-Bakersf	MFPC	PHD	73.	Miss	# * & 9-79
Badawi, Ibrahim M.	Prof	St John's	FMC	PHD	77	NYU	& 0-77
Baddour, Jamal	Inst	Yarmouk Univ	FGND	MS	93	Illinois	1993
Bader, Mary	Prof	Mn-Moorhead	LX	LLM	91	Wm Mitch	&2000
Badi, Mahmound Muhvadin		Saudia Arabi	1989	PHD	79.	Oklahoma	
Badren, Sanaa M.			FAM	PHD	83.	Arkansas	
Bae, Benjamin R.	Assoc	Central Wash	S	PHD	98.	Temple	2004
Bae, Byung-Han	Prof	Kyungpook Un	M	PHD	89	Keimyung	1981
Bae, Gil Soo	Assoc	Korea Univ	FM	PHD	94.	Minnesota	& 3-98
Baer, M. Elizabeth	Retir	Miami U-Ohio	2001	MBA	77	Miami U	& 9-78
Baey-Diez, Anibal	Asst	Puerto Rico	F	PHD	04.	Kent St	1-03
Baggett, Lawrence E.	Retir	Austin Peay	2004	MA	65	Alabama	&1965
Baggett, Walter O.	Assoc	Manhattan	ASP	PHD	73	N Carol	&1983
Baginski, Stephen P.	Prof	Georgia	FM	PHD	86.	Illinois	& 8-02
Herbert E. Miller Chair in Financial Accounting							
Bagley, Pennie	Asst	Texas Tech	AF	PHD	07.	Georgia	2007
Bagley, Rayment R.	Retir	Providence	1998	MA		Providen	&1955
Bagley, Ron N.	Retir	Sultan Qaboo	FM	PHD	70.	Minnesota	&1998
Baglia, David S.	C-Ac	Grove City	AF	DBA	99.	Clev St	&1995
Bagnani, Betty S.	Lect	Boston Coll	F	PHD	86	Mass	2004
Bagnoli, Mark	C-Pr	Purdue	FTX	PHD	85	Princeton	8-99
Bagranoff, Nancy A.	Dean	Old Dominion	SM	DBA	86.	Geo Wash	&2003
Bagur, Llorenc	Asst	Pompeu Fabra			05	UB	
Bagwell, Jennifer	Inst	Ohio Univ	M	MST		Alabama	& 9-03
Bahjatt, Mohammed F.		King Adbul U	1995	PHD	82.	Mich St	
King Abdul-Azia Univ; Atg Dept; PO Box 9031; Fac of Eco Adm; Jeddah Saudia Ar							
Bahmanziari, Tammy E.	Asst	Mid Tenn St	SM	PHD	06.	S Illinois	2006
Bahnson, Paul R.	Prof	Boise State	FTV	PHD	87.	Utah	&1999
Baik, Bok	Asst	Florida St	F	PHD	03.	Berkeley	8-03
Bailes, Jack C.	Retir	Oregon State	2004	PHD	73.	U Wash	1972
Bailetti, Antonio (Tony)	Retir	Carleton Un	2003	PHD	76	Cincinnati	1979
Bailey, Allan R.	Retir	San Diego St	XF	PHD	69.	UCLA	1968
Bailey, Andrew D. Jr.	Emer	Illinois	2003	PHD	71.	Ohio St	# * &1994
Securities and Exchange Commission							
Bailey, Charles D.	Prof	Memphis	MBCJ	PHD	81.	Geo St	* 8-03
Arthur Andersen Chair of Excellence							
Bailey, Eldon R.	Retir	McNeese St	2003	PHD	70.	LSU	&1964
Bailey, James A.	Prof	S Nevada	AME	PHD	92.	Nebraska	2004
MBA Director; Univ of Southern Nevada; email jbailey@usn.edu							
Bailey, K. Edwin			FM	PHD	76.	N Carol	&
Bailey, Larry P.	Retir	Rider	2004	PHD	74.	Penn	& 9-80
Bailey, Micaiah	Assoc	Cumberland	PX	MBA	72	Murray St	* & 8-73
Bailey, Richard L.	Prof	Oregon Tech	XMF	MACC	85	Utah St	&1991
Bailey, Sharla S.	Asst	SW Baptist	MZPG	MBA		Okla St	* &1994
Bailey, Wendy J.	Asst	So Carolina	F	PHD	00.	Pittsburgh	&2005
Bailey, William T.			FMCA	PHD	78.	Tx-Austin	&
Baillie, Courtney	Assoc	Nebraska Wes	FS	PHD	03	Nebraska	1999
Baiman, Stanley	Prof	Pennsylvania	F	PHD	74.	Stanford	1991
Ernst & Young Professor of Accounting							
Bain, Craig E.	Prof	No Arizona	FCP	PHD	87.	Tx A&M	&1991
Bainbridge, D. Raymond	Retir	Lehigh	2001	PHD	78.	Lehigh	& 9-72
Bainbridge, Ted A.			S	PHD	00.	Iowa	
Baird, Byron N.	Retir	Cleveland St	1994	MS	63	Penn St	&1967
Baird, Jane E.	Assoc	Mn St-Mankat	AP	PHD	94.	Cincinnati	&1993
Baird, Kevin M.	SLect	Macquarie Un	M	PHD	04	Macquarie	&1998

Name	Rank	School	Code	Degree	Yr	Deg School		
Baird, Michael	Asst	Dalhousie U		MBA	98	Bowl Gr		1997
Bait, El Mai Mahamed A.		Libya		DBA	78.	Kentucky		
Bajor, Lawrence H.	Asst	Bowling Gr	X	PHD	02.	Mich St		2001
Bakay, Virginia H.	Retir	Nev-L Vegas	1997	PHD	69.	Alabama		&1978
Baker, C. Richard	C-Pr	Adelphi	AF	PHD	75.	UCLA		&2005
Baker, Dennis M.	Prof	CS-Fresno	SM	PHD	73.	UCLA		& 8-84
Baker, Denton	Inst	Intl College		MBA				
Baker, Donna	C-Ac	Siena Height	AS	MBA	86	Mich St		&1990
Baker, George P. III			M	PHD	86.	Harvard		
Baker, Glen	Lect	U Lethbridge	F	BCOM	77	Calgary	*	7-02
Baker, J. W.	Retir	Bloomsburg	1984	MA	69	Wash St		1969
Baker, Jack D.	Retir	N Car-Wilmin	2003	PHD	80.	Missouri		&1986
Baker, James Weston		APO S FranCA	1988	DBA	63.	S Calif		
Baker, John	Assoc	NW Missouri	JKXL	LLM	77	Mo-Ks Cty		1977
Baker, Keith E.	Retir	Ogelthorpe	1999	ABD	66	Florida		&1983
Baker, Pam P.	Lect	Macquarie Un	M	MEC	95	Macquarie		1988
Baker, Pamela S.	Asst	Txs Woman's	STV	PHD	96.	North Tx		2002
Baker, Paul D.	Retir	West Georgia	2001	PHD	74.	Geo St		&9-77
Baker, Richard E.	Emer	No Illinois	2005	PHD	74.	Wisconsin		&6-79
Baker, Richard L.	C-Pr	Bloomsburg	NFV	PHD	84.	Penn St	# *	&1987
Baker, Robert L.			SM	PHD	78.	S Carol		
Baker, Ronald	Asst	Univ Regina		MBA	98	Athabasc		2003
Baker, Roy E.	Retir	Mo-KansasCty	1990	DBA	62.	Harvard		&1967
Baker, Susan	Lect	Mich-Dearbor	FM	MA	95	Michigan		9-05
Baker, Terry A.	Assoc	Wake Forest	PFT	PHD	98.	Kentucky		&9-98
PricewaterhouseCoopers Professor of Accountancy								
Baker, Timothy W.	Lect	CS-Fresno	PFMX	MSTX	93	San Joaq		&8-00
Baker, William M.	Prof	Appalach St	SCUR	PHD	87.	Va Tech	*	1991
Baker-Collins, Mae	H-SLe	Univ Leeds	FNH	PHD	94	Leeds		9-94
Bakini, Olfa	Asst	Univ Tunis	F	DEA	98	ISCAE		1998
Bakker, Patricia	Lect	So Cross Un	XF	MBUS	94	So Cross		&1991
Bakre, Owalabi M.	Lect	West Indies	M	MCOM		Rajastha		
Balachandran, Bala V.	Prof	Northwestern	AMS	PHD	73	Car Mellon	# *	&1973
J.L. Kellogg Distinguished Professor; Dir Atg Research Center								
Balachandran, I.	SLect	London Metro	CM	MBA				1998
Balachandran, K. R.	Prof	New York U	MYQC	PHD	68	Berkeley	*	1979
Balachandran, Sudhakar	Asst	Columbia	MF	PHD	01.	Harvard		2000
Baladouni, Vahe	Retir	New Orleans	2000	PHD	65.	Illinois		1966
Balakrishnan, Ramji	Prof	Iowa	MY	PHD	86.	Columbia	*	8-86
Ernst & Young Research Professor								
Balatbat, Maria	Lect	New So Wales	FA	PHD	98	Sydney		
Balch, John W.		Mt St MaryMD		MS		Geotown		&
Balcom, N. Jean	Assoc	Indianapolis	ACPX	PHD	91.	Arkansas		&1992
Balden, John A.	Assoc	Utah Valley	X	MACC	80	Brighm Yg		&1996
Baldenius, Tim	Assoc	Columbia	M	PHD	98	Vienna		1998
Baldiga, Nancy R.	C-Ac	Holy Cross	FA	MST	92	Bentley		&9-91
Baldvinsdottir, Gudrun	Lect	Dundee						2005
Baldwin, Amelia A.	Assoc	Alabama-Hunt	S	PHD	91.	Va Tech		2006
Baldwin, Bruce A.	C-Pr	Ariz St-West	F	PHD	79.	Ariz St		9-89
Baldwin, Duane E.	Retir	Nev-L Vegas	1996	DBA	75.	S Calif		&1975
Baldwin, Jane N.	Prof	Baylor	F	PHD	85.	Arkansas		&1986
Ernst & Young Teaching Fellow								
Baldwin, William T. Jr.	Prof	Transylvania	F	PHD	75	Kentucky		1988
Bale, Jill M.	Prof	Doane	FMC	PHD	93	Nebraska		1993
Bales, John E.	Retir	Manchester C	2001	MBA	61	Indiana		&1977
Balke, Thomas E.	Retir	Nebraska	2004	PHD	70.	Missouri		1970
Ball, Amanda	Prof	Canterbury	JNW	BA	85	CNAA		2006
Ball, Frazer	SLect	Bournemouth	MS	BA				9-95
Ball, Ian	Prof	Victoria NZ	FGMN	PHD	76	Birminghm		1995
Ball, J. T.		FASB	1994	PHD	71.	Tx-Austin		1973
Asst Director; FASB; 47 Wellingon Dr; Stamford CT 06903; 203-847-0700								
Ball, Nicholas L.	Inst	Brigham Yg	S	PHD	05	Minnesota		8-05
Ball, Raymond J.	Prof	Chicago	F	PHD	72.	Chicago		&2000
Sidney Davidson Professor of Accounting								
Ballard, Deborah	Asst	Dickinson St	FGNX	MBA	95	Plymouth		&8-03
Ballew, Van B.			MA	PHD	77.	Houston		&
Ballou, Brian	Prof	Miami U-Ohio	AM	PHD	96.	Mich St		&8-03
Balogun, Jacob O.	Prof	Fayetteville	GCL	PHD	80.	LSU		&1985
Balsam, Steven	Prof	Temple	FX	PHD	91.	Baruch		&1991
Merves Research Fellow								
Balsari, Cagnur				DBA	04.	Boston U		
Bamber, E. Michael	Prof	Georgia	AB	PHD	80.	Ohio St		1990
Harold M. Heckman Professor of Accounting								
Bamber, Linda S.	Prof	Georgia	CMF	PHD	83.	Ohio St		&1990
J.M. Tull Professor of Accounting								
Bame-Aldred, Charles	Asst	Northeastern	AFB	PHD	04.	Mass		9-07
Banatte, Jean-Marie	Prof	Norfolk St	XF	PHD	77.	Missouri		& 7-83

Name	Rank	School	Code	Degree	Year	Institution		Date
Bancroft, Patricia C.	C-Ac	Bridgewater	FLX	DBA				&9-98
Bandua, Frank	Asst	McNeese St	FAN	ABD		Rutgers		2004
Bandura, Randall P.	Prof	Frostburg St	VFP	MS	76	Penn St		&9-83
Bandy, Dale	Retir	Cen Florida	2006	PHD	72.	Tx-Austin		&8-85
Bandyopadhyay, Sati P.	Assoc	Un Waterloo	FAIZ	PHD	89.	Iowa		1989
Banham, Richard L.	Assoc	Tenn State	DISX	PHD	84.	Tx-Austin		1993
Banker, Rajiv D.	Prof	Temple	MSCQ	DBA	80.	Harvard	*	&2005
Banks, Doyle W.	Retir	St Louis	2003	PHD	79.	Iowa		&9-82
Banks, William	C-Ac	Wilfrid Laur	FS	PHD	92	McMaster		&1988
Bannister, James W.	C-Ac	Hartford	FI	PHD	88.	N Carol		1994
Bannon, Richard J.	Retir	DePaul	1987	PHD	54	Catholic		&1983
Banyi, Monica L.	Asst	Oregon State	F	PHD	04.	Arizona		&2004
Bao, Ben-Hsien	Assoc	HongKon Tech	FIT	PHD	84.	Missouri		1996
Bao, Da-Hsien	Prof	Rowan	MF	PHD	81.	S Calif		1995
Bao, Yan	Asst	Frostburg St	PFI	PHD	04.	Kent St		&8-02
Bar-Yosef, Sasson	C-Pr	Hebrew Univ	FM	PHD	73	Aston		1978
Julius Fienstein Chair in Accounting								
Baran, Arie		Israel	1990	PHD	76.	Berkeley		
Kfar Veradih; PO Box 42 Doer-Na; Mela-Galil 24960 Israel								
Barbeau, Debra	Inst	St Louis	F	MA	85	S Illinois		&1997
Barbee, Ronald F.	C-Ac	Alaska-Ancho	SFMG	PHD	93.	Wash St		&8-01
Barber, Brad M.	Prof	Cal-Davis	FQ	PHD	91	Chicago		1991
Barber, G. Russell Jr.	Retir	Mercer-Macon	2004	PHD	90	Miss		&9-73
Barber, James P.		Fort Wort TX	1000	PHD	01.	Tx-Austin	&	
Barbor, John F.	Asst	York-Penn	CDFV	MBA		Shippensb		&9-73
Barcal, John J.	Assoc	So Calif	X	JD	68	Stanford		&1975
Barclay, Roderick S.			GMSA	PHD	93.	Kent St	&	
Barcuh, D.	Asst	Touro	ACLP	JD		NYU		&2-91
Barden, Ronald S.	Retir	Georgia St	2005	PHD	71.	Tx-Austin	#	&9-81
Bardhan, Indranil R.	Asst	Texas-Dallas	SQM	PHD	95	Tx-Austin		2001
Bardin, John P.	Lect	Texas-Dallas	AEJ	MBA	98	Manhatten		&2006
Bardo, Frederic S.	Assoc	Shippensburg	AMPI	PHD	88	Stirling		&1-85
Barefield, Russell M.	Deces	Georgia	9-02	PHD	69.	Ohio St		&7-89
Bareket, Moshe			M	PHD	01.	Columbia		
Barfield, Jesse T.	Retir	Loyola-N Orl	ACFM	PHD	71.	LSU		&9-77
Barfitt, Laurie	Asst	Delta State	PCG	PHD	06.	Miss	*	&1998
Barger, James W.	Retir	Middle Tenn	1987	PHD	63.	Alabama		&1980
Baridwan, Zaki		Fak Economi	1992	DBA	89.	Kentucky		
Fak Economi Univraw; Jawa Timur Indonesia								
Bariff, Martin L.	Assoc	Illinois Tch	AS	PHD	73.	Illinois		&1983
Baril, Charles P.	Prof	Jms Madison	F	PHD	87.	Florida		&1-89
Frank & Co. Faculty Fellow								
Barker, Katherine J.	Assoc	S Fl-St Pete	AFC	PHD	99.	Arkansas		&8-07
Barker, Robert L.	Retir	CS-Northrdge	2005	PHD	74.	Alabama		&1981
Barkhi, Reza	Assoc	Virg Tech	S	PHD	95	Ohio St		8-97
Alumni Research Fellow								
Barkman, Arnold I.	Assoc	Tx Christian	SM	PHD	74.	Houston	*	&1974
Barkman, Beryl V.	Retir	Mass-Dartmou	2002	PHD	88.	S Carol	*	9-87
Barlev, Benzion	Prof	Hebrew Univ	F	PHD	70	NYU		&1972
Chaired Professorship								
Barlow, Daniel W.	Prof	Roberts Wesl	LPX	JD	87	Colorado		&1989
Barlow, H. A.	Retir	Lamar	1994	MBA	51	LSU		&1951
Barnes, B. L.	Retir	Iowa	1988	PHD	58.	Illinois		&1958
Barnes, Gregory D.	Retir	Clarion	5-00	MBA	73	Maryland		&8-76
Barnes, Jeffrey N.	Assoc	Srthrn Utah	AS	MACC	84	Brighm Yg		&1986
Barnett, Andrew H.	Emer	San Diego St	AF	PHD	76.	Tx Tech		&1983
Barnett, Donald J.	Prof	CS-Dominguez	BFM	PHD	73.	UCLA		1996
Barnett, James J.	D-Le	Un Waterloo	X	BCOM	75	Queens		&1990
Barnette, Glenn	Asst	Gustavus Ado	FCMV	PHD	98	Rensselaer		1997
Barney, Douglas K.	Prof	Indiana SE	FX	PHD	93.	Miss	*	&8-93
Barnhart, J. Robert			FM	DBA	68.	Indiana	&	
Barniv, Ran	Prof	Kent State	FI	PHD	83	Ohio St		8-90
Baron, C. David	Retir	New Mex St	D-01	PHD	70.	Illinois		&7-80
Barone, Gerhard J.			F	PHD	02.	Wisconsin		
Baroudi, Jack	Prof	Delaware	SB	PHD	84	NYU		2002
Barrack, John B.	Retir	Georgia	2001	PHD	75.	Okla St		&1972
Barragato, Charles A.	D-Pr	Lg Isl-Post	XFVN	PHD	02.	Baruch		&1986
Barrett, David J.	Asst	Maine	F	PHD	04	Indiana		2004
Barrett, Jeannie A.	Lect	Texas A&M	F	MBA	02	Sam Hous		1-03
Barrett, Kevin S.			XP	PHD	91.	Va Tech	# *	&
Barrett, M. Edgar (Ed)			FMZ	PHD	71.	Stanford		
Barrett, Michael J.	Deces	Neb-Omaha	8-90	DBA	69.	Colorado	#	1987
Barrett, William B.	Retir	Arizona	1995	PHD	62.	Illinois		&9-68
Barrick, John A.	Assoc	Brigham Yg	X	PHD	98.	Nebraska		&6-00
Barron, Orie E.	Assoc	Penn State	AFST	PHD	93.	Oregon		&8-97
Barron, Rhelda W.	Retir	Tenn-Martin	2003	DBA	78.	Miss St		&9-77
Barrone, Gerhard	Asst	Gonzaga	FS	PHD	02	Wisconsin		2006

Name	Rank	School		Deg		Univ		
Barsky, Noah P.	Assoc	Villanova	MU	PHD	98.	Conn	*	&1998
Bartczak, Norman J.		Harvard	1992	PHD	78.	U Wash		
Harvard Business School; 56 Craftsland Rd; Chestnut Hill MA 02167								
Bartenstein, Edwin	Retir	CS-Northrdge	1988	DBA	75.	S Calif	*	1975
Barth, Frank R.	Retir	Luther	1988	MBA	48	Nrthwstrn	# *	&1946
Barth, Mary E.	Prof	Stanford	F	PHD	89.	Stanford		&1995
Atholl McBean Professor of Accounting; Assoc Dean for Academic Affairs								
Bartkowski, Richard J.			BCM	PHD	82.	Pittsburgh		
Bartlett, Henry C. Jr.	Col	US Air Force		DBA	75.	Indiana		
Bartlett, Roger W.	Retir	CS-Sacrament	2004	PHD	80.	Houston		&1984
Bartlett, Sue	Tutor	Cardiff U	DFM	PHD	96	Cardiff		1990
Bartlett, Thomas E.	Clin	Alaska-Fairb	AF	MBA	69	Emory		&8-07
Bartley, Jon W.	Prof	N Carol St	FT	PHD	78.	N Carol		&8-87
Bartman, Richard J.	Assoc	CUNY-York						
Barton, Allan D.	Prof	Australian N	GPI	PHD	61	Cambridge		&1996
Barton, Jan J.	Assoc	Emory	F	PHD	98.	Alabama		&8-98
Barton, M. Frank Jr.	Deces	Memphis		PHD	75.	Miss		&1977
Barton, Peter	Prof	Wis-Whitewat	XM	JD	88	Wisconsin		&1983
Barton, Thomas L.	Prof	North Fla	FMT	PHD	84.	Florida		&1982
Barton, Thomas M.			F	PHD	86.	Geo St	*	
Barton, William E.	Retir	Colorado Col	1997	PHD	70.	Missouri		1958
Bartov, Eli	Prof	New York U	F	PHD	89.	Berkeley		1992
Barty, Scottie	Asst	No Kentucky	MF	MBA	78	Cincinnati		&8-82
Barua, Abhijit	Asst	Fla Internat	F	PHD	06.	LSU		2006
Bashir, Tariq H.	SLect	Un East Lond	F	BA				1991
Basi, Bart A.	Emer	So Illinois	1996	DBA	71.	Indiana		&1978
Basile, Anthony	Asst	Hofstra	APX	PHD	01	NYU		&1993
Baskett, James	Assoc	Loyola-N Orl	MFX	PHD	76	Arizona	*	&1982
Baskin, Elba F. (Bud)	Retir	Arthur Ander	1996	PHD	70.	Mich St		&6-79
Basoglu, Besalet	Assoc	Manhattan	CFM	DBA	79.	Fla St		1984
Bastable, Charles W.	Retir	Columbia	1986	PHD	52.	Columbia		&1952
773 Village Circle; Venice FL 34292								
Bastian, Nicole	Asst			PHD	05.	Stanford		
Basu, Atasi	Asst	Utica	AFMQ	PHD	05	Syracuse		2005
Basu, Onker N.			CFM	PHD	92.	Penn St		
Basu, Progyan	Asst	Georgia	FSM	PHD	92.	Nebraska		2001
on leave to University of Maryland								
Basu, Sanjoy (Joe)	Deces	McMaster	1-83	PHD	75.	Cornell	*	7-74
Basu, Sudipta	Assoc	Temple	F	PHD	95.	Rochester		2007
Basyouni, Mohamed	Asst	King Saud U	M	PHD	93	Alexandria		1996
Batchelder, Walter I.			SFX	PHD	88.	Va Tech		
Bate, J. Benedict	SLect	Napier Univ	M	MA			*	9-85
Bateman, David H.	Assoc	St Marys-Cdn	DSPE	MBA	83	Dalhousie		&9-80
Bates, Homer L.	Prof	North Fla	MFC	PHD	77.	Illinois		&1984
Bates, Ira W.	Asst	Florida A&M	FT	PHD	00.	Arkansas		2001
Bates, Kenneth	Lect	Un Warwick	FMSE	BA	76	Nottingh	&	
Bathke, Allen W. Jr.	Assoc	Florida St	F	DBA	82.	Fla St		8-84
Batta, George Eli		Natl Econ Re		DBA	05.	Harvard		
National Economic Research Association								
Battaglia, Samuel T.	Emer	Denver	2002	PHD	68.	SUNY-Buf		1969
Battelle, Peter E.	Retir	Vermont	5-07	MBA	63	Columbia		&1970
Batten, Jonathan	Prof	Deakin-Burwo	F	PHD	96	Sydney		2000
Battistel, George P.			FMS	PHD	92.	Oregon	#	&
Baucum, Richard P.	Assoc	Dillard		MA		Loyola		&
Baudin, Jerry J.			F	PHD	82.	LSU		&
Bauer, Kathleen	Asst	Midwest St	VPX	MA	72	Alabama		&9-81
Bauers, Ron	Inst	Neb-Omaha	FSCA	MPA	89	Ne-Omaha	# *	&1995
Bauman, Christine C.	Assoc	No Iowa	XF	PHD	97.	Wisconsin		&2005
Bauman, Mark P.	Assoc	No Iowa	F	PHD	97.	Wisconsin		2005
Baumann, Chris	Lect	Macquarie Un	IM	MBA	00	Simon Fr		2004
Baumler, John V.			M	DBA	70.	Harvard		
Baur, Lawrence E.	Retir	Cal Poly-SLO	1998	MBA	57	Michigan		&1-62
Bausch, Norbert G.				PHD	41.	Illinois		
Bavelaar, Anja	Lect	Vrije Univ	FP	MS	95	Christian		2003
Baxendale, Sidney J.	Prof	Louisville	MC	DBA	78.	Indiana	*	&1984
Baxter, George C.	Retir	Saskatchewan	2001	PHD	72.	Minnesota	#	&1966
Baxter, Jane A.	AProf	Univ Sydney	NNW	PHD	95	NS Wales		&2003
Baxter, Ryan	Asst	Bentley	S	PHD	07	Case Wes		8-07
Bay, Darlene D.	Assoc	Brock Univ	FM	PHD	97.	Wash St		&2004
Bayer, Frieda A.			FV	PHD	84.	Tx-Arlin	*	&
Bayerkohler, Glenn M.	Assoc	SW Minn St	VXPD	JD	79	Wm Mitch		&1988
Bayes, Paul E.	Retir	East Tenn St	2006	DBA	83.	Kentucky		1984
Bayler, Charles M.	Retir	Bloomsburg	1992	MBA	65	Bucknell		&1965
Bayley, Francis L. (Chip)	Deces	Sangamon St	1994	PHD	71	Bowl Gr		1973
Bayou, Mohamed E.	Prof	Mich-Dearbor	MF	PHD	83.	Cincinnati		1990
Bazaz, M. Sadegh	Prof	Oakland	FI	PHD	85.	Oklahoma		1987
Bazley, John D.	Prof	Denver	F	PHD	72.	Minnesota		&1976

Beagle, Chauncey M.	Retir	Colorado		1986	MA	40	Illinois	1957
2535 Dartmough Ave; Boulder CO 80303								
Bealing, William E. Jr.	Prof	Bloomsburg	FV		PHD	91.	Penn St	&1999
Beam, Thomas J.	Retir	F Dick-Madis		2000	PHD	76	NYU	&1982
Beaman, Burwell G.	Retir	Neb-Omaha		6-92	ABD		Kansas St	&1960
Beaman, Ian	SLect	Monash Univ	QD		PHD	77	Newcastle	1985
Beams, Floyd A.	Retir	Virg Tech		1995	PHD	68.	Illinois	1967
Beams, Joseph D.	Asst	New Orleans	MS		PHD	03.	Va Tech	& 8-03
Bean, Benjamin W.	Prof	Utah Valley	FMH		MBA	71	Utah	&1976
Bean, David F.	Prof	Iona	PV		PHD	94.	Temple	& 9-98
Bean, LuAnn G.	Prof	Fla Tech	PAFM		PHD	89.	Arkansas	# & 8-02
Bean, Russell D.			FX		DBA	74.	Colorado	* &
Bean, Virginia L.	Retir	No Colorado		1994	PHD	65.	Tx-Austin	&1990
Beard, Atha A.	Retir	Auburn		1995	MBA	65	Auburn	& 9-65
Beard, Deborah F.	Assoc	SE Missouri	PFIE		PHD	87.	Arkansas	* 1976
Beard, Larry H.	Retir	Emory	MCS		PHD	74.	Georgia	* 1981
Bearden, Cindi S.	Assoc	LaGrange	FPS		MACC	90	Alabama	& 8-01
Bearden, Laura	Asst	Siena Height	F		MBA	94	Toledo	&2006
Beasley, Mark S.	Prof	N Carol St	AF		PHD	94.	Mich St	&1994
Beattie, Vivien A.	Prof	Univ Glasgow	AFE		PHD	94	Southampt	&2004
Beatty, Anne L.	Prof	Ohio State	F		PHD	92.	MIT	&2004
Deloitte & Touche Chair in Accounting								
Beatty, Bernard L.	Assoc	Wake Fr-MBA	ACM		DBA	72.	Harvard	# * &1974
Beatty, Randolph P.	Dean	So Calif	F		PHD	82.	Illinois	2001
Alan Casden Dean's Chair								
Beauchesne, Alain	Prof	Sherbrooke	FT		LCOM	69	Laval	&1972
Beaulieu, Philip R.	C-Ac	Univ Calgary	FMBA		PHD	91.	U Wash	1991
Beaulieu, Suzanne	Prof	Sherbrooke	S		MS	92	HEC-Mont	&1986
Beauregard, Claude		Quebec a Hul	X		MSC			&
Beausejour, David	Prof	Bryant	XF		JD	89	Suffolk	& 8-84
Beaver, William H.	Emer	Stanford	F		PHD	65.	Chicago	&1969
Joan E. Horngren Professor of Accounting, Emeritus								
Beavers, Lorren H.	Retir	Central Okla		2003	EDD	74	Oklahoma	& 9-65
Beazley, Garnett F. Jr.	Retir	So Carolina		2000	PHD	63.	Pittsburgh	&1966
Bebbington, Jan	Prof	St Andrews	WETJ		PHD	99	Dundee	&2004
Bebee, Richard F.	Dean	Ohio U-Chill			DBA	71.	Colorado	&
Ohio Univ-Chillicothe; Chillicothe OH 45601; 740-774-7222; bebee@ohio.edu								
Beccalli, Elena	Lect	London Econ	FI		PHD	00	Milan	2000
Bechtel, Terence W.	Assoc	NW St of LA	FMX		PHD	96.	Oklahoma	&1994
Beck, Audrie M.	Retir	Bethune-Cook		2000	MPA	83	Loyola	& 8-93
Beck, Grant M.	Asst	Nev-L Vegas	S		PHD	04.	Missouri	2004
Beck, Paul J.	Prof	Illinois	AX		PHD	77.	Tx-Austin	8-83
Irwin Jecha Professor								
Becker, D'Arcy A.	C-Pr	Wis-Eau Clar	AF		PHD	92.	Wisconsin	& 8-95
Becker, Edward A.					PHD	84.	Penn St	* &
Becker, Helmut	Retir	Portland		1999	DBA	71	Indiana	&1973
Becker, Hilary	Inst	Carleton Un	F		MBA	90	Windsor	1996
Becker, Lana	Lect	East Tenn St	P		MBA	90	E Tn St	&1997
Becker, Steven A.	Retir	Wis-Plattev	FPX		MBA	70	Oregon	& 8-73
Beckman, Judy K.	Assoc	Rhode Island	FIT		PHD	91.	Tx Tech	&1992
Beckman, Ronald J.	Retir	Sam Houston	AFV		PHD	88.	North Tx	&
Beckon, Susan	Asst	Lk Superior	ACSU		MBA	96	Mich St	9-96
Bedard, Gaston	Assoc	Sherbrooke	X		MBA	57	McGill	&1989
Bedard, Gerald	Prof	Sherbrooke	X		MFIS	84	Sherbrook	2001
Bedard, Jean	Prof	Univ Laval	AS		PHD	86.	S Calif	&1985
Bedard, Jean C.	Prof	Bentley	AF		PHD	85.	Wisconsin	&2005
Bedell, Donald Paul	Retir	St Louis		1998	PHD	66.	St Louis	&1969
Bedford, Norton M.	Retir	Illinois		1987	PHD	50.	Ohio St	&1954
Bedient, John B.	Assoc	Albion	MFV		MBA	78	Indiana	&1985
Bedingfield, James P.	Emer	Maryland	MA		DBA	71.	Maryland	&1967
Bee, Sarah	Inst	Seattle	SP		MBA	93	Seattle	1999
Beechy, Thomas H.	Emer	York		2000	DBA	71.	Wash U	&1971
Beed, Teresa K.	Prof	Montana	FT		PHD	81.	Colorado	&1980
Beegle, John A.	Retir	W Carolina		2006	PHD	67.	St Louis	# * &1972
Beehler, John M.	Dean	Wichita St	X		PHD	85.	Indiana	& 8-00
Beekes, Wendy	Lect	U Lancaster	FM		PHD	00	Wales	2000
Beeler, Jesse D.	Prof	Millsaps	FTPB		PHD	94.	Tx-Arlin	&1994
H.F. McCarty Chair in Business Administration								
Beeler, Mary B.	Deces	Nicholls St		8-90	PHD	69.	LSU	1984
Beers, Richard H.	Retir	Drexel		1985	MBA	47	Drexel	1947
Beets, S. Douglas	Prof	Wake Forest	PA		PHD	87.	Va Tech	& 1-87
Befford, David	Lect	Tech-Sydney	M		BBUS	04	Tech-Sydn	2005
Begley, Joy	Assoc	British Colu	F		PHD	91.	Rochester	1989
Ronald L. Cliff Professor in Accounting								
Behgharbin, Salem M.					PHD	82.	LSU	
Behn, Bruce K.	Prof	Tennessee	F		PHD	94.	Ariz St	& 8-94
Ergen Professor of Business								

Behrens, Marcia	Asst	Nichols Col		MBA	89	Nichols		8-05
Beil, Frank	SLect	Minnesota	F	MS	77	N Dakota		&
Beirne, Thomas J. Jr.	Prof	CS-Sacrament	FTR	PHD	81.	Oklahoma		&1977
Bejan, Mary R.		Durham NC		PHD	85.	Berkeley		
Bejaoui, Raoudha	Inst	Univ Tunis	F	EXPC	99	ISCAE		1999
Belanger, France	Assoc	Virg Tech	S	PHD	97	S Fla		8-97
Alumni Research Fellow								
Belcher, Finley E.	Deces	Florida St	O-94	MS	48	Miss		&1949
Belk, Penelope A.	Lect	Loughborough	IF	MA	75	Lancaster		1987
Bell, Cody				PHD	78.	Syracuse		
Bell, Gordon E.	Retir	Fla Atlantic	1990	PHD	64.	Florida		&1964
Bell, Jan	Prof	Babson	FM	PHD	80.	UCLA		&2006
Bell, Linda Joyce	Prof	Wm Jewell	AFSX	MBA	83	Missouri		&9-85
Bell, Philip W.	Retir	Boston Univ	1992	PHD	54	Princeton		9-89
490 E Ireland Court; Hernando FL 32642								
Bell, Sharon	Asst	NC-Pembroke	P	MBA		Campbell	*	&1989
Bell, Timothy B.		KPMG	2000	PHD	81.	Okla St	*	&1987
KPMG Peat Marwick; Three Chestnut Ridge Rd; Montvale NJ 07645								
Bell, Tony	Inst	Thompson Riv	PFMA	MBA		Thom River		2006
Belski, William H.	Asst	Samford	FV	PHD	04.	Va Tech		&8-04
Belzile, Rejean	Prof	Quebec-Montr	M	PHD		Montreal		&7-81
Ben Amar, Walid	Asst	Univ Ottawa	FM	PHD	03	HEC-Mont		2004
Ben-Artzy, Anty				PHD	79.	NYU		
Ben-Daihan, Meshari	Asst	Kuwait Univ	F	PHD	03	Arkansas		2003
Benartzi, Shlomo	Assoc	UCLA	F	PHD	94.	Cornell		1996
Benco, Daniel C.	Assoc	SE Okla St	SGFM	PHD	04.	Tx-Arlin		&2002
Benecke, Robert W.	Retir	Neb-Omaha		DBA	66.	Colorado		
taught in the Finance Department at Nebraska at Omaha								
Benefield, Bruce S.	Dir	TRW	Fnce	DBA	68.	Harvard		
Beneish, Messod D. (Daniel)	Prof	Indiana	FJI	PHD	87.	Chicago		1996
Sam Frumer Professor of Accounting								
Benford, Tanya S.	Asst	Cen Florida	S	PHD	00.	S Fla		&8-04
Bengel, Ross	Prof	Loyola Marym	X	JD	75	S Carol		&1984
Beniluz, Yoel	Asst	Rutgers-N Br	FM	PHD	06.	Chicago		9-04
Benis, Martin	Retir	CUNY-Baruch	2004	PHD	72.	NYU		&1972
Benjamin, James J.	H-Pr	Texas A&M	F	DBA	72.	Indiana		&6-74
Andersen Professor								
Benjamin, Wahjudi P.		U Indonesia	1992	PHD	80.	Missouri		
Univ of Indonesia; Mgmt Prog/Fac of Grad Studies; JL Salemba 4 Sakarta Indone								
Benke, Ralph L. Jr.	Retir	Jms Madison	1998	DBA	78.	Fla St	*	9-81
Bennett, Earl D.	Retir	Texas A&M	6-90	PHD	59	Michigan		&8-68
Bennett, Gary K.	H-Ac	Fairmont	ACFX	MBA	75	W Virginia		&1980
Bennett, Hite	Deces	West Florida	1988	PHD	68	LSU		1969
Bennett, Jeffrey A.	Emer	Northwood	5-04	MBA	65	Mich St		1965
Bennett, Jerome V.	Prof	SC Upstate	CS	PHD	76.	S Carol	*	1986
Bennett, R. J.	Retir	Aquinas	1996	PHD		St Louis		1960
Bennett, Richmond Oliver Jr.	Retir	Lamar	1987	PHD	57.	Tx-Austin		&1957
Bennett, Robert E.	Retir	No Illinois	2001	PHD	72.	Missouri	*	&9-68
Bennett, Shelby D.			MX	PHD	79.	N Carol		
Benninger, Lawrence J.	Deces	Florida	1991	PHD	49.	Missouri		1956
Bens, Daniel A.	Assoc	Arizona	B	PHD	99.	Penn		8-05
BenSaoud, Nejib	Asst	Univ Tunis	AO	EXPC		IHEC		
Bensinger, Dennis D.	Retir	Youngstown	2003	MAC	68	Ohio St		&9-72
Benson, A.	Lect	Univ Hull	M	PHD	05	Hull		9-93
Benson, Frank D.	Prof	CS-San Bern	FMAO	PHD	84	Claremont	# *	&1986
Benson, Janice	Lect	Wyoming	FM	MBA	93	Kansas St		&1999
Benson, Karen	Lect	U Queensland	F	MCOM	95	Jms Cook		2002
Benson, M. Birger	Assoc	St Michaels		MBA		Harvard		
Benson, Vaughn L.	Dean	Wayne St Col	FG	PHD	85.	Nebraska		&1974
Benston, George J.	Prof	Emory	FM	PHD	63.	Chicago		&9-87
Bentancourt, Luis	Asst	Maryland		PHD	95.	Cen Fla		
Bentley, James R.	Retir	Portland St	1989	PHD	68.	U Wash		1968
Bentley, Kathleen	Inst	Miami U-Ohio	P	MBA	04	Franciscan		&8-06
Benton, Christian Y.	D-As	Oglethorpe	AFM	MA	84	Webster		&1999
Benton, James E.	Asst	Lander	XLJR	JD	00	Geo St		1-01
Bentz, William F.	Emer	Ohio State	FUMC	PHD	69.	Ohio St		&1988
Berberich, Greg	Asst	Wilfrid Laur	AEJ	PHD	05	Waterloo		2002
Berecz, Don L.	Clln	Geo Southern	PJ	MBA	81	W Illinois		2007
Berenbaum, Gerald J.	Assoc	Robt Morris	FCRM	MBA	68	Mass		&9-71
Beresford, Dennis R.	Exec	Georgia	FTI	BS	61	S Calif	*	&6-97
Ernst & Young Executive Professor								
Berg, Gary G.	Assoc	East Tenn St	FCM	PHD	87.	Tx A&M		&1987
Berg, Joyce E.	Assoc	Iowa	MF	PHD	88.	Minnesota		&1992
Pioneer Hi-Bred Fellow								
Berg, Kenneth B.	Emer	U Washington	1983	PHD	52.	Illinois		&1950
Berg, Warren G.	Retir	Luther	1988	PHD	60	Iowa		1948
Berger, Harold	Retir	NY Inst Tech	1993	MBA		NYU		&

Berger, Philip G.	Prof	Chicago	F	PHD	92.	Chicago		2002
Bergeron, Jacques	Assoc	HEC-Montreal	DS	MBA	03	HEC-Mont		&6-04
Bergevin, Peter M.	Assoc	Redlands	FM	PHD	85.	Ariz St		2005
Bergin, J. Lawrence	Prof	Winona State	FCM	ABD		Kent St		1981
Bergman, Lila	Retir	CUNY-Hunter	2000	MBA	79	Fordham		&9-85
Bergman, Ruthann	C-Ac	Pine Manor	DFN	MBA		Penn		1983
Berk, Joel L.		Fin Atg I NJ	1994	PHD	78.	Columbia		
Financial Accounting Institute; PO Box 120; Tenafly NJ 07670; 201-568-0249								
Berkowitz, C. S.	Lect	Touro	XP	MS				&2-01
Berkshire, Stewart Jr.	Retir	CS-Long Bch	1988	PHD	75.	Santa Cl		1974
Berman, Arnold L.	Prof	Pace-Westch	FX	LLM	76	NYU		&1974
Berman, Norman D.	Retir	New York U	1998	MBA	57	Columbia		1973
Bermudez, Andres	Deces		1980	DBA	76.	Kent St		
Bernard, Michel	Prof	Quebec-Montr	F	MBA		Montreal	*	8-73
Bernard, Victor L.	Deces	Michigan	N-95	PHD	82.	Illinois		&9-82
Bernardi, Richard A.	C-Pr	Roger Wm	FBJ	PHD	92.	Union-NY		&9-99
Bernstein, Leopold A.	Retir	CUNY-Baruch	1995	PHD	66.	NYU		&1960
Bernstein, Michael M.				PHD	70.	UCLA		
Bernstein, Richard F.	Retir	Toledo	1991	MBA	65	Toledo		&1965
Berrios-Burgos, Luis A.		Puerto Rico	1992	PHD	79.	Penn St		&
210 Street GS-55; Country Club PR 00924								
Berry, Delano Howard	Asst	Fayetteville	GMF	PHD	91.	Kentucky	*	8-05
Berry, G.	Adj	Southern-NO	TF	MS	99	N Orleans		&1998
Berry, Joseph W.	Asst	Campbell		MBA		Fayettev		1996
Berry, Kevin T.	Assoc	Alaska-Fairb	MZF	PHD	95.	Okla St		8-07
Berry, Leonard Eugene	Retir	Georgia St	6-97	PHD	76.	Colorado	#	&6-77
Berry, Lucille M.	Retir	Webster	F	PHD	87	St Louis		8-84
Berry, Maureen H.	Retir	Illinois	1997	PHD	76.	UCLA		&1-74
Berry, Nancy W.	Assoc	Lock Haven	FAX	MBA	78	Penn St	*	&9-84
Berry, Paul	Assoc	Mt Allison U	FQM	MBA	82	Queens	*	7-82
Berry, R. H.	Prof	U Nottingham	HQ	PHD	87	Warwick		1994
Berry, Walter W.	SLect	Old Dominion	PXC	MBA	77	Old Dom		&1977
Berry, Wilbur G.	Retir	Jacksonvl St	2000	MA	66	Alabama	#	&9-81
Berryman, Robert Glen	Retir	Minnesota	1995	PHD	58.	Illinois	#	&1958
Berthling-Hansen, Pal	Assoc	Norwegian Mg	CM	PHD	93	Southmptn		1994
Bertucelli, Robert E.	Prof	Lg Isl-Post	XF	MSTX	73	Long Isl		&1974
Besbes, Hichem	Asst	Univ Tunis	AR	EXPC		IHEC		
Beshara, Robert L.	Retir	LaSierra	PEHM	PHD	81.	Florida	*	7-96
Bess, Allen B.	Retir	Evansville	1996	ABD	56	Missouri		&1963
Besser, Lance J.			MPV	PHD	83.	Arkansas	#	
Best, Kathy T.	Dean	Mount Olive	ACPX	PHD		N Car St		&1981
Best, Peter J.	Assoc	Queensld Tec	AD	PHD	78	Newcastle		&4-88
Betancourt, Wanda	Inst	Puerto Rico	A	MBA				&2001
Bettinger, Cynthia A.			CX	DBA	82.	La Tech		&
Bettinghaus, Bruce	Lect	Michigan St	F	PHD	00.	Penn St		1-02
Bettis, J. Carr			F	PHD	92.	Indiana		&
Bettner, Mark S.	Assoc	Bucknell	FM	PHD	88.	Tx Tech		9-89
Christian R. Lindback Chair								
Betts, Jenny	Lect	Deakin-Warrn	FE	MBA	89	Monash		&1986
Betts, Norman M.	Assoc	New Brunswic	FTY	PHD	92	Queen's		&1992
Beverly, John G.	Retir	Notre Dame	1992	PHD	71.	N Carol		&1967
Bevington, Alexandra	Lect	U Portsmith		BA				2003
Bewley, Kathryn	Assoc	York Univ	AFST	PHD	98	Waterloo		&2002
Beyer, Anne	Asst	Stanford	F	PHD	06.	Nrthwstrn		2006
Bezdziecki, Lawrence J.	Retir	Moravian	CFPX	MBA	76	Lehigh	*	&9-79
Bezik, Mark H.	Asst	Idaho State	PF	MBA	78	Case Wes		&1999
Bhada, Yezdi K.	Retir	Georgia St	2001	PHD	68.	Florida	*	9-70
Bhamornsiri, Surasakdi	Assoc	N Car-Charl	FM	DBA	79.	Tennessee		&1978
Bhaskar, Ramamorthi				PHD	78.	Car Mellon		
Bhati, Shyam	Lect	U Wollongong	FI	PHD	94	Punjab		&1998
Bhatia, Ramesh C.	Prof	Millersville	M	PHD	78	W Virginia	*	1978
Bhattacharjee, Sudip	Asst	Virg Tech	ABM	PHD	97.	Mass		2001
Bhattacharya, Nilabhra	Asst	So Methodist	F	PHD	98.	Georgia		2004
Bhattacharya, Somnath	D-Ac	Fla Atlantic	SMA	PHD	94.	S Fla		1999
Bhimani, Alnoor	Prof	London Econ	BIM	PHD	92	London	*	1988
Bhojraj, Sanjeev	Assoc	Cornell	F	PHD	00.	Florida		&8-99
Bhushan, Ravi	Deces	MIT	4-94	PHD	87	Chicago		1986
Biagioni, Louis F.	Retir	Indiana	1996	PHD	64.	Missouri		&1974
Biankers, Beth	Asst	Buena Vista	PMX	JD	03	Minnesota	*	&2005
Bible, Lynn	Assoc	Berry	FB	PHD	99.	Conn		&8-05
Bice, Phillip	Inst	Wis-La Cross	FMA	MS	75	Wi-White		&8-81
Bichsel, Mark	Lect	St Marys-Cal		MBA				1999
Bidaya, Nantaporn	Lect	Chulalongkor	CM	MAS	71	Illinois		1968
Biddle, Gary C.	H-Pr	Hong Kong Sc	FIAM	PHD	80.	Chicago		&1996
Synergis-Geoffrey YEH Chair Professor of Accounting								
Bien, Frederick A.	Retir	Franklin	2004	MBA	63	Xavier	*	&1965
Bienenstoch, S.	Inst	Touro	AXP	MBA				&3-85

Name	Rank	School	Code	Degree	School2	Year
Bierman, Harold Jr.	Retir	Cornell	1996	PHD	55. Michigan	7-56
Bierstaker, James L.	Assoc	Villanova	ABEM	PHD	95. Conn	2004
Biggart, Timothy B.	Assoc	Berry	CMS	PHD	97. Fla St	8-05
Biggs, Stanley F.	Prof	Connecticut	BFA	PHD	78. Minnesota	9-84
KPMG Professor of Accounting						
Bigras, Diane		Quebec a Hul	FG	MSC		
Bilbeisi, Khamis	C-Ac	Troy-Dothan	AGM	PHD	89. Miss	1986
Bildersee, John S.	Prof	New York U	F	PHD	72. Chicago	1978
Billings, B. Anthony	Prof	Wayne State	XI	PHD	86. Tx A&M	1989
Billings, Bruce K.	Assoc	Florida St	F	PHD	96. Penn St	8-96
KPMG Fellow						
Billings, Mary	Asst	New York U		PHD	07 Indiana	2007
Billiot, Mary Jo	Assoc	New Mex St	FM	DBA	97. Miss St	&8-01
Bilodeau, Julien	Prof	Quebec-Montr	F	PHD	W Ontario	&6-87
Bindon, Kathleen R.	Assoc	Alabama	IX	PHD	81. Penn St	&1979
Bingham, Louise P.	Retir	S F Austin	1988	JD	52 Cumberl	&1963
Binkley, Max A.				PHD	53. Illinois	
Biondich, Nick	SLect	Minnesota	FA	MS	79 N Dakota	&1990
Biondo, John	C-Ac	SUNY Old Wes	FVXT	MBA	86 Hofstra	&1985
Bir, Poonam	Lect	Monash Univ	FAJO	MPHI	83 Delhi	&1996
Bird, Bruce M.	Prof	West Georgia	XP	JD	84 Cincinnati	&9-91
Bird, Cynthia E.			X	PHD	89. Georgia	&
Bird, Francis A.	Retir	Richmond	1994	PHD	68. Penn St	&1972
Bird, Karen S.	Lect	Michigan	F	MBA	88 Michigan	1988
Birk, Cynthia	Lect	Nevada-Reno	F	MA	86 Iowa	&1989
Birkett, Brenda S.	Retir	McNeese St	AF	PHD	80. LSU	&8-03
Birkett, William P.	Retir	New So Wales	ME	MEC	68 Sydney	&1962
Birnberg, Jacob G.	Emer	Pittsburgh	6-06	PHD	62. Minnesota	1964
Birr, Martin	SLect	Indiana-Indy	FVN	MBA	87 Indiana	* &1-89
Birrer, G. Eddy	Prof	Gonzaga	F	PHD	81 N Dakota	&1984
Birt, Jacqueline L.	Asst	Australian N	EF	MBUS	98 RMIT	2000
Birts, Anthony N.	SLect	Univ Bath	F	MBA	76 Manchest	1988
Biscontri, Robert G.	Asst	U Manitoba	MQ	PHD	02 Macquarie	2004
Bishop, Ashton C. Jr.	Retir	Jms Madison	2002	PHD	80. Okla St	2-81
Bishop, Bill J.			VF	PHD	61. Tx-Austin	&
Bishop, Helen E.	Lect	Massey-Alban	FY	MACC	96 Victoria	1999
Bishop, Ollie	Asst	NC-Pembroke	FD	MBA	N Carol	&1979
Bishop, Rachel A.			M	PHD	90. Arizona	
Bitenc, Sandra	Lect	Tx-Arlington	FM	MS	82 Wi-White	&8-05
Bitner, Larry N.	Prof	Shippensburg	MC	PHD	85. Geo Wash	* 1998
Bitter, Michael E.	Prof	Stetson	AFEF	PHD	94. Miss	&8-96
Bixler, Vencil J.	Retir	SW Missouri	1996	PHD	70. Missouri	1963
Finance Department						
Bizarro, Pascal A.	Asst	Mississippi	S	PHD	03. Alabama	2003
Bizzell, Allen H.	Retir	SW Texas St	2003	DBA	76. Miss St	&1999
Bjorndal, Endre	Assoc	Norwegian U	Q	DOEC	Norwegia	
Bjornenak, Trond	Prof	Norwegian U	M	DOEC		
Bjornson, Chris E.	Assoc	Indiana SE	FX	PHD	93. Illinois	&8-92
Blacconiere, Walter G.	Assoc	Indiana	F	PHD	88. U Wash	&1994
Ernst & Young Faculty Fellow						
Black, Angela	Prof	Aberdeen	FQ	PHD	95 Dundee	1999
Black, Clarence A.	Retir	Wis-Whitewat	1982	PHD	65. Missouri	&1964
Black, Ervin L.	Assoc	Brigham Yg	F	PHD	95. U Wash	9-00
Black, Homer A.	Retir	Florida St	1990	PHD	56. Michigan	&1957
407 North Ride; Tallahassee Florida 32303; 850-385-1095						
Black, Katherine D.	Prof	Utah Valley	X	LLM	89 Ca-Davis	&2005
Black, Martin L. Jr.	Deces	Duke	9-88	MBA	33 Nrthwstrn	&1930
Black, Robert L.	Retir	CS-S Marcos	2003	PHD	76. Minnesota	&1992
Black, Thomas G.	Prof	San Jose St	SMC	PHD	79. Missouri	* &1979
Blacker, Kelly	Asst	Mercy-NY	FMAV	MBA	87 Baruch	&9-98
Blackwell, Michael T.	Inst	West Liberty	AMPX	MBA	00 Wheeling	&2004
Blaine, Robert Earl	Retir	British Colu	1996	MBA	61 Berkeley	&1958
Blair, Allan G.			M	DBA	67. Harvard	
Blair, Bill	SLect	Macquarie Un	S	MEC	00 N Eng-Au	2000
Blair, Joe S.	Prof	Mars Hill	AMPF	MACC	73 S Carol	&1979
Blair, Ronald J.	SLect	Texas-Dallas	X	MBA	73 Oklahoma	&1999
Blakely, Edward J.	Retir	Wisconsin	1991	PHD	61. Tx-Austin	&1952
Blanc, Steven D.	Inst	No Illinois	X	JD	86 San Fran	&2006
Blanchard, Louis	Deces	Southern Ark	ACGP	MBA	Miss	&9-56
Blanchard, Phillip A.	SLect	Arizona	M	MBA	77 Fairl Dick	&1-98
Blanchette, Danielle	Prof	Sherbrooke	CFB	PHD	01 UQVAM	&1996
Blanchette, Michel		Quebec a Hul	FTVY	MBA		* &
Blanco, Huguette	Prof	Laurentian	FITY	PHD	94 Lancaster	7-84
Bland, Sandra	C-Pr	Bemidji St	XPS	PHD	02 E Illinois	&1992
Blank, Mark M.	Deces	San Fran St	SAB	PHD	84. Penn St	1987
Blankenbeckler, George M.			X	PHD	72. Georgia	&
Blankley, Alan I.	Assoc	N Car-Charl	FS	PHD	92. Tx A&M	1-04

Name	Rank	School	Code	Degree	Yr	University	Notes
Blann, Jack R.	Deces			PHD	78.	Wash U	
Blanthorne, Cynthia	Asst	Rhode Island	FX	PHD	00.	Ariz St	&2007
Blaskovich, Jennifer L.	Asst	Neb-Omaha	BCF	PHD	05.	Nebraska	&2005
Blattner, Emanuel	Lect	Norwegian Mg	FM	MBUS	81	Friboug	1991
Blatz, Robert E. Jr.	Assoc	Mich-Dearbor	LX	LLM	91	NYU	9-05
Blay, Allen D.	Asst	Florida St	AF	PHD	00.	Florida	& 8-07
Blazek, Michele M.			AFB	PHD	90.	Ariz St	* &
Blazer, Eric L.	C-Ac	Millersville		PHD	96	Va Tech	1996
Blazey, Lee	Lect	Case Western	X	BA	63	Case Wes	& 6-98
Bledsoe, Nancy L.			MCFP	PHD	93.	Alabama	
Blevins, Ronald	Retir	E New Mexico	C	PHD	01	N Mex St	2001
Blight, David	PLect	Coventry Un	DQ	MSC			9-71
Bline, Dennis M.	C-Pr	Bryant	BVFI	PHD	85.	Arkansas	1-92
Bliss, Mark	Asst	HongKon Tech	AF	PHD	06	City U	2004
Bloch, Fred A.	H	Adelaide	F	PHD	72	Adelaide	1969
Blocher, Edward J.	Prof	No Carolina	MAS	PHD	74.	Tx-Austin	* &1976
Block, Linda J.			FMP	PHD	78.	Purdue	&
Blocker, John G.	Retir	Kansas		PHD	34	Kansas	
Blommaert, Jos	Prof	Tilburg Univ	FE	PHD	95	Maastricht	&1997
Bloom, Robert	Prof	John Carroll	FIT	PHD	76.	NYU	1986
Bloomfield, Robert J.	Prof	Cornell	MTFB	PHD	92	Michigan	&9-91
Nicholas H. Noyes Professor of Management; Director of Graduate Studies							
Bloore, Ross	Asst	Bond Univ	ABFS	PHD	98	Bond	1992
Blosel, William F.	Assoc	Calif U Penn	CIP	MDA		Pittsburgh	1976
Blouch, William E.	Prof	Loyola-Maryl	FM	DBA	87.	Kent St	1984
Blouin, Jennifer	Asst	Pennsylvania	F	PHD	04.	N Carol	2003
Blount, Jimmie	Inst	Delta State	M	MPA		Delta St	&2004
Blount, Yvette	Lect	Macquarie Un	SM	MBA	00	N Eng-Au	&2005
Blue, Eugene R.	Asst	Howard	FMB	PHD	97.	Mich St	2000
Blue, Jon	Asst	Delaware	S	PHD	06	Va Comm	2006
Blue, Michael A.	Inst	Louisiana St	FCM	MS	91	LSU	& 8-95
Blue, Michael C.	Retir	Bloomsburg	2006	PHD	90	Idaho	* &1989
Blum, James D.	Dir	AICPA	1998	PHD	71	Mich St	&1983
1211 Ave of the Americas; New York NY 10036							
Blum, Lisa M.	Inst	Louisville	PLX	LLM	03	NYU	&1995
Blum, Marc P.		Law Frm-Balt		PHD	69.	Columbia	
Blumenfrucht, Israel	C-Pr	CUNY-Queens	XV	PHD	81	NYU	& 9-81
Boatsman, James R.	Prof	Arizona St	F	PHD	73.	Tx-Austin	&1986
KPMG Professor							
Bobek, Donna D.	Assoc	Cen Florida	FT	PHD	97.	Florida	& 1-97
Bochner, Paul	Asst	Fordham	XF	LLM	80	NYU	1997
Bockus, Keith A.				PHD	98.	Chicago	
Boczko, T.	Lect	Univ Hull	IFST	MA	95	Humbersi	9-01
Bodenhamer, Rosa M. B.		Self Employ		PHD	57.	Missouri	
Bodnar, George H.	Assoc	Duquesne	SC	PHD	75	Penn	1980
Boedigheimer, Michael	Prof	SW Minn St	SDG	MBA	68	St Cloud	* &1968
Boedker, C.	Lect	New So Wales		MCOM		NS Wales	
Boer, Germain B.	Prof	Vanderbilt	M	PHD	64.	LSU	& 9-77
Boersema, Jan M. J.				PHD	73.	Penn	
Boes, Richard F.	Prof	Idaho State	XMF	PHD	78.	Mich St	& 1-77
Bogart, Fred O.	Retir	Arizona	8-75	MS	44	Indiana	1946
Boggs, Robert E.	Retir	Miami U-Ohio	1984	DBA	66.	Indiana	&1962
Bohn, Helmut	LectA	Flinders Un	AY	BEC	96	Flinders	2-98
Bohs, George L.	Retir	St Joseph	1995	MBA	51	Temple	1984
Boisvert, Hugues	Prof	HEC-Montreal	BCMU	PHD	77	Stanford	* 6-86
Bokemeier, L. Charles	Lect	Michigan St	FG	DBA	83.	Kentucky	&2000
Boland, Richard J. Jr.	Retir	Case Western	MS	PHD	76.	Case Wes	& 8-90
Boldt, Margaret N.	Assoc	S Ill-Edward	MF	PHD	97.	Oklahoma	2006
Bolen, Dennis I.	Asst	Augustana SD	CFMN	PHD	00	N Dakota	* &1988
Boley, Richard	Retir	North Texas	2004	PHD	76.	Tx-Austin	&1989
Bolick, Bruce A.	C-Ac	Mary Hrdn-By	FXR	MS.	77	Tx Tech	&1987
Bollen, Laury	Assoc	Maastricht	FM	PHD	96	Maastricht	1985
Bolling, Rodger A.	Emer	No Illinois	2001	LLM	81	Florida	8-87
Bollinger, Everett R.			FM	DBA	62.	Indiana	&
Bollom, William J.	Retir	Wis-Oshkosh	1999	PHD	72.	Wisconsin	& 9-65
Bolt, Melesa A.		Kenan Sys	1999	PHD	99.	Va Tech	
Kenan Systems Corporation							
Bolt-Lee, Cynthia E.	Assoc	Citadel	PAX	MTX	88	S Carol	& 8-90
Bombera, Benedict B.	Retir	DePaul	1987	MBA	51	DePaul	1948
Bomeli, Edwin C.	Retir	Bowling Gr	1983	PHD	63.	Mich St	&1956
258 S. Church St; Bowling Green, OH 43402							
Bonawitz, Irving M.	Deces		3-03	DBA	64.	Mich St	&
Bonawitz, Mary Fenney			CPFJ	PHD	02.	Fla Intl	&
Bond, Christopher	Asst	St Joseph C	JLMR	JD		Maine	&2005
Bond, David	Lect	Tech-Sydney	FA	BBUS	02	Tech-Sydn	2003
Bond, James G.	Retir	Winthrop	2002	PHD	77.	S Carol	& 9-79
Bondhus, JoAnn	Prof	Wayne St Col	XL	LLM	83	Denver	1979

Name	Rank	School	Code	Degree	Yr	PhD School		Note
Boneck, Robin	Asst	Srthrn Utah	XL	JD	86	Brighm Yg		&2005
Boned, Josep Lluis	Asst	Pompeu Fabra			05	UB		
Bongiorni, Peter J.	Asst	Providence	FX	MS	56	Columbia		&1972
Bonner, Bill	Asst	Univ Regina		PHD	02	Calgary		&2003
Bonner, Sarah E.	Prof	So Calif	BFA	PHD	88.	Michigan		& 7-92
USC Accounting Associates Professor								
Bonnier, Carole	Assoc	ESCP deParis	CFMU	PHD	01	CNAT		1992
Boo, Hian Youn El'Fred	Assoc	Nanyang Tech	AF	PHD	01	Nanyang		&1993
Boockholdt, James L.	Retir	Samford	5-04	PHD	77	Alabama	*	& 8-91
122 Dewberry Drive; Lake Jackson, TX 77566; jlboockh@earthlink.net								
Boodai, Khalid M.		Kuwait	1989	PHD	80.	Missouri		
Booker, Donna M.	Asst	Cincinnati	BM	PHD	00.	Mich St		&2000
Booker, Jon A.	Prof	Tenn Tech	FAS	PHD	71.	North Tx	#	&1984
Booker, Quinton	C-Pr	Jackson St	FGN	DBA	84.	Miss St		&1981
Boon, Kym	Lect	Macquarie Un	A	BCOM	02	Macquarie		2003
Boone, Jeff P.	Assoc	Tx-S Antonio	F	PHD	94.	North Tx		&2005
Boone, Pieter W.	Lect	Vrije Univ	FM	MS	76	Vrije		1976
Boone, Ted	Lect	Kansas	S	MS	00	Penn St		2005
Boonlert-U-Thai, Kriengkrai	Lect	Chulalongkor	F	PHD	04.	Okla St		1995
Boonmak, Supattra	Assoc	Chulalongkor	DMS	MA	81	Detroit	#	1984
Boonyanet, Wachira	Asst	Chulalongkor	AFR	PHD	02	Southhamp		&1995
Boos, John D.	Prof	Ohio Wesley	VFMA	JD	66	Geo Wash		1983
Booth, W. Scott III	C-Pr	Pfeiffer	ACXG	MA	71	Appalach		& 8-82
Booth-Bell, Darlene	Inst	Benedict Col	M	MPM	95	Car Mellon		2000
Borden, James P.	Assoc	Villanova	MSCD	PHD	87.	Drexel		&1986
Borders, Barbara	Lect	Illinois St	MF	MS		Illinois		&2005
Borgia, Carl R.	Assoc	Fla Atlantic	VFI	PHD	74	Mass		&1987
Borini, Mario P.				PHD	64.	NYU		
Boritz, J. Efrim	Prof	Un Waterloo	SJAB	PHD	83.	Minnesota		&1983
Chartered Accountants Chair of Ontario								
Borke, John	Prof	Wis-Plattev	FPV	MAS	79	N Illinois		& 8-81
Borkowski, Susan C.	Prof	LaSalle	ICBS	PHD	88.	Temple		9-89
Borman, Robert G.	Retir	Duquesne	1995	MBA	64	Pittsburgh		&1964
Bornholtz, Evan F.	Retir	Kettering	DFM	MBA	66	Iowa		1966
Bornstein, Samuel	Asst	Kean	PXFM	MBA	76	NYU		&1978
Borovnjak, Juny	ALect	W Sydney	AFIF	MCOM	03	W Sydney		
Borowsky, Stuart	Assoc	Philadelphia	FPXM	MBA	67	Drexel		&1967
Borthick, A. Faye	Prof	Georgia St	S	DBA	82.	Tennessee	*	& 9-94
Bortz, Tiffany A.	SLect	Texas-Dallas	FPA	MSA	95	Tx A&M		&2001
Bos, Lawrence J.	Assoc	Cornerstone	PCM	MBA	74	Mich St		1-76
Boscia, Marian Larson	Assoc	King's Col	CMX	PHD	93.	Colorado		& 9-97
Boss, Scott	Asst	Bentley	S	PHD	07	Pittsburgh		8-07
Bossung, Sharon	Assoc	SUNY-Geneseo	AJX	MBA		Arkansas		& 9-88
Bost, Patricia J.	C-Ac	New Mex High	MCGN	PHD	92	Geo Wash	*	1998
Bostick, Lisa N.	Asst	Tampa	FA	DBA	01.	La Tech		&2001
Bostrom, Donald E.	Retir	North Dakota	1996	PHD	74.	North Tx		& 9-74
Bostrom, Warren	Asst	St John's-MN	NSPM	MBT	04	Minnesota		2004
Bostwick, Eric		Pensacola CC		PHD	03.	Miss		
Pensacola Christian College								
Bostwick, William J.	Retir	Geo Southern	2001	PHD	80	Geo St		&1980
Boterenbrood, D. Rob	Lect	Vrije Univ	FP	MS	02	Vrije		2004
Botica, Redmayne N.	Lect	Massey Univ	FQAV	MSC		Zagreb		1992
Botosan, Christine A.	Assoc	Utah	F	PHD	95.	Michigan		& 7-99
C. Roland Christensen Faculty Fellow								
Bottiglieri, William A.	Assoc	Iona	PX	JD	79	NYU Law		& 9-85
Bottin, Ronald R.	Dean	Missouri St	FSM	PHD	74.	Missouri		8-90
Bouattour, Mohamed	Asst	Univ Tunis	F	EXPC	91	IHEC		1995
Boubaker, Souheil	Inst	Univ Tunis	F	ECM	92	ISCAE		1998
Boucher, Joseph W.	SLect	Wisconsin	XL	JD	77	Wisconsin		1980
Bougen, Philip D.	Assoc	New Mexico	FI	PHD	87	LondonSE		1995
Bouillon, Marvin L.	C-Ac	Iowa State	CM	PHD	86.	Kansas		& 7-86
Boujos, Jocelyne	ALect	W Australia	T	LLB	90	W Austrl		1987
Bouley, Judith N.			I	PHD	91.	Alabama		&
Boulianne, Emilio	Asst	Concordia U	MS	PHD	00	Montreal		1999
Boumedienne, Emma	Asst	Univ Tunis	F	DEA	93	ISC		1993
Bourne, Amy	Inst	Oregon State	F	MS	96	Tx Tech		&2006
Bourne, Frances W.			M	PHD	78.	Okla St		
Bourne, Lowell D.			MC	PHD	77.	Wash U		
Bourouni, Mounira	Asst	Univ Tunis	M	DEA	98	ISCAE		1998
Bourque, Donald D.	Retir	SUNY-Albany	2001	PHD	65.	U Wash		1972
Bourret, Ralph	Asst	E New Mexico	A	PHD	05.	Miss St		2005
Boutell, Wayne S.	Retir	Cal-Berkeley	1993	PHD	63.	Berkeley		&1963
Bouwman, Marinus J.	Prof	Arkansas	BEMS	PHD	79.	Car Mellon		6-92
Bovee, Matthew	Asst	Vermont		PHD	04.	Kansas		
Mgt Information Systems Dept; 802-656-0502; bovee@bsad.uvm.edu								
Bowdery, A.	PLect	Liverpool JM	MF	ACA				1996
Bowen, Linda C.	Adj	No Carolina	F	PHD	72.	Geo St		& 9-74

Name	Rank	School		Degree		University	
Bowen, Paul L.	Assoc	Florida St	SA	PHD	92.	Tennessee	&1-06
Bowen, Robert M.	Prof	U Washington	MF	PHD	78.	Stanford	9-78
Bowens, William H. M.	Retir	Norfolk St	1989	MBA	59	NYU	9-72
Bower, James B.	Retir	Wisconsin	1988	PHD	60.	Tx-Austin	&1947
Bowers, William K.	Assoc	SC-Salkehatc	X	PHD	94.	S Carol	&
Bowhill, Bruce	PLect	U Portsmith	M	BSC			1984
Bowlby, G. Robert	Retir	Widener	1995	MBA	69	Temple	&1962
Bowles, Windell	Deces	Bellarmine	1993	MBA	62	Louisville	&1960
Bowlin, William F.	H-Pr	N Dakota St	CMNG	PHD	84.	Tx-Austin	2007
Bowman, Robert G. (Jerry)	Prof	U Auckland	F	PHD	78.	Stanford	&1987
Bowrey, Graham	Lect	U Wollongong	FTM	MCOM	05	Wollong	&2006
Bowrin, Anthony R.		West Indies		PHD	00.	S Illinois	
Bows, Albert J.	Retir	Emory	1979	MBA	35	Nrthwstrn	1975
Boyas, Elise A.	Asst	Robt Morris	F	PHD	91.	Rutgers	* &8-05
Boyce, Gordon	SLect	Macquarie Un	SA	BCOM	94	Deakin	1997
Boyce, L. Fred	Retir	NE Missouri	1991	MS	47	Dartmouth	&1985
Boyd, F. Virgil		Chicago IL	1988	PHD	56.	Nrthwstrn	&
Boyd, James H.	Retir	Arizona St	2001	PHD	76.	Tx-Austin	&1976
Boyd, Joseph L.	Dean	Txs Southern	X	PHD	77.	S Carol	&2001
Boyd, Ralph L.				PHD	42.	Illinois	
Boyd, Sanithia	Assoc	Am U Sharjah	FAO	DED	96	Grambling	* &2004
Boyd, Thomas	Prof	St John's	XP	MBA	62	NYU	&1975
Boyer, Benoit	C-Pr	Sacred Heart	F	PHD	87.	UCLA	&1997
Boyer, Glen L.	Retir	Brigham Yg	2000	PHD	72	N Dakota	9-67
Boyett, Arthur S.	Visit	Guilford	FAT	PHD	80.	Tx Tech	&2005
Boylan, Robert L.	D-As	Jacksonvil U	CEFX	PHD	90	Duke	&2003
Boylan, Scott J.	Assoc	Wash & Lee	F	PHD	95.	Ohio St	&1999
Boyle, Edmund J.	Assoc	Rhode Island	AO	PHD	90.	Penn St	&1988
Boyle, MT	Lect	Univ Ulster	F	BSC			2-90
Boyles, Jesse V.	Assoc	Florida	X	PHD	75.	Florida	&9-74
Boynton, Charles E. IV	Retir	North Texas	2000	PHD	85.	Illinois	&1990
Boynton, William C.			FA	PHD	76.	Mich St	&
Boys, Noel	Teach	U Melbourne	BEFY	BBUS	83	RMIT	2002
Bozanich, Peter	Deces		1976	PHD	76.	S Carol	
Boze, Ken M.	Prof	Alaska-Ancho	MCF	PHD	83	Arkansas	* &1989
Bozec, Richard	Assoc	Univ Ottawa	FG	PHD	01	Quebec	1997
Bozec, Yves	Asst	HEC-Montreal	FM	PHD	04	HEC-Mont	* 1-04
Brabazon, Anthony	SLect	Un Cl Dublin	CDM	MS	95	Kingston	* &1992
Brachen, Harry J.				DBA	63.	Harvard	
Bracken, Robert M.	Retir	So Alabama	2002	DBA	83.	Miss St	&1985
Brackner, James W.	Retir	Utah State	2001	PHD	84.	Alabama	* &9-81
Brackney, Kennard S. Jr.	Assoc	Appalach St	FI	PHD	90.	N Carol	&2003
Bradbury, Michael E.	Prof	Massey-Alban	FYI	PHD	90	Auckland	&2006
Bradely, EM	Lect	Univ Ulster	F	PHD			9-02
Bradford, Bruce M.	Assoc	Fairfield	FMT	DBA	89.	Memphis	&1994
Bradford, Jorja F.	Asst	Alabama St	AF	MBA	98	Aub-Mont	1999
Bradford, Marianne	Asst	N Carol St	S	PHD	01.	Tennessee	&2003
Bradish, Richard D.			XF	PHD	63.	U Wash	&
Bradley, Bryce T.		Private Prac		PHD	79.	Nebraska	
Bradley, Cassie F.			NSX	PHD	94.	Alabama	
Bradley, David B.	Prof	Lyndon State	MAX	MBA	82	Plymouth	# * 9-81
Bradley, Joseph	Asst	Mo-Rolla	FMA	PHD	04	Claremont	2006
Bradley, Michael P.	Retir	Augusta St	2002	PHD	87.	Ariz St	&1993
Bradley, Randy	Asst	Tennessee	S	PHD	06	Auburn	8-06
Bradley, Wray E.	Assoc	Tulsa	BXE	PHD	99.	Arkansas	* &8-98
Bradley-McKee, Linda J.	Assoc	Charleston	XFH	PHD	93.	North Tx	&1993
Bradshaw, John H.	Lect	Victoria NZ	CEM	MCOM	90	Port Eliz	1998
Bradshaw, Mark T.	Assoc	Harvard	F	PHD	00.	Michigan	2000
Bradshaw, Thornton F.				DCS	51.	Harvard	
Bradwick, Faye	Assoc	Indiana U-PA	X	LLM	88	Geotown	&1991
Brady, Joseph A.	Inst	Delaware	S	MBA	77	Drexel	9-90
Brady, Rodney H.				DBA	66.	Harvard	
Brady, Thomas J.	Assoc	Dayton	FS	PHD	82.	St Louis	1981
Braide, January				PHD	81.	Missouri	
Brailsford, Timothy J.	H-Pr	U Queensland	F	PHD	94	Monash	&2002
Braiotta, Louis Jr.	Assoc	SUNY-Bingham	AF	MBA	75	Iona	&1981
Brajcich, Daniel	Retir	Gonzaga	2004	JD	45	Gonzaga	&1946
Brand, Vivienne	LectB	Flinders Un	LWEJ	LLM	92	London	2-95
Brandon, Charles H.	Prof	Rollins	CM	PHD	72.	Georgia	&1982
Brandon, Chrisopher	CIAs	Ind/Pur-Col	2007	PHD	01.	Purdue	
Indiana-Purdue University; Columbus, Indiana							
Brandon, Dorothy M.	Retir	E Carolina	1987	MBA	62	U Wash	&1955
Brandon, Duane M.	Asst	Auburn	A	PHD	03.	Va Tech	8-03
Brandon-Pollard, Sonia	Lect	U Portsmith		MSC			2004
Brandt, Lloyd Jr.	Retir	Loyola-N Orl	2001	PHD	73.	LSU	& 9-81
Brannan, Rodger L.	Assoc	Minn-Duluth	GNEC	PHD	89.	Nebraska	& 8-89
Branson, Bruce C.	Assoc	N Carol St	FV	PHD	92.	Fla St	8-92

Branson, Leonard L.	C-Ac	Il-Springfld	BSMF	PHD	90.	St Louis	*	&1987
Brant, Steve	Inst	S Ill-Edward	FM	MS	79	Illin St		1999
Brashier, April	Asst	Freed Hardem	PC	ABD		Alabama		8-05
Brasseaux, J. Herman	Retir	New Orleans	1991	PHD	58.	LSU		&1959
Braswell, Daniel E.			F	PHD	00.	S Illinois		
Braswell, Michael	Asst	San Fran St	FA	PHD	07.	Missouri		2007
Brathen, Tore	H-Pr	Norwegian Mg	LX	DJUR	98	Oslo		1990
Brathwaite, Faye	Asst	Athens State		DBA	06	Nova SE		2005
Braun, Gary P.	Assoc	Txs-El Paso	ABFI	PHD	95.	Arizona		9-94
Braun, Karen Wilken	Asst	Case Western	FM	PHD	96.	Conn		& 7-06
Braun, Robert L.	Assoc	SE Louisiana	AF	PHD	94.	LSU	#	8-96
Braun, Robert M.				PHD	81.	NYU		&
Bravenec, Lorence L.	Prof	Texas A&M	X	LLM	66	NYU		&8-71
Bray, Warren C.	Deces	CS-L Angeles	6-80	PHD	58	NYU		&1959
Brazel, Joseph F.	Asst	N Carol St	AF	PHD	04.	Drexel		2003
Brazelton, Julia K.			X	PHD	85.	S Carol		
Brazina, Paul R.	Asst	LaSalle	FAM	MBA	72	Penn St	# *	&9-73
Breakfield, Robert H.	Prof	Winthrop	XL	LLM	75	Boston U		9-76
Breaux, Kevin	Asst	Nicholls St	CFM	PHD	04.	LSU		8-03
Brecha, Sonia A.	Deces	Wright State	3-98	DBA	83.	Kent St		&9-76
Brecht, H. David	Prof	CS-Sacrament	CM	PHD	74.	Tx-Austin		&9-75
Breen, Heimie E.				PHD	53.	Illinois		
Breitkreitz, Duane	Inst	Thompson Riv		MBA		City		1979
Bremser, Wayne G.	C-Pr	Villanova	BKEM	PHD	74.	Penn		&1974
Brenan, Kathleen	Assoc	Ashland	DP	MA	82	Bowl Gr		&9-84
Brennan, Edward W.	Retir	Pennsylvania	1987	PHD	66	Penn		1953
Brennan, Julia M.	Asst	Mass-Boston	X	PHD	03.	Kentucky		8-03
Brennan, Niamh	Prof	Un Cl Dublin	FIY	PHD	95	Warwick		&1980
Brennan, Paul J.	Asst	Mn St-Mankat	X	PHD	99.	S Illinois		2002
Brennan, W. John	Retir	Saskatchewan	2000	PHD	72.	Michigan		&1967
Brennen, Edward W.	Retir	Pennsylvania	1979	PHD	66	Penn		1953
Brenner, Vincent C.	Prof	Stetson	FZT	PHD	69.	Penn St		&8-98
David M. Beights Professor of Accountancy								
Brent, Averil R.			F	PHD	87.	Cornell		&
Bressler, Linda	Asst	Houston-Down	S	DBA	00	Sarasota		2001
Breton, Gaetan	Prof	Quebec-Montr	F	PHD		London		&6-90
Brett, Frederic A.	Deces			PHD	58.	Alabama		
Brewer, Carl W.	Assoc	Sam Houston	TM	PHD	81.	Houston		&9-88
Brewer, Peter C.	Assoc	Miami U-Ohio	M	PHD	94.	Tennessee		1994
Brewis, Joanna	Asst	Univ Essex	BM	PHD	96	Manchest		1999
Briand, Louise		Quebec a Hul	AJU	PHD				&
Bricker, Robert J.	Prof	Case Western	FABH	PHD	87.	Case Wes		&8-90
Ernst & Young Faculty Fellow								
Brickhouse, Frasier W.	Retir	Virginia St	2004	MBA	65	NYU		9-67
Brickler, Kim	Asst	Lindenwood	AFPS	MBA		St Louis		&2003
Brickman, Deborah	Asst	CUNY-Stn Isl	DA	MBA	85	CUNY-Brk		&1979
Brickner, Daniel R.	Assoc	E Michigan	FAM	PHD	02.	Kent St		&2000
Bridges, Alan	Lect	Tech-Sydney	BCEG	MA	81	Macquarie		1975
Bridges, Gary	SLect	Tx-S Antonio	FM	PHD	99	Co-Denve		&8-04
Bridges, Jack C.	Retir	Samford	1993	MBA	56	Auburn		&8-88
Bridges, Wilbur	Retir	SW Missouri	2000	MBA	60	Arkansas		9-65
Brief, Richard P.	Retir	New York U	2002	PHD	64	Columbia		1961
Briers, Michael L.	SLect	New So Wales	MB	PHD	97	NS Wales		1988
Briggs, Gary P.	Assoc	SUNY-Brockpo	CEFN	MBA	76	Indiana		&1979
Briggs, John W.	Asst	Jms Madison	SPD	PHD	04.	Va Tech		9-02
Brighton, Gerald D.	Emer	Illinois	1989	PHD	53.	Illinois		&1954
Briginshaw, John	Asst	Pepper-L Ang	FM	PHD	03	Berkeley		2004
Brill, Robert J.	Retir	St Bonaventu	2003	MBA	61	Pittsburgh	*	&1961
Briloff, Abraham J.	Retir	CUNY-Baruch	1991	PHD	65.	NYU		&1944
52 Gremercy Park; New York NY 10010								
Brimble, Mark	Lect	Griffith Un	FQ	BCOM	98	Griffith		2000
Brin, Clifford F.	Retir	No Michigan	2001	DBA	74	Ind No		&1971
Briner, Russell F.	Prof	Tx-S Antonio	AMF	PHD	76.	Okla St		&1988
Brinker, Thomas M.	Assoc	Arcadia	AX	MST	93	St Joe		&9-97
Brinkman, Sidney E.	Retir	Wichita St	1993	MS	66	Wichita St		&1958
Briscoe, Nat R.	Prof	NW St of LA	CFMG	PHD	88.	Fla St		&1997
Poindexter Fund Professor of Accounting								
Bristol, James T.			CN	PHD	78.	Tx-Austin	*	&
Briston, Richard J.	Retir	Univ Hull	TI	BSC	58	London		1-85
Broce, Patricia			F	DBA	91.	Kentucky		&
Brock, Barbara H.	Deces	Caninius	1992	PHD	79.	SUNY-Buf	#	1975
Brock, Glenda C.	Prof	CS-Pomona	XGN	PHD	89.	Miss		&9-92
Brock, Horace R.	Retir	North Texas	1994	PHD	54.	Tx-Austin		&1954
Broden, Barry C.	Prof	Hartford	X	DBA	77.	Maryland		&1983
Broderick, Dale G.			1994	PHD	73.	Columbia		&
Dale Broderick Associates; 173 Packers Falls Rd; Durham NH 03874								

Brodshatzer, Arthur		San Diego CA	1992	DBA	64.	S Calif	&
4502 New Hampshire St #5227; San Diego CA 92116							
Brody, Richard G.	Assoc	New Mexico	ABO	PHD	93.	Ariz St	&
Broers, Larry	Assoc	Myers	MA	MBA	87	Bald-Wal	&1988
Broeze, G. B. (Ed)	Lect	Vrije Univ	A	PHD		Amsterdam	2005
Broihahn, Michael A.	C-Ac	Barry	FAJ	MBA	73	Wisconsin	# * &8-88
Broman, Amy J.			X	PHD	87.	Michigan	
Bromley, Robert G.	Prof	Cen Michigan	SA	PHD	84.	Nebraska	&1983
Bromwich, Michael	Prof	London Econ	FMT	BSC	65	London	* 1985
Chartered Inst of Mgt Accountants Professor of Accounting & Financial Mgt							
Bronson, Scott N.	Asst	Michigan St	A	PHD	06.	Tennessee	&2006
Brook, George C.	Deces		6-76	PHD	48.	Chicago	
Brookhart, Jess	Assoc	Miss Vall St	AC	PHD		Alabama	2002
Brooks, Ann	Lect	New Mexico	F	MBA		New Mex	2002
Brooks, Eugene H.	Retir	Elon	5-92	PHD	83.	N Carol	&1988
403 Overland Drive; Chapel Hill NC 27514							
Brooks, John E.		Intel Corp	1995	PHD	81.	Mich St	
16011 N 49th Pl; Scottsdale AZ 85254							
Brooks, Kelli	Lect	Angelo State		MPAC	04	AngeloSt	2005
Brooks, Leonard J.	Prof	Univ Toronto	MWJ	MBA	67	Toronto	&1974
Brooks, Richard C.	Prof	W Virginia	FGN	PHD	91.	LSU	8-91
Brooks, William A.		Paola KS	1994	PHD	70.	Kansas	
932 Prairie; Paola KS 66071; 913-294-4967							
Brooks, William S.	Retir	SW Okla St	1995	MBA	49	SW Ok St	1983
Broom, Lowell S.	Prof	Alabama-Birm	AN	DBA	80.	La Tech	&1988
Broome, O. Whitfield	Prof	Virginia	FIV	PHD	71.	Illinois	& 9-67
Frank Kaulback Jr. Professor							
Brouard, Francois	Asst	Carleton Un	BEFX	DBA	04		&1999
Brough, Kathleen	Assoc	St Peters	FCMX	MBA		Rutgers	&1981
Brown, Bernard P.	Asst	Gallaudet		MBA		Gallaudet	
Brown, Betty C.	Prof	Louisville	AF	PHD	85.	Va Tech	# * &1983
Brown, Carol E.	Assoc	Oregon State	MS	PHD	89	Oregon St	&1978
Brown, Charles	Asst	Penn St-Erie	PM	PHD	02.	Kent St	& 8-01
Brown, Clifford D.	Prof	Clarkson	AGVX	PHD	68.	Mich St	* 2005
Brown, Clifton E.	Prof	Illinois	BCM	PHD	78.	Florida	8-78
H. T. Scovill Professor							
Brown, Darrell L.	D-Ac	Portland St	SBM	PHD	94.	Utah	1994
Les Fahey/KPMG Accounting Fellow							
Brown, Darryl L.	Asst	Illinois St	X	PHD	06.	Arizona	2005
Brown, David	SLect	Tech-Sydney	BCM	PHD	00	Tech-Sydn	2000
Brown, Donald W.	Retir	Iowa State	1990	MBA	47	Denver	&1951
2521 Northwood Drive; Ames IA 50010							
Brown, Douglas S.	Prof	Mont St-Bill	FAOL	MBA	79	Colorado	&1988
Brown, Elizabeth	Assoc	Keene State	CDFM	EDD	93	Mass	1987
Brown, Gerald C.	Retir	Otterbein	1995	PHD	67.	Ohio St	& 9-88
Brown, H. Donald	Asst	Brock Univ	EM	MSC	85	Saskatch	* &7-85
Brown, Helen	Asst	Boston Coll	ASF	PHD	03.	Wisconsin	2004
Brown, Homer A. Jr.	Retir	Oklahoma	1990	DBA	68.	Indiana	&1956
Brown, Howard J.	Retir	St Johns	1991	PHD	75	NYU	1981
Brown, James	Lect	Napier Univ		MSC			1999
Brown, James E.	Retir	No Kentucky		PHD	62.	Florida	
Brown, James F. Jr.	Prof	Nebraska	CM	DBA	81.	Tennessee	* 1980
Brown, Jennifer L.	Asst	Arizona St	X	PHD	07	Tx-Austin	2007
Brown, John A.	Inst	So Miss	FM	MPA	75	S Miss	& 8-01
Brown, Judy A.	Prof	Victoria NZ	FTW	PHD	95	Victoria	1988
Brown, Kenneth W.	Retir	SW Missouri	D-00	PHD	92.	Arkansas	& 8-88
Brown, Kevin F.	Asst	Wright State	AFT	PHD	01.	Case Wes	& 9-04
Brown, Larry	Inst	Oregon State	AF	BS	73	Oregon St	&2005
Brown, Lawrence D.	Prof	Georgia St	FM	PHD	75	Rochester	9-97
J. Mack Robinson Professor							
Brown, Michael	Lect	Mo-St Louis	FM	MS	78	Walsh	&2001
Brown, Michael H.	C-As	Millikin	FXV	PHD	94.	Miss	&2002
Brown, Michael R.	Retir	Montana	2004	JD	69	Montana	& 9-71
Brown, Molly G.	Inst	Jms Madison	FGN	MSA	99	Jms Mad	& 8-02
Brown, Nerissa C.	Asst	So Calif	M	PHD	05.	Maryland	2005
Brown, Nigel	SLect	U Glamorgan	BF	BA	79	Kent	& 9-98
Brown, Noel	SLect	So Queensind	DSXF	MEC	96	N Eng-Au	&1986
Brown, Paul J.	Lect	Tech-Sydney	FA	MBA	04	Tech-Sydn	2005
Brown, Paul R.	Dean	Lehigh	FA	PHD	79.	Tx-Austin	&2007
Brown, Pennye		Austin Peay	PF				
Brown, Philip A.	C-Ac	Harding	FTBR	PHD	99.	Miss	&1987
Brown, Philip R.	Prof	New So Wales	F	PHD	68.	Chicago	&
Brown, R. Gene	Exec	Bus-WoodsiCA	1994	PHD	61.	Ohio St	
3417 Woodside Rd; Woodside CA 94062							
Brown, Richard A.	SLect	Dundee	DQS	PHD	70	Newcastle	2001
Brown, Richard E.	C-Pr	Kent State	GMNO	DPA	68	Harvard	8-84

Name	Rank	Institution	Code	Degree	Yr	School	
Brown, Robert M.	H-Pr	Virg Tech	SM	PHD	77.	Geo St	1977
R. B. Pamplin Professor of Accounting and Information Systems							
Brown, Ronald D.	Deces	Wilfrid Laur	1998	PHD	77.	Syracuse	1973
Brown, Sarah Ruth			FGS	DBA	90.	Miss St	&
Brown, Stephen	Asst	Emory	F	PHD	01.	Nrthwstrn	&9-00
Brown, Sudro			FVD	PHD	79.	Wisconsin	&
Brown, Terra	Lect	Tx-Arlington	FM	MPA	05	Tx-Arlin	&1-07
Brown, Victor H.	Retir	George Mason	1999	PHD	57.	SUNY-Buf	* &1993
Brown, William D.	Asst	Syracuse	F	PHD	01.	Mass	&2003
Brown, William P.	C-Ac	Longwood	XS	PHD	85.	N Carol	& 8-87
Brownell, Peter			M	PHD	79.	Berkeley	
Brownell, Wede	Asst	Central Okla	CF	PHD	04.	Okla St	8-05
Browning, C. Edward	Retir	NW Missouri	2001	PHD	71.	Missouri	1961
Brownlee, E. Richard II	H-Pr	Virg-Grad	FMIT	PHD	75.	Geo St	& 8-75
Brozovsky, John A.	Assoc	Virg Tech	BFMX	PHD	90.	Colorado	&1989
William S. Gay Research Fellow							
Brubeck, Helen	Lect	San Jose St		ABD		Berkeley	1999
Bruce, E.	SLect	London Metro	AFX	BSC			2002
Brucker, William	Asst	Robt Morris	X	JD		Duquesne	& 9-82
Brudvik, Arthur	Assoc	Norwegian U	X				
Bruggen, Alexander	Asst	Maastricht	M	PHD	05	Maastricht	2001
Brugger, Karl A.			FMN	PHD	78.	Ariz St	&
Bruha, George R.		Arthur Ander		PHD	72.	Nrthwstrn	&1976
Bruington, Rex G.	Asst	Miss Women	A	MS		Miss St	&1994
Brumett, Clifford			ADF	PHD	93.	Kent St	
Brumm, Joan M.				PHD	96.	LSU	
Brummet, R. Lee	Retir	No Carolina	1986	PHD	57.	Michigan	&1970
Brunetti, Frank L.	Prof	F Dick-Teane	X	LLM		NYU	9-80
Brunn, David	Prof	Carthage	FMCV	MBA	62	Nrthwstrn	* &1993
Rogers Palmer Distinguished Professor of Business Administration							
Bruno, Joan D.	Prof	Houston-Cl L	FT	PHD	69.	LSU	& 9-75
Bruns, Sharon M.	Prof	Northeastern	FM	PHD	81.	Geo St	9-80
Bruns, William J. Jr.	Lect	Northeastern	FM	PHD	63.	Berkeley	2001
Bruton, Carol M.			ATFM	PHD	89.	U Wash	# * &
Bryan, Barry J.	Prof	Tx Christian	AJS	PHD	94.	Tx A&M	&
Bryan, Daniel M.	Asst	U Wash-Tacom	FSM	PHD	02.	Oregon	&2007
Bryan, E. Lewis	Retir	Suffolk	2005	DBA	80.	Geo Wash	&2002
Bryan, Lois D.	H-Ac	Robt Morris	FX	DSC	06	Rbt Morr	& 9-82
Bryan, Stephen H.	Assoc	Wake Fr-MBA	F	PHD	94.	NYU	8-99
Bryant, Jeffrey J.	D-Ac	Wichita St	X	PHD	93.	Tx Tech	&1993
BKD Faculty Fellow							
Bryant, Keith Jr.	Emer	Alabama-Birm	1995	PHD	67	Alabama	* 1969
Bryant, Linnae W.	Asst	Chicago St	LPNA	JD		DePaul	&1992
Bryant, Murray J.	Assoc	West Ontario	M	PHD	83.	Cincinnati	&1980
Bryant, Scott M.	Lect	Baylor	P	MACC	03	Baylor	2003
Bryant, Stephanie M.	D-Ac	South Fla	S	PHD	96.	LSU	& 8-91
Dan R. and Tina P. Johnson Distinguished Professor of Accounting							
Bryant-Kutcher, Lisa L.	Asst	Oregon	F	PHD	99.	Colorado	&2003
Bryer, Robert A.	Prof	Un Warwick	FHIT	PHD	77	Warwick	
Bryne, G.	Lect	Univ Ulster	B	BSC			1994
Bryson, R. Eugene	Assoc	Alabama-Hunt	FHV	PHD	76.	Geo St	&1976
Bubalo, Nigel	Lect	W Sydney-Nep	CFJX	MCOM	96	W Sydney	1998
Bublitz, Bruce O.	Prof	Mich-Dearbor	F	PHD	82.	Illinois	& 8-05
Buchan, Howard	Asst	SUNY-Oneonta	JBX	PHD	04.	SUNY-Bin	& 8-02
Buchan, Leslie J.	Deces			PHD	43.	Illinois	
Buchanan, Keith	Lect	Appalach St	PX	MS	79	Appalach	&2006
Buchanan, Phillip G.	Assoc	George Mason	FV	PHD	83.	Temple	&1981
Buche, Mari W.	Asst	Mich Tech	S	PHD	03.	Kansas	
Buchheit, Steve	Assoc	Texas Tech	CH	PHD	97.	Tx-Austin	9-01
Rawls Professor							
Buchin, Stanley I.				DBA	62.	Harvard	
Buchl, Carol E.	Retir	No Michigan	2001	MA	70	N Mich	&1973
Buchman, Thomas A.	Assoc	Colorado	F	PHD	76.	Illinois	&1974
Buchoff, Barry S.	Asst	Towson	CFMT	MBA		Loyola	&1972
Buck, Carroll	Lect	San Jose St	FM	MBA	82	Maine	2002
Buck, Paul M.	C-Pr	Plymouth St	FXAM	MS	68	Northeas	& 9-72
Buckby, Sherrena	Lect	Queensld Tec	A	MBUS	81	Queensl	& 1-90
Buckhoff, Thomas A.	Assoc	Geo Southern	PCJ	PHD	95.	Kentucky	&2004
Buckhold, Jerry W.			XF	PHD	86.	Ariz St	&
Buckland, Roger	Prof	Aberdeen	FGI	MPHL	85	York	1993
Buckless, Frank A.	H-Ac	N Carol St	AF	PHD	89.	Mich St	&1988
KPMG Professor							
Buckley, C. James	Retir	Mesa State	AF	MS	70	Colo St	&1972
Buckley, Charles	Retir	Scranton	1993	MBA	55	Scranton	1957
Buckley, John W.	Retir	UCLA	1999	PHD	64.	U Wash	1964
Buckman, A. Gregory	Retir	CS-Hayward	1990	PHD	72.	UCLA	1-76
Buckmaster, Dale A.	Prof	Delaware	FH	PHD	73.	Penn St	& 9-70

Buckner, Kathryn C.	Retir	Georgia St	1988	DBA	71.	Geo St	&9-66
Buckwell, Lloyd J.	Retir	Indiana NW	1995	PHD	69.	Minnesota	1985
Budd, Cassy JH	Assoc	Brigham Yg	FAX	MACC	02	Utah St	&2005
Budd, Charlene Spoede	Retir	Baylor	2005	PHD	82.	Tx-Austin	* &8-73
Buddensick, Janice	Asst	Wagner	PAQ	MBA	85	Pace	&
Budding, G. T. (Tjerk)	Inst	Vrije Univ	BGN	MS	97	Vrije	2001
Budge, Bruce P.	Retir	Montana	1999	PHD	68.	Minnesota	&1981
Budwitz, Peter A.	Retir	Central Conn	2003	MBA	63	Bucknell	&9-71
Buehlmann, David M.	Deces	Neb-Omaha	9-03	PHD	75.	Illinois	&1975
Buerger, Kurt H.	H-Pr$	Angelo State	FVGI	PHD	71	Kentucky	* &1983
Bueu, Kevin	Asst	Augustana SD	EFJX	MBA	86	USD	8-06
Bugeja, Martin	Lect	Univ Sydney	FY	PHD	04	Sydney	&1997
Buhr, Nola	Assoc	Saskatchewan	FHW	PHD	94	W Ontario	&2000
Buijink, Willem F. J.	Prof	Tilburg Univ	FE	PHD	77	Antwerp	&2001
Bujaki, Merridee L.	C-Ac	Univ Ottawa	FA	PHD	96	Queen's	&1995
Bukics, Rose Marie L.	C-Pr	Lafayette	TFIK	MBA	80	Lehigh	&1980
Thomas Roy and Lura Forrest Jones Professor							
Bukovinsky, David M.	Assoc	Wright State	MCPG	PHD	93.	Kentucky	&9-99
Bukowy, Stephen J.	Assoc	NC-Pembroke	MNCS	PHD	93.	Georgia	& 8-94
Bull, Ivan O.	Retir	Illinois	1998	PHD	87.	Illinois	&1987
Bullard, Ruth H.	Retir	Tx-S Antonio	1991	PHD	72.	Tx-Austin	& 7-74
Bullen, Maria Lombardi	Assoc	Clayton St	BAF	PHD	82.	UCLA	&2006
Buller, Lewis C.		F		PHD	66.	Illinois	&
Bullis, Debra A.			MCB	PHD	94.	Tx-Austin	&
Bulloch, James	Deces	Inst Mgt Act	9-95	PHD	61.	Ohio St	* &
Bullock, Charles	Dean	Houston-Vict	X	LLM	84	Denver	9-96
Bullock, James H.	Retir	New Mex St	1996	PHD	74.	Okla St	& 8-72
Bulmash, Gary F.	VAsst	Maryland	FMA	DBA	74.	Maryland	&2005
Bump, Edwin A.	Retir	East Wash	1999	PHD	70.	Missouri	* &1973
Bundy, Tracy L.	Asst	La-Lafayette	FX	ABD		La Tech	8-06
Bunker, Gaylen	Assoc	Westminst-UT	FMNU	MBA		Utah	&1989
Bunn, Radie G.	Prof	Missouri St	X	JD	77	Wm Mitch	8-84
Bunsis, Howard	Prof	E Michigan	FGN	PHD	93.	Chicago	& 5-98
Burba, David	Inst	Bowling Gr	P	MBA	90	Toledo	
Burch, John G.	Retir	Nevada-Reno	1998	PHD	68.	Alabama	1986
Burckel, Daryl V.	Prof	McNeese St	FX	DBA	86.	Miss St	&1992
Burdick, Keith H.		Laramie WY	1988	DBA	70.	Colorado	&
Burge, Christy A.	Inst	Louisville	PS	MBA	87	Bowl Gr	7-00
Burgess, Deanna O.	Assoc	Fl GulfCoast	F	PHD	91.	Cen Fla	&1997
Burgstahler, David C.	Prof	U Washington	FMA	PHD	81.	Iowa	&1980
Burilovich, Linda	Prof	E Michigan	XF	PHD	90	Michigan	& 1-91
Burke, Brian E.	Retir	British Colu	1980	DBA	63.	U Wash	1951
Burke, Jacqueline A.	Assoc	Hofstra	P	PHD	00	NYU	& 8-93
Burke, John L.	Assoc	Univ Otago	FQT	PHD	72	Toronto	1998
Burke, John T.	Retir	W Michigan	1990	PHD	58.	Mich St	&1962
Burke, Kimberly G.	D-Pr	Millsaps	ASFB	PHD	95.	Okla St	&1995
Kelly Gene Cook Chair of Business Administration							
Burke, Mimi			ACFM	PHD	78.	Tx A&M	&
Burke, Richard C.			FTEW	PHD	76.	U Wash	
Burkett, Homer H.	Retir	Mississippi	6-05	DBA	72.	Fla St	&1977
Burkett, Jimmy	Lect	So Carolina	MX	MX	95	S Carol	&1995
Burkett, Teresa	Assoc	Tiffin	PQ	MAC	85	Bowl Gr	&
Burkette, Gary D.	C-Ac	East Tenn St	A	PHD	94.	Va Tech	&1992
Burkey, Julie L.	C-Ac	Goldey-Beacm	FA	DBA	02	Sarasota	& 9-94
Burks, Bryan	Dean	Harding	SFPC	DBA	06	Nova SE	&1995
Burks, Eddy J.	Assoc	Troy	X	DBA	88.	La Tech	&2006
Burling, Shaylee	Asst	Hardin-Simm		MBA	99	HardSimm	2004
Burm, Karel	Asst	Tilburg Univ	FT	MBA	96	Tilburg	1998
Burnaby, Priscilla A.	Prof	Bentley	FO	PHD	82.	Tx A&M	&1976
Burnam, Paul W.	Retir	SW Louisiana	1979	PHD	59.	Alabama	1942
Burnell, Mary A.	Asst	Fairmont	DFMS	MPA	85	W Virginia	&1989
Burnett, John J.	Retir	Tenn-Martin	1992	MS	67	Miss	&9-67
Burnett, Mary Joyce	Retir	Txs Wesleyan	2002	EDD	72	North Tx	1963
Burnett, Royce D.	Asst	U Miami	M	PHD	03.	Okla St	* 2003
Burnett, Sharon K.			CNP	PHD	98.	Okla St	
Burney, J F	Retir	Austin Peay	1995	PHD	69.	Alabama	&1959
Burns, Cathleen S.	Inst	Colorado	CM	PHD	95	N Mex St	&2002
Burns, David C.	Prof	Cincinnati	FA	DBA	71.	Indiana	&1976
Ernst & Young Professor							
Burns, Jane O.	Retir	Texas Tech	6-97	PHD	76.	Penn St	& 7-86
Burns, John E.	Dean	Dundee	MTUS	PHD	96	Manchest	2004
Burns, Thomas J.	Deces	Ohio State	1996	PHD	63.	Minnesota	&1963
Burress, Joanne	Assoc	Ithaca	FM	PHD	94	SUNY-Buf	8-04
Burrill, Cecil L.				DCS	38.	Harvard	
Burritt, Roger L.	Assoc	Australian N	MNTI	MPHL	75	Oxon	&1989
Burrowes, Ashley W.	Assoc	Wis-La Cross	AOST	PHD	86.	Nebraska	* & 8-02
Burrows, Geoffrey H.	PFell	U Melbourne	M	MCOM		Melbourne	&1971

Name	Rank	School	Field	Degree	Year	University	Date
Burrows, Ron J.	C-Ac	Dayton	FI	PHD	80.	Penn St	8-81
Burrus, Patricia	Asst	Barton	FGVX	MBA	81	E Carol	& 8-94
Bursal, Nasuhi I.	Retir	Ohio State	1989	PHD	52	Zurick	1981
Burton, Arleigh R.	Retir	Arizona St	1974	PHD	44.	Nebraska	1941
Burton, Bruce M.	SLect	Dundee	FJMT	PHD	98	Dundee	1999
Burton, E. James	Dean	Mid Tenn St	BFMC	PHD	76.	Illinois	&1990
Burton, F. Greg	Assoc	Brigham Yg	M	PHD	94.	S Carol	& 7-01

Deloitte & Touche Research Fellow

Name	Rank	School	Field	Degree	Year	University	Date
Burton, Hughlene A.	Assoc	N Car-Charl	X	PHD	94.	Alabama	&1996
Burton, John C.	Retir	Columbia	2001	PHD	62.	Columbia	&1961
Burza, Vernon	Assoc	MD E Shore	FMX	JD	76	Loyl-Chgo	9-03
Busbee, Howard	Adj	Wm & Mary	X	JD	67	Wm&Mary	& 1-02
Busby, G. Steve	Retir	West Georgia	2003	MS	64	Miss	& 9-69
Busch, Suzanne M.	Lect	CS-East Bay	FA	MBA	77	CS-Haywa	* & 9-74
Bush, H. Francis	Prof	Va Military	AFMS	PHD	89.	Florida	&1994
Bush, James L. Jr.	Assoc	Mid Tenn St	CM	PHD	77.	Arkansas	&1985
Busham, Ravi	Deces	So Methodist	4-94	PHD	86	Chicago	1993
Bushee, Brian J.	Assoc	Pennsylvania	F	PHD	97.	Michigan	2000
Bushman, Robert M.	C-Pr	No Carolina	FM	PHD	89.	Minnesota	& 7-99

The Forensic Accounting Distinguished Professor

Name	Rank	School	Field	Degree	Year	University	Date
Bushong, J. Gregory	Assoc	N Car-Ashvil	FGNV	PHD	89.	LSU	* & 8-00
Bussman, John F.	Retir	South Fla	2003	DBA	73.	Fla St	& 9-77
Busta, Bruce	C-Pr	St Cloud St	FS	PHD	90.	Nebraska	&1988
Butler, Daniel L. Jr.	Retir	La St-Shreve	2000	PHD	76.	LSU	& 8-58
Butler, David H.	Retir	San Diego St	X	PHD	78.	Cincinnati	&1981
Butler, Janet B.	Asst	Tx St-S Marc	SCM	PHD	92.	Georgia	&2003
Butler, Marcus B.	Asst	Emory	FKX	PHD	03.	Chicago	&2004
Butler, Maureen	Asst	South Fla	F	PHD	06.	Arkansas	8-06
Butler, Robie S.	Asst	Campbell		MBA		Campbell	&1995
Butler, Stephen A.			2002	PHD	82.	Iowa	

427 East Main St; Washington, IA 52353; 319-653-2018; sbutler@iowatelcom.net

Name	Rank	School	Field	Degree	Year	University	Date
Butt, Don		Mt St MaryMD		MBA		Geo Wash	1996
Buttars, Thomas A.	Retir	South Dakota	2007	PHD	88.	Wisconsin	1991
Butterfield, Scott	Assoc	Clayton St	CX	PHD	02.	Geo St	8-06
Buttermilch, Rita	Assoc	SUNY Old Wes	GFPE	MS	79	Lgls-Post	&1984
Butterworth, John E.	Deces			PHD	67.	Berkeley	
Buttimer, Harry Raymond Jr.	Deces			PHD	59.	Stanford	
Buttross, Thomas E.	C-Ac	Penn St-Harr	CM	PHD	91.	Miss	* & 8-00
Butts, F. Eugene	Emer	Appalach St	1998	EDD	69	N Colo	&1977
Buzby, Stephen L.	Retir	Michigan St	2001	PHD	72.	Penn St	& 9-78
Byard, Donal A.	Assoc	CUNY-Baruch	F	PHD	98.	Maryland	9-02
Byars, Richard B.	Retir		XM	PHD	77.	North Tx	&
Byington, J. Ralph	Dean	So Car-Aiken	FV	PHD	85.	Arkansas	& 7-03
Bylinski, Joseph H.	Assoc	No Carolina	M	PHD	80.	Ohio St	& 1-80
Byrd, Clarence	Prof	Athabasca Un		MBA		Michigan	2000
Byrd, David B.	Prof	Missouri St	FER	PHD	79.	Arkansas	& 8-84
Byrd, Sandra D.	Prof	Missouri St	FTPE	PHD	79.	Arkansas	& 8-84
Byrne, Marann	SLect	Dublin City	EFT	PHD	92	Dublin Cty	&1982
Caban-Garcia, Maria T.	Asst	South Fla	PM	PHD	04.	Missouri	& 8-04

email caban@banshee.sar.usf.edu

Name	Rank	School	Field	Degree	Year	University	Date
Cable, Dawn	Lect	Macquarie Un	M	BCOM	75	Queensld	&1992
Cable, Roberta J.	Prof	Pace-Westch	CM	PHD	81	Columbia	* 1989
Caborle, Carla	Asst	Minot State	FXUP	MS	96	Colo St	&2004
Cadenhead, Gary M.		Texas	1992	PHD	68.	Stanford	

Dept of Mgt; 512-471-5289; gary.cadenhead@mccombs.utexas.edu

Name	Rank	School	Field	Degree	Year	University	Date
Cadle, Judith	Asst	Tarleton St	PSD	MBA	91	Tarleton	1993
Cadman, Brian	Asst	Northwestern	F	PHD	05.	Oregon	2005
Cagwin, Douglass			CMGN	PHD	99.	Arkansas	
Cahan, Steven F.	Prof	U Auckland	FA	PHD	88.	Colorado	&2004
Cain, Susan	Asst	So Oregon St	APV				&2004
Cainas, Jennifer	Inst	South Fla	F	MACC		S Fla	8-05
Caird, Kathryn G.	STut	U Auckland	MA	BCOM	78	Auckland	1979
Cairney, Timothy D.	Asst	Geo Southern	MS	PHD	95.	Va Tech	&2003
Cairns, Scott N.	Prof	Shippensburg	FX	PHD	83.	Illinois	&1990
Calaf, Jorge E.	Prof	Puerto Rico	CSQ	MAS	75	Duke	* &1982
Calcote, Roger D.	Deces	Jackson St		DBA	71.	Miss St	&1974
Calderisi, Matthew C.	Assoc	F Dick-Teane	AIFM	MBA	75	Iona	9-76
Calderon, Thomas G.	C-Pr	Akron	CM	PHD	87.	Va Tech	& 9-88
Caldwell, Charles W.	Prof	Tenn Tech	MF	DBA	79.	Fla St	* 8-91
Caldwell, James C.				PHD	70.	Alabama	&
Calegari, Mary F.	Asst	San Jose St	P	PHD	01.	Georgia	* 2003
Calegari, Michael J.	C-Ac	Santa Clara	FX	PHD	96.	Arizona	&2001
Calhoun, Charles H. III	C-Pr	North Fla	FXI	DBA	73.	Fla St	&1995
Caliendo, Charles	SLect	Minnesota	FX	MBA	93	Minnesota	&1995
Calk, Russell	Assoc	New Mex St	M	PHD	97.	Okla St	& 8-01
Call, Andrew C.	Asst	Georgia	F	PHD	07	U Wash	8-07
Call, Donald P.	Deces	CS-Northrdge	5-92	MBA	64	UCLA	&1983

Call, Dwight V.	Retir	CS-Northrdge	2003	PHD	66.	UCLA	&1962
Callaghan, Clare	H-SLe	U Portsmith	NIG	MSC			1992
Callaghan, David R.	Assoc	Bentley	FD	PHD	78.	Mass	
Callaghan, Joseph H.	Prof	Oakland	FMS	PHD	92.	Illinois	&1989
Callaghan, Sandra Renfro	Assoc	Tx Christian	FX	PHD	98.	Mich St	& 8-98
Callahan, Carolyn M.	Prof	Arkansas	FM	PHD	85.	Mich St	2001
Doris M. Cook Chair							
Callahan, John	Retir	Carleton Un	2003	PHD	71	Toronto	1980
Callen, Jeffrey L.	Prof	Univ Toronto	FM	PHD	76	Toronto	2000
Rotman Chair in Accounting							
Callen, Mindy				PHD	99.	Rutgers	
Callimaci, Antonello	Prof	Quebec-Montr	FT	PHD	97.	Florida	& 6-91
Calvasina, Richard V.	Prof	West Florida	CM	PHD	73.	Miss	* &1980
Calvert, Jane	Asst	Central Okla	MPF	MAC	84	Oklahoma	& 9-84
Cameron, Alan M.	SLect	Victoria NZ	LT	LLM	84	Victoria	1975
Cameron, Alex B.	Prof	East Wash	ASM	PHD	82.	Utah	* &1981
Cameron, James B.	Retir	Brigham Yg	1997	PHD	67	Mont St	&1969
Cameron, Paul A. Jr.	Assoc	Tx A&M-C Chr	FM	MS	65	Air Force	& 9-78
Cameron, Robyn	ALect	Griffith-GC	FT	BBUS	98	Griffith	1999
Camfferman, C. (Kees)	Prof	Vrije Univ	FHP	PHD	96	Vrije	1989
Camillus, John C.	Prof	Pittsburgh	MS	DBA	72.	Harvard	
Management Dept; University of Pittsburgh							
Cammack, Susan	Asst	Cameron	FGPV	PHD	02.	Missouri	2006
Camp, Graeme	STut	U Auckland	F	PHD	00	Auckland	1995
Camp, Margaret	Assoc	Neb-Kearney	P	EDD	85	Nebraska	8-76
Campbell, Alan D.			2007	PHD	88.	North Tx	* &
1547 Scotch Pine Dr; Brandon, FL 33511; 813-643-0718; fax 813-653-0931							
Campbell, Amy B.	Lect	Auburn	F	MAC	92	Auburn	& 1-94
Campbell, Annhenrie	Prof	CS-Stanislau	FC	PHD	91.	Colorado	* &1991
Campbell, Clarence E.	Retir	Wright State	1992	MA	69	Missouri	9-71
Campbell, David R.	C-Pr	Drexel		PHD	75.	Georgia	&2004
Campbell, Dennis	Asst	Harvard		DBA	04.	Harvard	2004
Campbell, J. Douglas	Retir	Temple	1997	LLM	81	Temple	&1976
Campbell, Jane E.	Prof	Kennesaw St	FEBT	DBA	81.	Tennessee	& 9-92
Campbell, Katherine	Assoc	North Dakota	F	PHD	96.	U Wash	& 8-03
Campbell, Linda M.	Assoc	Siena Height	APCV	MBA	87	Toledo	&2000
Campbell, Michael C.	C-Pr	Mont St-Bill	DNGS	MS	75	Colo St	&1978
Campbell, Richard J.	Asst	Rio Grande	MSC	MBA	81	Gannon	* & 8-93
Campbell, Robert J.	Prof	Miami U-Ohio	M	DBA	76.	Indiana	* 1-77
Campbell, Ronald L.	Asst	N Carol A&T	FN	PHD	89.	Tx A&M	&1993
Campbell, Sharon N.	C-Pr	No Alabama	FEP	DBA	95.	La Tech	&1996
Campbell, Steven V.			FM	PHD	93.	Oregon	&
Campbell, Terry L.			FMS	DBA	79.	Indiana	* &
Campbell, Walter M.	Prof	No Alabama	AFTE	PHD	82.	North Tx	&1994
Campbell, William D.	Retir	Clarion	2001	PHD	80	Pittsburgh	& 8-74
Campfield, William L.	Retir	Fla Intl	1986	PHD	51.	Illinois	&1981
Canavan, Martin J.	Assoc	Skidmore	PFWE	MS	75	SUNY-Alb	&1979
Canina, Linda	Assoc	Cornell-Hotl	F	PHD	90	NYU	1994
Canlar, Mehmet	Prof	Plymouth St	FMV	PHD	77	Hacettep	9-88
Cannata, Elizabeth A.	Asst	Johnson&Wale	FP	MBA	96	Providen	&2005
Canning, Mary	Dean	Golden Gate		LLM	82	Golden Gt	1988
Canning, Mary	SLect	Dublin City	AF	PHD	97	Wales	&1992
Cannon, David M.	Asst	Grand Valley	S	PHD	02.	Kent St	& 8-00
Cannon, Harold L.	Deces	SUNY-Albany	1988	PHD	65	Minnesota	1965
Cannon, Norman S.	Retir	Utah State	1984	PHD	58.	Columbia	&1947
Cantoria, Filomena M.	C-Pr	Guam	AFRM	DBA	84	Phillipe	&1991
Cao, Jian	Asst	Fla Atlantic		PHD	07	Kent St	8-07
Cao, Jin Wei	Asst	Delaware	S	PHD	95	Arizona	9-05
Cao, Zhiyan	Asst	U Wash-Tacom	FM	PHD	06	Yale	2007
Capatch, P. William	Retir	Kent State	1981	PHD	67.	Pittsburgh	&
Capettini, Robert J.	Prof	San Diego St	MCE	PHD	75.	Illinois	&1985
Capkun, Vedran	Asst	HEC Paris	FIAV	PHD	06	HEC Lausa	2006
Caplan, Dennis H.	Asst	Oregon State	ATM	PHD	94.	Berkeley	* &2004
Caplan, Edwin H.	Retir	New Mexico	1991	PHD	65.	Berkeley	&1967
8201 Harwood NE; Albuquerque NM 87110							
Caplan, Robert H. 3rd	Deces			DBA	68.	Harvard	
Capone, James J. Jr.	C-Pr	Kean	PLMC	JD	68	Rutgers	1975
Capozzoli, Ernst	Asst	Kennesaw St		PHD		Miss	
Capps, Robert				DBA	78.	Geo Wash	
Capriotti, Kim	Asst	Jacksonvil U	AFS	PHD	92.	Fla St	& 8-01
Capstaff, John	H-SLe	Strathclyde	FM	MSC	83	Strathcl	1983
Carberry, Pauline R.		Consultant		PHD	70.	Ohio St	
Carbone, Domenic	LectB	Adelaide	X	LLB		Adelaide	1992
Carcello, Joseph V.	Prof	Tennessee	AF	PHD	90.	Geo St	# * & 8-93
Ernst & Young Professor							
Cardegna, Thomas F.	Retir	Baltimore	1991	MA	51	Woodst	&1971
Cardwell, Paul H.			CMXY	PHD	91.	Tennessee	&

Cardwell, Paula M.	Inst	Elon	F	MACC				&2000
Carey, Peter	SLect	Monash Univ	AJO	MBA	93	Monash		&1990
Cargile, Barney R.	Retir	Alabama	8-03	PHD	79.	Missouri		&1978
Cargill, Willie N.	Prof	Tx A&M Intl	ASX	PHD	86.	Missouri		& 9-89
Carl, Lee	Assoc	St Thomas-TX	FP	MBA	74	N Illinois		& 8-74
Carlin, Madeleine J.	Assoc	Pittsburgh	FX	MBA	78	Temple		&1991
Carlini, Jeffrey	Lect	N Car-Charl	FM	MS	02	Lehigh		2005
Carlsen, Eric	Prof	Kean	VCNG	PHD	69	Cornell		&1976
Carlson, Arthur E.	Retir	Wash Univ	1988	PHD	54	Nrthwstrn		1952
Carlson, Carolyn	Lect	Dayton	MP	MBA	81	Dayton		&2007
Carlson, Marvin L.	Retir	So Methodist	MFT	PHD	64.	Wisconsin		&1974
Carlson, R. Loring	Assoc	W New Eng	PXTF	JD	72	Conn		&1984
Carlson, Ronald E.	Prof	St Cloud St	FV	PHD	73.	Wisconsin		&1972
Carlson, Steven J.	Assoc	North Dakota	FS	PHD	91.	Arkansas		& 7-94
Carlsson, Torbjorn	Asst	Univ of Umea	F	BSC	00	Umea		1-00
Carment, Thomas M.	Retir	NE St-Okla	5-04	PHD	91.	Okla St		& 9-79
Rogers State Univ; 918-343-7522; tcarment@rsu.edu								
Carmichael, Bobby J.	Prof	Tx A&M-Comm	XRFD	EDD	79	Florida		&1980
Carmichael, Douglas R.	Prof	CUNY-Baruch	A	PHD	68.	Illinois		&1983
Wollman Distinguished Professor of Accountancy								
Carmichael, Robert	Retir	CS-Northrdge	1988	PHD	74	UCLA		1983
Carmody, Robert	Assoc	Siena	FA	MBA		Siena		& 9-79
Carnaghan, Carla	Asst	U Lethbridge	BFS	PHD	99	Alberta		2006
Carnegie, Garry D.	Prof	Deakin-Geelg	FH	PHD	94	Flinders		&1988
Carnes, Gerald	Asst	Edinboro	FX	MBA	74	Gannon		&1976
Carnes, Gregory A.	Dean	Lipscomb	X	PHD	91.	Geo St		& 1-06
Carnes, Kay C.	D-Pr	Gonzaga	AN	PHD	90.	St Louis	#	&1979
Carnes, Thomas A.	Assoc	Berry	F	PHD	97.	Fla St		& 8-05
Caron, Marie-Andree	Prof	Quebec-Montr		PHD		HEC-Mont	*	
Carpenter, Brian W.	Prof	Scranton	FBHM	PHD	87.	Penn St	*	1987
Alperin Teaching Fellow								
Carpenter, Charles G.	Assoc	Fran Marion	F	PHD	69.	Illinois		& 8-05
Carpenter, Floyd W.	Prof	Murray State	FX	PHD	84.	Miss		&1987
Carpenter, Frances H.			F	PHD	85.	Illinois		&
Carpenter, Janice			F	PHD	86.	Tx A&M		&
Carpenter, Jon R.	Prof	South Dakota	FTC	PHD	81.	Va Tech		1989
Carpenter, Susan R. Whisnant			MA	PHD	76.	Tx-Austin		&
Carpenter, Tina D.	Asst	Georgia		PHD	04.	Fla St		& 8-04
Carpenter, Vivian L.			FG	PHD	85.	Michigan		&
Carpentier, Cecile	Prof	Univ Laval		PHD	98	Lille II		1999
Carper, William Brent			1998	PHD	73.	Alabama		&
American Univ in Cairo; Cairo 11511 Egypt; phone 20-2-357-6703								
Carr, Janice S.	Prof	Cal Poly-SLO	FXE	PHD	85.	Ariz St		& 9-83
Carr, John E. III	Emer	Longwood	1989	MBA	60	Syracuse		1966
Carr, Lawrence P.	Prof	Babson	CMU	PHD	89.	Union-NY		1989
Carr, Pamela S.	H-Ac	Ark Tech	PX	PHD	01.	Okla St		&1991
Carr, Rebecca	Inst	Arkansas St	FXP	MS	86	Illinois		& 8-88
Carr, Tyee	Inst	Portland St	FX	MBA		Oregon		2004
Carr, Virgil A.	Asst	Clark Atlant	AFN	MBA	72	Atlanta		&1988
Carraway, Ernest R.	Lect	N Carol St	LXR	JD	77	N Carol		&1985
Carrington, Donley	ALect	West Indies	MT	MSC		Iowa St		
Carrithers, James M.	Retir	Wash State	1984	PHD	42.	Illinois		&1982
Carroll, James J.	Prof	Georgian Ct	CAVU	DBA	87	Nova SE	*	&1991
Carroll, Joan M.	Assoc	SUNY Oswego	FEPW	MS	76	Clarkson		&1980
Carroll, Ray F.	Assoc	Dalhousie	FV	PHD	96	Dalhousie		&1987
Carroll, Thomas H.	Deces			DCS	39.	Harvard		
Carroll, Thomas J.	Lect	Iowa	F	PHD	88.	Michigan		& 1-89
Carruth, Paul J.	Prof	SE Louisiana	FMC	PHD	79.	LSU		& 8-79
Carslaw, Charles A.P.N.	Assoc	Nevada-Reno	VFI	MA	71	Oxford		&1990
Carson, Albert B.	Deces	UCLA	8-79	PHD	43.	Nebraska		1947
Carson, Elizabeth	Lect	New So Wales	F	MCOM	99	NS Wales		1998
Carstens, Robert H. K.	Retir	Tuskegee	2001	PHD	92.	Miss	*	8-94
Carter, B. Douglas	Retir	Cen Arkansas	2000	PHD	85.	Arkansas	*	& 8-82
Carter, Charles E.	Retir	Mo-Kansas Ct	2002	PHD	84.	Missouri		1974
Carter, Chris	Read	St Andrews	WTI	PHD	01	Aston		2002
Carter, Clairmont P. (Monty)	Prof	Mass-Lowell	FV	DBA	71.	Kent St		1982
Carter, David	Lect	Victoria NZ		LLB				
Carter, David T.	Retir	Un Waterloo	2003	MBA	69	Windsor		&1978
Carter, Donald G. A.		Inst Chrt Ac	1996	PHD	77.	Berkeley		
5553 Nancy Greene Way; N Vancouver V7R 4R6 Canada								
Carter, Fonda Long	Assoc	Columbus St	FPA	DBA	98.	Miss St		&1988
Carter, Forest C.	Retir	Tx-Pan Amer	1986	DBA	62.	Indiana		&1981
Carter, Gary W.			X	PHD	85.	Tx-Austin		&
Carter, Jack L.	Retir	Fla Internat	5-98	PHD	80.	Cincinnati		1-79
Carter, Lemuria D.	Asst	Miss State	S	PHD	06.	Va Tech		8-06
Management Information Systems Department								
Carter, Mary Ellen	Asst	Pennsylvania	F	PHD	98.	MIT		2002

Name	Rank	School					
Carter, Tollie L.	Assoc	Chicago St	FCVA	MBA	85	Illinois	&1986
Carter, William K.	Assoc	Virginia	CM	PHD	78.	Okla St	& 1-78
Carty, John J.	Retir	Stonehill	XFM	MBA	55	Harvard	& 9-63
Caruso, Karin	C-Ac	So New Hamp	PFMC	MBA		NewHamp	9-77
Carvell, Steven	Assoc	Cornell-Hotl	F	PHD	84	SUNY-Bin	1986
Carver, M. Robert Jr.	Prof	Fontbonne	AEFR	PHD	80.	Missouri	&2002
Carver, Patricia	Inst	Bellarmine	P	MBA	00	Bellarm	& 8-02
Casabona, Patrick A.	Prof	St John's	CP	PHD	79	Baruch	1982
Cascini, Karen T.	Prof	Sacred Heart	IFJ	PHD	88	Conn	&1992
Case, Al	H-Ac	So Oregon St	FX	MACC	93	Brighm Yg	&2001
Casello-Bouges, Janie C.	Asst	Mass-Lowell	FX	PHD	05	Mass	&2005
Casey, Cornelius J. Jr.	Deces	Dartmouth	1984	PHD	78.	Ohio St	1982
Casey, Rebecca	C-In	Pittsburg St	F	MBA	95	Pitt St	&2002
Casey-Baker, Donna	Asst	Mass Lib Art		MBA	02	SUNY-Alb	2004
Cash, Donald M.	Retir	Pittsburg St	1996	MBA	66	Denver	&1966
Cash, L. Stephen	Prof	Clemson	X	LLM	72	Wash U	&1982
Cashell, James D.	Prof	Miami U-Ohio	SA	PHD	84.	Cincinnati	&1986

C. Rolin Niswonger Professor of Accounting

Name	Rank	School					
Caskey, Judson	Asst	UCLA	F	PHD	06.	Michigan	&2006
Caslan, David F.			FMC	PHD	92.	St Louis	&
Casler, Darwin J.	Retir	Cen Michigan	1989	DBA	62.	Mich St	&1984

108 Alger Drive; Blue Springs, MO 64014

Name	Rank	School					
Caspari, John A.			1996	PHD	76	Missouri	*

Constraint Accounting Measurements

Name	Rank	School					
Cassar, Gavin	Asst	Pennsylvania	MC	PHDM	05	Berkeley	2005
Cassel, Herbert S.	Retir	Shippensburg	1994	PHD	69.	SUNY-Buf	9-74
Cassel, Michael N.	Assoc	Baylor	FG	PHD	76.	Georgia	9-80
Cassidy, Judith H.	Assoc	Mississippi	MSI	PHD	86.	Tx Tech	* &1-89
Cassill, Arthur D.	C-Pr	Elon	X	PHD	86.	Tennessee	&2002
Castaldi, Raymond J.	Retir	Towson	AFMD	MBA		Geo Wash	&1971
Castellano, Joseph F.	Prof	Dayton	GMF	PHD	71.	St Louis	1999
Caster, A. Bruce	Prof	Valdosta St	FM	PHD	88.	Georgia	&1985
Caster, Paul	Assoc	Fairfield	AFB	PHD	87.	North Tx	&1994
Casterella, Jeffrey R.	Assoc	Colorado St	F	PHD	95.	Colorado	&2000
Castle, John	Retir	Bishop's Un	1997	BCOM		McGill	&
Cataldo, Anthony J. II			M	PHD	96.	Va Tech	* &
Cataldo, James	Asst	Suffolk	F	PHD	86	Columbia	2006
Catanach, Anthony H. Jr.	Assoc	Villanova	FM	PHD	94.	Ariz St	* &1998
Catanese, Margaret E.	Retir	DePauw	2002	MBA	78	Mich St	& 8-79
Cathey, Jack M.	Assoc	N Car-Charl	CFS	PHD	89.	Va Tech	&1988
Cato, C. E.	Retir	Grambling St	ATX	PHD	72.	Miss	& 8-88
Cattanbach, Richard L.				PHD	72.	Ariz St	
Caufield, Charles F.	Retir	Loyola-Chicg	2000	JD	62	Loyola	& 9-62
Causey, Denzil Y. Jr. (Dan)			FA	DBA	72.	S Calif	&
Causse, Genevieve	Prof	ESCP deParis	CFUN	PHD	82	Paris I	1971
Causseaux, Wanda	Inst	Valdosta St	F	MBA		Valdosta	& 8-06
Cauvin, Christian	Prof	HEC Paris	ACFM	HECD	69	HEC Paris	&1970
Cavalluzzo, Ken S.			M	PHD	98.	Penn	
Cavanagh, W. Forbes	Assoc	York-Atkinsn	MC	PHD	85.	SUNY-Buf	&1976
Cavanagh, William F. Jr.	Retir	St Johns	1988	JD	54	St Johns	&1973
Caylor, Marcus L.	Asst	So Carolina	F	PHD	06.	Geo St	8-06
Cebenoyan, Fatma	Asst	CUNY-Hunter	FPX	PHD	98.	Maryland	1999
Cecchini, Mark	Asst	So Carolina	S	PHD	05	Florida	2005
Cecere, Ralph	Lect	McGill Univ	F	BCOM	88	McGill	&1993
Cecil, H. Wayne	Assoc	Fl GulfCoast	X	PHD	96.	Kentucky	* &2007
Cegelski, Ray Leo	Retir	Duquesne	2000	MBA	62	Duquesne	&1962
Cenedella, David	Asst	CUNY-Baruch	T	LLM	97	NYU	9-06
Cenker, William J.	Prof	John Carroll	AFX	PHD	89.	Kent St	&1987
Cerepak, John R.	Retir	F Dick-Teane	1995	PHD	71	Philathe	& 9-63
Cerf, Alan R.	Emer	Cal-Berkeley	1993	PHD	56	Stanford	1955
Cerf, Douglas C.	Prof	Cal Poly-SLO	FM	PHD	91	Ca-Davis	& 9-90
Cermignano, Gregory P.	Assoc	Widener	VLE	JD	84	Widener	* 1979
Cerullo, M. Virginia	Prof	Missouri St	FSO	PHD	90.	LSU	# & 8-88
Cerullo, Michael J.	Prof	Missouri St	S	PHD	71.	LSU	& 8-88
Cezair, Joan A.	Asst	Fayetteville		PHD			
Chabot, Marc	Prof	Quebec-Montr	M	PHD		Montreal	& 7-80
Chaderton, Robertine	H-Lec	West Indies	AI	PHD		Manchest	
Chadwick, Lester W.	Deces	Delaware	1999	PHD	73.	Syracuse	& 9-79
Chaffin, Royce E.	Retir	West Georgia	2004	MBA	73	Golden Gt	& 9-90
Chai, Deborah H. S.	Inst	City Univ HK	CMTJ	MSCA	99	UMIST	# 2004
Chakos, Peter J.	Deces	Niagara	1996	MBA		McMaster	1964
Chalermkanjana, Kotchakorn	Asst	Chulalongkor	CM	MACC	82	Chulalong	1976
Chalos, Peter	Prof	Ill-Chicago	M	PHD	82.	Illinois	1985
Chaloupecky, Kurt E.	Assoc	Missouri St	FA	PHD	77.	Missouri	& 8-73
Chamberlain, Don H.	C-Ac	Murray State	GSF	DBA	90.	Kentucky	1986
Chamberlain, Sandra L.	Assoc	British Colu	FM	PHD	91.	Chicago	2001

Deloitte and Touche Chair in Accounting

Name	Rank	School	Code	Degree	Yr	Degree School	Notes
Chamberlin, William A.	Retir	Embry-Riddle	1996	MBA	69	Stetson	& 9-79
Chambers, A. Milton	Retir	Berry	1995	MS	55	Tennessee	1953
Chambers, Dennis J.	Asst	Kentucky	F	PHD	96.	Tx-Austin	2003
Chambers, Donald R.		Lafayette		PHD	81	N Carol	
KPMG Peat Marwick Professor							
Chambers, Raymond J.	Deces	Sydney	9-99	DSC	73	Sydney	&1953
Chambers, Valrie	Assoc	Tx A&M-C Chr	XFM	PHD	00.	Houston	& 9-00
Chamisa, Edward E.	Lect	Un Zimbabwe	V	PHD			
Champion, John E.	Deces	Florida St	N-02	PHD	60.	Michigan	&1956
Chan, Andrew H. T.			FS	PHD	94.	Purdue	
Chan, C.	Lect	Massey Univ	EXJP	MBS		Massey	&1988
Chan, Canri	Assoc	Monterey	FIB	PHD	01	Flinders	&2001
Chan, Chris W. H.	Assoc	Un Hong Kong	MBI	PHD	93.	Missouri	* 1999
Chan, Derek K. W.	Assoc	Un Hong Kong	F	PHD	95	Brit Colum	2001
Chan, Hong Tak (Andy)	Assoc	Slippery Roc		PHD	94	Purdue	2000
Chan, Hung C. (Leon)	Asst	CS-Pomona	MS	PHD	06.	Houston	2006
Betty & Hayward Taff Faculty Fellow							
Chan, James L.	Prof	Ill-Chicago	GN	PHD	76.	Illinois	1981
Chan, K. Hung	D-Pr	Lingnan U	AIMX	PHD	74	Penn St	* &2000
J.K. Lee Chair Professor							
Chan, Kam C.	Prof	Pace-Westch	FP	PHD	91.	S Carol	1997
Chan, Kam Fong	Lect	U Auckland	F	PHD	06	Queenslnd	2005
Chan, Kelly	Lect	Tech-Sydney	FT	MCOM	95	NS Wales	1997
Chan, Lilian Him-Lai	Asst	Un Hong Kong	F	PHD	07	Tx-Dallas	2007
Chan, Philip	Lect	HongKon Tech	FT	MPHL	93	Wales	2004
Chan, Samuel	Assoc	HongKon Tech	XCJ	PHD	01	RMIT	1984
Chan, Siew H.	Asst	Wash State	SM	PHD	01.	Utah	2006
Chan, Y. C. Lilian	Assoc	McMaster Un	CFM	PHD	85.	Va Tech	* & 1-86
Chan, Yvonne	Inst	City Univ HK	A	MBA	03	HKUST	O-06
Chan-Ng, Ai Lin	Lect	Nanyang Tech		MBA	99	Nanyang	2006
Chand, Parmod	Lect	Macquarie Un	IFA	MA	03	S Pacific	2004
Chandar, Nandini	Asst	Drexel	FMH	PHD	97.	Case Wes	&2004
Chandler, John S.	Assoc	Illinois	UMS	PHD	77	Ohio St	8-78
Chandler, Roy A.	Prof	Cardiff U	AFHI	BSC	77	Cardiff	&1980
Chandra, Akhilesh	Prof	Akron	DS	PHD	93.	Memphis	* 9-01
Chandra, Gyan	Deces	Miami U-Ohio	5-05	PHD	71.	Ohio St	6-72
Chandra, Ramesh	Retir	Univ Windsor	2003	PHD	86.	Oklahoma	1984
Chandra, Uday	Assoc	SUNY-Albany	FVM	PHD	92.	Purdue	8-05
Chaney, Barbara A.	Assoc	Montana	GPF	PHD	97.	Georgia	&2003
Chaney, Melinda	Prof	Intl College		PHD			&
Chaney, Paul K.	Prof	Vanderbilt	F	PHD	83.	Indiana	* & 1-84
Chang, C. Janie	Prof	San Diego St	SFMA	PHD	95.	Ca-Irvine	2006
Vern Odmark Professor of Accountancy							
Chang, Catherine Chiichao				PHD	02.	Baruch	
Chang, Charles	Asst	Cornell-Hotl	F	PHD	03	Berkeley	2003
Chang, Chi	Lect	San Jose St		MBA		CS-Fresno	
Chang, Chiaho	Assoc	Montclair St	FMPC	PHD	97	NYU	2001
Chang, Chinfu	Asst	Nat Chengchi	FPQ	PHD	99.	Rutgers	2000
Chang, Chiou-Hsiung (Bear)	Prof	CS-Dominguez	MST	PHD	73.	LSU	* 1983
Chang, Chun-Chia	Asst	San Fran St	F	PHD	06.	Houston	2006
Chang, Chung-Yueh		Houston		PHD	93.	Houston	
Chang, Davis L.			FM	PHD	74.	Pittsburgh	* &
Chang, Emily C.	Retir	CS-L Angeles	1983	PHD	56	Michigan	&1959
Chang, Hsihui			MF	PHD	94.	Minnesota	&
Chang, Hung-Chun			FGN	PHD	89.	Maryland	&
Chang, James J.			F	PHD	99.	Harvard	
Chang, Linda	AsLec	New So Wales	M	MCOM	00	NS Wales	1998
Chang, Lucia S.	Retir	Fla Internat	1999	PHD	72.	Tx-Austin	1971
Chang, Millicent	Lect	W Australia	F	BCOM	90	W Austrl	1992
Chang, Otto H.	Prof	CS-San Bern	FMX	PHD	84.	Illinois	&1991
Chang, Philip				PHD	02.	Baruch	
Chang, Ruey-Dang				PHD	96.	S Illinois	
Chang, She-I	Asst	Ntl Chung Ch	DS	PHD	03	Queensland	2003
Chang, Stanley Y.			GNMO	PHD	87.	Tx Tech	# * &
Chang, Young H.			FT	PHD	88.	Va Tech	
Chant, Peter D.		Deloitte&Tou	1996	PHD	78.	Nrthwstrn	
Deloitte & Touche; 95 Wellington St West; Toronto Ont M5J 2P4 Canada							
Chapin, Wayne R.	Retir	CS-Fresno	1992	DBA	65.	S Calif	& 8-81
Chaplin, J. Richard	C-Pr	F Dick-Madis	CAS	ABD	69	Rutgers	* &1970
Chaplin, Sally	AcLec	Un Tasmania	BIS	01		Tasmania	2002
Chapman, Christopher S.	Read	Oxford Univ	MS	PHD	95	LondonSE	1996
Chapman, Gordon L.	Retir	East Wash	2005	PHD	73.	Ariz St	&1979
Chapman, Lowell	Retir	Ferris State	1981	DED		Penn St	1958
Chapman, William C.	Retir	Okla Baptist	FAX	PHD	82.	Oklahoma	& 8-02
Chapple, Sandra	Lect	U Wollongong	F	MCOM		Wollong	&2003
Charalambous, Chris	Prof	Cyprus	Q	PHD	71	McMaster	1993
Chari, Ramesh		Industry		PHD	98.	Wash U	

Name	Rank	School	Code	Degree	Yr	Institution	
Charitou, Andreas	C-Ac	Cyprus	FMI	PHD	86.	Penn St	* &1992
Charkey, Barbara	C-Pr	Keene State	VCFM	MS	85	Mass	&1987
Charland, Kimberly	Inst	Kansas State	AFMN	MACC	85	Kansas St	& 8-96
Ernst & Young Teaching Fellow							
Charles, Shannon	Asst	Brigham Yg	MF	PHD	00.	Okla St	2001
Charlton, Richard E.		Ann Arbor MI	1995	PHD	76.	Mich St	
2844 Oakdale Dr; Ann Arbor MI 48108; 313-973-2879							
Charpentier, Claes	Asst	Stockholm Ec	M	ED	92	Stockholm	1983
Charrier, Gretchen B.	Lect	Texas-Austin	FMX	MPA	96	Tx-Austin	& 6-97
Charron, Kimberly F.	Assoc	Nev-L Vegas	FNV	PHD	97.	Arizona	1997
Charron, Pierre		Quebec a Hul	CMF	MBA			&
Charters, Darren	Lect	Un Waterloo	ALJ	MBA	00	Wilfr Lau	2002
Chase, Bruce W.	Prof	Radford	FNG	PHD	91.	Va Comm	&1992
Chase, Linda	Asst	Baldwin-Wal	AFC	MBA	97	Bald-Wal	9-01
Chase, Michael D.	Prof	CS-Long Bch	FVS	PHD	84.	S Calif	1982
Chastain, Clark E.	Retir	Mich-Flint	1994	PHD	58.	Michigan	1968
Chasteen, Lanny G.	Prof	Oklahoma St	EF	PHD	70.	Arkansas	&1969
Kerr McGee Professor							
Chatfield, Michael	Retir	So Oregon St	PFHM	DBA	66.	Oregon	&1990
Chatham, Michael D.	Asst	Radford	PMC	PHD	04.	Okla St	&2004
Chatham, Thomas W.	Retir	NE Louisiana	1995	DBA	80.	La Tech	&
Chatman, Emanuel D.	Prof	Univ of D C	GF	EDD	80	S Calif	&1974
Chatraphorn, Pongprot	Asst	Chulalongkor	F	PHD	01.	Va Tech	1995
Chau, Chak-Tung	Assoc	Ixs Southern	FA	PHD	92.	Fla St	&2004
Chau, Gerald K.	Asst	HongKon Tech	A	PHD	00	Warwick	1984
Chavis, Betty M.	C-Pr	CS-Fullerton	FIX	PHD	90.	S Calif	&1996
Cheatham, Carole B.	Retir	NE Louisiana	1999	PHD	71.	Arkansas	* &1986
Chee, Yong Hee		Sobang		PHD	79.	U Wash	
Cheever, John K.	Retir	CS-Pomona	2000	DBA	75	S Calif	& 9-68
Cheh, John J.	Assoc	Akron	S	PHD	86.	Michigan	1999
Chen, Al Y. S.	Prof	N Carol St	MS	PHD	88.	Ga Tech	1988
Chen, Andrew N. K.	Asst	Kansas	S	PHD	99	Conn	2006
Chen, Andy H.	Asst	NE Illinois	S	PHD	90	Tennessee	& 9-90
Chen, C. Richard	Assoc	E Kentucky	SF	PHD	80.	Tx-Austin	&1989
Chen, Changling	Asst	Un Waterloo	F	PHD	04.	Wisconsin	2004
Chen, Charlene	ALect	Macquarie Un	F	BCOM	01	Macquarie	2001
Chen, Charles J. P.	H-Ac	City Univ HK	FM	PHD	95.	Houston	9-95
Chen, Chih-Ying	Asst	Hong Kong Sc	F	PHD	97.	Berkeley	&2000
Chen, Ching-Kuan	Asst	Brighm Yg-HI	FJWX	PHD	05.	Cen Fla	2005
Chen, Chong-Tong	C-Pr	NE Illinois	MCS	PHD	72	Illinois	* & 9-85
Chen, Clarra	Asst	Illinois	FM	PHD	06	UCLA	8-06
Chen, Clement C.	Assoc	Mich-Flint	MBCE	PHD	01.	Kentucky	2001
Chen, David M.		Fu Jen Univ	M	PHD	86.	Illinois	1989
Chen, Fulton T.				PHD	69.	Alabama	&
Chen, Hui	Asst	Vanderbilt	F	PHD	05.	Tennessee	2005
Chen, Huyaing "Lucy"	Asst	Ariz St West		PHD	05.	Temple	8-05
Chen, Jessica	ALect	Macquarie Un					
Chen, Jieping		City-Hong Ko	1996	PHD	95.	Houston	
Chen, Jiin-Feng	Assoc	Nat Chengchi	ADFS	PHD	91.	Wisconsin	&1991
Chen, Joyce T.	Retir	Ill-Chicago	2000	PHD	72	Illinois	* &1977
Chen, Keji	Asst	Alabama	F	PHD	03.	Ohio St	7-03
Chen, Kevin C. W.	Prof	Hong Kong Sc	Fl	PHD	85.	Illinois	&1996
Chair Professor							
Chen, Kung H.	Prof	Nebraska	UMBC	PHD	74.	Tx-Austin	1973
Steinhart Foundation Professor							
Chen, Kuo-Tay	Assoc	Nat Taiwan U	SMF	PHD	92	Tx-Austin	8-93
Chen, Lei (Tony)	Asst	Georgia St	M	PHD	04	Tx-Dallas	2005
Chen, Ming-Chin	Assoc	Nat Chengchi	FPX	PHD	97.	Ariz St	&1997
Chen, Peter F.	Assoc	Hong Kong Sc	F	PHD	98	Alberta	1998
Chen, Qi	Assoc	Duke	FM	PHD	00	Chicago	7-00
Chen, Raymond S.	Emer	CS-Northrdge	AFI	PHD	73.	Missouri	&1971
Chen, Ring D.	Asst	NE Illinois	VF	PHD	85.	Florida	& 9-87
Chen, Robert C. T.		Self Employe		PHD	74.	Santa Cl	
Chen, Rosita S.	Retir	CS-Fresno	2004	PHD	73.	Illinois	8-80
Chen, Sean	Assoc	Furman	FS	PHD	92	Pittsburgh	2006
Chen, Shimin	Assoc	HongKon Tech	FM	PHD	92.	Georgia	2005
Chen, Shuping (Michelle)	Asst	U Washington	F	PHD	02.	S Calif	2002
Chen, Tai Yuan	Asst	Hong Kong Sc	F	PHD	06	Tx-Dallas	2006
Chen, Xia	Asst	British Colu	F	PHD	04	Chicago	2003
Chen, Xiao	Assoc	Tsinghua Un	F	PHD	96.	Tulane	1996
Chen, Xiaolin (Clara)	Asst	Ill-Chicago		PHD	06.	S Calif	2006
Chen, Yao-Tse		Ntl Cheng Ku		PHD	01.	Syracuse	
National Cheng Kung Univereisty							
Chen, Yasheng	Asst	Simon Fraser	MI	PHD	05	W Ontario	2-05
Chen, Yining	Prof	W Kentucky	SA	PHD	93.	S Carol	2005
Mary R. Nixon Professor of Accounting							
Chen, Yunhao	Asst	Fla Internat	FM	PHD	07	Minnesota	2007

Name	Rank	School		Degree		University	
Chen, Zhihong	Asst	City Univ HK	F	PHD	05	HKUST	2006
Chene, Douglas	Asst	So Maine		PHD	95	Illinois	2007
Cheng, Alan	Inst	Chinese HK	F	MA	97	Charles S	&2007
Cheng, C.S. Agnes	Prof	Louisiana St	F	PHD	83.	Illinois	8-07
Ourso Distinguished Chair							
Cheng, June	Asst	HongKon Tech	AIS	PHD	05	Ohio St	2005
Cheng, Kang	Assoc	Howard	F	PHD	98.	Geo Wash	&2006
Cheng, Mandy M.	SLect	New So Wales	M	MCOM	00	NS Wales	1998
Cheng, Mei	Asst	Arizona	F	PHD	05.	S Calif	2006
Cheng, Nam Sang	Asst	Natl Singapo	AM	PHD	97	Bradford	&1999
Cheng, Payyu			FM	PHD	89.	Nebraska	
Cheng, Peter	Assoc	HongKon Tech	FMT	PHD	82.	Mich St	2001
Cheng, Philip C.			NCV	PHD	64.	LSU	&
Cheng, Qiang	Asst	British Colu	F	PHD	02.	Wisconsin	2003
Cheng, Rita H.	Prof	Wis-Milwauke	GFN	PHD	88.	Temple	&1988
A. O. Smith Teaching Professor							
Cheng, Sarah	Lect	HongKon Tech	FJ	MBA	98	Chinese U	2000
Cheng, Shijun	Asst	Michigan	M	PHD	01.	Pittsburgh	2001
Cheng, Thomas T.	Prof	St Marys-Cdn	MFA	PHD	81.	Missouri	# * &1992
Cheng, Ting-Wong	Prof	Nat Chengchi	FV	PHD	74.	Missouri	&1975
Cheng, Zhuo		HongKong Pol		PHD	05.	Ohio St	
Chenhall, Robert H.	Prof	Monash Univ	MBS	PHD	81	Macquarie	&1989
Cheniam, Supapon	Asst	Chulalongkor	DFMS	DBA	94	Miss St	1978
Chenier, Julie C.	Inst	Louisiana St	FM	MBA	79	Tulane	# &1983
Chenna, S. Raju	Assoc	Kentucky Wes	AFGX	MBA	81	W NewMex	&1988
Cheon, Youngsoon Susan	C-Ac	Chung-Ang	FIV	PHD	94.	Georgia	&2000
Cherrington, J. Owen	Deces	Brigham Yg	2005	PHD	72.	Minnesota	& 9-78
Cherry, Alan A.	C-Pr	Loyola Marym	FW	PHD	78.	UCLA	1983
Cherry, Donald C.	Assoc	Dalhousie	FEPU	MBA	73	McMaster	* 1978
Cherry, Julius	Lect	CUNY-Baruch	F	PHD	82	NYU	9-03
Chesler, Samuel	Retir	Mass-Lowell	2002	MBA	66	Suffolk	1969
Chesley, G. Richard	Emer	St Marys-Cdn	MFT	PHD	73.	Ohio St	&1989
Chesley, Julie	Prof	Colorado Col		PHD	96	Colorado	2007
Chesser, Delton L.	Retir	Baylor	2005	PHD	72	Arkansas	& 7-82
Chester, Michael C.	Assoc	Flagler	FT	PHD	91.	Va Comm	&
Chetwin, Maree C.	Assoc	Canterbury	LX	LLB	74	Canterbu	1979
Cheung, Daniel	Assoc	HongKon Tech	X	PHD	04	Chinese U	1984
Cheung, Esther	ALect	Macquarie Un					
Cheung, Joe	SLect	U Auckland	F	MSC	88	Wash	2000
Cheung, Joseph K.	Deces	HongKon Tech	6-99	PHD	77.	Michigan	&1995
Chevalier, Gilles	Assoc	HEC-Montreal	LJ	PHD	75.	Illinois	& 7-02
Chevis, Gia	Asst	Baylor	MFI	PHD	03.	Tx A&M	8-05
Chewning, Eugene G. Jr.			F	PHD	84.	S Carol	&
Chhatwal, Gurprit S.	Assoc	R Stockton	FV	PHD	80	Kansas St	1992
Chi, Charles C.			FM	PHD	89.	Florida	
Chi, Pham Bich	Asst	Natl Econ	FM	MBA	97	Boise St	1989
Chi, Sung K	Asst	Pusan-Korea	M	PHD	89.	U Wash	&1991
Chiang, Bih-Horng (Bea)	Assoc	C New Jersey	CM	PHD	99.	Drexel	1998
Chiang, Catherine	Asst	N Carol Cen	FGPS	PHD	01	CUNY	&2001
Chiang, Hung-Fu		Northrup Ind		PHD	75.	UCLA	
Chiao, Lin S.	Retir	SUNY-Bingham	1987	PHD	52.	Illinois	1963
Chiapello, Eve	H-Ac	HEC Paris	BMTW	PHD	94	Paris IX	1989
Chiarella, Carol L.	Lect	Skidmore		MS	85	SUNY-Alb	& 8-04
Chiasson, Michael A.	C-Ac$	Nicholls St	FMX	DBA	94.	La Tech	8-94
John C. Daigle Free Enterprise Endowed Professorship							
Chikondo, J. T. M.	H-Le	Un Zimbabwe	M	MACC			&
Childs, Bradley D.	Assoc	Belmont	FX	PHD	94.	Purdue	&2001
Chilton, Robert C.			1994	DBA	92.	Boston U	
37 Ledgewood Rd; Bedford NH 03110-5125; 603-472-3675							
Chimchome, Natasek	Retir	Chulalongkor	AJ	FCA	72	ICAEW	&1972
Ching, Chee Kiong	Fell	Natl Singapo	FM	PHD	00	Queensla	&2000
Chio, Chun Duek (Anthony)			X	PHD	67.	Utah	&
Chipalkatti, Niranjan	Assoc	Seattle	FI	PHD	93.	Mass	&2004
Chisarick, Cynthia J.	Assoc	Wilkes	XF	MBA	84	Scranton	& 8-81
Chisholm, Samuel W.	Retir	Texas Tech	1981	MBA	50	Tx Tech	&1957
Chiu, Edward K. C.	Asst	Un Hong Kong	FP	BEC	71	Monash	& 9-79
Chiu, James S. H.	Prof	CS-Northrdge	LF	PHD	73.	Missouri	* &1979
Chiu, Yu-Hsien	Inst	Mo-Rolla		MS	91	Wi-Milwa	2007
Chiwamit, Palida	Lect	Chulalongkor	FM	MS	03	Warwick	&2007
Chlala, Nadi	Prof	Quebec-Montr	F	MSC		Saskatch	* &1-78
Cho, Charles	Asst	Concordia	F	PHD	07.	Cen Fla	2007
Cho, Ik Soon	Retir	Korea Univ	1993	PHD	66	Korea U	
Cho, Jang Y.		Korea	1997	PHD	87.	Florida	&
Cho, Joong-Seok				PHD	05.	Wisconsin	
Cho, Myo Jung	Asst	Fordham	F	PHD	05.	Maryland	
Cho, Paek J.			T	PHD	77.	Illinois	
Cho, Seong Ha	Prof	Korea Univ	F	MBA	70	Houston	3-71

Name	Rank	School		Deg	Yr	University	
Cho, Seong-Pyo	H-Pr	Kyungpook Un	F	PHD	90	Yonsei	&1986
Cho, Seong-Yeon	Asst	Oakland	FMS	PHD	01.	SUNY-Buf	2007
Cho, Stella	Assoc	HongKon Tech	X	PHD	99	HongKong	&1983
Cho, Whajoon				PHD	92.	Indiana	
Choe, Jong-Min	Prof	Kyungpook Un	MS	PHD	93	KAIST	&1987
Choe, Kukhyun	Asst	Chung-Ang	FTA	PHD	99	Geo Wash	&2002
Choe, Kungyun				PHD	99.	Geo Wash	
Choe, Yong S.			X	PHD	90.	Florida	
Choi, Byeonghee (Ben)	Asst	McGill Univ	F	PHD	94.	Iowa	
Management Dept; McGill University							
Choi, Frederick D. S.	C-Pr	New York U	IFM	PHD	72.	U Wash	1981
Choi, Hyun-Dol				PHD	95.	Ga Tech	
Choi, Jong-Hag	C-Pr	Seoul Natl	AFIQ	PHD	00.	Illinois	2006
Choi, Jung Ho	Prof	Chung-Ang	FPQ	PHD	87.	Houston	1988
Choi, Kok-Kun				PHD	94.	Houston	
Choi, Kwan		King Sejong	1992	PHD	92.	Syracuse	
Dept Acctg; Sch of Mgt; King Sejong Univ; Kunja-Don Seoul Korea							
Choi, Mun Soo			FM	PHD	93.	Kansas	
Choi, Nahnhee			AFT	PHD	88.	N Carol	&
Choi, Sung K.			1992	PHD	85.	Iowa	
Dept of Bus Adm; College of Comm & Econ; Gyongsan S Korea							
Choi, TaeHee				PHD	02.	Ohio St	
Choi, Won W.			XVFR	PHD	00.	Columbia	
Choi, Woooook			F	PHD	04.	Mich St	
Choi, Yeong Chan	Assoc	St John's	CF	PHD	89.	Drexel	&1989
Choi, Young-Soo	Lect	U Lancaster	FQ	PHD	03	Lancaster	2005
Cholak, Michael	Lect	Wis-Parkside	FM	MBA	98	Marquette	8-03
Chong, Eng Heng	Lect	Nanyang Tech		MSC	97	Nanyang	&2001
Chong, H. Gin	Assoc	Prairie View	AMSJ	PHD	99	Sheffield	2005
Chong, Kar Ming	Lect	New So Wales	F	PHD		E Cowan	2000
Chong, Vincent K.	SLect	W Australia	M	PHD	99	W Austrl	&2000
Chong, Y. S. Sebastian	Assoc	Natl Singapo	FM	MECO	83	Sydney	&1980
Choo, Freddie	Prof	San Fran St	A	PHD	89	NS Wales	&1990
Choo, Hwi Suck		Yonsei U		PHD	74.	Georgia	
Choo, Teck Min	Assoc	Nanyang Tech	AF	PHD	93.	Pittsburgh	&1987
Chookhiatti, Sarun	Asst	Chulalongkor	ACDR	MACC	95	Chulalong	&1995
Chope, Roger A.	Inst	Portland St	FM	PHD	81.	Oregon	2002
Chou, Ling-Tai Lynette	Prof	Nat Chengchi	AFNO	PHD	85.	Houston	&1990
Chou, Shu-Chen	Lect	Ntl Chung Ch	FT	MA	96	Chengchi	2002
Chow, Charles	STut	U Auckland	FA	BCOM	85	Auckland	2007
Chow, Chee W.	Emer	San Diego St	MC	PHD	81.	Oregon	1984
Chow, Yee-Chuing		Honolulu HI	1988	PHD	43.	Illinois	
Choy, Amy	Asst	Univ Alberta	AF	PHD	05	U Wash	2005
Choy, Helen	Asst	Cal-Riversid	F	PHD	04.	Rochester	2003
Chrisman, Heidi Hadlich			F	PHD	90.	U Wash	
Christ, Leroy F. (Rick)	Assoc	No Iowa	XF	PHD	91.	Tx-Austin	&2007
Christ, Mary York	Assoc	No Iowa	FAO	PHD	88.	Tx-Austin	&2007
Christensen, Anne L.	C-Pr	Montana St	X	PHD	89.	Utah	8-02
Christensen, David S.	C-Pr	Srthrn Utah	MCJ	PHD	87.	Nebraska	* &8-98
Christensen, Elwyn L.	Retir	CS-Fresno	1993	DBA	68.	S Calif	&8-68
Christensen, Fred	Lect	Boise State	PGAF	MBA	81	Utah	&1-84
Christensen, John	Prof	U So Denmark	TMF	PHD	79.	Stanford	1973
Christensen, Linda F.			IMS	PHD	89.	S Carol	&
Christensen, Theodore E.	Assoc	Brigham Yg	M	PHD	95.	Georgia	&9-00
Christenson, Charles J.	Emer	Harvard	1996	DBA	61	Harvard	1957
Royal Little Professor of Business Administration							
Christian, Cal	Asst	East Carol	FA	PHD	00.	Fla St	&8-00
Christian, Charles W.	D-Pr	Arizona St	X	PHD	85.	Georgia	&1-85
Christiansen, Linda	Assoc	Indiana SE	FLJ	JD	87	Indiana	&8-98
Christianson, Charles	H-Pr	Luther	FMX	MBA	75	S Dakota	&1988
Christie, Andrew A.	Prof	Louisiana St	FCTM	PHD	81.	Stanford	1995
Christie, Nancy L.	Retir	Seattle Pac	2006	PHD	90.	Va Tech	&2003
Christmore, Patricia C.	Deces	New Mex St	5-80	PHD	75.	Oklahoma	&8-72
Christopher, Jeff	SLect	U Glamorgan	FS	MA	78	Manchest	* &9-78
Christopher, Jill R.	Prof	Ohio Northrn	PD	DBA	99.	Clev St	&1988
Chu, David	Assoc	Holy Cross	FCN	PHD	85	Indiana	9-91
Chu, Eric L.			FMV	PHD	92.	NYU	
Chu, Ling	Asst	Wilfrid Laur	XF				
Chu, Pai-Cheng	Assoc	Ohio State	S	PHD	87	Tx-Austin	1987
Chu, Sunnie			F	PHD	96.	Oregon	
Chua, Francis C. K.	Lect	Massey Univ	HEFT	MBS		Massey	1987
Chua, Wai Fong	Prof	New So Wales	MH	PHD	83	Sheffield	&1985
Chugh, Lal C.	Retir	Mass-Boston	2001	PHD	71	Harvard	1985
Chugh, S.	ALect	New So Wales		MBA		Ntl Sch	
Chukwuma, Emilia	Assoc	Gallaudet	CFPT	MS	87	Baltimore	&1988
Chumley, Delbert W.	Retir	La St-Shreve	2000	PHD	75.	Arkansas	&8-87
Chung, Chong A.	Dean	Yonsei Univ	FA	PHD	84	Yonsei	&1978

Chung, Dennis Y.	Assoc	Simon Fraser	AFT	PHD	91	Alberta	* &9-05
Chung, Hay Young		Kyung-Hee U		PHD	87.	Berkeley	
Chung, Hyeesoo "Sally"	Asst	Ariz St West		PHD	04.	Purdue	8-05
Chung, Janne O. Y.	Assoc	York Univ	ABEO	PHD	98	E Cowan	2000
Chung, Kee-Young		Keimyung Un	2004	PHD	85.	Tx-Austin	
Keimyung University; Chairman Korean Accounting Standards Board							
Chung, Kun Y.		Keimyung Un	1996	PHD	88.	Wisconsin	
Chung, Kwang-Hyun	Prof	Pace	DFTQ	PHD	90.	Baruch	1990
Chung, Lai Hong	Assoc	Nanyang Tech	CM	PHD	92.	Pittsburgh	&1987
Chung, Moon-Chong		Dong-A Korea		PHD	92.	Illinois	
Chung, Shifei	Assoc	Rowan	FA	PHD	95.	Memphis	&1997
Chung, Tsai-Yen				PHD	85.	Tx Tech	&
Chung, Yanghon			1995	PHD	94.	Geo St	1994
Tae Jeon Univ; Korea							
Chung, Yong-Keun	C-Pr	Dongguk U	FPV	PHD	86	Korea	3-80
Chung, Yu To				DBA	75.	Indiana	
Church, Bryan K.	Prof	Georgia Tech	ABF	PHD	86.	Florida	&9-96
Church, Kimberly	Asst	Oklahoma St		PHD	07.	Arkansas	2007
Church, Lisa	Assoc	Rhode Isl Cl	LXF	JD	92	NE Law	&9-00
Church, Pamela H.	C-Ac	Rhodes Coll	M	PHD	86.	Houston	&1988
Churchill, Neil C.	Prof	INSEAD	1994	PHD	62	Michigan	&
Churchman, Robert J.	Asst	Harding	FBR	MBA	03	Cen Ark	&2004
Churyk, Natalie T.	Assoc	No Illinois	F	PHD	01.	S Carol	&8-01
Catearpillar Professor of Accountancy							
Chwastiak, Michele E.	Assoc	New Mexico	MC	PHD	91.	Pittsburgh	1999
Ciancanelli, Penelope L.	SLect	Strathclyde	WIT	PHD	83	New Sch	1996
Cianci, Anna M.	Asst	Drexel	AF	PHD	00.	Duke	&2005
Cianciolo, S. Thomas A.	Retir	E Michigan	8-05	PHD	75.	Mich St	&1985
Ciccio, Star	Inst	Johnson&Wale	MP	MBA	05	John&Wal	2005
Ciftci, Mustafa	Asst	SUNY-Bingham	F	PHD	06	Tx-Dallas	2007
Cipriano, Angela	VInst	Cleveland St	FM	MACC	04	Clev St	2006
Cipriano, Michael C.	Asst	Charleston	AFJ	PHD	06.	S Carol	2006
Cirtin, Arnold L.	Retir	Ball State	1977	PHD	74.	Cincinnati	&9-67
Citarella, Victor	Retir	St Thomas-FL	1998	DCS	43	Havana	&1979
Claes, Paul C. M.	Lect	Vrije Univ	EFIM	MS	94	Maastricht	1999
Claiborne, M. Cathy	Prof	Colorado Spr	FGM	PHD	94.	Tennessee	* &2007
Claire, Alison L.	Retir	Clemson	2000	PHD	91.	Georgia	&
alibd@clemson.edu							
Clancy, Donald K.	Prof	Texas Tech	CM	PHD	76.	Penn St	1982
Clapin-Pepin, Daniel	Prof	Quebec-Montr	A	PHD		Quebec	&7-80
Clark, Benjamin E.	Retir	SW Baptist	1993	PHD	73.	LSU	1966
Clark, Corolyn E.	Retir	St Joseph	2007	PHD	85.	Temple	1978
Clark, Dixie L.			ASFG	DBA	91.	La Tech	&
Clark, Erlinda T.	Retir	CS-Sacrament	2004	PHD	71	Tx Tech	&1980
Clark, Fredrick A.	Retir	W Kentucky	1989	MPA	78	Miss St	1971
Clark, George S.	Deces	E Michigan	XF	LLM	75	Wayne St	&1975
Clark, Gloria	Assoc	Winston-Slm	XFM	EDD	87	Atlanta	&8-95
Clark, Greg	Lect	Wilfrid Laur	FM	CMA	90	McMaster	2001
Clark, Johnnie L.	Retir	Clark Atlant	1996	PHD	73.	Georgia	&9-62
2794 Chaucer Dr SW; Atlanta GA 30311; 404-691-5955							
Clark, Julie	Lect	Univ Leeds	FX	BA	88	Manchest	9-97
Clark, Kris	Inst	Georgia St	F	MAC	01	Arizona	&8-02
Clark, Lawrence S.	Assoc	Clemson	FV	MA	70	Georgia	* &1977
Clark, Murray B.	SLect	Lincoln-NZ	EFHP	MCOM	70	Canterbu	&1978
Clark, Myrtle W.	Assoc	Kentucky	FM	PHD	78.	S Carol	* 1977
Clark, Robert	Retir	Emporia St	1989	EDD	69	Okla St	8-87
Clark, Robert W.	Deces	Idaho	1991	MS	58	Idaho	&1956
Clark, Roger W.	Assoc	Austin Peay	PXI	PHD	92	Tennessee	&1992
Clark, Ronald L.	Prof	Auburn	S	PHD	83.	Alabama	&6-95
Clark, Stanley J.	Prof	So Miss	FTV	PHD	91.	Kentucky	&1990
Clark, Theresa	Prof	Methodist	LX	JM	71	N Carol	1992
Clark, Virginia	Inst	Cincinnati	F	MBA	80	Cincinnati	&1986
Clark, Wayne	C-As	SW Baptist	FPAX	MBA		Mo St	&1991
Clark, Wilbur Rhea	Assoc	S F Austin	NAM	PHD	80.	Missouri	&1984
Clark, Willard C. Jr.	Emer	Dayton	2001	MBA	60	Miami U	&9-63
Clarke, Alex	SLect	W Australia	F	MCOM	91	W Austrl	1983
Clarke, Bevan J.	Prof	Canterbury	DSFT	PHD	75	Brit Colum	&1963
Clarke, Brian	Lect	Monash Univ	MCAB	MBA	89	Monash	&1989
Clarke, Christine	STut	U Auckland	F	BCOM	82	Auckland	2002
Clarke, Douglas A.	Deces	Georgia	8-90	PHD	87.	Wisconsin	&1987
Clarke, Peter J.	H-Pr	Un Cl Dublin	EMH	PHD	84	Dublin	&1980
Clarke, Robert W.		Practice TX		PHD	67.	Illinois	1979
Clarke, Rose Marie		BDO Dunwoody		PHD	00.	NYU	
BDO Dunwoody LLP - National Office							
Clarke-Okah, Ann	Inst	Carleton Un	F	BA	73	Simon Fr	&1983
Clarkson, Peter M.	Prof	U Queensland	A	PHD	86	Brit Colum	2002
Clary, Duane A.	Retir	Nev-L Vegas	1996	DBA	69.	Tx Tech	&1973

Clatworthy, Mark A.	Lect	Cardiff U	FI	BSC	96	Cardiff	1996
Claus, James				PHD	00.	Columbia	
Clausen, Thomas S.	Asst	Il-Springfld	S	PHD	02	Conn	2007
Clay, Alvin A.	Retir	Villanova	1995	MBA	57	Drexel	1999
Clay, Raymond J. Jr.	Prof	North Texas	AFO	DBA	74.	Kentucky	&1983
Institute of Internal Auditors Professor							
Claypool, Gregory A.	Prof	Youngstown	FAEJ	PHD	88.	Kent St	9-86
Clayton, Bruce M.	SLect	Deakin-Geelg	CM	DCOM	84	Potchef	1982
Clayton, Penny R.	Prof	Drury	FG	PHD	90.	Okla St	&1990
Cleary, T.	SLect	London Metro	DS	MSC			1999
Cleaveland, M. Catherine	Asst	Kennesaw St	T	PHD	06.	Geo St	8-06
Clem, Anne M.	Lect	Iowa State	F	PHD	97.	Tx-Austin	& 8-95
Clement, Michael B.	Assoc	Texas-Austin	F	PHD	97.	Stanford	& 1-97
KPMG Faculty Fellowship in Accounting Education							
Clement, Robin P.	Inst	Oregon	F	PHD	94.	Mich St	&2003
Clements, A. Bruce	Assoc	Kennesaw St	XCF	PHD	89.	Florida	&1992
Clements, Curtis E.	Asst	Abilene Chr	AC	PHD	99.	Tx A&M	&2005
Clements, Lori	Lect	Un Waterloo	X	MTAX	99	Waterloo	&2007
Clements, Lynn H.	Prof	Fla Southern	PTVG	DBA	02	Nova SE	* &1990
Clendenon, Irel D.	Retir	Franklin	1997	MBA	83	Xavier	&1970
Cleveland, Frederick				PHD	67.	Columbia	
Cleveland, Gerald L.			FT	PHD	65.	U Wash	
Cleveland, Grover A.	Prof	Metro St-MN	XF	DBA	73.	Indiana	&1995
Clevenger, Barbara				PHD	95.	Cen Fla	&
Clevenger, Novella Noland	Assoc	Washburn	X	LLM	87	Wm&Mary	& 8-88
Clevenger, Thomas B.	Assoc	Washburn	AM	DBA	87.	Memphis	& 8-88
Cleverley, William O.	Retir	Ohio State	2003	PHD	71.	Berkeley	1974
Cliffe, Cheryl	SLect	U Auckland	F	PHD	03	Auckland	1987
Clifton, Gregory	Asst	Metro State		LLM			
Clifton, James W.	SLect	N Dakota St	NFXG	MS	88	N Dakota	&1998
Clifton, Norma	Asst	Roanoke	FPX	MBA	00	Radford	1-01
Clikeman, Paul M.	Assoc	Richmond	AFM	PHD	95.	Wisconsin	# &1995
Clinch, Gregory J.	Prof	Austral Grad	F	PHD	88.	Stanford	1991
Cline, Donald G.	Retir	Ind-So Bend	1988	MBA		Michigan	&1968
3504 Chevy Chase; South Bend IN46615							
Clingan, J. A. P.	SLect	Un East Lond	FM	BA			1978
Clinkenbeard, John A.	Retir	Saginaw Vall	1998	ABD	51	Chicago	&1969
Clinton, B. Douglas	Prof	No Illinois	CMU	PHD	94.	Tx-Arlin	* &8-01
Alta Via Consuiltng Professor of Management Accounting							
Clinton, Sarah	Asst	Tennessee	F	PHD	07.	Georgia	2007
Cloud, C. Douglas	Retir	Pepper-Malib	2003	DBA	71.	Ariz St	&1986
Clovey, Robert	Asst	CUNY-York					
Clowery, Grant M.			1994	PHD	83.	Chicago	&
Horst, Frisch, Clowery & Finan; 2445 M Street NW Suite 200; Wash DC 20037							
Cloyd, C. Bryan	Prof	Virg Tech	X	PHD	92.	Indiana	& 8-05
John E. Peterson, Jr. Professor of Accounting and Information Systems							
Clune, Richard R.	Asst	Kennesaw St	AFM	EDM	05	Case Wes	&2002
Clurman, Herman	Retir	New York U	1992	JD	52	Brooklyn	&1955
Cluskey, G. Robert Jr.	Assoc	Troy-Dothan	ACFM	DBA	94.	S Illinois	&2006
Clute, Ronald C.	Retir	Metro State	8-99	PHD	77	Notre Dm	9-88
Clutterbuck, Peter	Lect	U Queensland	S	MSC	95	Queenl Tc	
Clyde, Nita J.			1999	PHD	80.	Tx-Arlin	&
Clyde Associates; Dallas TX							
Coakley, James R.	Assoc	Oregon State	G	PHD	82.	Utah	1990
Coakley, Jerry	Prof	Univ Essex	FQ	PHD	92	Open	2001
Coarts, Darlene G.	Inst	No Iowa	CM	MBA	76	Maryland	&2006
Coate, Charles Joseph	C-Ac	St Bonaventu	AMJ	PHD	92.	Maryland	&2000
Coates, J. Dennis	Dean	Fla Atlantic	F	PHD	89.	LSU	& 8-89
Coats, Jay H.	Retir	W Virginia	2005	PHD	76.	Pittsburgh	1971
Cobb, Earl Kennedy	Retir	CS-L Angeles	1987	MBA	49	Nrthwstrn	&1958
PO Box 950519; Lake Mary FL 32795							
Cobb, Ian	Lect	Dundee	CDMS	PHD	97	Dundee	* 1989
Cobb, Janice	Inst	Tx Christian	F	MBA	86	Tx Chr	&1997
Cobb, Laurel G.	Assoc	Saint Leo-FL	FAEJ	PHD	93.	S Fla	&1986
Cobbin, Phillip E.	SLect	U Melbourne	FA	MCOM	02	Melbourne	&1989
Cocco, Anthony F.	Assoc	Nev-L Vegas	F	PHD	91.	Fla St	& 1-92
Cochran, Robert J.	Asst	Longwood	FM	PHD	01.	Va Comm	&2003
Cochrane, Dorothy	Lect	Monash Univ	FT	PHD	96	Waikato	&2000
Cockrum, Robert B.	Inst	South Fla	F	JD	74	Indiana	& 8-02
Coda, Bernard A. Jr.	Retir	North Texas	1994	PHD	62.	Illinois	&1965
Coe, Martin	Assoc	W Illinois	SV	MBA	92	St Ambro	# * &9-94
Coe, Teddy L.	Retir	North Texas	CF	PHD	72.	Tx A&M	&1980
Coenenberg, Adolf G.		Augsburg Un	CMU	PHD	68	Cologne	
Coffee, C. David	Prof	W Carolina	FT	DBA	83.	Kentucky	&1988
Coffer, Curtis A.			F	PHD	91.	Michigan	&
Coffey, James J.	Prof	SUNY-Plattsb	XL	JD	74	Suffolk	1981
Coffey, Mark A.	Deces	W New Eng	MC	MBA	76	Mass	* 1974

Name	Rank	School		Degree		School		
Coffman, Edward N.	C-Pr	Virg Comm	FT	DBA	73.	Geo Wash		1966
Coglitore, Frank J.	Assoc	St Thomas-MN	AF	MBA	65	Scranton		&9-82
Cohen, Alan H.	Assoc	Ithaca	FCMX	MS		SUNY-Bin		&8-76
Cohen, Albert H.	Retir	Tulane	1995	PHD	53.	Michigan		&1982
Cohen, Ann Burstein	VAsoc	SUNY-Buffalo	XF	MBA	82	SUNY-Buf		&1986
Cohen, Daniel A.	Asst	So Calif	F	PHD	04.	Nrthwstrn		2004
on leave to New York University								
Cohen, Edwin	Prof	DePaul	FTV	PHD	60.	Mich St		&1981
Cohen, Jacob	Affil	INSEAD	F					2003
Cohen, Jeffrey R.	Assoc	Boston Coll	BJIE	PHD	87.	Mass	*	1986
Cohen, Leslie	SLect	Arizona	F	MBA	90	Chicago		1994
Cohen, Ronnie	Prof	Chris Newpor	LX	LLM	88	Wm&Mary		1983
Cohen, Susan	Asst	Harvard		PHD	99.	Stanford		
Cohn, Gordon M.	Assoc	Touro	ACP	PHD	97	Baruch		7-98
Cojeen, Robert H.	Retir	Mich-Flint	1989	DBA	55	Indiana		1956
Coker, John W.	Assoc	Belmont	PFC	PHD	90.	Miss		&1991
Colabella, Patrick R.	Assoc	St John's	MX	MBA	80	Pace		&1987
Colantoni, Claude S.	Deces	Penn	1987	PHD	68	Purdue		1975
Colbert, Gary J.	Assoc	Colo-Denver	FAM	PHD	91.	Oregon		&9-93
Colbert, Janet L.	Prof	E Kentucky	A	PHD	84.	Georgia	#	&2006
Colburn, Steven C.	C-Ac	Maine	XF	PHD	89.	Georgia		&9-92
Cole, Cathy J.			FM	PHD	99.	Geo Wash		&
Cole, Elizabeth T.	Asst	Jms Madison	FCA	PHD	99.	Kent St		&9-02
Cole, Frederick M.	Retir	North Fla	2002	EDD	71	Florida		&1972
Cole, Sheldon N.				PHD	71.	Michigan		
Coleman, Clarence Jr.	Prof	Winthrop	AFC	PHD	90.	S Carol		&9-02
Coleman, Fred	Inst	Southern Ark	SE	MBA	03	Hend St		
Coleman, Jack W.		CS-Fullerton	1990	DBA	58.	Indiana		1968
Colgan, Joseph C.	Retir	Fort Lewis	2000	PHD	81.	North Tx		&1981
Coller, Maribeth			FM	PHD	91.	Indiana		1991
Collett, Nick J.	Lect	U Manchester	F	PHD	94	Manchest		1986
Collett, Peter H.	Lect	Un Tasmania	FT	MA	88	Tasmania		1990
Colley, J. Ronald	C-Pr	West Georgia	MSP	PHD	86.	Geo St		&9-89
Colliander, John	Inst	New Hampshir	X	JD	71	Boston U		1990
Collier, Boyd D.	Prof	Tarleton St	FV	PHD	70	Tx-Austin		&1983
Collier, Bruce E.			MAGC	PHD	75.	Okla St		& 3
Collier, Karen	Inst	Georgia Col						
Collier, Paul A.	Lect	Univ Exeter	DX	PHD	94	Exeter		&1984
Collier, Philip A.	AProf	U Melbourne	S	MSC	79	Essex		2001
Collier, Robert	TchAc	Univ Ottawa	CF	BAH	71	Carleton	*	2003
Collins, Allison B.	Inst	Memphis	FM	PHD	87.	Houston		&8-03
Collins, Daniel W.	Prof	Iowa	TF	PHD	73.	Iowa		9-77
Henry B. Tippie Research Chair in Accounting								
Collins, David	Asst	Univ Essex	BM	MSC	89	Strathcl		1999
Collins, David T.	Assoc	Bellarmine	FIS	PHD	93.	Geo St		&8-94
Collins, Dennis J.			AF	PHD	79.	Iowa		&
Collins, Denton L.	Assoc	Memphis	FM	PHD	95.	Colorado		8-03
Collins, Don E.	Deces	Ithaca	FCAS	MACC	76	Ohio St	*	&8-85
Collins, Frank	Prof	Tx A&M Intl	MB	PHD	74.	Houston		&6-04
Radcliffe Killam Distinguished Professor of Accounting								
Collins, J. Stephen	C-Ac	Mass-Lowell	FMGN	PHD	75	Boston C		&9-86
Collins, Jacklyn	Lect	U Miami		MPRA	03	U Miami		2006
Collins, James F.		U Galway Ire	1992	PHD	78.	Nrthwstrn		
Univ of Galway; Dept of Accounting; Galway Ireland								
Collins, James R.				DBA	79.	Tennessee		&
Collins, Jane	Inst	Millsaps	XFG	LLM	05	U Miami		2005
Collins, Joanne A.	Retir	CS-L Angeles	2004	PHD	76.	Nrthwstrn	*	&1982
Collins, Karen M.	Assoc	Lehigh	FB	PHD	88.	Va Tech		&1990
Collins, Lane G.	Retir	Baylor	FGNV	DBA	78.	S Calif		&9-71
Collins, Mary K.	Assoc	LeMoyne	FABC	PHD	91.	Syracuse		&9-84
Collins, Mike	Prof	Univ Leeds	FNH	PHD	72	LondonSE		9-74
Collins, Roger	Assoc	Thompson Riv	FPTS	MSC	81	LondonEc	*	1992
Collins, Ronald	Inst	Miami U-Ohio	P	MS	77	Missouri		&8-05
Collins, Thomas S.	C-Pr	Loras	AL	MA	85	Iowa		&1988
Collins, William	Assoc	Un Stirling	M	MBA	82	Glasgow		1979
Collins, William A.	Retir	N Car-Greens	2006	PHD	75.	U Wash		&8-89
Collinsworth, Carol	C-As	Tx-Brownsvil		MBA	83	Tx-PanAm		&1982
Collison, David J.	SLect	Dundee	FMTA	MACC	93	Dundee		&1989
Collum, Taleah	Inst	Jacksonvl St	FM	MACC	04	Fla St		&
Collura, Thomas	Lect	SUNY-Albany	X	JD	88	AlbanyLw		2001
Colon, Manuel	Retir	Puerto Rico	1992	MBA	62	NYU		&1970
Colquhoun, Philip	Lect	Victoria NZ	FGWH	PHD		Canterbu		1992
Colquitt, Denise	Lect	West Georgia	P	MPAC	96	W Geo		8-06
Colson, Robert H.		Grant Thornt	2006	PHD	80.	Ohio St		&2000
Colter, Norman	Lect	New Mexico	F	MBA		New Mex		&2001
Colvard, Robert G.	Prof	Mid Tenn St	ATF	PHD	81.	Georgia		&1-78
Coman, Carol Lynn	Assoc	Calif Luthrn	FMX	MS	84	CS-Nrthr		1986

Combs, Margaret D.	C-Ac	Cumberland	FAC	DBA	04	Sarasota	&2005
Comerford, Ellen	Prof	Kean	XADF	MBA	79	Seton Hall	&1988
Comerford, Richard	STut	U Melbourne		BCOM		Melbourne	1999
Comiskey, Eugene E.	Prof	Georgia Tech	FMIT	PHD	65.	Mich St	* &1980
Callaway Professor; Associate Dean of Faculty and Research							
Committe, Bruce E.			KFLG	PHD	83.	Alabama	* &
Comprix, Joseph	Asst	Arizona St	F	PHD	00.	Illinois	8-00
Compton, Ted R.			MCS	PHD	80.	Cincinnati	*
Comstock, S. Mark	Prof	Missouri So	AFM	PHD	91.	Oklahoma	&1993
Comtois, Jean	Prof	Sherbrooke	F	MCOM	67	Sherbrook	&1968
Comunale, Christie L.	Assoc	Lg Isl-Post	PF	PHD	99.	S Fla	&1999
Condie, Frank A.	Retir	Utah State	1999	PHD	69.	Ariz St	&1968
Cong, Nguyen Van	Lect	Natl Econ	FMCV	PHD	95	Natl Econ	1986
Cong, Yu	Asst	Towson	SMAD	PHD	04.	Rutgers	2005
Conheady, Brian	TchAc	Univ Ottawa	CM	MBA	77	McGill	* &2006
Conley, Raymond A.				PHD	68.	Ariz St	
Conn, Carolyn T.	Asst	St Edwards	MCN	PHD	78.	Arkansas	&2007
Conner, Elizabeth C.	SInst	Colo-Denver	FTX	MS	79	Colo St	& 9-89
Conner, Henry H.				DBA	71.	Harvard	
Connors, Elizabeth	Asst	Mass-Boston	SMB	PHD	04.	Mich St	
Conover, Teresa L.	Prof	North Texas	FI	PHD	88.	Tx A&M	&1989
Paden Neeley Professor of Accounting							
Conrad, Bruce	Assoc	Marshall	FF	MBA	73	SUNY-Buf	&
Conrad, Edward J.	Assoc	Akron	F	PHD	91.	Fla St	* & 8-91
Conrad, Lynne	PLect	U Portsmith	BCM	PHD		Essex	&
Conrod, Joan E. D.	Prof	Dalhousie	FT	MBA	86	Toronto	&1989
Considine, Brett A.	Lect	Macquarie Un	S	BCOM	99	Melbourne	
Constas, Michael	Prof	CS-Long Bch	CMLX	PHD	94	UCLA	1994
Conture, Lyne	Lect	Sherbrooke	F	MS	85	Sherbrook	2002
Conway, Grace M.	Assoc	Adelphi	CVGF	MA	77	NY Soc	&1978
Conway, Lucian G.			TS	PHD	75.	LSU	&
Conway, Robert	Prof	Wis-Plattev	PTM	PHD	92.	Wisconsin	8-90
Conway, Thomas E. Jr.			F	PHD	98.	Maryland	
Cooch, Francis A. III				DBA	72.	Geo Wash	
Cook, A. M.	SLect	Liverpool JM	FM	FCA			
Cook, Clifford G.	Retir	Ohio Wesley	VFMA	MBA	76	Drexel	* &1984
Cook, David	C-Pr	Calvin	FMX	MS	79	W Mich	& 9-85
Cook, Don R.	Retir	Tenn Tech	1995	PHD	70.	Alabama	&1956
Cook, Doris Marie	Retir	Arkansas	1998	PHD	68.	Tx-Austin	&1947
Cook, Ellen D.	H-Pr	La-Lafayette	XFE	MS	75	LSU	&1977
Cook, Gail L.	Assoc	Brock Univ	MCSE	PHD	90.	Utah	&2000
Cook, Harold B.	Retir	Lock Haven	5-02	PHD	86.	Michigan	9-94
hcookmi@aol.com							
Cook, James F.	Retir	Tx-Arlington	1989	MBA	54	North Tx	1963
Cook, Jay D. Jr.	Retir	Wash & Lee	1991	PHD	56	Ohio St	1953
905 Sunset Drive; Lexington VA 24450							
Cook, John K.	Asst	Wright State	X	LLM	96	Florida	9-04
Cook, John P. Jr.	Asst	Heidelberg	F	PHD	94	Kentucky	&1995
Cook, John W.	Retir	Georgia St	1991	PHD	63.	Alabama	& 9-56
2635 Hawthorne Place NE; Atlanta GA 30345							
Cook, N. Ellen	Prof	San Diego	MI	PHD	78.	UCLA	1975
Cook, Sally V.	Assoc	Tx Lutheran	LTXP	JD		Tx-Austin	&1997
Cook, Teresa	Inst	Ferris State		PHD		Capella	2002
Cook, Victor J.	Prof	Tulane		PHD	65.	Michigan	
Marketing Dept; Tulane University							
Cooke, Calvin L.	Retir	Howard	1991	MBA	54	Indiana	&1970
Cooke, Terence E.	H-Pr	Univ Exeter	FI	PHD	89	Exeter	&1980
Cooke, Thomas B.	Asst	Georgetown	LX	MLT	85	Geotown	1975
Distinguished Teaching Professor							
Coolbaugh, Carl W.	Asst	Adams State		MBA		Colorado	&
Cooley, Glen	Assoc	NW St of LA	EJPX	PHD		North Tx	& 8-81
Coolidge, Herbert	Retir	So Adventist	2002	PHD	70	Mich St	&1991
Coombs, Hugh M.	PLect	U Glamorgan	NMI	PHD	98	Glamorgan	& 1-87
Cooper, Christine	SLect	Strathclyde	F	MSC	84	LondonEc	1988
Cooper, David J.	Prof	Univ Alberta	WGH	PHD	79	Manchest	1989
Certified General Accountants Professor of Accounting							
Cooper, Jean C.	Assoc	Kentucky	MB	PHD	85.	N Carol	&1990
Cooper, Kathleen Anne	SLect	U Wollongong	HFLW	PHD	94	Wollong	1985
Cooper, R. J.	SLect	Un East Lond	FM	MSC			1984
Cooper, Robert	Prof	Methodist	VCXI	DBA	97	Nova SE	* &1989
Cooper, Robin	Prof	Emory	M	DBA	82.	Harvard	& 8-98
Cooper, Rolland	Lect	E Michigan	CFA	MBA	84	E Mich	&1980
Cooper, William D.	Prof	N Carol A&T	FAHV	PHD	80.	Arkansas	& 5-85
Cooper, William W.	Emer	Texas-Austin	1994	DSC	70	Ohio St	1980
Foster Parker Centennial Professor Emeritus of Finance and Management							
Cooperstein, Alice R.	Retir	Central Conn	2003	MBA	75	Hartford	9-69
Copeland, Benny R.	Retir	North Texas	2000	PHD	66.	Tx-Austin	# * &1963

Copeland, Cheryl	Lect	CS-Fresno	PMC	MBA	03	CS-Fresno	8-03
Copeland, Phyllis V.	Deces	New Orleans	2000	PHD	95.	LSU	&1994
Copeland, Richard W.	Assoc	Stetson	XL	LLM	72	U Miami	1976
Copeland, Ronald M.	Retir	Northeastern	1993	PHD	66.	Mich St	9-81
Copley, Paul A.	D-Pr	Jms Madison	AGV	PHD	88.	Alabama	&7-04
Hantzmon, Wiebel & Company Faculty Fellow							
Coppage, Richard E. (Rick)	Prof	Louisville	FVT	DBA	86.	Kentucky	* &1979
Coppinger, Richard J.	Retir	St John's	2004	MBA	64	NYU	&1975
Copple, Scott E.	Assoc	Neb-Omaha	X	LLM	82	Denver	&1990
Coppolella, Biagio G.	Retir	Bridgeport	2003	MBA	63	NYU	&1963
Coram, Paul	SLect	U Melbourne	ABE	MACC		W Aust	2004
Corbett, B. Dean	Retir	North Fla	1998	PHD	75.	Florida	&1973
Corbett, Rena	Asst	Barton	FACM	MBA	94	N Carol	&8-01
Corbin, Donald A.	Retir	Hawaii-Manoa	1986	PHD	54.	Berkeley	&9-60
Corcoran, A. Wayne			C	PHD	66.	SUNY-Buf	&
Cordery, Carolyn	ALect	Victoria NZ		MCOM			* &
Cordova, Kathryn	Lect	Arizona		MBA	00	Ariz St	2005
Core, John E.	Prof	Pennsylvania	M	PHD	95.	Penn	1996
Corkern, Sheree M.	Asst	Miss College	AFPS	PHD	04.	JacksonSt	1985
Corkum, Patricia E.	Asst	Acadia Univ	FX	MBA		Dalhousie	&
Corless, John C.	Prof	CS-Sacrament	AFTJ	PHD	71.	Minnesota	# &1984
Corman, Eugene J.	Retir	CS-Fullerton	1991	DBA	71.	S Calif	&1966
Cormier, Denis	Prof	Quebec-Montr	FT	DSC		Mons	# * &6-84
Cormier, Elise	Prof	Univ Laval		PHD	96	Laval	1999
Cornelius, Barbara H.	Prof	Univ of Umea	F	PHD	94	N Eng-Au	1-05
Cornell, David W.	Assoc	Mo-Kansas Ct	F	PHD	88.	LSU	* &1989
Cornell, Max T.		Real Esta CA		DBA	71.	S Calif	&1980
Cornell, Robert M.	Asst	Oklahoma St	BCUM	PHD	06.	Utah	2006
Cornelsen, Erin	Asst	Briar Cliff		MPA		Nebraska	&
Cornick, Michael F.	Assoc	Winthrop	DM	PHD	80.	N Carol	&9-02
Corning, Gerald L.	Assoc	Adams State		MBA		W NewMex	# * &
Corona, Carlos	Asst	Texas-Austin	TMFA	PHD	06.	Stanford	&7-06
Corr, Arthur V.	Retir	Wis-Parkside	1995	MBA	56	NYU	* 8-78
Correia, Ernst V.			FGT	PHD	77.	Miss	
Corriher, J. D.	Retir	Alabama	1987	PHD	76.	Alabama	1954
#9 Guilds Wood; Tuscaloosa AL 35401							
Corsini, Louis S.	Assoc	Boston Coll	FI	PHD	72.	LSU	&1971
Cortese, Corinne	Lect	U Wollongong	FIP	PHD			2006
Cory, Suzanne N.	Prof	St Marys-Tx	FB	PHD	88.	Maryland	&8-91
Cosgrove, Debra	Lect	Nebraska	S	MPA	89	Nebraska	2001
Coshell, J.	SLect	London Metro	Q	PHD			1989
Cossey, Tiffany J.	Asst	Missouri So	PXV	LLM	02	Mo-Ks Cty	&2005
Cossitt, Betty	Lect	Nevada-Reno	M	MBA	91	Nev-Reno	&2000
Costella, Salvatore	Deces			DBA	67.	Mich St	
Costello, Daniel E.	Retir	Colorado St	2003	PHD	68	Mich St	1996
Costigan, Michael L.	C-Pr	S Ill-Edward	MF	PHD	85.	St Louis	9-91
Costouros, George J.	Retir	San Jose St	2001	PHD	72.	Santa Cl	8-68
Cote, Gustave C.	Retir	Providence	1989	MBA	54	Penn	&1952
3423 SE 22nd Place; Cape Coral FL 33904							
Cote, Jane M.	Assoc	Wash State	MCNB	PHD	94.	Wash St	1-93
Cote, Louise	Assoc	HEC-Montreal	JMV	PHD	95	Quebec	&8-01
Cote, Marie	Lect	Sherbrooke	CMT	MS	95	Sherbrook	1995
Cote, Marie B.	Retir	Bryant	1994	EDD	72	Sarasota	9-54
Cote, Raymond	Retir	Johnson&Wale	2000	MSBA	66	Suffolk	&1982
Cote, Sean	Asst	Nichols Col		MBA	99	Nichols	8-05
Cottell, Philip G. Jr.	Prof	Miami U-Ohio	FE	DBA	82.	Kentucky	1982
Cotter, Julie	SLect	So Queenslnd	FTY	PHD	98	Queensld	1991
Cotton, William David J.	Retir	SUNY-Geneseo	2003	MCOM	65	Canterbu	* &9-85
Cottrell, David M.	Prof	Brigham Yg	FA	PHD	92.	Ohio St	9-92
Cottrell, James L.	Retir	Temple	FM	PHD	70	Penn	&1968
Cottrill, Michael D.	Lect	Northeastern	FVA	MAC	75	Va Tech	&9-85
Coulmas, Nancy E.	Prof	Bloomsburg	CPFM	PHD	89.	Penn St	1994
Coulombe, Daniel	Prof	Univ Laval	FT	PHD	87	Brit Colum	&1985
Coulson, Andrea	Lect	Strathclyde	FN	PHD		Durham	1999
Coulter, D.	Lect	Univ Ulster	AD	BSC			* D-03
Coulter, John M.	Prof	W New Eng	ABES	PHD	94.	Mass	&1997
Coulton, Jeffery J.	Lect	New So Wales	FAY	LLB	94	Sydney	
Counts, R. Wayne	Asst	Txs-Perm Bas	XC	PHD	05.	Tx Tech	2004
Courtenay, Stephen M.			F	PHD	82.	Arkansas	&
Courtis, John K.	Prof	City Univ HK	VTH	PHD	74.	Minnesota	&1992
Courtney, Harley M.	Retir	Tx-Arlington	2003	PHD	66.	Illinois	&1970
Covaleski, Mark A.	Prof	Wisconsin	N	PHD	79.	Penn St	&1-79
Robert Beyer Professor of Managerial Accounting and Control							
Cowan, Mark	Asst	Boise State	XL	JD	04	Conn	&2004
Cowan, Mickey W.	Assoc	OK Christian	VPX	MS	70	Okla St	&9-00
Cowen, Janet	Lect	W Sydney	EFJ	MEC	99	N Eng-Au	
Cowen, Scott S.	Prof	Tulane	MU	DBA	75.	Geo Wash	* 1998

Name	Rank	School	Jrnl	Degree	Yr	Deg School	Note
Cowgill, Kim	ALect	W Sydney	FJRX	BCOM	91	W Sydney	
Cowling, John F.	VAsst	Maryland	FM	PHD	89.	Indiana	2007
Cox, Bill D.	Retir	No Colorado	2004	PHD	80.	Missouri	&1988
Cox, Carol	Asst	Mid Tenn St		PHD	03	Va Comm	&2006
Cox, Clifford T.	Deces	Alaska-Fairb	O-94	PHD	81.	Iowa	& 8-80
Cox, Ellen F.			F	PHD	82.	Berkeley	
Cox, James S.	Emer	Ohio Univ	1999	PHD	74.	Pittsburgh	&1964
Cox, Michael A.	Pres	MBA Seminars	1996	PHD	82.	Okla St	&1989

MBA Intl Inc; 3455 Peachtree Indus Blvd Ste 305-262; Duluth GA 30136 476-2736

Name	Rank	School	Jrnl	Degree	Yr	Deg School	Note
Cox, Patty J.	Asst	Elon	FA	MS	87	NC-Green	&1987
Cox, Sharon P.			X	PHD	01.	Kentucky	&
Coy, David G.	Prof	Adrian	PCSV	MBA	83	Toledo	* &8-88
Coyle, William H.	Assoc	Babson	FAMI	PHD	93.	Tx A&M	* &1992
Coyne, Michael P.	Assoc	Bucknell	BHJW	PHD	02.	Conn	&9-00
Coyner, Randolph S.	Asst	Fla Atlantic	CMS	MBA	68	U Miami	* &1975
Coyte, Rodney	Lect	New So Wales	MB	MCOM	88	NS Wales	&1992
Cozort, Larry A.			XNG	PHD	86.	Va Tech	&
Crabtree, Aaron D.	Asst	Nebraska	XF	PHD	04.	Va Tech	2004
Cracraft, Scott	Retir	Albion	1997	MS	60	Miss	&1977
Craft, Clifford J.	Retir	CS-L Angeles	1987	PHD	84.	S Calif	* 9-73
Craig, Caroline K.	Prof	Illinois St	X	PHD	87.	Illinois	&1987
Craig, Darryl L.	Retir	Wis-Milwauke	2001	PHD	83.	Kansas	&1985
Craig, Quiester	Dean	N Carol A&T	FC	PHD	71.	Missouri	&8-72
Craig, Robert	Lect	Queensld Tec	F	MBA		Queensld	1995
Craig, Thomas R.	Prof	Illinois St	AT	PHD	84.	Illinois	&1981
Crain, Gilbert W.	Assoc	Il-Springfld	GF	PHD	78.	Illinois	2007
Crain, John L.			FXZ	PHD	88.	Miss	&
Crain, Terry L.	Assoc	Oklahoma	XZ	PHD	89.	Tx Tech	&9-89

Dale Looper Chair in Accounting

Name	Rank	School	Jrnl	Degree	Yr	Deg School	Note
Crall, Lamar	Retir	SW Okla St	1996	MBA	67	Arkansas	1967
Cram, Donald P.			MF	PHD	98.	Stanford	
Cramer, Donald H.	Retir	So Carolina	1991	MS	42	Indiana	&1980

25 Northlake Road; Columbia SC 29223

Name	Rank	School	Jrnl	Degree	Yr	Deg School	Note
Cramer, Joe J. Jr.	Deces	Howard	1986	DBA	63.	Indiana	&1981
Cramer, Lowell			FMV	PHD	94.	Fla Intl	
Crampton, John V.	Retir	SE Missouri	2000	PHD	70.	Missouri	1965
Crandall, Robert H.	Retir	Queen's Univ	1993	PHD	68.	Berkeley	&1968
Crane, Stuart R.				DBA	67.	Indiana	
Cranor, Rosalind N.	Retir	Virg Tech	2004	MA	66	Wstrn Ky	1965
Craswell, Allen T.	Prof	U Queensland	A	PHD	84	Sydney	&2001
Cratsley, Edward K.				DCS	43.	Harvard	
Craven, Albert L.	Deces	Jackson St	2-02	PHD	68.	Alabama	&1998
Craven, William	Assoc	NewJerseyCty	FGX	MBA	70	NYU	* &1989
Cravens, Karen S.	D-Pr	Tulsa	C	PHD	92.	Tx A&M	* &9-92

Chapman Professor of Accounting

Name	Rank	School	Jrnl	Degree	Yr	Deg School	Note
Crawford, Constance	C-Ac	Ramapo	AFT	MBA	86	Iona	1992
Crawford, Corinne L.	Asst	Marymt Manht		MBA	84	Pace	&2005
Crawford, Dean	C-Ac	LeMoyne	XFR	PHD	87.	Rochester	&9-06
Crawford, Jean G.	C-Pr	Alabama St	TAF	PHD	87.	Alabama	& 8-88
Crawford, Louise	Lect	Dundee	AESN	PHD	90	Edinburgh	2006
Cready, William M.	D-Pr	Texas-Dallas	CFM	PHD	85.	Ohio St	2004
Creasy, J. B.	Retir	Bloomsburg	1986	DED	73	Penn St	1960
Credle, Sid Howard	Dean	Hampton	FSH	PHD	89.	Tx-Austin	&9-99
Creech, Janie L.				PHD	74.	American	
Creighton, Cassie F.	C-Ac	Lyon College	FLXP	MBA	83	Ark St	&1984
Crespi, Cheryl	Assoc	Central Conn	FMX	JD	04	Conn	# &2005
Cress, James L.	Retir	Akron	5-96	DBA	80.	Kent St	&1973
Cress, William P.	Retir	Wis-La Cross	FP	PHD	80.	North Tx	& 8-85
Crichfield, Timothy R.				PHD	79.	Cornell	
Cripe, Bradrick L.	Asst	No Illinois	X	PHD	06.	Nebraska	&2006
Cripps, Jeremy G. A.	Prof	Am Un Kuwait	ACIN	PHD	92	Union-NY	&2004
Criscione, Eugene Richard	Asst	Morehead St	CJO	ABD		Miss	&2005
Crisostomo, Doreen	Inst	Guam	GFMS	MA	04	Phoenix	2005
Criss, Robert R.	Retir	Auburn	1993	LLM	88	Alabama	&9-66
Critchett, John D.	Assoc	Madonna	BWM	PHD	97.	Kentucky	&1994
Crockcroft, Sophie	Lect	U Queensland	S	PHD	99	Otago	2000
Crockett, James R.	Retir	So Miss	2006	DBA	74.	Miss St	# &1987
Croll, David B.	Retir	Virginia	2003	PHD	74.	Penn St	1-74
Crombie, Neil	Lect	Canterbury	CMU	MCOM	02	Canterbu	2004
Cron, William R.	Prof	Cen Michigan	FMV	PHD	73	Mich St	* 1982
Cronin, William	Asst	Il-Springfld	TL	LLM		Wash U	&2005
Crooch, G. Michael	FASB		2003	PHD	70.	Mich St	&

Financial Accounting Standards Board

Name	Rank	School	Jrnl	Degree	Yr	Deg School	Note
Crosby, Michael A.	Deces	Toledo	5-91	PHD	78.	Ohio St	1985
Crosby, William M.	Retir	Jacksonvil U		PHD	86.	Georgia	&1993
Cross, Joann Noe	Prof	Wis-Oshkosh	FHN	PHD	81.	Illinois	* &1980
Cross, Richard L.	Assoc	Bentley	RFCV	MBA	72	Northeas	&1969

Cross, William L.	Retir	Miss State	1989	MBA	50	Michigan		&1957
Crosser, Rick L.	Prof	Metro State	XJ	PHD	87.	Okla St		& 8-95
Crossland, Hugh J.	Lect	Northeastern	X	LLM	74	Boston U		9-94
Crow, Steven R.	Prof	CS-Sacrament	XM	PHD	90.	S Calif		&1989
Crowe, Lisa	Inst	Lindsey Wils	FA	MPA	96	Wstrn Ky		2001
Crowell, Steven J.		Tax Attorney	1998	PHD	87.	Georgia		&

Blanco Tackabery, Combs & Matamoros; Winston-Salem NC

Crowley, Robert M.	Retir	W Illinois	AXS	PHD	79.	Nebraska		& 9-69
Crowley, Steve M.	Asst	Fort Lewis	CMS	PHD	03.	Utah	*	&2007
Croxall, John R.				PHD	70.	American		
Cruden, Al	Retir	Siena	1995	MBA				&
Crum, Robert P.	Assoc	Penn State	MX	DBA	83.	Kentucky		& 9-83
Crum, William F.	Retir	CS-L Angeles	1983	PHD	51.	Tx-Austin		9-77
Crumbley, D. Larry	Prof	Louisiana St	XAZ	PHD	67.	LSU		& 8-96

KPMG LLP Endowed Professor

Crump, Zelma	Asst	Savannah St	AFI	ABD		JacksonSt		& 8-03
Crumpler, John R.	Retir	West Florida	2005	MBA	77	W Fla		9-77
Cruse, Rex B. Jr.		San Anton TX	1989	PHD	73.	Tx-Austin		&
Cubbage, Kenneth W.			XG	DBA	68.	Colorado		&
Cuccia, Andrew D.	Assoc	Oklahoma	X	PHD	90.	Florida		&1999

Grant Thornton Faculty Fellow

Cuccia, Cynthia	Lect	Oklahoma		PHD	91.	Florida		&2006
Cucumel, Guy	Prof	Quebec-Montr	M	DSC		Paris		6-91
Cui, Tracey	ALect	Macquarie Un						
Culbertson, Harold	Retir	Bemidji St	PF	PHD		U Wash		&1991
Cull, Michele	ALect	W Sydney	CFMX	BCOM	96	W Sydney		
Cullather, James L.	Retir	Notre Dame	1989	PHD	52	Colorado		1952
Cullen, John E.	Retir	Mercy-NY	F	JD	68	NY Law		& 9-71
Cullers, Sue	H-Ac	Tarleton St	MPV	PHD	89.	North Tx		&1985
Cullinan, Charles P.	Prof	Bryant	AMF	PHD	91.	Kentucky	# *	& 8-92
Culp, Richard I.	Inst	Ball State	F	BA	66	Fairmont		1-03
Culp, William H.	Retir	Mich-Dearbor	1991	PHD	61.	Michigan		&1965
Culpepper, Anthony	Asst	Pepper-Malib	CM	EDD	05	Pepperdi	*	&2005
Culpepper, David H.	Prof	Millsaps	PFXI	PHD	91.	Alabama		&1984

Kelly Gene Cook Chair of Business Administration

Culpepper, Robert C.	Emer	Ark-Ltl Rock	1998	PHD	69.	Arkansas		& 6-75
Culumovic, Louis	Assoc	Brock Univ	ADES	PHD	89	W Ontario		& 7-90
Cumby, Judy	Assoc	Memorial Un	F	MBA	94	Memorial		&1994
Cumming, John	Emer	Miami U-Ohio	FGN	PHD	73.	Illinois		& 8-77
Cummings, C. William	Assoc	No Illinois	SDM	PHD	86.	Missouri		& 8-84
Cummings, Lorne S.	Prof	Macquarie Un	JTW	PHD	02	Macquarie		&1996
Cummings, Lu Ann	Assoc	Findlay	MA	EDM		Case Wes		2000
Cummings, Richard	Asst	Wis-Whitewat	FX	PHD	95	Kansas St		&2002
Cummings, Robert R.		Practice		PHD	76.	Miss		&1979
Cunat, Vicente	Assoc	Pompeu Fabra		PHD	01	London SE		
Cunitz, Jonathan A.				DBA	68.	Harvard		
Cunningham, Billie M.	AcTch	Missouri	P	PHD	80.	North Tx		1994
Cunningham, Bobby R.	Retir	Grambling St	PO	DBA	96.	La Tech		8-90
Cunningham, Carolyn	Retir	Missouri So	1996	MBA	73	Pittsburgh		&1978
Cunningham, Gary M.	Prof	Univ of Umea	FIM	PHD	76.	Tx-Austin		& 9-06
Cunningham, Peter G.	Assoc	Bishop's Un	F	MBA		McGill		&
Cunningham, Reba	Retir	Texas-Dallas	2000	PHD	91.	North Tx		&1994
Cunningham, Roboe D.		Austin Coll	1992	PHD	92.	North Tx		
Cunnyngham, Jon S.	Retir	Ohio State	1989	PHD	64	Chicago		1966
Cuperus, Susann	Asst	Mary	ARX	MS	00	Mary		9-98
Cuppett, David	Retir	Saint Leo-FL		MBA		Utah		& 8-80
Curatola, Anthony P. (Tony)	Prof	Drexel	XB	PHD	81.	Tx A&M		9-89

Joseph F. Ford Professor of Accounting

Curbo, Lawrence W.	Retir	Memphis St	1989	MBA	50	Miss		&1958

5570 Lamar; Memphis TN 38118

Curbo, Robert S.	Retir	Memphis St	1989	MBA	58	Miss		&1962

PO Box 549; Olive Branch MS 38654

Curling, Michelle				PHD	06.	Penn St		
Curran, Joseph R.	Retir	Northeastern	1996	PHD	69.	Columbia	*	1966
Current, Frederick D.	Retir	Furman	6-99	MBA	66	Mich St	#	9-79
Currie, Edward M.	Retir	San Francisc	1991	PHD	67.	Minnesota	*	7-84

1135 Divisadero St #2; San Francisco CA 94115

Curry, Dudley W.	Retir	So Methodist	1980	PHD	69.	Stanford		&1937

2 Queensview Court; Dallas TX 75225

Curry, E. Lou	Retir	Tx-S Antonio	1996	LLM	75	Emory		9-75
Curry, Jeanie	Asst	Ouachita Bap	TF	ABD		Miss		&1988
Curry, Othel J.	Retir	No Texas St	6-74	PHD	39.	Michigan		1944
Curtis, A.	Lect	New So Wales	F	MCOM		NS Wales		
Curtis, Larry R.	Adj	Iowa State	P	JD	73	Iowa		1973
Curtis, Mary B.	Assoc	North Texas	ASDB	PHD	95.	Kentucky		& 8-98
Curtis, Robert E.	Retir	Minn-Duluth	1987	MS	63	Minnesota		&1963

2801 23rd Avenue SW Apt 221; Fargo ND 58103

Curtis, Susan M.	Lect	Illinois	BA	PHD	00.	Illinois	8-00
Curtner, David M.				PHD	93.	Okla St	
Cushing, Barry E.	Deces	Utah	3-05	PHD	69.	Mich St	&7-91
Custer, Henry L. Jr.			T	PHD	70.	Alabama	
Cutler, Ross	Inst	North Texas	F	MA	75	Brighm Yg	&8-04
Cutt, James	Retir	Victoria-Cdn	2003	PHD		Toronto	1977
Cycyota, Cynthia	Assoc	USAF Academy		PHD	03	Tx-Austin	&6-02
Cyze, Donald A.	D-Ac	Saint Xavier	TLXP	LLM		Valparaiso	&1985
Czaja, Rita J.	Asst	Wis-Whitewat	EF	PHD	95.	Nrthwstrn	&2005
Czarnecki, Richard E.	Retir	Mich-Dearbor	2004	PHD	65.	Mich St	&1968
Czarsty, Steven L.	Retir	Mary Wash	2000	DBA	75.	Geo Wash	9-78
Czernkowski, Robert M.	Lect	New So Wales	FQ	BCOM	88	Tasmania	&1989
Czyzewski, Alan B.	Assoc	Indiana St	PCR	PHD	85.	S Calif	&9-92
D'Allesandio, Gennaro E.	Retir	Wagner	1993	MBA	83	Wagner	&
D'Amore, Anthony	Inst	Intl College	XF	MBA	55	NYU	&1995
D'Aquila, Jill M.	Assoc	Iona	PA	PHD	97	NYU	&9-96
D'Augustine, Charles H.	Retir	Ohio Univ	1985	PHD	63	Fla St	&1981
d'Ouville, Edmond	Retir	Indiana NW	2004	PHD	87	Il-Chicago	&9-70
D'Souza, Julia M.	Assoc	Cornell	F	PHD	95.	Nrthwstrn	9-94
Dafashy, Wagih G.	Prof	Wm & Mary	FM	PHD	66.	Arkansas	1965
Daggett, Donald G.	Retir	Mn St-Mankat	2000	MBA	64	Denver	&1967
Dagwell, Ron	SLect	Griffith Un	FV	MFM	80	Queensld	&1981
Dahawy, Khaled		Egypt		PHD	98.	North Tx	
Daher, Ahmad				PHD	00.	Wisconsin	
Dahl, Gunnar A.	SLect	Norwegian U	F				
Dahlin, Laurie	Asst	Worcester St	PAJM	DBA		Nova SE	* 5-01
Dahlmans, Hanneke	Asst	Tilburg Univ	A	MBA	89	Maastricht	&1993
Dahmash, Naim H.				PHD	73.	Illinois	
Dai, Zhonglan	Asst	Texas-Dallas	XYM	PHD	05.	N Carol	2005
Daigle, Ronald J.	Asst	Sam Houston	S	PHD	02.	Tx Tech	&8-06
Daily, Cynthia M.	Asst	Ark-Ltl Rock	A	PHD	02.	La Tech	&6-04
Daily, R. Austin	ClPr	Texas A&M	F	PHD	70.	N Carol	&9-92
Deloitte & Touche Professional Program Director's Professor							
Dale, Karen	Asst	Univ Essex	BM				2002
Dale, Mary L.	SLect	Macquarie Un	F	MEC	84	Macquarie	&1991
Daley, Daniel H.				PHD	96.	Michigan	
Daley, Lane A.	Deces	Univ Alberta	8-98	PHD	81.	U Wash	&1992
Daley, Michele J.			M	PHD	95.	Rochester	&
Dallmus, John	Lect	Ariz St West	FS	MBA	94	Loyola	8-00
Dalton, Michael A.			XSM	PHD	79.	Geo St	* &
Dalton, Thomas M.	Prof	San Diego	FX	PHD	92.	Houston	& 1-92
Daly, Bonita L.			FB	PHD	90.	Illinois	&
Daly, Dan			MC	PHD	97.	Michigan	
Daly, Dennis C.	C-Ac	Metro St-MN	MC	MBA	62	Detroit	* 1993
Dambrin, Claire	Asst	HEC Paris	UMCB	PHD	05	Paris IX	2004
Damitio, James W.	Prof	Cen Michigan	PM	PHD	88	Mich St	* 1983
Dammak, Lotfi	Inst	Univ Tunis	F	EXPC			
Damtew, Desta	Prof	Norfolk St	CMI	DBA	79.	Kentucky	9-84
Danbolt, Jo	Prof	Univ Glasgow	F	PHD	97	Heriot-Wat	1998
Dancer, Terry	Assoc	Arkansas St	CMF	PHD	88.	Miss	8-78
Danese, Stephen P.	Inst	S Fl-St Pete	F	PHD	80.	Georgia	&8-01
Daneshfar, Alizera	Asst	New Haven	FMT	PHD	01	Concordia	1-01
Dang, Li	Assoc	Cal Poly-SLO	F	PHD	04.	Drexel	7-06
Daniel, C. Lee	Asst	Troy	P	MBA	76	Tx Tech	&1985
Daniel, Shirley J.	Prof	Hawaii-Manoa	AM	PHD	85.	Okla St	& 1-86
Henry A. Walker Jr. Professor of Business Enterprise							
Daniel, Troy E.	Retir	Miss State	1989	PHD	68.	Alabama	&1972
200 Colonial Circle; Starkville MS 39759-4206; 601-323-7579							
Daniels, Bobbie W.	Asst	Jackson St	GF	PHD	05.	JacksonSt	&2005
Daniels, Deanna	Assoc	Morningside	PCNG	PHD	85.	S Calif	&1991
Daniels, Howard M.	Deces			PHD	57.	Tx-Austin	
Daniels, James E.			FX	PHD	70.	Arkansas	&
Daniels, Janet D.			FGN	DBA	88.	Boston U	&
Daniels, Robert H.	Prof	San Fran St	XL	JD	72	Harvard	1983
Daniels, Roger B.	Assoc	Charleston	FHT	PHD	91.	Miss	&1992
Danile, Teresa M.	Assoc	St John's	PMA	EDD	06	St Johns	&1981
Danko, Dori	Inst	Grand Valley	FM	MBA	91	Gr Valley	& 8-98
Danko, Kenneth L.	Prof	San Fran St	BMCQ	DBA	82.	Indiana	* 1986
Danos, Paul	Dean	Dartmouth	F	PHD	74.	Tx-Austin	&6-95
Laurence F. Whittemore Professor of Business Administration							
Danvers, Kreag	Prof	Clarion	CMS	PHD	99.	Kent St	* &8-05
Darayseh, Musa M.	Prof	Purdue Calum	FCM	PHD	90.	Nebraska	1990
Darby, Mary Alice G.	D-As$	Southern	FLX	JD	90	Southern	&8-71
Darcy, John W.	Asst	Tx-Pan Amer	XIJL	PHD	02.	Oklahoma	&9-02
Daroca, Frank P.	Prof	Loyola Marym	AMG	PHD	81.	Illinois	&1986
Darrough, Masako N.	C-Pr	CUNY-Baruch	MY	PHD	75	Brit Colum	9-98
Das, Nandita	Assoc	Wilkes	F	PHD	04	Lehigh	8-05

Das, Somnath	Prof	Ill-Chicago	NFIM	PHD	88	Car Mellon		1996
Dasaro, George A.	Prof	Loyola Marym	FVX	MS	66	CS-L Ang		&1977
Dascher, Paul E.	Prof	Stetson	C	PHD	69.	Penn St		1993
M. E. Rinker Professor								
Dasgupta, Manilal	Retir	Saskatchewan	1988	PHD	65	Calcutta	*	1966
DaSilva Rosa, Raymond	Asst	W Australia	B	PHD	95	W Austrl		2001
Datar, Srikant M.	Prof	Harvard	FMA	PHD	85.	Stanford	*	&1996
Arthur Lowes Dickenson Professor of Accounting								
Datta, Yudhishter	Retir	No Kentucky	2000	PHD	71.	SUNY-Buf		8-73
Dau, Khalifa Ali		Arab Fund	1990	PHD	75.	LSU		
Dauber, Nicky	Lect	CUNY-Queens	A	MS	80	Long Isl		&2-76
Dauderis, Henry J.	Assoc	Concordia U	ASFI	MBA	72	McGill		&1967
Daugherty, Brian E.	Asst	Wis-Milwauke	FA	PHD	06.	Tx-SanAnt		&2006
Daughtery, William K.		Sul Ross St	AS	PHD	69.	Tx-Austin	#	&
Daughtrey, Zoel W.	Retir	Miss State	2002	PHD	70	N Car St		&1982
DaVault, James W.	Retir	Florida		PHD	40	Columbia		1947
Davenport, Shirley	Asst	Txs-Perm Bas	AM	PHD	02	Tx Tech		9-02
Davern, Michael J.	AProf	U Melbourne	BDMS	PHD	98	Minnesota		2003
Davey, Austin	Asst	Laurentian		BA	68	W Ontario		&7-75
Davey-Evans, Sue	Lect	U Portsmith						2006
David, Amy	Lect	CUNY-Queens		MS	06	Queens		&
David, Betty P.	Asst	Fran Marion	FMS	MBA	88	S Carol		8-00
David, Jeanne M.	Assoc	Detroit Merc	FMV	PHD	88.	Tx A&M	*	&1988
David, Julia Smith	Assoc	Arizona St	S	PHD	95.	Mich St		&8-95
David, Theodore M.	Assoc	F Dick-Teane	X	LLM		NYU		1982
Davidoff, Howard	Assoc	CUNY-Brookly	LXP	LLM	87	NYU		&9-86
Davidovits, Murray	Lect	CUNY-Queens	LR	JD	83	NY Law		2-98
Davids, Cindy	SLect	Macquarie Un	LJ	PHD	05	NS Wales		2003
Davidson, Alexander N.	Retir	W Illinois	1990	JD	55	Denver		&9-78
Davidson, David B.	Prof	CS-Long Bch	XFCA	PHD	82	N Colo		&1983
Davidson, Ephraim E.		Bus Mgr MS		PHD	66.	LSU		
Davidson, H. Justin	Retir	Ohio State	1991	MS	55	Car Mellon		&1979
Davidson, Leslie		Austin Peay	PC					2004
Davidson, Lewis F.	Prof	Fla Internat	FA	PHD	74.	Penn St		1984
Davidson, Ronald A.	Retir	Ariz St West	AFE	PHD	88.	Arizona		&8-96
Davidson, Sharon M.	Asst	Alfred	A	MS	83	Roch Tech		&1983
Davidson, Sidney	Emer	Chicago	1999	PHD	50.	Michigan		&1958
Davidson, Spring	Inst	Delaware	S	MBA	03	Delaware		1996
Davie, Elizabeth	Asst	Un Stirling	DEQ	PHD	71	Edinburgh		1991
Davies, J. R.	SLect	Strathclyde	F	BSC	64	LondonEc		1976
Davies, Jeff R.	PLect	U Glamorgan	SM	MA	69	Wansea	*	4-75
Davies, Jonathan J.	Partn	Coopers&Lybr	1995	DBA	75.	LSU		&
1100 Campanile; 1155 Peachtree St; Atlanta GA 30309; 404-870-1156								
Davies, Marlene	PLect	U Glamorgan	AN	BSC	74	Wales		&6-89
Grant Thornton Research Fellow								
Davies, Thomas L.	C-Pr	South Dakota	XF	LLM	92	Mo-Ks Cty		&1987
Davila, Antonio	Assoc	Univ Navarra	SM	DBA	98.	Harvard		9-04
Davila, Ruben A.	Clin	So Calif	FM	JD	00	Loyola		&1984
Davis, Alan B.	Assoc	Truman State	XP	JD	92	Geo St		&2004
Davis, Angela K.	Asst	Oregon	F	PHD	01.	U Wash		&2006
Davis, Barbara J.	Prof	Centenary-LA	F	DBA	95	La Tech	#	&8-86
Davis, Charles E.	C-Ac	Baylor	SMB	PHD	91.	N Carol		&1991
Walter Plumhoff Professor of Accounting								
Davis, Charles J.	Prof	CS-Sacrament	FM	PHD	79.	Illinois		&1982
Davis, Dale A.	Retir	Mich-Flint	1996	PHD	78	Michigan		1982
Davis, Darrel W.	Retir	No Iowa	2005	PHD	75.	Okla St		&1969
Davis, Dorothy A. (Dot)	Assoc	La-Monroe	SV	DBA	88.	Miss St		&1989
George T. Walker Professor of Entrepreneurship								
Davis, Earl F.	Retir	Georgia	1994	PHD	62.	Alabama		1966
Davis, Elizabeth B.	Prof	Baylor	MA	PHD	92.	Duke		&1992
Davis, Fred G.	Retir	Hawaii Pacif	1996	PHD	68.	Mich St		&8-91
Davis, Garistine	Asst	Fayetteville		JD				
Davis, Glenda	Lect	W Sydney	CDSX	BCOM	00	W Sydney		
Davis, Gordon B.	Retir	Minnesota	1997	PHD	59.	Stanford		&1961
Davis, Harold E.	Assoc	SE Louisiana	SDF	DBA	02.	La Tech		&1998
Davis, Harry Zvi	Prof	CUNY-Baruch	FATH	PHD	78.	Columbia		1974
Davis, Helen E.	Assoc	Johnson&Wale	MC	MBA	85	Bryant	*	1987
Davis, Henry H. (Hank)	Prof	E Illinois	FMTS	PHD	84.	N Carol		1991
Davis, James B.	Retir	West Tx A&M	1998	EDD	66	Okla St		&9-68
Davis, James R.	Prof	Anderson Col	CJS	PHD	74.	Geo St	*	2005
Davis, James W.	Prof	Mississippi	VH	PHD	72.	Miss		&1965
Peery Chair of Accountancy								
Davis, Jefferson T.	Assoc	Weber State	SAF	PHD	93.	Tennessee		1998
Davis, Jenny R.	Asst	Mary Hrdn-By	FCQ	MBA	99	AngeloSt		&2005
Davis, Jon S.	C-Pr	Wisconsin	XB	PHD	87.	Arizona		&2000
Davis, Larry R.	Assoc	Mich Tech	AFV	PHD	86.	Indiana		&9-93

Davis, Lee E.		Practice	1994	PHD	81. Georgia	
Tax Consultants Inc; 1200 Johnson Ferry Rd; Marietta GA 30068; 404-973-1544						
Davis, Michael L.	D-Ac	Alaska-Fairb	FV	PHD	86. Mass	&8-04
Davis, Murray L.	Deces	Univ Calgary	6-98	PHD	72 London	&1974
Davis, P. Michael	Retir	Baltimore	1999	PHD	69. Illinois	&1987
Davis, Richard O.	Prof	Susquehanna	XFL	LLM	92 Geotown	&9-92
Davis, Robert R.	Assoc	Canisius	AF	PHD	82. SUNY-Buf	&1967
Davis, Scott	Asst	High Point	CMXJ	MSA	NC-Green	&1996
Davis, Shawn M.			AS	PHD	02. Wash U	
Davis, Stanley B.	Assoc	Tenn-Chattan	M	PHD	00. Alabama	* &7-06
Davis, Stanley W.	Prof	Ind-Pur/FtWy	MTAJ	PHD	84. Penn St	&2000
Davis, Wayne J.	Retir	Indiana U-PA	2000	PHD	70 Rutgers	&1968
Davis-Friday, Paquita Y.	Assoc	CUNY-Baruch	F	PHD	96. Michigan	&2-06
Davison, Dale L.	ClPr	Thunderbird	FX	PHD	73. Georgia	&1990
Davisson, Kathleen E.	Lect	Denver	MS	MACC	91 Denver	2003
Davy, Anne R.	STut	U Auckland	FA	MCOM	91 Auckland	&1989
Dawes, N.	Lead	London Metro		MA		1992
Dawkins, Louis E.	Retir	Henderson St	2001	PHD	81. Arkansas	&1964
Dawkins, Mark C.	Assoc	Georgia	F	PHD	94. Fla St	* &8-94
Dawkins, Sarah C.	Retir	Mid Tenn St	FCM	PHD	78. LSU	&1987
Dawson, John W.	Emer	Chris Newpor	1999	MBA	78 Va Comm	&1979
Dawson, Julie A.	Asst	Carthage	FMX	MSA	93 Wisconsin	&2007
Dawson, Marie	Lect	Illinois St	MF	MS	80 Illin St	&2005
Day, Honry J. II	Aoooo	Mount Olive	CFOX	PhD	97. Va Tech	1995
Day, John S.				DCS	56. Harvard	
Day, Robert	SLect	Bournemouth	FGHT	MSC		9-88
Day, Ron L.	Lect	Sydney Un	FE	MCOM	90 NS Wales	&2004
Day, William E.	Retir	Manchester C	AX	MBA	73 Harvard	&1980
Daynes, Arief	Lect	U Portsmith	IF	PHD		1994
de Koning, Arie	Retir	Intl Mgt Dev	1999	DRS	63 Erasmus	1968
de la Rosa, Denise M.	Assoc	Grand Valley	FI	PHD	96. North Tx	8-03
Deacon, James	Lect	Napier Univ	X	BCOM		&F-85
Deakin, Edward B.	Deces	Texas	1-93	PHD	72. Illinois	&9-72
Deal, Keren H.	Asst	Auburn-Montg	FGM	PHD	07 Auburn	&2007
Deal, Stan	Asst	Azusa Pacif	XT	MS	Golden Gt	&9-84
Dean, B. Samuel	Retir	Macon State	2003	MACC	67 Georgia	&1973
Dean, Donald C.	Prof	St Rose	FCVA	PHD	91 Rensselaer	* &1979
Dean, Douglas L.	Assoc	Brigham Yg	S	PHD	85 Arizona	6-99
David & Knight Research Fellow						
Dean, Graeme W.	Prof	Univ Sydney	FHTA	MEC	76 Sydney	&1974
Dean, Joyce Clare	Retir	Baylor	1992	MBA	57 Tx-Austin	&1957
4121 Westchester; Waco TX 76710						
Dean, Passard	Asst	Albany State		PHD	04 Argosy	8-06
Dean, R. Gary	Retir	Creighton	1997	PHD	70. Nebraska	9-77
DeAngelo, Linda E.	Prof	S Calif	1998	PHD	80. U Wash	&
Finance Department; 213-740-3868; ldeangelo@sba.usc.edu						
Dear, James E.	Retir	Miss College	2000	PHD	65. LSU	&1991
Dearborn, DeWitt C.				DCS	58. Harvard	
Dearden, John	Deces	Harvard		MBA	46 Penn	&1959
Dearman, David T.	Assoc	Ark-Ft Smith	MCS	PHD	98. Memphis	*
DeBarthe, Linda M.	C-Pr	Graceland	PX	PHD	97 Iowa	&1990
DeBerg, Curtis L.	Prof	CS-Chico	FE	PHD	85. Okla St	&9-90
DeBerry, Thomas W.	Prof	Freed Hardem	PA	PHD	94 Tx Tech	&8-06
Debessay, Araya	Prof	Delaware	AFMI	PHD	79. Syracuse	# * &9-78
DeBoskey, David	Asst	San Diego St	F	PHD	06 Rutgers	&2006
Debreceny, Roger S.	Prof	Hawaii-Manoa	AFS	PHD	98 Australia	&2004
Shidler College Distinguished Professor						
DeBruine, Marinus	Assoc	Grand Valley	FT	PHD	91. Ohio St	&9-91
DeBusk, Gerald K.	Asst	Appalach St	M	PHD	04. Va Tech	* &8-04
DeCelles, Michael D.	Assoc	Angelo State	PTF	PHD	83. Oklahoma	2003
Dechow, Niels	Lect	Oxford Univ	MS	PHD	01 Copenhag	2004
Dechow, Patricia M.	Prof	Cal-Berkeley	F	PHD	93. Rochester	2007
Donald H. and Ruth F. Seiler Chair in Public Accounting						
Deck, Alan B.	Assoc	Bellarmine	CFP	PHD	84. Alabama	* &8-98
Decker, Jeffrey	Assoc	Il-Springfld	FMS	PHD	01. Arizona	* &2005
Decker, LaRita			MC	PHD	92. Indiana	
DeCoster, Don T.	Retir	Seattle	1994	PHD	61. Tx-Austin	&1986
Dee, Carol Callaway	Asst	Colo-Denver	FM	PHD	99. LSU	&8-06
Deehan, John P.	Retir	Seton Hall	1999	MBA	61 Seton Hall	&1959
DeFalguera, Jordi	Asst	Pompeu Fabra			02 UPF	
DeFatta, Joseph A.	Retir	La-Monroe	2003	PHD	70. LSU	&1975
Defenbach, James	Deces	Tx-Brownsvil		MS	55 Idaho	1996
Defeo, Victor J.	Lect	Pennsylvania	FM	PHD	83. Illinois	1999
DeFilippis, Robert A.	D-Ac	F Dick-Madis	FA	MBA	73 Rutgers	&1974
Defleise, Philip L.	Deces	Columbia	O-97	ABD	NYU	&1-78
DeFond, Mark L.	Prof	So Calif	FAI	PHD	87. U Wash	&1987
Joseph A. DeBell Professor of Business Administration						

DeFranceschi, James	Inst	SE Louisiana	FM	MS	94	LSU	& 8-96
DeFranco, Gaetano	Asst	Univ Toronto		PHD	04.	Penn	
Degnan, Donna M.	Assoc	Johnson&Wale	P	MS	95	John&Wal	1987
Degnan, Theodore E.			XA	PHD	83.	S Carol	
Dehning, Bruce	Assoc	Chapman	FS	PHD	99.	Colorado	9-02
Dehning, Lyle E.	Retir	Metro State	2001	MA	72	N Colo	& 9-68
Dein, Raymond C.	Deces	Nebraska	1989	PHD	44.	Minnesota	1948
Deines, Dan S.	Prof	Kansas State	F	PHD	85.	Nebraska	& 9-82
Ralph Crouch - KPMG Professor of Accounting							
Deinzer, Harvey T.	Retir	Florida	9-73	PHD	47	Michigan	1947
Deis, Donald R. Jr.	Prof	Tx A&M-C Chr	AG	PHD	88.	Tx A&M	& 9-04
Ennis & Virginia Joslin Endowed Chair of Accounting							
Deitrick, James W.	Prof	Texas-Austin	FEV	DBA	77.	Tennessee	6-77
KPMG Peat Marwich Centennial Fellow in Accounting							
DeJong, Douglas V.	Prof	Iowa	AFQ	PHD	80.	Michigan	& 9-80
John F. Murray Professor of Accounting							
DeJonge, A.	SLect	London Metro	F	MBA			1999
Dekker, Henri C.	Assoc	Vrije Univ	CM	PHD	03	Vrije	1997
Dekleva, Sasha	Assoc	DePaul	S	PHD	87	Belgrade	1986
Delancey, Howard	Deces			DBA	54.	Indiana	
Delaney, John	Asst	Augustana IL	AGNO	MBA	95	Iowa	# &
Delaney, John E.	C-Ac	Southwestern	FACP	PHD	89.	Tx-Austin	& 8-88
Delaney, Patrick	Lect	Concordia U	AF	BCOM	81	Concordia	&1997
Delaney, Patrick R.	Deces	No Illinois	5-00	PHD	71.	Illinois	& 1-70
DeLange, Paul	SLect	Monash Univ	FTVE	PHD		LaTrobe	1988
Delany, Tom	SLect	So Queenslnd	FXDE	MTAX	95	NS Wales	&1993
DeLaune, Laura D.	Inst	Louisiana St	FS	PHD	04	LSU	& 8-96
DeLaurell, Roxane	Asst	Charleston	IL	PHD	00	Tx-Dallas	2000
DeLeo, Wanda I.			FTD	PHD	85.	Geo St	&
DelGaudio, Richard	Prof	Merrimack	FAV	MBA	66	Northeas	&1972
DeLuca, Dorrie	Asst	Delaware	S	PHD	02	Temple	9-02
DelVacchio, James E.	Prof	St Peters	FX	MBA		Seton Hall	&1976
Delvaille, Pascale	Assoc	ESCP deParis	AFI	PHD	01	Paris IX	1984
Delvecchio, Stephen C.	Assoc	Cen Missouri	ASM	DBA	90.	S Illinois	&2000
deMagalhaes, Roberto	Asst	North Dakota	A	PHD	98.	Miss	& 8-05
DeMaris, E. Joe	Retir	North Texas	1989	PHD	55.	Illinois	&1975
600 Ridgecrest Circle; Denton TX 76205							
DeMayo, William	Retir	New Haven	1991	MBA			& 9-82
DeMers, David E.	Retir	Minot State	AX	MS	71	N Dakota	&1970
Demers, Elizabeth A.	Asst	INSEAD	F	PHD	99.	Stanford	2006
Deming, Robert H.				DBA	63.	Harvard	
Demosthendus, Maz	LectA	Flinders Un	TP	DIP	97	S Austr	2-98
Demotses, Andrew J.			FM	PHD	78.	Mass	&
DeMoville, Wig B.	Retir	Tx-Pan Amer	FXR	PHD	78.	Tx Tech	&1988
Dempsey, Stephen J.	Assoc	Vermont	FM	PHD	86.	Va Tech	1987
Demski, Joel S.	Prof	Florida	TMF	PHD	67.	Chicago	7-94
Frederick E. Fisher Eminent Scholar							
Den Adel, Kevin J.	Assoc	Central Col	FAS	PHD	99.	Iowa	2002
Deng, F. Johnny		Jinglun Elec	MS	PHD	98.	Memphis	
Jinglun Electornic Co., Ltd							
Deng, Zhen	Asst	CUNY-Baruch	F	PHD	00.	NYU	1999
Denham, Ross A.	Retir	Univ Alberta	1996	PHD	72.	Minnesota	&1963
Denis, Robert B.	Retir	Hartford	1994	PHD	72.	American	1977
Denna, Eric L.			SMGE	PHD	89.	Mich St	
Dennis, David K.	Prof	Otterbein	FSB	PHD	75.	Cincinnati	&1990
Dennis, David M.	Retir	South Fla	2004	PHD	72.	Missouri	& 9-72
Dennis, H. Lawrence	Retir	No Georgia	1999	DBA	76.	Kentucky	&1968
Dennis, Lynda M.	Lect	Cen Florida	FG	PHD	04	Cen Fla	& 8-05
Dennis-Escoffier, Shirley	Assoc	U Miami	X	PHD	81	U Miami	&1983
Dennler, Carl Jr.	Retir	Fla Atlantic	1988	PHD	62.	Wisconsin	1978
Denstel, Chris	Inst	Louisiana St	FM	MS	02	LSU	& 1-03
Dent D'Almuano, Roseline	Asst	European U		PHD	91.	Ariz St	
Deo, Hemant	SLect	U Wollongong	VW	PHD	99	Wollong	&1995
DePasquale, Robert J.	Prof	St Vincent	CMR	PHD	92	Pittsburgh	* &1978
Deppe, E. Devon	Prof	Weber State	X	JD	77	Brighm Yg	&1978
Deppe, Larry A.	Assoc	Weber State	FA	PHD	88.	Utah	* &1996
DePree, Chauncey M. Jr.	Prof	So Miss	M	DBA	87.	Kentucky	1988
Depusoir, Francisco	Assoc	Virgin Islan	AFGH	MBA	78	Missouri	&1989
Dereshiwsky, Mary			PMC	PHD	85.	Mass	
DeRidder, Jerome J.	Prof	Salisbury	FH	PHD	81.	Nebraska	1985
DerManelian, Guenther	Assoc	Johnson&Wale	P	MBA	85	Bryant	&1986
Dermer, Jerry D.	Prof	York	MS	PHD	69.	Illinois	1980
Derrick, Patricia L.	Asst	Salisbury	FXT	PHD	05.	Geo Wash	&2005
Derstine, Robert P.	Prof	Villanova	AF	PHD	73.	SUNY-Buf	&1972
Desai, Hemang A.	Prof	So Methodist		PHD	97.	Tulane	8-98
Desai, Renu V.	Asst	Fla Internat	FM	PHD	07	Cen Fla	2007
Desai, Vikram	Asst	Wilfred Laur	F	ABD		Cen Fla	

Name	Rank	School		Degree		School	
DeSantiago, Dominique	Lect	Florida	F	MACC	89	Florida	&5-94
Desfleurs, Aurelie	Prof	Univ Laval		PHD	04	Laval	2004
Deshmukh, Ashutosh	Prof	Penn St-Erie	SA	PHD	93.	Memphis	* &1993
DeSilva, Tracy-Anne	Lect	Lincoln-NZ	BE	BCOM		Lincoln	2004
DeSimpelare, James M.	Lect	Michigan	FX	MBA	92	Indiana	&1993
Desir, Rosemond	Asst	Niagara	FM	PHD	07	Mass	2007
Desjardins, Ivan	Inst	Thompson Riv	FPXV	MS		Sherbrook	* &1993
Deskins, James W.	Retir	Wichita St	2002	PHD	65.	Tx-Austin	&1985
Desmond, Nancy A.	Retir	Illinois	2000	MA	59	Illinois	&1955
Desselle, Bettye	Asst	Prairie View	NFA	MBA		Wisconsin	&2001
Determan, Thomas	Lect	Wis-Parkside	PM	MS	05	Card Str	8-06
Dettmann, John A.	Retir	Minn-Duluth	1987	PHD	55	Wisconsin	&1948
Detzel, F. Larry	C-Ac	CS-S Marcos	X	PHD	96.	Cen Fla	&1999
Deumes, R.	Asst	Maastricht	FM	PHD	05	Maastricht	1998
Deutsch, Robert A.	Asst	Campbell		PHD	91	Kentucky	&2000
Deutsch, Robert A.			CFGV	PHD	91.	Kentucky	&
deVidal, Douglas	Lect	Texas-Austin	FX	PHD	91.	Tx-Austin	9-92
DeVincenzi, Bill	Lect	San Jose St		MBA		Berkeley	1995
Devine, Carl T.	Deces	Florida St	9-98	PHD	40.	Michigan	&1965
Devine, E. A. (Dan)	Retir	E Michigan	2002	PHD	73.	LSU	&1976
Devine, John W.	Retir	Murray State	1991	PHD	62	Indiana	1963
Devine, Kevin M.	Prof	Xavier	BMU	PHD	90.	Nebraska	1989
Devine, Margaret D.	Assoc	Wis-Eau Clar	DF	PHD	92.	Wisconsin	& 8-82
Dovino, Wilfrod F.	Retir	Villanova	2002	PHD	85.	Temple	&1972
Devlin, R.	Lect	Univ Ulster	FM	BA			* 1-85
Devona, Sandra J.	Inst	No Illinois	F	MAS	94	N Illinois	& 8-94
DeVries, Delwyn D.	Asst	Belmont	SM	PHD	01.	Ariz St	&2007
DeVries, Joann A.			FTUJ	PHD	75.	Okla St	&
DeWaegenaere, Anja	Assoc	Tilburg Univ	M	PHD	93	Antwerp	1996
Dewhirst, John F.	Emer	York	1977	PHD	68	Michigan	1966
Dewing, I. P.	SLect	East Anglia	FG	BA			&
Dexter, Albert S.	Prof	British Colu	S	PHD	70.	Columbia	
Management Dept: University of British Columbia							
Dexter, John E.	Asst	Northwood	FMVX	MA	86	Webster	&1999
Dexter, Lee	C-Pr	Mn-Moorhead	EVF	PHD	86.	Nebraska	* &1988
Dey, Aiyesha	Asst	Chicago	F	PHD	05.	Nrthwstrn	2005
Dey, Colin	Lect	Dundee	WJDM	PHD		Edinburgh	1997
Dey, Mithu R.	Asst	Wm & Mary	FM	PHD	05.	Geo Wash	&2006
DeZoort, F. Todd	Prof	Alabama	ABJS	PHD	95.	Alabama	6-01
Professional Advisory Board Fellow							
DeZoysa, Anura	Lect	U Wollongong	FEM	PHD	03	Wollong	&2002
Dhaliwal, Dan S.	H-Pr	Arizona	FMT	PHD	77.	Arizona	1980
Louis A. Myers Professor							
Dhanani, Alpa	Lect	Cardiff U	IM	PHD	98	Cardiff	1998
Dhanani, Karim	Retir	Grambling St	M	DBA	86.	La Tech	&9-77
Dharan, Bala G.	Prof	Rice	FMT	PHD	81.	Car Mellon	&1982
J. Howard Creekmore Professor of Accounting							
Dhavale, Dileep G.	Prof	Clark	FM	PHD	75	Penn St	&9-87
Diamond, Michael A.	Prof	So Calif	FI	PHD	78.	UCLA	&1985
Diaz, Michelle C.	Asst	Louisiana St	S	PHD	06.	Tx A&M	& 8-06
Dibblee, David A.	Assoc	Benedictn-IL		MBA	79	N Illinois	&1982
DiBenedetto, Joseph C.	Prof	Pace-Westch	RJMC	JD	75	Brooklyn	* &1971
Dichev, Ilia D.	Assoc	Michigan	F	PHD	95.	U Wash	8-96
Michael and Joan Sakkinen Accounting Scholar							
Dicino, Carol Lynn			FMX	PHD	96.	Arkansas	&
Dick-Forde, Emily	Lect	West Indies	F	MPHL		Cambridge	
Dickens, Robert L.	Deces	Duke	1989	MS	50	N Carol	&1949
Dickens, Thomas L.	Prof	Clemson	XF	PHD	83.	Tx A&M	* &1984
University Alumni Professor							
Dickey, Ellen M.	Inst	South Dakota	MP	MA	99	Oklahoma	* &2004
Dickey, Robert I.	Retir	Illinois	8-77	PHD	42.	Illinois	&1940
Dickhaut, John W.	Prof	Minnesota	B	PHD	70.	Ohio St	1976
Curtis Carlson Professor							
Dickins, Denise E.	Asst	East Carol		PHD	06.	Fla Atl	& 8-06
Dickinson, Harry D.			PT	PHD	81.	Georgia	&
Dickinson, Victoria	Asst	Florida		PHD	05.	Wisconsin	& 8-06
Dieguez, Manuel	Lect	Fla Internat	FM	MSM	76	Fla Intl	&1976
Dierks, Paul A.	Retir	Wake Fr-MBA	2001	PHD	75	U Wash	&1987
Dietrich, J. Richard	C-Pr	Ohio State	F	PHD	81.	Car Mellon	2000
Dietz, Donna K.	Asst	N Dakota St	CMU	PHD	89	N Dakota	* &2000
Diggins, Bruce	Lect	W Sydney	FAMC	MACC	90	Wollong	
DiGregorio, Dean M.	Assoc	SE Louisiana	FGN	PHD	98.	Houston	&8-99
Dikolli, Shane S.	Asst	Duke	M	PHD	98	Waterloo	&2006
DiLernia, Cary	ALect	Macquarie Un					
Dilla, William N.	Assoc	Iowa State	AFB	PHD	87.	Tx-Austin	&8-98
Dillard, Jesse F.	Prof	Portland St	MBW	PHD	76.	S Carol	8-03
Retzlaff Chair							

Name	Rank	School	Code	Degree	Yr	Institution	Flag
Dillard-Eggers, Jane	Assoc	Belmont	FP	PHD	95.	Alabama	&1998
Dillaway, M. Peter	Retir	New Mex St	XJ	PHD	80.	Florida	&8-82
Dilley, David R.	Chrm	U.S. Steel		DBA	56.	Indiana	
Dilley, Steven C.	Prof	Michigan St	X	PHD	72.	Wisconsin	&9-72
Dillion, William B.	Retir	Carson-Newmn	FMAX	MS	79	Radford	1984
Dillon, Gadis J. (Buck)	Prof	Oakland	FT	PHD	77.	Michigan	&1987
Dillon, Ray D.	Retir	Georgia St	1999	PHD	74.	Tx Tech	&9-72
Dimian, Fawzi G.	Retir	Minn-Duluth	1994	PHD	68.	U Wash	&1974
Dimitrov, Vaneltin	Asst	Rutgers-Newk		PHD	03	Tulane	2003
Dimitry, Kenneth E.	Deces	Missouri	7-91	PHD	90.	Fla St	&8-90
Dimon, Annette	Retir	Utica	DGNP	MBA	78	Rensselaer	&1980
Dimovski, William	Lect	Deakin-Geelg	F	MBA	79	GSU	&1985
Ding, Rong	Lect	Vrije Univ	MI	BA	98	JiaoJong	2003
Dinger, Mark	Assoc	Kutztown	PSD	MBA		Lehigh	1980
Dinh, Nguyen Van	Asst	Natl Econ	FTMC	MBA	96	Boise St	1989
Dinius, Sara H.	Retir	Auburn	1993	PHD	74	Auburn	&5-68
Dinville, Pamela	C-Ac	Bellevue	VA	MBA	83	NW Mo St	* &1985
Diold, Christioua	Asst	Cyprus		BS	97	Oxford	&2002
DiPietro, Janice D.		Consulting	FA	DBA	89.	Boston U	&
Dirksen, Charles J.	Assoc	Dalhousie	MS	DBA	73.	Oregon	1979
Dirsmith, Mark W.	Prof	Penn State	AB	PHD	75.	Nrthwstrn	&9-75
Deloitte Touche Professor of Accounting							
Dithipyangkul, Pattarin	Asst	City Univ HK	MTO	PHD	05	Brit Colum	2005
Dittenhofer, Mortimer A.	Retir	Fla Internat	2001	PHD	74.	American	# 1986
Dittman, David A.	Prof	Cornell-Hotl	MCU	PHD	73.	Ohio St	7-90
The Hubert E. Westfall Professor of Accounting							
Dittrich, Norman E.	Retir	Tennessee	1993	PHD	66.	Ohio St	&9-68
Dixon, Glen	ALect	Griffith Un	FQZ	BSC	98	Queenslnd	2001
Dixon, Gordon	Retir	U Lethbridge	XG	MSC	80	Saskatch	* 8-79
Dixon, Hollis A.	Deces	Arizona	9-91	PHD	64.	Arkansas	&1963
Dixon, James	Inst	S Ill-Edward	FX	LLM	91	Wash U	1999
Dixon, Keith	SLect	Canterbury	BGHM	PHD	96	Massey	2007
Dixon, Robert L.	Retir	Michigan		PHD	41	Yale	&1942
Box 48 Cedar Crest; Lambertville NJ 08530							
Dmohowski, Stanley J.	Retir	Boston Coll	1996	MBA	58	NYU	&1945
Do, Sangho			CDFM	PHD	92.	Pittsburgh	
Dobiyanski, Alfreda	Inst	Prairie View	ACM	MS	84	Sam Hous	* &1992
Dobler, Philippe	Assoc	ESCP deParis	CM	MS	71	Paris-I	1979
Dockery, Everton	Lect	U Portsmith		PHD			2005
Dockweiler, Raymond C.	Retir	Missouri	2000	PHD	69.	Illinois	&1968
Dodd, James L.	Prof	Drake	PMT	PHD	92.	Georgia	&1992
Aliber Professor of Accounting							
Dodd, Joe				PHD	97.	Tx-Austin	
Dodd, P.	SLect	Liverpool JM	F	FCMA			2006
Dodd, Peter		Banking	F	PHD	80.	Rochester	
Warburg Dillon Read							
Dodson, Donald R.	Retir	Henderson St	1998	MBA	61	Tx A&M	&1957
Doering, James A.	Assoc	WI-Green Bay	LX	LLM	88	NYU	&1991
Dogar, Zulfiquar A.	Asst	Alcorn St	DS	MBA	87	NE La	&1987
Doherty, Michael	Lect	Wyoming	S	MBA	00	Wyoming	&2000
Doherty, Patricia A.	Inst	Boston Univ	FME	MS	77	Bentley	9-94
Doherty, Patricia M.	SLect	Old Dominion	PF	MBA	91	Golden Gt	&1985
Doing, Judith	SLect	Arizona	FX	MSA	94	Arkansas	1-95
Dole, Michael	Adj	Marquette	FMC	MS	81	Wi-Milwa	&1987
Dollar, Cecil			M	PHD	63.	LSU	&
Domanski, Robert R.	Retir	Slippery Roc	2005	MACC	71	S Fla	&9-76
Dombrowski, Robert F.	Prof	Salisbury	AMI	DBA	75.	La Tech	&1989
Domeny, John H.	Retir	SW Missouri	1993	MED	64	Missouri	9-65
Dominiak, Geraldine F.	Retir	Tx Christian	5-97	PHD	66.	Mich St	&1969
Domuta, Daniela	Lect	U Manchester	FIMT	PHD	01	Manchest	9-01
Donabedian, Bairj	Assoc	Pace-Westch	PM	PHD	89.	Columbia	1994
Donadio, Janette M.			AI	PHD	92.	Colorado	
Donadio, Paul J.			MCF	PHD	91.	Colorado	&
Donahue, Marlene S.			FV	PHD	79.	Nebraska	&
Donald, John	Lect	Deakin-Burwo	FM	MBA	86	Monash	1987
Donchess, Carleton M.	Prof	Bridgewater		MSA			* 9-84
Donegan, James J.	Assoc	Western Conn	F	PHD	95.	Arizona	&1999
Donelan, Joseph G.	Prof	West Florida	CPME	PHD	89.	St Louis	* &1999
Doney, Lloyd D.	Retir	Marquette	8-02	PHD	63.	LSU	1969
Dong, Bei	Asst	South Fla	F	PHD	07	Mich St	8-07
Dong, Nguyen Thi	Lect	Natl Econ	FMCV	PHD	91	Natl Econ	1976
Donis, Jack P.	Retir	South Fla	1989	PHD	49	Chicago	1982
Donley, Harvey E.	Retir	Bowling Gr	1984	PHD	53.	Missouri	&1959
Donnelly, David P.	C-Pr	Mo-Kansas Ct	AB	PHD	81.	Illinois	&7-04
Donnelly, Maureen E.	Assoc	Brock Univ	ELX	LLM	93	Toronto	&1984
Donnelly, William J.	Prof	San Jose St	FA	PHD	87	Golden Gt	&1975
Donohoe, Wendy	Lect	Santa Clara	FMX	MS	88	Golden Gt	&1998

Donohoo, Jim	Prof	CS-L Angeles	FX	LLM	84	SanDiego		& 9-78
Donovan, Shannon	Assoc	Bridgewater	M	PHD				
Dontoh, Alex	Assoc	New York U	M	PHD	84	NYU		1988
Doogar, Rajib K.	Asst	Illinois	FMT	PHD	94.	Penn St		8-98
Doonan, Deborah A.	Assoc	Johnson&Wale	P	MST	95	Bryant		&1990
Doost, Roger K.	Retir	Clemson	CM	PHD	84	Georgia		1983
Dopuch, Nicholas	Emer	Wash Univ	MA	PHD	61.	Illinois		&1983
Herbert C. & Dorothy R. Moog Professor of Accounting								
Doran, B. Michael	Assoc	Iowa State	FE	PHD	84.	Iowa		& 1-84
Doran, David T.	Assoc	Penn St-Erie	FMIN	PHD	85.	Pittsburgh		&1989
Doran, Jamie T.	Assoc	Muhlenberg	MDSE	MS	71	Duquesne		& 9-92
Doran, Martha S.	Assoc	San Diego St	AF	PHD	94	Ariz St		&1996
Dorata, Nina	Asst	St John's	FV	PHD	03.	Rutgers		&2006
Dorocak, John R.	Prof	CS-San Bern	X	LLM	90	Florida		&1991
Dorr, Patrick B.	Prof	Oklahoma St	XS	PHD	79.	North Tx		& 9-77
Haskell Cudd Professor								
Dorsey, Paul R.			DS	PHD	88.	Utah		
Dorsey, Roger	Inst	Ark-Ltl Rock	XLP	LLM	03	Florida		& 7-06
Doryland, Charles F.			MS	DBA	70.	Harvard		
Dosch, Jennifer	Asst	Metro St-MN	M	MBA	92	St Thom	*	2005
Dosch, Robert J.	Assoc	North Dakota	A	PHD	96.	Iowa		& 8-00
Dotan, Amihud	C-Ac	Tel Aviv Un	FM	PHD	77	Cornell		1978
Doty, Edwin A.	Assoc	East Carol	SACM	PHD	81.	Mass		&1988
Doucet, Mary S.	Prof	CS Bakersf	AJSF	PHD	83.	Arizona	#	& 9-98
Doucet, Thomas A.	Prof	CS-Bakersf	CFMS	PHD	92.	Georgia		9-98
Dougherty, Frank P.	Retir	St Marys-Cdn	1997	PHD	76.	Penn St	*	& 1-78
Dougherty, Gerald A.	Retir	Villanova	2002	MBA	68	Temple		&1963
Dougherty, Maureen	Adm	St Marys Pla		DBA	67.	Oregon		
Douglas, Alan V. S.	Assoc	Un Waterloo	FMTY	PHD	94	Queens		1995
Douglas, Patricia C.	Assoc	Loyola Marym	MFIJ	PHD	95.	Va Comm	*	1995
Douglas, Patricia P.	Retir	Montana	1999	PHD	67.	Berkeley		&1966
Douglas, Ronald D.	Asst	SW Minn St	ACP	MS	70	SUNY		2000
Douma, Irene K.	Prof	Montclair St	AFTV	PHD	82.	Baruch		&1973
Doupnik, Timothy S.	D-Pr	So Carolina	FI	PHD	83.	Illinois		&1982
Cramer Fellow of International Accounting								
Douthett, Edward B. Jr.	Asst	Geo Mason	AMI	PHD	95.	Georgia		&2002
Dow, Kathy J.	Assoc	Salem State	F	DBA	89.	Boston U		1994
Dow, Kevin E.	Asst	Kent State	S	PHD	00.	S Carol		8-02
Dowd, Joe E.	Assoc	East Wash	C	PHD	97.	Tx-Austin		&1999
Dowd, Richard				PHD	76.	NYU		
Dowdell, Thomas D.	Asst	N Dakota St	AF	PHD	04.	Temple	*	&2003
Dowell, C. Dwayne	Prof	Texas Tech	FTV	PHD	74.	Mich St		& 9-91
PricewaterhouseCoopers Professor								
Dowling, Carlin	STut	U Melbourne	ABES	BCOM	99	Tasmania		2003
Down, Alexis	Assoc	Emporia St	X	PHD	98	LSU		2005
Downer, Pauline	Assoc	Memorial Un	F	MBA	98	Memorial		&1998
Downes, David H.	Retir	Cal-Berkeley	2003	PHD	75.	Cornell		7-73
Downey, Angela	C-Ac	U Lethbridge	MQUB	PHD	00	W Ontario	*	1996
Downs, Susan R.			SFEI	PHD	88.	Utah		
Doyle, Gerardine	Lect	Un Cl Dublin	FIMN	BSC	85	Dublin		&1992
Doyle, Jeffrey T.	Assoc	Utah State	F	PHD	03.	Michigan		&2003
George S. Eccles Chair in Capital Markets Research								
Doyle, Leonard A.	Retir	Berkeley		PHD	43	Ohio St		1942
Doyle, Marion V.	Retir	Lethbridge	1990	BMA	79	Lethbridge	*	&1979
Doyle, Wendy	Prof	Mt St Vincen	VFGN	MBA	80	Dalhousie		& 7-74
Doyon, David	Asst	So New Hamp	FMI	MBA		S NwHamp		9-01
Dozier, Donald D.	Assoc	Loyola-N Orl	SFA	PHD	81.	Missouri		& 9-85
Dragoo, Amie	Inst	Edgewood	PM	MBA	91	Michigan		&1998
Draimin, K. Charles	Assoc	Concordia U	TWN	PHD	82	Concordia		&1973
Drake, Andrea R.	Assoc	Louisiana Te	BMF	PHD	99.	Mich St		2007
Drake, David F.		Am Hosp Asso	1989	PHD	63.	Chicago		&
Drake, Philip D.	Assoc	Arizona St	F	PHD	90.	Ohio St		&2006
Drebin, Allan R.	Prof	Northwestern	FG	PHD	62	Michigan		&1969
Drechsler, Christoph	Lect	Un Cl Dublin		PHD	02	Paris		2002
Drennan, A. Don	Retir	Abilene Chr	1988	MS	62	Abilene		1958
Drennan, James M.	Retir	St John's	2001	MBA	66	St Johns		&1966
Dresnack, William H.	C-Ac	SUNY-Brockpo	EFTX	JD	97	SUNY-Buf		&1989
Dressel, Norman X.	Deces	Georgia St	8-87	PHD	58	NYU	*	& 9-55
Drew, James	Prof	HEC-Montreal	X	LSCC	72	HEC-Mont		& 6-75
Driscoll, Donna A.	C-Pr	CS-Northrdge	S	PHD	84.	S Calif		1980
Driscoll, John	Retir	DePaul	1993	MBA	62	DePaul		1975
Driscoll, Philip T.	Retir	Syracuse	1989	BS	48	Ohio St		&1982
Driver, Betty A.	Inst	Murray State	F	MBA	83	Murray St		1983
Driver, Phyllis N.	Assoc	Carson-Newmn	PCFV	ABD		Tennessee		&1978
Drtina, Ralph E.	Prof	Rollins	CMU	PHD	80	Ohio St		&1984
Drucker, Meyer	Retir	Winthrop	LX	LLM	83	Emory		& 9-02
Druger, Pamela J.	C-Pr	Augustana IL	FCV	MS	86	Iowa	*	& 9-87

Name	Rank	School		Degree	Year	University	
Drumming, Saundra T.	Assoc	Florida A&M	FT	PHD	82.	Wisconsin	&1983
Drury, Donald H.	C-Pr	McGill Univ	MS	PHD	76.	Nrthwstrn	* 1976
Drymiotes, George C.	Asst	Houston	M	PHD	04.	Florida	9-04
Du, Chan	Asst	CS-Fresno	PFM	DBA	06.	Boston U	8-06
Du, Hongwei	Asst	CS-East Bay	SD	PHD	94	Fla Tech	9-01
Du, Hui	Asst	Houston-Cl L	AFS	PHD	02.	Rutgers	9-07
Du, Jianjun	Asst	Houston-Vict	F	PHD	02	St Louis	8-01
Du, Ning	Asst	DePaul		PHD	05.	Illinois	2005
Duangploy, Orapin S.	Prof	Houston-Down	F	PHD	77.	Missouri	&1987
Dubke, Marie E.	Retir	Memphis	1996	PHD	61.	Mich St	&1967
Dubois, Donald A.			M	PHD	74.	Missouri	&
Duchac, Jonathan E.	Assoc	Wake Forest	PF	PHD	93.	Georgia	& 9-93
Merrill Lynch Professor of Accountancy							
DuCharme, Larry L.	Lect	U Washington	DFMS	PHD	94.	U Wash	1972
Duckworth, Patricia Lynch	Retir	Metro State	1992	DBA	66.	Colorado	& 9-66
Dudley, Lola W.	Retir	E Illinois	2005	PHD	82.	Arkansas	&1989
Duellman, Scott	Asst	SUNY-Bingham	F	PHD	06.	Syracuse	8-06
Duffy, Cathy	Asst	Carthage	FMAX	MST	96	DePaul	&2001
Duffy, Jan	Adj	Iowa State	FM	MS	80	Penn St	&1985
Duffy, Michael L.	Dean	San Francisc	X	JD	83	Berkeley	8-07
Duffy, Wendy A.			FET	PHD	89.	Illinois	&
Dugan, Michael T.	Prof	Alabama	FT	DBA	82.	Tennessee	&1985
Ernst & Young Professor							
Dugar, Amitabh			FS	PHD	88.	Nrthwstrn	* &
Dugdale, David	Prof	Univ Bristol	CM	PHD	71	Hull	2003
Duh, Rong-Ruey	Prof	Nat Taiwan U	ABCM	PHD	86.	Minnesota	8-88
Duimstra, Frits	Lect	Vrije Univ	FM	MS			1988
Duke, Curtis C.	Retir	Virginia St	1988	MBA		NYU	& 9-53
20006 Oakland Avenue; Colonial Heights VA 23834							
Duke, Donald E.			X	PHD	74.	Georgia	&
Duke, Gordon Leon	Assoc	Minnesota	ASI	PHD	80.	Georgia	& 9-81
Duke, Joanne C.	Prof	San Fran St	VFT	PHD	87.	Penn St	* 1987
Dukes, Roland E. (Pete)	Prof	U Washington	FTI	PHD	74.	Stanford	1979
Dull, Richard B.	Assoc	Clemson	S	PHD	97.	Va Tech	&2001
Dunbar, Amy E.	Assoc	Connecticut	X	PHD	89.	Tx-Austin	& 1-99
Dunbar, David	SLect	Victoria NZ	FILX	LLM	79	Victoria	1995
Duncan, Alain C. B.	SLect	Simon Fraser	FM	MBA	75	York	& 9-95
Duncan, Carson M.	Retir	St Fran Xav	M	PHD	78	W Ontario	1967
Duncan, Clarence	Retir	Piedmont	2005	MBA	73	Jacksv St	1974
Duncan, Doris	Prof	CS-East Bay	SD	PHD	78	Golden Gt	4-76
Duncan, James R.	Assoc	Ball State	FA	PHD	97.	Kentucky	& 9-97
Duncan, John B.			CM	PHD	95.	Miss	&
Duncan, Keith R.	Assoc	Bond Univ	FTY	PHD	93	Bond	&1989
Duncan, William A.	Assoc	Ariz St-West	X	PHD	83.	Tx-Austin	& 9-91
Dungan, Chris W.	Retir	South Fla	1998	PHD	83.	Illinois	& 1-83
Dungan, Kelli	Lect	Michigan	F	MACC	93	Michigan	1998
Dunham, Clive F.	Retir	Illinois	8-77	PHD	35.	Illinois	&1965
605 W Delaware; Urbana IL 61801							
Dunigan, James P.	Retir	Wis-Stev Pt	5-01	MBA	59	Wisconsin	& 9-70
Dunmore, Paul V.	Prof	Massey-Welli	AFMQ	PHD	75	McMaster	2004
Dunn, Cheryl L.	Assoc	Grand Valley	SD	PHD	94.	Mich St	& 8-05
Dunn, Clarence L.	Retir	Virg Comm	1987	PHD	53.	Illinois	&1978
11800 Rochampton Sq; Richmond VA 23233							
Dunn, John	Lect	Strathclyde	AF	MACC	88	Glasgow	&1991
Dunn, Kimberly A.	Asst	Fla Atlantic	AF	PHD	97	Geo St	2001
Dunn, Laura Menzel			FMX	PHD	98.	Colorado	&
Dunn, Paul	Assoc	Brock Univ	FAJ	DBA	99.	Boston U	&1998
Dunn, Wm. Marcus	Retir	Tx-Arlington	2004	PHD	76.	Florida	& 6-79
Dunne, Kathleen M.	Assoc	Rider	VI	PHD	88.	Temple	1989
Dunne, Theresa	Lect	Dundee	BEFI	PHD	03	Dundee	2003
Dunning, Greg	LT	Univ Windsor	A	MBA	75	E Mich	2002
Dunstan, Judith	Inst	New Bruns-SJ		LLB	95	Toronto	&1999
Dunstan, Keitha	H-Pr	Victoria NZ	FGMT	PHD	98	Queenlsd	&2000
Dupree, Dempsey M.	Retir	Clarion	1993	PHD	65.	Mich St	& 8-67
DuPree, Jean M.			F	PHD	82.	Geo St	&
Winston-Salem NC							
Dupuis, Euclid A.	Prof	So New Hamp	XC	MS	77	Bentley	& 9-84
Durand, Robert	Lect	W Australia	F	MBA	97	Edinburgh	1998
Durkee, David A.	Assoc	Weber State	FSI	PHD	87.	Okla St	&1991
Durler, M. George	Assoc	Emporia St	AFS	PHD	97.	LSU	& 8-00
Durocher, Sylvain	Assoc	Univ Ottawa	FIN	PHD	03	Quebec	&2006
Durtschi, Cindy	Assoc	Utah State	FV	PHD	98.	Arizona	2003
Duru, Augustine	Assoc	American U	MF	PHD	97.	Maryland	& 9-98
Dusenbury, Richard B.	Assoc	Florida St	MB	PHD	89.	Florida	& 1-90
Dutta, Saurav K.	Assoc	SUNY-Albany	MA	PHD	91.	Kansas	* 1998
Dutta, Sunil	C-Ac	Cal-Berkeley	M	PHD	94.	Minnesota	1996
Egen and Joan von Kaschnitz Associate Professor of Atg & Intl Business							

Name	Rank	School	Code	Degree	Yr	Univ	Year
Duval, Marc A.	Retir	E Kentucky	1985	PHD	72	NYU	&1978
Duvall, Linda G.	Assoc	Sam Houston	FI	PHD	93.	Maryland	&1994
Duxbury, Darren	SLect	Univ Leeds	BMQ	PHD	96	Leeds	9-94
Dworetsky, Ephraim D.	Emer	Lg Isl-Brook	1990	MBA	49	CCNY	&1946
Dworin, Lowell			1994		77.	Michigan	1985
Dir, Office Tax Analysis; Rm 4064 Main Treasury; Wash DC 20220; 202-622-0269							
Dwyer, Peggy D.	Assoc	Cen Florida	FA	PHD	88.	Missouri	& 8-97
Dyball, Maria Cadiz	SLect	Macquarie Un	HEFS	PHD	03	NS Wales	2004
Dyckman, Samuel A.	Retir	CUNY-Baruch	1991	LLM	51	NYU	&1952
Dyckman, Thomas R.	Emer	Cornell	2007	PHD	62	Michigan	9-64
Ann Whitney Olin Professor of Accounting							
Dye, Charles F.	Retir	York-Penn	1998	MED		Shippensb	9-71
Dye, Janet L.	C-Pr	Alaska SE		PHD	94	Colum Pac	& 8-93
Dye, Ronald A.	C-Pr	Northwestern	FM	PHD	80	Car Mellon	1986
Leonard Spacek Professor of Accounting Information & Management							
Dye, Wilma R.	Assoc	Txs-Perm Bas	XF	PHD	98.	Tx Tech	&9-92
Dyer, Jack L.	Retir	E Kentucky	2002	DBA	73.	Kentucky	&1989
Dykxhoorn, Hans J.	Prof	W Michigan	AFO	PHD	78.	Mich St	&1979
Dyrnes, Sverre	IndPr	Norwegian Mg	CFM	MBUS	78	NHH Berg	&2001
Dyson, K.	Lect	Univ Ulster	F	MSC			9-92
Dyt, Robyn	ALect	Monash Univ	AF	BA			2001
Dzeng, Simon C.			S	PHD	92.	Drexel	
Eakin, Cynthia F.	Assoc	Pacific	FXM	PHD	93.	Fla St	&1996
Ealey, Thomas L.	Assoc	Alma		MAC	70	Bowl Gr	&2000
Eames, Michael J.	Assoc	Santa Clara	FM	PHD	95.	U Wash	&1996
Earles, Melanie James	Assoc	Tenn Tech	XC	DBA	97.	Miss St	& 8-98
Earley, Christine E.	Assoc	Bentley	A	PHD	98.	Pittsburgh	2005
Earner, William A.				DBA	73.	Harvard	
Earnest, Kenneth R.			CP	PHD	78.	Tx-Austin	* &
Earney, Charles L.	Asst	N Car-Wilmin	GF	MBA	70	Wisconsin	&1982
Eason, Catherine	Inst	Queens-Charl		MS	00	Charlest	&2002
Eason, James F.	Retir	Coast Carol	FM	MA	75	Appalach	1977
Eason, Patricia L.	Asst	Txs-El Paso	X	PHD	94.	Tx Tech	& 9-95
Eastergard, Alf M.			FMCS	PHD	88.	Nebraska	* &
Easterwood, Cintia M.	Inst	Virg Tech	FS	PHD	93.	Houston	8-92
Easton, Edison E.		Business		DBA	67.	S Calif	&
Easton, Peter	Prof	Notre Dame	F	PHD	84.	Berkeley	&2003
Alumni/Andersen Chair							
Easton, Reed W.	Assoc	Seton Hall	XKLO	LLM	82	NYU	& 9-89
Easton, Sandra W.	Retir	No Kentucky	2000	MBA	87	Xavier	8-72
Easton, Steve	Prof	U Newcastle	F	PHD	93	Monash	1991
Eaton, James O.			M	PHD	50.	Illinois	
Eaton, Ronald H.	Assoc	Christian Br	SA	PHD	73.	Arkansas	&2002
Eaton, Tim V.	Assoc	Miami U-Ohio	F	PHD	96.	Tennessee	& 8-05
Ebey, Carl F.			FG	DBA	80.	Indiana	&
Ebrahim, Ahmed	Asst	SUNY-N Paltz	CM	PHD	04.	Rutgers	1994
Ebrahim, M. Shahid	Read	U Nottingham	FQ	DBA	95	S Illinois	2003
Eccher, Elizabeth A.			FM	PHD	96.	Nrthwstrn	
Eckel, Leonard G.	Retir	Un Waterloo	2002	PHD	69	Michigan	&1981
Eckel, Norman L.	Assoc	Bowling Gr	MCU	PHD	82	W Ontario	1979
Ecker, Frank	Asst	Duke	F	PHD	05	Trier	2007
Eckstein, Claire			FT	PHD	88.	NYU	&
Ecton, William W.	Retir	Kentucky	1996	PHD	66.	Missouri	&1957
Eddey, Peter H.	Prof	Macquarie Un	F	MCOM	75	NS Wales	&1977
Eddie, Ian	C-Ac	N Eng-Austr	I	PHD		N Eng-Au	&1982
Eddlemon, Carlene V.			XF	PHD	96.	LSU	&
Edelson, Charles B.	Retir	Maryland	1991	MBA	50	Indiana	&1950
Edelson, Robert E.	Dean	Wilmington	BMQ	PHD	00	Claremont	2005
Eden, Ronald	Assoc	Univ Ottawa	MGN	PHD	94	SUNY	1988
Ederhof, Merle	Asst	Yale	MT	PHD	07	Stanford	7-07
Edgley, Carla	Tutor	Cardiff U	FX	MA	85	Oxford	&1998
Edmiston, G. Dean	Assoc	Emporia St	FMC	MS	67	EmporiaSt	& 8-78
Edmonds, Cindy	Retir	Alabama-Birm	MP	PHD	91.	Alabama	1989
Edmonds, Dwight M.	Retir	Wilfrid Laur	1996	PHD	69.	Wisconsin	* &1982
Edmonds, Thomas P.	Prof	Alabama-Birm	FP	PHD	79.	Geo St	1986
Alumni and Friends Professor of Accounting							
Edmunds, Wayne L.	Assoc	Virg Comm	X	MLT	84	Wm&Mary	&1984
Edney, Robert K.	Retir	Rider	2004	MBA	72	Temple	&1987
Edwards, Courtney H.	Adj	No Carolina	X	PHD	06.	N Carol	&2004
Edwards, Donald E.	Retir	Ark-Ltl Rock	2005	PHD	66.	Arkansas	& 8-91
Edwards, James B.	Prof	So Carolina	2005	PHD	71.	Georgia	# * &1971
Edwards, James Don	Emer	Georgia	1999	PHD	53.	Tx-Austin	&1972
Edwards, James E.	Retir	Truman State	1996	MA	61	NE Mo St	1965
Edwards, James W.	Retir	Tx A&M-Comm	FIE	PHD	66.	Mich St	&1998
Edwards, John D.			AF	PHD	65.	Alabama	# &
Edwards, John Richard	Prof	Cardiff	FH	MSC	75	Cardiff	&1971
Edwards, Lewis	Retir	Queensld Tec	1998	MBA	77	Queensld	& 1-73

Name	Rank	University		Deg	Yr	School	Date
Edwards, Pamela	SLect	U Manchester	FIMW MSC		93	Manchest	9-90
Edwards, Peter	Lect	Univ Sydney	BCDM BEC		92	Macquarie	&1994
Edwards, Randal K.	Dean	Appalach St	ANG	PHD	88.	Tennessee	&1981
Edwards, Wendell E.	H-Pr	Tx A&M-Comm	MCE	PHD	73.	North Tx	&1969
Efebera, Henry	Deces	Akron	FSX	PHD	99.	S Fla	&1999
Efendi, Jap	Asst	Tx-Arlington	FA	PHD	04.	Tx A&M	8-07
Egenolf, Robert V.	Retir	Texas-Austin	1999	PHD	74.	Tx A&M	& 9-90
Eger, Carol E.			MF	PHD	82.	Minnesota	
Eggleton, Ian R. C.	Prof	W Australia	BGM	PHD	79.	Chicago	1984
Eglem, Jean-Yves	H-Pr	ESCP deParis	FIMU	PHD	80	Paris I	1971
Eguae-Obazee, Gertrude	C-Ac	Albright	MCNG	MBA	80	JacksonSt	&1991
Ehab, Mohammed	Lect	Sultan Qaboo	FA	PHD	97	City-UK	1998
Ehlen, Craig R.	Prof	So Indiana	PAB	DBA	94.	S Illinois	&1991
Ehrenberg, James F.	Retir	Valparaiso	1996	MS	66	N Illinois	& 9-66
Ehrenreich, Keith B.	Retir	CS-Pomona	2000	DBA	75.	S Calif	&1970
Eichenseher, John W.	Prof	Wisconsin	FIA	PHD	80.	Michigan	& 8-83
Eid, Saleh	Assoc	King Saud U	FX	PHD	87	Cairo	1997
Eide, Barbara J.	C-Pr	Wis-La Cross	CM	PHD	98.	Va Comm	& 8-98
Eidson, Vicky	Assoc	Quincy	APV	DMGT	98	Webster	&2004
Eighme, Jan E.	Lect	Miami U-Ohio	S	PHD	01.	Fla St	8-00
Eikner, A. Elaine	Prof	Tx St-S Marc	FPV	PHD	94.	Arkansas	& 9-92
Eilifsen, K. Aasmund	Prof	Norwegian U	A	DOEC			
Einhorn, Ester	Asst	Tel Aviv Un	F	PHD	03	Tel Aviv	2003
Eining, Martha M.	Prof	Utah	SA	PHD	87.	Okla St	&1987
Eischen, Erick	Asst	Northern St					8-06
Eisenman, Seymour L.	Retir	CUNY-Baruch	2002	PHD	75.	Baruch	1970
Eiteman, Dean S.	Retir	Indiana U-PA	5-99	PHD	67.	Mich St	1988
Ekanayake, Samson	Lect	Deakin-Burwo	FM	MA	82	Lancaster	1992
Ekins, Gayle	Lect	East Wash	F	MA	04	E Wash	&2006
Ekmekjian, Elizabeth	Asst	Wm Paterson	XL	LLM	98	NYU Law	1999
El Fquir, Bayrem	Asst	Univ Tunis	F	DEA	99	ISCAE	1999
El-Adly, Yousef A.	Prof	Kuwait Univ	FM	PHD	70.	Illinois	9-95
El-Arabi, Adbussalam A.		Libya		PHD	77.	LSU	
El-Azma, Mohammed A.	Prof	Kuwait Univ	FVI	PHD	76	Manchest	1978
El-Badawi, Mohamed H.	C-Pr	CS-Dominguez	MF	PHD	80.	S Calif	&1986
El-Bahr, Hussa	Asst	Kuwait Univ	GS	PHD	85	Ain Shams	1985
El-Gallab, George Nashwa				PHD	87.	Baruch	
El-Gawhary, Ali M.		Tanta U Egyp	1995	PHD	80.	Mich St	

College of Commerce; Dept of Accounting; Tanta Univ; Tanta Egypt

Name	Rank	University		Deg	Yr	School	Date
El-Gazzar, Samir M.	Prof	Pace	F	PHD	84.	Baruch	1992

KPMG Peat Marwick Professor of Accounting

Name	Rank	University		Deg	Yr	School	Date
El-Gehawe, Adbelsalam				PHD	80.	Missouri	
El-Hashash, Hadeya			MCS	PHD	93.	Rutgers	1992
El-Hawary, Mohamed N. H.				PHD	61.	Illinois	
El-Hosseiny, Mohamed A.				PHD	88.	Baruch	
El-Leithy, Fouad M.			AF	PHD	82.	Okla St	
El-Masry, Hussein	Asst	CS-L Angeles	FS	PHD	03.	S Fla	9-03
El-Rajabi, Mohamed	Assoc	Kuwait Univ	CF	PHD	86	Wisconsin	2001
El-Rajabir, Md-Taysir A. H.				PHD	86.	Wisconsin	
El-Refadi, Idris	Deces			PHD	86.	North Tx	
El-Shamy, Mostafa	Assoc	Kuwait Univ	FI	PHD	89	NYU	1993
El-Sharif, Younis				PHD	78.	Missouri	
El-Sherazy, Abbas M.				PHD	66.	Illinois	
El-Sherif, Hassan Ahmed		Cairo, Egypt		PHD	51.	Chicago	
El-Zayaty, Ahmed I.	Assoc	Findlay	FGN	PHD	86.	Baruch	1993
Elam, Dennis	Inst	North Texas	FMA	PHD	03	Tx-Austin	&2006
Elam, Rick	Prof	Mississippi	CS	PHD	73.	Missouri	& 8-99

Reynolds Distinguished Professor

Name	Rank	University		Deg	Yr	School	Date
Elayan, Fayez	Assoc	Brock Univ					
Elbannan, Mohamed		Cairo Univ		PHD	03.	S Illinois	

Cairo University; Egypt

Name	Rank	University		Deg	Yr	School	Date
Eldahrawy, Kamal	Asst	Alexandria	1991	PHD	85.	North Tx	

Dept of Atg; Fac of Comm; Alexandria Univ; Alexandra Egypt

Name	Rank	University		Deg	Yr	School	Date
Eldenburg, Leslie G.	Assoc	Arizona	M	PHD	91.	U Wash	&1993
Elder, Randal J.	C-Pr	Syracuse	AG	PHD	93.	Mich St	&1992
Elderedge, Tom	Adj	Utah	FS	MBA	94	Utah	&2002
Eldridge, Susan	Asst	Neb-Omaha	FP	PHD	97.	N Carol	&2002
Eletr, Amr			CM	DBA	92.	Miss St	*
ElEuch, Sarra	Asst	Univ Tunis	CM	DEA	97	ISCAE	1997
Eley, Marion J.	Emer	Dayton	1996	MBA	64	Xavier	&1961
Eley, Robin	Lect	McGill Univ	FT	MBA	83	McGill	&1989
ElFekey, Mahmoud E.			1992	PHD	89.	Miss	

204 Alhegaz St #14; Misr Algadeeda; Cairo Egypt

Name	Rank	University		Deg	Yr	School	Date
ElFrink, John A.	C-Pr	W Illinois	F	PHD	87.	St Louis	& 8-06
Elgers, Pieter T.	Prof	Massachusett	FM	DBA	78.	Maryland	&1979
Elhamy, Mohamed A.		Cairo, Egypt	1990	PHD	65.	Illinois	
Elias, Nabil S.	Assoc	N Car-Charl	FM	PHD	70.	Minnesota	* 2001

Elias, Rafik Z.	Assoc	CS-L Angeles	FMC	DBA	97.	La Tech	&9-93
Eliezer, Supriya	ALect	Sydney Un	FIE	MTLW	03	UTS	2004
Elifoglu, Ibrahim H.	Assoc	St John's	MSA	PHD	76	New Sch	1999
Elijido-Ten, Evangeline	Lect	U Queensland	A	MBA	91	St Thomas	2002
Elikai, Fara M. H.	Assoc	N Car-Wilmin	MC	PHD	83.	Oklahoma	1986
Eliraqi, Iraqui				PHD	82.	Arkansas	
Elitzur, R. Ramy	Assoc	Univ Toronto	AF	PHD	88.	NYU	* &1988
Elkharouf, Farouk Wasef			1992	PHD	82.	Illinois	
Finance/Accountancy; PO Box 1506; 1211 Geneva Switzerland							
Elkhatib, Sobhy M.		Alexandria	1992	PHD	92.	Tx-Arlin	
Axexandria Univ; Dept of Accounting; Fac of Comm; Alexandria Egypt							
Ellert, James C.	Prof	Intl Mgt Dev		PHD	75	Chicago	1981
Ellett, John S. II	Retir	New Orleans	8-94	PHD	69.	N Carol	&1970
Ellingson, Dee Ann	Assoc	North Dakota	CMP	PHD	96.	Va Tech	&1993
Elliott, C. Orville	Retir	W Illinois	1977	PHD	58	Oklahoma	&9-67
Elliott, C. Williard	Retir	Southern	ASGN	PHD	64.	Arkansas	&1979
Elliott, Edward L.			C	PHD	64.	Illinois	
Elliott, John A.	Dean	CUNY-Baruch	XAF	PHD	82.	Cornell	&9-02
Elliott, Patrica C.	Retir	New Mexico	1997	DBA	73.	Colorado	&1977
Elliott, Terry G.	Assoc	Morehead St	CA	MSA	87	Morehead	&1989
Elliott, W. Brooke	Asst	Illinois	F	PHD	03.	U Wash	6-03
Ellis, Laura	Retir	Scranton	PA	PHD	97.	Oregon	&1994
Ellis, William M.	Retir	Central Conn	1992	JD		Conn	&9-75
Ellis, Yvonne	Asst	Morehouse	MFBV	PHD	05.	JacksonSt	2005
Ellison, David J.	Retir	Creighton	2001	PHD	74.	Arkansas	&9-81
Ellison, Mitchell	Prof	Quincy	CFMP	PHD	93	St Louis	* &1993
Ellison, Robert	Lect	Tx St-S Marc	CFM	MACY	01	SW Tx St	2003
Elloumi, Fathi	Assoc	Athabasca Un		PHD		Montreal	2000
Elloumi, Iyadh	Inst	Univ Tunis	RAV	EXPC	98	ISCAE	1999
Ellwood, Sheila	Prof	Univ Bristol	ACFG	PHD	95	Aston	2006
Elmadfai, Omar A.			FV	PHD	76.	LSU	
Elmallah, Amin A.	Dean	CS-Stanislau	CIGS	PHD	74.	Illinois	* & 7-00
Elmendorf, Richard G.	Assoc	Wyoming	FN	DBA	87.	Boston U	1989
Elmore, Robert C.	Prof	Tenn Tech	CMX	PHD	86.	Miss	&1988
Elmslie, Harry D.	Retir	Lakehead U	2002	ABD		Illinois	&1965
ElNaggar, A. Osh	Deces	Anderson	2005	PHD	96.	Kentucky	&1996
Elnathan, Dan			MI	PHD	89.	Penn	
Elnicki, Richard A.	Prof	Florida	1998	DBA	67.	Harvard	1971
Department of Management; 352-392-6640; dicke@nervm.nerdc.ufl.edu							
Elrod, Henry	C-As	Incarnate	AJFM	MBA	69	Tx Chr	&8-00
Elsayed-Ahmed, Sameh M.	Assoc	MD E Shore	VCFI	PHD	86.	North Tx	8094
Elsea, John E.	Retir	No Colorado	2004	PHD	74	N Colo	&9-78
Elshafie, Essam A.	Asst	Tx-Brownsvil		PHD	05.	Kent St	2005
Elshany, Mostafa			1991	PHD	89.	NYU	
500 Marboro Rd A4; Wood Ridge NJ 07075							
Elshazly, Talaat A.	Assoc	Charleston	CM	MSA	64	Illinois	* &1979
Elson, Raymond J.	Asst	Valdosta St	A	PHD	01	Sarasota	& 8-03
Elvik, Kenneth O.	Retir	Iowa State	1998	PHD	70.	Nebraska	1970
Ely, Kirsten M.	Assoc	Sonoma State	SA	PHD	88.	Chicago	2005
Emanuel, David M.	Prof	U Auckland	FA	PHD	84	Auckland	&1975
Emblen, Donald J.	Retir	Montana	6-71	PHD	44	Columbia	
Emby, Craig	Prof	Simon Fraser	AB	PHD	89	Alberta	& 1-87
Emenyonu, Emmanuel N.	C-Pr	So Conn St	VPT	PHD	93	Glasgow	&2000
Emerson, Mike	Asst	Harding	ATF	MS	89	Harding	&1985
Emery, Mary Ann	Assoc	St Olaf	PFM	MA	65	Minnesota	&1969
Emery, Richard F.	Prof	Linfield	XPT	MBA	71	E New Mex	& 8-86
Emig, James M.	Assoc	Villanova	CFME	PHD	87.	Tx A&M	&1983
Emmanuel, Clive R.	Prof	Univ Glasgow	FMS	PHD	72	Lancaster	1987
Emore, James R.	Assoc	Akron	UMC	DBA	84.	Kent St	9-73
KPMG Fellow; Associate Dean							
Empey, Philip H.	Assoc	Purdue Calum	FMAS	PHD	72	Purdue	&1970
Emsley, David	SLect	Univ Sydney	MWS	PHD	96	Macquarie	&2005
Endrawes, Medhat	Lect	W Sydney	AF	MCOM		NS Wales	
Eng, Li Li	Asst	Oklahoma St	F	PHD	95.	Michigan	&8-02
Engel, Ellen	Assoc	Chicago	F	PHD	97.	Stanford	&1996
Engelbret, William G.	Assoc	Penn St-Brch	EFM	PHD	91.	Penn St	&9-77
England, Thomas G.	Retir	East Tenn St	1992	PHD	98.	Pittsburgh	&1983
39120 Harbor Hills Blvd; Lady Lake FL 32159							
Englard, Baruch	Asst	CUNY-Stn Isl	CF	MBA	74	Long Isl	&1972
Engle, Howard	AdjLe	Illinois		MS	75	DePaul	1988
Engle, Terry J.	Prof	South Fla	AS	PHD	83.	Missouri	&1983
Advisory Council Professor							
Englebrecht, Ted D.	Prof	Louisiana Te	XF	PHD	76.	S Carol	2001
Smolinski Eminent Scholar Endowed Chair of Accounting							
Englehart, Jose'	Retir	Fla Atlantic	MCF	MBA	84	Fla Atl	&1990
Engler, Calvin	Retir	Iona	6-95	PHD	77.	Baruch	&1969
PO Box 103; Monsey NY 10952							

Name	Rank	School	Code	Degree	Yr	University	Marks
Englert, Lawrence R.	Emer	Indiana East	D-05				
English, Denise M.	C-Pr	Boise State	FAEO	PHD	88.	Indiana	# &1-88
English, Linda M.	SLect	Univ Sydney	EGF	BCOM	83	Monash	&1990
English, Richard D.	Assoc	Augustana SD	EFJX	MBA	68	Wash U	&1974
English, Thomas J.	Prof	Boise State	AOR	PHD	88.	Ariz St	&9-87
Engstrom, John H.	Emer	No Illinois	2004	DBA	77.	Indiana	&6-82
Enis, Charles R.	Assoc	Penn State	X	DBA	81.	Maryland	&9-81
Enke, Ernest L.	Retir	Alfred	7-01	PHD	67.	Illinois	# * &1973
Ennis, Kevin L.	Asst	Miss St-Mer	AX	PHD	05.	JacksonSt	# * & 8-95
Ennis, Leon M. Jr.	Adm	No Carolina		PHD	68.	N Carol	
Ennis, Thomas E. Jr.			AFMT	PHD	64.	Michigan	
Ennouri, Imed	Asst	Univ Tunis	AFK	EXPC	91	IHEC	1992
Enthoven, Adolf J. H.	Prof	Texas-Dallas	IMT	PHD	60	Netherl	&1975
Entwistle, Gary M.	Assoc	Saskatchewan	FAIW	PHD	97	W Ontario	&1990
Epaves, Richard A.			F	DBA	72.	Kent St	&
Epelle, Chuks T.			FM	PHD	92.	S Carol	
Epping, Lori L.	Inst	South Dakota	P	MBA	99	S Dakota	&2000
Epps, Kathryn K.	Asst	Kennesaw St	FA	PHD	01.	Geo St	2004
Epps, Ruth W.	Prof	Virg Comm	MGN	PHD	87.	Va Comm	&1987
Epstein, Marc J.	VProf	Rice	FM	PHD	73.	Oregon	1998
Research Professor of Management							
Eramus, Edward W.	Asst	SUNY-Brockpo	JLXY	JD	73	Case Wes	1977
Erb, Emerson C.	Retir	CS-Bakersf	7-91	DBA	61.	Indiana	&9-72
113 Parkway Drive; Wabash IN 46992							
Ericksen, Douglas C.	Retir	Mo-Kansas Ct	1992	PHD	68	Missouri	* &1986
Erickson, Merle M.	Prof	Chicago	FX	PHD	96.	Arizona	&9-96
Erickson, Paul R.	Prof	Baylor	XL	JD	81	Idaho	&1981
R. E. and Marilyn Reamer Professor of Accounting							
Erickson, Sheri	Asst	Mn-Moorhead	ACP	PHD	06	N Dak St	&1998
Eriksen, Scott	Asst	Co St-Pueblo	MC	PHD	87.	North Tx	* &2005
Erlach, David	Asst	CUNY-Queens	TC	PHD	95	SW Jose	2-78
Erlich, L.	Inst	Touro	PT	BS			& 1-97
Ernst, John D.				PHD	75.	Geo St	
Ertimur, Yonca	Asst	Duke	F	PHD	03.	NYU	2006
Erturk, Ismail	Lect	U Manchester	F	MA	85	NYU	1987
Esdaille, Eustace	C-Ac	Virgin Islan	CFM	PHD	95	U Wash	1999
Esernio, Robert J.	Retir	C W Post	1985	MBA	71	NYU	&1971
Eskew, Robert K.	Prof	Purdue	AFEK	PHD	73.	Purdue	1976
Esmond-Kiger, Connie L.	Assoc	Ohio Univ	FAGN	PHD	95.	Indiana	&9-99
Richard P. & Joan S. Fox Professor in Business							
Espahbodi, Hassanali	Prof	W Illinois	FM	PHD	81.	Alabama	&9-90
Espahbodi, Pouran T.	Prof	W Illinois	FM	PHD	81.	Alabama	&9-90
Espahbodi, Reza	Prof	Ind-So Bend	AFM	PHD	81.	Alabama	&8-98
Espenlaub, Susanne	Lect	U Manchester	FQTY	PHD		Oxford	1992
Espensen, Henry J.	C-Pr	Rockford	FRTX	MA		Iowa	* &1986
Essex, Patricia A.	Assoc	Bowling Gr	MS	PHD	93.	Mich St	* &1993
Essien, C.	SLect	London Metro	FI	MSC			2001
Estes, Ralph W.	Retir	American U	1997	DBA	67.	Indiana	&9-90
Estes, Thomas G. Jr.	Retir	Mercer-Macon	2005	PHD	71.	Arkansas	&1992
Estrin, Teviah L.	Retir	Univ Windsor	2000	PHD	73	UCLA	* 1984
Esworthy, Raymond W.				PHD	43.	Illinois	
Etebari, Ahmad	C-Pr	New Hampshir	MZE	PHD	79	North Tx	1980
Etheridge, Harlan L.	Asst	Western Wash	AMS	PHD	91.	LSU	&2007
Etherington, Lois D.	Retir	Simon Fraser	8-98	PHD	77.	U Wash	9-80
Ethridge, Jack R.	Prof	S F Austin	FTA	PHD	86.	Arkansas	&1983
Etienne, Margaret	Retir	Ferris State	2004	MSA	80	Cen Mich	&1984
Etnier, Donald E.	Retir	Wis-Eau Clar	1994	PHD	73.	Minnesota	&9-66
Etter, Edwin R.	Assoc	E Michigan	FV	PHD	92.	Ohio St	&2002
Ettredge, Michael L.	Prof	Kansas	FT	PHD	82.	Tx-Austin	1993
Crown/Sheff Professor							
Etzold, Michele	Asst	Johnson&Wale	F	MBA	95	Bryant	&2002
Eugene, Edward J. Jr.			FM	PHD	95.	Memphis	&
Euske, Kenneth J.	Prof	Naval Postgr	MB	PHD	78.	Ariz St	1978
Evanchik, Michael			FM	PHD	89.	U Wash	
Evans, Allison L.	Asst	N Car-Wilmin	X	PHD	06.	N Carol	2006
Evans, Elaine	SLect	Macquarie Un	HE	PHD	03	NS Wales	&2001
Evans, Hugh G. Jr.	Retir	Elizabethtwn	2002	MA	66	Penn St	1968
Evans, John H. III (Harry)	Prof	Pittsburgh	MTN	PHD	80.	Car Mellon	1978
Alumni Professor of Accounting							
Evans, Kevin	Lect	Cardiff U	Q	MSC	99	Warwick	2005
Evans, Lisa	Prof	Un Stirling	FHI	PHD	00	Reading	&2006
Evans, M.	SLect	Liverpool-JM	MF	MA			1992
Evans, Paul	Retir	York-Atkinsn	2004	DIP	66	Oxon	&1971
Evans, Thomas G.	Retir	Cen Florida	IT	PHD	69.	Mich St	8-90
Evans, William	Lect	Rochest Tech	M	MBA	84	Rochester	9-04
Everard, Andrea	Asst	Delaware	S	PHD	93	Pittsburgh	9-03
Everett, Jeffery	Asst	Univ Calgary	AEG	PHD	01	Calgary	2003

Everett, John O.	Prof	Virg Comm	X	PHD	78.	Okla St		&1982
Everitt, Mary	SLect	Un East Lond	FT	BA				1985
Evers, Pamela	Assoc	N Car-Wilmin	JL	LLM	99	Lewis&Cl		2001
Everson, Paul	Asst	Northern St	FMTV	MBA	78	S Dakota		&1977
Ewald, Albert A.	Retir	Temple	1985	PHD	68.	Mich St		1972
916 Sara Drive: Springfield PA 19064								
Ewer, Sid R.	Prof	Missouri St	GMIO	PHD	89.	Miss	# *	&8-88
Ewing, Janet S.	Assoc	Baldwinldwin	PFD	ABD		Va Comm		1977
Ewing-Chow, Frank	Retir	CS-Pomona	2004	DBA	77.	S Calif		&1980
Eyler, Kel-Ann S.	Assoc	Wesleyan-GA	AM	PHD	90.	Geo St		&2006
Eyster, James	Emer	Cornell-Hotl	2000	PHD	77	Cornell		1972
Ezzamel, Mahmoud A.	Prof	Cardiff U	BHMW	PHD	75	Southampt		1975
Faerber, LeRoy G.	Retir	Utah	1998	PHD	64	U Wash		1970
Fafatas, Stephan A.	Asst	Wash & Lee	FA	PHD	06.	Colorado		2006
Fahmy, Samir B.	Retir	St John's	2004	PHD	67.	Tx-Austin		9-81
Fahnestock, Robert T.	Prof	West Florida	TFMX	PHD	84.	Miss		&1974
Fahringer, Richard J.	Retir	So Conn St	1995	MBA	67	NYU	# *	&1982
Fahs, Janis K.	H-Ac	Manchester C	FRS	MIM	86	AGSIM		&1996
Fair, George W.	Retir	LSU	1980	PHD	60.	LSU		&1946
Fairchild, Joseph V.	Retir	Henderson St	2004	PHD	75.	LSU		&8-00
Faircloth, Archie W.	Assoc	Louisville	FNH	DBA	77.	Kentucky		&9-72
Faircloth, Terence A.	Retir	Roosevelt	2005	MSA	71	Roosevelt		&1974
Fairfield, Patricia M.	Assoc	Georgetown	F	PHD	86	Columbia		1989
Fairhall, Tim	SLect	Victoria NZ	AJS	BCA	73	Victoria		2002
Faisal, Abdullah M.				PHD	79.	Oklahoma		
Falcetto, Larry R.	Assoc	Emporia St	FP	MBA	76	Pittsburgh	*	&8-76
Falcon, Alan H.	Prof	Loyola Marym	FME	MAC	73	Arizona	# *	&1979
Falgiani, A. Anthony	Assoc	W Illinois	XML	JD	81	S Texas	*	9-89
Falk, Christopher W.	Lect	Fla State	F	MACC	96	Miami U		&8-06
Falk, Haim	Retir	Technion	2004	PHD	71	Hebrew		&
Technion, Israel Institute of Technology								
Fallan, Lars	Prll	Norwegian U	X	DOEC				
Fallatah, Yaser				PHD	06.	Fla Atl		
Falls, Robert G.	Prof	Anderson Col		DBA	54.	Indiana		
Falsetta, Diana	Asst	U Miami	X	PHD	02.	S Carol		&2006
Falu, Georgina	Retir	SUNY Old Wes	1997	EDD				1980
Fan, Joseph P. H.	Prof	Chinese HK	F	PHD	96	Pittsburgh		2004
Fan, Quintao	Asst	Cal-Berkeley	FM	PHD	04.	Stanford		2003
Fan, Weiguo (Patrick)	Assoc	Virg Tech	S	PHD	02	Michigan		2002
Fane, Gary R.	Retir	North Fla	5-07	PHD	74.	Florida	*	&1975
Fang, Chih-Chiang				PHD	93.	St Louis		
Fanning, Kurt	Assoc	Grand Valley	S	PHD	94.	Kansas	*	&8-00
Fantl, Irving L.	Deces	Fla Internat	1991	PHD	74.	NYU		&1975
Farag, Magdy	Asst	CS-Pomona	F	PHD	07	Kent St		2007
Farber, David B.	Asst	Missouri	AF	PHD	02.	Cornell		&2006
Farber, Irving	Retir	Ill-Chicago	1991	MBA	76	Loyola		1986
Farewell, Stephanie M.	Asst	Ark-Ltl Rock	SF	PHD	01	Oklahoma		7-01
Fargher, Neil L.	Prof	Macquarie Un	FA	PHD	93.	Arizona		&2004
Farina, Louis J.	Asst	Framingham	ACTV	MS	80	DePaul		&1991
Farinacci, Carl S.	Retir	Clarion	2005	JD	70	Akron		&8-83
Farlee, Mitchell A.			M	PHD	96.	Ohio St		&
Farley, Alan A.	Prof	Monash Univ	DMQE	PHD	86	Monash		&1976
Farlik, Terry E.			Edinboro		DSC	06	Rbt Morr		&2003
Farmer, Larry E.	Prof	Mid Tenn St	AFTG	DBA	75.	La Tech	# *	&1980
Farmer, Martha K.			Augusta	FT	PHD	77.	S Carol		&
Farmer, Timothy A.	Assoc	Mo-St Louis	MB	PHD	84.	Ohio St		&9-87
Farooqi, Nauman	Assoc	Mt Allison U	FM	PHD	93	St Louis		7-00
Farrar, Robert H.	Assoc	Bryant	MUF	PHD	78.	Mass		8-86
Farrell, Anne M.	Asst	Illinois	M	PHD	02.	Mich St		&6-02
Farrell, Barbara	Asst	Pace-Westch	DFRS	EDD	93	Columbia		&1993
Farrell, Brian	SLect	Tech-Sydney	DT	PHD	97	Tech-Sydn		1992
Farrell, John B.	Retir	UCLA	1998	MBA	50	UCLA		&1982
Farrelly, Gail E.	Retir	Rutgers-Newk	2002	DBA	81.	Geo Wash		&9-84
Fasci, Martha A.	Assoc	Tx-S Antonio	FM	PHD	77	Tx-Austin		&1977
Faubus, A. Overton	Retir	Abilene Chr	1985	PHD	69.	Arkansas		&1952
Faulkner, Robert	Assoc	St Ambrose	DGVF	DBA	61	Heed		1976
Favere-Marchesi, Michael	Asst	Simon Fraser	ABI	PHD	95.	S Calif	#	&7-00
Fay, Jack R.	Prof	Pittsburg St	XF	PHD	75.	Arkansas		&1996
Fayerman, G.	Lect	Concordia U	F	MBA	89	McGill		&1984
Fazzi, Charles	Prof	St Vincent	JNI	PHD	83.	Penn St		2002
Fearfull, Anne	Lect	St Andrews	WT	PHD	94	UMIST		2002
Fearnley, Stella	Prof	U Portsmith	A	BA				1994
Fedhila, Hassouna			Tunisia		PHD	90.	Colorado		
Fedje, Patti A.	Asst	Minot State	MPFD	MACC	87	N Dakota		&1987
Fedorowicz, Jane	Prof	Bentley	DS	PHD	81	Car Mellon		1994
Rae D. Anderson Chair in Accounting & Information Systems								
Fedoryshyn, Michael W.	Assoc	St John Fshr	ARPC	MBA	75	Rochester	*	&1989

Fedyk, Tatiana	Asst	Arizona St	M	PHD	07	Berkeley		&2007
Fee, H. M.	Lect	Univ Ulster	CFI	BSC				1-06
Fee, James C.	Retir	Villanova	1998	JD	61	Temple		&1982
Feeney, Charles F.	Prof	Mass-Lowell	FMX	MBA	70	Northeas		&1968
Feiden, Marci	Lect	Kansas	M	MBA	95	DePaul		1998
Feimson, Carla	Asst	Bethune-Cook	XA	MBA	79	Pace		&2001
Fekrat, M. Ali	Retir	Georgetown	FMI	PHD	69	Indiana		1967
Felber, Michael J.	Assoc	Baldwin-Wal	FMX	MS	75	Akron		& 9-83
Feldmann, Dorothy A.	Assoc	Bentley	F	DBA	92.	Boston U		&1991
Feldstein, Paul J.	Prof	Calif-Irvine		PHD	61.	Chicago		
Dept of Management; Univ of California-Irvine								
Felix, William L. Jr.	Prof	Arizona	A	PHD	70.	Ohio St		&1983
Eller Professor								
Fell, Robert S.	Retir	Clark Atlant	FTX	PHD	67	Brown		& 9-91
4343 Village Oaks Lane; Dunwood, GA 30338								
Feller, Anita L.	Lect	Illinois	EPX	PHD	89	Illinois		&1990
Feller, Robert E.		Belgium	FMX	PHD	75.	Arkansas		&
Fellingham, John C.	Prof	Ohio State	FM	PHD	75.	UCLA		1995
H.P. Wolfe Chair in Accounting								
Fellowes, Robert E.	Emer	Chris Newpor	1995	MS	57	MIT		&1979
Fellows, James A.	Prof	S Fl-St Pete	CXM	PHD	77	LSU		&1982
Felo, Andrew J.	Asst	Penn St GrVl	MFC	PHD	99.	SUNY-Bin	*	2001
Felt, Howard M.	Retir	Temple	FT	DBA	69.	S Calif		&1968
Feltham, Gerald A.	Emer	British Colu	2003	PHD	67.	Berkeley		&1971
Deloitte and Touche Emeritus Professor of Accounting								
Feltham, Glenn D.	Dean	U Manitoba	X	PHD	95	Waterloo		2004
Feltmate, Ian	Asst	Acadia Univ	FV	MBA		Dalhousie		7-91
Felton, Mark	Inst	St Thomas-MN		MBA	90	Minnesota		& 9-06
Felton, Sandra	Assoc	Brock Univ	EFH	PHD	88.	SUNY-Buf		&1976
Felts, Linda S.	Retir	Txs-Perm Bas	FTDS	MBA	75	Tx-PrmBs	*	& 9-75
Feltus, Oliver L.	C-As$	E Kentucky	GMS	PHD	86.	Alabama		&1991
Felty, William M.	Asst	Mo Bapitst	AFMP	MBA	91	SE Mo St	*	&
Feng, Mei	Asst	Pittsburgh	F	PHD	05.	Michigan		2004
Fenimore, John R.	Assoc	Wittenberg	FMA	MACC	73	Bowl Gr		& 8-01
Fenn, Christopher J.	Inst	Georgia St	X	MTX		Geo St		& 9-94
Fennema, Martin G. (Bud)	C-Ac	Florida St	MB	PHD	93.	Illinois	*	& 8-93
Ernst & Young Professor of Accounting								
Fenton, Edmund D. Jr.	Assoc	E Kentucky	X	DBA	86.	Kentucky		&2000
Ferguson, Andrew	SLect	New So Wales	AFOQ	PHD		Tech-Sydn		
Ferguson, Colin B.	Prof	U Melbourne	ASY	PHD	94	Deakin		&2004
Professor of Accounting and Business Information Systems								
Ferguson, Francis	Retir	Bryant	1989	MED	59	Rutgers		9-54
Ferguson, John	Lect	Dundee	ETWJ	MACC	02	Dundee		2005
Ferguson, Michael J.	Assoc	Chinese HK	BEF	PHD	97	Minnesota		1997
Ferguson, Richard K.	Retir	F Dick-Madis	2000	MBA	68	St Johns		& 9-71
Fergusson, Janice	Lect	So Carolina	FMS	MACC	01	S Carol		&2004
Ferlauto, Kimberly	ALect	W Sydney	AFST	MCOM	05	W Sydney		
Fern, Richard H.	Prof	E Kentucky	F	DBA	86.	Kentucky		&1986
Fernandez, Albert	Asst	Univ Navarra	SM	DBA	02.	Boston U		6-91
Fernandez, Leticia	Asst	Puerto Rico	TF	MBA	80	Geo Wash		&1982
Fernandez, Ramon	Asst	St Thomas-TX	XGMR	MBA	83	Houston	# *	& 8-83
Fernandez, Rudy	Assoc	Alaska-Ancho	FIX	JD	94	Colorado		&1988
Fernando, Guy	Asst	SUNY-Albany	FM	ABD		Syracuse		2007
Feroz, Ehsan H.	Prof	U Wash-Tacom	FKIG	PHD	82	Chicago	#	&2005
Ferrante, Claudia	Assoc	USAF Academy		PHD	03	Car Mellon		& 6-02
Ferrara, William L.	Emer	Stetson	1999	PHD	59.	Mich St		&1989
Ferraro, Fred	Retir	N Carol St	1993	JD	58	Union		1987
Ferreri, Linda B.			FC	PHD	85.	Case Wes	*	
Ferri, Fabrizio	Asst	Harvard	FM	PHD	04.	NYU		2004
Ferris, Kenneth R.	Prof	Claremont	FI	PHD	74.	Ohio St		2006
Ferry, Jerry W.	Assoc	No Alabama	MC	PHD	86.	Arkansas		9-91
Fertakis, John P.	Retir	Wash State	1993	PHD	67.	U Wash		1965
Fertig, Paul E.	Retir	Ohio State	6-80	PHD	52.	Ohio St		&1948
Fertuck, Len	Retir	Univ Toronto	2005	PHD	77.	Cornell		1974
Fesler, Robert D.	C-Pr$	Tenn Tech	AFM	DBA	86.	Miss St	# *	&1986
Fesmire, Walker E.	Retir	Mich-Flint	1999	PHD	82.	Miss		&1982
Fess, Philip E.	Retir	Illinois	1987	PHD	60.	Illinois		&1953
1340 Bald Eagle; Naples FL 33942								
Fess, Robert C.	Retir	San Fran St	1990	PHD	84.	Santa Cl		&1981
21028 Crocus Court; Sonoma CA 95476								
Fessler, Nicholas J.	Asst	Cen Missouri	CM	PHD	98.	Indiana	*	&2005
Fetters, Michael L.	Prof	Babson	F	PHD	73.	Wisconsin		& 9-77
Fettus, Sharon H.			MNFT	PHD	89.	Maryland		&
Fetyko, David F.	Retir	Kent State	D-01	PHD	72.	Mich St		& 8-81
Feucht, Fred	Asst	Prairie View	FXP	PHD	04	Tx A&M		2004
Fewson, V. R.	Lect	Univ Hull	X	BSC	88	Hull		9-94
Fidow, Margarret A.	Asst	City Univ HK	MSJ	MCOM	80	Auckland	*	8-89

Fiebelkorn, George A.	Retir	Marymount	2002	PHD	77. Geo St	&1986
Fiechtner, Susan B.	ClAc	Texas A&M		PHD	82. Oklahoma	1-99
Fiederlein, Kathleen J.			X	PHD	92. Indiana	&
Fields, Kent T.	Retir	Tx-Pan Amer	2006	PHD	77. Tx A&M	# * &9-04
Fields, Thomas D.	Lect	Wash Univ	F	PHD	04. Nrthwstrn	2006
Fifield, Suzanne	Lect	Dundee	FITZ	PHD	99 Dundee	2000
Figlewicz, Raymond E.			F	DBA	87. S Illinois	&
File, Richard G.	Prof	Neb-Omaha	FTYZ	PHD	81. Tx-Austin	&1988
Union Pacific Professor						
Files, James A.	Asst	Ouachita Bap	FS	PHD	05. Miss St	2005
Filipek, David	C-As	Rhode Isl Cl	FMPV	MBA	76 Babson	& 7-90
Filippelli, Michael F.	Prof	Bryant	FP	MBA	65 Rhode Isl	& 9-70
Filling, Steven M.	Assoc	CS-Stanislau	SF	PHD	96. LSU	&1994
Filter, William	Retir	Wayne St Col	2000	PHD	90. Nebraska	&1964
Finch, Elizabeth			IF	PHD	95. LSU	&
Finch, Michael L.	Asst	Maryland	AJV	PHD	94. Tennessee	& 9-00
Findlay, Robert W.	Retir	So Maine	1994	MBA	64 Boston U	&1967
Finger, Catherine A.	Lect	Ariz St West	FV	PHD	91. Berkeley	2004
Fink, Calvin	Inst	Bethune-Cook	FMC	MBA	83 N Fla	2004
Fink, Gregory	Assoc	R Stockton	FT	MBA	Rutgers	&
Fink, Milton A.	Retir	Alaska-Fairb	1992	MSBA	66 Denver	&1968
Fink, Philip R.	Prof	Toledo	XFM	JD	74 Ohio No	&1975
Finke, Carl A.	Retir	Missouri So	1993	JD	52 Oklahoma	&1970
Finkler, Steven A.	Retir	New York-Gr	CNF	PHD	78 Stanford	&1984
Finley, Angela	Retir	New Mex St	1988	MBA	78 Tx-ElPaso	& 8-78
Finley, David R.	Retir	Simon Fraser	2004	PHD	77 American	& 9-91
Finley, Jane B.	C-Ac	Belmont	SM	PHD	95 Fla St	&1995
Finn, Don W.	Prof	Arkansas	BJM	PHD	82. Arkansas	2003
Garrison/Wilson Chair						
Finn, Frank J.	Prof	U Queensland	F	PHD	81 Queensl	&1969
Finn, Mark W.	Asst	Northwestern	FM	PHD	95. Cornell	1996
Finn, Philip M.	Assoc	Pace-Westch	VPI	PHD	90. Baruch	&1983
Finnegan, Thomas R.	Lect	Illinois	MFX	PHD	93. Illinois	1993
Finney, Harrry Anson	Deces	Northwestern	5-66			1920
Finney, Sharon G.	C-Ac	Morgan State	FEJ	PHD	89. Geo St	&1999
Fiol, Michel	Prof	HEC Paris	BEMU	PHD	91 Paris IX	1985
Fioriti, Andrew A.	Retir	Dayton	1996	MBA	58 Detroit	& 9-65
Firmin, Peter A.	Emer	Denver	6-96	PHD	57. Michigan	& 7-74
Fisch, William H.	Retir	Georgia SW	3-97	MBA	Georgia	& 9-76
Fischer, Carol M.	Prof	St Bonaventu	FTXB	PHD	93. Penn St	&1985
Fischer, Cindy Ogden	Inst	Colo-Denver	FSG	MBA	80 Colorado	&1983
Fischer, Dov				PHD	03. Colorado	
Fischer, James H.	Lect	WI-Green Bay	FMX	PHD	71. Wisconsin	* &8-03
Fischer, Mary L.	Prof	Texas-Tyler	GFV	PHD	83 Conn	9-90
Fischer, Michael J.	Prof	St Bonaventu	FTA	PHD	93. Penn St	&1985
Fischer, Paul E.	Prof	Penn State	F	PHD	89 Rochester	& 8-99
Fischer, Paul M.	C-Pr	Wis-Milwauke	FC	PHD	69. Wisconsin	&1969
J. A. Leer Professor of Accounting						
Fischer, Wilbert R.	Retir	Moorhead St	1995	PHD	72 N Dakota	&1966
Fischman, Myrna L.	C-Pr$	Lg Isl-Brook	JMGA	PHD	76 NYU	&1968
Fish, Gary L.	Retir	Illinois St	1997	EDD	76 Illinois	&1966
Fisher, Allan J.				PHD	38. Pittsburgh	
Fisher, Dann G.	Assoc	Kansas State	XFJ	PHD	92. Missouri	& 6-91
Deloitte & Touche Faculty Fellow						
Fisher, I.	SLect	Liverpool JM	M	FCMA		1997
Fisher, Ingrid	Asst	SUNY-Albany	AS	PHD	02 SUNY-Alb	&1994
Fisher, James	Retir	Wilfrid Laur	2003	MSC	69 Minnesota	&1984
Fisher, Joseph G.	C-Pr	Indiana	FM	PHD	87. Ohio St	&1993
Fed Ex Faculty Fellow						
Fisher, Lance M.	Asst	Oklahoma St		PHD	07. Arizona	2007
Fisher, Marguerite H.		Tucson AR	1989	PHD	84. Illinois	&
Fisher, Richard T.	SLect	Canterbury	ABFS	MCM	95 Lincoln	&2004
Fisher, Steven A.	C-Pr	CS-Long Bch	CF	DBA	85. Kent St	* &1990
Fisher, Ted L.	Deces	NE St-Okla	3-03	PHD	77. Okla St	&1985
FitzGerald, Adrian A.	Lect	Napier Univ	FM	BCOM		1998
Fitzgerald, Gerald	Asst	LaSalle	FP	MA	76 Villanova	9-95
Fitzgerald, John M.	Retir	Massachusett	1987	MA	61 Conn	&1956
Fitzgerald, Lin	SLect	Un Warwick	CM	BA	71 Essex	
Fitzgerald, Michael N.		Fenton MO	1992	PHD	83. St Louis	
1742 Gilsinn Lane; Fenton MO 63026						
Fitzgibbon, Thomas	Inst	Alabama	F	MACC	06 Alabama	8-06
Fitzsimons, Adrian P.	Prof	St John's	AFK	PHD	84 New Sch	* &1990
Fizzell, Maureen R.	Lect	Simon Fraser	FM	MS	86 Saskatch	* 9-93
Fjell, Kenneth	Assoc	Norwegian U	MQ	DOEC		
Fladstad, Harald	SLect	Norwegian U	P			
Flagg, James C.	Assoc	Texas A&M	AFKO	PHD	88. Tx A&M	& 9-87
Flaherty, Daniel J.	Retir	Tx St-S Marc	VAFS	PHD	74. Tx A&M	# * &1997

Flaherty, Richard E.	Retir	Nev-L Vegas	2007	PHD	71.	Kansas	& 8-99
Flamholtz, Eric G.	Prof	UCLA	1998	PHD	69	Michigan	1969
Management Dept; phone 310-825-4956							
Flaming, Linda J.	Asst	Monmouth	FA	PHD	02	Oklahoma	2003
Flanagan, Robert J.				PHD	71.	Ariz St	
Flanigan, Mary A.	Prof	Longwood	CFI	PHD	95.	Va Comm	&1989
Fleak, Sandra K.	Prof	Truman State	FTP	PHD	88.	Missouri	&1984
Fleenor, William C.			SAF	PHD	78.	LSU	&
Fleischman, Gary M.	Assoc	Wyoming	X	PHD	95.	Tx Tech	* &2000
Fleischman, Richard K.	Retir	John Carroll	FHM	PHD	73	SUNY-Buf	& 9-83
Fleming, A. Scott	Asst	W Virginia	MFS	PHD	05.	Va Tech	&2005
Fleming, Damon M.	Asst	San Diego St	BFM	PHD	06.	Va Tech	* 1-07
Fleming, Larry D.	Retir	Grove City	F	MS	64	N Dakota	&1974
Fleming, Mary M. K.	Retir	CS-Fullerton	2003	DBA	79.	S Calif	* &1974
Fleming, Robert J.	Assoc	No Michigan	MFT	PHD	82.	Miss	&1977
Flesher, Dale L.	Prof	Mississippi	FHMO	PHD	75.	Cincinnati	# * & 9-77
Arthur Andersen Alumni Professer; Associate Dean							
Flesher, Tonya K.	Prof	Mississippi	XH	PHD	79.	Miss	&1979
Arthur Andersen Alumni Professor							
Fletcher, John C.		Willmette IL	1988	DBA	81.	Colorado	
Fletcher, Leslie B.	Prof	Geo Southern	FMI	PHD	93.	LSU	& 9-93
Flewellen, William C.	Retir	Georgia	1981	PHD	57.	Columbia	1968
Flinn, Ronald E.	Assoc	Creighton	CFXZ	DBA	89.	Kentucky	* & 9-86
Flint, Roger D.	Assoc	Okla Baptist	BPTV	MBA	80	SW Mo St	& 8-80
Flood, Barbara	Lect	Dublin City	EM	PHD	04	Loughbor	&1995
Flores, F. Brigg	Deces	Txs-El Paso	1988	PHD	68	Utah	9-71
Flores, Michael B.	Asst	Wichita St	BM	ABD		Tx Tech	&1998
Flory, Steven M.			FI	PHD	76.	LSU	* &
Flowers, Vincent S.				PHD	74.	North Tx	
Flowers, W. Baker	Deces	Alabama	9-75	PHD	59.	Tx-Austin	&1963
Flynn, Christopher J. Jr.	Retir	Boston Coll	1992	JD	52	Boston C	1957
Flynn, Kevin E.	Assoc	West Chester	XNF	PHD	03.	Drexel	9-97
Flynn, Lisa	Asst	SUNY-Oneonta	JB	PHD	01.	SUNY-Bin	8-00
Flynn, R. Steven	C-Pr	Thomas More	MNAS	PHD	87	Cincinnati	1997
Flynn, Robert	Assoc	Georgian Ct	TVXR	MBA	74	Pace	&1984
Flynt, Janie R.	Retir	La St-Shreve	1999	MBA	63	Tx Tech	& 6-62
Foerster, Al	Lect	Wilfrid Laur					
Fogarty, Timothy J.	Prof	Case Western	XABE	PHD	89.	Penn St	& 8-89
KPMG Peat Marwick Faculty Fellow							
Fogelberg, Graeme G.				PHD	69	W Ontario	
Fogg, Stephen L.	Assoc	Temple	SA	PHD	78	NYU	&1976
Folami, L. Buky	Asst	Bryant	FM	PHD	99.	Geo St	* &2006
Foley, Joseph T.	Assoc	Assumption	FTPR	MS	73	Northeas	&1979
Foley, William T.	Assoc	Saint Leo-FL	XCVS	MBA		S Fla	* & 1-83
Foltin, Craig				DBA	96.	Clev St	&
Mayor, City of Lorain, Ohio							
Foltz, Jack O.	Retir	Arizona	1986	MBA	49	Tx-Austin	&1957
Fonfeder, Robert	Prof	Hofstra	PM	PHD	80.	Baruch	* &1980
Fontaine, Marie		Quebec a Hul		PHD			
Fontaine, Richard	Prof	Quebec-Montr		PHD		Quebec	
Foo, See Liang	Assoc	Nangang Tech	AF	PHD	88	Hull	&1984
Foote, Paul S.	Prof	CS-Fullerton	SF	PHD	83.	Mich St	7-89
Foran, Michael F.	Prof	Mich-Dearbor	TFE	PHD	72.	U Wash	# * & 8-01
Foran, Nancy J.	Deces	Mich-Dearbor	2-02	PHD	85.	Okla St	&2000
Forbes, Ben L.	Retir	New Orleans	1993	PHD	62.	Illinois	&1966
Forbes, Renee	Asst	Bethune-Cook		PHD		Sarasota	2005
Ford, Amy	Inst	W Illinois	P	MACC	02	W Illinois	& 8-06
Ford, Caroline O.	Asst	Baylor	AB	PHD	06.	Tx Tech	2007
Ford, Donald H.	Retir	CS-Sacrament	1992	PHD	74	N Colo	& 9-75
Ford, Jeremiah G.	Retir	Seton Hall	1988	MBA	70	Seton Hall	&1971
Ford, Joseph F.	Retir	Drexel	1985	MBA	52	Penn	&1946
Ford, N. Allen	Prof	Kansas	X	PHD	70.	Arkansas	1976
Larry D. Horner/KPMG Peat Marwick Distinguished Professor							
Ford, Sharon K.	Assoc	Delta State	XM	PHD	96.	Miss	& 8-01
Ford, Tim	Asst	Southern Ark					2006
Ford, Wilhelmina H. (Mimi)	Assoc	Macon State	FLPX	JD	95	Mercer	&2000
Forde, John E.	Deces	CS-Hayward	1989	PHD	80	Santa Cl	6-75
Fordham, David R.	Prof	Jms Madison	SD	PHD	92.	Fla St	* & 9-92
PBGH Faculty Fellow							
Forehand, Thomas	Lect	SUNY-N Paltz	FX	MBA		Michigan	&1993
Foreman, Kimberley A.	Inst	Jms Madison	PCM	MSA	96	Jms Mad	& 9-96
Forget, Robert Sr.	Assoc	Marshall	P	MBA	89	NewHamp	
Forgione, Dana A.	Prof	Tx-S Antonio	NCM	PHD	87.	Mass	* & 8-06
Janey S. Briscoe Endowed Chair in the Business of Health							
Fornaro, James M.	Asst	SUNY Old Wes	FIPT	DPS	03	Pace	* &2003
Forney, Janet A.	Assoc	Piedmont	CF	DBA	94	Nova SE	8-01
Foroughi, Tahirih K.			CM	PHD	75.	Oregon	

Forrest, J. Patrick	Assoc	W Michigan	S	DBA	87.	Kentucky	&1982
Forsaith, David M.	LectC	Flinders Un	FI	MSC	75	London	7-90
Forsyth, Jay D.	Prof	Central Wash	CXTF	MS	64	Okla St	&9-69
Forsyth, Timothy B.	C-Ac	Appalach St	FM	PHD	91.	Alabama	1-89
Fort, C. Patrick	Assoc	Alaska-Ancho	FV	PHD	93.	Colorado	1993
Fortin, Anne	Prof	Quebec-Montr	F	PHD	86.	Illinois	6-83
Fortin, Jacques	Prof	HEC-Montreal	FLUV	MBA	77	HEC-Mont	&9-74
Fortin, Karen A.	Retir	Baltimore	1999	PHD	79.	S Carol	&8-94
Fortin, Steve	Asst	McGill Univ	F	PHD	01	Waterloo	&2001
Fortner, Richard W.	Emer	Mich-Flint	1999	DBA	64.	Indiana	&9-80
Fortner, Wesley O.	Retir	Austin Peay	2004	PHD	67.	Alabama	&1983
Fosbre, Anne	Prof	Georgian Ct	PFM	PHD	84	NYU	&1993
Foss, Emily W.	Asst	Gardner-Webb	FP	MBA	94	W Carol	1994
Foss, Helga B.	Retir	Ball State	1998	PHD	87.	Cincinnati	&9-83
Foss, Robert K.	Asst	Concordia C	FP	MACC		N Dakota	&8-90
Fossett, G. Craig	Asst	Mesa State	PMGV	MBA	89	Wstrn St	# * &2004
Foster, Benjamin P.	Assoc	Louisville	MCF	PHD	91.	Tennessee	* &8-94
Foster, Cecil G. Jr.				PHD	81.	Georgia	&
Foster, Christi	Inst	Tarleton St	FP	MBA	00	Tarleton	8-04
Foster, Cynthia	Inst	W Illinois	P	MACC	05	St Ambro	&8-06
Foster, G.	SLect	Liverpool JM	FG	CPFA			
Foster, George	Prof	Stanford	MFC	PHD	75.	Stanford	1978
Paul L. and Phyllis Wattis Professor of Management							
Foster, H.	Loot	Univ Ulster	TNX	DA			&9-02
Foster, Sheila D.	D-Pr	Citadel	FIMP	PHD	94.	Va Tech	&8-92
Foster, Taylor W. (Bill)	Retir	New Mex St	FTV	PHD	74.	Penn St	8-84
Foth, Edward C.	Assoc	DePaul	X	PHD	71.	Mich St	&1975
Fotheringham, Alun	Lect	Napier Univ		BA			1999
Fouch, Scott R.	C-Pr	Truman State	XP	PHD	90.	Okla St	&1985
Foulks, Steve	Assoc	No Michigan	AX	MBA	72	Chicago	&1975
Fountaine, Drew	Lect	CS-Northrdge	UFLM	MBA	97	CS-Nrthr	2007
Fourcade, Francois	Asst	ESCP deParis	CEMU	PHD	04	Ecole Pl	2004
Foust, Karen M.	ClPr	Tulane	FMPT	PHD	94.	Tulane	&2003
Fowler, Anna C.	Retir	Texas-Austin	2005	PHD	77.	Tx-Austin	&9-77
Fowler, Bill	C-Ac	Abilene Chr	ACX	MBA	83	Walsh	1992
Fowler, Carolyn	SLect	Victoria NZ	MSHG	MCOM	95	Canterbu	2002
Fowler, Kenneth	Lect	San Jose St	PX	PHD	97	Miss	# * &2000
Fowler, M. Lou	Asst	Missouri Wes	G	MS	86	NE Mo St	&1991
Fowler, Ray M.	Retir	Union		PHD	51.	Nebraska	
Fowlkes, Melinda I.	Asst	Longwood	P	MBA	94	Va Comm	&1996
Fox, Alison	Lect	Dundee	FX	BA	89	Dundee	&2000
Fox, Gary A.	Retir	Miami U-Ohio	2001	MA	67	Illinois	&9-70
Fox, James G.	Retir		1990	DBA	74.	Geo Wash	* &
445 Myers Ave; Harrisonburg VA 22801-4211							
Fox, Ken	Asst	Saskatchewan	FO	MPAC	01	Saskatch	2006
Fox, Kenneth L.	Retir	Kansas State	1989	PHD	66.	Illinois	&9-69
2105 Goodnow Circle; Manhattan KS 66502							
Fox, Wayne	Lect	No Arizona	AMP	MS	71	UCLA	&1983
Foxworth, James				PHD	55.	Columbia	
Frackelton, R. Leigh	Prof	Mary Wash	XL	JD	77	Richmond	&9-86
Fraedrich, Karl E.	Retir	Wis-Whitewat	1999	PHD	69.	Wisconsin	* &1968
Fraihat, Haidar M.	Asst	King Fahd Un	S	PHD	92	Illinois	2002
Frakes, Albert H.	Retir	Wash State	FA	PHD	74.	U Wash	&1972
Frakes, Joyce E.	Assoc	Denver	F	PHD	71	Stanford	&1977
France, Jim	Inst	Nev-L Vegas	M	MS	03	Nev-L Vg	2004
Francia, Arthur J.	Prof	Houston	M	PHD	69.	Minnesota	1974
KPMG Peat Marwick Professor							
Francis, Jennifer	Prof	Duke	F	PHD	87.	Cornell	&7-99
Douglas & Josie Breeden Doctoral Professor of Accounting & Senior Assoc Dean							
Francis, Jere R.	Prof	Missouri	FA	PHD	82	N Eng-Au	&1994
KPMG/Joseph A. Silvoso Distinguished Research Professor							
Francis, Rick N.	Asst	No Iowa	F	PHD	03.	Oklahoma	&1-06
Francis-Gladney, Laura E.	Asst	SUNY-Utica		PHD	04.	S Illinois	
Francisco, Albert K.	Retir	Friday HarWA	1995	PHD	72.	Mich St	
PO Box 2105; Friday Harbor WA 98250							
Francisco, Cherie	Inst	Portland St	FM	MBA	95	Bowl Gr	&2001
Francisco, William H.	Asst	Austin Peay	S	MS	75	S Miss	* &2006
Francoeur, Claude	Asst	HEC-Montreal	FM	PHD	03	Quebec	6-03
Frank, Allen J.	Inst	West Florida	FJ	MACC	88	W Fla	1988
Frank, Gary B.	Prof	Akron	FMA	PHD	73	Illinois	* &1-85
Frank, Mary M.	Asst	Virg-Grad	XFI	PHD	99.	N Carol	&2002
Frank, Sarah L.	Inst	West Florida	SDP	EDD	99	W Fla	&8-84
Frank, Werner G.	Retir	Wisconsin	1991	PHD	58.	Illinois	&1964
Frankel, George	Prof	San Fran St	X	LLM	89	NYU	&1991
Frankel, Micah P.	Prof	CS-East Bay	FQV	PHD	91.	Arizona	* &9-91
Frankel, Richard M.	Asst	Wash Univ	F	PHD	93.	Stanford	&
Franklin, Mitchell	Inst	Syracuse	FM	MS	00	Syracuse	&2004

Franklin, Paul	Asst	Benedictn-KS	S	MS	93	Mo-Ks Cty	&2003
Frantz, Pascal	Lect	London Econ	AFY	PHD	94	London	1993
Franz, David P.	Prof	San Fran St	MC	PHD	86.	Penn St	* 1987
Franz, Diana R.	C-Ac	Toledo	AF	PHD	92.	Tx Tech	&1992
Franzen, Laurel	Asst	Texas-Dallas	FX	PHD	00.	U Wash	2000
Fraser, Ian A. M.	Prof	Un Stirling	AF	MA	74	Glasgow	&2004
Fraser, J.	SLect	Liverpool JM	SG	CPFA			2002
Fraser, Michael	Lect	Victoria NZ	WMG	BCA	02	Victoria	2003
Fraser, Patricia	Prof	Aberdeen	FQ	PHD	89	City Bus	1995
Fraser, Steven G.	Asst	Australian N	MS	PHD	02	Melbourne	2003
Frashier, Ira Kaye	Asst	E New Mexico	A	MS	80	Miss	2006
Frasier, Charles E.	C-Ac	Lipscomb	PXFM	MA	67	Alabama	* &9-71
Fratto, Victoria A.	Asst	Robt Morris	CNM	MS		Rbt Morr	9-85
Frazer, J. Douglas	Prof	Millersville	MSTV	PHD	87.	Temple	&1979
Frazier, Jessica J.	Assoc	E Kentucky	MX	DBA	90.	Kentucky	1986
Frazier, Katherine Beal			FBTW	PHD	81.	S Carol	&
Frazier, William R.	Retir	Greensboro	1994	MS			&1959
Frazin, Alex	Lect	Redlands	FLX	BS	78	CS-Pomon	&2002
Frecka, Thomas J.	Prof	Notre Dame	FM	PHD	78.	Syracuse	& 7-90
Vincent and Rose Lizzadro Chair							
Fred, J. David	Assoc	Ind-So Bend	CFV	MS	75	Purdue	&1978
Frederick, David M.	Assoc	Colorado	BAF	PHD	86.	Michigan	&1986
Frederickson, James R.			BFM	PHD	90.	U Wash	&
Fredricks, Thomas P.	Lect	Carroll	FMT	MS	64	Wisconsin	9-97
Free, Clinton	Asst	Queen's Univ	FI	PHD	04	Oxford	2004
Freear, John	Retir	New Hampshir	2005	MA	67	Cambridge	&1983
Freed, Chrislynn	Clin	So Calif	FAE	MBA	92	S Calif	&1991
Freedman, Martin	Prof	Towson	TBWF	PHD	75.	Illinois	2000
Freeland, Susanne	Inst	Ohio Univ	F	MST	88	Capital	& 9-01
Freeman, Colin	Assoc	Australian N	DS	MSC	71	Sheffield	2001
Freeman, Gary R.	Assoc	NE St-Okla	FM	PHD	88.	Geo St	2004
Freeman, Jack L.	Prof	Univ Windsor	FM	PHD	81.	Mich St	1972
Freeman, Robert J.	Prof	Texas Tech	GN	PHD	66.	Arkansas	&1979
Distinguished Professor							
Freeman, Robert N.	Prof	Texas-Austin	F	PHD	77.	Tx-Austin	& 6-88
Arthur Andersen & Co. Alumni Centennial Professorship in Accounting							
Freix, Greg	Lect	Kansas	S	MBA	99	Kansas	1998
Freixas, Xavier	Dean	Pompeu Fabra	F	PHD	78	Toulouse	
Fremgen, James M.	Retir	Naval Postgr	2001	DBA	61.	Indiana	&1965
French, Daisy	Retir	E Kentucky	1989	EDD	69	Kentucky	1969
French, G. Richard	C-Pr	Indiana SE	MXE	PHD	90.	Miss	&1990
Frese, Philip B.			P	PHD	93.	Drexel	&
Frey, Karen	Assoc	Gettysburg	CFM	PHD	94.	Maryland	&1993
Frey, Ralph W.			MFT	DBA	72.	Maryland	&
Friar, Shirley A.	C-Ac	Clark Atlant	MF	PHD	86.	Tx-Austin	
Fried, Haim Dov	Assoc	New York U	MF	PHD	77	NYU	1979
Fried, Jacob M.	Retir	New Orleans	1994	MBA	46	Miss	&1980
Friedberg, Alan H.	Prof	Fla Atlantic	SCO	PHD	83.	Florida	&1989
Friedlan, John M.			F	PHD	90.	U Wash	&
Friedlob, G. Thomas	Retir	Clemson	2004	PHD	81.	Miss	* &1979
gtfrdlb@clemson.edu							
Friedman, Lauren A.		Daly City CA	1991	PHD	75.	Kansas	&
274 Greenview Dr; Daly City CA 94014							
Friedman, Mark E.	Assoc	U Miami	CDS	PHD	77	NYU	&1977
Fries, Clarence E.			M	DBA	83.	Tennessee	
Friest, Philip L.	Retir	Minn-Duluth	1987	PHD	72.	Minnesota	&1953
1055 Missouri Avenue; Duluth MN 55811							
Frigo, Mark L.	Prof	DePaul	MR	PHD	81	N Illinois	* &9-80
Ledger & Quill Distinguished Professor of Accounting							
Friis, Ole	Asst	U So Denmark	ATF	PHD	04	Odense	1999
Frimor, Hans	Prof	U So Denmark	TMF	PHD	96	Odense	1992
Frings, Virginia			F	PHD	98.	Memphis	
Frischmann, Peter J.	Prof	Idaho State	XM	PHD	92.	Ariz St	&2000
Frishkoff, Patricia A.	Retir	Oregon State	2002	DBA	74.	Kent St	* &1978
Frishkoff, Paul	Prof	Oregon	2000	PHD	70.	Stanford	&1967
Friske, Karyn B.			FAP	PHD	94.	Tx A&M	&
Fritsche, Steven R.	Assoc	Howard	EFIT	PHD	91.	Alabama	&2004
Fritz, Patricia	Lect	East Carol	FM	MSA	97	E Carol	2007
Fritzemeyer, Joe R.	Retir	Arizona St	1992	DBA	60.	Indiana	& 9-73
Fritzsch, Ralph B.	C-Ac	Midwest St	SCM	DBA	72	Geo Wash	& 9-84
Frizzell, Monica	C-Ac	Western Conn	MFMP	MSA	82	W Conn	* 1981
Frost, Carol A.	Prof	North Texas	F	PHD	89.	Michigan	2007
Bernard A. Coda Chair of Accounting							
Frost, Geoff	SLect	Univ Sydney	FW	PHD	00	N Eng-Au	2000
Froud, Julie	SLect	U Manchester	GNWF	PHD		Manchest	1996
Frucot, Veronique G.	Assoc	Chris Newpor	FI	PHD	87.	Tx A&M	1998
Frumer, Samuel	Retir	Indiana	1996	DBA	60.	Indiana	&1960

Name	Rank	School	Codes	Degree	Yr	Univ	Extra
Fry, Dovi	Inst	NW Missouri	FCP	MBA	94	NW Mo St	&2000
Fry, Nicholas E.	Retir	Nicholls St	2001	DBA	78.	Miss St	& 8-78
Frye, Randy L.	C-As	St Fran-Penn	PFC	EDD	97	Pittsburgh	* 1980
Fu, Huijing	Asst	Tx Christian	F	PHD	05	Minnesota	
Fu, Philip Y.	Retir	Chinese HK	1996	PHD	68.	Illinois	1968
Fuehrmeyer, James	Spec	Notre Dame	FA	MBA	80	Chicago	&2007
Fuentes, Henry L.	Assoc	F Dick-Teane	AF	MBA	74	Seton Hall	& 9-76
Fuerman, Ross D.	C-Ac	Suffolk	FM	PHD	96.	Cincinnati	&1997
Fuerst, Oren			FITM	PHD	97.	Columbia	
Fuglister, Jayne	Prof	Cleveland St	F	DBA	85.	Geo Wash	&1986
Fuhrmann, J. Stanley			S	PHD	91.	Tx-Austin	&
Fujita, Yukio			1990	PHD	68.	Illinois	
22-14 Takanodai; Kodaira-Shi; Tokyo 187 Japan							
Fukui, Yoshitaka		Tohoku U		PHD	98.	Car Mellon	
Fukukawa, Hironori	Assoc	Hitotsubashi	FA	DBA	02	Hitotsub	2007
Fulks, Daniel L.	D-Ac	Transylvania	XF	PHD	80.	Geo St	&1997
Fuller, B. J.	Retir	Nevada-Reno	1999	PHD	73.	Miss	1976
Fuller, Harlan	Lect	Illinois St	GMA	MS	79	Illin St	* &1982
Fuller, Lori R.	Asst	Widener	AS	PHD	96.	Ariz St	&2002
Fuller, Robert	Asst	Tennessee	S	PHD	03	Indiana	8-06
Fullerton, Rosemary R.	Assoc	Utah State	MF	PHD	98.	Utah	&1999
Fullwood, Virginia	Inst	Tx A&M-Comm	FDEP	MBA	89	Tx A&M-C	&2002
Fulmer, John G. Jr.	Prof	Tenn-Chattan	F	PHD	70	Alabama	9-77
Vieth Professor; Associate Dean							
Fults, Gail J.	Prof	CS-Humboldt	FM	PHD	87	Claremont	1986
Fung, Teresa	Lect	HongKon Tech	CMX	MBUS	02	Monash	2005
Fung, Yu Kit Simon	Asst	HongKon Tech	AF	PHD	06	City U	2004
Funk, Roland W.	Deces			PHD	51.	Chicago	
Funnell, Warwick N.	Prof	U Wollongong	MGH	PHD	94	Wollong	&1981
Furlong, William L.	Practice		1998	PHD	63.	Alabama	&
CPA Practice; 2623 N. Monroe; Tallahassee Florida; 904-386-2193							
Furze, Sally			A	PHD	94.	Oregon	&
Gaa, Charles J.	Deces	Mich State	D-91	PHD	40.	Illinois	&1958
Gaa, James C.	Prof	Univ Alberta	BJTW	PHD	82.	Illinois	1995
Gabbin, Alexander L.	Prof	Jms Madison	F	PHD	86.	Temple	& 9-85
KPMG Professor							
Gabehart, Keith	Retir	W Kentucky	1999	MA	60	Peabody	1964
Gabello, William	Retir	Scranton	1992	BS	49	Scranton	&1983
Gaber, Brian G.	Dir	York-Atkinsn	ABFS	PHD	83.	Wisconsin	&1993
Gaber, Mohamed K.	C-Pr	SUNY-Plattsb	FMI	PHD	85.	Baruch	1985
Gabhart, David R. L.	Deces	Bentley	N-93	PHD	78.	Mich St	1987
Gabre, Helen G.	Inst	Alabama A&M	PFXG	MBA	84	Alab A&M	& 9-99
Gabriel, E. Ann	Asst	Ohio Univ	MUF	PHD	93.	Ohio St	& 9-01
Gabsi, Abedrrazak	Asst	Univ Tunis	VR	EXPC		IHEC	
Gac, Edward J.	Retir	Colorado	LX	JD	68	Illinois	&1982
Gadd, H. Robert	Prof	So Adventist	FIT	PHD	00.	Tx-Arlin	2000
Gaddis, Marcus D.	Assoc	Troy-Dothan	C	PHD	93.	Kentucky	2002
Gaertner, James F.	Prof	Sam Houston	FI	PHD	77.	Tx A&M	&2002
Gaffikin, Michael J. R.	Emer	U Wollongong	FHTW	PHD	86	Sydney	&1988
Gaffney, Dennis J.	C-Pr	Cleveland St	XF	PHD	73.	Illinois	&2004
Gaffney, Mary Anne	Assoc	Temple	NFM	PHD	84.	Maryland	1983
Gage, Martin A.	Retir	Widener	1987	MBA	54	NYU	&1970
Gagne, Bridgett	Lect	Howard		MBA	88	Texas	&2006
Gagne, Gilles	Prof	HEC-Montreal	X	LSCC	61	HEC-Mont	& 9-80
Gagne, Lynda	Prof	Victoria-Cdn		PHD	02	Brit Colum	2001
Gagne, Margaret L.	Assoc	Marist	CMQ	PHD	89.	Indiana	2000
Gagnon-Valotaire, Danielle	Prof	Quebec-Montr	F	MBA		Montreal	& 8-79
Gaharan, Catherine	Assoc	Nicholls St	CF	PHD	88.	LSU	& 8-90
Gai, Pham Thi	Lect	Natl Econ	FMCV	PHD	88	Natl Econ	1976
Gaines, Michael R.	Retir	Portland St	1993	PHD	69.	U Wash	&1965
Gal, Graham	Assoc	Massachusett	SD	PHD	85.	Mich St	1985
Galante, Joseph	Assoc	Millersville	X	JD	92	Cooley	1998
Galantine, Carolyn A.	Asst	Pepper-Malib	TF	PHD	94.	S Calif	&2003
Galbraith, Clyde J.	C-Ac	West Chester	AFM	MBA	71	Drexel	& 9-74
Galbreath, Susan Coomer	Prof	Lipscomb	SAFP	PHD	93.	Tennessee	&2001
Galer, Willis F.	Retir	Lk Superior	1990	MBA	70	Mich St	9-70
Gallagher, Denise	STcFl	Univ Leeds	DEF	MSC	02	Huddersf	7-02
Gallagher, Lynn	SLect	Queensld Tec	F	MFM			&1982
Gallagher, Michael G.	Retir	George Wash	2000	LLM	71	Geo Wash	&1961
Gallant, Leo T.	Prof	St Fran Xav	FMH	FCA	71	Queens	&1973
Gallery, Gerry	SLect	New So Wales	FTLY	PHD	01	Queensl	
Gallery, Natalie	SLect	Univ Sydney	FT	PHD	99	Griffith	&2001
Galley, Lori J.	Assoc	Wash & Jeff	CFI	DBA	04	Nova SE	*
Gallhofer, Sonja	Prof	Dundee	EHIT	PHD	84	Austria	
Galliart, Willard H.	Retir	Loyola-Chicg	2000	PHD	72.	Illinois	& 9-79
Gallun, Rebecca A.	Retir	Houston-Cl L	2002	PHD	79.	Tx A&M	9-77

Name	Rank	School	Code	Degree	Yr	Institution		
Gallups, William C.	Retir	Florida St	4-94	PHD	68.	Michigan		&1966
Hwy 372; Panacea Florida; 850-984-5677								
Galvan, Abel	Lect	Ill-Chicago	ARFM	MBA	96	Il-Chicago		1997
Gamble, George O.	Prof	Houston	FM	PHD	80.	Penn St		1978
Robert Grinaker Professor								
Gammo, Mary Lou C.	Retir	East Tenn St	1998	MBA	59	Auburn		&1966
Gamra, Houcine	Inst	Univ Tunis	F	EXPC	99	ISCAE		1999
Gandhi, Natwar M.		Gov Atg Off		PHD	73.	LSU		
Gangolly, Jagdish S.	C-Ac	SUNY-Albany	ASF	PHD	77.	Pittsburgh	#	1990
Ganguli, Gouranga	Prof	Tx-Pan Amer	FCI	PHD	83.	Miss	# *	&8-90
Ganguly, Ananda R.	Assoc	Claremont	FM	PHD	95.	Pittsburgh		2007
Ganon, Michelle W.	Asst	Western Conn	X	PHD	96.	Arizona		&1991
Gantt, Elise	Retir	Jacksonvl St	2002	MBA	78	Jacksv St		&1-83
Gantt, Gamewell	Retir	Idaho State	2005	JD	72	Tx-Austin		&1982
Gantt, Karen	Asst	Hartford	XL	LLM	96	Baltimore		9-02
Ganz, David R.	Retir	Mo-St Louis	2004	ABD		Missouri		9-66
Gao, Lei	Asst	Nebraska	A	PHD	05.	Kansas		2005
Gao, Simon	Prof	Napier Univ		PHD				1999
Gao, Yanmin	Asst	Univ Alberta	FTY	PHD	06	Brit Colum		2006
Gara, Stephen C.	Assoc	Drake	X	PHD	98.	Memphis		&2005
Garceau, Linda R.	Dean	East Tenn St	SDAP	DBA	86	Boston U		&2000
Garcia, Andy	Asst	Bowling Gr	FA	PHD	05.	Tx Tech		2005
Garcia, Merced Juan	Assoc	Puerto Rico	AR	MBA	85	Wisconsin		&1982
Garcia, Norberto	D	De Cordoba		PHD		DeCordoba		
Gardener, Edward	Dir	Wales-Bangor	FM	PHD	79	Bangor		9-75
Gardner, Clare	Lect	Univ Otago	JESM	MCOM	96	Otago		1994
Gardner, George F.	Prof	Bemidji St	GPVR	MBA		Minnesota		&1989
Gardner, J. Randall	Assoc	Mo-Kansas Ct	X	LLM	86	Mo-Ks Cty		&1983
Gardner, John C.	Prof	New Orleans	FTM	PHD	83.	Mich St		8-04
KPMG Professor of Accounting								
Gardner, John C..	Prof	Wis-La Cross	XPJE	PHD	74	LSU		&8-85
Gardner, Larry D.	Deces	No Arizona	1989	MA	60	Missouri		&1965
Gardner, Penelope J.	SLect	Napier Univ	F	BSC				&9-87
Gardner, Robert L.	Prof	Brigham Yg	X	PHD	79.	Tx-Austin		9-79
Robert J. Smith Professor								
Gariboldi, Nicole	Asst	St Thomas-FL	FI	DBA	99	Nova SE		&2002
Garlick, John R. Sr.	Asst	Fayetteville	MX	PHD	89.	S Carol		
Garner, Don E.	Prof	CS-Stanislau	AF	DBA	72.	S Calif	#	&1987
Garner, Frank B.	Retir	Kennesaw	1990	PHD	77.	Geo St		&1987
Garner, R. Michael	Prof	Salisbury	VGI	PHD	86.	Arkansas		&1990
Garner, S. Paul	Deces	Alabama	O-96	PHD	40.	Tx-Austin		&1939
Garnsey, Margaret R.	Asst	Siena	SVM	PHD	01	SUNY-Alb		1997
Garrett, Charles S.	Retir	Kennesaw St	1993	MBA	73	Geo St		&1975
Garrett, Ian	Prof	U Manchester	FQTY	PHD		Brunel		1993
Garrett, Nathan T.	Retir	N Carol Cen	2002	JD	86	N Car Cen		&1987
Garrett, Randall	Asst	S Nazarene	PATJ	MSA	78	Okla Cty		&1976
Garris, Henry	Lect	Touro	CFMX	MS		Pace		&9-05
Garrison, Larry R.	Prof	Mo-Kansas Ct	X	PHD	86.	Nebraska		&1986
Garrison, Ray H.	Retir	Brigham Yg	1993	DBA	66.	Indiana		&1966
Garsombke, H. Perrin	Retir	Neb-Omaha	2005	PHD	76.	UCLA		&1986
Garstka, Stanley J.	Prof	Yale	FMT	PHD	70	Car Mellon		1978
Garverick, James E.	Assoc	Tx-Pan Amer	X	MS	64	Kent St		&2007
Garvin, Deborah R.	Lect	Florida	X	JD	78	N Carol		&8-83
Garvin, Jim	C-Ac	Brescia	QJ	ABD	75	Ohio St		&1985
Garvin, Sharon	Asst	Wayne St Col	SFPA	EDD	05	S Dakota		&1982
Gary, Robert F.	Asst	Iowa State	XF	PHD	05.	Arizona		&2005
Gately, Mary Sue	Retir	Texas Tech	8-98	PHD	81.	Houston		&1981
Gates, Sandra	Asst	Texas-Tyler		PHD		Ariz St		&
Gaudreau, Lucie	Asst	Sherbrooke	X	MFIS	02	Sherbrook		2002
Gaukel, Patricia	Inst	S Fl-St Pete	PC	MA	83	Florida		&8-04
Gaumnitz, Bruce R.	Prof	St Cloud St	F	PHD	82.	Wisconsin	# *	&1996
Gaumnitz, Carol B.	Prof	St Cloud St	FT	PHD	85.	Wisconsin		&2001
Gaunt, Clive	SLect	U Queensland	F	PHD	99	Queensld		2001
Gauntt, James E.	Retir	Ark-Ltl Rock	1999	PHD	86.	Miss		&9-82
Gauthier, Keith G.	C-As	American Int	VX	MS	84	Hartford		&1986
Gaver, Jennifer J.	Prof	Georgia	F	PHD	86.	Arizona		&1990
James Don Edwards Chair in Corporate Accounting Policy								
Gaver, Kenneth M.	Retir	Georgia	2005	PHD	74	Car Mellon		1990
Gavin, Thomas A.	Prof	Tenn-Chattan	FAO	DBA	82.	Tennessee		&9-71
Joseph Decosimo Professor of Accounting								
Gay, Grant E.	Assoc	Monash Univ	A	MEC				&1986
Gaynor, Lisa M.	Asst	South Fla	A	PHD	00.	Tx-Austin		&2006
Gayton, Robert J.		Peat Mar Cda		PHD	73.	Berkeley		
Gazur, Wayne M.	Assoc	Colorado	XL	LLM	84	Denver		&1986
Gbenedio, Pender	Prof	Benedict Col	FIS	PHD	77	Cincinnati		1999
Ge, Weili	Asst	U Washington	F	PHD	06.	Michigan		7-06
Gean, G. Farrell	Assoc	Pepper-Malib	F	PHD	81.	Geo St	*	&1981

Geary, K. Michael (Mike)	Assoc	Dayton	AEF	PHD	82.	Cincinnati		&9-76
Geary, William T.	Assoc	Wm & Mary	FM	PHD	76.	Nrthwstrn		&1978
Geddes, S.	Lect	N Eng-Austr	P	MEC		N Eng-Au		&1988
Geddes, Sheri	Inst	Andrews		MBA	99	Iowa		8-04
Geddiz, Mary	Assoc	CS-Chico	FG	ABD		Houston		8-06
Geerts, Guido L.	Assoc	Delaware	S	PHD	93	Free U		9-00
Geiger, Dale R.	Retir	CS-S Marcos	8-03	DBA	93.	Harvard		1992
Geiger, Karen	SLect	Arizona St	M	MS	92	Ariz St		1997
Geiger, Marshall A.	Prof	Richmond	AJST	PHD	88.	Penn St		&2000
Geile, Amy L.				PHD	07	Arizona		
Geiser, Eugene G.	Retir	Clarkson	1988	PHD	75.	NYU		&1973
5 Berkley Drive; Potsdam NY 13676								
Geisler, Charlene	Asst	Nanyang	ABF	PHD	04.	Tx-Austin		&1997
Geisler, Gregory G.	Assoc	Mo-St Louis	X	PHD	95.	N Carol		&2002
Gelardi, Alexander M. G.	Assoc	St Thomas-MN	MX	PHD	91.	Ariz St		&9-04
Gelb, David S.	C-Ac	Seton Hall	FAS	PHD	97.	NYU		&9-96
Gelinas, Francine	Prof	Quebec-Montr	M	BAA		Sherbrook		&8-79
Gelinas, Ulric J. Jr. (Joe)	Prof	Bentley	SAO	PHD	78.	Mass		1981
Geller, A. Neal	Prof	Cornell-Hotl	MA	PHD	77.	Syracuse		&1976
Robert H. Beck Professor of Hospitality Financial Management								
Geller, Louis	Retir	CUNY-Queens	2001	ABD		NYU		&2-55
Gellis, Harold C.	Prof	CUNY-York		MBA		Baruch		&1981
Gelman, Harry L.	Retir	Villanova	1998	MBA	58	Rutgers		&1962
Gelman, Wendy	Lect	Fla Internat	X	LLM	90	U Miami		2001
Gendeon, Yves	Prof	Univ Laval		PHD	97	Laval		2006
Generas, George P. Jr.	Asst	Hartford	FL	JD	90	Conn		&1979
Gentry, James A. Jr.	Retir	Emory	1999	PHD	66.	N Carol		&1965
George, Carolyn R.	Retir	N Carol Cen	2001	DBA	91.	Memphis		&1996
George, Nashwa E.	Prof	Montclair St	FMIC	PHD	88	Baruch	*	1999
Georgoutsos, Dimitris	Asst	Athens Univ	F	PHD	89	Essex		2002
Gerard, Gregory J.	Assoc	Florida St	S	PHD	98.	Mich St		&8-98
Gerard, Joseph	Lect	Wis-Whitewat	BCE	MS	96	Wi-Milwa		&2007
Gerber, Quentin N.	Prof	St John's-MN	MNFV	PHD	77.	Minnesota		&2000
Geren, Donald	Assoc	NE Illinois	P	MBA	69	DePaul		&9-78
Gerhardy, Peter G.	LectC	Flinders Un	AT	MEC	86	N Eng-Au		1-86
Geriesh, Lotfi H.	Asst	Southeastern		DBA	02	Nova SE		2000
Gerk, J.	Lect	N Eng-Austr	D	HONS		Cologne		2001
Germain, E. Samuel	Retir	Syracuse	1987	MBA	50	Columbia		&1951
140 Lewis Avenue; Syracuse NY 13224								
German, Louis T.	Retir	Rutgers-Newa	1988	MBA	68	Seton Hall		&1963
Gernon, Helen	C-Pr	Oregon	FXI	PHD	78.	Penn St		&1978
Lundquist Professor of Accounting (1994-2006); Associate Dean								
Gerrand, W.	Prof	Univ Leeds	FQ	PHD	95	York		9-95
Gerrard, Michael J.	LectC	Adelaide	D	PHD	76	London		1990
Gerrard, Ronald J.	Retir	Acadia	1995	MBA		McMaster		&
Gersich, Frank III	Prof	Monmouth IL	ACSV	EDD	93	N Illinois		&1998
Gessford, Glenn N.		Ernst & Whin		PHD	66.	UCLA		
Geu, Harold L.	Retir	Colorado St	1992	PHD	70.	Nebraska		&1969
Ghamni, Chiheb	Inst	Univ Tunis	F	EXPC	99	ISCAE		1999
Ghani, Waqar I.	Assoc	St Joseph	FM	PHD	94.	Drexel		&1990
Gharaibeh, Fawzi A. R.		U Jordan	1992	PHD	72.	Wisconsin		
Univ of Jordan; Fac of Econ & Adm Sci; Univ of Jordan; Amman Jordan								
Ghartey, James B. Jr.			EIG	PHD	73.	Illinois		&
Ghedamsi, Mohamed N.	Inst	Univ Tunis	F	ECM	97	ISCAE		1998
Gheyara, Kelly F.	Assoc	Concordia U	MS	PHD	79.	Okla St		&1986
Ghicas, Dimitrios C.	Prof	Athens Univ	FM	PHD	85.	Florida		1994
Ghobashy, Mohamed E.	Prof	Indiana U-PA	CF	PHD	63	Intl Com		&1976
Gholson, Marvin E.		Tx Regist Of		PHD	62.	Tx-Austin		
Ghosal, Monojit	Retir	Valdosta St	2001	PHD	64	Bihar	*	&1985
Ghosh, Aloke	Prof	CUNY-Baruch	FV	PHD	93.	Tulane		9-93
Ghosh, Dipankar	Prof	Oklahoma	MBC	PHD	91.	Penn St		1-91
Giacobbe, Francesco	Lect	Tech-Sydney	M	PHD	94	Tech-Sydn		1992
Giacoletti, Robert R.	Retir		FCMX	DBA	81.	Kentucky		&
8835 Bergeson; Indianapolis IN 46278								
Giacomino, Don E.	Prof	Marquette	FA	DBA	78.	Kentucky		&1977
Donald F. & Beverly L. Flynn Chair in Accounting								
Gibbins, Michael	Prof	Univ Alberta	FAB	PHD	76.	Cornell		&1984
Winspear Foundation Distinguished Chair in Professional Accounting								
Gibbs, Judith A.	Retir	Transylvania	1997	MBA	76	Fla Intl		&1978
Gibbs, Sharon	Asst	Roanoke	FAO	MA	95	Va Tech		8-02
Gibson, Ann M.	Prof	Andrews	AJ	PHD	92.	Wash St		9-92
Gibson, Charles H.	Retir	Toledo	1994	DBA	70.	Kent St		&1970
Gibson, Dana L.			FS	PHD	93.	Tx-Arlin		&
Gibson, Gary	Assoc	Lindsey Wils	FX	MAC	92	Tennessee		&2004
Gibson, Robert W.		Deakin Univ	1996	PHD	76.	Cincinnati		&
Gideon, Michael C.	C-Ac	St Martin	AU	MBA	74	U Wash		&1990
Gierlasinski, Norman J.	Prof	Central Wash	AEF	PHD	84	Nova SE	#	&3-86

Name	Rank	School		Degree		School	
Giese, J. W.	Retir	No Texas St	1986	PHD	62.	Illinois	&1966
Gifford, Richard H.	Assoc	SUNY-Geneseo	AF	PHD	02.	Temple	&9-01
Gifford, William R.	Retir	C W Post	1985	BS	47	Ohio St	&1961
Gift, Michael J.	Assoc	Bangkok	2000	PHD	83.	Florida	1996
Business; 66 1 8889-5508							
Gigler, Frank B.	Assoc	Minnesota	B	PHD	92.	Minnesota	2002
Giguere, Pierre	Prof	Quebec-Montr	M	LIC		Montreal	&8-80
Giladi, Kreindel	C-Ac	CUNY-Brookly	PCFM	MA	81	CUNY-Brk	&2-97
Gilbert, Arthur H. Jr.	Assoc	West Florida	MSU	DBA	95.	La Tech	&2004
Gilbert, Arthur L.	Retir	Manchester C	1998	MBA	54	Indiana	&1958
Gilbert, Julitta	Inst	No Illinois	MX	MAS	90	N Illinois	&8-00
Gilbert, Xavier F.	Prof	Intl Mgt Dev	IM	DBA	72.	Harvard	
Dept of Management; Intl Mgt Dev							
Gilbertson, David L.	Assoc	Western Wash	AF	PHD	97.	Utah	* &1998
Gilday, Thomas J.	Assoc	Thomas More	FXP	MBA	93	Xavier	1979
Gilders, Frank	SLect	W Australia	X	DIPE	88	Monash	1988
Giles, Gary N.	Retir	Srthrn Utah	2000	MACC	62	Brighm Yg	&1965
Giles, Jill P.			ABF	PHD	98.	Rutgers	&
Giles, John	Lect	N Carol St	MF	MS	84	N Car St	&1991
Gilfillan, Sally W.	Assoc	Longwood	VNI	MS	90	Virginia	&1986
Giljum, Joseph P.	Retir	Mo-St Louis	2001	LLM	65	NYU	&1968
Gill, Hubert W.	Inst	North Fla	FM	MACC	90	N Fla	&1992
Gill, John W.	Prof	Alcorn St	A	PHD	92.	Miss	&1998
Gill, Susan	Assoc	Wash State	FMC	PHD	94.	Mich St	&1994
Gillam, Helen	Lect	Tech-Sydney	FNW	MBUS	92	Tech-Sydn	1991
Gillard, Concetta		Athabasca Un		CA			
Gilles, Louis H. Jr.	Retir	S Car-Coastl	1983	PHD	69.	Missouri	
143 University Drive; Quail Creek; Conway SC 29526							
Gillespie, Jackson F.	C-Ac	Delaware	MC	PHD	78.	Va Tech	* 9-77
Gillespie, Janet D.	Lect	Texas-Austin	FSG	MBA	82	W Wash	&9-88
Gillespie, Lisa	Lect	Loyola-Chicg	FM	ABD	97	Notre Dm	9-03
Gillett, John W.	C-Pr	Bradley	FTV	PHD	83.	North Tx	&8-93
Gillett, Peter R.	Assoc	Rutgers-N Br	SDAB	PHD	96.	Kansas	&9-96
Gillick, J.	SLect	U Washington	AFS	BBA	57	Manhatten	1986
Gillies, Annette	Lect	U Portsmith		MBA			2003
Gillies, Kenneth R.	Assoc	F Dick-Teane	CMI	MBA	66	Rutgers	&9-74
Gilligan, C.	Assoc	Univ Ulster	FX	MSC			&9-03
Gilmore, JoAnn W.	Asst	Liberty	PX	MBA	91	Liberty	&1995
Gilmore, Joseph	Inst	Frostburg St	VAFN	ABD		Pace	&9-91
Gilmore, Philip N.	Assoc	Liberty	P	DBA	02	Nova SE	* &1980
Gilmore, Rufus III	Asst	Alabama A&M	PCF	MBA	76	Atlanta	1976
Gingras, Russell T.	Retir	Saginaw Vall	2006	DBA	74.	Mich St	&1985
Giove, Frank C.	Retir	Niagara	AFPX	MBA		Columbia	&1977
Giovinazzo, Vincent J.	Retir	Georgia St	MSC	PHD	71	NYU	* 6-76
Girard, Aline C.	Assoc	HEC-Montreal	BFIN	PHD	90.	Tennessee	&6-89
Giraud, Francoise	Assoc	ESCP deParis	BCMU	PHD	00	ESC Bord	1991
Girlando, Anthony	Asst	St Joseph C	JMF	DBA		Nova SE	1998
Girling, David T.				PHD	71.	Nrthwstrn	
Giroux, Gary A.	Prof	Texas A&M	GFN	PHD	79.	Tx Tech	&9-78
Shelton Professor							
Gist, Willie E.	Prof	Ohio Univ	FTA	PHD	88.	Tx A&M	&2003
O'Bleness Professor of Accounting							
Giullian, Marc A.	Asst	Montana St	FP	PHD	96.	Illinois	&8-01
Givens, Horace R.	Retir	Maine	1997	PHD	75	NYU	&1983
Givoly, Dan	C-Pr	Penn State	F	PHD	75.	NYU	&8-02
Ernst & Young Professor of Accounting							
Gjems-Onstad, Ole	Prof	Norwegian Mg	X	DRJU	84	Oslo	1985
Gjesdal, Froystein	C-Pr	Norwegian U	VT	PHD	79.	Stanford	
Gjonnes, Svein	Doct	Norwegian Mg	FM	MBA	92	NHH Berg	2004
Glader, Mats		Stockholm Ec	D	EL	71	Umea	1985
Gladstone-Millar, Charlotte	PLect	U Portsmith	E	BA			1988
Glandon, Sid	Asst	Txs-El Paso	FAB	DBA	97.	La Tech	&9-00
Glandon, Terry Ann	Asst	Txs-El Paso	SCB	PHD	00.	Tx-Arlin	&9-00
Glass, C.	Prof	Univ Ulster	F	MSC			8-87
Glass, Kathrine	VLect	Indiana	F	MBA	84	Indiana	2006
Glasscock, Lorraine	Assoc	No Alabama	FPC	MBA	77	N Alab	* 1979
Glatt, Janice	SLect	N Dakota St	PF	MBA	85	N Dak St	&1985
Glazer, Alan S.	C-Pr	Frank & Mars	AFT	PHD	78.	Penn	&1975
Stager Professor of Business							
Gleason, Cristi A.	Asst	Iowa	F	PHD	98.	Cornell	2004
Gleeson, Derek	ALect	W Sydney	CMT	MEC			
Gleim, Irvin N.		Gleim Public	1998	PHD	71.	Illinois	# * &
Gleim Publications; PO Box 12848; Gainesville FL 32604; 352-375-0772							
Glenski, Christine	Asst	Benedictn-KS	X	MS	93	Tx-Austin	* 2003
Glezen, G. William	Retir	Arkansas	2000	PHD	79.	Arkansas	&1979
Glick, John R.	Retir		1989	DBA	75.	Colorado	
14420 B Club Villa Dr; Colorado Springs CO 80921; 719-488-3517							

Name	Rank	School		Degree	Yr	Institution	Notes
Glodstein, David	VAsst	SUNY Old Wes	AFP	MS	89	Lgls-Post	&1999
Glover, Glenda B.	Dean	Jackson St	FS	PHD	90	Geo Wash	&1994
Glover, Hubert D.	C-Ac	Howard	AF	PHD	92.	Tx A&M	# * &2004
Glover, Jonathan C.	Prof	Carnegie Mel	TMF	PHD	92.	Ohio St	&1992
Glover, Robert I.			FI	PHD	75.	Arkansas	&
Glover, Steven M.	Prof	Brigham Yg	FAB	PHD	94.	U Wash	9-94
PricewaterhouseCoopers Research Fellow							
Glynn, Arthur L.	Retir	Boston Col	1986	JD	39	Boston C	&1952
Gnizak, Charles J.	Asst	Fort Hays St	XF	PHD	93.	Kent St	&2001
Gober, Jerald R.			XMF	PHD	94.	Tx Tech	&
Godbout, Luc	Prof	Sherbrooke	X	MRIS	95	Sherbrook	2002
Goddard, Scott	SLect	U Nottingham	F	MCOM	72	Birmingham	1990
Gode, Dhananjay K.	Asst	New York U	FM	PHD	94.	Car Mellon	1998
Godfrey, Earl	C-Ac	Gardner-Webb	ACF	DBA		Nova SE	& 8-92
Godfrey, James T.	Retir	George Mason	1999	PHD	67	Michigan	1988
Godfrey, Jayne M.	H-Pr	Monash Univ	FTIU	PHD	91	Queensl	&2002
Godfrey, L. Howard	Prof	N Car-Charl	X	PHD	75.	Alabama	&1974
Godfrey, Robert F.	Retir	Marshall	5-97	PHD	77	Ohio St	& 6-76
Godin, William N.		Hard Mfg		PHD	72.	SUNY-Buf	
Godwin, Joseph H.	Prof	Grand Valley	FI	PHD	88.	Wisconsin	&1995
Godwin, Larry B.			FA	DBA	74.	Colorado	&
Godwin, Norman H.	D-Ac	Auburn	F	PHD	96.	Mich St	& 9-96
Goedde, Harold			FAX	DBA	88.	Kentucky	* &
Goeddo, Richard	D-Ac	St Olaf	M	MBA	78	Wisconsin	* &1988
Goedono, Mohamed		Gadgahmada U		PHD	97.	Temple	
Goergen, Marc	Lect	U Manchester	FIY	PHD	97	Oxford	1-99
Goetz, Billy E.	Deces			PHD	49.	Chicago	
Goetz, Joe F. Jr.	Retir	La St-Shreve	7-02	PHD	74.	Nebraska	* 6-95
Goggans, Travis P.	Retir	Oklahoma	1988	PHD	63	Oklahoma	&1958
Goh, Alicia	ALect	W Australia	F	BCOM	99	W Austrl	2000
Goh, Chye Tee	Assoc	Nanyang Tech	CM	MCOM	79	NS Wales	&1980
Goh, Lisa	Lect	London Econ	FQ	PHD			2007
Gohlke, Gene Allan				PHD	68.	Wisconsin	
Gokarn, Rajul Y.	Assoc	Clark Atlant	FIMT	PHD	84.	Geo St	1994
Goktan, Erkut		Ankara Turke	1992	PHD	68.	N Carol	
20 Sok No 20/1; Bahcelievler 06490; Ankara Turkey							
Goldberg, Martin	Asst	New Haven	BL	LLM	79	NYU	9-01
Goldberg, Seymour	Retir	Lg Isl-Post	1998	JD	66	St Johns	&1955
Goldberg, Stephen R.	C-Pr	Grand Valley	AIF	PHD	88.	Wisconsin	&1996
Golden, Mary R.	Retir	Auburn-Montg	1999	DBA	79.	Miss St	&1973
Goldman, Arieh	Sen	Hebrew U		PHD	70.	Berkeley	
Goldman, Arthur H.	Lect	Kentucky	P	MBA	88	Wi-LaCros	&2003
Goldman, Donald	SLect	Arizona St	T	BS	74	Ariz St	2001
Goldsman, Larry	Lect	McGill Univ	F	BCOM	77	Concordia	&1997
Goldsmith, Geoffrey	Assoc	Belhaven	NPT	PHD	96.	Kent St	1993
Goldwater, Paul M.	Assoc	Cen Florida	MCQ	PHD	89.	LSU	* 7-89
Golemme, Joseph M.	Retir	Northeastern	1985	MA	40	Boston U	&1938
Golen, Steven P.	Assoc	Arizona St	F	PHD	79	Ariz St	1984
Goma, Ahmed Tawfik	Assoc	Manhattan	FM	PHD	85.	Baruch	1987
Gomaa, Ismail I.	Prof	King Saud U	FM	PHD	82.	Florida	1996
Gomaa, Mohamed	Asst	Suffolk		PHD	05	Maastrich	2007
Gomez, Sonia	Retir	Puerto Rico	1993	MBA	60	NYU	&1962
Gonedes, Nicholas J.	Prof	Pennsylvania	C	PHD	69.	Tx-Austin	1978
Gong, Guojin	Asst	Penn State	F	PHD	05.	Iowa	7-05
Gong, James	Asst	Illinois	FM	PHD	05	S Calif	8-05
Gonzalez Tobaoada, Jose A.	Prof	Puerto Rico	TFQ	DBA	81	Kent St	# * &1994
Gonzalez, Lillian	Asst	Wofford	CA	MPA	95	Clemson	& 9-01
Gooch, Roxanne L.	Assoc	Midwest St	FM	PHD	05.	Oklahoma	& 9-06
Goodacre, Alan	H-Pr	Un Stirling	AFQ	PHD	81	Exeter	&1981
Goodale, Denis	Retir	Univ Alberta	1993	PHD	73.	U Wash	&1950
Goode, Larry W.	Retir	Missouri So	5-01	MS	67	Pitt St	1968
Goode, Sigi	Asst	Australian N	DS	GRAD	97	Austr Natl	2000
Goodhart, Edward S.	Retir	Shippensburg	2004	PHD	82.	Penn St	9-84
Goodman, Leonard	Prof	Rutgers-N Br	GXH	PHD	82	NYU	&1976
Goodman, Sam				PHD	69.	NYU	
Goodman, Theodore	Asst	Arizona	F	PHD	05.	Penn	8-05
Goodman, William D.	Assoc	Bluefield St	CGNS	MA	77	Appalach	& 8-87
Goodpasture, James				PHD	99.	Fla St	
Goodrich, Mary Beth W.	SLect	Texas-Dallas	SA	MBA	94	LSU	# &2002
Goodspeed, Georgia M.	Retir	Saskatchewan	1985	MBA	49	Chicago	&1942
Goodyear, Alice	Lect	Denver	F	MACC	76	Denver	1978
Goosen, Kenneth R.	Retir	Ark-Ltl Rock	1998	PHD	69.	Tx-Austin	& 1-76
Goot, T van der	Asst	Un Amsterdam	FGKY	PHD	97	Amsterdm	1990
Goran, Ruth	Assoc	NE Illinois	X	MSA	76	Roosevelt	& 1-80
Gordan, Elizabeth				PHD	97.	Columbia	
Gorden, Paula	Inst	NE St-Okla	AX	MBA	98	NE Ok St	&2002
Gordon, Agnes M.	Deces	Ohio State		PHD	64.	Ohio St	1960

Gordon, Dennis	Retir	Akron	1981	MBA	38	Chicago		&1946
Gordon, Elizabeth A.	Assoc	Temple	FI	PHD	98.	Columbia		&2007
Gordon, Gus A.			AF	DBA	88.	La Tech	#	&
Gordon, Irene M.	Prof	Simon Fraser	FT	PHD	81	Simon Fr		&9-81
Gordon, Isabel	Lect	Univ Sydney	AFHI	MCOM	95	NS Wales		&1995
Gordon, Jay H.	Retir	Norwich	2001	MBA	59	NYU		&1990
Gordon, L.	SLect	Liverpool JM	FD	ICAE				1999
Gordon, Lawrence A.	Prof	Maryland	M	PHD	73.	Rensselaer		1980
Ernst & Young Alumni Professor of Managerial Accounting								
Gordon, Teresa P.	Assoc	Idaho	NMF	PHD	86.	Houston		&1986
Gore, Angela K.	Asst	George Wash	AFG	PHD	00.	SUNY-Buf		&2007
Gore, J. P. O.	Lect	U Lancaster	FA	PHD	89	Lancaster		1991
Gore, Richard A.	Assoc	Fort Lewis	FX	PHD	98.	Wash St		&2006
Gorelik, George	Retir	British Colu	1991	PHD	70.	Berkeley		&1963
Gorenberg, Hyman	Prof	CUNY-Baruch	X	LLM	60	NYU		&1960
Gorman, F. Barry	Prof	St Marys-Cdn	X	PHD	91	Bath		&1979
Gormly, C.	Lect	New So Wales		MEC	92	Sydney		
Gornik-Tomaszewski, Sylwia	Assoc	St John's	IFV	DBA	96.	Clev St	*	F-00
Gorton, Donald E.	Retir	Wayne State	1995	MBA	62	Wayne St	*	1961
Gosman, Martin L.	Prof	Quinnipiac	F	PHD	71.	Wisconsin		&1996
Goss, Betsy C.			F	PHD	91.	Wisconsin		&
Gosse, Darrel I.			MSC	PHD	89.	Mich St		&
Gosselin, David J.			SMC	PHD	86.	Arkansas		
Gosselin, Maurice	D-Pr	Univ Laval	MB	DBA	95	Boston U	*	&1988
Gotlob, David	Deces	Ind-Pur/FtWy	D-98	PHD	85.	Missouri		&8-91
Gottlieb, Max M.	Prof	CUNY-Stn Isl	SD	PHD		Gdansk		&9-87
Gould, Graham P.	LectB	Adelaide	F	MCOM	97	Adelaide		1997
Gould, John	ALect	W Australia	Q	BCOM	01	W Austrl		2001
Goulet, Bernard	Prof	Sherbrooke	X	MFIS	85	Sherbrook		1986
Goveia, John C.	Retir	Portland	2005	PHD	72	N Illinois	*	&1978
Govindaraj, Suresh	Assoc	Rutgers-Newk	CFM	PHD	90.	Columbia		2000
Govindarajan, Vijay	Prof	Dartmouth	M	DBA	78.	Harvard		1985
Daum Professor of International Management								
Gowing, Maureen	Asst	Univ Windsor	A	PHD	96	Queen's		2005
Goyal, Mahendra K.	Lect	Monash Univ	MF	PHD	84	Rajasthn		&1996
Goza, Nina M.	Asst	Ark Tech	GFM	PHD	05.	Miss		2004
Graber, Dean E.	Retir	NE St-Okla	5-04	PHD	70.	Missouri	*	&1993
Grabski, Severin V.	Assoc	Michigan St	SD	PHD	83.	Ariz St	*	&1983
Grace, Debra M.	Prof	CS-Long Bch	FX	PHD	80.	Okla St		&2001
Grace, Elizabeth V.	Prof	San Jose St	F	PHD	84	Penn		1986
Graci, Samuel P.	Prof	No Michigan	MFT	PHD	82.	Arkansas		&1980
Gracia, Louise	SLect	U Glamorgan	FX	BA	93	Glamorgan		7-93
Gradisher, Suzanne	Inst	Akron	FMX	JD	04	Akron		&8-04
Grafton, Jennifer	Lect	U Melbourne	MN	PHD	02	Melbourne		2002
Graham, Alan	Lect	U Portsmith		MA				2005
Graham, Allan W.	C-Ac	Rhode Island	MS	PHD	00.	Va Tech		2000
Graham, Cameron	Asst	York Univ	WGHT	PHD	05	Calgary		2005
Graham, Carol	Assoc	San Francisc	FM	PHD	95	Strathcl		9-98
Graham, Curtis C.	Retir	New Mex St	5-01	PHD	68.	Oklahoma		&7-79
Graham, James E.	Retir	Wis-Superior	D-89	MS				&
Graham, John	Retir	Morehead St	M	MHE	71	Morehead		1970
Graham, John R	Prof		2004	PHD	71.	Arkansas		
Kansas State Univ; Finance Dept; 785-532-3184; jgraham@ksu.edu								
Graham, Lynford E.	Partn	BDO Seidman	2003	PHD	76.	Penn		&1998
BDO Seidman; 330 Madison Ave; NY 10017-5001; 212-885-8551; fax 212-697-5076								
Graham, Roger C.	H-Pr	Oregon State	XF	PHD	90.	Oregon		&1991
Graham, Willard J.	Deces	No Carolina	1966	PHD	34.	Chicago		
Grambo, Ronald J.	Assoc	Scranton	AMCD	PHD	81.	Penn St		1977
Gramkow, Raymond C.	Retir	Ramapo	2003	MBA	80	Fairl Dick		&1981
Gramlich, Jeffrey D.	Prof	So Maine	XF	PHD	88.	Missouri		&2003
L.L. Bean Endowed Chair								
Gramling, Audrey A.	Assoc	Kennesaw St	PA	PHD	95.	Arizona	#	&8-05
Gramling, Lawrence J.	Asst	Connecticut	AFM	DBA	82.	Maryland		&9-80
Grams, Edsel	Retir	Wis-Eau Clar	1996	MS	57	Fla St		&9-63
Grandes, Maria J.	H-Pr	Univ Navarra	FM	DOCT		UPC		N-84
Grandorf, James	ClAso	Indiana	F	MBA	64	Indiana		&1998
Grange, E. Vance	Assoc	Utah State	XE	PHD	87.	Tx-Austin		&1978
Grange, Janet	Assoc	Chicago St	PMLX	JD	83	Illinois		&1989
Granger, Courtenay L.			A	PHD	75.	Florida		&
Granger, Ellsworth C. Jr.	Retir	Mn St-Mankat	2002	MBA	68	Indiana		&1968
Granger, H. Garland III	Assoc	Guilford	AF	MA	71	Appalach	#	&1983
Granger, M. Parker II	Retir	Jacksonvl St	2001	PHD	80.	Arkansas	*	&9-73
Granof, Michael H.	Prof	Texas-Austin	FG	PHD	72.	Michigan		&1-72
Ernst & Young Distinguished Centennial Professor of Accounting								
Grant, C. Terry	Prof	CS-Fullerton	FI	PHD	92.	Fla St		&2005
Grant, Delvin	Assoc	DePaul	S	PHD	91	SUNY-Bin		2000
Grant, Edward B.	Prof	Cen Michigan	FM	PHD	77.	Mich St		&1977

Grant, Gerry H.	Assoc	CS-Fullerton	SC	PHD	05	Miss			&2004
Grant, J. L.	Lect	Univ Ulster	FD	MSC				*	1-84
Grant, Julia E. S.	Assoc	Case Western	FMD	PHD	89.	Cornell			& 7-91
Grant, Rita H.	Assoc	Grand Valley	TF	MBA	82	Mich St			&1980
Grant, Thomas J.	C-Ac	Kutztown	CPM	MBA		Drexel		*	1987
Grasso, Lawrence P.	Assoc	Central Conn	CMS	DBA	89.	Boston U			&2003
Grasty, William J.	Retir	Mid Tenn St	2001	PHD	67.	Florida			&1980
Graul, Paul R.	Retir	East Wash	1999	PHD	75.	Berkeley			&1986
Graves, Mary			UMT	PHD	87.	North Tx		*	&
Graves, O. Finley	Prof	North Texas	FIW	PHD	85.	Alabama			& 8-02
Graves, Sharron Marlow	Asst	S F Austin	SF	MBED	75	SF Austin			&1975
Gray, C. Delano	Lect	Fla Internat	AIS	MS	92	NYU			1999
Gray, Dahli		Strayer	FMT	DBA	84.	Geo Wash		*	&
Gray, Furman R.	Retir	Clemson	1992	MBA	67	Georgia			&1957
206 Sirrine; Clemson SC 29631									
Gray, Glen L.	Prof	CS-Northrdge	S	PHD	88.	S Calif			&1987
Gray, Jack C.	Retir	Michigan St	2004	PHD	63.	Ohio St		*	&1990
Gray, O. Ronald	Prof	West Florida	AFHV	PHD	80.	Arkansas	#	*	&1982
Gray, Otha L.	Retir	Lander	6-94	PHD	61	Alabama			&1985
Gray, Phil	Assoc	U Queensland	F	PHD	00	NS Wales			1999
Gray, Ralph	Retir	DePauw	1997	PHD	62	Syracuse			8-65
Gray, Robert H.	Prof	St Andrews	WETJ	PHD	03	Glasgow			&2004
Gray, Sidney J.	H-Pr	Univ Sydney	IFT	PHD	76	Lancaster			& 7-03
Gray, Stephen F.	Prof	U Queensland	F	PHD	95	Stanford			1997
Grayson, Michael M.	Asst	Jackson St	AM	DBA	01.	La Tech			&2001
Greaney, Catherine			FM	PHD	99.	Geo Wash			&
Greco, Joseph A.	Retir	Montclair St	2001	PHD	72.	NYU			&1972
Green, Brian Patrick	Prof	Mich-Dearbrn	ANS	PHD	91.	Kent St			& 5-92
Green, Darien	Asst	Univ of D C	F	MBA	72	American			&1980
Green, David O.	Emer	CUNY-Baruch	1999	PHD	56.	Chicago			& 9-78
Green, Diane J.	Asst	Sam Houston	AX	MS	71	LSU			&1978
Green, Duncan L.	C-Ac	9900 Calgary	FM	MSC	89	Saskatch			&1989
Green, Eva S.	Assoc	Univ of D C	XFM	MBA	63	Cincinnati			&1969
Green, J. Peter	SLect	Univ Ulster	FQT	DPHL					1-86
Green, James S.	Inst	Tenn-Martin	P	MBA	68	Arkansas		*	& 9-98
Green, John Kevin	Retir	Wash & Lee	FM	PHD	69	Virginia		*	&1984
Green, John L.			XL	PHD	77.	Houston			&
Green, Joseph	Retir	Fairleigh Di	1985	PHD		NYU			1979
Green, Mitzi C.	Prof	West Alabama	ARPV	DBA	83.	Miss St			&2005
Green, Peter	Assoc	U Queensland	DS	PHD	97	Queensl			&1999
Green, Raymond A.	Retir	Texas Tech	1992	MS	51	HardSimm			1956
Green, Richard	Assoc	Incarnate	FCX	PHD	99.	St Louis			& 8-01
Green, Sharon L.	Assoc	Duquesne	BCM	PHD	89.	Pittsburgh			1993
Green, Steve G.	Prof	USAF Academy	CN	DBA	87	US Intl			6-88
Green, Wendy J.	SLect	New So Wales	AB	PHD	00	NS Wales			&1985
Greenan, K.	H-Pr	Univ Ulster	E	MBA					0-04
Greenawalt, Mary B.			AMOE	PHD	86.	Georgia	#		&
on leave Academic Fellow SEC 2003-2004; First Union Ntl Bank Professor of Atg									
Greenball, Melvin N.	Retir	Ohio State	1997	PHD	66	Chicago			&1968
Greenberg, Daniel	Asst	Centenary-NJ	CPVX	MBA		Pace			& 8-00
Greenberg, Ira S.			XF	PHD	83.	Missouri			&
Greenberg, Penelope Sue	Assoc	Widener	ASMU	PHD	82.	Ohio St		*	&1995
Greenberg, Ralph H.	Assoc	Temple	MSB	PHD	81.	Ohio St			& 9-88
Greenberg, Robert R.	Prof	Wash State	MCS	PHD	81.	Ariz St			1983
Greenberg, Rochelle	Lect	Florida St	FM	MBA	77	Ohio St			8-04
Greene, David	ClPr	Indiana	FM	JD	73	Indiana			&1997
Greene, William F.	Retir	Mid Tenn St	1994	MS	61	Tennessee			&1968
Greenfield, Chad	Inst	Txs-Perm Bas	PMV	ABD		Va Comm			9-05
Greenhalgh, Robert	Lect	East Anglia	CM	BA	82	Wales			&
Greenlee, Janet S.	Assoc	Dayton	NFSP	PHD	93.	Kentucky			&1999
Greenlees, E. Malcolm	Prof	Linfield	ACGR	PHD	72.	U Wash			&1984
Glenn L. & Helen S. Jackson Professor of Business									
Greenough, Paul W.	Retir	Assumption	2001	MBA	66	Northeas			1983
Greenspan, James W.	C-Pr	Wright State	AFMV	PHD	86.	Tx A&M			1-03
Greenstein, Brian R.	Assoc	Seton Hall	X	PHD	87.	Houston			9-93
Greenwell, Gregory A.	Assoc	Kennesaw St	XF	JD	93	Marshall			&1978
Greer, Carl C.				PHD	66.	Columbia			
Greer, Olen L.	Prof	Missouri St	MB	PHD	86.	Colorado			8-79
Greer, Susan	Lect	Macquarie Un	FW	PHD	06	Macquarie			1993
Greer, Willis R. Jr.	Retir	No Iowa	7-01	PHD	71.	Michigan		*	1996
Gregg, M. Ray	Assoc	Oral Roberts	PX	MBA	71	Tx Tech			& 8-73
Grego, Michael J.	Assoc	St John's	ADC	MBA	71	St Johns			&1979
Gregor, Shirley	C-Pr	Australian N	DS	PHD		Queenslnd			2001
Gregory, Robert H.	Retir	Lowell	1986	PHD	44.	Tx-Austin			&
Gregson, Terry L.			FB	PHD	87.	Arkansas			&
Greig, Anthony C.	ClLe	Purdue	F	PHD	92.	Rochester			2002
Grein, Barbara Murray	Asst	Drexel	F	PHD	02.	N Carol			2004

Name	Rank	School		Deg	Yr	Grad School	
Grenci, Anthony	Prof	Clarion	XM	PHD	03	Pittsburgh	# * &8-03
Greshik, Vicki	Asst	Jamestown	FTVX	MBA	92	Moorhead	&1989
Gress, Edward J.	Prof	Canisius	TFI	PHD	70.	Arizona	1976
Grey, Richard	Lect	Strathclyde	MW	BA	77	Manchest	1996
Greynolds, Elbert B.	Assoc	So Methodist	CSD	PHD	71.	Geo St	&1974
Gribbin, Donald W.	C-Pr	W Michigan	CM	PHD	89.	Okla St	&2006
Grice, J. Stephen	Assoc	Alabama-Birm	FA	PHD	97.	Alabama	&2007
Grief, Louis A.	Deces	Louisville	5-91	DBA	79.	Kentucky	&1966
Grierson, Peter R.	Retir	Slippery Roc	2005	PHD	81.	Geo St	& 1-88
Griffin, Carleton H.	Emer	Michigan	1996	JD	53	Michigan	&1985
Griffin, Charles H.	Retir	Texas-Austin	1991	PHD	53.	Tx-Austin	&1962
Griffin, Hariette	Lect	N Carol St	FS	ME	78	N Car St	&1978
Griffin, Lynn K.	Retir	N Carol A&T	CFQ	PHD	86.	S Carol	&1989
Griffin, Marilyn T.	Inst	Virg Tech	S	MA	01	Va Tech	2001
Griffin, Michael	Lect	Mass-Dartmou	M	MBA	81	Bryant	* 1986
Griffin, Nancy	Inst	Penn St-Harr	SP	BS	81	Penn St	&2006
Griffin, Paul A.	Prof	Cal-Davis	FT	PHD	74.	Ohio St	&1981
Griffin, Richard B.	Prof	Tenn-Martin	FVSM	PHD	79.	Miss	* 8-88
Griffith, Kenneth	Retir	E Kentucky	1998	MBA	68	Kentucky	&1965
Griffiths, Marion D.	Lect	Murdoch Univ	FX	MACC		W Austrl	1988
Griggs, Jack A.	Prof	Abilene Chr	F	PHD	71	Tx-Austin	1-91
Grigsby, William W.	Assoc	Winthrop	GNFV	DBA	73.	Oklahoma	& 9-87
Grimlund, Richard A.			MA	PHD	77.	U Wash	1-78
Grimsley, Larry J.	Retir	Fort Hays St	2003	MSA	72	Ft Hays	&1973
Grimstad, Clayton R.	Retir	Denver	1985	PHD	56.	Ohio St	1968
18826 Welk Drive; Sun City AZ 85373							
Grinaker, Robert L.	Retir	Virginia	FA	MBA	47	Harvard	& 9-86
Griner, Emmett H.			M	PHD	91.	Maryland	&
Grinnell, Dale Jacque	Retir	Vermont	2003	DBA	68.	Indiana	1978
Grippo, Frank	Assoc	Wm Paterson	AF	MBA	77	Fairl Dick	&1979
Griswold, Melissa	Dean	Quincy	F	PHD	96	Nebraska	1998
Grivette, Denise	Prof	Governors St		JD		DePaul	
Grobbelaar, Johan	STut	U Auckland	MA	BCOM	76	S Africia	2004
Groff, James E.	C-Pr	Tx-S Antonio	MSG	PHD	84.	Iowa	* 1988
Grollman, William K.				PHD	71.	NYU	&
Center for Video Education							
Groner, Michael I.	Assoc	Roosevelt	CF	PHD	77.	Illinois	&1981
Groomer, S. Michael	Prof	Indiana	AS	PHD	75.	Missouri	&1974
Grooms, Ferris L.	Deces	Baylor		PHD	71.	Tx Tech	& 6-70
Groot, Tom L. C. M.	C-Pr$	Vrije Univ	BCM	PHD	88	Groningn	1995
Grosch, Paul A.	Retir	Loyola Marym	1985	MA	50	Missouri	&1952
Gross, Norma Jean	Retir	St Louis	2002	PHD	86	St Louis	&1968
Grossman, Steven D.	Assoc	Texas A&M	F	PHD	72	Tufts	6-76
Grove, Hugh D.	Prof	Denver	FMZ	DBA	75.	S Calif	& 9-75
Groves, Roger E. V.	Prof	Cardiff	1992	PHD	70.	Purdue	1978
Univ of Wales College of Cardiff; Cardiff CF1 3EU Wales							
Grubbs, William A.	Prof	Guilford	RFC	MBA	65	N Carol	&1967
Sulon Bibb Stedman Professor of Accounting							
Gruber, Cindy	VInst	Marquette	FM	MBA	98	Wi-Milwa	&2000
Gruber, Robert A.	C-Pr	Wis-Whitewat	EGI	PHD	90.	Wisconsin	# * &1986
C.A. Black Professor of Accounting							
Gruber, William H.				PHD	65.	MIT	
Grubnic, Suzana	Lect	U Nottingham	M	PHD	00	Derby	2001
Grudnitski, Gary M.	Prof	San Diego St	S	PHD	75.	Mass	1988
Gruetzmacher, Vance S.	Retir	Wis-Stev Pt	2004	JD	72	Wisconsin	& 9-72
Grugle, Roger A.	Assoc	Baldwin-Wal	CDM	ABD		Kent St	& 9-87
Grunloh, Melvin P.	Prof	Quincy Col		PHD	62.	Chicago	
Gu, Feng	Asst	SUNY-Buffalo	FI	PHD	97	Wash U	2005
Gu, Zhaoyang	Assoc	Carnegie Mel	FM	PHD	99.	Tulane	&1999
Guan, Liming	Assoc	Hawaii-Manoa	SF	PHD	01.	Okla St	8-01
Guan, Yanling	Asst	Un Hong Kong	FM	PHD	06	London	2006
Guan, Yu Yan	Asst	City Univ HK	F	PHD	06	Toronto	2006
Guay, Wayne R.	Assoc	Pennsylvania	F	PHD	98.	Rochester	1997
Guenther, David A.	H-Pr	Oregon	FX	PHD	90.	U Wash	2005
Scharpf Professor of Accounting							
Guenther, Harry P.	Retir	No Michigan	1998	DBA	59	Indiana	1990
Guercio, John P.	Retir	Loyola-Maryl	1998	MBA	71	Loyola	&1967
Guerra, Flavio J.	Retir	St Louis	1990	MBA	50	LSU	&1955
Guess, A. Kay	C-Ac	St Edwards	AFXB	PHD	93.	North Tx	& 8-98
Guffey, Daryl M.	Prof	Clemson	FJ	PHD	89.	S Carol	# * &9-99
Guide, Vincent D. R.	Retir	Clemson	1993	MS	70	Clemson	1976
Guidry, Flora			FM	PHD	92.	Arizona	&
Guidry, Michele D.	Inst	Nicholls St	FLM	MBA	89	Nicholls	& 8-89
Guidry, Ronald P.	Asst	La-Monroe	F	PHD	04.	Miss St	&2003
Guilding, Chris	AProf	Griffith-GC	MW	PHD	91	Bradford	* 1996
Guindon, Michel	Prof	HEC-Montreal	BIMT	PHD	92	Montreal	6-78
Guinn, Robert E.	Assoc	N Car-Charl	AFR	PHD	73.	Alabama	&1976

Name	Rank	School				
Guithues-Amrhein, Denise M.	Assoc	St Louis	FQT	PHD	83. St Louis	&1997
Gujarathi, Mahendra R.	Prof	Bentley	MFI	PHD	81 India	&1989
Gul, Ferdinand A.	H-Pr	HongKon Tech	A	PHD	83 N Eng-Au	&2004
Guldemond, A. C.	Lect	Vrije Univ	UM	MS	99 Erasmus	2001
Gulden, Bror Petter	IndPr	Norwegian Mg	A	MBUS	78 NHH Berg	& 8-83
Gulledge, Dexter E. (Gene)	Prof	Ark-Monticel	NCFS	DBA	91. Miss St	* &2001
Gulley, Lawrence	Prof	Tuskegee	PFTC	PHD	86. Tx A&M	*
Gum, Burel	Retir	Bloomsburg	8-98	EDD	82 Pittsburgh	1970
Gumenik, Arthur J.	Asst	Bridgewater	FAX	PHD	93. Va Comm	&1990
Gunderson, Konrad E.	Asst	Missouri Wes	F	PHD	92. Nebraska	&2000
Gunewald, Sandra	Asst	Calif Luthrn	ACDF	MBA	91 Ca Luthr	&1992
Gunn, James A. Jr.		Self Employ		PHD	63. Arkansas	
Gunn, Sanford C.	Retir	SUNY-Buffalo	CMU	PHD	77. Ohio St	* 1973
Gunny, Katherine	Asst	Colorado	F	PHD	05 Berkeley	2005
Gunter, Marjorie E.	Retir	Birminghm So	1999	MBA	71 Samford	&1978
Gunther, Christopher	Fell	Bond Univ	M	BBUS	95 Capetown	& 5-02
Gunz, Sally P.	Prof	Un Waterloo	ALJ	LLB	75 Sydney	1981
Guo, Feng	ALect	Macquarie Un				
Guo, Hong-tao				PHD	02. Illinois	
Guo, Miin H.			FIPV	PHD	89. Arizona	&
Gupta, Mahendra	Dean	Wash Univ	MC	PHD	90. Stanford	1990
Gupta, Parveen P.	Assoc	Lehigh	FAIO	PHD	87. Penn St	1987
Gupta, Rameshwar D.	Assoc	Jackson St	GFN	PHD	84. Arkansas	1967
Gupta, Sanjay			X	PHD	90. Mich St	&
Gupta, Sanjay.	Assoc	Valdosta St	FM	PHD	97. Cen Fla	* & 8-97
Gupta, Vinay K.	Retir	CS-Pomona	2002	PHD	74 UCLA	&1973
Gurganus, Frankie E.	Retir	High Point	FGIM	PHD	91. Va Comm	&1994
Gurka, Geoffrey J.	Assoc	Mesa State	XP	PHD	92. Mich St	&2001
Gurley, A. Lee	H-Ac	Auburn-Montg	XF	PHD	96. Miss	&2000
Gurun, Umit G.	Asst	Texas-Dallas	F	PHD	04 Mich St	2004
Guskiewicz, Richard B.	Retir	St Vincent	1999	MSBA	57 Duquesne	&1962
Gustafson, George A.	Retir	CS-L Angeles	1983	DBA	71. S Calif	&1970
140 Shiras Points Drive; Manquette MI 49885						
Gustafson, Lyal			CF	PHD	89. Geo St	
Gutierrez, Elsa	Prof	Puerto Rico	EFV	MBA	79 P Rico	&1985
Gutierrez, Teresa K.			PX	PHD	93. North Tx	&
Gutmann, Jean	Prof	So Maine	DPS	MBA	74 Maine	1977
Gutterman, Paul	SLect	Minnesota	X	LLM	88 NYU	&1992
Guttikonda, Rama R.	Assoc	Tuskegee	F	PHD	84. Arkansas	1-03
Guttman, Amir			F	PHD	94. Berkeley	
Guttman, Ilan	Asst	Stanford		PHD	04 Hebrew	2004
Guven, P.	Lect	East Anglia	BCM	PHD	E Anglia	
Guy, Dan M.	VP	AICPA-Audit	1996	PHD	71. Alabama	& 6-79
1211 Avenue of the Americas; New York NY 10036						
Guy, Joseph F.	Deces	Georgia St	1990	PHD	71. Illinois	& 9-75
Guydan, Donna	Lect	Valparaiso	FXM	LLM	98 DePaul	&1987
Guyette, Roger W.	Asst	West Florida	X	LLM	77 Florida	&1980
Guyton, Diane T.	Retir	Mississippi	6-92	MBA	71 Delta St	&1976
Gvenin-Paracini, Henri	Prof	Univ Laval	ABD			2006
Gynther, Reginald S.	Deces	Queensland		DBA	66. U Wash	
Ha, Gook-Lak			FPS	PHD	94. Purdue	&
Habegger, Jerrell W.	C-Ac	Susquehanna	AFV	PHD	88. Va Tech	& 9-89
Tressler Chair of Accounting						
Haber, F. Barry	Retir	Fayetteville	2004	PHD	73 Ariz St	&1988
Haber, Jeffry R.	Assoc	Iona	PN	PHD	94 Rensselaer	& 9-00
Habib, Abo-El-Yazeed	Prof	Mn St-Mankat	FTV	PHD	83. North Tx	1988
Habib, Ahsan	Lect	Lincoln-NZ	AG	PHD	Hitotsub	2005
Hackenbrack, Karl E.	Assoc	Vanderbilt	A	PHD	88. Ohio St	&2004
Haddad, Amin N.		Najah Nat	1992	DBA	89. S Illinois	
Najah National Univ; PO Box 7; Nablus West Bank Isreal						
Hadden, Linda	Asst	Keene State	ACFM	PHD	02 Nova SE	2002
Hadidi, Hamed M.		Kuwait		PHD	73. Tx Tech	
Hadley, Galen D.	Retir	Neb-Kearney	2004	PHD	75. Nebraska	& 8-91
Hadlock, Bruce	Deces	So Carolina	1996	BS	59 Florida	&1988
Hafemeister, Lynn	Lect	Wis-Whitewat	FP	MS	82 Wi-White	&2002
Hagadorn, Michelle	Asst	Roanoke	FMN	MA	92 Va Tech	8-04
Hagan, Dan	Lect	Tx-Arlington	FM	MPA	85 Tx-Arlin	&2002
Hagan, Joseph M.	Assoc	East Carol	XM	PHD	90. Geo St	&1995
Hagen, Will	Prof	CS-East Bay	LX	SJD	04 Wisconsin	4-06
Hagendorff, Jeus	Lect	Univ Leeds	FMQ	MA	04 Leeds	9-06
Hagerman, Robert L.	Retir	SUNY-Buffalo	2003	PHD	72. Rochester	&1973
Haggqvist, Ann-Christin	Asst	Univ of Umea	F	MSC	82 Umea	7-88
Hagigi, Moshe	Prof	Boston Univ	FIVX	PHD	81 NYU	9-88
Hagler, J. Larry	Retir	East Carol	2004	PHD	72. Colorado	&1988
Hahn, F. James	Prof	Western St	PLJ	JD	66 Wisconsin	1969
Hahn, Randall L.	Assoc	So Illinois	XA	DBA	84. Kentucky	&1984
Hail, Luzi	Asst	Pennsylvania	F	PHD	96 Zurich	2005

Haining, Hazel E.	Deces	Ferris St	1988	PHD	72.	Nebraska	&1973
Hairrell, Bonnie H.	Retir	Birminghm So	APG	MAC	88	Alabama	&1988
Hajji, Nourredine	Asst	Univ Tunis	AO	EXPC		IHEC	
Haka, Susan F.	Prof	Michigan St	MBI	PHD	83.	Kansas	& 9-82
Ernst & Young Professor of Accounting							
Hakansson, Nils H.	Emer	Cal-Berkeley	2003	PHD	66	UCLA	&1969
Halabi, Abdel K.	Lect	Monash Univ	FE	MACC			1990
Hale, Dennis P.	Retir	Auburn	1985	MA	49	Peabody	9-57
Hale, Elton B.		Hale Oil Co		PHD	48.	Tx-Austin	
Hale, Jack A.			MS	PHD	75.	Cincinnati	&
Hale, Larzette G.	Retir	Utah State	1992	PHD	55.	Wisconsin	& 9-90
163 E 100 N; Logan UT 84321							
Hales, Jeffrey W.	Asst	Texas-Austin	BF	PHD	03.	Cornell	9-02
Hall, Charles				PHD	95.	Columbia	
Hall, Jack O.	Prof	W Kentucky	TRF	PHD	73.	Missouri	&1968
Hall, James A.	Assoc	Lehigh	DS	PHD	80.	Okla St	1979
Hall, Jason	Lect	U Queensland	F	BCOM	96	Queenslnd	1999
Hall, Linda A.	Asst	SUNY-Fredoni	FITV	PHD	99	SUNY-Buf	&2001
Hall, Matthew	Lect	London Econ	BM	PHD			2006
Hall, Sheila H.			BF	PHD	91.	S Carol	&
Hall, Steven C.	C-Ac	Neb-Kearney	CPM	PHD	90	Utah	& 8-01
Hall, Steven D.	Prof	Tx A&M-C Chr	FNGT	EDD	82	N Illinois	& 9-81
Hall, T. P.	Retir	Kennesaw St	1999	MS	58	Ga Tech	&1991
Hall, Thomas W.	Prof	Tx-Arlington	AFB	PHD	80.	Okla St	&1981
Public Accounting Professor							
Hall, W. Clayton	Retir	Illinois Tch	2001	PHD	64	Illinois	1967
Hallam, James A.	Retir	Ill Wesleyan	1998	PHD	65	Iowa	9-88
Hallam, Jolene J.			F	PHD	95.	Missouri	&
Hallbauer, Rosalie C.	Retir	Fla Internat	2006	PHD	73.	Florida	* &1972
Halperin, Robert M.	Retir	Illinois	2005	PHD	77.	Penn	& 8-97
Halsey, Robert F.	Assoc	Babson	F	PHD	97.	Wisconsin	1997
Halterman, John Fredereick	Retir	Cal-S Barbar		PHD	40.	Berkeley	
Halverson, Gaylon L.	Retir	No Iowa	1998	DBA	68.	Indiana	&1963
Hamberg, Mattias	AcII	Norwegian U	F	DREK	00	Uppsala	
Hamburg, Jared M.	Asst	Wichita St	F	ABD		Wash St	2007
Hamby, William L.			CDMS	PHD	92.	Alabama	
Hamdallah, Ahmed El-Sayed			FM	PHD	85.	Baruch	
Hameleers, Michel	Asst	Tilburg Univ	F	MBA	86	Tilburg	&1993
Hamer, John G.	Assoc	Mass-Lowell	FM	PHD	84.	Tx A&M	1982
Hamer, Michelle M.			FMTV	PHD	80.	Wisconsin	*
Hamill, James R.	C-Pr	New Mexico	X	PHD	87.	Ariz St	&1993
KPMG Professor of Accounting							
Hamill, Robert P.	Prof	Indiana Wes	PL	PHD	03	Ind St	&
Hamilton, Austin L.			1992	PHD	69.	Missouri	&
HC61 Box 57; Coleman OK 73432							
Hamilton, Charles T.	Assoc	Illinois Tch	AMF	PHD	87.	Illinois	&1991
Hamilton, Marshall L.			FA	PHD	74.	Ariz St	&
Hamilton, Robert E.			2007	DBA	75.	S Calif	&
6656 Baker Rd; Sommerville OH 45064; 513-726-7845; polygony@fuse.net							
Hamilton, Stewart	Prof	Intl Mgt Dev	IMF	MA	66	Edinburgh	&1985
Hamlen, Susan S.	C-Ac	SUNY-Buffalo	FMYV	PHD	73.	Purdue	* 1973
Hamm, Jeffrey L.	Assoc	Ark-Ltl Rock	FVX	PHD	95.	Tx Tech	& 7-00
Hammad, Ahmed Hany			1991	PHD	83.	North Tx	
Box 228 Zagazig; Zagazig Egypt							
Hammer, Lawrence H.			XCM	DBA	77.	Indiana	&
Hammer, Seth	Assoc	Towson	FCXB	PHD	93	Pittsburgh	* &1993
Hammersley, Jacqueline S.	Asst	Georgia	AB	PHD	03.	Illinois	& 8-03
Hammett, Ted M.	Assoc	Ark-Monticel	ACGF	DBA	94.	La Tech	&2000
Hammond, Michael	Inst	Missouri St	M	MACC	02	Mo St	8-02
Hammond, Theresa A.	Assoc	Boston Coll	BWJE	PHD	90.	Wisconsin	* 1990
Ernst and Young Research Fellow in Diversity Studies							
Hammond, W. Rogers	Retir	Georgia St	1982	DBA	54.	Indiana	& 6-56
Hammond, William A.	Retir	So Colorado	1987	MBA	56	Denver	1957
Hammons, Albert	Asst	Ark-Pine Blf	FV	MBA	76	Michigan	&1986
Hamood, Roger B.	C-Ac	Shepherd	CXVP	MBA	72	Marshall	&1978
Hampton, Jenny	Asst	LaGrange	ALV	JD	93	Chicago	&2000
Hampton, Joseph E.	Deces	American U		PHD	57.	Ohio St	& 9-61
Hampton, Lindsay F.	SLect	Canterbury	GJL	SJD	95	Wisconsin	1968
Hampton, Marcye S.	Inst	Cen Florida	F	MBA	96	Cen Fla	& 8-04
Hamre, James C.	Retir	Wisconsin	MSPC	PHD	71.	Wisconsin	&1972
Han, Bong-Heui	Assoc	Ajou Univ	FM	PHD	91.	Tx-Austin	&1995
Han, Ingoo	Prof	Korea Adv In	SMF	PHD	90.	Illinois	* &1992
Han, Jerry C. Y.			FMIT	PHD	86.	SUNY-Buf	&
Han, Jin-Soo	Prof	Dongguk U	SF	PHD	86.	Indiana	9-86
Han, Jongsoo	Asst	Rutgers-Camd	BAS	PHD	01.	Pittsburgh	2000
Han, Jun	Asst	Un Hong Kong	FMB	PHD	05	NTU	2005
Han, L.	Lect	Univ Hull	F	PHD	05	Warwick	8-04

Han, Soongsoo	Asst	Signapore Mg		PHD	06.	Illinois	2006
Hanbery, Glyn W.	Prof	Denver	FA	PHD	71.	Ariz St	&1973
Hand, John R. M.	Prof	No Carolina	F	PHD	87.	Chicago	9-93

The H. Allen Andrew Distinguished Professor of Entrepreneurial Education

Handlang, Alice		S Christian	CMSJ	DBA	91.	Kentucky	&

Southern Christian Univ; Montgomery AL; alicehandland@southernchristian.edu

Handley-Schachler, Ian Morri	Lect	Napier Univ		DPHL			1999
Handy, Charles B.	Retir	Iowa State	1992	PHD	70	Iowa St	&1958
Handy, Sheila	Asst	Lafayette	PEX	PHD	01	NYU	&1996
Haniffa, Roszaini M.	Lect	Univ Exeter	FI	PHD	99	Exeter	1999
Hankins, Kenneth P.	Retir	Youngstown	1996	PHD	70.	Arkansas	& 9-78
Hankins, Robert W.		SW Texas St	1992	PHD	85.	N Carol	

Dept of Health Adm; Southwest Texas St Univ; San Marcos TX 78666

Hanks, George F.	Retir	Ball State	2000	DBA	74.	Kentucky	* &9-74
Hanley, Philip M.	Inst	So Indiana	FP	MSA	69	Illinois	&2005
Hanlon, Michelle	Assoc	Michigan	FX	PHD	03.	U Wash	2002
Hann, Rebecca N.	Asst	So Calif	F	PHD	00.	Penn	2002
Hanna, J. Douglas	Assoc	So Methodist	FKQ	PHD	91.	Cornell	* &2004
Hanna, John R.	Retir	Un Waterloo	1996	PHD	71.	Michigan	&1980
Hanna, Richard B.	Retir	Ferris State	2001	MS	75	Cen Mich	&1981
Hannah, Gwen	Lect	Dundee	INLX	PHD	04	Dundee	2003
Hannan, R. Lynn	Assoc	Georgia St	M	PHD	00.	Pittsburgh	&8-00
Hanni, Kenneth J.	Retir	Utah	1998	JD	62	Utah	&1962
Hanno, Dennis M.			RAT	PHD	90	Mass	&
Hanouille, Leon J.	Asst	Syracuse	FAS	PHD	83	Syracuse	& 9-78
Hanratty, John J.	Retir	LaSalle	1995	EDD	74	Temple	& 9-67
Hansa, John J.			BM	PHD	94.	Illinois	
Hansen, Don R.	H-Pr	Oklahoma St	CM	PHD	77.	Arizona	* 1989

Kerr-McGee Professor

Hansen, Gary W.	Assoc	Brigham Yg	S	PHD	74	Indiana	9-83
Hansen, Glen A.			F	PHD	97.	Rochester	
Hansen, James	Asst	Ill-Chicago	F	PHD	04.	Georgia	2004
Hansen, James D.	Assoc	Mn-Moorhead	AP	PHD	93.	Nebraska	&2002
Hansen, James V.	Prof	Brigham Yg	S	PHD	73	U Wash	9-82
Hansen, Kathryn A.	Assoc	CS-L Angeles	FMG	PHD	96	Geo Wash	9-98
Hansen, Kenneth A.	Prof	North Dakota	LX	LLM	89	DePaul	& 9-91
Hansen, Robert E.	Retir	W Kentucky	1994	DBA	68.	Indiana	&1988
Hansen, Stephen C.	Asst	George Wash	M	PHD	88.	Car Mellon	2002
Hanson, Donald T.	C-Ac	Merrimack	JFCR	MBA	70	Northeas	&1970
Hanson, Ernest I.	Retir	Wisconsin	8-02	DBA	63.	Mich St	& 9-65
Hanson, Richard O.	Prof	So New Hamp	FUM	PHD		Nova SE	* & 9-83
Hanson, Scott	Asst	Dickinson St	ACFM	MACC	85	Georgia	& 8-02
Hanwell, Jerry W.	Assoc	Robt Morris	GX	JD	90	Duquesne	# * & 9-82
Hao, H. T.	Lect	McMaster Un	FM	ABD		SUNY-Buf	7-99
Haque, M. Shamsul	Retir	Howard	2002	PHD	67.	American	& 9-71
Harbecke, Paula Ann	Dir	MarylandAsia	1994	PHD	83.	Illinois	& 8-83

Univ of Maryland; Asian Division; APO NY 96328

Hardcastle, Rodney	Prof	Pacific Unio	OFAX	MBA	89	Golden Gt	&1989
Harden, J. William	Assoc	N Car-Greens	FX	PHD	97.	Kentucky	& 8-98
Harder, Wesley E.	Retir	CS-Chico	2004	PHD	73.	Ariz St	& 9-68
Hardin, J. Russell	C-Pr	So Alabama	XF	PHD	95.	Miss	&2007
Harding, Noel	SLect	New So Wales	A	MCOM	95	NS Wales	1994
Hardman, O. Clyde	Prof	CS-Fullerton	XFC	PHD	74.	Illinois	&1974
Hardy, John W.	Retir	Brigham Yg	2000	PHD	72.	Tx-Austin	&1969
Hardy, Leslie	ALect	Monash Univ	IFE	GRAD			1995
Hardy, Martine	ALect	Univ Sydney	BFJT	BCOM	98	Newcastle	2002
Hargadon, Joseph M.	H-Ac	Widener	VITF	PHD	93.	Drexel	* &1981
Haried, Andrew A.	Retir	Arizona St	1994	PHD	70.	Illinois	&1969
Harjo, Yvette	Prof	East Central	CLP	JD	84	Oklahoma	& 9-84
Harkins, Jeffrey L.	Assoc	Idaho	FT	PHD	80.	U Wash	&1983
Harkness, Michael D.	C-Ac	Mich-Dearbrn	SX	PHD	99.	S Fla	& 8-97
Harlan, Leonard M.				DBA	65.	Harvard	
Harlan, Neil Eugene				DBA	56.	Harvard	
Harline, N. Lavar	Assoc	Utah	X	PHD	82.	Nebraska	&1982
Harmelink, Philip J.	C-Pr	New Orleans	X	PHD	72.	Iowa	&1979

Ernst & Young Professor of Accounting

Harmon, Coby	Lect	Cal-Santa Br	VGFS	BA	82	Ca-SnBarb	&1988
Harmon, Michael R.	Assoc	Indiana St	LXR	JD	77	Indiana	& 7-86
Harmon, W. Ken	C-Pr	Kennesaw St	SA	DBA	82.	Tennessee	&
Harms, Bruce L.	SLect	Wisconsin	LX	JD	75	Wisconsin	&1975
Harned, W. Wallace	Retir	San Diego St	1978	PHD	64.	UCLA	1962
Harold, Linda	Lect	Univ Otago	EFW	MMS		Waikato	2006
Harper, Ashley B.	Inst	SE Louisiana	FM	MS	01	LSU	& 8-02
Harper, Betty S.	Assoc	Mid Tenn St	P	EDD	76	Miss St	&1982
Harper, James C.	Retir	Nev-L Vegas	1988	PHD	75.	Utah	&

5020 Pacific Grove Drive; Las Vegas NV 89130

Harper, Phil	Assoc	Mid Tenn St	XF	JD	70	Nashvil	&1966

Harper, Robert M. Jr.	Prof	CS-Fresno	PSFM	DBA	84.	Fla St	1-90
Harper, Thomas R.		Dallas TX	1992	PHD	74.	Tx-Austin	&
8906 Forest Hills; Dallas TX 75218							
Harr, David J.	Asst	George Mason	FMN	PHD	78.	Wisconsin	&1997
Associate Dean							
Harrast, Steven A.	Asst	No Iowa	S	PHD	99	Memphis	&2003
Harrell, Adrian M.	Emer	So Carolina	2005	PHD	75.	Tx-Austin	&1980
Harrell, Horace W. Jr.	Retir	Geo Southern	2002	PHD	76.	Georgia	&1972
Harrigan, Fiona	Lect	Un Cl Dublin					2001
Harrington, Jeannie D.	Assoc	Mid Tenn St	FM	PHD	95.	Kentucky	* &1988
Harrington, Kirstin		SW Adventist		PHD	03.	Nebraska	
SW Adventist; Keene, TX							
Harrington, Robert P.			FA	PHD	86.	Va Tech	&
Harrington, Stephen	Assoc	Dominican	F	JD	86	Notre Dm	
Harris, Cathryn A.	LectB	Adelaide	F	DAC		Flinders	1988
Harris, Cindy K.	Assoc	Ursinus	FMAP	MBA		Penn	&1984
Harris, David G.	Assoc	Syracuse	X	PHD	94.	Michigan	& 8-99
Harris, Ellen			MSC	PHD	91.	Utah	
Harris, Iris	Asst	S Nazarene	PCMJ	MBA	92	Cen Okla	&1982
Harris, Jean E.	Assoc	Penn St-Harr	GXHW	PHD	90.	Va Tech	&1990
Harris, John K.	Retir	Tulsa	1997	PHD	70.	Arkansas	& 9-75
Harris, Judith A.	Assoc	Nova SE	FMC	DBA	88.	Boston U	*
Harris, Lebrone C.	Retir	South Fla	2002	DBA	70.	Fla St	& 9-70
Harris, Michael	Prof	St Edwards	FMS	PHD	98	Tx-Austin	&1997
Harris, Peter	Assoc	NY Inst Tech	X	MBA		Columbia	&
Harris, Richard W.	Prof	Grand Valley	X	LLM	90	Geotown	&1995
L. William Seidman Professor of Accounting							
Harris, Ruth C.	Retir	Virg Union	5-97	EDD	77	Wm&Mary	& 9-49
Harris, Thomas D.	Asst	Indiana St	TFXP	PHD	89.	S Carol	& 7-88
Harris, Trevor S.			FIM	PHD	83.	U Wash	&
Harris, Wm. Thomas Jr.	Retir	Midwest St	2004	PHD	75.	LSU	* & 9-93
Harrison, David S.	Assoc	So Car-Aiken	PFC	PHD	98.	Va Tech	8-97
Harrison, Graeme L.	Prof	Macquarie Un	MI	PHD	90	Macquarie	&1974
Harrison, James J.	Assoc	St Peters	IJL	JD		Seton Hall	1976
Harrison, Keith E.	Assoc	Truman State	APS	PHD	99.	Kansas	&1987
Harrison, Kenneth E.				PHD	83.	Tx-Austin	&
Harrison, Lincoln J.	Deces	Southern U		PHD	53.	Ohio St	
Harrison, Patricia M.	Deces	New Orleans	D-92	PHD	91	N Orleans	&1975
Harrison, Paul D.	Prof	Wichita St	CM	PHD	82.	Ariz St	2000
H. Dene Heskett Chair in Accounting							
Harrison, Walter T. Jr.	Retir	Baylor	2005	PHD	76.	Mich St	& 9-85
Harsha, Phillip D.	Assoc	Missouri St	MCSO	PHD	83	Geo St	# 8-89
Harston, Mary E.			AEHN	PHD	91.	North Tx	&
Hart, Dennis	Assoc	Australian N	DS	PHD			2001
Harter, Charles I.	D-Pr	Geo Southern	FPT	PHD	91.	Nebraska	&2006
Hartgraves, Al L.	Prof	Emory	FM	PHD	75.	Geo St	* &1980
Hartl, Robert J.	C-Ac	St Scholasti	BM	MA	90	St Schol	8-01
Hartley, Carol A.	Asst	Providence	AFT	MBA		Rhode Isl	&1980
Hartley, Ronald V.	Retir	Bowling Gr	1998	PHD	67.	Illinois	1965
Hartman, Bart P.	Retir	St Joseph	2007	PHD	75.	Kentucky	* &1996
Hartman, Charles	Assoc	Cedarville	LX	JD	97	Dayton	1989
Hartman, Randall	Prof	Methodist	AFGS	JD	93	Widener	&1997
Hartman, Robert J.	Lect	Iowa	F	MAC	98	Iowa	& 8-99
Hartnett, Neil A.	Lect	U Newcastle	CFM	MCOM	91	Newcastle	&1986
Hartono, Jogiyanto		Gadgahmada U		PHD	97.	Temple	
Hartwell, Carolyn L.	Assoc	Wright State	FTS	PHD	93.	Cincinnati	& 9-01
Hartz-Hanssen, Petter	SLect	Norwegian U	X				
Harvey, Barron H.	Dean	Howard	FC	PHD	77	Nebraska	&1982
Harvey, David	H-Pr	So Queenslnd	AFMP	PHD	88	Bath	&2000
Harvey, David W.	Assoc	Georgia	FMTV	PHD	72.	Minnesota	* & 8-03
Harvey, Joann P.	Prof	Ohio Wesley	XFV	MBA	82	Ohio St	&1981
Harvey, Maryellen	Assoc	Ramapo	CIT	PHD	01	Nova SE	1993
Harvey, Patrick J.	AdjAc	Hong Kong Sc	BAX	PHD	94.	S Calif	&2000
Harvey, Samuel	Lect	Howard		JD	83	Geotown	2002
Harwell, Jeff L.	Asst	Sam Houston	FGVE	MBA	77	Tx A&M	& 9-81
Harwood, Dale S. Jr.			MS	DBA	57.	U Wash	
Harwood, Elaine			2004	PHD	93.	S Calif	&
Cornerstone Research							
Harwood, Gordon B.	Retir	Georgia St	CMBX	PHD	73.	Houston	& 9-72
Haselkorn, Michael	Assoc	Bentley	MF	PHD	81.	Chicago	1974
Haseman, Wilber C.	Retir	Missouri	1985	PHD	55	Syracuse	1960
Haskin, Daniel L.	Prof	Central Okla	FU	PHD	82.	Tx Tech	& 8-93
Haskins, Mark E.	Prof	Virg-Grad	IFMB	PHD	84.	Penn St	&1984
Haslam, James	Prof	Dundee	HGTW	PHD	92	Essex	&2004
Hass, Susan W.	Prof	Simmons	FM	MBA	75	Harvard	&1980
HassabElnaby, Hassan R.	Asst	Toledo	FI	PHD	98	Cairo U	&2003
Hassan, Abbas Shafie				PHD	65.	Wisconsin	

Hassan, Mahamood M.	Prof	CS-Fullerton	CF	PHD	89	Arizona		&2-90
Hassan, Nabil	Retir	Wright State	1995	PHD	69.	Alabama		1980
Hasseini, Ahmad	Lect	Santa Clara	FM	PHD	81	Missouri		&2007
Hassel, Lars G.	C-Pr	Univ of Umea	BCMI	PHD	92	Abo		7-98
Hasselback, James R.	Prof	West Florida	X	PHD	76.	Mich St		8-06
Mary Ball Washington Eminent Scholar								
Hasseldine, D. John	SLect	U Nottingham	XB	PHD	97.	Indiana		&1997
Hassell, John M.	Prof	Indiana-Indy	FBE	PHD	83.	Indiana		&8-96
OneAmerica Chair								
Hassey, Jum'a El		Libya		PHD	80.	Oklahoma		
Hassink, Harold	Prof	Maastricht	AFOU	PHD	01	Maastricht		&1990
Hassler, Eugene C.	Retir	West Chester	1993	MBA	54	Indiana		&9-69
Hasson, Naim	Assoc	Sultan Qaboo	M	PHD		Birminghm		1999
Hassouna, Fedhila		Tunisia	1995	PHD	90.	Colorado		
Haswell, Stephen	SLect	Macquarie Un	F	MEC	90	ANU		&2001
Hatanaka, Robert K.	Inst	Hawaii-Manoa	FA	MACC	83	Hawaii		&8-04
Hatcher, John W.	Asst	Purdue	XFR	MBA	62	Chicago		&1982
Hatfield, Richard C.	Asst	Alabama	XA	PHD	98.	Florida		&8-06
Hatheway-Dial, K. D.	Inst	Idaho	AFM	MACC		Idaho		2003
Hathorn, John M.	Asst	Metro State	FC	PHD	00.	Kent St		&8-04
Haugen, John D.	Asst	Wartburg	AFG	MS	73	N Dakota		&1979
Haugen, Susan D.	Retir	Wis-Eau Clar	2006	EDD	82	Okla St	# *	8-85
Haugland, Jerry L.	Retir	SE Missouri	2001	PHD	75.	Okla St	*	1966
Hauser, Rexford C.	Retir	SW Louisiana	1994	DBA	65	Harvard		1957
Hausman, Thomas	VAsst	Akron	X	LLM	76	NYU		9-06
Haven, Emmanuel	Asst	Univ Essex	PQ	PHD	01	Montrael		1999
Haverly, Frederick S.	Retir	Western St	1998	MBA	66	Syracuse		&1977
Haverty, John L.	Assoc	St Joseph	FMU	PHD	86	Temple		&1976
Havranek, Susan F.	Asst	LeMoyne	F	PHD	07	Ariz St		9-06
Haw, In-Mu G.	Prof	Tx Christian	FM	PHD	83.	Alabama		1990
Hawat, Prachit	Asst	Chulalongkor	ADQS	PHD	98	Calgary		&1986
Hawkes, L. C.	Lect	Massey Univ	JMW	MBS		Massey		1987
Hawkins, Charles E.	Retir	NW Missouri	1994	PHD	83.	Nebraska		&1975
Hawkins, David F.	Prof	Harvard	F	DBA	62.	Harvard		1960
Lovett-Learned Professor of Business Administration								
Hawkins, Ennis M.	Prof	Sam Houston	MC	DBA	74.	Tx Tech	# *	&1966
Hawkins, Jean L. G.	C-Pr	Wm Jewell	CTNM	MA	70	Cen Mo St	*	&9-76
Hawkins, Kyleen W.			A	DBA	92.	La Tech		&
Hawthorne, William H.	Retir	Wm & Mary	2004	PHD	74	Tennessee		1976
Hay, David C.	Assoc	U Auckland	FA	PHD	99	Auckland	#	&2000
Hay, Leon E.	Retir	Arkansas	6-93	PHD	54.	Illinois		&1980
Hay, Robert D.	Retir	Arkansas		PHD	54.	Ohio St		
Haydel, Jennifer A.	Inst	New Orleans		MS	03	N Orleans		&2005
Hayes, David C.	Asst	Jms Madison	BS	PHD	02.	S Fla		&8-07
Hayes, David C..		Consultant	M	PHD	75.	Ohio St		
Hayes, Gary W.	Asst	Cen Michigan	CM	DBA	94.	Miss St		&1993
Hayes, Louise	Asst	York-Atkinsn	AFS	MBA	74	Brit Colum		&2000
Hayes, Nancy T.	Assoc	NY Inst Tech	M	MBA		Long Isl		&
Hayes, Rachel M.	Assoc	Chicago	FM	PHD	96.	Stanford		9-00
Hayes, Randall B.	Prof	Cen Michigan	FM	PHD	78.	Michigan		1989
Hayes, Rick S.	Prof	CS-L Angeles	FBA	PHD	89	London		9-90
Hayes, Robert D.	Prof	Tenn State	FM	PHD	86.	Arkansas	*	&1990
Hayes, Ruby G.	Retir	Virginia St	1991	MBA	50	NYU		9-61
Hayes, Ruth		Private Prac		PHD	95.	Tx-Arlin		
Hayes, Thomas P. Jr.	Asst	Ark-Ft Smith	AP	PHD	06.	North Tx		&2006
Hayn, Carla K.	Assoc	UCLA	F	PHD	87.	Michigan		1997
Haynes, Christine M.	Prof	West Georgia	AFMP	PHD	93.	Tx-Austin		8-06
Hays, Charles T.	Prof	W Kentucky	XF	PHD	68.	Missouri		&1963
Hays, Larry L.				PHD	81.	St Louis		
Hays, Laurie	Inst	W Michigan	P	MSA	84	W Mich		&1995
Hays, Rita	Inst	SW Okla St	XFP	MACC	88	Oklahoma		&2004
Hays, Stanley W.	Asst	La St-Shreve	GPVX	DBA	00.	La Tech		&8-02
Hayward, D. R.	Retir	Cy London Pl	1989	MSC				&
Haywood, Dale M.	Deces	Northwood	F	PHD	80	North Tx		1965
Haywood, J. Otis Jr.	Retir	Winston-Sal	1991	PHD	76	Toledo		1970
Haywood-Sullivan, Betsy	Asst	Rider	MS	PHD	01.	Georgia	*	&2001
Hazelton, James C. P.	Lect	Macquarie Un	F	BEC	93	Macquarie		&1993
Hazen, Marinus	Deces	Cedarville	2002	ABD	93	Clev St		&1983
Hazera, Alejandro	Prof	Rhode Island	FIV	DBA	89.	Kentucky		&1989
He, Haihong	Asst	CS-L Angeles	FM	PHD	04.	Conn		9-04
He, Yi-Hong (Daniel)	Asst	Monmouth	FI	DBA	02.	Clev St	*	&2002
Head, Julie	Lect	Indiana	F	BS	82	Indiana		&9-92
Heagy, Cynthia D.	Prof	Houston-Cl L	MS	DBA	87.	Memphis	*	&9-90
Heakel, Mohamed S.	Partn		1994	PHD	68.	Illinois		
McGladrey & Pullen; 1440 Midwest Plz W; 801 Nicollet Av; Minneapolis MN 55402								
Heal, Inez	Retir	Youngstown	F	MBA	76	Youngstwn		&8-77
Heales, Jon	Lect	U Queensland	ADOS	PHD	98	Queensln		&1998

Healy, John C.	Lect	Wis-Milwauke	X	MS	92	Wi-Milwa		&1977
Healy, Patricia	Assoc	Pace-Westch	VC	MBA	75	NYU	*	&1977
Healy, Paul M.	C-Pr	Harvard	FM	PHD	83.	Rochester		&1997
MBA Class '49 Professor of Business Administration								
Healy-Burress, Joanne P.			FM	PHD	94.	SUNY-Buf	*	&
Hearn, Paula S.	Inst	Tenn-Martin	XL	MAC	03	Tennessee		8-04
Heaston, Patrick H.	Prof	Drake	FVT	PHD	82.	Nebraska	'	&1983
Aliber Professor of Accounting								
Heaston, William R.	Deces	Creighton	1989	MA	59	Creighton		&9-58
Heath, Loyd C.	Emer	U Washington	1998	PHD	65.	Berkeley		1962
Heath, Rebekah A.	Asst	Pittsburg St	FM	PHD	99.	Nebraska	#	&2005
Heaviside, Richard	Retir	Coventry Un	2000					9-75
Hebble, Annette	Assoc	St Thomas-TX	MXI	PHD	89.	Houston	*	&8-91
Hebblewhite, W. Marshall	Retir	Wayne State	1976	MA	33	Michigan		1959
Hebert, Marcel G.	Prof	Bryant	FNGC	PHD	87.	Tx Tech	*	&9-79
Hechmi, Abdelwahed	Asst	Univ Tunis	RAV	EXPC		IHEC		
Hecht, Gary W.	Asst	Emory	MB	PHD	05.	Illinois		&9-04
Heck, William Ross	Deces	Florida St	7-05	PHD	60.	LSU		&1959
Hedges, Thomas V.	Retir	So Methodist	1993	DBA	67.	Indiana		&1974
Hedley, Timothy P.		KPMG	2003	PHD	95	SUNY-Alb		&
KPMG Forensic Services; 1345 6th Ave; NY NY 10105; 202-872-3496								
Heely, James	Retir	Monmouth	2004	MBA	89	Fairl Dick		&1987
Heerema, Douglas L.	Retir	Indiana-Indy	2002	PHD	66	Iowa		&1979
Heesacker, Gary W.	Prof	Central Wash	FAJ	MBA	69	U Wash		&9-72
Heflin, Frank L.	Assoc	Florida St	F	PHD	92.	Purdue		8-05
Hefzi, Hassan	C-Pr	CS-Pomona	FVM	PHD	88.	Ariz St		&9-98
Mickey & Lee Segal Faculty Fellow								
Hegazy, Mohamed Abbas				PHD	65.	Wisconsin		
Hegstad, Larry P.	Retir	Pacific Luth	MF	PHD	78.	U Wash		1979
Hehre, Robert J.	Retir	Bryant	7-92	DBA	68	Indiana		&8-85
Meadowview; Rt 5 Box 427; Lexington VA 24450								
Heian, James B.	Assoc	Utica	AFS	PHD	85.	Utah		&2003
Heier, Jan Richard	Assoc	Auburn-Montg	MHC	DBA	86.	Miss St		&1986
Heimann, Stephen R.		Battelle Res	C	PHD	72.	Ohio St		
Heimbach, Raymond O.	Retir	Kutztown	2007	MBA		Temple		1970
Hein, Cheryl D.	Deces	Tx A&M-C Chr	2001	PHD	83.	Arkansas		9-83
Hein, Leonard W.	Retir	CS-L Angeles	1983	PHD	62.	UCLA		&1956
1225 N Granada #33; Alhambra CA 91801								
Heintz, James A.	D-Pr	Kansas	AF	DBA	72.	Wash U		&1998
Deloitte & Touche Faculty Fellow								
Heisz, Mary A.	Lect	West Ontario	F	MBA	02	W Ontario		&7-90
Heitger, Dan L.	Assoc	Miami U-Ohio	M	PHD	00.	Mich St		8-04
Heitger, Lester E.	Prof	Indiana	M	PHD	72.	Mich St		&1972
Heitzman, Shane M.	Asst	Rochester	FX	PHD	06.	Arizona		&2006
Hekimian, James S.			1990	DBA	63.	Harvard		
141 Rutledge Rd; Belmont MA 02178								
Helal, Samir Riad A. B.		Tanta U Egyp	1988	PHD	83.	Illinois		
Helfert, Erich A.				DBA	58.	Harvard		
Helleloid, Richard T.			XB	PHD	84.	Minnesota		&
Heller, Kenneth H.	Prof	George Mason	FX	PHD	77.	Tx-Austin		&7-87
Helliar, Christine V.	Prof	Dundee	ACFK	PHD	99	Dundee		&1990
Hellman, Niclas		Stockholm Ec	V	CE	90	Sundsvall		1990
Hellstrom, Katerina		Stockholm Ec	F	CE	97	Stockholm		1997
Helluin, Stella B.	Inst	SE Louisiana	FM	MBA	90	Houston		&8-93
Helmi, Medhat A.	Retir	Alabama-Birm	2000	PHD	76.	Illinois	*	1976
Helmkamp, John G.	Retir	Indiana-Indy	2002	DBA	68.	Indiana		&1973
Helms, Glenn L.	Prof	Elon	AF	PHD	84.	Houston	#	&2006
Helmuth, John A.	Dean	Mich-Flint	FIX	PHD	81	S Carol		7-07
Helquist, Joel H.	Asst	Utah Valley	SF	PHD	07	Arizona		&2007
Heltzer, Wendy	Asst	DePaul	FPQ	PHD	06	Chicago		2007
Helvey, Aubree L.	Asst	Cameron	LJ	JD	02	Oklahoma		&2002
Hemingway, James R.	Retir	S F Austin	F	PHD	79.	North Tx		&
Hemingway, Linda J.	C-Ac	Athens State	EGT	MACC	84	N Mex St		&9-91
Hemmer, Thomas	Prof	Houston	M	PHD	90	Odense		9-05
Charles McMahen Chair								
Henage, Richard T.	Assoc	Utah Valley	FS	PHD	95.	Utah		&2001
Henaidy, Hamid M.				PHD	80.	Missouri		
Henderson, B. Charlene	Asst	Arkansas	XF	PHD	96.	Ariz St		&2005
BKD Lecturer								
Henderson, Brian	Lect	U Nottingham	F	BA	97	Derby		2001
Henderson, James	Assoc	Golden Gate	XL	JD	81	San Fran		&1988
Henderson, James R.	Assoc	So Miss	FC	PHD	80.	Tx A&M		&1988
Henderson, James Y.		NS Wales Flm		PHD	72.	Berkeley		
Henderson, John W.	Retir	Georgia St	1994	MPA	73	Syracuse		1-81
Henderson, Linda R.	C-Ac	Coast Carol	FXIV	DBA	89.	La Tech		&1986
Henderson, M. Scott	Retir	Adelaide	2003	PHD	69.	UCLA		&1979
Henderson, Michele C.	C-As	Queens-Charl	ABM	PHD	98.	Georgia		&2002

Henderson, Porter W. Jr.	Deces	No Texas St	1973	PHD	63.	Tx-Austin	1959
Henderson, Robert F.	Retir	San Fran St	1991	JD	52	Berkeley	&1967
Hendricks, Ann	Asst	Wis-La Cross	AF	PHD	99.	Nebraska	# * &8-02
Hendricks, Arthur G.	Retir	Houston-ClLk	2001	PHD	77.	Houston	&1982
12589 Via Ravenna; Boynton Beach FL 33436; www.hendrickscpa.com							
Hendricks, James A.	Retir	No Illinois	5-99	PHD	74.	Illinois	&1-74
Hendrickson, Harvey S.	Deces	Fla Internat	2001	PHD	63.	Minnesota	&1972
Hendriksen, Eldon S.	Retir	Santa Clara	1983	PHD	56.	Berkeley	&1980
10510 Deodara Drive; Cupertino CA 95014							
Hendrix, Lynne	Assoc	Hope	A	MBA		Gr Valley	&1985
Hengel, H. G. (Hugo)	Asst	Vrije Univ	BGN	MS			2005
Heninger, William G.	Asst	Brigham Yg	S	PHD	97.	Georgia	&7-01
Henke, Emerson O.	Retir	Baylor	1991	DBA	53.	Indiana	&1948
Hennessee, Patrick A.	Prof	Tulsa	XPE	PHD	77.	North Tx	&7-81
Hennessey, John W.	Prov	Vermont		PHD	56.	U Wash	
Henney, Michele C.	Inst	Oregon	AFX	PHD	94.	Oregon	&2004
Hennig, Cherie J.	Prof	Fla Internat	X	PHD	80.	Colorado	&2005
Henning, Steven L.			FIT	PHD	94.	Wisconsin	&
Henri, Jean-Francois	Prof	Univ Laval		PHD	03	HEC-Mont	1999
Henrickson, Donald R.	Retir	St Norbert	1999	MBA	68	W Mich	&1972
Henry, Byron K.	Asst	Howard	FMG	PHD	99.	Tx A&M	&1997
Henry, Elaine R.	Asst	U Miami	F	PHD	05.	Rutgers	2005
Henry, Eleanor G.	Assoc	SE Missouri	CFMV	PHD	94.	St Louis	2002
Henry, Kenneth	VLect	Fla Internat	AFGS	MA	94	Fla Intl	&2000
Henry, Laurie J.	Assoc	Old Dominion	SFBG	PHD	93.	Miss	&1993
Henry, Linvol G.	Prof	CS-San Bern	FCX	MS	73	Long Isl	&9-85
Henry, Matthew R.	C-Ac	Ark-Pine Blf	VA	MBA	65	Atlanta	&1968
Henry, Theresa	Asst	Seton Hall	FP	PHD	03.	NYU	&1-03
Henschel, Don	Inst	Benedictn-IL		MBA		Chicago	&9-02
Hensler, Emil J. Jr.	Retir	Seton Hall	1992	MBA	66	Seton Hall	&1960
Hensley, Sanoa J.	Retir	Tx Christian	CM	MBA	68	So Meth	&1968
Hensold, Harold H.	Retir	Ill-Chicago	1991	BS	43	Illinois	&9-82
Henson, Sheri	Inst	W Kentucky	PC	MPA	98	Wstrn Ky	&8-01
Henton, Michael C.	Inst	Portland St	FP	MBA	73	Oregon	&1979
Hepp, John			F	PHD	04.	Wisconsin	
Hepworth, Samuel R.	Deces			PHD	54.	Michigan	
Her, Young-Won	Asst	Mo-St Louis	MB	PHD	06.	S Carol	2006
Herath, Hemantha	Assoc	Brock Univ		PHD		Auburn	
Herauf, Darrell	Inst	Carleton Un	F	BCOM	76	Alberta	&1985
Herbert, Leo	Deces	Va Tech	8-96	PHD	44.	LSU	&1975
Herbohn, Kathleen	Lect	U Queensland	FB	BCOM	93	Jms Cook	2001
Herbold, Joshua	Asst	Montana	FAP	PHD	05.	Illinois	&2004
Herbold, Marita I.	VAsst	SUNY Old Wes	VCPD	JD	98	Touro	&1995
Hereth, Russell H.	Retir	Wright State	2004	MBA	65	Miami U	&1-78
Herhold, Susan Baskin			1990	PHD	84.	Syracuse	
6 Glassford Lane; Durham NH 03824							
Herin, John S.	Retir	So Carolina	1988	MS	48	S Carol	&1946
Hermanson, Dana R.	Prof	Kennesaw St	AOME	PHD	93.	Wisconsin	1993
Dinos Eminent Scholar Chair of Private Enterprise							
Hermanson, Heather M.			FAB	PHD	93.	Wisconsin	
Hermanson, Roger H.	Retir	Georgia St	3-97	PHD	63.	Mich St	&7-73
Hernandez, Digna	Assoc	Puerto RicoM	CEMP	MBA	78	Florida	1-76
Heroux, Sylvie	Prof	Quebec-Montr		PHD		Quebec	
Herremans, Irene M.	Assoc	Univ Calgary	BIJM	PHD	89.	Kent St	&9-89
Herrera, Bravo Fernando		Santiago Chl	1992	PHD	77.	UCLA	
Diagonal Paraguay; 257 Torre 26 Oficinia; 1801 Santiago Chile							
Herrick, Theodore Pomeroy	Deces	Oklahoma		PHD	59.	Ohio St	&1958
Herrin, Glen Willis				PHD	65.	Alabama	
Herring, Clyde E.	D-Ac$	Miss State	FT	PHD	88.	Alabama	&1986
Bill Simmons Teaching Fellow							
Herring, Dora Rose	Retir	Miss State	1994	DBA	68.	Miss St	&9-64
Herring, Hartwell C. III	Retir	Utica	FGE	PHD	74.	Alabama	&2000
Herring, Nancy A.	Assoc	Oglethorpe	F	PHD	83.	Geo St	&2006
Herrmann, Donald R.	Assoc	Oklahoma St	AF	PHD	95.	Okla St	&7-05
Herron, Terri L.	C-Pr	Montana	AS	PHD	96.	Tx-Arlin	&1996
Hershberger, Melissa	Lect	N Car-Greens	F	MBA	05	Duke	8-05
Hertenstein, Julie H.	Assoc	Northeastern	FMB	DBA	84.	Harvard	9-92
Hertz, Daniel G.	Retir	Montana St	2002	EDD	72	Mont St	9-72
Hertzfeld, Patricia A.	Retir	Nichols Col	PX	MSAC	78	Mass	&1979
Herz, Paul J.	Assoc	Fort Lewis	EFV	PHD	94.	Utah	&2004
Herzlinger, Regina E.	Prof	Harvard		DBA	71.	Harvard	1971
General Management Dept; 617-495-6646; rherzlinger@hbs.edu							
Hesford, James W.	Asst	Cornell-Hotl	B	PHD	98.	S Calif	* 2004
Heslop, Gordon B.	Asst	Tx A&M-Comm	CM	DBA	86.	Miss St	*
Heslop, J.	Sen	Massey-Welli	NMWF	MBS		Massey	1999
Hess, David	Asst	Robt Morris	FXRA	MBA		Ohio St	&9-84
Hevas, Dimosthenis	Asst	Athens Univ	FT	PHD	85	Wales	1987

Hewitt, Leroy A.	Retir	Portland St	1978	PHD	68.	Minnesota		&1958
Hewitt, Max	Asst	Indiana	F	PHD	07	U Wash		&2007
Hibbets, Aleecia R.	Asst	La-Monroe	AM	PHD	06.	Alabama		&2003
Hibbitts, Wanda B.	Retir	So Indiana	1987	PHD	84	S Illinois		&1970
Hickerson, Truman O. Jr.	Retir	CS-Long Bch	1993	MBA	64	UCLA		&1965
Hickman, Charles	Asst	Alabama-Hunt		LLM	89	Mo-Ks Cty		2006
Hicks, Barry E.	Retir	Laurentian	1996	PHD	68.	Illinois		& 7-75
Hicks, Donald W.	Assoc	Chris Newpor	FTW	PHD	78.	Mich St		&1990
Hicks, Elizabeth	Asst	Mt St Vincen	FXWJ	MBA	94	StMry-Cd		& 9-85
Hicks, Ernest L.	Retir	Ohio State	1988	BS	39	Ohio St		& 9-78
Hicks, Harry E.	Prof	Butler	AXLJ	JD	79	Indiana		&1974
Hicks, James O. Jr.	Prof	Virg Tech	SDCM	PHD	76.	Geo St	*	1-76
Hicks, James R.	Lect	U Portsmith	EA	DPH				1989
Hicks, Joyce A.	Assoc	St Marys-Ind	VFX	MBA	90	Notre Dm		& 1-91
Hicks, Margaret	Assoc	Howard	CF	DBA	82.	Maryland		&1987
Hicks, Samuel A.	Assoc	Virg Tech	XS	PHD	76.	Wisconsin		&1979
Hicks, Truel D.	Retir	West Alabama	2003	MBA	60	S Miss		& 9-81
Hien, Vu Dinh	Asst	Natl Econ	FMCS	MBA	95	Boise St		1990
Higgins, Huong Ngo	Asst	Worcester Pl	FM	PHD	98.	Geo St		1998
Higgins, J. Warren	Retir	Connecticut	1995	MBA	61	Bucknell		& 9-67
Higgins, Larry	Prof	Rio Grande	AFS	MBA	75	Marshall		& 9-85
Higgins, Leslee N.	Assoc	Geo Southern	SAF	PHD	97	Cincinnati		1998
Higgins, Marie L.	Assoc	Johnson&Wale	PXL	JD	99	N Eng Cl		&2000
Higgins, Mark M.	Dean	Rhode Island	FX	PHD	89.	Tennessee		&1988
Higgs, Julia L.	Assoc	Fla Atlantic		PHD	98.	S Carol		1-98
Highsmith-Quick, Gwendolyn	Assoc	N Carol A&T	SEIR	PHD	88.	Houston		&1980
Higley, Wayne M.	Retir	Buena Vista	2001	PHD	62.	Illinois	*	&1986
Higson, Andrew W.	Lect	Loughborough	MA	PHD	87	Bradford		&1986
Higson, Christopher	Assoc	London Bus	FMT	PHD	93	London		&1986
Hiki, Fumiko	Prof	Hitotsubashi	MC	DBA	07	Hitotsubshi		1998
Hilary, Gilles	Assoc	Hong Kong Sc	FI	PHD	02	Chicago		2002
Hill, A J	Retir	Auburn	1985	MBA	49	Nrthwstrn		9-49
Hill, Alphonse G.	Asst	Howard	F	PHD	80	Union-NY		&1992
Hill, Aretha Y.	Asst	Flordia A&M	OAFB	PHD	01.	Tx A&M		&2002
Hill, Cecil L.	Asst	Jackson St	FS	PHD	02.	JacksonSt		&1995
Hill, Glenn	SLect	LaTrobe Univ	F	BBUS		Swinburn		&1990
Hill, John W.	Prof	Indiana	MCFA	PHD	86.	Iowa		1985
Hill, Mary Callahan	Prof	Kennesaw St	SAB	PHD	93.	Georgia		1997
Hill, Nancy Thorley	Prof	DePaul	MC	PHD	90.	Wisconsin	*	&1990
Hill, Neil F.	Retir	Wilfrid Laur	1995	PHD	84	York	*	&1987
Hill, Paula	Lect	Univ Leeds	FI	PHD	02	Leeds		D-00
Hill, Robert C.	Retir	Old Dominion	1993	DBA	65.	Harvard		1973
Hill, Robert W.			F	PHD	75.	S Calif		&
Hillegeist, Stephen A.	Asst	INSEAD	M	PHD	98.	Berkeley		2005
Hillier, David	Prof	Univ Leeds	FMQ	PHD	00	Strathcl		1-05
Hillier, David .	Lect	Strathclyde	F	BSC	92	Paisley		1998
Hillier, J.	Lect	N Eng-Austr	F	PHD	99	Otago		1999
Hillison, William A.	Prof	Florida St	AS	PHD	77.	Florida	*	& 1-77

Andersen Professor of Accounting

Hillman, A. Douglas	Prof	Drake	PSM	PHD	70.	Missouri	*	1970

Aliber Professor of Accounting

Hilmy, Joseph	Retir	George Wash	FIV	PHD	59	Aberdeen		1973
Hiltebeitel, Kenneth M.	Assoc	Villanova	AEFJ	PHD	85.	Drexel		&1986
Hiltner, Arthur A.	Retir	North Dakota	2005	PHD	75.	Nebraska		& 9-68
Hilton, Andrew (Sandy)	Asst	Univ Alberta	FI	PHD	03	Waterloo		&2002
Hilton, Carol Anne	Retir	Ohio Univ	2002	PHD	83.	Arkansas		1979
Hilton, Ian H.	Retir	U Melbourne	2002	MCOM		Melbourne		&1991
Hilton, Joseph N.	Retir	Ohio Univ	1999	PHD	80.	Arkansas		1979
Hilton, Ronald W.	Prof	Cornell	MQC	PHD	77.	Ohio St		9-77
Himes, Ella R.	Inst	Miami U-Ohio	P	MBA	79	Wright St		& 8-06
Hinds, John E.	Retir	CS-Long Bch	2000	DBA	81.	S Calif		&1981
Hiner, Ronald R.	Prof	West Tx A&M	FM	EDD	73	Okla St		& 9-84
Hines, Charles E. (Chip)	Assoc	W Michigan	F	PHD	79.	Mich St		&1976
Hines, Christopher	Inst	Pittsburg St	FA	MBA	01	Mo St	*	&2006
Hines, Danny Ray	Retir	East Carol	2000	PHD	75.	Florida		& 9-73
Hines, Robert L.	Retir	CS-Humboldt	2002	PHD	78	Ariz St		&1973
Hines, Tony	PLect	U Portsmith	FN	MSC				1986
Hinkelman, Harold I.				PHD	64.	NYU		
Hinrichs, Sue N.	Retir	Pacific	1995	PHD	74.	Santa Cl		&1977
Hinson, Dolan R.	Retir	N Car-Charl	1999	PHD	73	S Carol	*	1973
Hinson, Yvonne L.	Assoc	Wake Forest	PX	PHD	97.	Tennessee		& 9-97

PricewaterhouseCoopers Faculty Fellow; Director of Graduate Studies

Hinton, Joanne	SrTch	New Brunswic		BSC		Guelph		2005
Hintz, Arthur F.	Assoc	St John Fshr	VQF	MBA	76	Indiana		&1979
Hipscher, Aaron	ClPr	New York U	F	MBA	66	Rutgers		&2000
Hira, Labh S.	Dean	Iowa State	FX	PHD	75	Missouri		&1982
Hirojosa, Abel	Retir	Tx-Brownsvil		MBA	70	Houston		&1975

Hiromoto, Toshiro	Prof	Hitotsubashi	MC	DBA	93. Hitotsub	1981
Hirsch, A. Jay	Prof	CS-Fullerton	FM	PHD	62. Illinois	1966
Hirsch, Maurice L. Jr.	Retir	S Ill-Edward	2000	PHD	77. Wash U	1977
Hirst, D. Eric	Prof	Texas-Austin	BF	PHD	92. Minnesota	9-91
Ernst & Young Faculty Fellowship in Accounting						
Hirst, Mark K.	Prof	Austral Grad	M	PHD	87 NS Wales	1992
Hirunrusme, Tharee	Assoc	Chulalongkor	EFS	MS	72 Radford	1973
Hite, Peggy A.	Prof	Indiana	XBE	PHD	86. Colorado	&1988
Hitzig, Neal B.	Prof	CUNY-Queens	AQ	PHD	85. Baruch	&9-00
Hjelstrom, Tomas		Stockholm Ec	F	CE	95 Stockholm	1994
Hlyne, Ma				PHD	63. NYU	
Ho, Chi-Kun	VFell	HongKon Tech	AIJX	DBA	01 HK Poly	2002
Ho, Joanna L.	Prof	Calif-Irvine	FMB	PHD	86. Tx-Austin	* &7-86
Ho, Kathy S.	Assoc	Niagara	MF	PHD	88. Syracuse	9-96
Ho, Li-Chin Jennifer	Assoc	Tx-Arlington	FM	PHD	90. Tx-Austin	1-90
Ho, Mabel	Lect	HongKon Tech	F	MTAX	02 NS Wales	&2004
Ho, Sandra W.	Asst	Concordia U	AFM	PHD	00 HK Poly	&2004
Ho, Susanna	Lect	U Melbourne	DGI	PHD	Hong Kong	2004
Ho, Yew Kee	Asst	Natl Singapo	F	PHD	98. Car Mellon	&1998
Hoa, Nguyen Thi Phoung	Asst	Natl Econ	FAOM	MSC	98 London	1996
Hoagland, Descom D.	Retir	Babson	2002	MBA	63 Babson	&1966
Hobbes, Garry	SLect	Macquarie Un	FQ	PHD	99 UTS	1994
Hobbs, Dave	SLect	U Glamorgan	CM	MBA	94 Strathcl	* 1-91
Hobbs, Ed	Asst	SF Okla St	DXF	MT	90 Denver	&1993
Hobbs, James B.	Retir	Lehigh	1987	DBA	62 Indiana	1966
Hoben, William J.	Retir	Dayton	1992	MBA	60 Xavier	&9-56
Hobson, Jessen	Asst	Florida St		PHD	06. Tx-Austin	8-06
Hobson, L. Scott	Assoc	Brigham Yg	FM	MACC	83 Brighm Yg	&6-03
Hochman, Joel A.	Dean$	Yeshiva	MF	JD	82 Pace	&9-94
Philip H. Cohen Chair in Accounting						
Hock, Clayton A.	Prof	Miami U-Ohio	IF	PHD	74. Penn St	&1-74
Hocken, Mike	Lect	Queensld Tec	F	LLM	94 Queensld	1987
Hockenbury, Robert D.	SInst	Colo-Denver	FMTX	MTX	84 Houston	&6-87
Hocking, Deborah E.	Asst	Shippensburg	CFMA	MBA	98 Frostburg	&2004
Hockman, Kristen	AsTch	Missouri	GA	MACC	00 Missouri	2004
Hodder, Leslie D.	Asst	Indiana	F	PHD	01. Tx-Austin	&2003
Hodgdon, Christopher D.	Asst	Vermont	FM	PHD	04. Va Comm	2005
Hodge, Albert C.	Deces			PHD	22. Chicago	
Hodge, Frank D.	Assoc	U Washington	F	PHD	00. Indiana	2000
Hodge, Thomas G.	Assoc	La-Monroe	FXJ	PHD	91. Miss	# * &1990
John L. Luffey, Sr. Professor of Accounting						
Hodges, John P.	Asst	W Virg St	FCPA	MPA	81 W Virginia	&1984
Hodges, Richard L.	Assoc	W Michigan	NM	PHD	79. Nebraska	&1985
Hodges, Ron	H-Re	U Nottingham	FGN	MBA	91 Nottingh	&1992
Hodges, Stewart D.	Prof	Un Warwick	QMF	PHD	71 London	
Gsmee Fairbairn Professor of Accounting						
Hodgson, Allan	Prof	Griffith Un	FQT	PHD	95 Austr Natl	&1996
Hodieb, Mostafa A.		Cario, Egypt		PHD	85. S Carol	
Hoemberg, Reinhold	Prof	Aachen Univ	AXQ	PHD	73 Muenster	1994
Hoffa, Dara A.	Asst	Westminst-UT	PCMS	MACC	87 Utah St	&1990
Hofferd, Thomas J.			S	PHD	95. Cen Fla	&
Hoffman, Arthur C.			AV	PHD	72. Illinois	&
Hoffman, David E.	Deces	N Carolina	1998	PHD	75. Tx-Austin	& 1-75
Hoffman, MaryAnn		Andreus U		PHD	02. Ariz St	
Hoffman, Michael J. R.	Prof	Nova SE	X	DBA	83. Indiana	2007
Hoffman, Vicky B.	C-Ac	Pittsburgh	BAF	PHD	88. Michigan	&1988
Hoffman, William H.	Retir	Houston	2001	PHD	60. Tx-Austin	&1967
Hoffmans, Sharron R.	Retir	Txs-El Paso	2000	PHD	91. Okla St	&9-74
Hofmann, Mary Ann	Asst	Appalach St	FX	PHD	02. Ariz St	* &2006
Hofstedt, Thomas R.			FM	PHD	70. Stanford	
Hogan, Chris E.	Assoc	Michigan St	AF	PHD	94. Ohio St	&2006
Hogan, John	Asst	Aquinas	CS	MBA	00 Gr Valley	2002
Hogan, Thomas J.	Assoc	Mass-Boston	FA	PHD	86. Mass	&1992
Hohl, Katherine J.		Phillips Oil		PHD	77. Okla St	&1978
Hoitash, Rani	Asst	Bentley	AS	PHD	03. Rutgers	# 8-07
Holder, Dan	AdjLe	Illinois	X	JD	79 Loyola	8-06
Holder, William W.	Prof	So Calif	NGFA	DBA	74. Oklahoma	&1979
Ernst & Young Professor						
Holder-Webb, Lori L.	Asst	Wisconsin	F	PHD	02. Tx A&M	2002
Holdren, George C.	Retir		1995	PHD	61. Nebraska	&
Holifield, Suzanne M.				PHD	95. Ohio St	
Holland, Alexander	Inst	Metro State	P	MS	77 Colorado	&8-04
Holland, John B.	Prof	Univ Glasgow	IM	PHD	78 CNAA	1979
Holland, Michael L.	Prof	Valdosta St	XF	PHD	78. Georgia	&1987
Holland, Rodger G.	Prof	Fran Marion	MC	PHD	81. Ohio St	&2007
Hollander, Anita Sawyer	Lect	Tennessee	S	PHD	87. Tennessee	8-02
College of Business Reagan Scholar						

Hollander, T. Edward	Retir	Rutgers-Newk	FE	PHD	60.	Pittsburgh	&1990
Hollar, William R.	Retir	Frostburg St	PF	MA	74	Ball St	&9-85
Hollenbeck, R.		SUNY Oswego	VX	MS	95	SUNY-Osw	2005
Hollensbe, Ronda L.	Prof	Grand View	CFRX	MBA	88	Drake	* &
Holley, Charles L.	Retir	Virg Comm	SA	DBA	76.	Tennessee	&1975
Holley, Joyce H.	Retir	Txs Southern	FM	PHD	86.	Houston	&1992
Holley, Paul	Asst	No Alabama	MP	MBA	69	Memphis	&1981
Hollie, Dana			F	PHD	03.	Wash U	
Hollingsworth, Beverley A.	Asst	Fitchburg St					
Hollingsworth, Carl W.	Asst	Clemson	A	PHD	07	Tennessee	&2007
Hollingsworth, Danny P.	Dean	Miss State	FX	DBA	88.	Memphis	&7-00
H. Devon Graham, Jr. Professorship in Accounting							
Hollingsworth, Mont C.	Exec	Ohio Univ	MS	MS	73	Kent St	* &1-06
Hollins, Vera H.	Retir	Southern	FMV	MS	75	LSU	&8-72
Hollis, Joseph E.	Retir	Jms Madison	2002	EDD	76	Fla Atl	&9-76
Hollister, Joan	Asst	SUNY-N Paltz	FM	PHD	98.	Union-NY	* 2006
Holloman, Derek	Asst	Florida A&M	F	ABD		Grenoble	2006
Holloway, David A.	Lect	Murdoch Univ	FG	MBA		W Austrl	1988
Holloway, Delton R.	Retir	N Carol Cen	2002	MBA	71	Columbia	&1971
Holman, Vinita R.	Asst	Fisk	ATR	MBA	78	Berkeley	&1987
Holmen, Jay S.	Prof	Wis-Eau Clar	SM	PHD	81.	Minnesota	* &6-84
Holmes, D. D.		PPC	FA	PHD	81.	Tx Tech	&
VP Sales & Marketing; PPC; PO Box 966; Ft Worth Tx 76101; 817-251-4305							
Holmes, James R.	Assoc	Kentucky	CSM	PHD	77.	Missouri	&1975
Holmes, Janice R.	Inst	Louisiana St	FM	MS	98	LSU	&8-98
Holmes, Kevin J.	Prof	Victoria NZ	FTPX	MCOM	77	Auckland	
Holmes, Linda	Assoc	Wis-Whitewat	GFN	PHD	97.	Okla St	* 2000
Holmes, Raymond T.	Retir	Virg Comm	1995	MS	70	Va Comm	&1977
Holmes, Richard L.	Asst	Baylor	CFGM	PHD	93	N Carol	1993
US Army-Baylor Univ Grad Prog in Health Adm; San Antonio Tx; 210-221-6740							
Holmes, Roderick L.	Retir	Baylor	1986	PHD	62.	U Wash	&1950
Holmes, Sarah A.	C-Pr	East Central	F	PHD	84.	North Tx	&1-06
Holowaty, Thomas C.	Assoc	St Vincent	AXC	MBA	72	Duquesne	&1972
Holstrum, Gary L.		PCAOB	2006	PHD	70.	Iowa	&
Assoc Chief Auditor & Director of Research Public Company Atg Oversight Board							
Holt, Andrew	Assoc	Metro State		PHD			
Holt, Doris L.				PHD	84.	Michigan	&
Holt, Paul E.	Prof	Tx A&M-Kings	FIVP	PHD	92.	Okla St	&1990
Holt, Robert N.		Ivy Software	1999	PHD	77.	N Carol	&
Holter, Norma C.	Prof	Towson	NAMB	PHD	92	Geo Wash	# &1985
Holtfreter, Robert E.	Prof	Central Wash	FMA	PHD	78.	Nebraska	&1993
Distinguished Professor of Accounting & Research							
Holthausen, Robert W.	C-Pr	Pennsylvania	F	PHD	80.	Rochester	&1989
Nomura Securities Company Professor							
Holtzblatt, Mark A.	Assoc	Roosevelt	IF	PHD	84.	Arkansas	&1981
Holtzman, Mark P.	Asst	Seton Hall	MPF	PHD	97.	Tx-Austin	&9-03
Holub, Mark	Lect	W Australia	F	BCOM	88	W Austrl	1991
Holzer, H. Peter	Emer	Illinois	1992	DBA	51	Vienna	&1954
The University of Economics							
Holzmann, Oscar J.	Assoc	U Miami	IFV	PHD	74.	Penn St	1980
Honea, James H.	Retir	SE Louisiana	F	PHD	82.	LSU	&8-01
Hong, Changmok	Prof	Kookmin Univ	AMTY	PHD	90.	Tx-Austin	1991
Hong, Cheolkyu	Asst	Chung-Ang	CMQT	PHD	98	London SE	2002
Hong, Keejae P.	Asst	Ill-Chicago	FX	PHD	06.	Illinois	2006
Hong, S. Ted	Retir	West Chester	1993	PHD	72.	NYU	&1987
Hong, Sungbin Chu	Asst	Songang Univ	F	PHD	84.	Berkeley	
Hong, Yong-Sik		Hansung Univ	1995	PHD	89.	Mich St	
Dept of Bus Adm; Hansung Univ; 389, 2-ga, Samsun-dong, Sungbuk-gu; Seoul, Kor							
Honig, Susan	Asst	CUNY-Lehman	XCDS	MS		Pace	&1990
Honodel, David	Lect	Denver	FMC	MT	89	Denver	&1990
Hood, James T.	Retir	La-Monroe	2003	PHD	62.	LSU	1967
Hood, William C.	Prof	Cen Michigan	X	JD	86	Cooley	&1981
Hoogendoorn, Martin	Prof	Un Amsterdam	AFIP	PHD	82	Rotterdam	1991
Hooi, George	ALect	Griffith Un	FQT	BCOM	01	Griffith	2001
Hooks, Jill J.	Lect	Massey-Alban	FW	PHD	00	Waikato	1997
Hooks, Karen L.	Prof	Fla Atlantic	AB	PHD	81.	Geo St	&1996
Hooper, Cameron G.	Asst	Michigan	AF	PHD	03	NS Wales	2001
Hooper, Paul	Retir	Tulane	2003	PHD	76.	Tulane	&1997
Hoover, Gail A.	C-Ac	Rockhurst	SIME	EDD	95	N Illinois	&8-95
Hop, Gerrold	Asst	Tilburg Univ	F	MBA	90	Tilburg	&1993
Hope, Ole-Kristian	Asst	Univ Toronto	F	PHD	01.	Nrthwstrn	&2001
Hopewell, Rita J.			MF	DBA	75.	S Calif	*
Hopkins, A. Wayne			FTN	DBA	78.	Colorado	&
Hopkins, Bobbie H.			FR	PHD	75.	Arkansas	&
Hopkins, Debra R.	Fac	No Illinois	AR	MAS	87	N Illinois	# &1987
Hopkins, James M.	Prof	Morningside	AXDS	MA	73	Nebraska	&1986
Hopkins, Merle W.	Clin	So Calif	F	PHD	82.	Mich St	&1995

Hopkins, Patrick E.	Assoc	Indiana	ABFV	PHD	95. Tx-Austin	&1995
Deloitte Faculty Fellowship						
Hopkins, Ray F.				PHD	82. Okla St	
Hopley, Brian	AcLec	So QueensInd	MX	MFM	96 UCQ	1999
Hoppa, Donald A.	Asst	Roosevelt	FC	MSA	85 Roosevelt	&1985
Hoppe, Paul P.	Assoc	Golden Gate	FMQ	PHD	93. NYU	& 1-97
Hopper, Trevor M.	Prof	U Manchester	BCH	MPHL	78 Aston	1983
Hopwood, Anthony G.	Prof	Oxford Univ	MB	PHD	71 Chicago	1995
Hopwood, William S.	Prof	Fla Atlantic	SC	PHD	78. Florida	8-92
Hoque, Zahirul	Prof	LaTrobe Univ	BGMN	PHD	93 Manchest	*
Hor, Jamal	ALect	Univ Sydney	FI	BCOM	03 W Sydney	2004
Hora, Bambi A.	Prof	Central Okla	XCMG	JD	98 Okla Cty	& 8-90
Hora, Judith A.	Assoc	San Diego	FV	PHD	99. Va Comm	&1998
Horan, Margaret H.	Assoc	Wagner	PV	MBA	84 Wagner	&
Horlick, Geoffrey R.	C-Pr	St Fran-NY	PF	PHD	78. Tx A&M	&1980
Horn, Betty C.	Assoc	So Conn St	AS	PHD	87. Geo St	&1995
Horn, Frederick E.	Retir	Arthur Young	1974	PHD	52. Columbia	1952
Horne, Gilbert R.				PHD	54. Michigan	
Horngren, Charles T.	Emer	Stanford	1995	PHD	55. Chicago	&1965
Edmund W. Littlefield Professor of Accounting, Emeritus						
Horniachek, Dale	LT	Univ Windsor	FM	MBA	84 York	2003
Hornik, Steven R.	Lect	Cen Florida	FS	PHD	99 Fla Intl	& 5-06
Horning, Michele Y.	Assoc	Goshen	CPMX	MS	95 Drexel	& 7-98
Hornung, David	Lect	CUNY-Queens	F	MBA	75 Baruch	6-77
Horrigan, James O.	Retir	New Hampshir	1996	PHD	67. Chicago	1966
Horsman, Simon J.	SLect	Coventry Un	VBM	MSC	85 Warwick	& 9-80
Horton, Joanne	Lect	London Econ	FT	PHD	94 Aberystwyt	1997
Horwitz, Bertrand N.	Retir	SUNY-Bingham	1999	PHD	62. Minnesota	1972
Horwitz, Ronald M.	Retir	Oakland	2002	PHD	64 Mich St	&1979
Hosch, Gordon A.	Emer	New Orleans	2004	PHD	72. LSU	&1967
Hosegood, O. S.	Retir	Cy London Pl	1992	MA		
Hoshower, Leon B.	Prof	Ohio Univ	MC	PHD	83. Mich St	& 9-88
Hoskin, Keith W.	Prof	Un Warwick	HTEM	PHD	73 Penn	
Hoskin, Robert E.	Assoc	Connecticut	MF	PHD	81. Cornell	9-86
Hosking, Malcolm	SLect	Bournemouth	M	BA		8-01
Hoskins, Margaret A.	Prof	Henderson St	FTAJ	PHD	92. Miss	&1991
Don Dodson Professor						
Hoskins, William R.				DBA	59. Indiana	
Hossain, David	Asst	CS-L Angeles	FX	PHD	03. Rutgers	& 9-03
Hossain, Mahmud	Asst	Memphis	M	PHD	04. Baruch	&2006
Hossain, Mahmud.	Assoc	Nanyang Tech	F	PHD	98 Massey	1998
Hosseini, Ahmad	Retir	Sonoma St	2003	PHD	81. Missouri	&1990
Hossfeld, C.	Asst	ESCP deParis	AFI	PHD	96 Saar Bruck	2000
Hostak, Peter	Asst	Mass-Dartmou	F	PHD	05. Nrthwstrn	2005
Hotaling, Andrea	Assoc	Siena	FX	MS		SUNY-Alb & 9-80
Hoth, Gerald B.	Prof	CS-Fullerton	SMC	PHD	82. Colorado	* &1989
Houghton, Keith A.	Dean	Australian N	FA	PHD	84 W Austrl	&
Houle, Sylvain	Prof	Quebec-Montr		PHD	Laval	
Houser, Richard	Deces	No Arizona	2002	PHD	71. Wisconsin	&1973
Houston, Carol Olson			FI	PHD	86. U Wash	&
Houston, Joan E.	Asst	Minot State	PAC	MS	81 N Dakota	* &1984
Houston, Margaret A.	Lect	Wright State	SM	MBA	85 Wright St	* & 9-88
Houston, Richard W.	Prof	Alabama	AF	PHD	95. Indiana	&1995
Y. Boozer Faculty Fellow						
Houston, William S. Jr.			X	PHD	73. North Tx	&
Hove, Mfandaidza R.	SLect	Un Zimbabwe		MA		&
Hoverland, Hal	Emer	CS-San Bern	1999	PHD	63. Michigan	9-72
How, Janice C. Y.	Prof	U Auckland	F	PHD	94 W Austrl	2004
How, Shimin	Lect	Aberdeen	C	MSC	02 Manchester	2006
Howard, Arley A.	Retir	W Nex Mexico	2007	PHD	85. Nebraska	1992
Howard, C. Randy	Retir	Mont St-Bill	2000	MA	70 Missouri	&1973
Howard, Thomas P.	D-Pr	Missouri	AE	PHD	78. Ariz St	& 8-04
Joseph A. Silvoso Director						
Howe, Harry	C-Ac	SUNY-Geneseo	FSG	PHD	95. Union-NY	& 9-95
Howe, Keith R.			MOA	PHD	79. Ariz St	#
Howe, Martha	SLect	Bentley	F	PHD	99. Conn	1995
Howe, W. Asquith	Deces	Temple		PHD	54. Ohio St	1955
Howell, Curtis C.	Asst	Georgia SW	CX	EDD	96 N Illinois	* & 7-01
Howell, Robert A.	VProf	Dartmouth	FM	DBA	66. Harvard	&2000
Howell, Sharon K.	Asst	Txs-El Paso	AF	PHD	05. Cen Fla	& 9-05
Howell, Syd D.	Lect	U Manchester	Q	PHD	76 Manchest	1978
Hoyle, Joe B.	Assoc	Richmond	FV	MBA	72 Appalach	&1979
Hoyt, Hugh A.	Retir	Miami U-Ohio	2001	PHD	70. Mich St	& 9-73
Hrasky, Sue L.	Lect	Un Tasmania	FA	MSOC	95 Tasmania	1987
Hrazdil, Karel	Lect	Simon Fraser	F			7-07
Hribar, S. Paul	Prof	Iowa	F	PHD	00. Iowa	
Lloyd J. & Tholma W. Palmer Research Fellow						

Name	Rank	School		Degree	Yr	From	
Hrncir, Theresa	C-Ac	SE Okla St	AFJO	PHD	94	Oklahoma	&1996
Hronsky, Jane J. F.	Lect	U Melbourne	FA	MCOM	93	Melbourne	&1997
Hrubec, Thomas	C-Pr	Franklin	BCGM	EDD	04	Illin St	* &2005
Hsieh, James	SLect	Simon Fraser	F	MBA	74	Oregon	& 1-85
Hsieh, Pei-Gin	Asst	Ntl Chung Ch	FQM	PHD	05.	Case Wes	2004
Hsieh, Su-Jane	Prof	San Fran St	F	PHD	85.	Purdue	1992
Hsu, Charles	Asst	Hong Kong Sc	FIM	PHD	04.	Purdue	2004
Hsu, Ching-Ding (Stephen)			BS	PHD	88.	S Calif	* &
Hsu, Chung-Yuan	Assoc	Nat Chengchi	PTX	PHD	96.	Memphis	&1986
Hsu, H. Y. Kathy	Asst	Western Wash	FMI	PHD	94.	Houston	2007
Hsu, Ko-Cheng	Assoc	So Alabama	SA	PHD	93.	Memphis	&1993
Hsu, Ming Po				PHD	52.	Illinois	
Hsu, Sylvia H.	Asst	York Univ	CM	PHD	06	Wisconsin	2006
Hu, Kin Hoi Billy	Lect	Nanyang Tech	FM	MSC	96	Manchest	&1995
Hu, Xuesong	Asst	Oregon	F	PHD	05.	S Calif	2006
Huamon, Remi	Lect	Sherbrooke	F	MS	85	Sherbrook	
Huang, Alex Yuan Fu				PHD	01.	Baruch	
Huang, Allen R.	SLect	Griffith Un	IB	PHD	91	Griffith	1990
Huang, Chunghuey Linda		Nat Cheng Ku	1994	PHD	93.	SUNY-Buf	&

National Cheng Kung Univ; Tainan, Taiwan ROC; (06) 274-4104

Name	Rank	School		Degree	Yr	From	
Huang, Henry	Asst	Butler	PFM	PHD	05.	Houston	8-05
Huang, Jiunn C.	C-Pr	San Fran St	CFMI	PHD	80.	North Tx	* 1986
Huang, Rong	Asst	CUNY-Baruch	M	PHD	06	Tx-Dallas	9-06
Huang, Shi-Ming	C-Pr$	Ntl Chung Ch	ADMS	PHD	94	Sunderland	1999
Huang, Wenli	Asst	Boston Univ	FM	PHD	05.	Berkeley	9-05
Huang, Yuan	Asst	HongKon Tech	AF	PHD	06	HKUST	
Hubbard, Daniel J.	Assoc	Mary Wash	M	PHD	92	Va Tech	8-99
Hubbard, E. Dee	Retir	Brigham Yg	1992	PHD	67.	U Wash	* 9-59

2785 Marrcrest East; Provo UT 84604

Name	Rank	School		Degree	Yr	From	
Hubbard, Harold F.	Prof	Cumberland	FD	MBA	60	Kentucky	& 7-60
Hubbard, Thomas D.	Retir	Nebraska	8-98	PHD	69.	Missouri	& 9-77
Huber, C. Courtland Jr.	Retir	Texas-Austin	FCMT	PHD	78.	Stanford	6-88
Huber, Marsha M.	Assoc	Otterbein	ANFX	PHD	03	Ohio St	&1986
Hudack, Lawrence R.	Prof	Barry	FNXG	PHD	89.	North Tx	* & 8-98
Huddart, Steven J.	Prof	Penn State	MXY	PHD	91	Yale	& 8-99

KPMG Professor of Accounting

Name	Rank	School		Degree	Yr	From	
Hudson, Christopher	Lect	So Cross Un	SF	MBAM	95	So Cross	&1989
Hudson, Dennis H.	Assoc	Tulsa	FP	PHD	86.	Arkansas	9-82
Hudson, Jean Marie B.	Retir	Lamar	1994	PHD	84.	Tx-Austin	&1951
Hudson, John S.	Retir	Lk Superior	8-02	MBA	67	W Mich	8-70
Hudson, Mary	Lect	Western St	APM	MHCA	81	Minnesota	&2004
Hudson, Richard	H-Ac	Mt Allison U	JCQ	PHD	84	Ottawa	* 7-85
Hudson, Robert	SLect	Univ Leeds	MQ	PHD	06	Leeds	9-02
Huefner, Bernd	Asst	Aachen Univ	FCM	PHD	00	Aachen	1994
Huefner, Ronald J.	Prof	SUNY-Buffalo	FMV	PHD	68.	Cornell	* &1968

Distinguished Teaching Professor

Name	Rank	School		Degree	Yr	From	
Huerta, Esperanza E.	Asst	Txs-El Paso	MSB	PHD	03	Claremont	9-07
Huertas, Yvonne	Prof	Puerto Rico	CMS	MBA	72	P Rico	&1976
Huff, Kendra	Assoc	Tx A&M-Kings	PDF	PHD		Tx-PanAm	&1989
Huff, Patricia Lee	C-Pr$	CS-Fresno	CM	PHD	94.	Arkansas	& 8-93
Huff, Rita B.	Deces	Sam Houston	8-82	EDD	63	Houston	&1957
Huff, Thomas E.		New Cana CT	1992	PHD	81.	Columbia	

147 Fox Run Rd; New Canaan CT 06840

Name	Rank	School		Degree	Yr	From	
Huffman, William E.	Assoc	Missouri So	AEPG	PHD	98.	North Tx	&2000
Huffman, Wilmer E.	Retir	Pittsburg St	1997	PHD	75.	Kansas	&1978
Hughes, Barry J.	Assoc	St Rose	XVP	MAS	90	St Rose	&1985
Hughes, Diane Y.	Assoc	Rowan	LF	JD	87	Rutgers	&1983
Hughes, Harry N.	Lect	Tennessee	F	BS	75	Tennessee	& 4-76
Hughes, Hugh P.	Retir	Georgia St	2000	PHD	72.	Alabama	3-71
Hughes, Jesse W.	Retir	Old Dominion	1998	PHD	83.	Va Tech	# &1982
Hughes, John S.	Prof	UCLA	FMTY	PHD	74.	Purdue	& 7-99
Hughes, K. E. II (Skip)	Assoc	Louisiana St	FM	PHD	96.	Georgia	8-97

LeGrange Professor; Associate Dean

Name	Rank	School		Degree	Yr	From	
Hughes, Patricia J.	Retir	UCLA	2005	PHD	84	Brit Colum	8-95
Hughes, Peggy Ann	Asst	Montclair St	BIM	PHD	99.	Rutgers	9-05
Hughes, Stacie R.	Asst	Athens State		ABD		Alabama	2005
Hughes, Steward	SLect	Coventry Un	FM	MA	69	Manchest	9-71
Hughes, Susan B.	Assoc	Vermont	FMA	PHD	90.	Cincinnati	&2006
Hugon, J. Artur	Asst	Georgia St	F	PHD	04.	S Calif	2004
Huh, Sung-Kyoo	Prof	CS-San Bern	MC	PHD	88.	Kent St	1987
Huh, Sungkwan		Dong-A Univ	1991	PHD	86.	SUNY-Buf	

Dong-A Univ; 840 Hadan-Dong Saha-Gu; Pusan 604-714 South Korea

Name	Rank	School		Degree	Yr	From	
Huh, Youngpin	Prof	Chung-Ang	CMI	PHD	86	Korea	1984
Hui, Kai Wai	Asst	Hong Kong Sc	FIM	PHD	04.	Oregon	8-04
Hui, W. F.	Assoc	City Univ HK	V	MBA	89	Brunel	& 7-84
Huizingh, William	Retir	Arizona St	1985	PHD	63.	Michigan	&1959
Huizink, J. B.	Prof	Vrije Univ	LX	PHD	89	Groningen	2000

Hukai, Dawn	Assoc	Wis-Rvr Fall		PHD	98	Minnesota	1998
Hull, Rita P.	Retir	Virg Comm	2001	PHD	78.	Okla St #	&1982
Hulme, Richard D.	Retir	CS-Pomona	2006	PHD	91.	Wash St	&1991
Hulse, David S.	Assoc	Kentucky	X	PHD	93.	Penn St	1993
Deloitte and Touche Professor of Accountancy							
Humble, Thomas N.	Deces	Alabama	1990	PHD	63.	Tx-Austin	&1948
Hume, Evelyn C.	Prof	Longwood	XJ	PHD	88.	LSU	2004
Hummer, William R.	Lect	MD E Shore	FMX	MBA	77	Montana	1-01
Humphrey, Bill R.	Retir	Cen Arkansas	2001	PHD	69.	Arkansas	& 9-79
Humphrey, Christopher G.	H-Pr	U Manchester	ABCF	PHD		Manchest	&2001
Humphrey, Joseph L.	Prof	Tx St-S Marc	FM	PHD	71.	Tx Tech	&1972
Humphrey, Roberta L.	Inst	SE Missouri	PS	ABD		Miss	2006
Humphreys, David				PHD	95.	Temple	
Humphreys, K.	Lect	New So Wales		BCOM		NS Wales	
Humphreys, Peter	ALect	W Sydney	FINP	MCOM	04	N Eng-Au	
Hums, Edward F.	Spec	Notre Dame	FM	MBA	89	Ind-S Bn	&1992
Hung, Mingyi	Assoc	Chinese HK	FI	PHD	99.	MIT	2006
Hung, Yu-Chung	Assoc	Ntl Chung Ch	DFMS	PHD	95	Mo-Rolla	2005
Hunkins, Brett C.	Assoc	Northwood	AFMP	MBA	03	Cen Mich	&1999
Hunt, Alister L.			2004	PHD	96.	U Wash	
Charles Rivers Associates							
Hunt, Allen K.	650-2	S Ill-Edward	FT	PHD	01.	LSU	2006
Hunt, Atha	Assoc	Chicago St	XJL	JD	78	DePaul	1975
Hunt, Chris	SLect	Victoria NZ	F	PHD		QueensInd	2006
Hunt, George L.	Asst	S F Austin	XO	PHD	06.	Tx Tech	* &1984
Hunt, Herbert G.	Prof	CS-Long Bch	XF	PHD	82.	Colorado	&2002
Hunt, Ray C. Jr.	Retir	Virginia	1996	PHD	66.	NYU	& 9-58
Hunt, Steven C.	Assoc	W Illinois	AFB	PHD	91.	Florida	& 9-98
Hunter, Debra R.	Assoc	Kentucky Wes	CEFI	PHD	04.	La Tech	&2005
Hunter, R.	Lect	Univ Ulster	M	BA			1990
Hunter, Shirley	Asst	Tufts	FI	PHD	04.	Tx A&M	&
Tufts University; 617-627-2774; shirley.hunter@tufts.edu							
Hunthauser, John M.				PHD	74.	Missouri	
Huntington, Virginia Ruth	Retir	Arizona St	1980	PHD	62.	Tx-Austin	&1962
2625 E Southern #C101; Tempe AZ 85282							
Hunton, James E.	Prof	Bentley	SAB	PHD	94.	Tx-Arlin	&2002
Trustee Professor of Accounting							
Huntsman, Ronald O.	C-Ac	Tx Lutheran	AGMF	MBA		Mich St #	&1986
Elton Bohmann Professorship in Accounting							
Hurley, Catherine	Prof	New Bruns-SJ	MCFD	MBA		N Brunswk	&1997
Hurley, James F.	Assoc	Winona State	FIPT	PHD	83.	Nebraska	&1983
Hurley, Richard E.	Assoc	Connecticut	FXM	PHD	94.	Conn	& 9-99
Hurt, Robert L.	Prof	CS-Pomona	CMSU	PHD	91	Claremont	* 1987
Hurtt, David N.	Assoc	Baylor	F	PHD	98.	Tx A&M	&2005
Hurtt, R. Kathy	Asst	Baylor	S	PHD	99.	Utah	&2004
Huss, H. Fenwick	Dean	Georgia St	FA	DBA	82.	Tennessee	& 6-89
Hussain, Inam			FA	PHD	84.	Missouri	&
Hussayni, Musa Y.				PHD	59.	Michigan	
Hussein, Mohamed E. A.	H-Pr	Connecticut	MF	PHD	77.	Pittsburgh	9-78
Hussein, Mostaque	Lect	Sultan Qaboo	M	PHD	00	VASA	2000
Huston, Kevin E.	Assoc	Marian	FXAC	JD	80	Duke	&1989
Huston, Ryan	Asst	Florida St	X	PHD	07	Tx A&M	& 8-07
Huta, Randall	Retir	Utica	2002	MBA	65	Syracuse	&1965
Hutajulu, Sabam		Perthmina Co		PHD	02.	Case Wes	
Hutchinson, Ian R.	Assoc	Acadia Univ	IA	PHD	00	Queen's	&
Hutchinson, Marion	SLect	Deakin-Burwo	MQY	PHD	01	Deakin	&1998
Hutchinson, Patrick J.	Prof	N Eng-Austr	F	PHD		Bath	&1979
Hutchinson, R.	Dean	Univ Ulster	F	MA			4-90
Hutchinson, Robert	Asst	Oakland	MC	PHD	07	Ohio No	2007
Hutchison, Paul D.	Assoc	North Texas	FWBS	PHD	97.	Tx Tech	8-98
Hutton, Amy P.	Assoc	Boston Coll	F	PHD	92.	Rochester	2006
Hutton, Clifford E.	Retir	Tulsa	1992	PHD	61.	Tx-Austin	&1955
4637 S Lakewood; Tulsa OK 74135							
Hutton, Marguerite R. (Zite)	Prof	Western Wash	X	PHD	85.	Houston	&1989
Huxley, Sharon J.	C-Ac	Post	M	MBA	76	Hartford	1978
Hwang, Angela L. J.	Assoc	E Michigan	EFTV	PHD	97.	Houston	2002
Hwang, Dennis	Prof	Bloomsburg	FI	PHD	84	Oklahoma	* &1989
Hwang, Ho Chan		Korea	1992	PHD	92.	Ga Tech	
Hwang, In-Tae	Assoc	Chung-Ang	FI	PHD	94.	SUNY-Buf	&1995
Hwang, Iny	Asst	Mn St-Mankat	C	PHD	05	Tx-Dallas	2005
Hwang, Lee-Seok	Prof	Seoul Natl	FIQ	PHD	94.	NYU	2003
Hwang, Nen-Chen Richard	Prof	CS-S Marcos	FAC	PHD	91.	St Louis	* &1991
Hwang, Yuhchang	Assoc	Arizona St	FM	PHD	87.	Berkeley	8-95
Hwang, Yujong	Asst	DePaul	S	PHD	03	S Carol	2003
Hyatt, Troy A.	Asst	Wis-Oshkosh	AS	PHD	95.	Arizona	&2003
Hyde, Douglas F.	Retir	Temple	1988	MBA	61	Temple	&1956
Hyde, Julie	Asst	So Adventist	AF	MA	04	Tennessee	2006

Hyde, Stuart J.	Lect	U Manchester	FQTY	PHD		Newcastle	2000
Hyder, Syed N.	Retir	Indiana U-PA	2004	MTAX	82	Geo St	&1984
Hylton, Connie	Inst	Geo Mason	FM	MBA	81	Ariz St	&2000
Hylton, Delmer P.	Retir	Wake Forest	1991	MBA	49	Indiana	& 9-49

1856 Faculty Drive; Winston-Salem NC 27106

Hyman, Ladelle M.	Prof	Txs Southern	FM	PHD	75.	North Tx	&1981
Hyon, Yong-Ha			FHM	PHD	75.	NYU	&
Hypes, Gary	Asst	West Liberty	CP	JD	03	W Virginia	&2004
Iannucelli, Anthony V.	Retir	Roger Wm	2003	MS	70	Rhode Isl	9-70
Ibrahim, Adel	VAsst	Illinois	F	PHD	03.	Illinois	8-05
Ibrahim, Mohamed E.	Dean	Univ Sharjah	FAB	PHD	85.	North Tx	&2000
Ibrahim, Salma	Asst	Morgan State	FS	PHD	05.	Maryland	2006
Icerman, Joe D.	Assoc	Florida St	F	PHD	77.	N Carol	& 9-77
Icerman, Rhoda C.	Prof	Florida St	GA	DBA	83.	Fla St	& 1-83
Idowu, S.	SLect	London Metro	FM	MSC			2002
Ihrke, Frederic	C-Pr	Winona State	XGFL	JD	79	Wm Mitch	&1981
Ijiri, Yuji	Prof	Carnegie Mel	FM	PHD	63.	Car Mellon	&1967

Robert M. Trueblood University Professor of Accounting and Economics

Ikaheimo, Seppo	Prof	Helsinki Sch	BF	PHD	96	Turku	1999
Ikawa, Bruce E.	Assoc	Hillsdale	FMX	PHD	88.	Michigan	&1999

Brouwer D. & Jane E. McIntyre Chair in Business Administration

Ikin, Catherine	Asst	Australian N	FX	BEC	74	Tasmania	2003
Ikin, Chris	Asst	Australian N	AFT	MCOM	01	Melbourne	&2003
Ilacqua, Glen	Asst	Stonehill	AFXN	MST	87	Bentley	& 9-05
Ilcisin, Laura	Inst	Neb-Omaha	FM	MBA	80	Ne-Omaha	&1996
Ilett, Frank	Lect	Boise State	PSC	MBA	69	Chicago	& 9-94
Ilie, Virginia	Asst	Kansas	S	PHD	05	Cen Fla	2005
Ilyas, Irfan A.	Lect	King Fahd Un	S	MS	99	King Fahd	2000
Ilyas, Mohammad	Pres	Goldey-Beacm	F	PHD		Conn	9-75
Im, Jong-Gul			MF	PHD	89.	Penn	
Imdieke, Leroy F.	Retir		1991	PHD	68.	Illinois	&

14404 W Heritage Dr; Sun City West AZ 85375

Imhoff, Eugene A. Jr. (Gene)	Prof	Michigan	FI	PHD	73.	Mich St	& 8-77

Ernst & Young Professor of Accounting

Imke, Frank J.			1992	PHD	66.	Missouri	&

825 W Osborn 1013; Phoenix AZ 85013

Immelman, Abraham P. J.	Prof	Port Elizabe	1989	PHD	71.	Florida	
Imoisili, Olumhense A.		U Lagos	1988	PHD	85.	Pittsburgh	
Inberg, Carol	Retir	CS-East Bay	1988	PHD	70.	Berkeley	& 9-63
Indjejikian, Raffi J.	Prof	Michigan	MC	PHD	89.	Penn	& 8-96

Robert L. Dixon Collegiate Professor of Accounting

Indrianatoro, Nur	Asst	Gadjah Mada	1994	PHD	93.	Kentucky	1985
Ingalls, Wayne C.	Retir	Maine	AF	MBA	68	Wisconsin	&1980
Inge, Bobby M.				DBA	71.	Harvard	
Ingraham, Laura R.	Assoc	San Jose St	SMF	PHD	95.	Ariz St	&2003
Ingram, Robert W.	Prof	Alabama	FG	PHD	77.	Tx Tech	&1985

S. J. Ross-H. F. Culverhouse Chair

Iqbal, M. Zafar	Retir	Cal Poly-SLO	2005	PHD	79.	Nebraska	# * & 9-79
Irani, Afshad J.	Asst	New Hampshir	F	PHD	98.	Penn St	1998
Irish, Robert R.	Retir	Toledo	1992	PHD	70.	Tx-Austin	&1956

2924 Barrington Drive; Toledo OH 43606-3005

Irujo, Christine	Asst	Westfield St	PM	MS	85	Mass	
Irvin, Helen	SLect	U Wollongong	FN	PHD		Wollong	&2003
Irvine, Richard J.			AVM	DBA	89.	La Tech	&
Irvine, V. Bruce	Retir	Saskatchewan	2004	PHD	77.	Minnesota	* 1967
Irvine, Wayne	Inst	Univ Calgary	AF	BCOM	80	Calgary	&1992
Irving, James H.	Asst	Wm & Mary	FA	PHD	06.	N Carol	&2006
Irwin, Paula L.	C-Ac	Muhlenberg	JEBD	MBA	77	Lehigh	& 9-91
Isaac, Klepfish	Asst	Touro		JD		NYU	9-85
Isaacs, Patricia	C-Pr	Berea	EFJX	PHD	94.	Kentucky	&1989
Isaksson, Anders	Asst	Univ of Umea	SBYA	BSC	93	Umea	
Iselin, Errol R.	H-Pr	Bond Univ	BCM	PHD	82	Queensld	&2004
Ishikawa, Akira		Toyko, Japan	1992	PHD	72.	Tx-Austin	

2-2-39-219 Jingumae-Cho; Shibuya-Ku; Tokyo 150 Japan

Islam, A.	Lect	Massey-Welli		PHD		Wellingt	2003
Islam, Majidul	Asst	Concordia U	FMA	PHD	78	Moscow	2000
Islam, Muhammad S.	Lect	King Fahd Un	FS	MS	86	Boston U	1990
Isleib, R. Bruce	Lect	Houston-Cl L	FV	PHD	95.	Houston	& 9-93
Ismail, Badr E.	Prof	Syracuse	CM	PHD	74.	Illinois	1979
Ismail, Hamzah Bin		Malaysia	1989	DBA	78.	Indiana	
Ismail, Zakaria M.		Alexan Egypt	1988	PHD	83.	Baruch	
Issaevitch, Thomas	Asst	Minnesota		PHD	06.	Columbia	2006
Istvan, Donald F.	Retir	DePaul	1993	DBA	59.	Indiana	&1972
Itami, Hiroyuki	Prof	Hitotsubashi	MY	PHD	73.	Car Mellon	1973
Ito, Kunio	Prof	Hitotsubashi	FK	DBA	96	Hitotsub	1980
Ittner, Christopher D.	Prof	Pennsylvania	M	PHD	92.	Harvard	1991
Ivancevich, Daniel M.	Prof	N Car-Wilmin	FS	PHD	91.	Tx A&M	2000

Name	Rank	School	Code	Degree	Yr	University	
Ivancevich, Susan H.	Assoc	N Car-Wilmin	GFA	PHD	94.	Tx A&M	&2000
Iwok, Edet Robinson		U Calabar	1990	PHD	70.	Nrthwstrn	
Univ of Calabar; Dept of Mgt Studies; PMB 1115 Calabar Nigeria							
Iyengar, Raghavan J.	Assoc	N Carol Cen	FP	PHD	95.	Maryland	&2001
Iyenjar, Raj				PHD	96.	Maryland	
Iyer, Govind S.	Assoc	Arizona St	ST	PHD	94.	Geo St	&1998
Iyer, Venkataraman M.	Asst	N Car-Greens	AS	PHD	94.	Georgia	& 8-99
Izard, C. Douglass				PHD	81.	Miss	&1997
Izumi, Marleen M.		Consultant		PHD	77.	Ohio St	
Jabbour, Antoine	Retir	CS-Pomona	2001	PHD	75	Catholic	&1980
Jablonsky, Stephen F.	Emer	Penn State	2007	PHD	74.	Illinois	& 9-75
Jackling, Beverley	H-SL$	Deakin-Burwo	ME	PHD	01	Melbourne	&1991
Jackman, Susan	Lect	Canterbury	CEFM	MCOM	99	Canterbu	2005
Jackson, Alicia J.	Dean	Susquehanna	FM	PHD	97.	Tx-Austin	* 9-07
Jackson, Anthony W.	Retir	Hampton	BMT	PHD	85.	Cincinnati	1998
Jackson, Betty R.	Prof	Colorado	X	PHD	82.	Tx-Austin	&1983
Jackson, Cecil W.	Clin	So Calif	M	DCOM	93	Rhodes	1987
Jackson, Cynthia M.	Assoc	Northeastern	FS	PHD	92.	S Carol	& 7-98
Jackson, Dianne		Tx-San Anton		PHD	98.	Memphis	
Jackson, Gary Todd	Assoc	NE St-Okla	FAM	PHD	94.	Arkansas	* &2002
Jackson, George S.	Prof	Elizabeth Ct	XL	LLM	91	Geotown	&1998
Jackson, Gisele K.			FMB	PHD	95.	LSU	&
Jackson, Janet	ALect	Monash Univ	QA	BBUS			1005
Jackson, Kevin E.	Asst	Illinois	F	PHD	04.	Tx-Austin	& 8-04
Jackson, Pamela Z.	Prof	Augusta St	ASFM	PHD	90.	Georgia	& 1-89
Jackson, Robert E.	Asst	Geo Southern	FGNP	PHD	01	Kansas St	2005
Jackson, Scott B.	Asst	So Carolina	FM	PHD	97.	Nebraska	&2002
Jackson, Sharon S.	Asst	Samford	FM	MBA	84	Aub-Mont	& 8-97
Jackson, Steven R.	Assoc	So Miss	AM	PHD	93.	Ariz St	&2006
Jackson-Heard, Mary F.			F	PHD	87.	NYU	&
Jacob, John	Assoc	Colorado	FM	PHD	95.	Nrthwstrn	2000
Jacob, Rudolph A.	C-Pr	Pace		PHD	87.	NYU	1973
Jacobs, Fred A.	Retir	Georgia St	FM	PHD	73.	Georgia	* & 9-80
Jacobs, Fred H.	Assoc	Michigan St	MQ	PHD	77.	Illinois	& 3-76
Jacobs, Frederick R.	Retir	Minnesota	X	PHD	74.	Wisconsin	& 9-71
Jacobs, Norma M.			F	PHD	89.	Tx A&M	&
Jacobs, Paul	Asst	Elmhurst	FX	MS	95	DePaul	&2001
Jacobsen, David M.	Prof	Salem State	IM	JD	69	Boston U	1978
Jacobsen, Lyle E.	Retir	CS-Hayward	1991	PHD	58.	Illinois	&1985
]659 Allyn; St. Helena CA 94574							
Jacoby, C. Robert	Deces	Shippensburg	6-86	DED	75	Penn St	1965
Jacoby, Louis C.			F	DBA	72.	Mich St	
Jacoby, Louis R.	Asst	Saginaw Vall	SN	PHD	71	Michigan	&1980
Jacoby, Philip F.	Assoc	American U	AFB	DBA	80.	Geo Wash	& 9-72
Jacques, Marie	Assoc	Sherbrooke	X	MFIS	86	Sherbrook	1988
Jacques, Randolph	Prof	Alma	FGIM	MBA	72	Wayne St	1977
Jadallah, Salih M.		Deloitte Sau		PHD	78.	Tx Tech	
Jaedicke, Robert K.	Retir	Stanford	1992	PHD	57.	Minnesota	1961
Jaeger, David G.	Asst	North Fla	XL	JD	79	Cincinnati	1996
Jaenicke, Henry R.	Retir	Drexel	2003	PHD	63	Penn	& 9-80
Jaffer, Ashraf	Asst	No Carolina	FMT	PHD	07	LondonSE	2006
Jagetia, Lal C.	Retir	Cleveland St	2000	PHD	69	Alabama	&1975
Jaggi, Bikki L.	Prof	Rutgers-N Br	FM	PHD	68	Free U	7-82
Jagolinzer, Alan	Asst	Stanford		PHD	04.	Penn St	8-04
Jagolinzer, Philip	Retir	So Maine	2001	PHD	78.	Arizona	&1966
Jaikengkit, Aim-orn	Lect	Chulalongkor	F	PHD	03	Case Wes	1995
Jaikumar, V.				PHD	79.	Columbia	
Jain, Jagat P.	Prof	Niagara	ICFG	PHD	85	Patna	1979
Jain, Mahesh C.	Deces	Howard		PHD	74.	N Carol	&1976
Jain, Prem C.	C-Pr	Georgetown	F	PHD	84.	Florida	&2000
Jain, Rohit	Prof	Alabama A&M	MFI	PHD	80.	Florida	* 8-96
Jain, Tribhowan N.	Deces	Eastern Mich	1984	PHD	70.	Mich St	6-76
Jakubowski, Stephen T.	Prof	Ferris State	GFAM	PHD	88.	Kent St	&2001
Jamal, Karim	Prof	Univ Alberta	ABJK	PHD	91.	Minnesota	&1989
Chartered Accountants Chair							
James, David	Lect	Wales-Bangor	F	BA	75	Manchest	9-92
James, Kevin L.	Asst	Mid Tenn St	FA	PHD	00.	Tennessee	&2000
James, Lisa E.	SLect	U Glamorgan	NA	BA	87	Glamorgan	& 1-95
James, Marianne L.	Asst	CS-L Angeles	FM	PHD	98	Fla Intl	9-98
James, Origen J. Jr.	Retir	Geo Southern	1993	PHD	69.	Tx Tech	1974
James, Robert M.			M	PHD	51.	Illinois	
James, Stanley	ALect	W Sydney	MEOL	PHD	01	MSU	
James, Tyronne	C-As	Southern-NO	FACV	MACC	83	Florida	&1983
James, Walter F.	Retir	Washburn	1997	PHD	73.	Missouri	& 6-73
Jamison, Robert W.	Prof	Indiana-Indy	X	PHD	80.	Tx-Austin	& 8-98
Jan, Ching-Lih	Assoc	CS-East Bay	FM	PHD	88.	Berkeley	9-95
Janakiraman, Surya N.	Assoc	Texas-Dallas	MCS	PHD	94.	Penn	1998

Jancura, Elise G.	Retir	Cleveland St	6-94	PHD	71.	Case Wes	&1975
Janell, Paul A.	Retir	Northeastern	FA	PHD	74.	Mich St	&9-73
Janes, Clair W.	Retir	San Jose St	D-90	MBA	53	Ohio St	&9-58
Janes, Troy D.	Asst	Rutgers-Camd	FA	PHD	05.	Michigan	&2007
Jang, H. Jonathan		Inha Univ	1995	PHD	87.	Purdue	
Inha University; Inchon, Korea							
Jang, Jee In	Dean	Chung-Ang	FI	PHD	89.	SUNY-Buf	1990
Jang, Yeong M.			PAC	DBA	91.	Miss St	
Janiga, John M.	Prof	Loyola-Chicg	RX	LLM	91	DePaul	&9-88
Jankowitz, Irving	Retir	Pace	1991	MBA	67	NYU	&1968
Janowsky, Dale	Asst	Buffalo St	FMC	MS	75	Canisius	&9-81
Jansen, Ivo Ph.	Asst	Rutgers-Camd	FM	PHD	01.	Indiana	2007
Jansen, Nico A.	Lect	Vrije Univ	LX	MS	87	Utrecht	2002
Janson, Kenneth R.	Prof	No Michigan	ACM	PHD	79.	Wisconsin	&2001
Janssen, Fred L.	Retir	Columbus	1989	MBA	67	Xavier	&1973
Jantadej, Piyaratt	Asst	Thammasat		PHD	06.	Nebraska	2006
Thammasat University; Bangkok							
Janus, Frank A.	Prof	Pace	1998	PHD	74.	NYU	
Finance Department; Pace University							
Janvrin, Diane J.	Asst	Iowa State	S	PHD	01.	Iowa	&2000
Jarett, Irwin M.				PHD	64.	LSU	
Jarett, Steven B.	C-Ac	St Joseph-CT	FMAC	MPA	77	Tx-Austin	&1984
Jarnagin, Bill D.	Prof	Wichita St	F	PHD	76.	Arkansas	&1987
Allen, Gibbs & Houlik Faculty Fellow							
Jarusewic, Margaret	C-Ac	Bethel-IN	AFMX	MBA	89	Ind-S Bn	&8-81
Jarvie, Deborah	Lect	U Lethbridge	X	MSC	02	Lethbridge	7-00
Jasper, Harold W.	Retir	Miami U-Ohio	2001	MA	54	Miami U	&1959
Jayaraman, Sudarshan	Asst	Wash Univ	F	PHD	07	N Carol	2007
Jbarah, Hani Mahud Abu		Lebanon		PHD	72.	Wisconsin	
Jeacle, Ingrid	SLect	Edinbourgh		PHD			
Jeancola, Monica	Inst	Stetson	FSM	MBA	00	Stetson	&1998
Jeanjean, Thomas	Asst	HEC Paris	FAIV	PHD	02	Paris IX	2003
Jebeile, Sam	Lect	Macquarie Un	SM	MED	02	Macquarie	&2001
Jeffers, Agatha E.	Asst	Montclair St	ACMO	PHD	00.	Rutgers	&2004
Jeffords, Raymond	Retir	Tenn-Chattan	2005	PHD	89.	LSU	&9-88
Jeffrey, Cynthia G.	Assoc	Iowa State	FJIT	PHD	89.	Minnesota	&1988
Jelinek, Kate	Asst	Rhode Island	FA	PHD	05	Conn	&2005
Jenkel, Iris A.	C-Ac	St Norbert	CGMN	PHD	90.	Wisconsin	&1999
Jenkins, D. Ellis	PLect	U Glamorgan	NM	MSOC	79	Birminghm	&1-79
Jenkins, D. Randall			X	PHD	81.	Arizona	
Jenkins, David O.	Retir	CS-Stanislau	2003	DBA	63.	S Calif	&1970
Jenkins, David S.	Asst	Delaware	AF	PHD	02.	Maryland	9-02
Jenkins, Elizabeth K.	Prof	San Jose St	FBE	PHD	86.	Houston	&1985
Jenkins, J. Gregory	Assoc	Virg Tech	ABF	PHD	98.	Va Tech	&8-05
Jenkins, Nicole T.			F	PHD	02.	Iowa	&
Jenne, Stanley Earl	Dean	Utah Valley	FA	PHD	82.	Illinois	&2006
Jenner, Maurice	Lect	So Queenslnd	EFTY	MFM	86	Queensld	1991
Jenner, Paul	Lect	Touro	CFPX	MS		Baruch	&9-05
Jennings, David M.	Deces	Txs-San Ant		PHD	84.	Houston	1983
Jennings, James P.	Prof	St Louis	FK	PHD	70.	Missouri	* &1976
Jennings, Robert M.		Jefferson IN	1992	DBA	59.	Indiana	
Jennings & Co; 324 E Court Ave; Jeffersonville IN 47130							
Jennings, Ross G.	Prof	Texas-Austin	F	PHD	87.	Berkeley	1-87
PricewaterhouseCoopers Centennial Fellowship							
Jennings, William W.	Assoc	USAF Academy	FN	PHD	98	Michigan	&6-98
Jens, William G.	Prof	Stetson	FMA	PHD	92	Cen Fla	&1987
Lindback Professor							
Jensen, Daniel L.	Emer	Ohio State	2004	PHD	70.	Ohio St	&6-80
Jensen, David E.	Assoc	Bucknell	FVX	PHD	87.	Penn St	&1987
Jensen, Herbert L.			2003	PHD	78.	Tx A&M	* &
808-965-9647; herbjensen@lycos.com							
Jensen, Howard G.	Retir	Colorado	1986	PHD	63.	Minnesota	1957
Jensen, Kenneth R.	VPres	Cattallactie		PHD	74.	Chicago	
Jensen, Kevan L.	Assoc	Oklahoma	A	PHD	00.	Florida	1999
Jensen, Paul H.	Prof	Cen Arkansas	FM	DBA	95.	Memphis	&8-82
Jensen, Robert E.	Retir	Trinity	2007	PHD	66.	Stanford	&8-82
Jensen, Robert E..	Retir	Savannah St	2000	MBA	67	E Carol	1979
Jensen, Tilly		Athabasca Un		BCOM			*
Jenson, Richard L.	H-Pr	Utah State	S	PHD	88.	Utah	&1987
ATK Thiokol Professor							
Jeong, Seok Woo	Assoc	Korea Univ	FA	PHD	96.	SUNY-Buf	3-97
Jepperson, Mary	C-As	St John's-MN	AFPM	MBA	04	St Cloud	2003
Jeppson, Catherine T.	Lect	CS-Northrdge	XMCF	MS	75	CS-Nrthr	&1983
Jermakowicz, Eva K.	H-Pr	Tenn State	FIV	PHD	82	Warsaw	&2007
Jermias, Johnny	Asst	Simon Fraser	M	PHD	96	Waterloo	9-01
Jerome, William T. III				DCS	52.	Harvard	
Jerris, Scott I.	Prof	San Fran St	FE	PHD	87.	Purdue	1997

Jervis, Kathryn J.	Asst	Rhode Island	FG	PHD	97. Conn	&2007
Jessup, Carol	Asst	Il-Springfld	GSF	PHD	98 St Louis	&1998
Jeter, Debra C.	Assoc	Vanderbilt	F	PHD	90. Vanderbilt	&9-93
Jeter, John S.	Retir	Cameron	5-97	MBA	68 Arkansas	1968
Jetter, Ina	Prof	Puerto RicoM	EFPT	MACC	80 Va Tech	&1-78
Jetty, Juliana	Asst	Univ Glasgow	DF	PHD	03 Dundee	2002
Jewell, John	Inst	S Fl-St Pete	LX	LLM	93 Florida	&1-01
Ji, Xu-Dong	SLect	LaTrobe Univ	IHF	PHD	LaTrobe	1996
Jiambalvo, James J.	Dean	U Washington	MA	PHD	77. Ohio St	&1977
PricewaterhouseCoopers and Alumni Professor						
Jian, Ling	Asst	Lamar	F	PHD	06 Va Comm	2006
Jian, Ming	Asst	Nanyang Tech	FT	PHD	03 HKUST	2003
Jiang, John	Asst	Michigan St	F	PHD	05. Georgia	2005
Jiang, Wei	Asst	SUNY Old Wes	FPS	PHD	05. Rutgers	&2003
Jiang, Xiaowen	Asst	Cincinnati	F	DBA	05. Boston U	9-05
Jiang, Zhaodong	Assoc	Chinese HK	LX	SJD	92 Michigan	1995
Jin, Jong-Dae	Prof	MD E Shore	FMCX	PHD	89. Arizona	8-92
Jindanuwat, Niramol		Thailand		PHD	99. Ca-Irvine	
Jo, Seung Je	Assoc	Chosun Univ	CIJM	PHD	96 Sejong	1984
Joe, Jennifer R.	Assoc	Georgia St	A	PHD	99. Pittsburgh	&8-00
Joh, Gun-Ho	Assoc	San Diego St	F	PHD	88. Penn	1988
Johansson, Sven-Erik	Emer	Stockholm Ec	1995	ED	61 Stockholm	1953
John, Teresa A.	Assoc	New York U	F	PHD	86. NYU	1987
Johno, Christanta	Retir	Morgan State	1998	MBA	75 MorganSt	&1969
Johns, Leanne	Asst	Australian N	EHM	MPHL	01 Austr Natl	2002
Johns, Sharon			F	PHD	97. Tx A&M	&
Johnsen, Atle	Prof	Norwegian U	PF	LIC	Norwegia	
Johnson, Alan P.	Retir	CS-East Bay	1991	PHD	69. Illinois	&6-69
Johnson, Arthur H.			FM	PHD	61. Nrthwstrn	&
Johnson, Brad R.	C-Ac	Fran Marion	XLF	PHD	93. Houston	&8-03
Johnson, Bruce			CF	DBA	00. La Tech	
Johnson, Carol B.	Assoc	Oklahoma St	FI	PHD	93. Ariz St	&1992
Johnson, Charles E.	Deces			PHD	52. Minnesota	
Johnson, Christie W.	Assoc	Montana St	FVP	MBA	77 Wyoming	&9-80
Johnson, Darren	ALect	W Australia	M	BBUS	97 E Cowan	&2001
Johnson, Debra	Asst	Mont St-Bill	X	JD		2003
Johnson, Dena W.		Tarleton St	2003	PHD	97. Tx A&M	# &
Tarleton State Univ; Dept of Computer Info Sys; Stephenville TX 76402						
Johnson, Douglas A.	Retir	Arizona St	CMB	PHD	74. Tx-Austin	* &1974
Johnson, Eldred A.	Retir	Brigham Yg	1989	PHD	68. Utah	&9-55
Johnson, Elizabeth H.	Asst	Alderson Bro	ACFX	MBA		* &8-90
Johnson, Eric N.	Assoc	Indiana-Indy	ABS	PHD	89. Ariz St	* &1999
Johnson, Gary G.	Prof	SE Missouri	ANXS	PHD	89. Arkansas	* &1982
Johnson, Gene H.	Prof	Louisiana Te	BMI	PHD	86. Tx Tech	# * &9-90
Johnson, George A.	Assoc	Winston-Slm	FMVP	PHD	90. Va Tech	7-99
Johnson, Gerard G.		Industry		DBA	72. Harvard	
Johnson, Glenn L.	Retir	Wash State	2002	PHD	65. Berkeley	1979
Johnson, Grace F.	Prof	Marietta	FST	MA	88 S Fla	* &1989
McCoy Professor						
Johnson, H. Thomas	Prof	Portland St	HM	PHD	69 Wisconsin	&7-88
Johnson, Hans V.	Retir	Ark Tech	2003	PHD	73. Nebraska	# * &1992
Johnson, I. Richard	Prof	Utah State	FVT	PHD	84 Wisconsin	&1985
Larzette G. Hale Professor						
Johnson, James T.				PHD	58. LSU	
Johnson, Jaqueline	SLect	W Australia	S	MCOM	90 W Austrl	1985
Johnson, Jean	Retir	Angelo State	1993	MBA	56 Tx-Austin	1972
Johnson, John	Inst	Guam	FM	MBA	06 Am InterCo	2007
Johnson, Johnny	Inst	Florida A&M	FM	MBA	95 Fla A&M	2000
Johnson, Johnny R.	Deces			PHD	76. Va Tech	&
Johnson, Kenneth D.	Asst	OK Christian	OX	MBA	98 Cen Okla	&7-02
Johnson, Kenneth H. (Chuck)	Retir	Geo Southern	2005	PHD	89. Geo St	&1991
Johnson, Kenneth L.			AX	DBA	81. La Tech	&
Johnson, L. Todd		FASB	1994	PHD	72. Michigan	&1990
28 Governor's Lane; Bethel CT 06801						
Johnson, Laurence E.	Assoc	Colorado St	GAF	PHD	91. Tx Tech	&1990
Johnson, Lee L.	Retir			PHD	41. Missouri	
Johnson, Leigh	Asst	Murray State	J	JD	02 Kentucky	2006
Johnson, Linda M.	Retir		2006	PHD	90. Ariz St	&
Johnson, Lynn	Assoc	CS-Stanislau	F	PHD	98 Oregon	* &1995
Johnson, Marilyn	C-Ac	Wesley	FTV	MBA	96 Drexel	1982
Johnson, Marilyn F.	Assoc	Michigan St	F	PHD	92. U Wash	&2000
Johnson, Nicole	Asst	Cal-Berkeley	M	PHD	05 Stanford	2005
Johnson, Orace	Deces	Illinois	1991	PHD	66. Chicago	9-74
Johnson, Peter M.	Asst	Brigham Yg	FAM	PHD	03. Ariz St	&7-02
Johnson, Randy	Lect	Mich Tech	X	MS	85 Clarkson	1995
Johnson, Raymond E.	C-Ac	Guilford	XF	MBA	73 E Carol	&1988
Johnson, Raymond N.	Prof	Portland St	AEF	PHD	81. Oregon	&1980

Name	Rank	School	Dept	Degree	Year	University	Note
Johnson, Richard A.	Prof	Frostburg St	PFS	PHD	89.	Georgia	&9-87
Johnson, Richard V.	Retir	Ferris State	1999	MAS	63	Illinois	1966
Johnson, Robert T.	F			PHD	70.	NYU	&
Johnson, Rodney	Lect	Deakin-Burwo	FA	MEC	93	N Eng-Au	1978
Johnson, Ronald	SLect	So Queenslnd	FD	MACC	90	N Eng-Au	&1977
Johnson, Roxanne T.	Assoc	Scranton	IMF	PHD	87.	Penn St	&1993
Johnson, Scott	Prof	St Cloud St	FPX	LLM	82	Boston U	&1987
Johnson, Shondra	Inst	Bradley	FMS	MPA	93	Tx-Austin	& 8-04
Johnson, Sidney B.	F			DBA	78.	Miss St	&
Johnson, Steven B.	Deces	Bond Univ	4-89	PHD	79.	Wisconsin	&1988
Johnson, Steven D.	C-Ac	Utah Valley	MCB	PHD	91.	Va Tech	&2000
Johnson, Van E.	Retir		2005	PHD	92.	Ariz St	&
Johnson, W. Bruce	H-Pr	Iowa	F	PHD	75.	Ohio St	6-88
Arthur Andersen Professor of Accounting							
Johnson, Walter L.	Retir	Cen Florida	GN	PHD	74.	Tx-Austin	&9-79
Johnson, Wayne A.	Retir	Ind-Kokomo	1996	PHD	65.	Illinois	&8-92
Johnson-Dennis, Margaret	Asst	Hannibal-LaG	CVAX	MACC	88	W Illinois	* &1997
Johnston, Derek	Asst	Colorado St	F	PHD	01.	Colorado	&2002
Johnston, Gerald L.	Retir	CS-Fresno	1994	MBA	68	Kent St	& 8-71
Johnston, Holly H.	Asst	Mass-Boston	CMU	PHD	90	Car Mellon	
Johnston, James G.	Retir	Louisiana Te	2004	PHD	82.	Missouri	&1981
Johnston, Kenneth S.	Deces	Northwestern	1979	PHD	62.	Ohio St	1962
Johnston, Marvin A.				PHD	70.	Tx Tech	
Johnston, Ricky M.	Asst	Ohio State	F	PHD	04.	Penn	2004
Johnston, Roy W.	Retir	Ferris State	2001	MBA	62	Detroit	&1980
Johnston, Sheila A.	Inst	Louisville	PF	MST	92	Cincinnati	* &1-91
Johnston-Blair, Donna	Lect	Santa Clara	M	MBA	76	Toronto	&2001
Johnstone, Karla M.	Assoc	Wisconsin	AB	PHD	97.	Conn	&1997
Johnstone, Nathalie	Asst	Saskatchewan	FX	MPAC	00	Saskatch	&2005
Jolly, Stephen A.			FQT	PHD	78.	N Carol	
Jonas, Gregory	Asst	Case Western	FMS	ABD		Va Comm	* 7-07
Jones, Anne L.	Asst	Mass-Boston	F	DBA	03.	Boston U	2002
Jones, Becky	Lect	Baylor	P	MBA	78	Baylor	& 8-78
Jones, Christopher L.	Asst	George Wash	FM	PHD	98	Stanford	8-97
Jones, David T.	Assoc	Calif U-Penn	FMP	MS		W Virginia	1985
Jones, Deborah K.	SLect	Wayne State	FX	PHD	96.	Kent St	1994
Jones, Denise A.	Asst	Wm & Mary	F	PHD	00.	Colorado	2000
Jones, Don	LT	Univ Windsor	A	MBA	76		2004
Jones, Donald M.	Retir	North Texas	1983	MBA	49	North Tx	1955
Jones, Donald R.	Asst	Tx Tech	SAB	PHD	88.	Tx-Austin	&
Info Sys & Quant Sci Dept; Texas Tech University							
Jones, Elizabeth H.	Assoc	W Carolina	SFP	PHD	88	Indiana	&1994
Jones, Frederick L.	Prof	Mass-Dartmou	FA	DBA	91.	Boston U	& 9-82
Jones, Gardner M.	Retir	Mich State	1985	PHD	56.	LSU	&1956
2801 Hopkins Avenue; Lansing MI 48192							
Jones, H. Milton	Retir	Texas-Tyler	1995	DBA	67.	S Calif	& 8-86
Jones, Herbert C.	Retir	Mid Tenn St	2003	MA	67	Alabama	&1967
Jones, Howard E.	Retir	Tenn-Martin	1992	MS	58	Alabama	& 9-58
Jones, Jacqueline	Assoc	Miss College	FRVG	ABD	71	Miss St	&1971
Jones, James F.	Emer	Appalach St	1992	MA	52	E Carol	1956
Jones, Jane	LectB	Flinders Un	BM	MCOM	96	NS Wales	7-97
Jones, Jefferson P.	Assoc	Auburn	F	PHD	97.	Fla St	&9-97
Jones, Jennifer J.			FI	PHD	88.	Michigan	&
Jones, Judy L.	C-Pr	Transylvania	CAG	ABD		Anderson	&1980
Jones, Julian W.	Fell	U Manchester	M	MSC	96	Cardiff	1996
Jones, Keith	Asst	Geo Mason	AU	PHD	04.	Arizona	8-04
Jones, Keith T.	Assoc	Illinois St	MAF	PHD	01.	Kentucky	& 8-05
Jones, Kris Tina	Inst	SE Louisiana	FZ	MPA	85	Miss	& 8-87
Jones, Lynn C.	Asst	North Fla	FX	PHD	03.	Geo St	& 8-03
Jones, Michael A.	Prof	Linfield	TFV	MBA	74	Oregon	&1977
Jones, Mike	Prof	Cardiff U	FHIW	MA	75	Oxford	&1979
Jones, Nancy	Inst	CS-Chico	SM	MBA	01	CS-Chico	1-05
Jones, Pam	Asst	E Kentucky	FM	ABD			2005
Jones, Phillip A. Sr.	Retir	Richmond	2000	PHD	68.	Mich St	8-73
Jones, Ralph	Deces	Yale	1984				
Jones, Richard C.	Assoc	Hofstra	CP	PHD	01.	Rutgers	&8-97
Jones, Richard W.	Retir	Lamar	2002	PHD	75.	Arkansas	&1975
Jones, Rita C.	Assoc	Columbus St	FMT	DBA	94.	Miss St	* 2003
Jones, Roberta A.	Asst	Hawaii-Hilo	SAF	PHD	96.	Illinois	&2006
Jones, Roger G.	Inst	Wichita St	DS	MPA	92	Wichita St	1993
Jones, Royce D.	Retir	Ark Tech	2004	MBA	71	E Tx St	& 8-73
Jones, Sally M.	Retir	Virginia	2006	PHD	78.	Houston	& 8-92
Jones, Scott K.	Prof	Delaware	MC	PHD	88.	Drexel	1988
Jones, Seymour	ClPr	New York U	FA	MBA		NYU	1993
Jones, Stewart	Prof	Univ Sydney	FTI	PHD	91	Wellingt	&2001
Jones, Stuart H.	Assoc	Univ Calgary	FM	PHD	70	Wales	&1978
Jones, Vern	Dean$	Univ Calgary	SGMA	PHD	75	Brit Colum	1978

Jones, W. Elbert	Retir	So Carolina	1985	MS	57	S Carol				&1957
Jones, William J.	Retir	Seton Hall	FA	MBA	62	Fairl Dick				&1966
Joo, Hyunghwan				PHD	91.	Illinois				
Joo, In Ki	Prof	Yonsei Univ	FIA	PHD	86.	NYU				&1987
Joo, Jin-Kyu				PHD	88.	Berkeley				
Joos, Peter R.	Assoc	CUNY-Baruch	F	PHD	97.	Stanford				2-05
Joos, Philip	Asst	Tilburg	FT	PHD	00.	Stanford				2000
Jopling, Samuel H.	Retir	St Marys-Cdn	8-94	PHD	75.	Penn St		*		1976
Jordan, Charles E.	Prof	So Miss	FC	DBA	86.	La Tech				&1988
Jordan, Dan	Asst	Golden Gate	FA	MBA	76	Berkeley				&2000
Jordan, Hugues	Prof	HEC Paris	CUM	HECD	69	HEC Paris				1970
Jordan, Leland G.	C-Ac	Chris Newpor	MS	DBA	85.	Geo Wash				1999
Jordan, Louis H.	Retir	Fordham	1994	PHD	54.	Columbia				&1975
Jordan, Robert E.	Retir	Wis-Superior	2002	PHD	92.	Miss	#	*	&	1-92
Jordan, William F.	Retir	Florida St	5-03	PHD	74.	Geo St			&	9-74
Jordan, Win G.	Asst	Fort Hays St	MS	PHD	96	Mich St				1998
Jorgensen, Bjorn N.	Assoc	Columbia	MF	PHD	98.	Nrthwstrn				2002
Jorgenson, Maggie D.	Lect	N Dakota St	MS	MS	80	N Dakota		*		&2004
Joseph, George	Asst	Mass-Lowell	CM	PHD	97	Temple				&2005
Joseph, Gilbert W. (Joe)	Prof	Tampa	FGIS	PHD	92.	S Fla				&1986
Dana Professor										
Joseph, Harold W.	Retir	Clayton St	2001	DBA	78.	La Tech		*	&	6-87
Joseph, Jerry A.	Assoc	Indiana U-PA	FT	PHD	93.	Pittsburgh		*		&1990
Joseph, Joseph J. Jr.			FA	DBA	72.	Oklahoma		&		
Joy, Arthur C.	Retir	Columbus St	2002	PHD	85.	Illinois		*		&1991
Joy, David W.	Prof	Cen Missouri	PCX	PHD	84.	Nebraska				&1990
Joyce, Edward J.	Prof	Minnesota	BM	PHD	76.	Illinois				1981
Joyce, William B.	Assoc	E Illinois	CTFB	PHD	97	Nebraska				&1999
Jozsi, Celina L.	Inst	South Fla	F	MACC	77	S Fla			&	6-76
Juarez-Valdes, Luis F.	Asst	Univ America		PHD	99.	Tx A&M				
Jucius, Michael J.	Retir	Arizona-Mgt		PHD	42.	Chicago				1966
Judd, Andrew J.	Assoc	Cen Florida	X	PHD	85.	Florida			&	8-87
Judd, Mark	Lect	San Diego	FMA	IMBA	94	SanDiego				&1997
Juffernbruch, Mark	Assoc	Simpson	ACGX	JD		Iowa				1999
Julius, Edward H.	Prof	Calif Luthrn	FTV	MS	75	Penn				&1981
Jun, Aelee	AcLec	U Wollongong		PHD		Sydney				2007
Jung, Boo Chun	Asst	Hawaii-Manoa	FI	PHD	07	Colorado				8-07
Jung, Do Jin (James)			FAP	PHD	04.	Kentucky				
Jung, Kooyul	H-Pr	Korea Adv In	FM	PHD	87.	Florida				&2002
Jung, Woon-Oh	Prof	Seoul Natl	FQTX	PHD	86.	UCLA				1998
Juras, Paul E.	Assoc	Wake Forest	PCM	PHD	91.	Syracuse		*	&	9-91
Jurinski, James J.	Assoc	Portland	LX	JD	80	Lewis&Cl				&1987
Justice, Vera	Retir	Abilene Chr	1985	MA	80	Abilene				&1981
Juurmaa, Risto	Res	Helsinki Sch	FM	MS	92	Helsinki				1992
Kablan, Abdelsalam A.				PHD	82.	LSU				
Kabot, Alvin A.	Retir	CUNY-Hunter	1-99	LLM	63	NYU			&	9-67
Kachelmeier, Steven J.	Prof	Texas-Austin	AVFB	PHD	88.	Florida			&	1-88
Charles T. Zlatkovich Centennial Professorship in Accounting										
Kachur, Robert L.	Asst	R Stockton	CSUM	ABD		Capella				2004
Kaderabek, Joseph D.	Retir	Baldwin-Wal	FAX	MBA	70	Case Wes			&	9-76
Kadous, Hamdy M.		King Saud Un	1992	PHD	84.	Syracuse				
King Saud Univ; Acctg Dept; PO Box 2459; Riyadh Saudia Arabia										
Kadous, Kathryn	Assoc	Emory	AF	PHD	96.	Illinois			&	8-03
Kaenzig, Rebecca	Assoc	Appalach St	XP	PHD	87.	S Carol				1986
Kagaya, Tetsuyuki	Assoc	Hitotsubashi	FA	DBA		Hitotsub				2000
Kagle, Arthur R.	Retir	Cen Michigan	1989	PHD	75	Tx Tech	#	*		1981
Kahle, Jennifer B.	Asst	South Fla	FX	PHD	03.	S Carol			&	8-03
Kahn, David C.	Inst	Yeshiva	F	BS	73	Lng Isl			&	2-02
Kahn, Nathan			FM	PHD	79.	Columbia				
Kahya, Emel	Assoc	Rutgers-Camd	F	PHD	91.	Rice				1991
Kaiama, Cathy M.	Inst	Hawaii-Manoa	F	MACC	88	Hawaii			&	8-91
Kaidonis, Mary A.	H-Ac	U Woolongong	BTW	PHD	96	Wollong				&1989
Kaiser, Mark	Lect	SUNY-Plattsb	AFX	MBA	80	Clarkson				&1986
Kako, Yoshihito	Prof	Waseda Univ	FIN	PHD		Waseda				
School of Commerce; 1-6-1 Nishi-waseda, Shinjuku-ku; Tokyo 169-8050 Japan										
Kalagnanam, Suresh S.	Assoc	Saskatchewan	CMB	PHD	97.	Wisconsin		*		1996
Kalbers, Lawrence P.	Prof	Loyola Marym	JFAS	PHD	89.	Penn St				&2005
R. Chad Dreier Chair in Accounting Ethics										
Kalesnikoff, Doug	Asst	Saskatchewan	AFO	BCOM	77	Saskatch				&2004
Kalfayan, Garo	Prof	Cal Poly-SLO	X	JD	83	UCLA			&	9-06
Kalfon, Charles	Assoc	HEC Paris	FLNP	HECD	65	HEC Paris				1990
Kallapur, Sanjay G.			F	PHD	90.	Harvard				
Kallio, Larry	SLect	Minnesota	A	MBA		Minn-Dul				
Kalotay, Egon A.	Lect	Macquarie Un	F	PHD	02	AUSM				1991
Kalyta, Pavlo	Asst	Univ Ottawa	FMC	PHD	07	Concordia				2006
Kam, Thomas	Asst	Hawaii Pacif	MPE	MBA	78	Hawaii		*	&	8-86
Kam, Vernon T.	Emer	CS-East Bay	2000	PHD	68.	Berkeley			&	9-69

Name	Rank	School		Degree		Institution	
Kama, Itay	Asst	Tel Aviv Un	F	PHD	05	Tel Aviv	2006
Kamas, J. William	Lect	Texas-Austin		MBA	91	Chicago	&2002
Kamen-Friedman, Michelle	Asst	CUNY-Lehman	XPRA	MBA		St Johns	&1985
Kamia, Rania	Lect	Dundee	IJTW	PHD	05	Edinburgh	2006
Kamin, Jacob Y.			M	PHD	75.	NYU	
Kaminski, Kathleen A.	Asst	Mont St-Bill	FST	PHD	02.	Okla St	& 8-05
Kaminsky, Daniel	VInst	Cleveland St	AF	MSA	78	Cen Fla	&2006
Kamlet, Elliot	Lect	SUNY-Bingham	F	MS	77	SUNY-Bin	&1982
Kamniker, Judith A.	Prof	Auburn-Montg	FGN	PHD	82	Denver	&1985
Kamp-Roelands, Nancy	Asst	Tilburg Univ	A	MBA	86	Rotterdam	&1993
Kan, Shirley	Inst	Chinese HK	FVX	MA	91	Lancaster	&1999
Kana, Said M.		Geneva Switz	1992	PHD	70.	NYU	
10A Avenue Marc Peter; 1290 Versoix Switzerland							
Kanaan, George K.	Assoc	Concordia U	FMEV	PHD	84.	Wisconsin	1987
Kanagaretnam, Kiridaran	Assoc	McMaster Un	FM	PHD	00.	Syracuse	7-02
Kanan, Rief	Lect	SUNY-N Paltz	FM	MS	76	Syracuse	&1998
Kandelin, Nils A.			SO	PHD	90.	S Calif	
Kandiel, El-Sayed H. A.	Asst	SUNY-Plattsb	CFMV	PHD	85.	Baruch	1989
Kandunias, Chris	LectA	Flinders Un	DTQ	BCOM	92	Adelaide	1-93
Kane, Gregory D.	Prof	Delaware	FS	PHD	92.	Va Tech	& 2-93
Kaneda, Naoyuki	Asst		FMQX	PHD	02.	Car Mellon	
Gakushuin University							
Kang, Byung-Min A.		Korea		PHD	95.	Illinois	
Kang, Gerui	Asst	Minn-Duluth		ABD		North Tx	2007
Kang, Helen	Lect	New So Wales	MF	MCOM	00	NS Wales	1999
Kang, Ho-Young	Prof	Kyungpook Un	C	PHD	91	Pusan	1983
Kang, Jai S.	Prof	San Fran St	CSI	PHD	77.	Tx A&M	&1983
Kang, Joo Hun				DBA	94.	Miss St	
Kang, Jungpao	Assoc	Nat Chengchi	FQT	PHD	91	NYU	1991
Kang, Sok-Hyon	Prof	George Wash	FMY	PHD	88.	MIT	2000
Kang, Tony	Asst	Fla Atlantic		PHD	03.	Illinois	& 8-07
Kannenberg, Karen	Asst	Mo Bapitst	FM	DMGT	99	Webster	
Kanodia, Chandra	Prof	Minnesota	M	PHD	78.	Car Mellon	1981
Arthur Andersen-Duane Kullberg Land Grant Chair							
Kanter, Howard A.	Assoc	DePaul	SE	EDD	84	N Illinois	&1979
Kantor, Jeffrey	Prof	Univ Windsor	CM	PHD	84	Bradford	&1983
Kantorovitz, Bracha		Bar Illan Un		PHD	89.	Penn	
Kao, Jennifer L.	Prof	Univ Alberta	F	PHD	91	Brit Colum	&1998
Kaplan, Allen	Retir	Lg Isl-Brook	1992	MS	75	Long Isl	&1974
678 Fulton Street #V-8; Famington NY 11735							
Kaplan, Jane E.	Inst	Drexel	F	MSA	85	Drexel	&1994
Kaplan, Robert S.	Prof	Harvard	MC	PHD	68.	Cornell	1983
Marvin Bower Professor of Leadership Development							
Kaplan, Steven E.	Prof	Arizona St	M	PHD	82.	Illinois	1981
Kaplan, Steven N.	Prof	Chicago		PHD	88.	Harvard	
Dept of Finance; University of Chicago							
Kapoor, M. Rai	Assoc	Concordia U	FM	PHD	86	Toronto	* 1980
Karadbil, Laura L.	Retir	American U	1991	PHD	71.	American	& 9-58
Karamanou, Irene	Asst	Cyprus	FMI	PHD	00.	Penn St	2000
Karan, Vijay			SC	PHD	83.	Tx-Austin	
Karaoglu, N. Emre	Asst	So Calif		PHD	02.	Nrthwstrn	&2004
Karayan, John E.	Prof	CS-Pomona	MXIG	PHD	94	Claremont	1991
Karbens, John P.	Assoc	Hawaii Pacif	FPER	EDD	83	Hawaii	# * & 8-90
Karbhari, Yusuf	Read	Cardiff U	AGMN	PHD	97	Cardiff	1990
Karcher, Julia N.	Assoc	Louisville	FEJ	PHD	92.	Fla St	* 8-91
Karim Eldin, Ahmed	Asst	King Saud U	F	PHD	85	Birminghm	1989
Karim, A.K.M. Waresul	Lect	Victoria NZ	FMIW	PHD	95	Leeds	1997
Karim, Khondkar E.	Assoc	Rochest Tech	FCM	DBA	95.	Miss St	& 9-01
Kariuki-Mwangi, Benson	C-As	Alcorn St	FAN	DBA	00	Nova SE	&1986
Karl, Peter A. III	Prof	SUNY-Utica	XL	JD	78	AlbanyLw	&1981
Karlin, Arthur D.	Prof	Ark-Pine Blf	XF	PHD	64.	Illinois	1994
Karlin, Barbara H.	VP	Golden Gate	X	LLM	81	Golden Gt	&1986
Vice President Academic Affairs							
Karlinsky, Stewart S.	Prof	San Jose St	X	PHD	81.	NYU	& 8-88
Karmon, David J.	Prof	Cen Michigan	FV	PHD	84.	Nebraska	&1979
Karnes, Allan L.	Prof	So Illinois	X	JD	86	S Illinois	&1981
KPMG Tax Research Professor							
Karpik, Philip G.			MFNS	PHD	86.	Syracuse	
Karrenbrock, Roger E.			1992	PHD	56.	Illinois	&
12551 The Vista; Los Angeles CA 90049							
Karuga, Gilbert	Asst	Kansas	S	PHD	02	Conn	8-02
Karuna, Christo	Asst	Calif-Irvine	M	PHD	04.	Michigan	7-04
Karvel, George R.			FX	DBA	79.	Colorado	
Kaschmitter, Ursula	Lect	Santa Clara	FX	MBA	83	Golden Gt	&1987
Kasperski, Michael D.	Lect	St Bonaventu	CFMV	MBA	83	St Bonav	& 8-03
Kasputzys, Joseph				DBA	72.	Harvard	
Kass-Schraibman, Frimette	Asst	CUNY-Brookly	APF	MA			& 9-05

Name	Rank	School		Degree		Degree School	
Kassinis, George	Asst	Cyprus	FMW	PHD	97	Princeton	1997
Kast, Daniel K.	Retir	Iona	1990	JD	53	NYU	&1961
Kastantin, Joseph T.	Assoc	Wis-La Cross	VGPI	MBA	79	Butler	* &1-84
Kasznik, Ron	Assoc	Stanford	F	PHD	95.	Berkeley	1995
Katagiri, Catherine M.	Assoc	St Rose	PFCA	MS		SUNY	* &9-80
Katori, John N.	Retir	Nichols Col	2000	MBA	81	Nichols	1958
Kattelman, Lorsanne	Inst	Weber State	FT	MS	90	Weber St	1998
Kattelus, Susan C.	H-Pr	E Michigan	XGNF	PHD	90.	Mich St	&1990
Katter, Norm	SLect	Queensld Tec	F	PHD		Queensld	1987
Katz, Robert	Prof	Hofstra	X	LLM	71	NYU	1975
Katz, Sharon P.	Asst	Harvard		PHD	06.	Columbia	7-06
Kauder, W. Frank Jr.	Retir	Winston-Slm	5-99	PHD	82.	Georgia	1987
Kauffman, Joel	Retir	San Fran St	1995	LLM	67	NYU	&1989
Kauffman, Marvin	Retir	Temple	1992	MBA	60	Temple	&1956
Kauffman, N. Leroy	Assoc	W Carolina	CMPU	PHD	88.	Ohio St	&1994
Kaufman, Arnold	Retir	Fairleigh Di	1985	PHD	58	NYU	&9-59
Kaufman, Felix	Retir	Coopers&Lybr		PHD	60.	Chicago	&
Kaufman, Jerry M.	Retir	SW Okla St	2000	PHD	74.	Okla St	&1992
Kaulback, Frank S. Jr.	Retir	Virginia	1982	PHD	45	Virginia	1946
Kauppila, William	Clln	Seattle Pac	AFPX	MBA	70	W Mich	&9-06
Kausch, Darlene E.			AT	DBA	79.	Kent St	&
Kavanagh, M.	SLect	U Queensland	FM	PHD	01	Queensl	2000
Kavermann, Markus	Asst	Aachen Univ	FCM	MA	99	Aachen	1999
Kavusoanoo, Emmanuel	Prof	Athens Unlv	FQ	PHD	93	City-UK	2001
Kaye, R.	Prof	East Anglia	SCM	MSC		Sheffield	
Kayed, Metwally	Asst	Kuwait Univ	IF	PHD	90	Hull	1993
Kaylor, Norman R.	Retir	N Car-Wilmin	2001	PHD	71.	Miss	1971
Ke, Bin	Assoc	Penn State	X	PHD	99.	Mich St	&8-99
Kealey, Burch T.	Asst	Neb-Omaha	F	PHD	96.	Oklahoma	2001
Kearney, Linwood W.	Asst	Wichita St	F	ABD		Fla St	2007
Kearns, Francis E.	Asst	Rochest Tech	FA	PHD	86.	SUNY-Buf	&9-86
Kearns, Grover S.	Asst	S Fl-St Pete	S	PHD	97	Kentucky	&8-01
Kearns, Robert W.	Retir	Carroll	1995	MBA		Miami U	&9-72
Keasey, Kevin	Prof	Univ Leeds	FBMQ	PHD	81	Newcastle	9-90
Keasler, Hubert L. Jr.	Assoc	Wm Carey	CMGN	DBA	91.	Miss St	* 1999
Keating, A. Scott	VAsoc	MIT	FM	DBA	95.	Harvard	2007
Keating, Elizabeth K.		Harvard		PHD	99	MIT	
Public Policy Dept; 617-495-9856; elizabeth_keating@ksg.harvard.edu							
Keating, John L.	Deces			PHD	78.	Tx-Austin	&
Keating, Patrick J.			S	PHD	90.	Penn St	
Keck, John T.	Deces	High Point	FIJ	PHD	77.	Geo St	&2004
Kedia, Sushila	Asst	Grambling St	PMS	MBA	88	La Tech	* &1991
Kee, Robert C.	Prof	Alabama	CS	DBA	80.	Fla St	* 9-78
Keeling, Kermit O.	Assoc	Loyola-Maryl	XP	LLM	87	Houston	&1987
Keenan, Michael G.	SLect	U Auckland	FA	PHD	77	St Andre	1984
Keenan, Philip S.	Assoc	Wofford	XFC	MBA	78	Michigan	&9-81
Keenan, Sue	Lect	Indiana	F	BA	82	Dartmouth	1997
Keene, David	AsLec	So Queenslnd	ATW	MBS	97	Massey	1999
Keener, Mary	Asst	E Michigan	FEX	PHD	07.	Kent St	2005
Keeping, David	Inst	New Bruns-SJ		MBA	03	St Marys	&2003
Keerasuntonpong, Prae	Asst	Chulalongkor	CM	MBA	92	SASIN	1995
Keinath, Annemarie K.	Assoc	Indiana NW	AF	PHD	89.	Mich St	&8-92
Keister, Orville R. (Bud)	Retir	Akron	1995	PHD	64.	Illinois	9-66
Keith, Richard L.		Mass Medical	1996	DBA	82.	Fla St	* 1996
Univ of Massachusetts Medical Center							
Keith, Robert M.	Retir	South Fla	2007	PHD	69.	Alabama	&9-69
Keithley, John P.	Prof	St Louis	MVTW	PHD	72.	Missouri	&1968
Kell, Walter G.	Retir	Michigan	1987	PHD	52.	Illinois	&1961
Kellard, Neil	Asst	Univ Essex	F	PHD	00	Nottingh	2002
Keller, A. Craig	Asst	Missouri St	M	PHD	00.	Tx A&M	8-01
Keller, Carl E.	Asst	Ind-Pur/FtWy	CX	PHD	97.	Tennessee	&8-02
Keller, Donald E.	Retir	San Diego	2001	DBA	69.	S Calif	* &1997
Keller, Earl C.	Prof	Cal Poly-SLO	FGKV	PHD	73.	U Wash	&9-87
Keller, Francis C.	Retir	St Marys-Tx	1989	MBA	65	St MryTX	&9-64
Keller, J. Howard	SLect	Indiana-Indy	FM	MBA	78	Indiana	&1981
Keller, Rachel	Lect	Appalach St	P	MS	00	Appalach	&2006
Keller, Robert J.			TF	PHD	73.	LSU	&
Keller, Stuart B.	Retir	Kentucky	2002	PHD	81.	N Carol	1981
Keller, Thomas F.	Emer	Duke	F	PHD	60.	Michigan	&9-59
R. J. Reynolds Professor of Business Administration							
Kelley, Ann G.	Asst	Providence	FPVX	MBA		Northeas	&1986
Kelley, Claudia L.	Prof	Appalach St	X	PHD	91.	Alabama	&1994
Kelley, Dawn	Lect	Texas Tech	F	MBA	87	Tx Tech	1988
Kelley, Thomas	Inst	Seattle	ACFP	MBA	72	NewHamp	&2002
Kelley, Timothy	Prof	San Diego	F	PHD	84.	Houston	&1983
Kelliher, Charles F.	Assoc	Cen Florida	FBT	PHD	90.	Tx A&M	&8-85
Kellner, Rochelle	Prof	CS-Pomona	FP	PHD	85	UCLA	1979

Kellogg, Milford K.				PHD	55.	Illinois	
Kellogg, Robert L.			F	PHD	80.	Rochester	
Kelly, Andrea	Lect	Deakin-Geelg	F	BCOM	93	Deakin	1994
Kelly, Anne S.	Asst	Butler	APCF	PHD	86.	Cincinnati	&2006
Kelly, Chris F.	SLect	Deakin-Geelg	AF	MEC	81	N Eng-Au	&1977
Kelly, Elaine D.	Assoc	OK Christian	AT	MBA	89	Cen Okla	& 8-92
Kelly, J.		London Metro					
Kelly, J. Ann	Inst	Geo Southern	P	MBA	02	Ga Srthrn	2002
Kelly, Khim	Asst	Nanyang Tech	MB	PHD	03	S Calif	&1997
Kelly, Kirk P.			S	PHD	85.	Pittsburgh	
Kelly, Lauren	Assoc	Hawaii Pacif	MF	PHD	76.	Alabama	8-02
Kelly, M.	Lect	Univ Ulster	FM	MBA			&O-03
Kelly, M. B.	Assoc	Univ Ulster	AF	BA			&O-03
Kelly, Patrick T.	C-As	Providence	CMF	PHD	04.	Conn	2001
Kelsey, Richard L.	Assoc	St Thomas-FL	FCA	PHD	79.	U Wash	&2005
Kelting, William R.	Retir	SUNY-Plattsb	2006	PHD	87.	Arkansas	& 9-75
Kelton, Andrea	Asst	South Fla	S	PHD	06.	Tennessee	8-06
Keltyka, Pamela K.	Assoc	Akron	CM	PHD	99.	Ca-Irvine	9-97
KPMG Fellow							
Kemerer, Kevin L.		Fla Memorial	MFT	PHD	90.	Va Tech	&
Kemp, Patrick S.			FV	PHD	59.	Illinois	&
Kempner, Jack J.	Retir	Montana	1981	PHD	56.	Ohio St	&1956
Kemsley, Deen	Prof	Tulane	TX	PHD	95.	N Carol	&2004
Kenamond, Frederick D.	Retir	So Miss	1981	PHD	71.	Alabama	&1961
Kend, Michael	Asst	Australian N	AFT	PHD	02	Melbourne	2003
Kenis, Izzet	H-Ac	Rutgers-Camd	BCFM	PHD	74	NYU	9-72
Kennedy, Calvin E.			MP	PHD	63.	Nebraska	&
Kennedy, Dennis T.			FT	PHD	83.	Temple	
Kennedy, Duane B.	Assoc	Un Waterloo	MF	PHD	87.	Cornell	* 7-87
Kennedy, Frances A.	Assoc	Clemson	CM	PHD	02.	North Tx	&2001
Kennedy, Helen A.			F	PHD	79.	Okla St	
Kennedy, Henry A.	Retir	Univ Alberta	1993	PHD	73	U Wash	&1965
Kennedy, James Kevin	Assoc	Northern St	GCFI	DBA	94.	S Illinois	1999
Kennedy, Jeffrey L.			CM	PHD	87.	Tx A&M	
Kennedy, John	Assoc	ESCP deParis	AGI	MBA	66	Carleton	1988
Kennedy, Kathryn	Inst	Miami U-Ohio	P	MBA	82	Miami U	& 8-05
Kennedy, Paul E.	Retir	Alaska SE	2001	MBA	73	Idaho	&1979
Kennedy, S. Jane	Prof	U Washington	BF	PHD	92.	Duke	* 1-92
Kennedy, Tom	ClAc	Indiana	X	JD	71	Indiana	&2002
Kennelley, Michael D.		John Brown U	FIJT	PHD	83.	Okla St	& 8-00
John Brown Univ; Siloam Springs, AR 72761; 501-524-3131							
Kenner, Anne C.			FMCT	DBA	89.	La Tech	&
Kennett, Danny L.	Assoc	Emporia St	MP	DBA	83.	Miss St	1988
Kennon, Walter P.		IBM Corp		PHD	54.	Chicago	
Kenny, Mark	Lect	Un Cl Dublin	FIP	ACA			2004
Kenny, Paul	LectB	Flinders Un	XTI	MTAX	98	Deakin	2-95
Kenny, Robert	Prof	St Michaels		MBA		Vermont	&
Kenny, Sara York		IFC	2004	PHD	89.	North Tx	&
Kenny, William J.	Prof	Portland St	XL	JD	73	Gonzaga	&1985
Kenson, Donna K.			FA	PHD	95.	Tx-Arlin	&
Kent, D. Donald	Assoc	SUNY-Brockpo	ABES	PHD	96.	Union-NY	&1994
Kent, Martha	VAsst	West Alabama	PC	MBA	79	Auburn	&1979
Kent, Pamela F.	SLect	U Queensland	A	PHD	91	N Eng-Au	&1987
Kent, Ros	Lect	Queensld Tec	F	MFM	78	Queensld	& 1-76
Kenyon, Peter B.	Prof	CS-Humboldt	FC	PHD	85.	Santa Cl	* 1984
Kerby, Debra K.	Prof	Truman State	FMP	PHD	89.	Nebraska	* &1982
Kercsmar, John		E Stroudsbur	2001	PHD	84.	Houston	&
East Stroudsburg University							
Kerler, William A.	Asst	N Car-Wilmin	FA	PHD	05.	Va Tech	2005
Kermis, George F.	Assoc	Canisius	FC	PHD	82.	Syracuse	&1978
Kern, Beth B.	Assoc	Ind-So Bend	FX	PHD	86.	Indiana	&1995
Keros, John W.	Retir	E Michigan	D-98	MBA	60	Michigan	&1965
Kerr, David S.	Assoc	N Car-Charl	AS	PHD	89.	Mich St	2005
Kerr, Jennifer	Lect	U Auckland	MA	MCOM	88	Auckland	1997
Kerr, Rebecca A.	Lect	So Carolina	F	MACC	91	S Carol	&1999
Kerr, Stephen G.	Asst	Bradley	M	PHD	00	Alberta	* 8-07
Kerr, Stephen W.	Prof	Hendrix	XF	MBA	77	So Meth	&1979
Kerry, Mike	Lect	Deakin-Geelg	F	MCOM	92	Melbourne	&2002
Kershaw, Russell	Assoc	Butler	PMCS	PHD	96.	S Carol	1996
Carl K. Doty Professor of Accounting							
Kerstein, Joseph	Assoc	CUNY-Baruch	FC	PHD	90	Penn	1989
Claire & Eli Mason Scholar in Accountancy							
Kertz, Connie	C-Pr	Emory	XL	JD	75	Emory	1980
Kerwin, Frank P.	Retir	No Michigan	1998	MBA	74	NewHaven	&1977
Kesselman, Jerome J.	Retir	Denver	1994	JD	52	Denver	&1946
Kessler, Lara	Asst	Grand Valley	LMP	JD	95	Vanderbilt	8-07
Kessler, Lawrence	Retir	Furman	2005	PHD	77.	Tx-Austin	& 9-80

Name	Rank	School	Code	Degree	Yr	Institution	Mark	Year
Kestel, Joanne	Lect	Murdoch Univ	FM	MACC		Australia		1990
Ketchand, Alice A.	Prof	Sam Houston	BFI	PHD	94.	Houston		&1992
Kettering, Ronald C.	Prof	Columbus St	MFCP	DBA	77	La Tech	# *	&1986
Ketteriss, Holger	Asst	Aachen Univ	FCM	MA	99	Aachen		2000
Ketz, J. Edward	Assoc	Penn State	FJ	PHD	77.	Va Tech		9-81
Key, J. Henry	Retir	Tx Christian		PHD	56.	Tx-Austin		
Key, Kimberly G.	Assoc	Auburn	T	PHD	95.	Mich St		&9-99
Keys, David E.	Retir	No Illinois	2004	PHD	75.	Illinois	* &	1-75
Khaledi, Naser	Asst	Purdue Calmu		PHD		Temple		2005
Khalifa, Zakaa				PHD	92.	Rutgers		
Khallaf, Ashraf	Asst	So Indiana	FS	PHD	04.	Fla Atl		2003
Khalsa, Jodha Singh			M	PHD	87.	Ariz St	&	
Khan, Israr	Inst	King Fahd Un	S	PHD	85	Kanpur		1992
Khan, Mozaffav	Asst	MIT	FM	PHD	05	Toronto		2005
Khan, Radib	AsLec	LaTrobe Univ						2006
Khan, Zafar U.	Prof	E Michigan	MFCS	PHD	87.	LSU	# *	1989
Khanlarian, Cynthia J.	Lect	N Car-Greens	PF	MSA	95	NC-Green		&8-97
Khanna, Bhagwan S.	SLect	Victoria NZ	BCEF	PHD	92	Victoria	*	1986
Khanna, Haresh	Assoc	Alabama A&M	PFM	DBA	80	Miss St	*	9-77
Khasharmeh, Hussein	Asst	Yarmouk Univ	FM	PHD	95	Middlesex		1987
Khelifi, Ali	Asst	Univ Tunis	F	DEA	96	ISCAE		&1996
Khemakhem, Abdellatif	Retir	King Saud Un		PHD	66.	Ohio St		
Khoury, Paul	Asst	St Scholasti	MANS	MBA	92	Wright St		&8-96
Khumawala, Caleha D.	Assoc	Houston	FGI	PHD	70.	N Carol		&1078
Khurana, Inder K.	Prof	Missouri	F	PHD	89.	Ariz St		&1989
Deloitte Professor								
Khurshed, Arif	Lect	U Manchester	FQTY	PHD		Reading		1999
Kiani-Aslani, Rajabali	Prof	CS-Northrdge	M	PHD	75.	Oklahoma		1978
Kiattikulwattana, Prapaporn	Lect	Chulalongkor	F	MACC	00	Chulalong		&2001
Kickham, Lawrence J.	C-Pr	Saginaw Vall	AM	MS	72	Northeas		&1974
Kida, Thomas E.	Prof	Massachusett	BF	PHD	78.	Mass		1982
Kiddoo, Robert J.	Emer	CS-Northrdge	C	DBA	78	S Calif	*	1970
Kido, Nolan Y.	Lect	Chaminade	P	MBA	03	Hawaii		8-05
Kido, Richard Y.	D-As	Chaminade	EACN	MBA	97	Hawaii		&8-02
Kidwell, Linda A.	Assoc	Wyoming	AJB	PHD	93.	LSU		8-05
Kiefer, Dale L.	Retir	Cincinnati	1989	PHD	63	Cincinnati		&1954
Kiel, Mark	Assoc	N Carol A&T	FGN	PHD	78.	Georgia		&1980
Kieso, Donald E.	Emer	No Illinois	1993	PHD	63.	Illinois		&1963
Kiger, Jack E.	Prof	Tennessee	AF	PHD	71.	Missouri		& 6-76
Warren L. Slagle Professor of Accounting								
Kildal, Tor S.	IndPr	Norwegian Mg	X	MBUS	90	NHH Berg		&1993
Kile, Charles O.	Asst	Mid Tenn St	FP	PHD	93.	Wash U		2003
Kilgore, Alan	SLect	Macquarie Un	IF	MEC	89	Macquarie		&2001
Kilgore, Ronald W.	Prof	Tenn-Martin	FX	PHD	74.	Miss		9-75
Kilic, Emre				PHD	05.	Syracuse		
Killough, Larry N.	Prof	Virg Tech	CMB	PHD	69.	Missouri		&1969
KPMG Professor of Accounting and Information Systems								
Kilpatrick, Bob G.	C-Pr	No Arizona	XFM	PHD	84.	Okla St		& 1-88
Kilpatrick, Donna J.	Assoc	Alaska-Ancho	CMB	PHD	97.	U Wash		
Kilpatrick, Joyce C.	Retir	Austin Peay	2000	DBA	82.	Memphis	#	&9-85
Kilpatrick, William C.	Retir	Colorado St	5-95	PHD	72.	Illinois	*	&8-76
Kim, An-Gyu	Prof	Chosun Univ	ANPS	PHD	96	Seogang		1979
Kim, Byoung Ho	C-Ac	Kookmin Univ	CFMQ	PHD	91.	Nrthwstrn		&1992
Kim, Changsoo	C-Ac	Chung-Ang	AFS	PHD	93.	Fla Intl		1994
Kim, Chung Kweon			FMX	PHD	94.	Pittsburgh		
Kim, Dohyeong	Asst	Kwang Woon	F	PHD	95.	Penn St		9-95
Kim, Dong C.	Prof	Dongguk U	BCM	PHD	89.	Iowa		9-91
Kim, Francis C.	Assoc	Old Dominion	F	PHD	94	Baruch		2006
Kim, Gwon Hee				PHD	90.	Wisconsin		
Kim, Ho Joong			CFM	PHD	93.	Geo St		
Kim, Hoon		Industry		PHD	01.	Car Mellon		
Kim, Hwan			FM	PHD	90.	Illinois	&	
Kim, Hyuk (David) (David)		Korea	1989	PHD	85.	Indiana		&1989
Kim, Il-Woon	Prof	Akron	CMI	PHD	85.	Nebraska		1-86
Kim, Irene	Asst	Duke	F	PHD	04.	Michigan		& 7-04
Kim, Jae-Oh			F	PHD	87.	Iowa		
Kim, Jawon			FMI	PHD	96.	Houston		
Kim, Jeehong	Prof	Yonsei Univ	FI	PHD	87.	Berkeley		1989
Kim, Jeong				PHD	99.	S Carol		
Kim, Jeong Youn	VProf	Auburn-Montg	F	PHD	89.	Wash St		2007
Kim, Jeong-Bon	Prof	HongKon Tech	FIM	PHD	86.	Temple		&1995
Kim, Jeong-Jae		Korea	1995	PHD	92.	Geo St		
Tae Gu Univ; 6-896 Jang Wedd Dong; Seoul, Korea								
Kim, Jeongkuk		Korea-Indust		PHD	91.	Nebraska		
Kim, Jin-Sun	Assoc	Dongguk U	FPT	PHD	90.	Tx-Austin		9-95
Kim, Jinbae	Asst	Korea Univ	MC	PHD	97.	Car Mellon		9-00
Kim, John J.	Assoc	CUNY-Hunter	F	PHD	93.	Memphis		1994

Kim, Jong H.	Prof	CS-Sacrament	FM	PHD	88. Missouri	8-89
Kim, Jong-dae			F	PHD	95. Geo Wash	
Kim, Jooho		Seoul Korea	1992	PHD	86. Colorado	
94-8 Chung Daam Dong; Knag Nam Ku; Seoul Korea 135-100						
Kim, Joon Seuk	Prof	Yonsei Univ	MSBC	DBA	82. Indiana	1982
Kim, Joung	Assoc	Nova SE	FA	PHD	99 S Carol	2007
Kim, Kap-Soon	Asst	Dongguk U	XF	PHD	98 Seoul Ntl	3-02
Kim, Ki-Pyung	Prof	Chosun Univ	EPRX	PHD	91 Hanyang	1979
Kim, Kil-Cho	Prof	Chung-Ang	AS	PHD	80 Korea	1980
Kim, Kun J.	Prof	CS-Fullerton	MF	DBA	83. Kentucky	&1986
Kim, Kwang-Yoon	Prof	Ajou Univ	FX	PHD	90 Korea	&1983
Kim, Kwon-Jung	Asst	Sook Myung	FM	PHD	91. SUNY-Buf	&1990
Sook Myung Women's University						
Kim, Kyonghee	Asst	Ill-Chicago	FM	PHD	05. Pittsburgh	2005
Kim, Kyung Kyu			S	PHD	86. Utah	&
Kim, Kyungho		Hong-Ik Univ	1995	PHD	87. Purdue	
Hong-Ik University; Seoul, Korea						
Kim, Moonchul		Korea	1994	PHD	93. Illinois	
Kim, Moshe	Prof	Pompeu Fabra			82 Toronto	
Kim, Myung-Sun	Asst	SUNY-Buffalo	F	PHD	95. Purdue	
Kim, Neung-Jip	Assoc	CS-L Angeles	F	PHD	87. Temple	6-88
Kim, Oliver	Prof	Maryland	FM	PHD	90. Penn	9-95
Ernst & Young Professor of Accounting						
Kim, Seung Yong	C-Ac	Chosun Univ	BCMP	PHD	90 Junnam	1989
Kim, Song-Ki	Prof	Seoul Natl	FCMV	PHD	79. Tx-Austin	&1983
Kim, Soon Kee		Seoul Natl		PHD	83. Houston	
Kim, Soon Nam	Assoc	Saskatchewan	FMW	PHD	01 Wollong	2005
Kim, Sung-soo	Assoc	Rutgers-Camd	FVT	PHD	93. Baruch	1998
Kim, Tae-Yong				PHD	90. Baruch	
Kim, Tong Hun		Hong-Ik Univ	1992	PHD	88. U Wash	
Hong Ik Univ; Sch of Bus; 72-1 Sangsudong Mapoku; Seoul Korea 121						
Kim, Yong Hwan			F	PHD	93. Penn St	
Kim, Yongtae	Asst	Santa Clara	F	PHD	01. SUNY-Buf	2001
Kimball, Kevin C.	Assoc	Brighm Yg-HI	ASFD	MACC	90 Brighm Yg	& 8-97
Kimball, William L.	Retir	CS-Northrdge	2003	PHD	67. Nrthwstrn	&1981
Kimbell, James A. Jr.	Retir	Fran Marion	1995	DBA	78. La Tech	& 8-85
Kimbrell, Janet I.	Retir	Oklahoma St	D-06	PHD	79. Okla St	&1979
Kimbro, Marinilka B.	Asst	U Wash-Tacom	FI	PHD	99. Maryland	2005
Kimbrough, Michael D.	Assoc	Harvard		PHD	02. Indiana	8-02
Kimmel, Paul D.	Assoc	Wis-Milwauke	FA	PHD	89. Wisconsin	&1989
Kimmell, Dennis L.	Retir	Akron	1998	DBA	74. Kent St	& 9-76
Kimmell, Sharon L.	Assoc	Akron	FV	DBA	86. Kent St	& 9-81
KPMG Teaching Fellow						
Kimmle, Manfred				DBA	72. Harvard	
Kimura, Joseph				PHD	82. UCLA	
Kinard, James C.	Assoc	Ohio State	SMCY	PHD	69. Stanford	&1972
Kind, Clinton J.	Retir	Mankato St	1996	MS	63 Mankato	1963
Kinder, Richard	Asst	Wash & Jeff	FMP	MBA	Penn	2003
Kindig, Fred E.	Retir		1980	PHD	51 Pittsburgh	1962
Kinfu, Johannes	C	Addis Ababa	F	DBA	70. Mich St	
Addis Abba Univ; P.O. Box 30204; Addis, Ethiopia						
King'Ori, Judika				PHD	03. S Illinois	
King, Arthur Edward	Assoc	High Point	AFM	MBA	W Virginia	&1989
King, Barry G.	Retir	Hardin-Simm	1995	PHD	64. Ohio St	&1990
King, Chula G.	C-Pr	West Florida	F	PHD	83. LSU	&1981
King, Darwin L.	Prof	St Bonaventu	XSHA	MBA	71 Mich St	&1983
King, Ian	Asst	Univ Essex	BM	PHD	90 Liverpool	1990
King, J. William (Bill)	Prof	Wash & Lee	MCI	PHD	86. Fla St	1989
King, James B.	Deces	So Illinois	2004	PHD	88. Indiana	&1987
King, Jerry G.	Retir	So Miss	2002	PHD	75. Miss	&1983
King, Jimmie Jr.	Retir	Tuskgegee	1986	EDD	81 Iowa	9-62
King, Kurleigh				PHD	73. Columbia	
King, Martha			CMR	PHD	94. Tx-Arlin	&
King, Raymond D.	Prof	Oregon	F	PHD	80. Oregon	&1982
Rippey Professor of Accounting						
King, Ronald R.	Prof	Wash Univ	FA	PHD	86. Arizona	&1986
Myron Northrop Professor of Accounting						
King, Ruth M.	Lect	Loughborough	FE	BSC	77 Nottingh	&1989
King, Teresa T.			FGHM	PHD	89. Geo St	&
King, Thomas E.	Emer	S Ill-Edward	2005	PHD	73. UCLA	&1977
King, Wayne	Assoc	Memorial Un	F	MBA	69 McMaster	&1991
Kingery, Rita	Inst	Delaware	FM	MS	78 CS-Sacra	&1980
Kininmonth, Kirsten	Asst	Univ Glasgow	HM	BACC	98 Paisley	2002
Kinkle, Charas	Assoc	NE Illinois	XL	JD	77 Howard	9-84
Kinnersley, Randall L.	Assoc	W Kentucky	PNG	PHD	97. Tx Tech	& 1-03
Kinney, Michael R.	Assoc	Texas A&M	ICMX	PHD	90. Arizona	8-89
KPMG Faculty Fellowship						

Kinney, William R. Jr.	Prof	Texas-Austin	A	PHD	68.	Mich St	&1987
Charles & Elizabeth Prothro Regents Chair/PriceWaterhouseCoopers Fel in Audit							
Kinnunen, Juha	Prof	Helsinki Sch	F	PHD	88	Helsinki	1978
Kinserdal, Arne	Emer	Norwegian U	2003				
Kinsman, Michael D.	Retir	Pepper-L Ang	FX	PHD	75	Stanford	&1975
Kintzele, Marilyn R.	Prof	Ind-Kokomo	FAM	MBA	77	Indiana	&1977
Kintzele, Philip L.	C-Pr	Cen Michigan	FGV	DBA	73.	Indiana	&1981
Kirby Jones, Alison J.	C-Ac	Boston Univ	MC	PHD	86.	Stanford	7-94
Kirby, Floyd W.	Retir	Jacksonvl St	AFVS	MA	77	Alabama	& 9-79
Kirch, David P.	Prof	Ohio Univ	F	PHD	90.	Penn St	& 8-94
Kircher, Paul	Retir	UCLA	1986	PHD	49.	Michigan	&1952
5625 East Seaside Walk; Long Beach CA 90803							
Kirchner, Mary	C-Pr	Methodist	FPVJ	PHD	98	Tennessee	&1996
Kiringoda, Dayal			MCS	PHD	84.	Nebraska	
Kirk, Donald J.	Retir	Columbia	2000	MBA	61	NYU	&1987
Kirk, Florence R.	Assoc	SUNY Oswego	FT	PHD	88.	Cornell	9-93
Kirk, N.	Lect	Massey Univ	AFW	BBS		Massey	1998
Kirk, R. S.	Prof	Univ Ulster	FMI	BSC			& 1-92
Kirkey, Bernie	Inst	Univ Cariboo	DP	MBA		W Ontario	1992
Kirkland, Charles	Lect	Valparaiso	FGMS	MBA	80	Augusta	* &2002
Kirkpatrick, Donald C.				PHD	76.	Colorado	
Kirkpatrick, Thomas L.	Retir	Ambassador	1992	PHD	80.	North Tx	&1989
Kirsch, Robert J.	Prof	So Conn St	FI	PHD	86.	S Carol	&1993
Kircohbaum, Max	Retir	Pace	1990	MA	54	NYU	&1965
Kirschenheiter, Michael T.	Assoc	Purdue	FMT	PHD	95.	Nrthwstrn	&2004
Kirschman, Charles F.		DuPont		PHD	74.	Kansas	
Kissinger, John N.	Assoc	St Louis	FTS	PHD	74.	Mich St	&1985
Kistler, Linda H.	Retir	Mass-Lowell	2000	MS	66	Colo St	&1966
Kite, Devaun			AC	PHD	92.	Florida	&
Kitunen, Joan	SLect	Univ Toronto	X	BBM	77	Ryerson	&1990
Kizirian, Timothy G.	Assoc	CS-Chico	SAM	PHD	01.	Arizona	7-01
Klamm, Bonnie K.	Assoc	N Dakota St	DSF	PHD	99.	Va Comm	&2000
Klammer, Thomas P.	Prof	North Texas	MF	PHD	71.	Wisconsin	& 9-70
Regents Professor of Accounting							
Klassen, Kenneth J.	Assoc	Georgia	XF	PHD	95.	Stanford	&2006
Klassen, Mark	Asst	Saskatchewan	MS	MBA	94	Saskatch	* 2004
Kleen, Penny L.	AsTch	Missouri	F	PHD	96.	Missouri	&2007
Kleespie, Dee L.	Retir	Arizona	1988	PHD	61.	Ohio St	&1962
Klein, April	Assoc	New York U	F	PHD	83	Chicago	1987
Klein, Donald J.	Retir	Grand Valley	2001	DBA	64	Mich St	* &1973
Klein, Hans E.		Renss-Hartf	M	DBA	77.	Kentucky	*
Klein, Kyle H.		Practice		PHD	78.	Arkansas	&1980
Klein, Lawrence A.	Assoc	Bentley	MEUA	PHD	78.	Penn St	1984
Klein, Roberta	Lect	Rochest Tech	FMX	MBA	79	Roch Tech	& 9-95
Klein, Steven H.	Retir	Truman State	5-03	MS	62	Wash U	&1991
Kleinerman, David	Retir	Roosevelt	1995	MBA	59	Chicago	&1955
Kleinman, Gary	Prof	Robt Morris	ABF	PHD	92.	Rutgers	2007
Kleinsorge, Ilene K.	Dean	Oregon State	MC	PHD	87.	Kansas	&1987
Klemme, Dana F.				PHD	84.	Michigan	
Klemstine, Charles F.	Lect	Michigan	AM	PHD	91	Michigan	1987
Klersey, George F.	Assoc	Birminghm So	AFT	PHD	90.	S Calif	&1995
EBSCO Professor of Accounting; on leave							
Klett, Taylor	Assoc	Sam Houston	XL	JD	88	Houston	&1999
Klimek, Janice L.	Asst	Cen Missouri	FCX	PHD	96.	Nebraska	&2001
Klimesh, Michael	Asst	Gustavus Ado	C	MBA			2002
Kline, Adrian L.	Retir	St Marys-Tx	1993	PHD	70.	Mich St	&1984
3401 McHenry Drive; San Antonio, TX 78239							
Kline, Germain P.	C-Ac	Indiana U-PA	GNP	PHD	00	Walden	&1989
Kline, Stacey	Inst	Drexel	FMX	MBA	98	Temple	1997
Klingstedt, John P.	Decea	Oklahoma		PHD	69.	North Tx	&1987
Klonigsmaier, Heinz	Asst	Univ Graz	AFI	PHD	04	U Graz	1988
Klumpes, Paul J. M.	Prof	U Nottingham	FMN	PHD	96	NS Wales	&
Knapp, Carol A.	Asst	Oklahoma	MF	PHD	95.	Oklahoma	2001
Knapp, Jeffery J.	Lect	New S Wales	F	BEC	89	Macquarie	* &1992
Knapp, Michael C.	Prof	Oklahoma	ACF	PHD	83.	Oklahoma	* &1988
McLaughlin Chair in Business Ethics							
Knauf, Janine B.		Consultin NY	1992	PHD	81.	Columbia	&1985
12 Springwood Ln; Pittsford NY 14534							
Knechel, W. Robert	Prof	Florida	FA	PHD	81.	N Carol	& 8-81
Ernst & Young Professor of Accounting							
Kneer, Dan C.			ADS	PHD	81.	Missouri	&
Knerr, Charles W.	Retir	Shippensburg	MXP	DED	76	Penn St	1966
Knight, Barry A.	Retir	CS-San Bern	2002	DBA	76.	S Calif	& 9-90
Knight, Harry	Retir	So Oregon St	DMPX	MBA		S Calif	&1981
Knight, Lee G.	D-Pr	Wake Forest	PTFX	PHD	81.	Alabama	9-00
Hylton Professor of Accountancy							
Knight, Marilyn Y.	Asst	Saginaw Vall	FXEM	MT	88	Walsh	&1984

Knight, Ray A.		Capstone Pln	X	JD	81	Wake For		&1994
Capstone Planning Alliance, LLC; Winston-Salem NC								
Knight, Royal E.	Retir	No Alabama	1998	EDD	76	N Colo	*	1981
Knighton, Lennis M.		Brigham Yg	N	PHD	66.	Mich St		&
Institute of Public Mgt; Brigham Young Univ; Provo UT 84602								
Knivsfla, Kjell Henry	Assoc	Norwegian U	F	DOEC		Norwegia		
Knoblett, James A.	Emer	Kentucky	2000	PHD	63.	U Wash	*	&1968
Knowles, David	Prof	Acadia Univ	FV	MBA	95	Queen's		
Knowles, William	Inst	New Hampshir	F	MS		Mass	*	&1993
Knox, Trevor	Assoc	Muhlenberg	BMX	PHD	00	Conn		&9-00
Knutson, Dennis L.	Retir	Wis-Eau Clar	2005	DBA	77.	Kentucky	*	&8-87
Knutson, Peter H.	Retir	Pennsylvania	1996	PHD	65.	Michigan		&1965
Ko, Chen-en	Dean	Nat Taiwan U	ASM	PHD	87.	Minnesota	# *	&8-88
Ko, W. Matthew		Hankuk Univ		PHD	85.	Ohio St		
Kobelsky, Kevin	Asst	Baylor	SMDA	PHD	00	Ca-Irvine		&2004
Kober, Ralph	SLect	U Auckland	MA	PHD	06	Queensld		2005
Kocakulah, Mehmet C.	Prof	So Indiana	PMC	PHD	82	Istanbul		1987
Koch, Adam S.			FM	PHD	99.	Tx-Austin		
Koch, Barry W.	Lect	Strathclyde	F	MBL		SA		&1977
Koch, Bruce S.	VAsoc	Seattle	MFB	PHD	77.	Ohio St		&2002
Koch, Paula			1992	PHD	89.	Nrthwstrn		
80 Hogan Lane; Ambler PA 19002								
Koch, Robert F.	Assoc	St Peters	X	MBA		Fairl Dick		&1976
Koch, Susan R.			ADGS	PHD	93.	Alabama		
Kochanek, Richard Frank	Prof	Connecticut	FPV	PHD	72.	Missouri		9-72
Kociolik, Rev. Charles	Asst	King's Col	P	MBA		Notre Dm		9-81
Koechling, Sherrie	Asst	Lincoln	M	PHD		Webster		8-89
Koehler, Robert W.	Deces	Penn State		PHD	67.	Mich St		1963
Koehn, Jo Lynne	Prof	Cen Missouri	AP	PHD	95.	Wisconsin		&1995
Koen, Sandra	Asst	Athens Univ	C	PHD	01	Athens		2002
Koeplin, John P. S.J.	Assoc	San Francisc	FM	PHD	98.	North Tx		&9-98
Koeppen, David R.	Prof	Boise State	FTVM	PHD	83.	Wisconsin		&9-86
Koester, Robert J.			ACFT	PHD	75.	Nebraska	*	&
Koga, Kentaro	Asst	Illinois	M	DBA	99.	Harvard		1-02
Kogan, Alexander	Prof	Rutgers-Newk		PHD	88	USSR Acad		1993
Koh, Hian Chye			FQ	PHD	87.	Va Tech		&
Koh, Ping Sheng	Lect	U Queensland	FTY	PHD	01	Tasmania		2001
Koh, Seunghee	Asst	Chungbuk	FM	PHD	92.	Oklahoma		1992
Koh, Sung Sam	Prof	Chung-Ang	AX	PHD	99	Inha		&1978
Kohlbeck, Mark J.	Asst	Fla Atlantic	F	PHD	99.	Tx-Austin		&2005
Kohler, Paul A.	Retir	Missouri		PHD	50	Iowa		1947
Kohlmeier, John M.	Visit	DePaul	S	DBA	64	Harvard		1995
Kohlmeyer, James M. III	Asst	East Carol	MBC	PHD	01.	S Fla		&2002
Kohn, S. David	C-Ac	Bridgeport		PHD	95	NYU		&2002
Koivistoinen, Kari	Lect	Helsinki Sch	CM	MS	82	Helsinki		1983
Kojima, Koji	Asst			PHD	04.	U Wash		2004
Kwansie Gakuin University								
Kole, Michael A.	Retir	Rider	1999	PHD	78	Mass		1983
Kolenda, Stephen A.	Prof	Hartwick	FIJ	MBA	83	Conn		&1983
Kollar, Robert	Asst	Duquesne	AFV	MBA	94	Duquesne		2003
Kollaritsch, Felix P.	Retir	Ohio St	1989	PHD	52	Hoch F W		&1962
Komaratat, Duangmanee	Assoc	Chulalongkor	CDMU	MACC	73	Chulalong		1971
Kominis, George	Asst	Univ Glasgow	MB	PHD	02	Glasgow		2002
Komutphong, Thitiphol	Lect	Chulalongkor	F	MSPA	01	Mich St		&1998
Konkol, Charles A.	Lect	Wis-Milwauke	XFAM	MS	81	Wi-Milwa		&1983
Konrath, Larry F.	Retir	Toledo	1991	PHD	70.	Michigan		&1964
2631 Cheltenham Road; Toledo OH 43606								
Konstans, Constantine	Prof	Texas-Dallas	MSX	PHD	66.	Mich St	# *	&1993
Koo, Meihua	Asst	Nev-L Vegas	IF	PHD	01.	Okla St		2001
Koogler, Paul R.			CM	PHD	82.	Arizona		&
Koole, Willem	Retir	N Carol St	MS	BS	78	NC-Charl		1991
Koonce, Lisa	Prof	Texas-Austin	BF	PHD	90.	Illinois	*	&1-90
Deloitte & Touche Professor of Accounting								
Kopczynski, Frank J.	Assoc	Plymouth St	MCSJ	PHD	93	Union-NY		&9-90
Kopel, Roann R.	Prof	E Illinois	FE	PHD	86.	N Carol		1991
Kopitzke, Henry	Prof	Pacific Unio	FLXV	JD	80	Idaho		&1973
Koplin, Mara	Lect	U Wollongong	FQ	MEC	93	N Eng-Au		&1998
Kopp, Lori S.	Asst	U Lethbridge	ABME	PHD	00.	Alabama		&7-02
Koprowski, William R.	C-Ac	Charleston	NO	PHD	87	Temple		2005
Kopulsky, Marvin R.	Retir	Loyola-Chicg	1994	PHD	70.	Nrthwstrn		&9-63
Korb, Phillip J.	C-Ac	Baltimore	XVF	MBA	75	Maryland		&1976
Kordecki, Gregory S.	Assoc	Clayton St	AFBI	MPA	76	Geo St		&1976
Kordi, Khalil A.		Saudia Arab	1992	PHD	79.	Arizona		
PO Box 87703; Riyadh Saudi Arabia 11652								
Korte, Leon	Assoc	South Dakota	CMGN	PHD	92.	Nebraska	*	&1992
Koshiyama, Lynn K.	Prof	Alaska-Ancho	FM	MBA	91	Ak Pacif		&1988
Koski, Timothy R.	Assoc	Mid Tenn St	X	PHD	98.	Missouri		&2002

Kosnik, Kenneth R.				PHD	75.	Nrthwstrn		
Kostolansky, John W.	Assoc	Loyola-Chicg	FT	PHD	75	Columbia		&9-72
Kotchetova, Natalia V.	Asst	Un Waterloo	A	PHD	02.	Geo St	*	2002
Kotey, Bernice	SLect	N Eng-Austr	M	PHD		N Eng-Au		2000
Kothari, S. P.	C-Pr	MIT	F	PHD	86.	Iowa		1999
Kovacs, Gene				PHD	04.	Columbia		
Kovar, Stacy E.	Assoc	Kansas State	MS	PHD	95.	Okla St		&8-97
PricewaterhouseCoopers Faculty Fellow								
Kowalczyk, Tamara K.	Assoc	Appalach St	FXJ	PHD	96.	Tx A&M		&2005
Kowalczyk, William J.	Retir	St Peters	1995	BS		St Peter		&1965
Kowalski, Lawrence W.	C-As	Bowling Gr	X	JD	75	Toledo		1978
Kown, Soon-Chul	Prof	Kyungpook Un	X	PHD	85	Hanyang		1981
Kozbert, Anthony				PHD	01.	NYU		
Kozloski, Thomas M.	Asst	Wilfrid Laur	AB	PHD	02.	Drexel		&2003
Kozmetsky, George	Deces	Texas-Austin	2003	DCS	57.	Harvard		
Kozub, Robert M.	Assoc	Wis-Milwauke	XF	DBA	83.	Kentucky		&1983
Kraft, Arthur G.	Asst	London Bus	F	PHD	01	Chicago		2001
Kramer, Bonita K. Peterson	Prof	Montana St	AFR	PHD	94.	Wash St	# *	&8-94
Kramer, Charles				PHD	49.	NYU		
Kramer, John L.	Prof	Florida	X	PHD	75.	Michigan		9-79
Kramer, Robert F.	Retir	St Norbert	1991	MBA	67	Wi-Milwa		&1963
Kramer, Sandra S.	Assoc	Florida	X	PHD	79.	Tx-Austin		9-79
Kranacher, Mary-jo	Assoc	CUNY-York						
Kranowski, Nathan J.	Retir	Radford	2002	PHD	66	Columbia		&1977
Krasney, Melvin A.		Am Produc TX		PHD	77.	Berkeley		1980
Krasniewski, Raymond J.	Emer	Ohio State	XMN	PHD	72	Purdue		&1970
Kratchman, Stanley H.	Prof	Texas A&M	VFJ	PHD	73.	Penn St		9-77
Kraten, Michael	Asst	Suffolk	FMB	PHD	04.	Conn		&2005
Krause, James D.	C-Ac	Tampa	FMCU	DBA	97	Nova SE		&1985
Krause, Michael J.	Assoc	LeMoyne	PFCA	MS		Syracuse		&9-82
Krause, Paul	Retir	CS-Chico	MSC	PHD	74	Oklahoma	# *	&8-80
Kraut, Marla Myers	H-Ac	Idaho	AFX	PHD	92.	Arizona		&1991
Kravet, Robert W.	Asst	Fairfield	PM	MS	69	Mass		&1978
Krawczyk, Katherine A.	Prof	N Carol St	BXF	PHD	92.	Tx-Austin		&8-92
Kreander, Niklas	Asst	Univ Glasgow	FW	PHD	03	Glasgow		2002
Krebs, Joseph E.	Retir	Univ of D C	2006	DBA	74.	Miss St		&1983
Kreiner, Raymond F.	Asst	Piedmont		MS	91	Ball St		8-04
Kreiser, Lawrence A.	Emer	Cleveland St	2005	PHD	75.	Cincinnati	#	&1976
Kreissl, Laura J.			CM	PHD	01.	Miss		&
Kreitzman, Alan J.	Asst	Adelphi	MA	MBA	69	Adelphi		&1977
Kremer, Larvi	Asst	Lycoming	A	MBA		Wilkes		2006
Kren, Barbara	Inst	Marquette	FM	MS	85	Wi-Milwa		&1999
Kren, Leslie	Assoc	Wis-Milwauke	CM	PHD	88.	Houston		&1991
Kresse, William J.	Asst	Saint Xavier	AL	JD				&1996
Kretschmar, Carl G.		SC		DBA	70.	Indiana		
Kretschmar, Paula W.			1992	PHD	83.	S Carol		
112 Forty Love Point Rd; Chapin SC 29036								
Kreuze, Jerry G.	Prof	W Michigan	FT	PHD	83.	Missouri		&1983
Kriegman, Oscar M.	Retir	Pace	1994	PHD	58.	Illinois		&1965
Krippel, Gregory L.	Assoc	Coast Carol	AFS	PHD	91.	Fla St		1994
Krische, Susan D.	Asst	Illinois	FB	PHD	02.	Cornell		8-01
Krishnamoorthy, Ganesh	Assoc	Northeastern	ABFS	PHD	94.	S Calif		&9-00
Krishnamurthi, Sudhir			FM	DBA	84.	Harvard		
Krishnamurthy, Vasu			MF	PHD	93.	Car Mellon		
Krishnan, Gopal V.	Assoc	Geo Mason	FS	PHD	86.	North Tx		&1-04
VSCPA Nova Chapter Professorship in Accounting								
Krishnan, Jagan (Krish)	Assoc	Temple	AF	PHD	91.	Ohio St		&1991
Merves Research Fellow								
Krishnan, Jayanthi	Asst	Temple	AFM	PHD	90	Ohio St		9-00
Krishnan, Murugappa (Murgie)			FM	PHD	87.	Penn		
Krishnan, Ranjani	Assoc	Michigan St	M	PHD	98.	Pittsburgh		8-98
Krishnan, Sudha			F	PHD	01.	S Calif		
Krissek, Thomas J.	Asst	NE Illinois	CMQV	MBA	82	Loyola		&9-83
Kristensen, Roy	Lect	Norwegian Mg	FX	ABD	94	Oslo		2007
Krittaphol, Wanpen	Retir	Chulalongkor	ADOS	MACC	73	Chulalong		1980
Krivogorsky, Victoria	Assoc	San Diego St	AF	PHD	99.	Wisconsin		2005
Kroeker, Jeff	Lect	British Colu	FM	MBA	90	Queens	*	1998
Kroener, Peter H.		Siemens		DBA	73.	Indiana		
Krogstad, Jack L.	Prof	Creighton	A	PHD	75.	Nebraska		&9-80
Union Pacific Professor of Accountancy								
Krolick, Debra			2004	PHD	98	Chicago		&
Cornerstone Research								
Kromis, Stephen G.				DBA	89.	La Tech	#	&
Kross, William J.	Prof	Purdue	F	PHD	75.	Iowa		&1978
Kruck, Susan E.	Asst	Jms Madison		PHD	98.	Va Tech		
Computer Information Department								
Krueger, James M.	Asst	Mo-St Louis	FG	DBA	76.	Indiana		&1975

Krueger, Jerome R. (Jerry)	Retir	Kentucky St	XLAV	JD	70	Indiana	&1976
Krueger, Lavern E.	Assoc	Mo-Kansas Ct	FT	DBA	74.	Colorado	&1970
Krueger, Peter	Lect	Monash Univ	SD	GRAD			&1984
Kruglinski, John	Asst	Kutztown	FSX	MBA	05	NYU	&2005
Krull, George W. Jr.	Prof	Bradley	AFS	PHD	71.	Mich St	&1-01
Krull, Linda K.	Asst	Texas-Austin	FX	PHD	01.	Arizona	&2001
Krumwiede, Kip R.	Assoc	Boise State	CM	PHD	96.	Tennessee	* &2003
Krumwiede, Timothy G.	Assoc	Bryant	XF	PHD	93.	Tx Tech	&8-92
Kruse, Bruce T.	Retir	St Cloud St	1997	PHD	64.	LSU	1986
Kruse, Geraldine M.	Retir	E Michigan	1995	MBA	63	Michigan	&1997
Krzystofik, Anthony T.	Emer	Massachusett	1992	MA	61	Conn	&1958
Ktat, Sara	Asst	Univ Tunis	F	DEA	99	ISCAE	1999
Kuang, Jason Xi	Asst	Georgia Tech	BJM	PHD	05	Pittsburgh	8-05
Kubican, Terry R.	SLect	Old Dominion	PSAC	MSA	95	Old Dom	* &1995
Kubin, Konrad W.	Retir	Virg Tech	2003	PHD	72.	U Wash	&9-72
Kucic, A. Ronald	D-Ac	Denver	MSC	PHD	77.	NYU	* 1976
Kudar, Randolph P. (Randy)	Retir	West Ontario	SMCV	PHD	78	W Ontario	* 1979
Kuechler, Linda J.	C-Ac	Daemen	CSFI	PHD	96	SUNY-Buf	* &1984
Kuhn, Stephen D.	Assoc	Wash & Jeff	CDIN	MAC		Bowl Gr	&1987
Kuhns, Eldon F. II	Assoc	Lycoming	FXG	MAC	75	Oklahoma	&1979
Kuklis, Richard	Assoc	St Michaels		PHD		Syracuse	
Kulas, Ludwik	Retir	North Dakota	1989	JD	51	N Dakota	&9-46
Kulesza, Marie G.	Lect	Hartford	FMA	MS	99	Hartford	&9-05
Kulkarni, Joyce	Inst	Metro State	P	MBA	87	UCA	1-90
Kulp, Susan Cohen	Asst	George Wash	M	PHD	00	Stanford	2007
Kulsrud, William N.	Assoc	Indiana-Indy	X	PHD	80.	Tx-Austin	&1979
Kulzick, Raymond S.	Prof	St Thomas-FL	DMSU	DBA	90	Nova SE	1997
Kumar, Akhil		Hong Kong	1991	PHD	86.	North Tx	
Vice President Research, LG Caltex; Hong Kong							
Kumar, Gaurav	Asst	Ark-Ltl Rock	FTP	PHD	06.	Miss	&8-06
Kumar, Krishna R.	Prof	George Wash	FT	PHD	88.	Columbia	1992
Kunitake, Walter K.	Retir	Hawaii-Hilo	2000	PHD	80.	Arkansas	&1987
Kunkel, J. Gregory	C-Pr	CS-L Angeles	FV	PHD	81.	Berkeley	9-93
Kunpanitchakit, Danuja	Dean	Chulalongkor	CM	PHD	83	Wisconsin	1976
Kunskek, Rudy	Asst	Indiana East					2007
Kunz, Jeffrey T.	D-As	Carroll	FMPT	MS	76	Wisconsin	&9-81
Kuo, Horng-Ching	Prof	Nat Chengchi	CFM	PHD	84.	Miss	1992
Kurlander, Neale	Retir	Adelphi	1995	JD	68	NY Law	&1962
Kurtenbach, James M.	Assoc	Iowa State	FG	PHD	92.	Missouri	8-91
Kurtovich, Annamaria	Lect	U Wollongong	AO	PHD		Wollong	&2004
Kurtz, Frederick C.	Retir	George Wash	1992	MBA	49	Penn	&9-49
Kurunmaki, Liisa	Read	London Econ	BNM	PHD	00	Jyvaskyla	1999
Kuruvilla, Mohan	Assoc	Houston Bapt	AIP	PHD	96.	Houston	* &9-03
Kusama, Indra				PHD	98.	Kent St	
Kusel, Jimie	Prof	Ark-Ltl Rock	FM	PHD	73.	Mich St	&9-81
Kushel, Paul S.	Assoc	Fordham	X	PHD	81.	Tx-Austin	&1988
Kvaal, Erlend	Assoc	Norwegian Mg	TFI	CAND	94	Oslo	1991
Kvam, Robert L.	Retir	Missouri	1987	PHD	57.	LSU	&1960
Kwak, Byungjin	Asst	Yonsei Univ		PHD	04.	Purdue	
Kwak, Su-Keun	Prof	Seoul Natl	FMCW	PHD	87.	N Carol	1988
Kwak, Wikil	Prof	Neb-Omaha	CM	PHD	90.	Nebraska	1989
Distinguished Alumni Professor							
Kwan, Sabrina Y. S.	AdjAc	Hong Kong Sc	FIX	PHD	96	London	&1996
Kwiatkowski, Vernon E.	Prof	Cen Michigan	GF	DBA	86.	Kentucky	&1986
Kwon, Chan-Tae	Prof	Kyungpook Un	FA	PHD	85	Pusan	&1980
Kwon, Soo Young	Prof	Korea Univ	FV	PHD	92.	Wash U	3-93
Kwon, Soon-Yong	Asst	Yeungnam	1992	PHD	90.	Oklahoma	1992
Kwon, Sun-Kook	Assoc	Kyungpook Un	FA	PHD	89.	Oklahoma	* &7-95
Kwon, Sung-Soo			FD	PHD	89.	Mich St	
Kwon, Young K.	Retir	Illinois	2005	PHD	78.	Tx-Austin	5-85
Kwong, K. S.	TFell	Chinese HK	EM	MBA	81	ChinesHK	* &1986
Kyj, Larissa S.	Prof	Rowan	CM	PHD	85	Columbia	* &1992
Kykkanen, Tapani	Lect	Helsinki Sch	FM	MS	90	Helsinki	1983
Kylakoski, Kalevi	Prof	Helsinki Sch	CM	PHD	81	Helsinki	1970
Kyle, Daniel G.	Retir	Louisiana St	1989	PHD	68.	Arkansas	&1968
Kyle, Donald L.	Prof	Houston-Cl L	CM	PHD	69.	Arkansas	&6-74
Label, Wayne A.			AF	PHD	71.	UCLA	&
Labelle, Andre		Quebec a Hul	X	MFIS			&
Labelle, Real	Prof	HEC-Montreal	DLMT	DSC	84	Grenoble	&7-96
Labro, Eva	Lect	London Econ	MS	PHD	01	Leuven	2000
Lacey, John M.	Prof	CS-Long Bch	FTKJ	PHD	82.	UCLA	&1989
Ernst & Young Research Fellow							
Lachman, Ted	Retir	CUNY-Brookly	2003	MBA	74	Baruch	&9-82
Lacina, Michael J.	Asst	Houston-Cl L	CFM	PHD	98.	Purdue	&9-05
LaCombe, Amy	Lect	Boston Coll	FS	MBA	00	Boston C	2001
Lacoste, Jean M.	Inst	Virg Tech	S	MA		Va Tech	1997
Lacy, Bud	Assoc	Oklahoma St	X	PHD	83.	Colorado	&1981

Name	Rank	School	Code	Degree	Year	Deg-School	Extra
Lacy, Jo Y.	Asst	Cen Florida	ABF	PHD	02.	Geo Wash	& 8-02
Ladd, Dwight R.				DBA	56.	Harvard	
Ladley, Herbert Vern	Retir	Univ of D C	1981	PHD	71.	Geo Wash	&1969
1212 Burtonwood Ct; Alexandria VA 22307							
LaFave, Steven J.	Prof	Augsburg Col	EFC	MBA	89	Minnesota	&1991
Laferriere, Claude	Prof	Quebec-Montr	X	MFIS		Sherbrook	& 8-80
Lafferty, George W.		C,B,L&K TX		PHD	48.	Tx-Austin	
Lafleur, Lydia M.	Inst	Louisiana St	FO	MBA	00	LSU	& 6-00
Lafond, C. Andrew	Asst	Philadelphia	XMPE	PHD		Sarasota	&2001
LaFond, Ryan Z.	Asst	MIT	F	PHD	05.	Wisconsin	2005
Lafond-LaVallee, Carole	Prof	Quebec-Montr	F	MA		Montreal	& 6-78
LaFortune, Andree	Assoc	HEC-Montreal	BFMS	MBA	86	Laval	& 9-82
LaFrancois, Helen	Retir	Mass-Dartmou	2002	MBA	76	Bryant	& 9-82
LaGore, William	Asst	E Michigan	FGN	ABD		Fla St	2006
LaGrone, Paul G.	Retir	Geo Southern	1983	PHD	58.	Alabama	1962
LaGrone, R. Michael	Assoc	Cumberland	FMC	PHD	90.	S Carol	* & 8-98
LaGroue, Harold	VAsst	La-Lafayette	FS	PHD	06	LSU	& 8-06
Lahey, James M.	Retir	No Illinois	1993	PHD	69.	Illinois	& 9-70
Lai, David T. W.	Inst	City Univ HK	FXL	MTAX	04	Sydney	* &2005
Lai, Liona			FI	PHD	04.	Tx A&M	
Lai, Min Mei	Inst	City Univ HK	F	MBA	83	Ohio U	4-97
Lai, Richard T.	Assoc	St John's	X	LLM	83	NYU	&1987
Laibstain, Samuel	Retir	Rider	1991	PHD	66.	NYU	& 9-81
Laiken, Stanley N.	Prof	Un Waterloo	X	PHD	72	W Ontario	1981
Deloitte Professor of Taxation							
Laimon, Samuel	Retir	Saskatchewan	6-90	ABD		Chicago	* 1953
Lake, Robert C.	Retir	Auburn-Montg	1999	PHD	77.	La Tech	# * &1971
Lakefish, Sidney	Retir	Portland St	1989	MBA	63	Portland	&1956
Laksmana, Indrarini (Rini)	Asst	Kent State	CM	PHD	04.	Geo St	& 8-04
Lam, Edmund	Lect	San Jose St		MBA		Wyoming	1999
Lam, Francis	Lect	HongKon Tech	FT	MBA	92	Warwick	1987
Lam, Kevin	Assoc	Chinese HK	IMS	PHD	97	Toronto	* &1998
Lam, Peter	Lect	New So Wales	F	MBA		Chicago	
Lam, Wai P.	Emer	Univ Windsor	2002	PHD	74.	Mich St	&1973
Lamarra, Frank	Lect	Wayne State	M	MBA	99	Wayne St	8-02
Lamb, James	Lect	U Queensland	DS	BBUS	87	Deakin	1998
Lamb, Margaret	SLect	Un Warwick	XFH	PHD	01	Reading	
Lambert, Caroline	Asst	HEC Paris	UMBC	PHD	05	Paris IX	2004
Lambert, Cecilia	SLect	Griffith Un	FT	PHD	99	N Eng-Au	&1988
Lambert, Jane	SLect	Indiana-Indy	FM	MBA	84	Indiana	&1998
Lambert, Joyce C.	Prof	New Orleans	AFJ	PHD	73.	LSU	# & 8-84
Arthur Andersen Professor of Accounting							
Lambert, Kenneth E.	D-Pr	Memphis	FN	PHD	76.	Arkansas	1982
Lambert, Richard A.	Prof	Pennsylvania	FM	PHD	82.	Stanford	1999
Miller-Sherrerd Professor							
Lambert, S. Joseph III	Prof	New Orleans	CAFS	PHD	73.	LSU	& 8-84
Oil & Gas Professor of Accounting							
Lamberton, Barbara A.	Assoc	Hartford	MC	PHD	98	Mich St	&1999
Lamberton, Geoff	Lect	So Cross Un	MF	MBUS	94	So Cross	&1991
Lamden, Charles W.	Deces	San Diego St	5-92	PHD	49.	Berkeley	&1976
Lammers, Lucille E.	Retir	Illinois St	1998	PHD	75.	Wisconsin	&1981
Lamminmake, Dawne	ALect	Griffith-GC	M	MBA	92	England	* 1996
Lampe, James C.	Assoc	Missouri St	ASJO	PHD	70.	Michigan	& 8-06
Lan, George P. W.	C-Ac	Univ Windsor	F	PHD	91	Queens	1988
Lancaster, Kathryn A. S.	Assoc	Cal Poly-SLO	EFMW	PHD	97.	Tx A&M	& 9-97
Land, Judy K.	Asst	N Carol Cen	F	PHD	05.	N Carol	2005
Landau, Barbara	Asst	Nova SE	XL	LLM	86	NYU	2003
Lander, Gerald H.	Prof	S Fl-St Pete	MAF	DBA	80.	Kentucky	& 8-81
Landgraf, Ellen L.	Assoc	Loyola-Chicg	APRF	PHD	91	Il-Chicago	& 9-89
Landis, Mark	Asst	San Fran St	MS	PHD	06.	Missouri	2006
Landry, Horace J.	Retir	Syracuse	1996	MS	36	Syracuse	&1975
Landry, Maurice		Laval		PHD	69.	UCLA	
Landry, Raymond M.			SP	PHD	87.	Arkansas	
Landry, Steven P.	Prof	Monterey	MIGB	PHD	92.	Colorado	* &2000
Landry, Suzanne			X	PHD	99.	Florida	
Landsman, Wayne R.	Prof	No Carolina	F	PHD	84.	Stanford	9-90
KPMG Professor of Accounting							
Lane, Alison J.	SLect	U Glamorgan	NM	BA	86	Lancaster	&O-94
Lane, James E.	Retir	Indiana St	1993	DBA	62	Indiana	& 9-57
Lane, Jennifer	Lect	Univ Wales	FM	BSC	85	Aberystw	&2002
Lane, Joseph E.	Deces	Alabama	5-89	LLB	56	Alabama	&1949
Lane, Marguerite Bishop	Adj	Pennsylvania	F	PHD	95.	Nrthwstrn	1997
Lane, Michael R.			JAF	PHD	80.	Tx A&M	&
Lane, Scott J.	Asst	New Haven	MFU	PHD	99.	Kentucky	9-99
Lane, Susan	STut	U Auckland	FA	BA	85	Nottinghm	2007
Lanen, William N.	Prof	Michigan	MC	PHD	83.	Penn	1990
Michael and Joan Sakkinen Accounting Scholar							

Lanese, Karen B.			X	PHD	93.	S Fla		&
Lanfranconi, Claude P.			FMVI	PHD	76	W Ontario		&
Lang, Mark H.	Prof	No Carolina	FI	PHD	90.	Chicago		&9-94

Thomas W. Hudson Jr./Deloitte & Toughe LLP Distinguished Professor

Lang, Sandra	Asst	McKendrea	S	PHD	01.	S Illinois		2001
Lang, Teresa	Asst	Columbus St	SXP	PHD	04	Auburn		&2004
Langa, Leo	Lect	LaTrobe Univ	FT	MEC		LaTrobe		1993
Lange, Gerard A.	Assoc	St John's	PA	EDD	07	St Johns		&1985
Lange, Glen E.				PHD	69.	Missouri		
Langefeld, Phillip A.		Austin TX	1992	PHD	78.	Cornell		

4003 Brookview Road; Austin TX 78722

Langemeier, Brian			XF	PHD	87.	Nebraska	*	
Langenderfer, Harold Q.	Retir	No Carolina	1993	DBA	54.	Indiana		&1953
Langendijk, Henk P. A. J.	Prof	Un Amsterdam	A	PHD	94	Leiden		1980
Langer, B.	Inst	Touro	NAVG	MBA		Brooklyn		&9-01
Langer, Russell D.			FV	PHD	76.	Berkeley		&
Langevin, Marcel		Quebec Canad	1992	PHD	81.	Syracuse		

225 - 54E Ave; Lachine; Quebec H8T 3A2 Canada

Langfield-Smith, Ian A.	Lect	Monash Univ	FTV	LLB				&1999
Langfield-Smith, Kim	Prof	Monash Univ	MCB	PHD	92	Monash		&2002
Langholm, Odd	Emer	Norwegian U	1999	DOEC				
Langli, John Christian	Prof	Norwegian Mg	FI	DREC	93	NHH Berg		8-93
Langmead, Joseph	Exec	Loyola-Maryl	FJKU	MBA	73	Loyola		1-04
Langsam, Sheldon A.	Prof	W Michigan	AFG	PHD	89.	Arkansas		&1989
Langston, Carolyn		So Arkansas	1996	DBA	87.	La Tech		

Southern Ark - El Dorado Branch; 300 S W Ave; El Dorado AR 71730

Langstraat, Craig J.	Prof	Memphis	X	LLM	82	SanDiego		&1987
Langton, Robert J.	LectC	Adelaide	JL	PHD		Massey		1991
Lanham, James S.	Retir	NAA		PHD	42.	Tx-Austin		
Lanier, Danny	Asst	Tx Christian	F	PHD	03.	Georgia		& 8-03
Lanis, Roman	SLect	Tech-Sydney	FA	PHD	01	Newcastle		2004
Lankton, Nancy	Asst	Michigan St	S	PHD	00	Ariz St		1-01
Lannan, John	Prof	Salem State	CX	MBA	76	Suffolk		&1979
Lanoue, Nicole	Prof	Quebec-Montr	F	PHD	93	Laval		& 7-79
Lansford, Benjamin N.	Asst	Northwestern		PHD	05.	Penn St		8-05
Lanthier, Denise	Prof	Quebec-Montr	F	MBA		McGill		& 9-80
Lantry, Terry L.	Retir	Colorado St	1998	JD	61	Valparaiso		&1965
Lantz, Keith W.	C-Pr	Tx-Pan Amer	FMT	PHD	75.	Iowa		2006
Lanzillotti, Louis	Assoc	So New Hamp	FMNC	MBA		Northeas		& 9-75
LaPage, Peter Paul	Retir	CS-Long Bch	1993	MBA	49	S Calif		&1957
Lapidus, Arnold	Retir	Fairleigh Di	1985	PHD	67	NYU		1974
Laplante, Stacie O. Kelley	Asst	Georgia	XF	PHD	05.	U Wash		2005
Lara, Rafael M.	Asst	Concordia U	FM	PHD	03.	Colorado		2003
Larcker, David F.	Prof	Stanford	M	PHD	78.	Kansas		2005
Largay, James A. III	Prof	Lehigh	FVX	PHD	71.	Cornell		&1980
Laribee, Stephen F.	Prof	E Illinois	PABI	DBA	74.	Kent St		&1989
Larka, Anita	Inst	Univ Calgary	C	BCOM	87	Calgary		&1995
Larkin, Jim	LectA	Flinders Un	QAT	BA	91	SAIT		1-96
Larkin, Joseph M.	Assoc	St Joseph	FA	PHD	88.	Temple	# *	&1984
Larkin, Ryan E.	Lect	Utah State	FX	MPRA	02	Utah		&2006
Larkins, Ernest R.	Prof	Georgia St	X	PHD	82.	Va Tech		1-82

School of Accountancy Alumni Professor

Laroche, D.-Claude	Assoc	HEC-Montreal	AFO	MBA	80	HEC-Mont		& 8-78
Larsen, E. John	Prof	So Calif	KVFJ	DBA	67	S Calif		& 6-63
Larsen, Jytte G.	Assoc	U So Denmark	M	PHD	94	Odense		1992
Larson, Douglas A.	Prof	Salem State	VA	MBA	77	Conn	# *	&1979
Larson, John A.	Retir	Mich-Flint	1994	PHD	56	Nrthwstrn		&1976
Larson, Kermit D.	Emer	Texas-Austin	1994	DBA	66.	Colorado		&1966

Arthur Andersen and Co. Alumni Centennial Emeritus Professor of Accounting

Larson, Linda L.	Assoc	Central Wash	SOB	DBA	97.	Clev St	#	& 8-06
Larson, Lucy L.	Retir	St John's-MN	2000	MBA	72	St Cloud		&1972
Larson, Raymond L.	Emer	Appalach St	2004	PHD	70.	Oregon		9-72
Larson, Richard C.	Retir			PHD	68.	Mich St		
Larson, Robert K.	Assoc	Dayton	IFMV	PHD	93.	Utah	*	&2001
Larsson, Claes-Goran	Assoc	Univ of Umea	FTA	PHD	75	Umea		8-94
Larsson, Lars				PHD	78.	Cornell		
LaRue, David W.	Assoc	Virginia	X	PHD	84.	Houston		8-83
LaSalle, Randall E.	Assoc	West Chester	CFA	PHD	91.	Drexel		&1998
Lasater, David B.				PHD	82.	Tx-Austin		
Laska, Lewis L.	Prof	Tenn State	FL	PHD	78	Peabody		&1973
Lassar, Sharon S.	D-Ac	Fla Internat	X	PHD	88.	S Calif		2006
Lasseter, James Jr.	Retir	South Fla	2004	MBA	64	Chicago		&1966
Lassila, Dennis R.	Prof	Texas A&M	X	PHD	81.	Minnesota		& 7-83

Shelton Tax Professor

Laswad, Fawzi	H-Pr	Massey Univ	FIV	PHD	88	Sydney		&1989
Latham, Claire K.	Assoc	Wash State	FAS	PHD	94.	Geo St		&1994
Latham, Harold L.	Retir	E Kentucky	1988	MA	56	Kentucky		&1973

Name	Rank	School	Code	Degree	Yr	University	Year
Lathan, Malcolm H. (Mac)	Assoc	Virginia	FA	PHD	82.	N Carol	&8-83
Lathen, William C.	Prof	Boise State	XE	PHD	82.	Ariz St	&9-84
Latimar, Amy	VInst	Toledo	P	MBA	07	Toledo	2005
Latshaw, Craig A.	Assoc	St John's	CF	PHD	00.	Drexel	&1999
Lattimer, Lee L.	Retir	St John's	2000	DBA	76.	Geo Wash	&1978
Lau, Amy Hing-Ling	C-Pr	Un Hong Kong	CMIF	PHD	82.	Wash U	&6-03
Lau, Chew King	Lect	Nanyang Tech		MIB	98	Monash	2005
Lau, Chong Man	Asst	W Australia	M	PHD	98	W Austrl	&2000
Lau, Chor T.	Prof	CS-L Angeles	MC	PHD	76.	Oregon	1985
Lau, James	ALect	Macquarie Un					
Lau, Richard T.	Assoc	CS-L Angeles	FV	PHD	89.	LSU	9-89
Lau, Thomas	Asst	HongKon Tech	AF	PHD	99	Chinese	2000
Laubach, Peter B.				DCS	56.	Harvard	
Laudeman, Max A.				PHD	76.	Arkansas	* &
Lauderdale, Frank Junior	Retir	S F Austin	1985	PHD	66.	Tx-Austin	&1952
Laufer, Doug	Prof	Metro State	PAFJ	PHD	85.	Okla St	&8-95
Laughland, Alan R.	Retir	New Brunswic	BMQ	MBA	71	McMaster	* 1971
Laughlin, Eugene J.	Retir	Kansas State	1990	PHD	65	Illinois	&9-56
Lauly, Jean-Paul	Prof	Quebec-Montr		MBA		Paris	
Launstein, Howard C.	Deces	Marquette	4-97	PHD	56	Ohio St	1958
Lauriclla, Leonard	Asst	Montclair St	FX	LLM	86	NYU Law	2002
Laurin, Claude	Prof	HEC-Montreal	FMG	PHD	96	Brit Colum	* D-99
Laursen, Gary A. H.	Assoc	South Fla	XL	LLM	72	U Miami	&8-80
Laux, Judith A.	Prof	Colorado Col	FM	PHD	90	Colorado	1979
Laux, Volker	Asst	Texas-Austin		PHD	03	Frankfurt	7-06
Lauzon, Leo-Paul	Prof	Quebec-Montr	M	DSG		Grenoble	* 6-73
Laverdiere, Raymond G.			MCS	PHD	82.	Penn St	
Lavermicocca, Catriona	Lect	Macquarie Un	XL	MLAW	92	NS Wales	&1995
Laverty, Brian L.	Prof	Toledo	FXV	PHD	84.	Mich St	&1990
Lavery, Kenneth A.	Asst	High Point	FXM	ABD		La Tech	&1997
Lavin, David	Retir	Fla Internat	2006	PHD	74.	Illinois	&1974
Law, C. E.	Retir	Queen's Univ	1992	ABD		Brit Colum	1966
Law, Daniel	Asst	Gonzaga	CF	PHD	03.	Wash St	&2002
Law, David B.	Prof	Youngstown	F	DBA	95.	Clev St	&1-94
Law, Donald R.	Retir	Augusta	1993	PHD	72.	Florida	&1974
Lawler, William C.	Assoc	Babson	CM	PHD	81.	Mass	1979
Lawrence, Carol M.	Assoc	Richmond	CGMN	PHD	89.	Indiana	1996
Lawrence, Charles	Emer	Purdue	1986	PHD	52.	Illinois	&1967
Lawrence, Howard J.	ClPr	Mississippi	FM	PHD	72.	Miss	* &2005
Lawrence, Janice E.	Assoc	Nebraska	PEJI	PHD	92.	Tx A&M	&1992
Lawrence, Joan	Assoc	Fairmont	FGNV	MBA	73	W Virginia	&1973
Lawrence, Leonare			AM	PHD	97.	Nebraska	&
Lawrence, Mark L.	Prof	No Alabama	SXVT	DBA	01	Nova SE	* &2004
Lawrence, Robyn	C-Ac	Scranton	CMIF	PHD	88.	Houston	* 1993
Lawrence, S. C.	SLect	Un East Lond	FMI	MSC			&1984
Lawson, William M.	Retir	Carleton Un	2003	PHD	74	York	1975
Layne, Armand W.	Lect	West Indies	MT	PHD		Birminghm	
Layton, Rose	Clin	So Calif	PAF	MACC	83	DePaul	&1993
Lazar, Laura K.			F	PHD	86.	Indiana	&
Lazer, Ron	Asst	Houston	F	PHD	04.	NYU	9-04
Le Vourc'h, Joelle	Assoc	ESCP deParis	IFAC	MBA	73	ESCP	1985
Lea, Bih-Ru	Asst	Mo-Rolla		PHD	98	Clemson	2003
Lea, Kenneth R.	Prof	Tenn State	AMNO	DBA	80.	La Tech	&1975
Lea, Richard B.	Retir	CS-Chico	2004	PHD	70.	Minnesota	&8-89
Leach, Maria A.	Asst	Auburn-Montg	CSIM	DBA	02.	Miss St	&2004
Leahey, Anne L.	Asst	Txs-El Paso	FV	MBA	70	Hawaii	&9-76
Leahy, Alison	Teach	U Melbourne	M	BCOM	03	Melbourne	2004
Leaman, Richard S.	Assoc	Denver	X	JD	79	Chicago	&9-91
Leary, Carol A.			FM	PHD	03.	Va Comm	&
Lease, Terry M.	Prof	Sonoma State	PX	PHD	96.	S Calif	&2002
Leathart, Marilynn	Retir	John Carroll	EFH	PHD	75.	Alabama	&1985
Leathers, Park E.	Retir	Bowling Gr	1995	PHD	76	Penn	&1975
Leauby, Bruce A.	Assoc	LaSalle	FGAH	PHD	90.	Drexel	* &9-89
Leavins, John R.	C-Pr	St Thomas-TX	AS	PHD	87.	Houston	&8-03
Lebas, Michel J.	Retir	HEC Paris	CMUI	MBA	69	Dartmouth	1970
Lebensbaum, Louis	Retir	Adelphi	1992	JD	53	Brooklyn	&1968
42 Acorn Lane; Planview NY 11803							
Lebon, Claude	Prof	Laval		PHD	70.	Columbia	
LeBow, Marc I.	Asst	Hampton	ADX	PHD	91	Va Comm	&2004
Lechner, Thomas A.	Asst	Utah	AEFM	PHD	98.	SUNY-Buf	&2005
Lecky, Marcella Y.	Retir	La-Lafayette	2002	MS	63	Miss	&1972
LeClere, Marc J.	Asst	Valparaiso	FX	PHD	89	Penn St	&2007
Ledbetter, John	Asst	Ball State	FX	PHD	98.	Houston	&9-99
Ledgerwood, John	Asst	Embry-Riddle	FMPT	MACC			2006
Ledoux, Marie-Josee	Prof	Quebec-Montr	M	PHD		Waterloo	* 8-94
Lee, Ben B.	Emer	Lg Isl-Brook	2003	PHD	65	NYU	&1965
Lee, Bong Hack			FM	PHD	96.	Mass	

Lee, Brian	Assoc	Prairie View	MTV	PHD	94	Temple	2005
Lee, Buryung (Brian)			FS	PHD	94.	Temple	* &
Lee, Byung-chull	Asst	Korea	F	PHD	93.	Kansas	
Lee, Byunghwan	Asst	CS-Pomona	F	PHD	05.	Houston	2007
Lee, Chan M.		Dan-Kook U	1992	PHD	83.	Nebraska	
Dankook Univ; Col; of Bus & Econ; 8 Hannan-Dong Yongsan-Ku; Seoul Korea							
Lee, Chang-Woo	Prof	Seoul Natl	FIAX	PHD	87.	Berkeley	&1992
Lee, Chao-Hsiung	Asst	Ntl Chung Ch	BCM	PHD	02	Tsukuba	2002
Lee, Charles M. C.	Prof	Cornell	FB	PHD	90.	Cornell	& 8-96
Henrietta Johnson Louis Professor of Management							
Lee, Chi-Wen Jevons	Prof	Tulane	FMAI	PHD	77	Rochester	* &1988
Lee, Chia-Ling	Assoc	Ntl Chung Ch	CM	PHD	98	Sun Yat-se	1999
Lee, Chih-Chen	Asst	No Illinois	S	PHD	00.	S Illinois	& 8-05
Lee, Choongseop			FA	PHD	95.	Geo St	
Lee, Chun-Eui	Prof	Chosun Univ	BFHW	PHD	92	Sejong	1980
Lee, Chuo-Hsuan (Jason)	Asst	SUNY-Plattsb	FMP	PHD	03.	Kent St	* 8-06
Lee, Daisun		Sogang Univ	1992	PHD	87.	Nebraska	
Sogang Univ; CPO Box 1142; Seoul Korea							
Lee, Deanna S.			F	PHD	01.	Illinois	
Lee, Deborah	Inst	NE St-Okla	FS	MS	00	Okla St	&2000
Lee, Dong-Woo	Dean	CS-L Angeles	FI	PHD	95.	Michigan	9-95
Lee, Eunsang		Korea	M	PHD	90.	Stanford	1990
Lee, Foong Tow Marina	Assoc	Nanyang Tech	FM	MBA	80	Melbourne	&1985
Lee, Grace Meina			IMJ	PHD	96.	Utah	&
Lee, Harold O.	Retir	Houston	1996	PHD	69.	Tx-Austin	&1958
Lee, Heather	Lect	HongKon Tech	FM	MBA	96	York	2004
Lee, Ho Young			MS	PHD	00.	Oregon	
Lee, Hoseoup	Asst	SUNY-Utica	AF	PHD	00	Conn	&1996
Lee, Hua	Asst	Chinese HK	ACF	PHD	01	Ntl Taiwan	2004
Lee, Hyunkoo			FM	PHD	98.	Car Mellon	
Lee, Janet	Asst	Australian N	EFG	PHD	01	N Eng-Au	2001
Lee, Jason	Assoc	Univ Alberta	FI	PHD	91	Alberta	1998
Lee, Jaywon	Asst	CUNY-Baruch	F	ABD		Columbia	9-06
Lee, John Y.	Prof	Pace-Westch	CM	PHD	79.	LSU	1992
Schaeberle Professor of Accounting							
Lee, Johnny	Asst	Villanova	MS	PHD	06.	Utah	2006
Lee, Jong-Cheon		Korea	1989	PHD	89.	Illinois	
Lee, Kangil	Asst	Youngnam Un	FQ	PHD	95.	Nebraska	1995
Youngnam Univ; Daekoo City Korea							
Lee, Kent O. K.	VTcFl	Lingnan U	AEG	MBA	05	HongKong U	2006
Lee, Kin Wai	Asst	Nanyang Tech	AF	PHD	04	Nanyang	&2000
Lee, Kyung Joo		Korea	1992	PHD	90.	Arizona	1990
Dept of Acct; Col of Bus & Econ; Cheju 690-756 Korea							
Lee, Kyung Tae	Assoc	Yonsei Univ	MYCT	PHD	92.	UCLA	1994
Lee, Linden	Lect	Un Cl Dublin	D				&1992
Lee, Lip Nyean	Assoc	Nanyang Tech	AF	MBA	79	Strathcl	* &1987
Lee, Lucy Chao			C	PHD	68.	Illinois	
Lee, Manwoo	Prof	Korea Univ	AFVX	PHD	87.	Georgia	& 3-88
Lee, Meina Grace	Asst	Lingnan U	FIJ	PHD	97	Utah	2003
Lee, Michael T.	Lect	U Melbourne	DS	MCOM	98	Monash	2002
Lee, Minwoo	Assoc	W Kentucky	MV	PHD	93.	Pittsburgh	1993
Lee, Myung		Buk Univ	1992	PHD	90.	Missouri	
Kyung Buk Univ; Dept Acct; Col Econ & Bus; 1370 San Kyeg 702-701 Korea							
Lee, Nam Joo	Asst	Sogang Univ		PHD	88.	Tx-Austin	
Lee, Orland S.	Retir	SW Texas St	1994	PHD	78.	Okla St	&1978
Lee, P.	VInst	Cleveland St	FIC	PHD	01	Kyung-He	&2001
Lee, Patsy L.	Adj	Tx-Arlington	F	PHD	83.	North Tx	&1997
Lee, Philip J.	SLect	Univ Sydney	FS	PHD	03	Sydney	&1990
Lee, Picheng	Assoc	Pace	FM	PHD	00.	Rutgers	2000
Lee, Richard E.	Lect	U Melbourne	FY	BEC	74	Monash	&1992
Lee, Samuel S. O.	Retir	Hawaii	1985	PHD	64.	Columbia	& 9-55
Lee, Sang-Chul	Asst	Dongguk U	CM	PHD	02	Yonsei	9-04
Lee, Sang-Kyu	Asst	W New Eng	MC	DBA	05.	Boston U	8-04
Lee, Sangsoo	Prof	Troy-Montg		PHD	86.	Tx-Austin	
Lee, Seok-Young			MF	PHD	92.	Minnesota	
Lee, Suk Jun			FI	PHD	93.	Wash U	
Lee, Sung Han		Ill-Chicago		PHD	06.	S Calif	
Lee, Tae Hee	Asst	Kookmin Univ	FQS	PHD	94.	Illinois	1994
Lee, Tanya M.	Asst	Robt Morris	MS	PHD	99.	Ariz St	8-06
Lee, Thomas A.	Retir	Alabama	FAHW	DLIT	84	Strathcl	&1-91
Lee, Thomas A..	Retir	Winona State	2000	MBA	74	Mankato	&1978
Lee, William	Lect	HongKon Tech	FJ	MBT	87	S Calif	&1997
Lee, Yang Hyun	Prof	Chung-Ang	FX	PHD	85	Chung-Ang	1985
Lee, Yen-Jung	Asst	Georgia St		PHD	05.	Mich St	2005
Lee, Yong-Gyo	Asst	Houston-Vict	FM	PHD	93.	Geo St	9-01
Lee, Younghwa (Gabe)	Asst	Kansas	S	PHD	05	Colorado	2005

Name	Rank	School		Degree	Yr	University	
Lee, Yow-Min R.	Retir	CS-Northrdge	1990	PHD	73.	Missouri	&
10800 Cozycroft Ave; Chatsworth CA 91311							
Leech, Stewart A.	Prof	U Melbourne	S	MEC	76	Tasmania	&2000
Professor of Accounting and Business Information Systems							
Leeds, Kevin A.	C-Pr	St Peters	FX	MBA		Fairl Dick	&1981
Leekbhai, Chongchitt	Retir	Chulalongkor	A	MBA	75	Thammas	&1981
Leenaars, Hans	Prof	Un Amsterdam		PHD	93	Amsterdm	1994
Leer, J. A.	Retir	Wisc-Milwauk		MBA	49	Nrthwstrn	&1949
W 254 S8760 Hi-Lo Dr; Mukwonago WI 53149							
Leese, Wallace R.	Prof	CS-Chico	CFM	PHD	78.	Ariz St	* 9-78
Lefanowicz, Craig E.	Asst	Virginia	FM	PHD	90.	Tx-Austin	&9-04
Leflar, Charles J. F.	Clin	Arkansas	FA	PHD	95.	Missouri	&1993
Leftwich, Howard D.	Retir	OK Christian	1996	DBA	70.	Oklahoma	&6-67
Leftwich, Richard W.	Prof	Chicago	F	PHD	80.	Rochester	&1979
Fuji Bank and Heller Professor of Accounting and Finance							
Leftwich, Wallace G.	Deces	Loyola-N Orl	1989	MBA	50	Tulane	&1950
Legault, Michel	Retir	Univ Laval	2004	PHD	79.	Syracuse	1976
Leggett, Carl L.			A	PHD	90.	Miss	&
Legoria, Joseph	Assoc	Louisiana St	F	PHD	97.	Arkansas	&8-01
LeGuyader, Louis P.	Mgr	Pricewaterh	2000	PHD	98.	Columbia	&
PricewaterhouseCoopers; 1177 Ave of the Americas; NY 10036; 212-596-7891							
Lehavy, Reuven	Asst	Michigan	F	PHD	97.	Nrthwstrn	2002
Bank One Corporation Assistant Profesor in Business Administration							
Lehman, Cheryl R.	Prof	Hofstra	BHW	PHD	85	NYU	1979
Lehman, Mark W.	Assoc	Miss State	AS	PHD	95.	Miss	&1984
Tenneco Professorship in Accounting							
Lehmann, Constance M.	Asst	Houston-Cl L	ABFS	PHD	01.	Tx A&M	9-01
Lehtonen, Taru	Res	Helsinki Sch	CGMN	MS	95	Helsinki	1995
Leibowicz, Barry	Assoc	CUNY-Queens	XL	LLM	73	NYU	9-74
Leibowitz, Martin A.	Asst	Yeshiva	MF	PHD	96.	Columbia	&9-95
Kirzner Chair; leibowitz613@juno.edu							
Leinheiser, Frederick D.	Asst	York-Penn	AF	MBA		Shippensb	&9-80
Leinicke, Linda M.	Prof	Illinois St	F	PHD	87.	Miss	&1984
Leininger, Albert A.	Retir	CS-Northrdge	1987	MBA	48	Nrthwstrn	&1962
1507 Granite Shadow Drive; Prescott AZ 86301							
Leininger, Wayne E.	Retir	Virg Tech	2003	PHD	71.	Mass	1971
Leitch, Robert Alan	Prof	So Carolina	SMQ	PHD	73	Tennessee	&1989
Wilbur S. Smith Distinguished Foundation Fellow							
Leitch, Shirley	C-Pr	U Wollongong					2006
Leitsch, Deborah	Assoc	Goldey-Beacm	FM	DBA	03	Sarasota	2-95
Leledakis, George	Lect	Athens Univ	F	PHD	99	Warwick	2002
Lelievre, Clara Chambers	Retir	Cincinnati	1987	PHD	68.	Alabama	&1957
Lelievre, Thomas W.	Retir	Cincinnati	1985	PHD	68.	Alabama	&1957
5880 Winton Ridge Lane; Cincinnati OH 45232							
Lembke, Valdean C.	Retir	Iowa	2001	PHD	69.	Michigan	1968
Lemeron, Everett G.		Birmingha AL	1988	PHD	72.	Alabama	
Lemieux, Pierre A.	Prof	Sherbrooke	FRV	MBA	67	Sherbrook	* &1970
Lemke, Bernard C.	Deces	Mich State	1989	PHD	46.	Minnesota	1949
Lemler, Bradley K.	Assoc	Hardin-Simm	FMXA	PHD	90.	Indiana	&2006
Lemon, W. Morley	Retir	Un Waterloo	2004	PHD	75.	Tx-Austin	& 1-81
PricewaterhouseCoopers Professor in Auditing							
Lenard, Mary Jane	Assoc	Meredith	ACNS	PHD	95	Kent St	* 8-05
Lenk, Margarita M.	Assoc	Colorado St	MSBC	PHD	91.	S Carol	* 1991
Lennox, Clive S.	Assoc	Hong Kong Sc	AFM	PHD	98	Oxford	2001
Lenthen, Simon	ALect	W Sydney	DNST	BCOM	02	W Sydney	
Lentilhon, Robert W.	Retir	Massachusett	1987	MBA	63	Boston U	&1952
Leonard, Barbara Brockie	Assoc	Hawaii-Hilo	PFTI	PHD	91.	Okla St	* 2002
Leonard, Glenn	Inst	New Brunswic		MA		New Bruns	2006
Leonard, Valorie	Prof	Laurentian		MBA	87	Laurentian	& 7-83
Leone, Andrew J.	Assoc	Penn State	FMT	PHD	97.	Pittsburgh	* &9-05
Leone, Sara	Asst	St FrancisIL	CVFX	MS	87	N Illinois	&1992
Leong, Kenneth K.			CM	PHD	85.	Colorado	
Leong, Michele	ALect	W Australia	F	MEC	95	Macquarie	&2001
Leong, Scott S. W.	Asst	Illinois St	SF	PHD	03.	Utah	* &
Leppiniemi, Jarmo	Prof	Helsinki Sch	PFTX	PHD	85	Helsinki	1972
Leraghan, Rosemary	Asst	Il-Springfld	F	PHD	06	UIS	2006
Lere, John C.	Prof	St Cloud St	MC	PHD	76.	Wisconsin	&1983
LeRoux, Emile		Quebec a Hul	F	BCOM			&
Lesage, Cedric	Attac	HEC Paris	FABV	PHD	99	Rennes 1	2006
Leshinski, Dianne L.	Lect	Arizona St	F	MBA	93	Dayton	&2006
Lesiak, Michael J.	Retir	Tri State	FCM	MBA	67	Colorado	&1967
Lesmond, David A.	Assoc	Tulane	FMS	PHD	94.	SUNY-Buf	1997
Lessard, Camille	Asst	Bishop's Un	F	MA		Sherbrooke	&
Lessard, Nathalie	Lect	Sherbrooke	AR	MS	91	Sherbrook	1985
Letourneau, Angela	C-Ac	Winthrop	CMX	DBA	87.	La Tech	&9-88
Letsinger, Marion Clyde	Retir	Tennessee	1990	MS	59	Tennessee	&1956
Lett, Samuel L.	Retir	Auburn-Montg	2006	PHD	81.	S Carol	&1976

Name	Rank	School	Codes	Degree	Year	University	Extra
Letzkus, William C.	Retir	Arkansas	1997	PHD	73.	Tx-Austin	&1980
Leung, Kwok Wai	Asst	Catholic	CF	PHD	99.	Maryland	9-00
Leung, Olivia S. L.	Asst	City Univ HK	FMC	PHD	04	CityU HK	&2004
Leung, Patrick W. Y.	Asst	HongKon Tech	AM	PHD	02	NS Wales	&1995
Leung, Sidney C. M.	Assoc	City Univ HK	FYA	PHD	97	NS Wales	&1997
Leung, Tak Yan	Asst	City Univ HK	AF	PHD	04	PolyU HK	&2005
Leung, Victor	TFell	Chinese HK	CMBA	PHD	91	Arkansas	1980
Leuz, Christian	Prof	Chicago	M	PHD	96	Goethe	
Lev, Baruch	Prof	New York U	F	PHD	68.	Chicago	&1995
Phillip Bardes Chair in Accounting & Finance							
Levelle, Michael J.	Assoc	Flagler		MBA		Dayton	&
Levendowski, Glenda	Lect	Arizona St	FX	MS	83	Hou-ClLk	&2004
Leventhal, Brian	Lect	Ill-Chicago	FM	MBA	87	N Illinois	&1993
Leveson, Lynne	Lect	LaTrobe Univ	BEMC	MED		LaTrobe	1990
Levesque, Raymond J.	SLect	Bentley	XF	MST	78	Bentley	&1983
Levi, Shai	Asst	Cal-Berkeley	F	PHD	04.	NYU	2004
Levine, Carolyn B.	Assoc	Carnegie Mel	FTM	PHD	96.	Car Mellon	2001
Levine, Marc H.	Prof	CUNY-Queens	AF	PHD	83	Yeshiva	&2-75
Levine, Seth	Lect	U Miami	PM	MBA	89	U Miami	&2001
Levitan, Alan S.	Prof	Louisville	MS	DBA	83.	Kentucky	&1979
Levitt, Warren R.	Retir	C New Jersey	XFM	MBA	74	Pace	&1975
Levy, Arthur S.	Retir	Savannah St	P	BS	49	Pittsburgh	&1979
Levy, Elliott S.	Assoc	Bentley	FAEP	MA	78	Florida	# * &1980
Levy, Linda G.			BX	PHD	96.	Colorado	&
Levy, Philippe	Lect	McGill Univ	FM	MBA	90	McGill	&1990
Lew, Albert Y.			CFV	PHD	84.	Nebraska	&
Lewis, Barry L.	C-Pr	Colorado St		PHD	78.	Penn St	4-04
Lewis, Barry T.	Deces	SW Missouri	8-01	PHD	78	Missouri	& 8-87
Lewis, Daniel C. Jr.			DCS		54.	Harvard	
Lewis, Eddie M. Jr.	Assoc	Wm Carey	FIM	DBA	74.	Miss St	2003
Lewis, Eldon C.	Retir	CS-San Bern	2004	PHD	67.	Missouri	&1987
Lewis, Eric E.	C-Ac	Ithaca	AV	PHD	95.	Union-NY	8-02
Lewis, Johnston C.	Assoc	Troy-Dothan	X	MACC	82	Alabama	&2001
Lewis, Judy D.	Assoc	Angelo State	AP	PHD	96.	North Tx	&1999
Lewis, Karen	Lect	Canterbury	FHW	PHD	03	Canterbu	2004
Lewis, Lawrence D.	Prof	Portland	CM	PHD	84.	Nebraska	* 2001
Lewis, Merrill T.	Deces	CS-Pomona	1996	PHD	84.	S Calif	&1989
Lewis, Philip	Asst	E Michigan	IBF	PHD	01.	Cincinnati	&2005
Lewis, Roger	Inst	St Cloud St	P	MAC	88	Arizona	&2001
Lewis, Ronald J.	Retir	Cen Michigan	D-91	PHD	65.	Mich St	1981
Lewis, Stanley X.	D-Pr	So Miss	S	DBA	75.	Miss St	&1980
Lewis, Thomas D.	C-Ac	Creighton	FM	PHD	79.	Nebraska	* &9-81
Lewis, Timothy B.	Assoc	Srthrn Utah	XL	JD	79	Brighm Yg	1985
Lewis, William	Assoc	Rockford	CP	MBA		Illinois	&1992
Li, Aili		Hong Kong Sc	F	PHD	98.	Berkeley	
Li, Chunyan	Asst	Pace	FM	PHD	01.	Rutgers	2001
Li, David	Lect	HongKon Tech	FS	MBA	88	Iowa	&2000
Li, David H.		Bethesda MD	1992	PHD	53.	Illinois	&
17 Pepperell Court; Bethesda MD 20817							
Li, Fang Sherry	Asst	Rider	F	ABD		Mass	2007
Li, Feng	Asst	Michigan		PHD	05.	Chicago	
Li, Haidan	Asst	Iowa	F	PHD	02.	Tx-Austin	8-02
Li, Jennifer	Asst	Brock Univ	FT	PHD	03	Massey	2003
Li, John Q.	Asst	Suffolk	FI	PHD	00.	Wash U	2003
Li, June F.	Asst	Wis-Rvr Fall	EFPV	PHD	92.	Kentucky	&2006
Li, Karen	Inst	Chinese HK	AFD	MBA	90	SanFranSt	&1999
Li, Laura	Asst	Illinois	FM	PHD	06	Tulane	8-06
Li, Melody M. W.	TchFl	Lingnan U	AF	MA	05	City U	2006
Li, Oliver Zhen	Assoc	Arizona	FX	PHD	03.	Arizona	2007
Li, Shu-Hsing	Prof	Nat Taiwan U	FM	PHD	90.	NYU	8-93
Li, Siyi	Asst	Illinois	F	PHD	03.	Columbia	8-03
Li, Wei	Asst	Kent State	F	PHD	06.	Wash St	& 8-06
Li, Xu	Asst	Texas-Dallas	FX	PHD	04.	MIT	2004
Li, Ying	Asst	George Wash	F	PHD	02.	MIT	2007
Li, Ying-Hua	Asst	Purdue		PHD	05	Brit Colum	2005
Li, Yong	Asst	Un Stirling	AF	MSC	01	Stirling	2004
Li, Yu-Ku	Retir	SUNY-Brockpo	2001	PHD	68.	Berkeley	&1977
Li, Zining	Asst	So Methodist		PHD		Minnesota	
Liang, Jia-Wen	Asst	Nat Chengchi		PHD	02.	Oregon	2003
Liang, Lihong	Asst	George Wash	F	PHD	02.	Penn St	2002
Liang, Pierre Jinghong	Assoc	Carnegie Mel	TMF	PHD	98.	Florida	1998
Liao, Pei-Cheng	Asst	Nat Taiwan U	FIT	PHD	02	U Wash	& 2-03
Liao, Shu S.	Emer	Naval Postgr	2004	PHD	71.	Illinois	1977
Liao, Woody M.	Prof	Cal-Riversid	MQY	PHD	74.	Florida	* &1991
Libby, Patricia A.	Assoc	Ithaca	FETN	PHD	84.	Michigan	& 8-89
Libby, Robert	C-Pr	Cornell	FBA	PHD	74.	Illinois	& 7-89
David A. Thomas Professor of Management							

Name	Rank	School	Code	Degree	Yr	Institution		Year
Libby, Theresa	Assoc	Wilfrid Laur	MB	PHD	96	Waterloo		&1996
Licastro, Ralph D.	SLect	Penn State	AX	MS	71	Penn St		&9-72
Licata, Michael P.	Assoc	Villanova	AFMS	PHD	84.	Tx A&M		1983
Liddle, Stephen W.	Assoc	Brigham Yg	S	PHD	95	Brighm Yg		6-95
Grant & David Research Fellow								
Lieberman, Alvin H.	Assoc	Akron	XF	JD	64	Akron		&9-69
KPMG Fellow								
Liebling, Alexander	Dean	E Tx Baptist	MF	PHD	73.	Oklahoma		
East Texas Baptist University; Marshall Tx								
Liedtka, Stephen L.			M	PHD	99.	Maryland		
Liew, Angela	STut	U Auckland	MA	MCOM	03	Auckland		2007
Lightbody, Margaret	LectB	Adelaide	CMFA	PHD	00	S Austrl		&1997
Lighthouse, Wally D.	Assoc	Pacific Unio	FLX	JD	91			2007
Lightle, Susan S.	Prof	Wright State	A	PHD	91.	Cincinnati	#	&9-91
Lightner, Kevin M.	Emer	San Diego St	F	PHD	70.	UCLA		1968
Lightner, Sharon Douglas	D-Ac	San Diego St	F	PHD	77.	Oregon		&9-77
Lightner, Teresa A.	Asst	Texas Tech	FX	PHD	01.	Oklahoma		9-02
Lightstone, Karen	Asst	St Marys-Cdn	FEU	PHD		Portsmouth		&1999
Likierman, Sir Andrew	VProf	London Bus	MGJ	MA	65	Oxford		&1979
Lilien, Steven B.	Prof	CUNY-Baruch	CF	PHD	76	NYU		&1972
Irving Weinstein Professor of Accountancy								
Lillie, Rick		CS-San Bern						
Lillis, Anne M.	AProf	U Melbourne	M	PHD	98	Melbourne		1997
Lilly, Martha S.	Retir	No Colorado	2004	PHD	81.	Tx Tech		&1988
Lim, Changwoo P.	Assoc	Chung-Ang	CMY	PHD	89.	Purdue		1989
Lim, Chee Yeow	Asst	Nanyang Tech	F	PHD	00	Nanyang		2000
Lim, Chen	Tutor	Univ Exeter	CF	MSC	00	Lancaster		2001
Lim, Jee-Hae	Asst	Un Waterloo	S	PHD	06.	Kansas		2006
Lim, Kwang Soo	Assoc	Eastern Conn		PHD	94.	Purdue		
Lim, Nena	Lect	U Melbourne	BDJS	PHD	03	Queenslnd		2005
Lim, Nena	Lect	U Queensland	DS	MSC	95	Geo St		1999
Lim, Roslinda	ALect	Macquarie Un	FM	MFIN	00	UWA		2004
Lim, Selena	Lect	LaTrobe Univ	MDS	BEC		RMIT		1984
Lim, Stephen	SLect	Tech-Sydney	FTY	PHD	96	Tech-Sydn		1992
Lim, Steve C.	Assoc	Tx Christian	F	PHD	89.	Penn		1999
Lim, Suk Sig		Seoul City U	1991	PHD	90.	Minnesota		
Seoul City Univ; Dept of Atg; Jeonnong Dong Dongdaemun-Gu; Seoul 130-743 Kore								
Lim, Tayseop		Samsum Life		PHD	93.	N Carol		
Limacher, Joseph			F	PHD	97.	U Wash		
Limberg, Stephen T.	Prof	Texas-Austin	X	PHD	82.	Ariz St		9-82
PricewaterhouseCoopers Centennial Professor of Accountng; MPA/PPA Director								
Lin, Beixin	Asst	Montclair St	FM	PHD	04.	Rutgers		2003
Lin, Cecila H.	Asst	Portland	AFS	PHD	00.	North Tx		&2006
Lin, Chan-Jane	C-Pr	Nat Taiwan U	FIA	PHD	89.	Maryland		&D-90
Lin, Haijin	Asst	Florida		PHD	04.	Car Mellon		8-04
Grant Thornton Term Professor								
Lin, Hsiou-wei	Asst	Nat Chengchi		PHD	94.	Stanford		
Lin, Hwey-Jane	Assoc	Nat Taiwan U	CFME	MA	80	Penn		&8-84
Lin, Jean	Asst	St Joseph	FM	PHD	07	Tennessee		2007
Lin, Jerry W.	Assoc	Minn-Duluth	FASB	PHD	94.	North Tx		1999
Lin, Kenny Z. P.	Assoc	Lingnan U	AXF	PHD	96	Glasgow		2000
Lin, Liang-Feng	Lect	Nat Chengchi	PCF	MC	94	Temple		1984
Lin, Mei-Hwa	Prof	Nat Chengchi	FTV	PHD	87.	Drexel	*	&1989
Lin, Pao-Chuan (Paul)	Assoc	Wright State	S	PHD	88.	LSU		9-00
Lin, Ping	Asst	CS-Long Bch	CM	PHD	03.	Ca-Irvine	*	2006
Lin, Shu	Asst	CS-Fresno	PFM	PHD	06	Tx		8-06
Lin, Stephen W.	Assoc	Fla Internat	IF	PHD	99	Manchest		2005
Lin, Suming (Tim)	Assoc	Nat Taiwan U	XF	PHD	93	Ariz St		&8-93
Lin, Thomas W.	Prof	So Calif	MIA	PHD	75.	Ohio St	*	1975
Accounting Circle Professor								
Lin, Ting-Ting	Asst	Ntl Chung Ch	CM	DBA	04.	Boston U		2004
Lin, Wan-Yin	Assoc	Nat Chengchi	PCT	DBA	99.	Boston U		1986
Lin, Y. C. George	Asst	Ntl Chung Ch	BFQT	PHD	98	Syracuse		1999
Lin, Y. Robert	Assoc	CS-East Bay	CFM	PHD	89.	UCLA	*	1-89
Lind, Johnny	Asst	Stockholm Ec	M	ED	96	Uppsala		2000
Lindahl, Frederick W.	Assoc	George Wash	MCI	PHD	85.	Chicago		&9-93
Lindbeck, Rudolph S.	Retir	Louisiana Te	1996	PHD	69.	Alabama		&1989
Lindberg, Deborah L.	Assoc	Illinois St	AF	DBA	97.	Boston U		&1997
Lindberg, Erik	Asst	Univ of Umea	MA	LIPH	98	Lulea		8-98
Lindbergh, Lars	Asst	Univ of Umea	F	PHD	03	Umea		8-92
Lindblom, Cristi K.			FIJV	PHD	83.	Illinois	*	
Linden, Rowene F.	Fac	No Illinois	E	MS	95	N Illinois		7-98
Lindgren, Richard K.	D-Ac	Graceland	CJ	MBA	80	Michigan	*	&2002
Lindh, C. Ted	Retir	Indiana U-PA	7-01	MA	73	Duquesne		&1975
Lindhe, Richard	Retir	Northeastern	6-90	PHD	62.	Chicago		1966
Lindloff, Paul W. Jr.				PHD	65.	Tx-Austin		
Lindlolm, Gunnar		Stockholm Ec	M	CE	68	Stockholm		1994

Lindquist, Stanton C.	Prof	Grand Valley	AP	PHD	72.	Missouri	&1974
Lindquist, Timothy M.	Assoc	No Iowa	BFM	PHD	91.	Colorado	1991
Lindsay, David H.	C-Pr	CS-Stanislau	F	PHD	92	Kent St	&1991
Lindsay, R. Murray	Dean	U Lethbridge	BMST	PHD	88	Lancaster	* 2005
Lindsay, W. Daryl	Prof	Saskatchewan	AF	PHD	80.	Minnesota	&1971
Lindsey, Bradley	Asst	Wm & Mary	FX	PHD	06.	N Carol	&2006
Lindskog, Arlynn	Retir	Purdue Calum	2003	MBA		Purdue	&1978
Lindstrom, Craig J.	AsTch	Brigham Yg	S	MS	01	Utah St	8-02
Ling, Qianhua	Asst	Marquette	C	PHD	07	Okla St	8-07
Lingenfilter, Gabriele	Inst	Chris Newpor	PA	MBA	92	NW Mo St	&2004
Link, William R.	Lect	Mo-St Louis	FM	MBA	67	Missouri	&1981
Linn, Gary	Prof	Henderson St	FBX	DBA	97.	La Tech	&1995
Cecil Cupp Chair							
Linn, James J.	Retir	Tulane	1996	PHD	63.	Berkeley	1966
Linnegar, Gary J.			FMS	DBA	88.	Miss St	&
Linnell, Robert S.	Retir	Tulsa	1985	MBA	48	Denver	&1955
Lins, William C.	Retir	Rutgers-Newk	1993	PHD	62.	Columbia	&1964
Linsley, Colin A.	VAsst	Maryland	FM	PHD	86	Exxes	2007
Linsmeier, Thomas J.		FASB	F	PHD	85.	Wisconsin	&2006
Linthicum, Cheryl L.	Assoc	Tx-S Antonio	FIS	PHD	93.	Okla St	&1993
Linton, Sara M.	Assoc	Indiana NW	LCSX	PHD	92.	Houston	8-04
Linville, Mark E.	Asst	Kansas State	AF	PHD	95.	U Wash	& 8-02
BKD Faculty Fellow							
LiPari, Joseph	Asst	Montclair St	PTF	MBA	81	Fairl Dick	&1989
Lipe, Marlys Gascho	Prof	Oklahoma	MB	PHD	85.	Chicago	* & 8-97
Rath Chair in Accounting							
Lipe, Robert C.	Assoc	Oklahoma	F	PHD	85.	Chicago	& 1-98
KPMG Centennial Professor							
Lipka, Roland	Prof	Temple	XF	PHD	76	Rutgers	&1983
Lipman, Francine J.	Assoc	Chapman	FX	LLM	94	NYU	& 9-01
Lippincott, Barbara J.	Asst	Tampa	FG	PHD	98.	Missouri	&2004
Lippitt, Jeffrey W.	Assoc	Ithaca	CFM	PHD	82.	Penn St	8-02
Lippman, Ellen	Assoc	Portland	BF	PHD	91.	Oregon	&1983
Lipsig, Roberta M.	Retir	SUNY Oswego	2003	MS	78	Ariz St	&1978
Lirely, Roger L.	H-Ac	W Carolina	X	DBA	96.	S Illinois	1996
Lisciandro, Joseph A.	Retir	Slippery Roc	AFP	MBA	75	Clarion St	& 9-77
Lish, Rex		Las CrucesNM	1991	DBA	77.	Kentucky	&
405 E Amador; Las Cruces NM 88001							
Lisko, Mary K.	Retir	Augusta St	FMT	MBA	69	Arizona	* &1979
Lisowski, Paul	Asst	Edinboro	FV	MBA	75	Pittsburgh	1975
Litherland, Dorothy A.	Retir	Illinois	9-72	PHD	51.	Illinois	1946
Little, Harold T. Jr.	Assoc	W Kentucky	CFMP	PHD	99.	S Illinois	# * &1993
Little, Margaret	Retir	Arkansas	2003	MSA	86	Arkansas	&1986
Little, Philip L.	Prof	W Carolina	FT	DBA	86.	La Tech	&1993
Littleton, A. C.	Deces	Illinois	1974	PHD	31	Illinois	&1915
Littrell, Earl K.	Retir	Willamette	2005	PHD	73.	Oregon	* 1976
Litzler, Samuel J.	Retir	No Arizona	1988	MBA	61	Tx A&M	&1966
Liu, Caixing	Asst	CS-Sacrament	FA	PHD	04.	Hawaii	2004
Liu, Cathy Zishang	VAsst	Louisiana St		PHF	07	Houston	8-07
Liu, Chao M.	Assoc	Tarleton St	XV	PHD	82.	North Tx	&1984
Liu, Chao-Shin	Assoc	Notre Dame	FM	PHD	92.	Illinois	1992
Deloitte Faculty Fellow							
Liu, Chi-Chun	Prof	Nat Taiwan U	FM	PHD	94	NYU	8-97
Liu, Chiawen	Asst	Nat Taiwan U	AFT	PHD	97	Natl Taiw	& 2-02
Liu, Jiangxia Renee	Asst	W Carolina	FPT	PHD	06	Tx-Dallas	2006
Liu, Jing	Assoc	UCLA	F	PHD	99.	Columbia	1999
Liu, Michelle	Asst	Penn State	F	PHD	06.	MIT	7-06
Liu, Min-Hsin (Carol)	Asst	Oakland	FM	PHD	05.	SUNY-Buf	8-05
Liu, Ou	VLect	HongKon Tech	DS	PHD	06	City U	2006
Liu, Shuen-Zen	Assoc	Nat Taiwan U	PFN	PHD	93.	Pittsburgh	8-94
Liu, Suping				PHD	94.	Fla Intl	
Liu, Weimin	Lect	U Manchester	FQTY	PHD		Manchest	2000
Liu, Xiaohong	Asst	Hong Kong Sc	AFMT	PHD	02	Brit Colum	2002
Liu, Xiaohui Gloria	Asst	Texas-Dallas	F	PHD	04.	Nrthwstrn	2004
Liu, Zhen	Asst	Hong Kong U		PHD	03.	S Calif	
Liu, Zhu (Alfred)	Asst	Connecticut	FV	PHD	06.	Ca-Irvine	2006
Livermore, Douglas	Prof	Morningside	B	EDD	86	N Colo	1980
Liveson, Avi O.	Prof	CUNY-Hunter	LX	LLM	75	NYU	9-86
Livingston, Alex	Retir	NY-Geneseo	5-89	MBA	65	Syracuse	& 9-79
Livingstone, J. Leslie			1992	PHD	66.	Stanford	&
Litgation Consulting Atg Fin; 2300 Beach Lakes Blvd # 306; W Palm Bch FL33409							
Livingstone, Jane R.	Asst	N Car-Greens	XF	PHD	98.	Penn St	2004
Livnat, Joshua	Prof	New York U	FM	PHD	87	NYU	&1987
Livne, Gilad			F	PHD	96.	Berkeley	&
Liyanarachchi, Gregory	SLect	Univ Otago	FMA	PHD	04	Otago	1994
Ljungdahl, Philip W.	Deces			PHD	66.	Tx-Austin	& 9-87
Lloyd, Paul	Lect	W Australia	FC	BCOM	91	W Austrl	&1994

Name	Rank	School	Code	Degree	Yr	School	Note
Lloyd, William H.	Asst	Lock Haven		MBA	04	Lingnan	& 2004
Lo, Agnes W. Y.	Asst	Lingnan U	IX	PHD			2004
Lo, Kin	Assoc	British Colu	FQK	PHD	99.	Nrthwstrn	& 7-99
CA Professorship in Accounting							
Lo, May Hwa	Prof	W New Eng	FVM	PHD	92.	Drexel	1993
Loan, Dang Thi	Lect	Natl Econ	FMCV	PHD	91	Kiev	1976
Lobingier, Patricia G.	Inst	Virg Tech	F	PHD	97.	Va Tech	8-05
Lobo, Gerald J.	C-Pr	Houston	F	PHD	82.	Michigan	2004
Arthur Andersen Chair							
Locatelli, Paul L.	Retir	Santa Clara		DBA	71.	S Calif	&1974
Lockett, Peter Paul	Retir	CS-L Angeles	1994	DBA	73.	S Calif	&1969
Lockhart, Julie A.	C-Pr	Western Wash	M	MS	82	Illinois	* &1982
Lockridge, T. Maurice	Asst	Marshall	FMPU	PHD	04.	Memphis	&2006
Lockwood, Donald	Lect	British Colu	F	MBA	76	Chicago	&1976
Lockwood, M. Jill	Prof	Geo Southern	XL	LLM	79	Emory	&1984
Lodhia, Sumit K.	Asst	Australian N	CDS	MA	99	USP	2001
Loeb, Martin P.	C-Pr	Maryland	M	PHD	75	Nrthwstrn	8-82
Deloitte & Touche Faculty Fellow							
Loeb, Stephen E.	Prof	Maryland	JAG	PHD	70.	Wisconsin	&1970
Ernst & Young Alumni Professor of Accounting & Business Ethics							
Loebbecke, James K.	Retir	Utah	1999	BS	58	Berkeley	&1980
Loftus, Janice A.	SLect	Univ Sydney	FTI	MCOM	91	NS Wales	2002
Logan, Jennifer	Asst	Southern Ark		PHD		Oklahoma	2007
Logan, Lawrence B.	Assoc	Mass-Dartmou	FA	PHD	83	Wisconsin	1994
Logsdon, John J.	Assoc	Webber Coll	AGMS	MS	88	Cen Fla	&1986
Logue, James	Asst	St Fran-Penn		MS		Widener	1995
Loh, Lye Chye Alfred	Assoc	Natl Singapo	FMI	PHD	89	W Austrl	&1981
Lohmann, Rebecca	Inst	SE Missouri	P	MS	03	S Illinois	2005
Lohrke, Cynthia A.	Assoc	Samford	S	PHD	94.	Drexel	&2000
Loi, Nguyen	Lect	Natl Econ	FCT	PHD	96	Natl Econ	1997
Loken, Svein A.	IndPr	Norwegian Mg	ADO	MBUS	70	NHH Berg	1985
Lomax, Victor W.	Retir	Pikeville	1995	PHD	84.	Missouri	&1993
Lombard, J. Larry	Assoc	Metro State	PFAG	PHD	71.	Arkansas	9-80
London, Coy N.	Retir	Arkansas St	1996	PHD	71.	Missouri	& 8-70
Long, Brett J.	Assoc	So Indiana	XL	LLM	93	Missouri	&1993
Long, Kathleen G.	Asst	Tenn-Chattan	P	MBA	98	La-Lafay	& 1-00
Longfield, Henry W.	Retir	Indiana St	1992	PHD	70.	Ariz St	& 9-69
Lonie, Alasdair A.	Deces	Dundee	1999	MA	62	Glasgow	1982
Loning, Helene	Assoc	HEC Paris	MBCI	PHD	94	HEC Paris	1989
Lont, David	SLect	Univ Otago	DEQF	PHD	01	Otago	1-89
Lookabill, Larry L.			F	PHD	75.	Stanford	&
Lopez, Dennis	Asst	Tx-S Antonio	MA	PHD	07.	Arkansas	& 8-06
Lopez, Kathrine J.	Asst	Trinity	BJTE	MS	01	Trinity	& 8-07
Lopez, Thomas J.	Assoc	So Carolina	F	PHD	98.	Ariz St	* &2004
Loraas, Tina M.	Asst	Auburn	S	PHD	04.	Tx A&M	
Lorange, Peter	Pres	Intl Mgt Dev	IM	DBA	72.	Harvard	1993
Lord, Alan T.	Prof	Bowling Gr	ABS	PHD	89.	Case Wes	&1995
Ernst & Young Professor of Accounting							
Lord, Beverley R.	SLect	Canterbury	FMQ	PHD	01	Waikato	1991
Lord, Robert J. A.	Deces			DBA	73.	Harvard	&1974
Lordi, Frank C.	Assoc	Widener	FMEH	MBA	70	Penn St	# * &1976
Lorek, Kenneth S.	Prof	No Arizona	FMC	PHD	75.	Illinois	& 8-96
Ralph M. Bilby Endowed Professor							
Loschen, Leslie R.	Retir	E New Mexico	1990	PHD	63.	U Wash	* &1987
Losell, Donna	SLect	Univ Toronto	FA	MBA	78	Toronto	&1981
Loss, David E.	Retir	Central Conn	2003	MBA	63	Northeas	& 9-70
Lossett, Ronald D.				DBA	73.	S Calif	&
Loster, Donald R.	Lect	Cal-Santa Br	MA	BS	69	Woodbury	&1979
Loudder, Martha L.	Assoc	Texas A&M	F	PHD	90.	Ariz St	9-88
PricewaterHouseCoopers Fellowship							
Louderback, Joseph G.	Retir	Clemson	2000	PHD	70.	Florida	&1982
Loudon, Geoffrey F.	Prof	Macquarie Un	F	PHD	96	AGSM	&1985
Lougee, Barbara A.	Asst	San Diego	F	PHD	99.	Cornell	2007
Loughlin, Brian	Assoc	Maryland UC	AOF	MBA	88	Maryland	# * &1999
Louhi, Kullervo	Deces	Mich State	4-76	PHD	55.	Chicago	1958
Louie, Charles F.	Retir	Santa Clara	1997	PHD	63.	Berkeley	1963
Louie, Judy	AsLec	LaTrobe Univ					2005
Louis, Henock	Asst	Penn State	F	PHD	01.	Ohio St	8-01
Lourens, Laurie	Reitr	LaTrobe Univ	1993	MA		Kent	&1988
Lousteau, Carolyn L.			CF	PHD	97.	Tx-Arlin	&
Louwers, Timothy J.	Prof	Jms Madison	ASD	PHD	93.	Fla St	# & 9-05
Jackson E. Ramsey Centennial Professor							
Lovata, Linda M.	Prof	S Ill-Edward	MS	PHD	83.	Indiana	&1989
Lovatt, D. A.	Lect	East Anglia	FM	PHD		Cambridge	
Love, Dianne B.	Assoc	Houston-Cl L	MF	PHD	84.	Arkansas	1981
Love, William H.	Assoc	Wis-Stev Pt	FA	PHD	86.	Arkansas	# * & 8-82
Loveland, Terry L.	Retir	Missouri St	FI	ABD	72	Missouri	& 8-72

Low, Bernardine	Asst	Nanyang Tech	ABF	PHD	04.	Cornell	1997
Low, Kin-Yew	Asst	Nanyang Tech	AB	PHD	01.	Illinois	&1993
Low, Pek Yee	VFell	City Univ HK	IV	PHD	96.	Nebraska	&1996
Lowe, D. Jordan	Assoc	Ariz St West	AFM	PHD	92.	Ariz St	& 9-03
Lowe, Howard D.	Retir	Hawaii-Manoa	1992	DBA	57.	Indiana	& 9-66
Lowe-Ardoin, Letti	Inst	Louisiana St	FX	MS	83	LSU	& 8-98
Lowenfeld, George	Asst	Concordia U	XA	ABD		Toronto	&1976
Lowensohn, Suzanne H.	Asst	Colorado St	ABGM	PHD	96.	U Miami	&2002
Lowenthal, Franklin	Prof	CS-East Bay	CMSQ	PHD	65	Stanford	9-78
Lowry, Paul B.	Asst	Brigham Yg	S	PHD	02	Arizona	5-02
Lowry, Wallace M.	Retir	Sonoma State	1999	MBA	69	Berkeley	& 9-69
Loyland, Mary J.	Assoc	North Dakota	AF	PHD	89.	Nebraska	& 1-87
Lrang, Xinghua	Asst	McMaster Un	F	PHD	07	Toronto	7-06
Lu, Debra Hua	Retir	St Cloud St	1999	PHD	73	Minnesota	&1973
Lu, Hai	Asst	Univ Toronto	FM	PHD	04.	S Calif	2004
Lu, Tong	Asst	Houston	F	PHD	04	Minnesota	9-04
Lu, Wei	SLect	Monash Univ	IH	PHD	99	LaTrobe	1994
Lu, Yvonne	Asst	So Calif		PHD	04.	Stanford	2003
Lu, Zemin	VAsst	Un Hong Kong	IF	PHD	98.	Tulane	2006
Lu, Zhou	Asst	Hong Kong U	FX	PHD	00.	S Calif	9-00
Lubberink, Martien	Lect	U Lancaster	F	MSC	92	Groningen	2000
Lubell, Myron S. (Mike)	Retir	Fla Internat	2006	DBA	78.	Maryland	&1975
Lubich, Bruce H.	Assoc	Maryland UC	XFJ	PHD	91.	Penn St	& 7-03
Lubwama, Christopher W. K.	C-Pr	CS-East Bay	CIMU	PHD	89	Simon Fr	9-87
Lucas, Marcia J.	Prof	W Illinois	FEP	PHD	91.	St Louis	& 9-79
Lucas, William H.	Retir	So Miss	1995	PHD	66.	Alabama	&1990
Luchs, Christopher	Asst	Ball State	FM	PHD	03.	Kent St	8-06
Lucido, Peter	Asst	SUNY Old Wes					
Luckett, Peter F.	Assoc	New So Wales	MB	PHD	84	Sydney	&1983
Luckie, William V.	Retir	Mercer-Macon	2002	MBA	68	Miss	&1976
Ludwig, Stephen E.	Asst	NW Missouri	AS	PHD	99.	Arkansas	&2001
Lueders, Susan	Inst	DePaul	PFGQ	MSA	90	Illinois	&2001
Luehlfing, Michael S.	Assoc	Louisiana Te	FTA	PHD	90.	Georgia	* &1998
Max P. Watson, Jr. Endowed Professor							
Luft, Joan L.	Prof	Michigan St	MB	PHD	92.	Cornell	1992
Eli Broad Professor of Accounting							
Luh, Frank F. S.	Retir	Lehigh	1995	PHD	65.	Ohio St	1965
Luh, Troy V.	Assoc	Webster	FA	PHD	03	St Louis	&2002
Lui, Daphne	Lect	U Lancaster	F	PHD	05	London	2005
Luing, Gary A.	Retir	Fla Atlantic	2002	MAS	61	Illinois	&1965
Lukawitz, James M.	Assoc	Memphis	F	PHD	89.	Fla St	& 1-89
Luli, Roger	Asst	Baldwin-Wal	AFS	MBA	75	Bald-Wal	9-96
Lulseged, Ayalew Ali	Asst	Florida St	CMF	PHD	99.	LSU	8-02
Lumbattis, Catherine E.	Inst	So Illinois	F	MBA	75	S Illinois	&1981
Luna, LeAnn	Asst	Tennessee	FC	PHD	00.	Tennessee	& 6-05
Lund, Reuel I.	Deces	Minnesota		PHD	40.	Minnesota	
Lundblad, Heidemarie	Prof	CS-Northrdge	MF	PHD	86.	U Wash	1982
Lundholm, Russell J.	C-Pr	Michigan	F	PHD	87.	Iowa	1993
Arthur Andersen Professor of Accounting							
Lundquist, Richard E.	Retir			PHD	55.	Minnesota	
Lundsford, Dale L.			DBS	PHD	96.	Ohio St	
Lundy, William T.	Assoc	SUNY Oswego	FTR	MS	84	SUNY-Bin	&1978
Luneski, Chris J.	Retir	Oregon	1993	PHD	65.	Minnesota	1961
Lunn, H. Nelson				PHD	70.	Illinois	&
Luo, Rebecca K. W.	SLect	Lingnan U	XFL	MBA	94	Toronto	2002
Luoma, Gary A.	Retir	So Carolina	2005	DBA	66.	Wash U	* & 7-86
Luoma, Raymond G.	Retir	East Tenn St	1988	ABD		Mich St	1967
Lupino, Joseph F.	Assoc	St Marys-Cal	ADGP	MBA	69	Armstron	&1977
Lusher, Anna	Assoc	Slippery Roc		EDD		Marshall	&2006
Lusk, Edward J.	Prof	SUNY-Plattsb	AMSG	PHD	72.	Nrthwstrn	& 8-06
Lussier, Madeleine		Quebec a Hul	ACM	BCOM			&
Lustgarten, Steven	Prof	CUNY-Baruch	F	PHD	71	UCLA	1988
Luthy, David H.	Retir	Utah State	S	DBA	75.	Indiana	&1975
Luttman, Suzanne M.	Assoc	Santa Clara	XF	PHD	88.	Illinois	1991
Lutz, Cederic W.			DCS		39.	Harvard	
Lutz, Edward O.	Retir	CUNY-Brookly	1996	BS	40	Columbia	& 9-48
Lutz, Jennifer L.	Assoc	Manchester C	DMP	MAS	96	Illinois	1999
Luzi, Andrew D.	Prof	CS-Fullerton	S	PHD	78.	Kansas	1990
Lye, Joanne M.	Lect	LaTrobe Univ	FM	MBS	96	Massey	2001
Lyken, Herbert L.	Retir	Mass-Boston	1990	MBA	51	Harvard	&1975
Lyle, Harry C.	Deces	Miami U-Ohio		PHD	60.	Ohio St	&1968
Lyle, Johanna D.	Inst	Kansas State	FLG	MACC	83	Kansas St	& 9-83
Ernst & Young Teaching Fellow							
Lynch, Antoinette L.	Asst	Fla Internat		PHD	04.	S Fla	8-06
Lynch, Howell J.	C-Pr	Lamar	XJ	PHD	91.	Tx A&M	& 1-97
Lynch, Luann J.	Assoc	Virg-Grad	FMU	PHD	98.	N Carol	1998
Robert F. Vandell Research Chair; Assoc Dean for Intellectual Capital							

Name	Rank	School				
Lynch, Mariah	Inst	So Carolina	FM	MACC	03	NC-Wilm	2005
Lynch, Michael F.	Prof	Bryant	X	JD	80	NE Law	& 1-77
Lynch, Nancy Pennoyer	Lect	W Virginia	PA	MS	86	Colorado	* & 8-91
Lynch, Patrick M.	VAsst	Loyola-N Orl		MS		N Orleans	
Lynch, Thomas E.	Retir	Golden Gate	2000	DBA	71.	S Calif	&1997
Lyne, Stephen R.	SLect	Univ Bristol	CUBM	PHD			& 8-79
Lynn, Bernadette E.	Retir	McMaster Un	MC	PHD	74	McMaster	* 7-80
Lynn, Edward S.	Retir	Arizona	1985	PHD	55.	Tx-Austin	&1965
825 W Golf View Drive; Oro Valley AZ 85737							
Lynn, Quepha	Lect	Texas Tech	FCH	MSA	88	North Tx	& 9-91
Lynn, Stephen G.	Assoc	City Univ HK	IMV	PHD	97	NYU	1997
Lynn, Susan A.	Assoc	Baltimore	FBE	DBA	82.	Maryland	& 1-89
Lyon, Chris S.	Inst	Fort Lewis	FX	MS	90	Colorado	&2002
Lyon, John D.	Prof	Austral Grad	AFS	PHD	91.	Ohio St	&1999
Lyon, Robert A.	SLect	Dundee	IMVZ	MA	69	Dundee	* &1976
Lyons, J.	PLect	London Metro	FMNE	MBA			1990
Lyons, Kimberly	Inst	Wis-La Cross	PX	MS	94	Illinois	& 1-97
Lyons, Lyndon	Lect	Griffith Un	FQ	MCOM	79	NS Wales	1989
Lys, Thomas Z.	Prof	Northwestern	FM	PHD	82.	Rochester	1981
Eric L. Kohler Chair in Accounting							
Ma, Alfred K. W.	Asst	City Univ HK	MF	MBA	86	ChinesHK	9-89
Ma, Chenghu	Asst	Univ Essex	FQ	PHD	92	Montreal	1999
Ma, Qing Zhong	Asst	Cornell-Hotl	F	PHD	06	S Calif	2006
Ma, Ronald	Prof	Griffith Un	FI	MBA	64	Brit Colum	&1990
Ma, Sheree Shiow-Ru	Prof	Nat Chengchi	AMOV	PHD	89.	Alabama	&1989
Ma, Zhongming	Asst	Pomona		PHD	07.	Utah	
Maas, Jayne D.	Asst	Loyola-Maryl	FM	EDD	02	Nova SE	&2002
Maas, William	Asst	Wis-Stev Pt	FM	JD	92	N Illinois	&2002
Maass, Lisa E.	Lect	Cal-Santa Br	CFNP	BA	85	Ca-SnBarb	&1989
MacArthur, John B.	Prof	North Fla	MUCI	PHD	85	Wales	&1994
MacAskill, Donald	Lect	Napier Univ	M	BA			* 4-87
MacAulay, Ken	Assoc	St Fran Xav	FTW	PHD	97	Queen's	&1992
Maccarrone, Eugene T.	Assoc	Hofstra	A	MBA	81	Hofstra	& 5-80
Maccracken, Harriet	SLect	Arizona St	F	MA	80	Ariz St	& 8-95
Macdonald, Anne	SLect	Simon Fraser	FM	MACC	98	Monash	& 9-98
Macdonald, David	Adj	Victoria NZ	AGFI	BCOM	63	NZealand	2002
MacDonald, David F.	Retir	Concordia	1994	BCOM	60	Geo Wm	&1964
MacDonald, Larry Keith				PHD	69.	Utah	
MacDonald, Laura D.	Assoc	Wilfrid Laur	MH	PHD	99	Queen's	* 1998
MacDonald, Michael	Lect	Wis-Whitewat	CFX	MS	76	Wi-White	&1997
MacFee, Raymond D.	Inst	Colorado	FAN	MBA	70	Penn St	&1987
MacGregor, Jason E.	Asst	Baylor	A	PHD	07	Florida	2007
MacHaffie, Fraser G.	Retir	Marietta	CMV	MBA	82	Clev St	&1982
Machande, Kenneth D.	Asst	Mary Wash	FP	MBA	98	Albany St	1-03
Machfoedz, Masud	Prof	Gadjah Mada	1994	PHD	94.	Kentucky	1979
Machlan, George O.	Retir	Susquehanna	MCR	MS	66	Penn St	& 9-66
Machuga, Susan	Asst	Hartford	FA	PHD	96.	Mass	& 9-06
Maciariello, Joseph A.	Retir	Claremont	2003	PHD	73	NYU	1979
Macintosh, John C. C.	Assoc	York-Atkinsn	VFTN	PHD	84	S Africa	& 7-90
Macintosh, Norman B.	Retir	Queen's Univ	1998	MBA	63	W Ontario	&1967
PHD 2001 Univ of Gotenburg							
Macione, Kyle	Inst	Emory Henry	FALV	JD		Miss	2007
MacIver, Brian H.	Assoc	Bentley	FA	EDD		Mass	&1975
MacKenzie, John	Lect	Napier Univ	M	CIMA			* 1991
Mackey, James T.	Prof	CS-Sacrament	CM	PHD	81.	Illinois	* & 9-87
Mackie, James J. (Jay)	Assoc	Shippensburg	CFM	PHD	86.	Tx A&M	2003
Mackintosh, Brandy	Asst	Saskatchewan	FA	BCOM	97	Saskatch	2006
Macklin, James H.	Lect	CS-Northrdge	A	MA	66	Ohio St	& 1-83
MacLean, Bruce W.	Asst	Dalhousie	SA	MBA	72	Dalhousie	&1977
MacLeod, Barbara	C-Ac	Ohio Wesley	FJV	MBA	86	Nrthwstrn	1999
John J. Joseph Professor of Economics							
MacMillan, Allistair R. (Al)		Practice		PHD	77.	Missouri	1983
Macnaughton, Alan	Assoc	Un Waterloo	X	PHD	83	Brit Colum	1985
KPMG Professor in Accounting							
Macniven, Louise	ResAc	Cardiff U	F	BSC	01	Cardiff	2001
MacQuarrie, Allan J.			SFMC	PHD	89.	Penn St	* &
Macur, Kenneth M.	C-Pr	Edgewood	STFC	PHD	88.	Illinois	&2003
Macve, Richard H.	Prof	London Econ	FHP	MSC	76	London	&1996
Madani, Haider H.	Asst	King Fahd Un	FA	PHD	96	Henley	1996
Madden, Deborah	Inst	Morehead St	CA	MBA	98	Kentucky	&1999
Madden, Donald L.	Emer	Kentucky	2000	PHD	67.	Tx-Austin	* &1968
Madden, Robert F.	Prof	St Fran Xav	MF	FCA	71	Queens	&1971
Maddocks, P. Merle	Retir	Alabama-Hunt	ACM	PHD	89.	Florida	&1993
Madeo, Silvia A.	Retir	Georgia	8-05	PHD	77.	North Tx	& 8-00
Madera, F. Robert	Retir	Midwest St	1989	DBA	71.	Harvard	& 9-51
3113 Milby Avenue; Wichita Falls TX 76308							
Madison, Roland L.	Prof	John Carroll	CFU	PHD	78.	Nebraska	&1983

Madison, Thomas F.	C-Ac	St Marys-Tx	FBCM	PHD	99.	Tx Tech	* &8-98
Madlinger, Lisa L.	Inst	No Illinois	F	MBA	00	N Illinois	&6-01
Madray, J. Russell	SLect	Clemson	PF	MPAC	88	Clemson	# * &8-94
Madrid, Daniel G.	Asst	Pacific Unio	CIFN	ABD		Golden Gt	1991
Madura, Jeffrey M.	Prof	Benedictn-IL		MBA	71	Nrthwstrn	&1971
Maeder, Raymond	Retir	HEC Paris	AFOT	HECD	64	HEC Paris	&1969
Magann, Julia H.			F	PHD	81.	S Carol	
Magee, Robert P.	Prof	Northwestern	MQ	PHD	74.	Cornell	1976

Keith I. DeLashmutt Professor of Accounting; Associate Dean

Magen, Shimon D.	Retir	Univ of D C	1992	PHD	69	NYU	1973

2756 Riverview Drive; Ria MD 21140

Maggio, Michele	Asst	Westfield St					
Magilke, Matthew J.	Asst	Utah	F	PHD	04.	Wisconsin	8-04
Magill, Harry T.	Retir	Arizona St	1998	MS	48	Illinois	&8-84
Magliolo, Joseph III	C-Pr	So Methodist	F	PHD	86.	Stanford	9-93

Distinguished Professor of Accounting

Magnall, Paul	Assoc	Wartburg	DSXF	MBA	82	N Iowa	&1983
Magnan, Michel L.	Prof	Concordia U	FMES	PHD	89.	U Wash	&2000
Magner, Nace Richard	Prof	W Kentucky	MCB	DBA	90.	S Illinois	* 1989

J. C. Holland Professor of Accounting

Magner, Richard	Retir	Youngstown	1992	MS	57	W Minist	&9-64
Magrath, Lorraine K.	Assoc	Troy	MS	PHD	99.	Alabama	&1998
Magratten, Joan	Retir	Pace-Westch	PM	MBA	67	Fordham	1969
Magro, Anne M.			BAX	PHD	98.	Illinois	
Maguire, Karen A.	Asst	Coast Carol	FM	PHD	04.	Alabama	2004
Mah, Edwin			AFS	PHD	98.	Memphis	
Mahama, Habib	Lect	New So Wales	M	PHD		NS Wales	2001
Mahapatra, Sitikantha	Prof	CS-Long Bch	FTM	PHD	74	Case Wes	1983
Mahenthiran, Sakthi	C-Ac	Butler	BCMS	PHD	91.	Temple	1995
Maher, Elin	Prof	New Brunswic	CMI	MBA	93	Maine	&1988
Maher, John J.	Prof	Virg Tech	SF	PHD	85.	Penn St	1989

L. Mahlon Harrel Research Fellow

Maher, Michael W.	Prof	Cal-Davis	MA	PHD	75.	U Wash	&1987
Maher, Michel	Assoc	HEC-Montreal	X	LLD	03	Ottawa	6-04
Maher, Robert	Prof	New Brunswic	IVF	MBA	75	McGill	&1988
Maheshwari, Suneel	Prof	Marshall	CMP	PHD	98.	Fla Atl	1999
Mahlig, Harvey	Retir	Cleveland St	1984	JD	53	Clev St	&1975
Mahmoud, Amal A. W.				PHD	85.	Wisconsin	
Mahoney, Daniel P.	Prof	Scranton	FVG	PHD	90	Syracuse	&1989

Alperin Teaching Fellow

Mahoney, Lois S.	Assoc	E Michigan	FMCW	PHD	97.	Cen Fla	* &8-04
Mahsua, Amos	Prof	Myers	FMX	MBA	76	Gannon	&1977
Maiello, Dominic J.	Retir	Manhattan	1985	MBA	49	NYU	1947
Maier, Thomas B.	Retir	Santa Clara	1983	EDD	58	Temple	&1967
Maier-Lytle, Jeannette	Inst	So Indiana	PFM	MBA	97	S Indiana	&1995
Maiga, Adam S.	Asst	Fla Internat	FM	PHD	98.	Memphis	2007
Mailett, Catherine	Assoc	ESCP deParis	AFX	PHD	87	Paris IX	1985
Mailibayeva, Zhanel D.	Asst	Fla Atlantic		PHD	07	Purdue	8-07
Main, Daphne	Assoc	Salem State	FAB	PHD	90.	Ohio St	&8-06
Maindiratta, Ajay	Assoc	New York U	MCYN	PHD	84	Car Mellon	1985
Maines, Laureen A.	Prof	Indiana	FM	PHD	90.	Chicago	&1997

PricewaterhouseCoopers Faculty Felllow

Maingot, Michael	Assoc	Univ Ottawa	FA	PHD	81	Belfast	&1981
Majoor, Barbara	Asst	Un Amsterdam	A	PHD	97	Amsterdm	1991
Major, Richard D.		Controlle-OH		PHD	73.	Pittsburgh	
Major, Robert	Lect	U Portsmith	EI	BSC			1994
Mak, Kelvin P. L.	Inst	City Univ HK	X	MAIA	98	CityUnHK	N-00
Mak, Wai Yeong	Asst	Nanyang Tech	M	PHD	03	Nanyang	&2006
Mak, Yuen Teen	C-Ac	Natl Singapo	FM	PHD	94	Victoria	&1996
Makar, Stephen D.	Assoc	Wis-Oshkosh	FMC	PHD	94.	Kent St	&1994
Makkawi, Bilal	Assoc	Morgan State	FA	PHD	98	Fla Intl	&1998
Makowski, James S.	Asst	Flagler		MBA		Notre Dm	&
Maksy, Mostafa M.	Prof	NE Illinois	FM	PHD	83.	Baruch	&9-89
Malaga, Stanley L.	Retir	Lg Isl-Post	2002	MBA	71	Baruch	&1971
Malamud, Richard	Prof	CS-Dominguez	XL	LLM	79	NYU	&1990
Malandra, Marco	Inst	Temple	FX	MTAX	83	Golden Gt	&1992
Malandro, Rudolph	Retir		1978	PHD	65.	Pittsburgh	&
Malcom, Robert E.	Retir	Penn State	1991	PHD	62.	Ohio St	&1962
Maldonado, Edwin	Inst	Puerto Rico	X	LLM	02	Geotown	&2000
Maldonado, Peter	Retir	Findlay	2006	PHD	70	Loyola	1984
Maletta, Mario J.	Assoc	Northeastern	FB	PHD	89.	Mass	9-97

Cowan Research Professor of Accounting

Malgeri, Linda M.	Asst	Kennesaw St	FVE	MBA	77	Stetson	&1989
Malgwi, Charles	Asst	Bentley	FMLI	PHD	93	Reading	1999
Malik, Mohamed	Asst	King Saud U	F	PHD	83	Reading	1991
Malina, Mary A.			M	PHD	01.	Colorado	
Malinowski, Carolyn	SLect	Un East Lond	F	BA			1987

Mallek, J. Randolph			FMS	PHD	86.	Tx-Austin	&
Mallenby, Michel				PHD	88.	Nebraska	
Maller, Ross	Asst	W Australia	Q	PHD	76	W Austrl	1999
Malleret, Veronique	Dean$	HEC Paris	CUMN	PHD	93	Paris IX	1987
Mallie, Tina Y.			SFA	PHD	93.	Tennessee	
Mallouk, Brenda	Retir	Univ Toronto	FM	MBA	71	York	* 1977
Malloy, John M.	Prof	Memphis	X	PHD	70.	LSU	& 1-88
Malmgren, Edward G.	Assoc	N Car-Charl	MQ	PHD	72	Iowa	&1972
Malmi, Teemu	Prof	Helsinki Sch	CM	PHD	97	Helsinki	1990
Malone, Charles F.	Assoc	N Carol A&T	AF	PHD	92.	Missouri	&1982
Malone, Fannie L.	Prof	Txs Southern	ASEM	PHD	84.	Tx A&M	& 1-85
Malone, J. David	Assoc	Texas Tech	FIS	PHD	87.	Arkansas	1997
Maloney, David M.	Prof	Virginia	X	PHD	84.	Illinois	& 1-84
Carmen Blough Professor							
Maloney, Robert C.	Prof	Alaska-Ancho	FE	MBA	72	Miami U	&1988
Maloney, Suzanne	Lect	So Queenslnd	AM	MPHL	96	Griffith	&1991
Maloo, Man Chand	Prof	Towson	CFM	DBA	77.	Fla St	1988
Manao, Hekinus		U Prasada		DBA	95.	Clev St	
Manasa, Harold J.	Assoc	Winthrop	PX	MA	85	Oklahoma	# &
Mandai, Katsunobu	Prof	Hitotsubashi	FH	DBA		Hitotsub	1996
Mande, Vivek	Prof	CS-Fullerton	FI	PHD	91.	UCLA	&2002
Mandel, James P.	Lect	Rice	FMT	PHD	73.	Illinois	&1988
Mandl, Gerwald	Prof	Univ Graz	AF	PHD	77	Vienna	1978
Manooroj, Parinda	Loot	Chulalongkor	F	MSA	07	Illinoio	&1905
Manegold, James G.	Assoc	So Calif	F	PHD	78.	Stanford	1982
Manes, Rene P.	Retir	Florida St	D-95	PHD	61	Purdue	& 8-84
Mangold, Nancy R.	Prof	CS-East Bay	MF	PHD	84.	Berkeley	9-84
Manion, John J.	Retir	Temple	1994	MBA	64	Temple	&1964
Mankin, Jeff A.	Asst	Lipscomb	MPCX	PHD	00.	Miss	* & 1-91
Manktelow, Loretta M.	Inst	Jms Madison	FPM	MBA	87	U Miami	& 8-05
Manley, Michael	Asst	American Int	F	MBA	93	Am Intl	&2003
Manly, Tracy S.	Assoc	Tulsa	XF	PHD	00.	Arkansas	& 7-01
A. Charles Funai Faculty Fellow							
Mann, Gary J.	Emer	Txs-El Paso	2006	PHD	86.	Tx Tech	& 1-86
Mann, Harvey	Deces	Brock Univ	8-95	PHD	72.	NYU	& 7-87
Mann, Lucretia S.	D-Ac	Mercy-NY	FAVT	MBA	78	Iona	& 9-82
Mann, M. Herschel	Prof	Texas Tech	TF	PHD	71.	Alabama	&1972
KPMG Professor							
Manners, George E.	Prof	Kennesaw St	M	PHD		Geo St	1996
Manning, Chris	Lect	U Queensland	A	BSC	90	Tasmania	2001
Mannino, Laura Lee	Asst	St John's	X	LLM	01	NYU	2002
Mannino, Ronald C.	C-Ac	Massachusett	MN	DBA	77.	Colorado	&1974
Mano, Ronald M.	C-Pr	Weber State	FA	PHD	78.	Nebraska	&1985
Willard Eccles Research Fellow							
Manowan, Pavinee	Lect	Chulalongkor	F	MSPA	02	Mich St	2002
Manrique-Gutierrez, Justo	Asst	Houston-Down	M	PHD	91	Iowa St	2002
Manry, David	Assoc	New Orleans	FTKV	PHD	92.	Tx-Austin	2001
Energy Accounting Conference Professsor							
Manson, Stuart	Asst	Univ Essex	AFT	MA	79	Strathcl	&1988
Mansour, Fathi A.	Deces	West Georgia	1979	PHD	76.	Miss	&1976
Mantzke, Katrina L.	Assoc	No Illinois	X	PHD	01.	Wisconsin	& 8-01
Kieso Professor of Accountancy							
Manzon, Gil B. Jr.	Assoc	Boston Coll	FX	DBA	90.	Boston U	1989
Manzoni, Jean-Francois			MB	DBA	93.	Harvard	&
Mao, Chunlin	Asst	Un Hong Kong	F	PHD	06.	Penn St	8-06
Maples, Andrew J.	SLect	Canterbury	LX	LLM	95	Canterbu	1998
Maples, Larry	Prof	Tenn Tech	X	DBA	76.	Miss St	&1985
Foundation Professor of Accounting							
Mapp, Johnnie A.	Prof	Norfolk St	FI	PHD	81.	Georgia	9-83
Marais, M. Laurentius			1992	PHD	85.	Stanford	
We Wecker Assoc; 505 San Martin Dr; Novato CA 94945							
Marakas, George	Assoc	Kansas	S	PHD	95	Fla Intl	8-05
Marchant, Garry	Dean	Bond Univ	MCU	PHD	87.	Michigan	&O-04
Marcheggiani, Joseph	Retir	Butler	2004	MBA	72	Bridgepr	&1981
Marcinek, George	Asst	Marywood	CV	MBA	81	Scranton	&1986
Marcinkewciz, Carolyn S.	Retir	Ferris State	2003	MA	69	Cen Mich	1980
Marcinko, David J.	Assoc	Skidmore	M	PHD	73	Boston C	2007
Marcuccio, Elizabeth	Asst	Siena	FL	JD		AlbanyLw	2004
Marcum, Sue	Asst	American U	F	MST	86	American	& 9-06
Marden, Ronald E.	Prof	Appalach St	AF	PHD	95.	S Fla	& 8-95
Mareeta, F.	Lect	Un Zimbabwe		MBA			
Margavio, Geanie W.	Assoc	Missouri St	FX	PHD	90	Alabama	& 8-90
Margheim, Loren L.	Prof	San Diego	F	PHD	84.	Ariz St	&1984
Marginson, David E. W.	Prof	Cardiff U	M	PHD	97	Lancaster	2005
Margiotta, Mary M.			MF	PHD	92.	Car Mellon	
Margret, Julie	Lect	Deakin-Geelg	FM	MCOM	94	Deakin	1992
Margrif, Frederick D.	Retir	No Michigan	2001	PHD	72.	Missouri	* 1972

Marie, Adb Elhay		Alexandria U	1995	PHD	69.	Mich St	
Faculty of Commerce; Alexandria Univ; Alexandria Egypt							
Marin, Jose	Prof	Pompeu Fabra	F	PHD	94	Penn	
Marino, Frank A.	Assoc	Assumption	VAP	MST	82	Bentley	&1981
Marita, Riadh	Asst	Univ Tunis	F	DEA	99	ISCAE	1999
Mark, Richard S.	Assoc	Tx-Arlington	XLZ	LLM	81	Denver	&1981
Markarian, Garen	Asst	Concordia U	MF	PHD	04.	Case Wes	2004
Markelevich, Ariel	Asst	Lg Isl-Post	CFP	PHD	04.	Baruch	2003
Markell, William	Retir	Delaware	1993	EDD	59	Columbia	&9-58
Markmann, Joseph G.	Retir	LaSalle	2001	BS	49	LaSalle	&9-49
Markov, Stanimir	Asst	Emory	F	PHD	02.	Rochester	2001
Marks, Barry R.	C-Pr	Houston-Cl L	FGX	PHD	75	Purdue	9-84
Marks, Marcus F.		Tampa FL	1992	PHD	78.	Florida	
5034 Paloma Dr; Tampa FL 33624							
Markwalder, Alice S.	Retir	Portland	6-96	PHD	82.	Georgia	&1988
Marmon, Richard	Assoc	Rowan	FXR	JD	90	Widener	* &1985
Maron, Matthew	Asst	Bridgeport	X	MS	97	NewHamp	2004
Maroney, James J.	Assoc	Northeastern	F	PHD	94.	Conn	&9-93
Marples, Lynn W.	Lect	Northeastern	MF	MBA		Stanford	* 6-90
Marquardt, Carol A.	Assoc	CUNY-Baruch	F	PHD	97.	Cornell	9-06
Marquardt, John D.	Retir	Mich-Flint	2001	PHD	75.	Illinois	&1980
Marques, Ana C.		Noa de Lisb	2007	PHD	05.	Tx-Austin	
Universidade Nova de Lisbon; Portugal							
Marquette, R. Penny			FGHN	DBA	79.	Kent St	&
Marquis, Linda M.	Prof	No Kentucky	MC	DBA	78.	Kentucky	* &7-86
Marrero, Rafael	Inst	Puerto Rico	EFP	MBA	91	P Rico	&1995
Marriot, Pru	SLect	U Glamorgan	FS	BA	89	Glamorgan	&9-91
Marriott, Lisa	ALect	Victoria NZ		MBA			2006
Marsden, Alastair	Assoc	U Auckland	F	PHD	97	Auckland	1991
Marsden, Stephen	Lect	Queensld Tec	F	MBUS	94	Queensld	&1-92
Marsh, George	Retir	N Carol St	1999	MDIV	79	SE Bapt	&1970
Marsh, Treba A.	C-Ac	S F Austin	FGN	DBA	97.	La Tech	&1996
Marshall, A. Richard	Retir	McGill Univ	1993	ABD		Wisconsin	&1955
Marshall, Andrew P.	Lect	Strathclyde	F	MPHL	95	Strathcl	1992
Marshall, Byron	Asst	Oregon State	S	PHD	05	Arizona	2005
Marshall, Clifford L.	Assoc	Ark-Pine Blf	F	PHD	83.	North Tx	2000
Marshall, David	SLect	Bournemouth	CDFP	MBA			&9-90
Marshall, David H.	Retir	Millikin	1992	MBA	67	Nrthwstrn	* &9-67
155 Glencoe Avenue; Decatur IL 62522							
Marshall, Donald C.	Retir	CS-Fullerton	1996	PHD	67.	LSU	&1989
1649 Camelot Dr; Redlands CA 92374; 504-763-6409							
Marshall, Leisa L.	Prof	Valdosta St	FES	DBA	93.	Miss St	* &9-93
Marshall, P. Douglas	Prof	Salisbury	CMP	PHD	96	Maryland	&1976
Marshall, Rex L.	Lect	Murdoch Univ	X	BEC		W Austrl	1989
Marshall, Ronald M.	Emer	Michigan St	2003	PHD	69.	Ohio St	&1969
Marshall, Sandra			CM	PHD	98.	Kent St	
Marsicovetere, Dominic A.	Asst	Hofstra	PF	MBA	73	Pace	&1978
Marsland, Bruce D.	Retir	Goldey-Beacm	2004	MBA	67	Delaware	&9-79
Martel, Louise	C-Pr	HEC-Montreal	ADFJ	MSC	81	HEC-Mont	9-78
Martin, Alvin				PHD	71.	Nrthwstrn	
Martin, Barry	Asst	CUNY-Stn Isl	TX	MS	72	Long Isl	&1978
Martin, Carrick A.			F	PHD	74.	Minnesota	&
Martin, Charles L. Jr.	Prof	Towson	FTAE	DBA	81.	Geo Wash	&1988
Martin, Dale R.	Prof	Wake Forest	FTI	DBA	76.	Kentucky	9-82
The Wayne Calloway Professor of Accountancy							
Martin, Donald D.	Retir	Cen Missouri	2002	PHD	72.	Missouri	1986
Martin, Edward	Retir	Iona	1996	MBA	72	Iona	&1971
Martin, G.	Lect	Univ Ulster	BJ	BSC			9-02
Martin, George R.			MAS	PHD	67.	Berkeley	* &
Martin, Harold	Asst	Wm & Mary					
Martin, Herbert	Assoc	Hope	XS	MA	79	Arkansas	&8-82
Martin, James R.	Retir	South Fla	2004	PHD	76	Alabama	* 1982
Martin, Jim	Lect	Washburn	XF	MTX	83	Tx-Austin	8-04
Martin, Jimmy W.	Prof	Montevallo	FAK	PHD	78.	Alabama	&1984
Martin, Kris R.	Asst	Bob Jones	F	PHD	02.	Va Tech	2002
Martin, L. Ann	Assoc	Colo-Denver	FMIZ	PHD	93.	Minnesota	&9-94
Martin, Lisa C.				PHD	86.	Geo St	
Martin, Lisa H.			FM	PHD	97.	Tx-Austin	
Martin, Peter	Asst	Univ of D C	VX	MBA	71	American	&1972
Martin, R. Keith	Prof	Fairfield	Sys	PHD	73	U Wash	1979
Martin, Randall P.		Peat Marwick		PHD	70.	Geo St	
Martin, Roger D.	Assoc	Virginia	FA	PHD	96.	Tx-Austin	* &9-03
Martin, Rose	Prof	CS-Pomona	FS	PHD	96.	S Calif	&9-99
Martin, Spencer J.	Prof	Rhode Island	FT	PHD	70.	Illinois	&9-70
Martin, Steven	Asst	Capital	LXM	JD		Ohio St	1994
Martin, Susan W.	Prof	Mich-Dearbor	NGX	PHD	88.	Mich St	# * &
Martin, Xiumin	Asst	Wash Univ	F	PHD	07	Missouri	2007

Martindale, Bobbie C.	Prof	Dallas Bapt	XM	PHD	89.	North Tx	&1993
Martinelli, Alvaro	Prof	Appalach St	CHI	PHD	74.	North Tx	9-74
Martinelli, John T.	Retir	CS-Long Bch	1993	MBA	53	Chicago	1965
Martinez Colon, Juan L.	Prof	Puerto Rico	IRX	ABD		NYU	# * &1976
Martinez-Jerez, Francisco	Asst	Harvard	FM	PHD	02.	Harvard	2002
Marting, Edward D.			FV	PHD	74.	Ariz St	
Martinis, Karen	Prof	Central Wash	FM	MBA	80	Puget Sd	& 9-79
Martino, Peter A. III	Asst	Johnson&Wale	PGN	MBA	96	Bryant	&2002
Martinov, Nonna	Lect	New So Wales	AB	PHD		NS Wales	&1990
Martinson, Otto B.	Prof	Old Dominion	CJM	DBA	70.	Geo Wash	* &1989
Marts, John A.	Deces	N Car-Wilmin	FX	PHD	75	S Carol	&1986
Martzoukos, Spyros	Asst	Cyprus	FQT	PHD	95	Geo Wash	1998
Marudas, Nicholas P.	Prof	Auburn-Montg	AND	PHD	01.	Geo St	# &2002
Marx, Lewis	C-As	St Ambrose	ASGM	MA	86	W Illinois	&1989
Marxen, Dale E.			F	PHD	88.	Colorado	&
Masasi, M.	Lect	Un Zimbabwe	F	MBL			
Mascha, Maureen F.	Asst	Marquette	ASM	PHD	98.	Kentucky	&2003
Maschmeyer, Richard A.			CGMI	DBA	82.	Kentucky	
Mashaw, Bijan	Prof	CS-East Bay	SD	PHD	76	Clemson	9-84
Mashruwala, Raj	Asst	Wash Univ	M	PHD	02	Tx-Dallas	2001
Masimba, Roderick		Dar es Salaa	1995	PHD	90.	Colorado	
Univ of Dar es Salaam, Tanzania							
Masocha, Walter	Asst	Un Stirling	AFO	PHD	00	Strathcl	&2001
Mason, Carlton W.	Retir	Ferris St	1991	PHD	74	N Colo	1978
Mason, J. David	Assoc	Alaska-Ancho	MX	PHD	93.	Colorado	&
Mason, John O. Jr.	Prof	Alabama	AD	PHD	69.	Missouri	&1968
Mason, Paul T.	Lect	Kansas	FAVM	MBA	76	Conn	# * &1998
Mason, Richard	Asst	Nevada-Reno	X	PHD	01	Conn	2000
Masoner, Michael M.	Assoc	So Illinois	SM	PHD	75	Minnesota	&1978
Massa, Niel	Retir	Ithaca	1995	MBA	64	Michigan	& 8-65
Masselli, John J.	Assoc	Texas Tech	X	PHD	98.	Geo St	& 9-98
Haskell Taylor Professor							
Massey, Dawn W.	C-Ac	Fairfield	FJBV	PHD	98.	Conn	&1997
Massimini, Al	Asst	LaSalle	FV	MBA		Drexel	& 9-81
Massoud, Marcos F. (Marc)	D-Pr	Claremont	FTI	PHD	73	NYU	* 1980
Robert A. Day Distinguished Professor of Accounting							
Massuglia, David	Asst	Bemidji St	PAM	MBA		St Thomas	&2006
Master, Joseph J.	Retir	Stetson	1998	MA	57	Stetson	&1964
Mastracchio, Nicholas J.	Lect	South Fla	FA	PHD	93.	Union-NY	& 8-06
Mastro, Anthony J.	Retir	George Wash	1995	MA	62	Notre Dm	&1967
Matejka, Michal	Asst	Michigan	M	PHD	02	Tilburg	2004
Mather, Paul	Assoc	Monash Univ	F	PHD			&1991
Matherly, C. Michele	Asst	N Car-Charl	S	PHD	94.	Alabama	&2001
Mathew, Zacharian			FMAT	PHD	73.	American	&
Mathieu, Robert	Assoc	Wilfrid Laur	F	PHD	95	Waterloo	&1998
Mathis, Harry R.	Retir	Univ of D C	1992	EDD	72	N Car St	* &1972
Mathur, Rohit				PHD	01.	Columbia	
Matika, Lawrence A.				PHD	88.	Kent St	&
Matolcsy, Zoltan P.	Prof	Tech-Sydney	F	PHD	83	NS Wales	1982
Matoney, Joseph P.	Prof	Rhode Island	FX	PHD	73.	Penn St	&1973
Matson, Diane M.	Assoc	St Thomas-MN	ABF	PHD	97	Minnesota	* & 9-01
Matsumoto, Dawn A.	Assoc	U Washington	FM	PHD	98.	U Wash	2000
Matsumura, Ella Mae	Assoc	Wisconsin	MAT	PHD	84	Brit Colum	9-85
Matsunaga, Steven R.	Assoc	Oregon	FX	PHD	92.	U Wash	&1992
Mattei-Ballester, Wanda M.	D-Ac	Puerto Rico	FIE	PHD	02.	Tx A&M	&1995
Mattessich, Richard V.	Emer	British Colu	1988	DRP	45	Vienna	&1967
Matthew, Dianna L.	Retir	Ball State	2001	MA	77	Ball St	& 9-77
Matthews, Richard M.	Retir	Pace	1989	MSA	54	NYU	&1949
Matthews, Robert J.	Assoc	NewJerseyCty	ACFV	MBA	84	Pace	&1988
Matthews, Thomas	Asst	Univ Alberta	XFIM	PHD	02	Waterloo	2001
Mattimoe, Ruth	Lect	Dublin City	M	PHD	03	Manchest	&1986
Mattison, Dorothy M.	Assoc	MD E Shore	FMNP	PHD	90.	Geo Wash	8-93
Mattoney, Don	Asst	Scranton	F	PHD	90.	Syracuse	
Mattson, Lucretia W.	Retir	Wis-Eau Clar	2007	DBA	84.	Kentucky	& 8-75
Matulich, Serge	Retir	Rollins	2001	PHD	71.	Berkeley	&1984
Matuszewski, Linda J.	Asst	No Illinois	F	PHD	07	Cincinnati	&2006
Matz, Adolph	Deces	Pennsylvania	F-87	PHD	37	Penn	1936
Mauldin, D. Shawn	Dean	Nicholls St	BFVX	PHD	97.	Miss	* & 6-00
Betsy Ayo Endowed Professorship							
Mauldin, Elaine G.	Assoc	Missouri	SA	PHD	97.	Nebraska	&1997
BKD Professor							
Maupin, Rebekah J.			FC	PHD	81.	Arkansas	&
Maurer, Linda	C-As	Fontbonne	CDMX	JD	83	St Louis	&1999
Maurer, Robert J.	Assoc	Central Col		MBA	68	Indiana	1968
Maurer, Wayne O.	Assoc	Wittenberg	VCM	MBA	74	Wright St	* 9-74
Maurice, Jacques	Inst	Carleton Un	FC	MBA	99	McGill	* &1988

Mauriello, Joseph A.	Retir	Seton Hall	1987	PHD	44.	NYU	&1978
45 Springfield Ave; Springfield, NJ 07081; 973-564-6322;j.a.mauriello@att.net							
Maus, Marilyn E.			FS	DBA	91.	Miss St	&
Maust, Robert S.	Prof	W Virginia	FT	ABD		Michigan	&1959
Louis F. Tanner Distinguished Professor of Public Accounting							
Mautz, R. David Jr.	Assoc	N Car-Wilmin	AF	PHD	87.	Tennessee	&2007
Mautz, Robert K.	Retir	Salt Lake Cy	1992	PHD	42.	Illinois	&
684 East 4149 South; Salt Lake City UT 84107							
Mavrides, Costas	Lect	Cyprus	F	PHD	95.	Houston	1995
Mavrinac, Sarah C.			M	DBA	96.	Harvard	
Mawani, Amin	Assoc	York Univ	TM	PHD	95	Waterloo	* 2000
Maxey, Charles	Dean	Calif Luthrn	B	PHD	82	Illinois	1991
Maxfield, Jodie	ALect	Monash Univ	DF	GRAD			&1993
Maxson, Lisa	Lect	San Jose St	SMF	MBA	82	Pepperdi	2000
May, D.	Inst	Suffolk	ACFX	MS	94	Bentley	&2004
May, Gordon S.	Retir	Georgia	2002	PHD	72.	Mich St	&1977
May, John M.	C-In	SW Okla St	PF	MBA	75	Okla Cty	&2002
May, Phillip T.	Retir	Wichita St	2005	PHD	67.	Wisconsin	&1974
May, Robert G.	Prof	Texas-Austin	FM	PHD	70.	Mich St	6-79
KPMG Centennial Professor of Accounting							
Mayberry, Robert C.	Retir	Mont St-Bill	RPXF	MMAC	67	Fla St	&1989
Maydew, Edward L.	Prof	No Carolina	X	PHD	94.	Iowa	& 7-99
David E. Hoffman Distinguished Professor							
Maydew, Gary L.	Retir	Iowa State	2000	PHD	78.	Illinois	&1977
Mayer, Richard D.	Prof	Bemidji St	CPMR	MBA		Iowa	&1981
Mayer-Sommer, Alan P.	Assoc	Georgetown	FJH	PHD	76.	Geo St	* &1981
Mayes, Sarah E.	Lect	N Car-Ashvil	FPX	MBA	82	W Carol	& 8-86
Mayew, William J.	Asst	Duke	F	PHD	06.	Tx-Austin	& 7-06
Mayfield, Vicki	Lect	Tennessee	XL	JD		Tennessee	8-07
Mayhew, Brian W.	Assoc	Wisconsin	A	PHD	97.	Arizona	&1999
Maynard, Gilbert P.	Deces	Iowa		PHD	51	Iowa	1946
Maynard, Jennifer	SLect	Coventry Un	AFX	BSC	84	Exeter	&N-94
Mayne, Frank A.	Asst	Txs-El Paso	CFMX	PHD	82	Arizona	& 9-78
Mayorga, Diane	Lect	New So Wales		MCOM		NS Wales	
Mayper, Alan G.	Prof	North Texas	FTAB	PHD	81.	Florida	&1987
Mays, Robert L. Jr.		San Anton-TX	1992	PHD	79.	Purdue	1984
6512 Fox Run; San Antonio TX 78233							
Mazachek, JuliAnn	Assoc	Washburn	M	PHD	93.	Kansas	* 8-92
Mazhandu, STSM	Lect	Un Zimbabwe		BACC			&
Mazhin, Reza	Prof	CS-Dominguez	MF	PHD	84.	Indiana	&1984
Mazza, Cheri L.			F	PHD	94.	North Tx	* &
Mazzitelli, James R.	Adj	Iowa State	FC	MBA	71	Drake	&1971
Mazzocchi, Henry L.				PHD	71.	NYU	
Mbagwu, Chima	Lect	Wilfrid Laur	F	MSC	03	Saskatch	2006
Mboya, Fratern M.				PHD	81.	Arizona	
McAllister, Brian C.	Asst	St Bonaventu	FDMV	MBA	81	St Bonav	&1977
McAllister, Brian P.	Asst	Colorado Spr	FA	PHD	05.	Nebraska	&2007
McAllister, John P.	Dean	North Fla	FAI	PHD	80.	Penn St	& 7-05
McAllister, Leray L.	Retir	Brigham Yg	1993	PHD	71.	Ariz St	& 9-63
McAlum, Harry G.	Prof	Macon State	APS	DBA	83.	La Tech	&2001
McAnally, Mary Lea	Assoc	Texas A&M	F	PHD	94.	Stanford	# & 9-02
May Faculty Fellowship							
McAree, D.	Lect	Univ Ulster	F	BA			2-95
McAuley, Laurie	Lect	Loughborough	MD	PHD	93	Loughbor	* 1997
McBeth, Kevin H.			FTX	PHD	89.	Utah	&
McBrayer, Phillip D.	Inst	N Carol A&T	XP	MBA		NC-Green	# * &2003
McBride, Freda D.	Dean	Elizabeth Ct	FB	PHD	98.	Va Tech	&2002
McBride, Gary R.	Prof	CS-East Bay	X	JD	81	Hastings	& 1-88
McBride, Karen	Lect	U Portsmith	MBF	BSC			1997
McCabe, John C.	Retir	Ball State	2003	DBA	82.	Indiana	& 9-72
McCabe, Robert K.	Retir	CS-Fullerton	2005	PHD	73.	Colorado	&1990
McCaffrey, Suzanne	Inst	Mississippi	P	MACC	97	Miss	& 8-00
McCallig, John	Lect	Un Cl Dublin	DMF	PHDM	03	Lancaster	* &1993
McCallum, Brent	Asst	Am U Sharjah	FPCX	MS	93	American	* &1999
McCameron, Fritz A.	Retir	Louisiana St	1996	PHD	54.	Alabama	&1959
McCann, C.	Lect	Univ Ulster	F	MSC			9-98
McCarron, Karen B.		Gordon Coll	F	PHD	88.	Alabama	
Barnesville, GA 30304; 770-358-5031; kmccarron@falcon.gdn.peachnet.edu							
McCarthy, Ann	Lect	East Carol	F	MBA	85	Winthrop	&1993
McCarthy, Franklin L.	Retir	Pittsburgh	2000	PHD	71.	Minnesota	&1977
McCarthy, Irene N.	Prof	St John's	EJFV	PHD	93	NYU	&1975
McCarthy, Mark	Asst	DePaul	XMFR	JD	85	Illinois	* &1979
McCarthy, Mark G.	Prof	East Carol	FM	PHD	92.	S Carol	& 8-91
McCarthy, Neil T.	Assoc	Kettering	F	PHD	77	Rensselaer	1973
McCarthy, Simon D. I.	SLect	U Glamorgan	FS	BSC	90	Cardiff	&O-94
McCarthy, William E.	Prof	Michigan St	S	PHD	78.	Mass	1-78
McCartney, Jean	Lect	W Sydney-Nep	EF	BCOM	76	Witwaters	&1989

Name	Rank	School					
McCartney, Mark W.	Prof	Saginaw Vall	FA	PHD	95.	Memphis	&8-99
McCartney, Sean	Asst	Univ Essex	AFTX	MSC	90	LondonEc	&1991
McCarty, Naomi J.		Tulsa OK	1988	PHD	74.	Arkansas	&
McCarty, T. Michael	Deces		X	PHD	83.	North Tx	
McCaslin, Thomas E.	Assoc	Nev-L Vegas	FAS	DBA	82.	Tennessee	&1988
McClaflin, John	Inst	Benedictn-KS		EMBA	01	Benedict	&2002
McClain, Bruce W.	Assoc	Cleveland St	XL	JD	82	Case Wes	&6-87
McClain, Guy	Asst	Auburn	FA	PHD	07.	Arkansas	8-07
McClain, Lois M.	Retir	CS-L Angeles	1993	MBA	75	CS-L Ang	&9-76
McClain, Michael	Lect	Hampton	FT	PHD	98	Nova SE	1998
McClary, Ray H.	Retir	No Illinois	1993	DBA	67.	Indiana	1969
McClellan, William	Retir	Ben Franklin	1986	MCS	48	Ben Frnk	&1956
McClendon, Thurrell O.	Retir	SE Louisiana	1996	PHD	81.	Arkansas	&8-80
McClure, Jean S.	Retir	Maine	1986	MS	63	Wisconsin	1963
McClure, Malcolm M.	Assoc	Illinois St	FI	PHD	83.	Illinois	&1982
McClure, Melvin T.	Retir	Maine	1994	PHD	68.	Illinois	1961
McClure, Nancy L.	Inst	Penn State	FM	MS	87	Penn St	8-94
McClure, Ronnie C.			X	PHD	87.	North Tx	&
McCluskey, Tom	Lect	Dublin City	FX	BCOM	77	NUI	&1982
McClymont, Trevor L.		N Caribbean	FPRV	DBA	88	Intl Grad	&
McColl, Anna	Visit	Tulsa	XFP	MAC	98	Tx-Dallas	&8-00
McCollough, Elzy V.	Retir	Ohio State	1985	PHD	51.	Iowa	1959
McCombie, Kellie	Lect	U Wollongong	TW	MCOM	96	Wollong	1996
McCombs, Gary D.	Assoc	C Michigan	DCFG	MDA	00	Michigan	&1982
McComiskey, Terese	AcLec	So Queenslnd	W	BCOM	94	Griffith	1997
McConnell, Allen W.	Prof	No Colorado	FVP	MS	66	N Dakota	&1968
McConnell, Cheryl A.	Assoc	Rockhurst	XAF	MPA	84	Wichita St	&1988
McConnell, Donald K. Jr.	Assoc	Tx-Arlington	AF	PHD	81.	North Tx	&1978
McConnell, James L.	Retir	St Fran-Penn	1994	EDD	67	Penn St	1957
McConomy, Bruce J.	Assoc	Wilfrid Laur	FTA	PHD	96	Queen's	&1999
McCord, Kenneth R.	Retir	East Txs St	1994	PHD	67.	Oklahoma	1950
McCormack, G. Edward	Prof	Berea	AMD	MBA	88	Estrn Ky	&1986
McCormack, Vincent F.	Retir	Shippensburg	2005	PHD	77.	Mich St	1981
McCosh, Andrew M.		Scotland Eng	1992	DBA	66.	Harvard	&
The Grange; 12 Wyvern Park; Edinburgh EH9 2JY Scotland							
McCosh, R. Bruce				DBA	58.	Indiana	
McCoskey, Melanie G.	Assoc	Tenn-Chattan	XF	PHD	96.	Georgia	&8-98
Brice L. Holland Associate Professor of Taxation							
McCoster, Joseph		U Conception		PHD	68.	UCLA	
McCowen, George B.				PHD	40.	Illinois	
McCoy, Carl	Retir	SE Okla St	1989	EDD	59	Oklahoma	1950
McCoy, Timothy L.			FMJT	PHD	94.	Miss	&
McCracken, Susan A.	Asst	Univ Toronto	AM	PHD	98	Waterloo	&1998
McCrae, Michael S.	Retir	U Wollongong	SFG	PHD	86	Austr Natl	&1993
McCrary, J. Michael	App	Tulsa	AF	MAC	74	Okla St	&8-96
McCraw, J. Harrison	Prof	West Georgia	CMP	PHD	87.	Georgia	9-85
McCray, John H.			AC	PHD	71.	Georgia	&
McCullers, Levis D.		Hagyard D-KY	1992	PHD	69.	Florida	&
1965 Blairmore Rd; Lexington KY 40502							
McCulloch, Brian			1998	PHD	97.	U Wash	
The Treasury, New Zealand							
McCullough, Margaret A.			MC	PHD	88.	Cincinnati	
McCutcheon, John	Assoc	Wilfrid Laur	FMV	ABD		Manchest	* 1980
McDaniel, Linda S.	Prof	Kentucky	AB	PHD	88.	Michigan	&2002
Von Allmen Chair of Accountancy							
McDermott, Eugene W.	Asst	Charlestn So	MF	PHD	94.	S Carol	&1994
McDermott, Richard E.	Prof	Weber State	CM	PHD	84.	Okla St	1989
McDevitt, Anthony A.	Retir	U Queensland	1994	MECO	73	Queensl	1973
McDevitt, Rosalie		Mount Olive					2007
McDevitt, Roselie E.	Asst	Fairfield	MFJ	SCD	01	NewHaven	&1984
McDonald, Charles L.	Lect	Florida	F	PHD	72.	Mich St	&5-01
McDonald, Daniel L.	Retir	Simon Fraser	1993	PHD	67.	Stanford	&9-74
McDonald, Frederick	Lect	Central Wash	FX	MBA	91	Port St	2002
McDonald, Robert	Assoc	New Haven	MCF	MBA		NYU	# * &9-84
McDonald, Thomas	SLect	Deakin-Burwo	DF	MCOM	91	Deakin	1978
McDonough, Helen L.	Prof	Quebec-Montr	M	MBA		Concordia	* 6-85
McDonough, John J.	Retir	UCLA	1995	DBA	69.	Harvard	1968
McDougal, Karen	Asst	St Joseph	CB	ABD		Temple	8-06
McDowell, Evelyn	Asst	Rider	F	PHD	06	Case Wes	8-05
McDowell, Wyatt	Assoc	Louisville	XL	LLM	89	Capital	8-91
McDuffie, R. Steve	Prof	Missouri St	ASG	DBA	90.	La Tech	8-88
McEacharn, E. Michelle	H-Pr	La-Monroe	GNAF	DBA	94.	La Tech	# &1989
Hood/DeFatta Professor of Accounting							
McEldowney, John E.	Assoc	North Fla	FAO	DBA	84.	Miss St	# * &1980
McElhaney, Monica	Assoc	Bellevue	TFSC	MBA	95	Northeas	* &8-96
McElroy, Barbara W.	Assoc	Susquehanna	MF	PHD	97.	Penn St	&9-02
McElroy, Julie	ALect	Newcastle	ESM	BBUS	01	Charles S	2005

McElroy, Trefor	H-Ple	Bournemouth	FPM	MSC			4-89
McEnerney, JoAnn	Asst	R Stockton	ARV	MBA	82	NYU	&1982
McEnroe, John E.	Prof	DePaul	FTA	DBA	77.	Kentucky	&1981
Deloitte Distinguished Professor							
McEwen, Ruth Ann	Prof	Suffolk	F	PHD	86.	Ga Tech	&1998
McFadden, Gwendolyn	Assoc	N Carol A&T	XP	LLM	90	Florida	&1990
McFall, Donald	Lect	Kent State	F	MS	91	Kent St	& 8-00
McFarlan, F. Warren	Retir	Harvard	1996	DBA	65.	Harvard	1964
McFarland, Walter B.				PHD	39.	Stanford	
McFerrin, W. Don	Retir	CS-Fresno	2003	PHD	78	US Intl	8-76
McFesters, M.	Asst	Grove City	CF	MS	98	Grove Cy	2007
McGahran, Kathleen T.			F	PHD	82.	NYU	&
McGarvey, Raymond L.				PHD	59.	Illinois	
McGee, JoAnn		LSU-Shreve	FM	DBA	89.	La Tech	&
McGee, Linda	Assoc	W New Mexico	XPJF	MBA	72	W NewMex	1980
McGee, Paul F.	C-Pr	Salem State	AT	MS	76	Bentley	&1984
McGee, Robert W.	Prof	Barry	FJI	PHD	86	Warwick	# * & 8-02
McGhee, Thomas M. (Mitch)	Assoc	CS-Stanislau	XI	PHD	89.	S Carol	8-06
McGill, Gary A.	D-Ac	Florida	XI	PHD	88.	Tx Tech	& 8-86
PricewaterhouseCoopers Professor of Accounting							
McGillis, Sheila	Asst	Laurentian		MBA	87	Laurentian	* 7-85
McGillivray, Robert E.	Retir	Guam	1996	PHD	74.	North Tx	&1990
McGilsky, Debra E.	Prof	Cen Michigan	X	PHD	86.	Mich St	&1989
McGinley, Leslie	SLect	Deakin-Burwo	F	MEC	78	Monash	1988
McGonigle, William	Assoc	East Wash	FXL	JD	76	Gonzaga	&1978
McGowan, Annie S.	Assoc	Texas A&M	M	PHD	94.	North Tx	9-93
Carroll Phillips Fellowship							
McGowan, John J.	Assoc	King's Col	ACP	MBA	66	Scranton	* & 9-70
McGowan, John R.	Assoc	St Louis	XFI	PHD	88	S Illinois	&1987
McGrail, George R.	Retir	Wyoming	1995	PHD	72.	Arkansas	&1965
McGrath, G.	Lect	Univ Ulster	FM	MSC			1-91
McGregor, Calvert C. (Buck)	Assoc	Elon	FM	PHD	87.	Va Tech	&1990
McGregor, Scott			1998	PHD	96.	Fla St	
Institute for Vaishnava Studies, Director of Development							
McGregor-Lowndes, M.	Prof	Queensld Tec	F	PHD		Madmin Qld	1984
McGrew, William Clement	Retir	Oklahoma	1986	PHD	67.	Arkansas	&1947
McGuigan, Craig	Lect	Lincoln-NZ		BCM		Canterbu	2006
McGuire, Brian L.	C-Pr	So Indiana	CMS	PHD	96.	Cen Fla	* &1995
McGuire, Chester C. Jr.				PHD	74.	Chicago	
McGurr, Paul T.	C-As	Fort Lewis	AMS	PHD	96	Purdue	&2004
McHugh, Joseph A.	Retir	Bentley	1999	PHD	70.	Mich St	9-90
McHugh, Marion	VAsst	Illinois	A	PHD	05.	Arkansas	1-07
McIff, Lyle Hatch	Retir	Arizona	1985	DBA	66.	S Calif	&1965
McInnes, Morris	Prof	Suffolk	FMB	DBA	69.	Harvard	1987
McInnes, William M.	Prof	Un Stirling	AFET	PHD	87	Glasgow	&1994
McIntyre, D. David	Asst	Mercer-Macon	F	PHD	01.	Kentucky	&2004
McIntyre, Edward V.	Retir	Florida St	D-02	PHD	71.	N Carol	&1970
McKay, Britton A.	Asst	Geo Southern	PI	ABD		S Illinois	2007
McKay, Duane W.	Retir	Wis-Oshkosh	1998	MBA	66	Wi-Milwa	* &1969
McKay, F. Ellen			FVJA	PHD	81.	Mass	&
McKay, Tim	H-Le	Napier Univ	XF	BSC			&1989
McKeag, Christine L.	Asst	Evansville	FS	MBA	75	Pittsburgh	&1981
McKean, Gerald W.	C	Illinois St	S	PHD	85	Illin St	1974
McKee, A. James	Assoc	Tx-Pan Amer	ACM	PHD	82.	Okla St	* &2007
McKee, Stephen K.	LectC	Adelaide	D	PHD		Flinders	1991
McKee, Thomas E.	Prof	East Tenn St	TAOE	PHD	75.	Geo St	# * &1976
McKee, Tim C.	Assoc	Old Dominion	XLJP	LLM	81	DePaul	& 1-85
McKeever, John L.	Retir		1995	PHD	61.	Mich St	
2700 Harvard; Fort Collins CO 80525							
McKell, Lynn J.	Prof	Brigham Yg	SQMD	PHD	73	Purdue	8-74
McKenzie, Claudel B.	C-Ac	N Car-Ashvil	FJTP	MBA	80	W Carol	* & 8-81
McKenzie, Judy	Asst	Freed Hardem	PXV	MS	90	Memphis	& 8-87
McKenzie, Karen S.	Prof	Nova SE	MG	PHD	89.	LSU	&2007
McKenzie, Patrick B.	Retir	Arizona St	1997	PHD	70.	Mich St	&1970
McKeon, Joseph M.	Retir	Cleveland St	1992	DBA	79.	Kent St	&1982
McKeown, James C.	Prof	Penn State	FST	PHD	69.	Mich St	8-89
Mary Jean & Frank P. Smeal Professor of Accounting							
McKernan, John F.	Asst	Univ Glasgow	F	PHD	01	Glasgow	1990
McKie, Anita R.			PFC	PHD	96.	S Carol	&
McKillop, Paul	Lect	Salve Regina	PSF	MS		Salve Rg	
McKinley, Brian	Deces	Kentucky St		DBA	95.	Kent St	1996
McKinney, James E.	Retir	Valdosta St	2000	MA	70	Fla St	&1970
McKinney, James J.	VAsst	Maryland	SABH	PHD	02.	Maryland	2007
McKinney, Lisa	Inst	Alabama	F	MTA	95	Alabama	8-03
McKinnon, Jill L.	Asst	Macquarie Un	FI	PHD	84	Macquarie	&1979
McKnight, Constance	Asst	Ark Tech	FA	PHD	02.	Arkansas	&2003
McKnight, D. Harrison	Asst	Michigan St	S	PHD	97	Minnesota	2001

McKnight, Reed			FMC	PHD	81.	Oregon	&
McLaughlin, Thomas D.			FC	DBA	90.	Miss St	* &
McLaurin, Rayford J.	Retir	Tenn-Chattan	1989	MBA	51	Alabama	9-55
McLean, C. W. S.	Lect	Univ Ulster	B	BA			1990
McLean, James H.	Retir	Virg Comm	1985	PHD	67.	Ohio St	&1981
Route 3 Box 790; Glen Allen VA 23060							
McLean, John P.	Retir	Scranton	1990	BS	40	Scranton	1940
1036 Wheeler Avenue; Scranton PA 18510							
McLeay, Stuart	Prof	Wales-Bangor	F	PHD	88	Lancaster	& 1-88
McLelland, Andrew J.	Asst	Auburn	FKAG	PHD	03.	Tx A&M	* & 8-02
McLelland, Malcolm J.	CIAs	Indiana	F	PHD	99.	Mich St	&2007
McLeod, Rose Anne	SenFl	Victoria NZ		MBA		Massey	2006
McLeod, Thomas E.	Retir	Alabama-Birm	1987	PHD	71.	Alabama	&1957
McLintock, Alyson J.	Teach	U Nottingham	M	BCOM	73	Edinburgh	2000
McMahan, John W.				PHD	39.	Illinois	
McMahon, C.	SLect	Liverpool JM	FP	MA			1993
McMahon, Richard G. P.	H-Pr	Flinders Un	IF	PHD	98	N Eng-Au	& 1-78
McManus, Lisa	Lect	Griffith-GC	A	BBUS	97	Griffith	1993
McMath, H. Kent			CM	PHD	85.	S Carol	*
McMeeking, Kevin P.	Lect	Univ Exeter	A	PHD	00	Lancaster	1999
McMenimen, Leo J.	Retir	Montclair St	2005	PHD	76.	Penn St	&1980
McMichael, John H.	Retir	Pennsylvania	1986	MBA	49	Penn	&1948
McMickle, Peter L.	Prof	Memphis	DS	PHD	77.	Alabama	&1978
McMillan, Jeffrey J.	Prof	Clemson	FABO	PHD	00.	S Carol	1000
McMillan, Keith P.	Lect	London Econ	HJW	PHD	98	London	&2000
McMillan, Michael G.	Lect	Johns Hopkin		PHD	02.	Geo Wash	
Department of Finance; mcmillan@jhu; (202)588-5192							
McMullen, Dorothy A.	Assoc	Rider	AT	PHD	93.	Drexel	&1991
McMullen, Kyle G.	Retir	Marshall	1995	MBA	69	W Virginia	& 9-66
McMurtrie, Anthony J. E.	LectB	Adelaide	MF	MCOM	99	Flinders	1997
McNabb, Patrick J.	Prof	Ferris State	XFP	MBA	78	Geo Wash	&1981
McNair, Carol J.			M	PHD	86.	Columbia	*
McNair, Frances E.	Prof	Miss State	XMP	PHD	87.	Miss	&1987
KPMG Peat Marwick Professorship in Accounting							
McNamara, Frances M.	Retir	Adelaide	1988	BA		Sydney	1967
McNamara, James B.			TFM	PHD	78.	Arkansas	&
McNamara, Raymond P.	Assoc	Bond Univ	ABFS	PHD	91	Queensld	* &1989
McNamee, Alan H.	Prof	Lyon College	BCMS	PHD	88.	N Carol	&1994
Frank & Marion Bradley Lyon Professor of Accounting							
McNeill, I. Eugene	Retir	Houston Bapt		PHD	53.	Tx-Austin	1976
McNeill, Neil E.	Retir	Mo-Kansas Ct	1992	DBA	73.	Harvard	* 1982
10061 Hardy Drive; Overland Park KS 66212							
McNelis, L. Kevin	Asst	New Mex St	FMS	PHD	97.	Tx-Arlin	& 8-97
McNelis, Leslie L.	Retir	Tx-San Ant	1987	PHD	70.	Oklahoma	& 5-73
McNellis, Casey	Lect	East Wash	FM	MA	03	Gonzaga	&2004
McNerney, J. Peter				DBA	59.	Harvard	
McNett, Stephen A.			DSVX	PHD	87.	Missouri	
McNichols, Maureen F.	Prof	Stanford	FN	PHD	84.	UCLA	& 1-84
Marriner S. Eccles Professor of Public and Private Management							
McPeak, Charles	Lect	Pepper-L Ang	FM	MBA	66	S Calif	&1990
McPhail, Kenneth J.	Prof	Univ Glasgow	JEN	PHD	97	Dundee	1997
McQuade, Ralph J. Jr.	Assoc	Bentley	FTXE	MBA	72	Babson	&1975
McQueen, Patricia D.			MF	PHD	93.	NYU	
McQuilkin, John	Asst	Salve Regina	A	JD		Lewis&Cl	&2004
McQuitter-Banks, Bonnie	Asst	Alabama A&M	PM	MBA	84	Alab A&M	1984
McRae, Issac	Asst	Southeastern		MST	86	Southeas	
McStraw, T.	Assoc	Univ Ulster	FM	BA			& 9-03
McSwain, Dwayne N.	Asst	Mid Tenn St		PHD	02.	Tx-Arlin	&2003
McSweeney, Brendan M.	Prof	Univ Essex	AFBM	PHD	95	LondonEc	1999
McTague, Edward P.	Assoc	CUNY-Brookly	PNFR	MBA	81	Fairl Dick	& 9-82
McTeer, William E.				PHD	69.	Missouri	
McVay, Gloria	Assoc	Winona State	FMP	PHD	01.	Kentucky	2000
McVay, Sarah E.	Asst	New York		PHD	04.	Michigan	2004
McWall, D. M.	Lect	Univ Ulster	AOJ	BSC			1-06
McWhorter, Laurie B.	Asst	Miss State	M	PHD	01.	Kentucky	* &2004
McWilliams, John	Prof	San Fran St	XL	JD	72	Duke	&1976
McWilliams, Mallory L.	Lect	San Jose St	FM	MBA	78	San Jose	&1980
Mead, George C.	Retir	Michigan St	1999	PHD	62.	Illinois	&1962
Mead, Howard R.	Dir	Va Comm		PHD	78.	S Carol	
Mead, Stuart B.	Deces	Mich State	1990	DBA	50.	Indiana	
Meade, Janet A.	Assoc	Houston	X	PHD	87.	Ariz St	&1988
Meador, Anna Lee	Retir	Marshall	2001	DBA	89.	Memphis	& 8-89
Means, Kathryn M.	Prof	Fla Atlantic	F	PHD	79.	Geo St	&1985
Meares, Irene	Asst	W New Mexico	APRX	DBA	02	Sarasota	2002
Mecimore, Charles D.	Retir	N Car-Greens	6-98	PHD	66.	Alabama	* & 1-80
Medalen, Rodney E.	Retir	North Dakota	2000	MS	67	N Dakota	& 9-67
Meddaugh, E. James	Emer	Ohio Univ	2006	PHD	74.	Penn St	& 9-87

Name	Rank	School		Deg		Year	School		Year
Medema, Robert	Assoc	Calvin	FMP	MBA	72	Michigan			1999
Medinets, Ann F.	Assoc	Wm Paterson	ACM	PHD	04.	Rutgers			2006
Medlar, Deborah	SLect	U Washington	X	LLM	84	NYU			&2000
Medlin, John J.	Retir	Boise State	2001	MBA	64	Denver			&7-70
Meek, Gary K.	Prof	Oklahoma St	IF	PHD	80.	U Wash			&1980
Oscar S. Gellein/Deloitte & Touche Professor									
Meek, Joseph C.	Retir	St Louis	5-97	MBA	68	Wash U	*	&1968	
Meeting, David T.	Prof	Winthrop		DBA	86.	Kent St			&
Megaard, Susan L.	Prof	East Wash	XL	LLM	82	Geotown			1984
Mehl, Arthur G.	Retir	Bradley	1988	MBA	51	Wisconsin			&9-57
1216 N Elmwood; Peoria IL 61606									
Meier, Heidi H.	Assoc	Cleveland St	AFO	DBA	87.	Kent St			&1986
Meier, Robert A.	Retir	San Diego	1999	PHD	57.	Chicago			&1987
Meigs, Robert F.	Retir	San Diego St	1999	DBA	72.	S Calif			&1972
Meigs, Walter B.	Retir	So Calif	1978	PHD	44	S Calif			&1945
2881 Forrester Drive; Los Angeles CA 90064									
Meisel, Scott I.	Asst	Morehead St	FLM	PHD	01.	Kent St			&2002
Meisinger, Ken	Retir	Colorado Spr	2004	PHD	72	Tx A&M	*	1980	
Meixner, Wilda F.	Prof	Tx St-S Marc	BF	PHD	85.	Tx A&M			&1986
Mejri, Malek	Asst	Univ Tunis	F	DEA	97	ISCAE			1997
Melcher, Trini U.	Retir	CS-S Marcos	2003	PHD	77.	Ariz St			&1990
Melendrez, Kevin D.	Asst	Louisiana St	FM	PHD	04.	Arizona			7-04
KPMG LLP Developing Scholar									
Melendy, Sara R.	Asst	Gonzaga	FA	PHD	05.	SUNY-Buf			&2005
Mellett, Howard J.	H-Pr	Cardiff U	GNH	MSC	84	Cardiff			&1974
Mellman, Martin	Retir	Hofstra	1997	PHD	61.	NYU			& 8-93
Mello-e-Souza, Carlos A.	Asst	Seattle	FI	PHD	89.	Cornell			2002
Mellon, Mark J.	Prof	New Bruns-SJ		MBA		StMry-Cd			
Mellum, Steven D.	C-Ac	Capital	FGCM	MBA		Ohio St			&1991
Melnick, Arnold M.	Retir	Saginaw Vall	1998	PHD	62	Oklahoma			1982
Melnik, Steven V.	Assoc	CUNY-Baruch	X	LLM	00	NYU			2000
Melton, Howard W.		Evanston IL	1988	PHD	72.	Nrthwstrn			&
Melton, Paul D.	Assoc	W Virg Tech	CGPA	MBA					&
Melumad, Nahum D.	Prof	Columbia	MAF	PHD	85.	Berkeley			&1993
James L. Dohr Professor of Accounting & Business Law									
Menard, Louis	Prof	Quebec-Montr	F	MBA		Montreal			& 8-82
Mendelson, Sheldon	Retir	Governors St	1994	PHD	74	Colo St			& 1-74
Mendes, Margaret	Lect	West Indies	AE	MA		W Indies			
Mendola, Edward	Assoc	Calif U-Penn	PXG	MS	82	Rbt Morr			1989
Mendoza, Carla	Prof	ESCP deParis	BCMU	PHD	91	HEC			1987
Menefee, Opal P.	Retir	La St-Shreve	1993	MBA	49	LSU			8-47
Menn, Herbert C. Jr.		Dept Ment-TX		PHD	57.	Tx-Austin			
Mennicken, Andrea	Lect	London Econ	AGPI	PHD	00	London			2006
Menocal, Enrique V.	Reitr	Trenton St	1993	DCS	60	Havana			&1972
Menon, Gopenathan	Inst	King Fahd Un	S	MS	90	Monash			1992
Menon, Krishnagopal	Prof	Boston Univ	FM	PHD	82.	Penn St			9-82
Mensah, Michael O.	Dean	Scranton	FTS	PHD	89.	Houston			1987
Alperin Teaching Fellow									
Mensah, Yaw M.	Prof	Rutgers-N Br	FM	PHD	79.	Illinois	*	1984	
Mensching, James R.	Prof	CS-Chico	SF	PHD	76	Chicago			& 9-91
Menyah, Kojo	SLect	London Metro	M	PHD					1990
Meonske, Norman R.	Prof	Kent State	FM	PHD	72.	Missouri			&1972
Merced, Gregoria				PHD	73.	Tx-Austin			
Mercer, Charles R.	Deces	Drury	1995	PHD	67.	Arkansas			
Mercer, Molly	Assoc	Arizona St	F	PHD	01.	Tx-Austin			2007
Merchant, Kenneth A.	Prof	So Calif	MB	PHD	78.	Berkeley			&1990
Deloitte & Touche LLP Chair of Accountancy									
Mercincavage, Janet	Assoc	King's Col	FPR	MBA	84	Temple			& 9-80
Mereba, Janice R.			FS	PHD	94.	Penn St			
Meredith, John W.	Retir	Mary Hrdn-By	2000	PHD	75	North Tx			1-88
Meredith, Vicki Banet	Prof	Indiana SE	FES	DBA	85.	Kentucky	*	&1983	
Merei, Issam J. (Sam)			FS	PHD	77.	Tx Tech			
Merino, Barbara D.	C-Pr	North Texas	FHT	PHD	75.	Alabama			&1983
Horace Brock Chair & Regents Professor of Accounting									
Merriam, Kemper W.			XFC	PHD	57.	Tx-Austin			&
Merrill, Gregory B.		National Un	CFS	PHD	80.	Tx A&M			
National University									
Merrill, Joseph S.	Assoc	Srthrn Utah	VTFM	PHD	67.	Wisconsin			& 1-94
Merritt, Martha E.	Asst	No Georgia	AF	MACC	84	S Carol			&1988
Merryman, Maryann	C-Pr	St Marys-Ind	AFN	MSA	80	Notre Dm			& 8-83
Mersereau, Alexander	Assoc	HEC-Montreal	CMU	PHD	99	Paris	*	D-96	
Merz, C. Michael	Retir	Boise State	2000	DBA	74.	S Calif	*	& 9-74	
Mescall, Devan	Asst	Hawaii-Manoa		PHD	07	Waterloo			8-07
Meservy, Rayman D.	Assoc	Brigham Yg	SADG	PHD	85.	Minnesota			9-89
Messer, Jean F.	Deces	Wyoming	1981	PHD	49	Iowa			&1949
Messere, Carl J.	Retir	N Carol St	2004	PHD	76.	S Carol			1976
Messier, Jean R.	Retir	Quebec a Hul	1999	MSC					

Name	Rank	School	Code	Degree	Yr	University	Last
Messier, William F. Jr.	Prof	Georgia St	AFB	DBA	79.	Indiana	&1-98
Deloitte & Touche LLP Professor							
Messina, Frank M.	C-Ac	Alabama-Birm	SX	DBA	93.	Miss St	&1993
Ernst & Young Scholar							
Messing, Janet K.	Retir	CUNY-Lehman	1990	PHD	59.	NYU	&1969
35-23 171 Street; Flushing LI NY 11358							
Messmer, Victor C.	Retir	E Kentucky	1988	DBA	81.	Kentucky	&1961
Messner, Martin	Asst	HEC Paris	UCMB	PHD	06	Innsbruck	2006
Mest, David P.	Asst	Seton Hall	FKST	PHD	95.	Tx-Austin	&9-03
Metcalf, Christopher C.	Inst	Miami U-Ohio	P	MBA	74	Indiana	8-00
Metcalf, Richard W.	Deces	Arizona	2002	DBA	68.	Indiana	&1997
Metrejean, Cheryl T.	Asst	Geo Southern	XS	PHD	97.	Tx A&M	&2005
Metrejean, P. Eddie	Asst	Geo Southern	AS	PHD	04.	Miss	&2005
Metzger, Lawrence M.	Prof	Loyola-Chicg	MN	PHD	87	Il-Chicago	* &9-85
Metzger, Patricia L.	Deces	Mary Wash	2001	PHD	96	Berne	# * &9-85
Meuwissen, Roger H. G.	H-Pr	Maastricht	A	PHD	99	Maastricht	&1992
Meyer, Dan W.	Assoc	Austin Peay	FMGP	PHD	88.	Missouri	&2004
Meyer, Jean A.	Inst	Xavier-LA	FMGV	MBA		LSU	&
Meyer, Kent W.	Prof	CS-Sacrament	XI	PHD	80.	Tx-Austin	1980
Meyer, Michael J.	Asst	Ohio Univ	M	DBA	97.	Miss St	&1-05
Meyer, Pamela	Inst	La-Lafayette	FMS	MBA	98	USL	&8-98
Meyer, Philip E.	Retir	Boston Univ	2005	DBA	70.	Maryland	&1970
Meyers, Philip T.	Retir	Rochester	1993	MS	51	Okla St	&1962
Meyers, Stephen L.	Deces	Wash Univ	D-75	PHD	70	Penn	0 71
Meyler, Bernard W.	Retir	Suffolk	1996	MBA	65	Northeas	&1971
Mgwenya, J.	Lect	Un Zimbabwe		MBA			
Mia, Lokman	Prof	Griffith-GC	M	PHD	85	Queensld	&1994
Miah, Zaman	Lect	W Sydney-Nep	CFGI	MEC	85	Sydney	1989
Miano, Edward	Prof	Mass Lib Art	M	MBA	78	Pace	1985
Micet, Paul	Lect	W Sydney-Nep	ADES	MCOM	02	W Sydney	1998
Michael, James R.	Retir	Louisiana Te	1998	DBA	73.	La Tech	1968
Michael, Rodney R.			ATP	PHD	92.	North Tx	
Michaelsen, Robert H.	Retir	North Texas	X	PHD	82.	Illinois	&1986
Michaelson, Rosa	Fello	Dundee	DQSE	MSC	83	Heriot W	1990
Michalka, William J.	Retir	Odessa Col	M	PHD	76.	North Tx	
Michel, Kevin A.	Assoc	Maryland UC	NG	EDD	99	Nova SE	&1998
Michel, Mary	C-As	Manhattan	FM	PHD	97.	Columbia	1998
Michelman, Jeffrey E.	Assoc	North Fla	FSNM	PHD	87.	Wisconsin	* &1990
Michenzi, Alfred R.	C-Ac	Loyola-Maryl	AFS	PHD	74	Case Wes	&1989
Mickhail, George M. E.	SLect	U Wollongong	DSA	MIS	90	LondonEc	1994
Middaugh, J. Kendall II	Assoc	Wake Fr-MBA	MU	PHD	81.	Ohio St	7-87
Middlemist, Melanie R.	Retir	Colorado St	2002	PHD	86.	Okla St	&1985
Middleton, Joyce M.	Prof	Frostburg St	XPF	PHD	92.	Georgia	&1-90
Middleton, Mary A.	VAsst	Richmond	FM	PHD	88.	Georgia	&2000
			PX	PHD	99.	St Louis	&
Mielke, Carol A.							
Mielke, David E.	Dean	E Michigan	FI	PHD	81.	Wisconsin	7-04
Mihalek, Paul H.	Assoc	Hartford	FMA	PHD	86	Conn	&1986
Mikhail, Michael B.	Asst	Arizona St	F	PHD	97	Chicago	&2006
Mikol, Alain	Prof	ESCP deParis	AHJ	PHD	89	Paris I	1982
Milacek, Emil C.	Retir	Winona State	1998	PHD	86.	North Tx	&1989
Milam, Edward E.	Retir	Miss State	2006	PHD	71.	LSU	&1990
Milam, Lorie	Inst	No Colorado	CFGX	MPA	95	Tx-Austin	&2005
Milani, Kenneth W.	Prof	Notre Dame	XMN	PHD	72.	Iowa	&1-72
Milano, Duane R.	Deces	SW Assem God	3-02	PHD	79.	Mich St	*
Milanova, Elena	Asst	Univ Essex	BMI	DIP	92	HIE	2000
Milbrath, Robert S.	VAsst	Houston	FM	PHD	86	Michigan	1993
Milburn, John S.				PHD	77.	Illinois	
Milcic, Edward A.	Retir	Duquesne	1988	MS	51	Duquesne	&1949
Miles, Catherine E.	Retir	Georgia St	1980	PHD	53.	Alabama	9-52
4904 Commwealth Road; Palmetto FL 34221							
Milich, Marvin M.	Assoc	CUNY-Queens	LR	JD	71	NYU	&9-87
Millanta, Brian	Lect	Macquarie Un	F	MEC	87	Macquarie	&1993
Millar, James A.	Prof	Arkansas	F	PHD	71	Oklahoma	* 1971
Department of Finance							
Miller, Allie F.	Asst	Rutgers-Camd	FM	PHD	86.	Ariz St	&
Miller, Angharad	SLect	Bournemouth	X	MSC			1-96
Miller, Bruce L.	Prof	UCLA	MF	PHD	67	Stanford	1984
Miller, Cathleen L.	Assoc	Wayne State	MBAB	PHD	98.	Kentucky	&1-07
Miller, Charles R. (Tad)	Prof	Cal Poly-SLO	FA	PHD	87.	Arizona	&9-87
Miller, Elwood L.	Retir	St Louis	1991	PHD	70.	St Louis	&1975
Miller, Gary A.	Prof	CS-Bakersf	FI	PHD	85.	Santa Cl	&2005
Miller, Gerald J.	Assoc	C New Jersey	FGV	PHD	94.	Kentucky	&1995
Miller, Gibbes U.		TallahasseFL	1991	PHD	70.	Michigan	&1981
Miller, Gregory S.	Assoc	Harvard	F	PHD	98.	Michigan	1998
Miller, Helen J.	Lect	Baylor	P	MBA	72	Baylor	&8-73
Miller, Henry C.				PHD	71.	Illinois	&
Miller, Herbert E.	Retir	Georgia	1989	PHD	44.	Minnesota	&1978

Miller, J. Glenn	Assoc	Piedmont	QM	PHD	02	Ga Tech	&2002	
Miller, James E.	D-As	Gannon	FMAX	DBA	96	Gannon	&1997	
Miller, James J.		Manhattan KS	1990	PHD	78.	Missouri	&	
1815 Cedar Crest Dr; Manhattan KS 66502								
Miller, Jeffrey R.	Assoc	Augusta St	ADFP	PHD	85.	LSU	&1993	
Miller, Jeffrey S.	Assoc	Notre Dame	F	PHD	00.	Tx-Austin	&2000	
Miller, Jerome	Asst	4Asst astern		MBA	89	Southeas		
Miller, Karen C.	Asst	Union-TN		PHD	06.	Miss	1998	
Miller, Kim	Asst	Tri State		MBA		Indiana	&	
Miller, Macy J.	Inst	New Haven	F	MBA	06	NewHamp	9-05	
Miller, Malcolm C.	Assoc	New So Wales	FI	MCOM	73	NS Wales	&1964	
Miller, Paul B. W.	Prof	Colorado Spr	FJ	PHD	71.	Tx-Austin	&1988	
Miller, Peter B.	C-Pr	London Econ	MW	PHD	83	London	1987	
Miller, Robert L. C.	Prof	CS-Fullerton	FG	PHD	73.	Oregon	1974	
Miller, Roger O.	VPres	Georgia St	1992	PHD	74.	Geo St		
Miller, Sandra K.	Prof	Widener	XLF	LLM	90	Villanova	&1991	
Miller, Scott E.	Asst	Gannon	FXLP	JD	97	Pittsburgh	&1998	
Miller, Thomas I. (Tim)	Prof	Murray State	F	PHD	73.	Arkansas	&1967	
Miller, Thomas K.	Retir	Central Okla	PFC	MBA	68	Penn	&9-83	
Milles, Richard J.	Retir	So Ill-Edwar	1983	PHD	71.	St Louis	&1960	
Milliron, Valerie C.	Prof	CS-Chico	XE	PHD	84.	S Calif	&9-90	
Mills, Annette J.	SLect	Canterbury	SDM	PHD	96	Waikato	1998	
Mills, Donald	Retir	Alabama	1983	PHD	61.	Alabama	1954	
1210 Oakwood Avenue; Tuscaloosa AL 35401								
Mills, John R.	Prof	Nevada-Reno	F	PHD	79.	Colorado	&1982	
Mills, Kathleen D.			AM	PHD	93.	Arizona	&	
Mills, Lillian F.	Assoc	Texas-Austin	X	PHD	96.	Michigan	&2006	
Mills, Patricia	Clin	So Calif		LLM	86	SanDiego	2002	
Mills, Robert H.	Retir	Lehigh	1991	PHD	60.	Wisconsin	&	
Mills, Sherry K.	Prof	New Mex St	BM	PHD	88.	Tx Tech	&8-88	
Mills, Timothy H.	Prof	E Illinois	FG	DBA	89.	La Tech	&1989	
Milne, Markus J.	Prof	Canterbury	JW	MA	88	Lancaster	2006	
Milne, Ronald A.	Retir	Nev-L Vegas	2000	PHD	81.	Illinois	1983	
Milner, Margaret M.	Asst	Univ Glasgow	QS	MACC	87	Glasgow	1986	
Milroy, Robert R.	Retir	Indiana	1978	PHD	38	Iowa	&1944	
Min, Han Ki			CF	PHD	74.	Oklahoma	* &	
Minars, David	Retir	CUNY-Brookly	XL	JD	70	NY Law	& 1-71	
Minbiole, Elizabeth	C-Ac	Northwood	PFCM	MBA	84	Cen Mich	&1982	
Minch, Roland A.	Retir	SUNY-Albany	1997	PHD	70	Rensselaer	# *	1977
Mini, Donald L.		Redding CA	1992	PHD	64.	Illinois		
PO Box 790; Redding CA 96099								
Minke, Susan	Lect	Ind-Pur/FtWy	FMP	MBA	88	W Mich	9-98	
Minmier, George S.	Prof	Memphis	F	PHD	74.	Arkansas	* &1976	
Mintchik, Natalia	Asst	Mo-St Louis		PHD	05.	North Tx	2005	
Minter, Frank C.	Exec	Samford	T	MBA	67	Memphis	&9-88	
Mints, Frederick E.	Retir	CS-L Angeles	1-82	DBA	72	S Calif	&1970	
Mintz, Jack	Prof	Univ Toronto	X	PHD	80	Essex	1989	
Mintz, Seymour	Asst	CUNY-Queens		JD		Touro	&	
Mintz, Steven M.	Prof	Cal Poly-SLO	FJ	PHD	78.	Geo Wash	&9-06	
Minyard, Donald H.			FMV	PHD	88.	Illinois	&	
Miranda, Jose	Asst	Monterrey Tc		PHD	06.	Tx Tech		
Miranti, Paul J. Jr.	Prof	Rutgers-Newk	AFH	PHD	85	J Hopkins	&1982	
Mirghani, Mohamed Ali	Assoc	King Fahd Un	MS	DBA	79.	Indiana	1983	
Miro, Abdelradi	Asst	King Saud U	FX	PHD	84	Birminghm	1987	
Mirza, Malik	SLect	Queensld Tec	F	MCOM	76	Queensld	&7-90	
Misch, Marilyn B.	Assoc	Pepper-Malib	FI	PHD	99.	Ariz St	&1997	
Misener, David L.	Retir	Acadia	1995	MS		Illinois	&	
Mishra, Birendra K. (Barry)	Asst	Texas-Dallas	SM	PHD	96.	Tx-Austin	2000	
on leave at University of California, Riverside								
Misic, Milica	ALect	Macquarie Un	FA	BCOM	99	Macquarie	2002	
Misiewicz, Kevin M.	Assoc	Notre Dame	XJ	PHD	74.	Mich St	&9-78	
Mister, William G.	Prof	Colorado St	CMFV	PHD	73.	Berkeley	1989	
Mistry, Jamshed J.	Asst	Suffolk	FM	DBA	99.	Boston U	2007	
Mitchell, Albert R.	Retir	Jms Madison	8-95	PHD	66.	Missouri	&1-90	
Mitchell, E. Carla	Asst	Elizabeth Ct	FC	PHD	03	Old Dom	&2003	
Mitchell, Graeme	SLect	W Sydney	BCEJ	GDIP	94	NS Wales		
Mitchell, James L.	Retir	Saginaw Vall	1993	DBA	67.	Mich St	1977	
Mitchell, Jennie L.	Assoc	St Mary Wood	F	MBA	86	Ind St	* &8-86	
Saint Mary-of-the-Woods College								
Mitchell, John D.	Deces			PHD	67.	UCLA		
Mitchell, John M.	Retir	Geneva	1995	MBA	62	Pittsburgh	&1962	
Mitchell, Laurel B.	Assoc	Redlands	FAS	PHD	97.	Columbia	&2003	
Mitchell, LeRoy W.	Assoc	Iona	PG	DPA	85	NYU	&9-72	
Mitchell, Lloyd A.	C-As	St Thomas-FL	FCA	MBA	81	U Miami	&1984	
Mitchell, Maria	Asst	Thomas More	FVCM	MBA	95	Xavier	2003	
Mitchell, Naomi C.		Consulting	FAM	DBA	94.	Clev St	&	
Mitchell, T.	Adj	Southern-NO	FA	MBA	99	N Orleans	&1999	

Name	Rank	School		Deg	Yr	Where	Year
Mitchell, Tiffany	Asst	Mary Hrdn-By	AFM	MBA	03	MryHrd-B	2005
Mitchell, Wiley S.	Retir	Kansas	1987	MBA	47	Kansas	&1946
Mitchem, Cheryl E.	Assoc	Virginia St	FCI	PHD	90.	Va Comm	* &8-91
Mitewa, Helen	AcLec	Un Tasmania		MBUS	02	Victoria	2003
Mitra, Santanu	Assoc	Wayne State	FM	PHD	02.	LSU	1-07
Mitschow, Mark C.	Prof	SUNY-Geneseo	FJV	PHD	94.	Maryland	9-94
Mitsudome, Toshiaki	Asst	CUNY-Hunter		PHD	01.	Baruch	9-00
Mittelstaedt, H. Fred	C-Pr	Notre Dame	F	PHD	87.	Illinois	&1992
PricewaterhouseCoopers Faculty Fellow							
Mittendorf, Brian	Assoc	Yale	AMFT	PHD	02.	Ohio St	7-02
Mittermaier, Linda J.	Prof	Capital	FMX	PHD	87.	Indiana	&1994
Mittler, Dale L.	Prof	Capital	XAV	MBA		Capital	&1978
Mixon, Jesse D.	Retir	S F Austin	1988	MBA	53	So Meth	1965
Mladenovic, Rosina	SLect	Univ Sydney	FEW	PHD	01	NS Wales	&2002
Mlynarczyk, Francis A.	Partn			PHD	69.	Purdue	
Prospect Advisors							
Mo, Phyllis Lai Lan	H-Pr	Lingnan U	AXY	PHD	99	HongKong C	2006
Moalla, Hannene	Asst	Univ Tunis	F	DEA	97	ISCAE	1997
Moalla, Mohamed	Inst	Univ Tunis	F	EXPC	99	ISCAE	1999
Mobley, Sybil C.	Retir	Florida A&M	6-03	PHD	64.	Illinois	&1963
Mobus, Janet Luft			AFMH	PHD	97.	North Tx	&
Mock, Theodore J.	Prof	So Calif	ABS	PHD	69.	Berkeley	1973
Arthur Andersen Alumni Professor of Accounting							
Modisette, James P.	Retir	Arkansas	1997	PHD	62.	LCU	&1960
Moe, Bonnie M.	Retir	Il-Springfld	F	PHD	96.	St Louis	&1990
Moeckel, Cindy L.	Retir	Arizona St	2002	PHD	87.	N Carol	&1987
Moehrle, Stephen R.	Assoc	Mo-St Louis	F	PHD	97.	Indiana	&1999
Moellenberndt, Richard A.	Prof	Washburn	F	PHD	73.	Nebraska	&8-76
Moeller, Hans Peter	C-Pr	Aachen Univ	FCIA	PHD	72	Cologne	1990
Moerman, Lee	Lect	U Wollongong	FT	MCOM	00	Wollong	2001
Moers, Frank	Prof	Maastricht	M	PHD	01	Maastricht	6-97
Moersen, Leo C.	Assoc	George Wash	LIJK	JD	81	Wm&Mary	&1984
Moet, Lisa K.			AFS	PHD	97.	Colorado	&
Moffat, Andrew	Lect	Napier Univ	MF	BA			&1991
Moffeit, Katherine S.	Prof	West Georgia	AFGN	PHD	85.	North Tx	&8-01
Moffie, Robert P.	L-Ac	N Carol Cen	AXFH	PHD	78.	N Carol	&1987
Moffitt, Jackie S.	Assoc	Louisiana St	F	PHD	01.	Fla St	8-01
Mogus, Taffere		Levittown PA	1991	PHD	78.	Syracuse	
11 Maplewood Dr; Levittown PA 19056							
Mohamed Massoud Farag, S.				PHD	67.	Illinois	
Mohamed, Emad			F	PHD	02.	Geo St	
Mohammadi, Hamid Reza	Asst	Saint Xavier	CQPD	PHD	90	Ill Tech	&1989
Mohammed, Emad	Asst	McMaster Un	F	PHD	03	Geo St	7-04
Mohanram, Partha S.	Assoc	Columbia	F	PHD	98.	Harvard	2003
Mohr, Rosanne M.			FG	PHD	81.	Wisconsin	&
Mohrman, Mary Beth	C-Ac	Mo-St Louis	F	PHD	91.	Wash U	1990
Mohrweis, Lawrence C.	Prof	No Arizona	AFPE	PHD	86.	Wisconsin	&8-92
Moiz, Syed	Asst	Wis-Plattev		MBA	94	Minn St	8-06
Moizer, Peter	Prof	Univ Leeds	ABJ	PHD	93	Manchest	4-89
Mok, Annie Y. N.	Inst	City Univ HK	FMAX	MBA		CityU HK	
Molisa, Pala	Lect	Victoria NZ		BCA			
Molloy, Karen H.	Assoc	Illinois	X	PHD	80.	Va Tech	&1-81
Molony, Jospeh T.	Lect	Elizabethtwn	MF	MS		American	2001
Molyneaux, David	SLect	Aberdeen	NAJ	PHD	01	Edinburgh	2001
Molyneux, Philip	Prof	Wales-Bangor	FQ	PHD	96	Bangor	9-98
Molyneux, Steve	STcFl	Univ Leeds	CFMQ	MBA	98	Leicester	8-02
Momin, M.	Lect	Massey Univ		PHD		Glasgow	2005
Monahan, Steven J.	Asst	INSEAD	F	PHD	99.	N Carol	2003
Monahan, Thomas F. (Tim)	Prof	Villanova	FTM	PHD	81.	Temple	&1981
Monborne, Edward H.	Retir	St Fran-Penn	1998	MS	72	Duquesne	&1966
Moncada, Susan M.	Prof	Indiana St	FGSR	PHD	90	Illinois	&8-90
Moncada, Thomas P.	Assoc	E Illinois	XEM	JD	75	IIT Kent	&1980
Monden, Yasuhiro	H-Pr	Univ Tsukuba	CMQ	PHD	90	Tsukuba	3-83
Moneef, Abdullah Ali		King Saud U	1991	PHD	81.	S Carol	
King Saud Univ; PO Box 21208; Riyadh Saudi Arabia							
Monem, Reza	Lect	U Queensland	A	PHD	00	Queenslnd	2000
Monger, Rod R.				PHD	80.	Houston	
Monical, Earl	Retir	Wis-Rvr Fall	1997	MACC		S Calif	&1970
Monippallil, Matthew M.	D-Pr	E Illinois	XL	JD	84	S Illinois	&1986
Monk, D.	SLect	London Metro	DFS	BSC			1999
Monk, Ellen	Inst	Delaware	S	MBA	87	Delaware	1989
Monk, Lissa	Fello	Dundee	DQSE	BA	87	Liverpool	1997
Monks, Thomas	Assoc	Western Conn	LX	LLM	92	Quinnipi	2004
Monllau, Teresa	Asst	Pompeu Fabra			98	UPC	
Monroe, Gary S.	Prof	Australian N	ABEJ	PHD	78.	Mass	2002
Monsen, Norvald	Assoc	Norwegian U	G	DOEC			
Monson, Wesley L.	Retir	Moorhead St	1992	MS	67	N Dakota	1968

Name	Rank	School	Code	Degree	Yr	Degree School		Year
Monsour, Edward L.	Asst	CS-L Angeles	FX	JD	82	Clev St		& 9-02
Montalvo, Manuel L.	Retir	Puerto Rico	1990	MBA	62	NYU		&
Montgomery, Andrew T.	Deces	San Fran St	1986	PHD	71.	Stanford		1971
Montgomery, James B.	Retir	Fla Atlantic	1997	PHD	65.	Florida		&1964
Montgomery, Patrick	Asst	Wis-Plattev		MAS	02	St Ambro		8-06
Montgomery, S. John				PHD	66.	NYU		
Montgomery, Walter	Asst	Alabama St	CFA	MBA	74	Atlanta		&1993
Montondon, Lucille M.	Prof	Tx St-S Marc	GFNO	PHD	90.	Houston		1989
Montreuil, Francis	Prof	Quebec-Montr	X	MFIS		Sherbrook		& 1-84
Montrone, Paul				PHD	65.	Columbia		
Moody, Janette W.	Assoc	Citadel	SPE	PHD	93	S Fla		& 1-93
Moody, Ray	Lect	Troy	F	MBA	68	Fla St		1-01
Moody, Sharon M.			MCF	PHD	87.	Miss		&
Moon, James E.	Prof	Illinois St	2006	PHD	70.	Alabama		& 8-94
Mooncroft, D.	SLect	Liverpool JM	M	CPFA				2006
Moonen, Hans	Prof	Tilburg Univ	AD					&1986
Mooney, J. Lowell	Prof	Geo Southern	SMC	PHD	89.	Georgia	*	&1989
Mooney, Kate	Prof	St Cloud St	FS	PHD	89.	Tx A&M		&1986
Moonitz, Maurice W.	Retir	Berkeley	7-78	PHD	41.	Berkeley		&1947
555 Pierce St Apt 16234; Albany CA 94706								
Moore, Carl L.	Retir	Lehigh	6-86	MA	48	Pittsburgh		&1948
Moore, Charles K. (Ken)	Retir	Akron	2000	PHD	73.	Tx Tech		& 1-73
Moore, David	Lect	Un Tasmania	F	MBUS	02	RMIT		2004
Moore, Debra	Asst	Dallas Bapt	FS	PHD	07	Touro		&2001
Moore, Dennis P.	Prof	Worcester St	CVXP	MST		Bentley		9-83
Moore, Dolores W.	Retir	Ohio Northrn	M	MBA		Ohio U	*	1974
Moore, Erin A.	Asst	Lehigh	F	PHD	06.	Mass		2005
Moore, J. Thomas	Retir	Kennesaw St	2000	DBA	82.	Kentucky		&1984
Moore, Jared A.	Asst	Oregon State	XF	PHD	06.	Ariz St		&2006
Moore, John C.	Asst	Queen's Univ	BCME	MBA	76	Queen's	*	1980
Moore, John O.	Retir	Central Wash	2002	PHD	81.	Houston		& 9-80
Moore, John W.	Assoc	Virginia St	FS	PHD	92.	Va Comm		& 1-91
Moore, Louella	Prof	Arkansas St	GHF	PHD	86.	Arkansas	*	& 8-79
Moore, Mark	SLect	W Australia	Q	PHD	00	Rutgers		&2001
Moore, Michael J.			FA	PHD	93.	Alabama		&
Moore, Michael L.	Retir	CS-Fullerton	2005	PHD	71.	Penn St		&1998
Moore, P. Michael	Prof	Cen Arkansas	F	PHD	82.	Arkansas	*	& 7-89
Moore, Perry G.	Prof	Lipscomb	OAVP	PHD	92.	Georgia	#	& 8-82
Moore, Ronald K.		NW Nazarene	M	PHD	88.	North Tx		
Moore, Sandra A.	Asst	Mo Baptist	FMP	MBA	81	Wash U		
Moore, Tom C.	Assoc	Georgia Col	LXP	PHD	84	Georgia		1987
Moore, Walter B.	D-Ac	Nova SE	AMF	PHD	89.	Nebraska		&1996
Moore, William T..	Inst	Geo Southern	FMP	MBA	84	Auburn	#	1993
Moores, C. Tommy	Prof	Nev-L Vegas	FET	PHD	82.	LSU		&1989
Moores, Kenneth J.	Prof	Bond Univ	MBE	PHD	82	Birminghm	*	&1988
Moraglio, Joseph	Inst	Geo Mason	FM	BS	57	Holy Cr		&2000
Morakul, Supitcha	Deces			PHD	99.	North Tx		
Moran, Timothy	Asst	Aurora	AFTW	MBA	99	St Johns		2003
Moreau, John R.	Retir	McNeese St	2003	MS	76	S Miss		&1976
Morecroft, Susan E.			F	PHD	96.	Va Comm		
Morehead, William	C-As	Delta State	GIJN	ABD		S Miss		&2007
Morehouse, Wade A. Jr.	Retir	CS-Hayward	1993	PHD	65.	Berkeley		& 1-82
Moreland, Keith A.	Prof	Mich-Flint	AFE	PHD	92.	Cincinnati	*	&1994
Morell, Robert W.	Retir	Virginia		PHD	57	St Louis		
Moreno, Kimberly K.	Asst	Northeastern	AF	PHD	98.	Mass		9-07
Morf, Duffy A.	ClAs	Mississippi	CFGH	PHD	00.	Miss		& 8-00
Morgan, Carmen	Assoc	Oregon Tech	FVA	MBA	91	Port St	*	&1989
Morgan, Donald Ace	Prof	Neb-Kearney	APF	PHD	78	Iowa		& 8-88
Morgan, Jerold J.	Retir	So Miss	1992	PHD	65.	Alabama		&1969
Box 5178-SS; Hattiesburg MS 39401								
Morgan, John D.	Assoc	Winona State	FS	PHD	92.	Nebraska	*	&2006
Morgan, Mark	Asst	Miss College	PAFM	PHD	07	JacksonSt		2006
Morgan, Robert G.	Prof	East Tenn St	FXM	PHD	74.	Georgia	*	&1985
Morgret, Andrew J.	Inst	Memphis	F	MBA	86	Memphis		&1997
Mori, Joseph E.	Retir	San Jose St	VF	PHD	72.	Santa Cl		&1964
Moriarity, James	Assoc	Mass Lib Art		MBA	80	Am Intl		1980
Moriarity, Shane R.	Retir	U Auckland	CM	PHD	73.	Illinois		2001
Morin, Danielle	Assoc	HEC-Montreal	AMUY	PHD	99	ENAP		& 8-99
Morin, Robert J.	Prof	Sherbrooke	X	MFIS	78	Sherbrook		&1982
Morissette, Raymond	Asst	HEC-Montreal	AMU	PHD	97	Waterloo	*	& 4-04
Morita, Tetsuya	Retir	Hitotsubashi	1993	DBA	62	Hitotsub		1959
Morley, Rachel	Assoc	Victoria NZ		PHD		Otago		&
Morley, Susan	Inst	Colorado	XL	JD	00	Colorado		2004
Moroni, J. Alfred	Retir	Christian Br	1992	MS	54	St Louis		1954
Morrill, Cameron K. J.	Assoc	U Manitoba	FM	PHD	91	Alberta		1997
Morrill, Janet	Asst	U Manitoba	AF	PHD	94	Alberta		1997
Morris, Barbara S.			AINF	PHD	85.	Georgia	#	&

Morris, Bonnie W.	Assoc	W Virginia	SOA	PHD	92. Pittsburgh	&1-90
Morris, David E.	Assoc	No Georgia	CX	PHD	93. American	&1983
Morris, Deigan	C-Pr	INSEAD	M	PHD	72. Warwick	1972
Morris, Everett L. Jr.	Pres			DBA	71. Geo Wash	
Public Service Electric & Gas; 80 Park Pl #7200; Newark NJ 07101						
Morris, Janice T.	Lect	San Diego	EFS	MBA	88 Hou-CILk	&2003
Morris, Joseph L.	Assoc	SE Louisiana	FT	PHD	86. Miss	&8-84
Morris, Michael H.	Prof	Notre Dame	MCQ	PHD	80. Cincinnati	* &9-79
Morris, Paula H.	Assoc	Kennesaw St	FA	MPA	79 Geo St	&1981
Morris, Philip W.	C-As	Sam Houston	MF	PHD	03. Tx Tech	&2000
Morris, Richard D.	SLect	New So Wales	FH	PHD	88 NS Wales	&1974
Morris, Roselyn E.	C-Pr	Tx St-S Marc	AFX	PHD	93. Houston	&1993
Morris, Stephanie	Lect	Mercer-Macon	F	MACC	01 Georgia	&2006
Morris, Susan B.	Asst	Wm & Mary	XFG	MBA	95 Old Dom	&
Morris, William C.	Retir	W Michigan	2004	MBA	57 Nrthwstrn	&1961
Morris, William J. Jr.	Retir	North Texas	2000	PHD	71. Mich St	&1-71
Morrison, Lloyd F.	Retir	LSU	1977	PHD	48. Michigan	&1949
Morrison, Theodore D. III	Assoc	Wingate	FVAM	DBA	92. Miss St	&
Morrison, Thomas A.	Retir	Hartford	1999	PHD	67. Penn St	* &1989
Morrissey, Leonard E. Jr.	Retir	Dartmouth	1991	MBA	48. Dartmouth	&1951
36 Occum Ridge; Hanover NH 03755						
Morrow, Mitchel C.			BM	PHD	92. Georgia	
Morse, Barry	Tutor	Cardiff U	EMP	MA	71. Oxford	&1997
Morse, Dale C.	Prof	Oregon	FM	PHD	78. Stanford	1991
Charles E. Johnson Memorial Professor of Accounting						
Morse, Judith M.	Asst	Providence	MCXF	MST	Bryant	&1989
Morse, Wayne J.	Prof	Rochest Tech	CMS	PHD	71. Mich St	&7-01
Morsfield, Suzanna G.			F	PHD	98. Arizona	
Mortensen, Tony	ALect	Canterbury	BFP	BCOM	93 Lincoln	2005
Mortimer, Dell L.	Retir	CS-Fresno	8-91	DBA	68. Colorado	8-68
Mortimer, Greta	Retir	CS-Fresno	1991	MBA	51 Berkeley	&8-84
Mortimer, John W.	Asst	Coast Carol	SFMT	PHD	01. Fla Atl	2002
Morton, James R.			MV	DBA	73. S Calif	&
Morton, Jane E.	Assoc	Merrimack	ACFJ	PHD	93. Arizona	&2001
Morton, Richard M.	Assoc	Florida St	F	PHD	94. Penn St	&8-94
Deloitte Professor of Accounting						
Mosakowski, Joe	Asst	No Alabama	MP	ABD	Miss	1972
Moschetti, Tom	Lect	San Jose St	X	MST	San Jose	1989
Moscove, Stephen A.	Retir	New Haven	SM	PHD	71. Okla St	&1-01
Mosebach, Janet	VAsst	Illinois	X	PHD	06 Arkansas	&8-06
Mosebach, Michael	VAsst	Illinois	F	PHD	96. Oklahoma	&8-06
Moseley, Owen B.	Retir	Arkansas St	2001	PHD	76. Okla St	&8-86
Moser, Donald V.	Prof	Pittsburgh	FBM	PHD	86. Wisconsin	&9-86
Moser, Duane	Prof	Western Conn		PHD	84. Ohio St	&1990
Moser, William J.	Asst	Missouri	X	PHD	05. Arizona	&2005
Moses, O. Douglas	D-Ac	Naval Postgr	FM	PHD	83. UCLA	1985
Moshier, Michelle R.	Lect	SUNY-Albany	X	MSA	87 Hartford	1998
Mosich, Anelise N.	Retir	So Calif	1993	PHD	63. UCLA	&1964
Moss, Gisele J.	Assoc	Lamar	PMV	PHD	95. LSU	&2000
Moss, Henry	Retir	DePaul	1992	MSA	55 Long Isl	&1985
Most, Kenneth S.	Retir	Fla Internat	1994	PHD	70. Florida	&1975
Mostafa, Ghaleb	Lect	Kuwait Univ	PC	PHD	90 Kent	1993
Motekat, Ula K.	Retir	Old Dominion	2000	DBA	71. Colorado	&1980
Moten, Sebrena	Asst	Troy	LR	JD	80 Alabama	1994
Motluck, Mark	Asst	Anderson	FXLM	JD	85 U Miami	2000
Mott, Charles H.	Retir	West Chester	2000	PHD	79 American	&9-88
Mottice, H. Jay		Real Esta-FL	1998	PHD	64. Ohio St	&1979
300 Summerbrooke Dr.; Tallahassee FL 32301; 850-668-2254						
Motyka, Wolodymyr	SLect	U Newcastle	DHIM	PHD	94 NS Wales	1988
Mouck, Tom	Retir	New Mexico	FG	PHD	87 Okla St	&1989
Moughan, Michael	Inst	Temple	F	PHD	98 Delaware	2006
Mould, P.	Lect	Univ Hull	XF	MSC	04 Humbersi	O-01
Mounce, Patricia H.	C-Ac$	Cen Arkansas	X	PHD	98. Miss	&8-04
Mount, Dan	Assoc	Penn St-Hotl	FIQM	PHD	94 US Intl	8-95
Mouritsen, Matthew L.	Assoc	Weber State	FS	PHD	97 Utah St	&2001
Moussalli, Stephanie D.	Asst	West Fla	AF	PHD	05. Miss	&8-06
Moustafa, Mohamed E.	Retir	CS-S Marcos	2003	PHD	65. Illinois	2000
Moustafa, Salah		Ritsumeikan		PHD	82. North Tx	
Ritsumeikan Asia Pacific University; Japan						
Movdawalla, Pirooz P.				PHD	98. Car Mellon	
Mowen, Maryanne M.	Assoc	Oklahoma St	MCB	PHD	79 Ariz St	* 1980
Mowrey, Megan E.	Asst	Clemson		PHD		
Moyer, C. A.	Retir	Illinois	3-72	PHD	38 Illinois	1931
Moyes, Glen D.	Assoc	Tx-Pan Amer	AS	DBA	91 US Intl	9-01
Mozes, Haim A.	Assoc	Fordham	FPQV	PHD	89. NYU	1989
Mucklow, Belinda	Lect	Wisconsin	F	PHD	90. Cornell	1990
Mudalige, Nihal	SLect	Monash Univ	MC	MBA	86 Monash	* &1988

Mudrinich, Andrew K.	Asst	West Liberty	PR	JD		96	Akron	&2006
Muehlmann, Brigitte	Asst	Suffolk		PHD		95	Vienna	
Muehsam, Valerie P.	Asst	Sam Houston		PHD		98.	Tx A&M	
Economics Dept								
Mueller, Frank	Prof	St Andrews	WTI	PHD		91	Oxford	2004
Mueller, Fred J.	Retir	U Washington	1987	PHD		56	Ohio St	&1956
Mueller, Gerhard G.	Emer	U Washington	1996	PHD		62.	Berkeley	&1960
Mueller, Jennifer M.	Assoc	Auburn	FAS	PHD		00.	Va Tech	8-00
Mufrig, Nasser	Asst	West Bank	1992	DBA		92.	S Illinois	1992
Mugan, Can Simga		Bilkent Univ	2000	PHD		87.	Illinois	
Dept of Management; Bilkent Univ Pks; 06533 Bilkent Ankara Turkey								
Muhanna, Waleed A.	Assoc	Ohio State	S	PHD		87	Wisconsin	1987
Mukherji, Arijit	Deces	Minnesota	2000	PHD		91.	Pittsburgh	& 1-91
Mulchandani, Prakash	SLect	Ohio State	CM	MACC		01	Ohio St	2001
Mulford, Charles W.	Prof	Georgia Tech	F	DBA		83.	Fla St	& 1-83
Invesco Chair								
Mulig, Elizabeth	Asst	S Fl-St Pete	PF	DBA		96.	La Tech	& 7-05
Mullen, Louis E.	Retir	Tenn State	2001	PHD		64.	Illinois	&1984
Muller, Barbara	SLect	Ariz St-West	TF	MBA		91	Ariz St	& 9-91
Muller, Karl A. III	Assoc	Penn State	FI	PHD		97.	Illinois	8-02
Mulling, Frank H.	Deces			PHD		64.	Alabama	
Munn, Patricia P.	Inst	So Miss	FM	MPA		86	S Miss	&1986
Munro, Lois	Lect	Queensld Tec	F	MFM		93	Queensld	& 1-89
Munro, Michelle C.	Inst	Montana St	FPM	MPAC		96	Mont St	& 8-05
Munshi, Persy	SLect	Arizona St	AS	MBA		88	Ohio St	7-03
Munter, Paul			FA	PHD		78.	Colorado	&
Muntoro, Ronny		Indonesia		PHD		86.	S Calif	
Murdoch, Alastair J.			X	PHD		92.	U Wash	&
Murdoch, Brock G.	Prof	CS-Chico	FT	PHD		84.	Ca-Irvine	& 9-85
Murdock, Richard J.	Assoc	Ohio State	FK	PHD		77.	Cornell	&1974
Murir, Rahat	ALect	Macquarie Un						
Murphy, Ann B.	Assoc	Metro State	CM	PHD		96.	Arkansas	* 1-02
Murphy, Brian	Lect	U Wollongong	OU	MCOM			CSU	&2004
Murphy, Brid	Lect	Dublin City	AEM	MACC		95	NUI	&2002
Murphy, Daniel P.	H-Pr	Tennessee	X	PHD		90.	N Carol	& 8-90
Deloitte & Touche Professor								
Murphy, David S.	C-Ac	Lynchburg	AFGI	PHD		89.	Wash St	& 8-02
Murphy, Dennis M.	Prof	CS-L Angeles	XFM	MBA		65	Michigan	&1975
Murphy, Elizabeth A.	Assoc	DePaul	FTVR	PHD		95.	Kentucky	&1994
Murphy, George J.	Retir	Saskatchawan	1994	PHD		70.	Mich St	&1962
4817 Sea Ridge Drive; Victoria BC, Canada V8Y 3B6								
Murphy, John A. D.	Assoc	Palm Bch CC	MXS	PHD		91.	Fla Atl	8-87
Murphy, K.	Assoc	Univ Ulster	XF	MBA				& 1-04
Murphy, Kevin E.	Assoc	Oklahoma St	X	PHD		83.	Wisconsin	&1981
Murphy, Pam	Asst	Queen's Univ	AF	PHD		07	Wisconsin	2007
Murphy, Roger P.	Retir	Iowa State	2002	MS		69	Colo St	&1969
Murphy, William J. F.	Retir	So New Hamp	2005	MA		70	Rhode Isl	& 9-75
Murray, Dennis F.	Prof	Colo-Denver	FB	PHD		81.	Mass	&1983
Murray, Molly	Retir	Colorado St	D-89	MS		53	Wyoming	1966
Murray, Sister Mary Jude	Retir	St Joseph	2000	MBA			Suffolk	1972
Murray-Jackson, Lynda H.	Assoc	Goldey-Beacm	FX	PHD		97.	Temple	& 8-02
Murrell, F. Anthony	Lect	CUNY-Lehman						&1994
Murtaza, Mirza			SM	PHD		92.	Houston	
Murthy, Uday S.	Prof	South Fla	ASD	PHD		89.	Indiana	& 8-02
Jim and Leacy Quinn Eminent Scholar Chair								
Murtuza, M. Athar (Art)	Assoc	Seton Hall	BCEH	PHD		77	Wash St	* 1988
Musa, G.	SLect	London Metro	D	MA				1989
Musazi, Buagu	Asst	Florida A&M	X	PHD		97	Wayne St	&2006
Muse, Judith E.			F	PHD		64.	LSU	&
Musigchai, Chatchwed		Gov Off-Thai		DBA		65.	S Calif	
Muslu, Volkan	Asst	Texas-Dallas	FI	PHD		05.	MIT	2005
Musser, Thomas H.	Prof	DePauw	FM	MA		80	Arizona	&2001
Mustafa, Sameer	Asst	Concordia U	AM	PHD		03	Clev St	2001
Mutchler, Jane F.	Prof	Georgia St	A	PHD		83.	Illinois	& 7-99
J. W. Holloway/Ernst & Young Professor; Associate Dean								
Muzatko, Steven R.	Asst	WI-Green Bay	FA	PHD		00.	Wisconsin	8-99
Mwaura, Muroki	Assoc	Wm Paterson	FM	PHD		94	Illinois	1994
Myers, Adam	SLect	Texas A&M	PX	JD		85	Harvard	9-07
Myers, Gerald M.	Prof	Pacific Luth	MC	PHD		84.	Iowa	1982
Myers, James N.	Assoc	Texas A&M	F	PHD		97.	Michigan	8-05
Myers, Joan K.	Assoc	LeMoyne	CFMP	PHD		93.	Syracuse	& 9-89
Myers, John H.	Deces	Indiana	1994	PHD		43	Nrthwstrn	&1968
Myers, Jon W.	C-Ac	Woodbury	ACFP	MBA		60	Berkeley	& 3-83
Myers, Linda A.	Asst	Texas A&M	AF	PHD		01.	Michigan	8-05
PricewaterhouseCoopers Faculty Fellow								
Myers, Louis A. Jr.	Retir	Arizona	1984	MS		50	Arizona	1948
Myers, Mary D.	C-Pr	Shippensburg	CFMV	PHD		88.	Maryland	&1985

Name	Rank	School	Code	Degree	Yr	School	Misc
Myers, Patricia M.	Assoc	Brock Univ	AOSE	PHD	95.	Arizona	&2003
Mykleburst, Harold N.	Deces	So Colorado	2-86	PHD	75.	American	&1985
Mynatt, Patricia G.			FQT	PHD	89.	N Carol	&
Myring, Mark J.	Assoc	Ball State	FS	PHD	01.	Kent St	8-00
George and Franaes Ball Distinguished Professor of Accounting							
Myrtle, Jamie	Assoc	MidAmer Naz	U	MBA		Kansas	&2001
Na'im, Ainun		Gadgahmada U		PHD	96.	Temple	
Na, Chongkil	Asst	U Ulsan-Kore	FM	PHD	93.	Wash St	1-94
Univ of Ulsan; Ulsan, Kyunghan, S Korea; 522-78-2807							
Na, Young	Assoc	Chung-Ang	CPQT	PHD	93.	Rutgers	1993
Nabar, Sandeep M.	Asst	Oklahoma St	FM	PHD	97.	Tx-Austin	8-02
Nabors, Carl W.	Retir	Mississippi	1992	MBA	52	Miss	&1961
Nabulsi, Mahmound	Inst	Jackson St	GM	MPA	86	JacksonSt	&2004
Naciri, M. Ahmed	C-Pr	Quebec-Montr	M	PHD		Laval	8-82
Nagar, Venkatesh (Venky)	Asst	Michigan	M	PHD	99	Penn	1998
Auerbach Faculty Fellow							
Nagarajan, Nandu J.	Prof	Pittsburgh	CMY	PHD	84.	Nrthwstrn	* 1-84
Nagell, Terje	SLect	Norwegian U	A				
Naggar, Ali K.	Prof	West Chester	XC	PHD	75.	Oklahoma	9-77
Nagle, Brian M.	Assoc	Duquesne	AFN	PHD	94.	St Louis	&1993
Nagoda, Robert J.	Assoc	Webber Coll	XFJS	PHD	82.	Arizona	1997
Nagy, Albert L.	Assoc	John Carroll	APF	PHD	99.	Tennessee	&8-99
Nagy, Charles F.	Retir	Cleveland St	1993	PHD	59.	Alabama	&1968
Nagy, Judy	Lect	Deakin-Burwo	M	BCOM	80	Melbourne	&1998
Nahartyo, Ertambang				PHD	03.	Kentucky	
Gadjah Mada University							
Naidoo, Krish	Lect	U Newcastle		BCOM	84	S Africa	2004
Nainar, S. M. Khalid	Prof	McMaster Un	FZJI	PHD	89	Florida	7-88
Nair, R. D.	Prof	Wisconsin	F	PHD	77.	Michigan	& 1-78
PricewaterhouseCoopers Professor of Accounting							
Nakamura, Tadashi	Retir	Hitotsubashi	1994	DBA		Hitotsub	&1970
Nalepka, William T.	Assoc	Adrian	PXDC	MBA	76	E Mich	&8-96
Nam, Sang-Oh	Prof	Seoul Natl	FMA	PHD	81	Seoul Natl	&1974
Nam, Seungham	Asst	Korea Adv In		PHD	05.	NYU	
Nam, Young Ho	Asst	Kookmin Univ	CMNU	PHD	90.	Mich St	1996
Namazi, Mohammad		Shiraz-Iran	MF	PHD	83.	Nebraska	
Nammer, Helmi M.				PHD	57.	Illinois	
Nan, Lin	Asst	Carnegie Mel	FY	PHD	04.	Florida	2004
Nanayakkara, Gemunu	ALect	Griffith Un	CMN	MBA	99	USQ	2001
Nance, Jon R.	Retir	SW Missouri	5-02	PHD	81.	Georgia	* &8-86
Nance, Michelle	Inst	NW Missouri	FP	MBA	03	NW Mo St	2004
Nanda, Dhananjay (DJ)	Assoc	Duke	M	PHD	97	Rochester	7-02
Nanni, Alfred J. Jr.	C-Pr	Babson	UBMC	PHD	81.	Mass	1993
Naoum, Christos		Univ Pizaeus	1996	PHD	77.	Penn St	
Pireaus Grad Sch Bus Studies; 40 Karaoli & Dimitriou; Pireaus 185 32 Greece							
Naples, Gregory J.	Assoc	Marquette	XLI	LLM	83	DePaul	1984
Narasimhan, Ramesh	Assoc	Montclair St	ABIO	PHD	88.	Va Tech	# * &8-98
Narayan, Venkat	Lect	Macquarie Un	MUF	BCOM	02	Macquarie	2003
Narayanamoorthy, Ganapathi	Asst	Illinois	F	PHD	02.	Rochester	1-07
Narayanan, V. G.	Prof	Harvard	MF	PHD	96.	Stanford	1994
Narayanaswamy, Sivakumar				PHD	89.	Rice	
Narktabtee, Kanogporn	Asst	Kasetsart U	2001	PHD	00.	Arkansas	2000
Bangkok, Thailand							
Narumanchi, Radha R. M.	Assoc	So Conn St	CAFT	MBA	74	CUNY	* &1977
Narz, Marvin J.	Assoc	Montevallo	XLF	LLM	89	Alabama	&1978
Naser-Tavakolian, Mohsen	Prof	San Fran St	FMS	PHD	80.	Missouri	* 1978
Nash, Claire Y.	C-Ac	Christian Br	XMF	PHD	99.	Miss	&1998
Nash, John F.	Retir	East Tenn St	2002	PHD	64	London	1982
Nash, Joseph V.			1991	PHD	73.	UCLA	
279 S Beverly Dr #1195; Beverly Hill CA 90212							
Nasralla, Ali	Lect	U Manchester	M	BA	72	Baghdad	&1985
Nassiripour, Sia	Assoc	Wm Paterson	CF	PHD	93.	Wash St	&2001
Natan, R.	Lect	London Metro	FM	BA			2001
Natarajan, Ashok	Lect	CS-Pomona	FM	PHD	02.	Ca-Irvine	2004
Natarajan, Ram	Assoc	Texas-Dallas	MCS	PHD	92.	Penn	1998
Nath, N.	Lect	Massey Univ		MA			2003
Nathan, Edward C.	VAsst	Houston	FB	PHD	81.	Tx-Austin	&1980
Nathan, Kevin S.			MF	PHD	84.	Oregon	
Nathan, Siva	Assoc	Georgia St	FT	PHD	88.	SUNY-Buf	9-93
Natho, Kermit C. Jr.	Retir	Georgia St	2001	PHD	70.	LSU	& 9-66
Natovich, Joseph			AS	PHD	96.	Rutgers	&
Naud, Marjolaine	Assoc	HEC-Montreal	FXW	MFIS	90	Sherbrooke	&6-92
Naulleau, Gerard	Prof	ESCP deParis	CEMU	PHD	90	EHESS	1986
Ndlovu, S.	Lect	Un Zimbabwe	C	MBL			
Ndubizu, Gordian A.	Prof	Drexel	FI	PHD	85.	Temple	1-87
Neal, David	Lect	North Wales	BIF	BA	80	Leeds	9-94

Name	Rank	School					
Neal, George H.	Retir	Univ Windsor	1991	DBA	71.	Mich St	1970
595 Barrington Road; Grosse Pointe Park MI 48230							
Neal, Philip G.	Asst	NE Illinois	XL	JD	78	S Illinois	& 9-89
Neal, Terry L.	Assoc	Tennessee	A	PHD	98.	Tennessee	& 8-03
William & Sara Clark Professor							
Nearing, Dudley W.	Retir	Pace	1994	MBA	49	Dartmouth	& 6-73
Nedri, Bechir	Inst	Univ Tunis	F	EXPC	97	ISCAE	1999
Nee, Laura M.	Lect	Denver	FM	MACC	01	Denver	&2007
Needham, Robert A.	Assoc	Bucknell	FM	MS	79	Youngstwn	& 9-94
Needles, Belverd E. Jr.	Prof	DePaul	AFI	PHD	69.	Illinois	* &1978
Ernst & Young Alumni Distinguished Professor							
Neeley, L. Paden	Retir	North Texas	2000	PHD	61.	Arkansas	&1960
Neeraj, Mittal		India		PHD	04.	Ohio St	
Public Serivde in Indian							
Neffinger, George G.	Retir	Clark Atlant	1991	PHD	70.	Maryland	& 9-71
Nefzaoui, Ali	Asst	Univ Tunis	VR	EXPC		IHEC	
Nehari-Talet, Amine	Asst	King Fahd Un	MIS	PHD	02	Tlemcen	2001
Nehdi, Bechir	Inst	Univ Tunis	C	EXPC			
Nehmer, Robert A.	Asst	Oakland	FMS	PHD	88.	Illinois	2005
Neidermeyer, Adolph A. (Ade)	Prof	W Virginia	FX	PHD	74.	Iowa	1971
Neidermeyer, Presha E.	Assoc	Union	ABI	PHD	97	Va Comm	& 9-96
Neidert, Kalo E.	Retir	Nevada-Reno	1990	MSBA	50	Wash U	&1962
Neill, John D. III	Prof	Abilene Chr	FAV	PHD	90.	Florida	& 8-00
Neilson, Denis P.	Prof	San Francisc	SM	PHD	74.	Berkeley	& 9-80
Neimark, Marilyn D.	Prof	CUNY-Baruch	PS	PHD	83	NYU	1983
Nekrasz, Frank Jr.	Lect	Illinois	A	PHD	93.	Illinois	& 8-99
Nellen, Annette	Prof	San Jose St	XP	JD	87	Loyola	& 5-90
Nelms, Linda L.	Prof	N Car-Ashvil	CSMP	MBA	78	N Carol	* & 8-78
Nelsestuen, Linda B.	Assoc	Tampa	XCM	PHD	96.	S Fla	* & 8-06
Nelson, A. Tom	Retir	Utah	1998	PHD	62.	Mich St	&1962
Nelson, Carl L.	Retir	Cal-Santa Br	1994	PHD	44.	Minnesota	&1984
Nelson, Clifford	Asst	Connecticut	MS	DBA	63	Illinois	8-97
Nelson, Donald A.	Assoc	Merrimack	KM	MS	71	Mass	&1975
Nelson, Douglas	Retir	Augustana SD	FMXL	JD	74	Iowa	&1992
Nelson, Edwin R.	Inst	New Hampshir	AFM	ABD		Boston U	# * &1994
Nelson, G. Kenneth	Deces	Penn State	1996	PHD	53.	Illinois	&1950
Nelson, Irvin T.	Assoc	Utah State	CEFT	PHD	92.	Nebraska	&1992
Nelson, Jacob			F	PHD	92.	Wash U	
Nelson, John	Retir	Luther	5-98	MBA	65	Iowa	&1992
Nelson, Karen K.	Assoc	Rice	F	PHD	96.	Michigan	2003
Nelson, Mark W.	Prof	Cornell	FBA	PHD	90.	Ohio St	& 7-90
Eleanora and George Landew Professor of Management							
Nelson, Martha K.	Assoc	Frank & Mars	MBCF	PHD	90.	Pittsburgh	& 1-91
Nelson, Ramona F.	Prof	Luther	AFX	MBT	85	Minnesota	& 9-90
Nelson, Toni L.	Assoc	U Lethbridge	EFMQ	PHD	92.	Oregon	&1990
Nemrow, Norman R.	Prof	Brigham Yg	F	MACC	79	Brighm Yg	9-92
Neslund, Kristofer	Assoc	Golden Gate	XKF	LLM	85	NYU	&2005
Ness, Lee J.	Retir	North Dakota	LX	LLM	86	Denver	& 6-86
Nestor, Joseph M.	Retir	Rutgers-Newk	1994	MBA	75	Baruch	1975
Nethercott, Leslie J.	Assoc	Monash Univ	FX	MEC			&1970
Neu, Dean	Prof	Univ Calgary	B	PHD	89	Queen's	&1989
Future Fund Professor of Accounting; Director, Centre for Public Interest Atg							
Neubig, Robert D.	Deces	W Michigan	9-04	PHD	61.	Ohio St	&1967
Neumann, Bruce R.	D-Pr	Colo-Denver	MNCB	PHD	75.	Illinois	1984
Neumann, Frederick L.	Emer	Illinois	2002	PHD	67.	Chicago	# &1965
Neumann, Reuben	Retir	Nev-L Vegas	1993	PHD	74.	Ariz St	&1962
Neurath, James H.	Inst	Cen Michigan	PX	MS	84	Cen Mich	&1984
Nevicky, Barbara	Lect	Macquarie Un	MFS	BCOM	02	Macquarie	2003
Neville, Joyce Jeannine				DBA	73.	Colorado	
Newberry, Kaye J.	Prof	Houston	X	PHD	94.	Ariz St	& 9-05
C. T. Bauer Professor							
Newberry, Susan	AProf	Univ Sydney	FG	PHD	02	Canterbu	2005
Newby, Rick	Lect	W Australia	F	MPHL	96	Murdoch	2001
Newcombe, Leo	Retir	DePaul	1990	MBA	47	Michigan	&1979
Newell, Deborah	Asst	Union-TN		MBA	81	Murray St	1988
Newell, Gale E.	Retir	W Michigan	2004	PHD	68.	Mich St	* 1968
Newell, Randall	Asst	Adams State		DBA		Nova SE	&
Newhouse, Benjamin	Prof	N Carol Cen	AF	PHD	82.	Michigan	&2004
Newhouse, Bertha S.	Retir	CUNY-Baruch	1985	MS	39	Columbia	&1945
Newlove, George H.	Deces	Texas	1984	PHD		Illinois	
Newman, Bernard H.	Prof	Pace	AVGN	PHD	66	NYU	&1975
Newman, D. Paul	Prof	Texas-Austin	FT	PHD	77.	Tx-Austin	9-77
Clark W. Thompson Jr., Chair of Accounting Education							
Newman, Harry A.	Assoc	Fordham	CM	PHD	84.	Nrthwstrn	1995
Newman, Leslie	Lect	Napier Univ	M	BSC			* 3-81
Newman, Maurice S.	Retir	Alabama	1987	PHD	72	NYU	* & 1-77
38 Ridgeland; Tuscaloosa AL 35406							

Name	Rank	School	Field	Degree	Yr	Degree School	
Newman, Michael	VAsst	Houston	FMX	MBA	00	Houston	9-06
Newman, Michael	Read	U Manchester	DMS	PHD		Bcolom	1981
Newman, Monica D.	C-Pr	Western St	XPCT	PHD	88.	Tx-Austin	&1990
Newman, Scott G.	Prof	Western St	PFVR	PHD	86.	Tx-Austin	&1989
Newmark, Richard I.	D-Ac	No Colorado	PXSE	PHD	96.	U Miami	&2001
Newton, David	Lect	U Manchester	F	PHD	79	Salford	1990
Newton, Grant W.	Retir	Pepper-Malib	2001	PHD	74.	NYU	* &1984
Newton, James D.			FMT	PHD	72.	U Wash	
Newton, Sherwood W.	Retir	Kansas	1978	MBA	52	Kansas	&1953
Neyer, Stanley R.	Retir	Elizabethtwn	5-98	MBA	76	Shippensb	& 9-64
Neyhart, Charles A.	Retir	Oregon State	2002	PHD	73.	Penn St	1973
Ng, Andy	TFell	Chinese HK	AF	MBA	82	Ottawa	&1991
Ng, Bu Peow	Assoc	Nanyang Tech	AB	PHD	03	Nanyang	&1993
Ng, Chew	C-Pr	Griffith Un	BFT	PHD	93	Melbourne	&1995
Ng, David S. P.		Hong Kong	FM	PHD	75.	Berkeley	
Ng, Eng Juan	Assoc	Nanyang Tech	CM	MBA	78	S Calif	&1987
Ng, Hock Guan	SLect	W Australia	Q	PHD		Stanford	1999
Ng, Juliana	SLect	W Australia	AM	PHD	95	W Austrl	&1996
Ngoc, Le Thi Bich	Asst	Natl Econ	FPTM	MBA	95	Boise St	1988
Nguyen, Loc T.	Assoc	CS-Long Bch	FXI	MST	89	SanDiego	&1986
Nibbelin, Michael C.		State Farm	CDMS	PHD	88.	Fla St	* &
State Farm; Bloomington, Illinois							
Nicholas, Lee H.	Retir	No Iowa	M	MBA	70	Tulsa	* &1974
Nichols, Alice B.	Retir	Florida St	D-93	MS	54	Illinois	&1956
3386 Lakeshore Dr; Tallahassee Florida 32312; 850-385-9218							
Nichols, D. Craig	Asst	Cornell	F	PHD	05.	Indiana	2005
Nichols, Dave Leroy	Assoc	Mississippi	FA	PHD	92.	Okla St	& 1-91
Nichols, David L.				PHD	78.	Arkansas	&
Nichols, Donald R.	Prof	Tx Christian	AF	PHD	70.	Oklahoma	&1984
Nichols, Gerald E.	Retir	CS-Stanislau	1993	PHD	67.	LSU	&1984
Nichols, Linda M.	D-Pr	Texas Tech	FZA	PHD	89.	LSU	& 7-89
Nichols, Nancy B.	Assoc	Jms Madison	X	PHD	97.	North Tx	& 9-97
Deloitte & Touche Faculty Fellow							
Nichols, Richard L.	Retir	SW Missouri	2000	PHD	80.	Arkansas	8-74
Nichols, William D.	Prof	Notre Dame	F	DBA	78.	Fla St	& 9-77
Nicholson, Brian	Lect	U Manchester	BDW	PHD		Salford	1999
Nicholson, John T.	Deces	W Ontario	8-80	DBA	63.	Harvard	1953
Nickerson, Charles A.	Retir	Fla Internat	1991	PHD	71.	Georgia	&1980
Nickerson, Clarence B.	Retir	Harvard		DCS	35.	Harvard	1930
Nicol, Robert E. G.	Retir	U Melbourne	1998	PHD	69.	UCLA	
Nicolaou, Andreas I.	Assoc	Bowling Gr	MS	DBA	93.	S Illinois	&2000
Niece, Jennifer M.	Asst	Assumption	CPS	MBA	98	Boston C	&2001
Nielsen, Gordon L.	Retir	Tulsa	8-95	PHD	67.	Tx-Austin	& 9-77
Nielsen, Mogens	Assoc	U So Denmark	TF	PHD	86	Odense	1983
Nielsen, Oswald	Deces	Stanford		PHD	36.	Minnesota	1948
Niemann, Ranier	Prof	Univ Graz	FX	PHD	04	Tuebingen	2004
Niemeyer, Ronald D.	Prof	Cen Missouri	PVT	DBA	74.	Miss St	1980
Niemi, Lasse	Res	Helsinki Sch	A	MS	96	Helsinki	1996
Nieminsky, Arthur C.	Retir	CS-Northrdge	1988	PHD	75.	UCLA	1967
Nieschwietz, Robert J.	Asst	Colo-Denver	FA	PHD	01.	Ariz St	& 8-01
Nieuw Ammerongen, Niels van	Lect	Vrije Univ	AB	MS	95	Vrije	2000
Nigrini, Mark J.	Asst	St Michaels	CX	PHD	93.	Cincinnati	&
Nikias, Anthony D.	Asst	Tx A&M-Kings	MPS	PHD	02.	Ohio St	2005
Nikitkov, Alexia	Asst	Brock Univ	SM	PHD	04.	Missouri	8-04
Nikolai, Loren A.	Prof	Missouri	F	PHD	73.	Minnesota	&1976
Ernst & Young Professor							
Niles, Marcia S.	Retir	Idaho	FA	PHD	84.	U Wash	&1991
Nilsson, Henrik	Asst	Univ of Umea	FT	PHD	03	Umea	8-95
Nilsson, Stellan	Assoc	Univ of Umea	AF	LIPH	95	Umea	9-90
Nindi, Nitham	Assoc	Miles Coll	FM	DBA	91.	Miss St	1991
Nini, Eugene A.	Retir	Txs-Perm Bas	1996	PHD	66.	LSU	&1973
Ninsuvannakul, Pianchai				PHD	68.	Illinois	
Ninsuvannakul, Prawit	Retir	Chulalongkor	AFM	PHD	74.	Illinois	&1981
Nisiotis, George	VAsst	Cyprus	FQ	PHD	99	Nrthwstrn	2001
Nissan, Samir I.	Prof	CS-Chico	IVFM	PHD	71	Illinois	& 9-80
Nissim, Doron	C-Ac	Columbia	F	PHD	98.	Berkeley	1997
Nissing, Burton J.	Retir	St Louis	1996	PHD	76.	St Louis	& 7-76
Niswander, Frederick D.	Dean	East Carol	FI	PHD	93.	Tx A&M	&1993
Niswonger, C. Rollin	Deces	Miami U-Ohio	2-80	PHD	50.	Ohio St	1935
Nitkin, Mindell	Asst	Simmons	F	DBA	06.	Boston U	9-06
Nitta, Tadachika	Prof	Hitotsubashi	FA	DBA	87	Hitotsub	1994
Nitterhouse, Denise	Assoc	DePaul	SBN	DBA	81.	Harvard	1985
Niu, Flora	Asst	Wilfrid Laur	F	PHD	04	Waterloo	2003
Nix, Harold M.	Retir	Bradley	2000	PHD	74.	Okla St	* & 8-86
Nix, Paul E.	Retir	Montana St	2003	PHD	77.	North Tx	& 9-72
Nix, Wayne E.	Asst	Miss College	AFPS	DBA	95.	Miss St	&2004
Nixon, Bill	Prof	Dundee	MBSC	PHD	95	Dundee	&1982

Nixon, Clair J.	Prof	Texas A&M	X	PHD	80	Tx A&M		&9-80
PricewaterhouseCoopers Professor								
Nixon, Mark R.	C-Ac	Bentley	X	PHD	95.	Tx A&M		&1993
Njoroge, Joyce	Asst	Drake	FM	PHD	01.	Wash St		2000
Nobes, Christopher W.	Prll	Norwegian Mg	FI	PHD	83	Exeter		2003
Noble, Paul E.	Retir	U Miami	1989	PHD	52.	Ohio St		&1980
Nodoushani, Patricia	Prof	Hartford	X	PHD	87.	Houston		&1995
Noe, Christopher F.		Charles Rive	2004	PHD	96.	Rochester		
Charles River Associates Inc.								
Noel, James C.			MA	PHD	81.	Ohio St		
Noel, Roger	Dean	Sherbrooke	FR	MS	70	Sherbrook		&
Noga, Tracy J.	Asst	Bentley	X	PHD	01.	Tx Tech		&2005
Nogara, Carmine	Asst	St Fran-NY	FGSV	MBA	93	St Johns		&2002
Nogler, George E.	Assoc	Mass-Lowell	AF	DBA	87.	Boston U		&2001
Nohl, Thomas	C-As	Intl College	POA	MS	89	Wisconsin		&1996
Noke, Christopher	SLect	London Econ	FH	MSC	78	London		&1976
Noland, Thomas G.	Assoc	Geo Southern	A	PHD	00.	Miss	*	&2002
Noland, Thomas R.	Assoc	Houston	F	PHD	92.	Illinois		&9-92
Nolder, Christine	Inst	Bentley	F	MBA	01	Bentley		&2005
Nondorf, Maria E.	Asst	Cal-Berkeley	F	PHD	03.	N Carol		2003
Nordhauser, Fred	Retir	Tx-S Antonio	2003	PHD	71	Purdue		&9-79
Nordhauser, Susan L.	Retir	Tx-S Antonio	2003	PHD	78.	Tx-Austin	*	&1978
Noreen, Eric W.	Emer	U Washington	2005	PHD	77.	Stanford		1976
Norgaard, Corine T.	Retir	Hartford	2004	PHD	65.	Tx-Austin		&1996
Norman, Carolyn Strand	Assoc	Virg Comm	SM	PHD	98.	Tx A&M		&2002
Normand, Carol J.	Assoc	Wis-Whitewat	MS	EDD	98	N Illinois		&2002
Norris, Barbara	Asst	Johnson&Wale	DP	MBA	88	Bryant		2001
Norris, Daniel M.			AS	PHD	82.	Missouri	# *	&
Norris, Gweneth	SLect	Deakin-Geelg	BCM	MCOM	93	Deakin		&1983
Norris, Kathleen B.			F	PHD	93.	Oklahoma		
Norstrom, Carl J.	Emer	Norwegian U	2004	DOEC				
Northcut, W. Dana			F	PHD	94.	S Calif		&
Northrup, Richard V.	Retir	Ohio State	1989	MA	47	Ohio St		1956
Northup, Michael	Inst	NW Missouri	FP	MS	88	Mo-Ks Cty		&1999
Norton, Arthur J.	Retir	Cen Missouri	6-93	PHD	73.	Missouri		&1965
Norton, Curtis L.	Emer	No Illinois	2005	PHD	76.	Ariz St		9-76
Norton, David P.		Industry		DBA	72.	Harvard		
Norton, Simon	Lect	Cardiff U	AFI	PHD		Cardiff		1996
Norvelle, Joan W.	Retir	Arizona	1996	PHD	78	Arizona		1978
Norwood, Fred W.	Retir	Txs-El Paso	1985	PHD	52.	Tx-Austin		&9-80
Nosari, John S.	Retir	Il-Springfld	2005	PHD	84.	St Louis		&1978
Nourallah, Fayez S.		Prac-El Paso		PHD	66.	Illinois		1-79
Nourayi, Mahmoud M.	Prof	Loyola Marym	MCQ	PHD	89.	S Calif	*	&9-87
Nouri, Hossein	C-Pr	C New Jersey	ABF	PHD	92.	Temple		1992
Novack, Garth	Asst	Utah State	XF	PHD	03.	Arizona		8-03
Novak, E. Shawn	Assoc	Boise State	PXR	PHD	91.	Houston		&9-96
Novin, Adel M.	Asst	Clayton St	SCMG	PHD	82.	Georgia		8-01
Nowlin, Tanya S.			FM	PHD	99.	LSU		&
Noxon, George	C-As	High Point	ACFJ	MBA		Tulane		&1993
Nugent, David A.	Assoc	Slippery Roc		PHD	92.	Pittsburgh		&2007
Nunamaker, Thomas R.	Assoc	Wash State	FN	PHD	83.	Wisconsin		&1982
Nunez, Karen R.	Asst	N Carol St	CFM	PHD	02.	Oklahoma	*	2001
Nunley, Terry J.	Retir	N Car-Charl	2000	PHD	83.	Alabama		&1984
Nunn, George E.	Deces			DBA	53.	Indiana		
Nunthirapakorn, Ted	Lect	Natl Inst Dv	1998	PHD	84.	Arkansas		1988
National Institute of Development Adm; Bangkok Thailand								
Nurnberg, Hugo	Prof	CUNY-Baruch	FMT	PHD	68.	Columbia		&1980
Nutter, David E.			FA	DBA	74.	S Calif		&
Nutter, Sarah E.	C-Ac	George Mason	FMX	PHD	93.	Mich St		1995
Nwaeze, Emeka T.	Assoc	Tx-S Antonio	CMF	PHD	92.	Conn		8-06
Nyaboga, Andrew	Assoc	Wm Paterson	SFM	PHD	00	Stevens		1996
Nyadroh, Emmanuel M. K.	Asst	NE Illinois	FM	PHD	81.	Nrthwstrn		9-87
Nycum, Vicki L.			FT	PHD	85.	Nebraska		&
Nye, Cynthia	Assoc	Bellevue	MC	MS	84	S Calif	*	&1995
Nyunt, Khin Ohn Thant				PHD	67.	Wisconsin		
O'hOgartaigh, Ciaran	SLect	Dublin City	BFHI	PHD	97	Leeds		&1992
O'Brien, Ann D.	Lect	Wisconsin	FX	MBA	85	Tx-Austin		&1999
O'Brien, Francis J.	Retir	Un Cl Dublin	FI	PHD	78.	Pittsburgh		&1970
O'Brien, John R.	Assoc	Carnegie Mel	FM	PHD	85.	Minnesota		1984
O'Brien, John T.	Retir	Staten Isl	1988	MBA	51	NYU		1963
O'Brien, Marcia L.	Asst	Roberts Wesl	MPJ	MBA	90	Rochester		2002
O'Brien, Patricia C.	Prof	Un Waterloo	FIK	PHD	85.	Chicago		&2000
Ernst & Young Professor								
O'Brien, Paul	Lect	U Queensland	S	BSC	90	Queenslnd		2000
O'Brien, Paul R.	Retir	Governors St	XCM	PHD	78	Ill Tech		&1982
O'Brien, William	Lect	Santa Clara	FM	MBA	79	Pepperdi		&1992
O'Bryan, David W.	Prof	Pittsburg St	FU	PHD	92.	Missouri	*	&1992

O'Callaghan, Susanne	Assoc	Pace	AVGN	PHD	94.	Cincinnati	&9-94
O'Clock, Priscilla M.	Prof	Xavier	BMX	PHD	91.	Nebraska	&1992
O'Connell, Brendan T.	Assoc	Deakin-Geelg	F	PHD	99	Monash	&2002
O'Connell, James P.	Emer	Massachusett	1994	JD	73	W New Eng	&9-65
O'Connell, John D.	Assoc	Holy Cross	FVX	MBA	58	Boston U	&9-57
O'Connor, Debra	Asst	Holy Cross	FX	PHD	06	Mass	8-06
O'Connor, Eugene	Assoc	Canisius	LX	JD	59	SUNY-Buf	1976
O'Connor, John T.	Prof	Worcester Pl	FM	PHD	70	Notre Dm	1986
O'Connor, Melvin C.	Retir	Michigan St	2001	PHD	71.	Kansas	&1970
O'Connor, Neale G.	Assoc	Un Hong Kong	CM	PHD	96	Griffith	2006
O'Connor, W.	SLect	Un East Lond	F	MSC			1986
O'Connor, Walter F.	C-Pr	Fordham	XI	PHD	76.	Baruch	&9-87
O'Dea, William A.	Lect	Un Cl Dublin	CM	MCOM	80	Dublin	* 1991
O'Dell, Michael A.	Retir	Arizona St	2005	PHD	80.	Tx-Austin	&1980
O'Doherty, Brian A.	Assoc	East Carol	M	PHD	78.	Florida	1984
O'Donnell, Edward F.	Asst	Kansas	A	PHD	95.	North Tx	&2006
O'Donnell, Joseph B.	Asst	Niagara	AS	PHD	02	SUNY-Buf	2007
O'Donovan, Gary	C-Ac	Un Tasmania		PHD		Victoria	&2003
O'Grady, Winnie	Lect	9900ckland	BMS	MBS	93	Massey	2000
O'Hanlon, John F.	H-Pr	U Lancaster	F	MA	84	Lancaster	&1984
O'Keefe, Daniel E.	Deces	North Fla	1993	DBA	72.	Miss St	&1981
O'Keefe, Herbert A. Jr.	Retir	Geo Southern	1997	PHD	74.	Geo St	&1978
O'Keefe, Ruth R.	Prof	Jacksonvil U	LX	JD	79	SUNY-Buf	&1982
O'Keefe, Terrence D.	Prof	Oregon	AF	PHD	70	Purdue	1980
also Professor at University of Queensland							
O'Keefe, W. Timothy	Prof	West Florida	CM	DBA	78.	Fla St	&1998
O'Kelly, Peggy	Lect	Northeastern	AFV	MS	74	Northeas	&9-81
O'Leary, Connor	Lect	Queensld Tec	AO	MBUS	93	Queensld	&6-89
O'Leary, Daniel E.	Prof	So Calif	S	PHD	86.	Case Wes	# * &9-85
Elaine and Kenneth Leventhal Research Fellow							
O'Leary, Ted	Prof	U Manchester	BCH	PHD	83	Warwick	2001
O'Mara, Daniel J.	Assoc	Villanova	TF	MBA	71	Fordham	&1976
O'Mara, Daniel J..	Retir	Quinnipiac	1998	BS	61	Quinnipi	&1968
O'Meara, James W.	Prof	St John's-MN	CMXF	MS	71	Minnesota	&1974
O'Neil, Thomas J.	Retir	American Int	1997	MBA	66	Am Intl	&1967
O'Neill, Michael J.	C-As$	Gannon	MXJL	JD	83	Syracuse	* 1991
O'Neill, Sharron	SLect	W Sydney	BFJM	MCOM	02	NS Wales	&1996
O'Reilly, Dennis M.			FA	PHD	00.	S Carol	&
O'Reilly, Vin	Exec	Boston Coll	HJI	MBA	59	Penn	&1997
O'Reilly-Allen, Margaret	C-Ac	Rider	F	PHD	97.	Drexel	&1997
O'Rouke, Joseph J.	Deces	Portland St		PHD	64.	U Wash	&1968
O'Shaughnessy, John	Prof	San Fran St	AFO	PHD	90	Golden Gt	# * &1982
O'Shaughnessy, Patrick R.	Retir	Central Wash	1999	MBA	59	Wash St	&9-64
O'Sullivan, Noel	Lect	Loughborough	FK	PHD	00	Nottingh	1994
O'Tousa, Janet L.	Spec	Notre Dame	FM	MBA	88	Notre Dm	2001
O, Sewon	Asst	Txs Southern	FM	PHD	01.	Miss St	&1-05
Oakes, Leslie S.	Assoc	New Mexico	FHN	PHD	88.	Wisconsin	1995
Oates, Lynn	Lect	Un Warwick		PHD	00	W Austrl	
Oatsvall, Rebecca J.	Prof	Meredith	XFP	PHD	78.	S Carol	1984
Obata, Hiroshi	C-Pr	Hitotsubashi	CM	DBA		Hitotsub	1987
Obersteiner, Erich	Retir	Cleveland St	1994	PHD	72	Columbia	1977
Ocariz, Jose	Emer	Univ Navarra	2004	DOCT		ETSIN	9-63
Ochu, Jean M.	Assoc	St John's-MN	PMF	MBA	74	St Cloud	&1982
Ockree, Kanalis A.	Assoc	Washburn	FTSM	PHD	93.	Kansas	* &8-85
Odaiyappa, Ramasamy	Assoc	Alcorn St	CMP	PHD	85.	Florida	2000
Oddo, Alfonso R.	C-Pr	Niagara	F	MBA		SUNY-Buf	&1973
Odedra, S.	SLect	London Metro	F	MSC			
Oden, Debra H.	Prof	Missouri St	X	LLM	81	Mo-Ks Cty	&8-89
Odmark, Vernon E.	Deces	San Diego St	1991	PHD	53.	Missouri	1952
Odom, Gary L.			CM	PHD	86.	S Carol	
Odom, Marcus Dean	D-Ac	So Illinois	ABOS	PHD	93.	Okla St	&5-98
Deloitte & Touche Faculty Fellow							
Oehlers, Peter F.	Asst	West Chester	SMPE	DBA	03.	La Tech	* &9-04
Oestreich, Nathan	Prof	San Diego St	X	PHD	81.	Houston	&1985
Offeren, Dick H. van	Asst	Un Amsterdam	INPT	MBA	78	Amsterdm	1979
Ofobike, Emeka	Assoc	Akron	FVI	PHD	84.	Oregon	* &9-89
Ogan, Pekin	Retir	Indiana	2000	PHD	74.	N Carol	1974
Ogazon, Agueda	Asst	St Thomas-FL	BEMN	EDD	96	Fla Intl	2002
Ogden, Judith	Asst	Clayton St	X	JD	79	Duquesne	8-04
Ogden, Stuart G.	Prof	U Manchester	MN	MA	71	Warwick	9-00
Ogilby, Suzanne M.	Prof	CS-Sacrament	IFGH	PHD	91.	Wisconsin	&1-90
Oglesbee, Thomas W. Jr.			AMS	PHD	83.	S Carol	
Oglesby, Rodney A.	Prof	Drury	CGS	PHD	91	Missouri	* 2002
Ogundele, Babatunde O.	H-Pr	U Ilorin	1992	PHD	70.	Illinois	1982
Univ of Ilorin; P M Bag 1515; Ilorin Nigeria; Abiola Endowed Professorship							
Ogunjim, Emmanuel O.				PHD	80.	Arkansas	
Oh, Joon-Whan	Asst	Univ Hongik	PF	PHD	95.	Va Comm	&1995

Ohene-Nyako, Eric	Asst	Alabama A&M	CPMF	MBA	82	Alab A&M		1983
Ohlson, James A.	Prof	Arizona St	FT	PHD	72.	Berkeley		2004
W. P. Carey Chair in Accountancy								
OhOgartaigh, Ciaran	Assoc	Victoria NZ		PHD		NUI		2006
Ohta, Yasuhiro	Asst	York-Atkinsn	F	PHD	03.	SUNY-Buf		2002
Oien, M. Burton	Retir	Alaska-Fairb	1993	PHD	76.	Oklahoma		&1980
Okamoto, Kiyoshi	Retir	Hitotsubashi	1993	DBA	64	Hitotsub		1961
Okcabol, Fahrettin			FM	PHD	89.	Baruch		
Okleshen, Marilyn	Assoc	Mn St-Mankat	CMP	PHD	91.	Nebraska		&1983
Okopny, D. Robert	Prof	E Michigan	IAO	PHD	85.	Tx A&M	# *	1988
Okpechi, Simeon O.			IM	PHD	76.	Ohio St		
Okunev, John	Prof	Macquarie Un	F	PHD	89	Aust Natl		&2005
Okyere, Kofi Appiah	Asst	Syracuse	F	PHD	05.	Wisconsin		2005
Olach, Thomas J.	Asst	Mn St-Mankat	AP	PHD	05.	Miss St		2005
Olds, Nanne	Asst	Nebraska Wes	PXM	MPA			*	&1999
Olds, Philip R.	Assoc	Virg Comm	F	PHD	82.	Geo St		&1981
Oler, Derek K.	Asst	Indiana	F	PHD	04.	Cornell		&7-04
Oler, Mitchell J.	Asst	Virg Tech		PHD	06.	U Wash		2007
Oleson, Michael D.	Deces	No Iowa	5-04	PHD	99.	Illinois		8-00
Oleyere, Peter	H-As	Sultan Qaboo		PHD		Queen's		
Olibe, Kingsley	Asst	Kansas State	F	PHD	99.	Tx A&M		8-07
Oliva, Robert R.	C-Pr	Ark-Ltl Rock	X	PHD	93	Fla Intl		&7-05
Oliva, Suzanne	Inst	St Marys-Tx	PXL	JD	96	St MryTX		&9-05
Olive, Franklin T.	Assoc	Manchester C	FGNP	MBA	80	Maryland		&1999
Olive, Russell W.	Retir	Northeastern	1996	DBA	67	Harvard		1970
Oliver, Bruce L.	Prof	Rochest Tech	FJV	PHD	69.	U Wash		9-85
Oliver, E. Eugene	Retir	Elon	1990	EDD	77	NC-Green		1981
Oliver, Elizabeth G.	H-Pr	Wash & Lee	F	PHD	92.	Tx A&M		&1991
Oliver, Joseph R.	Retir	Tx St-S Marc	2005	PHD	76.	Missouri	*	&1980
Oliver, Robert	Retir	SE Okla St	2001	PHD	74	Colo St		&1984
Oliver, Thomas W.	C-Pr	Clarion	FT	PHD	83.	Mass		8-92
Olivera, Herbert E.	Retir	Towson State	1996	PHD	75.	Arizona		&1988
Oliveras, Esster	Assoc	Pompeu Fabra		PHD	99	Lancashire		
Oliverio, Mary Ellen	Retir	Pace	2004	PHD	54	Columbia		&1980
Olliff, Edie A.	Inst	Geo Southern	P	MBA	98	Ga Srthrn		&1999
Olsavsky, John	Asst	SUNY-Fredoni	CDEF	MS	82	Rbt Morr		&1982
Olsberg, Michael D.	Asst	St Cloud St	P	MS	67	N Dakota		&1967
Olsen, Gary L.	Assoc	Carroll	SFAC	PHD	86	Marquette		&9-75
Olsen, J. Christian III			F	PHD	84.	Stanford		
Olsen, Lori			F	PHD	01.	Oklahoma		&
Olshewsky, Steven J.			PLX	PHD	04.	Tx A&M		
Olson, Angela	Inst	South Dakota	F	MPA	02	S Dakota		&2004
Olson, Carol A.			FX	PHD	89.	Florida		
Olson, David R.	Retir	Il-Springfld	GF	PHD	87.	Illinois		&1980
Olson, Gerald A.	Prof	Ill Wesleyan	AFVR	MS	86	Illin St		&9-86
Olson, Olov	Prll	Norwegian U	MG	DREK		Gothenbu		
Olson, Ronald L.		System Group		DBA	65.	Indiana		
Olson, Ronnie G.				PHD	74.	Ariz St		
Olson, Stevan K.	Prof	Missouri St	FMBN	PHD	74.	Wisconsin		&8-87
Olson, William			1992	PHD	87.	North Tx		
500 Mariah Bay Drive; Rockwall Tx 76087								
Olson, William C.	Assoc	Wagner	CMQ	MBA	73	Pace		&9-85
Olsson, Per M.	Assoc	Duke	F	PHD	98	Stockholm		7-01
Olsson, Rickard	Asst	Univ of Umea	FT	MSC	95	Umea		8-95
Oltikar, Pratima	Asst	Puerto RicoM	PCM	MBA	91	P Rico		&1-91
Oman, Patsy	Retir	Illinois St	1995	MS	70	Illin St		&1974
Omer, Khursheed	C-Pr	Houston-Down	MCS	DBA	90.	Memphis		&1991
Omer, Thomas C.	Prof	Texas A&M	X	PHD	86.	Iowa		8-05
Ernst & Young Professor								
Omonuk, Joseph Ben	Asst	Southern		ABD		LSU		
Omps, James R.	Retir	Hawaii-Manoa	1988	PHD	61.	Pittsburgh		&9-67
Omundson, Janet S.	Retir	Txs-El Paso	2000	MS	71	Miss		&9-79
Ong, April W. Y.	Inst	City Univ HK	FX	MA	03	CityU HK		&2005
Ong, Audra	Asst	Univ Windsor	FM	PHD	00	W England		2000
Onifade, Emmanuel O.	Assoc	Morehouse	MCBF	PHD	93.	S Carol		&1994
Onsi, Mohamed	Retir	Syracuse	MBNQ	PHD	64.	Illinois		9-66
Onyeocha, Joseph	Asst	So Carol St	FA	MBA	81	Wright St		&1987
Ophir, Tsvi	Assoc	Hebrew Univ	F	PHD	60.	MIT		1966
Opong, Kwaku K.	H-Pr	Univ Glasgow	F	PHD	89	Glasgow		2002
Oppegard, Anne M.	Assoc	Augustana SD	DEFT	PHD	97	Nebraska		&1988
Oppong, Andrews	Prof	Dalhousie	MT	PHD	76.	Iowa		1978
Orapin, Duangsamorn	Asst	Chulalongkor	F	MS	77	S Illinois		1978
Orbach, Kenneth N.	Prof	Fla Atlantic	X	PHD	78.	Tx A&M		&1990
Orchard, Lou X.	Asst	Wis-Eau Clar	FM	PHD	98.	Arizona		&8-07
Ormsby, Susan Young	Prof	S F Austin	CEMQ	PHD	82.	Arkansas		&1981
Orsini, Larry L.	Retir	St Bonaventu	2002	MBA	81	St Bonav		&1979
Ortega, William R.	Assoc	Winona State	MAC	PHD	95.	Fla St	*	2003

Ortegren, Alan K.	Prof	S Ill-Edward	FT	PHD	82.	Arkansas	&1982
Ortiz, Dennis S.	Asst	Tx-Brownsvil		PHD	00.	North Tx	1998
Ortiz, Eulalio	Prof	Puerto RicoM	CFMX	MBA	76	Syracuse	& 8-73
Ortman, Richard F.	Prof	Neb-Omaha	MCU	PHD	71.	Wisconsin	* & 8-79
Hockett Professor							
Orton, Bryce B.	Retir	Brigham Yg	1989	PHD	62.	U Wash	9-61
Osaghae, Vincent	Assoc	Chicago St	MSVT	MBA	86	Gov St	&1989
Osborn, John P.	Prof	CS-Fresno	XA	PHD	81.	Georgia	& 8-79
Osborne, Edward H.	C-Pr	Marietta	AFX	MBA	65	Indiana	&1971
McCoy Professor							
Osman, Adam	Asst	Australian N	FG	MPHL	02	Austr Natl	2003
Ossman, Edward T.	Emer	CS-East Bay	2001	PHD	71	Ill Tech	& 9-72
Ostendorf, Harry	Retir	Wis-Oshkosh	1994	MA	63	Iowa	* 1964
Ostergren, Katarina	Assoc	Norwegian U	B	PHD			
Osterheld, Karen	SLect	Bentley	FS	MBA	78	Wisconsin	&1990
Ostman, Lars	Prof	Stockholm Ec	T	ED	73	Stockholm	1968
Ostrosky, Joyce A.	Prof	Illinois St	FCE	PHD	87.	Miss	* & 9-74
Ostrowski, Barbara A.			XF	PHD	83.	Illinois	&
Oswald, Dennis R.	Asst	London Bus	M	PHD	00	Chicago	1999
Otero, Kathy F.	Lect	Txs-El Paso	FM	MACC	95	Tx-ElPaso	* 9-95
Otley, David T.	Prof	U Lancaster	MB	PHD	76	Manchest	1972
Ott, Richard L.	H-Ac	Kansas State	XFB	PHD	86	Tx Tech	& 0-86
Grant Thornton Faculty Fellow							
Otte, Randon C.	Asst	Clarion	ANP	MBA	74	Clarion St	& 8-76
Ottinger, Lisa L.	Asst	Kansas	S	PHD	94	Tx A&M	&2000
Otto, Karen A.	SLect	Arizona	FA	DBA	99.	Boston U	8-99
Ou, Chin-Shyh	Prof	Ntl Chung Ch	CMS	PHD	93.	Minnesota	# * &1998
Ou, Jane A.	Assoc	Santa Clara	FV	PHD	84.	Berkeley	1984
Ounapu, Arnold J.	Retir	Ball State	1993	MS	61	N Illinois	& 9-62
Outslay, Edmund	Prof	Michigan St	XI	PHD	81.	Michigan	& 1-81
Deloitte/Michael Licata Teaching Fellow							
Ouyang, Zhao (Joseph)			MI	PHD	02.	Maryland	
Overbey, John T.			MS	PHD	76.	Tx-Austin	&
Overmyer, Wayne S.	Retir	Cincinnati	1983	MA	47	Ohio St	1947
Overton, John H.	Retir	New Hampshir	1993	MS	72	Wisconsin	&1984
Owen, Eugene K. (Ken)	Retir	Delta State	ALGR	MBA	67	Loyl-NOr	&1977
Owen, Glenn E.	Lect	Cal-Santa Br	SF	BA	75	UCLA	&1979
Owen, Heather	Lect	Napier Univ	M	BSC			* 1991
Owen, James M.	Deces			PHD	53.	LSU	
Owen, Will H. Jr.	Retir	Miss State	2000	MPA	58	Miss St	&1958
Owens, Garland C.	Retir	Mercer-Macon	1994	PHD	56.	Columbia	&1984
Owens, Lisa A.	Asst	Clemson	FM	PHD	01.	Okla St	&2004
Owens, Robert W.	Assoc	SW Missouri		PHD	78.	U Wash	
Finance Department							
Owhoso, Vincent E.	Assoc	No Kentucky	AF	PHD	98.	Florida	1-06
Owings, Guy W.	Retir	Pittsburg St	2005	PHD	80.	Missouri	&1971
Owsen, Dwight M.	Inst	Lg Isl-Brook	SFAM	ABD		U Portsm	8-03
Owusu-Ansah, Stephen	Assoc	Tx-Pan Amer	FIQ	PHD	98	Middlesex	9-01
Oxner, Karen	Asst	Hendrix	AF	DBA	94.	S Illinois	&1997
Oxner, Mary	Asst	St Fran Xav	FC	PHD	06	Alberta	&2000
Oxner, Thomas H.	Prof	Cen Arkansas	AFS	PHD	77.	Georgia	& 7-97
Ozair, Merav	Asst	Tel-Aviv		PHD	04.	NYU	
Ozbilgin, Mehmet	Asst	CUNY-Baruch	M	PHD	02.	Purdue	9-02
Ozkan, A.	Prof	Univ Hull	F	PHD	96	York	2-07
Ozzello, Lawrence M.	Retir	Wis-Eau Clar	1998	PHD	67	Mich St	* 6-71
Paananen, Mari		Hertfordshir	FI	PHD	03.	North Tx	
Paapanen, William H.	Retir	Missouri So	8-00	MA	75	Oklahoma	&1976
Pabst, Donald F.	Retir	Wright State	1995	PHD	61.	Ohio St	&1967
Pace, Ryan	Asst	Weber State	X	JD	92	Washburn	2004
Pacharn, Parunchana	Asst	SUNY-Buffalo	FM	PHD	02.	Car Mellon	2002
Pacini, Carl J.	Prof	Fl GulfCoast	AFI	PHD	97.	Fla St	&2000
Marguerite and Guy Howard Professorship in Business							
Packee, Jennifer	Lect	Wis-Whitewat	FM	MS	02	Marquette	&2007
Pacter, Paul A.		Deloitte	2004	PHD	67.	Mich St	&
Paddock, Harold E.			VD	PHD	55.	Tx-Austin	&
Pae, Jinhan	Asst	Queen's Univ		PHD	99.	Brit Colum	2002
Paek, Wonsun	Asst	Sung Kyun Kw	FITX	PHD	96.	Temple	3-97
Kung Kyun Kwan University; Seoul, Korea: (02)760-0415							
Pagach, Donald P.	Assoc	N Carol St	FT	PHD	92.	Fla St	8-94
Pagas, Paraskevas	Lect	U Portsmith		MSC			2004
Page, Charles	Retir	SW Okla St	1999	EDD	70	N Carol	&1970
Page, John R.	Assoc	Tulane	FMS	PHD	75	Tulane	&1984
Page, Michael J.	Prof	U Portsmith	AFT	PHD			1990
Page, R. Frank	Retir	Mo-St Louis	2001	PHD	67.	Illinois	&1968
Paige, Kenneth L.			FBN	PHD	85.	Pittsburgh	&
Paik, Chei-Min	Prof	George Wash	CUM	DBA	63.	Harvard	1964
Paik, Gyung H.	Asst	Brigham Yg	M	PHD	01.	Illinois	1-01

Name	Rank	School	Codes	Degree	Grad	Year
Paik, Tae-Young			MYPF	PHD	89. Berkeley	
Paisley, Christopher B.	Exec	Santa Clara	F	MBA	77 UCLA	2001
Pak, Hong S.	Prof	CS-Pomona	F	PHD	91. Memphis	&1991
Pak, Hyung				DBA	93. Memphis	
Palas, Rimona			F	PHD	98. Rutgers	
Palencia, Luis Enrique	Asst	Univ Navarra	MF	PHD	99. Berkeley	9-92
Palepu, Krishna G.	Prof	Harvard	FM	PHD	83. MIT	1983
Ross Graham Walker Professor; Senior Associate Dean; Director Research						
Pallot, June	Deces	Canterbury	2004	PHD	91 Victoria	1996
Palmer, Glen O.	Retir	Brigham Yg	2000	ABD	S Calif	& 9-64
Palmer, Richard J.	Prof	E Illinois	MSC	DBA	90. S Illinois	&2000
Lumpkin Distinguished Professor of Business						
Palmer, Robert D.	Retir	Troy State	1998	MBA	64 Cincinnati	1972
Palmer, Walter S. Jr.	Retir	Nevada-Reno	1980	PHD	54. Stanford	1946
Palmon, Dan	C-Pr	Rutgers-Newk	F	PHD	74. NYU	1980
Palmrose, Zoe-Vonna	Prof	So Calif	AF	PHD	82. U Wash	&1989
PricewaterhouseCoopers Auditing Professor; on leave SEC						
Pan, Alexander		Coopers & Ly	1989	PHD	86. S Calif	1988
Pan, Gary	Lect	U Melbourne	MSI	PHD	04 Manchest	2005
Pan, Sheng-Der	Retir	CS-Fresno	2004	PHD	74. Illinois	8-80
Pandit, Ganesh M.	Assoc	Adelphi	MF	DBA	94. La Tech	* &2004
Pandit, Shailendra	VAsst	Ohio State	F	PHD	06. Rochester	2006
Panich, Richard L.	Deces	Pepper-L Ang	1993	PHD	85. Ariz St	& 8-92
Panichi, Vincent M.	Retir	John Carroll	F	MBA	59 Case Wes	&1961
Pannell, Richard L.	Retir	Monmouth	1991	PHD	79 NYU	&
11 Andover Lane; Aberdeen NJ 07747						
Pannese, Danny A.	Assoc	Sacred Heart	XAF	MST	84 NewHaven	&1985
Pant, Laurie W.	Prof	Suffolk	MCJ	DBA	86. Boston U	* 1991
Panten, Robert A.	Deces	Georgian Ct	1993	BS	Manhatten	&1961
Panther, John H.	PLect	Coventry Un	VM	MSC	71 Warwick	9-73
Panukcu, Omer	Asst	Un Waterloo	F	BSC	98 Car Mellon	2003
Pany, Kurt J.	Prof	Arizona St	AF	PHD	78. Illinois	& 1-78
Paolasini, Arnold L.	Retir	Fla Atlantic	1995	PHD	76. Illinois	&1973
Papadaki, Aphroditi	Asst	Athens Univ	FT	PHD	97 Athens	1998
Papadakis, George	Asst	Boston Univ	F	PHD	07 MIT	9-07
Paperman, Jacob B.	Retir	CS-Fullerton	7-93	PHD	76. Cincinnati	&1988
Papiernik, Janet C.	Assoc	Ind-Pur/FtWy	FT	DBA	97. Clev St	& 8-99
Paquette, Laurence R.	Prof	Fran Marion	CSQ	PHD	85. Mass	* 2006
Paquette, Suzanne M.	Prof	Univ Laval	TY	PHD	94 Waterloo	&1994
Paradza, P.	Lect	Un Zimbabwe	T	MSC		
Pare, Paul-Victor	Prof	Univ Laval	FM	PHD	83. Michigan	1981
Parent, Beauregard J. Jr.	Inst	Tulane	FASC	ABD	LSU	&1977
Paretta, Robert L.	Assoc	Delaware	F	PHD	73. Syracuse	& 9-72
Parham, Abbie Gail	Asst	Geo Southern	PC	MBA	88 Ga Srthrn	* &1990
Pariser, David B.	Prof	W Virginia	FGNI	PHD	70 S Illinois	* &1989
Parish, Beth	Exec	No Colorado	FMP	MS	85 Colo St	2006
Park, Changgil	Prof	Kookmin Univ	FHJP	PHD	84 Seoul Ntl	&1982
Park, Changhun		Korean Telec		PHD	93. Purdue	
Park, Charles A.	Retir	Lander	1991	MBA	60 S Carol	&1960
Park, Chul W.			F	PHD	94. Wash U	&
Park, Colin I.				PHD	55. Chicago	
Park, Gil-Young	Asst	Chosun Univ	GNPR	ME	82 Chosun	1979
Park, Gwanghoon	Asst	South Korea	F	PHD	91. Georgia	
Park, Hai G.			FM	PHD	83. Oklahoma	
Park, Jaewan	Assoc	Dongguk U	ACM	PHD	95. Tx-Austin	9-96
Park, James W.	Retir	Belhaven	5-01	PHD	74 Alabama	1977
Park, Jeongdae	Asst	Hanyaung U		PHD	84. Fla St	
Park, Jinyonng (Jeanne)	Asst	La Tech	FM	PHD	05. Purdue	&9-05
Park, Jong Chool	Asst	Rensselaer	F	PHD	06. Car Mellon	2006
Park, Jongchan	Asst	Univ Seoul	F	PHD	04. Wisconsin	8-04
Park, June				PHD	97. Geo Wash	
Park, Kyungjoo			CFM	PHD	90. Baruch	
Park, L. Jane	Prof	CS-L Angeles	F	PHD	65 Illinois	&9-89
Park, Manyong			FMA	PHD	88. Tx-Austin	
Park, Myung S.	Asst	Virg Comm	FS	PHD	99. Purdue	2004
Park, Sechoul	Deces	Morgan St	FM	PHD	92. Maryland	&1992
Park, Seong W.			S	PHD	90. Geo St	
Park, Soong H.			FMCA	PHD	77. Iowa	
Park, Taewoo			F	PHD	96. Purdue	
Park, Yonpae			FM	PHD	02. Nebraska	
Park, Young			A	PHD	98. Pittsburgh	
Parkash, Mohinder	C-Ac	Oakland	FT	PHD	87. Arizona	&1991
Parker, Diane	Asst	So Alabama	AP	PHD	04. Miss St	&2003
Parker, Dorothy J.	SLect	U Wash-Tacom	MXFS	PHD	92. Arkansas	&1997
Parker, Frederick R. Jr.	Assoc	La St-Shreve	JLX	LLM	88 NYU	& 8-98
Parker, Hugh J.			A	PHD	82. Okla St	&
Parker, James E.	Retir	Missouri	2000	PHD	69. Mich St	&1969

Parker, Larry M.	C-Ac	Case Western	ABFM	PHD	81.	Houston	&7-85
Parker, Lee D.	Prof	Adelaide	MGHJ	PHD	83	Monash	&1997
Parker, M. Virginia	C-Pr$	Metro State	FV	PHD	82.	Colorado	&9-87
Parker, Robert H.	Prof	Univ Exeter	FHI	BSC	54	London	&1976
Parker, Robert J.	Assoc	New Orleans	CM	PHD	92.	Temple	&2002
Parker, Seth K.	Retir	Kentucky Wes	2004	PHD	74.	Mich St	&2000
Parker, Susan	Assoc	Santa Clara	AF	PHD	98.	Oregon	1998
Parker, Walter A.	Retir	Central Conn	1996	MBA	64	NYU	&9-69
Parkes, Alison	Lect	U Melbourne	S	MBS	01	Massey	2001
Parkinson, John M.	Assoc	York-Atkinsn	CIM	PHD	84	Bradford	* &1984
Parkison, Paul W.	Retir	Ball State	2001	DBA	67.	Indiana	&9-66
Parks, Charles	Lect	N Car-Ashvil	AS	MS		NC-Green	
Parks, Sandra	Asst	Miss College	PAFM	MBA	76	Miss Col	&1976
Parks, Virginia L.	Retir	Seattle	2005	PHD	71	Houston	&1972
Parmer, Jerold A.			XF	PHD	73.	Tx Tech	&
Parmley, William K.	Deces	SW Missouri	1987	PHD	79.	Okla St	&8-82
Parrish, Barbara K.	Assoc	Central Okla	FMPT	PHD	94.	Arkansas	&8-99
Parrish, Lillian C.	Retir	Georgia SW	2000	PHD	77.	Miss	&9-96
Parrish, Sharon R.	Assoc	Kentucky St	FG	DBA	86.	Kentucky	&1985
Parrott, William H.	Assoc	South Fla	F	PHD	71.	Illinois	1-77
Parry, Robert W. Jr. (Rob)	Prof	Indiana	FNEG	PHD	79.	Lehigh	1979
Parsegian, Elsa V.	Prof	Youngstown	FMI	PHD	85.	Pittsburgh	* &9-98
email: evparsegian@cs.com							
Parsons, James W.	Retir	Baylor	1966	PHD	55.	LSU	&1955
Parsons, Kristine	Assoc	Ashland	MSVC	PHD	95.	Kent St	* 2005
Parsons, Linda M.	Asst	Geo Mason	SGN	PHD	01.	Houston	&2001
Pasch, Kenneth W.	Inst	Penn State	M	MBA	82	N Colo	1-98
Paschke, Randolph C.	C-Le	Wayne State	XI	BBA	71	Michigan	&8-02
Pasewark, William R.	Prof	Texas Tech	MF	PHD	86.	Tx A&M	&9-00
Pastena, Victor S.	Deces	SUNY-Buffalo	7-99	PHD	76.	NYU	&1990
Pastoria, L. Gail			CMI	PHD	93.	Kent St	* &
Pate, Gwen R.	Assoc	So Miss	FMV	PHD	91.	Tennessee	&1990
Pate, John G. Jr.	Retir	SC-Spartanbu	1992	PHD	68.	Columbia	&1988
106 Lori Circle; Spartenburg SC 29303							
Patel, Chris	H-Pr	Macquarie Un	FI	PHD	99	Macquarie	* &1995
Patell, James M.	Prof	Stanford	FMC	PHD	77.	Car Mellon	9-75
Herbert Hoover Professor of Public & Private Management							
Paterson, Jeffrey S.	Assoc	Florida St	XF	PHD	95.	Georgia	8-95
Andersen Professor							
Pathak, Chandra P.	Retir	E Michigan	9-04	PHD	71	Tennessee	&1981
Pathak, Jagdish	Asst	Univ Windsor	AS	PHD	95	Goa	2002
Paton, William A.	Deces	Michigan	4-91	PHD	17	Michigan	&1915
Paton, William A. Jr.	Retir	Windsor	1986	PHD	54.	Michigan	1979
5601 Prarie Road; Saline MI 48176							
Patrick, Albert W.	Deces	Kentucky	1982	PHD	56.	Michigan	&1968
Patrick, Patricia	Asst	Kutztown	ANO	PHD	06	Penn St	&
Patrick, Patricia A.	Retir	New Orleans	4-96	PHD	79	Miss	1973
Patten, Dennis M.	Prof	Illinois St	MGW	PHD	87.	Nebraska	&1985
Patten, James A.	Assoc	CS-Bakersf	F	MBA	70	DePaul	&9-82
Patten, Ronald J.	Retir	DePaul	2000	PHD	63.	Alabama	&7-89
Patterson, Carolyn	Asst	NE St-Okla	XF	PHD	94.	Okla St	&1994
Patterson, David W.	Asst	SW Minn St	CFMP	PHD	01	Nev-L Vg	* &2005
Patterson, Denise M.	Prof	CS-Fresno	AF	PHD	94.	Geo St	&8-94
Patterson, Evelyn R.	Assoc	Indiana-Indy	AF	PHD	87.	Tx-Austin	&8-05
Patterson, Jeffrey L.	Prof	Grove City	FGHX	PHD	83.	Penn St	&1995
Patterson, Robert D.	Inst	Penn St-Erie	PCFQ	MBA	88	Penn St	&1988
Pattillo, James W.	Deces	Ind-So Bend	8-97	PHD	63.	LSU	* &6-81
Pattison, Diane D.	D-Pr	San Diego	CJM	PHD	81.	U Wash	1986
Patton, James M.	Retir	Pittsburgh	2005	PHD	76.	Wash U	&1976
Patton, R.	SLect	Univ Ulster	J	MBA			1-04
Patton, Terry K.		GASB	2004	PHD	99.	Tx Tech	&
Patz, Dennis H.	Deces	Oklahoma St	O-06	PHD	75.	Tx-Austin	&1986
Paul, Amanda	Asst	Troy	F	MBA	00	Troy	2007
Paul, Diane	Assoc	HEC-Montreal	AJMT	MSC	93	HEC-Mont	&9-86
Paul, John W.	Prof	Lehigh	AM	PHD	78.	Lehigh	&9-74
Pauley, C. Edman	Asst	W Virg St	FPTX	MBA	74	W Virginia	&1982
Pauly, Deborah M.	Prof	Loras	CM	MBA	92	N Iowa	* &1983
Pava, Moses L.	Prof	Yeshiva	MF	PHD	90.	NYU	9-87
Alvin H. Einbender Chair in Business Ethics							
Pavelka, Deborah D.	D-Pr	Roosevelt	FT	PHD	85.	Missouri	&1989
Pavlock, Ernest J.	Retir	Virg Tech	2000	PHD	65.	Michigan	&1980
Pawliczek, Ronald B.	Assoc	Boston Coll	FE	PHD	75.	Mass	1974
Paxson, Dean A.	Lect	U Manchester	Z	DBA	70	Harvard	1974
Paxton, William E.			F	DBA	83.	Kent St	&
Payne, Carolyn	Inst	Union-KY	ST	MBA	02	Morehead	&2001
Payne, Elizabeth A.	Asst	Mississippi	AF	PHD	02.	Kentucky	&2005
Payne, Jeff L.	Assoc	Kentucky	AFS	PHD	95.	Florida	&2004

Payne, Ronald	Asst	Brescia		MS		Tulsa	2003
Pazmandy, Greg	SLect	Tech-Sydney	CDFS	MBUS	93	Tech-Sydn	1990
Peace, Robert L.	Prof	N Carol St	XL	JD	74	NYU	1982
Peacock, Eileen	Dean	Mass-Dartmou	CM	PHD	74	Birminghm	* &8-04
Peacock, Kenneth E.	Prof	Appalach St	XF	PHD	79.	LSU	&1983
University Chancellor							
Pearce, W. Leon			SD	PHD	73.	Missouri	&
Pearl, Daniel	Retir	Mass-Lowell	1992	PHD	69.	Minnesota	&1987
200 Market St Apt 411; Lowell MA 01852							
Pearlman, Leslie	Lect	Harvard	NP	DBA	96.	Boston U	1998
John F. Kennedy School of Gov; 79 JFK St; Cambridge MA 02138; 617-496-0811							
Pearlman, Sy	Lect	CS-Long Bch	FX	JD	66	DePaul	&1996
Pearson, David B.	Prof	Case Western	AF	DBA	64.	Indiana	& 1-99
Pearson, Della A.			FZ	PHD	78.	Tx A&M	&
Pearson, Michael A.	Prof	Kent State	AJ	DBA	79.	Kent St	* &6-83
Pearson, Thomas C.	Prof	Hawaii-Manoa	XJK	LLM	05	NYU	& 1-89
Pearson, Timothy A.	D-Ac	W Virginia	FAS	PHD	90.	Wisconsin	& 7-91
Peasnell, Kenneth V.	Prof	U Lancaster	F	PHD	75	Lancaster	&1970
Peck, Cynthia L.	Assoc	Anderson	FAN	MBA	88	Indiana	&1984
Peck, Milo W. Jr.	Asst	Fairfield	GFXR	LLM	80	Boston U	&1990
Peden, Vicki	Prof	CS-Pomona	AFS	PHD	94.	Tx-Arlin	&1995
Pedersen, Ronald	Lect	Wyoming	PM	MS	02	Wyoming	&2003
Pedwell, Kathryn	Asst	Univ Ottawa	X	PHD	00	Calgary	1996
Peebler, Richard G.	Retir	Drake	1996	MA	59	Drake	&1965
Peecher, Mark E.	Prof	Illinois	BAF	PHD	94.	Illinois	6-98
Peek, Erik	Assoc	Maastricht	F	PHD	01	Vrije	1999
Peek, George S.	Prof	W Illinois	MS	PHD	90.	Georgia	* &9-87
Peek, Lucia E.	Prof	W Illinois	AM	PHD	87.	Georgia	& 9-87
Peel, Michael J.	Prof	Cardiff U	AF	MBA	87	Bradford	* 1987
Peery, Harry Eugene	Deces	Mississippi	6-93	MA	47	Nebraska	&1951
Peetathawatchai, Pimpana	Lect	Chulalongkor	FI	DBA	96	Boston U	1996
Peeyawan, Polpadhoo	Asst	Chulalongkor	S	MBA	86	Arizona	1981
Peffer, Sean A.	Assoc	Kentucky	CMF	PHD	96.	Indiana	&1997
Chelgren Professor of Accounting							
Pefkaros, Kenneth	Prof	CS-East Bay	SDQ	PHD	72	Delaware	9-84
Pegum, R. H.	PLect	Liverpool JM	AFM	FCCA			
Pei, Buck K. W.	Prof	Arizona St	SBA	PHD	85.	North Tx	1986
Peirce, Richard F.				PHD	57.	Illinois	
Peirson, C. Graham	Emer	Monash Univ	2002	MEC			&1963
Peles, Yoram C.	Prof	Hebrew Univ	M	PHD	69	Chicago	1971
Pelesh, Jeffrey N.	Inst	Villanova	AF	MBA	88	Villanova	&1991
Pelfrey, Sandra H.	Assoc	Oakland	NOG	MBA	74	Wright St	&1986
Pellegrino, Kathleen B.	Retir	Westfield St	2001	MBA	76	W New Eng	&1978
Pelletier, Laurence	C-Pr	So New Hamp	FPMN	EDD		Nova SE	9-88
Pelletier, Mary-Joan	Lect	Suffolk	ACFK	MSA	04	Suffolk	&2005
Peltier-Rivest, Dominic	Assoc	Concordia	F	PHD	96.	Fla St	2000
Pelz, Ulrich		Sacrament CA	1989	DBA	76.	Colorado	&
Penafiel, Lorenzo V.	Retir	Angelo State	1992	PHD	70.	Tx Tech	& 9-70
Penalva, Fernando	Asst	Univ Navarra	F	PHD	98.	Berkeley	9-98
Penaranda, Francisco	Asst	Pompeu Fabra			03	CEMFI	
Pence, Diana Kay	Assoc	Houston-Down	F	PHD	96.	North Tx	2006
Pendarvis, Deborah			F	PHD	98.	Florida	&
Pendergast, Susanna D.	Inst	W Illinois	P	MACC	95	W Illinois	& 9-94
Pendlebury, Maurice	Prof	Cardiff U	NGE	PHD	86	Cardiff	&1977
Pendleton, Nichole	Asst	Friends	X	MACC	01	Kansas St	N-04
Pendley, John A.	Asst	Alabama-Hunt	SFA	PHD	94	Georgia	&1998
Peng, Jacob	Asst	Mich-Flint	S	PHD	05.	Tx Tech	9-05
Peng, Yan (Emma)	Asst	Fordham	F	PHD	05.	Oregon	8-05
Penman, Stephen H.	Prof	Columbia	F	PHD	78.	Chicago	&1999
George O. May Professor of Accounting							
Penner, Nancy	Assoc	SW Okla St	P	PHD	99	North Tx	1986
Pennington, Robin R.	Asst	N Carol St	BS	PHD	02.	S Carol	8-07
Penno, Mark C.	Prof	Iowa	FM	PHD	83.	Nrthwstrn	&2004
Soumyo Sarkar Fellow in Accounting							
Pentland, Brian T.	Prof	Michigan St	S	PHD	91	MIT	2000
Penz, Anton J.	Retir	Alabama	8-71	PHD	47	Ohio St	1947
800 Rice Valley Rd F-31; Tuscaloosa AL 35406							
Peragallo, Edward	Retir	Holy Cross					
Percy, Majella	SLect	Queensld Tec	F	MFM	90	Queensld	& 4-88
Pereira, Emilio		Nicaragua		PHD	91.	Houston	
Minister of Finance, Nicaragua							
Pereira, Fernando	Emer	Univ Navarra	2004	DOCT		ETSIC	9-58
Pereira, Raynolde	Assoc	Missouri	X	PHD	01.	Arizona	2000
Andersen/Joseph A. Silvoso Professor							
Perera, Ryle	Lect	Macquarie Un	FQ	PHD	02	NS Wales	2002
Perera, Sujatha	Prof	Macquarie Un	M	PHD	00	Macquarie	* 1991
Peres, Andre	Prof	HEC-Montreal	DOSV	LSCC	73	HEC-Mont	&O-75

Name	Rank	School	Code	Degree	Yr	School	Note
Peretz, Moshe	Lect	Tel Aviv Un	F	MA		Tel Aviv	&1998
Perez, Candido	C-Pr	Puerto RicoM	ADFS	MSA	85	Mass	# * &6-83
Perez, Mario	Lect	U Miami		MST		Fla Intl	2006
Perez-Lopez, Juan		IESE		DBA	70.	Harvard	
Pergola, Teresa M.	Inst	Tampa	FM	ABD		Nova SE	&2002
Perkins, Carlton	Asst	Txs Southern	FLX	JD	78	Houston	&1982
Perkins, Jon D.	Lect	Illinois	ABXM	PHD	03.	Illinois	* &8-07
Perkins, W. David	Assoc	Abilene Chr	AC	PHD	91.	Tx A&M	* &1999
Perlow, Mickey R.	Retir	Tampa	1998	MS	66	Rhode Isl	* &1980
Perman, James	Lect	Napier Univ	X	BSC			&1989
Perreau, D.	Tutor	Massey-Alban		BBS			
Perret, Marie-Solange		Business		PHD	82	W Ontario	1985
Perrin, Ronald W.	Lect	U Wollongong	FTW	MCOM	91	Wollong	&1991
Perry, Jacqueline A.	Assoc	W Virg Tech	EPV	PHD			&1999
Perry, Kenneth W.	Retir	Illinois	1985	PHD	53.	Illinois	&1950
Perry, Linda	SLect	Texas A&M	F	MS	71	Illinois	&6-87
Persellin, Mark B.	Prof	St Marys-Tx	X	PHD	87.	Houston	&8-91
Persoff, Ilene L.	Assoc	Lg Isl-Post	VF	MS	78	Lgls-Post	&1984
Persons, Obeau S.	Assoc	Rider	F	PHD	91.	Tx-Austin	&1991
Pescow, Jerome K.	Retir	Hofstra	1990	MS	57	Columbia	&1962
Petchesky, Joseph	Retir	Lg Isl-Brook	1995	JD	49	St Johns	&1967
Peterlin, Edward L.	Retir	So Colorado	1995	MA	59	N Colo	&1963
Peters, David H.	C-Ac	Southeastern		MJ	82	American	&
Peters, Gary F.	Asst	Arkansas	FA	PHD	98.	Oregon	&2003
Peters, James M.		Loyola	SANB	PHD	89.	Pittsburgh	&
Peters, Michael F.	Asst	Villanova	FB	PHD	96.	Indiana	&2004
Peters, Richard M.	Prof	Fort Hays St	FMT	PHD	76.	Penn St	&1994
Peters, Robert M.	Retir	DePaul	2004	PHD	72	Kentucky	&1975
Petersen, Clinton	Retir	Babson	1990	MBA		Babson	&1946
Petersen, Michael J.	Asst	Arizona St	M	PHD	02.	Iowa	2001
Petersen, Russell J.	Retir	Tx-Arlington	2000	PHD	71.	U Wash	&8-94
Peterson, Fredric G.	Asst	Brigham Yg	Q	PHD	73	Utah	9-75
Peterson, Judy	C-Ac	Monmouth IL	FMXV	MBA	80	Mankato	&1998
Peterson, Scott	C-As	Northern St	FS	MPA	87	S Dakota	&1987
Peterson, Timothy	Asst	Gustavus Ado	FXM	MBA	76	Wisconsin	&1997
Peterson, William A.				PHD	63.	Michigan	
Petra, Steven	Assoc	Hofstra	CFMX	PHD	02.	Rutgers	&2002
Petravick, Simon P.	Assoc	Bradley	AS	PHD	94	Il-Chicago	&8-94
Petri, Enrico	Deces	SUNY-Albany	2002	PHD	73	NYU	&1966
Petrie, A. George	Retir	Southern-NO	2004	PHD	70.	LSU	&1999
Petro, Fred A.	Prof	Pepper-L Ang	IFME	PHD	73.	Arkansas	* 1980
Petro, Louis W.	Sess	Univ Windsor	ASMF	PHD	74.	Michigan	# * &1998
Petrone, Franca	LectB	Flinders Un	IJLM	MBA	98	Adelaide	1-93
Petrone, Grace	Retir	Staten Isl	1991	MBA	62	Rutgers	&1959
43 St Mary's Avenue; Staten Island N:Y 10305							
Petroni, Kathy R.	C-Pr$	Michigan St	FA	PHD	90.	Michigan	&9-90
Deloitte/Michael Licata Professor of Accounting							
Petrovits, Christine M.	Asst	New York U	F	PHD	05.	N Carol	&2005
Petru, James W.				PHD	75.	Nrthwstrn	
Petruzzi, Christopher R.	Prof	CS-Fullerton	X	PHD	84	S Calif	7-89
Petrych, William	Retir	Youngstown	1992	MA	57	Ohio St	9-57
Petty, John	Lect	Tech-Sydney	CMU	MBUS	97	Tech-Sydn	1993
Petty, Richard M.	TFell	Un Hong Kong	AFT	MCOM	96	NS Wales	* &1998
Peyvandi, Ali A.	Prof	CS-Fresno	FCRI	PHD	80.	Missouri	8-80
Pfeffenberger, Dyne L.	Retir	Ind-Pur/FtWy	2001	MA	67	Ball St	&8-72
Pfeiffer, F.	Inst	Touro	ACB	MS			&2-93
Pfeiffer, Glenn M.	C-Pr	Chapman	FM	PHD	80.	Cornell	9-95
Pfeiffer, Ray J.	Assoc	Massachusett	F	PHD	94.	N Carol	1994
Pflugrath, G.	Lect	New So Wales		MBA		Melbourne	
Pforsich, Hugh	Asst	CS-Sacrament	C	PHD	95.	Wash St	&2004
Phadoongsidhi, Maruey		Thailand		PHD	72.	Wisconsin	
Phadoongsitthi, Monvika	Asst	Thammasat U		PHD	02.	Maryland	2003
Thammasat University; Thailand							
Pham, H. Dang	Prof	HEC Paris	FTIE	HECD	67	HEC Paris	1968
Phelan, Marilyn E.		Tx Tech Law		PHD	71.	Tx Tech	1975
Phelan, Tamara	Inst	No Illinois	FMS	MM	86	Nrthwstrn	1-02
Pheny, Monica	VLect	HongKon Tech	JX	MTAX	02	NS Wales	&2005
Philbrick, Donna R.	Prof	Portland St	F	PHD	84.	Cornell	&1989
Philhours, Joel E.	Retir	W Kentucky	2003	PHD	91.	Kentucky	* &1977
Philipich, Kirk L.	Asst	Mich-Dearbor	FAV	DBA	84.	Indiana	9-05
Philips, G. Edward	Retir	New Mexico	1994	PHD	60.	Mich St	&1982
Phillips, ALee	Lect	Kansas	FM	MAIS	98	Kansas	2001
Phillips, Cynthia		Mn-Moorhead		JD	76	N Dakota	1979
Phillips, Donna			MAF	PHD	91.	Tx A&M	&
Phillips, Fred	Assoc	Saskatchewan	AFB	PHD	96.	Tx-Austin	&1996
Phillips, Janet F.	Prof	So Conn St	FGNM	SCD	97	NewHaven	&1991
Phillips, Jeffrey Joseph			FMST	PHD	86.	Georgia	&

Phillips, Jillian	Lect	So Cross Un	FE	DIP	90	Victoria		&1981
Phillips, John D.	Assoc	Connecticut	X	PHD	99.	Iowa		1-99
Phillips, John M.	Assoc	Guam	JVC	MBA	83	Guam		&1981
Phillips, Jon	ALect	Monash Univ	FCM	BBUS				2001
Phillips, Lawrence C.	Prof	U Miami	X	PHD	66.	Ohio St		&1985
Phillips, Mary	Prof	N Carol Cen	CFJ	PHD	83.	N Carol		1983
Phillips, Mary E.	Asst	Mid Tenn St	F	PHD	04.	Kentucky		&2004
Phillips, Mary Ellen	Retir	Oregon State	1994	MBA	73	Oregon St		&1973
Phillips, Robert H. Jr.			ADPS	PHD	89.	Va Tech		&
Phillips, Samuel H.	Asst	Geo Mason	AFNS	PHD	91.	Houston		&
Phillips, Thomas E.	Retir	Cen Florida	2000	PHD	74.	Nebraska		&6-77
Phillips, Thomas J. Jr.	D-Pr	Louisiana Te	FBTJ	PHD	84.	Geo St		&1987
KPMG Endowed Professor								
Phinney, Theresa	Lect	Texas A&M	S	MS	84	Tx A&M		9-05
Phipps, David W.	Retir	Alabama	1988	MBA	48	Denver		&1975
6 Rollingwood; Tuscaloosa AL 35406								
Phoonphiphat, Veravan	Retir	Chulalongkor	C	MACC	68	Chulalong		1968
Phuong, Nguyen Minh	Lect	Natl Econ	FMCV	PHD	91	Natl Econ		1976
Piaker, Philip M.	Retir	SUNY-Bingham		MBA	49	CUNY		&1952
Picard, Robert R.	C-Pr	Idaho State	MVS	PHD	94.	Kentucky		&1994
Picart, Justo				PHD	78.	Arkansas		
Picconi, Marc P.	Asst	Indiana	F	PHD	04.	Cornell		7-04
Pickard, Andrew	Inst	St Marys-Tx	FC	MACC	93	St MryTX		&9-94
Pickering, Joanne	Lect	Univ Sydney	FI	MSC	92	Saskatch	*	&1992
Picur, Ronald D.	Prof	Ill-Chicago	GFTN	PHD	73.	Nrthwstrn		&1978
Pier, Charles A.	Asst	Tx St-S Marc	FX	PHD	04.	Tx-Arlin		2006
Pierce, Aileen	SLect	Un Cl Dublin	FIP	PHD	75	Dublin		&1979
Pierce, Barbara Gugliotta	Assoc	Fla Tech	FV	PHD	92.	Indiana		&8-99
Pierce, Bernard	Dean$	Dublin City	JM	PHD	93	Lancaster		&1982
Pierce, Bethane Jo (Becky)	Assoc	Tx-Arlington	X	PHD	87.	North Tx		&1985
Pierce, Ronald L.	Retir	CS-L Angeles	2001	MA	65	Brighm Yg		&9-72
Pierce-Brown, Rhoda	Lect	Un Warwick		PHD	00	Warwick		
Piercey, David	Asst	Massachusett	AF	PHD	06.	Illinois		2006
Pierides, Yiannis	Asst	Cyprus	F	PHD	94	MIT		1994
Pierno, Ronald J.	Lect	Florida St	FC	JD	81	Fla St		&8-94
Pierpont, Wilbur K.	Retir	Michigan	1982	PHD	42.	Michigan		1-77
Pike, Debra	Inst	St Louis	FA	MBA	92	St Louis		&2006
Pike, Eileen	Retir	New Bruns-SJ	MCF	MBA	88	Dalhousie	*	1979
Pike, Gene E.	Inst	Tampa	FM	MBA	77	Tampa	*	&2001
Pike, Joel E.	Asst	Illinois	FM	PHD	03.	Wisconsin		8-03
Pillai, Kesan P.				PHD	55.	NYU		
Pillsbury, Ceil M.	Assoc	Wis-Milwauke	SA	PHD	84.	Okla St		&1984
Pillsbury, Wilbur F.	Dean	Knox Coll		DBA	54.	Indiana		
Pilote, Claude	Prof	Quebec-Montr	S	PHD	90.	S Calif		&7-94
Pincus, Karen V.	Prof	Arkansas	ABE	PHD	84.	Maryland		&8-95
S. Robson Walton Chair								
Pincus, Morton	C-Pr	Calif-Irvine	FX	PHD	82.	Wash U		&7-05
Pinello, Arianna S.	Asst	Georgia St	F	PHD	04.	Fla St		8-04
Pineno, Charles J.	Prof	Shenandoah	CM	PHD	79	Penn St		2004
Pinney, Hubert R.	Retir	Mount Union	1996	MA	62	Ohio St		&1967
Pinnuck, Matthew L.	SLect	U Melbourne	FA	PHD	03	Melbourne		1997
Pinny, J.	STuto	Massey-Welli		BCA		Wellingt		2005
Pinsker, Robert	Asst	Old Dominion	MF	PHD	02.	S Fla		&8-02
Pinson, Kathleen	VAsst	Mercer-Atlan	PVX	MBA	82	Mercer		&2005
Pinto, Edwin I.	Retir	San Jose St	2001	DBA	66.	S Calif		&1963
Pinto, JoAnn	Assoc	Montclair St	FMIC	PHD	99.	Rutgers		9-99
Pion, Nelson E.	Emer	Massachusett	1997	EDD	83	Mass		1964
Piotroski, Joseph D.	Assoc	Chicago	F	PHD	99.	Michigan		1999
Piper, Beverly	Assoc	Ashland	PMC	MS	78	Toledo	*	&9-79
Piper, Thomas R.	Prof	Harvard	FJ	DBA	70	Harvard		1970
Industrial Bank of Japan Professor								
Pippin, Sonja	Asst	Nevada-Reno	X	PHD	06	Tx Tech		2006
Pirkul, Hasan	Dean	Texas-Dallas	SQ	PHD	83	Rochester		1996
Pirrong, Gordon D.	Retir	Boise State	2002	DBA	72.	Ariz St	*	&9-78
Pitman, Marshall K.	Assoc	Tx-S Antonio	AFM	PHD	83.	Miss	*	&1984
Pitre, Richard	Prof	Txs Southern	EF	PHD	78.	Houston		&1991
Pitre, Terence J.	Asst	St Thomas-MN	BF	PHD	04.	Mich St		9-07
Pitt, H. Ronald	Retir	No Arizona	2003	PHD	78.	Okla St		&1981
Pitt, Kay C.	SLect	No Arizona	PFGM	MS	73	Okla St		&1981
Pitt, Max	Asst	Graceland	AJM	MBA	93	Tx-Brown		2004
Pittman, Jeffrey A.	Assoc	Memorial Un	F	PHD	00	Waterloo	*	&2000
Pittman, Travis D.	Retir	Txs Southern	1995	MBA	58	Houston		&1969
Pitts, Marianne	Lect	Un Warwick	H	BA	63	Oxford		
Pizzini, Mina J.	Asst	So Methodist	MC	PHD	02.	Penn		&8-05
Plachta, Leonard E.	Retir	Cen Michigan	8-02	PHD	64.	Mich St		1972
Placid, Raymond	Asst	Fl GulfCoast	X	JD	90	U Miami		&2002
Pladson, Paul R.	Prof	St John's-MN	PMFX	MBA	71	St Cloud		&1975

Plagman, Carol	Lect	Arizona		MAC	94	Arizona	2001
Plante, Catherine A.	Assoc	New Hampshir	FG	PHD	91.	Ohio St	&1991
Platau, Steven M.	Prof	Tampa	FXL	JD	84	Cincinnati	&1984
Platt, David E.	SLect	Texas-Austin	CM	PHD	97.	Cornell	& 9-96
Platt, Marjorie B.	H-Pr	Northeastern	BCEM	PHD	77	Michigan	* 1982
Plesko, George A.	Assoc	Connecticut	XM	PHD	85	Wisconsin	2005
Plewa, Franklin J.	Prof	Idaho State	VF	PHD	83.	LSU	1984
Plucinski, Daniel M.	Retir	Frostburg St	2002	MBA	75	Pittsburgh	* &9-75
Plucinski, Kenneth J.	Asst	SUNY-Fredoni	AFM	MBA	79	Pittsburgh	&1984
Plum, Charles W.	Retir	Texas A&M	1988	MBA	51	Case Wes	& 1-78
Plumlee, Marlene A.	Asst	Utah	FI	PHD	97.	Michigan	&1997
Plumlee, R. David	Prof	Utah	SA	PHD	82.	Florida	&1997
Plummer, C. Elizabeth	Assoc	North Texas	X	PHD	94.	Tx-Austin	& 8-03
KPMG Faculty Fellow							
Plunkett, Linda M.			VFT	PHD	81.	Geo St	&
Poe, C. Douglas	Retir	Kentucky	2003	PHD	85.	Tx A&M	1985
Pofahl, James W.	Inst	Wis-Oshkosh	F	MBA	66	Chicago	&1998
Poff, J. Kent	Assoc	No Georgia	X	PHD	91.	Va Tech	&1995
Pogach, Kenneth S.	VInst	Purdue Calmu	FM	MBA		Chicago	
Pogacnik, Ruth C.	Asst	Mount Union	MC	MBA	97	Youngstwn	2007
Pogogeff, Andrew D.	Assoc	St Peters	AF	MBA		Fair Dick	&1978
Pogue, Elizabeth	Asst	St Ambrose	AOPC	MA	04	St Ambro	* &2004
Pogue, M. A.	Lect	Univ Ulster	FM	MBA			0-04
Poli, Paul P. H.	Asst	City Univ HK	M	MBA	89	Henley	2-90
Pointer, Larry Gene	Deces	Texas A&M	1994	PHD	69.	Florida	& 1-69
Pointer, Martha M.	Assoc	East Tenn St	FMI	PHD	92.	S Carol	& 9-91
Poirier, Gilles	H	Quebec a Hul	CEMJ	PHD			*
Poirier, Kevin W.	C-Ac	Johnson&Wale	ADS	ABD	97	Salve Rg	&1990
Poland, Leo A.				DBA	62.	Indiana	1958
Polejewski, Shirley A.	Prof	St Thomas-MN	ICMU	PHD	83	Minnesota	9-76
Poletti, Elena	Lect	Univ Otago	FM	PHD	87	Otago	1988
Poli, Patricia M.	Assoc	Fairfield	FI	PHD	94	NYU	&1996
Polimeni, Ralph S.	Prof	Hofstra	C	PHD	73.	Arkansas	& 9-73
Polinski, Paul W.	Asst	Grant Thonto	AFS	PHD	00.	Alabama	& 1-02
Poliski, Mindy	Inst	Lk Superior	ACPX	MBA	05	Lawrence	9-07
Pollack, Robert C.	VAsst	Purdue Calmu	LFN	JD		Valparaiso	
Pollack, Sheldon D.	Prof	Delaware	XL	PHD	79	Cornell	1994
Pollado, Donna S.	Asst	SE Louisiana	F	MBA	02	N Orleans	& 8-07
Pollanen, Raili M.	Asst	Carleton Un	MU	PHD	97	Lancaster	2000
Pollard, William B.	Prof	Appalach St	XM	PHD	81.	S Carol	1981
Pollastrini, Raymond	Asst	Dominican		ABD		Nrthwstrn	
Polledo, Donna	VAsst	Loyola-N Orl		ABD		Miss St	
Polley, Roy J.	Retir	Puget Sound	5-99	MBA	64	Puget Sd	# &1963
Pollock, Kathy S.	C-Ac	Ind-Pur/FtWy	A	PHD	98.	Kentucky	& 8-96
Pomerantz, Lawrence S.		Univ Heig OH	1992	PHD	72.	Wisconsin	
2472 Dysart Rd; University Heights OH 44118							
Pomeranz, Felix	Retir	Fla Internat	2005	PHD	92	Birminghm	&1985
Pommerich, Robert G.	Retir	Loras	1999	MBA	65	Wisconsin	&1962
Pomroy, H. Marshall	Retir	Elizabethtwn	5-99	MAD	71	Penn St	& 9-64
Pond, Lallon	Assoc	Mary Baldwin	PF	ABD		Fla St	1992
Ponder, Jimmy N.	Retir	Nicholls St	7-96	PHD	72.	Arkansas	& 9-68
Ponemon, Lawrence A.			AF	PHD	89.	Union-NY	# * &
Pongpun, Jirada	Lect	Chulalongkor	FM	MSPA	03	Mich St	&2007
Ponko, Duane M.	Asst	Indiana U-PA	VAF	MS	75	Duquesne	&1978
Pontius, Vernon E.		Hacienda CA	1992	PHD	70.	UCLA	
PO Box 389; Alhambra CA 91802							
Poon, Margaret C. C.	Assoc	City Univ HK	EMB	PHD	96	Bradford	9-87
Poon, Pak-lok	Asst	HongKon Tech	DS	PHD	00	Melbourne	1999
Poon, Ser-Huang		U Manchester	FQ	PHD	91	Lancaster	
Poon, Wing W.	Assoc	Montclair St	FMIC	PHD	96.	LSU	1997
Poonakasem, Pornsiri		Chulalongkor	1992	PHD	87.	Florida	
Chulalongkorn Univ; Faculty of Comm; Bangkok 10500 Thailand							
Pope, Jennings B.				PHD	42.	Tx-Austin	
Pope, Kelly R.	Asst	DePaul	BCJM	PHD	01	Va Tech	2006
Pope, Peter F.	Prof	U Lancaster	FM	MA	77	Lancaster	1977
Pope, Thomas R.	Assoc	Kentucky	X	DBA	76.	Kentucky	&1984
Ernst & Young Professor of Accounting							
Popelka, Carl B.	Assoc	Wis-Rvr Fall	FCS	MBA		Roosevelt	* &1981
Popowits, Michael T.	Lect	Ill-Chicago	DSJ	MSA	83	Illinois	&1988
Porcano, Thomas M.	Prof	Miami U-Ohio	XI	DBA	76.	Indiana	& 1-77
Arthur Andersen & Co. Alumni Professor of Accounting							
Porch, Mike G.	SLect	U Glamorgan	XFM	BSC	86	Wansea	& 1-96
Pornupatham, Sompong	Lect	Chulalongkor	AFSX	PHD	06	Cardiff	&2000
Porporato, Marcela	Prof	De Cordoba		MS		Suffolk	
Porreca, Albert	Retir	Staten Isl	1988	MS	52	Columbia	1961
Portelli, Frank	Lect	Tech-Sydney	FIMS	MCOM	79	NS Wales	1975
Porter, Brenda	Prof	Victoria NZ	AFM	PHD	90	Victoria	2003

Name	Rank	School		Degree		Institution	
Porter, Gary A.			FTPE	PHD	77.	Colorado	&
Porter, Grover L.	Prof	Tenn State	FM	PHD	73.	LSU	&2001
Porter, Jason	Asst	Idaho	F	PHD	06.	Georgia	2006
Porter, Leslie R.	Clin	So Calif	DS	PHD	80	UCLA	1994
Porter, Mattie C.	Prof	Houston-Cl L	AFM	PHD	79.	Tx A&M	&1986
Porter, R. Alan	Retir	E New Mexico	1997	PHD	66.	Arkansas	&1992
Porter, Susan L.	Assoc	Massachusett	FX	PHD	94.	U Wash	& 9-98
Porter, Thomas L.			FT	PHD	92.	U Wash	&
Porter, W. Thomas Jr.		Touche Ross		PHD	64.	Columbia	&1975
Portnoff, Linda		Stockholm Ec	M	CE	00	Goteborg	1994
Portz, Kristin	Assoc	St Cloud St	FS	PHD	00.	Nebraska	&2000
Posey, Clyde L.	Prof	Alcorn St	MA	PHD	78.	Okla St	&2005
Posey, Imogene A.	Retir	Tennessee	1997	MS	62	Tennessee	* &1966
Posey, J. Marion	Retir	Pace	FRX	PHD	68.	Arkansas	& 9-84
Posey, Roderick B.	Prof	So Miss	MGN	PHD	80.	Okla St	& 9-79
Jerold J. Morgan Professor							
Poskitt, Russell	SLect	U Auckland	F	PHD	01	Auckland	2002
Poston, Kay M.		South Univ	CM	DBA	84.	Tennessee	&
Poston, Robin S.	Asst		S	PHD	03	Mich St	&
Univ of Memphis; Dept of Management Information Systems							
Poteau, Raymond	Prof	Philadelphia	AEFG	MBA	73	Geo Wash	&1984
Potratz, Wendy K.	Inst	Wis-Oshkosh	FM	MBA	88	Wi-Oshko	* &2007
Potter, Bradley N.	SLect	U Melbourne	F	PHD	03	Deakin	2003
Potter, Gordon S.	Assoc	Cornell-Hotl	FM	PHD	86.	Wisconsin	&1994
Potter, Thomas	Lect	SUNY-Oneonta	GNX	BS	69	SUNY-Alb	&1978
Potts, Andrew J.	Prof	So Maine	FM	EDD	77	Geo Wash	&1985
Potts, Bill L.	Retir	Wis-Plattev	2002	MBA	72	Colorado	& 8-79
Potts, James H.	Retir	Cen Florida	2001	PHD	76.	Alabama	& 8-90
Poullaos, Chris	AProf	Univ Sydney	FHW	PHD	93	NS Wales	&2004
Poulson, Linda L.	Assoc	Elon	FX	PHD	99.	St Louis	& 1-98
Pourciau, Susan G.			F	PHD	88.	Ariz St	&
Pourjalali, Hamid	Prof	Hawaii-Manoa	CMFI	PHD	92.	Okla St	8-96
Powell, Cindy	Asst	S Nazarene	PXFJ	MBA	91	Cen Okla	&1985
Powell, Norma C.	Retir	Mass-Lowell	2002	PHD	82.	Tx A&M	&1991
Powell, Ray M.	Retir	Notre Dame	1993	DBA	59.	Indiana	&1959
Powell, Richard W.	C-Ac	Pepper-L Ang	XF	PHD	97.	Arkansas	&1996
Power, David M.	Prof	Dundee	FQTI	PHD	92	Dundee	1987
Power, Jacqueline Lou	Retir	Tx A&M Intl	2002	PHD	93.	Tx A&M	9-93
Power, Jeffrey	Asst	St Marys-Cdn	MCE	PHD	91.	Purdue	* 1995
Power, Michael K.	Prof	London Econ	AFTO	PHD	84	Cambridge	&1987
Powers, Marian			FIX	PHD	82.	Illinois	
Powers, Ollie S.	Assoc	Alabama-Birm	FV	MA	71	Alabama	* 1976
Powers, Victor	Retir	Cs-Chico	1995	PHD	71.	U Wash	&
Pownall, Grace	Prof	Emory	FI	PHD	85.	Chicago	8-93
Poynter, Harry V.	Retir	Cen Missouri	PS	MBA	75	Missouri	&1981
Poznanski, Peter John	Assoc	Cleveland St	BCM	PHD	91.	Tx Tech	* &1991
Prachyl, Cheryl L.	Adj	Tx-Arlington	S	PHD	96.	Tx-Arlin	& 6-03
Prado, Edwin	Assoc	Puerto Rico	X	LLM	91	NYU	&1991
Pragasam, John	SLect	So Queenslnd	AIB	MSC	80	Hull	&1992
Prakash, Prem	Prof	Pittsburgh	FM	PHD	71	MIT	1977
Prater, George I.				PHD	63.	Stanford	&1965
Prater, Mary Ann M.	SLect	Clemson	FMP	MS	83	Clemson	&1985
Prather-Kinsey, Jenice J.	Assoc	Missouri	CHI	PHD	85.	Alabama	&1984
Pratt, James W.	Prof	Houston	X	DBA	72.	S Calif	&1972
PricewaterhouseCoopers Professor							
Pratt, Jamie H.	Prof	Indiana	BAEI	DBA	77.	Indiana	&1990
KPMG Professor of Accounting							
Prawitt, Douglas F.	Prof	Brigham Yg	AB	PHD	93.	Arizona	& 1-93
Warnick/Deloitte & Touche Research Fellow							
Preda, Paul	ALect	Univ Sydney	FMT	BBUS	97	UTS	&2001
Preis, Nancy J.		Kleinwort Be	1991	PHD	82.	Michigan	
Kleinwort Benson; 200 Park Ave 25th Floor; New York NY 10166							
Premo, Patrick M.	Retir	St Bonaventu	FGNP	MS	73	St Bonav	&1970
Premont, Marion	Retir	Siena	1996	MS			& 9-75
Prentice, Charles A.	Retir	Calgary	1989	PHD	71.	Berkeley	1972
Prentice, Deborah	Asst	Mass-Dartmou	FA	PHD	99	Alabama	&2001
Prescott, Gregory L.	Inst	So Alabama	P	MACC	93	S Alabama	&1994
Preslar, Tina	Asst	Pfeiffer	AFPM	MA	00	NC-Charl	8-01
Press, Eric G.	C-Ac	Temple	F	PHD	88.	Oregon	&1992
Pressly, Thomas R.			FM	PHD	89.	Kent St	&
Prestigiacomo, Chris	AsTch	Missouri	FM	PHD	96	Missouri	* 2004
Preston, Alistair M.	Prof	New Mexico	MBS	PHD	82	Bath	1992
Grant Thornton Professor of Accounting							
Preston, R.	SLect	London Metro	X				&
Presutti, Anthony H. Jr.	Asst	Miami U-Ohio	SMC	PHD	88.	Cincinnati	&1989
Previts, Gary John	Prof	Case Western	FHKE	PHD	72.	Florida	& 7-79
Price, Agnes J.	Retir	N Car-Greens	6-97	ME	70	NC-Green	& 8-81

Price, Charles E.	Retir	Auburn	2007	PHD	87.	Georgia	&9-87
Price, Dennis W.	Asst	Samford	X	JD	88	Alabama	&2003
Price, Harry R.	Retir	U Miami	1985	PHD	54	Nrthwstrn	1947
Price, Jay H. Jr.	Prof	Utah State	FTVG	DACC	93	Utah St	&9-88
Arthur Andersen Executive Professor							
Price, Jean B.	Assoc	Marshall	PFVE	PHD	92.	Indiana	2002
Price, John E.	Prof	North Texas	X	PHD	81.	North Tx	&1987
Vice Provost, UNT at Dallas; area code (972)							
Price, Renee A.	Asst	Nebraska	FM	PHD	93.	Tx A&M	&2000
Price, Richard A. III	Asst	Rice	FD	PHD	05.	Stanford	2005
Price, Theresa	Inst	South Fla	AP	MACC	92	Florida	&8-92
Prieur, Nicole	Assoc	HEC-Montreal	X	LLM	00	HEC-Mont	6-99
Primiano, Lee	Retir	Montclair St	2001	MBA	74	Rutgers	&1975
Prince, Thomas R.	Prof	Northwestern	MSF	PHD	62.	Illinois	&1962
Pringle, Lynn M.	CIAs	Iowa	AM	PHD	87.	Colorado	&9-98
Pritchard, Joan	Deces	Cen Arkansas	G	MSE	75	Tennessee	&8-80
Privo, A.	Asst	Touro	PMF	PHD			2-87
Prober, Larry M.	Assoc	Rider	F	PHD	85.	Temple	* &1987
Probst, Frank R.	Retir	Marquette	5-05	PHD	69.	Florida	&1964
Proctor, Raymond	SLect	Coventry Un	M	MBA	90	Warwick	9-98
Proctor, Richard J.	Prof	Western Conn	AUVX	MBA	70	Columbia	&1983
Proctor, Thomas	C-Pr	Union-TN	X	PHD	00	Memphis	1996
Proimos, Alex	ALect	Macquarie Un	FM	BAF	03	Macquarie	2004
Prosch, Marilyn M.	Assoc	Ariz St West	SF	PHD	91.	Temple	&8-00
Provost, Robert A.	Deces	Bryant	1997	BS	61	Rhode Isl	&9-67
Pruis, Donald E.	Retir	Calvin	1993	ABD		Michigan	&1957
Pryor, Charlotte A.	Assoc	So Maine	MSGN	PHD	96.	Penn St	&1999
Pryor, Leroy J.	Retir	CS-Chico	1999	DBA	72.	S Calif	&9-80
Przybyla, Jane	Assoc	Rhode Isl Cl	AEFS	MBA	73	Rutgers	&9-85
Psaros, Jim	Prof	U Newcastle	A	PHD	97	NS Wales	&1982
Puig, Xavier	Asst	Pompeu Fabra			02	UPF	
Pulliam, Dale R.	Retir	West Tx A&M	1998	PHD	79.	North Tx	&9-79
Pumphrey, Lela M. (Kitty)	Retir	Idaho State	D-06	PHD	84.	Missouri	# * &1988
Purcell, Harold I.	Retir	CS-Bakersf	7-91	DBA	71.	S Calif	&9-71
508 Portsmouth St; Bakersfield CA 93311							
Purcell, Thomas J. III	Assoc	Creighton	XLI	PHD	88.	Nebraska	&9-79
Purdy, Charles R.	Retir	Denver	1990	PHD	63.	Minnesota	&1988
Puretz, Elliott H.	Assoc	Merrimack	FXTR	MBA	74	Boston U	&1974
Purisky, John C.	Assoc	Salem State	MN	MBA	89	Rider	* &9-90
Purnell, Allan	Lect	Deakin-Burwo	F	BBUS	76	VColl	&1984
Puro, Marsha			FX	PHD	83.	Wash U	
Pursifull, Charles	Inst	Central Okla	PFM	MBA	58	Oklahoma	&1-95
Purvis, S. E. C.	Asst	Nevada-Reno	F	PHD	85.	Columbia	&2006
Pushkin, Ann B.	Prof	W Virginia	ADOS	PHD	78.	Va Tech	&1981
Pusker, Henri C.	Retir	Savannah St	1994	DBA	62.	Indiana	&1987
2032 Skyview Lane; Kent OH 44240; 330-678-5754							
Pustorino, Anthony R.	Retir	Pace	2002	MBA	54	NYU	&9-65
Putman, Robert L.	Prof	Tenn-Martin	GFC	DBA	88.	Memphis	&8-90
Putnam, Donald F.	Retir	CS-Pomona	2006	PHD	76	Claremont	&9-79
Putnam, Karl B.	Assoc	Txs-El Paso	FMGR	PHD	80.	Okla St	6-86
Putney, Frederick B.	P&S	Columbia		PHD	68.	Stanford	1969
Puttee, Colleen	Lect	W Sydney	ABEF	MCOM	94	Wollong	
Pye, Malcolm L.	Retir	Temple	1985	PHD	54.	Illinois	&1-75
Pyke, C. J.	H-PLe	Liverpool JM	FG	MPHL			1995
Pyo, Youngin		Kangwon Univ	1995	PHD	87.	Purdue	
Kangwon University; Chuncheon, Korea							
Pyper, Rhonda	Asst	Univ Ottawa	MB	MBA	03	Laurentian	* 2006
Pyrah, Bradan D.	Assoc	Manchester C	LPX	JD	86	Brighm Yg	&1995
Qagish, Mahmoud	Assoc	Yarmouk Univ	CM	PHD	87	Rensselaer	1987
Qi, Daqing D.			FM	PHD	96.	Mich St	
Qiang, Xinrong			FIMS	PHD	04.	SUNY-Buf	
Qu, Sandy Q.	Asst	York Univ	FM	PHD	06	Alberta	2006
Quadackers, Luc L. M.	Lect	Vrije Univ	AB	MS	92	Maastricht	2004
Quan, Daniel	Assoc	Cornell-Hotl	F	PHD	90	Berkeley	1999
Quarles, N. Ross	Prof	Sam Houston	SAM	PHD	88.	North Tx	&1994
Quattrone, Paolo	Lect	Oxford Univ	MS	PHD	96	Catania	2003
Que, Antonio L.	Retir	Clarion	5-02	PHD	85.	NYU	&8-85
Quigley, Behnaz Z.	Prof	Marymount		PHD	87.	Maryland	2002
Quilliam, William C.	Inst	South Fla	AB	PHD	91.	Florida	# &8-92
Quinn, Tina Steward	C-Ac	Arkansas St	FX	PHD	96.	Miss	&8-96
Quinones, Eva Z.	Assoc	Puerto RicoM	CFPR	MPA	88	Tx-Austin	&1-90
Quintana, Olga	Assoc	U Miami	MNG	DBA	75.	Geo Wash	&1979
Quintanilla, Hector	Dean$	Txs Wesleyan	BFX	PHD	96.	Tx-Arlin	&1995
Quire, Catherine DeMotte	Deces			PHD	37.	Berkeley	
Quirin, Jeffrey J.	Assoc	Wichita St	CMF	PHD	98.	Nebraska	2000
W. Frank Barton Distinguished Chair in Business							
Quirke, B.	SLect	Liverpool-JM	F	MPHL			1992

Quon, John P.	Retir	Delta State	CMFP	MBA	65	Miss		&1971
Quon, Pamela	C-As	Athabasca Un		BCOM		Alberta		2001
Qureshi, Anique Ahmed			MA	PHD	93.	Rutgers		&
Qureshi, Mahmood A.	Retir	CS-Northrdge	2004	PHD	69.	UCLA		1979
Quynh, Nguyen Quang	Dean	Natl Econ	AOFM	PHD	82	Karel Mark		1968
Raabe, William A.	SLect	Ohio State	XIE	PHD	79.	Illinois		&2003
Raar, Jean	Lect	Deakin-Burwo	EM	PHD	99	RMIT		&1993
Rabe, Craig	Asst	Luther	FMC	MBA	04	Minnesota		&2004
Rabe, Elizabeth	Inst	NE St-Okla	FS	MS	01	SMSU		&2006
Rabinowitz, Allan M.	Prof	Pace	FOUB	MBA	62	NYU		&1962
Raby, William L.	Retir	Arizona St	1993	PHD	71.	Arizona		&1990
Radcliffe, Vaughan S.	C-Ac	West Ontario	AOPS	PHD	95	Alberta		2003
Radebaugh, Lee H.	Prof	Brigham Yg	IFM	DBA	73	Indiana		9-80
KPMG Professor								
Radford, Jack J.	SLect	Lincoln-NZ	BCMW	BCOM	74	Otago		&1987
Radhakrishna, Bal			F	PHD	95.	Michigan		&
Radhakrishnan, Suresh	Prof	Texas-Dallas	FCMA	PHD	92.	NYU		&1999
Radice, Gerard V.	Retir	DePaul	1989	MBA	49	Chicago		&1969
Radich, Renee	Prof	Macquarie Un	A	PHD	02	Bond		&1999
Radig, William J.	Retir	Marshall	1998	DBA	88.	Miss St		& 9-72
Radoll, Peter	Asst	Australian N	S	MIT	03	Canberra		2003
Radtke, Robin R.	Asst	Fla Atlantic	BCJ	PHD	92.	Florida		8-07
Raedy, Jana Smith	Assoc	No Carolina	F	PHD	98.	Penn St		& 7-97
Raedy, Kevin M.	Adj	No Carolina	AF	PHD	98.	Penn St		&2002
Raffield, Janice M.	Assoc	St Thomas-MN	FAE	MPAC	91	Clemson		& 9-92
Ragan, Joseph M.	C-Ac	St Joseph	MVSU	MBA	75	Penn	*	&1977
Rager, Larry	Asst	St Fran-Penn		DBA	04	Nova SE		1999
Raghavan, Kamala	Asst	Robt Morris	CF	DBA	04	Clev St		8-04
Raghunandan, K.	Prof	Fla Internat	FA	PHD	90.	Iowa	*	2003
Raghunathan, Bhanu	Prof	Toledo	MC	PHD	86.	Pittsburgh		&1985
Raghurandam, Moolchand	Lect	West Indies	C	MSC		W Indies		
Ragothaman, Srinivasan C.	Prof	South Dakota	ASF	PHD	91.	Kansas		&1991
Ragsdale, Robert W.	Asst	Johnson&Wale	IXF	MBA	79	Fairl Dick		&1994
Ragunthan, Vanitha	Lect	U Queensland	QI	PHD	99	RMIT		1999
Rahaman, Abu Shiraz	Assoc	Univ Calgary	SB	PHD	98	Waikato		&2002
Rahman, Asheq Razaur	Prof	Massey-Alban	F	PHD	88	Sydney		2006
Rahman, Mawdudur	Prof	Suffolk	FCBS	PHD	76	Manchest		1981
Rahman, Monsurur	Prof	Indiana U-PA	FC	DBA	92.	S Illinois		
Rahman, Sheikh F.	Asst	Southern-NO	PFXG	MBA	69	Tx So		&1969
Rai, Atul	Asst	Wichita St	F	PHD	96.	NYU		2007
Raiborn, Cecily A.	Prof	Tx St-S Marc	FCJM	PHD	75.	LSU	*	&2006
McCoy Professor of Accounting								
Raiborn, Mitchell H.	Prof	Bradley	FM	PHD	70.	Missouri	*	& 8-81
Raisty, Lloyd B.	Retir	Fed Reser-CA		PHD	34.	Tx-Austin		
Rajan, Madhav V.	C-Pr	Stanford	M	PHD	90.	Car Mellon		2001
Rajgopal, Shivaran	Prof	U Washington	F	PHD	98.	Iowa		2003
Rakotonjanahary, Philemon	Asst	HEC-Montreal	ABFI	PHD	99	HEC-Mont		6-01
Rakow, Jessica	Inst	Louisiana St	FM	MS	00	Miss		& 8-07
Rakow, K. C.	Asst	Louisiana St	FM	PHD	05.	Georgia		& 8-05
Rall, Deforest J.	Retir	Montana St	1993	PHD	74	N Dakota		9-71
Ralston, Frances M. B.	Deces	Ark St		PHD	98.	Miss		&
Rama, Dasaratha V.	Prof	Fla Internat	S	PHD	90	Iowa	*	2003
Ramage, Judy Anne	Prof	Christian Br	FM	DBA	95	Nova SE		&1992
Ramaglia, Judith A.	D-Pr	Pacific Luth	FI	PHD	88.	U Wash		&1982
Ramakrishnan, Ram T. S.	H-Pr	Ill-Chicago	FMT	PHD	81.	Nrthwstrn		1994
Ernst & Young Professor of Accounting								
Ramalingegowda, Santhosh	Asst	Georgia	FM	PHD	06.	Penn St		8-06
Ramamoorti, Sridhar (Sri)		Ernst & Youn	2004	PHD	95	Ohio St		& 8-98
Ernst & Young LLP								
Ramamurthy, Rama	Asst	Wm & Mary	CFM	MAS	91	Illinois		2006
Raman, K. K.	Prof	North Texas	FGN	PHD	79.	Indiana		&1981
O. J. Curry Professor								
Ramanan, Ramachandran	Prof	Notre Dame	FM	PHD	86.	Nrthwstrn		1991
Ramanathan, K. V.	Emer	U Washington	CMU	PHD	70.	Nrthwstrn		&1971
Ramanauskas, Helene M. A.	Retir	DePaul	1989	PHD	48	Munich		&1959
Ramaswamy, K. P.	AdjAc	Hong Kong Sc	CFM	PHD	93.	Kansas		1994
Ramaswamy, Vinita M.	Assoc	St Thomas-TX	FVT	PHD	94.	Houston		8-95
Rambo, Robert G.	Asst	Providence	FV	PHD	94.	Fla St		&2006
Ramesh, Krishnamoorthy	Prof	Michigan St	FK	PHD	91.	Mich St		8-03
Plante & Moran Teaching Fellow								
Ramnath, Sundaresh	Asst	Georgetown	F	PHD	96.	Penn St		2001
Ramos-Alexander, Jeannette	Assoc	NewJerseyCty	ACDF	MBA	79	Fairl Dick	*	&1989
Ramsaran, Tara	Lect	Concordia U	T	MBA	00	Concordia		&2001
Ramsay, Alan L.	Assoc	Monash Univ	EF	MEC				1981
Ramsay, Louis P.	Retir	Clemson	2000	DBA	75.	Kent St		&1980
Ramsay, Robert J.	Assoc	Kentucky	AB	PHD	91.	Indiana		&1995
Arthur Andersen & Co. Professor of Accounting								

Name	Rank	University		Degree	Yr	School		
Ramsey, Donald D.	Assoc	Univ of D C	EPS	MBA	69	American		&1972
Rand, Richard S. Jr.	Assoc	Tenn Tech	AFO	PHD	89.	S Carol		&1989
Randall, Boyd C.	Prof	Brigham Yg	X	PHD	72.	Minnesota		9-74
Ernst & Young Professor								
Randall, Clyde N.	Deces	Utah		PHD	46.	Stanford		&1931
Randall, Reed H.	Retir	Utah	1999	PHD	69	Berkeley		1969
Randall, Taylor R.	Asst	Utah	M	PHD	99	Penn		1999
Randolph, David W.	Asst	Dayton	XF	PHD	00.	Indiana		&2003
Rangan, Srinivasan			F	PHD	95.	Penn		&
Ranganathan, Krishnan	Assoc	Angelo State	XMP	PHD	90.	North Tx	*	&1997
Rangarajan, A. V.	Inst	Cen St-Ohio	VFDM	MS	69	Wash U		9-70
Ranirez, Carlos	Asst	HEC Paris	AHIJ	PHD	03	EHESS Pari		2002
Rankin, D. C.	SLect	Univ Ulster	FX	FCA				&1-72
Rankin, Debbie	Asst	Lincoln	F	MS		Missouri		& 8-86
Rankin, Frederick W.	Assoc	Colorado St	M	PHD	99.	Tx A&M		2005
Rankin, Larry J.	Assoc	Miami U-Ohio	AE	PHD	82.	Mich St		&1980
Rankin, Michaela	Lect	So Queenslnd	TFW	MEC	97	N Eng-Au		1994
Rankine, Graeme W.	C-Ac	Thunderbird	FI	PHD	87.	U Wash		1995
Rans, D. Lynn	Retir	CS-L Angeles	2000	DBA	72.	Indiana		&1984
Ransom, Charles R. (Chuck)	Assoc	Oklahoma St	FIT	PHD	83.	Wisconsin		&1981
Ransopher, Tad D.	Asst	Georgia St	X	JD		Geo St		9-94
Rao, Arundhati S. (Aru)	Assoc	Morgan State	FS	PHD	96.	Cincinnati		2001
Rao, Gita			F	PHD	90.	Rochester		
Rao, H. V. Vasudeva			FC	PHD	74.	Tx A&M		&
Rao, Hema	Asst	SUNY Oswego	AFGN	DBA	90.	Miss St		&2000
Rao, Kailas J.			SF	PHD	74.	Oklahoma		1981
Rapaccioli, Donna	Assoc	Fordham	V	PHD	88.	NYU		&1986
Rapp, Lucille	Retir	Quincy	5-92	MBA		W Illinois		&1972
Rappaport, Alfred	Retir	Northwestern	1996	PHD	63.	Illinois		&1967
Ras, Gerard	Inter	Wayne St Col	APG	MBA	03	Wayne Co		&2005
Rasaratnam, S.	Lect	Univ Ulster	F	MSC				4-98
Rasch, Ronald H.	Retir	Auburn	2004	PHD	80.	Tx-Austin		9-93
Raschke, Robyn L.	Asst	Nev-L Vegas	S	PHD	07	Ariz St		&2007
Raslan, Maher M.	Asst	King Saud U	1991	PHD	83.	Arkansas		
Acct Dept; Col of Admin Sci; POB 2459 King Saud Univ; Riyadh 11451 Saudi-Arab								
Rasmussen, David J.	Assoc	St Martin	MP	MBA	73	Utah		&1993
Rasmussen, Janicke	SLect	Norwegian Mg	FM	CPA	90	NHH Berg		2000
Rassi, Faouzi	Prof	Quebec-Montr	M	DSCE		Geneva		6-83
Ratcliffe, Thomas A.	Retir	Troy	2006	PHD	78.	Alabama		&1986
Rathe, Hjalmar J.	Retir	Portland St	1989	MBA	55	Oregon		&1964
Ratliff, Dennis J.	Assoc	Jacksonvil U	CFXV	MBA	76	Wright St		&1978
Ratliff, James R.	Retir	New York U	2002	PHD	70.	NYU		&1964
Ratliff, Richard L.	Retir	Utah State	AO	PHD	79.	N Carol	#	1990
Ratliff-Miller, Paulette A.	Asst	Grand Valley	CFM	PHD	01.	Oklahoma		8-07
Ratnatunga, Janek	Prof	Monash Univ	MC	PHD	90			&1990
Ratti, Barbara B.		Cen Florida		PHD	95.	Cen Fla		
Rau, Stephen E.	C-Ac	Duquesne	AFMS	PHD	97	Pittsburgh		1999
Frandk & Ann Cahouet Professor								
Rauch, Susan L.	Retir	Shippensburg	2003	MS	82	Southeas		& 9-83
Raun, Donald L.	Retir	CS-Northrdge	1992	MBA	49	Stanford		&1959
Raux, Donald	Asst	Siena	FGN	PHD	02	SUNY-Alb		&
Raval, Vasant H.	Prof	Creighton	SMIC	DBA	76.	Indiana		9-80
Raven, John	Lect	Monash Univ	EF	MBA				1995
Ravenscroft, Sue P.	Prof	Iowa State	MFBE	PHD	89.	Mich St		& 8-98
Raver, Daniel H.	Assoc	Geneva	PFM	MBA	85	Pittsburgh		&1980
Raverta, Eusebia Louis		Springfie MA	1992	PHD	71.	NYU		
2495 Wilbraham Rd; Springfield MA 01129								
Ravi, Indumathi			F	PHD	90.	SUNY-Buf		&
Ravia, David				PHD	01.	NYU		
Analysis Group/Economics								
Rawashdeh, Mufeed			FM	PHD	94.	St Louis		
Ray, Amy W.			S	PHD	89.	Va Tech		
Ray, Delmas D.	Deces	Florida	6-98	PHD	56.	Florida		&1948
Ray, Graham H.	Retir	Univ Bath	1996	PHD	81	Bath		1964
Ray, J. C.	Retir	CS-L Angeles	1989	MBA	57	Tulsa		&1957
303 30th Street; Hermosa Beach CA 90254								
Ray, J. O. III		Troy State	1990	DBA	85.	Miss St		
430 Cecilla Dr; Memphis TN 38117								
Ray, Korok	Asst	Chicago	CMTY	PHD	04	Stanford		2004
Ray, Manash R.			M	PHD	89.	Penn St		
Rayburn, Frank R.	Emer	Alabama-Birm	1998	PHD	74.	Alabama	*	&1990
Rayburn, Judy D.	C-Pr	Minnesota	F	PHD	85.	Iowa		&1985
Rayburn, L. Gayle	Deces	SE Missouri	2000	PHD	66.	LSU	# *	&1993
Rayburn, William	D	Austin Peay	DecS	MBA	82	Vanderbilt		1989
Raymond, Robert H.	Retir	Nebraska	1991	PHD	64.	Mich St		&1958
Raza, Syed A.	Lect	King Fahd Un	MIS	MS	00	King Fahd		2001
Razaki, Khalid A.	Prof	Illinois St	M	PHD	86.	Illinois		1980

Name	Rank	School	Code	Deg	Yr	Deg School		Last
Razeed, Abdul J.	Lect	Univ Sydney	FWS	BCOM	98	Murdoch		&2005
Razek, Joseph R.	Retir	New Orleans	2003	PHD	73.	Illinois		&1977
Read, William J.	Prof	Bentley	FA	PHD	84.	Va Tech		&1984
Reardon, John F.	Retir	LaSalle	2002	EDD	72	Temple		9-62
Rearick, Thomas R.	Lect	Indiana	F	BA	87	Indiana		2002
Rebber, Dennis L.			MF	PHD	79.	S Carol		
Rebele, James E.	Prof	Robt Morris	AFS	PHD	84.	Indiana		1-04
Reber, Beat	Lect	U Nottingham	M	PHD	00	Nottingh		2001
Rebmann-Huber, Zelma	Retir	Simon Fraser	8-99	PHD	88.	U Wash		1-87
Rebovich, Joseph	Retir	New York U	2002	PHD	72	NYU		1991
Reburn, James P.	D-Pr	Samford	FNS	DBA	88.	La Tech		&1996
Rechtschaffen, Glenn	STut	U Auckland	FA	JD	82	UCLA		2001
Reck, Jacqueline L.	Assoc	South Fla	GMF	PHD	96.	Missouri		&8-96

James E. Rooks Distinguished Professor

Name	Rank	School	Code	Deg	Yr	Deg School		Last
Reckers, Philip M. J.	Prof	Arizona St	FAB	PHD	78.	Illinois		1980
Redding, Rodney J.	Assoc	Am U Sharjah	FPT	PHD	79.	Penn St		&2003
Redemske, Mike	Inst	Connecticut	X	MS		DePaul		2001
Redenbaugh, Margaret	Assoc	Buena Vista	PXCA	MBA	74	NW Mo St	*	&1982
Redfield, James E.		Nacogdoch TX	1992	PHD	60.	Tx-Austin		

PO Drawer 1402; Nacogdoches TX 75961

Name	Rank	School	Code	Deg	Yr	Deg School		Last
Redhead, Keith J.	PLect	Coventry Un	P	MPHL	75	Warwick		9-72
Redinbaugh, Donna			FM	PHD	86.	Nebraska		
Reding, Kurt F.	Prof	Friends	OAF	PHD	88.	Tennessee	# *	&1-07
Redmer, Timothy A. O.	Prof	Regent Univ	MFN	PHD	88.	Va Comm	*	5-91
Redpath, Ian J.	C-Ac	Canisius	XL	LLM	86	Wisconsin		1985
Reeb, David	Prof	Temple	M	PHD	96	S Carol		2006
Reece, James S.	Prof	Michigan	M	DBA	70.	Harvard	*	1975

Professor of Accounting & Operations Management

Name	Rank	School	Code	Deg	Yr	Deg School		Last
Reece, William T.	Retir	Old Dominion	1988	MBA	56	N Carol		&1969
Reed, Anita	Asst	North Texas	ASM	PHD	07	S Fla		2006
Reed, Arthur E.	Inst	Bentley	X	MST	85	Bentley		&1989
Reed, Barbara L.			FI	PHD	82.	Ariz St		
Reed, Bradford J.	Assoc	S Ill-Edward	FA	PHD	95.	Arizona		&1995
Reed, Connie	SLect	Univ Toronto	FM	MBA	96	Leicester	*	1989
Reed, Donna S.			FNA	DBA	99.	Miss St	#	
Reed, I. Max	Deces	E Kentucky	1989	PHD	76.	Missouri	*	1974
Reed, Margaret P.	Asst	Cincinnati	X	PHD	97.	Kansas		&8-97
Reed, Randy M.			MSV	DBA	98.	La Tech		&
Reed, Richard E.	Retir	Augustana IL	2001	MBA	73	Bowl Gr		&9-73
Reed, Ronald O.	Prof	No Colorado	APFJ	PHD	81.	Tx Tech		&1988
Reeder, Craig	Inst	Florida A&M	FM	MBA				
Reeder, David B.	Retir	Evansville	FXA	DBA	80.	Kentucky		&1-68
Reeder, Janis R.	Retir	Delaware	X	PHD	78.	S Carol		&1981
Rees, D.	Lect	London Metro	DS	MSC				2001
Rees, David A.	Prof	Srthrn Utah	FGT	PHD	82.	Tx Tech		&1985
Rees, Lynn L.	Prof	Houston	FI	PHD	94.	Ariz St		9-05

C. T. Bauer Professor

Name	Rank	School	Code	Deg	Yr	Deg School		Last
Reese, Craig E.	Prof	St Thomas-FL	XGAT	PHD	79.	Tx-Austin		8-92
Reese, Otis G.	Retir	SW Texas St	1990	MA	56	SW Tx St		&1956
Reese, Sara F.	Asst	Virg Union	SCM	MACC	80	Miss		&8-87
Reeve, James M.			M	PHD	80.	Okla St		&
Regel, Roy W.	Prof	Montana	MC	PHD	85.	Colorado	*	&9-85
Regev, Tomer		Morgan Stanl		PHD	01.	Columbia		
Regier, Philip R.	Assoc	Arizona St	F	PHD	87.	Illinois		&1987
Rego, Sonja Olhoft	Assoc	Iowa	FX	PHD	99.	Michigan		&8-99

Lloyd J. and Thelma W. Palmer Research Fellow

Name	Rank	School	Code	Deg	Yr	Deg School		Last
Reichardt, Karl E.	Assoc	Valparaiso	CSME	PHD	71.	Missouri	*	1988
Reichelstein, Stefan	Prof	Stanford	MF	PHD	84	Nrthwstrn		2001

William R. Timken Professor of Accounting

Name	Rank	School	Code	Deg	Yr	Deg School		Last
Reichelt, Kenneth	Asst	Louisiana St	FM	PHD	05	Missouri		&8-05
Reichert, Charles J.	Prof	Wis-Superior	FX	MST	77	Colo St	#	&1977
Reid, George R.	Retir	Savannah St	1999	PHD	83.	Missouri		1987
Reid, Graeme C.	Lect	Univ Hull	FD	BSC	82	Hull		9-92
Reid, K.	PLect	London Metro	FA	MBA				1989
Reid, Linda W.	Asst	Adams State	S	DBA	05	Nova SE		&
Reid, Mark E.	Assoc	New Orleans	X	PHD	98.	Geo St		&1997
Reider, Barbara P.	Prof	Montana	FM	PHD	91.	Kent St	# *	&2001
Reilly, Terence J.	Prof	Albright	F	MS	67	Northeas		&1975
Reimers, Jane L.	Prof	Rollins	MB	PHD	86.	Michigan		&8-03
Reingold, Theodore	Assoc	Lenoir-Rhyne	F	DBA	95	Golden Gt		&1998
Reininga, Warren H.	Emer	Ohio Univ	1988	MS	47	Indiana		&1950
Reinoso, Richardo C.	Retir	Lynchburg	1999	PHD	71.	N Carol		&1995
Reinstein, Alan	Prof	Wayne State	AF	DBA	80.	Kentucky		&1987

George R. Husband Professor of Accounting

Name	Rank	School	Code	Deg	Yr	Deg School		Last
Reinstein, Todd R.	Emer	CS-Northrdge	X	JD	62	UCLA		&1967
Reis, Priscilla R.	Assoc	Idaho State	MS	PHD	91	Rensselaer	*	&1994
Reis, Ricardo	Asst	Portuguese U		PHD	05.	Penn		

Name	Rank	School		Degree	Yr	School		
Reisch, John T.	Assoc	East Carol	ABC	PHD	97.	S Carol		&8-99
Reisch, Michele	Lect	East Carol	FM	MBA	99	Fla Atl		2002
Reisig, Raymond	Asst	Pace-Westch	AF	MBA	76	Pace		&1979
Reitenga, Austin L.	Asst	Alabama	D	PHD	98.	Kentucky	*	&8-06
Reiter, Sara A.	C-Ac	SUNY-Bingham	F	PHD	85.	Missouri		&1990
Remmele, David A.	Retir	Wis-Whitewat	FM	PHD	85.	Wisconsin		&1981
Renault, Micheline	Prof	Quebec-Montr	M	DSC		Mons		&6-89
Renders, Annelies	Asst	Maastricht	F	PHD	06	Leuven		2006
Reneau, J. Hal	Deces	Arizona St	2000	PHD	75.	Missouri		&1975
Renner, Celia J.	Assoc	Boise State	SCM	PHD	95.	Colorado		&2002
Rennie, Morina D.	Prof	Univ Regina	ABEF	PHD	89	Alberta	*	&1982
Renshaw, Claude D.	Prof	St Marys-Ind	XIP	MBA	70	Mich St		&1-77
Rentfro, Randy W.	Asst	Nova SE	SFCE	PHD	00.	Fla Atl	*	&2006
Resler, William M.	SLect	U Washington	X	LLM	73	NYU		1982
Reveley, T R (Tom)	Deces	St Thomas-TX	7-95	PHD	78.	Houston		&9-85
Revoir, Richard L.	Asst	St Scholasti	PFSX	MBA	96	Ariz St		8-04
Revsine, Lawrence	Prof	Northwestern	FTI	PHD	68.	Nrthwstrn		&1971
John & Norma Darling Distinguished Professor of Financial Accounting								
Rexer, Marianne M.	C-Pr	Wilkes	AS	PHD	97.	Drexel		&8-90
Rexroad, W. Max	Retir	Illinois St	2004	PHD	78.	Illinois		&1969
Reynolds, Don	Assoc	Calvin		PHD	03	Sarasota		2003
Reynolds, Issac N.	Retir	No Carolina	1988	PHD	57.	N Carol		1949
312 Estes Drive; Chapel Hill NC 27514								
Reynolds, J. Kenneth			AS	PHD	99.	Missouri		
Reynolds, Mary Ann	Assoc	Western Wash	FWJ	PHD	88	Utah		1995
Reynolds, Ruthie G.	Prof	Tenn State	CFLX	PHD	81.	Geo St		&1998
Reynolds-Moehrle, Jennifer	Assoc	Mo-St Louis	F	PHD	97.	Indiana		&1999
Rezac, Reg N.	Prof	Txs Woman's	XTV	PHD	74	N Colo		1983
Rezaee, Zabihollah	Prof	Memphis	MA	PHD	85.	Miss	# *	&2001
Thompson-Hill Chair of Excellance								
Rhame, Susan R.	Asst	Austin Col		PHD	95.	Tx-Arlin		8-95
Rhoades-Catanach, Shelley C.	Assoc	Villanova	XM	PHD	95.	Tx-Austin		&1998
Rhode, John Grant			AFXB	PHD	69.	Minnesota		&
Rhodes, William R.	ClAs	Mississippi	LX	JD	82	Miss		&1-97
Riahi-Belkaoui, Ahmed	Retir	Ill-Chicago	2006	PHD	72.	Syracuse	*	1980
Ricchiute, David N.	Prof	Notre Dame	A	DBA	77.	Kentucky		&9-77
Deloitte Chair								
Rice, E. Barry	Emer	Loyola-Maryl	2003	MBA	75	Maryland		&1975
Rice, John D.	Assoc	Trinity	XP	JD	79	Tx Tech		&1-84
Rice, John F.	SLect	Monash Univ	EPF	MEC	77	Monash		&1988
Rice, Sarah	Asst	Connecticut	ASB	PHD	06	Ohio St		2006
Rice, Steven J.	SLect	U Washington	X	PHD	74.	Tx-Austin		&1985
Rich, Anne J.	Prof	Central Conn	FMT	PHD	78.	Mass	*	&2007
Rich, Anne N.	Assoc	Cedarville	P	MS	78	Cen Fla		&2000
Rich, Dave	Asst	Kentucky St	MS	MBA		W Virginia		1985
Rich, Jay S.	Assoc	Illinois St	ABF	PHD	97.	Illinois		&2004
Rich, John C.	Assoc	Emporia St	FP	PHD	85.	North Tx		&9-68
Richard, J. Roland	Retir	Mass-Dartmou	2002	MBA	67	Boston C		&9-73
Richards, Claire			FPM	PHD	01.	Utah		
Richards, Don-Rice	Retir	Jms Madison	1993	PHD	78.	St Louis		9-78
Richards, E. William		Consulting	1989	PHD	76.	Mich St	# *	&1989
PO Box 808; Collegedale TN 37315								
Richards, James D.	Lect	Murdoch Univ	FM	BCOM		W Austrl		1986
Richards, Ralph J.				DBA	65.	Harvard		
Richards, Robert W.	Inst	Georgia St	X	MTX	81	Geo St		&8-84
Richards, Roy W.	Retir	Ind-Purdue	1989	DBA	67.	Indiana		&8-68
Richardson, A. William	Retir	McMaster Un	F	PHD	66	McMaster	*	7-04
Richardson, Alan J.	C-Pr	York Univ	BHM	PHD	85	Queen's		&2003
Richardson, Alex	Asst	Australian N	S	BIT	99	C Queensln		2003
Richardson, Clara L.	Assoc	McMurry	FMA	PHD	85.	Tx A&M		&1998
Richardson, Frederick M.	Prof	Virg Tech	FMT	PHD	80.	N Carol		1980
Richardson, Gordon D.	C-Pr	Univ Toronto	F	PHD	83.	Cornell		&2002
Richardson, Grant	Asst	City Univ HK	X	PHD	02	Monash		&2003
Richardson, Keith W.	C-Ac	Bellarmine	PFB	PHD	95.	Oregon		&8-97
Richardson, Robert C.	Assoc	Jms Madison	AP	PHD	98.	Va Tech		&9-01
Richardson, Scott A.			F	PHD	03.	Michigan		
Richardson, Vernon J.	C-Pr	Arkansas	SF	PHD	97.	Illinois		&2005
Ralph L. McQueen Chair								
Richardson, William M.	Lect	Monash Univ	CEM	MEC	84	Monash	*	1987
Richardson, Willie			AF	PHD	78.	Georgia		
Richardson, Wm. Eddie	C-Ac	Wofford	DF	PHD	92	Tennessee		9-02
Richeson, Leslie R.			SBM	PHD	89.	Tx Tech		
Richman, Vincent	Prof	Sonoma State	CM	PHD	97.	Columbia	*	2002
Richmond, Kelly A.			MIJ	PHD	01.	Va Tech		
Richtermeyer, Sandra B.	C-Ac	Xavier	FMN	PHD	97.	Colorado	*	&2004
IMA Professor in Residence								
Ricigliano, Daniel	Asst	Buffalo St	FMX	MBA	75	SUNY-Buf		&9-79

Ricketts, Donald E.	Deces	Cincinnati	8-96	DBA	71.	Indiana	1976
Ricketts, Jeri B.	Assoc	Cincinnati	F	PHD	86.	Cincinnati	&1982
Ricketts, Robert C.	Prof	Texas Tech	X	PHD	88.	North Tx	&1988
Frank Burke Chair in Taxation							
Ricks, William E.			1992	PHD	80.	Berkeley	&
575 Dalewood Dr; Orinda CA 94563							
Riechman, Edward J.	Assoc	Cen St-Ohio	AXFM	MBA	66	Xavier	&9-86
Riedl, Edward J.	Assoc	Harvard	F	PHD	02.	Penn St	2002
Rieman, Mark	Asst	East Carol	MSU	PHD	03.	Wash St	2003
Riess, F. Kelleher	ClPr	Tulane	X	LLM	72	Boston U	&1974
Riffe, Susan M.	SLect	So Methodist	F	PHD	92.	S Calif	1992
Riggs, William H.	Deces	Indiana SE	1992	MBA	64	New Mex	1969
Rigoli, Raymond C.	Assoc	Ramapo	AFT	MBA	83	Fairl Dick	&1983
Rigone, Anne	Inst	Mt St Mary's		MS		S Calif	&
Rigsby, John T.	Assoc	Miss State	FA	DBA	86.	Memphis	&1989
Riise, Arne J.	Retir	Norwegian U	2003	PHD	78.	Illinois	
Riistama, Veijo	Adj	Helsinki Sch	AFI	PHD	78	Helsinki	&1963
Riley, Anne C.	Retir		2001	DBA	87.	Geo Wash	&9-81
Riley, C. Allison	Assoc	Thomas Univ		PHD	06.	Fla St	&8-06
Riley, Donald B.	Emer	Chris Newpor	1992	MBA	63	N Carol	&1963
Riley, Mark E.	Asst	No Illinois	FX	PHD	07	Tx Tech	&2007
Riley, Richard A.	Assoc	W Virginia	FTU	PHD	98.	Tennessee	&8-98
Louis F. Tanner Distinguished Professor of Public Accounting							
Riley, Robert				PHD	62.	NYU	
Riner, Sam	Assoc	Southern Ark	AMSG	DBA	97.	La Tech	&1999
Rinke, Dolores F.	Prof	Purdue Calum	FIAK	EDD	90	N Illinois	&1987
Rinke, Patricia	C-Ac	Grand View	LQS	JD		Iowa	&
Riordan, Diane A.	Prof	Jms Madison	XI	PHD	88.	Va Tech	&9-89
Journal of Accounting Education Research Professor							
Riordan, Michael P.	Prof	Jms Madison	FM	PHD	89.	Va Tech	&9-89
Cherry, Bekaert & Holland Faculty Fellow							
Rios, Arcadio	Assoc	Puerto RicoM	FPRV	MS	82	Mass	&1-82
Riportella, Terrie L.	Inst	Elizabethtwn	AFM	MBA		St Joe	&2002
Ristau, Jack E.	Retir	Miami U-Ohio	9100	MBA	71	Miami U	&9-72
Ritchie, Pamela C.	Prof	New Brunswic	HFTY	PHD	89	Lancaster	1984
Riter, William R.	Assoc	Cornerstone	ASVX	MS	71	Illinois	&8-85
Ritsema, Christina M.	Asst	Hope	X	PHD	01.	Arkansas	&2001
Ritson, Philip A.	LectA	Adelaide	MF	BCOM	89	Flinders	1997
Rittenberg, Larry E.	Prof	Wisconsin	AO	PHD	75.	Minnesota	# &1976
Ernst & Young Professor of Accounting							
Ritter, David E.			DCXS	DBA	86.	La Tech	&
Ritter, Jeffrey D.	Assoc	St Norbert	AFRV	MBA	74	Miami U	&1983
Ritts, Blaine A.	Retir	Bowling Gr	1996	PHD	71.	Mich St	1978
Rivera, Donato			MF	PHD	72.	NYU	
Rivera, Gonzalo Jr.	Assoc	Tx A&M-Kings	ILPX	JD	88	Baylor	&1989
Rivera, Juan M.	Assoc	Notre Dame	FI	PHD	75.	Illinois	&9-83
Rivers, Richard A.	Prof	So Illinois	MFS	DBA	76.	Kent St	&6-78
Rix, James A.			F	PHD	73.	Arkansas	&
Ro, Byung T.	Prof	Purdue	F	PHD	76.	Mich St	1976
Roark, Donald E.	Retir	San Jose St	1988	DBA	58.	Indiana	&1955
Roark, Stephen J.	Retir	Missouri So	2003	PHD	86.	Ariz St	&1992
Robb, Alastair	Lect	U Queensland	DS	BBUS	97	Queenslnd	1994
Robb, Sean W. G.	Asst	Cen Florida	F	PHD	95.	Florida	&8-05
Robbins, Donald J.	Retir	Indiana U-PA	CF	MS	71	Ind-Penn	1969
Robbins, Walter A.	Prof	Alabama	NF	DBA	82.	Tennessee	&1981
Roberson, Sandy	Assoc	Furman	AF	MPA	81	W Virginia	&1-99
Robert, Anne-Marie	Prof	Sherbrooke	MNS	PHD	91	Laval	&1985
Roberts, Alfred R.			FHIT	PHD	71.	Alabama	
Roberts, Andrea Alston	Asst	Boston Coll	FN	PHD	00.	Geo Wash	&1999
Roberts, Arthur T.	Retir	Baltimore	1994	PHD	55.	LSU	&1979
Roberts, Aubrey C.	Retir	Wayne State	1981	MBA	42	Michigan	&1957
Roberts, Bruce J.	Asst	Edgewood	AUF	MBA	64	Wisconsin	&1997
Roberts, Clare	Prof	Aberdeen	FIW	PHD	88	Glasgow	1997
Roberts, Clyde A.	Prof	Calif U-Penn	CSX	DBA	88.	Kentucky	&1992
Roberts, David J.	Assoc	DePaul	XR	JD	82	DePaul	&1977
Roberts, Diane H.	C-Pr	San Francisc	AFM	PHD	95.	Ca-Irvine	* &9-94
Roberts, F. Douglas	Asst	Appalach St	S	PHD	02.	Tennessee	&2002
Roberts, Hanno	Prll	Norwegian Mg	M	PHD	93	Maastricht	O-96
Roberts, Howard V.	C-Ac	Pikeville	FCRV	MBA	78	Marshall	1984
Roberts, Martin B.	Retir	Mercer-Atlan	1994	PHD	80.	Geo St	1989
Roberts, Michael L.	Assoc	Colo-Denver	XAB	PHD	88.	Geo St	&2004
Roberts, Ray	Retir	CS-Hayward	2003	PHD	78.	Santa Cl	# &9-85
Roberts, Richard S.	Retir	Akron	D-89	PHD	66.	Ohio St	&
Roberts, Robin W.	D-Pr	Cen Florida	G	PHD	87.	Arkansas	&6-98
Burnett Eminent Scholar Chair							
Roberts, Roydon A.	Lect	Cardiff U	AH	BSC	72	Cardiff	&1976
Robertson, Darroch A.	Assoc	West Ontario	XFMT	PHD	87	W Ontario	&1985

Name	Rank	School	Code	Degree	Yr	Institution	
Robertson, J. S.	Lect	Massey Univ	AH	MBS		Massey	&1987
Robertson, Jack C.	Retir	Texas-Austin	2003	PHD	70.	N Carol	&1970
Robertson, James W.	Dean	Sonoma State		PHD	63.	U Wash	2004
Robertson, John	Asst	Arkansas St	X	LLM	99	Alabama	2000
Robertson, Paul J. (Jep)	Prof	Henderson St	FCN	DBA	88.	Miss St	&2004
Robey, James T.	Retir	Old Dominion	1995	PHD	69.	Florida	&1975
Robichaud, Yves	Assoc	Laurentian		PHD	01	Aixlmars	7-90
Robichek, Alexander A.		Stanford	fnce	PHD	62.	Berkeley	1960
Robinson, Andrew	SLect	Univ Leeds	MQ	PHD	98	Bradford	D-00
Robinson, Dahlia	Asst	South Fla	F	PHD	00.	Georgia	5-07
Robinson, Diana W.	Asst	N Carol A&T	FM	PHD	02.	Okla St	&1989
Robinson, E. Thomas	Emer	Alaska-Fairb	2005	MSA	71	Wisconsin	* &8-74
Robinson, John R.	Prof	Texas-Austin	XV	PHD	81.	Michigan	&9-85
C. Aubrey Smith Professor of Accounting							
Robinson, Leonard A.	Retir	Alabama-Birm	1987	DBA	65.	Geo St	1981
Robinson, Leslie A.	Asst	Dartmouth	XF	PHD	06.	N Carol	&2006
Robinson, Linda	Lect	Un Waterloo	A	BCOM	82	Manitoba	&2003
Robinson, Loudell Ellis	Deces	Alabama-Birm	2005	PHD	73.	Alabama	* &1970
Robinson, Michael A.	Prof	Baylor	CM	PHD	81.	Illinois	1991
Robinson, Patricia A.	Assoc	Johnson&Wale	P	MSA	94	Bentley	1994
Robinson, Peter	Lect	W Australia	F	MED	80	W Austrl	1990
Robinson, Robert Jr.			F	PHD	70.	Ariz St	
Robinson, Sandra	Lect	Concordia U	AF	MBA	76	NYU	&1980
Robinson, Sharon L.	C-Pr	Frostburg St	AP	MPA	70	Tx Chr	&9-72
Robinson, Thomas R.			F	PHD	92.	Case Wes	&
Robinson-Backmon, Ida B.	C-Ac	N Carol A&T	CM	PHD	93.	Okla St	&2005
Robison, Jack C.	Retir	Cal Poly-SLO	2005	PHD	82.	Arizona	&1-85
Robison, K. Wayne	Prof	Wash & Jeff	AFTX	MBA	79	Ohio St	&1979
Robson, Gary S.	Assoc	Bloomsburg	CDFM	PHD	90.	Arizona	&2006
Robson, Julie	Lect	Un Waterloo	X	MACC	92	Waterloo	&2001
Robson, Keith	Prof	Cardiff U	MFAB	PHD	88	Manchest	2005
Roca, Eduardo	SLect	Griffith Un	FIQ	PHD	99	Griffith	1999
Roche', Quentin C.	Deces	Auburn-Montg	1984	PHD	68.	Alabama	&1969
Rochlin, Robert E.	Emer	Lg Isl-Brook	2002	MBA	65	NYU	* &1964
Rock, Steven K.	Assoc	Colorado	F	PHD	96.	Penn St	# * 8-98
Rockness, Howard O.	Prof	N Car-Wilmin	MCU	PHD	73.	U Wash	8-93
Rockness, Joanne W.	Prof	N Car-Wilmin	FJV	PHD	80.	N Carol	&1993
Cameron Professor							
Rockwell, Stephen R.	Assoc	Tulsa	AS	PHD	93.	Mich St	8-98
Rod, Michael O.	Deces	No Iowa	1988	PHD	84.	Minnesota	* &1972
Rodgers, Fay H.	Retir	Kennesaw St	1993	DBA	76.	Geo St	&1973
Rodgers, Jacci L.	C-Ac	Okla City	CME	PHD	88.	Oklahoma	* &8-92
Rodgers, Theodore C.	Asst	So Carolina	AFM	PHD	06.	Arizona	&2006
Rodgers, Thomas H.	Retir	Tenn State	1999	MBA	60	Georgia	&1976
Rodgers, Waymond	C-Pr	Cal-Riversid	FBAJ	PHD	84.	S Calif	&1992
Rodriguez de Marrero, Aurea	Prof	Puerto Rico	FP	JSD	01	Compluten	1986
Rodriguez, Ada	Lect	CUNY-Lehman		MBA		Columbia	1994
Rodriguez, Juan M.	Lect	U Miami	PXI	MPA	03	U Miami	&1991
Rodriguez, Leonardo	Retir	Fla Internat	2005	DBA	75	Fla St	1973
Rodwanna, Pannipa	Asst	Chulalongkor	ABFS	PHD	96	Chulalong	&1996
Roe, George	ClAc	Ill-Chicago	JL	JD	80	DePaul	1977
Roe, Helen	Lect	Ill-Chicago	XL	JD	72	DePaul	1989
Roebuck, Peter J.	SLect	New So Wales	AB	MCOM	88	NS Wales	&1985
Roehm, Harper A.	Emer	Dayton	2001	DBA	72.	Fla St	&1992
Roemmich, Roger A.		Bus-Athen GA	2002	PHD	75.	Mich St	1985
Quantum Financial Strategists; 1551 Jennings Mill; Bogart GA 30622							
Rogers, Alan	Prof	Westminst-UT	PF	MBA	77	Utah	&1979
Rogers, David E.	Prof	Mesa State	MC	MBA	72	Golden Gt	&1975
Rogers, Donald R.			F	PHD	70.	Oregon	&
Rogers, Jonathan L.	Asst	Chicago	FM	PHD	05.	Penn	2004
Rogers, Richard L.	Assoc	Indiana-Indy	FA	PHD	81.	Penn St	&1981
Rogers, Rodney K.	Dean	Bowling Gr	FHS	PHD	95.	Case Wes	&7-06
Rogers, Violet C.	Dean	S F Austin	FBA	PHD	93.	North Tx	&1991
Rogoff, Donald L.	Prof	CS-Northrdge	FM	DBA	64	Mich St	&1977
Rogow, Robert B.	Dean	E Kentucky	GFA	PHD	76.	Arkansas	&1998
Rohde, Fiona H.	SLect	U Queensland	FM	PHD	00	Queensl	1990
Rohde, Lynn O.	Retir	Norfolk St	1990	MBA	56	Indiana	&9-81
Rohlfing, Harry J.	Retir	Villanova	1989	BS	50	Villanova	&1960
Rohrbach, Kermit J.		Lingnan U		PHD	83.	Illinois	&
Rohrs, Brian	Inst	Bowling Gr	P	MBA	97	Indiana	&1998
Roig, Reed	Asst	W Carolina	MS	ABD		Case Wes	1-06
Rolen, Charles O.	Retir	Tenn State	1994	PHD	69.	Arkansas	&1974
Rolfe, Robert J. (Rob)			XIBZ	PHD	83.	Oklahoma	&
Rolfes, Mary S.	C-Ac	Mn St-Mankat	CFQ	MAS	71	Illinois	1979
Roline, Alan C.	C-Ac	Minn-Duluth	JKL	JD	87	Minnesota	1993
Rolland, Beatrice	Asst	West Chester	FAVC	MBA	95	Temple	&9-94
Roller, Julius A.	Retir	U Washington		MA	60	Michigan	1945

Rolleri, Michael	Assoc	New Haven	F	MBA		Conn		&9-80
Rollins, Theresa P.			VT	PHD	89.	Temple		&
Romal, Jane B.	Assoc	SUNY-Brockpo	MCV	DBA	00.	Clev St	*	&2000
Roman, Damian	Prof	Puerto Rico	T	MBA	63	NYU		1960
Roman, Francisco J.	Asst	Texas Tech	M	PHD	03.	Arizona		2007
Roman, Mark A.	Assoc	Maryville	FV	MS	87	Truman St		&1999
Romanus, Robin	Asst	Texas Tech	F	PHD	07	Va Tech		2007
Romeo, George C.	Prof	Rowan	F	PHD	91.	Drexel	# *	&1979
Romero, Mary	Visit	New Mex High	DPMG	MBA	91	Nw Mx Hi		&2001
Romine, Jeffrey M.	Prof	Truman State	AS	PHD	92.	Memphis		&1976
Romney, Marshall B.	C-Pr	Brigham Yg	2006	PHD	77.	Tx-Austin		&9-77
John & Nancy Hardy Professor								
Ronen, Joshua	Prof	New York U	TABX	PHD	70.	Stanford		&1973
Roof, Bradley M.	Prof	Jms Madison	A	PHD	85	Virginia	*	&9-77
Roohani, Saeed J.	Prof	Bryant	SAF	DBA	92.	Miss St		8-91
Rooney, Cynthia J.			FAIB	PHD	90.	Tennessee	*	&
Root, Peggy	Retir	Dayton	1989	MBA	78	Dayton		&1979
Roper, Barbara E.	Asst	Chicago St	PMXF	MST	82	DePaul		&1988
Rorem, C. Rufus	Deces			PHD	29.	Chicago		
Rosacker, Kirsten	Asst	South Dakota	PS	PHD	05	Nebraska	*	2005
Rosacker, Robert E.	Prof	South Dakota	FS	PHD	89.	Nebraska		&1992
Rosanes, M. Josep	Prof	Univ Navarra	JM	PHD	77.	Nrthwstrn		7-71
Roscher, Richard A.	Asst	N Car-Wilmin	AFM	MBA	72	Denver		&1982
Roscoe, W.	Lect	Concordia U	AF	BCOM	79	Concordia		&1986
Rose, Ania M.	Asst	So Illinois	ATF	PHD	98.	Tx A&M		8-05
Rose, Jacob M.	Assoc	So Illinois	SB	PHD	98.	Tx A&M		1-06
Rose-Green, Ena	Asst	S Ill-Edward	FT	PHD	94.	Fla St		2004
Rosen, L. S. (Al)	Emer	York	2001	PHD	66.	U Wash		&1972
Rosen, Louis I.		Cost Atg Std		DBA	74.	Maryland		&1972
Rosenbaum, Allen S.	Asst	Metro State		PHD	68.	Illinois		
Rosenberg, Donald L.	Prof	Towson	FMXL	JD		Baltimore	*	&1984
Rosencrants, Lydia	C-Ac	LaGrange	FMP	PHD	99.	Mich St	*	&6-99
Boatwright Professor of Accounting								
Rosenfeld, Gerald I.	Retir	Robt Morris	2002	MS	73	Duquesne		&9-70
Rosenzweig, Kenneth Y.	Emer	Dayton	2001	PHD	77.	Mich St	# *	&1981
Roser, Sherman R.	Retir	St Cloud St	1999	PHD	79.	Nebraska		1979
Rosett, Joshua G.	Assoc	Claremont	FTV	PHD	89	Princeton		2003
Roshto, Patricia G.	Inst	La-Monroe	P	MBA	80	La-Monroe		&1986
Rosman, Andrew J.	Assoc	Connecticut	BFV	PHD	89.	N Carol		&1-89
Rosner, Rebecca L.	Assoc	Lg Isl-Post	AS	PHD	99.	Baruch		&1999
Ross, Barbara W.	Prof	E Michigan	ESA	PHD	97.	Mich St		&2003
Ross, D.	Retir	Cy London Pl	1992					&1989
Ross, Dianna			FMIN	PHD	93.	Va Tech		&
Ross, Frank	Visit	Howard	A	MBA	68	Long Isl		&2003
Ross, Gary	Asst	Harding	FMVP	MBA	94	Tx Tech		2000
Ross, James U.	Retir	Tx-S Antonio	1999	JD	65	Tx-Austin		&9-75
Ross, John B.	Deces	Tennessee	6-76	PHD	60.	Alabama		
Ross, Kenton E.	Retir	Central Okla	1995	EDD	61	UCLA		&8-91
Ross, Mark T.	Asst	W Kentucky	PF	PHD	96.	Arizona		&1994
Ross, Marshall	Lect	CUNY-Lehman						
Ross, Phillip	SLect	W Sydney	AU	PHDM	94	UTS		
Ross, Ronald L.	Assoc	Frostburg St	MF	MBA	81	Frostburg		&8-82
Ross, Ronald S.			XF	PHD	78.	Tx-Austin		&
Ross, Sherry K.	Lect	Tx St-S Marc	PFM	MBA	87	SW Tx St		&1-00
Ross, Timothy L.			F	PHD	69.	Mich St		&
Ross, Wilbur R. (Bill)	Retir	Tx-Arlington	1996	PHD	65.	Tx-Austin		&1974
Rossell, James H.	Retir	Pittsburgh	1988	MLIT	46	Pittsburgh		&1937
Rossi, John D. III	Assoc	Moravian	CFNP	MBA	97	Moravian	*	&5-96
Rosson, Gerald W.	Assoc	Lynchburg	ACEX	MAC	72	Va Tech		&1980
Rotch, William	Retir	Virg-Grad	1999	DBA	59.	Harvard		1-59
Rotenberg, Wendy D.	Prof	Univ Toronto	FI	PHD	87	Toronto		1990
Rotfort, Donald B.	Retir	Babson	2004	JD	71	Suffolk		&1968
Roth, Harold P.	Prof	Tennessee	M	PHD	80.	Va Tech	*	&1-81
Rothenberg, Naomi				PHD	01.	Ohio St		
Rothwell, James C.	Asst	Ouachita Bap	FA	MBA	79	La Tech		&1981
Rotondi, Robert T.	C-Pr	Norwich	FX	MBA	71	Fordham		&9-77
Roubi, Raafat R.	Prof	Brock Univ	CFUV	PHD	85.	North Tx	*	1-91
Roudaki, Jamal	SLect	Lincoln-NZ	EJP	PHD		Wollong		2007
Roulstone, Darren T.	Assoc	Chicago	F	PHD	00.	Michigan		2000
Rountree, Brian R.	Asst	Rice	M	PHD	03.	N Carol		2003
Rouse, Pamela	Lect	Butler	PF	MBA	88	Indiana		1996
Rouse, Paul A.	Assoc	U Auckland	MA	PHD	96.	Auckland		&1987
Rouse, Robert W.	Retir	Charleston	2006	PHD	74.	S Carol	*	&1992
Roush, Charles H. Jr.				DBA	71.	Harvard		
Roush, Melvin L.	Assoc	Pittsburg St	CM	PHD	03	Victoria		&2005
Roush, Pamela B.	Assoc	Cen Florida	FAO	PHD	89.	Geo St	*	7-89
Roussey, Robert S.	Clin	So Calif	FAI	BS	57	Fordham		&1992

Routledge, James	Asst	Bond Univ	FT	PHD	00	UNI Sun		&9-03
Rovelstad, Richard G.	Assoc	Montevallo	FNH	PHD	86.	Alabama		&1982
Rovetta, Charles A.	Deces	Florida St	N-04	MBA	37	Chicago		1953
Rowe, Beverly J.			M	PHD	00.	Tx A&M		&
Rowe, Casey	Asst	Arizona St	M	PHD	01.	Pittsburgh		2001
Rowe, Stephen	Lect	So Cross Un	AFE	MA	92	So Austrl		&1986
Rowe, Thomas M.	Retir	Sam Houston	2002	PHD	85.	Tx A&M		&1978
Rowlands, Terrence	Lect	U Queensland	S	PHD	97	NS Wales		2000
Rowley, C. Stevenson	Retir	Minn-Duluth	2000	PHD	70.	Wisconsin	*	&1986
Rowley, Thomas H.			SM	PHD	87.	Utah		&
Roxas, Maria L.	Prof	Central Conn	CMSJ	PHD	88.	Georgia		&1992
Roy, Chantale	Prof	Sherbrooke	CMT	DSC	94	Montpell		&1986
Roy, Daniel			D	PHD	92.	Illinois		&
Roy, S. Paul	Assoc	York	M	PHD	79.	Iowa		&1986
Royalty, Kent W.	Prof	St Marys-Tx	XL	LLM	94	Houston		&8-86
Roybark, Helen M.	Asst	Radford	AMS	PHD	03.	Va Comm		2002
Roychowdhury, Sugata	Asst	MIT	F	PHD	03	Rochester		2003
Royehowdhury, Sugata			F	PHD	04.	Rochester		
Royer, J. Everett	Retir	U Miami		EDD	55	Indiana		1946
Rozanski, Eugene R.	Retir	Illinois St	2002	PHD	75.	LSU	*	&1976
Rozelle, David L.	Assoc	W Michigan	XP	MS	70	W Mich	*	&1974
Rozen, Etzmun S.	Assoc	Cleveland St	F	PHD	86.	NYU		1981
Rubenfield, Allen J.	Asst	Clark Atlant	EFJX	JD	76	Pittsburgh		&1998
Rubenfield, Ronald R.	Assoc	Robt Morris	FMC	MBA		Shippensb	*	&9-87
Rubenstein, Henry	Retir	Pace	D-89	MBA	61	NYU		&1958
39 Gramercy Park North; New York NY 10010								
Rubin, Marc A.	C-Pr	Miami U-Ohio	FG	PHD	85.	Tx-Austin		&1990
PricewaterhouseCoopers Professor of Accountancy								
Rubio, Gonzalo	Prof	Pompeu Fabra			85	UCB		
Ruble, Michael R.	Asst	Central Wash	AFG	PHD	84.	Ariz St		&1998
Ruble, Vickie			FM	PHD	90.	Ariz St		
Ruby, Richard	Asst	Roosevelt		JD	78	J Marshal		1980
Ruchala, Linda V.	Assoc	Nebraska	MBCN	PHD	91.	Indiana		1991
Ruddock, C.	Lect	New So Wales		LLB		UTS		
Rude, John A.	Assoc	Bloomsburg	GITV	PHD	90.	Kent St		&1997
Rudkin, Kathy	Lect	U Wollongong	PTW	PHD	02	Wollong		&1996
Rudnick, Martin	Assoc	Wm Paterson	FVM	MS	73	Alabama		&1978
Rudolf, Uwe J.	Prof	Luther	FVI	ABD		Cincinnati		&1971
Rudolph, Holly R.	Assoc	Murray State	F	DBA	94.	S Illinois		&1980
Rue, Joseph C.	Prof	Fl GulfCoast	F	PHD	79.	Penn St		&1997
Rueschhoff, Donald S.			FV	PHD	81.	Nebraska		
Rueschhoff, Norlin G.	Retir	Notre Dame	FI	PHD	68.	Nebraska		&1969
Ruf, Bernadette M.	Prof	Delaware St	DS	PHD	90.	Va Tech		&2004
Ruffner, Roy A.		Westminister		PHD	74.	Missouri		
Ruggieri, Lynn	Asst	Roger Wm	XAF	MS	91	Bryant		&9-04
Ruggieri, Margaret	Asst	Providence		MST		Bryant		1995
Ruggle, Leo A.	Retir	Mankato St	CEJP	PHD	77	Iowa St		1981
Ruh, Lorraine	Inst	No Kentucky	PM	MBA	75	Kentucky		8-96
Ruhe, Nancy C.	Lect	W Virginia	FP	MPA	82	W Virginia		&1987
Ruhl, Jack M.	Prof	W Michigan	M	PHD	91.	Case Wes		1993
Rui, Oliver M.	Assoc	Chinese HK	F	PHD	97.	Houston		2003
Ruiz, Janis	Prof	CS-Bakersf	FMZ	PHD	86.	UCLA		3-89
Ruiz, Rosemarie	Assoc	CUNY-York						
Rujoub, Mohamad A.	C-Pr	Eastern Conn	CFIS	PHD	88.	Arkansas		8-99
Ruland, Robert G.		Ruland Mfg	1996	PHD	82.	Illinois		&1996
380 Pleasant; Watertown MA 02172; 617-924-8000; rruland@ruland.com								
Ruland, William J.	Prof	CUNY-Baruch	F	PHD	76.	SUNY-Buf		9-81
Rullan, Jose (Tony)	Retir	Rochest Tech	1998	MBA	75	Roch Tech		&6-76
Rummell, Janice	Asst	Pitts-Johnst		MA		StFran-NY		1998
Rumpel, Joan H.	Asst	Fort Hays St	PMC	MBA	77	Ft Hays		&1977
Rundall, James	Inst	Wis-Eau Clar	F	MS	74	Illin St	*	&8-82
Runyan, Bruce W.	Asst	Texas-Tyler	FMI	PHD	05.	Tx A&M	*	&9-05
Rupert, Lyle M.	Prof	Hendrix	DSM	MBA	85	Chicago		&1987
Rupert, Timothy J.	Assoc	Northeastern	BX	PHD	94.	Penn St		9-92
Joseph M. Golemme Professor of Accounting								
Rupley, Kathleen Hertz	Asst	Portland St	F	PHD	06.	U Wash		9-06
Rupp, Galen L.	Assoc	Pittsburg St	CMF	PHD	82.	Okla St	*	1985
Rupp, Russ	Assoc	Goshen	FAD	MBA	84	Notre Dm		&9-95
Rusbarsky, Mark K.			AMF	PHD	86.	Arizona		&
Rusch, Nancy E.	Inst	Cen Michigan	PF	MS	79	Cen Mich		&1981
Rushinek, Avi	Assoc	U Miami	SM	PHD	79	Tx-Austin		1980
Rushing, Reginald	Retir	Texas Tech	1971	PHD	48.	Tx-Austin		&1939
Russ, Robert W.	Asst	No Kentucky	F	PHD	05.	Va Comm		&8-05
Russell, Grant W.	Assoc	Un Waterloo	M	MBA	70	McMaster	*	1974
Russell, John D.			BFW	PHD	98.	Penn St		&
Russell, Keith A.	Dean	St Marys-Tx	ICPF	PHD	80.	Arkansas	*	1-05
Russell, Louisa L.	Inst	Miss Women	FP	MPA	02	Miss St		2004

Russell, P. O.	SLect	East Anglia	AGN	MA		Manchest		&1981
Russell, Richard	Asst	Jackson St	X	JD	97	Iowa		&1-97
Russo, Charles J.	Assoc	Bloomsburg	BX	PHD	02	Penn St		2003
Russo, Joseph A. Jr.	Prof	Pace	AB	PHD	94.	Rutgers		&1968
Rusth, Douglas B.	Assoc	Houston-Cl L	VIJE	PHD	91.	Houston		&9-91
Rusticus, Tjomme O.	SLect	Northwestern	MC	PHD	06.	Penn		2006
Ruswinckel, John W.	Retir	Mich State		MBA	31			1939
Rutledge, Robert W.	Prof	Tx St-S Marc	FMBJ	PHD	89.	S Carol		&1-01
Rutledge, Walter K.	Retir	West Florida	1996	PHD	70.	Alabama		&1969
Ruttanaporn, Supapun	Retir	Chulalongkor	CMUV	MBA	69	Mich St		&1966
Ruud, T. Flemming			AU	PHD	88	Utah		&
Ruzengwe, C. M.	Lect	Un Zimbabwe	A	BSC				&
Rwegasira, Kami				PHD	79.	Columbia		
Ryack, Kenneth N.	Asst	Eastern Conn	F	ABD		Mass		&
Ryan, Christine	SLect	Queensld Tec	F	MFM	80	Queensld		&7-76
Ryan, D. William			MIS	PHD	84.	S Calif		
Ryan, David H.	Assoc	Temple	XF	PHD	89.	S Carol		&1989
Ryan, Huldah A.	Prof	Iona	PI	PHD	90.	Houston		9-96
Ryan, James R.	Retir	Mary	1997	MS	79	N Dakota		&9-79
Ryan, John B.	Assoc	W Sydney	TFH	PHDM	02	Wollong	*	&1990
Ryan, Stephen G.	Assoc	New York U	F	PHD	88.	Stanford		1990
Ryerson, Frank E. III	Assoc	Macon State	ACFV	PHD	83.	Alabama		2005
Ryker, Kirsty	ALect	Macquarie Un	AS	BBA	03	Macquarie		2005
Rylander, Wilfrid F.	Retir	Tx A&M-C Chr	1994	PHD	69.	Tx-Austin		&8-73
Rymer, Victoria S.			FT	PHD	83.	Maryland		&
Ryu, Tae Ghil	Assoc	Metro State	FMT	PHD	93.	Rutgers		&8-93
Saadouni, Brahim	SLect	U Manchester	FIM	MSC	84	Glasgow		1-00
Saaydah, Mansour I.			1991	PHD	91.	St Louis		
Sal PO Box 647; Salt Jordan								
Sabac, Florin	Asst	Univ Alberta	MTY	PHD	01	Brit Colum		2000
Sabbagh, Hashem M.	Assoc	Jordan		PHD	71.	Arizona		
Sabino, Jowell S.			F	PHD	96.	Nrthwstrn		
Sachs, Kevin D.			F	PHD	99.	SUNY-Buf		
Sack, Robert J.	Emer	Virg-Grad	2001	BS	56	Miami U		&1987
Sadan, Simcha	Retir	Tel Aviv	2006	PHD	72.	Berkeley		1974
Sadeghi, Mehdi	Lect	Macquarie Un	F	PHD	82	Kentucky		2001
Sadhwani, Arjan T.	Prof	San Jose		PHD	71.	Mich St		&2000
San Jose State Univ; MIS Dept								
Sadka, Gil	Asst	Columbia	FIL	PHD	05	Chicago		2005
Sadowski, Susan T.			CT	PHD	94.	Geo Wash		&
Saemann, Georgia C.	Assoc	Wis-Milwauke	BFA	PHD	87.	Mich St		&1991
Safik, Issa	Retir	U Cairo		PHD	64.	Ohio St		
Saftner, Donald V.	Prof	Toledo	SF	PHD	80.	Penn St		1987
Sage, Judith A.	Assoc	Il-Springfld	XF	PHD	87.	Okla St		&2005
Sage, Lloyd G.	Retir	Governors St	6-05	PHD	84.	Nebraska		&2001
Sager, Clayton R.	Assoc	Wis-Whitewat	FM	PHD	81.	Iowa		1983
Saghafi, Ali				PHD	79.	Missouri		
Sagrillo, Marilyn	Assoc	Wl-Green Bay	SAM	PHD	95.	Wisconsin		&8-94
Sahay, Savita A.			M	PHD	97.	Berkeley		
Said, Amal A.	Asst	Toledo	MI	PHD	03.	Va Comm		2003
Said, Hassan A.	Assoc	Austin Peay	MFCX	PHD	94	Alabama		
Said, Kamal E.	Retir	Tx-Brownsvil	2006	PHD	71.	Tx-Austin	#	&2003
Sailors, J. Franklin			CFA	PHD	85.	Georgia		
Sailors, William M. (Skip)	Assoc	Western Wash	FS	MBA	71	S Calif		&1974
Sainty, Barbara J.	Assoc	Brock Univ	MF	PHD	95.	Ohio St	*	&1999
Saksena, Pankaj	Assoc	Ind-So Bend	AEIM	PHD	97	Geo St		&1995
Sala, Francisco	Retir	Christian Br	1992	DCS	49	Havana		1961
Salama, Yehia A.	Lect	Ill-Chicago	CFIM	PHD	83.	Alabama		2002
Salamasick, Mark L.	SLect	Texas-Dallas	ADOF	MBA	76	Cen Mich	#	2003
Salamon, Gerald L.	Prof	Indiana	FM	PHD	71.	Ohio St		&1986
Prickett Professor of Accounting								
Salamone, Diane M.			T	PHD	92.	St Louis		&
Salatka, William K.	Assoc	Wilfrid Laur	FTV	PHD	84.	Iowa		&1993
Salbador, Debra A.	Assoc	Virg Tech	X	PHD	93.	S Carol		&8-94
Saldana, Cesar			1991	PHD	82.	Nrthwstrn		
Univ of Phillipines; Col of Bus; Diliman, Quezon City 3004 Phillipines								
Saldin, Theodore R.	Retir	Wash State	1987	JD	52	U Wash		1947
Sale, C.	PLect	London Metro	FMN	MSC				&1991
Sale, Geraldine W.	Retir	Florida St	4-06	PHD	79.	Florida		&1982
Sale, J. Timothy	C-Pr	Cincinnati	MQIS	PHD	70.	Cincinnati		&1964
Sale, Martha L.	Asst	Sam Houston	CM	DBA	99.	La Tech		&2005
Salem, Aziza Ahmed			1991	PHD	86.	Miss		
8 Nasirkhisro St; 7th Districk; Nasr City Apt 11; Cairo Egypt								
Salem, Fawzi Amin El-Sayed			FM	PHD	72.	Wisconsin		
Salim, Monir Mahmound				PHD	65.	Wisconsin		
Salimi, Anwar Y.	Prof	CS-Pomona	FSDM	PHD	84.	UCLA	*	1981
Salisbury, Donald M.	Retir	Neb-Kearney	1991	ABD		N Colo		1987

Sallee, Larry	Prof	Winona State	FX	DBA	91	US Intl	* &1985
Salley, Walter B.	Retir	Virginia	1986	BS	54	Clemson	&1957
Salmela, Karen E.	Inst	Minn-Duluth	M	MBA	91	Minnesota	1989
Salmon, Errol D.	Asst	Univ of D C	RDA	MBA	71	American	&1975
Salmon, Suzanne	Lect	LaTrobe Univ	M	BEC		LaTrobe	&1991
Salmonson, Roland F.	Deces	Mich State	7-97	PHD	56.	Michigan	&1955
Salter, John H.	Retir	Cen Florida	2004	PHD	75.	LSU	& 9-75
Salter, Marilyn P.	Retir	Cen Florida	2004	MS	81	Cen Fla	& 8-81
Salter, Stephen B.	Prof	Txs-El Paso	IF	PHD	91.	S Carol	9-07
Salterio, Steven E.	Prof	Queen's Univ	AF	PHD	93.	Michigan	&2003
Saltz, S.	Lect	Touro	CVT	BS			& 2-84
Salvary, Stanley C. W.	Retir	Canisius	2005	PHD	77	NYU	&1979
Salvucci, Debra M.	C-Ac	Stonehill	XCFM	MS	79	Bentley	& 9-84
Saly, P. Jane	C-Ac	St Thomas-MN	FM	PHD	91	Brit Colum	9-99
Salyer, Robert	Inst	No Kentucky	X	MS	84	Cincinnati	& 8-01
Salzarulo, W. Peter	Prof	Miami U-Ohio	X	PHD	73.	Colorado	& 9-73
Ernst & Young Professor of Accountancy							
Sambamurthy, V.	Prof	Michigan St	S	PHD	89	Minnesota	8-02
Eli Broad Professor of Information Technology							
Samelson, Donald P.	Assoc	Colorado St	AX	PHD	92.	Va Tech	&1998
Sami, Heibatollah	Prof	Lehigh	F	PHD	84.	LSU	2005
Mercy Professor							
Samidi, Juhari		Malaysia	1989	PHD	89.	Arkansas	
Samiolo, Riva	JLect	London Econ	ACPI	MSC			2000
Sampson, Michael P.	Prof	American U	X	LLM	73	Geotown	& 9-83
Sampson, Wesley C.			AFD	PHD	85.	Missouri	&
Samson, William D.	Deces	Alabama	9-05	PHD	81.	N Carol	* & 8-84
Samuel, Sajay	Clln	Penn State	AB	PHD	95.	Penn St	8-03
Samuels, Janet A.	Asst	Ariz St West	SCM	PHD	04.	Ariz St	9-03
Samuelson, Bruce A.	Prof	Pepper-L Ang	FMS	PHD	78.	S Calif	& 9-83
Samuelson, Richard A.	Retir	San Diego St	2005	PHD	71.	UCLA	&1973
Samy, Martin	ALect	Monash Univ	F	MED		Monash	2000
San Miguel, Joseph G.	Prof	Naval Postgr	BCMU	PHD	73.	Tx-Austin	&1982
Sanborn, Robert H.	Assoc	Richmond	FTPK	PHD	82.	Georgia	1988
Sanchez, Della	Lect	Tx-Pan Amer	FM	MS	06	Tx-PanAm	2007
Sanchez, Juan Manuel	Asst	Arkansas	FMS	PHD	06.	Tx-SanAnt	2006
Sanchez, Maria H.	Asst	Rider	AT	PHD	03.	Drexel	&2002
Sandberg, Angela H.	Assoc	Jacksonvl St	CFAP	DBA	90.	Miss St	# * & 9-82
Sandelin, Mikko	Res	Helsinki Sch	CMU	MS	02	Helsinki	2003
Sander, Henry C.	Lect	Cal-Santa Br	FXP	BA	76	Conn	&1980
Sander, James F.	Assoc	Butler	PFT	PHD	87.	Illinois	&1990
Sanders, Allen B.	Retir	Elon College	1987	PHD	73.	N Carol	* 1965
Sanders, Bevie Truett	Retir	Arizona St	1982	PHD	57.	Tx-Austin	&1957
703 Solana Drive; Tempe AZ 85281							
Sanders, D. Elaine	Assoc	Tx-S Antonio	CMB	PHD	95.	Oklahoma	8-94
Sanders, Debra L.	Prof	Wash State	XB	PHD	86.	Ariz St	&1985
Sanders, George D.	Prof	Western Wash	FGN	PHD	89.	Alabama	&1995
Sanders, Howard P.	Retir	So Carolina	1993	PHD	67.	Florida	* &1966
Sanders, Joan	Lect	Texas A&M	S	MS	90	Tx A&M	& 9-00
Sanders, John	Assoc	So Maine	PF	MBA	77	S Maine	* &1982
Sanders, Joseph C.	C-Pr	Indiana St	RPFV	PHD	92.	Kentucky	& 9-92
Sanders, William C.	Retir	So Car-Aiken	1987	MS	64	S Carol	1966
Sanderson, George C.	Prof	Mn-Moorhead	NFM	PHD	85.	Nebraska	&1976
Sanderson, Glen R.	Retir	Illinois St	1995	PHD	68.	Mich St	&1981
Sanderson, Marlane K.	Retir	Mn-Moorhead	9-07	MBA	78	Moorhead	* &1983
Sandifer, Lisa	Inst	Delta State	SPAF	MBA	90	Miss	&1998
Sandin, Ariel	Prof	De Cordoba		ABD		DeCordoba	
Sandino, Tatiana	Asst	So Calif	M	PHD	04.	Harvard	2004
Sandler, John	Asst	CUNY-Stn Isl	TX	JD	96	Lgls-Post	&1998
Sandler, Mel	Retir	New Hampshir	1992	MA	47	Nrthwstrn	&1972
Sandlin, Petrea K.	D-Ac	Trinity	FBE	PHD	87.	Tx-Austin	8-88
Sandretto, Michael J.	Lect	Illinois	FM	PHD	79.	Illinois	& 8-98
Sands, John Stephen	Lect	Griffith Un	ABEI	MCOM	89	GCUCGU	1990
Sandstrom, Scott	Assoc	Holy Cross	FLX	JD	83	Suffolk	& 9-83
Sangeladji, Mohammad A.	Emer	CS-Northrdge	M	PHD	75.	Oklahoma	* 1979
Sangster, Carol Lee	Retir	Sam Houston	1999	MA	63	Alabama	& 9-67
Sanguanchart, Dusadee	Retir	Chulalongkor	FPTV	MACC	73	Chulalong	1968
Sankaraguruswamy, Srini	Asst	Georgetown	FM	PHD	96.	Purdue	1996
Sankaranarayanan, S.			F	PHD	86.	Pittsburgh	
Sannella, Alexander J.	Assoc	Rutgers-Newk	ACFV	PHD	84	NYU	& 9-87
Sansing, Richard C.	Prof	Dartmouth	XMT	PHD	90.	Tx-Austin	1998
Santomero, Nicole G.	Inst	Widener		MST	97	Widener	&2004
Santos, Dante E.		San Franc-CA	1992	PHD	76.	Santa Cl	
2626 23rd Ave; San Francisco CA 94116							
Saouma, Richard	Asst	UCLA	M	PHD	06	Stanford	2006
Sapienza, Samuel R.	Retir	Penn	1987	PHD	56	Penn	&1948
Sapp, Richard W.	Retir	Portland St	MC	PHD	78.	Houston	&1978

Name	Rank	School		Degree		University	
Sapra, Haresh	Assoc	Chicago	FMT	PHD	00	Minnesota	2000
Sara, Graham L.	H-Pl	Coventry Un	VSF	MSOC	80	Birminghm	&4-74
Sarath, Bharat	Assoc	CUNY-Baruch	M	PHD	88.	Stanford	9-97
Saravanamuthu, Kala	SLect	N Eng-Austr	M	PHD		SA	2002
Sardinas, Joseph L. Jr.	Emer	Massachusett	2004	PHD	75.	Penn St	9-75
Sardinha, Carlos				PHD	80.	S Calif	
Saremejeanne, Jacques	Prof	Quebec-Montr		PHD		Quebec	
Sargant, C.	D-PLe	Liverpool JM	FG	MA			
Sarhan, Mostafa H.	Dean	Savannah St	MCU	PHD	83.	Arkansas	* 1-99
Sarikas, Robert H. S. (Zeke)	Assoc	Ohio Univ	FI	PHD	92.	Illinois	&2002
Sarin, Madhuri	C-Ac	W Virg Tech	FPXM	MBA			* 1988
Sarkar, Ratna G.			M	PHD	97.	Stanford	
Sasaki, Takashi	Prof	Hitotsubashi	FA	DBA		Hitotsub	1997
Sasovova, Zuzana	Lect	Vrije Univ	MB	MS	99	Comenius	1999
Satava, David R.	Assoc	Houston-Vict	AFP	DBA	94.	Miss St	&8-95
Sathe, Richard	Assoc	St Thomas-MN	JEFH	EDD	00	StThomMN	&9-90
Satin, Diane C.	Prof	CS-East Bay	FMC	PHD	92.	Berkeley	1990
Satterfield, Naomi L.	Retir	West Georgia	6-89	MBE	62	Geo St	9-62
Saubert, Lynn K.	Prof	Radford	FCT	PHD	77.	Wisconsin	* &1985
Saubert, R. Wayne	Prof	Radford	XLP	JD		Drake	1985
Sauceda, Mary Jane	Assoc	Tx-Brownsvil		PHD	01.	Tx A&M	&1992
Saudagaran, Shahrokh M.	Dean	U Wash-Tacom	FIG	PHD	86.	U Wash	&2004
Sauerlender, Karin M.			NFM	PHD	93.	Penn St	&
Saulpic, Olivier	H-Pr	ESCP deParis	BMSU	PHD	00	Ecole Pl	1997
Sauls, Eugene H.	Retir	CS-Sacrament	CMF	PHD	69.	Mich St	* &1984
Saunders, Gary J.	Prof	Marshall	PMCT	DBA	77.	Kentucky	&1990
Savage, Allan H.	Retir	New Mex St	1988	PHD	66.	Tx-Austin	&8-74
905 Conway St #27; Las Cruces NM 88005							
Savage, Arline	Assoc	Cal Poly-SLO	SF	DCOM	99	Port Eliz	&9-04
Savage, Helen M.			SFX	PHD	89.	Kent St	*
Savage, Kathryn S.	Prof	No Arizona	CM	PHD	93.	Penn St	&1-91
Savage, Linda J.	Retir	Cen Florida	AFO	PHD	76.	Florida	# &9-80
Savchak, John F.	Retir	Drexel	1995	MBA	66	Drexel	&1964
Savey, Ronald N.	Retir	Western Wash	2000	MBA	64	Denver	&1976
Savich, Richard S.	Prof	CS-San Bern		PHD	73.	Illinois	&
Savoie, Leonard M.	Deces	Notre Dame	1-91	BS	46	Illinois	&1980
Savoth, Paul	Assoc	Monmouth	XL	LLM	84	Villanova	&1986
Sawers, Kimberly M.	Asst	Seattle Pac	BMN	PHD	02.	U Wash	9-06
Sawyer, Adrian J.	Assoc	Canterbury	FLX	MCOM	93	Canterbu	1991
Sawyer, Broadus E.				PHD	55.	NYU	
Sawyer, Rebecca S.	Asst	N Car-Wilmin	SMF	MBA	75	Duquesne	&1978
Sawyers, Roby B.	Prof	N Carol St	MXB	PHD	90.	Ariz St	&1989
Saxunova, Darina		Edgewood	AFJ	PHD	07	Comenius	2007
Sayed, Naqi	Asst	Lakehead U	FM	PHD	02	Wollong	2002
Sayers, David L.			AF	PHD	85.	Nebraska	&
Sayre, Julian R.	Retir		1993	PHD	81.	Arizona	&
7120 N Edgewood Pl; Tucson AZ 85704							
Sayre, Todd L.	Assoc	San Francisc	SM	PHD	94.	Arizona	&9-98
Sbaraglea, Andrew	Asst	Fla Internat		PHD		Penn St	2006
Scallen, David	Lect	Wilfrid Laur	FM	MBA	99	Wilfr Lau	1999
Scanlan, D. M. S.	Lect	Univ Hull	M	BSC	66	Leeds	9-90
Scanlan, Michael J.		Peat Marw-CO	1992	PHD	73.	Tx-Austin	
6813 So Detroit Cir; Littleton CO 80122							
Scanlon, Kevin P.		Indiana NW	FK	PHD	85.	Florida	&8-92
Scapens, Robert W.	Prof	U Manchester	BCIM	PHD		Manchest	&1970
Scarbrough, D. Paul	Assoc	Brock Univ	M	PHD	87.	Va Tech	1995
Scarinci, Cynthia	Asst	CUNY-Stn Isl	S	MBA	88	Pace	&2001
Scarpati, Stephen	Asst	Sacred Heart	FJPU	MBA	77	Fordham	
Scerbinski, Vincent	Assoc	Lg Isl-Brook	X	MBA		St Johns	&1990
Schachner, Leopold	Retir	CUNY-Baruch	1991	PHD	64	NYU	&1964
Schader, Gary	Assoc	Kean	MXPD	MBA	73	Penn	&1980
Schadewald, Michael S.	Assoc	Wis-Milwauke	X	PHD	88.	Minnesota	&1992
Schaeberle, Frederick W.	Retir	W Michigan	1996	PHD	73.	Missouri	&1965
Schaefer, Hadley P.	Prof	Florida	MCU	PHD	63.	Michigan	8-80
Schaefer, James C.	Prof	Evansville	AGN	DBA	90.	S Illinois	&1990
Schaefer, Thomas F.	Prof	Notre Dame	F	PHD	83.	Illinois	&8-98
KPMG Chair							
Schaer, Kurt	Prof	Intl Mgt Dev		DBA	76	Harvard	1973
Schafer, Brad A.	Asst	South Fla	S	PHD	03.	Utah	8-03
Schafer, Eldon L.	Retir	Arizona	1998	PHD	63.	Nebraska	&1992
Schafer, John	Prof	Hannibal-LaG	TE	PHD	91	Missouri	&1987
Schain, Linda J.	Asst	Hofstra	PV	MBA	78	Iona	&1984
Schalow, Christine M.			FSJ	PHD	92.	Arkansas	&
Schamber, Sharon B.	Inst	Wm Carey	AFVX	MPA	80	S Miss	2004
Scharf, W. F.	SLect	Univ Ulster	I	BSC			1981
Scharlach, Robert A.	Clin	So Calif	X	BS	61	Illinois	&1994
Schattke, Rudolph W.	Retir	Colorado	6-97	PHD	59.	Illinois	&1961

Schatzberg, Jeffrey W.	Prof	Arizona	AM	PHD	86.	Iowa		& 1-87
Schatzel, John A.	Prof	Stonehill	VFS	DBA	88.	Boston U		& 9-93
Schauer, Paul C.	Assoc	Bowling Gr	AFS	PHD	99.	Temple		&1999
Schaupp, L. Christian	Asst	N Car-Wilmin	S	PHD	05.	Va Tech		2005
Schaze, Vincent J.	Emer	San Fran St	2004	MS	56	SanFranSt		1956
Scheerens, Joseph D.	Retir	Ferris State	1991	MA	69	Missouri		&1960
Scheidt, Marsha A.	Prof	Tenn-Chattan	MCS	DBA	91.	Miss St	*	9-90
UC Foundation Professor								
Scheiner, James H.	Dean	Stetson	AS	PHD	75.	Ohio St		& 7-04
Scheiwe, Dan J.	Lect	Queensld Tec	AF	MACC	93	N Eng-Au		& 7-93
Schell, Wayne M.	Assoc	Chris Newpor	X	PHD	84.	Va Tech		&1976
Schelleman, C.	Asst	Maastricht	AFOS	PHD	03	Maastricht		1997
Schelluch, Peter	Prof	Monash Univ	BAFO	MCOM	78	NS Wales		&1989
Schelps, Clarence		Tulane		PHD	43.	LSU		
Schenk, Robert B.	Assoc	Bishop's Un	M	MBA		SUNY	*	& 6-78
Schenk-Hoppe, K.	Prof	Univ Leeds	VFQB	PHD	96	Bremen		1-05
Schepper, Ruth P.	Retir	Hampton	1997	MS	79	Old Dom		&1981
Scheuermann, Sandra	Inst	La-Lafayette	F	MBA	84	Nicholls		&1985
Schieb, Richard	Inst	Penn St-Harr	LPX	LLM	93	Geotown		2006
Schiehll, Eduardo	Asst	HEC-Montreal	FM	PHD	02	HEC-Mont		6-01
Schier, Lewis	Prof	Pace	F	PHD	71	NYU		1965
Schiff, Allen I.	Prof	Fordham	FPC	PHD	73	NYU		1976
Schiff, Andrew	Prof	Towson	SMB	PHD	93.	Rutgers		&2000
Schiff, Jonathan B.	Prof	F Dick-Teane	CMF	PHD	84	NYU	# *	9-86
Schiff, Michael	Retir	Yeshiva	1992	PHD	47	NYU		& 2-87
Schiffel, Lee	Asst	SUNY-Geneseo	S	PHD	03.	Missouri		9-05
Schilder, Arnold	Prof	Un Amsterdam	AJDR	PHD	94	Groningn		1991
Schilit, Howard M.	Pres	Ctr Fin Res	2002	DBA	81.	Maryland		&
Center for Financial Research & Analysis Inc; Rockville, MD								
Schindler, James S.	Deces	SUNY-Buffalo	D-77	PHD	55.	Michigan		&1948
Schipper, Katherine	C-Pr	Duke	F	PHD	77.	Chicago		2006
Thomas F. Keller Professor Business Administration								
Schirger, Joseph F.	Retir	Wis-Oshkosh	1999	PHD	71.	NYU		1976
Schisler, Dan L.	C-Pr	East Carol	XF	PHD	92.	Memphis		&1992
Schisler, Debra	Lect	East Carol	FG	MAC	89	Auburn		2006
Schlachter, Paul J.	Asst	St Thomas-FL	BCMA	PHD	86.	N Carol	*	5-94
Schlatter, William J.	Retir	McMaster Un	1982	PHD	47	Illinois		& 7-67
Schleicher, Debra	Assoc	Loras	XL	MACC	87	S Illinois		&2000
Schleicher, Thomas	Lect	U Manchester	FQ	MPHL		Manchest		1996
Schleifer, Lydia L.	Assoc	Clemson	FA	PHD	88.	Georgia		1985
Schleifer, Michael	Lect	CUNY-Hunter	AF	MBA	84	Pace		9-98
Schlesinger, Warren	Assoc	Ithaca	FCMT	MBA		Cornell		& 8-82
Schlichting, David K.	Assoc	Carthage	FMX	PHD	88.	Wisconsin		&1997
Schloemer, Paul G.	Assoc	Ashland	MVX	PHD	91.	Va Tech		& 8-01
Schlorff, H. Lee	Prof	Bentley	FAE	PHD	73.	Missouri		1978
Schloss, Leo	Deces	Lg Isl-Brook	1989	MS	61	St Johns		&1938
Schlosser, Robert E.	Retir	Rutgers-Newk	1996	PHD	55.	Illinois		&1981
Schmeltz, William F.	Retir	Bowling Gr	1976	PHD	66.	Case Wes	*	&1947
845 Scott Blvd; Bowling Green OH 43402								
Schmelzle, George D.	Assoc	Missouri St	MS	PHD	92.	Miss		& 8-06
Schmerling, Shirley	Lect	Massachusett	SD	PHD	94	Mass		2005
Schmid, Lauran	Lect	Tx-Brownsvil		MBA	88	Tx-PanAm		&2004
Schmidgall, Raymond J.	Prof	Michigan St	M	PHD	80.	Mich St		
Hilton Hotels Professor; School of Hospitality Mgt; schmidga@bus.msu.edu								
Schmidt, Andrew P.	Asst	Columbia	FX	PHD	04.	Ariz St		&2004
Schmidt, Bunney L.	Asst	Utah Valley	AMCF	DBA	06	Nova SE	*	&1998
Schmidt, Dennis R.	Prof	Montana St	XS	PHD	85.	Nebraska		& 8-05
Schmidt, George L.	Asst	Ark-Ft Smith	F	PHD	96.	North Tx		
Schmidt, Lee L.	Retir	Tx A&M-Comm	2001	PHD	71.	Arkansas		&1996
Schmidt, Leo A.	Deces	Michigan		MA	24			1947
Schmidt, Richard J.	Retir	Saint Leo-FL	2002	PHD	79.	Santa Cl	# *	& 8-96
Schmidt, Tom W.			BFXT	PHD	93.	Missouri		&
Schmuhl, William	Spec	Notre Dame	FM	MBA	72	Chicago		&2006
Schmukler, Nathan	Retir	Lg Isl-Post	1992	PHD	52.	NYU		&1982
81-06 229th Street; Queens Village; Queens NY 11427								
Schmutte, James L.	Prof	Ball State	FA	DBA	83.	Kentucky		& 9-81
Schneck, W.	Asst	Touro	ACPX	MBA		Pace		& 8-84
Schnee, Edward J.	Prof	Alabama	X	PHD	73.	Mich St		& 6-82
Culverhouse Professor of Accounting								
Schneible, Richard A. Jr.	Asst	Tx Christian	M	PHD	03.	Syracuse		8-03
Schneider, Arnold	C-Pr	Georgia Tech	AMBO	PHD	82.	Ohio St		& 1-82
Schneider, Douglas K.	Prof	East Carol	FTC	PHD	89.	Georgia		&1991
Schneider, Gary P.	Assoc	San Diego	SMB	PHD	93.	Tennessee		&1992
Information Systems Department								
Schneider, Harold C.			F	PHD	81.	Missouri		&
Schneider, Kent N.	Prof	East Tenn St	XDE	JD	78	Missouri		&1984

Schneider, Manfred	Tut	Univ Toronto	FA	MBA	86	York		&1985
Schneider, Nancy W.	Prof	Lynchburg	ACFT	MPA	78	Geo St	*	&7-90
Schneider, Richard	Prof	Winona State	FSX	MS	71	Ariz St		&1981
Schnoor, Barbara K.	Retir	Mankato St	1999	MBA	72	Mankato		&1971
Schoch, Herbert P.	Retir	Macquarie Un	MF	PHD	74.	American		&1996
Schoderbek, Michael P.	Assoc	Rutgers-N Br	FH	PHD	92.	Indiana		1991
Schoeffler, Charlton G.	Retir	Detroit Merc	1991	PHD	60.	Illinois		1946
24050 Norwood; Oak Park MI 48237								
Schoenebeck, Karen P.	Asst	Southwestern	FMCX	MBA	82	Minnesota		&2001
email: kschoene@sckans.edu; Southwestern College; Winfield KS 67156								
Schoener, Robert B.	Asst	New Mex St	FM	MBA	69	Penn		&1-04
Schoenfeld, Hanns-Martin	Emer	Illinois	1994	PHD	54	Hamburg		6-62
Scholl, Leonard	Asst	Aurora	ACFT	MBA	62	Xavier		2001
Scholz, Susan	Assoc	Kansas	FAV	PHD	97.	S Calif		1997
Harper Faculty Fellow								
Schonbeck, Harold	Assoc	Fitchburg St		MBA		Clark		&
Schorg, Chandra A.	Asst	Loyola-N Orl	FM	MBA	86	Tx Woman		&8-02
Schoute, Martin	Lect	Vrije Univ	QMB	MS	97	Vrije		1998
Schrader, Richard W.	Assoc	Bellarmine	FGV	PHD	93.	Fla St	#	&8-99
Schrader, William J.	Retir	Penn State	D-91	PHD	59.	U Wash		&1954
Schraeder, Donald P.	C-Pr	Greensboro	PFSV	ABD		Mich St		&1989
Schramer, Joe	Retir	St Thomas-MN	1998	BA		StThomMN		&9-67
Schrand, Catherine M.	Assoc	Pennsylvania	F	PHD	94.	Chicago		1994
Schreiner, Paul W.	Prof	Troy-Dothan	MS	PHD	76.	Illinois		&1993
Schrimper, Richard	Lect	Indiana	F	MBA	85	Indiana		&1984
Schroeder, Angelika		Boulder CO	1992	PHD	88.	Colorado		
1668 Bear Mountain Dr; Boulder CO 80303								
Schroeder, Douglas A.	Assoc	Ohio State	FM	PHD	81.	Kansas		1986
Schroeder, Jack D.	Deces	Wayne State	O-00	PHD	75.	Mich St		1970
Schroeder, Joan G.			CF	PHD	65.	Wisconsin		&
Schroeder, Nicholas W.	Prof	Toledo	MCF	DBA	84.	Colorado		&1985
Schroeder, Richard G.	Prof	N Car-Charl	BFT	PHD	74.	Ariz St		&1991
Schroeder, Roger G.	Lect	Wisconsin	X	BBA	64	Wisconsin		&2000
Schuchardt, Robert A.	Retir	Mo-St Louis	1992	DBA	67.	Wash U		1966
Schuele, Karen	Assoc	John Carroll	PFS	PHD	91.	Kent St		&1989
KPMG Associate Professor of Accounting								
Schueler, Robert H.			FC	PHD	73.	Missouri		
Schugart, Gary L.	Assoc	Houston	FZI	PHD	74	Kansas		1989
Schulte, Arthur A. Jr.	VPres	Portland	Fnce	DBA	64.	Oregon		
Schultz, Joseph J. Jr.	Prof	Arizona St	ABM	PHD	74.	Tx-Austin		&1983
Schultz, Norman O.	Retir	Colorado St	2001	PHD	82.	Utah		1983
Schultz, Sally M.	Assoc	SUNY-N Paltz	FTH	PHD	87.	Penn St		1984
Schultz, Thomas D.	Asst	Miami U-Ohio	XF	PHD	04.	Ariz St		&8-06
Schultz, Tim	Prof	Tiffin	PC	MBA		Wash U		
Schulz, Axel K-D.	AProf	U Melbourne	MB	PHD	98	NS Wales		1999
Schulz, Diane	Retir	Montclair St	2000	MBA	63	Harvard		&1985
Schulzke, Kurt S.	Assoc	Kennesaw St	XIPM	JD	98	Geo St		&9-90
Schumacher, Michael G.	Assoc	Gardner-Webb	CM	PHD	03.	Miss	*	2006
Schurrer, Phillip	Inst	Bowling Gr	P	MBA	98	Toledo		8-03
Schuster, Michael	Inst	Portland St	M	MBA		City U		
Schuster, Walter	Asst	Stockholm Ec	P	ED	89	Stockholm		1981
Schwab, Richard D.	Retir	Capital	1994	MLT	61	Wm&Mary		&1956
Schwaig, Kathy S.	Assoc	Kennesaw St	S	PHD	96	S Carol		2002
Schwan, Edward S.	Retir	Susquehanna	7-02	PHD	73.	Colorado		&9-85
Schwartz, Bill N.			EJ	PHD	78.	UCLA		&
Schwartz, James	C-As	Golden Gate	FIV	MS	75	Wisconsin		&1996
Schwartz, James R.	Retir	Montana St	1996	PHD	74.	Nebraska	*	&9-76
Schwartz, Kenneth B.	Assoc	Boston Coll	FTK	PHD	82.	Syracuse		1986
Schwartz, Rachel	Assoc	Illinois	A	PHD	94.	Nrthwstrn		2003
Schwartz, Steven T.	Assoc	SUNY-Bingham	FMA	PHD	97.	Ohio St		&1998
Schwartz, William C.	Asst	Arizona	F	PHD	01.	Iowa		2001
Schwarzbach, Henry R.	Prof	Rhode Island	MQS	DBA	76.	Colorado		&1976
Schwarzkopf, David L.	Asst	Bentley	BFMA	PHD	02.	Conn		&1991
Schweikart, James A.	Dir	Rhode Isl Cl	MCI	PHD	84	Indiana		&9-98
Schwencke, Hans Robert	Prof	Norwegian Mg	TFI	DJUR	02	Oslo		&1990
Schwer, Pamela	Assoc	Saint Xavier	PTCV	MBA			*	1983
Schwersenz, Jack	Retir	Pace-Westch	1999	MBA	59	NYU		&1977
Schwieger, Bradley J.	Prof	St Cloud St	AFOP	DBA	70.	Indiana		&1976
Schwinghammer, Paul H.	Prof	Mn St-Mankat	F	PHD	86.	Arkansas		&1986
Scofield, Barbara W.	Assoc	Dallas	VFDS	PHD	89.	Tx-Austin		&2004
Scofield, Stephen B.	Deces	Tx A&M-Kings	2001	DBA	97.	La Tech		&1987
Scott, Bert G.			VF	DBA	85.	Miss St		&
Scott, Edgar W.	Retir	Dalhousie	2002	ABD		Toronto	*	&1962
Scott, Edward R.				PHD	74.	Illinois		&
Scott, George M.	Prof	Connecticut	S	DBA	68.	U Wash		&
Dept of Management; University of Connecticut								
Scott, Irana J.	Inst	Jms Madison	FPM	MACC	01	E Tn St		&8-05

Scott, Keith B.	Retir	SW Missouri	1989	PHD	72.	Missouri	&9-69
Scott, Mary R.			AFSP	DBA	96.	La Tech	* &
Scott, Richard A.	Retir	Virginia	2004	PHD	70.	American	&8-78
Scott, Stanley J.	Retir	So Methodist	1987	MBA	41	Tx-Austin	&1-82
Scott, Thomas W.	Prof	Univ Alberta	FM	PHD	88	Queens	1985
Scott, William R.	Retir	Un Waterloo	1996	PHD	73.	Chicago	&1983
Scott, Winifred D.				PHD	00.	Fla St	&
Scott-Morton, Michael S.	Prof	MIT	1994	DBA	67.	Harvard	1966

Behavioral & Policy Science Dept; MIT; 617-253-7175; Forrester Prof of Mgt

Scovill, Hiram Thompson	Deces	Illinois	O-62				
Scribner, Edmund A.	Prof	New Mex St	STJ	PHD	85.	Okla St	&8-83
Scribner, John	Prof	CS-San Bern	FP	MABA	74	Ca-Rivers	&9-78
Scudiero, Dominic J.	Retir	Elmhurst	1996	MBA	55	DePaul	&1966
Seago, W. Eugene	Prof	Virg Tech	X	PHD	70.	Georgia	&1970

R. B. Pamplin Professor of Accounting and Information Systems

Seal, William	Prof	Univ Essex	FM	PHD	91	Sheffield	1998
Seaman, Alfred E.	Asst	McMaster Un	MA	PHD	95	Queens	* 7-01
Seaman, James L.	Deces			DBA	64.	S Calif	
Seamer, Michael	Lect	U Newcastle		BCOM	99	Newcastle	1998
Searchfield, Chris	Lect	Macquarie Un	SM	MCOM	98	Macquarie	&2001
Searcy, DeWayne L.	Asst	Auburn	CSM	PHD	02.	Tennessee	# * &8-05
Searfoss, D. Gerald	Retir	Utah	2007	PHD	72.	Indiana	&1994
Sears, Thomas G.	Prof	Hartwick	MXQ	MBA	87	Syracuse	&1978
Seat, Donald L.	Prof	Valdosta St	XF	DBA	80.	Kentucky	&1985
Seaton, Lloyd (Pat)	Assoc	Neb-Kearney	PS	PHD	91.	Nebraska	&8-01
Seaton, Lloyd Jr.	Retir	Arkansas	1993	PHD	68.	Arkansas	&1971
Seawell, Lloyd Vann	Retir	Indiana	1994	DBA	58.	Indiana	&1957
Seay, Robert A.	Prof	Murray State	A	DBA	86.	Miss St	&1985
Seay, Sharon S.	Assoc	Macon State	ACFV	PHD	92.	Georgia	2005
Secord, Peter C.	C-Ac	St Marys-Cdn	FVIH	PHD	03	Reading	# * 1989
Secoy, Thomas G.			F	PHD	59.	Illinois	&
Sedaghat, Ali M.	Assoc	Loyola-Maryl	CFM	DBA	86.	Geo Wash	* 1986
Sedatole, Karen L.	Assoc	Michigan St	M	PHD	00.	Michigan	&2006
Sedki, S. Sam	Prof	St Marys-Tx	FM	PHD	73	N Colo	* &8-81
Sedor, Lisa M.	Asst	U Washington	AF	PHD	01.	U Wash	&7-07
Sedzro, Komlan	Retir	Quebec a Hul	1999	PHD			
Seese, Larry P.	Asst	East Carol	ICFB	PHD	00.	S Carol	&8-00
Seethamraju, Chandra			F	PHD	01.	NYU	&
Seetharaman, A.	Asst	Sultan Qaboo	FM	PHD	00	Madris	1987
Seetharaman, Ananth	C-Ac	St Louis	XMI	PHD	91.	Geo St	&1-92
Sefcik, Stephan E.	Prof	U Washington	FWP	PHD	83.	Illinois	&1986
Segal, Benjamin	Asst	INSEAD	F	PHD	03.	NYU	2006
Segal, Dan	Asst	Univ Toronto	F	PHD	00.	NYU	&2000
Segal, Mark A.	Prof	So Alabama	X	MLT	82	Emory	&1986
Seglund, Ragnor J.	Retir	CS-Sacrament	2001	DBA	71.	Colorado	1984
Segovia, Joann R.	Assoc	Mn-Moorhead	SVPB	PHD	03.	Tx Tech	&2002
Segovia, Juan J.	Assoc	Concordia U	FM	PHD	79	Paris	1983
Seida, Jim A.	Assoc	Notre Dame	FX	PHD	97.	Tx A&M	&8-01

Ernst & Young Faculty Fellow

Seidler, Lee J.			1992	PHD	66.	Columbia	&

5001 Joewood Dr; Sanibel Island FL 33957

Seifert, Deborah	Asst	Illinois St	FCG	PHD	06.	Wash St	&2007
Seiler, Robert E.	Retir	Houston	1998	PHD	53.	Alabama	&1966
Seiler, Thomas G.	Prof	Franklin	FAHO	JD	98	Capital	&2002
Seipel, Cindy L.	Assoc	New Mex St	AF	PHD	90.	Okla St	&8-90
Selby, Daniel	Asst	Florida A&M	FM	ABD		Fla St	2007
Selin, J. Roger	Prof	Wis-Eau Clar	FP	PHD	74	Minnesota	&1-66
Selk, Ann	Lect	Wl-Green Bay	FMNG	MBA	83	Wi-Milwa	&8-83
Sellers, Fred E.	Assoc	Southwestern	FGTV	PHD	84.	Kansas	&1987
Sellers, James H.	Retir	Texas-Tyler	2003	PHD	70.	Arkansas	&9-78
Sellers, Keith F.	Prof	No Alabama	XF	DBA	89.	Memphis	&2006

LaGrange Eminent Scholar of Business Valuations & Director, Center Bus Val

Selling, Thomas I.			FMIK	PHD	82.	Ohio St	&
Sellner, Mark	Lect	Minnesota					
Selph, C. Jason	Retir	Appalach St	1994	DBA	80.	Fla St	&1978
Selto, Frank H.	C-Pr	Colorado	M	PHD	77.	U Wash	1985
Selvy, Patricia M.	Assoc	Bellarmine	FA	PHD	91	Geo St	&8-86
Semenza, Robert A.	Retir	Quinnipiac	APV	BBA	56	Iona	&1989
Sen, Kaustav	Assoc	Pace	FM	PHD	94.	Rutgers	1996
Sen, Pradyot K.	Prof	Cincinnati	M	PHD	85.	Columbia	2000
Sen, Tarun K.	Prof	Virg Tech	S	PHD	85	Iowa	1985
Senatra, Phillip T.	Retir	Lewis & Clrk	2003	PHD	76.	Iowa	&1985
Seng, Dyna	Lect	Univ Otago	FI	MCOM	96	Otago	1994
Senge, Stephen V.	D-Pr	Simmons	MGN	DBA	85.	Kent St	* 2000
Sengupta, Partha	Assoc	Geo Mason	FM	PHD	95.	Florida	
Senkow, David W.	Prof	Univ Regina	CFM	PHD	92.	Minnesota	1992

Senn, Alan R.			1992	PHD	70.	UCLA	&
17661 San Rouqe Lane; Huntington Beach CA 92647							
Sennetti, John T.	Prof	Nova SE	TAS	PHD	73	Va Tech	&1996
Senteney, David L.	Assoc	Ohio Univ	PMI	PHD	87.	Illinois	&9-94
Seol, Inshik	Asst	Clark	FM	PHD	96	Conn	2001
Seow, Gim S.	Assoc	Connecticut	FT	PHD	85.	Oregon	9-91
Seow, Jean Lin	Assoc	Nanyang Tech	AF	MSC	96	Manchest	&1993
Sepe, James F.	Assoc	Santa Clara	F	PHD	80.	U Wash	&1979
Seppanen, Harri J.	Asst	Helsinki Sch	FI	PHD	99	Helsinki	1987
Sergeant, Anne M. A.			FM	PHD	94.	Arizona	
Sergenian, Gail K.	Assoc	Suffolk	FAB	PHD	94.	Conn	& 1-93
Serhan, Ali		Saudia Arabi		PHD	05.	Arkansas	
Serocki, James	Asst	Oakland	LX	LLM		Wayne St	2005
Serraino, William J.	Retir	Miami U-Ohio	1998	PHD	62.	Ohio St	&1963
Retired Dept of Finance; Miami Univ; Oxford OH 45056; 513-529-1567							
Serrato, Darlene Bohac	C-Ac	Houston Bapt	MCFP	PHD	87.	Houston	* 1987
Serrett, Randall K.	Assoc	Houston-Down	G	PHD	86.	Houston	&2000
Serry, Alan J.	ALect	Monash Univ	FD	BEC			&1991
Serva, Mark A.	Asst	Delaware	S	PHD	94	Tx-Austin	9-99
Seshie, Godwin O.	C-Ac	Virg Union	PFT	PHD	88.	Geo St	8-97
Seth, Shirish B.	Prof	CS-Fullerton	MC	PHD	69.	Mich St	1976
Sevalstad, Suzanne	Inst	Nev-L Vegas	F	MS	72	Mont St	&1979
Sevcik, Galen R.	D-Pr	Georgia St	M	PHD	91.	Minnesota	* &6-97
Severance, Robert L.	Lect	Tx St-S Marc	PFM	MBA	00	SW Tx St	# &2001
Sevigny, Kathleen	Prof	Bridgewater	CFTA	MBA			# * 1-83
Seville, Mary Alice	Retir	Oregon State	2002	PHD	83.	Illinois	&1983
Sevin, Suzanne K.	Clin	N Car-Charl	F	PHD	02.	Georgia	2001
Seward, Henry H.	Retir	CUNY-Baruch	2004	DBA	73.	Harvard	9-97
Sexton, Clifton Jr.	Retir	Nebraska Wes	2001	MA	72	Houston	&1985
Shaaban, Hamed A.	Assoc	Zagazila Egy		PHD	83.	Nebraska	
Shabahang, Reza		Teharan Iran		PHD	70.	Syracuse	
Shackelford, Douglas A.	Prof	No Carolina	X	PHD	90.	Michigan	& 7-90
Meade H. Willis Professor of Accounting							
Shackell-Dowell, Margaret B.	Asst	Notre Dame	M	PHD	99.	Michigan	2000
Shackleton, J. Kendrick	Retir	Univ Glasgow	HMB	MSC	74	Bradford	&1974
Shadbolt, Michael	Prof	Midland Luth	F	PHD	90.	Nebraska	1975
Shady, Aly M.				PHD	63.	Illinois	
Shafer, Glenn	Prof	Rutgers-Newk	SAQ	PHD	73	Princeton	9-93
Shafer, Patricia M.	Dean$	W Virg St	CFGT	MBA	75	WVCOGS	&1980
Shafer, Steve	Asst	Simpson	ACGT				2004
Shafer, William E.	Assoc	Lingnan U	AJW	PHD	94.	Houston	* &2003
Shaff, Greg	Asst	Roanoke	APU	MA	84	Jms Mad	8-04
Shaffer, Kathie J.	Prof	Frostburg St	C	MBA	85	Frostburg	* 1-86
Shaffer, Raymond J.	Prof	Youngstown	FXG	PHD	90.	Kentucky	& 9-90
Shafik, Issa		Cario		PHD	64.	Ohio St	
Shaftel, Timothy L.	Prof	Kansas	SQFM	PHD	72	Car Mellon	1988
Jordan Haines Distinguished Professor							
Shah, Arish			F	PHD	96.	Car Mellon	
Shah, Jaymeen			S	PHD	93.	Houston	
Shah, Syed Zultiqar Ali	Lect	Univ Exeter	CF	MBA	97	Peshawap	2001
Shahid, Abdus	Assoc	C New Jersey	F	PHD	92.	Temple	1990
Shailer, Gregory E. P.	Assoc	Australian N	ABQT	PHD	96	Adelaide	&1990
Shakespeare, Catherine M.	Asst	Michigan	F	PHD	02.	Illinois	2001
Shakun, Harlan J.	Asst	Central Conn	FMX	MSPA	76	Hartford	&9-81
Shalaby, Afaf A.	Assoc	NewJerseyCty	DFV	PHD	96.	Rutgers	1992
Shalchi, Hossein	Prof	CS-San Bern	FTQ	PHD	81.	Illinois	1989
Shalev, Ron	Asst	Wash Univ	F	PHD	07	Columbia	2007
Shamsuddin, Abdul	Assoc	N Eng-Austr	Q	PHD		Simon Fr	1998
Shanahan, Yvonne	H-Ac	Canterbury	CFMN	PHD	02	Syracuse	1991
Shane, Philip B.	Assoc	Colorado	F	PHD	82.	Oregon	& 8-97
Shangguan, Zhaoyun	Assoc	Mass-Dartmou		PHD	05.	Conn	2004
Shanholtzer, Dennis D.			FMS	DBA	89.	Miss St	&
Shank, John K.	Deces	Dartmouth	M	PHD	69.	Ohio St	&1984
Shankar, Geeta R.	Lect	Dayton	P	MBA	01	Dayton	&2001
Shankar, Premila G.	Assoc	Nanyang Tech	AB	PHD	03	Nanyang	&1994
Shanklin, Stephen B.	Asst	So Indiana	FP	PHD	99.	St Louis	&2007
Shannon, Donald S.	Prof	DePaul	FT	PHD	72	N Carol	&1981
Shannon, Robert P.	SLect	N Eng-Austr	A	MEC	85	N Eng-Au	&1993
Shannon, Susan S.	Lect	Boise State	PX	MBA	85	Boise St	&1985
Shanthikumar, Devin M.	Asst	Harvard	FM	PHD	04	Stanford	7-04
Shaoul, Jean E.	SLect	U Manchester	HIGW	PHD		Salfird	1983
Shapeero, Mike P.	Prof	Bloomsburg	ABPJ	PHD	96.	Va Tech	* &1997
Shapiro, Brian P.	Assoc	St Thomas-MN	FWSH	PHD	90.	Minnesota	1-04
Shapiro, Howard M.	Retir	East Wash	TA	MS	68	Mass	&1970
Shapiro, Robert E.	Assoc	Seton Hall	X	LLM	61	NYU	&1981
Shapland, Julie	Lect	Illinois	X	MS	97	Illinois	& 8-99
Sharaf, Hussein A.		Cario		PHD	59.	Illinois	

Name	Rank	School	Code	Degree	Yr	Institution	
Sharav, Itzhak	Retir	CUNY-Lehman		PHD	71	CUNY	&9-67
Shareef, Ghouse A.			ABM	PHD	71.	Alabama	# *
Sharifi, Mohsen	Prof	CS-Fullerton	SFM	PHD	75.	LSU	* 8-01
Sharkas, Wagdy K.				PHD	72.	Missouri	
Sharma, Divesh S.	Assoc	Fla Internat	FA	PHD	99	Griffith	2007
Sharma, Hari	Assoc	Virginia St	F	PHD	89	Agra Un	2003
Sharma, Vineeta	VProf	Fla Internat	F	PHD	06	UAUS	2007
Sharp, Andrew D.		Spring Hill	1992	PHD	90.	Miss	
4311 The Cedars; Mobile AL 36608							
Sharp, David J.	Assoc	West Ontario	IMJE	PHD	87	MIT	8-92
Sharp, Douglas	Retir	Wichita St	2000	PHD	69.	Missouri	&1969
Sharp, Durwin L.		Business	MS	PHD	79.	UCLA	1981
Sharp, Florence C.	Emer	Ohio Univ	2003	PHD	82.	Illinois	&9-88
Sharp, Kevin	Lect	Monash Univ	BMN	MEC			&1988
Sharp, Robert F.	Emer	Ohio Univ	1999	PHD	78.	Tx-Austin	&9-88
Shastri, Karen A.	Assoc	Pittsburgh	FNM	PHD	90.	Pittsburgh	&1998
Shastri, Trimbak	Asst	Louisville	AS	PHD	92.	Oklahoma	# * &8-01
Shaub, Michael K.	ClPr	Texas A&M	A	PHD	89.	Tx Tech	&6-06
Shaver, Carol G.	Inst	Louisiana Te	FM	MBA	85	La-Monroe	# &2002
McCallister Endowed Teaching Professor							
Shaver, James H.	Retir	Missouri So	2004	DBA	85.	La Tech	&1989
Shaver, John E. Jr.	Retir	Louisiana Te	2003	DBA	73.	La Tech	&1967
Shaw, Gail Allan	Emer	W Virginia	2002	PHD	71.	Missouri	&1973
Shaw, H.	SLect	London Metro	FM	PHD			1999
Shaw, J. Riley	Asst	Mississippi	FX	PHD	02.	Okla St	&8-02
Shaw, Kenneth W.	Assoc	Missouri	F	PHD	95.	Wisconsin	&2002
CBIZ/MHM Scholar							
Shaw, Lewis	Assoc	Suffolk	SF	PHD	02	Durham	* 1996
Shaw, Pamela E.	ClPr	Tulane	FA	PHD	89.	Florida	&2000
Shaw, Wayne H.	Prof	So Methodist	XF	PHD	85.	Tx-Austin	& 8-95
Robert B. Cullum Distinguished Professor							
Shawver, Tara J.	Asst	King's Col	FPV	DBA	02	Nova SE	1-03
Shawver, Todd	Asst	Lock Haven					
Shearer, Teri L.	Assoc	Queen's Univ	WTM	PHD	96.	Iowa	&1997
Shearon, Winston T. Jr.	Prof	Texas A&M	MS	DBA	74	Virginia	8-75
Ernst & Young Professor							
Sheehan, Norman T.	Assoc	Saskatchewan	MUB	PHD	02	Norwegia	* 2002
Sheets, Mary	Prof	Central Okla	PSF	PHD	95	Oklahoma	&9-88
Sheetz, Steven D.	Assoc	Virg Tech	S	PHD	96	Colorado	8-96
Sheffield, Susie E.	Lect	Appalach St	P	MS	85	Appalach	&1998
Shehata, Mohamed	C-Pr	McMaster Un	FM	PHD	88.	Florida	7-87
Sheikh, Aamer	Asst	Quinnipiac	FA	PHD	01.	Georgia	2006
Sheikholeslami, Mehdi	Assoc	Wis-Eau Clar	FMI	PHD	86	Tx-Dallas	* 8-88
Shekib, Aida A. H.	Prof	Governors St	AMC	PHD	70	Illinois	* &1973
Sheldahl, Terry K.	Retir	Saint Leo-FL	2004	PHD	79.	Alabama	0-95
Sheldon, Debra R.	Prof	George Wash	FG	DBA	80.	Geo Wash	&9-80
Sheldon, George	Retir	Clarkson	8-92	PHD	71	Mass	&1981
Shellard, Elaine	SLect	U Glamorgan	MG	CPFA	77		&9-91
Shellenberger, John S.	Retir	Delaware	1985	MA	62	Penn	&9-63
Shelley, Marjorie K.	Assoc	Texas A&M	BM	PHD	89.	Tx-Austin	* &8-05
Shelton, Fred A.		Camarillo CA	1992	PHD	78.	Iowa	&
990 Jay Ave; Camarillo CA 93010							
Shelton, James B.	Prof	Liberty	PCA	PHD	93.	Va Comm	&1995
Shelton, James G.			ACF	PHD	98.	Miss	&
Shelton, Margaret L.	Assoc	Houston-Down	F	PHD	86.	Houston	&1989
Shelton, Sandra W.	Assoc	DePaul	AB	PHD	94.	Wisconsin	&8-94
Shen, Dabai	Assoc	Soochow Univ	F	PHD	92.	Tulane	1992
Shen, Min	Asst	Geo Mason	F	PHD	05.	Mich St	2005
Sheng, William		Taiwan		PHD	94.	Purdue	
Shenkir, William G.	Retir	Virginia	2007	PHD	64.	Tx-Austin	&7-77
Shepard, Eugene H.	Retir	Delta State	1995	PHD	77.	Arkansas	&1991
Sheppard, John D.	Retir	W Michigan	1993	PHD	70.	Missouri	1965
Sherer, Michael J.	Prof	Univ Essex	AFMN	MA	72	Manchest	&1984
Sheridan, Joanne	Retir	Mont St-Bill	2002	MBA	80	U Wash	&1978
Sheridan, Kaye F.	H-Ac	Tenn-Chattan	X	DBA	98.	Miss St	&8-02
Sherif, Hanaa				PHD	87.	Baruch	9-84
Sheriff, Jimmy D.	Retir	Clemson	2002	PHD	76.	Georgia	1974
Sherman, Eugene H.	Deces	Troy State	FG	MA	53	Alabama	1963
Sherman, H. David	Prof	Northeastern	MU	DBA	81.	Harvard	&9-85
Sherman, Karl J.	Retir	Lk Superior	5-00	MS	67	S Illinois	9-71
Sherman, W. Richard	Prof	St Joseph	XFI	LLM	91	Villanova	&1989
Shetewi, Idris				PHD	81.	Missouri	
Shetty, Shanker	Retir	DePauw	1997	PHD	73	Minnesota	8-79
Shevlin, Susan E.			FT	PHD	89.	Rochester	&
Shevlin, Terry	C-Pr	U Washington	FX	PHD	86.	Stanford	1-86
Piggot-PACCAR Professor							
Shi, Charles	Asst	Calif-Irvine	F	PHD	00	Minnesota	7-00

Shi, Yari	Asst	West Ontario	IFMV	ABD		Concordia	7-07	
Shiarappa, Barbara J.			FTV	PHD	87.	Temple		
Shibano, Toshi			MAI	PHD	89.	Stanford		
Shieh, Tony	Asst	City Univ HK	IF	PHD	99.	NYU	1999	
Shields, Jeffrey F.	Assoc	So Maine	CM	PHD	91.	Pittsburgh	2001	
Shields, Michael D.	Prof	Michigan St	M	PHD	78.	Pittsburgh	1997	
Schaberg Endowed Chair in Accounting								
Shields, P. David	Dean	W Michigan	FM	PHD	80.	Michigan	&2006	
Shifflett, Eileen M.	Inst	Jms Madison	FCM	MBA	98	Jms Mad	& 1-02	
Shih, S. H. Michael	Assoc	Natl Singapo	M	PHD	88.	Minnesota	&1996	
Shillinglaw, Gordon	Retir	Columbia	1991	PHD	52	Harvard	1961	
196 Villard Ave; Hastings-on-Hudson NY 10706								
Shim, E. Daniel	Assoc	Sacred Heart	FM	PHD	93.	Rutgers	1997	
Shim, Eun Sup			FME	PHD	93.	Rutgers		* &
Shim, Jae K.	Prof	CS-Long Bch	CM	PHD	73	Berkeley	1981	
Shim, Kyu-Young				PHD	90.	Kent St		
Shima, Kim	Asst	CS-East Bay	FI	PHD	07	Hawaii	9-07	
Shimawi, Ahmemd A. K.	Dir	Grains Saud		DBA	70.	S Calif		
Shimeld, Sonia	AcLec	Un Tasmania	F	MCOM	02	Newcastle	2003	
Shimerda, Thomas A.	Assoc	Creighton	CMS	PHD	78.	Nebraska	* &9-80	
Shin, Doug Y.			FM	PHD	89.	Iowa		
Shin, Haeyoung	Asst	Houston-Cl L	F	PHD	07	Tx-Dallas	9-07	
Shin, Hong-Chul		Seoul Korea	1992	PHD	85.	Tx-Austin		
32-35 Choong-Jung; RO 3-KA Seedaemoon-Ku; Seoul Korea								
Shin, Jae Yong	Asst	Illinois	FM	PHD	06	Wisconsin	8-06	
Shin, Joon Y.	Prof	Korea Univ	MY	PHD	83.	Minnesota	3-85	
Shin, Yong-Chul	Asst	Rensselaer	F	PHD	00.	MIT	2004	
Shipley, Vicki	Inst	Ball State	FM	MA	76	Ball St	3-79	
Shiraz, Adam				PHD	84	Simon Fr		
Shishoff, John W.	Lect	Dayton	MP	ABD		Penn St	&1999	
Shiue, F. Norman			T	PHD	90.	Geo Wash	&	
Shivakumar, Lakshmanan	Asst	London Bus	F	PHD	96	Vanderbilt	* 1996	
Shivaswamy, Melkote K.	Retir	Ball State	FM	PHD	70	India	9-76	
Shoaf, Victoria	C-Ac	St John's	FE	PHD	97.	Baruch	1997	
Shockley, Randolph A. (Skip)	Retir	Georgia	2005	PHD	78.	N Carol	&1979	
Shoemaker, Bill	Asst	Dallas	XAM	MBA	73	Golden Gt	&	
Shoemaker, Paul A.	D-Ac	Nebraska	FXH	PHD	89.	Penn St	&1989	
Nebraska CPAs Distinguished Professor								
Shoenthal, Edward R.	Retir	CUNY-Brookly	2003	PHD	85	NYU	& 2-73	
Shoesmith, D. E.	SLect	Liverpool JM	FT	MA				
Shome, Anamitra	Assoc	Brock Univ	MS	PHD	98	Concordia	1997	
Shon, John J.	Asst	CUNY-Baruch	F	PHD	04.	Chicago	9-03	
Shook, Carol L.	Inst	Arkansas	FM	MBA	94	Arkansas	&1999	
Shook, Charles H.	Prof	Mercy-NY	GCNR	PHD	79.	Okla St	&9-80	
Shores, D.	Assoc	U Washington	F	PHD	86.	Stanford	1986	
Shorney, Mayda			FA	PHD	88.	Tx A&M		
Short, Daniel G.	Dean	Tx Christian	F	PHD	77.	Michigan	&8-04	
Short, Helen	SLect	Univ Leeds	BMQ	PHD	96	Leeds	9-90	
Shortridge, Rebecca T.	Asst	No Illinois	F	PHD	99.	Mich St	&8-05	
Shough, Evan	Asst	N Car-Greens	FM	PHD	05.	Oklahoma	8-05	
Shough, J. Stuart	Inst	SC Upstate	FC	MACC	86	S Carol	&1986	
Shoulders, Craig D.	Prof	NC-Pembroke	FG	PHD	82.	Tx Tech	&2004	
Showalter, Jerry E.	Assoc	Indiana Wes	XP	MA	67	Ball St	&1966	
Showalter, Scott	VLect	Illinois						
Showers, Robert	Asst	Cen Missouri	PM	MBA	82	S Dakota	&2001	
Shriver, Keith A.	Retir	Arizona St	2000	PHD	83.	Tx-Austin	& 1-83	
Shroff, Pervin K.	Assoc	Minnesota	FA	PHD	92.	Columbia	1998	
Shu, Susan Z.	Assoc	Boston Coll	AKF	PHD	00.	Rochester	1999	
Shulman, James S.				DBA	67.	Harvard		
Shulman, Milton D.	Retir	DePaul	1991	PHD	54	Illinois	1968	
Shuman, Franklin	SLect	Utah State	FMCR	MACC	89	Utah St	# * &1992	
Shutibhinyo, Wasatorn	Lect	Chulalongkor	ACM	MACC	04	Chulalong	&2004	
Shwayer, Keith R.		Samsonite		PHD	68.	Stanford	&	
Siagian, Ferdinand	Asst	Maine	AF	PHD	02.	Oregon	2007	
Siam, J.	Asst	McMaster Un	F	PHD	01	Concordia	7-02	
Sian, Suki	Lect	Cardiff U	H	PHD	06		2004	
Sidaway, David D.	Retir	Oakland	FA	MACC	68	Ohio St	&1977	
Sidhu, Baljit K.	SLect	Austral Grad	FI	PHD	93	Sydney	& 1-99	
Sidler, Paul D.				PHD	73.	Arkansas	&	
Siebel, Jerry D.	Retir	South Fla	2006	PHD	70.	Iowa	&9-72	
Sieg, Herbert C.	Retir	Illinois St	2005	MS	65	Illinois	&1966	
Siegel, Gary H.	Retir	DePaul	MB	PHD	77	Illinois	&1980	
Siegel, Joel G.	Prof	CUNY-Queens	FM	PHD	78.	Baruch	&9-74	
Siegel, Philip H.			AFMB	DBA	85.	Memphis	&	
Siegel, Rachel S.	Prof	Lyndon State	QF	MBA	89	Yale	9-90	
Sievewright, Douglas J. A.	SLect	Napier Univ	AF	FCCA			&3-80	
Siganos, Antonios	Asst	Univ Glasgow	F	MA	01	Exeter	2004	

Sigler, John N.	Assoc	Baltimore	LXFS	JD	76	Maryland	&1970
Sigloch, Berndt A.	Inst	Univ Cariboo	PMQ	MBA		Brit Colum	1980
Sigmond, Norman C.	Asst	Kutztown	APX	MST	99	Temple	&1995
Sih, Kwang C.	Retir	Seton Hall	1995	PHD	52.	Illinois	1983
Sikes, Helen B.	Prof	Centenary-LA	T	DBA	95	La Tech	* &8-90
Sikka, Prem N.	H-Pr	Univ Essex	AEFW	PHD	91	Sheffield	&1996
Sil, Amar N.			QS	PHD	84.	Columbia	
Silaen, Parulian	Lect	U Wollongong	CMU	MCOM		Wollong	2004
Silhan, Peter A.	Assoc	Illinois	SMI	DBA	80.	Tennessee	* 8-79
Silkoff, Richard	Assoc	Eastern Conn	FX	SCD	02	NewHaven	&
Silliman, Benjamin	Asst	CUNY-Queens	TF	EDD	04	NYU	&9-04
Silowati, Isabelly	Lect	Univ Sydney	FIM	BCOM	03	NS Wales	2004
Silver, Donald P.	Retir	Lg Isl-Post	1998	MBA	61	Columbia	&1984
Silverman, Harold	Prof	Bridgewater	FLX	LLM			&8-83
Silvester, Katherine J.	Assoc	Siena	CM	PHD	92.	Maryland	2003
Silvester, Mark	AcLec	So Queenslnd	ADFQ	BBUS	93	S Queens	1996
Silvester, W. Harold	Retir	Saskatchewan	1994	PHD	78.	Missouri	&1973
Silvoso, Joseph A.	Deces	Missouri	2-98	PHD	51.	Missouri	&1955
Sim, Khim Ling	Assoc	Roger Wm	MC	PHD	96.	Drexel	8-05
Simanjuntak, Binsar				DBA	94.	Clev St	
Assistant State School of Government Accountants							
Simasathien, Panas		Thailand	1991	PHD	58.	Illinois	
Ministry of Finance; Rama Vi Rd; Bangkok 10400 Thailand							
Simini, Joseph Peter	Retir	U San Fran	1985	MBA	57	Berkeley	&9-54
Simione, Kathleen	Asst	Quinnipiac	CP	MBA	80	Bentley	&1989
Simkins, Allen F.	Prof	Weber State	MCQF	PHD	76.	Ariz St	&1976
Simko, Paul J.	Assoc	Virg-Grad	FMTX	PHD	96.	Tx-Austin	&2002
Simmonds, Kendall L.	Clin	So Calif	AFPX	MBA	77	Berkeley	1992
Simmons, Bonnie A.	Assoc	Elmhurst	FM	MBA	82	Ill Tech	&2002
Simmons, Cynthia V.	Assoc	Univ Calgary	BMW	PHD	89.	Houston	1988
Simmons, Donald C.	Prof	Frostburg St	CPF	MBA	77	Jms Mad	&9-78
Simmons, John K.	Retir	Florida	2005	PHD	67.	Ohio St	& 7-74
Simmons, John S.	Retir	Nicholls St	1988	JD	72	Loyola	9-76
Simmons, Joseph T.	Retir	South Dakota		PHD	74.	Nebraska	&
Department of Finance							
Simmons, Laura E.				PHD	97.	N Carol	
Cornerstone Research							
Simmons, Richard S.	Asst	Lingnan U	AX	PHD	02	London	&1991
Simmons, Sharelle	Lect	U Queensland	A	MCOM	91	NS Wales	2000
Simms, Jack	Asst	St Thomas-TX	M	PHD	06.	Houston	9-06
Simms, Walter	Inst	Miss Vall St		MPA		Delta St	8-98
Simnett, Roger	H-Pr	New So Wales	AB	PHD	92	NS Wales	&1987
Simon, Abraham J.	Prof	CUNY-Queens	FTGN	PHD	71	Penn	&9-75
Simon, Claude	Prof	ESCP deParis	TM	PHD	92	CPA	1990
Simon, Daniel T.	Retir	Notre Dame	2004	PHD	83.	Nrthwstrn	& 8-89
Simon, J. B.	H-Lec	Univ Hull	EF	MBA	88	Cardiff	9-89
Simon, John R.	Emer	No Illinois	2001	PHD	74.	Illinois	&9-73
Simon, Milton	Retir	Lg Isl-Post	1990	BA	44	Penn St	&1947
Simon, Ronald				PHD	68.	Columbia	
Simons, Donald R.	C-Pr	Wis-Oshkosh	NMG	PHD	72.	Wisconsin	&1985
Simons, Harry	Retir	UCLA	1975	MA	36	UCLA	1935
Simons, Kathleen A.	Prof	Bryant	F	DBA	91.	Boston U	& 8-84
Simons, Robert L.	Prof	Harvard	MBU	PHD	84	McGill	&1984
Charles M. Williams Professor of Business Administration							
Simonsen, Lori	Inst	Neb-Omaha	FM	MACC	06	Ne-Omaha	2006
Simpkins, Kevin	SenFl	Victoria NZ		BCOM			2007
Simpson, Aua	Lect	London Econ	FIQ	PHD	06	London	2006
Simpson, Ben	Retir	CS-Humboldt	6-90	MBA	59	Kansas	&1963
Simpson, Richard H.	Assoc	Massachusett	F	PHD	67.	N Carol	&1967
Simpson, Rick	H-Ac	SE Louisiana	FX	PHD	96.	Houston	& 8-96
Simunic, Dan A.	C-Pr	British Colu	AFMI	PHD	79.	Chicago	&1979
Certified General Accountants Professor							
Simyar, Farhad	Dean	Chicago St	EIM	DBA	75.	S Calif	&2005
Sin, Samantha	SLect	Macquarie Un	E	MCOM	92	Macquarie	1990
Sinason, David H.	Assoc	No Illinois	SA	PHD	96.	Fla St	# & 8-96
PricewaterhouseCoopers Professor of Accountancy							
Sinclair, Debra T.	Asst	Geo Southern	P	PHD	05.	Temple	* 2004
Sinclair, John McInnes		Brookline MA	1992	DBA	67.	Harvard	&
77 Pond Ave C601; Brookline MA 02146							
Sinclair, Kenneth P.	C-Pr	Lehigh	M	PHD	72.	Mass	9-72
Sinclair, Scott	Lect	British Colu	AF	BCO	79	Brit Colum	&2006
Singer, Frank A.	Retir	Clarion	1988	DBA	55.	Indiana	8-86
Singer, Robert	Assoc	Quincy	FI	PHD	96	St Louis	&1998
Singer, Ronald M.	Retir	Wis-Parkside	2002	PHD	89.	Wisconsin	& 8-73
Singh, Vidyapati	Retir	St Ambrose	CMUP	PHD	61	Case Wes	&1982
Singhal, Raj B.			FVM	PHD	91.	S Carol	
Singhasaneh, Phayon				PHD	57.	Illinois	

Name	Rank	School	Field	Degree	Yr	School	
Singhasaneh, Suthee				PHD	57.	Illinois	
Singhvi, Surendra S.	VPres	Edison Bros	1991	PHD	67.	Columbia	* &
Edison Brothers Stores, St. Louis MO; 513-748-2569							
Single, Louise E.	Asst	St Edwards	XF	PHD	95.	Florida	&2007
Singleton, Lawrence G.	Assoc	George Wash	FMI	PHD	85.	LSU	&1984
Singleton, Roger L.			F	PHD	70.	Missouri	
Singleton, Tommie W.	Assoc	Alabama-Birm	AEOS	PHD	95.	Miss	* &2003
Singleton, W. Ron	Prof	Western Wash	XFI	PHD	83	Hawaii	& 1-76
Sinha, Nishi	Asst	Boston Univ	FM	PHD	94.	Purdue	9-01
Sinha, Praveen	Assoc	Chapman	FM	PHD	92	Car Mellon	9-04
Sinha, Ranjan			FM	PHD	92.	Berkeley	
Sinkin, Charlene	Asst	Bryant		ABD		Okla St	
Sinnadurai, Philip T.	Lect	Macquarie Un	F	PHD	04	Sydney	1993
Sinning, Kathleen E.	Prof	W Michigan	XI	PHD	78.	Mich St	8-79
Sipes, Daniel E. Sr.	Assoc	Mary	PFVT	MS	71	N Dakota	&9-73
Sipes, Kimberly A.	Asst	Kentucky St	FM	MSA	82	Kentucky	&2000
Sipple, Stanley		Doane Coll	F	PHD	85.	Nebraska	&
Sisaye, Seleshi	Prof	Duquesne	BCM	PHD	88.	Pittsburgh	1985
Sisco, William T.	Retir	Eastern Conn	ADFX	MST	89.	Suffolk	&1985
Sisneros, Craig	Asst	Wichita St	F	PHD	06.	Ariz St	2007
Sitchawat, Sadwanne		Thammasat U	1990	DBA	81.	Kentucky	
Thammasat Univ; Faculty of Comm & Acctcy; Bangkok Thailand 10200							
Sithole, J. S.	Lect	Un Zimbabwe	X	MSC			
Sitkiewicz, Adolph L.	Retir	DePaul	FP	MBA	56	DePaul	* &1957
Siu, David	ALect	Macquarie Un					
Siva, Velayutham	Asst	Sultan Qaboo	FM	PHD	96	Massey	1998
Sivabalan, Prabhu	Lect	Tech-Sydney	CSI	BBUS	90	Tech-Sydn	2001
Sivakumar, Kumar N.	Assoc	Boston Univ	FH	PHD	89.	Rice	9-01
Sivaramakrishnan, K. (Shiva)	Prof	Houston	FM	PHD	88.	Nrthwstrn	1-03
C.T. Bauer Endowed Chair							
Sjoblom, Leif M.	Prof	Intl Mgt Dev	MUFI	PHD	93.	Stanford	* 1993
Skadden, Donald H.	Deces		2-05	PHD	55.	Illinois	& 1-87
Skadden, Karin M.			1997	PHD	82.	Michigan	&
3112 Chipping Wedge Ct; Sanford NC 27330; 919-499-1292							
Skaggs, Charles P.	Retir	W Virginia	1988	MS	63	W Virginia	&1954
Skaife, Hollis	Assoc	Wisconsin	F	PHD	97.	Iowa	* &1997
Skalberg, Randall	Asst	Minn-Duluth	JLX	LLM	96	Case Wes	2001
Skaldehaug, Espen	SLect	Norwegian Mg	CM	MSCR	83	Linkoping	1989
Skalpe, Ole	Assoc	Norwegian Mg	FM	DOEC	96	NHH Berg	2003
Skandera, Rudolf			MS	PHD	65.	Columbia	
Skantz, Don	Retir	SUNY Oswego	1994	JD	65	Tx-Austin	&1979
Skantz, Terrance R.	Assoc	Fla Atlantic	MC	PHD	79.	Okla St	* 1992
Skapski, Tomasz	Deces	Quebec a Hul	Q	PHD			
Skarbnik, John H.	Asst	F Dick-Madis	X	LLM	87	NYU	&1988
Skaro, Matthew M.		Chicago IL	1992	PHD	87.	Nebraska	
2912 E 78th St; Chicago IL 60649							
Skekel, Ted D.	Assoc	Tx-S Antonio	FTVE	PHD	77.	Oregon	&1986
Skelly, Ralph E.	Retir	Missouri	1987	PHD	64.	Alabama	# 1957
Skender, C. J.	Adj	No Carolina	FM	MBA	81	Duke	# * &1999
Skinner, Douglas J.	Prof	Chicago	F	PHD	89.	Rochester	2005
Skipper, Joseph F.				PHD	81.	Tx A&M	
Sklar, Albert	C-Pr	Touro	PANV	ABD		NYU	&9-71
Skogsvik, Kenth	Prof	Stockholm Ec	P	ED	94	Stockholm	1977
KPMG Professor of Business Administration							
Skogsvik, Stina		Stockholm Ec	F	CE	90	Stockholm	1990
Skolnick, Gerald	Deces	CUNY-Baruch	1991	JD	64	CUNY	1963
Skougstad, David	Asst	Metro State	CMP	MS	73	Colo St	3-76
Skousen, Chris	Asst	Utah State	S	PHD	04.	Okla St	2007
Skousen, Clifford R.	Prof	Utah State	MI	PHD	79	Golden Gt	* &9-78
Ernst & Young Professor							
Skousen, K. Fred	Prof	Brigham Yg	F	PHD	68.	Illinois	&9-70
Vice President							
Skousen, Karl M.	Retir	Brigham Yg	1981	PHD	62.	Mich St	&1958
424 W 230 N; Orem UT 84057							
Skully, Michael	Prof	Monash Univ	FI	GRAD			&1992
Slade, Priscilla D.			F	PHD	90.	Tx-Austin	
Slager, Raymond L.	Prof	Calvin	SVAM	MS	70	W Mich	&1982
Slagle, Warren L.	Retir	Tennessee	1989	MS	50	Tennessee	&1948
Slater, Robert D.	Asst	Tx A&M-C Chr	FS	PHD	07.	S Fla	&9-05
Slattery, Dennis	Asst	So Oregon St	CMN	MBA	97	S Oregon	&2004
Slaubaugh, Michael D.	Assoc	Ind-Pur/FtWy	MFNG	PHD	92.	Indiana	&8-95
Slaughter, D. French III	Retir	Virg-Grad	X	JD	80	Virginia	1987
Slaughter, Raymond L.	C-Ac	Richmond	XLP	LLM	91	Wm&Mary	&1977
Slavin, Nathan S.	Prof	Hofstra	F	PHD	80.	Baruch	&9-74
Slaymaker, Adrianne E.	Assoc	Metro St-MN		DBA	84.	Kentucky	&
Sleenkamp, N.	Lect	Massey-Alban		PHD			2006
Sletten, Ewa	Asst	MIT	F	PHD	07	Nrthwstrn	2007

Name	Rank	School		Degree	Yr	Institution	
Slipkowsky, John N.	Retir	Merrimack	1999	MBA	65	Boston C	* &1971
Sliwoski, Leonard J.	Prof	Mn-Moorhead	F	PHD	88	N Dakota	* &1982
Sloan, Richard G.			F	PHD	92.	Rochester	
Sloboda, William P.	Assoc	Gallaudet	AFNS	MBA	72	Geo Wash	&1969
Slocum, Elliott L.	Retir	Georgia St	2003	PHD	72.	Missouri	9-66
Slotnick, Mitchell L.		NorthbrookIL	1992	PHD	68.	Nrthwstrn	
1418 Ridge Rd; Northbrook Il 60062							
Slowey, William E.	Retir	Notre Dame	1990	MBA	52	Michigan	&1946
Slusarz, George	Asst	NE St-Okla	AL	JD	00	Memphis	&2005
Slutsky, Joanne	Lect	Illinois		MBA	94	Tulane	8-97
Smalley, Robert	Asst	Augusta St		MBA	73	Georgia	2002
Smalt, Steven W.	Assoc	Kennesaw St	FA	PHD	99	Union-NY	&1988
Smark, Ciorstan	SLect	U Wollongong	JNE	PHD		Wollong	&2004
Smedley, Georgia A.	Asst	Mo-Kansas Ct	S	PHD	01.	Okla St	2007
Smetana, Joan G.	Assoc	Marywood	PM	EDD		Temple	
Smieliauskas, Wally	Prof	Univ Toronto	A	PHD	80.	Wisconsin	&1979
Smigla, John E.	C-Ac	Myers	FM	MS		Kent St	&2005
Smillie, Donald	Inst	Missouri St	F	MACC	01	Mo St	8-02
Smith, Abbie J.	Prof	Chicago	F	PHD	81.	Cornell	1980
Boris and Irene Stern Professor of Accounting							
Smith, Aileen	Prof	S F Austin	BFIJ	PHD	92.	LSU	&1993
Smith, Alan F.		E Windsor NJ	1992	DBA	68.	Colorado	&
460 Fairfield Rd; Twin Rivers; East Windsork NJ 08520							
Smith, Andrew M. C.	Assoc	Victoria NZ	FX	MCA	84	Victoria	1982
Smith, Anne	Asst	St Marys-Cal		EDD		N Illinois	* 2006
Smith, Austin M.			MA	PHD	67.	Illinois	&
Smith, Barney M. Jr.	Retir	W Illinois	1989	JD	54	Tx-Austin	&9-67
Smith, Barry	Lect	Dublin City	DFS	MECO	01	NUI	&2001
Smith, Becky L.	C-As	York-Penn		PHD	94	US Intl	&9-97
Smith, Bernandette	AcLec	Un Tasmania	F	BCOM	03	Tasmania	2002
Smith, Bruce W.	Retir	Mn St-Mankat	2004	MS	67	N Dakota	&1967
Smith, C. Aubrey	Deces	Texas	N-94	PHD	33	Columbia	
Smith, C. Ray	Retir	Virg-Grad	1997	MBA	58	Virginia	&1961
Smith, Carl S.	Assoc	Hartford	CS	PHD	88	Conn	* &9-81
Smith, Carl S..	Retir	West Chester	2006	MBA	71	Temple	&9-71
Smith, Charles H.	Emer	Penn State	F	PHD	68.	Penn St	& 1-87
KPMG Professor Emeritus of Accounting							
Smith, Charles R.	Assoc	Millikin	FMO	PHD		Amer-Lond	&1992
Smith, Christine	AProf	Griffith-GC					
Smith, Claude K.	Retir	E Kentucky	1989	MBA	66	Kentucky	&1964
Smith, Clinton A.	Retir	Tarleton St	1994	MBA	58	Houston	&1961
Smith, Darlene A.	Prof	West Tx A&M	XF	PHD	87.	North Tx	&8-97
Smith, David	SLect	U Melbourne	BCMQ	PHD		Monash	2003
Smith, David B.	Prof	Nebraska	F	PHD	79.	Illinois	&2005
Raymond C. Dein Professor & Deloitte & Touche Scholar							
Smith, David M.	C-Ac	Missouri So	FCSM	PHD	97.	North Tx	&1995
Smith, Donna	Asst	Cen Arkansas	CS	MBA		Okla St	* 8-78
Smith, Douglas L.	Asst	Samford	AM	PHD	01	Al-Birm	# * &2000
Smith, E. Daniel	Prof	Georgia	FEY	PHD	74.	Ohio St	1991
Smith, Ephraim P.	Prof	CS-Fullerton	X	PHD	68.	Illinois	8-90
Smith, Fred W.	Inst	Kansas State	FM	MACC	88	Kansas St	&8-94
Ernst & Young Teaching Fellow							
Smith, G. Robert Jr.	Assoc	Mid Tenn St	GF	PHD	95.	Tx Tech	&8-99
Smith, G. Stevenson	Prof	SE Okla St	CM	PHD	78.	Arkansas	* &2006
Smith, Gary	ALect	W Australia	F	BCOM	96	Curtin	1998
Smith, Gaylord N.	Prof	Albion	FXA	MBA	67	Mich St	&1976
Smith, Gene	C-As	E New Mexico	A	PHD	05	N Cen Un	2002
Smith, Gerald	Prof	No Iowa	AF	PHD	74.	Oklahoma	# &1989
Smith, Henry C. III	Assoc	Otterbein	MC	PHD	94.	Va Comm	* 2001
Smith, Howard G.	Retir	Tx St-S Marc	CDGS	PHD	85.	Tx Tech	&1988
Smith, J. David			CM	PHD	79.	Nebraska	
Smith, J. Reed	Assoc	Indiana-Indy	SM	PHD	89.	Ohio St	8-02
Smith, Jack L.	Retir	South Fla	2003	PHD	69.	Miss	&9-69
Smith, James A.	Assoc	St Cloud St	PGI	DBA	94.	La Tech	&1994
Smith, James E.	Prof	Wm & Mary	X	PHD	72.	Arizona	&1970
John S. Quinn Professor of Accounting							
Smith, James F.	Assoc	Massachusett	BMF	PHD	80.	U Wash	& 1-87
Smith, James K.	Assoc	San Diego	X	PHD	95.	Arizona	&2001
Smith, Janet Rosalea M.		Quebec Canad		PHD	74.	Berkeley	
Smith, Janice A.	Retir	Bryant	2002	PHD	75.	LSU	1-70
Smith, Jay M. Jr.			FAE	PHD	65.	Stanford	&
Smith, Jill A.	Asst	Missouri So	PAF	MBA	87	Minnesota	&1986
Smith, Jill M.	Asst	Idaho State	PF	MBA	75	Idaho St	&1986
Smith, John H.	Retir	No Illinois	1994	PHD	67.	Illinois	&8-87
Smith, Joseph R.	Retir	So Oregon St	1990	EDD		N Colo	1964
Smith, Joyce van der laan	Asst	Virginia St	FIW	PHD	05	Va Comm	8-05

Smith, Julian D.	Retir	NE Louisiana		1990	PHD	75.	LSU	&1976
2701 Anita Lane; Monroe LA 71201								
Smith, Karen A.				FAVI	PHD	94.	Tx-Austin	&
602-366-7995								
Smith, Kathleen J.	Prof	Neb-Kearney		XLP	LLM	89	McGeorge	&8-89
Smith, Keith	Prof	Freed Hardem		PSGN	PHD	88.	Miss	&8-00
Smith, Keith E.	C-Ac	George Wash		XF	LLM	78	Florida	&1984
Smith, Ken A.	Asst	Willamette		MGN	PHD	01.	Missouri	&2004
Smith, Kenneth A.	Prof	Idaho State		ARM	PHD	71.	Tx-Austin	&1970
Smith, Kenneth J.	C-Pr	Salisbury		FMT	DBA	86.	Geo Wash	# * &8-92
Trice, Geary, & Myers Professor of Accounting								
Smith, Kevin R.	Asst	Kansas			PHD	05.	Arizona	8-05
Smith, Kimberly J.	Assoc	Wm & Mary		MFU	PHD	89.	Maryland	&1988
Smith, L. Murphy	Prof	Texas A&M		JISA	DBA	83.	La Tech	& 6-84
Smith, Langford Wheaton		Palo Alto CA		1992	PHD	62.	Stanford	
243 Ely Place; Palo Alto CA 94306								
Smith, Lute	Assoc	Chicago St		LJ	JD	62	J Marshal	1978
Smith, Margaret C.				FP	PHD	86.	Duke	&
Smith, Mark E.	Inst	Louisville		PL	JD	82	Louisville	&1984
Smith, Michael J.	Assoc	Boston Univ		FM	PHD	98.	Stanford	9-04
Smith, Milo	Retir	Berkeley		1984	JD	50	Iowa St	1951
Smith, Nancy E.	Retir	W Illinois		FT	PHD	86.	Nebraska	&9-82
Smith, Ola	Asst	W Michigan		M	PHD	02.	Mich St	&2000
Smith, Pamela A.	Prof	No Illinois		FIJ	PHD	93.	North Tx	& 1-94
KPMG LLP Professor of Accountancy								
Smith, Pamela C.	Asst	Tx-S Antonio		X	PHD	01.	Va Tech	9-01
Smith, Patricia	Inst	DePaul		AFP	MBA	92	DePaul	&1995
Smith, Patricia	Retir	Tarleton St		FPA	MBA	84	Tarleton	&1984
Smith, Paul H.		McKendree		1991	PHD	85.	Arkansas	
McKendree College; Lebanon IL 62254								
Smith, Ralph E.	Retir	Arizona St		2004	PHD	70.	Kansas	&1975
Smith, Richard L.	Retir	Utah State		1989	DCS	56.	Harvard	& 3-77
Smith, Robert J.		Provo UT		1989	DBA	57.	Indiana	9-49
Smith, Rodney E.	Assoc	CS-Long Bch		FMS	PHD	00.	Ca-Irvine	* &2006
Smith, S. Duane	Prof	Brescia		AFGM	PHD	91.	Tx A&M	* &2001
Smith, Sammie L.	Retir	S F Austin		F	PHD	72.	Arkansas	&1980
Smith, Sarah H.	Assoc	Cedarville		GF	PHD	82.	Va Tech	1980
Smith, Sharon	Retir	Tx-Brownsvil		2002	MA	69	Arizona	1973
Smith, Sheldon R.	Prof	Utah Valley		MFVE	PHD	93.	Mich St	# * &2001
Smith, Sondra	Lect	West Georgia		P	MPAC	96	W Geo	& 9-03
Smith, Steven D.	Asst	Illinois		F	PHD	05.	Cornell	8-04
Smith, Steven H.	Asst	Western Wash		MX	PHD	00.	Ariz St	&2000
Smith, Toni				XF	PHD	99.	Case Wes	&
Smith, Tracy L.	Asst	Coast Carol		FI	PHD	01.	Alabama	&2006
Smith, V. Scott	Inst	Cen Florida		M	MBA	83	Loyola	& 8-98
Smith, Virginia G.	C-Le	St Marys-Cal		PMX	MBA		CS-Haywa	&1985
Smith, W. Robert	Assoc	So Miss		XFM	PHD	88.	LSU	&1995
Smith, Walter P.	Asst	Siena		CM	PHD	98.	Ohio St	* 2004
Smith, Wilbur I.	Assoc	Florida A&M		MC	PHD	84.	Wisconsin	1984
Smith, William E.	Retir	Xavier		2002	MBA	57	Xavier	&1956
Smith, William L.	Asst	New Mex St		F	PHD	04	N Mex St	& 1-05
Smith-Banks, Betty	C-Ac	Aquinas		AVN	MBA	75	Atlanta	&1994
Smith-Gaffney, Maureen H.	Asst	SUNY-Utica			PHD	79.	Ohio St	
Smolarski, John	Assoc	Tx-Pan Amer		CFM	PHD	96.	North Tx	&2007
Smolinski, H. Carl	Assoc	La St-Shreve		FCT	DBA	87.	La Tech	& 8-87
Smolinski, Harold J.	Retir	Louisiana Te		D-85	MBA	40	LSU	&1941
1502 Shelor Drive; Ruston LA 71270								
Smyth, M. J.	Lect	Univ Ulster		FI	BSC			& 1-78
Snavely, H. Jim	Retir	Wright State		1995	DBA	68.	Colorado	& 6-88
Snead, Kenneth C.	Assoc	Bowling Gr		MB	PHD	88.	S Carol	1988
Sneathen, L. Dwight Jr.	Asst	Geo Southern		FV	PHD	01.	Arizona	2005
Sneed, Cynthia Smith	Assoc	Jacksonvl St		M	PHD	94.	Alabama	8-01
Sneed, Florence R.	Retir			A	PHD	79.	North Tx	&
Sneed, Joel	Inst	Oregon		FX	PHD	01.	Arizona	&2000
Sneed, John E.	Assoc	Jacksonvl St		F	PHD	94.	Alabama	& 9-01
Snider, Helen					PHD	01.	NYU	
Snider, Lois A.	C-As	Hannibal-LaG		FPM	MA	85	NE Mo St	1982
Snow, Charles G. Jr.	Assoc	Rhode Isl Cl		FCM	PHD	93.	Drexel	* &9-92
Snow, Charles J.	Dean	Touro		AFVX	PHD	80.	NYU	* 9-04
Snow, Nancy	Inst	Toledo		P	MS	95	Toledo	&1998
Snowball, Doug	Prof	Florida		MFB	PHD	75.	U Wash	& 3-75
J. Michael Cook/Deloitte & Touche Professor of Accounting								
Snudden, Leslie W.	Retir	San Diego St		1990	DBA	65.	S Calif	&1959
Snyder, Debra	Assoc	Mt Vernon Nz			PHD	03.	Kent St	
Snyder, Herbert	Assoc	N Dakota St		AJS	PHD	94	Syracuse	2003
Snyder, John P.					PHD	85.	S Carol	&
Snyder, Willard S. Jr.	Lect	San Diego St		XF	MBA	76	S Calif	&1990

Snyir, Andrew G. (Drew)	Prof	E Michigan	MCFS	PHD	81.	Purdue	6-84
Sobery, Julie S.	Assoc	So Illinois	FT	PHD	82.	St Louis	&1985
Soczek, Mark E.	Lect	Wash Univ	FT	ABD		Nrthwstrn	1997
Soderstrom, Gosta	Asst	Univ of Umea	FT	BSC	84	Umea	8-85
Soderstrom, Naomi S.	Assoc	Colorado	SM	PHD	90.	Nrthwstrn	2000
Soel, Inshik			MB	PHD	97.	Conn	
Soffer, Leonard C.	Assoc	Ill-Chicago	PERF	PHD	91.	Berkeley	&2000
Soh, Joseph	ALect	Macquarie Un					
Sohail, Tashfeen	Asst	Inst Empresa		PHD	06.	Maryland	
Sohlinger, Jean				PHD	01.	U Wash	
Sohn, B. Charlie	Asst	City Univ HK	AFT	PHD	06	Seoul Ntl	2006
Sohn, Min	Prof	Ajou Univ	AFMX	PHD	86	Hong-Ik	&1984
Sohn, Pyung Sik		Industry	F	PHD	93.	Tx-Arlin	
Sohn, Sungkyu	Assoc	Yonsei Univ	FA	PHD	92.	Nrthwstrn	&1993
Solano, James	Assoc	Philadelphia	XFMP	MS	67	Temple	&1977
Solcher, Charles J.	SLect	Texas-Dallas	LX	JD	71	S Tx Law	&1995
Solcum, William N.	Deces		1962	PHD	61.	Ohio St	
Sole, Andreu	Prof	HEC Paris	MJSW	PHD	81	Nancy II	1979
Soled, Jay A.	Prof	Rutgers-Newk	X	LLM	89	NYU	1-95
Solheim, Perry	Asst	Montana St	F	PHD	07.	Utah	8-07
Solieri, Steven A.			AS	PHD	00.	SUNY-Bin	&
Soliman, Mahmond E.		Alexandria U	1992	PHD	89.	Georgia	
Alexandria Univ; Fac of Comm; Acct Dept; Alexandria Egypt							
Soliman, Mark T.	Assoc	U Washington	FB	PHD	03.	Michigan	&6-07
Soliman, Soliman Y.	Assoc	Tulane	CMFS	PHD	79.	Georgia	* &1979
Soll, Roy	Retir	Fla Atlantic	1995		41	NYU	&1977
Sollenberger, Harold M.	Prof	Michigan St	MI	DBA	67.	Indiana	&1967
Solomon, Howard B.	Prof	CUNY-Brookly	LX	LLM	67	NYU	9-74
Solomon, Ira	H-Pr	Illinois	AB	PHD	79.	Tx-Austin	&8-83
RC Evans Endowed Chair in Business							
Solomon, Jill	Lect	Cardiff U	FIJW	PHD	96	Manchest	2000
Solomon, Lanny M.	Prof	Mo-Kansas Ct	CM	PHD	74.	Case Wes	* 8-98
Solomon, Paul E.	Assoc	W New Eng	FTME	PHD	81.	Minnesota	2006
Solomon, Sandra K.			FMB	PHD	06.	Ariz St	&
Solomons, David	Deces	Pennsylvania	2-95	DSC	66	London	1959
Sommerfeld, Ray M.	Deces	Texas-Austin	8-95	PHD	63	Iowa	&1963
Sommers, Gregory A.	Asst	So Methodist		PHD	02.	Ohio St	8-02
Sommerville, Patricia M.				PHD	91.	St Louis	
Sompayrac, Joanie	Assoc	Tenn-Chattan	FLPX	JD	91	Cincinnati	&8-98
UC Foundation Associate Professor of Accounting							
Son, Myungsoo	Assoc	CS-Fullerton	FM	PHD	05.	Nebraska	2007
Soncharoen, Sonthilaksn	Lect	Chulalongkor	FMP	MBA	81	Wisconsin	1970
Song, Chang Joon	Asst	Virg Tech	F	PHD	04.	Mich St	1-07
Song, In-Man		Sung Kyun K	1996	PHD	86.	Wisconsin	
Sung Kyun Kwan University							
Song, Ja	Retir	Yonsei Univ	1997	DBA	67.	Wash U	1976
Song, Xiaofei	Prof	St Marys-Cdn	F	PHD	99	Baruch	1998
Sonnier, Blaise M.	VAsst	La-Lafayette	F	PHD	07	Grenoble	2007
Soo, Billy S.	C-Ac	Boston Coll	AFK	PHD	91.	Nrthwstrn	1990
Soo, Lisa Gilbert			FI	DBA	88.	Boston U	&
Soobaroyen, Teeroven	Lect	Univ Wales	FM	MB	96	Lancaster	2004
Soonawalla, Kazbi	Lect	London Econ	FIQ	PHD	02.	Stanford	2002
Soongswang, Oranuj	H-As	Chulalongkor	DS	DBA		Miss St	1975
Sopariwala, Parvez R.	Prof	Grand Valley	M	PHD	85.	Mich St	&8-92
Sorathia, Vali M.	Assoc	Briar Cliff	CGVX	ABD	72	Indiana	1974
Sorcinelli, Gino	Lect	Massachusett	S	MS	75	Mass	1994
Sorensen, James E.	Prof	Denver	MCG	PHD	65.	Ohio St	&1965
Sorensen, Susan M.	Asst	Houston-Cl L	FXI	PHD	03	Minnesota	& 1-03
Sorenson, Chester A.	Deces			DBA	65.	U Wash	
Soriano, Beverly A.	Asst	Framingham	CFM	MS	80	Bentley	&1984
Sorkin, Horton L.	Retir	Howard	2001	PHD	77.	Minnesota	# 1986
Soroosh, Jalal	Prof	Loyola-Maryl	FM	PHD	81.	Miss	* 1983
KPMG LLP Faculty Fellow							
Sorter, George H.	Retir	New York U	2005	PHD	63.	Chicago	&9-74
Soubliere, Richard	Retir	Quebec a Hul	1999	MSC			
Sougiannis, Theodore	Prof	Illinois	F	PHD	90.	Berkeley	1990
KPMG Distinguished Professor							
Souissi, Mottsen	Asst	Fayetteville		PHD			
Soukhovtseva, Olga	Asst	Carleton Un	A	PHD	79	Moscow St	2004
Soutar, Louise	Lect	Napier Univ	A	BCOM			&1991
Souza, Carlos M.	Asst	INSEAD	F	PHD	89.	Cornell	
Sowell, Ellis Mast	Deces			PHD	44.	Tx-Austin	
Soybel, Virginia E.	Asst	Babson	FM	PHD	89.	Columbia	1995
Soyode, Afolabi		Olabisi Onab	2007	PHD	73.	Penn	
Olabisi Onabanyo University; Nigeria							
Spalding, Albert D. Jr.	Assoc	Wayne State	JLX	JD	79	Geo Wash	&1983
Spanswick, Ralph S.	Retir	CS-L Angeles	2000	EDD	67	N Illinois	9-88

Sparks, H. Charles			SADF	PHD	96.	Iowa	&
Sparks, Shelby	Lect	East Tenn St	P	MACC	98	E Tn St	&1998
Spasich, Connie	Lect	U Wollongong	FTW	MCOM	95	Wollong	&1992
Spear, Nasser A.	H-Pr	U Melbourne	FI	PHD	92.	North Tx	1996
G. L. Wood Professor of Accounting							
Spear, Robert K.			FNM	PHD	88.	Va Tech	
Specdtor, Stephen	Lect	Simon Fraser	FMA	ANA	82	Simon Fr	9-06
Spece, Paul S.	Deces	Cen Michigan	1999	PHD	69.	Mich St	1958
Specht, James	Assoc	Concordia C	AC	PHD	88.	Geo St	&2000
Specht, Linda B.	Assoc	Trinity	AFEJ	JD	85	St Marys	&8-88
Speciale, Raymond		Mt St MaryMD		MBA		Maryland	&1996
Spector, Charles A.	Prof	SUNY Oswego	FPTE	MS	74	Clarkson	&1974
Spede, Edward C.	Assoc	Virg Comm	F	PHD	82.	Va Tech	&1981
Speer, Charles C.	Retir	Appalach St	2002	MBA	68	E Tn St	&1970
Speer, Derek M.	Lect	U Auckland	MA	MCOM	81	Auckland	&1984
Speier, Cheri	Prof	Michigan St	S	PHD	96	Indiana	8-98
Spencer, Angela W.	Asst	Oklahoma St	F	PHD	06.	Arkansas	2006
Spencer, Charles H.	Retir	Hawaii		DBA	53.	Indiana	9-68
Spencer, Darin	Lect	Catawba	FPCE	MACC	99	NC-Charl	8-05
Spero, Abba V.	Assoc	Cleveland St	F	PHD	76.	NYU	&1973
Spero, Andrew E.			M	PHD	94.	Car Mellon	
Sperry, John B.	Retir	Virg Comm	1996	PHD	66.	American	&1971
Spiceland, J. David	Prof	Memphis	F	PHD	76.	Arkansas	&1981
Spiceland, Jesse W.	Retir	Memphis St	D-85	MS	48	Wash U	1949
Spicer, Barry H.	Dean	U Auckland	MA	PHD	76.	U Wash	1989
Spikes, Pamela A.	Prof	Cen Arkansas	X	PHD	93.	Miss	&8-80
Spilker, Brian C.	Prof	Brigham Yg	XB	PHD	93.	Tx-Austin	&6-93
Glen Ardis Research Fellow							
Spiller, Earl A. Jr.	Emer	So Carolina	1999	PHD	60.	Michigan	&9-89
Spindle, Roxanne M.	Assoc	Virg Comm	XJ	PHD	90.	Colorado	&1-90
Spires, Eric E.	Assoc	Ohio State	ABF	PHD	87.	Illinois	&1985
Spivck, Dara	Asst	Bellevue	XGN	MPA	95	N Orleans	&1990
Spizewski, A.	ALect	N Eng-Austr	D	BFIN		N Eng-Au	2001
Splettstoesser, Ingrid	Asst	York-Atkinsn	ADS	PHD	96	Waterloo	&1991
Spoule, Robert	Lect	Un Waterloo	M	MBA	78	Calgary	* 2003
Spraakman, Gary P.	Assoc	York-Atkinsn	AMN	PHD	96	Concordia	* 1991
Spradling, Dale W.		Business	2000	PHD	88.	Houston	&
www.drta.com; 4747 Research Forest Dr. 108-256; The Woodlands TX 77381							
Springer, Carol W.	Inst	Georgia St	FM	MS	82	Virginia	&6-98
Springer, Elizabeth H.	Inst	Alabama-Birm	F	MACC	82	Alabama	&2006
Springer, Kathleen A.	Assoc	Doane	TVX	ABD		Missouri	1998
Sprinkle, Geoffrey B.	Assoc	Indiana	M	PHD	96.	Iowa	&1999
Deere & Company Faculty Fellow							
Sprohge, Hans Dieter	Prof	Wright State	FM	PHD	74	SUNY-Buf	&9-88
Sprou, Spyros	Lect	Athens Univ	F	PHD	97	Brunel	2001
Sprouse, Robert T.	Retir	Stanford	1990	PHD	56.	Minnesota	
465 El Rancho Vista North; Chula Vista CA 91910							
Spruill, Wanda G.	Retir	SUNY-Geneseo	2004	MBA	81	Ms Women	&9-87
Spurrell, Lloyd	Assoc	N Brit Col	1996	PHD	88.	Nebraska	7-93
Univ Northern British Columbia, Prince George, BC Canada V2N 4Z9 250-960-6497							
Spurrier, Randall R.	SLect	Old Dominion	PFAS	MBA	68	Hawaii	&1999
Squires, Karen D.	Assoc	Tampa	FMCT	MBA	76	Alabama	&1978
Sribunnak, Visarut	Asst	Chulalongkor	F	PHD	04	Berkeley	1994
Sridhar, Sri S.	Prof	Northwestern	FM	PHD	90.	Pittsburgh	&1990
John L. and Helen Kellog Distinguished Professor of Accounting Info & Mgt							
Srinidhi, Bin N.	Prof	SUNY-Albany	FMA	PHD	84.	Columbia	2005
Srinivasan, Cadambi A. (Cas)	Retir	Drexel	1994	PHD	72	Illinois	1972
Srinivasan, Dhinu	Asst	Pittsburgh	M	PHD	97	Minnesota	1996
Srinivasan, Suraj	Asst	Chicago	FIKM	DBA	04.	Harvard	2004
Sriram, Ram S.	Prof	Georgia St	S	PHD	87.	North Tx	&9-95
Controllers Roundtable Professor of Information Systems							
Srisawadi, Pimpana			1998	DBA	96.	Boston U	
Royal Chulalongkoan University; Thailand							
Srivastava, Rajendra P.	Prof	Kansas	MA	PHD	82.	Oklahoma	1982
Ernst & Young Distinguished Prof & Dir. of Center Audit Res. & Adv Tech							
St. Clair, Kenneth	Retir	Cedarville	2001	MS	63	Illinois	&1959
St. John, William C.	SLect	Rensselaer	FSPC	PHD	89	Rensselaer	1-90
St. Pierre, E. Kent	Prof	Delaware	FTE	PHD	81.	Wash U	&7-93
Stabler, Henry Francis	Retir	Georgia St	1999	PHD	68.	Alabama	&9-71
Stagliano, A. J.	Prof	St Joseph	XN	PHD	77.	Illinois	1985
Stahl, Charles E. III	Prof	Madonna	XLF	LLM	91	Wayne St	&1991
Staikouras, Christos	Lect	Athens Univ	F	PHD	01	City-UK	2002
Staley, Andrew B.	Assoc	Bloomsburg	DFX	DBA	97	Nova SE	2003
Stallings, Billy G.			SM	DBA	70.	Miss St	&
Stallman, James C.	Retir	Missouri	2000	PHD	69.	Illinois	1968
Stallworth, H. Lynn	Assoc	Appalach St	F	PHD	98.	LSU	&2006
Stamatelatos, Anna	STut	U Melbourne	M	BBUS	95	Monash	2003

Stambaugh, Clyde T.	Prof	Murray State	AS	DBA	81.	Kentucky	&1986
Stamm, Janis	Prof	Edinboro	X	JD	71	Ohio No	1988
Stammerjohan, William W.	Assoc	Louisiana Te	MC	PHD	95.	Wash St	&2004
George E. Breazel Family Endowed Professor							
Stamp, Edward	Deces	Lancaster	1-86				
Stancil, John L.	Assoc	Fla Southern	ACPX	DBA	89.	Memphis	# * &1998
Stanford, Mary Harris	Prof	Tx Christian	F	PHD	94.	Michigan	&2002
Stanga, Keith G.	Prof	Tennessee	F	PHD	74.	LSU	& 7-77
Andersen Professor of Accounting							
Stanger, Anthony M. J.	LectB	Flinders Un	AFQ	MCOM	98	N Eng-Au	2-89
Stangl, Robert	Asst	Heritage	1995	PHD	93.	Kansas	
Stanhope, Donald F.	Retir	Il-Springfld	5-00	MA	60	N Dakota	&1972
Stanko, Brian B.	C-Pr	Loyola-Chicg	FTBR	PHD	92.	Kentucky	&9-91
Stanley, A. Denise	Assoc	Emory Henry	FALV	PHD		Regent	&8-92
Stanley, Charles W.	Assoc	Baylor	SA	PHD	84.	Okla St	& 1-83
Stanley, Curtis H.	Retir	CS-Sacrament	2002	PHD	63.	Michigan	&1983
Stanley, Jonathan D.	Asst	Clemson	AF	PHD	07	Alabama	&2007
Stanley, Trevor	Lect	Queensld Tec	FE	MSC	85	Griffith	& 1-79
Stanny, Elizabeth	C-Pr	Sonoma State	FM	PHD	96.	Chicago	&1998
Stanton, F. Victor	Retir	CS-East Bay	AF	MBA	73	Golden Gt	* & 4-81
Stanton, Patricia A.	H-SLe	U Newcastle	FET	PHD	95	Newcastle	1989
Stanton, Thomas C.	Retir	Fran Marion		DBA	74.	Geo Wash	
Stanwick, Sarah A.	Assoc	Auburn	CW	PHD	93.	Fla St	&9-92
Staples, Catherine L.	Asst	Randolph-Mac	1997	PHD	90.	N Carol	&1995
Randolph-Macon College; Ashland VA 23005-5005; 804-752-7204							
Stapleton, Richard C.		U Manchester	FQ	PHD	72	Sheffield	
Stapleton, Thomas M.	Retir	St Johns	1989	MBA	49	NYU	&1965
Stara, Nancy J.	Retir	Nebraska	XL	LLM	85	Denver	&1985
Starbuck, George	Inst	McMurry	PX	MBA		Tx Chr	&1995
Stark, Andrew W.	Prof	U Manchester	F	PHD	83	Manchest	1995
Stark, Leonard L.	Retir	Hofstra	1988	JD	52	Brooklyn	&1950
Stark, Maurice E.	Retir	Kansas State	1998	PHD	72.	Missouri	& 6-76
Starr, Douglas A.	Asst	Tx Southern	M	PHD	78.	Penn St	
Stasny, Mary	Lect	Texas A&M	FP	MBA	83	Tx A&M	9-99
Staubus, George J.	Emer	Cal-Berkeley	1993	PHD	54.	Chicago	&1952
Steadman, Mark E.	Assoc	East Tenn St	FEJW	PHD	90.	Tennessee	* &1989
Stec-Helstad, Nancy	Inst	Colorado	X	MS	96	Colorado	2002
Stedry, Andrew C.	Deces			PHD	59.	Car Mellon	
Steed, Steve A.	Retir	Tarleton St	DV	PHD	85.	North Tx	&1971
Steedle, Lamont F.	Prof	Towson	CFMT	PHD	78.	Penn St	* 1990
Steele, Allan T.	Deces			PHD	60.	Tx-Austin	
Steele, Anthony	Prof	Un Warwick	AQ	MA	79	Lancaster	
Steele, Dennis	Asst	So Adventist	PS	MBA	98	Kennesaw	1999
Stefanescu, Monica L.	Asst	Arizona	F	PHD	06.	Penn St	8-06
Stefano, Denise	Asst	Mercy-NY	CDNU	MBA	02	Iona	&9-06
Stein, Douglas M.			DS	PHD	92.	Wisconsin	* &
Stein, Michael T.	Assoc	Old Dominion	AF	PHD	88	Brit Colum	2006
Steinbart, Paul John	Prof	Arizona St	S	PHD	85.	Mich St	&8-97
Steinke, Greg L.	Asst	Laurentian		MBA	86	Laurentian	&8-82
Stellenwerf, Anita L.	Assoc	Ramapo	CDX	MBA	78	Rutgers	&1984
Stemkoski, Michael J.	Prof	Utah Valley	IMFC	MACC	72	Utah St	1992
Stemsrudhagen, Jan-Ivar	Assoc	Norwegian U	M	DOEC		Norwegia	
Stent, W. J.	Lect	Massey-Alban		BCOM		Rhodes	2005
Stephan, Jens A.	Assoc	Cincinnati	F	PHD	85.	Cornell	1989
Stephens, Lynn	Prof	East Wash	FTN	PHD	83.	Nebraska	&1981
Stephens, Matthew J. Jr.	Retir	Pennsylvania	1996	PHD	64	Penn	&1956
Stephens, Ray G.	D-Pr	Ohio Univ	KFAV	DBA	78.	Harvard	* &8-99
James E. Daley Professor of Accounting							
Stephens, William L.	Retir	South Fla	2006	DBA	71.	Fla St	&9-71
Stephenson, C. B.	Emer	Ohio Univ	1988	MBA	59	Geo Wash	&1964
Stephenson, Teresa M.	Asst	Wyoming	TM	PHD	05.	Kentucky	2005
Sterling, Genevieve	Inst	Intl College		MS			
Sterling, Robert R.			1997	PHD	65.	Florida	
5618 Chaucer; Houston TX 77005; 713-528-5743; Fax 528-2107							
Stern, Jerrold J.	Prof	Indiana	X	PHD	79.	Tx A&M	1979
Stern, Lorraine	Asst	CUNY-York					
Stern, Myles S.	Assoc	Wayne State	MS	PHD	74.	Mich St	* 1971
Sternbach, Joseph	Retir	CS-Long Bch	1982	PHD	37	NYU	&1976
Sternburg, Thomas J.	Lect	Illinois	X	PHD	93.	Ariz St	&5-93
Stetson, T. Beth	Asst	Okla City	X	PHD	06.	Oklahoma	8-05
Stettler, David M.		DeKalb IL	1989	PHD	84.	Arkansas	
Stettler, Howard F.	Retir	Kansas	1984	MS	42	Illinois	&1947
1330 Spencer Dr; Lawrence KSA 66044							
Steven, Graham L.	Lect	Napier Univ		BA			* 1992
Stevens, Douglas E.	Assoc	Florida St	FMB	PHD	96.	Indiana	8-05
Stevens, Flumo Y.	Retir	Lawrence Tec	1998	PHD	74	Nebraska	1987

Name	Rank	School		Degree	Yr	University	
Stevens, Kevin T.	D-Pr	DePaul	TVX	DBA	89.	Kentucky	&1989
Ledger & Quill Director							
Stevens, Mary	Lect	Txs-El Paso	FX	MACC	87	Tx-ElPaso	& 8-88
Stevens, Michael	Assoc	CUNY-Queens		LLM		NYU	& 9-82
Stevens, R. Jim	LT	Univ Windsor	FS	BCOM	75	Windsor	2003
Stevens, Robert G.			CFMP	PHD	58.	Illinois	&
Stevens, William P.			FVRE	PHD	80.	Illinois	&
Stevens, William Thomas	Retir	Western Conn	1998	PHD	70.	Florida	&1994
Stevenson, Bill	Retir	Wisconsin	1997	PHD	67.	Missouri	&1967
Stevenson, Frank L.			FMT	PHD	84.	Oregon	&
Stevenson, Joanna	Asst	Un Stirling	AI	MA	84	Edinburgh	&1995
Stevenson, John W.	Retir	Corpus Chris	1993	PHD	68.	Tx-Austin	& 9-76
Stevenson, Lorna A.	SLect	Dundee	EFJW	BA	89	Strathcl	&2000
Stevenson-Clarke, Peta	Lect	Griffith Un	FIQ	PHD	02	Griffith	1999
Stewart, Barbara R.	Prof	Towson	VFBE	PHD	69	Columbia	&1988
Stewart, Cheryl	Asst	Union-KY	F	MBA	89	Kentucky	* 2000
Stewart, Dave N.	Prof	Brigham Yg	X	PHD	80.	Florida	& 9-80
Rachel Martin Professor							
Stewart, John R.	Retir	No Colorado	2004	PHD	77	N Colo	& 9-75
Stewart, Louis J.	Assoc	Kean	ACN	PHD	98	Wisconsin	&2005
Stewart, Ross E.	C-Pr	Seattle Pac	THFM	PHD	87	Glasgow	1986
Stice, Earl K.	Prof	Brigham Yg	F	PHD	88.	Cornell	9-98
PricewaterhouseCoopers Professor							
Stice, James D.	Prof	Brigham Yg	F	PHD	89.	U Wash	9-88
Distinguished Professor							
Stickel, Scott E.	Prof	LaSalle	MF	PHD	85	Chicago	& 7-92
Joseph Markmann Accounting Alumni Professor							
Stickney, Clyde P.	Emer	Dartmouth	2004	DBA	70.	Fla St	&1977
Ormond Beach, FL; 386-677-9712							
Still, Kelley	Assoc	Drury	CT	PHD	97	Oklahoma	&1995
Stillabower, Linda M.	Assoc	Brock Univ	X	PHD	82.	Case Wes	& 7-93
Stimpert, Larry	C-Pr	Colorado Col	FM	PHD	92	Illinois	1996
Stine, Linda	Inst	Heidelberg		MBA		Heidelbg	2004
Stiner, Frederic M. Jr.	Prof	F Dick-Teane	FSV	PHD	76.	Nebraska	&
Stiner, M. Susan	Retir	Villanova	XJD	LLM	86	Temple	&1988
Stinnette, Undine M.	Asst	Roosevelt	FC	MSA	76	Roosevelt	&1978
Stinson, Christopher H.			X	PHD	93.	Stanford	
Stinson, James B.	VAsst	Houston	FMS	PHD	00	Houston	5-02
Stinson, Terrye A.	Assoc	Southern Ark	FPR	DBA	89.	La Tech	&1980
Stipe, Sharon	Asst	West Alabama	PLX	LLM		NYU	1965
Stirk, Christina	SLect	Un East Lond	X	BA			1990
Stittle, John	Asst	Univ Essex	AFW	MSC	88	London	2001
Stitts, Randal H.		Sul Ross	1992	PHD	91.	Tx Tech	&
PO Box 420788; Del Rio TX 78842							
Stivason, Charles T.	Asst	Marshall	SAMO	PHD	98.	Va Tech	&
Stivers, Bonnie P.	Prof	Morehouse	MCB	PHD	83.	Geo St	&
Stives, Douglas	Spec	Monmouth	X	MBA	69	Lehigh	&2006
Stober, Thomas L.	Assoc	Notre Dame	F	PHD	83.	Chicago	&1995
Stock, Toby	Assoc	Ohio Univ	XF	PHD	95.	Indiana	& 9-01
Robert H. Freeman Professor of Accounting							
Stock, William J.	Retir	Mankato St	1992	MBA	51	Denver	1963
Stockard, Jane B.	Retir	Georgia Col	2003	ABD		Kansas St	&1983
Stocken, Mary Eliz			F	PHD	00.	Penn St	
Stocken, Phillip C.	Assoc	Dartmouth	F	PHD	98.	Penn St	2003
Stocks, Kevin D.	D-Pr	Brigham Yg	MC	PHD	81.	Okla St	& 6-83
Steve Albrecht Professor							
Stocks, Morris H.	Prof	Mississippi	FCB	PHD	91.	S Carol	& 8-91
Stockstill, Lowell E.	Prof	Wittenberg	FL	JD	82	Toledo	9-81
Stoel, Michael				PHD	06.	Ohio St	
Stokes, Carolyn R.			MC	DBA	84.	Kentucky	*
Stokes, Donald J.	Prof	Tech-Sydney	FA	PHD	90	NS Wales	&1997
Stokes, Leonard E.	Prof	Siena	FMPV	PHD	97.	Union-NY	& 9-86
Stokes, Sally	Asst	Wilmington	EFPX	MS	97	WilminDE	&1995
Stolar, Robert W.	Retir	Wilfrid Laur	1996	PHD	78.	Florida	* &1973
Stolle, Carlton D.	Retir	Texas A&M	2007	PHD	73.	Tx A&M	& 9-65
Stoller, Stuart M.	Assoc	Augsburg Col		MS		Long Isl	
Stolowy, Herve	Prof	HEC Paris	FIVA	PHD	90	Paris I	&1994
Stolt, Susan M.		Phoenix AZ	1990	PHD	86.	Ariz St	
12233 S. Warpaint Court; Phoenix AZ 85044							
Stoltzfus, Ronald L.	Assoc	E Mennonite		PHD	01.	Va Comm	1984
Eastern Mennonite Univ; 540-432-4155; Stoltzfr@emu.edu							
Stone, Clifford E.	Retir	Evansville	1986	PHD	68	Iowa	&1958
Stone, Dan N.	Prof	Kentucky	BEMS	PHD	87.	Tx-Austin	&2000
Gatton Chair of Accounting							
Stone, Donald E.	Emer	Massachusett	1996	PHD	65.	Wisconsin	&1970
Stone, Joan	Inst	Central Okla	FM	MBA	86	Cen Okla	& 8-05
Stone, Kenneth E.	C-Pr$	Cen Missouri	PF	PHD	76.	Missouri	&1969

Stone, Mary F.			MC	PHD	93.	Va Tech	
Stone, Mary S.	D-Pr	Alabama	FT	PHD	81.	Illinois	&1981
Hugh F. Culverhouse Professor							
Stone, Ronald S.	Prof	CS-Northrdge	AFPS	PHD	83.	UCLA	&1986
Stone, Virgil F.			CVQ	PHD	68.	Arkansas	&
Stone, Williard E.	Deces	Florida		PHD	57	Penn	&1960
Stone1 Olivia J.	Inst	Geo Southern	P	MACC	02	Ga Srthrn	2002
Stoneback, Jane Y.	Prof	Central Conn	CMBI	PHD	92.	Kansas	1992
Stonelake, Bernadette	SLect	Bournemouth	AFM	MA			9-02
Stoner, Gregory N.	Asst	Univ Glasgow	MS	BSC	78	Lancaster	&1984
Stopforth, David P.	Prof	Un Stirling	X	PHD	89	Glasgow	* &1980
Storey, Reed K.	Deces	FASB-Stamfor	4-99	PHD	58.	Berkeley	&
Storrer, Philip P.	Retir	CS-East Bay	2005	MBA	75	Golden Gt	& 9-73
Stott, David	Assoc	Bowling Gr	AF	PHD	00.	Wash St	&1999
Stout, David E.	Prof	Youngstown	MCE	PHD	82.	Pittsburgh	9-03
Stout, Gary R.	Prof	CS-Northrdge	X	DBA	77.	S Calif	&1985
Stout, William D.	D-Ac	Louisville	FN	PHD	97.	S Fla	& 8-96
Stovall, Dennis	Inst	Grand Valley	FM	MBA	97	Gr Valley	8-05
Stovall, Scott	Assoc	Abilene Chr	AC	PHD	03.	North Tx	&1998
Stower, Alwyn E.	SLect	So Queensnd	CM	MACC	93	N Eng-Au	&1989
Strachan, Beverly	Prof	Troy-Montg		MBA	93	Aub-Mont	
Strachan, James L.	Inst	S Fl-St Pete	PNG	PHD	76	Tx-Austin	* 8-03
Strand, Rolf Gunnar	Lect	Norwegian Mg	FM	ABD	74	NHH Berg	1992
Stratopoulos, Theophanis	Asst	Un Waterloo	FS	PHD	94	NewHamp	2006
Stratton, William O.	Retir	Pepper-L Ang	MDFC	PHD	77	Claremont	* & 9-01
Strauser, Shirl D.	Retir	Arkansas St	1994	PHD	69.	Missouri	& 8-66
Strauss, Norman	SInst	CUNY-Baruch	A	MA	69	Baruch	9-01
Strawser, Jeffrey W.	Assoc	Sam Houston	MS	PHD	97.	Tx A&M	1998
Strawser, Jerry R.	Dean	Texas A&M	AF	PHD	85.	Tx A&M	& 7-01
Leland/Weinke Chair							
Strawser, Joyce A.	Assoc	Seton Hall	FM	PHD	89.	LSU	9-95
Strawser, Robert H.	Prof	Texas A&M	PTBA	DBA	69.	Maryland	& 7-73
Andersen Chair							
Strayer, Richard L.	Retir	CS-Northrdge	2000	DBA	70.	S Calif	* &1968
Strecker, Mary F.			GC	PHD	74.	Missouri	
Streer, Paul J.	Prof	Georgia	X	PHD	78.	Illinois	&1978
Street, Donna L.	Prof	Dayton	FIT	PHD	87.	Tennessee	2002
Mahrt Chair in Accounting							
Streetman, H. Vaden	Retir	S F Austin	1989	DBA	66.	S Calif	&1983
2225 Ridgecrest Circle; Waco TX 76710							
Strefeler, John M.	Prof	Mount Union	XVP	PHD	77.	Arizona	* &1997
Streuling, G. Fred	Retir	Brigham Yg	2003	PHD	71.	Iowa	& 9-76
Streuly, Carolyn A.			F	PHD	87.	Wisconsin	&
Strickland, Pamela	Asst	Methodist	FPM	MBA	02	Phoenix	&2002
Strickland, Sherre	Assoc	Mass-Lowell	AS	PHD	81.	Tx A&M	&1991
Strickland, Sue	Retir	Tx-Arlington	FM	MBA	67	Arkansas	&1972
Stringer, Carolyn	SLect	Univ Otago	BM	PHD	06	Otago	1998
Strittmatter, Robert G.	C-Ac	Iona	PC	MBA	71	NYU	& 9-71
Strobel, Caroline D.	Prof	So Carolina	XM	PHD	78.	Georgia	* &1981
Strong, Joel M.	Assoc	St Cloud St	FS	PHD	99.	Nebraska	&1999
Strong, Norman C.	Prof	U Manchester	FQTY	MA		Newcastle	1989
Stroope, John C.	Retir	Il-Springfld	D-04	PHD	88.	North Tx	&1993
Stroud, J. B. Jr.	Retir	Nicholls St	2005	DBA	85.	Miss St	& 8-86
Strupeck, C. David	Assoc	Indiana NW	FDM	PHD	81	S Illinois	& 8-93
Stryker, Judson P.	C-Pr	Stetson	XF	DBA	81.	Miss St	&1976
Eugene M. Lynn Professor							
Stuart, Gloria J.	Inst	Geo Southern	P	MACC	99	Ga Srthrn	2004
Stuart, Iris C.			AJ	PHD	93.	Iowa	&
Stuart, Nathan V.	Asst	South Fla	M	PHD	01.	Indiana	8-05
Stubben, Stephan	Asst	No Carolina	F	PHD	06.	Stanford	2006
Stuchell, Donald V.	Emer	Ohio Univ	1995	MAS	61	Illinois	&1969
Stuebs, Martin T. Jr.	Asst	Baylor	JM	PHD	05.	Arkansas	2005
Stuerke, Pamela S.	Asst	Mo-St Louis	F	PHD	98.	Indiana	&
Stumbaugh, Charles C.	Retir	Central Okla	2004	PHD	75	Oklahoma	9-66
Stunda, Ronald A.	D-Ac	Birminghm So	FXC	PHD	96.	Fla St	* &1995
Sturby, Chris	Lect	West Ontario	F	MBA			
Sturm, Karen K.	Prof	Loras	AS	MA	81	Iowa	&1982
Styles, Alan K.	Assoc	CS-S Marcos	FIH	PHD	98.	North Tx	1998
Styron, W. Joey	Assoc	Augusta St	FX	PHD	93.	Tx A&M	&1991
Su, Lixin (Nancy)	Asst	HongKon Tech		PHD	05	Tx-Dallas	2005
Su, Robert K.	C-Pr	Nat Chengchi	FTMI	PHD	87.	LSU	1992
Su, Wei		Industry		PHD	06.	UCLA	
Su, Xijia	Assoc	City Univ HK	AFIT	PHD	96	Concordia	9-96
Suadi, Arief				PHD	81.	Missouri	
Suberly, Lynn A.	Asst	So Alabama	CGM	PHD	02.	Fla St	* & 8-06
Subramaniam, Chandra	Assoc	Tx-Arlington	F	PHD	93.	Minnesota	* & 6-03
Subramaniam, Nava	Lect	Griffith-GC	M	PHD		Griffith	&1990

Name	Rank	School	Code	Degree	Yr	School		Year
Subramanyam, K. R.	Assoc	So Calif	CFQ	PHD	93.	Wisconsin		1993
Sudano, Holly A.	Lect	Florida St	M	MACC	98	Fla St		&8-01
Sudarwan, M.		Indonesia		PHD	95.	Case Wes		
State Accounting School; Indonesia								
Sudderth, Tara N.	Assoc	Birminghm So	FLX	PHD	99.	Miss	*	&1998
Donald C. Brakston Professor of Accounting								
Sudibyo, Bambang				DBA	85.	Kentucky		
Sudit, Ephraim F.	Prof	Rutgers-Newk	F	PHD	73	NYU		1976
Sugiyanto, Bambang		GadgahMada U		PHD	97.	Temple		
Suh, Chung Woo	Prof	Kookmin Univ	FNT	PHD	88.	Illinois		&1988
Suh, Yoon S.	Prof	Ajou Univ	MFT	PHD	85.	Tx-Austin		&1995
Suijs, Jeroen	Assoc	Tilburg Univ	FM	PHD	98	Tilburg		1998
Suk, Inho	Asst	York Univ	F	PHD	06.	Purdue		
Suleiman, Nader A.			CFGM	PHD	81.	S Carol		
Sullens, Robert T.	Retir	Kent State	1990	DBA	74.	Kent St		&8-88
3883 Princeton Blvd; South Euclid OH 44121								
Sullivan, Carol E.	Asst	Central Wash	AS	PHD	92.	Tx A&M	#	&2004
Sullivan, Gene	C-Ac	Liberty	FPJ	PHD	04	Regent		&1987
Sullivan, Julie H.	Prov	Cal-SanDiego	X	PHD	83.	Florida		&7-03
University of California, San Diego; LaJolla CA 92093; jcollins@ucsd.edu								
Sullivan, Kathryn.			FMC	PHD	95.	Geo Wash		&
Sullivan, Mark J.	Assoc	DePaul	XF	PHD	79.	Wisconsin		&1976
Sullivan, Mary	Asst	George Wash	M	PHD		Chicago		2004
Sullivan, Stephen	Lect	St Joseph	FM	MBA		Temple		&2002
Sullivan, William N.	Asst	Assumption	XPF	MBA	75	Babson		&9-80
Sumi, Barbara E.	Prof	Northwood	PFMS	MS	80	Cen Mich		1980
Summa, Don J.	Retir	Monmouth	1992	MBA	72	Columbia		&9-90
Summers, Barbara	Lect	Univ Leeds	MQ	PHD	02	Bradford		7-98
Summers, Edward L.	Retir	Texas-Austin	2005	PHD	65.	Tx-Austin		&1968
Summers, George F.	Asst	Salisbury		PHD	03.	Houston		
Summers, Scott L.	Assoc	Brigham Yg	S	PHD	95.	Tx A&M		6-99
Summers, Suzanne B.	Assoc	Furman	CMX	PHD	92.	Georgia		9-99
Sumners, Glenn E.	Prof	Louisiana St	O	DBA	81.	Tennessee		&1-80
U.J. LeGrange Endowed Prof; Director, Center for Internal Auditing								
Sumutka, Alan R.	Assoc	Rider	XA	MBA	77	Seton Hall		&1977
Sun, Amy Xue	Asst	Penn State	F	PHD	05.	Car Mellon		7-05
Sun, Huey-Lian	Prof	Morgan State	FM	PHD	91.	Houston	*	&1990
Sun, Jialin (Kevin)	Asst	Hawaii-Manoa	IF	PHD	05.	Colorado		8-05
Sun, Li	Asst	Ball State	FM	PHD	07.	Okla St		1-07
Sun, Lili	Asst	Rutgers-Newk	A	PHD	04.	Kansas		
Sundarrajan, Sankar	Prof	Tarleton St	FP	PHD	94	Alabama		1992
Sundby, Lawrence C.	Retir	St Cloud St	2000	PHD	75.	Nebraska		&1975
Sundem, Gary L.	Prof	U Washington	CM	PHD	71.	Stanford		1971
Julius A. Roller Professor								
Sunder, Jayanthi	Asst	Northwestern	F	PHD	02	NYU		2003
Sunder, Shyam	Prof	Yale	FTM	PHD	73.	Car Mellon		1999
James L. Frank Professor of Accounting, Economics and Finance								
Sunder, Shyam V.	Asst	Northwestern	F	PHD	02.	NYU		2002
Sunderman, Norman A.	Prof	Angelo State	FCP	DMA	69	Michigan		&1987
Sundgren, Stefan	Prof	Univ of Umea	AFIT	PHD	95	Swedish		7-04
Suneson, Scott	Asst	Lk Superior	ACSX	MBA	93	Lake Sup		9-96
Sung, Heekyung Michael			CPF	PHD	93.	Oklahoma		
Sung, Kyu-Young			MCY	PHD	88.	U Wash		&
Sung, Steven			F	PHD	95.	Car Mellon		
Supattarakul, Somchai	Asst	Thammasat U		PHD	03	Tx-Austin		5-03
Superina, Susan C.	LectB	Flinders Un	FDS	MBA	95	Adelaide		2-88
Supviyadi,	Asst	Gudhahmada		PHD	98.	Kentucky		
Suraweera, Theek	Lect	Canterbury	SDM	MBA	91	Sri Jayewa		2002
Surdick, John J.	Prof	Xavier	VFMN	PHD	88.	Wisconsin		&1986
Surysekar, Krishnamurthy	Assoc	Fla Internat	FM	PHD	94.	Maryland		2001
Susanto, Djoko		Gadjah Mada	1992	PHD	92.	Arkansas		
Sutley, Kenneth R.			F	PHD	94.	Chicago		
Sutter, Mark D.			FMN	PHD	90.	Missouri		&
Suttle, Clyde T.	Retir	CS-Long Bch	9-81	DBA	68.	S Calif	*	1961
Sutton, Bernice R.	Asst	Fla Southern	ABDP	MBA	88	Fla So		2001
Sutton, Steve G.	Prof	Cen Florida	SAW	PHD	87.	Missouri		&8-05
KPMG Professor								
Sutton, Timothy G.	VProf	Univ Navarra	F	PHD	80.	U Wash		
Suver, James D.	Deces	Kentucky	1995	DBA	71.	Harvard	*	1990
Suzuki, Tomo	Lect	Oxford Univ	FIS	PHD	01	Oxford		2002
Svanstrom, Tobias	Asst	Univ of Umea	AMU	MSC	00	Umea		1-02
Svihla, William H.	Asst	Indiana St	APR	PHD	02.	Miss St		&8-96
Sviokla, John J.			SMW	PHD	86.	Harvard		
Swad, Randy G.	Retir	CS-Fullerton	2005	PHD	79.	LSU		&1977
Swage, S. H.	Retir	Cy London Pl	1992	BA				&
Swain, Monte R.	Prof	Brigham Yg	MSB	PHD	92.	Mich St	*	&9-91
Deloitte & Touche Research Fellow								

Swang, Axel W.	Retir	David Lipsco	1993	PHD	56.	Alabama	&9-47
Swanger, Susan L.	Assoc	W Carolina	ABJK	PHD	98.	S Carol	&1997
Swanson, Edward P.	Prof	Texas A&M	FTYI	PHD	77.	Wisconsin	&5-82
Nelson Durst Chair							
Swanson, G. A.	Prof	Tenn Tech	FMT	PHD	82.	Geo St	&1982
Swanson, James J.	Assoc	Worcester St	PAMX	MST		Bryant	1984
Swanson, Nancy J.	Asst	Valdosta St	F	ABD		Miss St	&8-07
Swanson, Robert D.	Retir	Iowa State	2002	PHD	78.	Iowa	* &1982
Swanson, Zane L.	Assoc	Emporia St	FTV	PHD	91.	Oklahoma	&1997
Swanz, Donald J.	Retir	St Bonaventu	2003	JD	58	Geotown	1981
Swartzlander, Jason	Asst	Bluffton		MBA	05	Tiffin	
Swary, Itzhak	Prof	Tel Aviv Un	F	PHD	79	Rochester	&1989
Swayze, James P.	Assoc	Nev-L Vegas	XF	PHD	92.	Houston	1991
Swearingen, James G.	Prof	Weber State	AF	PHD	82.	U Wash	&1985
Swearingen, Sandy	Asst	Weber State	FT	MPAC	86	Weber St	&1988
Sweeney, Daniel L.				PHD	58.	Michigan	
Sweeney, Henry W.				PHD	32.	Pittsburgh	
Sweeney, John T.	C-Pr	Wash State	FBJ	PHD	92.	Missouri	&1998
Sweeney, Michael P.	Assoc	Hillsdale	FXM	PHD	95.	Kentucky	&1996
Evert McCabe/UPS Professor							
Sweeney, Peter J.	Retir	LaSalle	1993	MBA	49	Penn	9-49
Sweeney, Robert B.	Deces	Memphis	5-95	PHD	60.	Tx-Austin	&1983
Sweet, Franklyn H.	Retir	So Alabama	1983	PHD	62.	Tx-Austin	&1966
500 Ridgelawn Dr West; Mobile AL 36608							
Sweet, Richard F.	Retir	So Alabama	5-04	DBA	94.	Miss St	&9-84
Sweeting, J.	SLect	Queensld Tec	F	MEC	84	N Eng-Au	&9-87
Swenson, Charles W.	Prof	So Calif	X	PHD	84.	S Calif	&1987
Elaine & Kenneth Leventhal Research Fellow							
Swenson, Dan W.	Assoc	Ariz St West	MC	PHD	93.	Miss	* &8-00
Swick, Ralph D.	Retir	So Illinois	1978	DBA	54.	Indiana	&1955
Swieringa, Robert J.	Dean	Cornell	FB	PHD	69.	Illinois	7-97
The Anne and Elmer Lindseth Dean							
Swift, Christopher	Asst	Nebraska Wes	ACP	MPA		Nebraska	&2001
Swift, Kenton D.			XF	PHD	91.	Wisconsin	&
Swindle, C. Bruce	Prof	McNeese St	F	PHD	79.	LSU	&1980
Swingen, Judyth A.	Prof	Ark-Ltl Rock	MX	PHD	84.	Wisconsin	&6-01
Swinney, Laurie S.	Prof	Neb-Kearney	PGNJ	PHD	93.	Nebraska	&8-91
Swirsky, Steve	Asst	Florida A&M	MCS	PHD	04.	Fla St	2002
Switzer, Ralph V.	Retir	Colorado St	1998	JD	72	Illinois	&1973
Swyers, William E.	Retir	So Miss	1990	PHD	62.	LSU	&1985
Syck, Lawrence J.	Retir	Minn-Duluth	2001	PHD	76.	Arizona	* &1973
Sykes, Ethel	Retir	San Diego	1989	MS	66	SanDiego	1968
Sykes, Viceola D.	C-Ac$	So Carol St	FX	PHD	89.	Florida	&1997
Sylvestre, A. Jeannette	Prof	So Alabama	FV	PHD	79.	Georgia	1-77
Sylvestre, Glenys	Inst	Univ Regina		BADM	94	Saskatch	2000
Sylvestre, Marilyn S.	Assoc	Rhode Isl Cl	IXF	MS	75	Rhode Isl	* &9-76
Symes, Christopher	LectC	Flinders Un	IJL	LLM	96	Adelaide	1-93
Symon, Iain W.	Retir	Dundee	AFQX	MA	59	St Andrew	&1965
Syversen, Jan	Pfll	Norwegian U	X				
Szendi, Joseph Z.	Asst	Fla Tech	GFVX	PHD	88.	La Tech	8-06
Szimayer, Alex	Lect	W Australia	Q	PHD	99	Bonn	2003
Sztajer, Jean C.	Retir	Augustana IL	XAS	MBA	84	Iowa	&9-81
Szwejkowski, Rafal			FT	PHD	01.	Arizona	
Tabak, Karen G.	Assoc	Maryville	CMS	PHD	97.	St Louis	&1996
Tabor, John G.	Retir	Loyola-Chicg	2003	PHD	78.	Nrthwstrn	&9-74
Tabor, Richard H.	Prof	Auburn	CA	PHD	80.	Florida	&9-85
Charles M. Taylor, Jr. Professor of Accounting							
Tabor, Robert C.	Retir	Emporia St	1996	MBA	60	LSU	&9-66
Tacchino, Kenn B.	Prof	Widener	XL	LLM	94	Widener	1990
Tachamontrikul, Suphamit	Lect	Chulalongkor	AIO	DBA	97	Chulalong	&1988
Tackett, James A.	Prof	Youngstown	F	PHD	83.	Ohio St	&9-84
Taft, Harry J.	Asst	Stetson	FX	MBA	72	Stetson	&1975
Tagerstein, D.	Inst	Touro	AV	JD		Brkyn-Law	&9-01
Taggart, Herbert F.	Deces	Michigan	3-83	PHD	28	Michigan	1920
Tagliaferri, Lee	Asst	Pace	M	MBA	58	Chicago	1975
Tagoe, Noel	Lect	Un Cl Dublin	M	PHD		Dundee	2001
Taher, Abdul-Hady H.		Gov Gen-Saud		PHD	64.	Berkeley	
Tahir, Mohammad I.	SLect	Griffith Un	FQT	PHD	01	N Eng-Au	&1999
Tahoun, Mohamed	Assoc	King Saud U	F	PHD	92	Alexandria	1997
Tai, Benjamin Y.	Prof	CS-Fresno	AF	PHD	81.	Missouri	* &8-85
Takeda-Brown, Carolyn				PHD	94.	Florida	
Talarczyk, Alan B.	Prof	Edgewood	X	JD	78	Wisconsin	&1979
Talbert, William L.		Corpus Ch-TX	1990	PHD	73.	Tx-Austin	&
701 Louisiana Ave; Corpus Christi TX 78404							
Talbott, John C.	Prof	Wright State	MX	DBA	74.	Kentucky	* 9-75
Talib, Ameen A.	Asst	Natl Singapo	FM	MSC	85	London	&1981
Talib, Moechtar				PHD	75.	Illinois	

Name	Rank	School		Degree		Institution		Year
Talib, Sayjda	Lect	U Lancaster	F	PHD	06	Lancaster		2006
Tallapally, Pavani	Assoc	Slippery Roc		ABD		La Tech		2007
Talmor, Eli	Prof	London Bus	F	PHD	81	N Carol		2000
Talukdar, Mohammed Yusuf	Assoc	Georgia SW	AIFS	PHD	79	City-UK		&7-02
Tam, Kinsum	Asst	SUNY-Albany	FS	PHD	99.	Conn		1999
Tamayo, Ane	Asst	London Bus	F	PHD	01	Rochester		2001
Tan, Andrew	Lect	U Wollongong						2007
Tan, Christine E. L.	Asst	CUNY-Baruch	FA	PHD	00	Melbourne		1999
Tan, Hun-Tong	Prof	Nanyang Tech	ABF	PHD	92	Michigan		&1987
Tan, Kai Guan Clement	Assoc	Nanyang Tech	DS	MSC	90	London		&1989
Tan, Kim B.	Asst	CS-Stanislau	MF	PHD	98	Temple		&1998
Tan, Lin Mei	Sen	Massey Univ	CEFX	MA		Lancaster		&1987
Tan, Mui Siang Patricia	H-Ac	Nanyang Tech	FQ	PHD	94	Brit Colum		&1987
Tan, Rebecca	Asst	Australian N	FTW	PHD	03	Murdoch		2003
Tan, Seet Koh	Asst	Nanyang Tech	ABDO	MSC	99	NUS		&1999
Tandy, Paulette R.	C-Ac	Nev-L Vegas	AOF	PHD	87.	Tx A&M		&8-89
Tanewski, George	SLect	Monash Univ	QBMW	PHD	95			1995
Tang, Charles Y.	Assoc	Pace	FMA	PHD	94	Baruch		1997
Tang, Donald L.	Retir	Portland St	1992	MA	61	N Dakota		&1966
Tang, Nancy O.	Retir	Portland St	1993	MBA	73	Port St		&1978
Tang, Qingliang	SLect	W Sydney-Nep	AFI	PHD	93	Glasgow		&1999
Tang, Roger Y. W.	Prof	W Michigan	MI	PHD	77.	Nebraska	# *	1988
Upjohn Chair of Business Administration								
Tang, Vicki	Asst	Georgetown	F	PHD	05.	Michigan		2005
Tangenes, Tor	SLect	Norwegian Mg	CM	ABD		NHH Berg		1999
Tanju, Deborah W.	Prof	Alabama-Birm	FO	PHD	81.	Georgia	# *	1982
Tanju, Murat N.	Prof	Alabama-Birm	FM	PHD	77.	Georgia	*	&1977
Tanlamai, Uthai	Prof	Chulalongkor	DS	PHD	83	Illinois		1995
Tanna, Wayne M.	Prof	Chaminade	LPNX	LLM	90	McGeorge		1-93
Tanner, Diane L.	Inst	North Fla	FP	MACC	80	N Fla		&1984
Tanner, Margaret M.	Assoc	Ark-Ft Smith	F	PHD	92.	North Tx		&
Tannery, Fladger F.	Retir	Frito Lay		PHD	41.	Tx-Austin		
Tansey, James N.	Prof	Christian Br	AC	MBA	69	Memphis		&1977
Tant, Kevin	SLect	Monash Univ	FIJ	MBA	96	S Cross		&1990
Tapp, Marvin L.	Asst	Taylor	PFJ	MBA	88	St Fran		&2001
Tarabzune, Muhiadin R.		King Abdulaz	1992	PHD	75.	Arkansas		
PO Box 3177; Jeddah Saudi Arabia								
Tarallo, Anthony E.	Deces	Ramapo		MBA	63	NYU		&1972
Tarantino, Kimberly A.	Lect	CS-Fullerton	AF	MS	83	Ca-SnDgo		&1993
Taranto, Karen A.	Asst	Georgetown	FM	ABD		Geo Wash		2004
Tarasovich, Barbara	Asst	Sacred Heart	FMUS	MBA	82	Sacred H		&2006
Tarca, Ann	Lect	W Australia	FI	MACC	97	W Austrl		1998
Tarpley, Robin L.	Assoc	George Wash	F	PHD	00.	Cornell		2000
Tasker, Sarah			F	PHD	97.	MIT		&
Tassin, Maurice F.	Retir	Louisiana Te	2003	PHD	75.	LSU		&1975
Tate, Stefanie	Asst	New Hampshir	AF	PHD	01.	Mich St		2001
Tatikonda, Lakshmi U.	Prof	Wis-Oshkosh	CMOQ	PHD	66	Tx-Austin	# *	&1978
Tatman, William	Lect	Wis-Whitewat	AF	MS	05	Wi-Milwa		&2005
Tatum, Cheryl L.	Inst	Geo Southern	P	MACC	06	Ga Srthrn		2007
Tatum, Kay W.	C-Ac$	U Miami	A	PHD	86.	Tx Tech		&1986
Tauber, Linda	Lect	CUNY-Lehman		MBA				&1990
Tauer, Ritamarie C.	Dean$	Houston Bapt	FCMP	MACC	85	Hou Bapt		&1986
Tauringana, Vern	SLect	Bournemouth	FA	PHD				9-02
Taussig, Russell A.	Retir	Hawaii	1978	PHD	62.	Berkeley		&9-64
2801 Coconut Avenue Apt 6-B; Honolulu HI 96815								
Tawadros, Milad A.	Retir	Ind-So Bend	1996	PHD		Iowa		&1967
Tawfik, Mohamed Sherif			1992	PHD	82.	Penn St		
17 Anas Ibn Malik St Apt 8; Mohandssen; Cairo Egypt								
Tayles, M. E.	Prof	Univ Hull	M	PHD	00	Bradford	*	O-03
Taylor, Audrey G.	Asst	Western Wash	MC	PHD	02	Wayne St		&2002
Taylor, Barbara G.			AF	PHD	83.	Tx Tech		&
Taylor, Charles Wallace	Retir	Mississippi	6-01	PHD	70.	Tx-Austin		&1965
Taylor, Cynthia	Assoc	Ark-Ltl Rock	IG	PHD	98.	Okla St		8-99
Taylor, Dale H.	Retir	Brigham Yg	1991	PHD	63.	Nrthwstrn		&9-73
Taylor, Dennis W.	Prof	Adelaide	FGIM	PHD		HongKong		&2003
Taylor, Donald H.	Retir	Arkansas	1998	PHD	67.	LSU		&1969
Taylor, Ed	Lect	Boston Coll	FMX	MST	93	Bentley		1986
Taylor, Eileen	Asst	N Carol St	ABS	PHD	06.	S Fla		2006
Taylor, Gary K.	Assoc	Alabama	FT	PHD	96.	Ohio St		&1996
PricewaterhouseCoopers Fellow								
Taylor, Henry	Inst	Sonoma State	CF	MBA	79	Santa Cl		&1982
Taylor, James D.	SLect	Claremont	XLPR	JD	74	Wayne St		&1989
Taylor, Lary	Assoc	Pacific Unio	FMP	MBA	76	Maryland		1978
Taylor, Mark H.	Assoc	Creighton	ABMS	PHD	94.	Arizona		&9-02
Begley Endowed Chair in Accounting								
Taylor, Martin E.	Prof	Tx-Arlington	AF	PHD	74.	Tx-Austin		&6-88
Taylor, Nicholas	ResFl	Cardiff U	MQ	PHD		London		2000

Taylor, Paul A.	Lect	U Lancaster	FVQ	MA	77	Lancaster	&1978
Taylor, Robert D.	Retir	Fla Atlantic	6-03	PHD	74.	Colorado	& 5-83
Taylor, Robert George		Assoc Atg-DC	1992	PHD	63.	Chicago	
1612 K Street NW Suite 900; Washington DC 20006							
Taylor, Ronald L.	Deces		X	DBA	78.	Tennessee	
Taylor, Sarah J.	Lect	U Melbourne	F	BCOM	99	Sydney	2003
Taylor, Sharon	SLect	W Sydney	F	MCOM	82	NS Wales	
Taylor, Stephen L.	Prof	New So Wales	FA	PHD	91	NS Wales	&
Taylor, Stuart D.	Lect	New So Wales	F	MCOM		Melbourne	
Taylor, Sue	Lect	Queensld Tec	F	MBUS	93	Queensld	& 1-87
Taylor, Suetlana	Lect	Cardiff U	MQ	PHD	06	Cardiff	2006
Taylor, Sydney S.	Retir	Temple	1995	MBA	60	Temple	&1963
Taylor, Thomas C.	Retir	Wake Forest	2004	PHD	70.	LSU	& 9-71
Taylor, Ulysses	C-Pr	Fayetteville	XL	JD	92	N Car Cen	1992
Taylor, William J.	Retir	Wis-Milwauke	FA	PHD	74.	Geo St	&1973
Teal, Mary	Asst	Central Okla	XZF	JD	05	Okla Cty	8-05
Teall, Howard D.			MU	PHD	87	W Ontario	&
Tearney, Michael G.	Emer	Kentucky	2005	PHD	71.	Missouri	&1983
Techavichit, Joseph V.				PHD	79.	Missouri	&1980
Tecklenburg, Donald	Asst	Ohio Wesley	VFMA	MBA	78	Virginia	2007
Tee, Kai-Hong	Lect	Aberdeen	FQ	MBA	06	Heriot W	2004
Teed, Dan	Asst	Troy-Dothan		MPA	73	Tx-Austin	&2006
Teeter, Steven C.	Prof	Utah Valley	FMSC	MBA	87	Phoenix	1987
Teets, Walter R.	Assoc	Gonzaga	F	PHD	89.	Chicago	&1994
Tegarden, David P.	Assoc	Virg Tech	S	PHD	91	Colorado	8-94
Teh, Seng Thiam	Asst	Australian N	AEFT	BCOM	91	W Austrl	2003
Teichman, Ronald J.	Retir	S Fl-St Pete	2004	PHD	77.	Nrthwstrn	8-98
Teitel, Karen	Asst	Holy Cross	FM	PHD	02.	Mass	& 8-04
Tejura, C.	SLect	London Metro	M	MSC			2001
Telford, C.	Assoc	Univ Ulster	F	MSC			N-04
Tellefsen, Jan Terje	Deces	Norwegian Mg	1999	MA		NHH Berg	
Teloian, George	Retir	New Hamp Col	1999	MBA	70	Northeas	& 9-62
Temme, Kim	Assoc	Maryville	AX	MBA	92	Notre Dm	&1993
Tennyson, B. Mack			FGN	PHD	82.	S Carol	* &
Teo, Pin Pin Susan			FT	PHD	89.	Wisconsin	
Teoh, Siew Hong	Prof	Calif-Irvine	F	PHD	88.	Chicago	7-06
Tepalagul, Nopmanee	Lect	Chulalongkor	F	MBA	03	Imperial	&2005
Tepper, Robert	Lect	New Mexico	FL	JD	83	New Mex	2004
Terando, William D.	Asst	Iowa State	XF	PHD	93.	Illinois	& 8-01
Terlouw, Charles D.	Assoc	Drake	PA	BS	71	Drake	&2004
Terre, Norbert C.	Deces			DBA	67.	Wash U	
Terrell, Junius H.	Retir	Catawba	1994	PHD	66.	Tx-Austin	& 8-90
Terrell, Katherene P.	C-Pr	Central Okla	F	EDD	94	Okla St	& 8-90
Terrell, Marian	Retir	Ft Valley St	EP	PHD	79	Geo St	9-77
Terrell, Robert L.	Prof	Central Okla	VAF	EDD	92	Okla St	# & 1-86
Terrill, William A.	Deces	No Carolina	6-74	PHD	52.	Illinois	1951
Teruya, Jenny N.	D-Ac	Hawaii-Manoa	CFM	PHD	98.	Arizona	& 8-97
Tervo, Wayne	Asst	Murray State	CM	PHD	06	Tx-SanAnt	&2006
Terzian, Susan E.	Lect	Wright State	F	MBA	79	Cincinnati	* & 9-98
Tessoni, Daniel D.	Asst	Rochest Tech	FT	PHD	86.	Syracuse	& 9-77
Testa, Gary J.	Assoc	CUNY-Brookly	TXP	MBA	78	St Johns	& 9-79
Teti, Robert	Lect	St Joseph	XFM	MBA	72	Drexel	&2001
Tew, Glade K.	C-Ac	Brighm Yg-HI	IMF	PHD	97.	Okla St	& 8-96
Thacker, Ronald J.	Deces	New Orleans	5-02	PHD	61.	LSU	&1962
Thames, Earl Glenn			1992	PHD	64.	Miss	
711 Hancock; Natchitoches LA 71457							
Thanh, Chu	Lect	Natl Econ	AOFM	MS	94	Illinois	1988
Tharrington, Angel	Asst	Greensboro	PFAX	MS		NC-Green	&1999
Thatcher, Jan C.	C-Ac	Lakehead U	FVA	MSC	88	Saskatch	&1983
Thatcher, Joseph W.	Assoc	Shepherd	FGP	MBA	80	SF Austin	&1983
Theisen, Barbara A.	Retir	Oakland	2002	MTX	85	Walsh	&1984
Theivananthampillai, Paul	Lect	Univ Otago	FMVQ	PHD	96	Otago	1989
Theuri, Peter M.	Assoc	No Kentucky	F	DBA	99.	Miss St	& 8-99
Thevaranjan, Alex	Assoc	Syracuse	M	PHD	93.	Minnesota	1993
Thiagarajah, Tirukumar	ALect	Tech-Sydney		BBUS	02	Tech-Sydn	2003
Thiagarajan, S. Ramu			FM	PHD	89.	Florida	&
Thibadoux, Gregory M.	Prof	Tenn-Chattan	MC	PHD	84.	Houston	9-86
Thibodeau, Jay C.	Assoc	Bentley	A	PHD	97.	Conn	&1996
Thibodeau, Nicole.	Asst	Naval Postgr	MFGN	PHD	03	Pittsburgh	2005
Thibodeaux, Francis A.	Retir	Nicholls St	5-96	MBA	59	LSU	& 9-61
Thies, James B.			FS	PHD	72.	Nrthwstrn	
Thiru, Yaso	C-Ac	Alaska Pacif	MIEF	EDD	02	Fielding	* 1989
Thoede, Steven W.	Lect	Tx St-S Marc	P	MBA	81	SW Tx St	* &1993
Thoman, Lynda	Asst	Purdue	M	PHD	84	Stanford	1986
Thomas, Arthur L.		Lawrence KS		PHD	63.	Michigan	&
Thomas, Bob D.	Asst	West Tx A&M	AGS	PHD	07	Tx Tech	2007

Name	Rank	School	Codes	Degree	Yr	University	Misc
Thomas, C. William	Prof	Baylor	A	PHD	78.	Tx-Austin	&6-71
J.E. Bush Professor of Accounting; KPMG-Thomas L. Holton Chair of Accounting							
Thomas, Charles	Lect	Illinois St	M	MS	97	Illin St	&1998
Thomas, Charles		Industry		PHD	96.	Tx-Arlin	
Thomas, David A.	Deces	Cornell	6-04	PHD	56.	Michigan	&1956
Thomas, Deborah W.	Assoc	Arkansas	X	JD	78	Vanderbilt	&1983
Nolan E. Williams Lecturer							
Thomas, Frank	Assoc	R Stockton	FXS	MBA	79	St Johns	&1979
Thomas, Gwen	Tutor	Cardiff U	FX	MA	80	Oxford	&2000
Thomas, Hardy M.	Asst	Univ Essex	DFMQ	PHD	94	Ulster	1991
Thomas, Jacob K.	Prof	Yale	FC	PHD	84.	Michigan	* 7-03
Ernst & Young Professor of Accounting & Finance							
Thomas, James	Lect	Indiana NW	BUXE	MBA	77	N Illinois	8-00
Thomas, Johnny	Dean	LaSierra	QFI	PHD	02	Claremont	1994
Thomas, Lynn R.	Assoc	Kansas State	F	PHD	80.	Kansas	&1-86
Thomas, Michael F.	Assoc	CS-Humboldt	M	PHD	85.	Wisconsin	* 2005
Thomas, Paula B.	C-Pr	Mid Tenn St	FT	DBA	87.	Miss St	* &1989
Advisory Board Distinguished Professor of Accounting							
Thomas, Phyllis L.			CMD	PHD	83.	Tx A&M	* &
Thomas, Robin	Lect	N Carol St	FM	MS	89	N Carol	1991
Thomas, Stuart	Assoc	U Lethbridge	BM	PHD	98	Fla Intl	7-98
Thomas, Wayne B.	Assoc	Oklahoma	FI	PHD	95.	Okla St	&2000
John T. Steed Chair							
Thomas, William E.	Retir	Illinois	1981	PHD	42.	Illinois	1945
Thomas, William F.			ACFS	PHD	85.	N Carol	
Thompson, Billy D.			F	PHD	74.	Arkansas	
Thompson, Carolyn L.	Retir	Ferris State	CMP	PHD	80	Arkansas	1972
Thompson, Charles F.	Assoc	Mass-Lowell	NFGS	MBA	69	Northeas	&1969
Thompson, Dan	Asst	Thompson Riv	PFMV	MBA		Queens	* 1988
Thompson, David W.	Retir	Virginia	1985	MS	40	Indiana	&8-76
1020 Park Avenue; New York NY 10028							
Thompson, Ferron	Inst	Rhodes	F	MBA	75	Memphis	&2001
Thompson, Forrest	C-Ac	Florida A&M	FAGV	PHD	78.	Tx A&M	# * &1989
Thompson, George C.	Retir	Columbia	1994	JD	49	Columbia	1949
Thompson, James H.	Prof	Okla City	FVT	PHD	82.	Oklahoma	&8-91
Thompson, James T.	Retir	Memphis St	1991	MBA	49	Indiana	&1955
545 Primrose Cove; Memphis TN 38117							
Thompson, James W.	Prof	St John's	TNF	EDD	81	Columbia	&1980
Thompson, Joel E.	Prof	No Michigan	FQHT	PHD	82.	Mich St	&1988
Thompson, John A.	Prof	Murray State	FA	PHD	74.	Arkansas	&8-66
Thompson, M.	Lect	Univ Ulster	FD	MSC			&9-88
Thompson, Mary S.	Prof	Mo Bapitst	FP	DMGT	03	Webster	
Thompson, Melanie	Asst	Tx Lutheran	JRSV	MBA		Tx A&M-C	&2003
Thompson, Raphael N.	Retir	N Carol Cen	1999	MBA	52	NYU	1960
Thompson, Ray	Assoc	Pitts-Johnst	MS	DBA	84	Nova SE	* 1980
Thompson, Robert B.	Assoc	American U	F	PHD	84.	Florida	&9-00
Thompson, Steven C.	Prof	Tx St-S Marc	X	PHD	84.	Houston	&8-04
McCoy Professor							
Thompson, Steven W.	Lect	Hartford	MS	MS	05	Hartford	&9-06
Thompson, T.	PLect	London Metro	CDE				&
Thomsen, C. Torben			FTS	PHD	73.	Mich St	* &
Thomson, Dianne	Lect	Deakin-Burwo	F	BCOM	88	LaTrobe	2002
Thomson, Genevieve	Lect	U Melbourne	BCM	PHD	98	Melbourne	2003
Thomson, Ian	Lect	Strathclyde	PN	BAW	83	Hentwatt	1997
Thornburg, Steven W.	Asst	Wash State	CM	PHD	05.	Cen Fla	2005
Thorne, Daniel T.	Assoc	E Kentucky	F	DBA	86.	Kentucky	&1986
Thorne, Jack F.	Retir	Auburn	1989	PHD	68.	Alabama	&9-72
Thorne, Jerry	Assoc	N Carol A&T	CM	PHD	98.	Tx A&M	&1980
Thorne, Joe A.				PHD	67.	Alabama	
Thorne, Linda	Assoc	York Univ	ABIJ	PHD	97	McGill	&1-97
Thorne, Lynn Bergold	Retir	N Carol St	9-92	MBA	64	Baylor	&1975
Thornton, Daniel B.	Prof	Queen's Univ	F	PHD	78	York	&1993
Thornton, Fred A. Jr.	Retir	West Florida	2001	PHD	70.	Ohio St	&1967
Thornton, John M.	Asst	Wash State	FMJ	PHD	96.	Wash St	&2000
Thornton, Lanie	SLect	Texas A&M	FP	MS	89	Tx A&M	&9-89
Thornton, Phillip W.	VInst	Cleveland St	FM	PHD	93.	North Tx	2004
Thorsell, Anna	Asst	Univ of Umea	FU	MSC	05	Umea	1-05
Throneberry, Mary Beth			POX	PHD	93.	Miss	&
Tian, Gary	Assoc	U Wollongong	FIU	PHD	94	Macquarie	2007
Tian, Joyce	Asst	Univ Alberta	AMTY	PHD	06.	Florida	2006
Tibbits, Garry E.	C-Pr	W Sydney	MJTU	MCOM	70	Auckland	&
Tibbits, Hendrika	Lect	W Sydney	DEFS	MBA	95	Wollong	
Tiburzi, D. James	Lect	Mo-St Louis	FX	JD	74	Illinois	&2002
Tichich, Mary C.	Assoc	Wis-Rvr Fall	CFMV	PHD	89.	Tx A&M	&2000
Tickell, Geoff	Assoc	Indiana U-PA	F	GRAD		Vic	
Tidd, Ronald R.	C-As	Central Wash	AS	PHD	92.	Minnesota	&2001

Name	Rank	School		Degree	Year	Institution		
Tidrick, Donald E.	Prof	No Illinois	AM	PHD	87.	Ohio St	# * & 8-00
Deloitte Professor of Accountancy							
Tidwell, Sam B.	Retir	Mich Tech	D-83	MA	42	Vanderbilt	&1956
Tidwell, Victor H.	Retir	Arizona St	6-99	DBA	66.	Indiana	& 1-72
Tidyman, Clayton R.	Retir	CS-Fresno	1979	PHD	57	S Carol	&1957
Tierney, Cecilia V.			F	PHD	70.	Tx-Austin	&
Tierney, Cornelius E.	Retir	George Wash	2000	PHD	92	Bryant	&1992
Tierney, Thomas G.	Lect	Wisconsin	X	BBA	72	Wisconsin	&1991
Tiessen, Peter	C-Pr	Univ Alberta	MF	PHD	75.	Minnesota	&1975
Tietz, Wendy	Lect	Kent State	M	PHD	07	Kent St	* & 8-00
Tiger, Dennis D.	Retir	Indiana U-PA	D-91	EDD	65	Pittsburgh	1973
Tiggeman, Theresa	Prof	Incarnate	FMPX	MBA	87	Incarnate	& 4-87
Till, Ada	Inst	Prairie View	FCJ	MS	87	Tx A&M	2005
Tilleman, William A.	Retir	Univ Calgary	8-97	PHD	72	Utah	1974
Tiller, Mikel G.	Assoc	Indiana	FMBE	DBA	80.	Indiana	1985
Tilley, J. Rod	Assoc	Mt St Vincen	FIMP	MBA	87	Dalhousie	& 7-83
Tillinger, Janet W.	C-Pr	Tx A&M-C Chr	XF	PHD	89.	Houston	& 9-95
Tillman, Talmadge C. Jr.	Retir	CS-Long Bch	1991	DBA	68.	S Calif	& 9-68
4578 Don Miguel Dr; Los Angeles CA 90006							
Tilt, Carol A.	LectC	Flinders Un	CDW	PHD	98	Flinders	1-93
Timinis, Loizos	Inst	Cyprus	FMA	BS	87	LondonEc	&1994
Tinaikar, Surjit	Asst	Florida		PHD	07	Toronto	8-06
Tinius, David E.	Prof	Seattle	MBC	PHD	77	U Wash	&1971
Tinkelman, Daniel P.	Prof	Pace	FA	PHD	97.	NYU	&1996
Tinker, Tony	Prof	CUNY-Baruch	PWMB	PHD	75	Manchest	&1983
Tinsley, Steve	Inst	SW Okla St					
Tipgos, Manuel A.	Prof	Indiana SE	FIAB	PHD	74.	LSU	& 8-90
Tippett, Mark J.	Prof	Univ Exeter	CMQ	PHD	79	Edinburgh	&1997
Tiras, Samuel L.	Assoc	Louisiana St	F	PHD	94.	Ohio St	& 8-07
KPMG Endowed Professor							
Tishlias, Dennis P.	Deces	Loyola-Chicg	3-92	PHD	84.	Cincinnati	& 9-88
Tisone, A. Anthony Jr.	Asst	Southeastern		MBA	76	Geo Wash	&
Titard, Pierre L.	Assoc	SE Louisiana	FMC	PHD	70.	LSU	& 1-00
Titus, Charles B.	Retir	CS-Fresno	1993	PHD	65.	Tx-Austin	8-63
Tng, Cheong	AcLec	Un Tasmania	F	MFIN	01	Queenslnd	2004
Tobbell, Graham	SLect	Un East Lond	FM	BSC			1991
Tocco, Anthony L.	Prof	Rockhurst	MF	PHD	86.	St Louis	1969
Todd, Christine	Lect	Co St-Pueblo	FP	MS	98	Co-Denve	2005
Todd, John	Lect	CS-Long Bch	FA	MBA	64	UCLA	&1995
Todd, Rebecca			FW	PHD	86.	N Carol	
Todorova, Nelly	SLect	Canterbury	DMQS	MSC	94	Sunderla	1998
Toerner, Michael C.	Prof	Southern	FEOT	PHD	90.	LSU	& 8-90
Tofteland, Elmer H.	Assoc	Northwood	PFGN	MBA	78	Cen Mich	&1982
Togo, Dennis F.	Prof	New Mexico	CMS	PHD	86.	Ariz St	* & 8-87
Toiviainen, Kari	Lect	Helsinki Sch	ADFC	MS	83	Helsinki	1983
Toledo, Marcia L.	Assoc	Pacific Unio	FMP	MED	89	Boston U	1984
Toledo, Moshe				DBA	04.	Boston U	
Toler, Loomis H.	Retir	Miss State	1989	PHD	63.	LSU	1963
Tolikas, Kostus	Asst	Cardiff U	MQ	PHD	05		2006
Tolleson, Thomas D.	Assoc	Txs Wesleyan	ACM	PHD	96.	North Tx	&1996
Tollett, Annette	Asst	Saint Leo-FL		MBA		W Fla	& 8-88
Tolliver, R. Wayne	Assoc	Berea	FT	DBA	87	Kentucky	1976
Tomassini, Lawrence A.	Prof	Ohio State	FM	PHD	74.	UCLA	& 8-93
Tomcal, Michael P.	Inst	Oregon	FCX	MACC	05	Oregon	2005
Tomczyk, Stephen H.	Assoc	Central Conn	FIMS	DBA	76.	Kentucky	* 2003
Toms, Steven	Prof	U Nottingham	FH	PHD	96	Nottingh	&1994
Tondkar, Rasoul H.	Prof	Virg Comm	FIH	PHD	80.	North Tx	8-80
Tong Wu, Marian	Assoc	Chinese HK	AEF	MPA	77	Tx-Austin	1989
Tong, Yen Hee	Asst	Nanyang Tech	F	PHD	05	U Wash	1999
Tonge, Richard	PLect	U Portsmith	MGN	MA			1989
Tonge, Stanley D.	Deces	Minn-Duluth	1993	DBA	88.	Memphis	&
Tongtharadol, Vajana			MF	PHD	87.	Ariz St	&
Toole, Howard R.	Emer	San Diego St	SMC	PHD	76.	Iowa	&1972
Tooley, S.	Assoc	Massey Univ	WGEF	MBS	91	Massey	1990
Toolson, Richard B.	Prof	Wash State	XI	PHD	87.	Ariz St	&1987
Toommanon, Vorasak	Lect	Chulalongkor	F	PHD	92.	Okla St	1983
Toon, Ian	Lect	U Portsmith		BSC			2005
Tooze, Michael J.	SLect	Dundee	MBT	MA	66	St Andrew	1966
Topple, M.	PLect	London Metro	QMD	MSC			1983
Topple, Stephen	SLect	Tech-Sydney	AFT	PHD	02	Sydney	1980
Torres, Donna K.	Inst	Louisiana St		MS	97	LSU	& 8-97
Torres, Paul D.	Retir	So Miss	2001	PHD	71.	Alabama	&1971
Tosanguan, Prayoon		City Bank	1988	PHD	83.	Indiana	
127 S. Sathorn Rd; Bangkok 10120 Tailand							
Tosh, David E.	Deces	Syracuse	3-88	PHD	85.	Penn St	1985
Totterdale, Gwen			MB	PHD	85.	Oregon	&
Tovey, Joseph				PHD	69.	NYU	

Tower, Margaret	Inst	DePaul	FMP	MBA	94	DePaul		&2003
Tower, Ralph B.	Prof	Wake Forest	PX	PHD	78.	N Carol		& 9-80
The Wayne Calloway Professor of Taxation								
Towle, Richard R.	Retir	Boston Univ	1988	BS	39	Boston U		& 9-46
Townsend, Eileen	Lect	Dublin City	AF	MBS	95	Dublin Cty		&2001
Townsend, Richard L.	Assoc	Tennessee	F	PHD	72.	Tx-Austin		& 9-69
Accounting Excellence Teaching Scholar								
Townsend, William L.	Retir	Ferris State	PCM	MBA	79	Gr Valley		1980
Towry, Kristy L.	Asst	Emory	MB	PHD	02.	Tx-Austin		9-02
Tozer, L. E.	Lect	Massey Univ	JOPA	MBS		Massey		&1997
Traas, L.	Retir	Vrije Univ	1995	PHD	67	Erasmus		1969
Trabelsi, Samir	Asst	Brock Univ	FT	PHD	05	HEC-Mont		2004
Tracey, Ann marie	Asst	Xavier	LR	JD	75	Cincinnati		2003
Tracy, John A.	Emer	Colorado	2000	PHD	61.	Wisconsin		&1965
Trafford, Pam	Lect	Massachusett	F	ABD		Mass		1997
Trammell, Vicki	Inst	NE St-Okla	MS	MBA	97	NE St		&2000
Tran, Alfred V. H.	Assoc	Australian N	FITX	PHD	97	Austr Natl		&1991
Tranter, Terry	SLect	Minnesota	F	PHD	78.	U Wash		&1979
Trapani, Teresa D.			UTF	PHD	90.	Kansas		&
Trapnell, Jerry E.		AACSB	2004	PHD	77.	Georgia		&
AACSB Chief Accreditation Officer								
Traub, Jack	Retir	CUNY-Brookly	2000	PHD	76.	Baruch		& 9-82
Traugh, Helen M.	Retir	Alabama-Birm	1998	PHD	81.	Okla St		1981
Treadwell, Gregory	C-In	Cameron	SACF	MSA	92	Oklahoma		1994
Trebby, James P.	Assoc	Marquette	X	DBA	81.	Kentucky		&1983
Trebesh, Michael F.	Retir	Alma	2007	MBA	76	Mich St		&1982
Treece, Darla	Inst	So Illinois	F	MACC	00	S Illinois		& 8-00
Trekell, Leon	Retir	West Tx A&M	2000	MBE	58	Oklahoma		9-60
Tremain, Harold W.	Retir	Cen Michigan	1988	MA	59	Mich St		&1967
Tremblay, Doria	Retir	Univ Laval	IWT	PHD	66.	Illinois		&1963
Trenchard, William H.	Prof	Catawba	FPCE	MS	72	Va Comm		& 8-88
Trenholm, Barbara A.	Prof	New Brunswic	AF	MBA	85	Maine		&1980
Trent, Miles	Lect	Lincoln-NZ	D	BCOM		Canterbu		1997
Trepo, Georges X.		IWSEAD		DBA	72.	Harvard		
Trewin, Janet	Assoc	Neb-Kearney	XP	PHD	91.	Mich St	# *	& 8-04
Trezevant, Robert H.	Assoc	So Calif	X	PHD	89.	Arizona		8-90
Elaine & Kenneth Leventhal Research Fellow								
Tribunella, Heidi	SLect	Rochester	A	MS	03	SUNY-IT		&2005
Tribunella, Thomas	Assoc	SUNY Oswego	SC	PHD	98	SUNY-Alb		&2006
Trigeorgis, Lenos	Prof	Cyprus	F	PHD	86	Harvard		1993
Trigg, Rodger R.	Retir	Columbus St	2001	PHD	81.	Arkansas	# *	&1975
Trimble, Charlie J.			XFC	DBA	91.	La Tech		&
Trine, J. Arden	Retir	Wis-Oshkosh	2003	PHD	69.	Illinois		&1970
Trinkle, Bradley S.	Asst	Charleston	DQS	PHD	06.	Alabama		8-06
Tripathy, Arindam	Asst	SUNY-Albany	FAS	PHD	06	Tx-Dallas		2007
Tripp, John C.	Prof	Denver	X	PHD	80.	Houston		&1979
Trippeer, Donald R.	Asst	SUNY-Oneonta	MX	PHD	93.	S Carol		&
Tritschler, Charles A.	Emer	Purdue	1999	PHD	67.	Stanford		&1967
Trivedi, Viswanath U.	Assoc	York Univ	ABSX	PHD	97.	Ariz St		&2002
Troberg, Pontus	Prof	Helsinki Sch	AFI	PHD	82.	Oklahoma		2000
Trodden, D.	PLect	London Metro	MN	MSC				&1990
Trombley, Mark A.	Prof	Arizona	F	PHD	90.	U Wash	*	& 1-91
Beach Fleischman Profesor								
Trompeter, Gregory M.	Assoc	Boston Coll	AEBF	PHD	88.	Wisconsin	*	&1992
Trotman, Ken T.	Prof	New So Wales	AB	PHD	84	NS Wales		&1974
Trott-Williams, Valerie C.	Asst	Duquesne	AMS	MBA	94	Pittsburgh	*	&2001
Trotter, Ben B.	Retir	Texas Tech	FA	ABD		Oklahoma		& 1-82
Troutman, Amy	SLect	Texas-Dallas	FPA	MPA	97	Tx-Austin		2001
Troutman, Coleen S.	Assoc	Bradley	FX	PHD	93.	Okla St		& 8-92
Trow, Donald G.	Retir	Victoria NZ	AF	BCOM	59	NZealand		1965
Trowbridge, Deborah W.	Adj	Alabama	AB	MACC	89	Alabama		&1992
Trowell, John R.	SLect	Univ Sydney	FM	MEC	78	N Eng-Au		&2003
Troy, Carmelita	Asst	Naval Postgr	FM	PHD	03.	Maryland		2003
Trudeau, Gregory P.	C-Pr	Wis-Superior	FCMA	EDD	01	Minnesota	# *	&1988
Trueman, Brett	C-Pr	UCLA	F	PHD	81	Columbia		2003
Truitt, Jack F.	Retir	Wash State	1994	PHD	76.	Illinois		&1978
Trumpfheller, Sheri L.	Inst	Colorado Spr	FM	MBA	00	Colo Spr		&2000
Trung, Pham Quang	Asst	Natl Econ	FTMP	MBA	95	Boise St		1988
Truong, Cameron	Lect	U Auckland	F	PHD	07	Auckland		2006
Truong, Thu Phyong	ALect	Victoria NZ		BCOM				2006
Trussel, John M.	Assoc	Penn St-Harr	FAN	PHD	93.	Geo Wash		&1998
Truuvert, Toomas	Lect	Macquarie Un	F	MCOM	92	NS Wales		2001
Tsaggari, Harithini	VAsst	Cyprus	QF	PHD	00	Penn St		2000
Tsai, Chih-Fong	Asst	Ntl Chung Ch	DS	PHD	05	Sunderla		2005
Tsai, Yann-Ching	Prof	Nat Taiwan U	FKP	PHD	89.	UCLA		2-90
Tsakumis, George T.	Asst	Drexel	ACB	PHD	03.	S Carol		2003
Tsang, Desmond	Asst	McGill Univ	F	PHD	06	Berkeley		2006

Tsay, Bor-Yi	Prof	Alabama-Birm	SM	PHD	86. Houston		&1986
Tsay, Jeffrey J.	Assoc	Tx-Arlington	SM	PHD	73. Missouri	*	&1974
Tsay, Jimmy Yang-Tzong	Prof	Nat Taiwan U	FMS	PHD	88. Maryland	#	&1988
Tschopp, Daniel J.	Assoc	Daemen	FACX	MBA	96 SUNY-Buf		2000
Tse, John Y. D.			M	DCS	57. Harvard		
Tse, Senyo Y.	Prof	Texas A&M	FM	PHD	83. Berkeley		&2004
KPMG Professor							
Tsui, Christina	Lect	HongKon Tech	VF	MBA	95 Brunel		1974
Tsui, Judy S. L.	Dean	HongKon Tech	AJIE	PHD	94 Chinese U		&2002
Chair Professor							
Tubbs, Richard M.	Emer	Iowa	2006	PHD	88. Florida		& 8-88
Tucker, Barbara L.	Prof	Heidelberg	TADR	MSA	83 Jms Mad		&1989
Tucker, James J. III	Assoc	Widener	TFMH	PHD	85. Penn St		&1990
Tucker, Jennifer W. (Jenny)	Asst	Florida	F	PHD	04. NYU		& 8-04
Prida Term Professor							
Tucker, John M.	Retir	Kent State	1998	MAS	63 Illinois		& 1-91
Tucker, Marvin W.	Emer	So Illinois	1996	PHD	66. Alabama		7-66
Tucker, Michael J.	Prof	Quinnipiac	XL	PHD	80. Houston		&1993
Tucker, Robert H.	Retir	Roosevelt	1978	MBA	49 Nrthwstrn		&
Tucker, Robert R.	Adj	Florida	A	PHD	87. Fla St	#	& 8-05
Tue, Ngo Tri	Asst	Natl Econ	FAOM	PHD	96 Acad Sci		1997
Tull, Guy L.	Deces	New Orleans	1984	PHD	82. LSU		&1982
Tully, Gregory J.	Assoc	Marist	FMC	PHD	83. Berkeley		1996
Tumer, Erol	Retir	Wis-Stev Pt	1999	PHD	73. Illinois		9-86
Tummins, Marvin	Retir	Houston-Cl L	1990	PHD	53. LSU		& 9-83
Tuna, Irem	Asst	Pennsylvania	F	PHD	03. Michigan		2002
Tung, Samuel S. L.			FM	PHD	87. Wisconsin		&
Tunlayadechanont, Suchitra	Asst	Chulalongkor	FM	PHD	91. Geo Wash		&1981
Tunnell, P. Larry	H-Ac	New Mex St	X	PHD	90. Okla St		& 8-94
Tuntiwongpiboon, Naronk	Deces	Thammasat Un	1993	PHD	90. Alabama		
Tuoriniemi, Joel C.	Lect	Mich Tech	XL	JD	87 Detroit		2001
Turbide, Johanne	Assoc	HEC-Montreal	FMNU	PHD	97 Warwick		& 6-95
Turchetta, Alexander	Asst	Johnson&Wale	P	MS	95 John&Wal		2001
Turcotte, William G.				DBA	72. Harvard		
Turetsky, Howard	Prof	San Jose St	FM	PHD	97. Va Comm		&2000
Turkenburg, Dirk	Lect	Vrije Univ	FM	MS	77 Vrije		2001
Turki, Hedi				PHD	81. Illinois		
Turley, W. Stuart	Prof	U Manchester	AFI	MA	Manchest		&1978
Turman, G. Thomas			FX	PHD	95. Va Comm		&
Turmel, Francine	Prof	Sherbrooke	FT	PHD	91 Laval		&1990
Turner, Cynthia Williams	Lect	Illinois	F	PHD	95. Ohio St		& 8-95
Turner, Deborah H.	Assoc	Georgia Tech	FXMI	PHD	85. Geo St		& 1-85
Turner, Emery C.	Retir	Grand Valley	1998	DBA	66. Wash U		1994
Turner, James A. Jr.	Retir	Clemson	1994	JD	66 S Carol		&1968
Turner, James M.	Assoc	Oglethorpe	FMX	PHD	96. Geo St		&1995
Turner, James R.	Assoc	Truman State	LP	JD	81 Missouri		&1982
Turner, Jerry L.	Assoc	Memphis	MSA	PHD	94. Tx A&M		& 8-99
Turner, Joanne H.			1992	PHD	84. Minnesota		
114 Emjay Lane; Rochester NY 14612							
Turner, Karen F.	Asst	No Colorado	FTJD	PHD	95. Tx-Arlin		&2005
Turner, Kim A.	Asst	Tenn-Chattan	F	MBA	Tn-Chatt		8-98
Turner, Laurie M.	Asst	Truman State	FGP	MS	75 Missouri		&1983
Turner, Leslie D.	C-Pr	No Kentucky	SM	DBA	88. Kentucky	*	8-88
Turner, Mark A.	Assoc	Tx St-S Marc	XM	DBA	87. Memphis	*	&2006
Turner, Martha J.	Assoc	Tiffin	CM	PHD	91. Cornell		
Turner, Martin	SenFl	Victoria NZ		MBA	AGSM		2006
Turner, Marvel A.	Asst	Jackson St	AF	PHD	04 JacksonSt		&2004
Turner, Patrick	SLect	Ohio State	AFJK	BS	76 Ohio St		2002
Turner, Robert M.	Assoc	Babson	FNE	DBA	92. Boston U		1990
Turner, Thomas C.	Emer	N Car-Charl	1993	MBA	55 N Carol		& 8-61
Turner, William Jr.	Retir	Jacksonvl St	1993	MBA	77 Alab A&M		& 5-78
Turney, Peter B. B.			1992	PHD	72. Minnesota		&
Cost Technology; PO Box 25124; Portland OR 97221							
Turpen, Richard A.	Assoc	Alabama-Birm	FA	PHD	87. Alabama		&1993
PricewaterhouseCoopers Scholar							
Turpin, Richard A. (Rick)	Assoc	Tenn-Chattan	FM	PHD	94. Alabama		& 8-93
UC Foundation Associate Professor of Accounting							
Tussing, Robert Theodore	Retir	Illinois St	1986	PHD	57. Tx-Austin		&1968
Tuthill, William C.	Retir	Emory	1989	PHD	59. Michigan		1963
Tutticci, Irene	Lect	U Queensland	F	PHD	01 Queenslnd		1996
Tuttle, Brad M.	Prof	So Carolina	SMA	PHD	91. Ariz St		& 1-92
Cramer Fellow of Accounting Information Systems							
Tuttle, Roy E.	Retir	Wisconsin	1991	PHD	59. Minnesota		&1955
Twedt, Ronald G.	Asst	Concordia C	XT	MTAX	Minnesota		&1991
Twombly, John R.			MF	PHD	80. Chicago		&
Twomey, Heather C.	Assoc	Manchester C	DPS	MA	97 Manchest		&2000
Tyler, Jonathan	Assoc	Tech-Sydney	AJX	MCOM	87 NS Wales		1985

Name	Rank	School	Interests	Degree	Year	University	Extra
Tyler, June D.			MSA Adv Mfg	1988	DBA	79. Indiana	
3445 Peachtree Rd; Atlanta GA 30326							
Tyler, Michael	Prof	Barry	FMT	PHD	95	Fla Intl	1-94
Typpo, Eric W.	Asst	Pacific	AFS	PHD	94.	Fla St	& 8-98
Tyra, Anita I.			FI	PHD	68.	U Wash	
Tyree, L. Mark	Prof	Shenandoah	PXMV	EDD	84	Wm&Mary	&1987
Yount, Hyde and Barbour Professor of Accounting							
Tyska, Claudia R.	Asst	R Stockton	ACMV	PHD	00.	Rutgers	&2004
Tyson, Thomas N.	C-Pr	St John Fshr	CHJM	PHD	87.	Geo St	* 9-90
Tzavalis, Elias	Prof	Athens Univ	FQ	PHD	93	London	2001
Tzur, Joseph			FC	PHD	83.	Columbia	&
Uddin, M. Jamir	Retir	Wis-Plattev	MCQ	EDD	77	N Illinois	8-77
Uddin, Nancy	Asst	Monmouth	AS	PHD	00.	Rutgers	1999
Uddin, Shahzad	Asst	Univ Essex	AEFW	PHD	97	Manchest	2002
Ude, Pamela	Lect	CS-Fresno	FM	MBA	02	CS-Fresno	& 1-05
Udpa, Suneel C.	Prof	St Marys-Cal	FM	PHD	90.	Wash U	8-93
Uecker, Wilfred C.	Prof	Rice	BMC	PHD	73.	Tx-Austin	&1984
Harmon Whittington Professor of Management; Assoc Dean for Executive Ed							
Ueno, Susumu	Prof	Konan Univ	CIMU	DBA	91.	S Illinois	1995
Konan University, Japan; ueno@konan-u.ac.jp; 81-78-431-4341 phone							
Ugras, Yusuf Joseph	Assoc	LaSalle	FCM	PHD	91.	Temple	* 9-84
Ukaegbu, B.	SLect	London Metro		PHD			
Ulinski, Michael	Asst	Pace-Westch	CM	PHD	87	NYU	&1984
Uliss, Barbara Turk	Prof	Metro State	FSAH	PHD	91.	Case Wes	& 8-96
Ullrich, Mark J.	Deces	Naval Postgr	2000	PHD	00.	S Carol	2000
Ulmer, Donna K.	Assoc	Webster	MD	PHD	99	St Louis	&2005
Ulseth, George W.	Retir	Rensselaer	1989	PHD	72	Minnesota	&1971
Ulstad, Ingrid	Inst	Wis-Eau Clar	P	MBA	79	Minnesota	& 1-98
Umansky, Philip H.	Assoc	Virg Union	VFGA	PHD	94.	Va Comm	& 1-89
Umar, Ahson			A	PHD	95.	Drexel	
Unni, Sanjay	Lect	Strathclyde	F	PHD	94	So Meth	1994
Unruh, Terry M.	Asst	Oral Roberts	VFC	MBA	80	Oral Rob	& 8-80
Unseth, Allan D.	Retir	Norfolk St	2006	MA	68	Minn St	& 9-73
Upchurch, Vernon Hill	Deces	Oklahoma	3-75	PHD	54.	Tx-Austin	1955
Updyke, Karel Ann	Assoc	Butler	FTM	PHD	87.	Purdue	&1986
Upneja, Arun U.	Assoc	Penn St-Hotl	CFIM	PHD	96.	Houston	8-96
Upton, David R.	Asst	N Car-Greens	BC	PHD	06.	Indiana	8-05
Urbancic, Frank R.	Prof	So Alabama	F	DBA	77.	Kent St	&1990
Ernest G. Cleverdon Professor of Business							
Uretsky, Myron	Prof	New York	1998	PHD	65.	Ohio St	&1970
Dept of Information Systems; New York Univ; 212-998-0844							
Urquhart, William	Inst	Fla Atlantic		MPA	79	Tx-Austin	8-98
Urrutia, Ingacio	Asst	Univ Navarra	SM	DOC	99	UC Madrid	1-04
Ushman, Neal L.	Assoc	Santa Clara	F	PHD	83.	Cornell	&1982
Usoff, Catherine A.			MC	PHD	94.	Ohio St	&
Usry, Milton F.	Emer	West Florida	D-05	PHD	64.	Tx-Austin	&1986
Utama, Suddharta	Asst	Indonesia	F	PHD	96.	Tx A&M	8-96
Utzman, Glen G.	Assoc	Idaho	X	LLM	94	NYU	&1973
Vaassen, Eddy	Prof	Maastricht	AMOS	PHD	94	Maastricht	&1994
Vaello, Linda	Lect	Tx-S Antonio	MFX	MBA	80	Tx-SanAnt	&2001
Vafeas, Nikos	Assoc	Cyprus	FMI	PHD	94.	Kansas	&1994
Vaidyanathan, Ganesh	C-Ac	Saskatchewan	BCDS	PHD	91	Waterloo	* 2001
Vaillement, Benoit	Prof	Sherbrooke	X	MRIS	00	Sherbrook	2001
Vaish, Ramesh C.			Practi-India		PHD	72.	Florida	
Vaivio, Juhani	Asst	Helsinki Sch	CMU	PHD	01	Helsinki	1989
Valades, Karyn	Lect	Tennessee	F	MACC	02	Tennessee	8-02
Valenti, Donald W.	Retir	GMI	1988	MBA	68	Michigan	1967
Valentine, Erick G.	Asst	Kansas State	M	PHD	03.	Memphis	& 8-02
Valenzuela, John	Lect	CS-Long Bch	FCM	MBA	81	CS-LgBch	&2000
Valiete, Felina J.				PHD	67.	LSU	
Vallely, Mark	AcLec	So Queenslnd	FTI	BBUS	84	S Queens	&1990
Valliant, Bill	Lect	McGill Univ	F	BSC	69	Holy Cr	&1994
Van den Brand, Bob	Asst	Tilburg Univ	BE	MBA	96	Tilburg	1996
Van der Laan, Joyce	Lect	Univ Sydney	FWA	MCOM	00	Wollong	&2001
Van der Stede, Wim A.	Prof	London Econ	BM	PHD	97	Ghent	2006
Van der Zanden, Peter	Prof	Tilburg Univ	AFM	MBA	84	Tilburg	1993
Van Es, Wim	Asst	Tilburg Univ	M				&1993
Van Os, Jerry A.	D-Pr	Westminst-UT	MSD	PHD	90	Brighm Yg	* &1988
Van Roy, Yvonne	Assoc	Victoria NZ	GL	LLB	84	Victoria	1980
Van Staden, C.	Sen	Massey-Alban	FW	DM		Pract SA	&1999
Van The, Nhut	Assoc	HEC-Montreal	BFM	PHD	82.	Illinois	& 8-76
Van Veen-Dirks, Paula	Asst	Tilburg Univ	BC	MBA	91	Eindhoven	1993
van Zijl, Tony	Prof	Victoria NZ	FPT	PHD	86	Victoria	&1978
VanAlst, Lucinda L.	C-Ac	Ball State	FX	DBA	89.	Kentucky	& 3-86
Vanasse, Robert W.	Retir	CS-Long Bch	1995	PHD	66.	Minnesota	&1987
VanBreda, Michael F.	Assoc	So Methodist	FMT	PHD	79.	Stanford	1981
VanBuskirk, Andrew	Asst	Chicago	F	PHD	05.	Penn	2004

Vance, Danny	Inst	Cen Arkansas	FMA	BBA	70	Cen Ark	&8-02
Vance, David	Asst	Rutgers-Camd	LF	JD	87	Rutgers	2003
Vance, Lawrence L.	Deces	Berkeley	6-78	PHD	47.	Minnesota	&1941
Vance, Susan M.	Prof	St Marys-Ind	LC	JD	77	Cooley	&9-81
Vancil, Richard F.	Retir	Harvard	1991	DBA	60.	Harvard	&1958
VanDaniker, Relmond P.	Retir	Kentucky	2002	DBA	70.	Maryland	&1970
Vandenberg, Amy T.	Asst	St Norbert	FVX	MST	92	Wi-Milwa	&1992
Vandenburg, Amy				PHD	98.	Wisconsin	
VanDenburgh, William M.	Asst	Jms Madison	XGF	PHD	04.	LSU	&8-06
Vander Bosch, Nancy	Lect	Un Waterloo	AF	MACC	86	Waterloo	* &2002
Vander Vyver, Mark	ALect	W Australia	FQ	BCOM	91	UTS	1996
Vander Weele, Ray			MCBF	PHD	72.	Wisconsin	* &
VanDerBeck, Edward J.	Prof	Xavier	CM	MS	68	SUNY-Alb	&1976
Vandervelde, Scott D.	Asst	So Carolina	ASFC	PHD	02.	Iowa	&2002
Vandevere, Wayne E.	Retir	S Col 7th Dy	1996	PHD	67.	Mich St	&1956
VanDiver, William M.			FM	DBA	73.	Geo St	
VanDongen, William O.	Retir	St Norbert	2002	PHD	81.	North Tx	&1990
Vanecek, Michael T.			S	PHD	78.	Tx-Austin	
VanEekelen, Antonie	Lect	Deakin-Burwo	EF	BED	85	VColl	1989
VanGelderen, Cynthia G.	Dean	Aquinas	XP	MBA	84	W Mich	&1980
Vangermeersch, Richard G.	Emer	Rhode Island	2004	PHD	70.	Florida	* &9-71
VanHelleman, Johan	Prof	Tilburg Univ	FIK	PHD	77	Rotterdam	&1996
VanHise, Joan	Assoc	Fairfield	PFJV	PHD	97	NYU	&1998
VanHoof, Hubert B.	D-Pr	Penn St-Hotl	MI	PHD	96	Ariz St	8-04
VanHorn, Lawrence G.			1992	PHD	73.	NYU	
PO Box 75; East Orleans MA 02643							
VanKessel, Paul	Prof	Tilburg Univ	AD	MBA	85	Tilburg	&1991
VanKollenburg, John	Prof	Tilburg Univ	A	MBA	80	Tilburg	&1985
VanLeer, Michael	Inst	Delaware	FM	MBA	78	Drexel	&9-86
VanLent, Laurence	Prof	Tilburg Univ	FM	PHD	99	Tilburg	1993
VanOrnam, Don	Dean	So Adventist	MP	PHD	95	Claremont	&1997
VanPatten, Michael R.	Retir	Siena	CFMX	MS		SUNY-Alb	&9-75
VanRegenmorter, Robert J.	Retir	CS-Stanislau	2004	PHD	73.	Okla St	&1981
VanRoekel, Arlan W.	Prof	Grand View	FPTV	MBA		Iowa	&
VanSantvoord, John C.	Prof	So New Hamp	MFCX	MBA	75	NewHamp	&9-80
VanSchaik, Frans	Prof	Tilburg Univ	AD	MBA	82	Groningen	&1999
VanSeventer, Antonie		Palo Alto CA	1992	PHD	66.	Michigan	&
2335 Waverley St; Palo Alto CA 94301							
Vanstraelen, Ann	Assoc	Maastricht	FA	PHD	00	Antwerp	1999
VanSyckle, Larry D.				DBA	85.	Kentucky	&
VanVlodrop, Jacques	Asst	Tilburg Univ	M				1993
VanVuren, Kenneth W.	Asst	Tenn-Martin	C	PHD	03.	Miss	8-03
VanWyhe, Glenn	Assoc	Pacific Luth	FA	PHD	91	U Wash	* &1979
VanZante, Neal R.	Assoc	Tx-Pan Amer	CFMG	PHD	76.	Okla St	* &2007
Varas, J.	Lect	Univ Wales					2006
Vargo, John J.	SLect	Canterbury	DMS	PHD	01	Canterbu	&1981
Vargo, Richard J.	Prof	Pacific	FCIM	PHD	69.	U Wash	1981
Vargus, Mark E.	Asst	Texas-Dallas	FM	PHD	96.	Penn	2002
Varick, Celia B.	Assoc	Lamar	FGP	PHD	95.	Arkansas	&1995
Varnell, Karen D.	Asst	Tarleton St	ACJP	MBA	98	Tarleton	1998
Varnon, Anthony N.	Assoc	SE Missouri	STIX	DBA	91.	Miss St	&1979
Varosi, Terry R.			CJX	PHD	95.	Va Comm	&
Vasarhelyi, Miklos A.	Prof	Rutgers-Newk	FSA	PHD	73	UCLA	1989
Vasquez, Marilyn	Assoc	Indiana NW	XL	JD	88	Valparaiso	&1979
Vasquez, Stephen W.	Retir	St Louis	1986	MBA	50	Tulane	&1953
Vass, Peter	Assoc	Univ Bath	FGU	MSC	70	London	1990
Vassilatou-Thanopoulou, Eli	Retir	Athens Univ	1997	DBA	63.	Indiana	1973
Vatter, William J.	Deces	Berkeley	1990	PHD	46.	Chicago	1957
Vaughan, D. Michael	Retir	Colorado St	2003	PHD	70.	Tx Tech	&1969
Vaughan, Jo Ann	Asst	Campbell		MA		N Carol	&1989
Vaughn, Thomas E.	Assoc	Chicago St	LJPX	JD	78	Kansas	&1982
Vautier, Allen D.	Retir	Central Wash	AX	JD	73	U Wash	&9-74
Vawter, Charles L.		Glendale CC		PHD	75.	Ariz St	
Vaysman, Igor	Assoc	INSEAD	M	PHD	93.	Stanford	2001
on leave to CUNY-Baruch							
Vazquez-Dodero, Juan-Carlos	Prof	Univ Navarra	JM	DOCT		IESE	8-69
Veazey, Richard E.	Assoc	Grand Valley	MC	PHD	81.	St Louis	&9-79
Vecchio, Nerina	ALect	Griffith-GC	W	MECO	96	Queensind	1998
Vedd Rishma	Asst	CS-Northrdge	PFMV	PHD		Dundee	2006
Veit, Marcia R.	Inst	Cen Florida	FV	MBA	76	Arkansas	&9-80
Veitschegger, Rodney D.	Retir	W Kentucky	1989	MBA	59	U Wash	&1964
Velayutham, Sivakumar	H-Ac	Univ Sharjah	FMHT	PHD	97	Massey	&2000
Veldman, J. F. (Hanne)	Lect	Vrije Univ	AJEF	MS	97	Vrije	1999
Velilla, Manuel	Prof	Univ Navarra	JMS	DOCT		IESE	7-71
Velkovitz, Dale M.	Retir	Governors St	1995	ABD		Illinois	* &9-80
Velury, Uma K.	Assoc	Delaware	F	PHD	99.	S Carol	9-99
Venable, Carol F.	Prof	San Diego St	BJE	PHD	88.	Arizona	&1988

Venables, Philip	Deces	U Wollongong	ADS	MCOM	95	Curtain		&2000
Vendrzyk, Valaria P.	Assoc	Richmond	AM	PHD	93.	Tx A&M		&2003
Venezia, Robert A.	Retir	Fla Atlantic	2004	MA	66	Florida	#	& 8-88
Venieris, George	Prof	Athens Univ	MS	PHD	75	Birminghm		1977
Venkatachalam, Mohan	Assoc	Duke	F	PHD	96.	Iowa		7-02
Venkataraman, Ram	Asst	Minnesota	F	PHD	01.	Penn St		&2001
Venkataraman, Ramgopal	Asst	So Methodist		PHD				
Venkateswar, Sankaran	Assoc	Trinity	FNIC	PHD	89.	Georgia		8-89
Vent, Glenn A.	Assoc	Nev-L Vegas	CF	PHD	83.	Arizona		&1982
Venugopalan, Raghu			TYFM	PHD	01	Minnesota		
Venuti, Elizabeth K.	Assoc	Hofstra	TV	PHD	97.	Columbia		&1999
Vera-Munoz, Sandra C.	Assoc	Notre Dame	BM	PHD	94.	Tx-Austin		&1994
KPMG Faculty Fellow								
Verbeeten, Marja J.	Asst	Penn St-Hotl	MI	EDD	04	NAU		1-05
Verdi, Rodrigo	Asst	MIT	F	PHD	06.	Penn		2006
Verduzco, David	Lect	Texas-Austin	F	MPA	93	Tx-Austin		& 9-00
Vergauwen, Philip	Assoc	Maastricht	M	PHD	98	Leuven		6-97
Verghese, Thomas			DS	PHD	87.	Columbia		&
Vergoossen, Ruud G. A.	Prof	Maastricht	FI	PHD	94	Vrije		&1999
Verhoeven, Peter	SLect	U Auckland	F	PHD	04	W Austr		2004
Verma, Kiran	Assoc	Mass-Boston	M	PHD	87.	Mich St		1992
Vermeer, Thomas E.	Assoc	Baltimore	AFNS	PHD	98.	North Tx		&2000
Ernst & Young Distinguished Professor								
Vernooij, A. T. J. (Fons)	Assoc	Vrije Univ	EMF	PHD	93	Erasmus		2002
Veronneau, Pierre	Prof	Quebec-Montr	F	PHD		Montreal		& 7-81
Verreault, Daniel A.	Assoc	Tampa	MJO	PHD	84.	Tx A&M		&2004
Verreault, Kathryn M.	Dean	Mass-Lowell	FM	PHD	82.	Tx A&M		1986
Verrecchia, Robert E.	Prof	Pennsylvania	F	PHD	76	Stanford		1983
Elizabeth F. Putzel Professor								
Verschoor, Curtis C.	Retir	DePaul	1995	EDD	77	N Illinois	# *	& 9-74
Vert, David	Lect	Un Waterloo	EFLQ	HBBA	83	Wilfr Lau		&2006
Vertigan, Michael J.		W Australia	M	PHD	74.	Berkeley		
Vessel, Herbert	Prof	Southern	FAT	PHD	86.	Missouri		& 8-93
Veuleman, Malcolm W.	Prof	Lamar	FCP	PHD	71.	Arkansas		&1970
Vezina, Michel	Prof	HEC-Montreal	MSU	DSC	95	Montpell		& 9-85
Viator, Ralph E.	Prof	Texas Tech	S	PHD	86.	Tx A&M		& 9-00
Vichitlekarn, Stan		Kasetsart Un		PHD	01.	Oregon		
Vichitsarawong, Thanyaluk	Lect	Chulalongkor	F	MBA	01	Illinois		&1997
Vickers, Tom	Retir	SE Okla St	1993	MS		SE Okla		1971
Vicknair, David B.	Assoc	Rockhurst	FTV	DBA	83.	Tennessee		&1993
Vickrey, Don W.	Prof	Ariz St-West	TF	PHD	75.	Tx-Austin		& 8-92
Vickrey, Donn W.			FM	PHD	93.	Okla St		&
Vicq, Jack G.	Retir	Saskatchewan	2000	MSC	69	Saskatch		&1967
Vidal, Jean-Pierre	Assoc	HEC-Montreal	GX	PHD	90	Montreal		& 6-02
Vidulich, Barbara B.			FM	DBA	79.	Colorado		&
Viebig, V. Richard Jr.	Lect	Rice	XAPZ	MAC	77	Rice		&1969
Viele, Daniel F.	Assoc	Webster	CMS	MS	79	Colo St	*	&1998
Vienne, Margaret W.	Inst	NW St of LA	P	MBA		La Tech		& 1-07
Viens, Donna J.	Inst	Johnson&Wale	CMX	MBA	96	John&Wal		2005
Viet, Sheila	Lect	Wis-Milwauke	FM	MS	79	Wi-Milwa		&2006
Vigeland, Robert L.	C-Pr	Tx Christian	F	PHD	77.	Columbia		& 8-89
Viger, Chantal	Prof	Quebec-Montr	F	PHD	96	Drexel		& 6-89
Viger, George W.	Retir	Notre Dame	1991	MBA	49	LSU		&1950
Vijayakumar, Jayaraman	Assoc	Virg Comm	MGN	PHD	90.	Pittsburgh		1997
Vijayan, Anil			FT	PHD	93.	Rutgers		
Villeneuve, Guy	Prof	Quebec-Montr	S	PHD		Laval		& 7-80
Vimuktanandana, Boonserm	Asst	Chulalongkor	FIMP	MBA	83	Ariz St		1970
Vincent, Carolyn	ALect	Queensld Tec	X	BCOM	89	Queensld		1994
Vincent, Linda	Assoc	Northwestern	F	PHD	95.	Nrthwstrn		1999
Vincent, Michael	SLect	Monash Univ	FMSW	MEI	92		*	1990
Vincent, Vern H.		Austin TX	1988	PHD	57.	Michigan		&
Vinciguerra, Barbara M.	Asst	Moravian	ABCP	PHD	01	Drexel		& 9-05
Vinciquerra, Barbara				PHD	01.	Drexel		
Vines, Cynthia C.	Assoc	Kentucky	X	PHD	92.	S Calif		& 8-98
Viney, Christopher W.	Lect	Deakin-Burwo	F	MBAS	96	Monash		1999
Vinning, Russell	Lect	Deakin-Burwo	F	MBA	91	Monash		&1988
Vinson, Michael	Asst	Golden Gate	X	LLM	86	NYU		&2006
Violet, William	Prof	Mn-Moorhead	LI	JD	97	N Dakota	# *	&1981
Violette, George R.	Prof	So Maine	XBF	PHD	87.	Ariz St		&1988
Virchick, John M.	Assoc	Chapman	ACFM	MBA	74	E New Mex		& 9-83
Virgil, Robert L.			FM	DBA	67.	Wash U		
Virtanen, Kalervo	C-Pr	Helsinki Sch	CMU	PHD	80	Helsinki		&1965
Virtanen, Tuija	Asst	Helsinki Sch	CM	MS	95	Helsinki		1990
Visse, Richard H.	Emer	Portland St	2003	PHD	74.	Ariz St		&1976
Visvanathan, Gnanakumar	Asst	Geo Mason	F	PHD	96.	NYU		&2002
Vito, Marilyn	Asst	R Stockton	AFT	MBA	85	Monmouth		&1994

Name	Rank	School	Code	Degree	Yr	University	
Vives, Antonio		Great Fal VA		1990	PHD	76. Car Mellon	
9417 Meadowshire Ln; Great Falls VA 22066							
Vives, Evangelina		Hillside PR		1988	PHD	70. NYU	&
Vlittis, Adamos		Univ Cyprus			PHD	06. Florida	
Vlotman, Fred	Prof	Tilburg Univ	CMU	PHD	81	Amsterdm	&1993
Vluggen, Mark	Asst	Maastricht	SM	PHD	06	Maastricht	6-97
Voege, Herbert W.	Retir	Ferris State	2004	PHD	71	Michigan	&1972
Vogel, Alan	Lect	Mass-Boston	FT	MBA	84	Bryant	&1999
Vogel, Mark A.	Assoc	Denver	X	LLM	76	Denver	&1976
Vogel, Nicholas C.	Retir	Hofstra	1989	JD	53	Brooklyn	&1949
Vogel, Thomas J.	C-Ac	W New Eng	FMVT	PHD	93	Penn St	&1998
Vogt, Rodney L.	Inst	Kansas State	FATM	MACC	91	Kansas St	&8-01
Ernst & Young Teaching Fellow							
Voigt, Dennis	Assoc	St Michaels	FMS	MBA		Vermont	1990
Volk, Gary A.	H-Ac	Wayne St Col	FTM	PHD	86.	Nebraska	1992
Volkan, Ara G.	C-Pr	Fl GulfCoast	FINT	PHD	79.	Alabama	&8-04
Moorings Park Chair in Managerial Accounting							
Volkert, James F.			F	PHD	81.	Illinois	
Vollmers, Gloria Lucey	Assoc	Maine	CFM	PHD	94.	North Tx	&1992
Volmer, Frans G.	Asst	Maastricht	FH	PHD	92	Rotterdam	&1986
Volz, William H.	Prof	Wayne State	JLX	JD	75	Wayne St	1978
VonDohlen, Gerald H.	VPres	Chemical Bk		PHD	69.	Columbia	
Vonsiatsky, Andre' A.	Asst	Salem Colleg	XM	MBA	78	Wake For	&1990
Salem College; Dept of Econ & Mgt; Winston-Salem NC 27108; 919-721-2743							
Vooren, Wim M. van der	Lect	Vrije Univ	FM	MS	66	Vrije	1966
Vorherr, Philip H.	Retir	Dayton	2000	PHD	75.	Cincinnati	&6-80
Voskuil, Julie	Asst	Calvin	MIF	MBA	02	W Mich	1999
Voss, James A.	C-In	Penn St-Erie	ABXF	ABD		Pittsburgh	&1984
Voss, William M.	Emer	Ohio Univ	1995	PHD	67.	Chicago	1971
Vosseberg, G.	Lect	Univ Hull	F	MBA	93	Hull	9-93
Vostok, Gary J.	Asst	Fitchburg St		MBA		Babson	* &1979
Voth, Melvin H.	VPres	Hesston Mfg		DBA	64.	Indiana	
Vousten-Sweere, Annemarie	Asst	Tilburg Univ	CD	MBA	94	Rotterdam	1997
Vreeland, Jannet M.	Assoc	Nevada-Reno	CFGM	PHD	92.	Tx A&M	1-91
Vruwink, Carol J.	Retir	Central Col	2003	MS	81	Drake	1979
Vruwink, David R.	Assoc	Kansas State	F	PHD	82.	Arkansas	9-82
Vyrtveit, Ingunn	Assoc	Norwegian Mg	CDMQ	DREC	95	NHH Berg	8-87
Wa, Jeanette H. S.	Asst	City Univ HK	A	MBA	94	Henley	9-86
Wachtel, Joshua	Retir	Fairleigh Di	1984	PHD	59.	NYU	&9-72
Wachtel, Rosina	Asst	Marymt Manht	XFL	LLM	78	NYU	&9-81
Wacker, DuWayne M.	Deces	North Dakota	1998	MS	66	N Dakota	&9-67
Wacker, Raymond F.	Assoc	So Illinois	XJ	PHD	89.	Houston	&9-89
Groennert/Emerson Electric Teaching Excellence Professor							
Waddell, Joella				PHD	96.	Memphis	
Waddington, James	Asst	Hawaii Pacif	FPG	MBA	82	Hawaii	&8-86
Wade, Daniel E.	Prof	So Indiana	XF	DBA	81.	Kentucky	&1986
Wade, George A.	Pres	Wade & Brady		PHD	75.	U Wash	
Wade & Brady Intl; 601 Valley St; Seattle WA 98109							
Wade, Kenneth S.			FM	PHD	67.	UCLA	
Wade, Linda G.	Asst	Tarleton St	FCP	MBA	82	Tarleton	&1982
Wade, Stacy R.	Asst	W Kentucky	FX	PHD	03.	Kentucky	&2003
Wade, Steven	Exec	Santa Clara	FM	MBA	73	W Ontario	&1994
Wadhwa, Darshan L. (Dash)	Prof	Houston-Down	X	DBA	88.	La Tech	&1984
Waegelein, James F.	C-Pr	Emporia St	AS	PHD	82.	Penn St	&2006
Wagaman, David	Assoc	Kutztown	PXT	MS		Drexel	&1984
Wagenhofer, Alfred	Prof	Univ Graz	YIMF	PHD	90	Vienna	1991
Wagner, Charles R.	Retir	Mankato St	1988	PHD	76.	Nebraska	# * &1984
Wagner, I. Warren	Retir	Ashland	5-99	MBA	65	Indiana	&9-71
Wagner, John W.	Deces	St Louis		PHD	64.	Illinois	&9-73
Wagner, Robin M.	Assoc	San Fran St	FT	PHD	82.	Berkeley	1986
Wagoner, W. J.	Retir	Ball State	1987	PHD	54	Iowa	9-63
Wahba, Sami	Assoc	Kuwait Univ	F	PHD	80	Sterling	1998
Wahlen, James M.	Prof	Indiana	FM	PHD	91.	Michigan	1997
Ford Motor Company Teaching Fellow							
Wahlstrom, Fedrick	Asst	Univ of Umea	CM	MSC	95	Stockholm	9-96
Wahlund, Jay L.	C-As	Minot State	FPNG	MPA	94	Nebraska	&1990
Wahrmann, Sally A.	Retir	Lg Isl-Post	8-07	MS	77	Long Isl	&1985
Wai, Miranda				PHD	03.	Rutgers	
Wailoo, Bert A.	Prof	Kean	CMTF	MBA	79	Pace	* &1985
Wain, Charles A.	Lect	Babson	FCM	MBA	70	Harvard	1999
Wakefield, Nelson D.	Retir	Illinois		PHD	52.	Illinois	1938
Wakefield, Robin	Asst	Baylor	S	PHD	01.	Miss	&
Information Systems Department; robin_wakefield@baylor.edu; 254-710-4240							
Walberg, Glenn	Asst	N Car-Wilmin	LX	LLM	04	Geotown	2001
Walczuch, R.	Assoc	Maastricht	S	PHD	94	Georgia	1996
Walden, Risto	Res	Helsinki Sch	X	MS	93	Helsinki	1997
Walden, Robert E.	Retir	Indiana		PHD	39	Iowa	1937

Name	Rank	Institution	Code	Degree	Yr	School		Year
Walden, W. Darrell	Assoc	Richmond	FMS	PHD	94.	Va Comm		&1994
Waldman, Erwin	SLect	Monash Univ	ECM	PHD	00	Monash	*	&1989
Waldron, Marilyn A.			FMJ	DBA	88.	La Tech		
Waldrup, Bobby E.	Assoc	North Fla	SFJ	PHD	97.	Miss		&2003
Wales, Stephen H. Sr.	Retir	Ferris State	1988	MBA	60	Indiana		&1968
Walgenbach, Paul H.	Retir	Wisconsin	1988	PHD	58.	Illinois		&1953
Walker, Arthur H.				DBA	67.	Harvard		
Walker, Charles G.				PHD	70.	Alabama		
Walker, David F.	D $	S Fl-St Pete	AK	MBA	80	Chicago		&D-02
Walker, Edward R.	Asst	McNeese St	FAN	PHD	96.	Houston		&2003
Walker, George T.				PHD	48.	LSU		
Walker, J. C.	Inst	SW Baptist	SM					2006
Walker, John P.	Prof	CUNY-Queens	AG	PHD	76.	Cincinnati		& 9-98
Walker, Julie	SLect	U Queensland	FM	PHD	94	Queensl		1990
Walker, Kenton B.	Prof	Wyoming	SMV	PHD	86.	Tx A&M		1985
Walker, Lauren M.	Retir	U Washington	1982	MBA	43	U Wash		&1946
Walker, Martin	Prof	U Manchester	FQY	PHD	80	Newcastle		1989
Walker, Norman	Assoc	St Michaels	FMC	MBA		NYU		&1984
Walker, Paul L.	Assoc	Virginia	FAS	PHD	94.	Colorado		& 9-94
Walker, Rhonald D.	Retir	So Methodist	2002	JD	68	So Meth		&1966
Walker, Robert A. (Robin)			XMC	PHD	91.	Tx-Austin		&
Walker, Robert D.	Retir	San Jose St	1988	EDD	59	S Calif		1956
Walker, Robert G.	Prof	Univ Sydney	FGHP	PHD	77	Sydney		&2004
Walker, Robert W.	Retir	Ball State	1997	MA	66	Ball St		& 9-66
Walker, Sara K.	Asst	Drake	P	JD	83	Drake		&1992
Walker, Stephen P.	Prof	Cardiff U	HF	PHD				&2003
Walker, Weldon H.	Retir	Harden-Simm	1991	PHD	68.	Missouri		
Wall, T.	Lect	Univ Ulster	FNM	BA				1-99
Wallace, Edward L.	Retir	SUNY-Bufallo	1984	PHD	57.	Chicago		1958
Wallace, James S.	Assoc	Claremont	FM	PHD	96.	U Wash		
Wallace, Linda G.	Assoc	Virg Tech	S	PHD	99	Geo St		2000
Wallace, R. S. Olusegun	Deces	King Fahd Un	2003	PHD	87	Exeter		1997
Wallace, Richard	Deces	Ark-Monticel	FPXV	MBA	67	Fayettev		&1968
Wallace, Sandra	Lect	U Queensland	CM	MFM	96	Queensland		1999
Wallace, Sarah R.	Prof	Lenoir-Rhyne	P	MA	66	Appalach		
Wallace, Wanda A.	Retir	Wm & Mary	2005	PHD	78.	Florida	# *	&1991
Wallace, William D.	Retir	Mississippi	1994	PHD	78.	Okla St		& 8-76
Wallage, Philip	Prof	Un Amsterdam	AIR	PHD	91	Amsterdm		1982
Waller, Thomas C.	Retir	Houston-Cl L	1991	PHD	77.	Houston		1-75
Waller, William T.	Prof	Arizona	CA	PHD	81.	U Wash		&1981
Deloitte & Touche Professor								
Wallin, David E.	Assoc	Ohio State	ABFM	PHD	90.	Arizona		&1989
Wallis, Kenneth	Assoc	SUNY-Utica	XM	MS	78	Akron	*	&1978
Walo, Judith C.	C-Pr	Central Conn	AFB	PHD	90.	Mich St		&1994
Walsh, Cassandra	Asst	Providence		ABD		Conn		2004
Walsh, Eamonn J.	Prof	Un Cl Dublin	FIP	PHD	83	Glasgow		1999
Walsh, Joseph G.	Prof	Golden Gate	X	LLM	78	NYU		&1984
Walsh, Mike	Retir	Northern St	AFMX	MS	76	N Dakota		&1976
Walsh, Robert J.	Assoc	Dallas	XF	PHD	95	Notre Dm		&2006
Walsh, William	Inst	Syracuse	FMAX	MBA	90	Syracuse		1997
Walter, Richard M.	Prof	Louisville	X	PHD	88.	Tennessee		& 8-93
Walter, T. Beth			FM	PHD	95.	Tennessee		&
Walters, L. Melissa	Assoc	Tampa	SMB	PHD	93.	Cen Fla		
Walters, Sharon T.	Assoc	Morehead St	RX	MBA	74	Morehead		&1989
Walther, Beverly R.	Assoc	Northwestern	FM	PHD	95.	Chicago	*	&1995
Walther, Larry M.	C-Ac	Tx-Arlington	F	PHD	80.	Okla St	*	&1980
Walton, H. Charles	Assoc	Gettysburg	SF	PHD	81	Fla St		&1989
Walts, Charles	Asst	Hardin-Simm		MPA	73	Tx-Austin		&1968
Walz, Karen S.	Asst	Minot State	FPV	MS	80	N Dakota		&1980
Wambsganss, Jacob R.	Deces	North Dakota	2-07	PHD	85.	Nebraska		& 8-92
Wampler, Bruce M.	Assoc	La St-Shreve	AFP	DBA	94.	La Tech		& 1-03
Wan, Huishan	Asst	CS-East Bay	F	PHD	07	Iowa		9-97
Wandler, Scott A.	Asst	New Orleans	FM	PHD	07	LSU		&2006
Wang, Dechun	Asst	Nebraska	FA	PHD	04.	Missouri		2004
Wang, Doris		Nat Chung Hs	1992	PHD	91.	Kentucky		
Wang, Hewei (Wendy)	Asst	Alabama A&M		DBA		Nova SE		
Wang, Isabel	Asst	Michigan St	F	PHD	05.	Georgia		2005
Wang, Jiannan	Asst	Delaware	S	PHD	06	Arizona		2006
Wang, Karl J.	Asst	Mississippi	AB	PHD	03.	S Carol		&2003
Wang, Kun	Asst	Txs Southern	FCG	PHD	05.	Tx A&M		2005
Wang, Li	Asst	Akron	FA	PHD	06.	Kent St	*	&9-07
Wang, Peijie J.	Read	Univ Hull	F	PHD	02	Manchest		O-04
Wang, Shiing-Wu	Assoc	So Calif	X	PHD	88.	Michigan		1996
Wang, Shiyun	Lect	Aberdeen	FQ	PHD	02	Cambridge		2007
Wang, Tay-Chang	Prof	Nat Taiwan U	FT	PHD	88	Penn	#	& 2-88
Wang, Ting (TJ)			SC	PHD	99.	Rutgers		
Wang, Weimin	Asst	St Louis	F	PHD	00.	Wash U		2006

Wang, Wen-Ying	Asst	Nat Chengchi	CIM	PHD	98	Hitotsub		&1999
Wang, Xin	Asst	Chinese HK	F	PHD	06.	Duke		2006
Wang, Xue	Asst	Emory	F	PHD	05	Chicago		8-05
Wang, Yang-Ruoh	Prof	Nat Chengchi	ACF	MC	77	Chengchi		1977
Wang, Zhemin M. (Jamie)	Prof	Wis-Parkside	FV	PHD	91.	Wisconsin		8-98
Wang, Zheng	Asst	CS-S Marcos	F	PHD	06.	Maryland		2007
Wannamaker, John M.	Retir	Clemson	1988	PHD	66.	LSU	*	&1963
Waples, Elaine	Assoc	Purdue Calum	XMCF	MST	88	Iowa		&1991
Ward, Bart H.	Prof	Okla City	A	PHD	73.	Nrthwstrn		&1-00
Ward, Burke T.	Prof	Villanova	JLWX	LLM	78	NYU		1977
Ward, D. Dewey	Emer	Michigan St	2006	PHD	79.	Tx-Austin		9-78
Ward, Dan R.	Prof	La-Lafayette	XFE	DBA	79.	La Tech		1981
Ward, J.	Prof	Univ Ulster	FXT	BA				&1-84
Ward, John R.	Retir	Pace	1990	MBA	36	NYU		&1961
Ward, Suzanne Pinac	Prof	La-Lafayette	FTE	PHD	87.	LSU		&1979
Ward, Terry J.	Prof	Mid Tenn St	F	PHD	91.	Tennessee		&1994
Wardlow, Penelope S.		GASB	1996	PHD	85.	Georgia		
10 1/2 Toilsome Ave; Norwalk CT 06851								
Warfield, Terry D.	Assoc	Wisconsin	FT	PHD	89.	Iowa		1989
Waring, Glen	Asst	Lindenwood	FMP	MBA		Lindenwo		&1999
Warne, Rick				PHD	07.	Utah		
Warner, Paul D.	C-Pr	Hofstra	ADOS	PHD	81.	NYU		&1991
Warren, Audrey A.	Retir	San Fran St	1992	MBA	69	Puget Sd		&1972
561 Marlin Cf; Redwood City CA 94065								
Warren, Carl S.	Retir	Georgia	6-02	PHD	73.	Mich St	# *	& 6-73
Warren, D. Lee	Assoc	Belmont	MP	PHD	95.	Georgia		&1998
Warren, Hugh E.	Prof	CS-L Angeles	FMC	PHD	66	Michigan		1-76
Warren, J. Donald			AO	PHD	04.	Tx A&M		
Warren, Robert L.			FG	PHD	73.	Arkansas		&
Warren, Sanford D.	Inst	Millsaps	GFPX	MBA	65	S Miss		&1994
Warrick, Shane	Inst	Southern Ark	PJV	MBA	99	Ark-LtlR		2002
Warrington, Ann	Lect	Mich Tech	CFM	MS		La Tech		&1999
Warsame, Hussein	Assoc	Univ Calgary	X	PHD	95	Calgary		2000
Warsame, Mohamed	Asst	Howard	F	PHD	06	MorganSt		&2006
Warsono, Sony				PHD	04.	Kentucky		
Gadjah Mada University								
Warth, Robert J.	Retir	Rochest Tech	7-02	MBA	87	Rochester		& 9-82
Wartick, Martha L.	H-Ac$	No Iowa	XF	PHD	91.	Penn St		1998
Warwick, David	SLect	N Eng-Austr	M	MSC		Bath		&1973
Wasan, Sonia	Asst	Virg Comm	F	PHD	06.	LSU		2006
Washburn, Mark	Lect	Texas-Tyler	XFS	MS	97	Tx-Arlin		& 9-04
Washburn, Wilbur L.	Retir	Tenn-Martin	1990	MS	64	Alabama		& 9-64
Washington, Aubrey	Asst	Virgin Islan	CDFX	MBA	83	Michigan		&1989
Washington, Joseph B.				PHD	66.	Alabama		
Washington, Kimberly	Asst	Dillard		MA		Southern		
Washington, Mary T.	Prof	Governors St	FPMX	PHD	87.	S Calif		&1993
Washington-Arnold, Liz	Asst	Citadel	FEPA	PHD	06	Rutgers		8-05
Wasley, Charles E.	C-Ac	Rochester	FT	PHD	87.	Iowa		1999
Wasley, Robert S.	Deces	Colorado		PHD	50.	Ohio St		1946
Watanabe, Judith E.	Assoc	Neb-Omaha	FX	PHD	85.	Nebraska		&1983
Waterbury, Lawrence	Retir	Quinnipiac	M	MBA	64	Chicago		&1977
Waterhouse, John H.			M	PHD	72.	U Wash		
Waters, Brenda N.			FMO	DBA	93.	La Tech	# *	&
Waters, Edwin D.	Retir	Tenn Tech	1990	PHD	71.	Alabama		&1971
Waters, Gary L.		Auburn	2004	DBA	81.	Tennessee		
Executive Director of Corp & Student Services; Finance Dept								
Waters, John M. II	Assoc	Anderson	AF	PHD	88.	Tennessee		&2006
Wates, Kathleen W.	SInst	So Car-Aiken	PFCV	MACC	91	S Carol	*	&1991
Watkins, Ann L.	Asst	N Car-Greens	AFI	PHD	95.	LSU		& 8-04
Watkins, Ceri	Asst	Univ Essex	MI	MA				2002
Watkins, Frank E. Jr.	Assoc	Alabama-Birm	X	PHD	73.	LSU		&1980
Watkins, Herbert N.	Assoc	Alabama St	CGF	PHD	70.	Wisconsin		&1999
Watkins, Larry E.	Prof	No Arizona	FTP	PHD	84.	Okla St		&1985
Watkins, Paul R.			SBA	PHD	80.	Ariz St	*	
Watne, Donald A.	Emer	Portland St	2001	PHD	77	Berkeley		&1976
Watson, David J. H.		Queensland	1990	PHD	72.	Ohio St		&1990
Member of Parliment Queensland Australia								
Watson, Iain D.	SLect	W Australia	F	PHD	96	Ulster		1998
Watson, John	Assoc	W Australia	F	PHD	96	W Austrl		1976
Watson, Richard B.	Lect	Cal-Santa Br	TMC	PHD	81	Ca-SnBarb		1981
Watson, Robert.	Lect	Napier Univ		ACII				1999
Watson, Stephanie F.	Asst	Cen Arkansas	OSP	PHD	04.	LSU	#	8-03
Watters, Michael Paul	Prof	Henderson St	FTA	DBA	89.	Miss St		&1996
Louis Dawkins Professor								
Watts, Edward J.	SLect	Macquarie Un	F	PHD	88	N Eng-Au		1988
Watts, James C.	Asst	McNeese St	MC	MS	68	LSU		&1968
Watts, John S.			MF	PHD	88.	Car Mellon		

Watts, Michael	Assoc	Ark-Ltl Rock		XFP	JD	90 Ark-LtlR	&9-79
Watts, Olga	Inst	McNeese St		FO	MBA	93 McNeese #	&1999
Watts, Ross L.	Prof	MIT		FHT	PHD	71. Chicago	&2006
Watts, Susan G.	Assoc	Purdue		FMT	PHD	91. Iowa	&1997
Watts, Ted	SLect	U Wollongong		CMUP	PHD	UTS	&2004
Waugh, James B.	Retir	Carleton	1994		MBA	64 Calif	&1965
Waymire, Gregory B.	Prof	Emory		F	PHD	84. Chicago	8-99
Candler Professor							
Wayne, William C.	Retir	CS-Fresno	1993		EDD	58 S Calif	8-54
Wayron, Paul W.	Inst	Bradley		FMJ	MBA	92 Mich St	&1-04
Wearing, Robert T.	Assoc	Univ Essex		FGNI	PHD	91 Essex	&1980
Weatherholt, Nancy D.	Assoc	Mo-Kansas Ct		FPA	PHD	88 Kansas	&1991
Weathers, Henry T.				AP	PHD	72. Missouri	&
Weatherwax, Roy C.	Prof	Wis-Whitewat		FC	PHD	74. Wisconsin	&1976
Weaver, Connie D.	Assoc	Texas A&M		X	PHD	97 Ariz St	&7-06
Webb, Alan	Asst	Un Waterloo		BM	PHD	01 Alberta	&2000
PricewaterhouseCoopers Fellow							
Webb, Charles D.	Retir	Marshall	5-97		MBA	69 W Virginia	&9-67
Webb, Judith L.				FM	PHD	88. U Wash	
Webb, Juliette Adams				ABS	PHD	01. Ariz St	* &
Webb, Kim	Visit	Txs Wesleyan		ASV	MA	96 Tx-Arlin	&2002
Webb, Laurie	SLect	Monash Univ		T	MADM		&1980
Webb, Teresa J.	Inst	Arkansas		F	DBA	04. La Tech	
Webber, Sally A.	Assoc	No Illinois		SME	PHD	94. Tx-Arlin	&8-99
HSBC Professor of Accountancy							
Weber, Catherine K.	Lect	Houston			PHD	06. Tx A&M	
Weber, David P.	Asst	Connecticut		FX	PHD	05. Colorado	&2005
Weber, Eric C.	Assoc	Univ Navarra		M	PHD	98. Nrthwstrn	6-87
Weber, Gary J.	Assoc	Gonzaga		X	PHD	97. Ariz St	1995
Weber, Joseph A.	Prof	Montana		XFP	PHD	84. Minnesota	&1983
Weber, Joseph P.	Assoc	MIT		FM	PHD	00. Penn St	&2000
Weber, Margaret (Peggy)	Asst	Ill-Chicago		F	PHD	04. Tx-Austin	8-04
Weber, Richard P.	Assoc	Michigan St		X	PHD	75. Michigan	&9-82
Weber, Ron A.	Prof	U Queensland		SA	PHD	77 Minnesota	&1979
Weber, Sandra L.	Prof	Truman State		MRFP	PHD	90. Missouri	* &1976
Webster, Carly	ALect	Monash Univ		MA	BBUS		2001
Webster, Phyllis Ann	Retir	N Car-Greens	1990		EDD	66 N Illinois	&1978
Webster, Robert L.	C-Ac	Ouachita Bap		CFN	DBA	93. La Tech	1993
George Young Chair of Business							
Webster, Stuart K.	Prof	Wyoming		F	PHD	75. Iowa	&1994
Webster-Poole, Kristine	Asst	LaSierra		XCR	MBA	91 LomaLinda	&2006
Wee, Marvin Ge Way	Lect	W Australia		F	MFIN	99 W Austrl	1999
Wee, Warren Y. F.	Assoc	Hawaii Pacif		AN	PHD	82. U Wash	&8-88
Wegman, David E.	Retir	Fla Atlantic	2001		DBA	79. Fla St	&9-77
Wehle, Mary M.					DBA	72. Harvard	
Wei, Donna				M	PHD	01. Berkeley	
Weickgenannt, Andrea	Asst	No Kentucky		FA	MBA	94 Maryland	&8-00
Weiden, Kathleen	Asst	Fairfield		FX	PHD	01. Baruch	&2002
Weidenmier, Marcia L.	Asst	Miss State		S	PHD	00. Tx-Austin	2004
Weidman, Stephanie M.	Assoc	Rowan		BMSJ	PHD	02. Drexel	* 1995
Weihrich, Susan G.	C-Ac	Seattle		XF	PHD	86. Houston	&1989
Weil, Roman L.	Prof	Chicago		FM	PHD	66. Car Mellon	* &1965
V. Duane Rath Professor of Accounting							
Weil, Sidney H.	Assoc	Lincoln-NZ		EF	PHD	89 WestnCape	&1995
Weimer, Daniel	Lect	Wayne State		F	MACC	05 Michigan	* 8-05
Weinberg, Frank F.	Retir	Golden Gate	1996		MBA	78 Golden Gt	&1956
Weiner, David P.	Prof	San Francisc		AFM	PHD	72. Michigan	&9-70
Weinstein, Gerald P.	C-Ac	John Carroll		FXE	PHD	90. Kent St	&1988
Weintrop, Joseph	Prof	CUNY-Baruch		F	PHD	84. Oregon	&9-93
Stan Ross Professorship in Accountancy							
Weirich, Thomas R.	Prof	Cen Michigan		AKF	PHD	76. Missouri	&1976
Weis, Frederick	Exec	Claremont		FAQ	ABD	Claremont	2003
Weis, William L.	Retir	Seattle	1999		PHD	79. U Wash	&1973
Weisel, James A.	Assoc	Mercer-Atlan		CEMU	DBA	91. Kentucky	&2000
Weisenfeld, Leslie W.	Prof	Winston-Slm		FABE	PHD	87. Va Tech	* 8-93
Sara Lee Professor							
Weiser, Herbert J.	Retir	Lg Isl-Brook		MTRC	ABD	Baruch	&1965
Weishar, Judy K.				SFM	PHD	97. Arkansas	&
Weisler, Raymond S.	Retir	CS-Dominguez	1989		MBA	63 Chicago	&1978
Weispfenning, William W.	Inst	Jamestown		AFG			&2006
Weiss, Aron	Assoc	CUNY-Stn Isl		ASF	MBA	63 CUNY	&1971
Weiss, Charles J.	Retir	Seton Hall	1990		MBA	54 Rutgers	&1951
42 North Mitchell Avenue; Livingston NJ 07039							
Weiss, Dan	Asst	Tel Aviv Un		M	PHD	01 Tel Aviv	2003
Weiss, Dieter H.	Retir	Ferris State	1995		PHD	76. American	&1982
Weiss, Earl	Prof	CS-Northrdge		XF	JD	74 Southwes	&1984
Weiss, Ira R.	Dean	N Carol St		SDMA	PHD	76 UCLA	D-04

Weiss, Ira S.	VAsst	Chicago	FX	PHD	01.	Chicago	&
Weiss, Jane M.	Asst	Wash & Lee	FM	PHD	01.	Wisconsin	2006
Weiss, Lawrence A.	Assoc	Georgetown	FM	DBA	89.	Harvard	&2006
Weiss, Mira			XF	PHD	05.	Case Wes	
Weiss, Neil S.				PHD	67.	Columbia	
Weiss, Renee E.	Asst	St Thomas-MN	AK	PHD	06.	Baruch	9-07
Welborn, Stephen I.	Prof	Redlands	M	MPA	68	Miss St	&1981
Welch, David	Prof	Franklin	FMXJ	MBA	86	E Tn St	&2007
Welch, George D.	Retir	Drake	1992	DBA	64.	Indiana	&1967
Welch, Judith K.	Assoc	Cen Florida	FGVS	PHD	85.	Fla St	& 9-88
Welch, Paul R.		Rollins	1998	PHD	81.	Florida	&
Technical Information Consultant; Rollins College							
Welch, Sandra T.	Prof	Tx-S Antonio	AFHO	PHD	91.	Tx A&M	&1991
Weld, Leonard G.	H-Pr	Valdosta St	FX	PHD	89.	Tx A&M	7-02
Welden, Mary Ann	Lect	Wayne State	M	MBA	78	Notre Dm	8-05
Welfley, Mark	Inst	Akron	D	MBA	04	CS-Domin	1-04
Welke, William R.	Retir	W Michigan	1998	PHD	62.	Wisconsin	&1967
Welker, Michael	Assoc	Queen's Univ	FT	PHD	93.	Iowa	&1996
Welker, Michael G.	Inst	Drexel	AFM	MBA	73	Drexel	* &1988
Welker, Robert B.	Prof	So Illinois	FMTB	PHD	77.	Ariz St	1987
Wellborn, Joe				PHD	69.	Arkansas	
Wellman, Delores	Asst	St Ambrose	VFXP	MS		Drake	&1984
Wells, Donald W.			FA	PHD	93.	Tx A&M	&
Wells, Jane B.	Assoc	Kentucky	F	MS	86	Kentucky	&1987
Wells, Peter	Assoc	Tech-Sydney	F	PHD	01	Sydney	1992
Wells, Steve C.	Dean$	Alcorn St	FX	PHD	94.	Miss	* &1996
Wells, Wayne R.	Prof	St Cloud St	XL	LLM	81	Pacific	1983
Wells, William L.	SLect	U Washington	F	MPAC	89	U Wash	1988
Wells-Jessup, Jean	Asst	Howard		JD	98	Geo Wash	2002
Welsch, Gemma M.	Retir	DePaul	2005	PHD	81.	Nrthwstrn	* &1972
Welsch, Glenn A.	Deces	Texas-Austin	O-04	PHD	52.	Tx-Austin	&1949
Welsh, Carol N.	C-As	Rowan	VF	EDD	07	Delaware	# &1983
Welsh, Mary Jeanne	C-Pr	LaSalle	FTB	PHD	87.	LSU	& 9-91
Welton, Ralph E.	D-Pr	Clemson	FTJ	PHD	82.	LSU	1983
Wempe, William F.	Asst	Tx Christian	M	PHD	98.	Tx A&M	&2001
Wendell, John P.	Prof	Hawaii-Manoa	SA	PHD	89.	Union-NY	& 8-89
Wendler, Clifford				PHD	64.	Tx-Austin	
Wendorf, Michelene D.	Inst	DePaul	FCP	MSED	76	Wisconsin	&1997
Wensley, Anthony K. P.	Assoc	Univ Toronto	S	PHD	89	Waterloo	&1988
Wentworh, Gerald O.	Deces	Stanford	9-96	PHD	60.	Stanford	1954
Wentworth, Jon	Assoc	So Adventist	MX	MTX	79	Tennessee	&1996
Wentzel, Kristin	Assoc	LaSalle	MB	PHD	98.	Temple	9-00
Wenzel, Hans	Analy	Grace Ind		PHD	66.	Columbia	
Wenzel, Loren A.	H-Pr	Marshall	PFGV	DBA	90.	Memphis	2000
Wermert, John G.	Asst	Mid Tenn St	SA	PHD	95	Indiana	* &2002
Werner, Charles A.	Assoc	Loyola-Chicg	ADR	JD	61	Chicago	& 9-82
Werner, Edward M.	Asst	Drexel	FX	PHD	05.	Ariz St	2005
Werner, Michael L.	Lect	U Miami	PFM	MPA	83	U Miami	&1984
Werner, R. Budd	Exec	Ohio Univ					& 7-98
Werner, Robert H.	Assoc	Rutgers-N Br	GA	PHD	89	NYU	&1977
Wertheim, Paul	Prof	Abilene Chr	FA	PHD	87.	Kansas	& 8-00
Wescott, Shari H.	Prof	Houston Bapt	SFV	PHD	82.	S Carol	1990
Wesnerli, Edward M.	Asst	Drexel		PHD	05	Ariz St	2005
Wessels, Susan B.	H-Pr	Meredith	AMCV	PHD	05	Sarasota	&1978
West, Alice	Lect	Tennessee	S	MACC	86	Tennessee	8-07
West, Cathy	Lect	Massachusett	F	MBA	01	Mass	2006
West, Robert J.	Retir	South Fla	1999	MS	62	Fla St	&1964
West, Robert N.	Asst	Villanova	SAMF	PHD	88.	S Calif	&1994
West, Ron	Asst	F Dick-Madis	X	LLM	92	NYU	&1997
West, Stephen L.	Lect	Arizona St	M	MBA	78	Nova SE	2006
West, Sue H.			SM	PHD	82.	Georgia	* &
West, Timothy D.	Assoc	Arkansas	MC	PHD	93.	Tennessee	&2002
Westbrook, L. Curtis	Retir	CS-San Bern	2004	PHD	92.	Georgia	* &1989
Westen, Cheryl	Inst	W Illinois	P	MBA	00	W Illinois	& 9-01
Westfall, Othel D.	Deces			PHD	54.	Tx-Austin	
Westort, Peter J.	Assoc	Wis-Oshkosh	FX	PHD	90.	Oregon	&2003
Westphal, Catherine M.			X	PHD	87.	Illinois	&
Westrup, Chris	SLect	U Manchester	BDW	PHD	96	UMIST	1993
Wetzel, T. Sterling (Tom)	Prof	Oklahoma St	A	PHD	80.	Okla St	1986
Wetzel, William E.	Retir	New Hampshir	1993	MBA	67	Chicago	1967
Weygandt, Jerry J.	Prof	Wisconsin	F	PHD	68.	Illinois	&1968
Arthur Andersen & Co. Alumni Chair in Accounting							
Weyns, Guy		Goldman Sach	1995	PHD	93.	Stanford	
Goldman Sachs; London							
Whalen, Tom	CLAs	Suffolk	FM	MS	01	Boston C	2001
Whang, Yong-Ho	Retir	Dongguk U	CMN	PHD	82	Hanyang	3-78
Whatley, Maliece	Asst	Savannah St	FM	MS	83	Georgia	& 8-03

Wheatley, Clark M.	Assoc	Fla Internat	F	PHD	94.	Va Tech	& 8-94
Wheeler, James E.	Retir	Michigan	1999	PHD	69.	Illinois	&1972
Wheeler, John T.	Retir	Berkeley	1991	PHD	47	MIT	1954
Wheeler, Lyn F.	Prof	Wash & Lee	FXM	DBA	74.	Geo Wash	&1983
Wheeler, Patrick R.	Asst	Missouri	S	PHD	99.	Geo St	&2002
Wheeler, Stephen W.	Prof	Pacific	FAMV	PHD	88.	Ariz St	& 6-94
Neven C. Hulsey Chair in Business Excellence							
Wheeling, Barbara M.	Asst	Mont St-Bill	FP	PHD	99	Alberta	& 8-04
Whelan, Adelaide			FX	PHD	90.	Baruch	
Whelan, Catherine	Asst	Georgia Col	F	PHD	04	Bond	2003
Whelan, Joseph M.	C-Ac	Maryland UC	FIV	MS	88	Geo Wash	&1993
Wheldon, Brett	SLect	W Sydney	CEFP	MCOM	94	W Sydney	
Whinston, Andrew B.		Texas-Austin		PHD	62.	Car Mellon	
Dept of Management; University of Texas-Austin							
Whisenant, J. Scott	Assoc	Houston	FAT	PHD	97	Oklahoma	* & 9-01
White, Amanda	Lect	Tech-Sydney	CSI	BBUS	90	Tech-Sydn	2002
White, Clinton E. Jr. (Skip)	Prof	Delaware	SA	DBA	81.	Indiana	9-87
White, Craig G.	Assoc	New Mexico	X	PHD	98.	Tx Tech	1998
White, David	Assoc	Victoria NZ	ILX	PHD	97	Sydney	2000
White, Gary E.	Retir	Texas Tech	8-99	PHD	69.	U Wash	&1979
White, Godwin T. (Tom)	Prof	Wm & Mary	FA	PHD	84.	Va Tech	&1983
White, Gwendolen B.	Assoc	Ball State	MA	PHD	89.	Indiana	& 9-86
White, J. Morgan	Retir	Brigham Yg	1993	MS	58	Brighm Yg	& 9-67
White, Jackson A.	Retir	Arkansas	1998	PHD	64.	LSU	# &1985
White, John Arch	Deces	Texas	5-80	PHD	37.	Tx-Austin	
White, John H.	ClPr	Denver	DSF	PHD	96	Co Mines	2000
White, John J.	Assoc	Elmhurst	F	PHD	99.	Arkansas	8-00
White, Laura	Inst	Emory Henry	FALV	MS		Webster	2003
White, Lourdes Ferreira	Assoc	Baltimore	MBC	DBA	89.	Harvard	9-92
White, Paul	Lect	Minnesota	M	ABD		Minnesota	
White, R. Dean	Retir	Loyola-Chic	1980	PHD	64.	Nrthwstrn	& 9-67
White, Richard A.	Prof	So Carolina	X	PHD	81.	Ariz St	&1985
Moore Faculty Fellow							
White, Scott	Assoc	Lindenwood	CMFX	MACC		Missouri	&2002
White, Stanford W.	Emer	St Marys-Cal	1996	MBA	72	Golden Gt	&1963
White, Steven D.			MS	PHD	88.	Arkansas	&
White, Thomas D.				PHD	69.	Illinois	
Whitecotton, Stacey M.	Assoc	Arizona St	MB	PHD	93.	Oklahoma	& 8-97
Whitehurst, Frederick D.	Retir	Old Dominion	1995	PHD	68.	Florida	&1972
Whiteman, Michael J.	VAsoc	Massachusett	X	LLM	75	Boston U	9-81
Whiting, Ros	SLect	Univ Otago	FES	PHD	07	Otago	1993
Whitis, Robert E.			FP	DBA	84.	La Tech	&
Whitley, William	Prof	Athens State	XVC	EDD	97	Alabama	# &1987
Whitman, J.	Lect	N Eng-Austr	F	MA		Canterbu	2002
Whitney, James R.	Retir	Citadel	1996	MBA	60	N Carol	& 9-58
Whitt, Dalton	Retir	Arkansas St	1997	MBA	68	Memphis	& 8-68
Whitt, John Doyle	Retir	S F Austin	1984	PHD	68.	Miss	&1969
Whitt, Sue Yeager			FMI	PHD	75.	Arkansas	* &
Whittaker, Gerald F.	Retir	South Fla	2003	PHD	73.	Nrthwstrn	# * 6-74
Whittaker, John	Lect	Loughborough	FN	MA	80	Manchest	&1976
Whitten, Alan F.	Retir	Alabama-Hunt	SD	MED	76	Harding	&1981
Whitten, Ruth A.			M	PHD	93.	U Wash	
Whittenburg, Gerald E.	Retir	San Diego St	X	PHD	76.	Houston	* &1976
Whittington, Mark	Lect	Aberdeen	ME	MBA	94	Open	2006
Whittington, O. Ray	Dean	DePaul	AF	PHD	78.	Houston	# * &1997
Whittington, William E.	Retir	Texas Tech	1975	PHD	57.	Illinois	1947
Whittred, Gregory P.	Prof	Austral Grad	F	PHD	86	NS Wales	&1990
Wichmann, Henry Jr.	Prof	Alaska-Fairb	GNMV	PHD	72	N Colo	& 1-86
Wick, Madalyn	Prof	Bemidji St	FP	PHD	93.	Nebraska	&1984
Wickramanayake, J.	Lect	Monash Univ	F	PHD			&1990
Widdison, Elizabeth	Lect	U Washington	FM	BS	92	City U	1999
Widener, Sally K.	Asst	Rice	FM	PHD	99.	Colorado	# &2001
Widman, Robert A.	Assoc	CUNY-Brookly	FPX	MBA	73	Rutgers	& 9-78
Wiecek, Irene	Tut	Univ Toronto	FPBV	BCOM	79	Toronto	& 7-91
Wieder, Bernhard	Assoc	Tech-Sydney	DMSU	PHD	98	Vienna	1998
Wiedman, Christine I.	Assoc	Un Waterloo	FP	PHD	94.	Cornell	&2006
Wiegand, Daniel G.	Lect	Miami U-Ohio	P	MBA	76	Miami U	2003
Wieland, Matthew	Asst	Georgia	FX	PHD	05.	Indiana	2005
Wielhouwer, Jacco L.	Asst	Tilburg Univ					
Wienecke, Richard E.	Asst	Lycoming	AX	MBA	79	Lgls-Post	&1982
Wier, Benson	Prof	Virg Comm	MB	PHD	92.	Tx Tech	&1992
Wier, Heather A.	Assoc	Univ Alberta	CF	PHD	94.	Cornell	&1992
Wiersma, Eelke	Lect	Vrije Univ	BM	PHD	03	Groningn	1997
Wiest, David N.	Asst	Merrimack	F	PHD	92.	N Carol	2006
Wiggins, Casper E. Jr.	C-Pr	N Car-Charl	ADS	DBA	82.	Tennessee	& 8-99
Wightman, Priscella Z.	Asst	Hartwick	AFC	MS	90	SUNY-Alb	&1985
Wijewardena, Hema	Retir	U Wollongong	EP	PHD	82	Sri J	&1987

Name	Rank	Institution		Degree	Yr	School	
Wijn, Martin	Assoc	Tilburg Univ	CMU	PHD	88	Tilburg	&1978
Wilberfoss, Caroline	STut	U Auckland	FA	BSC	81	Leichest	2002
Wilburn, Nancy L.	Prof	No Arizona	FPEV	PHD	87.	Tx A&M	& 1-88
Wilcox, Kirkland A.	Assoc	Colorado Spr	FA	PHD	72.	Tx-Austin	&1972
Wilcox, William E.	Asst	Bradley	FTV	PHD	97.	Nebraska	& 8-99
Wild, John J.	Prof	Wisconsin	FT	PHD	83.	Wisconsin	1989
Robert and Monica Beyer Professor of Accounting							
Wilde, Harold H.	C-Ac	North Dakota	AFG	PHD	81.	Nebraska	& 8-82
Wilder, W. Mark	Dean$	Mississippi	FGN	PHD	94.	Fla St	& 8-93
Wildey, Edwin	Retir	East Anglia	1999	MSC			&
Wilguess, John H.	Prof	Oklahoma St	X	PHD	79.	Arkansas	&1979
Wilhelm, Jana	VAsst	Kentucky St	PMA	MBA		Wayne St	
Wilk, Edward F.	Assoc	Gallaudet	FPTV	MBA	85	Gallaudet	&1985
Wilkerson, Jack E. Jr.	Dean	Wake Forest	PVN	PHD	84.	Tx-Austin	& 9-89
Wilkie, Macil C. Jr.	Retir	Grambling St	PMV	PHD	68.	LSU	7-85
Wilkie, Patrick J.	Assoc	Virginia	FX	PHD	84.	Michigan	9-02
Wilkie, R. Sue Legge	Retir	Rhodes Col	2003	PHD	88.	Miss	* &
Wilkin, Carla	Lect	U Melbourne	DS	PHD	01	Deakin	2003
Wilkins, Michael S.	Assoc	Texas A&M	F	PHD	94.	Arizona	9-94
PricewaterhouseCoopers Fellowship							
Wilkins, Trevor A.	Assoc	Natl Singapo	FIM	PHD	89	Queensla	1989
Wilkinson, Brett R.	Asst	Baylor	X	PHD	02.	Tx Tech	9-02
Roderick L. Holmes Chair of Accountancy							
Wilkinson, Christine A.	Asst	Iowa State	M	PHD	06.	Iowa	&2006
Wilkinson, Joseph W.	Retir	Arizona St	1997	DBA	66.	Oregon	&1964
Wilks, T. Jeffrey	Assoc	Brigham Yg	F	PHD	00.	Cornell	9-00
Will, Hartmut J.	Prof	Victoria-Cdn		PHD	69.	Illinois	* 1979
Willcocks, Geoff	PLect	Bournemouth	FXQ	PHD			7-88
Willenborg, Michael	Prof	Connecticut	AF	PHD	96.	Penn St	& 9-96
Ackerman Scholar							
Willett, Caroline	PLect	U Portsmith	FAJ	BA			1990
Willett, Roger J.	Prof	Queensld Tec	AFM	PHD	86	Aberdeen	&1996
Williams, Barry H.	C-Ac	King's Col	XVP	JD	95	Widener	& 9-89
Williams, Belinda	AcLec	Un Tasmania	FX	BCOM	91	Tasmania	2002
Williams, Bernard C.	H-SL	East Anglia	SAD	PHD			&
Williams, Brian G.	Lect	Deakin-Warrn	FHE	GDAC	80	Deakin	&1988
Williams, Dan	Assoc	Shepherd	ADP	MSA	91	Ferris	&2000
Williams, David D.	Assoc	Ohio State	A	PHD	84.	Penn St	&1984
Williams, Deborah	Asst	W Virg St	FMPT	MPA	82	W Virginia	&2005
Williams, Doyle Z.	Retir	Arkansas	FANE	PHD	65.	LSU	&1993
Doyle Z Williams Chair							
Williams, Elizabeth G.	Retir	Auburn	1987	MS	53	Auburn	9-46
Williams, H. James	Dean	Grand Valley	AFIX	PHD	82.	Georgia	* & 7-04
Williams, Heather	C-In	Univ Cariboo	AM	MBA	04	Athabasc	* &
Williams, Hywel D.	SLect	U Glamorgan	XMF	BA	77	Glamorgan	& 9-86
Williams, J. Richard (Dick)	D-Ac	Missouri St	FI	PHD	93.	Miss	& 8-90
Williams, Jackie G.	Retir	Virg Comm	1992	MS	57	Va Comm	1957
Williams, Jan L.	Asst	Baltimore	EF	PHD	06	MorganSt	&2006
Williams, Jan R.	Dean	Tennessee	FTE	PHD	70.	Arkansas	& 7-77
Pilot Chair of Excellance							
Williams, Jefferson	Lect	Michigan	FX	MA	96	Michigan	6-96
Williams, Joanne D.	Assoc	Babson	F	PHD	87.	Tx A&M	&1992
Williams, John J.			BFHM	PHD	78.	Penn St	*
Williams, Jonathan	Lect	Wales-Bangor	FQ	PHD	02	Bangor	D-92
Williams, Karel	Prof	U Manchester	HIMW	BSC		LondonEc	1993
Williams, Kent	Asst	Indiana Wes	ACJM	MBA	02	Ball St	&
Williams, Kitty B.	Retir	Geo Southern	2004	MBA	73	Ga Srthrn	&1978
Williams, L. K.	Prof	Morehead St	FMR	DBA	87.	Kentucky	&1988
Williams, Marvin	Assoc	2Prof n-Down	X	JD	86	Houston	* &1988
Williams, Megan	Lect	Univ Wales	FM	BSC	87	Aberystw	&2000
Williams, Mel C.	SLect	U Glamorgan	BF	MSC	79	Bath	* & 9-89
Williams, Michael	Lect	West Indies	C	MSC		W Indies	
Williams, Michael G.	Asst	Oregon	TXF	PHD	92	Princeton	2004
Williams, Michael G.			MX	PHD	96.	S Calif	
Williams, Nolan Eugene	Retir	Arkansas	1987	PHD	57.	Tx-Austin	&1951
Williams, P. Richard	Assoc	Tenn-Martin	FGM	PHD	95.	Arkansas	& 8-01
Williams, Patricia A.	Assoc	Fordham		DBA	92.	Boston U	1992
Williams, Patricia Elliott	Retir	Friends	FCMX	PHD	68	LSU	* &1995
Williams, Paul F.	Prof	N Carol St	MFT	PHD	77.	N Carol	1985
Williams, Ralph		West Indies	F	PHD	80.	S Calif	&
Williams, Randolph	Prof	West Indies	X	PHD		Colorado	
Williams, Ray E.	Retir	Mn St-Mankat	2004	DBA	87.	Memphis	&1992
Williams, Ron	Inst	Am U Sharjah	FCX	MBA	98	Lincoln	# &2001
Williams, S. Mitchell		Singapore Mg	IW	PHD	98	Murdoch	2000
Williams, Sarah	Lect	Deakin-Geelg	F	MCOM	96	Deakin	&1983
Williams, Satina	Asst	Marist	FA	PHD	03.	Va Comm	&

Name		Rank	School		Degree	Year	University	
Williams, Susan Perry		C-Pr	Virginia	FMV	PHD	90.	Wisconsin	* &9-90
KPMG Professor								
Williams, Thomas H.		Retir	Virginia	2002	PHD	61.	Illinois	&9-96
Williamson, Delbert E.		Deces	CS-Long Bch		PHD	60.	Stanford	1960
Williamson, Donald T.		C-Pr	American U	X	LLM	83	Geotown	&9-85
Williamson, James E.		Prof	San Diego St	MX	PHD	68.	Minnesota	&1968
Williamson, Joan W.		Assoc	Delaware St	FACN	PHD	97	Delaware	&1976
Williamson, Michael G.		Asst	Texas-Austin	M	PHD	05.	Indiana	7-05
Williamson, Richard L.		Retir	Loyola Marym	1987	DBA	56.	Indiana	
4571 Blanchard Road; Placerville CA 95667								
Williamson, Robert W.		Retir	Notre Dame	2000	PHD	71.	Chicago	&9-67
Willinger, G. Lee		Prof	Oklahoma	FTV	DBA	82.	Fla St	&1-83
John F. Y. Stambaugh Centennial Professor								
Willingham, John J.		Retir	Texas-Austin	1996	PHD	63.	Ohio St	&9-93
Willis, Betsy		Lect	Baylor	PX	MTAX	87	Baylor	&1983
Willis, David M.		Assoc	Ill Wesleyan	ACFV	PHD	92.	Cincinnati	&9-95
Willis, Eugene		Emer	Illinois	2003	PHD	75.	Cincinnati	&9-75
Willis, G. W. Ketchel			Baylor		PHD	77.	Tx A&M	
Management Information Systems Dept								
Willis, H. David		Retir	Virg Comm	1990	MED	54	Va Tech	1956
Willis, Marilyn		Assoc	Tenn-Chattan	F	EDD	76	Kentucky	&9-76
Willis, Pauline		C-Le$	Dublin City	EFX	BCOM	82	NUI	&1987
Willis, Richard H.		Assoc	Vanderbilt	MF	PHD	98.	Chicago	&2006
Willis, Veronda		Asst	Tx-S Antonio	F	PHD	05.	Colorado	&2005
Willits, Stephen D.		Assoc	Bucknell	AF	PHD	86.	Tx Tech	&1-86
Willms, Matthias		Asst	Aachen Univ	FCM	MA	05	Aachen	2005
Wilmshurst, Trevor		SLect	Un Tasmania		MED		N Eng-Au	2003
Wilner, Neil A.		Assoc	North Texas	FMB	PHD	80.	Ohio St	&1987
Wilson, A. W.		Lect	Univ Ulster	FX	BSC			&1-81
Wilson, Arlette C.		Prof	Auburn	FMA	PHD	83.	Arkansas	# * &6-85
Charles M. Taylor Jr. Professor of Accounting								
Wilson, Beverley M.		Retir	Kansas	1998	PHD	83.	Arizona	1987
Wilson, Carol		Retir	Oral Roberts	2005	MS	63	Kansas St	8-75
Wilson, David A.			Ernst&Young	1994	PHD	72.	Illinois	&1978
Ernst & Young; 2000 National City Center; Cleveland OH 44114								
Wilson, Earl R.		Retir	Missouri	2003	PHD	82.	Missouri	&1982
Wilson, G. Peter		Prof	Boston Coll	FTE	PHD	85.	Car Mellon	1997
Joseph E. Sweeney Chair in Accounting								
Wilson, George R.		Asst	Louisiana St	FM	PHD	06.	Georgia	8-06
Wilson, Harold O.		Prof	Mid Tenn St	FMAQ	PHD	68.	Alabama	&1983
Wilson, James E.				FM	DBA	81.	Miss St	&
Wilson, John		Read	St Andrews	QF	PHD	99	Wales	2000
Wilson, Katherine A.		Retir	Embry-Riddle	FMPT	MBA	77	Stetson	&9-84
Wilson, Kerrie		ALect	W Sydney	AFOJ	BECO	98	Macquarie	
Wilson, Michael		Asst	Metro St-MN	F	MBA	94	Minnesota	&2001
Wilson, Michael D.		Retir	Wis-Eau Clar	FG	PHD	83.	Missouri	1-78
Wilson, Milton		Deces	Howard	2003	DBA	51.	Indiana	&1970
Wilson, Nicholas		Prof	Univ Leeds	MQ	PHD		Nottingh	7-98
Wilson, Paula A.				ATV	PHD	89.	U Wash	&
Wilson, Peter R.		Assoc	Duke	F	PHD	84.	N Carol	9-91
Wilson, R. Alan		Lect	Strathclyde	MD	MS	80	Durham	&1981
Wilson, R. Tim		Asst	Alcorn St	AF	PHD	06.	Miss	&1975
Wilson, Richard M. S.		H-Pr	Loughborough	EM	MSC	69	Bradford	* &1995
Wilson, Sonja B.		Asst	SC Upstate	X	JD	98	S Carol	2000
Wilson, Thomas E. Jr.		Prof	La-Lafayette	AFEG	PHD	91.	LSU	&8-90
Wilson, W. Tony		Asst	Delta State	FXVM	MBA	79	Delta St	# * &1981
Wilson, Wendy M.		Asst	So Methodist	FI	PHD	05.	N Carol	&8-05
Wilton, Robert		SLect	U Auckland	F	MCOM	78	Auckland	1996
Winborne, Marilyn G.					PHD	62.	Tx-Austin	
Wind, Emagene		Retir	S F Austin	1988	MBA	73	SF Austin	# * &1978
Windal, Floyd W.		Retir	Georgia	1995	PHD	59.	Illinois	&7-92
2704 Charlestowne Drive West; Mobile AL 36693; 334-660-6085								
Windham, Philip W.		Retir	No Carol St	1985	MS	58	Alabama	&1973
810 Emory Drive; Chapel Hill NC 27514								
Windler, John		Inst	Neb-Omaha	FM	MBA	89	Ne-Omaha	&1999
Windram, Brian		Lect	Napier Univ	A	BCOM			&1991
Windsor, Carolyn A.		SLect	Griffith Un	ABJT	PHD	95	Queensln	1990
Wines, Graeme		Assoc	Deakin-Warrn	AFT	MEC	92	N Eng-Au	&1984
Wingfield, Mervyn W.		Retir	Jms Madison	1993	PHD	63.	Illinois	&9-80
Winjum, James O.				F	PHD	70.	Illinois	&
Wink, Geri B.		Lect	Co St-Pueblo	FP	MBA	78	Sam Hous	&2004
Winkelman, Kenneth		Asst	SUNY Old Wes	CLMT	LLM	04	NYU	2004
Winkle, Gary M.		Deces	Georgia St	1-00	DBA	70.	Fla St	&9-70
Winsen, Joseph K.		Prof	U Newcastle	F	PHD	73.	Ohio St	&1977
Winston, Ralph J.			San Diego CA	1988	DBA	65.	Wash U	&
Winter, Kenneth M.		Assoc	Wis-La Cross	FPH	PHD	88.	Wisconsin	* &8-88
Winters, Alan J.		Prof	Clemson	AP	PHD	74.	Tx Tech	&1994

Wintgerbotham, Glyn J.	Asst	Tx-Arlington	FA	ABD		Oklahoma	& 8-07
Wirtz, Patrick T.	C-Ac	Detroit Merc	FMA	MBA	74	Detroit	&1985
Wise, Spence L.	Retir	Geo Southern	2005	MBA	66	Ohio U	&1988
Wise, Trevor D.	SLect	U Melbourne	FA	PHD	02	Melbourne	* &1988
Wiseman, Donald E.	Retir	Saginaw Vall	2000	PHD	71	Michigan	1979
Wiseman, Dorsey E.	Retir	CS-Fullerton	1992	PHD	57.	Illinois	&1961
Wisner, Priscilla S.	Asst	Montana St	M	PHD	97.	Tennessee	8-05
Witherspoon, Aaron	Asst	Grambling St	F	ABD		JacksonSt	& 8-88
Withsde, Elbert	Lect	Virje Univ	MFIU	MS	79	Erasmus	1982
Witmer, Philip R.	Assoc	Appalach St	AF	PHD	93.	Geo Wash	&1992
Witner, Lawrence H.	Assoc	Bryant	X	LLM	76	Geo Wash	& 8-92
Witt, Terry J.	Retir	Tx-Arlington	2000	MA	68	Oklahoma	&1968
Wittenbach, James L.	Prof	Notre Dame	X	DBA	71.	Oklahoma	& 5-72
Wittenberg Moerman, Regina	Asst	Pennsylvania	F	PHD	06	Chicago	2006
Witty, Michael J.	Deces	Central Conn	1990	MBA	73	Baruch	& 9-74
Wixon, Rufus	Retir	Pennsylvania	6-80	PHD	45.	Michigan	1949
Wnek, Robert	C-Pr	New Haven	XL	LLM		Boston U	& 9-78
Woan, Ronald J.	Assoc	Indiana U-PA	FS	PHD	88.	Fla St	1991
Woehrle, Stephen L.	Prof	Mn St-Mankat	MCG	PHD	78	Nebraska	1976
Woelfel, Charles J.	Retir	N Car-Greens	1993	PHD	57.	Tx-Austin	&1978
Wojdak, Joseph F.	Exec	Suffolk	AF	PHD	68.	LSU	2006
Wojdat, Kurt V.	SLect	Rochester	F	PHD	99.	SUNY-Buf	2000
Wolcott, Susan K.		WolcottLynch	FA	PHD	93.	Nrthwstrn	* &
Wolf, Allen E.				DBA		Harvard	
Wolf, James	Asst			PHD	06.	Ohio St	
Wolfe, Christopher J.	Prof	Texas A&M	S	DBA	84.	Kent St	& 1-85
KPMG Faculty Fellowship							
Wolfe, Glenn	Assoc	Toledo	S	PHD	84	Va Tech	1989
Wolfe, Singleton B.	Retir	Tennessee	1988	BS		Va Tech	1-81
Wolff, Bernard C.				PHD	76.	Arkansas	
Wolff, Eric D.			FTM	PHD	98.	MIT	
Wolfson, Mark A.	Consu	Stanford	FX	PHD	77.	Tx-Austin	&1977
Wolgamott, Charles W.	Prof	Ferris State	CGRN	PHD	87	Michigan	# * &1978
Wolinsky, Daniel	Retir	C W Post	1986	MBA		NYU	* &1940
Wolitzer, Philip	Emer	Lg Isl-Brook	2001	MBA	61	NYU	&1965
Wolk, Allan	Retir	Rochester	2004	JD	60	Syracuse	1962
Wolk, Carel M.			BFAJ	PHD	92.	Missouri	&
Wolk, Harry I.	Retir	Drake	2000	PHD	68.	Mich St	1968
Wollman, Jack B.			XF	PHD	71.	Illinois	&
Wolnizer, Peter W.	Dean	Univ Sydney	AFHI	PHD	86	Sydney	&1999
Wolverton, Janet Bear	Assoc	Oregon Tech	DSM	MS	89	Colorado	&1994
Wong, Betty	Asst	Athabasca Un		BCOM		Alberta	1991
Wong, Brossa	Asst	Lingnan U	XE	PHD	00	Xiamen	2002
Wong, David W. S.	Asst	Un Hong Kong	CM	MBA	82	York	9-76
Wong, Edmund	Inst	Chinese HK	AS	MBA	97	HKUST	&2001
Wong, Hannah C.			FMV	PHD	96.	UCLA	
Wong, Jeffrey	Asst	Nevada-Reno	M	PHD	99.	Oregon	2006
Wong, Jenny S. F.	Inst	City Univ HK	F	MA	98	HKUST	1-07
Wong, Jilnaught	H-Pr	U Auckland	FA	PHD	87	Auckland	&1992
Wong, Jody	Lect	HongKon Tech	X	MSC	00	HK Poly	2001
Wong, Jonathan W.			FM	PHD	92.	Ohio St	* &
Wong, M. H. Franco	Assoc	Univ Toronto	F	PHD	97.	Penn	2006
Wong, Moon-hung Franco				PHD	97.	Penn	
Wong, Norman	Assoc	U Auckland	FA	PHD	00	Auckland	1992
Wong, Percy	Lect	HongKon Tech	X	MBA	98	City U	2000
Wong, Raymond	Inst	Chinese HK	AF	MSC	04	HKU	2007
Wong, Raymond M. K.	TCons	Un Hong Kong	AF	PHD	05	Poly U	2005
Wong, Rita	Lect	HongKon Tech	AF	MSC	95	London	&2001
Wong, Sai On	TFell	City Univ HK	FM	MBA	83	Alberta	* 2002
Wong, Shu-Lun	Assoc	Memorial Un	MFEC	MSC	74	Durham	* 1985
Wong, Sunny T. M.	TFell	City Univ HK	VM	MBA	92	Heriot-W	* 1998
Wong, Tak Jun	C-Pr	Chinese HK	F	PHD	90.	UCLA	2004
Wong-Boren, Adrian			MFC	PHD	82.	Va Tech	&
Wong-On-Wing, Bernard	Prof	Wash State	SBCM	PHD	86.	Ariz St	1986
Wongwanich, Suree	Asst	Chulalongkor	CFMU	MACC	84	Arkansas	1971
Wood, Andrew	Asst	Univ Essex	FI	PHD	00	London	2001
Wood, Carol	Asst	Lander		MS		S Carol	
Wood, Dorothy	Lect	W Sydney	BFW	PHD	02	W Sydney	
Wood, Edwin A.	Deces	North Fla		PHD	76.	Florida	&1979
Wood, Lynette I.	Asst	Virg Tech	B	PHD	03.	Indiana	&2004
Wood, Rahnl A.	Assoc	NW Missouri	CMP	PHD	93.	St Louis	&1993
Wood, Robert	Lect	Ariz St West	SD	PHD	69	Berkeley	8-05
Wood, Thomas D.				PHD	71.	Florida	
Wood, Wallace R.	Assoc	Cincinnati	SM	DBA	80	Tennessee	&1980
Woodfield, Leon W.	Retir	Brigham Yg	2000	DBA	65.	Mich St	& 9-60
Wooding, Giles C.			MA	DBA	84.	Geo Wash	* &
Woodland, Angela M.	Asst	Louisiana St	SAF	PHD	01.	Missouri	& 8-04

Name	Rank	School		Degree		University	
Woodliff, David R.	Asst	W Australia	F	PHD	96	W Austrl	1991
Woodlock, Peter D.	C-Pr	Youngstown	CF	PHD	90.	Ohio St	&9-95
Woodman, Martha (Marti)	Lect	Vermont	MCF	MBA	78	Mo-Ks Cty	* 1984
Woodroof, Jonathan B.	Assoc	Tennessee	S	PHD	94	Tx Tech	&8-99
Woodruff, Gregg S.	Assoc	W Illinois	X	PHD	03	Memphis	&9-01
Woods, Dexter R.	Prof	Ohio Northrn	LXPR	LLM	84	Florida	&1987
Woods, Janet	Assoc	Macon State	CFM	MBA	79	Georgia	&1989
Woods, Janet L.	Lect	Appalach St	P	MS	00	Appalach	&2001
Woods, Margaret M.	SLect	U Nottingham	M	MSC	80	London	&2001
Woods, Monica	Inst	Kansas State	FM	MACC	00	Kansas St	8-05
Woods, Richard S.	Retir	Pennsylvania	1987	PHD	57	Penn	&1947
62 Snyder Lane; Springfield PA 19064							
Woods, Roger	Asst	NW Missouri	CPFV	MBA	81	NW Mo St	* &1981
Woodward, Philip L.	Assoc	Biola	MPVX	MBT	81	S Calif	1990
Woollen, Mary	Inst	Hawaii-Manoa	FM	MACC	97	Hawaii	&8-02
Woolley, Darryl J.	Asst	Idaho	FS	PHD	02.	Utah	&2007
Woolley, James W.	Retir	Utah	2005	PHD	65.	Tx-Austin	&1968
Woolsey, Samuel M.	Retir	Houston	1981	PHD	54.	Tx-Austin	&1957
Woon, P. P.	Tutor	Massey Univ					
Wooten, Thomas C.	Assoc	Belmont	AP	PHD	94.	Geo St	&1994
Wootton, Charles W. (Bill)	Prof	E Illinois	FHV	DBA	82.	Miss St	1988
Workman, Jan	Lect	East Carol	FM	MBA	90	E Carol	1995
Worrells, Cecil E.		Redmond WA	1991	PHD	74.	Illinois	
20336 NE 34th Ct; Redmond WA 98053							
Worsham, Ronald G. Jr.	Assoc	Brigham Yg	X	PHD	94.	Florida	1-94
LeAnn Albrecht Fellow							
Worthington, James S.	Retir	Auburn	2000	PHD	76.	Missouri	&9-76
Worthington, Michael	Lect	Elizabeth Ct	AF	MBA		E Carol	&1983
Woudstra, Andrew	Retir	Athabasca Un		MBA	78	W Ontario	1981
Wragge, John H.	Assoc	Delaware	AS	PHD	75.	Houston	&1981
Wrege, William T.	Assoc	Ball State	FGN	DBA	84.	Kentucky	&9-87
Wright, Albert W.	Deces	CS-Northrdge		PHD	65	UCLA	&1965
Wright, Allan R.	Retir	Jackson CC		PHD	72.	Mich St	
7111 Kirkglade Ct; Houston TX 77095							
Wright, Anna	SLect	Tech-Sydney		PHD	05	Tech-Sydn	2000
Wright, Arnold M.	Prof	Northeastern	ABIE	PHD	79.	S Calif	&9-07
Joseph M. Golemme Research Professor of Accounting							
Wright, Brian	Lect	Univ Exeter	CF	MSC	98	Aberyst	2001
Wright, Carl N.	C-Ac	Virginia St	AM	PHD	03.	JacksonSt	&9-76
Wright, Charlotte J.	Prof	Oklahoma St	MCB	PHD	82.	North Tx	&1982
Wilton T. Anderson Professor of Accounting							
Wright, Chris	Prof	Lincoln-NZ	GST	PHD	92	Simon Fr	* 2006
Wright, Clifford S.	Prof	Xavier-LA	FAXL	MBA		Loyola	&
Wright, David W.	Assoc	Michigan	AF	PHD	86.	Mich St	&1984
Wright, Diane	Inst	Delaware	S	MS	94	Delaware	2001
Wright, Frank J.	Retir	Duquesne	1988	PHD	61.	Pittsburgh	1949
Wright, Gail B.	Retir	Bryant	2007	PHD	85.	Geo Wash	&8-94
Wright, Gail E.	Prof	Albright	XAI	MBA	75	Pittsburgh	# &1989
Wright, Iain A.	SLect	Napier Univ	FA	MACC			&2-75
Wright, Jennifer J.	Inst	Drexel	FX	MST	94	Villanova	&1995
Wright, Lorraine W.	Assoc	N Carol St	BXM	PHD	92.	Va Tech	1992
Wright, Michael E.	Assoc	Univ Calgary	FIZW	PHD	89	Queen's	1989
Wright, Mike	Prof	U Nottingham	FU	PHD	86	Nottingh	1978
Wright, Orville	Deces	Morgan State	2007	JD	85	Baltimore	&1994
Wright, Sally	Prof	Mass-Boston	MAB	DBA	93.	Boston U	&1991
Wright, Susan J.	SLect	Macquarie Un	F	PHD	97	Macquarie	1985
Wright, Suzanne A.	Inst	Penn State	F	MBA	92	Penn St	&8-96
Wright, William B.	Asst	Albany State	PX	MBA	78	Valdosta	9-82
Wright, William E.	Retir	Abilene Chr	2001	PHD	56.	Tx-Austin	&1956
Wright, William F.	VAsst	Illinois	M	PHD	75.	Berkeley	8-05
Wruck, Karen Hopper			F	PHD	88.	Rochester	
Wu, Anne	Prof	Nat Chengchi	MFQ	PHD	90.	Geo Wash	* &1990
Wu, Chung-Fern (Rebecca)	Prof	Nat Taiwan U	ADMS	PHD	87	UCLA	& 1-90
Wu, Donghui	Asst	HongKon Tech	AFI	PHD	03	CUHK	2005
Wu, Eng C.	Asst	Boston Univ	FCM	DBA	96.	Boston U	9-05
Wu, Frederick H.	Retir	North Texas	SM	PHD	75.	Tx Tech	* 1993
Wu, Jia	Asst	Mass-Dartmou	F	PHD	06	Rutgers	2005
Wu, Jirong				DBA	00.	Clev St	
Internal Audit; Eaton Corporation							
Wu, Joanna S.	Assoc	Rochester	FT	PHD	99.	Tulane	1999
Wu, Martin G. H.	Asst	Illinois	FM	PHD	95	Brit Colum	08-0
Wu, Min	Asst	Hong Kong Sc	IF	PHD	02.	NYU	2002
Wu, Se-Hwa	Prof	Nat Chengchi		PHD	84	Chungchi	1983
Wu, Steven	ALect	Macquarie Un					
Wu, Tsing Tzai			FSMP	PHD	87.	Baruch	
Wu, Woody	Prof	Chinese HK	FM	PHD	92.	NYU	1995
Wuller, Charles Edgar	Retir	St Louis	1988	PHD	54	St Louis	1943

Wunder, Haroldene F. (Deenie)	Prof	CS-Sacrament	FX	PHD	78.	S Carol	&8-93
Wurst, Christian	Inst	Temple	FMX	MBA	96	Rutgers	1998
Wyatt, Anne	Asst	Tech-Sydney	F	PHD	02	Tech-Sydn	* 2007
Wyatt, Arthur R.	Emer	Illinois		PHD	53.	Illinois	&1993
Wyatt, Kim	SLect	Monash Univ	EFX	MTAX	92	Melbourne	&1989
Wyatt, Robert L.	Dir	Drury	C	PHD	93.	Memphis	# * &1996
Wyer, Jean C.		Coopers&Lybr	2003	EDD	80	Wm&Mary	&1978

Coopers & Lybrand; 1251 Ave of Americas; NY NY 10020; 212-536-3270

Wygal, Donald E.	Assoc	Rider	FMEI	PHD	77.	Pittsburgh	1984
Wyler, Wayne E.	Retir	CS-Sacrament	1992	PHD	75	N Colo	&1973
Wyman, Harold E.	Retir	Fla Internat	2001	PHD	67	Stanford	1990
Wyndelts, Robert W.	Retir	Arizona St	2004	PHD	74.	Georgia	&1974
Wynn-Williams, Kate	H-SLe	Univ Otago	NME	PHD	99	Otago	1994
Wysocki, Peter D.	Assoc	MIT	F	PHD	99.	Rochester	2001
Wysong, Earl M. Jr.	Retir	Loyola-Maryl	1989	DBA	72.	Geo Wash	&1980
Xiao, Jason Zezhong	Prof	Cardiff U	I	PHD	95	Napier	1987
Xie, Hong	Asst	Illinois	FM	PHD	98.	Iowa	7-01
Xie, Jia-Zheng James	D-Pr	Chinese HK	AFMT	PHD	91	Brit Colum	1999
Xie, Shibin		HongKongSci	F	PHD	04.	Iowa	
Xie, Yuan	VAsst	Tulane		PHD	06.	Utah	
Xiong, Yan	Asst	CS-Sacrament	S	PHD	03.	Wash St	8-02
Xu, Bixia	Asst	Wilfrid Laur		PHD	03	Concordia	2002
Xu, Gary	Prof	Cardiff U	Q	PHD	93	Lancaster	2005
Xu, Le (Emily)	Asst	New Hampshir	F	PHD	03.	Mass	2003
Xu, Li	Asst	Morgan State	F	PHD	06.	Duke	2006
Xu, Lianzan	C-Pr	Wm Paterson	FVM	PHD	96.	Kentucky	1996
Xu, Wei	Asst	Wm Paterson	FTM	PHD	07	Rutgers	2004
Xu, Weihong	Asst	SUNY-Buffalo	F	PHD	00.	Wash U	2004
Xu, Yin	Asst	Old Dominion	BMF	PHD	01.	S Carol	2001
Xu, Zhaohui	Asst	Houston-Cl L	AF	PHD	07	Alabama	9-07
Xue, Jian	Asst	Hong Kong Sc		PHD	06.	Car Mellon	
Xue, Yanfeng	Asst	Texas-Austin	F	PHD	04.	MIT	8-04
Xydias, Maria	LectB	Flinders Un	SCM	MCOM	97	Adelaide	1-93
Yaansah, Robert A.	Assoc	Univ Ottawa	FM	PHD	90	Lancaster	&2001
Yaari, Varda	Assoc	Morgan State	T	PHD	89.	NYU	
Yadav, Pradeep K.	Prof	Strathclyde	F	PHD	92	Strathcl	1988
Yaekura, Takashi	Asst	Hosey Univ	2004	PHD	01.	Illinois	
Yager, E. Ben	Retir	Miami U-Ohio	1989	DBA	57.	Indiana	&1955
Yahr, Robert B.	Assoc	Marquette	FGVT	PHD	79.	Nebraska	&9-77
Yahya-Zadeh, Massood	Assoc	Geo Mason	FM	PHD	92.	Syracuse	&
Yakhou, Mehenna	Prof	Georgia Col	MI	PHD	85	Ca-Irvine	1994
Yallapragada, RamMohan R.	Assoc	Fayetteville		PHD	82.	Houston	&
Yamamura, Jeanne H.	Assoc	Nevada-Reno	AS	PHD	95.	Wash St	&1993
Yamashita, Gary A.		Fremont CA	1988	PHD	70.	Columbia	
Yammeesri, J.	Lect	Massey-Alban		PHD		Wollong	2004
Yampuler, Michael E.	Asst	Houston	F	PHD	04	Harvard	9-04
Yan, Meng		Fordham	FM	DBA	05.	Boston U	9-06
Yan, Yun-chia	Asst	CS-Pomona	FSA	PHD	07	Fla Intl	2007
Yancey, William F.			X	PHD	93.	Tx-Austin	&

www.willyancey.com; 6848 Mldrest Dr; Dallas TX 75240; 972-387-8558

Yandow, Thomas H.	Asst	Norwich	ACF	MBA	98	Lincoln	&2000
Yang, David C.	Prof	Hawaii-Manoa	FI	PHD	85.	Columbia	* 1-85
Yang, Dong-Hoon				PHD	99.	Syracuse	

Information and Communications University

Yang, James G. S.	Prof	Montclair St	XVFM	ABD		NYU	* &1982
Yang, Jing-Wen (Margaret)	Asst	CS-East Bay	F	PHD	07	Maryland	
Yang, Joon S.	Asst	Minn-Duluth	FMS	PHD	02.	Temple	2002
Yang, Rong	Asst	SUNY-Brockpo	FIKT	PHD	04.	Rutgers	&2004
Yang, Simon S. M.	Asst	Adelphi	MN	PHD	00	Houston	&2000
Yang, Sunny	Asst	Texas-Austin	F	PHD	06.	Colorado	&7-06
Yang, Ya-wen	Asst	U Miami	F	PHD	03.	Tennessee	&2004
Yang, Yong	Asst	Chinese HK	F	PHD	05.	Nrthwstrn	2005
Yang, Zhi Feng	Asst	City Univ HK	F	PHD	06	Alberta	8-06
Yankee, Glen G.	Retir	Cleveland St	1979	PHD	52.	Illinois	&1968
Yap, Christine L.	STut	U Newcastle	CFP	MCOM	99	Newcastle	&1989
Yapa, Premasiri	SLect	LaTrobe Univ	AEJ	PHD	02	RMIT	2003
Yarbrough, Kathryn	Lect	N Car-Charl	F	MBA	83	Winthrop	2003
Yardley, James A.	Assoc	Virg Tech	AF	PHD	86.	Illinois	&1986
Yares, Jerry R.	Retir	West Florida	2002	ABD		Alabama	&1-73
Yarr, Margaret	Lect	U Portsmith		MSC			2003
Ye, Cheong Heon				PHD	97.	UCLA	
Ye, Jianming	Assoc	CUNY-Baruch	F	PHD	92	Chicago	2001
Ye, Zhongxia (Shelly)				PHD	06.	Temple	
Yeakel, John A.	Retir	New Mexico	7-90	PHD	71.	Florida	&1965
Yeargan, Percy B. (Skip)	Retir	Alabama-Birm	1982	PHD	57.	Alabama	&9-77

209 Wheeler Street; Alexander City AL 35010

Yeary, James D.	Retir	SW Texas St	1997	PHD	75.	Okla St	&1974

Yeaton, Kathryn G.	Asst	Ramapo	FM	PHD	94.	S Fla	&2003
Yee, Helen	Lect	Deakin-Geelg	F	MA	84	Dundee	1992
Yee, Kenton K.	Asst	Columbia	FLT	PHD	01.	Stanford	2001
Yeh, Shu	Assoc	Nat Taiwan U	FM	PHD	90.	UCLA	2-93
Yehuda, Nir	Asst	Cornell		PHD	05.	Columbia	2005
Yei, Maywa				PHD	99.	S Fla	
Yellin, William	Prof	St Fran-NY	FXAC	MBA	61	NYU	&1972
Yelvington, Brenda	Asst	Ark St		PHD	98.	Miss	&
Arkansas State University - Fort Smith							
Yen, Alex C.	Asst	Suffolk	AFB	PHD	04.	Tx-Austin	&2005
Yeo, Gillian H. H.	Prof	Nanyang Tech	FT	PHD	90.	Illinois	&1984
Yeo, Julian J. L.	Asst	Columbia	F	PHD	03	Melbourne	2004
Yerep, Stanley J.	Asst	Pitts-Johnst	FAM	MED	72	Ind-Penn	&2004
Yerkes, Russell E.	Retir	Roosevelt	1992	PHD	75.	SUNY-Buf	&1985
305 55th St NW; Bradenton Fl 34209							
Yetman, Michelle H.	Asst	Cal-Davis	FT	PHD	01.	N Carol	&2003
Yetman, Robert J.	Assoc	Cal-Davis	FA	PHD	00.	N Carol	&2003
Yetmar, Scott A.	Asst	Cleveland St	BDJX	PHD	95.	Okla St	* &2002
Yeung, Daniel	Lect	W Sydney-Nep	SEMB	MCOM	96	Wollong	1997
Yeung, Ping Eric	Asst	Georgia	FS	PHD	03.	Oregon	8-03
Yeutter, John P.	Asst	NE St-Okla	XFJC	PHD	96.	Oklahoma	&1995
Yhin, Hark Ppin				DBA	94.	Miss St	
Yi, Cheong H.	Asst	HongKon Tech	VF	PHD	97	UCLA	1997
Yi, Han S.	Asst	Oklahoma	F	PHD	06.	Mich St	2006
Yi, Hwa D.				PHD	94.	UCLA	
Yi, Jaekyung	Assoc	Kookmin Univ	FKPV	PHD	92.	Tx-Austin	8-93
Yim, Andrew T. L.	Asst	City Univ HK	AMT	PHD	95	Yale	2001
Yin, Qin Jennifer	Asst	Tx-S Antonio	FM	PHD	99.	Houston	&2005
Yip, David S. O.	VAsoc	City Univ HK	CMT	MSC	87	LondonEc	9-89
Yoder, Timothy R.	Asst	Miss State	X	PHD	06.	Penn St	8-06
Yohn, Teri Lombardi	Assoc	Indiana	F	PHD	91.	Indiana	&2007
Yon, Donna-Lynn			AFM	PHD	85.	Tx A&M	&
Yoo, Chung-Eul		Kyunggi Univ	1995	PHD	88.	Purdue	
Kyunggi University; Seoul, Korea							
Yoo, Kwan H.	Prof	Korea Univ	MC	PHD	85.	Indiana	3-95
Yoo, Seung-Weon			AMT	PHD	97.	Wisconsin	
Yoo, Yong K.		Singapore Mg		PHD	04.	Columbia	
Yoon, Myung Ho	Assoc	NE Illinois	CMQS	PHD	88.	Houston	1-89
Yoon, Soon Suk		Chonnam Natl	1996	PHD	87.	Wisconsin	
Chonnam National University							
Yoon, Sung Sig		Korea	1989	PHD	87.	Berkeley	1988
Yoon, Sung-Soo			M	PHD	95.	Illinois	
Yoon, SungWook	Asst	Winona State	FV	PHD	04.	Colorado	2004
Yori, Robert P.			XCAI	PHD	84.	Penn St	&
Yost, Gregory C.	Prof	West Florida	A	EDD	85	Fla St	&1977
Yost, Jeffrey A.	Assoc	Charleston	MVY	PHD	89.	Ohio St	&2000
Young, Allister	C-Ac	Brock Univ	X	LLM	01	Toronto	* 1982
Young, Arthur E.	Asst	Fort Hays St	AXF	PHD	02.	Tx Tech	&2006
Young, Danqing	Assoc	Chinese HK	BCM	PHD	98.	Conn	1998
Young, David W.	Retir	Boston Univ	NMCU	DBA	77	Harvard	9-85
Young, Elmer R.	Retir	Utah	7-80	PHD	53	Columbia	1948
Young, Gail T.				DBA	86.	Geo Wash	&
Young, George R.	Assoc	Fla Atlantic	ABFX	PHD	96.	Tx-Arlin	&1996
Young, Harding B.				DBA	55.	Harvard	
Young, James C.	C-Pr	No Illinois	X	PHD	88.	Mich St	&8-00
Crowe Chizek Professor of Accountancy							
Young, Joni J.	Prof	New Mexico	FH	PHD	91.	Illinois	&1992
REDW Lecturer							
Young, Laura	Inst	Cen Arkansas	F	MAC	81	Cen Ark	&1-00
Young, Marilyn N.	Assoc	Belmont	PX	PHD	00.	Miss	&2001
Young, Nicola	Prof	St Marys-Cdn	FVP	MBA	82	Dalhousie	&1993
Young, Raymond	ALect	Macquarie Un					
Young, Richard A.	Prof	Ohio State	BCMY	PHD	84.	Ohio St	1990
Young, Roger D.	Prof	Bluffton		MBA	64	Xavier	&2001
Young, Ronald M.	Assoc	New Orleans	S	PHD	92.	Tx Tech	&1991
Energy Accounting and Tax Conference Profesor							
Young, S. David	Prof	INSEAD	F	PHD	85	Virginia	&1989
Young, S. Mark	Prof	So Calif	BCM	PHD	83.	Pittsburgh	7-92
KPMG Foundation Professor							
Young, Steven	SLect	U Lancaster	FM	PHD	95	Lancaster	2000
Young, Susan M.	Assoc	CUNY-Baruch	F	PHD	00.	S Calif	9-05
Youngberg, Suzanne	Inst	No Illinois	FX	MST	91	DePaul	&8-00
Younkins, Edward	Prof	Wheeling Col		PHD	84.	Miss	
Youssef, Leon A.	Retir	CS-Northrdge	1989	PHD	70.	Minnesota	1966
21525 Pch; Malibu CA 90265							
Yu, Carol Shaokun	Asst	No Illinois	FA	PHD	07.	Houston	&2007
Yu, Hung-Chao	Assoc	Nat Chengchi	ACFM	PHD	96.	Wisconsin	1996

Name	Rank	School		Degree		School	
Yu, Jeff Jiewei	Asst	MIT	F	PHD	07	Ohio St	2007
Yu, Lichen	ALect	Macquarie Un					
Yu, Minna	Asst	Ball State	F	ABD		Kent St	8-06
Yu, Se Hwan	Retir	Korea Univ	2003	PHD	64.	Wash U	3-56
Yu, Seongjae	Prof	Korea Adv In	CFM	PHD	72.	Minnesota	9-02
Yu, Shih Cheng	Retir	Florida	D-88	PHD	52	Iowa	9-67
Yu, Sui-Hua	Asst	Ntl Chung Ch	CFM	PHD	03	Chengchi	2003
Yu, Wayne	Assoc	HongKon Tech	F	PHD	97	Alberta	1999
Yu, Wen	Asst	St Thomas-MN	KFE	PHD	07.	Case Wes	9-07
Yu, Yong	Asst	Texas-Austin	F	PHD	06.	Penn St	8-06
Yue, Li	Assoc	Univ Toronto	FM	PHD	95	Queen's	1994
Yuen, Alexander E. C.	Prof	San Fran St	AGNI	PHD	89	Golden Gt	&9-80
Yuen, Kam-por	Lect	HongKon Tech	FT	MBA	91	Sheffield	2000
Yuen, Susana	Assoc	HongKon Tech	CMU	PHD	98	Bond	&1997
Yuhas, Michael A.	Prof	Grand Valley	X	LLM	80	Geotown	&1985
Yui, Shin Min Sherman				PHD	45.	LSU	
Yun, Joo-Kwang			FM	PHD	89.	Wisconsin	
Yundt, Charles L.	Deces	Tx-Pan Amer	2-89	PHD	85	Alabama	1967
Yunker, Penelope J.	Retir	W Illinois	D-04	PHD	82.	St Louis	&9-76
Yurkovac, William	Inst	Intl College		MS			
Yurkow, John	Retir	Delta State	1988	MBA	50	Miss	&1958
Yuschak, Marjorie E.	Inst	Rutgers-N Br	FM	MBA	84	Fairl Dick	* 2002
Yuthas, Kristi	Assoc	Portland St	MSWJ	PHD	91.	Utah	1999
Swigert Professor Information Systems							
Zabriskie, Fern	Asst	Pacific Luth	MF	PHD	02.	U Wash	* &2001
Zach, Tzachi	Asst	Wash Univ	F	PHD	04.	Rochester	2002
Zachry, Benny R.	Prof	Nicholls St	AFMS	DBA	85.	La Tech	&8-93
Zachry, Earl	Retir	Houston-Cl L	2002	LLM	84	Florida	1984
Zacur, Howard A.	Retir	U Miami-Fla		PHD	53	Pittsburgh	1947
Zagier, Allen F.V.	Prof	St Peters	C	MBA		Geo Wash	&1978
Zahi, Lotfi	Inst	Univ Tunis	FG	ECM	97	ISCAE	1999
Zaiac, Manuel	Retir	U Miami	1988	JD	54	U Miami	&1947
Zaid, Omar A.	Prof	King Fahd Un	HAE	PHD	78	CS-Humbo	2002
Zaidi, Baqar A.	Deces	CS-Sacramen	1984	DBA	66	U Wash	1969
Zakrzewski, Dorothea	ALect	W Sydney	EIMF	MINT	02	Bond	
Zakrzwski-Smiach, Deborah	Assoc	Pitts-Johnst	FADN	MBA	89	Pittsburgh	&1986
Zaman, Mahbub	Lect	U Manchester	FA	MA	95	Essex	&
Zammeeruddin, Rizvanna	Asst	Wis-Parkside	LX	JD	01	DePaul	8-03
Zamora, Valentina L.	Asst	Boston Coll	FM	PHD	03.	U Wash	2003
Zandarski, Joseph R.	Retir	Scranton	2004	PHD	64	Pittsburgh	&1951
Zang, Amy	Asst	Rochester	F	PHD	06.	Duke	2006
Zani, William M.		Industry		DBA	68.	Harvard	
Zanibbi, Louis	Prof	Laurentian	BCMU	PHD	89	Bradford	* 7-77
Zant, Robert F.				PHD	71.	Florida	
Zanzig, Jeffrey S.	Asst	Jacksonvl St	S	PHD	98.	Miss	# * &8-00
Zapalski, Christopher	Asst	Warner So		JD	02	Nova SE	2002
Zappala, Frederick J.	Retir	Boston Coll	1996	MBA	47	Penn	&1948
Zarb, Bert	Asst	Embry-Riddle	FMPI	DBA	04	Argosy	&1998
Zarowin, Paul A.	Assoc	New York U	F	PHD	85.	Chicago	1984
Zarrouk, Ridha	H-As	Univ Tunis	SAV	DOC	90	IGR France	&1994
Zarzeski, Marilyn T.	Retir	Mississippi	2004	PHD	94.	Florida	&8-99
Zaumeyer, David J.	Assoc	Rutgers-N Br	A	PHD	79	Columbia	&1982
Zaunbrecher, Hilary C.			FX	PHD	74.	LSU	&
Zavgren, Christine V.			FMJ	PHD	81.	Nebraska	&
Zawati, Abdel K.		Lakewood CO	1990	PHD	77.	LSU	
1808 S Union Ct; Lakewood CO 80228							
Zaziri, Lassaad	Inst	Univ Tunis	F	EXPC	99	ISCAE	1999
Zebda, Awni M.	Prof	Tx A&M-C Chr	BCM	PHD	82.	Va Tech	9-94
Zeff, Stephen A.	Prof	Rice	FHT	PHD	62.	Michigan	1978
Herbert S. Autrey Professor							
Zeghal, Daniel	Prof	Univ Ottawa	FM	PHD	79	Laval	1977
Zehms, Karl M.	C-Ac	Wl-Green Bay	FG	PHD	70.	Wisconsin	&9-70
Zeidan, Rabih	Asst	Am U Sharjah		PHD	07.	Houston	8-07
Zeigler, James F.	Inst	Bowling Gr	P	MBA	84	Toledo	&2001
Zeisel, Gerald A.		Jerusalem In	M	PHD	72.	Ohio St	&1978
Zekany, Kay E.	Asst	Ohio Northrn	FCMP	PHD	94.	S Carol	* 1998
Zelcer, Moishe	Assoc	CUNY-Brookly	DMF	PHD	91.	Baruch	&2-77
Zelin, Robert C. II	Assoc	Mn St-Mankat	MD	PHD	91.	Indiana	* &1993
Zeller, Thomas L.	Prof	Loyola-Chicg	CMS	PHD	91.	Kent St	&9-91
Zeng, Tao	Assoc	Wilfrid Laur	XF	PHD	00	Queen's	1998
Zenios, Stavros A.	Prof	Cyprus	F	PHD	86	Princeton	1993
Zetts, Jerome E.	Retir	Youngstown	2000	MBA	67	Wayne St	&9-67
Zhan, Ran				PHD	06.	Colorado	
Zhang, Frank X.	Asst	Yale	XT	PHD	06	Chicago	7-05
Zhang, Guochang	Prof	Hong Kong Sc	FMT	PHD	92	Brit Colum	1993
Zhang, Helen	Asst	Ohio State	F	PHD		Minnesota	2006
Zhang, Huai	Assoc	Nanyang Tech	F	PHD	00.	Columbia	2006

Zhang, Ivy Xiying	Asst	Minnesota	IF	PHD	06.	Rochester	2005
Zhang, Jian				PHD	05.	Ariz St	
Zhang, Jieying	Asst	So Calif	F	PHD	05.	MIT	2005
Zhang, Li	Asst	UCLA	FM	PHD	99.	Car Mellon	7-99
Zhang, Liping	Asst	Cincinnati		PHD	06.	Geo Wash	
Zhang, May H.	Asst	Missouri	F	PHD	05.	Tx-Austin	2005
Zhang, Mingshan	Asst	Hong Kong Sc	F	PHD	05.	UCLA	2005
Zhang, Ping	Assoc	Univ Toronto	A	PHD	94	Waterloo	&2000
Zhang, Sanjian (William)	Asst	Lehigh		PHD	06.	Ca-Irvine	
Zhang, Suning	Asst	Geo Mason		PHD		Minnesota	
Zhang, Tianyu	Asst	City Univ HK	F	PHD	05	HKUST	2005
Zhang, Wei	Assoc	SUNY-Albany	FM	PHD	00.	Nebraska	2007
Zhang, Xiao-Jun	C-Ac	Cal-Berkeley	F	PHD	98.	Columbia	1998

Emile R. Niemela Associate Professor of Accounting

Zhang, Yan	Asst	SUNY-Bingham	F	PHD	04.	LSU	2004
Zhang, Yifeng	Asst	SUNY-Albany	FS	ABD		Tx-Dallas	2007
Zhang, Yinglei	Asst	Chinese HK	F	PHD	05.	Ohio St	2005
Zhang, Yinqi	Asst	American U	F	PHD	06.	Temple	&9-06
Zhang, Yong	Asst	Hong Kong Sc	F	PHD	06.	Rochester	2005
Zhang, Yuan	Asst	Columbia	F	PHD	03.	S Calif	2003
Zhang, Yue (May)	Asst	Northeastern	MB	PHD	06.	Pittsburgh	9-06
Zhang, Yun (Clement)	Asst	Duke	M	PHD	04	Yale	2003
Zhao, Limount	Asst	Southern Ark		PHD		Miss St	2002
Zhao, Ronald	Asst	Monmouth	FMI	PHD	94.	Tx Tech	* &2002
Zhao, Yijiang	Asst	Alaska-Fairb	F	PHD	05.	Nebraska	8-06
Zheng, Lin (Sandy)	Asst	NE Illinois	FA	PHD	04.	Alabama	9-04
Zheng, Liu	Asst	Un Hong Kong	FM	PHD	03	S Calif	2003
Zhong, Ke	Asst	Texas-Tyler		PHD	05.	S Illinois	2004
Zhou, Flora	Lect	Illinois	FM	PHD	07	Cornell	8-06
Zhou, Haiyan	Asst	Tx-Pan Amer	FA	PHD	03.	Temple	9-03
Zhou, Jian	Asst	SUNY-Bingham	F	PHD	00.	Syracuse	&2001
Zhou, Lei	Asst	McGill Univ	M	PHD	02.	Maryland	2004
Zhou, Ling	Asst	Tulane	FM	PHD	04	Yale	2004
Zhou, Nan	Assoc	SUNY-Bingham	F	PHD	00	Minnesota	1999
Zhou, Ping			E	PHD	02.	Geo St	
Zhou, Yibin	Asst	Texas-Dallas	FMY	PHD	06	Toronto	2006
Zhu, Hong	Asst	Loyola-MD	FM	PHD	05.	Missouri	2003
Zhuang, Zili	Asst	Chinese HK	FM	PHD	01	Car Mellon	2006
Ziebart, David A.	D-Pr	Kentucky	NFT	PHD	83.	Mich St	&8-05
Ziebell, Mary			MFB	PHD	78.	U Wash	
Ziegenfuss, Douglas E.	C-Ac	Old Dominion	AOJS	PHD	89.	Va Comm	# * &1988
Ziegler, Richard E.	Emer	Illinois	2002	PHD	73.	N Carol	&9-72
Ziegler, Teresa	SLect	Ohio State	F	MBA	88	Ohio St	&1998
Zieha, Eugene L.	Retir	Maryland	6-90	PHD	52.	Illinois	* 8-85

500 Nichols Road Suite 403; Kansas City MO 64112

Zilca, Shlomi	SLect	U Auckland	F	PHD	03	Tel Aviv	2002
Zimbelman, Mark F.	Assoc	Brigham Yg	A	PHD	96.	Arizona	8-99

Selvoy J. Boyer Research Fellow

Zimmer, Robert K.	Emer	Denver	2000	PHD	64.	Ohio St	1983
Zimmerman, Jerold L.	Prof	Rochester	FTM	PHD	74.	Berkeley	1974

Ronald L. Bittner Professor of Business Administration

Zimmerman, John C.	Assoc	Nev-L Vegas	XF	JD	89	Southwes	&1989
Zimmerman, Vernon K.	Deces	Illinois	N-96	PHD	54.	Illinois	&1949
Zimmermann, Harvey	Inst	North Texas	AFO	MBA	72	North Tx	&8-02
Zimmermann, Raymond A.	C-Ac$	Txs-El Paso	LX	PHD	91.	Tx Tech	9-92
Zin, Michael	Deces	Univ Windsor		PHD	62.	Mich St	9-56
Zinck, George E. R.	Retir	Dalhousie	1989	BCOM	61	Dalhousie	&1964
Ziv, Amir			FMAT	PHD	90.	Stanford	
Zlatkovich, Charles P.			F	PHD	76	Tx-Austin	
Zlatkovich, Charles T.	Deces	Texas-Austin	2002	PHD	52.	Tx-Austin	&1940
Zmijewski, Mark E.	Prof	Chicago	FDP	PHD	83.	SUNY-Buf	1984

Leon Carroll Marshall Prof of Atg; Deputy Dean Part-Time MBA Prog; 312 area

Zoky, David C.	Prof	Mount Union	ACFP	MBA	79	Youngstwn	&1979
Zollo, Raynard	Assoc	St John's	FAS	MBA	82	St Johns	&9-82
Zook, John	Asst	LaSalle	FX	MBA		Drexel	&1-79
Zordan, Anthony	Prof	St FrancisIL	PAFX	DBA	98	Nova SE	* &1983
Zorr, William G.	Retir	Wis-Oshkosh	1998	MBA	58	Nrthwstrn	1966
Zorski, Christopher	Assoc	Detroit Merc	FM	PHD	74	Warsaw	&1985
Zoubi, Taisier A.	Prof	Am U Sharjah	FMIZ	PHD	92.	North Tx	2004
Zrihen, Robert	Asst	ESCP deParis	BCMU	PHD	02	Paris Daup	1996
Zuaiter, Farouq A.		Kuwait		PHD	74.	Tx Tech	
Zubaidah, Ismail	Asst	Natl Singapo	AF	PHD	93	NS Wales	&1994
Zuber, Jill	Asst	Wash State	M	ABD		Arkansas	2006
Zucca, Linda J.	Assoc	Kent State	F	PHD	89.	Case Wes	&8-88
Zuckerman, Gilroy J.	Prof	N Carol St	CQ	PHD	74	N Car St	1979
Zulauf, Dwight J.	Retir	Pacific Luth	1992	PHD	65.	Minnesota	&1949

710 South 120th St; Tacoma WA 98444

Zuliani, Elisa	Tut	Univ Toronto	FM	BBA	87	Ryerson	1991
Zupanc, Thomas	Assoc	St Cloud St	XL	LLM	82	Geo Wash	2000
Zurek, Danette	Assoc	LaSierra	AXON	MBA	98	Andrews	&2006
Zutshi, Ajay		Industry		PHD	95.	NYU	
Zvinakis, Kristina	Lect	Texas-Austin	X	PHD	99.	Tx-Austin	& 9-05
Zwicker, Charles H.	Retir	Lg Isl-Post	2004	MBA	50	NYU	&1942
Zwicker, Robert P.	Asst	Pace-Westch	FRV	EDD	91	Bridgepr	&1983
Zysman, Simon J.				DBA	73.	Harvard